Thirty Years' View
(Vol. 2)
Or, A History of the Working of the American Government for Thirty Years From 1820 to 1850

Thomas Hart Benton

Alpha Editions

This edition published in 2023

ISBN : 9789357949361

Design and Setting By
Alpha Editions
www.alphaedis.com
Email - info@alphaedis.com

VOL. II.

CHAPTER I.

INAUGURATION OF MR. VAN BUREN.

March the 4th of this year, Mr. Van Buren was inaugurated President of the United States with the usual formalities, and conformed to the usage of his predecessors in delivering a public address on the occasion: a declaration of general principles, and an indication of the general course of the administration, were the tenor of his discourse: and the doctrines of the democratic school, as understood at the original formation of parties, were those professed. Close observance of the federal constitution as written—no latitudinarian constructions permitted, or doubtful powers assumed—faithful adherence to all its compromises—economy in the administration of the government—peace, friendship and fair dealing with all foreign nations—entangling alliances with none: such was his political chart: and with the expression of his belief that a perseverance in this line of foreign policy, with an increased strength, tried valor of the people, and exhaustless resources of the country, would entitle us to the good will of nations, protect our national respectability, and secure us from designed aggression from foreign powers. His expressions and views on this head deserve to be commemorated, and to be considered by all those into whose hands the management of the public affairs may go; and are, therefore, here given in his own words:

> "Our course of foreign policy has been so uniform and intelligible, as to constitute a rule of executive conduct which leaves little to my discretion, unless, indeed, I were willing to run counter to the lights of experience, and the known opinions of my constituents. We sedulously cultivate the friendship of all nations, as the condition most compatible with our welfare, and the principles of our government. We decline alliances, as adverse to our peace. We desire commercial relations on equal terms, being ever willing to give a fair equivalent for advantages received. We endeavor to conduct our intercourse with openness and sincerity; promptly avowing our objects, and seeking to establish that mutual frankness which is as beneficial in the dealings of nations as of men. We have no disposition, and we disclaim all right, to meddle in disputes, whether internal or foreign, that may molest other countries; regarding them, in their actual state, as social communities, and preserving a strict neutrality in all their controversies. Well knowing the tried valor of our people, and our exhaustless resources, we neither anticipate nor fear any designed aggression; and, in the consciousness of our own just conduct, we feel a security that we shall never be called upon to exert our determination, never to permit an invasion of our rights, without punishment or redress."

These are sound and encouraging views, and in adherence to them, promise to the United States a career of peace and prosperity comparatively free from the succession of wars which have loaded so many nations with debt and taxes, filled them with so many pensioners and paupers, created so much necessity for permanent fleets and armies; and placed one half the population in the predicament of living upon the labor of the other. The stand which the United States had acquired among nations by the vindication of her rights against the greatest powers—and the manner in which all unredressed aggressions, and all previous outstanding injuries, even of the oldest date, had been settled up and compensated under the administration of President Jackson—authorized this language from Mr. Van Buren; and the subsequent conduct of nations has justified it. Designed aggression, within many years, has come from no great power: casual disagreements and accidental injuries admit of arrangement: weak neighbors can find no benefit to themselves in wanton aggression, or refusal of redress for accidental wrong: isolation (a continent, as it were, to ourselves) is security against attack; and our railways would accumulate rapid destruction upon any invader. These advantages, and strict adherence to the rule, to ask only what is right, and submit to nothing wrong, will leave us (we have reason to believe) free from hostile collision with foreign powers, free from the necessity of keeping up war establishments of army and navy in time of peace, with our great resources left in the pockets of the people (always the safest and cheapest national treasuries), to come forth when public exigencies require them, and ourselves at liberty to pursue an unexampled career of national and individual prosperity.

One single subject of recently revived occurrence in our domestic concerns, and of portentous apparition, admitted a departure from the generalities of an inaugural address, and exacted from the new President the notice of a special declaration: it was the subject of slavery—an alarming subject of agitation near twenty years before—quieted by the Missouri compromise—resuscitated in 1835, as shown in previous chapters of this View; and apparently taking its place as a permanent and most pestiferous element in our presidential elections and federal legislation. It had largely mixed with the presidential election of the preceding year: it was expected to mix with ensuing federal legislation: and its evil effect upon the harmony and stability of the Union justified the new President in making a special declaration in relation to it, and even in declaring beforehand the cases of slavery legislation in which he would apply the qualified negative with which the constitution invested him over the acts of Congress. Under this sense of duty and propriety the inaugural address presented this passage:

"The last, perhaps the greatest, of the prominent sources of discord and disaster supposed to lurk in our political condition, was the institution of domestic slavery. Our forefathers were deeply impressed with the delicacy of this subject, and they treated it with a forbearance so evidently wise, that, in spite of every sinister foreboding, it never, until the present period disturbed the tranquillity of our common country. Such a result is sufficient evidence of the justice and the patriotism of their course; it is evidence not to be mistaken, that an adherence to it can prevent all embarrassment from this, as well as from every other anticipated cause of difficulty or danger. Have not recent events made it obvious to the slightest reflection, that the least deviation from this spirit of forbearance is injurious to every interest, that of humanity included? Amidst the violence of excited passions, this generous and fraternal feeling has been sometimes disregarded; and, standing as I now do before my countrymen in this high place of honor and of trust, I cannot refrain from anxiously invoking my fellow-citizens never to be deaf to its dictates. Perceiving, before my election, the deep interest this subject was beginning to excite, I believed it a solemn duty fully to make known my sentiments in regard to it; and now, when every motive for misrepresentations have passed away, I trust that they will be candidly weighed and understood. At least, they will be my standard of conduct in the path before me. I then declared that, if the desire of those of my countrymen who were favorable to my election was gratified, 'I must go into the presidential chair the inflexible and uncompromising opponent of every attempt, on the part of Congress, to abolish slavery in the District of Columbia, against the wishes of the slaveholding States; and also with a determination equally decided to resist the slightest interference with it in the States where it exists.' I submitted also to my fellow-citizens, with fulness and frankness, the reasons which led me to this determination. The result authorizes me to believe that they have been approved, and are confided in, by a majority of the people of the United States, including those whom they most immediately affect. It now only remains to add, that no bill conflicting with these views can ever receive my constitutional sanction. These opinions have been adopted in the firm belief that they are in accordance with the spirit that actuated the venerated fathers of the republic, and that succeeding experience has proved them to be humane, patriotic, expedient, honorable and just. If the agitation of this subject was intended to reach the stability of our institutions, enough has occurred to show that it has signally failed; and that in this, as in every other instance, the apprehensions of the timid and the hopes of the wicked for the destruction of our government, are again destined to be disappointed."

The determination here declared to yield the presidential sanction to no bill which proposed to interfere with slavery in the States; or to abolish it in the District of Columbia while it existed in the adjacent States, met the evil as it then presented itself—a fear on the part of some of the Southern States that their rights of property were to be endangered by federal legislation: and against which danger the veto power was now pledged to be opposed. There was no other form at that time in which slavery agitation could manifest itself, or place on which it could find a point to operate—the ordinance of 1787, and the compromise of 1820, having closed up the Territories against it. Danger to slave property in the States, either by direct action, or indirectly through the District of Columbia, were the only points of expressed apprehension; and at these there was not the slightest ground for fear. No one in Congress dreamed of interfering with slavery in the States, and the abortion of all the attempts made to abolish it in the District, showed the groundlessness of that fear. The pledged veto was not a necessity, but a propriety;—not necessary, but prudential;—not called for by anything in congress, but outside of it. In that point of view it was wise and prudent. It took from agitation its point of support—its means of acting on the fears and suspicions of the timid and credulous: and it gave to the country a season of repose and quiet from this disturbing question until a new point of agitation could be discovered and seized.

The cabinet remained nearly as under the previous administration: Mr. Forsyth, Secretary of State; Mr. Woodbury, Secretary of the Treasury; Mr. Poinsett, Secretary at War; Mr. Mahlon Dickerson, Secretary of the Navy; Mr. Amos Kendall, Postmaster General; and Benjamin F. Butler, Esq. Attorney General. Of all these Mr. Poinsett was the only new appointment. On the bench of the Supreme Court, John Catron, Esq. of Tennessee, and John McKinley, Esq. of Alabama, were appointed Justices; William Smith, formerly senator in Congress from South Carolina, having declined the appointment which was filled by Mr. McKinley. Mr. Butler soon resigning his place of Attorney General, Henry D. Gilpin, Esq. of Pennsylvania (after a temporary appointment of Felix Grundy, Esq. of Tennessee), became the Attorney General during the remainder of the administration.

CHAPTER II.

FINANCIAL AND MONETARY CRISIS: GENERAL SUSPENSION OF SPECIE PAYMENTS BY THE BANKS.

The nascent administration of the new President was destined to be saluted by a rude shock, and at the point most critical to governments as well as to individuals—that of deranged finances and broken-up treasury; and against the dangers of which I had in vain endeavored to warn our friends. A general suspension of the banks, a depreciated currency, and the insolvency of the federal treasury, were at hand. Visible signs, and some confidential information, portended to me this approaching calamity, and my speeches in the Senate were burthened with its vatication. Two parties, inimical to the administration, were at work to accomplish it—politicians and banks; and well able to succeed, because the government money was in the hands of the banks, and the federal legislation in the hands of the politicians; and both interested in the overthrow of the party in power;—and the overthrow of the finances the obvious means to the accomplishment of the object. The public moneys had been withdrawn from the custody of the Bank of the United States: the want of an independent, or national treasury, of necessity, placed them in the custody of the local banks: and the specie order of President Jackson having been rescinded by the Act of Congress, the notes of all these banks, and of all others in the country, amounting to nearly a thousand, became receivable in payment of public dues. The deposit banks became filled up with the notes of these multitudinous institutions, constituting that surplus, the distribution of which had become an engrossing care with Congress, and ended with effecting the object under the guise of a deposit with the States. I recalled the recollection of the times of 1818-19, when the treasury reports of one year showed a superfluity of revenue for which there was no want, and of the next a deficit which required to be relieved by a loan; and argued that we must now have the same result from the bloat in the paper system which we then had. I demanded—

"Are we not at this moment, and from the same cause, realizing the first part—the illusive and treacherous part—of this picture? and must not the other, the sad and real sequel, speedily follow? The day of revulsion must come, and its effects must be more or less disastrous; but come it must. The present bloat in the paper system cannot continue: violent contraction must follow enormous expansion: a scene of distress and suffering must ensue—to come of itself out of the present state of things, without being stimulated and helped on by our unwise legislation."

Of the act which rescinded the specie order, and made the notes of the local banks receivable in payment of all federal dues, I said:

"This bill is to be an era in our legislation and in our political history. It is to be a point on which the view of the future age is to be thrown back, and from which future consequences will be traced. I separate myself from it: I wash my hands of it: I oppose it. I am one of those who promised gold—not paper. I promised the currency of the constitution, not the currency of corporations. I did not join in putting down the Bank of the United States to put up a wilderness of local banks. I did not join in putting down the paper currency of a national bank, to put up a national paper currency of a thousand local banks. I did not strike Cæsar to make Antony master of Rome."

The condition of our deposit banks was desperate—wholly inadequate to the slightest pressure on their vaults in the ordinary course of business, much less that of meeting the daily government drafts and the approaching deposit of near forty millions with the States. The necessity of keeping one-third of specie on hand for its immediate liabilities, was enforced from the example and rule of the Bank of England, while many of our deposit banks could show but the one-twentieth, the one-thirtieth, the one-fortieth, and even the one-fiftieth of specie in hand for immediate liabilities in circulation and deposits. The sworn evidence of a late Governor of the Bank of England (Mr. Horsely Palmer), before a parliamentary committee, was read, in which he testified that the average proportion of coin and bullion which the bank deems it prudent to keep on hand, was at the rate of the third of the total amount of all her liabilities—including deposits as well as issues. And this was the proportion which that bank deemed it prudent to keep—that bank which was the largest in the world, situated in the moneyed metropolis of Europe, with its list of debtors within the circuit of London, supported by the richest merchants in the world, and backed by the British government, which stood her security for fourteen millions sterling, and ready with her supply of exchequer bills (the interest to be raised to insure sales), at any moment of emergency. Tested by the rule of the Bank of England, and our deposit banks were in the jaws of destruction; and this so evident to me, that I was amazed that others did not see it—those of our friends who voted with the opponents of the administration in rescinding the specie order, and in making the deposit with the States. The latter had begun to take effect, at the rate of about ten millions to the quarter, on the first day of January preceding Mr. Van Buren's inauguration: a second ten millions were to be called for on the first of April: and like sums on the first days of the two remaining quarters. It was utterly impossible for the banks to stand these drafts; and, having failed in all attempts to wake up our friends, who were then in the majority, to a sense of the danger which was impending, and to arrest their ruinous voting with the opposition members (which most of them did), I determined to address myself to the President elect, under the belief that, although he would not be able to avert the blow, he might do much to soften its force and avert its consequences, when it did come. It was in the month of February, while Mr. Van Buren was still President of the Senate, that I invited him into a committee room for that purpose, and stated to him my opinion that we were on the eve of an explosion of the paper system and of a general suspension of the banks—intending to follow up that expression of opinion with the exposition of my reasons for thinking so: but the interview came to a sudden and unexpected termination. Hardly had I expressed my belief of this impending catastrophe, than he spoke up, and said, "Your friends think you a little exalted in the head on that subject." I said no more. I was miffed. We left the room together, talking on different matters, and I saying to myself, "*You will soon feel the thunderbolt.*" But I have since felt that I was too hasty, and that I ought to have carried out my intention of making a full exposition of the moneyed affairs of the country. His habitual courtesy, from which the expression quoted was a most rare departure, and his real regard for me, both personal and political (for at that time he was pressing me to become a member of his cabinet), would have insured me a full hearing, if I had shown a disposition to go on; and his clear intellect would have seized and appreciated the strong facts and just inferences which would have been presented to him. But I stopped short, as if I had nothing more to say, from that feeling of self-respect which silences a man of some pride when he sees that what he says is not valued. I have regretted my hastiness ever since. It was of the utmost moment that the new President should have his eyes opened to the dangers of the treasury, and my services on the Committee of Finance had given me opportunities of knowledge which he did not possess. Forewarned is forearmed; and never was there a case in which the maxim more impressively applied. He could not have prevented the suspension: the repeal of the specie circular and the deposit with the States (both measures carried by the help of votes from professing friends), had put that measure into the hands of those who would be sure to use it: but he could have provided against it, and prepared for it, and lessened the force of the blow when it did come. He might have quickened the vigilance of the Secretary of the Treasury—might have demanded additional securities from the deposit banks—and might have drawn from them the moneys called for by appropriation acts. There was a sum of about five millions which might have been saved with a stroke of the pen, being the aggregate of sums drawn from the treasury by the numerous disbursing officers, and left in the banks in their own names for daily current payments: an order to these officers would have saved these five millions, and prevented the disgrace and damage of a stoppage in the daily payments, and the spectacle of a government waking up in the morning without a dollar to pay the day-laborer with, while placing on its statute book a law for the distribution of forty millions of surplus. Measures like these, and others which a prudent vigilance would have suggested, might have enabled the government to continue its payments without an extra session of Congress, and without the mortification of capitulating to the broken banks, by accepting and paying out their depreciated notes as the currency of the federal treasury.

CHAPTER III.

PREPARATION FOR THE DISTRESS AND SUSPENSION.

In the autumn of the preceding year, shortly before the meeting of Congress, Mr. Biddle, president of the Pennsylvania Bank of the United States (for that was the ridiculous title it assumed after its resurrection under a Pennsylvania charter), issued one of those characteristic letters which were habitually promulgated whenever a new lead was to be given out, and a new scent emitted for the followers of the bank to run upon. A new distress, as the pretext for a new catastrophe, was now the object. A picture of ruin was presented, alarm given out, every thing going to destruction; and the federal government the cause of the whole, and the *national* recharter of the defunct bank the sovereign remedy. The following is an extract from that letter.

> "The Bank of the United States has not ceased to exist more than seven months, and already the whole currency and exchanges are running into inextricable confusion, and the industry of the country is burdened with extravagant charges on all the commercial intercourse of the Union. And now, when these banks have been created by the Executive, and urged into these excesses, instead of gentle and gradual remedies, a fierce crusade is raised against them, the funds are harshly and suddenly taken from them, and they are forced to extraordinary means of defense against the very power which brought them into being. They received, and were expected to receive, in payment for the government, the notes of each other and the notes of other banks, and the facility with which they did so was a ground of special commendation by the government; and now that government has let loose upon them a demand for specie to the whole amount of these notes. I go further. There is an outcry abroad, raised by faction, and echoed by folly, against the banks of the United States. Until it was disturbed by the government, the banking system of the United States was at least as good as that of any other commercial country. What was desired for its perfection was precisely what I have so long striven to accomplish—to widen the metallic basis of the currency by a greater infusion of coin into the smaller channels of circulation. This was in a gradual and judicious train of accomplishment. But this miserable foolery about an exclusively metallic currency, is quite as absurd as to discard the steamboats, and go back to poling up the Mississippi."

The lead thus given out was sedulously followed during the winter, both in Congress and out of it, and at the end of the session had reached an immense demonstration in New York, in the preparations made to receive Mr. Webster, and to hear a speech from him, on his return from Washington. He arrived in New York on the 15th of March, and the papers of the city give this glowing account of his reception:

> "In conformity with public announcement, yesterday, at about half past 3 o'clock, the Honorable DANIEL WEBSTER arrived in this city in the steamboat Swan from Philadelphia. The intense desire on the part of the citizens to give a grateful reception to this great advocate of the constitution, set the whole city in motion towards the point of debarkation, for nearly an hour before the arrival of the distinguished visitor. At the moment when the steamboat reached the pier, the assemblage had attained that degree of density and anxiety to witness the landing, that it was feared serious consequences would result. At half past 3 o'clock Mr. Webster, accompanied by Philip Hone and David B. Ogden, landed from the boat amidst the deafening cheers and plaudits of the multitude, thrice repeated, and took his seat in an open barouche provided for the occasion. The procession, consisting of several hundred citizens upon horseback, a large train of carriages and citizens, formed upon State street, and after receiving their distinguished guest, proceeded with great order up Broadway to the apartments arranged for his reception at the American Hotel. The scene presented the most gratifying spectacle. Hundreds of citizens who had been opposed to Mr. Webster in politics, now that he appeared as a private individual, came forth to demonstrate their respect for his private worth and to express their approbation of his personal character; and thousands more who appreciated his principles and political integrity, crowded around to convince him of their personal attachment, and give evidence of their approval of his public acts. The wharves, the

shipping, the housetops and windows, and the streets through which the procession passed, were thronged with citizens of every occupation and degree, and loud and continued cheers greeted the great statesman at every point. There was not a greater number at the reception of General Jackson in this city, with the exception of the military, nor a greater degree of enthusiasm manifested upon that occasion, than the arrival upon our shores of Daniel Webster. At 6 o'clock in the evening, the anxious multitude began to move towards Niblo's saloon, where Mr. Webster was to be addressed by the committee of citizens delegated for that purpose, and to which it was expected he would reply. A large body of officers were upon the ground to keep the assemblage within bounds, and at a quarter past six the doors were opened, when the saloon, garden, and avenues leading thereto were instantly crowded to overflowing.

The meeting was called to order by Alderman Clark, who proposed for president, David B. Ogden, which upon being put to vote was unanimously adopted. The following gentlemen were then elected vice-presidents, viz: Robert C. Cornell, Jonathan Goodhue, Joseph Tucker, Nathaniel Weed; and Joseph Hoxie and G. S. Robins, secretaries.

Mr. W. began his remarks at a quarter before seven o'clock, P.M. and concluded them at a quarter past nine. When he entered the saloon, he was received with the most deafening cheers. The hall rang with the loud plaudits of the crowd, and every hat was waving. So great was the crowd in the galleries, and such was the apprehension that the apparently weak wooden columns which supported would give way, that Mr. W. was twice interrupted with the appalling cry "*the galleries are falling*," when only a window was broken, or a stove-pipe shaken. The length of the address (two and a half hours), none too long, however, for the audience would with pleasure have tarried two hours longer, compels us to give at present only the heads of a speech which we would otherwise now report in detail."

Certainly Mr. Webster was worthy of all honors in the great city of New York; but having been accustomed to pass through that city several times in every year during the preceding quarter of a century, and to make frequent sojourns there, and to speak thereafter, and in all the characters of politician, social guest, and member of the bar,—it is certain that neither his person nor his speaking could be such a novelty and rarity as to call out upon his arrival so large a meeting as is here described, invest it with so much form, fire it with so much enthusiasm, fill it with so much expectation, unless there had been some large object in view—some great effect to be produced—some consequence to result: and of all which this imposing demonstration was at once the sign and the initiative. No holiday occasion, no complimentary notice, no feeling of personal regard, could have called forth an assemblage so vast, and inspired it with such deep and anxious emotions. It required a public object, a general interest, a pervading concern, and a serious apprehension of some uncertain and fearful future, to call out and organize such a mass—not of the young, the ardent, the heedless—but of the age, the character, the talent, the fortune, the gravity of the most populous and opulent city of the Union. It was as if the population of a great city, in terror of some great impending unknown calamity, had come forth to get consolation and counsel from a wise man—to ask him what was to happen? and what they were to do? And so in fact it was, as fully disclosed in the address with which the orator was saluted, and in the speech of two hours and a half which he made in response to it. The address was a deprecation of calamities; the speech was responsive to the address—admitted every thing that could be feared—and charged the whole upon the mal-administration of the federal government. A picture of universal distress was portrayed, and worse coming; and the remedy for the whole the same which had been presented in Mr. Biddle's letter—the recharter of *the* national bank. The speech was a manifesto against the Jackson administration, and a protest against its continuation in the person of his successor, and an invocation to a general combination against it. All the banks were sought to be united, and made to stand together upon a sense of common danger—the administration their enemy, the national bank their protection. Every industrial pursuit was pictured as crippled and damaged by bad government. Material injury to private interests were still more vehemently charged than political injuries to the body politic. In the deplorable picture which it presented of the condition of every industrial pursuit, and especially in the "war" upon the banks and the currency, it seemed to be a justificatory pleading in advance for a general shutting up of their doors, and the shutting up of the federal treasury at the same time. In this sense, and on this point, the speech contained this ominous sentence, more candid than discreet, taken in connection with what was to happen:

"*Remember, gentlemen, in the midst of this deafening din against all banks, that if it shall create such a panic, or such alarm, as shall shut up the banks, it will shut up the treasury of the United States also.*"

The whole tenor of the speech was calculated to produce discontent, create distress, and excite alarm—discontent and distress for present sufferings—alarm for the greater, which were to come. This is a sample:

> "Gentlemen, I would not willingly be a prophet of ill. I most devoutly wish to see a better state of things; and I believe the repeal of the treasury order would tend very much to bring about that better state of things. And I am of opinion, gentlemen, that the order will be repealed. I think it must be repealed. I think the east, west, north and south, will demand its repeal. But, gentlemen, I feel it my duty to say, that if I should be disappointed in this expectation, I see no immediate relief to the distresses of the community. I greatly fear, even, that the worst is not yet. I look for severer distresses; for extreme difficulties in exchange; for far greater inconveniences in remittance, and for a sudden fall in prices. Our condition is one not to be tampered with, and the repeal of the treasury order being something which government can do, and which will do good, the public voice is right in demanding that repeal. It is true, if repealed now, the relief will come late. Nevertheless its repeal or abrogation is a thing to be insisted on, and pursued till it shall be accomplished."

The speech concluded with an earnest exhortation to the citizens of New York to do something, without saying what, but which with my misgivings and presentiments, the whole tenor of the speech and the circumstances which attended it—delivered in the moneyed metropolis of the Union, at a time when there was no political canvass depending, and the ominous omission to name what was required to be done—appeared to me to be an invitation to the New York banks to close their doors! which being done by them would be an example followed throughout the Union, and produce the consummation of a universal suspension. The following is that conclusion:

> "Whigs of New York! Patriotic citizens of this great metropolis!—Lovers of constitutional liberty, bound by interest and affection to the institutions of your country, Americans in heart and in principle! You are ready, I am sure, to fulfil all the duties imposed upon you by your situation, and demanded of you by your country. You have a central position; your city is the point from which intelligence emanates, and spreads in all directions over the whole land. Every hour carries reports of your sentiments and opinions to the verge of the Union. You cannot escape the responsibility which circumstances have thrown upon you. You must live and act on a broad and conspicuous theatre either for good or for evil, to your country. You cannot shrink away from public duties; you cannot obscure yourselves, nor bury your talent. In the common welfare, in the common prosperity, in the common glory of Americans, you have a stake, of value not to be calculated. You have an interest in the preservation of the Union, of the constitution, and of the true principles of the government, which no man can estimate. You act for yourselves, and for the generations that are to come after you; and those who, ages hence, shall bear your names, and partake your blood, will feel in their political and social condition, the consequences of the manner in which you discharge your political duties."

The appeal for action in this paragraph is vehement. It takes every form of violent desire which is known to the art of entreaty. Supplication, solicitation, remonstrance, importunity, prayer, menace! until rising to the dignity of a debt due from a moneyed metropolis to an expectant community, he demanded payment as matter of right! and enforced the demand as an obligation of necessity, as well as of duty, and from which such a community could not escape, if it would. The nature of the action which was so vehemently desired, could not be mistaken. I hold it a fair interpretation of this appeal that it was an exhortation to the business population of the commercial metropolis of the Union to take the initiative in suspending specie payments, and a justificatory manifesto for doing so; and that the speech itself was the first step in the grand performance: and so it seemed to be understood. It was received with unbounded applause, lauded to the skies, cheered to the echo, carefully and elaborately prepared for publication,—published and republished in newspaper and pamphlet form; and universally circulated. This was in the first month of Mr. Van Buren's presidency, and it will be seen what the second one brought forth.

The specie circular—that treasury order of President Jackson, which saved the public lands from being converted into broken bank paper—was the subject of repeated denunciatory reference—very erroneous, as the event has proved, in its estimate of the measure; but quite correct in its history, and amusing in its reference to some of the friends of the administration who undertook to act a part for and against the rescission of the order at the same time.

> "Mr. Webster then came to the treasury circular, and related the history of the late legislation upon it. 'A member of Congress,' said he, 'prepared this very treasury order in 1836, but the only vote he got for it was his own—he stood 'solitary' and 'alone' (a laugh); and yet eleven days after Congress had adjourned—only six months after the President in his annual message had congratulated the people upon the prosperous sales of the public lands,—this order came out in known and direct opposition to the wishes of nine-tenths of the members of Congress.'"

This is good history from a close witness of what he relates. The member referred to as having prepared the treasury order, and offered it in the shape of a bill in the Senate, and getting no vote for it but his own,—who stood solitary and alone on that occasion, as well as on some others—was no other than the writer of this View; and he has lived to see about as much unanimity in favor of that measure since as there was against it then. Nine-tenths of the members of Congress were then against it, but from very different motives—some because they were deeply engaged in land speculations, and borrowed paper from the banks for the purpose; some because they were in the interest of the banks, and wished to give their paper credit and circulation; others because they were sincere believers in the paper system; others because they were opposed to the President, and believed him to be in favor of the measure; others again from mere timidity of temperament, and constitutional inability to act strongly. And these various descriptions embraced friends as well as foes to the administration. Mr. Webster says the order was issued eleven days after that Congress adjourned which had so unanimously rejected it. That is true. We only waited for Congress to be gone to issue the order. Mr. Benton was in the room of the private secretary (Mr. Donelson), hard by the council chamber, while the cabinet sat in council upon this measure. They were mostly against it. General Jackson ordered it, and directed the private Secretary to bring him a draft of the order to be issued. He came to Mr. Benton to draw it—who did so: and being altered a little, it was given to the Secretary of the Treasury to be promulgated. Then Mr. Benton asked for his draft, that he might destroy it. The private secretary said no—that the time might come when it should be known who was at the bottom of that Treasury order: and that he would keep it. It was issued on the strong will and clear head of President Jackson, and saved many ten millions to the public treasury. Bales of bank notes were on the road to be converted into public lands which this order overtook, and sent back, to depreciate in the vaults of the banks instead of the coffers of the treasury. To repeal the order by law was the effort as soon as Congress met, and direct legislation to that effect was proposed by Mr. Ewing, of Ohio, but superseded by a circumlocutory bill from Mr. Walker and Mr. Rives, which the President treated as a nullity for want of intelligibility: and of which Mr. Webster gave this account:

> "If he himself had had power, he would have voted for Mr. Ewing's proposition to repeal the order, in terms which Mr. Butler and the late President could not have misunderstood; but power was so strong, and members of Congress had now become so delicate about giving offence to it, that it would not do, for the world, to repeal the obnoxious circular, plainly and forthwith; but the ingenuity of the friends of the administration must dodge around it, and over it—and now Mr. Butler had the unkindness to tell them that their views neither he, lawyer as he is, nor the President, could possibly understand (a laugh), and that, as it could not be understood, the President had pocketed it—and left it upon the archives of state, no doubt to be studied there. Mr. W. would call attention to the remarkable fact, that though the

Senate acted upon this currency bill in season, yet it was put off, and put off—so that, by no action upon it before the ten days allowed the President by the constitution, the power over it was completely in his will, even though the whole nation and every member of Congress wished for its repeal. Mr. W., however, believed that such was the pressure of public opinion upon the new President, that it must soon be repealed."

This amphibology of the bill, and delay in passing it, and this dodging around and over, was occasioned by what Mr. Webster calls the delicacy of some members who had the difficult part to play, of going with the enemies of the administration without going against the administration. A chapter in the first volume of this View gives the history of this work; and the last sentence in the passage quoted from Mr. Webster's speech gives the key to the views in which the speech originated, and to the proceedings by which it was accompanied and followed. "*It is believed that such is the pressure of public opinion upon the new President that it must soon be repealed.*"

In another part of his speech, Mr. Webster shows that the repealing bill was put by the whigs into the hands of certain friends of the administration, to be by them seasoned into a palatable dish; and that they gained no favor with the "bold man" who despised flinching, and loved decision, even in a foe. Thus:

"At the commencement of the last session, as you know, gentlemen, a resolution was brought forward in the Senate for annulling and abrogating this order, by Mr. Ewing, a gentleman of much intelligence, of sound principles, of vigorous and energetic character, whose loss from the service of the country, I regard as a public misfortune. The whig members all supported this resolution, and all the members, I believe, with the exception of some five or six, were very anxious, in some way, to get rid of the treasury order. But Mr. Ewing's resolution was too direct. It was deemed a pointed and ungracious attack on executive policy. Therefore, it must be softened, modified, qualified, made to sound less harsh to the ears of men in power, and to assume a plausible, polished, inoffensive character. It was accordingly put into the plastic hands of the friends of the executive, to be moulded and fashioned, so that it might have the effect of ridding the country of the obnoxious order, and yet not appear to question executive infallibility. All this did not answer. The late President is not a man to be satisfied with soft words; and he saw in the measure, even as it passed the two houses, a substantial repeal of the order. He is a man of boldness and decision; and he respects boldness and decision in others. If you are his friend, he expects no flinching; and if you are his adversary, he respects you none the less, for carrying your opposition to the full limits of honorable warfare."

Mr. Webster must have been greatly dissatisfied with his democratic allies, when he could thus, in a public speech, before such an audience, and within one short month after they had been co-operating with him, hold them up as equally unmeritable in the eyes of both parties.

History deems it essential to present this New York speech of Mr. Webster as part of a great movement, without a knowledge of which the view would be imperfect. It was the first formal public step which was to inaugurate the new distress, and organize the proceedings for shutting up the banks, and with them, the federal treasury, with a view to coerce the government into submission to the Bank of the United States and its confederate politicians. Mr. Van Buren was a man of great suavity and gentleness of deportment, and, to those who associated the idea of violence with firmness, might be supposed deficient in that quality. An experiment upon his nerves was resolved on—a pressure of public opinion, in the language of Mr. Webster, under which his gentle temperament was expected to yield.

CHAPTER IV.

PROGRESS OF THE DISTRESS, AND PRELIMINARIES FOR THE SUSPENSION.

The speech of Mr. Webster—his appeal for action—was soon followed by its appointed consequence—an immense meeting in the city of New York. The speech did not produce the meeting, any more than the meeting produced the speech. Both were in the programme, and performed as prescribed, in their respective places—the speech first, the meeting afterwards; and the latter justified by the former. It was an immense assemblage, composed of the elite of what was foremost in the city for property, talent, respectability; and took for its business the consideration of the times: the distress of the times, and the nature of the remedy. The imposing form of a meeting, solemn as well as numerous and respectable, was gone through: speeches made, resolutions adopted: order and emphasis given to the proceedings. A president, ten vice-presidents, two secretaries, seven orators (Mr. Webster not among them: he had performed his part, and made his exit), officiated in the ceremonies; and thousands of citizens constituted the accumulated mass. The spirit and proceedings of the meeting were concentrated in a series of resolves, each stronger than the other, and each more welcome than the former; and all progressive, from facts and principles declared, to duties and performances recommended. The first resolve declared the existence of the distress, and made the picture gloomy enough. It was in these words:

> "Whereas, the great commercial interests of our city have nearly reached a point of general ruin—our merchants driven from a state of prosperity to that of unprecedented difficulty and bankruptcy—the business, activity and energy, which have heretofore made us the polar star of the new world, is daily sinking, and taking from us the fruits of years of industry—reducing the aged among us, who but yesterday were sufficiently in affluence, to a state of comparative want; and blighting the prospects, and blasting the hopes of the young throughout our once prosperous land: we deem it our duty to express to the country our situation and desires, while yet there is time to retrace error, and secure those rights and perpetuate those principles which were bequeathed us by our fathers, and which we are bound to make every honorable effort to maintain."

After the fact of the distress, thus established by a resolve, came the cause; and this was the condensation of Mr. Webster's speech, collecting into a point what had been oratorically diffused over a wide surface. What was itself a condensation cannot be farther abridged, and must be given in its own words:

> "That the wide-spread disaster which has overtaken the commercial interests of the country, and which threatens to produce general bankruptcy, may be in a great measure ascribed to the interference of the general government with the commercial and business operations of the country; its intermeddling with the currency; its destruction of the national bank; its attempt to substitute a metallic for a credit currency; and, finally, to the issuing by the President of the United States of the treasury order, known as the 'specie circular.'"

The next resolve foreshadowed the consequences which follow from governmental perseverance in such calamitous measures—general bankruptcy to the dealing classes, starvation to the laboring classes, public convulsions, and danger to our political institutions; with an admonition to the new President of what might happen to himself, if he persevered in the "*experiments*" of a predecessor whose tyranny and oppression had made him the scourge of his country. But let the resolve speak for itself:

> "That while we would do nothing which might for a moment compromit our respect for the laws, we feel it incumbent upon us to remind the executive of the nation, that the government of the country, as of late administered, has become the oppressor of the people, instead of affording them protection—that his perseverance in the experiment of his predecessor (after the public voice, in every way in which that voice could be expressed, has clearly denounced it as ruinous to the best interests of the country) has already caused the ruin of thousands of merchants, thrown tens of thousands of mechanics and laborers out of employment, depreciated the value of our great staple millions of dollars, destroyed the internal exchanges,

and prostrated the energies and blighted the prospects of the industrious and enterprising portion of our people; and must, if persevered in, not only produce *starvation* among the laboring classes, but inevitably lead to disturbances which may endanger the stability of our institutions themselves."

This word "*experiment*" had become a staple phrase in all the distress oratory and literature of the day, sometimes heightened by the prefix of "*quack*," and was applied to all the efforts of the administration to return the federal government to the hard money currency, which was the currency of the constitution and the currency of all countries; and which efforts were now treated as novelties and dangerous innovations. Universal was the use of the phrase by one of the political parties some twenty years ago: dead silent are their tongues upon it now! Twenty years of successful working of the government under the hard money system has put an end to the repetition of a phrase which has suffered the fate of all catch-words of party, and became more distasteful to its old employers than it ever was to their adversaries. It has not been heard since the federal government got divorced from bank and paper money! since gold and silver has become the sole currency of the federal government! since, in fact, the memorable epoch when the Bank of the United States (former sovereign remedy for all the ills the body politic was heir to) has become a defunct authority, and an "obsolete idea."

The next resolve proposed a direct movement upon the President—nothing less than a committee of fifty to wait upon him, and "*remonstrate*" with him upon what was called the ruinous measures of the government.

> "That a committee of not less than fifty be appointed to repair to Washington, and remonstrate with the Executive against the continuance of "the specie circular;" and in behalf of this meeting and in the name of the merchants of New York, and the people of the United States, urge its immediate repeal."

This formidable committee, limited to a minimum of fifty, open to a maximum of any amount, besides this "*remonstrance*" against the specie circular, were also instructed to petition the President to forbear the collection of merchants' bonds by suit; and also to call an extra session of Congress. The first of these measures was to stop the collection of the accruing revenues: the second, to obtain from Congress that submission to the bank power which could not be obtained from the President. Formidable as were the arrangements for acting on the President, provision was discreetly made for a possible failure, and for the prosecution of other measures. With this view, the committee of fifty, after their return from Washington, were directed to call another general meeting of the citizens of New York, and to report to them the results of their mission. A concluding resolution invited the co-operation of the other great cities in these proceedings, and seemed to look to an imposing demonstration of physical force, and strong determination, as a means of acting on the mind, or will of the President; and thus controlling the free action of the constitutional authorities. This resolve was specially addressed to the merchants of Philadelphia, Boston and Baltimore, and generally addressed to all other commercial cities, and earnestly prayed their assistance in saving the whole country from ruin.

> "That merchants of Philadelphia, Boston, Baltimore, and the commercial cities of the Union, be respectfully requested to unite with us in our remonstrance and petition, and to use their exertions, in connection with us, to induce the Executive of the nation to listen to the voice of the people, and to recede from a measure under the evils of which we are now laboring, and which threatens to involve the whole country in ruin."

The language and import of all these resolves and proceedings were sufficiently strong, and indicated a feeling but little short of violence towards the government; but, according to the newspapers of the city, they were subdued and moderate—tame and spiritless, in comparison to the feeling which animated the great meeting. A leading paper thus characterized that feeling:

> "The meeting was a remarkable one for the vast numbers assembled—the entire decorum of the proceedings—and especially for the deep, though subdued and restrained, excitement which evidently pervaded the mighty mass. It was a spectacle that could not be looked upon without emotion,—that of many thousand men trembling, as it were, on the brink of ruin, owing to the measures, as they verily believe, of their own government, which should be their

friend, instead of their oppressor—and yet meeting with deliberation and calmness, listening to a narrative of their wrongs, and the causes thereof, adopting such resolutions as were deemed judicious; and then quietly separating, to abide the result of their firm but respectful remonstrances. But it is proper and fit to say that this moderation must not be mistaken for pusillanimity, nor be trifled with, as though it could not by any aggravation of wrong be moved from its propriety. No man accustomed, from the expression of the countenance, to translate the emotions of the heart, could have looked upon the faces and the bearing of the multitude assembled last evening, and not have felt that there were fires smouldering there, which a single spark might cause to burst into flame."

Smouldering fires which a single spark might light into a flame! Possibly that spark might have been the opposing voice of some citizen, who thought the meeting mistaken, both in the fact of the ruin of the country and the attribution of that ruin to the specie circular. No such voice was lifted—no such spark applied, and the proposition to march 10,000 men to Washington to demand a redress of grievances was not sanctioned. The committee of fifty was deemed sufficient, as they certainly were, for every purpose of peaceful communication. They were eminently respectable citizens, any two, or any one of which, or even a mail transmission of their petition, would have commanded for it a most respectful attention. The grand committee arrived at Washington—asked an audience of the President—received it; but with the precaution (to avoid mistakes) that written communications should alone be used. The committee therefore presented their demands in writing, and a paragraph from it will show the degree to which the feeling of the city had allowed itself to be worked up.

"We do not tell a fictitious tale of woe; we have no selfish or partisan views to sustain, when we assure you that the noble city which we represent, lies prostrate in despair, its credit blighted, its industry paralyzed, and without a hope beaming through the darkness of the future, unless the government of our country can be induced to relinquish the measures to which we attribute our distress. We fully appreciate the respect which is due to our chief magistrate, and disclaim every intention inconsistent with that feeling; but we speak in behalf of a community which trembles upon the brink of ruin, which deems itself an adequate judge of all questions connected with the trade and currency of the country, and believes that the policy adopted by the recent administration and sustained by the present, is founded in error, and threatens the destruction of every department of industry. Under a deep impression of the propriety of confining our declarations within moderate limits, we affirm that the value of our real estate has, within the last six months, depreciated more than forty millions: that within the last two months, there have been more than two hundred and fifty failures of houses engaged in extensive business: that within the same period, a decline of twenty millions of dollars has occurred in our local stocks, including those railroad and canal incorporations, which, though chartered in other States, depend chiefly upon New York for their sale: that the immense amount of merchandise in our warehouses has within the same period fallen in value at least thirty per cent.; that within a few weeks, not less than twenty thousand individuals, depending on their daily labor for their daily bread, have been discharged by their employers, because the means of retaining them were exhausted—and that a complete blight has fallen upon a community heretofore so active, enterprising and prosperous. The error of our rulers has produced a wider desolation than the pestilence which depopulated our streets, or the conflagration, which laid them in ashes. We believe that it is unjust to attribute these evils to any excessive development of mercantile enterprise, and that they really flow from that unwise system which aimed at the substitution of a metallic for a paper currency—the system which gave the first shock to the fabric of our commercial prosperity by removing the public deposits from the United States bank, which weakened every part of the edifice by the destruction of that useful and efficient institution, and now threatens to crumble it into a mass of ruins under the operations of the specie circular, which withdrew the gold and silver of the country from the channels in which it could be profitably employed. We assert that the experiment has had a fair—a liberal trial, and that disappointment and mischief are visible in all its results—that the promise of a regulated currency and equalized exchanges has been broken, the currency totally disordered, and internal exchanges almost entirely discontinued. We, therefore, make our earnest appeal to the Executive, and ask whether it is not time to interpose the paternal authority of the government, and abandon the policy which is beggaring the people."

The address was read to the President. He heard it with entire composure—made no sort of remark upon it—treated the gentlemen with exquisite politeness—and promised them a written answer the next day. This was the third of May: on the fourth the answer was delivered. It was an answer worthy of a President—a calm, quiet, decent, peremptory refusal to comply with a single one of their demands! with a brief reason, avoiding all controversy, and foreclosing all further application, by a clean refusal in each case. The committee had nothing to do but to return, and report: and they did so. There had been a mistake committed in the estimate of the man. Mr. Van Buren vindicated equally the rights of the chief magistrate, and his own personal decorum; and left the committee without any thing to complain of, although unsuccessful in all their objects. He also had another opportunity of vindicating his personal and official decorum in another visit which he received about the same time. Mr. Biddle called to see the President—apparently a call of respect on the chief magistrate—about the same time, but evidently with the design to be consulted, and to appear as the great restorer of the currency. Mr. Van Buren received the visit according to its apparent intent, with entire civility, and without a word on public affairs. Believing Mr. Biddle to be at the bottom of the suspension, he could not treat him with the confidence and respect which a consultation would imply. He (Mr. Biddle) felt the slight, and caused this notice to be put in the papers:

"Being on other business at Washington, Mr. Biddle took occasion to call on the President of the United States, to pay his respects to him in that character, and especially, to afford the President an opportunity, if he chose to embrace it, to speak of the present state of things, and to confer, if he saw fit, with the head of the largest banking institution in the country—and that the institution in which such general application has been made for relief. During the interview, however, the President remained profoundly silent upon the great and interesting topics of the day; and as Mr. Biddle did not think it his business to introduce them, not a word in relation to them was said."

Returning to New York, the committee convoked another general meeting of the citizens, as required to do at the time of their appointment; and made their report to it, recommending further forbearance, and further reliance on the ballot box, although (as they said) history recorded many popular insurrections where the provocation was less. A passage from this report will show its spirit, and to what excess a community may be excited about nothing, by the mutual inflammation of each other's passions and complaints, combined with a power to act upon the business and interests of the people.

"From this correspondence it is obvious, fellow-citizens, that we must abandon all hope that either the justice of our claims or the severity of our sufferings will induce the Executive to abandon or relax the policy which has produced such desolating effects—and it remains for us to consider what more is to be done in this awful crisis of our affairs. Our first duty under losses and distresses which we have endured, is to cherish with religious care the blessings which we yet enjoy, and which can be protected only by a strict observance of the laws upon which society depends for security and happiness. We do not disguise our opinion that the pages of history record, and the opinions of mankind justify, numerous instances of popular insurrection, the provocation to which was less severe than the evils of which we complain. But in these cases, the outraged and oppressed had no other means of redress. Our case is different. If we can succeed in an effort to bring public opinion into sympathy with the views which we entertain, the Executive will abandon the policy which oppresses, instead of protecting the people. Do not despair because the time at which the ballot box can exercise its healing influence appears so remote—the sagacity of the practical politician will perceive the change in public sentiment before you are aware of its approach. But the effort to produce this change must be vigorous and untiring."

The meeting adopted corresponding resolutions. Despairing of acting on the President, the move was to act upon the people—to rouse and combine them against an administration which was destroying their industry, and to remove from power (at the elections) those who were destroying the industry of the country. Thus:

> "*Resolved*, That the interests of the capitalists, merchants, manufacturers, mechanics and industrious classes, are dependent upon each other, and any measures of the government which prostrate the active business men of the community, will also deprive honest industry of its reward; and we call upon all our fellow-citizens to unite with us in removing from power those who persist in a system that is destroying the prosperity of our country."

Another resolve summed up the list of grievances of which they complained, and enumerated the causes of the pervading ruin which had been brought upon the country. Thus:

> "*Resolved*, That the chief causes of the existing distress are the defeat of Mr. Clay's land bill, the removal of the public deposits, the refusal to re-charter the Bank of the United States, and the issuing of the specie circular. The land bill was passed by the people's representatives, and vetoed by the President—the bill rechartering the bank was passed by the people's representatives, and vetoed by the President. The people's representatives declared by a solemn resolution, that the public deposits were safe in the United States Bank; within a few weeks thereafter, the President removed the public deposits. The people's representatives passed a bill rescinding the specie circular: the President destroyed it by omitting to return it within the limited period; and in the answer to our addresses, President Van Buren declares that the specie circular was issued by his predecessor, omitting all notice of the Secretary of the Treasury, who is amenable directly to Congress, and charged by the act creating his department with the superintendence of the finances, and who signed the order."

These two resolves deserve to be noted. They were not empty or impotent menace. They were for action, and became what they were intended for. The moneyed corporations, united with a political party, were in the field as a political power, to govern the elections, and to govern them, by the only means known to a moneyed power—by operating on the interests of men, seducing some, alarming and distressing the masses. They are the key to the manner of conducting the presidential election, and which will be spoken of in the proper place. The union of Church and State has been generally condemned: the union of Bank and State is far more condemnable. Here the union was not with the State, but with a political party, nearly as strong as the party in possession of the government, and exemplified the evils of the meretricious connection between money and politics; and nothing but this union could have produced the state of things which so long afflicted the country, and from which it has been relieved, not by the cessation of their imputed causes, but by their perpetuation. It is now near twenty years since this great meeting was held in New York. The ruinous measures complained of have not been revoked, but become permanent. They have been in full force, and made stronger, for near twenty years. The universal and black destruction which was to ensue their briefest continuance, has been substituted by the most solid, brilliant, pervading, and abiding prosperity that any people ever beheld. Thanks to the divorce of Bank and State. But the consummation was not yet. Strong in her name, and old recollections, and in her political connections—dominant over other banks—bribing with one hand, scourging with the other—a long retinue of debtors and retainers—desperate in her condition—impotent for good, powerful for evil—confederated with restless politicians, and wickedly, corruptly, and revengefully ruled: the Great Red Harlot, profaning the name of a National Bank, was still to continue a while longer its career of abominations—maintaining dubious contest with the government which created it, upon whose name and revenues it had gained the wealth and power of which it was still the shade, and whose destruction it plotted because it could not rule it. Posterity should know these things, that by avoiding bank connections, their governments may avoid the evils that we have suffered; and, by seeing the excitements of 1837, they may save themselves from ever becoming the victims of such delusion.

CHAPTER V.

ACTUAL SUSPENSION OF THE BANKS: PROPAGATION OF THE ALARM.

None of the public meetings, and there were many following the leading one in New York, recommended in terms a suspension of specie payments by the banks. All avoided, by concert or instinct, the naming of that high measure; but it was in the list, and at the head of the list, of the measures to be adopted; and every thing said or done was with a view to that crowning event; and to prepare the way for it before it came; and to plead its subsequent justification by showing its previous necessity. It was in the programme, and bound to come in its appointed time; and did—and that within a few days after the last great meeting in New York. It took place quietly and generally, on the morning of the 10th of May, altogether, and with a concert and punctuality of action, and with a military and police preparation, which announced arrangement and determination; such as attend revolts and insurrections in other countries. The preceding night all the banks of the city, three excepted, met by their officers, and adopted resolutions to close their doors in the morning: and gave out notice to that effect. At the same time three regiments of volunteers, and a squadron of horse, were placed on duty in the principal parts of the city; and the entire police force, largely reinforced with special constables, was on foot. This was to suppress the discontent of those who might be too much dissatisfied at being repulsed when they came to ask for the amount of a deposit, or the contents of a bank note. It was a humiliating spectacle, but an effectual precaution. The people remained quiet. At twelve o'clock a large mercantile meeting took place. Resolutions were adopted by it to sustain the suspension, and the newspaper press was profuse and energetic in its support. The measure was consummated: the suspension was complete: it was triumphant in that city whose example, in such a case, was law to the rest of the Union. But, let due discrimination be made. Though all the banks joined in the act, all were not equally culpable; and some, in fact, not culpable at all, but victims of the criminality, or misfortunes of others. It was the effect of necessity with the deposit banks, exhausted by vain efforts to meet the quarterly deliveries of the forty millions to be deposited with the States; and pressed on all sides because they were government banks, and because the programme required them to stop first. It was an act of self-defence in others which were too weak to stand alone, and which followed with reluctance an example which they could not resist. With others it was an act of policy, and of criminal contrivance, as the means of carrying a real distress into the ranks of the people, and exciting them against the political party to whose acts the distress was attributed. But the prime mover, and master manager of the suspension, was the Bank of the United States, then rotten to the core and tottering to its fall, but strong enough to carry others with it, and seeking to hide its own downfall in the crash of a general catastrophe. Having contrived the suspension, it wished to appear as opposing it, and as having been dragged down by others; and accordingly took the attitude of a victim. But the impudence and emptiness of that pretension was soon exposed by the difficulty which other banks had in forcing her to resume; and by the facility with which she fell back, "solitary and alone," into the state of permanent insolvency from which the other banks had momentarily galvanized her. But the occasion was too good to be lost for one of those complacent epistles, models of quiet impudence and cool mendacity, with which Mr. Biddle was accustomed to regale the public in seasons of moneyed distress. It was impossible to forego such an opportunity; and, accordingly, three days after the New York suspension, and two days after his own, he held forth in a strain of which the following is a sample:

> "All the deposit banks of the government of the United States in the city of New York suspended specie payments this week—the deposit banks elsewhere have followed their example; which was of course adopted by the State banks not connected with the government. I say of course, because it is certain that when the government banks cease to pay specie, all the other banks must cease, and for this clear reason. The great creditor in the United States is the government. It receives for duties the notes of the various banks, which are placed for collection in certain government banks, and are paid to those government banks in specie if requested. From the moment that the deposit banks of New York, failed to comply with their engagements, it was manifest that all the other deposit banks must do the same, that there must be a universal suspension throughout the country, and that the treasury itself in the midst of its nominal abundance must be practically bankrupt."

This was all true. The stoppage of the deposit banks was the stoppage of the Treasury. Non-payment by the government, was an excuse for non-payment by others. Bankruptcy was the legal condition of non-payment; and that condition was the fate of the government as well as of others; and all this was perfectly known before by those who contrived, and those who resisted the deposit with the States and the use of paper money by the federal government. These two measures made the suspension and the bankruptcy; and all this was so obvious to the writer of this View that he proclaimed it incessantly in his speeches, and was amazed at the conduct of those professing friends of the administration who voted with the opposition on these measures, and by their votes insured the bankruptcy of the government which they professed to support. Mr. Biddle was right. The deposit banks were gone; the federal treasury was bankrupt; and those two events were two steps on the road which was to lead to the re-establishment of the Bank of the United States! and Mr. Biddle stood ready with his bank to travel that road. The next paragraph displayed this readiness.

> "In the midst of these disorders the Bank of the United States occupies a peculiar position, and has special duties. Had it consulted merely its own strength it would have continued its payments without reserve. But in such a state of things the first consideration is how to escape from it—how to provide at the earliest practicable moment to change a condition which should not be tolerated beyond the necessity which commanded it. The old associations, the extensive connections, the established credit, the large capital of the Bank of the United States, rendered it the natural rallying point of the country for the resumption of specie payments. It seemed wiser, therefore, not to waste its strength in a struggle which might be doubtful while the Executive persevered in its present policy, but to husband all its resources so as to profit by the first favorable moment to take the lead in the early resumption of specie payments. Accordingly the Bank of the United States assumes that position. From this moment its efforts will be to keep itself strong, and to make itself stronger; always prepared and always anxious to assist in recalling the currency and the exchanges of the country to the point from which they have fallen. It will co-operate cordially and zealously with the government, with the government banks, with all the other banks, and with any other influences which can aid in that object."

This was a bold face for an eviscerated institution to assume—one which was then nothing but the empty skin of an immolated victim—the contriver of the suspension to cover its own rottenness, and the architect of distress and ruin that out of the public calamity it might get again into existence and replenish its coffers out of the revenues and credit of the federal government. "Would have continued specie payments, if it had only consulted its own strength"—"only suspended from a sense of duty and patriotism"—"will take the lead in resuming"—"assumes the position of restorer of the currency"—"presents itself as the rallying point of the country in the resumption of specie payments"—"even promises to co-operate with the government:" such were the impudent professions at the very moment that this restorer of currency, and rallying point of resumption, was plotting a continuance of the distress and suspension until it could get hold of the federal moneys to recover upon; and without which it never could recover.

Indissolubly connected with this bank suspension, and throwing a broad light upon its history, (if further light were wanted,) was Mr. Webster's tour to the West, and the speeches which he made in the course of it. The tour extended to the Valley of the Mississippi, and the speeches took for their burden the distress and the suspension, excusing and justifying the banks, throwing all blame upon the government, and looking to the Bank of the United States for the sole remedy. It was at Wheeling that he opened the series of speeches which he delivered in his tour, it being at that place that he was overtaken by the news of the suspension, and which furnished him with the text for his discourse.

> "Recent evils have not at all surprised me, except that they have come sooner and faster than I had anticipated. But, though not surprised, I am afflicted; I feel any thing but pleasure in this early fulfilment of my own predictions. Much injury is done which the wisest future counsels can never repair, and much more that can never be remedied but by such counsels and by the lapse of time. From 1832 to the present moment I have foreseen this result. I may safely say I have foreseen it, because I have presented and proclaimed its approach in every

important discussion and debate, in the public body of which I am a member. We learn to-day that most of the eastern banks have stopped payment; deposit banks as well as others. The experiment has exploded. That bubble, which so many of us have all along regarded as the offspring of conceit, presumption and political quackery, has burst. A general suspension of payment must be the result; a result which has come, even sooner than was predicted. Where is now that better currency that was promised? Where is that specie circulation? Where are those rupees of gold and silver, which were to fill the treasury of the government as well as the pockets of the people? Has the government a single hard dollar? Has the treasury any thing in the world but credit and deposits in banks that have already suspended payment? How are public creditors now to be paid in specie? How are the deposits, which the law requires to be made with the states on the 1st of July, now to be made."

This was the first speech that Mr. Webster delivered after the great one before the suspension in New York, and may be considered the epilogue after the performance as the former was the prologue before it. It is a speech of exultation, with bitter taunts to the government. In one respect his information was different from mine. He said the suspension came sooner than was expected: my information was that it came later, a month later; and that he himself was the cause of the delay. My information was that it was to take place in the first month of Mr. Van Buren's administration, and that the speech which was to precede it was to be delivered early in March, immediately after the adjournment of Congress: but it was not delivered till the middle of that month, nor got ready for *pamphlet* publication until the middle of April; which delay occasioned a corresponding postponement in all the subsequent proceedings. The complete shutting up of the treasury—the loss of its moneys—the substitution of broken bank paper for hard money—the impossibility of paying a dollar to a creditor: these were the points of his complacent declamation: and having made these points strong enough and clear enough, he came to the remedy, and fell upon the same one, in almost the same words, that Mr. Biddle was using at the same time, four hundred miles distant, in Philadelphia: and that without the aid of the electric telegraph, not then in use. The recourse to the Bank of the United States was that remedy! that bank strong enough to hold out, (unhappily the news of its suspending arrived while he was speaking:) patriotic enough to do so! but under no obligation to do better than the deposit banks! and justifiable in following their example. Hear him:

> "The United States Bank, now a mere state institution, with no public deposits, no aid from government, but, on the contrary, long an object of bitter persecution by it, was at our latest advices still firm. But can we expect of that Bank to make sacrifices to continue specie payment? If it continue to do so, now the deposit banks have stopped, the government will draw from it its last dollar, if it can do so, in order to keep up a pretence of making its own payments in specie. I shall be glad if this institution find it prudent and proper to hold out; but as it owes no more duty to the government than any other bank, and, of course, much less than the deposit banks, I cannot see any ground for demanding from it efforts and sacrifices to favor the government, which those holding the public money, and owing duty to the government, are unwilling or unable to make; nor do I see how the New England banks can stand alone in the general crush."

The suspension was now complete; and it was evident, and as good as admitted by those who had made it, that it was the effect of contrivance on the part of politicians, and the so-called Bank of the United States, for the purpose of restoring themselves to power. The whole process was now clear to the vision of those who could see nothing while it was going on. Even those of the democratic party whose votes had helped to do the mischief, could now see that the attempt to deposit forty millions with the States was destruction to the deposit banks;—that the repeal of the specie circular was to fill the treasury with paper money, to be found useless when wanted;—that distress was purposely created in order to throw the blame of it upon the party in power;—that the promptitude with which the Bank of the United States had been brought forward as a remedy for the distress, showed that it had been held in reserve for that purpose;—and the delight with which the whig party saluted the general calamity, showed that they considered it their own passport to power. All this became visible, after the mischief was over, to those who could see nothing of it before it was done.

CHAPTER VI.

TRANSMIGRATION OF THE BANK OF THE UNITED STATES FROM A FEDERAL TO A STATE INSTITUTION.

This institution having again appeared on the public theatre, politically and financially, and with power to influence national legislation, and to control moneyed corporations, and with art and skill enough to deceive astute merchants and trained politicians,—(for it is not to be supposed that such men would have committed themselves in her favor if they had known her condition,)—it becomes necessary to trace her history since the expiration of her charter, and learn by what means she continued an existence, apparently without change, after having undergone the process which, in law and in reason, is the death of a corporation. It is a marvellous history, opening a new chapter in the necrology of corporations, very curious to study, and involving in its solution, besides the biological mystery, the exposure of a legal fraud and juggle, a legislative smuggle, and a corrupt enactment. The charter of the corporation had expired upon its own limitation in the year 1836: it was entitled to two years to wind up its affairs, engaging in no new business: but was seen to go on after the expiration, as if still in full life, and without the change of an attribute or feature. The explanation is this:

On the 19th day of January, in the year 1836, a bill was reported in the House of Representatives of the General Assembly of Pennsylvania, entitled, "*An act to repeal the State tax, and to continue the improvement of the State by railroads and canals; and for other purposes.*" It came from the standing committee on "*Inland navigation and internal improvement*;" and was, in fact, a bill to repeal a tax and make roads and canals, but which, under the vague and usually unimportant generality of "*other purposes*," contained the entire draught of a charter for the Bank of the United States—adopting it as a Pennsylvania State bank. The introduction of the bill, with this addendum, colossal tail to it, was a surprise upon the House. No petition had asked for such a bank: no motion had been made in relation to it: no inquiry had been sent to any committee: no notice of any kind had heralded its approach: no resolve authorized its report: the unimportant clause of "*other purposes*," hung on at the end of the title, could excite no suspicion of the enormous measures which lurked under its unpretentious phraseology. Its advent was an apparition: its entrance an intrusion. Some members looked at each other in amazement. But it was soon evident that it was the minority only that was mystified—that a majority of the elected members in the House, and a cluster of exotics in the lobbies, perfectly understood the intrusive movement:—in brief, it had been smuggled into the House, and a power was present to protect it there. This was the first intimation that had reached the General Assembly, the people of Pennsylvania, or the people of the United States, that the Bank of the United States was transmigrating! changing itself from a national to a local institution—from a federal to a State charter—from an imperial to a provincial institution—retaining all the while its body and essence, its nature and attributes, its name and local habitation. It was a new species of metempsychosis, heretofore confined to souls separated from bodies, but now appearing in a body that never had a soul: for that, according to Sir Edward Coke, is the psychological condition of a corporation—and, above all, of a moneyed corporation.

The mystified members demanded explanations; and it was a case in which explanations could not be denied. Mr. Biddle, in a public letter to an eminent citizen, on whose name he had been accustomed to hang such productions, (Mr. John Quincy Adams,) attributed the procedure, so far as he had moved in it, to a "*formal application on the part of the legislature to know from him on what terms the expiring bank would receive a charter from it*;" and gave up the names of two members who had conveyed the application. The legislature had no knowledge of the proceeding. The two members whose names had been vouched disavowed the legislative application, but admitted that, in compliance with suggestions, they had written a letter to Mr. Biddle in their own names, making the inquiry; but without the sanction of the legislature, or the knowledge of the committees of which they were members. They did not explain the reason which induced them to take the initiative in so important business; and the belief took root that their good nature had yielded to an importunity from an invisible source, and that they had consented to give a private and bungling commencement to what must have a beginning, and which could not find it in any open or parliamentary form. It was truly a case in which the first step cost the difficulty. How to begin was the puzzle, and so to begin as to conceal the beginning, was the desideratum. The finger of the bank must not be seen in it, yet, without the touch of that finger, the movement could not begin. Without something from the Bank—without some request or application from it, it would have been gratuitous and impertinent, and might have been insulting and offensive, to have offered it a State charter. To apply openly for a charter was to incur a publicity which would be the defeat of the whole movement. The answer of Mr. Biddle to the two members, dexterously treating their private letter, obtained by solicitation, as a formal legislative application, surmounted the difficulty! and got the Bank before the legislature, where there were friends enough secretly prepared for the purpose to pass it through. The terms had been arranged with Mr. Biddle beforehand, so that there was nothing to be done but to vote. The principal item in these terms was the stipulation to pay the State the sum of $1,300,000, to be expended in works of internal improvements; and it was upon this slender connection with the subject that the whole charter referred itself to the committee of "*Inland navigation and internal improvement*,"—to take its place as a proviso to a bill entitled, "*To repeal the State tax, and to continue the improvements of the State by railroads and canals*;"—and to be no further indicated in the title to that act than what could be found under the addendum of that vague and flexible generality, "*other purposes*;" usually added to point attention to something not worth a specification.

Having mastered the first step—the one of greatest difficulty, if there is truth in the proverb—the remainder of the proceeding was easy and rapid, the bill, with its proviso, being reported, read a first, second, and third time, passed the House—sent to the Senate; read a first, second, and third time there, and passed—sent to the Governor and approved, and made a law of the land: and all in as little time as it usually requires to make an act for changing the name of a man or a county. To add to its titles to infamy, the repeal of the State tax which it assumed to make, took the air of a bamboozle, the tax being a temporary imposition, and to expire within a few days upon its own limitation. The distribution of the bonus took the aspect of a bribe to the people, being piddled out in driblets to the inhabitants of the counties: and, to stain the bill with the last suspicion, a strong lobby force from Philadelphia hung over its progress, and cheered it along with the affection and solicitude of parents for their offspring. Every circumstance of its enactment announced corruption—bribery in the members who passed the act, and an attempt to bribe the people by distributing the bonus among them: and the outburst of indignation throughout the State was vehement and universal. People met in masses to condemn the act, demand its repeal, to denounce the members who voted for it, and to call for investigation into the manner in which it passed. Of course, the legislature which passed it was in no haste to respond to these demands; but their successors were different. An election intervened; great changes of members took place; two-thirds of the new legislature demanded investigation, and resolved to have it. A committee was appointed, with the usual ample powers, and sat the usual length of time, and worked with the usual indefatigability, and made the usual voluminous report; and with the usual "lame and impotent conclusion." A mass of pregnant circumstances were collected, covering the whole case with black suspicion: but direct bribery was proved upon no one. Probably, the case of the Yazoo fraud is to be the last, as it was the first, in which a succeeding general assembly has fully and unqualifiedly condemned its predecessor for corruption.

The charter thus obtained was accepted: and, without the change of form or substance in any particular, the old bank moved on as if nothing had happened—as if the Congress charter was still in force—as if a corporate institution and all its affairs could be shifted by statute from one foundation to another;—as if a transmigration of corporate existence could be operated by legislative enactment, and the debtors, creditors, depositors, and stockholders in one bank changed, transformed, and constituted into debtors, creditors, depositors and stockholders in another. The illegality of the whole proceeding was as flagrant as it was corrupt—as scandalous as it was notorious—and could only find its motive in the consciousness of a condition in which detection adds infamy to ruin; and in which no infamy, to be incurred, can exceed that from which escape is sought. And yet it was this broken and rotten institution—this criminal committing crimes to escape from the detection of crimes—this "counterfeit presentment" of a defunct corporation—this addendum to a Pennsylvania railroad— this whited sepulchre filled with dead men's bones, thus bribed and smuggled through a local legislature—that was still able to set up for a power and a benefactor! still able to influence federal legislation—control other banks—deceive merchants and statesmen—excite a popular current in its favor—assume a guardianship over the public affairs, and actually dominate for months longer in the legislation and the business of the country. It is for the part she acted—the dominating part—in contriving the financial distress and the general suspension of the banks in 1837—the last one which has afflicted our country,—that renders necessary and proper this notice of her corrupt transit through the General Assembly of the State of Pennsylvania.

CHAPTER VII.

EFFECTS OF THE SUSPENSION: GENERAL DERANGEMENT OF BUSINESS: SUPPRESSION AND RIDICULE OF THE SPECIE CURRENCY: SUBMISSION OF THE PEOPLE: CALL OF CONGRESS.

A great disturbance of course took place in the business of the country, from the stoppage of the banks. Their agreement to receive each others' notes made these notes the sole currency of the country. It was a miserable substitute for gold and silver, falling far below these metals when measured against them, and very unequal to each other in different parts of the country. Those of the interior, and of the west, being unfit for payments in the great commercial Atlantic cities, were far below the standard of the notes of those cities, and suffered a heavy loss from difference of exchange, as it was called (although it was only the difference of depreciation,) in all remittances to those cities:—to which points the great payments tended. All this difference was considered a loss, and charged upon the mismanagement of the public affairs by the administration, although the clear effect of geographical position. Specie disappeared as a currency, being systematically suppressed. It became an article of merchandise, bought and sold like any other marketable commodity; and especially bought in quantities for exportation. Even metallic change disappeared, down to the lowest subdivision of the dollar. Its place was supplied by every conceivable variety of individual and corporation tickets—issued by some from a feeling of necessity; by others, as a means of small gains; by many, politically, as a means of exciting odium against the administration for having destroyed the currency. Fictitious and burlesque notes were issued with caricatures and grotesque pictures and devices, and reproachful sentences, entitled the "*better currency*:" and exhibited every where to excite contempt. They were sent in derision to all the friends of the specie circular, especially to him who had the credit (not untruly) of having been its prime mover—most of them plentifully sprinkled over with taunting expressions to give them a personal application: such as—"This is what you have brought the country to:" "the end of the experiment:" "the gold humbug exploded:" "is this what was promised us?" "behold the effects of tampering with the currency." The presidential mansion was infested, and almost polluted with these missives, usually made the cover of some vulgar taunt. Even gold and silver could not escape the attempted degradation—copper, brass, tin, iron pieces being struck in imitation of gold and silver coins—made ridiculous by figures and devices, usually the whole hog, and inscribed with taunting and reproachful expressions. Immense sums were expended in these derisory manufactures, extensively carried on, and universally distributed; and reduced to a system as a branch of party warfare, and intended to act on the thoughtless and ignorant through appeals to their eyes and passions. Nor were such means alone resorted to to inflame the multitude against the administration. The opposition press teemed with inflammatory publications. The President and his friends were held up as great state criminals, ruthlessly destroying the property of the people, and meriting punishment—even death. Nor did these publications appear in thoughtless or obscure papers only, but in some of the most weighty and influential of the bank party. Take, for example, this paragraph from a leading paper in the city of New York:

> "We would put it directly to each and all of our readers, whether it becomes this great people, quietly and tamely to submit to any and every degree of lawless oppression which their rulers may inflict, merely because *resistance* may involve us in trouble and expose those who resist, to censure? We are very certain their reply will be, '*No*, but at what point is "resistance to commence?"—is not the evil of resistance greater "than the evil of submission?"' We answer promptly, that resistance on the part of a free people, if they would preserve their freedom, should always commence whenever it is made plain and palpable that there has been a deliberate violation of their rights; and whatever temporary evils may result from such resistance, it can never be so great or so dangerous to our institutions, as a blind submission to a most manifest act of oppression and tyranny. And now, we would ask of all—what shadow of right, what plea of expediency, what constitutional or legal justification can MARTIN VAN BUREN offer to the people of the United States, for having brought upon them all their present difficulties by a continuance of the *specie circular*, after two-thirds of their representatives had declared their solemn convictions that it was injurious to the country and should be repealed? Most assuredly, none, and we unhesitatingly say, that it is a more high-

handed measure of *tyranny* than that which cost *Charles* the 1st his crown and his head—more illegal and unconstitutional than the act of the British ministry which caused the patriots of the revolution to destroy the tea in the harbor of Boston—and one which calls more loudly for resistance than any act of Great Britain which led to the Declaration of Independence."

Taken by surprise in the deprivation of its revenues,—specie denied it by the banks which held its gold and silver,—the federal government could only do as others did, and pay out depreciated paper. Had the event been foreseen by the government, it might have been provided against, and much specie saved. It was now too late to enter into a contest with the banks, they in possession of the money, and the suspension organized and established. They would only render their own notes: the government could only pay in that which it received. Depreciated paper was their only medium of payment; and every such payment (only received from a feeling of duresse) brought resentment, reproach, indignation, loss of popularity to the administration; and loud calls for the re-establishment of the National Bank, whose notes had always been equal to specie, and were then contrived to be kept far above the level of those of other suspended banks. Thus the administration found itself, in the second month of its existence, struggling with that most critical of all government embarrassments—deranged finances, and depreciated currency; and its funds dropping off every day. Defections were incessant, and by masses, and sometimes by whole States: and all on account of these vile payments in depreciated paper. Take a single example. The State of Tennessee had sent numerous volunteers to the Florida Indian war. There were several thousands of them, and came from thirty different counties, requiring payments to be made through a large part of the State, and to some member of almost every family in it. The paymaster, Col. Adam Duncan Steuart, had treasury drafts on the Nashville deposit banks for the money to make the payments. They delivered their own notes, and these far below par—even twenty per cent. below those of the so-called Bank of the United States, which the policy of the suspension required to be kept in strong contrast with those of the government deposit banks. The loss on each payment was great—one dollar in every five. Even patriotism could not stand it. The deposit banks and their notes were execrated: the Bank of the United States and its notes were called for. It was the children of Israel wailing for the fleshpots of Egypt. Discontent, from individual became general, extending from persons to masses. The State took the infection. From being one of the firmest and foremost of the democratic States, Tennessee fell off from her party, and went into opposition. At the next election she showed a majority of 20,000 against her old friends; and that in the lifetime of General Jackson; and contrary to what it would have been if his foresight had been seconded. He foresaw the consequences of paying out this depreciated paper. The paymaster had foreseen them, and before drawing a dollar from the banks he went to General Jackson for his advice. This energetic man, then aged, and dying, and retired to his beloved hermitage,—but all head and nerve to the last, and scorning to see the government capitulate to insurgent banks,—acted up to his character. He advised the paymaster to proceed to Washington and ask for solid money—for the gold and silver which was then lying in the western land offices. He went; but being a military subordinate, he only applied according to the rules of subordination, through the channels of official intercourse: and was denied the hard money, wanted for payments on debenture bonds and officers of the government. He did not go to Mr. Van Buren, as General Jackson intended he should do. He did not feel himself authorized to go beyond official routine. It was in the recess of Congress, and I was not in Washington to go to the President in his place (as I should instantly have done); and, returning without the desired orders, the payments were made, through a storm of imprecations, in this loathsome trash: and Tennessee was lost. And so it was, in more or less degree, throughout the Union. The first object of the suspension had been accomplished—a political revolt against the administration.

Miserable as was the currency which the government was obliged to use, it was yet in the still more miserable condition of not having enough of it! The deposits with the States had absorbed two sums of near ten millions each: two more sums of equal amount were demandable in the course of the year. Financial embarrassment, and general stagnation of business, diminished the current receipts from lands and customs: an absolute deficit—that horror, and shame, and mortal test of governments—showed itself ahead. An extraordinary session of Congress became a necessity, inexorable to any contrivance of the administration: and, on the 15th day of May—just five days after the suspension in the principal cities—the proclamation was issued for its assembling: to take place on the first Monday of the ensuing September. It was a mortifying concession to imperative circumstances; and the more so as it had just been refused to the grand committee of Fifty—demanding it in the imposing name of that great meeting in the city of New York.

CHAPTER VIII.

EXTRA SESSION: MESSAGE, AND RECOMMENDATIONS.

The first session of the twenty-fifth Congress, convened upon the proclamation of the President, to meet an extraordinary occasion, met on the first Monday in September, and consisted of the following members:

SENATE.

NEW HAMPSHIRE—Henry Hubbard and Franklin Pierce.

MAINE—John Ruggles and Ruel Williams.

VERMONT—Samuel Prentiss and Benjamin Swift.

MASSACHUSETTS—Daniel Webster and John Davis.

RHODE ISLAND—Nehemiah R. Knight and Asher Robbins.

Connecticut—John M. Niles and Perry Smith.

New York—Silas Wright and Nathaniel P. Tallmadge.

New Jersey—Garret D. Wall and Samuel L. Southard.

Delaware—Richard H. Bayard and Thomas Clayton.

Pennsylvania—James Buchanan and Samuel McKean.

Maryland—Joseph Kent and John S. Spence.

Virginia—William C. Rives and William H. Roane.

NORTH CAROLINA—Bedford Brown and Robert Strange.

SOUTH CAROLINA—John C. Calhoun and Wm. Campbell Preston.

GEORGIA—John P. King and Alfred Cuthbert.

ALABAMA—Wm. Rufus King and Clement C. Clay.

MISSISSIPPI—John Black and Robert J. Walker.

LOUISIANA—Robert C. Nicholas and Alexander Mouton.

TENNESSEE—Hugh L. White and Felix Grundy.

KENTUCKY—Henry Clay and John Crittenden.

ARKANSAS—Ambrose H. Sevier and William S. Fulton.

MISSOURI—Thomas H. Benton and Lewis F. Linn.

ILLINOIS—Richard M. Young and John M. Robinson.

INDIANA—Oliver H. Smith and John Tipton.

OHIO—William Allen and Thomas Morris.

MICHIGAN—Lucius Lyon and John Norvell.

HOUSE OF REPRESENTATIVES.

MAINE—George Evans, John Fairfield, Timothy J. Carter, F. O. J. Smith, Thomas Davee, Jonathan Cilley, Joseph C. Noyes, Hugh J. Anderson.

NEW HAMPSHIRE—Samuel Cushman, James Farrington, Charles G. Atherton, Joseph Weeks, Jared W. Williams.

MASSACHUSETTS—Richard Fletcher, Stephen C. Phillips, Caleb Cushing, Wm. Parmenter, Levi Lincoln, George Grinnell, jr., George N. Briggs, Wm. B. Calhoun, Nathaniel B. Borden, John Q. Adams, John Reed, Abbott Lawrence, Wm. S. Hastings.

RHODE ISLAND—Robert B. Cranston, Joseph L. Tillinghast.

CONNECTICUT—Isaac Toucey, Samuel Ingham, Elisha Haley, Thomas T. Whittlesey, Launcelot Phelps, Orrin Holt.

VERMONT—Hiland Hall, William Slade, Heman Allen, Isaac Fletcher, Horace Everett.

NEW YORK—Thomas B. Jackson, Abraham Vanderveer, C. C. Cambreleng, Ely Moore, Edward Curtis, Ogden Hoffman, Gouverneur Kemble, Obadiah Titus, Nathaniel Jones, John C. Broadhead, Zadoc Pratt, Robert McClelland, Henry Vail, Albert Gallup, John I. DeGraff, David Russell, John Palmer, James B. Spencer, John Edwards, Arphaxad Loomis, Henry A. Foster, Abraham P. Grant, Isaac H. Bronson, John H. Prentiss, Amasa J. Parker, John C. Clark, Andrew D. W. Bruyn, Hiram Gray, William Taylor, Bennett Bicknell, William H. Noble, Samuel Birdsall, Mark H. Sibley, John T. Andrews, Timothy Childs, William Patterson, Luther C. Peck, Richard P. Marvin, Millard Fillmore, Charles F. Mitchell.

NEW JERSEY—John B. Aycrigg, John P. B. Maxwell, William Halstead, Jos. F. Randolph, Charles G. Stratton, Thomas Jones Yorke.

PENNSYLVANIA—Lemuel Paynter, John Sergeant, George W. Toland, Charles Naylor, Edward Davies, David Potts, Edward Darlington, Jacob Fry, jr., Matthias Morris, David D. Wagener, Edward B. Hubley, Henry A. Muhlenberg, Luther Reilly, Henry Logan, Daniel Sheffer, Chas. McClure, Wm. W. Potter, David Petriken, Robert H. Hammond, Samuel W. Morris, Charles Ogle, John Klingensmith, Andrew Buchanan, T. M. T. McKennan, Richard Biddle, William Beatty, Thomas Henry, Arnold Plumer.

DELAWARE—John J. Milligan.

MARYLAND—John Dennis, James A. Pearce, J. T. H. Worthington, Benjamin C. Howard, Isaac McKim, William Cost Johnson, Francis Thomas, Daniel Jenifer.

VIRGINIA—Henry A. Wise, Francis Mallory, John Robertson, Charles F. Mercer, John Taliaferro, R. T. M. Hunter, James Garland, Francis E. Rives, Walter Coles, George C. Dromgoole, James W. Bouldin, John M. Patton, James M. Mason, Isaac S. Pennybacker, Andrew Beirne, Archibald Stuart, John W. Jones, Robert Craig, Geo. W. Hopkins, Joseph Johnson, Wm. S. Morgan.

NORTH CAROLINA—Jesse A. Bynum, Edward D. Stanley, Charles Shepard, Micajah T. Hawkins, James McKay, Edmund Deberry, Abraham Rencher, William Montgomery, Augustine H. Shepherd, James Graham, Henry Connor, Lewis Williams, Samuel T. Sawyer.

SOUTH CAROLINA—H. S. Legare, Waddy Thompson, Francis W. Pickens, W. K. Clowney, F. H. Elmore, John K. Griffin, R. B. Smith, John Campbell, John P. Richardson.

GEORGIA—Thomas Glascock, S. F. Cleveland, Seaton Grantland, Charles E. Haynes, Hopkins Holsey, Jabez Jackson, Geo. W. Owens, Geo. W. B. Townes, W. C. Dawson.

TENNESSEE—Wm. B. Carter, A. A. McClelland, Joseph Williams, (one vacancy,) H. L. Turney, Wm. B. Campbell, John Bell, Abraham P. Maury, James K. Polk, Ebenezer J. Shields, Richard Cheatham, John W. Crockett, Christopher H. Williams.

KENTUCKY—John L. Murray, Edward Rumsey, Sherrod Williams, Joseph R. Underwood, James Harlan, John Calhoun, John Pope, Wm. J. Graves, John White, Richard Hawes, Richard H. Menifee, John Chambers, Wm. W. Southgate.

OHIO—Alexander Duncan, Taylor Webster, Patrick G. Goode, Thomas Corwin, Thomas L. Hamer, Calvary Morris, Wm. K. Bond, J. Ridgeway, John Chaney, Samson Mason, J. Alexander, jr., Alexander Harper, D. P. Leadbetter, Wm. H. Hunter, John W. Allen, Elisha Whittlesey, A. W. Loomis, Matthias Shepler, Daniel Kilgore.

ALABAMA—Francis S. Lyon, Dixon H. Lewis, Joab Lawler, Reuben Chapman, J. L. Martin.

INDIANA—Ratliff Boon, John Ewing, William Graham, George H. Dunn, James Rariden, William Herrod, Albert S. White.

ILLINOIS—A. W. Snyder, Zadoc Casey, Wm. L. May.

LOUISIANA—Henry Johnson, Eleazer W. Ripley, Rice Garland.

MISSISSIPPI—John F. H. Claiborne, S. H. Gholson.

ARKANSAS—Archibald Yell.

MISSOURI—Albert G. Harrison, John Miller.

MICHIGAN—Isaac E. Crary.

FLORIDA—Charles Downing.

WISCONSIN—George W. Jones.

In these ample lists, both of the Senate and of the House, will be discovered a succession of eminent names—many which had then achieved eminence, others to achieve it:—and, besides those which captivate regard by splendid ability, a still larger number of those less brilliant, equally respectable, and often more useful members, whose business talent performs the work of the body, and who in England are well called, the working members. Of these numerous members, as well the brilliant as the useful, it would be invidious to particularize part without enumerating the whole; and that would require a reproduction of the greater part of the list of each House. Four only can be named, and they entitled to that distinction from the station attained, or to be attained by them:—Mr. John Quincy Adams, who had been president; *Messrs.* James K. Polk, Millard Fillmore and Franklin Pierce, who became presidents. In my long service I have not seen a more able Congress; and it is only necessary to read over the names, and to possess some knowledge of our public men, to be struck with the number of names which would come under the description of useful or brilliant members.

The election of speaker was the first business of the House; and Mr. James K. Polk and Mr. John Bell, both of Tennessee, being put in nomination, Mr. Polk received 116 votes; and was elected—Mr. Bell receiving 103. Mr. Walter S. Franklin was elected clerk.

The message was delivered upon receiving notice of the organization of the two Houses; and, with temperance and firmness, it met all the exigencies of the occasion. That specie order which had been the subject of so much denunciation,—the imputed cause of the suspension, and the revocation of which was demanded with so much pertinacity and such imposing demonstration,—far from being given up was commended for the good effects it had produced; and the determination expressed not to interfere with its operation. In relation to that decried measure the message said:

> "Of my own duties under the existing laws, when the banks suspended specie payments, I could not doubt. Directions were immediately given to prevent the reception into the Treasury of any thing but gold and silver, or its equivalent; and every practicable arrangement was made to preserve the public faith, by similar or equivalent payments to the public creditors. The revenue from lands had been for some time substantially so collected, under the order issued by the directions of my predecessor. The effects of that order had been so salutary, and its forecast in regard to the increasing insecurity of bank paper had become so apparent, that, even before the catastrophe, I had resolved not to interfere with its operation. Congress is now to decide whether the revenue shall continue to be so collected, or not."

This was explicit, and showed that all attempts to operate upon the President at that point, and to coerce the revocation of a measure which he deemed salutary, had totally failed. The next great object of the party which had contrived the suspension and organized the distress, was to extort the re-establishment of the Bank of the United States; and here again was an equal failure to operate upon the firmness of the President. He reiterated his former objections to such an institution—not merely to the particular one which had been tried—but to any one in any form, and declared his former convictions to be strengthened by recent events. Thus:

> "We have seen for nearly half a century, that those who advocate a national bank, by whatever motive they may be influenced, constitute a portion of our community too numerous to allow us to hope for an early abandonment of their favorite plan. On the other hand, they must indeed form an erroneous estimate of the intelligence and temper of the American people, who suppose that they have continued, on slight or insufficient grounds, their persevering opposition to such an institution; or that they can be induced by pecuniary pressure, or by any other combination of circumstances, to surrender principles they have so long and so inflexibly maintained. My own views of the subject are unchanged. They have been repeatedly and unreservedly announced to my fellow-citizens, who, with full knowledge of them, conferred upon me the two highest offices of the government. On the last of these occasions, I felt it due to the people to apprise them distinctly, that, in the event of my election, I would not be able to co-operate in the re-establishment of a national bank. To these sentiments, I have now only to add the expression of an increased conviction, that the re-establishment of such a bank, in any form, whilst it would not accomplish the beneficial purpose promised by its advocates, would impair the rightful supremacy of the popular will; injure the character and diminish the influence of our political system; and bring once more into existence a concentrated moneyed power, hostile to the spirit, and threatening the permanency, of our republican institutions."

Having noticed these two great points of pressure upon him, and thrown them off with equal strength and decorum, he went forward to a new point—the connection of the federal government with any bank of issue in any form, either as a depository of its moneys, or in the use of its notes;—and recommended a total and perpetual dissolution of the connection. This was a new point of policy, long meditated by some, but now first brought forward for legislative action, and cogently recommended to Congress for its adoption. The message, referring to the recent failure of the banks, took advantage of it to say:

> "Unforeseen in the organization of the government, and forced on the Treasury by early necessities, the practice of employing banks, was, in truth, from the beginning, more a measure of emergency than of sound policy. When we started into existence as a nation, in addition to the burdens of the new government, we assumed all the large, but honorable load, of debt which was the price of our liberty; but we hesitated to weigh down the infant industry of the country by resorting to adequate taxation for the necessary revenue. The facilities of banks, in return for the privileges they acquired, were promptly offered, and perhaps too readily received, by an embarrassed treasury. During the long continuance of a national debt, and the intervening difficulties of a foreign war, the connection was continued from motives of convenience; but these causes have long since passed away. We have no emergencies that make banks necessary to aid the wants of the Treasury; we have no load of national debt to provide for, and we have on actual deposit a large surplus. No public interest, therefore, now requires the renewal of a connection that circumstances have dissolved. The complete organization of our government, the abundance of our resources, the general harmony which prevails between the different States, and with foreign powers, all enable us now to select the system most consistent with the constitution, and most conducive to the public welfare."

This wise recommendation laid the foundation for the Independent Treasury—a measure opposed with unwonted violence at the time, but vindicated as well by experience as recommended by wisdom; and now universally concurred in—constituting an era in our financial history, and reflecting distinctive credit on Mr. Van Buren's administration. But he did not stop at proposing a dissolution of governmental connection with these institutions; he went further, and proposed to make them safer for the community, and more amenable to the laws of the land. These institutions exercised the privilege of stopping payment, qualified by the gentle name of suspension, when they judged a condition of the country existed making it expedient to do so. Three of these general suspensions had taken place in the last quarter of a century, presenting an evil entirely too large for the remedy of individual suits against the delinquent banks; and requiring the strong arm of a general and authoritative proceeding. This could only be found in subjecting them to the process of bankruptcy; and this the message boldly recommended. It was the first recommendation of the kind, and deserves to be commemorated for its novelty and boldness, and its undoubted efficiency, if adopted. This is the recommendation:

> "In the mean time, it is our duty to provide all the remedies against a depreciated paper currency which the constitution enables us to afford. The Treasury Department, on several former occasions, has suggested the propriety and importance of a uniform law concerning bankruptcies of corporations, and other bankers. Through the instrumentality of such a law, a salutary check may doubtless be imposed on the issues of paper money, and an effectual remedy given to the citizen, in a way at once equal in all parts of the Union, and fully authorized by the constitution."

A bankrupt law for banks! That was the remedy. Besides its efficacy in preventing future suspensions, it would be a remedy for the actual one. The day fixed for the act to take effect would be the day for resuming payments, or going into liquidation. It would be the day of honesty or death to these corporations; and between these two alternatives even the most refractory bank would choose the former, if able to do so.

The banks of the District of Columbia, and their currency, being under the jurisdiction of Congress, admitted a direct remedy in its own legislation, both for the fact of their suspension and the evil of the small notes which they issued. The forfeiture of the charter, where the resumption did not take place in a limited time, and penalties on the issue of the small notes, were the appropriate remedies;—and, as such were recommended to Congress.

There the President not only met and confronted the evils of the actual suspension as they stood, but went further, and provided against the recurrence of such evils thereafter, in four cardinal recommendations: 1, never to have another national bank; 2, never to receive bank notes again in payment of federal dues; 3, never to use the banks again for depositories of the public moneys; 4, to apply the process of bankruptcy to all future defaulting banks. These were strong recommendations, all founded in a sense of justice to the public, and called for by the supremacy of the government, if it meant to maintain its supremacy; but recommendations running deep into the pride and interests of a powerful class, and well calculated to inflame still higher the formidable combination already arrayed against the President, and to extend it to all that should support him.

The immediate cause for convoking the extraordinary session—the approaching deficit in the revenue—was frankly stated, and the remedy as frankly proposed. Six millions of dollars was the estimated amount; and to provide it neither loans nor taxes were proposed, but the retention of the fourth instalment of the deposit to be made with the States, and a temporary issue of treasury notes to supply the deficiency until the incoming revenue should replenish the treasury. The following was that recommendation:

> "It is not proposed to procure the required amount by loans or increased taxation. There are now in the treasury nine millions three hundred and sixty-seven thousand two hundred and fourteen dollars, directed by the Act of the 23d of June, 1836, to be deposited with the States in October next. This sum, if so deposited, will be subject, under the law, to be recalled, if needed, to defray existing appropriations; and, as it is now evident that the whole, or the principal part of it, will be wanted for that purpose, it appears most proper that the deposits should be withheld. Until the amount can be collected from the banks, treasury notes may be temporarily issued, to be gradually redeemed as it is received."

Six millions of treasury notes only were required, and from this small amount required, it is easy to see how readily an adequate amount could have been secured from the deposit banks, if the administration had foreseen a month or two beforehand that the suspension was to take place. An issue of treasury notes, being an imitation of the exchequer bill issues of the British government, which had been the facile and noiseless way of swamping that government in bottomless debt, was repugnant to the policy of this writer, and opposed by him: but of this hereafter. The third instalment of the deposit, as it was called, had been received by the States—received in depreciated paper, and the fourth demanded in the same. A deposit demanded! and claimed as a debt!—that is to say: the word "*deposit*" used in the act admitted to be both by Congress and the States a fraud and a trick, and distribution the thing intended and done. Seldom has it happened that so gross a fraud, and one, too, intended to cheat the constitution, has been so promptly acknowledged by the high parties perpetrating it. But of this also hereafter.

The decorum and reserve of a State paper would not allow the President to expatiate upon the enormity of the suspension which had been contrived, nor to discriminate between the honest and solvent banks which had been taken by surprise and swept off in a current which they could not resist, and the insolvent or criminal class, which contrived the catastrophe and exulted in its success. He could only hint at the discrimination, and, while recommending the bankrupt process for one class, to express his belief that with all the honest and solvent institutions the suspension would be temporary, and that they would seize the earliest moment which the conduct of others would permit, to vindicate their integrity and ability by returning to specie payments.

CHAPTER IX.

ATTACKS ON THE MESSAGE: TREASURY NOTES.

Under the first two of our Presidents, Washington, and the first Mr. Adams, the course of the British Parliament was followed in answering the address of the President, as the course of the sovereign was followed in delivering it. The Sovereign delivered his address in person to the two assembled Houses, and each answered it: our two first Presidents did the same, and the Houses answered. The purport of the answer was always to express a concurrence, or non-concurrence with the general policy of the government as thus authentically exposed; and the privilege of answering the address laid open the policy of the government to the fullest discussion. The effect of the practice was to lay open the state of the country, and the public policy, to the fullest discussion; and, in the character of the answer, to decide the question of accord or disaccord—of support or opposition—between the representative and the executive branches of the government. The change from the address delivered in person, with its answer, to the message sent by the private secretary, and no answer, was introduced by Mr. Jefferson, and considered a reform; but it was questioned at the time, whether any good would come of it, and whether that would not be done irregularly, in the course of the debates, which otherwise would have been done regularly in the discussion of the address. The administration policy would be sure to be attacked, and irregularly, in the course of business, if the spirit of opposition should not be allowed full indulgence in a general and regular discussion. The attacks would come, and many of Mr. Jefferson's friends thought it better they should come at once, and occupy the first week or two of the session, than to be scattered through the whole session and mixed up with all its business. But the change was made, and has stood, and now any bill or motion is laid hold of, to hang a speech upon, against the measures or policy of an administration. This was signally the case at this extra session, in relation to Mr. Van Buren's policy. He had staked himself too decisively against too large a combination of interests to expect moderation or justice from his opponents; and he received none. Seldom has any President been visited with more violent and general assaults than he received, almost every opposition speaker assailing some part of the message. One of the number, Mr. Caleb Cushing, of Massachusetts, made it a business to reply to the whole document, formally and elaborately, under two and thirty distinct heads—the number of points in the mariner's compass: each head bearing a caption to indicate its point: and in that speech any one that chooses, can find in a condensed form, and convenient for reading, all the points of accusation against the democratic policy from the beginning of the government down to that day.

Mr. Clay and Mr. Webster assailed it for what it contained, and for what it did not—for its specific recommendations, and for its omission to recommend measures which they deemed necessary. The specie payments—the disconnection with banks—the retention of the fourth instalment—the bankrupt act against banks—the brief issue of treasury notes; all were condemned as measures improper in themselves and inadequate to the relief of the country: while, on the other hand, a national bank appeared to them to be the proper and adequate remedy for the public evils. With them acted many able men:—in the Senate, Bayard, of Delaware, Crittenden, of Kentucky, John Davis, of Massachusetts, Preston, of South Carolina, Southard, of New Jersey, Rives, of Virginia:—in the House of Representatives, Mr. John Quincy Adams, Bell, of Tennessee, Richard Biddle, of Pennsylvania, Cushing, of Massachusetts, Fillmore, of New York, Henry Johnson, of Louisiana, Hunter and Mercer, of Virginia, John Pope, of Kentucky, John Sargeant, Underwood of Kentucky, Lewis Williams, Wise. All these were speaking members, and in their diversity of talent displayed all the varieties of effective speaking—close reasoning, sharp invective, impassioned declamation, rhetoric, logic.

On the other hand was an equal array, both in number and speaking talent, on the other side, defending and supporting the recommendations of the President:—in the Senate, Silas Wright, Grundy, John M. Niles, King, of Alabama, Strange, of North Carolina, Buchanan, Calhoun, Linn, of Missouri, Benton, Bedford Brown, of North Carolina, William Allen, of Ohio, John P. King, of Georgia, Walker, of Mississippi:—in the House of Representatives, Cambreleng, of New York, Hamer, of Ohio, Howard and Francis Thomas, of Maryland, McKay, of North Carolina, John M. Patton, Francis Pickens.

The treasury note bill was one of the first measures on which the struggle took place. It was not a favorite with the whole body of the democracy, but the majority preferred a small issue of that paper, intended to operate, not as a currency, but as a ready means of borrowing money, and especially from small capitalists; and, therefore, preferable to a direct loan. It was opposed as a paper money bill in disguise, as germinating a new national debt, and as the easy mode of raising money, so ready to run into abuse from its very facility of use. The President had recommended the issue in general terms: the Secretary of the Treasury had descended into detail, and proposed notes as low as twenty dollars, and without interest. The Senate's committee rejected that proposition, and reported a bill only for large notes—none less than 100 dollars, and bearing interest; so as to be used for investment, not circulation. Mr. Webster assailed the Secretary's plan, saying—

> "He proposes, sir, to issue treasury notes of small denominations, down even as low as twenty dollars, not bearing interest, and redeemable at no fixed period; they are to be received in debts due to government, but are not otherwise to be paid until at some indefinite time there shall be a certain surplus in the treasury beyond what the Secretary may think its wants require. Now, sir, this is plain, authentic, statutable paper money; it is exactly a new emission of old continental. If the genius of the old confederation were now to rise up in the midst of us, he could not furnish us, from the abundant stores of his recollection, with a more perfect model of paper money. It carries no interest; it has no fixed time of payment; it is to circulate as currency, and it is to circulate on the credit of government alone, with no fixed period of redemption! If this be not paper money, pray, sir, what is it? And, sir, who expected this? Who expected that in the fifth year of the *experiment for reforming the currency*, and bringing it to an absolute gold and silver circulation, the Treasury Department would be found recommending to us a regular emission of paper money? This, sir, is quite new in the history of this government; it belongs to that of the confederation which has passed away. Since 1789, although we have issued treasury notes on sundry occasions, we have issued none like these; that is to say, we have issued none not bearing interest, intended for circulation, and with no fixed mode of redemption. I am glad, however, Mr. President, that the committee have not adopted the Secretary's recommendation, and that they have recommended the issue of treasury notes of a description more conformable to the practice of the government."

Mr. Benton, though opposed to the policy of issuing these notes, and preferring himself a direct loan in this case, yet defended the particular bill which had been brought in from the character and effects ascribed to it, and said:

> "He should not have risen in this debate, had it not been for the misapprehensions which seemed to pervade the minds of some senators as to the character of the bill. It is called by some a paper-money bill, and by others a bill to germinate a new national debt. These are serious imputations, and require to be answered, not by declamation and recrimination, but by facts and reasons, addressed to the candor and to the intelligence of an enlightened and patriotic community.

> "I dissent from the imputations on the character of the bill. I maintain that it is neither a paper-money bill, nor a bill to lay the foundation for a new national debt; and will briefly give my reasons for believing as I do on both points.

> "There are certainly two classes of treasury notes—one for investment, and one for circulation; and both classes are known to our laws, and possess distinctive features, which define their respective characters, and confine them to their respective uses.

> "The notes for investment bear an interest sufficient to induce capitalists to exchange gold and silver for them, and to lay them by as a productive fund. This is their distinctive feature, but not the only one; they possess other subsidiary qualities, such as transferability only by indorsement—payable at a fixed time—not re-issuable—nor of small denomination—and to be cancelled when paid. Notes of this class are, in fact, loan notes—notes to raise loans on, by selling them for hard money—either immediately by the Secretary of the Treasury, or, secondarily, by the creditor of the government to whom they have been paid. In a word, they possess all the qualities which invite investment, and forbid and impede circulation.

"The treasury notes for currency are distinguished by features and qualities the reverse of those which have been mentioned. They bear little or no interest. They are payable to bearer—transferable by delivery—re-issuable—of low denominations—and frequently reimbursable at the pleasure of the government. They are, in fact, paper money, and possess all the qualities which forbid investment, and invite to circulation. The treasury notes of 1815 were of that character, except for the optional clause to enable the holder to fund them at the interest which commanded loans—at seven per cent.

"These are the distinctive features of the two classes of notes. Now try the committee's bill by the test of these qualities. It will be found that the notes which it authorizes belong to the first-named class; that they are to bear an interest, which may be six per cent.; that they are transferable only by indorsement; that they are not re-issuable; that they are to be paid at a day certain—to wit, within one year; that they are not to be issued of less denomination than one hundred dollars; are to be cancelled when taken up; and that the Secretary of the Treasury is expressly authorized to raise money upon them by loaning them.

"These are the features and qualities of the notes to be issued, and they define and fix their character as notes to raise loans, and to be laid by as investments, and not as notes for currency, to be pushed into circulation by the power of the government; and to add to the curse of the day by increasing the quantity of unconvertible paper money."

Though yielding to an issue of these notes in this particular form, limited in size of the notes to one hundred dollars, yet Mr. Benton deemed it due to himself and the subject to enter a protest against the policy of such issues, and to expose their dangerous tendency, both to slide into a paper currency, and to steal by a noiseless march into the creation of public debt, and thus expressed himself:

"I trust I have vindicated the bill from the stigma of being a paper currency bill, and from the imputation of being the first step towards the creation of a new national debt. I hope it is fully cleared from the odium of both these imputations. I will now say a few words on the policy of issuing treasury notes in time of peace, or even in time of war, until the ordinary resources of loans and taxes had been tried and exhausted. I am no friend to the issue of treasury notes of any kind. As loans, they are a disguised mode of borrowing, and easy to slide into a currency: as a currency, it is the most seductive, the most dangerous, and the most liable to abuse of all the descriptions of paper money. 'The stamping of paper (by government) is an operation so much easier than the laying of taxes, or of borrowing money, that a government in the habit of paper emissions would rarely fail, in any emergency, to indulge itself too far in the employment of that resource, to avoid as much as possible one less auspicious to present popularity.' So said General Hamilton; and Jefferson, Madison Macon, Randolph, and all the fathers of the republican church, concurred with him. These sagacious statesmen were shy of this facile and seductive resource, 'so liable to abuse, and so certain of being abused.' They held it inadmissible to recur to it in time of peace, and that it could only be thought of amidst the exigencies and perils of war, and that after exhausting the direct and responsible alternative of loans and taxes. Bred in the school of these great men, I came here at this session to oppose, at all risks, an issue of treasury notes. I preferred a direct loan, and that for many and cogent reasons. There is clear authority to borrow in the constitution; but, to find authority to issue these notes, we must enter the field of constructive powers. To borrow, is to do a responsible act; it is to incur certain accountability to the constituent, and heavy censure if it cannot be justified; to issue these notes, is to do an act which few consider of, which takes but little hold of the public mind, which few condemn and some encourage, because it increases the quantum of what is vainly called money. Loans are limited by the capacity, at least, of one side to borrow, and of the other to lend: the issue of these notes has no limit but the will of the makers, and the supply of lamp-black and rags. The continental bills of the Revolution, and the assignats of France, should furnish some instructive lessons on this head. Direct loans are always voluntary on the part of the lender; treasury note loans may be a forced borrowing from the government creditor—as much so as if the bayonet were put to his breast; for necessity has no law, and the necessitous claimant must take what is tendered, whether with or without interest—whether ten or fifty per cent. below par. I distrust, dislike, and would fain eschew, this treasury note resource. I prefer the direct loans of 1820-'21. I could only bring myself to acquiesce in this measure when it was urged that there was not time to carry a loan through its forms; nor even then could I consent to it, until every feature of a currency character had been eradicated from the face of the bill."

The bill passed the Senate by a general vote, only Messrs. Clay, Crittenden, Preston, Southard, and Spence of Maryland, voting against it. In the House of Representatives it encountered a more strenuous resistance, and was subjected to some trials which showed the dangerous proclivity of these notes to slide from the foundation of investment into the slippery path of currency. Several motions were made to reduce their size—to make them as low as $25; and that failing, to reduce them to $50; which succeeded. The interest was struck at in a motion to reduce it to a nominal amount; and this motion, like that for reducing the minimum size to $25, received a large support—some ninety votes. The motion to reduce to $50 was carried by a majority of forty. Returning to the Senate with this amendment, Mr. Benton moved to restore the $100 limit, and intimated his intention, if it was not done, of withholding his support from the bill—declaring that nothing but the immediate wants of the Treasury, and the lack of time to raise the money by a direct loan as declared by the Secretary of the Treasury, could have brought him to vote for treasury notes in any shape. Mr. Clay opposed the whole scheme as a government bank in disguise, but supported Mr. Benton's motion as being adverse to that design. He said:

"He had been all along opposed to this measure, and he saw nothing now to change that opinion. Mr. C. would have been glad to aid the wants of the Treasury, but thought it might have been done better by suspending the action of many appropriations not so indispensably necessary, rather than by resorting to a loan. Reduction, economy, retrenchment, had been recommended by the President, and why not then pursued? Mr. C.'s chief objection, however, was, that these notes were mere post notes, only differing from bank notes of that kind in giving the Secretary a power of fixing the interest as he pleases.

"It is, said Mr. C., a government bank, issuing government bank notes; an experiment to set up a government bank. It is, in point of fact, an incipient bank. Now, if government has the power to issue bank notes, and so to form indirectly and covertly a bank, how is it that it has not the power to establish a national bank? What difference is there between a great government bank, with Mr. Woodbury as the great cashier, and a bank composed of a corporation of private citizens? What difference is there, except that the latter is better and safer, and more stable, and more free from political influences, and more rational and more republican? An attack is made at Washington upon all the banks of the country, when we have at least one hundred millions of bank paper in circulation. At such a time, a time too of peace, instead of aid, we denounce them, decry them, seek to ruin them, and begin to issue paper in opposition to them! You resort to paper, which you profess to put down; you resort to a bank, which you pretend to decry and to denounce; you resort to a government paper currency, after having exclaimed against every currency except that of gold and silver! Mr. C. said he should vote for Mr. Benton's amendment, as far as it went to prevent the creation of a government bank and a government currency."

Mr. Webster also supported the motion of Mr. Benton, saying:

"He would not be unwilling to give his support to the bill, as a loan, and that only a temporary loan. He was, however, utterly opposed to every modification of the measure which went to stamp upon it the character of a government currency. All past experience showed that such a currency would depreciate; that it will and must depreciate. He should vote for the amendment, inasmuch as $100 bills were less likely to get into common circulation than $50 bills. His objection was against the old continental money in any shape or in any disguise, and he would therefore vote for the amendment."

The motion was lost by a vote of 16 to 25, the yeas and nays being:

YEAS—Messrs. Allen, Benton, Clay, of Kentucky, Clayton, Kent, King, of Georgia, McKean, Pierce, Rives, Robbins, Smith, of Connecticut, Southard, Spence, Tipton, Webster, White—16.

NAYS—Messrs. Buchanan, Clay, of Alabama, Crittenden, Fulton, Grundy, Hubbard, King, of Alabama, Knight, Linn, Lyon, Morris, Nicholas, Niles, Norvell, Roane, Robinson, Smith, of Indiana, Strange, Swift, Talmadge, Walker, Williams, Wall, Wright, Young—25.

————————

CHAPTER X.

RETENTION OF THE FOURTH DEPOSIT INSTALMENT.

The deposit with the States had only reached its second instalment when the deposit banks, unable to stand a continued quarterly drain of near ten millions to the quarter, gave up the effort and closed their doors. The first instalment had been delivered the first of January, in specie, or its equivalent; the second in April, also in valid money; the third one demandable on the first of June, was accepted by the States in depreciated paper: and they were very willing to receive the fourth instalment in the same way. It had cost the States nothing,— was not likely to be called back by the federal government, and was all clear gains to those who took it as a deposit and held it as a donation. But the Federal Treasury needed it also; and likewise needed ten millions more of that amount which had already been "*deposited*" with the States; and which "*deposit*" was made and accepted under a statute which required it to be paid back whenever the wants of the Treasury required it. That want had now come, and the event showed the delusion and the cheat of the bill under which a distribution had been made in the name of a deposit. The idea of restitution entered no one's head! neither of the government to demand it, nor of the States to render back. What had been delivered, was gone! that was a clear case; and reclamation, or rendition, even of the smallest part, or at the most remote period, was not dreamed of. But there was a portion behind—another instalment of ten millions—deliverable out of the "*surplus*" on the first day of October: but there was no surplus: on the contrary a deficit: and the retention of this sum would seem to be a matter of course with the government, only requiring the form of an act to release the obligation for the delivery. It was recommended by the President, counted upon in the treasury estimates, and its retention the condition on which the amount of treasury notes was limited to ten millions of dollars. A bill was reported for the purpose, in the mildest form, not to repeal but to postpone the clause; and the reception which it met, though finally successful, should be an eternal admonition to the federal government never to have any money transaction with its members—a transaction in which the members become the masters, and the devourers of the head. The finance committee of the Senate had brought in a bill to repeal the obligation to deposit this fourth instalment; and from the beginning it encountered a serious resistance. Mr. Webster led the way, saying:

> "We are to consider that this money, according to the provisions of the existing law, is to go equally among all the States, and among all the people; and the wants of the Treasury must be supplied, if supplies be necessary, equally by all the people. It is not a question, therefore, whether some shall have money, and others shall make good the deficiency. All partake in the distribution, and all will contribute to the supply. So that it is a mere question of convenience, and, in my opinion, it is decidedly most convenient, on all accounts, that this instalment should follow its present destination, and the necessities of the Treasury be provided for by other means."

Mr. Preston opposed the repealing bill, principally on the ground that many of the States had already appropriated this money; that is to say, had undertaken public works on the strength of it; and would suffer more injury from not receiving it than the Federal Treasury would suffer from otherwise supplying its place. Mr. Crittenden opposed the bill on the same ground. Kentucky, he said, had made provision for the expenditure of the money, and relied upon it, and could not expect the law to be lightly rescinded, or broken, on the faith of which she had anticipated its use. Other senators treated the deposit act as a contract, which the United States was bound to comply with by delivering all the instalments.

In the progress of the bill Mr. Buchanan proposed an amendment, the effect of which would be to change the essential character of the so called, deposit act, and convert it into a real distribution measure. By the terms of the act, it was the duty of the Secretary of the Treasury to call upon the States for a return of the deposit when needed by the Federal Treasury: Mr. Buchanan proposed to release the Secretary from this duty, and devolve it upon Congress, by enacting that the three instalments already delivered, should remain on deposit with the States until called for by Congress. Mr. Niles saw the evil of the proposition, and thus opposed it:

"He must ask for the yeas and nays on the amendment, and was sorry it had been offered. If it was to be fully considered, it would renew the debate on the deposit act, as it went to change the essential principles and terms of that act. A majority of those who voted for that act, about which there had been so much said, and so much misrepresentation, had professed to regard it—and he could not doubt that at the time they did so regard it—as simply a deposit law; as merely changing the place of deposit from the banks to the States, so far as related to the surplus. The money was still to be in the Treasury, and liable to be drawn out, with certain limitations and restrictions, by the ordinary appropriation laws, without the direct action of Congress. The amendment, if adopted, will change the principles of the deposit act, and the condition of the money deposited with the States under it. It will no longer be a deposit; it will not be in the Treasury, even in point of legal effect or form: the deposit will be changed to a loan, or, perhaps more properly, a grant to the States. The rights of the United States will be changed to a mere claim, like that against the late Bank of the United States; and a claim without any means to enforce it. We were charged, at the time, of making a distribution of the public revenue to the States, in the disguise and form of a deposit; and this amendment, it appeared to him, would be a very bold step towards confirming the truth of that charge. He deemed the amendment an important one, and highly objectionable; but he saw that the Senate were prepared to adopt it, and he would not pursue the discussion, but content himself with repeating his request for the ayes and noes on the question."

Mr. Buchanan expressed his belief that the substitution of Congress for the Secretary of the Treasury, would make no difference in the nature of the fund: and that remark of his, if understood as sarcasm, was undoubtedly true; for the deposit was intended as a distribution by its authors from the beginning, and this proposed substitution was only taking a step, and an effectual one, to make it so: for it was not to be expected that a Congress would ever be found to call for this money from the States, which they were so eager to give to the States. The proposition of Mr. Buchanan was carried by a large majority—33 to 12—all the opponents of the administration, and a division of its friends, voting for it. Thus, the whole principle, and the whole argument on which the deposit act had been passed, was reversed. It was passed to make the State treasuries the Treasury *pro tanto* of the United States—to substitute the States for the banks, for the keeping of this surplus until it was wanted—and it was placed within the call of a federal executive officer that it might be had for the public service when needed. All this was reversed. The recall of the money was taken from the federal executive, and referred to the federal legislative department—to the Congress, composed of members representing the States—that is to say, from the payee to the payor, and was a virtual relinquishment of the payment. And thus the deposit was made a mockery and a cheat; and that by those who passed it.

In the House of Representatives the disposition to treat the deposit as a contract, and to compel the government to deliver the money (although it would be compelled to raise by extraordinary means what was denominated a surplus), was still stronger than in the Senate, and gave rise to a protracted struggle, long and doubtful in its issue. Mr. Cushing laid down the doctrine of contract, and thus argued it:

"The clauses of the deposit act, which appertain to the present question, seem to me to possess all the features of a contract. It provides that the whole surplus revenue of the United States, beyond a certain sum, which may be in the Treasury on a certain day, shall be deposited with the several States; which deposit the States are to keep safely, and to pay back to the United States, whenever the same shall be called for by the Secretary of the Treasury in a prescribed time and mode, and on the happening of a given contingency. Here, it seems to me, is a contract in honor; and, so far as there can be a contract between the United States and the several States, a contract in law; there being reciprocal engagements, for a valuable consideration, on both sides. It is, at any rate, a quasi-contract. They who impugn this view of the question argue on the supposition that the act, performed or to be performed by the United States, is an inchoate gift of money to the States. Not so. It is a contract of deposit; and that contract is consummated, and made perfect, on the formal reception of any instalment of the deposit by the States. Now, entertaining this view of the transaction, I am asked by the administration to come forward and break this contract. True, a contract made by the government of the United States cannot be enforced in law. Does that make it either honest or honorable for the United States to take advantage of its power and violate its pledged faith? I refuse to participate in any such breach of faith. But further. The administration solicits Congress to step in between the United States and the States as a volunteer, and to violate a contract, as the means of helping the administration out of difficulties, into which its own madness and folly have wilfully sunk it, and which press equally upon the government and the people. The object of the measure is to relieve the Secretary of the Treasury from the responsibility of acting in this matter as he has the power to do. Let him act. I will not go out of my way to interpose in this between the Executive and the several States, until the administration appeals to me in the right spirit. This it has not done. The Executive comes to us with a new doctrine, which is echoed by his friends in this House, namely, that the American government is not to exert itself for the relief of the American people. Very well. If this be your policy, I, as representing the people, will not exert myself for the relief of your administration."

Such was the chicanery, unworthy of a *pie-poudre* court—with which a statute of the federal Congress, stamped with every word, invested with every form, hung with every attribute, to define it a deposit—not even a loan—was to be pettifogged into a gift! and a contract for a gift! and the federal Treasury required to stand and deliver! and all that, not in a low law court, where attorneys congregate, but in the high national legislature, where candor and firmness alone should appear. History would be faithless to her mission if she did not mark such conduct for reprobation, and invoke a public judgment upon it.

After a prolonged contest the vote was taken, and the bill carried, but by the smallest majority—119 to 117;—a difference of two votes, which was only a difference of one member. But even that was a delusive victory. It was immediately seen that more than one had voted with the majority, not for the purpose of passing the bill, but to gain the privilege of a majority member to move for a reconsideration. Mr. Pickens, of South Carolina, immediately made that motion, and it was carried by a majority of 70! Mr. Pickens then proposed an amendment, which was to substitute definite for indefinite postponement—to postpone to a day certain instead of the pleasure of Congress: and the first day of January, 1839, was the day proposed; and that without reference to the condition of the Treasury (which might not then have any surplus), for the transfer of this fourth instalment of a deposit to the States. The vote being taken on this proposed amendment, it was carried by a majority of 40: and that amendment being concurred in by the Senate, the bill in that form became a law, and a virtual legalization of the deposit into a donation of forty millions to the States. And this was done by the votes of members who had voted for a deposit with the States; because a donation to the States was unconstitutional. The three instalments already delivered were not to be recalled until Congress should so order; and it was quite certain that it never would so order. At the same time the nominal discretion of Congress over the deposit of the remainder was denied, and the duty of the Secretary made peremptory to deliver it in the brief space of one year and a quarter from that time. But events frustrated that order. The Treasury was in no condition on the first day of January, 1839, to deliver that amount of money. It was penniless itself. The compromise act of 1833, making periodical reductions in the tariff, until the whole duty was reduced to an *ad valorem* of twenty per cent., had nearly run its course, and left the Treasury in the condition of a borrower, instead of that of a donor or lender of money. This fourth instalment could not be delivered at the time appointed, nor subsequently;—and was finally relinquished, the States retaining the amount they had received: which was so much clear gain through the legislative fraud of making a distribution under the name of a deposit.

This was the end of one of the distribution schemes which had so long afflicted and disturbed Congress and the country. Those schemes began now to be known by their consequences—evil to those they were intended to benefit, and of no service to those whose popularity they were to augment. To the States the deposit proved to be an evil, in the contentions and combinations to which their disposition gave rise in the general assemblies—in the objects to which they were applied—and the futility of the help which they afforded. Popularity hunting, on a national scale, gave birth to the schemes in Congress: the same spirit, on a smaller and local scale, took them up in the States. All sorts of plans were proposed for the employment of the money, and combinations more or less interested, or designing, generally carried the point in the universal scramble. In some States a pro rata division of the money, per capite, was made; and the distributive share of each individual being but a few shillings, was received with contempt by some, and rejected with scorn by others. In other States it was divided among the counties, and gave rise to disjointed undertakings of no general benefit. Others, again, were stimulated by the unexpected acquisition of a large sum, to engage in large and premature works of internal improvement, embarrassing the State with debt, and commencing works which could not be finished. Other States again, looking upon the deposit act as a legislative fraud to cover an unconstitutional and demoralizing distribution of public money to the people, refused for a long time to receive their proffered dividend, and passed resolutions of censure upon the authors of the act. And thus the whole policy worked out differently from what had been expected. The States and the people were not grateful for the favor: the authors of the act gained no presidential election by it: and the gratifying fact became evident that the American people were not the degenerate Romans, or the volatile Greeks, to be seduced with their own money—to give their votes to men who lavished the public moneys on their wants or their pleasures—in grain to feed them, or in shows and games to delight and amuse them.

CHAPTER XI.

INDEPENDENT TREASURY AND HARD MONEY PAYMENTS.

These were the crowning measures of the session, and of Mr. Van Buren's administration,—not entirely consummated at that time, but partly, and the rest assured;—and constitute in fact an era in our financial history. They were the most strenuously contested measures of the session, and made the issue completely between the hard money and the paper money systems. They triumphed—have maintained their supremacy ever since—and vindicated their excellence on trial. Vehemently opposed at the time, and the greatest evil predicted, opposition has died away, and given place to support; and the predicted evils have been seen only in blessings. No attempt has been made to disturb these great measures since their final adoption, and it would seem that none need now be apprehended; but the history of their adoption presents one of the most instructive lessons in our financial legislation, and must have its interest with future ages as well as with the present generation. The bills which were brought in for the purpose were clear in principle—simple in detail: the government to receive nothing but gold and silver for its revenues, and its own officers to keep it—the Treasury being at the seat of government, with branches, or sub-treasuries at the principal points of collection and disbursement. And these treasuries to be real, not constructive—strong buildings to hold the public moneys, and special officers to keep the keys. The capacious, strong-walled and well-guarded custom houses and mints, furnished in the great cities the rooms that were wanted: the Treasury building at Washington was ready, and in the right place.

This proposed total separation of the federal government from all banks—called at the time in the popular language of the day, the divorce of Bank and State—naturally arrayed the whole bank power against it, from a feeling of interest; and all (or nearly so) acted in conjunction with the once dominant, and still potent, Bank of the United States. In the Senate, Mr. Webster headed one interest—Mr. Rives, of Virginia, the other; and Mr. Calhoun, who had long acted with the opposition, now came back to the support of the democracy, and gave the aid without which these great measures of the session could not have been carried. His temperament required him to have a lead; and it was readily yielded to him in the debate in all cases where he went with the recommendations of the message; and hence he appeared, in the debate on these measures, as the principal antagonist of Mr. Webster and Mr. Rives.

The present attitude of Mr. Calhoun gave rise to some taunts in relation to his former support of a national bank, and on his present political associations, which gave him the opportunity to set himself right in relation to that institution and his support of it in 1816 and 1834. In this vein Mr. Rives said:

> "It does seem to me, Mr. President, that this perpetual and gratuitous introduction of the Bank of the United States into this debate, with which it has no connection, as if to alarm the imaginations of grave senators, is but a poor evidence of the intrinsic strength of the gentleman's cause. Much has been said of argument *ad captandum* in the course of this discussion. I have heard none that can compare with this solemn stalking of the ghost of the Bank of the United States through this hall, to 'frighten senators from their propriety.' I am as much opposed to that institution as the gentleman or any one else is, or can be. I think I may say I have given some proofs of it. The gentleman himself acquits me of any design to favor the interest of that institution, while he says such is the necessary consequence of my proposition. The suggestion is advanced for effect, and then retracted in form. Whatever be the new-born zeal of the senator from South Carolina against the Bank of the United States, I flatter myself that I stand in a position that places me, at least, as much above suspicion of an undue leaning in favor of that institution as the honorable gentleman. If I mistake not, it was the senator from South Carolina who introduced and supported the bill for the charter of the United States Bank in 1816; it was he, also, who brought in a bill in 1834, to extend the charter of that institution for a term of twelve years; and none were more conspicuous than he in the well-remembered scenes of that day, in urging the restoration of the government deposits to this same institution."

The reply of Mr. Calhoun to those taunts, which impeached his consistency—a point at which he was always sensitive—was quiet and ready, and the same that he had often been heard to express in common conversation. He said:

"In supporting the bank of 1816, I openly declared that, as a question *de novo*, I would be decidedly against the bank, and would be the last to give it my support. I also stated that, in supporting the bank then, I yielded to the necessity of the case, growing out of the then existing and long-established connection between the government and the banking system. I took the ground, even at that early period, that so long as the connection existed, so long as the government received and paid away bank notes as money, they were bound to regulate their value, and had no alternative but the establishment of a national bank. I found the connection in existence and established before my time, and over which I could have no control. I yielded to the necessity, in order to correct the disordered state of the currency, which had fallen exclusively under the control of the States. I yielded to what I could not reverse, just as any member of the Senate now would, who might believe that Louisiana was unconstitutionally admitted into the Union, but who would, nevertheless, feel compelled to vote to extend the laws to that State, as one of its members, on the ground that its admission was an act, whether constitutional or unconstitutional, which he could not reverse. In 1834, I acted in conformity to the same principle, in proposing the renewal of the bank charter for a short period. My object, as expressly avowed, was to use the bank to break the connection between the government and the banking system gradually, in order to avert the catastrophe which has now befallen us, and which I then clearly perceived. But the connection, which I believed to be irreversible in 1816, has now been broken by operation of law. It is now an open question. I feel myself free, for the first time, to choose my course on this important subject; and, in opposing a bank, I act in conformity to principles which I have entertained ever since I have fully investigated the subject."

Going on with his lead in support of the President's recommendations, Mr. Calhoun brought forward the proposition to discontinue the use of bank paper in the receipts and disbursements of the federal government, and supported his motion as a measure as necessary to the welfare of the banks themselves as to the safety of the government. In this sense he said:

"We have reached a new era with regard to these institutions. He who would judge of the future by the past, in reference to them, will be wholly mistaken. The year 1833 marks the commencement of this era. That extraordinary man who had the power of imprinting his own feelings on the community, then commenced his hostile attacks, which have left such effects behind, that the war then commenced against the banks, I clearly see, will not terminate, unless there be a separation between them and the government,—until one or the other triumphs— till the government becomes the bank, or the bank the government. In resisting their union, I act as the friend of both. I have, as I have said, no unkind feeling toward the banks. I am neither a bank man, nor an anti-bank man. I have had little connection with them. Many of my best friends, for whom I have the highest esteem, have a deep interest in their prosperity, and, as far as friendship or personal attachment extends, my inclination would be strongly in their favor. But I stand up here as the representative of no particular interest. I look to the whole, and to the future, as well as the present; and I shall steadily pursue that course which, under the most enlarged view, I believe to be my duty. In 1834 I saw the present crisis. I in vain raised a warning voice, and endeavored to avert it. I now see, with equal certainty, one far more portentous. If this struggle is to go on—if the banks will insist upon a reunion with the government, against the sense of a large and influential portion of the community—and, above all, if they should succeed in effecting it—a reflux flood will inevitably sweep away the whole system. A deep popular excitement is never without some reason, and ought ever to be treated with respect; and it is the part of wisdom to look timely into the cause, and correct it before the excitement shall become so great as to demolish the object, with all its good and evil, against which it is directed."

Mr. Rives treated the divorce of bank and State as the divorce of the government from the people, and said:

"Much reliance, Mr. President, has been placed on the popular catch-word of divorcing the government from all connection with banks. Nothing is more delusive and treacherous than catch-words. How often has the revered name of liberty been invoked, in every quarter of the globe, and every age of the world, to disguise and sanctify the most heartless despotisms. Let us beware that, in attempting to divorce the government from all connection with banks, we do not end with divorcing the government from the people. As long as the people shall be satisfied in their transactions with each other, with a sound convertible paper medium, with a due proportion of the precious metals forming the basis of that medium, and mingled in the current of circulation, why should the government reject altogether this currency of the people, in the operations of the public Treasury? If this currency be good enough for the masters it ought to be so for the servants. If the government sternly reject, for its uses, the general medium of exchange adopted by the community, is it not thereby isolated from the general wants and business of the country, in relation to this great concern of the currency? Do you not give it a separate, if not hostile, interest, and thus, in effect, produce a divorce between government and people?—a result, of all others, to be most deprecated in a republican system."

Mr. Webster's main argument in favor of the re-establishment of the National Bank (which was the consummation he kept steadily in his eye) was, as a regulator of currency, and of the domestic exchanges. The answer to this was, that these arguments, now relied on as the main ones for the continuance of the institution, were not even thought of at its commencement—that no such reasons were hinted at by General Hamilton and the advocates of the first bank—that they were new-fangled, and had not been brought forward by others until after the paper system had deranged both currency and exchanges;—and that it was contradictory to look for the cure of the evil in the source of the evil. It was denied that the regulation of exchanges was a government concern, or that the federal government was created for any such purpose. The buying and selling of bills of exchange was a business pursuit—a commercial business, open to any citizen or bank; and the loss or profit was an individual, and not a government concern. It was denied that there was any derangement of currency in the only currency which the constitution recognized—that of gold and silver. Whoever had this currency to be exchanged—that is, given in exchange at one place for the same in another place—now had the exchange effected on fair terms, and on the just commercial principle—that of paying a difference equal to the freight and insurance of the money: and, on that principle, gold was the best regulator of exchanges; for its small bulk and little weight in proportion to its value, made it easy and cheap of transportation; and brought down the exchange to the minimum cost of such transportation (even when necessary to be made), and to the uniformity of a permanent business. That was the principle of exchange; but, ordinarily, there was no transportation in the case: the exchange dealer in one city had his correspondent in another: a letter often did the business. The regulation of the currency required an understanding of the meaning of the term. As used by the friends of a National Bank, and referred to its action, the paper currency alone was intended. The phrase had got into vogue since the paper currency had become predominant, and that is a currency not recognized by the constitution, but repudiated by it; and one of its main objects was to prevent the future existence of that currency—the evils of which its framers had seen and felt. Gold and silver was the only currency recognized by that instrument, and its regulation specially and exclusively given to Congress, which had lately discharged its duty in that particular, in regulating the relative value of the two metals. The gold act of 1834 had made that regulation, correcting the error of previous legislation, and had revived the circulation of gold, as an ordinary currency, after a total disappearance of it under an erroneous valuation, for an entire generation. It was in full circulation when the combined stoppage of the banks again suppressed it. That was the currency—gold and silver, with the regulation of which Congress was not only intrusted, but charged: and this regulation included preservation. It must be saved before it can be regulated; and to save it, it must be brought into the country—and kept in it. The demand of the federal treasury could alone accomplish these objects. The quantity of specie required for the use of that treasury—its large daily receipts and disbursements—all inexorably confined to hard money—would create the demand for the precious metals which would command their presence, and that in sufficient quantity for the wants of the people as well as of the government. For the government does not consume what it collects—does not melt up or hoard its revenue, or export it to foreign countries, but pays it out to the people; and thus becomes the distributor of gold and silver among them. It is the greatest paymaster in the country; and, while it pays in hard money, the people will be sure of a supply. We are taunted with the demand: "*Where is the better currency?*" We answer: "*Suppressed by the conspiracy of the banks!*" And this is the third time in the last twenty years in which paper money has suppressed specie, and now suppresses it: for this is a game—(the war between gold and paper)—in which the meanest and weakest is always the conqueror. The baser currency always displaces the better. Hard money needs support against paper, and that support can be given by us, by excluding paper money from all federal receipts and payments; and confining paper money to its own local and inferior orbit: and its regulation can be well accomplished by subjecting delinquent banks to the process of bankruptcy, and their small notes to suppression under a federal stamp duty.

The distress of the country figured largely in the speeches of several members, but without finding much sympathy. That engine of operating upon the government and the people had been over-worked in the panic session of 1833-'34 and was now a stale resource, and a crippled machine. The suspension appeared to the country to have been purposely contrived, and wantonly continued. There was now more gold and silver in the country than had ever been seen in it before—four times as much as in 1832, when the Bank of the United States was in its palmy state, and was vaunted to have done so much for the currency. Twenty millions of silver was then its own estimate of the amount of that metal in the United States, and not a particle of gold included in the estimate. Now the estimate of gold and silver was eighty millions; and with this supply of the precious metals, and the determination of all the sound banks to resume as soon as the Bank of the United States could be forced into resumption, or forced into open insolvency, so as to lose control over others, the suspension and embarrassment were obliged to be of brief continuance. Such were the arguments of the friends of hard money.

The divorce bill, as amended, passed the Senate, and though not acted upon in the House during this called session, yet received the impetus which soon carried it through, and gives it a right to be placed among the measures of that session.

CHAPTER XII.

ATTEMPTED RESUMPTION OF SPECIE PAYMENTS.

The suspension of the banks commenced at New York, and took place on the morning of the 10th of May: those of Philadelphia, headed by the Bank of the United States, closed their doors two days after, and merely in consequence, as they alleged, of the New York suspension; and the Bank of the United States especially declared its wish and ability to have continued specie payments without reserve, but felt it proper to follow the example which had been set. All this was known to be a fiction at the time; and the events were soon to come, to prove it to be so. As early as the 15th of August ensuing—in less than one hundred days after the suspension—the banks of New York took the initiatory steps towards resuming. A general meeting of the officers of the banks of the city took place, and appointed a committee to correspond with other banks to procure the appointment of delegates to agree upon a time of general resumption. In this meeting it was unanimously resolved: "*That the banks of the several States be respectfully invited to appoint delegates to meet on the 27th day of November next, in the city of New York, for the purpose of conferring on the time when specie payments may be resumed with safety; and on the measures necessary to effect that purpose.*" Three citizens, eminently respectable in themselves, and presidents of the leading institutions—*Messrs.* Albert Gallatin, George Newbold, and Cornelius W. Lawrence—were appointed a committee to correspond with other banks on the subject of the resolution. They did so; and, leaving to each bank the privilege of sending as many delegates as it pleased, they warmly urged the importance of the occasion, and that the banks from each State should be represented in the proposed convention. There was a general concurrence in the invitation; but the convention did not take place. One powerful interest, strong enough to paralyze the movement, refused to come into it. That interest was the Philadelphia banks, headed by the Bank of the United States! So soon were fallacious pretensions exploded when put to the test. And the test in this case was not resumption itself, but only a meeting to confer upon a time when it would suit the general interest to resume. Even to unite in that conference was refused by this arrogant interest, affecting such a superiority over all other banks; and pretending to have been only dragged into their condition by their example. But a reason had to be given for this refusal, and it was—and was worthy of the party; namely, that it was not proper to do any thing in the business until after the adjournment of the extra session of Congress. That answer was a key to the movements in Congress to thwart the government plans, and to coerce a renewal of the United States Bank charter. After the termination of the session it will be seen that another reason for refusal was found.

CHAPTER XIII.

BANKRUPT ACT AGAINST BANKS.

This was the stringent measure recommended by the President to cure the evil of bank suspensions. Scattered through all the States of the Union, and only existing as local institutions, the federal government could exercise no direct power over them; and the impossibility of bringing the State legislatures to act in concert, left the institutions to do as they pleased; or rather, left even the insolvent ones to do as they pleased; for these, dominating over the others, and governed by their own necessities, or designs, compelled the solvent banks, through panic or self-defence, to follow their example. Three of these general suspensions had occurred in the last twenty years. The notes of these banks constituting the mass of the circulating medium, put the actual currency into the hands of these institutions; leaving the community helpless; for it was not in the power of individuals to contend with associated corporations. It was a reproach to the federal government to be unable to correct this state of things—to see the currency of the constitution driven out of circulation, and out of the country; and substituted by depreciated paper; and the very evil produced which it was a main object of the constitution to prevent. The framers of that instrument were hard-money men. They had seen the evils of paper money, and intended to guard their posterity against what they themselves had suffered. They had done so, as they believed, in the prohibition upon the States to issue bills of credit; and in the prohibition upon the States to make any thing but gold and silver a tender in discharge of debts. The invention of banks, and their power over the community, had nullified this just and wise intention of the constitution; and certainly it would be a reproach to that instrument if it was incapable of protecting itself against such enemies, at such an important point. Thus far it had been found so incapable; but it was a question whether the fault was in the instrument, or in its administrators. There were many who believed it entirely to be the fault of the latter—who believed that the constitution had ample means of protection, within itself, against insolvent, or delinquent banks—and that, all that was wanted was a will in the federal legislature to apply the remedy which the evil required. This remedy was the process of bankruptcy, under which a delinquent bank might be instantly stopped in its operations—its circulation called in and paid off, as far as its assets would go—itself closed up, and all power of further mischief immediately terminated. This remedy it was now proposed to apply. President Van Buren recommended it: he was the first President who had had the merit of doing so; and all that was now wanted was a Congress to back him: and that was a great want! one hard to supply. A powerful array, strongly combined, was on the other side, both moneyed and political. All the local banks were against it; and they counted a thousand—their stockholders myriads;—and many of their owners and debtors were in Congress: the (still so-called) Bank of the United States was against it: and its power and influence were still great: the whole political party opposed to the administration were against it, as well because opposition is always a necessity of the party out of power, as a means of getting in, as because in the actual circumstances of the present state of things opposition was essential to the success of the outside party. Mr. Webster was the first to oppose the measure, and did so, seeming to question the right of Congress to apply the remedy rather than to question the expediency of it. He said:

> "We have seen the declaration of the President, in which he says that he refrains from suggesting any specific plan for the regulation of the exchanges of the country, and for relieving mercantile embarrassments, or for interfering with the ordinary operation of foreign or domestic commerce; and that he does this from a conviction that such measures are not within the constitutional province of the general government; and yet he has made a recommendation to Congress which appears to me to be very remarkable, and it is of a measure which he thinks may prove a salutary remedy against a depreciated paper currency. This measure is neither more nor less than a bankrupt law against corporations and other bankers.

> "Now, Mr. President, it is certainly true that the constitution authorizes Congress to establish uniform rules on the subject of bankruptcies; but it is equally true, and abundantly manifest that this power was not granted with any reference to currency questions. It is a general power—a power to make uniform rules on the subject. How is it possible that such a power

can be fairly exercised by seizing on corporations and bankers, but excluding all the other usual subjects of bankrupt laws! Besides, do such laws ordinarily extend to corporations at all? But suppose they might be so extended, by a bankrupt law enacted for the usual purposes contemplated by such laws; how can a law be defended, which embraces them and bankers alone? I should like to hear what the learned gentleman at the head of the Judiciary Committee, to whom the subject is referred, has to say upon it. How does the President's suggestion conform to his notions of the constitution? The object of bankrupt laws, sir, has no relation to currency. It is simply to distribute the effects of insolvent debtors among their creditors; and I must say, it strikes me that it would be a great perversion of the power conferred on Congress to exercise it upon corporations and bankers, with the leading and primary object of remedying a depreciated paper currency.

"And this appears the more extraordinary, inasmuch as the President is of opinion that the general subject of the currency is not within our province. Bankruptcy, in its common and just meaning, is within our province. Currency, says the message, is not. But we have a bankruptcy power in the constitution, and we will use this power, not for bankruptcy, indeed, but for currency. This, I confess, sir, appears to me to be the short statement of the matter. I would not do the message, or its author, any intentional injustice, nor create any apparent, where there was not a real inconsistency; but I declare, in all sincerity, that I cannot reconcile the proposed use of the bankrupt power with those opinions of the message which respect the authority of Congress over the currency of the country."

The right to use this remedy against bankrupt corporations was of course well considered by the President before he recommended it and also by the Secretary of the Treasury (Mr. Woodbury), bred to the bar, and since a justice of the Supreme Court of the United States, by whom it had been several times recommended. Doubtless the remedy was sanctioned by the whole cabinet before it became a subject of executive recommendation. But the objections of Mr. Webster, though rather suggested than urged, and confined to the *right* without impeaching the *expediency* of the remedy, led to a full examination into the nature and objects of the laws of bankruptcy, in which the right to use them as proposed seemed to be fully vindicated. But the measure was not then pressed to a vote; and the occasion for the remedy having soon passed away, and not recurring since, the question has not been revived. But the importance of the remedy, and the possibility that it may be wanted at some future time, and the high purpose of showing that the constitution is not impotent at a point so vital, renders it proper to present, in this View of the working of the government, the line of argument which was then satisfactory to its advocates: and this is done in the ensuing chapter.

CHAPTER XIV.

BANKRUPT ACT FOR BANKS: MR. BENTON'S SPEECH.

The power of Congress to pass bankrupt laws is expressly given in our constitution, and given without limitation or qualification. It is the fourth in the number of the enumerated powers, and runs thus: "Congress shall have power to establish a uniform rule of naturalization, and uniform laws on the subject of bankruptcies throughout the United States." This is a full and clear grant of power. Upon its face it admits of no question, and leaves Congress at full liberty to pass any kind of bankrupt laws they please, limited only by the condition, that whatever laws are passed, they are to be uniform in their operation throughout the United States. Upon the face of our own constitution there is no question of our right to pass a bankrupt law, limited to banks and bankers; but the senator from Massachusetts [Mr. WEBSTER] and others who have spoken on the same side with him, must carry us to England, and conduct us through the labyrinth of English statute law, and through the chaos of English judicial decisions, to learn what this word bankruptcies, in our constitution, is intended to signify. In this he, and they, are true to the habits of the legal profession—those habits which, both in Great Britain and our America, have become a proverbial disqualification for the proper exercise of legislative duties. I know, Mr. President, that it is the fate of our lawyers and judges to have to run to British law books to find out the meaning of the phrases contained in our constitution; but it is the business of the legislator, and of the statesman, to take a larger view—to consider the difference between the political institutions of the two countries—to ascend to first principles—to know the causes of events—and to judge how far what was suitable and beneficial to one might be prejudicial and inapplicable to the other. We stand here as legislators and statesmen, not as lawyers and judges; we have a grant of power to execute not a statute to interpret; and our first duty is to look to that grant, and see what it is; and our next duty is to look over our country, and see whether there is any thing in it which requires the exercise of that grant of power. This is what our President has done, and what we ought to do. He has looked into the constitution, and seen there an unlimited grant of power to pass uniform laws on the subject of bankruptcies; and he has looked over the United States, and seen what he believes to be fit subjects for the exercise of that power, namely, about a thousand banks in a state of bankruptcy, and no State possessed of authority to act beyond its own limits in remedying the evils of a mischief so vast and so frightful. Seeing these two things—a power to act, and a subject matter requiring action—the President has recommended the action which the constitution permits, and which the subject requires; but the senator from Massachusetts has risen in his place, and called upon us to shift our view; to transfer our contemplation—from the constitution of the United States to the British statute book—from actual bankruptcy among ourselves to historical bankruptcy in England; and to confine our legislation to the characteristics of the English model.

As a general proposition, I lay it down that Congress is not confined, like jurists and judges, to the English statutory definitions, or the Nisi Prius or King's Bench construction of the phrases known to English legislation, and used in our constitution. Such a limitation would not only narrow us down to a mere lawyer's view of a subject, but would limit us, in point of time, to English precedents, as they stood at the adoption of our constitution, in the year 1789. I protest against this absurdity, and contend that we are to use our granted powers according to the circumstances of our own country, and according to the genius of our republican institutions, and according to the progress of events and the expansion of light and knowledge among ourselves. If not, and if we are to be confined to the "usual objects," and the "usual subjects," and the "usual purposes," of British legislation at the time of the adoption of our constitution, how could Congress ever make a law in relation to steamboats, or to railroad cars, both of which were unknown to British legislation in 1789; and therefore, according to the idea that would send us to England to find out the meaning of our constitution, would not fall within the limits of our legislative authority. Upon their face, the words of the constitution are sufficient to justify the President's recommendation, even as understood by those who impugn that recommendation. The bankrupt clause is very peculiar in its phraseology, and the more strikingly so from its contrast with the phraseology of the naturalization clause, which is coupled with it. Mark this difference: there is to be a uniform rule of naturalization: there are to be uniform laws on the subject of bankruptcies. One is in the singular, the other in the plural; one is to be a rule, the other are to be laws; one acts on individuals, the other on the subject; and it is bankruptcies that are, and not bankruptcy that is, to be the objects of these uniform laws.

As a proposition, now limited to this particular case, I lay it down that we are not confined to the modern English acceptation of this term *bankrupt*; for it is a term, not of English, but of Roman origin. It is a term of the civil law, and borrowed by the English from that code. They borrowed from Italy both the name and the purpose of the law; and also the first objects to which the law was applicable. The English were borrowers of every thing connected with this code; and it is absurd in us to borrow from a borrower—to copy from a copyist—when we have the original lender and the original text before us. *Bancus* and *ruptus* signifies a broken bench; and the word *broken* is not metaphorical but literal, and is descriptive of the ancient method of cashiering an insolvent or fraudulent banker, by turning him out of the exchange or market place, and breaking the table bench to pieces on which he kept his money and transacted his business. The term *bankrupt*, then, in the civil law from which the English borrowed it, not only applied to bankers, but was confined to them; and it is preposterous in us to limit ourselves to an English definition of a civil law term.

Upon this exposition of our own constitution, and of the civil law derivation of this term *bankrupt*, I submit that the Congress of the United States is not limited to the English judicial or statutory acceptation of the term; and so I finish the first point which I took in the argument. The next point is more comprehensive, and makes a direct issue with the proposition of the senator from Massachusetts, [Mr. WEBSTER.] His proposition is, that we must confine our bankrupt legislation to the usual objects, the usual subjects, and the usual purposes of bankrupt laws in England; and that currency (meaning paper money and shin-plasters of course), and banks, and banking, are not within the scope of that legislation. I take issue, sir, upon all these points, and am ready to go with the senator to England, and to contest them, one by one, on the evidences of English history, of English statute law, and of English judicial decision. I say English; for, although the senator did not mention England, yet he could mean nothing else, in his reference to the usual objects, usual subjects, and usual purposes of bankrupt laws. He could mean nothing else. He must mean the English examples and the English practice, or nothing; and he is not a person to speak, and mean nothing.

Protesting against this voyage across the high seas, I nevertheless will make it, and will ask the senator on what act, out of the scores which Parliament has passed upon this subject, or on what period, out of the five hundred years that she has been legislating upon it, will he fix for his example? Or, whether he will choose to view the whole together; and out of the vast chaotic and heterogeneous mass, extract a general power which Parliament possesses, and which he proposes for our exemplar? For myself, I am agreed to consider the question under the whole or under either of these aspects, and, relying on the goodness of the cause, expect a safe deliverance from the contest, take it in any way.

And first, as to the acts passed upon this subject; great is their number, and most dissimilar their provisions. For the first two hundred years, these acts applied to none but aliens, and a single class of aliens, and only for a single act, that of flying the realm to avoid their creditors. Then they were made to apply to all debtors, whether natives or foreigners, engaged in trade or not, and took effect for three acts: 1st, flying the realm; 2d, keeping the house to avoid creditors; 3d, taking sanctuary in a church to avoid arrest. For upwards of two hundred years—to be precise, for two hundred and twenty years—bankruptcy was only treated criminally, and directed against those who would not face their creditors, or abide the laws of the land; and the remedies against them were not civil, but criminal; it was not a distribution of the effects, but corporal punishment, to wit: imprisonment and outlawry.[1] The statute of Elizabeth was the first that confined the law to merchants and traders, took in the unfortunate as well as the criminal, extended the acts of bankruptcy to inability as well as to disinclination to pay, discriminated between innocent and fraudulent bankruptcy; and gave to creditors the remedial right to a distribution of effects. This statute opened the door to judicial construction, and the judges went to work to define by decisions, who were traders, and what acts constituted the fact, or showed an intent to delay or to defraud creditors. In making these decisions, the judges reached high enough to get hold of royal companies, and low enough to get hold of shoemakers; the latter upon the ground that they bought the leather out of which they made the shoes; and they even had a most learned consultation to decide whether a man who was a landlord for dogs, and bought dead horses for his four-legged boarders, and then sold the skins and bones of the horse carcases he had bought, was not a trader within the meaning of the act;

and so subject to the statute of bankrupts. These decisions of the judges set the Parliament to work again to preclude judicial constructions by the precision, negatively and affirmatively, of legislative enactment. But, worse and worse! Out of the frying-pan into the fire. The more legislation the more construction; the more statutes Parliament made, the more numerous and the more various the judicial decisions; until, besides merchants and traders, near forty other descriptions of persons were included; and the catalogue of bankruptcy acts, innocent or fraudulent, is swelled to a length which requires whole pages to contain it. Among those who are now included by statutory enactment in England, leaving out the great classes comprehended under the names of merchants and traders, are bankers, brokers, factors, and scriveners; insurers against perils by sea and land; warehousemen, wharfingers, packers, builders, carpenters, shipwrights and victuallers; keepers of inns, hotels, taverns and coffee-houses; dyers, printers, bleachers, fullers, calendrers, sellers of cattle or sheep; commission merchants and consignees; and the agents of all these classes. These are the affirmative definitions of the classes liable to bankruptcy in England; then come the negative; and among these are farmers, graziers, and common laborers for hire; the receivers general of the king's taxes, and members or subscribers to any incorporated companies established by charter of act of Parliament. And among these negative and affirmative exclusions and inclusions, there are many classes which have repeatedly changed position, and found themselves successively in and out of the bankrupt code. Now, in all this mass of variant and contradictory legislation, what part of it will the senator from Massachusetts select for his model? The improved, and approved parts, to be sure! But here a barrier presents itself—an impassable wall interposes—a veto power intervenes. For it so happens that the improvements in the British bankrupt code, those parts of it which are considered best, and most worthy of our imitation, are of modern origin—the creations of the last fifty years— actually made since the date of our constitution; and, therefore, not within the pale of its purview and meaning. Yes, sir, made since the establishment of our constitution, and, therefore, not to be included within its contemplation; unless this doctrine of searching into British statutes for the meaning of our constitution, is to make us search forwards to the end of the British empire, as well as search backwards to its beginning. Fact is, that the actual bankrupt code of Great Britain—the one that preserves all that is valuable, that consolidates all that is preserved, and improves all that is improvable, is an act of most recent date—of the reign of George IV.; and not yet a dozen years old. Here, then, in going back to England for a model, we are cut off from her improvements in the bankrupt code, and confined to take it as it stood under the reign of the Plantagenets, the Tudors, the Stuarts, and the earlier reigns of the Brunswick sovereigns. This should be a consideration, and sufficiently weighty to turn the scale in favor of looking to our own constitution alone for the extent and circumscription of our powers.

But let us continue this discussion upon principles of British example and British legislation. We must go to England for one of two things; either for a case in point, to be found in some statute, or a general authority, to be extracted from a general practice. Take it either way, or both ways, and I am ready and able to vindicate, upon British precedents, our perfect right to enact a bankrupt law, limited in its application to banks and bankers. And first, for a case in point, that is to say, an English statute of bankruptcy, limited to these lords of the purse-strings: we have it at once, in the first act ever passed on the subject—the act of the 30th year of the reign of Edward III., against the Lombard Jews. Every body knows that these Jews were bankers, usually formed into companies, who, issuing from Venice, Milan, and other parts of Italy, spread over the south and west of Europe, during the middle ages; and established themselves in every country and city in which the dawn of reviving civilization, and the germ of returning industry, gave employment to money, and laid the foundation of credit. They came to London as early as the thirteenth century, and gave their name to a street which still retains it, as well as it still retains the particular occupation, and the peculiar reputation, which the Lombard Jews established for it. The first law against bankrupts ever passed in England, was against the banking company composed of these Jews, and confined exclusively to them. It remained in force two hundred years, without any alteration whatever, and was nothing but the application of the law of their own country to these bankers in the country of their sojournment—the Italian law, founded upon the civil law, and called in Italy *banco rotto*, broken bank. It is in direct reference to these Jews, and this application of the exotic bankrupt law to them, that Sir Edward Coke, in his institutes, takes occasion to say that both the name and the wickedness of bankruptcy were of foreign origin, and had been brought into England from foreign parts. It was enacted under the reign of one of the most glorious of the English princes—a reign as much distinguished for the beneficence of its civil administration as for the splendor of its military achievements. This act of itself is a full answer to the whole objection taken by the senator from Massachusetts. It shows that, even in England, a bankrupt law has been confined to a single class of persons, and that class a banking company. And here I would be willing to close my speech upon a compromise—a compromise founded in reason and reciprocity, and invested with the equitable mantle of a mutual concession. It is this: if we must follow English precedents, let us follow them chronologically and orderly. Let us begin at the beginning, and take them as they rise. Give me a bankrupt law for two hundred years against banks and bankers; and, after that, make another for merchants and traders.

The senator from Massachusetts [Mr. WEBSTER] has emphatically demanded, how the bankrupt power could be fairly exercised by seizing on corporations and bankers, and excluding all the other usual subjects of bankrupt laws? I answer, by following the example of that England to which he has conducted us; by copying the act of the 30th of Edward III., by going back to that reign of heroism, patriotism, and wisdom; that reign in which the monarch acquired as much glory from his domestic policy as from his foreign conquests; that reign in which the acquisition of dyers and weavers from Flanders, the observance of law and justice, and the encouragement given to agriculture and manufactures, conferred more benefit upon the kingdom, and more glory upon the king, than the splendid victories of Poictiers, Agincourt, and Cressy.

But the senator may not be willing to yield to this example, this case in point, drawn from his own fountain, and precisely up to the exigency of the occasion. He may want something more; and he shall have it. I will now take the question upon its broadest bottom and fullest merits. I will go to the question of general power—the point of general authority—exemplified by the general practice of the British Parliament, for five hundred years, over the whole subject of bankruptcy. I will try the question upon this basis; and here I lay down the proposition, that this five hundred years of parliamentary legislation on bankruptcy establishes the point of full authority in the British Parliament to act as it pleased on the entire subject of bankruptcies. This is my proposition; and, when it is proved, I shall claim from those who carry me to England for authority, the same amount of power over the subject which the British Parliament has been in the habit of exercising. Now, what is the extent of that power? Happily for me, I, who have to speak, without any inclination for the task; still more happily for those who have to hear me, peradventure without profit or pleasure; happily for both parties, my proposition is already proved, partly by what I have previously advanced, and fully by what every senator knows. I have already shown the practice of Parliament upon this subject, that it has altered and changed, contracted and enlarged, put in and left out, abolished and created, precisely as it pleased. I have already shown, in my rapid view of English legislation on this subject, that the Parliament exercised plenary power and unlimited authority over every branch of the bankrupt question; that it confined the action of the bankrupt laws to a single class of persons, or extended it to many classes; that it was sometimes confined to foreigners, then applied to natives, and that now it comprehends natives, aliens, denizens, and women; that at one time all debtors were subject to it; then none but merchants and traders; and now, besides merchants and traders, a long list of persons who have nothing to do with trade; that at one time bankruptcy was treated criminally, and its object punished corporeally, while now it is a remedial measure for the benefit of the creditors, and the relief of unfortunate debtors; and that the acts of the debtor which may constitute him a bankrupt, have been enlarged from three or four glaring misdeeds, to so long a catalogue of actions, divided into the heads of innocent and fraudulent; constructive and positive; intentional and unintentional; voluntary and forced; that none but an attorney, with book in hand, can pretend to enumerate them. All this has been shown; and, from all this, it is incontestable that Parliament can do just what it pleases on the subject; and, therefore, our Congress, if referred to England for its powers, can do just what it pleases also. And thus, whether we go by the words of our own constitution, or by a particular example in England, or deduce a general authority from the general practice of that country, the result is still the same: we have authority to limit, if we please, our bankrupt law to the single class of banks and bankers.

The senator from Massachusetts [MR. WEBSTER] demands whether bankrupt laws ordinarily extend to corporations, meaning moneyed corporations. I am free to answer that, in point of fact, they do not. But why? because they ought not? or because these corporations have yet been powerful enough, or fortunate enough, to keep their necks out of that noose? Certainly the latter. It is the power of these moneyed corporations in

England, and their good fortune in our America, which, enabling them to grasp all advantages on one hand, and to repulse all penalties on the other, has enabled them to obtain express statutory exemption from bankrupt liabilities in England; and to escape, thus far, from similar liabilities in the United States. This, sir, is history, and not invective; it is fact, and not assertion; and I will speedily refresh the senator's memory, and bring him to recollect why it is, in point of fact, that bankrupt laws do not usually extend to these corporations. And, first, let us look to England, that great exemplar, whose evil examples we are so prompt, whose good ones we are so slow, to imitate. How stands this question of corporation unliability there? By the judicial construction of the statute of Elizabeth, the partners in all incorporated companies were held subject to the bankrupt law; and, under this construction, a commission of bankrupt was issued against Sir John Wolstenholme, a gentleman of large fortune, who had advanced a sum of money on an adventure in the East India Company's trade. The issue of this commission was affirmed by the Court of King's Bench; but this happened to take place in the reign of Charles II.—that reign during which so little is found worthy of imitation in the government of Great Britain—and immediately two acts of Parliament were passed, one to annul the judgment of the Court of King's Bench in the case of Sir John Wolstenholme, and the other to prevent any such judgments from being given in future. Here are copies of the two acts:

FIRST ACT, TO ANNUL THE JUDGMENT.

"Whereas a verdict and judgment was had in the Easter term of the King's Bench, whereby Sir John Wolstenholme, knight, and adventurer in the East India Company, was found liable to a commission of bankrupt only for, and by reason of, a share which he had in the joint stock of said company: Now, &c., Be it enacted, That the said judgment be reversed, annulled, vacated, and for naught held," &c.

SECOND ACT, TO PREVENT SUCH JUDGMENTS IN FUTURE.

"That whereas divers noblemen and gentlemen, and persons of quality, no ways bred up to trade, do often put in great stocks of money into the East India and Guinea Company: Be it enacted, That no persons adventurers for putting in money or merchandise into the said companies, or for venturing or managing the fishing trade, called the royal fishing trade, shall be reputed or taken to be a merchant or trader within any statutes for bankrupts."

Thus, and for these reasons, were chartered companies and their members exempted from the bankrupt penalties, under the dissolute reign of Charles II. It was not the power of the corporations at that time—for the Bank of England was not then chartered, and the East India Company had not then conquered India—which occasioned this exemption; but it was to favor the dignified characters who engaged in the trade—noblemen, gentlemen, and persons of quality. But, afterwards, when the Bank of England had become almost the government of England, and when the East India Company had acquired the dominions of the Great Mogul, an act of Parliament expressly declared that no member of any incorporated company, chartered by act of Parliament, should be liable to become bankrupt. This act was passed in the reign of George IV., when the Wellington ministry was in power, and when liberal principles and human rights were at the last gasp. So much for these corporation exemptions in England; and if the senator from Massachusetts finds any thing in such instances worthy of imitation, let him stand forth and proclaim it.

But, sir, I am not yet done with my answer to this question; do such laws ordinarily extend to corporations at all? I answer, most decidedly, that they do! that they apply in England to all the corporations, except those specially excepted by the act of George IV.; and these are few in number, though great in power—powerful, but few—nothing but units to myriads, compared to those which are not excepted. The words of that act are: "Members of, or subscribers to, any incorporated commercial or trading companies, established by charter act of Parliament." These words cut off at once the many ten thousand corporations in the British empire existing by prescription, or incorporated by letters patent from the king; and then they cut off all those even chartered by act of Parliament which are not commercial or trading in their nature. This saves but a few out of the hundreds of thousands of corporations which abound in England, Scotland, Wales, and Ireland. It saves, or rather confirms, the exemption of the Bank of England, which is a trader in money; and it confirms, also, the exemption of the East India Company which is, in contemplation of law at least, a commercial company; and it saves or exempts a few others deriving charters of incorporation from Parliament; but it leaves subject to the law the whole wilderness of corporations, of which there are thousands in London alone, which derive from prescription or letters patent; and it also leaves subject to the same laws all the corporations created by charter act of Parliament, which are not commercial or trading. The words of the act are very peculiar—"charter act of Parliament;" so that corporations by a general law, without a special charter act, are not included in the exemption. This answer, added to what has been previously said, must be a sufficient reply to the senator's question, whether bankrupt laws ordinarily extend to corporations? Sir, out of the myriad of corporations in Great Britain, the bankrupt law extends to the whole, except some half dozen or dozen.

So much for the exemption of these corporations in England; now for our America. We never had but one bankrupt law in the United States, and that for the short period of three or four years. It was passed under the administration of the elder Mr. Adams, and repealed under Mr. Jefferson. It copied the English acts including among the subjects of bankruptcy, bankers, brokers, and factors. Corporations were not included; and it is probable that no question was raised about them, as, up to that time, their number was few, and their conduct generally good. But, at a later date, the enactment of a bankrupt law was again attempted in our Congress; and, at that period, the multiplication and the misconduct of banks presented them to the minds of many as proper subjects for the application of the law; I speak of the bill of 1827, brought into the Senate, and lost. That bill, like all previous laws since the time of George II., was made applicable to bankers, brokers, and factors. A senator from North Carolina [Mr. BRANCH] moved to include banking corporations. The motion was lost, there being but twelve votes for it; but in this twelve there were some whose names must carry weight to any cause to which they are attached. The twelve were, Messrs. Barton, Benton, Branch, Cobb, Dickerson, Hendricks, Macon, Noble, Randolph, Reed, Smith of South Carolina, and White. The whole of the friends of the bill, twenty-one in number, voted against the proposition, (the present Chief Magistrate in the number,) and for the obvious reason, with some, of not encumbering the measure they were so anxious to carry, by putting into it a new and untried provision. And thus stands our own legislation on this subject. In point of fact, then, chartered corporations have thus far escaped bankrupt penalties, both in England, and in our America; but ought they to continue to escape? This is the question—this the true and important inquiry, which is now to occupy the public mind.

The senator from Massachusetts [Mr. WEBSTER] says the object of bankrupt laws has no relation to currency; that their object is simply to distribute the effects of insolvent debtors among their creditors. So says the senator, but what says history? What says the practice of Great Britain? I will show you what it says, and for that purpose will read a passage from McCulloch's notes on Smith's Wealth of Nations. He says:

> "In 1814-'15, and '16, no fewer than 240 country banks stopped payment, and ninety-two commissions of bankruptcy were issued against these establishments, being at the rate of one commission against every seven and a half of the total number of country banks existing in 1813."

Two hundred and forty stopped payment at one dash, and ninety-two subjected to commissions of bankruptcy. They were not indeed chartered banks, for there are none such in England, except the Bank of England; but they were legalized establishments, existing under the first joint-stock bank act of 1708; and they were banks of issue. Yet they were subjected to the bankrupt laws, ninety-two of them in a single season of bank catalepsy; their broken "promises to pay" were taken out of circulation; their doors closed; their directors and officers turned out; their whole effects, real and personal, their money, debts, books, paper, and every thing, put into the hands of assignees; and to these assignees, the holders of their notes forwarded their demands, and were paid, every one in equal proportion—as the debts of the bank were collected, and its effects converted into money; and this without expense or trouble to any one of them. Ninety-two banks in England shared this fate in a single season of bank mortality; five hundred more could be enumerated in other seasons, many of them superior in real capital, credit, and circulation, to our famous chartered banks, most of which are banks of moonshine, built upon each other's paper; and the whole ready to fly sky-high the moment any one of the concern becomes sufficiently inflated to burst. The immediate effect of this application of the bankrupt laws to banks in England, is two-fold: first, to save the general currency from depreciation, by stopping the issue and circulation of irredeemable notes; secondly, to do equal justice to all creditors, high and low, rich and poor, present and absent, the widow and the orphan, as well as the cunning and the powerful, by distributing their effects in proportionate amounts to all who hold demands. This is the operation of bankrupt laws upon banks in England, and all over the British empire; and it happens to be the precise check upon the issue of broken bank paper, and the precise remedy for the injured holders of their dishonored paper which the President recommends. Here is his recommendation, listen to it:

"In the mean time, it is our duty to provide all the remedies against a depreciated paper currency which the constitution enables us to afford. The Treasury Department, on several former occasions, has suggested the propriety and importance of a uniform law concerning bankruptcies of corporations and other bankers. Through the instrumentality of such a law, a salutary check may doubtless be imposed on the issues of paper money, and an effectual remedy given to the citizen, in a way at once equal in all parts of the Union, and fully authorized by the constitution."

The senator from Massachusetts says he would not, intentionally, do injustice to the message or its author; and doubtless he is not conscious of violating that benevolent determination; but here is injustice, both to the message and to its author; injustice in not quoting the message as it is, and showing that it proposes a remedy to the citizen, as well as a check upon insolvent issues; injustice to the author in denying that the object of bankrupt laws has any relation to currency, when history shows that these laws are the actual instrument for regulating and purifying the whole local paper currency of the entire British empire, and saving that country from the frauds, losses, impositions, and demoralization of an irredeemable paper money.

The senator from Massachusetts says the object of bankrupt laws has no relation to currency. If he means hard-money currency, I agree with him; but if he means bank notes, as I am sure he does, then I point him to the British bankrupt code, which applies to every bank of issue in the British empire, except the Bank of England itself, and the few others, four or five in number, which are incorporated by charter acts. All the joint-stock banks, all the private banks, all the bankers of England, Scotland, Wales, and Ireland, are subject to the law of bankruptcy. Many of these establishments are of great capital and credit; some having hundreds, or even thousands of partners; and many of them having ten, twenty, or thirty, and some even forty branches. They are almost the exclusive furnishers of the local and common bank note currency; the Bank of England notes being chiefly used in the great cities for large mercantile and Government payments. These joint-stock banks, private companies, and individual bankers are, practically, in the British empire what the local banks are in the United States. They perform the same functions, and differ in name only; not in substance nor in conduct. They have no charters, but they have a legalized existence; they are not corporations, but they are allowed by law to act in a body; they furnish the actual paper currency of the great body of the people of the British empire, as much so as our local banks furnish the mass of paper currency to the people of the United States. They have had twenty-four millions sterling (one hundred and twenty millions of dollars) in circulation at one time; a sum nearly equal to the greatest issue ever known in the United States; and more than equal to the whole bank-note circulation of the present day. They are all subject to the law of bankruptcy, and their twenty-four millions sterling of currency along with them; and five hundred of them have been shut up and wound up under commissions of bankruptcy in the last forty years; and yet the senator from Massachusetts informs us that the object of bankrupt laws has no relation to currency!

But it is not necessary to go all the way to England to find bankrupt laws having relation to currency. The act passed in our own country, about forty years ago, applied to bankers; the bill brought into the House of Representatives, about fifteen years ago, by a gentleman then, and now, a representative from the city of Philadelphia, [Mr. SERGEANT,] also applied to bankers; and the bill brought into this Senate, ten years ago, by a senator from South Carolina, not now a member of this body, [General HAYNE,] still applied to bankers. These bankers, of whom there were many in the United States, and of whom Girard, in the East, and Yeatman and Woods, in the West, were the most considerable—these bankers all issued paper money; they all issued currency. The act, then, of 1798, if it had continued in force, or the two bills just referred to, if they had become law, would have operated upon these bankers and their banks—would have stopped their issues, and put their establishments into the hands of assignees, and distributed their effects among their creditors. This, certainly, would have been having some relation to currency: so that, even with our limited essays towards a bankrupt system, we have scaled the outworks of the banking empire; we have laid hold of bankers, but not of banks; we have reached the bank of Girard, but not the Girard Bank; we have applied our law to the bank of Yeatman and Woods, but not to the rabble of petty corporations which have not the tithe of their capital and credit. We have gone as far as bankers, but not as far as banks; and now give me a reason for the difference. Give me a reason why the act of 1798, the bill of Mr. SERGEANT, in 1821, and the bill of General HAYNE, in 1827, should not include banks as well as bankers. They both perform the same function—that of issuing paper currency. They both involve the same mischief when they stop payment—that of afflicting the country with a circulation of irredeemable and depreciated paper money. They are both culpable in the same mode, and in the same degree; for they are both violators of their "promises to pay." They both exact a general credit from the community, and they both abuse that credit. They both have creditors, and they both have effects; and these creditors have as much right to a *pro rata* distribution of the effects in one case as in the other. Why, then, a distinction in favor of the bank? Is it because corporate bodies are superior to natural bodies? because artificial beings are superior to natural beings? or, rather, is it not because corporations are assemblages of men; and assemblages are more powerful than single men; and, therefore, these corporations, in addition to all their vast privileges, are also to have the privilege of being bankrupt, and afflicting the country with the evils of bankruptcy, without themselves being subjected to the laws of bankruptcy? Be this as it may—be the cause what it will—the decree has gone forth for the decision of the question—for the trial of the issue—for the verdict and judgment upon the claim of the banks. They have many privileges and exemptions now, and they have the benefit of all laws against the community. They pay no taxes; the property of the stockholders is not liable for their debts; they sue their debtors, sell their property, and put their bodies in jail. They have the privilege of stamping paper money; the privilege of taking interest upon double, treble, and quadruple their actual money. They put up and put down the price of property, labor, and produce, as they please. They have the monopoly of making the actual currency. They are strong enough to suppress the constitutional money, and to force their own paper upon the community, and then to redeem it or not, as they please. And is it to be tolerated, that, in addition to all these privileges, and all these powers, they are to be exempted from the law of bankruptcy? the only law of which they are afraid, and the only one which can protect the country against their insolvent issues, and give a fair chance for payment to the numerous holders of their violated "promises to pay!"

I have discussed, Mr. President, the right of Congress to apply a bankrupt law to banking corporations; I have discussed it on the words of our own constitution, on the practice of England, and on the general authority of Parliament; and on each and every ground, as I fully believe, vindicated our right to pass the law. The right is clear; the expediency is manifest and glaring. Of all the objects upon the earth, banks of circulation are the fittest subjects of bankrupt laws. They act in secret, and they exact a general credit. Nobody knows their means, yet every body must trust them. They send their "promises to pay" far and near. They push them into every body's hands; they make them small to go into small hands—into the hands of the laborer, the widow, the helpless, the ignorant. Suddenly the bank stops payment; all these helpless holders of their notes are without pay, and without remedy. A few on the spot get a little; those at a distance get nothing. For each to sue, is a vexatious and a losing business. The only adequate remedy—the only one that promises any justice to the body of the community, and the helpless holders of small notes—is the bankrupt remedy of assignees to distribute the effects. This makes the real effects available. When a bank stops, it has little or no specie; but it has, or ought to have, a good mass of solvent debts. At present, all these debts are unavailable to the community—they go to a few large and favored creditors; and those who are most in need get nothing. But a stronger view remains to be taken of these debts: the mass of them are due from the owners and managers of the banks—from the presidents, directors, cashiers, stockholders, attorneys; and these people do not make themselves pay. They do not sue themselves, nor protest themselves. They sue and protest others, and sell out their property, and put their bodies in jail; but, as for themselves, who are the main debtors, it is another affair! They take their time, and usually wait till the notes are heavily depreciated, and then square off with a few cents in the dollar! A commission of bankruptcy is the remedy for this evil; assignees of the effects of the bank are the persons to make these owners, and managers, and chief debtors to the institutions, pay up. Under the bankrupt law, every holder of a note, no matter how small in amount, nor how distant the holder may reside, on forwarding the note to the assignees, will receive his ratable proportion of the bank's effects, without expense, and without trouble to himself. It is a most potent, a most proper, and most constitutional remedy against delinquent banks. It is an equitable and a brave remedy. It does honor to the President who recommended it, and is worthy of the successor of Jackson.

Senators upon this floor have ventured the expression of an opinion that there can be no resumption of specie payments in this country until a national bank shall be established, meaning, all the while, until the present miscalled Bank of the United States shall be rechartered. Such an opinion is humiliating to this government, and a reproach upon the memory of its founders. It is tantamount to a declaration that the government, framed by the heroes and sages of the Revolution, is incapable of self-preservation; that it is a miserable image of imbecility, and must take refuge in the embraces of a moneyed corporation, to enable it to survive its infirmities. The humiliation of such a thought should expel it from the imagination of every patriotic mind. Nothing but a dire necessity—a last, a sole, an only alternative—should bring this government to the thought of leaning upon any extraneous aid. But here is no necessity, no reason, no pretext, no excuse, no apology, for resorting to collateral aid; and, above all, to the aid of a master in the shape of a national bank. The granted powers of the government are adequate to the coercion of all the banks. As banks, the federal government has no direct authority over them; but as bankrupts, it has them in its own hands. It can pass bankrupt laws for these delinquent institutions. It can pass such laws either with or without including merchants and traders; and the day for such law to take effect, will be the day for the resumption of specie payments by every solvent bank, and the day for the extinction of the abused privileges of every insolvent one. So far from requiring the impotent aid of the miscalled Bank of the United States to effect a resumption, that institution will be unable to prevent a resumption. Its veto power over other banks will cease; and it will itself be compelled to resume specie payment, or die!

Besides these great objects to be attained by the application of a bankrupt law to banking corporations, there are other great purposes to be accomplished, and some most sacred duties to be fulfilled, by the same means. Our constitution contains three most vital prohibitions, of which the federal government is the guardian and the guarantee, and which are now publicly trodden under foot. No State shall emit bills of credit; no State shall make any thing but gold and silver coin a tender in payment of debts; no State shall pass any law impairing the obligation of contracts. No State shall do these things. So says the constitution under which we live, and which it is the duty of every citizen to protect, preserve, and defend. But a new power has sprung up among us, and has annulled the whole of these prohibitions. That new power is the oligarchy of banks. It has filled the whole land with bills of credit; for it is admitted on all hands that bank notes, not convertible into specie, are bills of credit. It has suppressed the constitutional currency, and made depreciated paper money a forced tender in payment of every debt. It has violated all its own contracts, and compelled all individuals, and the federal government and State governments, to violate theirs; and has obtained from sovereign States an express sanction, or a silent acquiescence, in this double violation of sacred obligations, and in this triple annulment of constitutional prohibitions. It is our duty to bring, or to try to bring, this new power under subordination to the laws and the government. It is our duty to go to the succor of the constitution—to rescue, if possible, these prohibitions from daily, and public and permanent infraction. The application of the bankrupt law to this new power, is the way to effect this rescue—the way to cause these vital prohibitions to be respected and observed, and to do it in a way to prevent collisions between the States and the federal government. The prohibitions are upon the States; it is they who are not to do these things, and, of course, are not to authorize others to do what they cannot do themselves. The banks are their delegates in this three-fold violation of the constitution; and, in proceeding against these delegates, we avoid collision with the States.

Mr. President, every form of government has something in it to excite the pride, and to rouse the devotion, of its citizens. In monarchies, it is the authority of the king; in republics, it is the sanctity of the laws. The loyal subject makes it the point of honor to obey the king; the patriot republican makes it his glory to obey the laws. We are a republic. We have had illustrious citizens, conquering generals, and victorious armies; but no citizen, no general, no army, has undertaken to dethrone the laws and to reign in their stead. This parricidal work has been reserved for an oligarchy of banks! Three times, in thrice seven years, this oligarchy has dethroned the law, and reigned in its place. Since May last, it has held the sovereign sway, and has not yet vouchsafed to indicate the day of its voluntary abdication. The Roman military dictators usually fixed a term to their dictatorships. I speak of the usurpers, not of the constitutional dictators for ten days. These usurpers usually indicated a time at which usurpation should cease, and law and order again prevail. Not so with this new power which now lords it over our America. They fix no day; they limit no time; they indicate no period for their voluntary descent from power, and for their voluntary return to submission to the laws. They could agree in the twinkling of an eye—at the drop of a hat—at the crook of a finger—to usurp the sovereign power; they cannot agree, in four months, to relinquish it. They profess to be willing, but cannot agree upon the time. Let us perform that service for them. Let us name a day. Let us fix it in a bankrupt law. Let us pass that law, and fix a day for it to take effect; and that day will be the day for the resumption of specie payments, or for the trial of the question of permanent supremacy between the oligarchy of banks, and the constitutional government of the people.

We are called upon to have mercy upon the banks; the prayer should rather be to them, to have mercy upon the government and the people. Since May last the ex-deposit banks alone have forced twenty-five millions of depreciated paper through the federal government upon its debtors and the States, at a loss of at least two and a half millions to the receivers, and a gain of an equal amount to the payers. The thousand banks have the country and the government under their feet at this moment, owing to the community upwards of an hundred millions of dollars, of which they will pay nothing, not even ninepences, picayunes, and coppers. Metaphorically, if not literally, they give their creditors more kicks than coppers. It is for them to have mercy on us. But what is the conduct of government towards these banks? Even at this session, with all their past conduct unatoned for, we have passed a relief bill for their benefit—a bill to defer the collection of the large balance which they still owe the government. But there is mercy due in another quarter—upon the people, suffering from the use of irredeemable and depreciated paper—upon the government, reduced to bankruptcy—upon the character of the country, suffering in the eyes of Europe—upon the character of republican government, brought into question by the successful usurpation of these institutions. This last point is the sorest. Gentlemen speak of the failure of experiments—the failure of the specie experiment, as it is called by those who believe that paper is the ancient and universal money of the world; and that the use of a little specie for the first time is not to be attempted. They dwell upon the supposed failure of "the experiment;" while all the monarchists of Europe are rejoicing in the failure of the experiment of republican government, at seeing this government, the last hope of the liberal world, struck and paralyzed by an oligarchy of banks—seized by the throat, throttled and held as a tiger would hold a babe—stripped of its revenues, bankrupted, and subjected to the degradation of becoming their engine to force their depreciated paper upon helpless creditors. Here is the place for mercy—upon the people—upon the government—upon the character of the country—upon the character of republican government.

The apostle of republicanism, Mr. Jefferson, has left it as a political legacy to the people of the United States, never to suffer their government to fall under the control of any unauthorized, irresponsible, or self-created institutions of bodies whatsoever. His allusion was to the Bank of the United States, and its notorious machinations to govern the elections, and get command of the government; but his admonition applies with equal force to all other similar or affiliated institutions; and, since May last, it applies to the whole league of banks which then "shut up the Treasury," and reduced the government to helpless dependence.

It is said that bankruptcy is a severe remedy to apply to banks. It may be answered that it is not more severe here than in England, where it applies to all banks of issue, except the Bank of England, and a few others; and it is not more severe to them than it is to merchants and traders, and to bankers and brokers, and all unincorporated banks. Personally, I was disposed to make large allowances for the conduct of the banks. Our own improvidence tempted them into an expansion of near forty millions, in 1835 and 1836, by giving them the national domain to bank upon; a temptation which they had not the fortitude to resist, and which expanded them to near the bursting point. Then they were driven almost to a choice of bankruptcy between themselves and their debtors, by the act which required near forty millions to be distributed in masses, and at brief intervals, among the States. Some failures were inevitable under these circumstances, and I was disposed to make liberal allowances for them; but there are three things for which the banks have no excuse, and which should forever weigh against their claims to favor and confidence. These things are, first, the political aspect which the general suspension of payment was permitted to assume, and which it still wears; secondly, the issue and use of shinplasters, and refusal to pay silver change, when there are eighty millions of specie in the country; thirdly, the refusal, by the deposit banks to pay out the sums which had been severed from the Treasury, and stood in the names of disbursing officers, and was actually due to those who were performing work and labor, and rendering daily services to the government. For these three things there is no excuse; and, while memory retains their recollection, there can be no confidence in those who have done them.

CHAPTER XV.

DIVORCE OF BANK AND STATE: MR. BENTON'S SPEECH.

The bill is to divorce the government from the banks, or rather is to declare the divorce, for the separation has already taken place by the operation of law and by the delinquency of the banks. The bill is to declare the divorce; the amendment is to exclude their notes from revenue payments, not all at once, but gradually, and to be accomplished by the 1st day of January, 1841. Until then the notes of specie-paying banks may be received, diminishing one-fourth annually; and after that day, all payments to and from the federal government are to be made in hard money. Until that day, payments from the United States will be governed by existing laws. The amendment does not affect the Post Office department until January, 1841; until then, the fiscal operations of that Department remain under the present laws; after that day they fall under the principle of the bill, and all payments to and from that department will be made in hard money. The effect of the whole amendment will be to restore the currency of the constitution to the federal government—to re-establish the great acts of 1789 and of 1800—declaring that the revenues should be collected in gold and silver coin only; those early statutes which were enacted by the hard money men who made the constitution, who had seen and felt the evils of that paper money, and intended to guard against these evils in future by creating, not a paper, but a hard-money government.

I am for this restoration. I am for restoring to the federal treasury the currency of the constitution. I am for carrying back this government to the solidity projected by its founders. This is a great object in itself—a reform of the first magnitude—a reformation with healing on its wings, bringing safety to the government and blessings to the people. The currency is a thing which reaches every individual, and every institution. From the government to the washer-woman, all are reached by it, and all concerned in it; and, what seems parodoxical, all are concerned to the same degree; for all are concerned to the whole extent of their property and dealings; and all is all, whether it be much or little. The government with its many ten millions of revenue, suffers no more in proportion than the humble and meritorious laborer who works from sun to sun for the shillings which give food and raiment to his family. The federal government has deteriorated the currency, and carried mischief to the whole community, and lost its own revenues, and subjected itself to be trampled upon by corporations, by departing from the constitution, and converting this government from a hard-money to a paper money government. The object of the amendment and the bill is to reform these abuses, and it is a reform worthy to be called a reformation—worthy to engage the labor of patriots—worthy to unite the exertions of different parties—worthy to fix the attention of the age—worthy to excite the hopes of the people, and to invoke upon its success the blessings of heaven.

Great are the evils,—political, pecuniary, and moral,—which have flowed from this departure from our constitution. Through the federal government alone—through it, not by it—two millions and a half of money have been lost in the last four months. Thirty-two millions of public money was the amount in the deposit banks when they stopped payment; of this sum twenty-five millions have been paid over to government creditors, or transferred to the States. But how paid, and how transferred? In what? In real money, or its equivalent? Not at all! But in the notes of suspended banks—in notes depreciated, on an average, ten per cent. Here then were two and a half millions lost. Who bore the loss? The public creditors and the States. Who gained it? for where there is a loss to one, there must be a gain to another. Who gained the two and a half millions, thus sunk upon the hands of the creditors and the States? The banks were the gainers; they gained it; the public creditors and the States lost it; and to the creditors it was a forced loss. It is in vain to say that they consented to take it. They had no alternative. It was that or nothing. The banks forced it upon the government; the government forced it upon the creditor. Consent was out of the question. Power ruled, and that power was in the banks; and they gained the two and a half millions which the States and the public creditors lost.

I do not pretend to estimate the moneyed losses, direct and indirect, to the government alone, from the use of local bank notes in the last twenty-five years, including the war, and covering three general suspensions. Leaving the people out of view, as a field of losses beyond calculation, I confine myself to the federal government, and say, its losses have been enormous, prodigious, and incalculable. We have had three general stoppages of the local banks in the short space of twenty-two years. It is at the average rate of one in seven years; and who is to guaranty us from another, and from the consequent losses, if we continue to receive their bills in payment of public dues? Another stoppage must come, and that, reasoning from all analogies, in less than seven years after the resumption. Many must perish in the attempt to resume, and would do better to wind up at once, without attempting to go on, without adequate means, and against appalling obstacles. Another revulsion must come. Thus it was after the last resumption. The banks recommenced payments in 1817—in two years, the failures were more disastrous than ever. Thus it was in England after the long suspension of twenty-six years. Payments recommenced in 1823—in 1825 the most desolating crash of banks took place which had ever been known in the kingdom, although the Bank of England had imported, in less than four years, twenty millions sterling in gold,—about one hundred millions of dollars, to recommence upon. Its effects reached this country, crushed the cotton houses in New Orleans, depressed the money market, and injured all business.

The senators from New York and Virginia (Messrs. Tallmadge and Rives) push this point of confidence a little further; they address a question to me, and ask if I would lose confidence in all steamboats, and have them all discarded, if one or two blew up in the Mississippi? I answer the question in all frankness, and say, that I should not. But if, instead of one or two in the Mississippi, all the steamboats in the Union should blow up at once—in every creek, river and bay—while all the passengers were sleeping in confidence, and the pilots crying out all is well; if the whole should blow up from one end of the Union to the other just as fast as they could hear each other's explosions; then, indeed, I should lose confidence in them, and never again trust wife, or child, or my own foot, or any thing not intended for destruction, on board such sympathetic and contagious engines of death. I answer further, and tell the gentlemen, that if only one or two banks had stopped last May in New York, I should not have lost all confidence in the remaining nine hundred and ninety-nine; but when the whole thousand stopped at once; tumbled down together—fell in a lump—lie there—and when ONE of their number, by a sign with the little finger, can make the whole lie still, then, indeed, confidence is gone! And this is the case with the banks. They have not only stopped altogether, but in a season of profound peace, with eighty millions of specie in the country, and just after the annual examinations by commissioners and legislative committees, and when all was reported well. With eighty millions in the country, they stop even for change! It did not take a national calamity—a war—to stop them! They fell in time of peace and prosperity! We read of people in the West Indies, and in South America, who rebuild their cities on the same spot where earthquakes had overthrown them; we are astonished at their fatuity; we wonder that they will build again on the same perilous foundations. But these people have a reason for their conduct; it is, that their cities are only destroyed by earthquakes; it takes an earthquake to destroy them; and when there is no earthquake, they are safe. But suppose their cities fell down without any commotion in the earth, or the air—fell in a season of perfect calm and serenity—and after that the survivors should go to building again in the same place; would not all the world say that they were demented, and were doomed to destruction? So of the government of the United States by these banks. If it continues to use them, and to receive their notes for revenue, after what has happened, and in the face of what now exists, it argues fatuity, and a doom to destruction.

Resume when they will, or when they shall, and the longer it is delayed the worse for themselves, the epoch of resumption is to be a perilous crisis to many. This stopping and resuming by banks, is the realization of the poetical description of the descent into hell, and the return from it. *Facilis descensus Averni—sed revocare gradum— hic opus, hic labor est.* Easy is the descent into the regions below, but to return! this is work, this is labor indeed! Our banks have made the descent; they have gone down with ease; but to return—to ascend the rugged steps, and behold again the light above how many will falter, and fall back into the gloomy regions below.

Banks of circulation are banks of hazard and of failure. It is an incident of their nature. Those without circulation rarely fail. That of Venice has stood seven hundred years; those of Hamburgh, Amsterdam, and others, have stood for centuries. The Bank of England, the great mother of banks of circulation, besides an actual stoppage of a quarter of a century, has had her crisis and convulsion in average periods of seven or eight years, for the last half century—in 1783, '93, '97, 1814, '19, '25, '36—and has only been saved from repeated failure by the powerful support of the British government, and profuse supplies of exchequer bills. Her numerous progeny of private and joint stock banks of circulation have had the same convulsions; and not being supported by the government, have sunk by hundreds at a time. All the banks of the United States are banks of circulation; they are all subject to the inherent dangers of that class of banks, and are, besides, subject to new dangers peculiar to themselves. From the quantity of their stock held by foreigners, the quantity of other stocks in their hands, and the current foreign balance against the United States, our paper system has become an appendage to that of England. As such, it suffers from sympathy when the English system suffers. In addition to this, a new doctrine is now broached—that our first duty is to foreigners! and, upon this principle, when the banks of the two countries are in peril, ours are to be sacrificed to save those of England!

The power of a few banks over the whole presents a new feature of danger in our system. It consolidates the banks of the whole Union into one mass, and subjects them to one fate, and that fate to be decided by a few, without even the knowledge of the rest. An unknown divan of bankers sends forth an edict which sweeps over the empire, crosses the lines of States with the facility of a Turkish firman, prostrating all State institutions, breaking up all engagements, and levelling all law before it. This is consolidation of a kind which the genius of Patrick Henry had not even conceived. But while this firman is thus potent and irresistible for prostration, it is impotent and powerless for resurrection. It goes out in vain, bidding the prostrate banks to rise. A *veto* power intervenes. One voice is sufficient to keep all down; and thus we have seen one word from Philadelphia annihilate the New York proposition for resumption, and condemn the many solvent banks to the continuation of a condition as mortifying to their feelings as it is injurious to their future interests.

Again, from the mode of doing business among our banks—using each other's paper to bank upon, instead of holding each other to weekly settlements, and liquidation of balances in specie, and from the fatal practice of issuing notes at one place, payable at another—our banks have all become links of one chain, the strength of the whole being dependent on the strength of each. A few govern all. Whether it is to fail, or to resume, the few govern; and not only the few, but the weak. A few weak banks fail; a panic ensues, and the rest shut up; many strong ones are ready to resume; the weak are not ready, and the strong must wait. Thus the principles of safety, and the rules of government, are reversed. The weak govern the strong; the bad govern the good; and the insolvent govern the solvent. This is our system, if system it can be called, which has no feature of consistency, no principle of safety, and which is nothing but the floating appendage of a foreign and overpowering system.

The federal government and its creditors have suffered great pecuniary losses from the use of these banks and their paper; they must continue to sustain such losses if they continue to use such depositories and to receive such paper. The pecuniary losses have been, now are, and must be hereafter great; but, great as they have been, now are, and may be hereafter, all that loss is nothing compared to the political dangers which flow from the same source. These dangers affect the life of the government. They go to its existence. They involve anarchy, confusion, violence, dissolution! They go to deprive the government of support—of the means of living; they strip it in an instant of every shilling of revenue, and leave it penniless, helpless, lifeless. The late stoppage might have broken up the government, had it not been for the fidelity and affection of the people to their institutions and the eighty millions of specie which General Jackson had accumulated in the country. That stoppage presented a peculiar feature of peril which has not been brought to the notice of the public; it was the stoppage of the sums standing in the names of disbursing officers, and wanted for daily payments in all the branches of the public service.—These sums amounted to about five millions of dollars. They had been drawn from the Treasury, they were no longer standing to the credit of the United States; they had gone into the hands of innumerable officers and agents, in all parts of the Union, and were temporarily, and for mere safe-keeping from day to day, lodged with these deposit banks, to be incessantly paid out to those who were doing work and labor, performing contracts, or rendering service, civil or military, to the country. These five millions were stopped with the rest! In an instant, as if by enchantment, every disbursing officer, in every part of the Union, was stripped of the money which he was going to pay out! All officers of the government, high and low, the whole army and navy, all the laborers and contractors, post offices and all, were suddenly, instantaneously, left without pay; and consequently without subsistence. It was tantamount to a disbandment of the entire government. It was like a decree for the dissolution of the body politic. It was celebrated as a victory—as a conquest—as a triumph, over the government. The least that was expected was an immediate civil revolution—the overthrow of the democratic party, the change of administration, the reascension of the federal party to power, and the re-establishment of the condemned Bank of the United States. These consequences were counted upon; and that they did not happen was solely owing to the eighty millions of hard money which kept up a standard of value in the country, and prevented the dishonored bank notes from sinking too low to be used by the community. But it is not merely stoppage of the banks that we have to fear: collisions with the States may ensue. State legislatures may sanction the stoppage, withhold the poor right of suing, and thus interpose their authority between the federal government and its revenues. This has already happened, not in hostility to the government, but in protection of themselves; and the consequence was the same as if the intention had been hostile. It was interposition between the federal government and its depositories; it was deprivation of revenue; it was an act the recurrence of which should be carefully guarded against in future.

This is what we have seen; this is a danger which we have just escaped; and if these banks shall be continued as depositories of public money, or, which is just the same thing, if the government shall continue to receive their "paper promises to pay," the same danger may be seen again, and under far more critical circumstances. A similar stoppage of the banks may take place again—will inevitably take place again—and it may be when there is little specie in the country, or when war prevails. All history is full of examples of armies and navies revolting for want of pay; all history is full of examples of military and naval operations miscarried for want of money; all history is full of instances of governments overturned from deficits of revenue and derangements of finances. And are we to expose ourselves recklessly, and with our eyes open, to such dangers? And are we to stake the life and death of this government upon the hazards and contingencies of banking—and of such banking as exists in these United States? Are we to subject the existence of this government to the stoppages of the banks, whether those stoppages result from misfortune, improvidence, or bad faith? Are we to subject this great and glorious political fabric, the work of so many wise and patriotic heads, to be demolished in an instant, and by an unseen hand? Are we to suffer the machinery and the working of our boasted constitution to be arrested by a spring-catch, applied in the dark? Are men, with pens sticking behind their ears, to be allowed to put an end to this republic? No, sir! never. If we are to perish prematurely, let us at least have a death worthy of a great nation; let us at least have a field covered with the bodies of heroes and of patriots, and consecrated forever to the memory of a subverted empire. Rome had her Pharsalia—Greece her Chæronca—and many barbarian kingdoms have given immortality to the spot on which they expired; and shall this great republic be subjected to extinction on the contingencies of trade and banking?

But what excuse, what apology, what justification have we for surrendering, abandoning, and losing the precise advantage for which the present constitution was formed? What was that advantage—what the leading and governing object, which led to the abandonment of the old confederation, and induced the adoption of the present form of government? It was revenue! independent revenue! a revenue under the absolute control of this government, and free from the action of the States. This was the motive—the leading and the governing motive—which led to the formation of this government. The reason was, that the old confederation, being dependent upon the States, was often left without money. This state of being was incompatible with its existence; it deprived it of all power; its imbecility was a proverb. To extricate it from that condition was the design—and the cardinal design—of the new constitution. An independent revenue was given to it—independent, even, of the States. Is it not suicidal to surrender that independence, and to surrender it, not to States, but to money corporations? What does history record of the penury and moneyed destitution of the old confederation, comparable to the annihilation of the revenues of this government in May last? when the banks shut down, in one night, upon a revenue, in hand, of thirty-two millions; even upon that which was in the names of disbursing officers, and refuse a nine-pence, or a picaillon in money, from that day to this? What is there in the history of the old confederation comparable to this? The old confederation was often reduced low—often near empty-handed—but never saw itself stripped in an instant, as if by enchantment, of tens of millions, and heard the shout of triumph thundered over its head, and the notes of exultation sung over its supposed destruction! Yet, this is what we have seen—what we now see—from having surrendered to corporations our moneyed independence, and unwisely abandoned the precise advantage which led to the formation of this federal government.

I do not go into the moral view of this question. It is too obvious, too impressive, too grave, to escape the observation of any one. Demoralization follows in the train of an unconvertible paper money. The whole community becomes exposed to a moral pestilence. Every individual becomes the victim of some imposition;

and, in self-defence, imposes upon some one else. The weak, the ignorant, the uninformed, the necessitous, are the sufferers; the crafty and the opulent are the gainers. The evil augments until the moral sense of the community, revolting at the frightful accumulation of fraud and misery, applies the radical remedy of total reform.

Thus, pecuniary, political, and moral considerations require the government to retrace its steps, to return to first principles, and to restore its fiscal action to the safe and solid path of the constitution. Reform is demanded. It is called for by every public and by every private consideration. Now is the time to make it. The connection between Bank and State is actually dissolved. It is dissolved by operation of law, and by the delinquency of these institutions. They have forfeited the right to the deposits, and lost the privilege of paying the revenue in their notes, by ceasing to pay specie. The government is now going on without them, and all that is wanting is the appropriate legislation to perpetuate the divorce which, in point of fact, has already taken place. Now is the time to act; this the moment to restore the constitutional currency to the federal government; to restore the custody of the public moneys to national keepers; and to avoid, in time to come, the calamitous revulsions and perilous catastrophes of 1814, 1819, and 1837.

And what is the obstacle to the adoption of this course, so imperiously demanded by the safety of the republic and the welfare of the people, and so earnestly recommended to us by the chief magistrate? What is the obstacle—what the power that countervails the Executive recommendation, paralyzes the action of Congress, and stays the march of reform? The banks—the banks—the banks, are this obstacle, and this power. They set up the pretension to force their paper into the federal Treasury, and to force themselves to be constituted that Treasury. Though now bankrupt, their paper dishonored, their doors closed against creditors, every public and every private obligation violated, still they arrogate a supremacy over this federal government; they demand the guardianship of the public moneys, and the privilege of furnishing a federal currency; and, though too weak to pay their debts, they are strong enough to throttle this government, and to hold in doubtful suspense the issue of their vast pretensions.

The President, in his message, recommends four things: first, to discontinue the reception of local bank paper in payment of federal dues; secondly, to discontinue the same banks as depositories of the public moneys; thirdly, to make the future collection and disbursement of the public moneys in gold and silver; fourthly, to take the keeping of the public moneys into the hands of our own officers.

What is there in this but a return to the words and meaning of the constitution, and a conformity to the practice of the government in the first years of President Washington's administration? When this federal government was first formed, there was no Bank of the United States, and no local banks, except three north of the Potomac. By the act of 1789, the revenues were directed to be collected in gold and silver coin only; and it was usually drawn out of the hands of collectors by drafts drawn upon them, payable at sight. It was a most effectual way of drawing money out of their hands; far more so than an order to deposit in banks; for the drafts must be paid, or protested, at sight, while the order to deposit may be eluded under various pretexts.

The right and the obligation of the government to keep its own moneys in its own hands, results from first principles, and from the great law of self-preservation. Every thing else that belongs to her, she keeps herself; and why not keep that also, without which every thing else is nothing? Arms and ships—provisions, munitions, and supplies of every kind—are kept in the hands of government officers; money is the sinew of war, and why leave this sinew exposed to be cut by any careless or faithless hand? Money is the support and existence of the government—the breath of its nostrils, and why leave this support—this breath—to the custody of those over whom we have no control? How absurd to place our ships, our arms, our military and naval supplies in the hands of those who could refuse to deliver them when requested, and put the government to a suit at law to recover their possession! Every body sees the absurdity of this; but to place our money in the same condition, and, moreover, to subject it to the vicissitudes of trade and the perils of banking, is still more absurd; for it is the life blood, without which the government cannot live—the oil, without which no part of its machinery can move.

England, with all her banks, trusts none of them with the collection, keeping, and disbursement of her public moneys. The Bank of England is paid a specific sum to manage the public debt; but the revenue is collected and disbursed through subordinate collectors and receivers general; and these receivers general are not subject to the bankrupt laws, because the government will not suffer its revenue to be operated upon by any law except its own will. In France, subordinate collectors and receivers general collect, keep, and disburse the public moneys. If they deposit any thing in banks, it is at their own risk. It is the same thing in England. A bank deposit by an officer is at the risk of himself and his securities. Too much of the perils and vicissitudes of banking is known in these countries to permit the government ever to jeopard its revenues in their keeping. All this is shown, fully and at large, in a public document now on our tables. And who does not recognize in these collectors and receivers general of France and England, the ancient Roman officers of quæstors and proquæstors? These fiscal officers of France and England are derivations from the Roman institutions; and the same are found in all the modern kingdoms of Europe which were formerly, like France and Britain, provinces of the Roman empire. The measure before the Senate is to enable us to provide for our future safety, by complying with our own constitution, and conforming to the practice of all nations, great or small, ancient or modern.

Coming nearer home, and looking into our own early history, what were the "continental treasurers" of the confederation, and the "provincial treasurers and collectors," provided for as early as July, 1775, but an imitation of the French and English systems, and very near the plan which we propose now to re-establish! These continental treasurers, and there were two of them at first, though afterwards reduced to one, were the receivers general; the provincial treasurers and collectors were their subordinates. By these officers the public moneys were collected, kept, and disbursed; for there were no banks then! and all government drafts were drawn directly upon these officers. This simple plan worked well during the Revolution, and afterwards, until the new government was formed; and continued to work, with a mere change of names and forms, during the first years of Washington's administration, and until General Hamilton's bank machinery got into play. This bill only proposes to re-establish, in substance, the system of the Revolution, of the Congress of the confederation, and of the first years of Washington's administration.

The bill reported by the chairman of the Committee on Finance [Mr. WRIGHT of New York] presents the details of the plan for accomplishing this great result. That bill has been printed and read. Its simplicity, economy, and efficiency strike the sense of all who hear it, and annihilate without argument, the most formidable arguments of expense and patronage, which had been conceived against it. The present officers, the present mints, and one or two more mints in the South, in the West, and in the North, complete the plan. There will be no necessity to carry masses of hard money from one quarter of the Union to another. Government drafts will make the transfer without moving a dollar. A government draft upon a national mint, will be the highest order of bills of exchange. Money wanted by the government in one place, will be exchanged, through merchants, for money in another place. Thus it has been for thousands of years, and will for ever be. We read in Cicero's letters that, when he was Governor of Cilicia, in Asia Minor, he directed his *quæstor* to deposit the tribute of the province in Antioch, and exchange it for money in Rome with merchants engaged in the Oriental trade, of which Antioch was one of the emporiums. This is the natural course of things, and is too obvious to require explanation, or to admit of comment.

We are taunted with these treasury notes; it seems to be matter of triumph that the government is reduced to the necessity of issuing them; but with what justice? And how soon can any government that wishes it, emerge from the wretchedness of depreciated paper, and stand erect on the solid foundations of gold and silver? How long will it take any respectable government, that so wills it, to accomplish this great change? Our own history, at the close of the Revolution, answers the question; and more recently, and more strikingly, the history of France answers it also. I speak of the French finances from 1800 to 1807; from the commencement of the consulate to the peace of Tilsit. This wonderful period is replete with instruction on the subject of finance and currency. The whole period is full of instruction; but I can only seize two views—the beginning and the end— and, for the sake of precision, will read what I propose to present. I read from Bignon, author of the civil and diplomatic history of France during the consulate and the first years of the empire; written at the testamentary request of the Emperor himself.

After stating that the expenditures of the republic were six hundred millions of francs—about one hundred and ten millions of dollars—when Bonaparte became First Consul, the historian proceeds:

"At his arrival at power, a sum of 160,000 francs in money [about $32,000] was all that the public chests contained. In the impossibility of meeting the current service by the ordinary receipts, the Directorial Government had resorted to ruinous expedients, and had thrown into circulation bills of various values, and which sunk upon the spot fifty to eighty per cent. A part of the arrearages had been discharged in bills two-thirds on credit, payable to the bearer, but which, in fact, the treasury was not able to pay when due. The remaining third had been inscribed in the great book, under the name of consolidated third. For the payment of the forced requisitions to which they had been obliged to have recourse, there had been issued bills receivable in payment of the revenues. Finally, the government, in order to satisfy the most imperious wants, gave orders upon the receivers general, delivered in advance to contractors, which they negotiated before they began to furnish the supplies for which they were the payment."

This, resumed Mr. B., was the condition of the French finances when Bonaparte became First Consul at the close of the year 1799. The currency was in the same condition—no specie—a degraded currency of assignats, ruinously depreciated, and issued as low as ten sous. That great man immediately began to restore order to the finances, and solidity to the currency. Happily a peace of three years enabled him to complete the great work, before he was called to celebrate the immortal campaigns ending at Austerlitz, Jena, and Friedland. At the end of three years—before the rupture of the peace of Amiens—the finances and the currency were restored to order and to solidity; and, at the end of six years, when the vast establishments, and the internal ameliorations of the imperial government, had carried the annual expenses to eight hundred millions of francs, about one hundred and sixty millions of dollars; the same historian copying the words of the Minister of Finance, thus speaks of the treasury, and the currency:

"The resources of the State have increased beyond its wants; the public chests are full; all payments are made at the day named; the orders upon the public treasury have become the most approved bills of exchange. The finances are in the most happy condition; France alone, among all the States of Europe, has no paper money."

What a picture! how simply, how powerfully drawn! and what a change in six years! Public chests full—payments made to the day—orders on the treasury the best bills of exchange—France alone, of all Europe, having no paper money; meaning no government paper money, for there were bank notes of five hundred francs, and one thousand francs. A government revenue of one hundred and sixty millions of dollars was paid in gold and silver; a hard money currency, of five hundred and fifty millions of dollars, saturated all parts of France with specie, and made gold and silver the every day currency of every man, woman and child, in the empire. These great results were the work of six years, and were accomplished by the simple process of gradually requiring hard money payments—gradually calling in the assignats—increasing the branch mints to fourteen, and limiting the Bank of France to an issue of large notes—five hundred francs and upwards. This simple process produced these results, and thus stands the French currency at this day; for the nation has had the wisdom to leave untouched the financial system of Bonaparte.

I have repeatedly given it as my opinion—many of my speeches declare it—that the French currency is the best in the world. It has hard money for the government; hard money for the common dealings of the people; and large notes for large transactions. This currency has enabled France to stand two invasions, the ravaging of 300,000 men, two changes of dynasty, and the payment of a *milliard* of contributions; and all without any commotion or revulsion in trade. It has saved her from the revulsions which have afflicted England and our America for so many years. It has saved her from expansions, contractions, and ruinous fluctuations of price. It has saved her, for near forty years, from a debate on currency. It has saved her even from the knowledge of our sweet-scented phrases: "sound currency—unsound currency; plethoric, dropsical, inflated, bloated; the money market tight to-day—a little easier this morning;" and all such verbiage, which the haberdashers' boys repeat. It has saved France from even a discussion on currency; while in England, and with us, it is banks! banks! banks!—morning, noon, and night; breakfast, dinner, and supper; levant, and couchant; sitting, or standing; at home, or abroad; steamboat, or railroad car; in Congress, or out of Congress, it is all the same thing: banks—banks—banks; currency—currency—currency; meaning, all the while, paper money and shin-plasters; until our very brains seem as if they would be converted into lampblack and rags.

The bill before the Senate dispenses with the further use of banks as depositories of the public moneys. In that it has my hearty concurrence. Four times heretofore, and on four different occasions, I have made propositions to accomplish a part of the same purpose. *First*, in proposing an amendment to the deposit bill of 1836, by which the mint, and the branch mints, were to be included in the list of depositories; *secondly*, in proposing that the public moneys here, at the seat of Government, should be kept and paid out by the Treasurer; *thirdly*, by proposing that a preference, in receiving the deposits, should be given to such banks as should cease to be banks of circulation; *fourthly*, in opposing the establishment of a bank agency in Missouri, and proposing that the moneys there should be drawn direct from the hands of the receivers. Three of these propositions are now included in the bill before the Senate; and the whole object at which they partially aimed is fully embraced. I am for the measure—fully, cordially, earnestly for it.

Congress has a sacred duty to perform in reforming the finances, and the currency; for the ruin of both has resulted from federal legislation, and federal administration. The States at the formation of the constitution, delivered a solid currency—I will not say sound, for that word implies subject to unsoundness, to rottenness, and to death—but they delivered a solid currency, one not liable to disease, to this federal government. They started the new government fair upon gold and silver. The first act of Congress attested this great fact; for it made the revenues payable in gold and silver coin only. Thus the States delivered a solid currency to this government, and they reserved the same currency for themselves; and they provided constitutional sanctions to guard both. The thing to be saved, and the power to save it, was given to this government by the States; and in the hands of this government it became deteriorated. The first great error was General Hamilton's construction of the act of 1789, by which he nullified that act, and overturned the statute and the constitution together. The next great error was the establishment of a national bank of circulation, with authority to pay all the public dues in its own paper. This confirmed the overthrow of the constitution, and of the statute of 1789; and it set the fatal example to the States to make banks, and to receive their paper for public dues, as the United States had done. This was the origin of the evil—this the origin of the overthrow of the solid currency which the States had delivered to the federal government. It was the Hamiltonian policy that did the mischief; and the state of things in 1837, is the natural fruit of that policy. It is time for us to quit it—to return to the constitution and the statute of 1789, and to confine the federal Treasury to the hard money which was intended for it.

I repeat, this is a measure of reform, worthy to be called a reformation. It goes back to a fundamental abuse, nearly coeval with the foundation of the government. Two epochs have occurred for the reformation of this abuse; one was lost, the other is now in jeopardy. Mr. Madison's administration committed a great error at the expiration of the charter of the first Bank of the United States, in not reviving the currency of the constitution for the federal Treasury, and especially the gold currency. That error threw the Treasury back upon the local bank paper. This paper quickly failed, and out of that failure grew the second United States Bank. Those who put down the second United States Bank, warned by the calamity, determined to avoid the error of Mr. Madison's administration: they determined to increase the stock of specie, and to revive the gold circulation, which had been dead for thirty years. The accumulation of eighty millions in the brief space of five years, fifteen millions of it in gold, attest the sincerity of their design, and the facility of its execution. The country was going on at the rate of an average increase of twelve millions of specie per annum, when the general stoppages of the banks in May last, the exportation of specie, and the imposition of irredeemable paper upon the government and the people, seemed to announce the total failure of the plan. But it was a seeming only. The impetus given to the specie policy still prevails, and five millions are added to the stock during the present fiscal year. So far, then, as the counteraction of the government policy, and the suppression of the constitutional currency, might have been expected to result from that stoppage, the calculation seems to be in a fair way to be disappointed. The spirit of the people, and our hundred millions of exportable produce, are giving the victory to the glorious policy of our late illustrious President. The other great consequences expected to result from that stoppage, namely, the recharter of the Bank of the United States, the change of administration, the overthrow of the republican party, and the restoration of the federal dynasty, all seem to be in the same fair way to total miscarriage; but the objects are too dazzling to be abandoned by the party interested, and the destruction of the finances and the currency, is still the cherished road to success. The miscalled Bank of the United States, the soul of the federal dynasty, and the anchor of its hopes—believed by many to have been at the bottom of the stoppages in May, and known by all to be at the head of non-resumption—now displays her policy on this floor; it is to compel the repetition of the error of Mr. Madison's administration! Knowing that from the repetition of this error must come the repetition of the catastrophes of 1814, 1819, and 1837; and out of these catastrophes to extract a new clamor for the revivification of herself. This is her line of conduct; and to this line, the conduct of all her friends conforms. With one heart, one mind, one voice, they labor to cut off gold and silver from the federal government, and to impose paper upon it! they labor to deprive it of the keeping of its own revenues, and to place them again where they have been so often lost! This is the conduct of that bank and its friends. Let us imitate their zeal, their unanimity, and their perseverance. The amendment and the bill now before the Senate, embodies our policy. Let us carry them, and the republic is safe.

The extra session had been called to relieve the distress of the federal treasury, and had done so by authorizing an issue of treasury notes. That object being accomplished, and the great measures for the divorce of Bank and State, and for the sole use of gold and silver in federal payments, having been recommended, and commenced, the session adjourned.

CHAPTER XVI.

FIRST REGULAR SESSION UNDER MR. VAN BUREN'S ADMINISTRATION: HIS MESSAGE.

A brief interval of two months only intervened between the adjournment of the called session and the meeting of the regular one; and the general state of the public affairs, both at home and abroad, being essentially the same at both periods, left no new or extraordinary measures for the President to recommend. With foreign powers we were on good terms, the settlement of all our long-standing complaints under General Jackson's administration having left us free from the foreign controversies which gave trouble; and on that head the message had little but what was agreeable to communicate. Its topics were principally confined to home affairs, and that part of these affairs which were connected with the banks. That of the United States, as it still called itself, gave a new species of disregard of moral and legal obligation, and presented a new mode of depraving the currency and endangering property and contracts, by continuing to issue and to use the notes of the expired institution. Its currency was still that of the defunct bank. It used the dead notes of that institution, for which, of course, neither bank was liable. They were called resurrection notes; and their use, besides the injury to the currency and danger to property, was a high contempt and defiance of the authority which had created it; and called for the attention of the federal government. The President, therefore, thus formally brought the procedure to the notice of Congress:

"It was my hope that nothing would occur to make necessary, on this occasion, any allusion to the late national bank. There are circumstances, however, connected with the present state of its affairs that bear so directly on the character of the government and the welfare of the citizen, that I should not feel myself excused in neglecting to notice them. The charter which terminated its banking privileges on the 4th of March, 1836, continued its corporate powers two years more, for the sole purpose of closing its affairs, with authority 'to use the corporate name, style, and capacity, for the purpose of suits for a final settlement and liquidation of the affairs and acts of the corporation, and for the sale and disposition of their estate, real, personal and mixed, but for no other purpose or in any other manner whatsoever.' Just before the banking privileges ceased, its effects were transferred by the bank to a new State institution then recently incorporated, in trust, for the discharge of its debts and the settlement of its affairs. With this trustee, by authority of Congress, an adjustment was subsequently made of the large interest which the government had in the stock of the institution. The manner in which a trust unexpectedly created upon the act granting the charter, and involving such great public interests, has been executed, would, under any circumstances, be a fit subject of inquiry; but much more does it deserve your attention, when it embraces the redemption of obligations to which the authority and credit of the United States have given value. The two years allowed are now nearly at an end. It is well understood that the trustee has not redeemed and cancelled the outstanding notes of the bank, but has reissued, and is actually reissuing, since the 3d of March, 1836, the notes which have been received by it to a vast amount. According to its own official statement, so late as the 1st of October last, nineteen months after the banking privileges given by the charter had expired, it had under its control uncancelled notes of the late Bank of the United States to the amount of twenty-seven millions five hundred and sixty-one thousand eight hundred and sixty-six dollars, of which six millions one hundred and seventy-five thousand eight hundred and sixty-one dollars were in actual circulation, one million four hundred and sixty-eight thousand six hundred and twenty-seven dollars at State bank agencies, and three millions two thousand three hundred and ninety dollars *in transitu*; thus showing that upwards of ten millions and a half of the notes of the old bank were then still kept outstanding. The impropriety of this procedure is obvious: it being the duty of the trustee to cancel and not to put forth the notes of an institution, whose concerns it had undertaken to wind up. If the trustee has a right to reissue these notes now, I can see no reason why it may not continue to do so after the expiration of the two years. As no one could have anticipated a course so extraordinary, the prohibitory clause of the charter above quoted was not accompanied by any penalty or other special provision for enforcing it; nor have we any general law for the prevention of similar acts in future.

"But it is not in this view of the subject alone that your interposition is required. The United States, in settling with the trustee for their stock, have withdrawn their funds from their former direct ability to the creditors of the old bank, yet notes of the institution continue to be sent forth in its name, and apparently upon the authority of the United States. The transactions connected with the employment of the bills of the old bank are of vast extent; and should they result unfortunately, the interests of individuals may be deeply compromised. Without undertaking to decide how far, or in what form, if any, the trustee could be made liable for notes which contain no obligation on its part; or the old bank, for such as are put in circulation after the expiration of its charter, and without its authority; or the government for indemnity, in case of loss, the question still presses itself upon your consideration, whether it is consistent with duty and good faith on the part of the government, to witness this proceeding without a single effort to arrest it."

On the subject of the public lands, and the most judicious mode of disposing of them—a question of so much interest to the new States—the message took the view of those who looked to the domain less as a source of revenue than as a means of settling and improving the country. He recommended graduated prices according to the value of the different classes of lands in order to facilitate their sale; and a prospective permanent pre-emption act to give encouragement to settlers. On the first of these points he said:

"Hitherto, after being offered at public sale, lands have been disposed of at one uniform price, whatever difference there might be in their intrinsic value. The leading considerations urged in favor of the measure referred to, are, that in almost all the land districts, and particularly in those in which the lands have been long surveyed and exposed to sale, there are still remaining numerous and large tracts of every gradation of value, from the government price downwards; that these lands will not be purchased at the government price, so long as better can be conveniently obtained for the same amount; that there are large tracts which even the improvements of the adjacent lands will never raise to that price; and that the present uniform price, combined with their irregular value, operates to prevent a desirable compactness of settlement in the new States, and to retard the full development of that wise policy on which our land system is founded, to the injury not only of the several States where the lands lie, but of the United States as a whole.

"The remedy proposed has been a reduction of prices according to the length of time the lands have been in market, without reference to any other circumstances. The certainty that the efflux of time would not always in such cases, and perhaps not even generally, furnish a true criterion of value; and the probability that persons residing in the vicinity, as the period for the reduction of prices approached, would postpone purchases they would otherwise make, for the purpose of availing themselves of the lower price, with other considerations of a similar character, have hitherto been successfully urged to defeat the graduation upon time. May not all reasonable desires upon this subject be satisfied without encountering any of these objections? All will concede the abstract principle, that the price of the public lands should be proportioned to their relative value, so far as that can be accomplished without departing from the rule, heretofore observed, requiring fixed prices in cases of private entries. The difficulty of the subject seems to lie in the mode of ascertaining what that value is. Would not the safest plan be that which has been adopted by many of the States as the basis of taxation; an actual valuation of lands, and classification of them into different rates? Would it not be practicable and expedient to cause the relative value of the public lands in the old districts, which have been for a certain length of time in market, to be appraised, and classed into two or more rates below the present minimum price, by the officers now employed in this branch of the public service, or in any other mode deemed preferable, and to make those prices permanent, if upon the coming in of the report they shall prove satisfactory to Congress?

Cannot all the objects of graduation be accomplished in this way, and the objections which have hitherto been urged against it avoided? It would seem to me that such a step, with a restriction of the sales to limited quantities, and for actual improvement, would be free from all just exception."

A permanent prospective pre-emption law was cogently recommended as a measure just in itself to the settlers, and not injurious to the public Treasury, as experience had shown that the auction system—that of selling to the highest bidder above the prescribed minimum price—had produced in its aggregate but a few cents on the acre above the minimum price. On this point he said:

"A large portion of our citizens have seated themselves on the public lands, without authority, since the passage of the last pre-emption law and now ask the enactment of another, to enable them to retain the lands occupied, upon payment of the minimum government price. They ask that which has been repeatedly granted before. If the future may be judged of by the past, little harm can be done to the interests of the Treasury by yielding to their request. Upon a critical examination, it is found that the lands sold at the public sales since the introduction of cash payments in 1820, have produced, on an average, the net revenue of only six cents an acre more than the minimum government price. There is no reason to suppose that future sales will be more productive. The government, therefore, has no adequate pecuniary interest to induce it to drive these people from the lands they occupy, for the purpose of selling them to others."

This wise recommendation has since been carried into effect, and pre-emptive rights are now admitted in all cases where settlements are made upon lands to which the Indian title shall have been extinguished; and the graduation of the price of the public lands, though a measure long delayed, yet prevailed in the end, and was made as originally proposed, by reductions according to the length of time the land had been offered at sale. Beginning at the minimum price of $1 25 per acre, the reduction of price went down through a descending scale, according to time, as low as 12½ cents per acre. But this was long after.

CHAPTER XVII.

PENNSYLVANIA BANK OF THE UNITED STATES. ITS USE OF THE DEFUNCT NOTES OF THE EXPIRED INSTITUTION.

History gives many instances of armies refusing to be disbanded, and remaining in arms in defiance of the authority which created them; but the example of this bank presents, probably, the first instance in which a great moneyed corporation refused to be dissolved—refused to cease its operations after its legal existence had expired;—and continued its corporate transactions as if in full life. It has already been shown that its proviso charter, at the end of a local railroad act, made no difference in its condition—that it went on exactly as before. Its use of the defunct notes of the expired institution was a further instance of this conduct, transcending any thing conceived of, and presenting a case of danger to the public, and defiance of government, which the President had deemed it his duty to bring to the attention of Congress, and ask a remedy for a proceeding so criminal. Congress acted on the recommendation, and a bill was brought in to make the repetition of the offence a high misdemeanor, and the officers and managers of the institution personally and individually liable for its commission. In support of this bill, Mr. Buchanan gave the fullest and clearest account of this almost incredible misconduct. He said:

"The charter of the late Bank of the United States expired, by its own limitation, on the 3d of March, 1836. After that day, it could issue no notes, discount no new paper, and exercise none of the usual functions of a bank. For two years thereafter, until the 3d of March, 1838, it was merely permitted to use its corporate name and capacity 'for the purpose of suits for the final settlement and liquidation of the affairs and accounts of the corporation, and for the sale and disposition of their estate, real, personal, and mixed; *but not for any other purpose, or in any other manner, whatsoever.*' Congress had granted the bank no power to make a voluntary assignment of its property to any corporation or any individual. On the contrary, the plain meaning of the charter was, that all the affairs of the institution should be wound up by its own president and directors. It received no authority to delegate this important trust to others, and yet what has it done? On the second day of March, 1836, one day before the charter had expired, this very president and these directors assigned all the property and effects of the old corporation to the Pennsylvania Bank of the United States. On the same day, this latter bank accepted the assignment, and agreed to 'pay, satisfy, and discharge all debts, contracts, and engagements, owing, entered into, or made by this [the old] bank, as the same shall become due and payable, *and fulfil and execute all trusts and obligations whatsoever arising from its transactions, or from any of them,* so that every creditor or rightful claimant shall be fully satisfied.' By its own agreement, it has thus expressly created itself a trustee of the old bank. But this was not necessary to confer upon it that character. By the bare act of accepting the assignment, it became responsible, under the laws of the land, for the performance of all the duties and trusts required by the old charter. Under the circumstances, it cannot make the slightest pretence of any want of notice.

"Having assumed this responsibility, the duty of the new bank was so plain that it could not have been mistaken. It had a double character to sustain. Under the charter from Pennsylvania, it became a new banking corporation; whilst, under the assignment from the old bank, it became a trustee to wind up the concerns of that institution under the Act of Congress. These two characters were in their nature separate and distinct, and never ought to have been blended. For each of these purposes it ought to have kept a separate set of books. Above all, as the privilege of circulating bank notes, and thus creating a paper currency is that function of a bank which most deeply and vitally affects the community, the new bank ought to have cancelled or destroyed all the notes of the old bank which it found in its possession on the 4th of March, 1836, and ought to have redeemed the remainder at its counter, as they were demanded by the holders, and then destroyed them. This obligation no senator has attempted to doubt, or to deny. But what was the course of the bank? It has grossly violated both the old and the new charter. It at once declared independence of both, and appropriated to itself all the notes of the old bank,—not only those which were then still in circulation, but those which had been redeemed before it accepted the assignment, and were then lying dead in its vaults. I have now before me the first monthly statement which was ever made by the Bank to the Auditor-general of Pennsylvania. It is dated on the 2d of April, 1836, and signed J. Cowperthwaite, acting cashier. In this statement, the Bank charges itself with 'notes issued,' $36,620,420 16; whilst, in its cash account, along with its specie and the notes of State banks, it credits itself with 'notes of the Bank of the United States and offices,' on hand, $16,794,713 71. It thus seized these dead notes to the amount of $16,794,713 71, and transformed them into cash; whilst the difference between those on hand and those issued, equal to $19,825,706 45, was the circulation which the new bank boasted it had inherited from the old. It thus, in an instant, appropriated to itself, and adopted as its own circulation, all the notes and all the illegal branch drafts of the old bank which were then in existence. Its boldness was equal to its utter disregard of law. In this first return, it not only proclaimed to the Legislature and people of Pennsylvania that it had disregarded its trust as assignee of the old Bank, by seizing upon the whole of the old circulation and converting it to its own use, but that it had violated one of the fundamental provisions of its new charter."

Mr. Calhoun spoke chiefly to the question of the *right* of Congress to pass a bill of the tenor proposed. Several senators denied that right others supported it—among them Mr. Wright, Mr. Grundy, Mr. William H. Roane, Mr. John M. Niles, Mr. Clay, of Alabama, and Mr. Calhoun. Some passages from the speech of the latter are here given.

"He [Mr. Calhoun] held that the right proposed to be exercised in this case rested on the general power of legislation conferred on Congress, which embraces not only the power of making, but that of repealing laws. It was, in fact, a portion of the repealing power. No one could doubt the existence of the right to do either, and that the right of repealing extends as well to unconstitutional as constitutional laws. The case as to the former was, in fact, stronger than the latter; for, whether a constitutional law should be repealed or not, was a question of expediency, which left us free to act according to our discretion; while, in the case of an unconstitutional law, it was a matter of obligation and duty, leaving no option; and the more unconstitutional, the more imperious the obligation and duty. Thus far, there could be no doubt nor diversity of opinion. But there are many laws, the effects of which do not cease with their repeal or expiration, and which require some additional act on our part to arrest or undo them. Such, for instance, is the one in question. The charter of the late bank expired some time ago, but its notes are still in existence, freely circulating from hand to hand, and reissued and banked on by a bank chartered by the State of Pennsylvania, into whose possession the notes of the old bank have passed. In a word, our name and authority are used almost as freely for banking purposes as they were before the expiration of the charter of the late bank. Now, he held that the right of arresting or undoing these after-effects rested on the same principle as the right of repealing a law, and, like that, embraces unconstitutional as well as constitutional acts, superadding, in the case of the former, obligation and duty to right. We have an illustration of the truth of this principle in the case of the alien and sedition acts, which are now conceded on all sides to have been unconstitutional. Like the act incorporating the late bank, they expired by their own limitation; and, like it, also, their effects continued after the period of their expiration. Individuals had been tried, convicted, fined, and imprisoned under them; but, so far was their unconstitutionality from being regarded as an impediment to the right of arresting or undoing these effects, that Mr. Jefferson felt himself compelled on that very account to pardon those who had been fined and convicted under their provisions, and we have at this session passed, on the same ground, an act to refund the money paid by one of the sufferers under them. The bill is limited to those only who are the trustees, or agents for winding up the concerns of the late bank, and it is those, and those only, who are subject to the penalties of the bill for reissuing its notes. They are, *pro tanto*, our officers, and, to that extent, subject to our jurisdiction, and liable to have their acts controlled as far as they relate to the trust or agency confided to them; just as much so as receivers or collectors of the revenue would be. No one can doubt that we could prohibit them from passing off any description of paper currency that might come into their hands in their official character. Nor is the right less clear in reference to the persons who may be comprehended in this bill. Whether Mr. Biddle or others connected with this bank are, in fact, trustees, or agents, within the meaning of the bill, is not a question for us to decide. They are not named, nor referred to by description. The bill is very properly drawn up in general terms, so as to comprehend all cases of the kind, and would include the banks of the District, should Congress refuse to re-charter them. It is left to the court and jury, to whom it properly belongs, to decide, when a case comes up, whether the party is, or is not, a trustee, or agent; and, of course, whether he is, or is not, included in the provisions of the bill. If he is, he will be subject to its penalties, but not otherwise; and it cannot possibly affect the question of the constitutionality of the bill, whether Mr. Biddle, and others connected with him, are, or are not, comprehended in its provisions, and subject to its penalties."

The bill was severe in its enactments, prescribing both fine and imprisonment for the repetition of the offence—the fine not to exceed ten thousand dollars—the imprisonment not to be less than one nor more than five years. It also gave a preventive remedy in authorizing injunctions from the federal courts to prevent the circulation of such defunct notes, and proceedings in chancery to compel their surrender for cancellation. And to this "complexion" had the arrogant institution come which so lately held itself to be a *power*, and a great one, in the government—now borne on the statute book as criminally liable for a high misdemeanor, and giving its name to a new species of offence in the criminal catalogue—*exhumer and resurrectionist of defunct notes*. And thus ended the last question between the federal government and this, once so powerful moneyed corporation; and certainly any one who reads the history of that bank as faithfully shown in our parliamentary history, and briefly exhibited in this historic View, can ever wish to see another national bank established in our country, or any future connection of any kind between the government and the banks. The last struggle between it and the government was now over—just seven years since that struggle began: but its further conduct will extort a further notice from history.

CHAPTER XVIII.

FLORIDA INDIAN WAR: ITS ORIGIN AND CONDUCT.

This was one of the most troublesome, expensive and unmanageable Indian wars in which the United States had been engaged; and from the length of time which it continued, the amount of money it cost, and the difficulty of obtaining results, it became a convenient handle of attack upon the administration; and in which party spirit, in pursuit of its object, went the length of injuring both individual and national character. It continued about seven years—as long as the revolutionary war—cost some thirty millions of money—and baffled the exertions of several generals; recommenced when supposed to be finished; and was only finally terminated by changing military campaigns into an armed occupation by settlers. All the opposition presses and orators took hold of it, and made its misfortunes the common theme of invective and declamation. Its origin was charged to the oppressive conduct of the administration—its protracted length to their imbecility—its cost to their extravagance—its defeats to the want of foresight and care. The Indians stood for an innocent and persecuted people. Heroes and patriots were made of their chiefs. Our generals and troops were decried; applause was lavished upon a handful of savages who could thus defend their country; and corresponding censure upon successive armies which could not conquer them. All this going incessantly into the Congress debates and the party newspapers, was injuring the administration at home, and the country abroad; and, by dint of iteration and reiteration, stood a good chance to become history, and to be handed down to posterity. At the same time the war was one of flagrant and cruel aggression on the part of these Indians. Their removal to the west of the Mississippi was part of the plan for the general removal of all the Indians, and every preparation was complete for their departure by their own agreement, when it was interrupted by a horrible act. It was the 28th day of December, 1835, that the United States agent in Florida, and several others, were suddenly massacred by a party under Osceola, who had just been at the hospitable table with them: at the same time the sutler and others were attacked as they sat at table: same day two expresses were killed: and to crown these bloody deeds, the same day witnessed the destruction of Major Dade's command of 112 men, on its march from Tampa Bay to Withlacootchee. All these massacres were surprises, the result of concert, and executed as such upon unsuspecting victims. The agent (Mr. Thompson), and some friends were shot from the bushes while taking a walk near his house: the sutler and his guests were shot at the dinner table: the express riders were waylaid, and shot in the road: Major Dade's command was attacked on the march, by an unseen foe, overpowered, and killed nearly to the last man. All these deadly attacks took place on the same day, and at points wide apart—showing that the plot was as extensive as it was secret, and cruel as it was treacherous; for not a soul was spared in either of the four relentless attacks.

It was two days after the event that an infantry soldier of Major Dade's command, appeared at Fort King, on Tampa Bay, from which it had marched six days before, and gave information of what had happened. The command was on the march, in open pine woods, tall grass all around, and a swamp on the left flank. The grass concealed a treacherous ambuscade. The advanced guard had passed, and was cut off. Both the advance and the main body were attacked at the same moment, but divided from each other. A circle of fire enclosed each—fire from an invisible foe. To stand, was to be shot down: to advance was to charge upon concealed rifles. But it was the only course—was bravely adopted—and many savages thus sprung from their coverts, were killed. The officers, courageously exposing themselves, were rapidly shot—Major Dade early in the action. At the end of an hour successive charges had roused the savages from the grass, (which seemed to be alive with their naked and painted bodies, yelling and leaping,) and driven beyond the range of shot. But the command was too much weakened for a further operation. The wounded were too numerous to be carried along: too precious to be left behind to be massacred. The battle ground was maintained, and a small band had conquered respite from attack: but to advance or retreat was equally impossible. The only resource was to build a small pen of pine logs, cut from the forest, collect the wounded and the survivors into it, as into a little fort, and repulse the assailants as long as possible. This was done till near sunset—the action having began at ten in the morning. By that time every officer was dead but one, and he desperately wounded, and helpless on the ground. Only two men remained without wounds, and they red with the blood of others, spirted upon them, or stained in helping the helpless. The little pen was filled with the dead and the dying. The firing ceased. The expiring lieutenant told the survivors he could do no more for them, and gave them leave to save themselves as they could. They asked his advice. He gave it to them; and to that advice we are indebted for the only report of that bloody day's work. He advised them all to lay down among the dead—to remain still—and take their chance of being considered dead. This advice was followed. All became still, prostrate and motionless; and the savages, slowly and cautiously approaching, were a long time before they would venture within the ghastly pen, where danger might still lurk under apparent death. A squad of about forty negroes—fugitives from the Southern States, more savage than the savage—were the first to enter. They came in with knives and hatchets, cutting throats and splitting skulls wherever they saw a sign of life. To make sure of skipping no one alive, all were pulled and handled, punched and kicked; and a groan or movement, an opening of the eye, or even the involuntary contraction of a muscle, was an invitation to the knife and the tomahawk. Only four of the living were able to subdue sensations, bodily and mental, and remain without sign of feeling under this dreadful ordeal; and two of these received stabs, or blows—as many of the dead did. Lying still until the search was over, and darkness had come on, and the butchers were gone, these four crept from among their dead comrades and undertook to make their way back to Tampa Bay—separating into two parties for greater safety. The one that came in first had a narrow escape. Pursuing a path the next day, an Indian on horseback, and with a rifle across the saddle bow, met them full in the way. To separate, and take the chance of a divided pursuit, was the only hope for either: and they struck off into opposite directions. The one to the right was pursued; and very soon the sharp crack of a rifle made known his fate to the one that had gone to the left. To him it was a warning, that his comrade being despatched, his own turn came next. It was open pine woods, and a running, or standing man, visible at a distance. The Indian on horseback was already in view. Escape by flight was impossible. Concealment in the grass, or among the palmettos, was the only hope: and this was tried. The man laid close: the Indian rode near him. He made circles around, eyeing the ground far and near. Rising in his stirrups to get a wider view, and seeing nothing, he turned the head of his horse and galloped off—the poor soldier having been almost under the horse's feet. This man, thus marvellously escaping, was the first to bring in the sad report of the Dade defeat—followed soon after by two others with its melancholy confirmation. And these were the only reports ever received of that completest of defeats. No officer survived to report a word. All were killed in their places—men and officers, each in his place, no one breaking ranks or giving back: and when afterwards the ground was examined, and events verified by signs, the skeletons in their places, and the bullet holes in trees and logs, and the little pen with its heaps of bones, showed that the carnage had taken place exactly as described by the men. And this was the slaughter of Major Dade and his command—of 108 out of 112: as treacherous, as barbarous, as perseveringly cruel as ever was known. One single feature is some relief to the sadness of the picture, and discriminates this defeat from most others suffered at the hands of Indians. There were no prisoners put to death; for no man surrendered. There were no fugitives slain in vain attempts at flight; for no one fled. All stood, and fought, and fell in their places, returning blow for blow while life lasted. It was the death of soldiers, showing that steadiness in defeat which is above courage in victory.

And this was the origin of the Florida Indian war: and a more treacherous, ferocious, and cold-blooded origin was never given to any Indian war. Yet such is the perversity of party spirit that its author—the savage Osceola—has been exalted into a hero-patriot; our officers, disparaged and ridiculed; the administration loaded with obloquy. And all this by our public men in Congress, as well as by writers in the daily and periodical publications. The future historian who should take these speeches and publications for their guide, (and they are too numerous and emphatic to be overlooked,) would write a history discreditable to our arms, and reproachful to our justice. It would be a narrative of wickedness and imbecility on our part—of patriotism and heroism on the part of the Indians: those Indians whose very name (Seminole—wild,) define them as the fugitives from all tribes, and made still worse than fugitive Indians by a mixture with fugitive negroes, some of whom became their chiefs. It was to obviate the danger of such a history as that would be, that the author of this View delivered at the time, and in the presence of all concerned, an historical speech on the Florida Indian war, fortified by facts, and intended to stand for true; and which has remained unimpeached. Extracts from that speech will constitute the next chapter, to which this brief sketch will serve as a preface and introduction.

CHAPTER XIX.

FLORIDA INDIAN WAR: HISTORICAL SPEECH OF MR. BENTON

A senator from New Jersey [Mr. SOUTHARD] has brought forward an accusation which must affect the character of the late and present administrations at home, and the character of the country abroad; and which, justice to these administrations, and to the country, requires to be met and answered upon the spot. That senator has expressly charged that a fraud was committed upon the Florida Indians in the treaty negotiated with them for their removal to the West; that the war which has ensued was the consequence of this fraud; and that our government was responsible to the moral sense of the community, and of the world, for all the blood that has been shed, and for all the money that has been expended, in the prosecution of this war. This is a heavy accusation. At home, it attaches to the party in power, and is calculated to make them odious; abroad, it attaches to the country, and is calculated to blacken the national character. It is an accusation, without the shadow of a foundation! and, both, as one of the party in power, and as an American citizen, I feel myself impelled by an imperious sense of duty to my friends, and to my country, to expose its incorrectness at once, and to vindicate the government, and the country, from an imputation as unfounded as it is odious.

The senator from New Jersey first located this imputed fraud in the Payne's Landing treaty, negotiated by General Gadsden, in Florida, in the year 1832; and, after being tendered an issue on the fairness and generosity of that treaty by the senator from Alabama [Mr. CLAY], he transferred the charge to the Fort Gibson treaty, made in Arkansas, in the year 1833, by Messrs. Stokes, Ellsworth and Schermerhorn. This was a considerable change of locality, but no change in the accusation itself; the two treaties being but one, and the last being a literal performance of a stipulation contained in the first. These are the facts; and, after stating the case, I will prove it as stated. This is the statement: The Seminole Indians in Florida being an emigrant band of the Creeks, and finding game exhausted, subsistence difficult, and white settlements approaching, concluded to follow the mother tribe, the Creeks, to the west of the Mississippi, and to reunite with them. This was conditionally agreed to be done at the Payne's Landing treaty; and in that treaty it was stipulated that a deputation of Seminole chiefs, under the sanction of the government of the United States, should proceed to the Creek country beyond the Mississippi—there to ascertain first whether a suitable country could be obtained for them there; and, secondly, whether the Creeks would receive them back as a part of their confederacy: and if the deputation should be satisfied on these two points, then the conditional obligation to remove, contained in the Payne's Landing treaty, to become binding and obligatory upon the Seminole tribe. The deputation went: the two points were solved in the affirmative the obligation to remove became absolute on the part of the Indians; and the government of the United States commenced preparations for effecting their easy, gradual, and comfortable removal.

The entire emigration was to be completed in three years, one-third going annually, commencing in the year 1833, and to be finished in the years 1834, and 1835. The deputation sent to the west of the Mississippi, completed their agreement with the Creeks on the 28th of March, 1833; they returned home immediately, and one-third of the tribe was to remove that year. Every thing was got ready on the part of the United States, both to transport the Indians to their new homes, and to subsist them for a year after their arrival there. But, instead of removing, the Indians began to invent excuses, and to interpose delays, and to pass off the time without commencing the emigration. The year 1833, in which one-third of the tribe were to remove, passed off without any removal; the year 1834, in which another third was to go, was passed off in the same manner; the year 1835, in which the emigration was to have been completed, passed away, and the emigration was not begun. On the contrary, on the last days of the last month of that year, while the United States was still peaceably urging the removal, an accumulation of treacherous and horrible assassinations and massacres were committed. The United States agent, General Thompson, Lieutenant Smith, of the artillery, and five others, were assassinated in sight of Fort King; two expresses were murdered; and Major Dade's command was massacred.

In their excuses and pretexts for not removing, the Indians never thought of the reasons which have been supplied to them on this floor. They never thought of alleging fraud. Their pretexts were frivolous; as that it was a long distance, and that bad Indians lived in that country, and that the old treaty of Fort Moultrie allowed them twenty years to live in Florida. Their real motive was the desire of blood and pillage on the part of many

Indians, and still more on the part of the five hundred runaway negroes mixed up among them; and who believed that they could carry on their system of robbery and murder with impunity, and that the swamps of the country would for ever protect them against the pursuit of the whites.

This, Mr. President, is the plain and brief narrative of the causes which led to the Seminole war; it is the brief historical view of the case; and if I was speaking under ordinary circumstances, and in reply to incidental remarks, I should content myself with this narrative, and let the question go to the country upon the strength and credit of this statement. But I do not speak under ordinary circumstances; I am not replying to incidental and casual remarks. I speak in answer to a formal accusation, preferred on this floor; I speak to defend the late and present administrations from an odious charge; and, in defending them, to vindicate the character of our country from the accusation of the senator from New Jersey [Mr. SOUTHARD], and to show that fraud has not been committed upon these Indians, and that the guilt of a war, founded in fraud, is not justly imputable to them.

The Seminoles had stipulated that the agent, Major Phagan, and their own interpreter, the negro Abraham, should accompany them; and this was done. It so happened, also, that an extraordinary commission of three members sent out by the United States to adjust Indian difficulties generally, was then beyond the Mississippi; and these commissioners were directed to join in the negotiations on the part of the United States, and to give the sanction of our guarantee to the agreements made between the Seminoles and the Creeks for the reunion of the former to the parent tribe. This was done. Our commissioners, Messrs. Stokes, Ellsworth, and Schermerhorn, became party to a treaty with the Creek Indians for the reunion of the Seminoles, made at Fort Gibson, the 14th of February, 1833. The treaty contained this article:

> "ARTICLE IV. It is understood and agreed that the Seminole Indians of Florida, whose removal to this country is provided for by their treaty with the United States, dated May 9, 1832, shall also have a permanent and comfortable home on the lands hereby set apart as the country of the Creek nation; and they, the Seminoles, will hereafter be considered as a constituent part of the said nation, but are to be located on some part of the Creek country by themselves, which location shall be selected for them by the commissioners who have seen these articles of agreement."

This agreement with the Creeks settled one of the conditions on which the removal of the Seminoles was to depend. We will now see how the other condition was disposed of.

In a treaty made at the same Fort Gibson, on the 28th of March, 1833, between the same three commissioners on the part of the United States, and the seven delegated Seminole chiefs, after reciting the two conditions precedent contained in the Payne's Landing treaty, and reciting, also, the convention with the Creeks on the 14th of February preceding, it is thus stipulated:

> "Now, therefore, the commissioners aforesaid, by virtue of the power and authority vested in them by the treaty made with the Creek Indians on the 14th of February, 1833, as above stated, hereby designate and assign to the Seminole tribe of Indians, for their separate future residence for ever, a tract of country lying between the Canadian River and the south fork thereof, and extending west to where a line running north and south between the main Canadian and north branch will strike the forks of Little River; provided said west line does not extend more than twenty-five miles west from the mouth of said Little River. And the undersigned Seminole chiefs, delegated as aforesaid, on behalf of the nation, hereby declare themselves well satisfied with the location provided for them by the commissioners, and agree that their nation shall commence the removal to their new home as soon as the government will make the arrangements for their emigration satisfactory to the Seminole nation."

This treaty is signed by the delegation, and by the commissioners of the United States, and witnessed, among others, by the same Major Phagan, agent, and Abraham, interpreter, whose presence was stipulated for at Payne's Landing.

Thus the two conditions on which the removal depended, were complied with; they were both established in the affirmative. The Creeks, under the solemn sanction and guarantee of the United States, agree to receive back the Seminoles as a part of their confederacy, and agree that they shall live adjoining them on lands designated for their residence. The delegation declare themselves well satisfied with the country assigned them, and agree that the removal should commence as soon as the United States could make the necessary arrangements for the removal of the people.

This brings down the proof to the conclusion of all questions beyond the Mississippi; it brings it down to the conclusion of the treaty at Fort Gibson—that treaty in which the senator from New Jersey [Mr. SOUTHARD] has located the charge of fraud, after withdrawing the same charge from the Payne's Landing treaty. It brings us to the end of the negotiations at the point selected for the charge; and now how stands the accusation? How stands the charge of fraud? Is there a shadow, an atom, a speck, of foundation on which to rest it? No, sir: Nothing—nothing—nothing! Every thing was done that was stipulated for; done by the persons who were to do it; and done in the exact manner agreed upon. In fact, the nature of the things to be done west of the Mississippi was such as not to admit of fraud. Two things were to be done, one to be seen with the eyes, and the other to be heard with the ears. The deputation was to see their new country, and say whether they liked it. This was a question to their own senses—to their own eyes—and was not susceptible of fraud. They were to *hear* whether the Creeks would receive them back as a part of their confederacy; this was a question to their own *ears*, and was also unsusceptible of fraud. Their own eyes could not deceive them in looking at land; their own ears could not deceive them in listening to their own language from the Creeks. No, sir: there was no physical capacity, or moral means, for the perpetration of fraud; and none has ever been pretended by the Indians from that day to this. The Indians themselves have never thought of such a thing. There is no assumption of a deceived party among them. It is not a deceived party that is at war—a party deceived by the delegation which went to the West—but that very delegation itself, with the exception of Charley Emarthla, are the hostile leaders at home! This is reducing the accusation to an absurdity. It is making the delegation the dupes of their own eyes and of their own ears, and then going to war with the United States, because their own eyes deceived them in looking at land on the Canadian River, and their own ears deceived them in listening to their own language from the Creeks; and then charging these frauds upon the United States. All this is absurd; and it is due to these absent savages to say that they never committed any such absurdity—that they never placed their objection to remove upon any plea of deception practised upon them beyond the Mississippi, but on frivolous pretexts invented long after the return of the delegation; which pretexts covered the real grounds growing out of the influence of runaway slaves, and some evilly disposed chiefs, and that thirst for blood and plunder, in which they expected a long course of enjoyment and impunity in their swamps, believed to be impenetrable to the whites.

Thus, sir, it is clearly and fully proved that there was no fraud practised upon these Indians; that they themselves never pretended such a thing; and that the accusation is wholly a charge of recent origin sprung up among ourselves. Having shown that there was no fraud, this might be sufficient for the occasion, but having been forced into the inquiry, it may be as well to complete it by showing what were the causes of this war. To understand these causes, it is necessary to recur to dates, to see the extreme moderation with which the United States acted, the long time which they tolerated the delays of the Indians, and the treachery and murder with which their indulgence and forbearance was requited. The emigration was to commence in 1833, and be completed in the years 1834 and 1835. The last days of the last month of this last year had arrived, and the emigration had not yet commenced. Wholly intent on their peaceable removal, the administration had despatched a disbursing agent, Lieutenant Harris of the army, to take charge of the expenditures for the subsistence of these people. He arrived at Fort King on the afternoon of the 28th of December, 1835; and as he entered the fort, he became almost an eye-witness of a horrid scene which was the subject of his first despatch to his government. He describes it in these words:

> "I regret that it becomes my first duty after my arrival here to be the narrator of a story, which it will be, I am sure, as painful for you to hear, as it is for me, who was almost an eye witness to the bloody deed, to relate to you. Our excellent superintendent, General Wiley Thompson, has been most cruelly murdered by a party of the hostile Indians, and with him Lieutenant

Constant Smith, of the 2d regiment of artillery, Erastus Rogers, the suttler to the post, with his two clerks, a Mr. Kitzler, and a boy called Robert. This occurred on the afternoon of the 28th instant (December), between three and four o'clock. On the day of the massacre, Lieutenant Smith had dined with the General, and after dinner invited him to take a short stroll with him. They had not proceeded more than three hundred yards beyond the agency office, when they were fired upon by a party of Indians, who rose from ambush in the hammock, within sight of the fort, and on which the suttler's house borders. The reports of the rifles fired, the war-whoop twice repeated, and after a brief space, several other volleys more remote, and in the quarter of Mr. Rogers's house, were heard, and the smoke of the firing seen from the fort. Mr. Rogers and his clerks were surprised at dinner. Three escaped: the rest murdered. The bodies of General Thompson, Lieutenant Smith, and Mr. Kitzler, were soon found and brought in. Those of the others were not found until this morning. That of General Thompson was perforated with fourteen bullets. Mr. Rogers had received seventeen. All were scalped, except the boy. The cowardly murderers are supposed to be a party of Micasookees, 40 or 50 strong, under the traitor Powell (Osceola), whose shrill, peculiar war-whoop, was recognized by our interpreters, and the one or two friendly Indians we have in the fort, and who knew it well. Two expresses (soldiers) were despatched upon fresh horses on the evening of this horrid tragedy, with tidings of it to General Clinch; but not hearing from him or them, we conclude they were cut off. We are also exceedingly anxious for the fate of the two companies (under Major Dade) which had been ordered up from Fort Brooke, and of whom we learn nothing."

Sir, this is the first letter of the disbursing agent, specially detached to furnish the supplies to the emigrating Indians. He arrives in the midst of treachery and murder; and his first letter is to announce to the government the assassination of their agent, an officer of artillery, and five citizens; the assassination of two expresses, for they were both waylaid and murdered; and the massacre of one hundred and twelve men and officers under Major Dade. All this took place at once; and this was the beginning of the war. Up to that moment the government of the United States were wholly employed in preparing the Indians for removal, recommending them to go, and using no force or violence upon them. This is the way the war was brought on; this is the way it began; and was there ever a case in which a government was so loudly called upon to avenge the dead, to protect the living, and to cause itself to be respected by punishing the contemners of its power? The murder of the agent was a double offence, a peculiar outrage to the government whose representative he was, and a violation even of the national law of savages. Agents are seldom murdered even by savages; and bound as every government is to protect all its citizens, it is doubly bound to protect its agents and representatives abroad. Here, then, is a government agent, and a military officer, five citizens, two expresses, and a detachment of one hundred and twelve men, in all one hundred and twenty-one persons, treacherously and inhumanly massacred in one day! and because General Jackson's administration did not submit to this horrid outrage, he is charged with the guilt of a war founded in fraud upon innocent and unoffending Indians! Such is the spirit of opposition to our own government! such the love of Indians and contempt of whites! and such the mawkish sentimentality of the day in which we live—a sentimentality which goes moping and sorrowing about in behalf of imaginary wrongs to Indians and negroes, while the whites themselves are the subject of murder, robbery and defamation.

The prime mover in all this mischief, and the leading agent in the most atrocious scene of it, was a half-blooded Indian of little note before this time, and of no consequence in the councils of his tribe; for his name is not to be seen in the treaty either of Payne's Landing or Fort Gibson. We call him Powell; by his tribe he was called Osceola. He led the attack in the massacre of the agent, and of those who were killed with him, in the afternoon of the 28th of December. The disbursing agent, whose letter has been read, in his account of that massacre, applies the epithet *traitor* to the name of this Powell. Well might he apply that epithet to that assassin; for he had just been fed and caressed by the very person whom he waylaid and murdered. He had come into the agency shortly before that time with seventy of his followers, professed his satisfaction with the treaty, his readiness to remove, and received subsistence and supplies for himself and all his party. The most friendly relations seemed to be established; and the doomed and deceived agent, in giving his account of it to the government, says: "The result was that we closed with the utmost good feeling; and I have never seen Powell and the other chiefs so cheerful and in so fine a humor, at the close of a discussion upon the subject of removal."

This is Powell (Osceola), for whom all our sympathies are so pathetically invoked! a treacherous assassin, not only of our people, but of his own—for he it was who waylaid, and shot in the back, in the most cowardly manner, the brave chief Charley Emarthla, whom he dared not face, and whom he thus assassinated because he refused to join him and his runaway negroes in murdering the white people. The collector of Indian curiosities and portraits, Mr. Catlin, may be permitted to manufacture a hero out of this assassin, and to make a poetical scene of his imprisonment on Sullivan's island; but it will not do for an American senator to take the same liberties with historical truth and our national character. Powell ought to have been hung for the assassination of General Thompson; and the only fault of our officers is, that they did not hang him the moment they caught him. The fate of Arbuthnot and Ambrister was due to him a thousand times over.

I have now answered the accusation of the senator from New Jersey [Mr. SOUTHARD]. I have shown the origin of this war. I have shown that it originated in no fraud, no injustice, no violence, on the part of this government, but in the thirst for blood and rapine on the part of these Indians, and in their confident belief that their swamps would be their protection against the pursuit of the whites; and that, emerging from these fastnesses to commit robbery and murder, and retiring to them to enjoy the fruits of their marauding expeditions, they had before them a long perspective of impunity in the enjoyment of their favorite occupation. This I have shown to be the cause of the war; and having vindicated the administration and the country from the injustice of the imputation cast upon them, I proceed to answer some things said by a senator from South Carolina [Mr. PRESTON], which tended to disparage the troops generally which have been employed in Florida; to disparage a particular general officer, and also to accuse that general officer of a particular and specified offence. That senator has decried our troops in Florida for the general inefficiency of their operations; he has decried General Jesup for the general imbecility of his operations, and he has charged this General with the violation of a flag, and the commission of a perfidious act, in detaining and imprisoning the Indian Powell, who came into his camp.

I think there is great error and great injustice in all these imputations, and that it is right for some senator on this floor to answer them. My position, as chairman of the Committee on Military Affairs, would seem to assign that duty to me, and it may be the reason why others who have spoken have omitted all reply on these points. Be that as it may, I feel impelled to say something in behalf of those who are absent, and cannot speak for themselves—those who must always feel the wound of unmerited censure, and must feel it more keenly when the blow that inflicts the wound falls from the elevated floor of the American Senate. So far as the army, generally, is concerned in this censure, I might leave them where they have been placed by the senator from South Carolina [Mr. PRESTON], and others on that side of the House, if I could limit myself to acting a political part here. The army, as a body, is no friend of the political party to which I belong. Individuals among them are friendly to the administration; but, as a body, they go for the opposition, and would terminate our political existence, if they could, and put our opponents in our place, at the first general election that intervenes. As a politician, then, I might abandon them to the care of their political friends; but, as an American, as a senator, and as having had some connection with the military profession, I feel myself called upon to dissent from the opinion which has been expressed, and to give my reasons for believing that the army has not suffered, and ought not to suffer, in character, by the events in Florida. True, our officers and soldiers have not performed the same feats there which they performed in Canada, and elsewhere. But why? Certainly because they have not got the same, or an equivalent, theatre to act upon, nor an enemy to cope with over whom brilliant victories can be obtained. The peninsula of Florida, where this war rages, is sprinkled all over with swamps, hammocks, and lagoons, believed for three hundred years to be impervious to the white man's tread. The theatre of war is of great extent, stretching over six parallels of latitude; all of it in the sultry region below thirty-one degrees of north latitude. The extremity of this peninsula approaches the tropic of Capricorn; and at this moment, while we speak here, the soldier under arms at mid-day there will cast no shadow: a vertical sun darts its fiery rays direct upon the crown of his head. Suffocating heat oppresses the frame; annoying insects sting the body; burning sands, a spongy morass, and the sharp cutting saw grass, receive the feet and legs; disease follows the summer's exertion; and a dense foliage covers the foe. Eight months in the year military exertions are impossible; during four months only can any thing be done. The Indians well understand this; and, during these four months, either give or receive an attack, as they please, or endeavor to consume the season in wily parleys. The possibility of splendid military exploits does not exist in such a country, and against such a foe: but there is room there, and ample room there, for the exhibition of the highest qualities of the soldier. There is room there for patience, and for fortitude, under every variety of suffering, and under every form of privation. There is room there for courage and discipline to exhibit itself against perils and trials which subject courage and discipline to the severest tests. And has there been any failure of patience, fortitude, courage, discipline, and subordination in all this war? Where is the instance in which the men have revolted against their officers, or in which the officer has deserted his men? Where is the instance of a flight in battle? Where the instance of orders disobeyed, ranks broken, or confusion of corps? On the contrary, we have constantly seen the steadiness, and the discipline, of the parade maintained under every danger, and in the presence of massacre itself. Officers and men have fought it out where they were told to fight; they have been killed in the tracks in which they were told to stand. None of those pitiable scenes of which all our Indian wars have shown some— those harrowing scenes in which the helpless prisoner, or the hapless fugitive, is massacred without pity, and without resistance: none of these have been seen. Many have perished; but it was the death of the combatant in arms, and not of the captive or the fugitive. In no one of our savage wars have our troops so stood together, and conquered together, and died together, as they have done in this one; and this standing together is the test of the soldier's character. Steadiness, subordination, courage, discipline,—these are the test of the soldier; and in no instance have our troops, or any troops, ever evinced the possession of these qualities in a higher degree than during the campaigns in Florida. While, then, brilliant victories may not have been seen, and, in fact, were impossible, yet the highest qualities of good soldiership have been eminently displayed throughout this war. Courage and discipline have shown themselves, throughout all its stages, in their noblest forms.

From the general imputation of inefficiency in our operations in Florida, the senator from South Carolina [Mr. PRESTON] comes to a particular commander, and charges inefficiency specifically upon him. This commander is General Jesup. The senator from South Carolina has been lavish, and even profuse, in his denunciation of that general, and has gone so far as to talk about military courts of inquiry. Leaving the general open to all such inquiry, and thoroughly convinced that the senator from South Carolina has no idea of moving such inquiry, and intends to rest the effect of his denunciation upon its delivery here, I shall proceed to answer him here— giving speech for speech on this floor, and leaving the general himself to reply when it comes to that threatened inquiry, which I undertake to affirm will never be moved.

General Jesup is charged with imbecility and inefficiency; the continuance of the war is imputed to his incapacity; and he is held up here, on the floor of the Senate, to public reprehension for these imputed delinquencies. This is the accusation; and now let us see with how much truth and justice it is made. Happily for General Jesup, this happens to be a case in which we have data to go upon, and in which there are authentic materials for comparing the operations of himself with those of other generals—his predecessors in the same field—with whose success the senator from South Carolina is entirely satisfied. Dates and figures furnish this data and these materials; and, after refreshing the memory of the Senate with a few dates, I will proceed to the answers which the facts of the case supply. The first date is, as to the time of the commencement of this war; the second, as to the time that General Jesup assumed the command; the third, as to the time when he was relieved from the command. On the first point, it will be recollected that the war broke out upon the assassination of General Thompson, the agent, Lieutenant Smith, who was with him; the sutler and his clerks; the murder of the two expresses; and the massacre of Major Dade's command;—events which came together in point of time, and compelled an immediate resort to war by the United States. These assassinations, these murders, and this massacre, took place on the 28th day of December, 1835. The commencement of the war, then, dates from that day. The next point is, the time of General Jesup's appointment to the command. This occurred in December, 1836. The third point is, the date of General Jesup's relief from the command, and this took place in May, of the present year, 1838. The war has then continued—counting to the present time—two years and a half; and of that period, General Jesup has had command something less than one year and a half. Other generals had command for a year before he was appointed in that quarter. Now, how much had those other generals done? All put together, how much had they done? And I ask this question not to disparage their meritorious exertions, but to obtain data for the vindication of the officer now assailed. The senator from

South Carolina [Mr. PRESTON] is satisfied with the operations of the previous commanders; now let him see how the operations of the officer whom he assails will compare with the operations of those who are honored with his approbation. The comparison is brief and mathematical. It is a problem in the exact sciences. General Jesup reduced the hostiles in the one year and a half of his command, 2,200 souls: all his predecessors together had reduced them 150 in one year. Where does censure rest now?

Sir, I disparage nobody. I make no exhibit of comparative results to undervalue the operations of the previous commanders in Florida. I know the difficulty of military operations there, and the ease of criticism here. I never assailed those previous commanders; on the contrary, often pointed out the nature of the theatre on which they operated as a cause for the miscarriage of expeditions, and for the want of brilliant and decisive results. Now for the first time I refer to the point, and, not to disparage others, but to vindicate the officer assailed. His vindication is found in the comparison of results between himself and his predecessors, and in the approbation of the senator from South Carolina of the results under the predecessors of General Jesup. Satisfied with *them*, he must be satisfied with *him*; for the difference is as fifteen to one in favor of the decried general.

 Besides the general denunciation for inefficiency, which the senator from South Carolina has lavished upon General Jesup, and which denunciation has so completely received its answer in this comparative statement; besides this general denunciation, the senator from South Carolina brought forward a specific accusation against the honor of the same officer—an accusation of perfidy, and of a violation of flag of truce, in the seizure and detention of the Indian Osceola, who had come into his camp. On the part of General Jesup, I repel this accusation, and declare his whole conduct in relation to this Indian, to have been *justifiable*, under the laws of civilized or savage warfare; that it was *expedient* in point of policy; and that if any blame could attach to the general, it would be for the contrary of that with which he is blamed; it would be for an excess of forbearance and indulgence.

The justification of the general for the seizure and detention of this half-breed Indian, is the first point; and that rests upon several and distinct grounds, either of which fully justifies the act.

1. *This Osceola had broken his parole; and, therefore, was liable to be seized and detained.*

The facts were these: In the month of May, 1837, this chief, with his followers, went into Fort Mellon, under the cover of a white flag, and there surrendered to Lieutenant Colonel Harney. He declared himself done with the war, and ready to emigrate to the west of the Mississippi, and solicited subsistence and transportation for himself and his people for that purpose. Lieutenant Colonel Harney received him, supplied him with provisions, and, relying upon his word and apparent sincerity, instead of sending him under guard, took his parole to go to Tampa Bay, the place at which he preferred to embark, to take shipping there for the West. Supplied with every thing, Osceola and his people left Fort Mellon, under the pledge to go to Tampa Bay. He never went there! but returned to the hostiles; and it was afterwards ascertained that he never had any idea of going West, but merely wished to live well for a while at the expense of the whites, examine their strength and position, and return to his work of blood and pillage. After this, he had the audacity to approach General Jesup's camp in October of the same year, with another piece of white cloth over his head, thinking, after his successful treacheries to the agent, General Thompson, and Lieut. Colonel Harney, that there was no end to his tricks upon white people. General Jesup ordered him to be seized and carried a prisoner to Sullivan's Island, where he was treated with the greatest humanity, and allowed every possible indulgence and gratification. This is one of the reasons in justification of General Jesup's conduct to that Indian, and it is sufficient of itself; but there are others, and they shall be stated.

2. *Osceola had violated an order in coming in, with a view to return to the hostiles; and, therefore, was liable to be detained.*

The facts were these: Many Indians, at different times, had come in under the pretext of a determination to emigrate; and after receiving supplies, and viewing the strength and position of the troops, returned again to the hostiles, and carried on the war with renewed vigor. This had been done repeatedly. It was making a mockery of the white flag, and subjecting our officers to ridicule as well as to danger. General Jesup resolved to put an end to these treacherous and dangerous visits, by which spies and enemies obtained access to the bosom of his camp. He made known to the chief, Coi Hadjo, his determination to that effect. In August, 1837, he declared peremptorily to this chief, for the information of all the Indians, that none were to come in, except to remain, and to emigrate; that no one coming into his camp again should be allowed to go out of it, but should be considered as having surrendered with a view to emigrate under the treaty, and should be detained for that purpose. In October, Osceola came in, in violation of that order, and was detained in compliance with it. This is a second reason for the justification of General Jesup, and is of itself sufficient to justify him; but there is more justification yet, and I will state it.

3. *Osceola, had broken a truce, and, therefore, was liable to be detained whenever he could be taken.*

The facts were these: The hostile chiefs entered into an agreement for a truce at Fort King, in August, 1837, and agreed: 1. Not to commit any act of hostility upon the whites; 2. Not to go east of the St. John's river, or north of Fort Mellon. This truce was broken by the Indians in both points. A citizen was killed by them, and they passed both to the east of the St. John's and far north of Fort Mellon. As violators of this truce, General Jesup had a right to detain any of the hostiles which came into his hands, and Osceola was one of these.

Here, sir, are three grounds of justification, either of them sufficient to justify the conduct of General Jesup towards Powell, as the gentlemen call him. The first of the three reasons applies personally and exclusively to that half-breed; the other two apply to all the hostile Indians, and justify the seizure and detention of others, who have been sent to the West.

So much for justification; now for the expediency of having detained this Indian Powell. I hold it was expedient to exercise the right of detaining him, and prove this expediency by reasons both *a priori* and *a posteriori*. His previous treachery and crimes, and his well known disposition for further treachery and crimes, made it right for the officers of the United States to avail themselves of the first justifiable occasion to put an end to his depredations by confining his person until the war was over. This is a reason *a priori*. The reason *a posteriori* is, that it has turned out right; it has operated well upon the mass of the Indians, between eighteen and nineteen hundred of which, negroes inclusive, have since surrendered to Gen. Jesup. This, sir, is a fact which contains an argument which overturns all that can be said on this floor against the detention of Osceola. The Indians themselves do not view that act as perfidious or dishonorable, or the violation of a flag, or even the act of an enemy. They do not condemn General Jesup on account of it, but no doubt respect him the more for refusing to be made the dupe of a treacherous artifice. A bit of white linen, stripped, perhaps from the body of a murdered child, or its murdered mother, was no longer to cover the insidious visits of spies and enemies. A firm and manly course was taken, and the effect was good upon the minds of the Indians. The number since surrendered is proof of its effect upon their minds; and this proof should put to blush the lamentations which are here set up for Powell, and the censure thrown upon General Jesup.

No, sir, no. General Jesup has been guilty of no perfidy, no fraud, no violation of flags. He has done nothing to stain his own character, or to dishonor the flag of the United States. If he has erred, it has been on the side of humanity, generosity, and forbearance to the Indians. If he has erred, as some suppose, in losing time to parley with the Indians, that error has been on the side of humanity, and of confidence in them. But has he erred? Has his policy been erroneous? Has the country been a loser by his policy? To all these questions, let results give the answer. Let the twenty-two hundred Indians, abstracted from the hostile ranks by his measures, be put in contrast with the two hundred, or less, killed and taken by his predecessors. Let these results be compared; and let this comparison answer the question whether, in point of fact, there has been any error, even a mistake of judgment, in his mode of conducting the war.

The senator from South Carolina [Mr. PRESTON] complains of the length of time which General Jesup has consumed without bringing the war to a close. Here, again, the chapter of comparisons must be resorted to in order to obtain the answer which justice requires. How long, I pray you, was General Jesup in command? from December, 1836, to May, 1838; nominally he was near a year and a half in command; in reality not one year, for the summer months admit of no military operations in that peninsula. His predecessors commanded from December, 1835, to December, 1836; a term wanting but a few months of as long a period as the command of General Jesup lasted. Sir, there is nothing in the length of time which this general commanded, to furnish matter for disadvantageous comparisons to him; but the contrary. He reduced the hostiles about one-half in a year and a half; they reduced them about the one-twentieth in a year. The whole number was about 5,000; General Jesup diminished their number, during his command, 2,200; the other generals had reduced them about 150. At the rate he proceeded, the work would be finished in about three years; at the rate they proceeded, in about twenty years. Yet he is to be censured here for the length of time consumed without bringing the war to a close. He, and he alone, is selected for censure. Sir, I dislike these comparisons; it is a disagreeable task for me to make them; but I am driven to it, and mean no disparagement to others. The violence with which General Jesup is assailed here—the comparisons to which he has been subjected in order to degrade him— leave me no alternative but to abandon a meritorious officer to unmerited censure, or to defend him in the same manner in which he has been assailed.

The essential policy of General Jesup has been to induce the Indians to come in—to surrender—and to emigrate under the treaty. This has been his main, but not his exclusive, policy; military operations have been combined with it; many skirmishes and actions have been fought since he had command; and it is remarkable that this general, who has been so much assailed on this floor, is the only commander-in-chief in Florida who has been wounded in battle at the head of his command. His person marked with the scars of wounds received in Canada during the late war with Great Britain, has also been struck by a bullet, in the face, in the peninsula of Florida; yet these wounds—the services in the late war with Great Britain—the removal of upwards of 16,000 Creek Indians from Alabama and Georgia to the West, during the summer of 1836—and more than twenty-five years of honorable employment in the public service—all these combined, and an unsullied private character into the bargain, have not been able to protect the feelings of this officer from laceration on this floor. Have not been sufficient to protect his feelings! for, as to his character, that is untouched. The base accusation—the vague denunciation—the offensive epithets employed here, may lacerate feelings, but they do not reach character; and as to the military inquiry, which the senator from South Carolina speaks of, I undertake to say that no such inquiry will ever take place. Congress, or either branch of Congress, can order an inquiry if it pleases; but before it orders an inquiry, *a probable cause has to be shown for it*; and that probable cause never has been, and never will be, shown in General Jesup's case.

The senator from South Carolina speaks of the large force which was committed to General Jesup, and the little that was effected with that force. Is the senator aware of the extent of the country over which his operations extended? that it extended from 31 to 25 degrees of north latitude? that it began in the Okefenokee swamp in Georgia, and stretched to the Everglades in Florida? that it was near five hundred miles in length in a straight line, and the whole sprinkled over with swamps, one of which alone was equal in length to the distance between Washington City and Philadelphia? But it was not extent of country alone, with its fastnesses, its climate, and its wily foe, that had to be contended with; a new element of opposition was encountered by General Jesup, in the poisonous information which was conveyed to the Indians' minds, which encouraged them to hold out, and of which he had not even knowledge for a long time. This was the quantity of false information which was conveyed to the Indians, to stimulate and encourage their resistance. General Jesup took command just after the presidential election of 1836. The Indians were informed of this change of presidents, and were taught to believe that the white people had *broke* General Jackson—that was the phrase— had *broke* General Jackson for making war upon them. They were also informed that General Jesup was carrying on the war without the leave of Congress; that Congress would give no more money to raise soldiers to fight them; and that he dared not come home to Congress. Yes, he dared not come home to Congress! These poor Indians seem to have been informed of intended movements against the general in Congress, and to have relied upon them both to stop supplies and to punish the general. Moreover, they were told, that, if they surrendered to emigrate, they would receive the worst treatment on the way; that, if a child cried, it would be thrown overboard; if a chief gave offence, he would be put in irons. Who the immediate informants of all these fine stories were, cannot be exactly ascertained. They doubtless originated with that mass of fanatics, devoured by a morbid sensibility for negroes and Indians, which are now *Don Quixoting* over the land, and filling the public ear with so many sympathetic tales of their own fabrication.

General Jesup has been censured for writing a letter disparaging to his predecessor in command. If he did so, and I do not deny it, though I have not seen the letter, nobly has he made the amends. Publicly and officially has he made amends for a private and unofficial wrong. In an official report to the war department, published by that department, he said:

> "As an act of justice to all my predecessors in command, I consider it my duty to say that the difficulties attending military operations in this country, can be properly appreciated only by those acquainted with them. I have advantages which neither of them possessed, in better preparations and more abundant supplies; and I found it impossible to operate with any prospect of success, until I had established a line of depots across the country. If I have at any time said aught in disparagement of the operations of others in Florida, either verbally or in writing, officially or unofficially, knowing the country as I now know it, I consider myself bound as a man of honor solemnly to retract it."

Such are the amends which General Jesup makes—frank and voluntary—full and kindly—worthy of a soldier towards brother soldiers; and far more honorable to his predecessors in command than the disparaging comparisons which have been instituted here to do them honor at his expense.

The expenses of this war is another head of attack pressed into this debate, and directed more against the administration than against the commanding general. It is said to have cost twenty millions of dollars; but that is an error—an error of near one-half. An actual return of all expenses up to February last, amounts to nine and a half millions; the rest of the twenty millions go to the suppression of hostilities in other places, and with other Indians, principally in Georgia and Alabama, and with the Cherokees and Creeks. Sir, this charge of expense seems to be a standing head with the opposition at present. Every speech gives us a dish of it; and the expenditures under General Jackson and Mr. Van Buren are constantly put in contrast with those of previous administrations. Granted that these expenditures are larger—that they are greatly increased; yet what are they increased for? Are they increased for the personal expenses of the officers of the government, or for great national objects? The increase is for great objects; such as the extinction of Indian titles in the States east of the Mississippi—the removal of whole nations of Indians to the west of the Mississippi—their subsistence for a year after they arrive there—actual wars with some tribes—the fear of it with others, and the consequent continual calls for militia and volunteers to preserve peace—large expenditures for the permanent defences of the country, both by land and water, with a pension list for ever increasing; and other heads of expenditure which are for future national benefit; and not for present individual enjoyment. Stripped of all these heads of expenditure, and the expenses of the present administration have nothing to fear from a comparison with other periods. Stated in the gross, as is usually done, and many ignorant people are deceived and imposed upon, and believe that there has been a great waste of public money; pursued into the detail, and these expenditures will be found to have been made for great national objects—objects which no man would have undone, to get back the money, even if it was possible to get back the money by undoing the objects. No one, for example, would be willing to bring back the Creeks, the Cherokees, the Choctaws, and Chickasaws into Alabama, Mississippi, Georgia, Tennessee and North Carolina, even if the tens of millions which it has cost to remove them could be got back by that means; and so of the other expenditures: yet these eternal croakers about expense are blaming the government for these expenditures.

Sir, I have gone over the answers, which I proposed to make to the accusations of the senators from New Jersey and South Carolina. I have shown them to be totally mistaken in all their assumptions and imputations. I have shown that there was no fraud upon the Indians in the treaty at Fort Gibson—that the identical chiefs who made that treaty have since been the hostile chiefs—that the assassination and massacre of an agent, two government expresses, an artillery officer, five citizens, and one hundred and twelve men of Major Dade's command, caused the war—that our troops are not subject to censure for inefficiency—that General Jesup has been wrongfully denounced upon this floor—and that even the expense of the Florida war, resting as it does in figures and in documents, has been vastly overstated to produce effect upon the public mind. All these things I have shown; and I conclude with saying that cost, and time, and loss of men, are all out of the question; that, for outrages so wanton and so horrible as those which occasioned this war, the national honor requires the most ample amends; and the national safety requires a future guarantee in prosecuting this war to a successful close, and completely clearing the peninsula of Florida of all the Indians that are upon it.

CHAPTER XX.

RESUMPTION OF SPECIE PAYMENTS BY THE NEW YORK BANKS.

The suspension commenced on the 10th of May in New York, and was followed throughout the country. In August the New York banks proposed to all others to meet in convention, and agree upon a time to commence a general resumption. That movement was frustrated by the opposition of the Philadelphia banks, for the reason, as given, that it was better to await the action of the extra session of Congress, then convoked, and to meet in September. The extra session adjourned early in October, and the New York banks, faithful to the promised resumption of specie payments, immediately issued another invitation for the general convention of the banks in that city on the 27th of November ensuing, to carry into effect the object of the meeting which had been invited in the month of August. The 27th of November arrived; a large proportion of the delinquent banks had accepted the invitation to send delegates to the convention: but its meeting was again frustrated—and from the same quarter—the Bank of the United States, and the institutions under its influence. They then resolved to send a committee to Philadelphia to ascertain from the banks when they would be ready, and to invite them to name a day when they would be able to resume; and if no day was definitely fixed, to inform them that the New York banks would commence specie payments without waiting for their co-operation. The Philadelphia banks would not co-operate. They would not agree to any definite time to take even initiatory steps towards resumption. This was a disappointment to the public mind—that large part of it which still had faith in the Bank of the United States; and the contradiction which it presented to all the previous professions of that institution, required explanations, and, if possible, reconciliation with past declarations. The occasion called for the pen of Mr. Biddle, always ready, always confident, always presenting an easy remedy, and a sure one, for all the diseases to which banks, currency, and finance were heir. It called for another letter to Mr. John Quincy Adams, that is to say, to the public, through the distinction of that gentleman's name. It came—the most elaborate and ingenious of its species; its burden, to prove the entire ability of the bank over which he presided to pay in full, and without reserve, but its intention not to do so on account of its duty to others not able to follow its example, and which might be entirely ruined by a premature effort to do so. And he concluded with condensing his opinion into a sentence of characteristic and sententious brevity: "*On the whole, the course which in my judgment the banks ought to pursue, is simply this: The banks should remain exactly as they are—prepared to resume, but not yet resuming.*" But he did not stop there, but in another publication went the length of a direct threat of destruction against the New York banks if they should, in conformity to their promise, venture to resume, saying: "Let the banks of the Empire State come up from their Elba, and enjoy their hundred days of resumption! a Waterloo awaits them, and a Saint Helena is prepared for them."

The banks of New York were now thrown upon the necessity of acting without the concurrence of those of Pennsylvania, and in fact under apprehension of opposition and counteraction from that quarter. They were publicly pledged to act without her, and besides were under a legal obligation to do so. The legislature of the State, at the time of the suspension, only legalized it for one year. The indulgence would be out on the 15th of May, and forfeiture of charter was the penalty to be incurred throughout the State for continuing it beyond that time. The city banks had the control of the movement, and they invited a convention of delegates from all the banks in the Union to meet in New York on the 15th of April. One hundred and forty-three delegates, from the principal banks in a majority of the States, attended. Only delegates from fifteen States voted—Pennsylvania, Maryland and South Carolina among the absent; which, as including the three principal commercial cities on the Atlantic board south of New York, was a heavy defalcation from the weight of the convention. Of the fifteen States, thirteen voted for resuming on the 1st day of January, 1839—a delay of near nine months; two voted against that day—New York and Mississippi; and (as it often happens in concurring votes) for reasons directly opposite to each other. The New York banks so voted because the day was too distant—those of Mississippi because it was too near. The New York delegates wished the 15th of May, to avoid the penalty of the State law: those of Mississippi wished the 1st of January, 1840, to allow them to get in two more cotton crops before the great pay-day came. The result of the voting showed the still great power of the Bank of the United States. The delegates of the banks of ten States, including those with which she had most business, either refused to attend the convention, or to vote after having attended. The rest chiefly voted the late day, "*to favor the views of Philadelphia and Baltimore rather than those of New York.*" So said the delegates, "*frankly avowing that their interests and sympathies were with the former two rather than with the latter.*" The banks of the State of New York were then left to act alone—and did so. Simultaneously with the issue of the convention recommendation to resume on the first day of January, 1839, they issued another, recommending all the banks of the State of New York to resume on the 10th day of May, 1838; that is to say, within twenty-five days of that time. Those of the city declared their determination to begin on that day, or earlier, expressing their belief that they had nothing to fear but from the opposition and "deliberate animosity of others"—meaning the Bank of the United States. The New York banks all resumed at the day named. Their example was immediately followed by others, even by the institutions in those States whose delegates had voted for the long day; so that within sixty days thereafter the resumption was almost general, leaving the Bank of the United States uncovered, naked, and prominent at the head of all the delinquent banks in the Union. But her power was still great. Her stock stood at one hundred and twelve dollars to the share, being a premium of twelve dollars on the hundred. In Congress, which was still in session, not a tittle was abated of her pretensions and her assurance—her demands for a recharter—for the repeal of the specie circular—and for the condemnation of the administration, as the author of the misfortunes of the country; of which evils there were none except the bank suspensions, of which she had been the secret prime contriver and was now the detected promoter. Briefly before the New York resumption, Mr. Webster the great advocate of the Bank of the United States, and the truest exponent of her wishes, harangued the Senate in a set speech in her favor, of which some extracts will show the design and spirit:

"And now, sir, we see the upshot of the experiment. We see around us bankrupt corporations and broken promises; but we see no promises more really and emphatically broken than all those promises of the administration which gave us assurance of a better currency. These promises, now broken, notoriously and openly broken, if they cannot be performed, ought, at least, to be acknowledged. The government ought not, in common fairness and common honesty, to deny its own responsibility, seek to escape from the demands of the people, and to hide itself, out of the way and beyond the reach of the process of public opinion, by retreating into this sub-treasury system. Let it, at least, come forth; let it bear a port of honesty and candor; let it confess its promises, if it cannot perform them; and, above all, now, even now, at this late hour, let it renounce schemes and projects, the inventions of presumption, and the resorts of desperation, and let it address itself, in all good faith, to the great work of restoring the currency by approved and constitutional means.

"What say these millions of souls to the sub-treasury? In the first place, what says the city of New York, that great commercial emporium, worthy the gentleman's [Mr. Wright] commendation in 1834, and worthy of his commendation and my commendation, and all commendation, at all times? What sentiments, what opinions, what feelings, are proclaimed by the thousands of merchants, traders, manufacturers, and laborers? What is the united shout of all the voices of all her classes? What is it but that you will put down this new-fangled sub-treasury system, alike alien to their interests and their feelings, at once, and for ever? What is it, but that in mercy to the mercantile interest, the trading interest, the shipping interest, the manufacturing interest, the laboring class, and all classes, you will give up useless and pernicious political schemes and projects, and return to the plain, straight course of wise and wholesome legislation? The sentiments of the city cannot be misunderstood. A thousand pens and ten thousand tongues, and a spirited press, make them all known. If we have not already heard enough, we shall hear more. Embarrassed, vexed, pressed and distressed, as are her citizens at this moment, yet their resolution is not shaken, their spirit is not broken; and, depend upon it, they will not see their commerce, their business, their prosperity and their happiness, all sacrificed to preposterous schemes and political empiricism, without another, and a yet more vigorous struggle.

"Sir, I think there is a revolution in public opinion now going on, whatever may be the opinion of the member from New York, or others. I think the fall elections prove this, and that other more recent events confirm it. I think it is a revolt against the absolute dictation of party, a revolt against coercion on the public judgment; and, especially, against the adoption of new mischievous expedients on questions of deep public interest; a revolt against the rash and unbridled spirit of change; a revolution, in short, against further revolution. I hope, most sincerely, that this revolution may go on; not, sir, for the sake of men, but for the sake of measures, and for the sake of the country. I wish it to proceed, till the whole country, with an imperative unity of voice, shall call back Congress to the true policy of the government.

"I verily believe a majority of the people of the United States are now of the opinion that a national bank, properly constituted, limited, and guarded, is both constitutional and expedient, and ought now to be established. So far as I can learn, three-fourths of the western people are for it. Their representatives here can form a better judgment; but such is my opinion upon the best information which I can obtain. The South may be more divided, or may be against a national institution; but, looking again to the centre, the North and the East, and comprehending the whole in one view, I believe the prevalent sentiment is such as I have stated.

"At the last session great pains were taken to obtain a vote of this and the other House against a bank, for the obvious purpose of placing such an institution out of the list of remedies, and so reconciling the people to the sub-treasury scheme. Well, sir, and did those votes produce any effect? None at all. The people did not, and do not, care a rush for them. I never have seen, or heard, a single man, who paid the slightest respect to those votes of ours. The honorable member, to-day, opposed as he is to a bank, has not even alluded to them. So entirely vain is it, sir, in this country, to attempt to forestall, commit, or coerce the public judgment. All those resolutions fell perfectly dead on the tables of the two Houses. We may resolve what we please, and resolve it when we please; but if the people do not like it, at their own good pleasure they will rescind it; and they are not likely to continue their approbation long to any system of measures, however plausible, which terminates in deep disappointment of all their hopes, for their own prosperity."

All the friends of the Bank of the United States came to her assistance in this last trial. The two halls of Congress resounded with her eulogium, and with condemnation of the measures of the administration. It was a last effort to save her, and to force her upon the federal government. Multitudes of speakers on one side brought out numbers on the other—among those on the side of the sub-treasury and hard money, and against the whole paper system, of which he considered a national bank the citadel, was the writer of this View, who undertook to collect into a speech, from history and experience, the facts and reasons which would bear upon the contest, and act upon the judgment of candid men, and show the country to be independent of banks, if it would only will it. Some extracts from that speech make the next chapter.

CHAPTER XXI.

RESUMPTION OF SPECIE PAYMENTS: HISTORICAL NOTICES: MR. BENTON'S SPEECH: EXTRACTS.

There are two of those periods, each marking the termination of a national bank charter, and each presenting us with the actual results of the operations of those institutions upon the general currency, and each replete with lessons of instruction applicable to the present day, and to the present state of things. The first of these periods is the year 1811, when the first national bank had run its career of twenty years, and was permitted by Congress to expire upon its own limitation. I take for my guide the estimate of Mr. Lloyd, then a senator in Congress from the State of Massachusetts, whose dignity of character and amenity of manners is so pleasingly remembered by those who served with him here, and whose intelligence and accuracy entitle his statements to the highest degree of credit. That eminent senator estimated the total currency of the country, at the expiration of the charter of the first national bank, at sixty millions of dollars, to wit: ten millions of specie, and fifty millions in bank notes. Now compare the two quantities, and mark the results. Our population has precisely doubled itself since 1811. The increase of our currency should, therefore, upon the same principle of increase, be the double of what it then was; yet it is three times as great as it then was! The next period which challenges our attention is the veto session of 1832, when the second Bank of the United States, according to the opinion of its eulogists, had carried the currency to the ultimate point of perfection. What was the amount then? According to the estimate of a senator from Massachusetts, then and now a member of this body [Mr. WEBSTER], then a member of the Finance Committee, and with every access to the best information, the whole amount of currency was then estimated at about one hundred millions; to wit: twenty millions in specie, and seventy-five to eighty millions in bank notes. The increase of our population since that time is estimated at twenty per cent.; so that the increase of our currency, upon the basis of increased population, should also be twenty per cent. This would give an increase of twenty millions of dollars, making, in the whole, one hundred and twenty millions. Thus, our currency in actual existence, is nearly one-third more than either the ratio of 1811 or of 1832 would give. Thus, we have actually about fifty millions more, in this season of ruin and destitution, than we should have, if supplied only in the ratio of what we possessed at the two periods of what is celebrated as the best condition of the currency, and most prosperous condition of the country. So much for quantity; now for the solidity of the currency at these respective periods. How stands the question of solidity? Sir, it stands thus: in 1811, five paper dollars to one of silver; in 1822, four to one; in 1838, one to one, as near as can be! Thus, the comparative solidity of the currency is infinitely preferable to what it ever was before; for the increase, under the sagacious policy of General Jackson, has taken place precisely where it was needed—at the bottom, and not at the top; at the foundation, and not in the roof; at the base, and not at the apex. Our paper currency has increased but little; we may say nothing, upon the bases of 1811 and 1832; our specie has increased immeasurably; no less than eight-fold, since 1811, and four-fold since 1832. The whole increase is specie; and of that we have seventy millions more than in 1811, and sixty millions more than in 1832. Such are the fruits of General Jackson's policy! a policy which we only have to persevere in for a few years, to have our country as amply supplied with gold and silver as France and Holland are; that France and Holland in which gold is borrowed at three per cent. per annum, while we often borrow paper money at three per cent. a month.

But there is no specie. Not a ninepence to be got for a servant; not a picayune for a beggar; not a ten cent piece for the post-office. Such is the assertion; but how far is it true? Go to the banks, and present their notes at their counter, and it is all too true. No gold, no silver, no copper to be had there in redemption of their solemn promises to pay. Metaphorically, if not literally speaking, a demand for specie at the counter of a bank might bring to the unfortunate applicant more kicks than coppers. But change the direction of the demand; go to the brokers; present the bank note there; no sooner said than done; gold and silver spring forth in any quantity; the notes are cashed; you are thanked for your custom, invited to return again; and thus, the counter of the broker, and not the counter of the bank, becomes the place for the redemption of the notes of the bank. The only part of the transaction that remains to be told, is the per centum which is shaved off! And, whoever will submit to that shaving, can have all the bank notes cashed which he can carry to them. Yes, Mr. President, the brokers, and not the bankers, now redeem the bank notes. There is no dearth of specie for that purpose. They have enough to cash all the notes of the banks, and all the treasury notes of the government into the bargain. Look at their placards! not a village, not a city, not a town in the Union, in which the sign-boards do not salute the eye of the passenger, inviting him to come in and exchange his bank notes, and treasury notes, for gold and silver. And why cannot the banks redeem, as well as the brokers? Why can they not redeem their own notes? Because a *veto* has issued from the city of Philadelphia, and because a political revolution is to be effected by injuring the country, and then charging the injury upon the folly and wickedness of the republican administrations. This is the reason, and the sole reason. The Bank of the United States, its affiliated institutions, and its political confederates, are the sole obstacles to the resumption of specie payments. They alone prevent the resumption. It is they who are now in terror lest the resumption shall begin and to prevent it, we hear the real shout, and feel the real application of the rallying cry, so pathetically uttered on this floor by the senator from Massachusetts [Mr. WEBSTER]—*once more to the breach, dear friends, once more!*

Yes, Mr. President, the cause of the non-resumption of specie payments is now plain and undeniable. It is as plain as the sun at high noon, in a clear sky. No two opinions can differ about it, how much tongues may differ. The cause of not resuming is known, and the cause of suspension will soon be known likewise. Gentlemen of the opposition charge the suspension upon the folly, the wickedness, the insanity, the misrule, and misgovernment of the outlandish administration, as they classically call it; expressions which apply to the people who created the administration which have been so much vilified, and who have sanctioned their policy by repeated elections. The opposition charge the suspension to them—to their policy—to their acts—to the veto of 1832—the removal of the deposits of 1833—the Treasury order of 1836—and the demand for specie for the federal Treasury. This is the charge of the politicians, and of all who follow the lead, and obey the impulsion of the denationalized Bank of the United States. But what say others whose voice should be potential, and even omnipotent, on this question? What say the New York city banks, where the suspension began, and whose example was alleged for the sole cause of suspension by all the rest? What say these banks, whose position is at the fountain-head of knowledge, and whose answer for themselves is an answer for all. What say they? Listen, and you shall hear! for I hold in my hand a report of a committee of these banks, made under an official injunction, by their highest officers, and deliberately approved by all the city institutions. It is signed by Messrs. Albert Gallatin, George Newbold, C. C. Lawrence, C. Heyer, J. J. Palmer, Preserved Fish, and G. A. Worth,—seven gentlemen of known and established character; and not more than one out of the seven politically friendly to the late and present administrations of the federal government. This is their report:

> "The immediate causes which thus compelled the banks of the city of New York to suspend specie payments on the 10th of May last, are well known. The simultaneous withdrawing of the large public deposits, and of excessive foreign credits, combined with the great and unexpected fall in the price of the principal article of our exports, with an import of corn and bread stuffs, such as had never before occurred, and with the consequent inability of the country, particularly in the south-western States, to make the usual and expected remittances, did, at one and the same time, fall principally and necessarily, on the greatest commercial emporium of the Union. After a long and most arduous struggle, during which the banks, though not altogether unsuccessfully, resisting the imperative foreign demand for the precious metals, were gradually deprived of a great portion of their specie; some unfortunate incidents of a *local* nature, operating in concert with other previous exciting causes, produced distrust and panic, and finally one of those general runs, which, if continued, no banks that issue paper money, payable on demand, can ever resist; and which soon put it out of the power of those of this city to sustain specie payments. The example was followed by the banks throughout the whole country, with as much *rapidity* as the news of the suspension in New York reached them, without waiting for an *actual run*; and principally, if not exclusively, on the alleged grounds of the effects to be apprehended from that suspension. Thus, whilst the New York city banks were almost *drained* of their specie, those in other places preserved the *amount* which they held before the final catastrophe."

These are the reasons! and what becomes now of the Philadelphia cry, re-echoed by politicians and subaltern banks, against the ruinous measures of the administration? Not a measure of the administration mentioned!

not one alluded to! Not a word about the Treasury order; not a word about the veto of the National Bank charter; not a word about the removal of the deposits from the Bank of the United States; not a word about, the specie policy of the administration! Not one word about any act of the government, except that distribution act, disguised as a deposit law, which was a measure of Congress, and not of the administration, and the work of the opponents, and not the friends of the administration, and which encountered its only opposition in the ranks of those friends. I opposed it, with some half dozen others; and among my grounds of opposition, one was, that it would endanger the deposit banks, especially the New York city deposit banks,—that it would reduce them to the alternative of choosing between breaking their customers, and being broken themselves. This was the origin of that act—the work of the opposition on this floor; and now we find that very act to be the cause which is put at the head of all the causes which led to the suspension of specie payments. Thus, the administration is absolved. Truth has performed its office. A false accusation is rebuked and silenced. Censure falls where it is due; and the authors of the mischief stand exposed in the double malefaction of having done the mischief, and then charged it upon the heads of the innocent.

But, gentlemen of the opposition say, there can be no resumption until Congress "*acts upon the currency.*" Until Congress acts upon the currency! that is the phrase! and it comes from Philadelphia; and the translation of it is, that there shall be no resumption until Congress submits to Mr. Biddle's bank, and recharters that institution. This is the language from Philadelphia, and the meaning of the language; but, happily, a different voice issues from the city of New York! The authentic notification is issued from the banks of that city, pledging themselves to resume by the 10th day of May. They declare their ability to resume, and to continue specie payments; and declare they have nothing to fear, except from "*deliberate hostility*"—an hostility for which they allege there can be no motive—but of which they delicately intimate there is danger. Philadelphia is distinctly unveiled as the seat of this danger. The resuming banks fear hostility—deliberate acts of hostility—from that quarter. They fear nothing from the hostility, or folly, or wickedness of this administration. They fear nothing from the Sub-Treasury bill. They fear Mr. Biddle's bank, and nothing else but his bank, with its confederates and subalterns. They mean to resume, and Mr. Biddle means that they shall not. Henceforth two flags will be seen, hoisted from two great cities. The New York flag will have the word resumption inscribed upon it; the Philadelphia flag will bear the inscription of non-resumption, and destruction to all resuming banks.

I have carefully observed the conduct of the leading banks in the United States. The New York banks, and the principal deposit banks, had a cause for stopping which no others can plead, or did plead. I announced that cause, not once, but many times, on this floor; not only during the passage of the distribution law, but during the discussion of those famous land bills, which passed this chamber; and one of which ordered a peremptory distribution of sixty-four millions, by not only taking what was in the Treasury, but by reaching back, and taking all the proceeds of the land sales for years preceding. I then declared in my place, and that repeatedly, that the banks, having lent this money under our instigation, if called upon to reimburse it in this manner, must be reduced to the alternative of breaking their customers, or of being broken themselves. When the New York banks stopped, I made great allowances for them, but I could not justify others for the rapidity with which they followed their example; and still less can I justify them for their tardiness in following the example of the same banks in resuming. Now that the New York banks have come forward to redeem their obligations, and have shown that sensibility to their own honor, and that regard for the punctual performance of their promises, which once formed the pride and glory of the merchant's and the banker's character, I feel the deepest anxiety for their success in the great contest which is to ensue. Their enemy is a cunning and a powerful one, and as wicked and unscrupulous as it is cunning and strong. Twelve years ago, the president of that bank which now forbids other banks to resume, declared in an official communication to the Finance Committee of this body, "*that there were but few State banks which the Bank of the United States could not DESTROY by an exertion of its POWER.*" Since that time it has become more powerful; and, besides its political strength, and its allied institutions, and its exhaustless mine of resurrection notes, it is computed by its friends to wield a power of one hundred and fifty millions of dollars! all at the beck and nod of one single man! for his automaton directors are not even thought of! The wielding of this immense power, and its fatal direction to the destruction of the resuming banks, presents the prospect of a fearful conflict ahead. Many of the local banks will doubtless perish in it; many individuals will be ruined; much mischief will be done to the commerce and to the business of different places; and all the destruction that is accomplished will be charged upon some act of the administration—no matter what—for whatever is given out from the Philadelphia head is incontinently repeated by all the obsequious followers, until the signal is given to open upon some new cry.

Sir, the honest commercial banks have resumed, or mean to resume. They have resumed, not upon the fictitious and delusive credit of legislative enactments, but upon the solid basis of gold and silver. The hundred millions of specie which we have accumulated in the country has done the business. To that hundred millions the country is indebted for this early, easy, proud and glorious resumption!—and here let us do justice to the men of this day—to the policy of General Jackson—and to the success of the experiments—to which we are indebted for these one hundred millions. Let us contrast the events and effects of the stoppages in 1814, and in 1819, with the events and effects of the stoppage in 1837, and let us see the difference between them, and the causes of that difference. The stoppage of 1814 compelled the government to use depreciated bank notes during the remainder of the war, and up to the year 1817. Treasury notes, even bearing a large interest, were depreciated ten, twenty, thirty per cent. Bank notes were at an equal depreciation. The losses to the government from depreciated paper in loans alone, during the war, were computed by a committee of the House of Representatives at eighty millions of dollars. Individuals suffered in the same proportion; and every transaction of life bore the impress of the general calamity. Specie was not to be had. There was, nationally speaking, none in the country. The specie standard was gone; the measure of values was lost; a fluctuating paper money, ruinously depreciated, was the medium of all exchanges. To extricate itself from this deplorable condition, the expedient of a National Bank was resorted to—that measure of so much humiliation, and of so much misfortune to the republican party. For the moment it seemed to give relief, and to restore national prosperity; but treacherous and delusive was the seeming boon. The banks resumed—relapsed—and every evil of the previous suspension returned upon the country with increased and aggravated force.

Politicians alone have taken up this matter and have proposed, for the first time since the foundation of the government—for the first time in 48 years—to compel the government to receive paper money for its dues. The pretext is, to aid the banks in resuming! This, indeed, is a marvellous pretty conception! Aid the banks to resume! Why, sir, we cannot prevent them from resuming. Every solvent, commercial bank in the United States either has resumed, or has declared its determination to do so in the course of the year. The insolvent, and the political banks, which did not mean to resume, will have to follow the New York example, or die! Mr. Biddle's bank must follow the New York lead, or die! The good banks are with the country: the rest we defy. The political banks may resume or not, as they please, or as they dare. If they do not, they die! Public opinion, and the laws of the land, will exterminate them. If the president of the miscalled Bank of the United States has made a mistake in recommending indefinite non-resumption, and in proposing to establish a confederation of broken banks, and has found out his mistake, and wants a pretext for retreating, let him invent one. There is no difficulty in the case. Any thing that the government does, or does not—any thing that has happened, will happen, or can happen—will answer the purpose. Let the president of the Bank of the United States give out a tune: incontinently it will be sung by every bank man in the United States; and no matter how ridiculous the ditty may be, it will be celebrated as superhuman music.

But an enemy lies in wait for them! one that foretells their destruction, is able to destroy them, and which looks for its own success in their ruin. The report of the committee of the New York banks expressly refers to "*acts of deliberate hostility*" from a neighboring institution as a danger which the resuming banks might have to dread. The reference was plain to the miscalled Bank of the United States as the source of this danger. Since that time an insolent and daring threat has issued from Philadelphia, bearing the marks of its bank paternity, openly threatening the resuming banks of New York with destruction. This is the threat: "*Let the banks of the Empire State come up from their Elba, and enjoy their hundred days of resumption; a Waterloo awaits them, and a St. Helena is prepared for them.*" Here is a direct menace, and coming from a source which is able to make good what it threatens. Without hostile attacks, the resuming banks have a perilous process to go through. The business of resumption is always critical. It is a case of impaired credit, and a slight circumstance may excite a panic which may be fatal to the whole. The public having seen them stop payment, can readily believe in the mortality of their nature, and that another stoppage is as easy as the former. On the slightest alarm—on the stoppage of a few inconsiderable banks, or on the noise of a groundless rumor—a general panic may break out. *Sauve qui peut*— save himself who can—becomes the cry with the public; and almost every bank may be run down. So it was in England after the long suspension there from 1797 to 1823; so it was in the United States after the suspension from 1814 to 1817; in each country a second stoppage ensued in two years after resumption; and these second stoppages are like relapses to an individual after a spell of sickness: the relapse is more easily brought on than the original disease, and is far more dangerous.

The banks in England *suspended* in 1797—they *broke* in 1825; in the United States it was a *suspension* during the war, and a *breaking* in 1819-20. So it may be again with us. There is imminent danger to the resuming banks, without the pressure of premeditated hostility; but, with that hostility, their prostration is almost certain. The Bank of the United States can crush hundreds on any day that it pleases. It can send out its agents into every State of the Union, with sealed orders to be opened on a given day, like captains sent into different seas; and can break hundreds of local banks within the same hour, and over an extent of thousands of miles. It can do this with perfect ease—the more easily with resurrection notes—and thus excite a universal panic, crush the resuming banks, and then charge the whole upon the government. This is what it can do; this is what it has threatened; and stupid is the bank, and doomed to destruction, that does not look out for the danger, and fortify against it. In addition to all these dangers, the senator from Kentucky, the author of the resolution himself, tells you that these banks must fail again! he tells you they will fail! and in the very same moment he presses the compulsory reception of all the notes on all these banks upon the federal treasury! What is this but a proposition to ruin the finances—to bankrupt the Treasury—to disgrace the administration—to demonstrate the incapacity of the State banks to serve as the fiscal agents of the government, and to gain a new argument for the creation of a national bank, and the elevation of the bank party to power? This is the clear inference from the proposition; and viewing it in this light, I feel it to be my duty to expose, and to repel it, as a proposition to inflict mischief and disgrace upon the country.

But to return to the point, the contrast between the effects and events of former bank stoppages, and the effects and events of the present one. The effects of the former were to sink the price of labor and of property to the lowest point, to fill the States with stop laws, relief laws, property laws, and tender laws; to ruin nearly all debtors, and to make property change hands at fatal rates; to compel the federal government to witness the heavy depreciation of its treasury notes, to receive its revenues in depreciated paper; and, finally, to submit to the establishment of a national bank as the means of getting it out of its deplorable condition—that bank, the establishment of which was followed by the seven years of the greatest calamity which ever afflicted the country; and from which calamity we then had to seek relief from the tariff, and not from more banks. How different the events of the present time! The banks stopped in May, 1837; they resume in May, 1838. Their paper depreciated but little; property, except in a few places, was but slightly affected; the price of produce continued good; people paid their debts without sacrifices; treasury notes, in defiance of political and moneyed combinations to depress them, kept at or near par; in many places above it; the government was never brought to receive its revenues in depreciated paper; and finally all good banks are resuming in the brief space of a year; and no national bank has been created. Such is the contrast between the two periods; and now, sir, what is all this owing to? what is the cause of this great difference in two similar periods of bank stoppages? It is owing to our gold bill of 1834, by which we corrected the erroneous standard of gold, and which is now giving us an avalanche of that metal; it is owing to our silver bill of the same year, by which we repealed the disastrous act of 1819, against the circulation of foreign silver, and which is now spreading the Mexican dollars all over the country; it is owing to our movements against small notes under twenty dollars; to our branch mints, and the increased activity of the mother mint; to our determination to revive the currency of the constitution, and to our determination not to fall back upon the local paper currencies of the States for a national currency. It was owing to these measures that we have passed through this bank stoppage in a style so different from what has been done heretofore. It is owing to our "*experiments*" on the currency—to our "*humbug*" of a gold and silver currency—to our "*tampering*" with the monetary system—it is owing to these that we have had this signal success in this last stoppage, and are now victorious over all the prophets of woe, and over all the architects of mischief. These *experiments*, this *humbugging*, and this *tampering*, has increased our specie in six years from twenty millions to one hundred millions; and it is these one hundred millions of gold and silver which have sustained the country and the government under the shock of the stoppage—has enabled the honest solvent banks to resume, and will leave the insolvent and political banks without excuse or justification for not resuming. Our experiments—I love the word, and am sorry that gentlemen of the opposition have ceased to repeat it—have brought an avalanche of gold and silver into the country; it is saturating us with the precious metals, it has relieved and sustained the country; and now when these experiments have been successful—have triumphed over all opposition—gentlemen cease their ridicule, and go to work with their paper-money resolutions to force the government to use paper, and thereby to drive off the gold and silver which our policy has brought into the country, destroy the specie basis of the banks, give us an exclusive paper currency again, and produce a new expansion and a new explosion.

Justice to the men of this day requires these things to be stated. They have avoided the errors of 1811. They have avoided the pit into which they saw their predecessors fall. Those who prevented the renewal of the bank charter in 1811, did nothing else but prevent its renewal; they provided no substitute for the notes of the bank; did nothing to restore the currency of the constitution; nothing to revive the gold currency; nothing to increase the specie of the country. They fell back upon the exclusive use of local bank notes, without even doing any thing to strengthen the local banks, by discarding their paper under twenty dollars. They fell back upon the local banks; and the consequence was, the total prostration, the utter helplessness, the deplorable inability of the government to take care of itself, or to relieve and restore the country, when the banks failed. Those who prevented the recharter of the second Bank of the United States had seen all this; and they determined to avoid such error and calamity. They set out to revive the national gold currency, to increase the silver currency, and to reform and strengthen the banking system. They set out to do these things; and they have done them. Against a powerful combined political and moneyed confederation, they have succeeded; and the one hundred millions of gold and silver now in the country attests the greatness of their victory, and insures the prosperity of the country against the machinations of the wicked and the factious.

CHAPTER XXII.

MR. CLAY'S RESOLUTION IN FAVOR OF RESUMING BANKS, AND MR. BENTON'S REMARKS UPON IT.

After the New York banks had resolved to recommence specie payments, and before the day arrived for doing so, Mr. Clay submitted a resolution in the Senate to promote resumption by making the notes of the resuming banks receivable in payment of all dues to the federal government. It was clearly a movement in behalf of the delinquent banks, as those of New York, and others, had resolved to return to specie payments without requiring any such condition. Nevertheless he placed the banks of the State of New York in the front rank for the benefits to be received under his proposed measure. They had undertaken to recommence payments, he said, not from any ability to do so, but from compulsion under a law of the State. The receivability of their notes in payment of all federal dues would give them a credit and circulation which would prevent their too rapid return for redemption. So of others. It would be a help to all in getting through the critical process of resumption; and in helping them would benefit the business and prosperity of the country. He thought it wise to give that assistance; but reiterated his opinion that, nothing but the establishment of a national bank would effectually remedy the evils of a disordered currency, and permanently cure the wounds under which the country was now suffering. Mr. Benton replied to Mr. Clay, and said:

This resolution of the senator from Kentucky [Mr. CLAY], is to aid the banks to resume—to aid, encourage, and enable them to resume. This is its object, as declared by its mover; and it is offered here after the leading banks have resumed, and when no power can even prevent the remaining solvent banks from resuming. Doubtless, immortal glory will be acquired by this resolution! It can be heralded to all corners of the country, and celebrated in all manner of speeches and editorials, as the miraculous cause of an event which had already occurred! Yes, sir—already occurred! for the solvent banks have resumed, are resuming, and will resume. Every solvent bank in the United States will have resumed in a few months, and no efforts of the insolvents and their political confederates can prevent it. In New York the resumption is general; in Massachusetts, Rhode Island, Maine, and New Jersey, it is partial; and every where the solvent banks are preparing to redeem the pledge which they gave when they stopped—*that of resuming whenever New York did.* The insolvent and political banks will not resume at all, or, except for a few weeks, to fail again, make a panic and a new run upon the resuming banks—stop them, if possible, then charge it upon the administration, and recommence their lugubrious cry for a National Bank.

The resumption will take place. The masses of gold and silver pouring into the country under the beneficent effects of General Jackson's hard-money policy, will enable every solvent bank to resume; a moral sense, and a fear of consequences, will compel them to do it. The importations of specie are now enormous, and equalling every demand, if it was not suppressed. There can be no doubt but that the quantity of specie in the country is equal to the amount of bank notes in circulation—that they are dollar for dollar—that the country is better off for money at this day than it ever was before, though shamefully deprived of the use of gold and silver by the political and insolvent part of the banks and their confederate politicians.

The solvent banks will resume, and Congress cannot prevent them if it tried. They have received the aid which they need in the $100,000,000 of gold and silver which now relieves the country, and distresses the politicians who predicted no relief, until a national bank was created. Of the nine hundred banks in the country, there are many which never can resume, and which should not attempt it, except to wind up their affairs. Many of these are rotten to the core, and will fall to pieces the instant they are put to the specie test. Some of them even fail now for rags; several have so failed in Massachusetts and Ohio, to say nothing of those called wild cats—the progeny of a general banking law in Michigan. We want a resumption to discriminate between banks, and to save the community from impositions.

We wanted specie, and we have got it. Five years ago—at the veto session of 1832—there were but twenty millions in the country. So said the senator from Massachusetts who has just resumed his seat [Mr. WEBSTER]. We have now, or will have in a few weeks, one hundred millions. This is the salvation of the country. It compels resumption, and has defeated all the attempts to scourge the country into a submission to a national bank.

While that one hundred millions remains, the country can place at defiance the machinations of the Bank of the United States, and its confederate politicians, to perpetuate the suspension, and to continue the reign of rags and shin-plasters. Their first object is to get rid of these hundred millions, and all schemes yet tried have failed to counteract the Jacksonian policy. Ridicule was tried first; deportation of specie was tried next; a forced suspension has been continued for a year; the State governments and the people were vanquished, still the specie came in, because the federal government created a demand for it. This firm demand has frustrated all the schemes to drive off specie, and to deliver up the country to the dominion of the paper-money party. This demand has been the stumbling block of that party; and this resolution now comes to remove that stumbling block. It is the most revolting proposition ever made in this Congress! It is a flagrant violation of the constitution, by making paper money a tender both to and from the government. It is fraught with ruin and destruction to the public property, the public Treasury, and the public creditors. The notes of nine hundred banks are to be received into the Treasury, and disbursed from the Treasury. They are to be paid out as well as paid in. The ridiculous proviso of willingness to receive them on the part of the public creditor is an insult to him; for there is no choice—it is that or nothing. The disbursing officer does not offer hard money with one hand, and paper with the other, and tell the creditor to take his choice. No! he offers paper or nothing! To talk of willingness, when there is no choice, is insult, mockery and outrage. Great is the loss of popularity which this administration has sustained from paying out depreciated paper; great the deception which has been practised upon the government in representing this paper as being willingly received. Necessity, and not good will, ruled the creditor; indignation, resentment, and execrations on the administration, were the thanks with which he received it. This has disgraced and injured the administration more than all other causes put together; it has lost it tens of thousands of true friends. It is now getting into a condition to pay hard money; and this resolution comes to prevent such payment, and to continue and to perpetuate the ruinous paper-money payments. Defeat the resolution, and the government will quickly pay all demands upon it in gold and silver, and will recover its popularity; pass it, and paper money will continue to be paid out, and the administration will continue to lose ground.

The resolution proposes to make the notes of 900 banks the currency of the general government, and the mover of the resolution tells you, at the same time, that all these banks will fail! that they cannot continue specie payments if they begin! that nothing but a national bank can hold them up to specie payments, and that we have no such bank. This is the language of the mover; it is the language, also, of all his party; more than that—it is the language of Mr. Biddle's letter—that letter which is the true exposition of the principles and policy of the opposition party. Here, then, is a proposition to compel the administration, by law, to give up the public lands for the paper of banks which are to fail—to fill the Treasury with the paper of such banks—and to pay out such paper to the public creditors. This is the proposition, and it is nothing but another form of accomplishing what was attempted in this chamber a few weeks ago, namely, a direct receipt of irredeemable paper money! That proposition was too naked and glaring; it was too rank and startling; it was rebuked and repulsed. A circuitous operation is now to accomplish what was then too rashly attempted by a direct movement. Receive the notes of 900 banks for the lands and duties; these 900 banks will all fail again;—so says the mover, because there is no king bank to regulate them. We have then lost our lands and revenues, and filled our Treasury with irredeemable paper. This is just the point aimed at by the original proposition to receive irredeemable paper in the first instance: it ends in the reception of such paper. If the resolution passes, there will be another explosion: for the receivability of these notes for the public dues, and especially for the public lands, will run out another vast expansion of the paper system—to be followed, of course, by another general explosion. The only way to save the banks is to hold them down to specie payments. To do otherwise, and especially to do what this resolution proposes, is to make the administration the instrument of its own disgrace and degradation—to make it join in the ruin of the finances and the currency—in the surrender of the national domain for broken bank paper—and in producing a new cry for a national bank, as the only remedy for the evils it has produced.

[The measure proposed by Mr. CLAY was defeated, and the *experiment* of a specie currency for the government was continued.]

CHAPTER XXIII.

RESUMPTION BY THE PENNSYLVANIA UNITED STATES BANK; AND OTHERS WHICH FOLLOWED HER LEAD.

The resumption by the New York banks had its effect. Their example was potent, either to suspend or resume. All the banks in the Union had followed their example in stopping specie payments: more than half of them followed them in recommencing payments. Those which did not recommence became obnoxious to public censure, and to the suspicion of either dishonesty or insolvency. At the head of this delinquent class stood the Bank of the United States, justly held accountable by the public voice for the delinquency of all the rest. Her position became untenable. She was compelled to descend from it; and, making a merit of necessity, she affected to put herself at the head of a general resumption; and in pursuance of that idea invited, in the month of July, through a meeting of the Philadelphia banks, a general meeting in that city on the 25th of that month, to consult and fix a time for resumption. A few banks sent delegates; others sent letters, agreeing to whatever might be done. In all there were one hundred and forty delegates, or letters, from banks in nine States; and these delegates and letters forming themselves into a general convention of banks, passed a resolution for a general resumption on the 13th of August ensuing. And thus ended this struggle to act upon the government through the distresses of the country, and coerce it into a repeal of the specie circular—into a recharter of the United States Bank—the restoration of the deposits—and the adoption of the notes of this bank for a national currency. The game had been overplayed. The public saw through it, and derived a lesson from it which put bank and state permanently apart, and led to the exclusive use of gold and silver by the federal government; and the exclusive keeping of its own moneys by its own treasurers. All right-minded people rejoiced at the issue of the struggle; but there were some that well knew that the resumption on the part of the Bank of the United States was hollow and deceptive—that she had no foundations, and would stop again, and for ever I said this to Mr. Van Buren at the time, and he gave the opinion I expressed a better acceptance than he had accorded to the previous one in February, 1837. Parting from him at the end of the session, 1838-'39, I said to him, this bank would stop before we meet again; that is to say, before I should return to Congress. It did so, and for ever. At meeting him the ensuing November, he was the first to remark upon the truth of these predictions.

CHAPTER XXIV.

PROPOSED ANNEXATION OF TEXAS: MR. PRESTON'S MOTION AND SPEECH: EXTRACTS.

The republic of Texas had now applied for admission into the federal Union, as one of its States. Its minister at Washington, Memucan Hunt, Esq., had made the formal application to our executive government. That was one obstacle in the way of annexation removed. It was no longer an insult to her to propose to annex her; and she having consented, it referred the question to the decision of the United States. But there was still another objection, and which was insuperable: Texas was still at war with Mexico; and to annex her was to annex the war—a consequence which morality and policy equally rejected. MR. PRESTON, of South Carolina, brought in a resolution on the subject—not for annexation, but for a legislative expression in favor of the measure, as a basis for a tripartite treaty between the United States, Mexico and Texas; so as to effect the annexation by the consent of all parties, to avoid all cause of offence; and unite our own legislative with the executive authority in accomplishing the measure. In support of this motion, he delivered a speech which, as showing the state of the question at the time, and presenting sound views, and as constituting a link in the history of the Texas annexation, is here introduced—some extracts to exhibit its leading ideas.

"The proposition which I now submit in regard to this prosperous and self-dependent State would be indecorous and presumptuous, had not the lead been given by Texas herself. It appears by the correspondence of the envoy extraordinary of that republic with our own government, that the question of annexation on certain terms and conditions has been submitted to the people of the republic, and decided in the affirmative by a very large majority; whereupon, and in pursuance of instructions from his government, he proposes to open a negotiation for the accomplishment of that object. The correspondence has been communicated upon a call from the House of Representatives, and thus the proposition becomes a fit subject for the deliberation of Congress. Nor is it proposed by my resolution, Mr. President, to do any thing which could be justly construed into cause of offence by Mexico. The terms of the resolution guard our relations with that republic; and the spirit in which it is conceived is entirely averse to any compromise of our national faith and honor, for any object, of whatever magnitude. More especially would I have our intercourse with Mexico characterized by fair dealing and moderation, on account of her unfortunate condition, resulting from a long-continued series of intestine dissensions, which all who have not been born to liberty must inevitably encounter in seeking for it. As long, therefore, as the pretensions of Mexico are attempted to be asserted by actual force, or as long as there is any reasonable prospect that she has the power and the will to resubjugate Texas, I do not propose to interfere. My own deliberate conviction, to be sure, is, that that period has already passed; and I beg leave to say that, in my judgment, there is more danger of an invasion and conquest of Mexico by Texas, than that this last will ever be reannexed to Mexico.

"I disavow, Mr. President, all hostile purposes, or even ill temper, towards Mexico; and I trust that I impugn neither the policy nor principles of the administration. I therefore feel myself at liberty to proceed to the discussion of the points made in the resolution, entirely disembarrassed of any preliminary obstacle, unless, indeed, the mode by which so important an act is to be effected may be considered as interposing a difficulty. If the object itself be within the competency of this government, as I shall hereafter endeavor to show, and both parties consent, every means mutually agreed upon would establish a joint obligation. The acquisition of new territory has heretofore been effected by treaty, and this mode of proceeding in regard to Texas has been proposed by her minister; but I believe it would comport more with the importance of the measure, that both branches of the government should concur, the legislature expressing a previous opinion; and, this being done, all difficulties, of all kinds whatsoever, real or imaginary, might be avoided by a treaty tripartite between Mexico, Texas, and the United States, in which the assent and confirmation of

Mexico (for a pecuniary consideration, if you choose) might be had, without infringing the acknowledged independence and free agency of Texas.

"The treaty, Mr. President, of 1819, was a great oversight on the part of the Southern States. We went into it blindly, I must say. The great importance of Florida, to which the public mind was strongly awakened at that time by peculiar circumstances, led us precipitately into a measure by which we threw a gem away that would have bought ten Floridas. Under any circumstances, Florida would have been ours in a short time; but our impatience induced us to purchase it by a territory ten times as large—a hundred times as fertile, and to give five millions of dollars into the bargain. Sir, I resign myself to what is done; I acquiesce in the inexorable past; I propose no wild and chimerical revolution in the established order of things, for the purpose of remedying what I conceive to have been wrong originally. But this I do propose: that we should seize the fair and just occasion now presented to remedy the mistake which was made in 1819; that we should repair as far as we can the evil effect of a breach of the constitution; that we should re-establish the integrity of our dismembered territory, and get back into our Union, by the just and honorable means providentially offered to us, that fair and fertile province which, in an evil hour, we severed from the confederacy.

"But the boundary line established by the treaty of 1819 not only deprives us of this extensive and fertile territory, but winds with "a deep indent" upon the valley of the Mississippi itself, running upon the Red River and the Arkansas. It places a foreign nation in the rear of our Mississippi settlements, and brings it within a stone's throw of that great outlet which discharges the commerce of half the Union. The mouth of the Sabine and the mouth of the Mississippi are of a dangerous vicinity. The great object of the purchase of Louisiana was to remove all possible interference of foreign States in the vast commerce of the outlet of so many States. By the cession of Texas, this policy was, to a certain extent, compromised.

"The committee, it appears to me, has been led to erroneous conclusions on this subject by a fundamental mistake as to the nature and character of our government; a mistake which has pervaded and perverted all its reasoning, and has for a long time been the abundant source of much practical mischief in the action of this government, and of very dangerous speculation. The mistake lies in considering this, as to its nature and powers, a consolidated government of one people, instead of a confederated government of many States. There is no one single act performed by the people of the United States, under the constitution, *as one people*. Even in the popular branch of Congress this distinction is maintained. A certain number of delegates is assigned to each State, and the people of each State elect for their own State. When the functionaries of the government assemble here, they have no source of power but the constitution, which prescribes, defines, and limits their action, and constitutes them, in their aggregate capacity, a trust or agency, for the performance of certain duties confided to them by various States or communities. This government is, therefore, a confederacy of sovereign States, associating themselves together for mutual advantages. They originally came together as sovereign States, having no authority and pretending to no power of reciprocal control. North Carolina and Rhode Island stood off for a time, refusing to join the confederacy, and at length came into it by the exercise of a sovereign discretion. So too of Missouri, who was a State fully organized and perfect, and self-governed, before she was a State of this Union; and, in the very nature of things, this has been the case with all the States heretofore admitted, and must always continue to be so. Where, then, is the difficulty of admitting another State into this confederacy? The power to admit new States is expressly given. "New States may be admitted by the Congress into this Union." By the very terms of the grant, they must be *States* before they are admitted; when admitted, they become States *of the Union*. The terms, restrictions, and principles upon which new States are to be received, are matters to be regulated by Congress, under the constitution.

"Heretofore, in the acquisition of Louisiana and Florida, France and Spain both stipulated that the inhabitants of the ceded territories should be incorporated in the Union of the United States as soon as may be consistent with the principles of the federal constitution, and admitted to all the privileges, rights, and immunities of the citizens of the United States. In compliance with this stipulation, Louisiana, Arkansas, and Missouri have been admitted into the Union, and at no distant day Florida will be. Now, if we contract with France and Spain for the admission of States, why shall we not with Texas? If France can sell to us her subjects and her territory, why cannot the people of Texas give themselves and their territory to us? Is it more consistent with our republican notions that men and territory can be transferred by the arbitrary will of a monarch, for a price, than that a free people may be associated with us by mutual consent?

"It is supposed that there is a sort of political impossibility, resulting from the nature of things, to effect the proposed union. The committee says that "the measure is in fact the union of *two* independent governments." Certainly the *union* of twenty-seven "independent governments;" but the committee adds, that it should rather be termed the dissolution of both, and the formation of a new one, which, whether founded on the same or another written constitution, is, as to its identity, different from either. This can only be effected by the *summum jus*, &c.

"A full answer to this objection, even if many others were not at hand, as far as Texas is concerned, is contained in the fact that the *summum jus* has been exercised.

"Her citizens, by a unanimous vote, have decided in favor of annexation; and, according to the admission of the committee, this is sufficiently potent to dissolve their government, and to surrender themselves to be absorbed by ours. To receive this augmentation of our territory and population, manifestly does not dissolve this government, or even remodel it. Its identity is not disturbed. There is no appeal necessary to the *summum jus populi* for such a political arrangement on our part, even if the *summum jus populi* could be predicated of this government, which it cannot. Now, it is very obvious that two free States may associate for common purposes, and that these common purposes may be multiplied in number or increased in importance at the discretion of the parties. They may establish a common agency for the transaction of their business; and this may include a portion or all of their political functions. The new creation may be an agency if created by States, or a government if created by the people; for the people have a right to abolish and create governments. Does any one doubt whether Texas could rejoin the republic of Mexico? Why not, then, *re*join this republic?

"No one doubts that the States now composing this Union might have joined Great Britain after the declaration of independence. The learned committee would not contend that there was a political impossibility in the union of Scotland and England, or of Ireland and Britain; or that, in the nature of things, it would be impossible for Louisiana, if she were a sovereign State out of this Union, to join with the sovereign State of Texas in forming a new government.

"There is no point of view in which the proposition for annexation can be considered, that any serious obstacle in point of form presents itself. If this government be a confederation of States, then it is proposed to add another State to the confederacy. If this government be a consolidation, then it is proposed to add to it additional territory and population. That we can annex, and afterwards admit, the cases of Florida and Louisiana prove. We can, therefore, deal with the people of Texas for the territory of Texas, and the people can be secured in the rights and privileges of the constitution, as were the subjects of Spain and France.

"The Massachusetts legislature experience much difficulty in ascertaining the mode of action by which the proposed annexation can be effected, and demand "in what form would be the practical exercise of the supposed power? In what department does it lie?" The progress of events already, in a great measure, answers this objection. Texas has taken the initiative. Her minister has introduced the subject to that department which is alone capable of receiving communications from foreign governments, and the executive has submitted the correspondence to Congress. The resolutions before you propose an expression of opinion by Congress, which, if made, the executive will doubtless address itself earnestly, in conjunction with the authorities of Texas, to the consummation of the joint wishes of the parties, which can be accomplished by treaty, emanating from one department of this government, to be carried into effect by the passage of all needful laws by the legislative department, and by the exercise of the express power of Congress to admit new States."

The proposition of Mr. Preston did not prevail; the period for the annexation of Texas had not yet arrived. War still existing between Mexico and Texas—the *status* of the two countries being that of war, although hostilities hardly existed—a majority of the Senate deemed it unadvisable even to take the preliminary steps towards annexation which his resolution proposed. A motion to lay the proposition on the table prevailed, by a vote of 24 to 14.

CHAPTER XXV.

DEBATE BETWEEN MR. CLAY AND MR. CALHOUN, PERSONAL AND POLITICAL, AND LEADING TO EXPOSITIONS AND VINDICATIONS OF PUBLIC CONDUCT WHICH BELONG TO HISTORY.

For seven years past Mr. Calhoun, while disclaiming connection with any party, had acted on leading measures with the opposition, headed by Messrs. Clay and Webster. Still disclaiming any such connection, he was found at the extra session co-operating with the administration. His co-operation with the opposition had given it the victory in many eventful contests in that long period; his co-operation with the Van Buren administration might turn the tide of victory. The loss or gain of a chief who in a nearly balanced state of parties, could carry victory to the side which he espoused, was an event not to be viewed without vexation by the party which he left. Resentment was as natural on one side as gratification was on the other. The democratic party had made no reproaches—(I speak of the debates in Congress)—when Mr. Calhoun left them; they debated questions with him as if there had been no cause for personal complaint. Not so with the opposition now when the course of his transit was reversed, and the same event occurred to themselves. They took deeply to heart this withdrawal of one of their leaders, and his appearance on the other side. It created a feeling of personal resentment against Mr. Calhoun which had manifested itself in several small side-blows at the extra session; and it broke out into systematic attack at the regular one. Some sharp passages took place between himself and Mr. Webster, but not of a kind to lead to any thing historical. He (Mr. Webster) was but slightly inclined towards that kind of speaking which mingles personality with argument, and lessens the weight of the adversary argument by reducing the weight of the speaker's character. Mr. Clay had a turn that way; and, certainly, a great ability for it. Invective, mingled with sarcasm, was one of the phases of his oratory. He was supreme at a *philippic* (taken in the sense of Demosthenes and Cicero), where the political attack on a public man's measure was to be enforced and heightened by a personal attack on his conduct. He owed much of his fascinating power over his hearers to the exercise of this talent—always so captivating in a popular assembly, and in the galleries of the Senate; not so much so in the Senate itself; and to him it naturally fell to become the organ of the feelings of his party towards Mr. Calhoun. And very cordially, and carefully, and amply, did he make preparation for it.

The storm had been gathering since September: it burst in February. It had been evidently waiting for an occasion: and found it in the first speech of Mr. Calhoun, of that session, in favor of Mr. Van Buren's recommendation for an independent treasury and a federal hard-money currency. This speech was delivered the 15th of February, and was strictly argumentative and parliamentary, and wholly confined to its subject. Four days thereafter Mr. Clay answered it; and although ready at an extemporaneous speech, he had the merit, when time permitted, of considering well both the matter and the words of what he intended to deliver. On this occasion he had had ample time; for the speech of Mr. Calhoun could not be essentially different from the one he delivered on the same subject at the extra session; and the personal act which excited his resentment was of the same date. There had been six months for preparation; and fully had preparation been made. The whole speech bore the impress of careful elaboration and especially the last part; for it consisted of two distinct parts—the first, argumentative, and addressed to the measure before the Senate: and was in fact, as well as in name, a reply. The second part was an attack, under the name of a reply, and was addressed to the personal conduct of Mr. Calhoun, reproaching him with his desertion (as it was called), and taunting him with the company he had got into—taking care to remind him of his own former sad account of that company: and then, launching into a wider field, he threw up to him all the imputed political delinquencies of his life for near twenty years—skipping none from 1816 down to the extra session;—although he himself had been in close political friendship with this alleged delinquent during the greater part of that long time. Mr. Calhoun saw at once the advantage which this general and sweeping assault put into his hands. Had the attack been confined to the mere circumstance of quitting one side and joining the other, it might have been treated as a mere personality; and, either left unnoticed, or the account settled at once with some ready words of retort and justification. But in going beyond the act which gave the offence—beyond the cause of resentment, which was recent, and arraigning a member on the events of almost a quarter of a century of public life, he went beyond the limits of the occasion, and gave Mr. Calhoun the opportunity of explaining, or justifying, or excusing all that had ever been objected to him; and that with the sympathy in the audience with which attack for ever invests the rights of defence. He saw his advantage, and availed himself of it. Though prompt at a reply, he chose to make none in a hurry. A pause ensued Mr. Clay's conclusion, every one deferring to Mr. Calhoun's right of reply. He took the floor, but it was only to say that he would reply at his leisure to the senator from Kentucky.

He did reply, and at his own good time, which was at the end of twenty days; and in a way to show that he had "smelt the lamp," not of Demades, but of Demosthenes, during that time. It was profoundly meditated and elaborately composed: the matter solid and condensed; the style chaste, terse and vigorous; the narrative clear; the logic close; the sarcasm cutting: and every word bearing upon the object in view. It was a masterly oration, and like Mr. Clay's speech, divided into two parts; but the second part only seemed to occupy his feelings, and bring forth words from the heart as well as from the head. And well it might! He was speaking, not for life, but for character! and defending public character, in the conduct which makes it, and on high points of policy, which belonged to history—defending it before posterity and the present age, impersonated in the American Senate, before which he stood, and to whom he appealed as judges while invoking as witnesses. He had a high occasion, and he felt it; a high tribunal to plead before, and he rejoiced in it; a high accuser, and he defied him; a high stake to contend for, his own reputation: and manfully, earnestly, and powerfully did he defend it. He had a high example both in oratory, and in the analogies of the occasion, before him; and well had he looked into that example. I happened to know that in this time he refreshed his reading of the Oration on the Crown; and, as the delivery of his speech showed, not without profit. Besides its general cast, which was a good imitation, there were passages of a vigor and terseness—of a power and simplicity—which would recall the recollection of that masterpiece of the oratory of the world. There were points of analogy in the cases as well as in the speeches, each case being that of one eminent statesman accusing another, and before a national tribunal, and upon the events of a public life. More happy than the Athenian orator, the American statesman had no foul imputations to repel. Different from Æschines and Demosthenes, both himself and Mr. Clay stood above the imputation of corrupt action or motive. If they had faults, and what public man is without them? they were the faults of lofty natures—not of sordid souls; and they looked to the honors of their country—not its plunder—for their fair reward.

When Mr. Calhoun finished, Mr. Clay instantly arose, and rejoined—his rejoinder almost entirely directed to the personal part of the discussion, which from its beginning had been the absorbing part. Much stung by Mr. Calhoun's reply, who used the sword as well as the buckler, and with a keen edge upon it, he was more animated and sarcastic in the rejoinder than in the first attack. Mr. Calhoun also rejoined instantly. A succession of brief and rapid rejoinders took place between them (chiefly omitted in this work), which seemed running to infinity, when Mr. Calhoun, satisfied with what he had done, pleasantly put an end to it by saying, he saw the senator from Kentucky was determined to have the last word; and he would yield it to him. Mr. Clay, in the same spirit, disclaimed that desire; and said no more. And thus the exciting debate terminated with more courtesy than that with which it had been conducted.

In all contests of this kind there is a feeling of violated decorum which makes each party solicitous to appear on the defensive, and for that purpose to throw the blame of commencing on the opposite side. Even the one that palpably throws the first stone is yet anxious to show that it was a defensive throw; or at least provoked by previous wrong. Mr. Clay had this feeling upon him, and knew that the *onus* of making out a defensive case fell upon him; and he lost no time in endeavoring to establish it. He placed his defence in the forepart of the attack. At the very outset of the personal part of his speech he attended to this essential preliminary, and found the justification, as he believed, in some expressions of Mr. Calhoun in his sub-treasury speech; and in a couple of passages in a letter he had written on a public occasion, after his return from the extra session—commonly called the Edgefield letter. In the speech he believed he found a reproach upon the patriotism of himself and friends in not following his (Mr. Calhoun's) "*lead*" in support of the administration financial and currency measures; and in the letter, an impeachment of the integrity and patriotism of himself and friends if they got into power; and also an avowal that his change of sides was for selfish considerations. The first reproach, that of lack of patriotism in not following Mr. Calhoun's lead, he found it hard to locate in any definite part of the speech; and had to rest it upon general expressions. The others, those founded upon passages in the letter, were definitely quoted; and were in these terms: "*I could not back and sustain those in such opposition in whose wisdom, firmness and patriotism I had no reason to confide."*—*"It was clear, with our joint forces (whigs and nullifiers) we could utterly overthrow and demolish them; but it was not less clear that the victory would enure, not to us, but exclusively to the benefit of our allies, and their cause."* These passages were much commented upon, especially in the rejoinders; and the whole letter produced by Mr. Calhoun, and the meaning claimed for them fully stated by him.

In the speeches for and against the crown we see Demosthenes answering what has not been found in the speech of Eschines: the same anomaly took place in this earnest debate, as reported between Mr. Clay and Mr. Calhoun. The latter answers much which is not found in the published speech to which he is replying. It gave rise to some remark between the speakers during the rejoinders. Mr. Calhoun said he was replying to the speech as spoken. Mr. Clay said it was printed under his supervision—as much as to say he sanctioned the omissions. The fact is, that with a commendable feeling, he had softened some parts, and omitted others; for that which is severe enough in speaking, becomes more so in writing; and its omission or softening is a tacit retraction, and honorable to the cool reflection which condemns what passion, or heat, had prompted. But Mr. Calhoun did not accept the favor: and, neither party desiring quarter, the one answered what had been dropt, and the other re-produced it, with interest. In his rejoinders, Mr. Clay supplied all that had been omitted—and made additions to it.

This contest between two eminent men, on a theatre so elevated, in which the stake to each was so great, and in which each did his best, conscious that the eye of the age and of posterity was upon him, was an event in itself, and in their lives. It abounded with exemplifications of all the different sorts of oratory of which each was master: on one side—declamation, impassioned eloquence, vehement invective, taunting sarcasm: on the other—close reasoning, chaste narrative, clear statement, keen retort. Two accessories of such contests (disruptions of friendships), were missing, and well—the pathetic and the virulent. There was no crying, or blackguarding in it—nothing like the weeping scene between Fox and Burke, when the heart overflowed with tenderness at the recollection of former love, now gone forever; nor like the virulent one when the gall, overflowing with bitterness, warned an ancient friend never to return as a spy to the camp which he had left as a deserter.

There were in the speeches of each some remarkable passages, such only as actors in the scenes could furnish, and which history will claim. Thus: Mr. Clay gave some inside views of the concoction of the famous compromise act of 1833; which, so far as they go, correspond with the secret history of the same concoction as given in one of the chapters on that subject in the first volume of this work. Mr. Clay's speech is also remarkable for the declaration that the protective system, which he so long advocated, was never intended to be permanent: that its only design was to give temporary encouragement to infant manufactures: and that it had fulfilled its mission. Mr. Calhoun's speech was also remarkable for admitting the power, and the expediency of incidental protection, as it was called; and on this ground he justified his support of the tariff of 1816—so much objected against him. He also gave his history of the compromise of 1833, attributing it to the efficacy of nullification and of the military attitude of South Carolina: which brought upon him the relentless sarcasm of Mr. Clay; and occasioned his explanation of his support of a national bank in 1816. He was chairman of the committee which reported the charter for that bank, and gave it the support which carried it through; with which he was reproached after he became opposed to the bank. He explained the circumstances under which he gave that support—such as I had often heard him state in conversation; and which always appeared to me to be sufficient to exempt him from reproach. At the same time (and what is but little known), he had the merit of opposing, and probably of defeating, a far more dangerous bank—one of fifty millions (equivalent to one hundred and twenty millions now), and founded almost wholly upon United States stocks—imposingly recommended to Congress by the then secretary of the Treasury, Mr. Alexander J. Dallas. The analytical mind of Mr. Calhoun, then one of the youngest members, immediately solved this monster proposition into its constituent elements; and his power of generalization and condensation, enabled him to express its character in two words—*lending our credit to the bank for nothing, and borrowing it back at six per cent. interest.* As an alternative, and not as a choice, he supported the national bank that was chartered, after twice defeating the monster bank of fifty millions founded on paper; for that monster was twice presented to Congress, and twice repulsed. The last time it came as a currency measure—as a bank to create a national currency; and as such was referred to a select committee on national currency, of which Mr. Calhoun was chairman. He opposed it, and fell into the support of the bank which was chartered. Strange that in this search for a national bank, the currency of the constitution seemed to enter no one's head. The revival of the gold currency was never suggested; and in that oblivion of gold, and still hunting a substitute in paper, the men who put down the first national bank did their work much less effectually that those who put down the second one.

The speech of each of these senators, so far as they constitute the personal part of the debate, will be given in a chapter of its own: the rejoinders being brief, prompt, and responsive each to the other, will be put together in another chapter. The speeches of each, having been carefully prepared and elaborated, may be considered as fair specimens of their speaking powers—the style of each different, but each a first class speaker in the branch of oratory to which he belonged. They may be read with profit by those who would wish to form an idea of the style and power of these eminent orators. Manner, and all that is comprehended under the head of delivery, is a different attribute; and there Mr. Clay had an advantage, which is lost in transferring the speech to paper. Some of Mr. Calhoun's characteristics of manner may be seen in these speeches. He eschewed the studied exordiums and perorations, once so much in vogue, and which the rhetorician's rules teach how to make. A few simple words to announce the beginning, and the same to show the ending of his speech, was about as much as he did in that way; and in that departure from custom he conformed to what was becoming in a business speech, as his generally were; and also to what was suitable to his own intellectual style of speaking. He also eschewed the trite, familiar, and unparliamentary mode (which of late has got into vogue) of referring to a senator as, "my friend," or, "the distinguished," or, "the eloquent," or, "the honorable," &c. He followed the written rule of parliamentary law; which is also the clear rule of propriety, and referred to the member by his sitting-place in the Senate, and the State from which he came. Thus: "the senator from Kentucky who sits farthest from me;" which was a sufficient designation to those present, while for the absent, and for posterity the name (Mr. Clay) would be put in brackets. He also addressed the body by the simple collective phrase, "senators;" and this was, not accident, or fancy, but system, resulting from convictions of propriety; and he would allow no reporter to alter it.

Mr. Calhoun laid great stress upon his speech in this debate, as being the vindication of his public life; and declared, in one of his replies to Mr. Clay, that he rested his public character upon it, and desired it to be read by those who would do him justice. In justice to him, and as being a vindication of several measures of his mentioned in this work, not approvingly, a place is here given to it.

This discussion between two eminent men, growing out of support and opposition to the leading measures of Mr. Van Buren's administration, indissolubly connects itself with the passage of those measures; and gives additional emphasis and distinction to the era of the crowning policy which separated bank and state—made the government the keeper of its own money—repulsed paper money from the federal treasury—filled the treasury to bursting with solid gold; and did more for the prosperity of the country than any set of measures from the foundation of the government.

CHAPTER XXVI.

DEBATE BETWEEN MR. CLAY AND MR. CALHOUN: MR. CLAY'S SPEECH: EXTRACTS.

"Who, Mr. President, are the most conspicuous of those who perseveringly pressed this bill upon Congress and the American people? Its drawer is the distinguished gentleman in the white house not far off (Mr. VAN BUREN); its indorser is the distinguished senator from South Carolina, here present. What the drawer thinks of the indorser, his cautious reserve and stifled enmity prevent us from knowing. But the frankness of the indorser has not left us in the same ignorance with respect to his opinion of the drawer. He has often expressed it upon the floor of the Senate. On an occasion not very distant, denying him any of the noble qualities of the royal beast of the forest, he attributed to him those which belong to the most crafty, most skulking, and the meanest of the quadruped tribe. Mr. President, it is due to myself to say, that I do not altogether share with the senator from South Carolina in this opinion of the President of the United States. I have always found him, in his manners and deportment, civil, courteous, and gentlemanly; and he dispenses, in the noble mansion which he now occupies, one worthy the residence of the chief magistrate of a great people, a generous and liberal hospitality. An acquaintance with him of more than twenty years' duration has inspired me with a respect for the man, although, I regret to be compelled to say, I detest the magistrate.

"The eloquent senator from South Carolina has intimated that the course of my friends and myself, in opposing this bill, was unpatriotic, and that we ought to have followed in his lead; and, in a late letter of his, he has spoken of his alliance with us, and of his motives for quitting it. I cannot admit the justice of his reproach. We united, if, indeed, there were any alliance in the case, to restrain the enormous expansion of executive power; to arrest the progress of corruption; to rebuke usurpation; and to drive the Goths and Vandals from the capital; to expel Brennus and his horde from Rome, who, when he threw his sword into the scale, to augment the ransom demanded from the mistress of the world, showed his preference for gold; that he was a hard-money chieftain. It was by the much more valuable metal of iron that he was driven from her gates. And how often have we witnessed the senator from South Carolina, with woful countenance, and in doleful strains, pouring forth touching and mournful eloquence on the degeneracy of the times, and the downward tendency of the republic? Day after day, in the Senate, have we seen the displays of his lofty and impassioned eloquence. Although I shared largely with the senator in his apprehension for the purity of our institutions, and the permanency of our civil liberty, disposed always to look at the brighter side of human affairs, I was sometimes inclined to hope that the vivid imagination of the senator had depicted the dangers by which we were encompassed in somewhat stronger colors than they justified.

"The arduous contest in which we were so long engaged was about to terminate in a glorious victory. The very object for which the alliance was formed was about to be accomplished. At this critical moment the senator left us; he left us for the very purpose of preventing the success of the common cause. He took up his musket, knapsack, and shot-pouch, and joined the other party. He went, horse, foot, and dragoon; and he himself composed the whole corps. He went, as his present most distinguished ally commenced with his expunging resolution, *solitary and alone.* The earliest instance recorded in history, within my recollection, of an ally drawing off his forces from the combined army, was that of Achilles at the siege of Troy. He withdrew, with all his troops, and remained in the neighborhood, in sullen and dignified inactivity. But he did not join the Trojan forces; and when, during the progress of the siege, his faithful friend fell in battle, he raised his avenging arm, drove the Trojans back into the gates of Troy, and satiated his vengeance by slaying Priam's noblest and dearest son, the finest hero in the immortal Iliad. But Achilles had been wronged, or imagined himself wronged, in the person of the fair and beautiful Briseis. We did no wrong to the distinguished senator from South Carolina. On the contrary, we respected him, confided in his great and acknowledged ability, his uncommon genius, his extensive experience, his supposed patriotism; above all, we confided in his stern and inflexible fidelity. Nevertheless, he left us, and joined our common opponents, distrusting and distrusted. He left us, as he tells us in the Edgefield letter, because the victory which our common arms were about to achieve, was not to enure to him and his party, but exclusively to the benefit of his allies and their cause. I thought that, actuated by patriotism (that noblest of human virtues), we had been contending together for our common country, for her violated rights, her threatened liberties, her prostrate constitution. Never did I suppose that personal or party considerations entered into our views. Whether, if victory shall ever again be about to perch upon the standard of the spoils party (the denomination which the senator from South Carolina has so often given to his present allies), he will not feel himself constrained, by the principles on which he has acted, to leave them, because it may not enure to the benefit of himself and his party, I leave to be adjusted between themselves.

"The speech of the senator from South Carolina was plausible, ingenious, abstract, metaphysical, and generalizing. It did not appear to me to be adapted to the bosoms and business of human life. It was aerial, and not very high up in the air, Mr. President, either—not quite as high as Mr. Clayton was in his last ascension in his balloon. The senator announced that there was a single alternative, and no escape from one or the other branch of it. He stated that we must take the bill under consideration, or the substitute proposed by the senator from Virginia. I do not concur in that statement of the case. There is another course embraced in neither branch of the senator's alternative; and that course is to do nothing,—always the wisest when you are not certain what you ought to do. Let us suppose that neither branch of the alternative is accepted, and that nothing is done. What, then, would be the consequence? There would be a restoration of the law of 1789, with all its cautious provisions and securities, provided by the wisdom of our ancestors, which has been so trampled upon by the late and present administrations. By that law, establishing the Treasury department, the treasure of the United States is to be received, kept, and disbursed by the treasurer, under a bond with ample security, under a large penalty fixed by law, and not left, as this bill leaves it, to the uncertain discretion of a Secretary of the Treasury. If, therefore, we were to do nothing, that law would be revived; the treasurer would have the custody, as he ought to have, of the public money, and doubtless he would make special deposits of it in all instances with safe and sound State banks; as in some cases the Secretary of the Treasury is now obliged to do. Thus, we should have in operation that very special deposit system, so much desired by some gentlemen, by which the public money would remain separate and unmixed with the money of banks.

"There is yet another course, unembraced by either branch of the alternative presented by the senator from South Carolina; and that is, to establish a bank of the United States, constituted according to the old and approved method of forming such an institution, tested and sanctioned by experience; a bank of the United States which should blend public and private interests, and be subject to public and private control; united together in such manner as to present safe and salutary checks against all abuses. The senator mistakes his own abandonment of that institution as ours. I know that the party in power has barricaded itself against the establishment of such a bank. It adopted, at the last extra session, the extraordinary and unprecedented resolution, that the people of the United States should not have such a bank, although it might be manifest that there was a clear majority of them demanding it. But the day may come, and I trust is not distant, when the will of the people must prevail in the councils of her own government; and when it does arrive, a bank will be established.

"The senator from South Carolina reminds us that we denounced the pet bank system; and so we did, and so we do. But does it therefore follow that, bad as that system was, we must be driven into the acceptance of a system infinitely worse? He tells us that the bill under consideration takes the public funds out of the hands of the Executive, and places them in the hands of the law. It does no such thing. They are now without law, it is true, in the custody of the Executive; and the bill proposes by law to confirm them in that custody, and to convey new and enormous powers of control to the Executive over them. Every custodary of the public funds provided by the bill is a creature of the Executive, dependent upon his breath, and subject to the same breath for removal, whenever the Executive—from caprice, from tyranny, or from party motives—shall choose to order it. What safety is there for the public money, if there were a hundred subordinate executive officers charged with its care, whilst the doctrine of the absolute unity of the whole executive power, promulgated by the last administration, and persisted in by this, remains unrevoked and unrebuked?

"Whilst the senator from South Carolina professes to be the friend of State banks, he has attacked the whole banking system of the United States. He is their friend; he only thinks they are all unconstitutional! Why? Because the coining power is possessed by the general government; and that coining power, he argues, was intended to supply a currency of the precious metals; but the State banks absorb the precious metals, and withdraw them from circulation, and, therefore, are in conflict with the coining power. That power, according to my view of it, is nothing but a naked authority to stamp certain pieces of the precious metals, in fixed proportions of alloy and pure metal prescribed by law; so that their exact value be known. When that office is performed, the power is *functus officio*; the money passes out of the mint, and becomes the lawful property of those who legally acquire it. They may do with it as they please,—throw it into the ocean, bury it in the earth, or melt it in a crucible, without violating any law. When it has once left the vaults of the mint, the law maker has nothing to do with it, but to protect it against those who attempt to debase or counterfeit, and, subsequently, to pass it as lawful money. In the sense in which the senator supposes banks to conflict with the coining power, foreign commerce, and especially our commerce with China, conflicts with it much more extensively.

"The distinguished senator is no enemy to the banks; he merely thinks them injurious to the morals and industry of the country. He likes them very well, but he nevertheless believes that they levy a tax of twenty-five millions annually on the industry of the country! The senator from South Carolina would do the banks no harm; but they are deemed by him highly injurious to the planting interest! According to him, they inflate prices, and the poor planter sells his productions for hard money, and has to purchase his supplies at the swollen prices produced by a paper medium. The senator tells us that it has been only within a few days that he has discovered that it is illegal to receive bank notes in payment of public dues. Does he think that the usage of the government under all its administrations, and with every party in power, which has prevailed for nigh fifty years, ought to be set aside by a novel theory of his, just dreamed into existence, even if it possess the merit of ingenuity? The bill under consideration, which has been eulogized by the senator as perfect in its structure and details, contains a provision that bank notes shall be received in diminished proportions, during a term of six years. He himself introduced the identical principle. It is the only part of the bill that is emphatically his. How, then, can he contend that it is unconstitutional to receive bank notes in payment of public dues? I appeal from himself to himself."

"The doctrine of the senator in 1816 was, as he now states it, that bank notes being in fact received by the executive, although contrary to law, it was constitutional to create a Bank of the United States. And in 1834, finding that bank which was constitutional in its inception, but had become unconstitutional in its progress, yet in existence, it was quite constitutional to propose, as the senator did, to continue it twelve years longer."

"The senator and I began our public career nearly together; we remained together throughout the war. We agreed as to a Bank of the United States—as to a protective tariff—as to internal improvements; and lately as to those arbitrary and violent measures which characterized the administration of General Jackson. No two men ever agreed better together in respect to important measures of public policy. We concur in nothing now."

CHAPTER XXVII.

DEBATE BETWEEN MR. CLAY AND MR. CALHOUN: MR. CALHOUN'S SPEECH; EXTRACTS.

"I rise to fulfil a promise I made some time since, to notice at my leisure the reply of the senator from Kentucky farthest from me [Mr CLAY], to my remarks, when I first addressed the Senate on the subject now under discussion.

"On comparing with care the reply with the remarks, I am at a loss to determine whether it is the most remarkable for its omissions or misstatements. Instead of leaving not a hair in the head of my arguments, as the senator threatened (to use his not very dignified expression), he has not even attempted to answer a large, and not the least weighty, portion; and of that which he has, there is not one fairly stated, or fairly answered. I speak literally, and without exaggeration; nor would it be difficult to establish to the letter what I assert, if I could reconcile it to myself to consume the time of the Senate in establishing a long series of negative propositions, in which they could take but little interest, however important they may be regarded by the senator and myself. To avoid so idle a consumption of the time, I propose to present a few instances of his misstatements, from which the rest may be inferred; and, that I may not be suspected of having selected them, I shall take them in the order in which they stand in his reply.

[The argumentative part omitted.]

"But the senator did not restrict himself to a reply to my arguments. He introduced personal remarks, which neither self-respect, nor a regard to the cause I support, will permit me to pass without notice, as adverse as I am to all personal controversies. Not only my education and disposition, but, above all, my conception of the duties belonging to the station I occupy, indisposes me to such controversies. We are sent here, not to wrangle, or indulge in personal abuse, but to deliberate and decide on the common interests of the States of this Union, as far as they have been subjected by the constitution to our jurisdiction. Thus thinking and feeling, and having perfect confidence in the cause I support, I addressed myself, when I was last up, directly and exclusively to the understanding, carefully avoiding every remark which had the least personal or party bearing. In proof of this, I appeal to you, senators, my witnesses and judges on this occasion. But it seems that no caution on my part could prevent what I was so anxious to avoid. The senator, having no pretext to give a personal direction to the discussion, made a premeditated and gratuitous attack on me. I say having no pretext; for there is not a shadow of foundation for the assertion that I called on him and his party to follow my lead, at which he seemed to take offence, as I have already shown. I made no such call, or any thing that could be construed into it. It would have been impertinent, in the relation between myself and his party, at any stage of this question; and absurd at that late period, when every senator had made up his mind. As there was, then, neither provocation nor pretext, what could be the motive of the senator in making the attack? It could not be to indulge in the pleasure of personal abuse—the lowest and basest of all our passions; and which is so far beneath the dignity of the senator's character and station. Nor could it be with the view to intimidation. The senator knows me too long, and too well, to make such an attempt. I am sent here by constituents as respectable as those he represents, in order to watch over their peculiar interests, and take care of the general concern; and if I were capable of being deterred by any one, or any consequence, in discharging my duty, from denouncing what I regarded as dangerous or corrupt, or giving a decided and zealous support to what I thought right and expedient, I would, in shame and confusion, return my commission to the patriotic and gallant State I represent, to be placed in more resolute and trustworthy hands.

"If, then, neither the one nor the other of these be the motive, what, I repeat, can it be? In casting my eyes over the whole surface I can see but one, which is, that the senator, despairing of the sufficiency of his reply to overthrow my arguments, had resorted to personalities, in the hope, with their aid, to effect what he could not accomplish by main strength. He well knows that the force of an argument on moral or political subjects depends greatly on the character of him who advanced it; and that to cast suspicion on his sincerity or motive, or to shake confidence in his understanding, is often the most effectual mode to destroy its force. Thus viewed, his personalities may be fairly regarded as constituting a part of his reply to my argument; and we, accordingly, find the senator throwing them in front, like a skilful general, in order to weaken my arguments before he brought on his main attack. In repelling, then, his personal attacks, I also defend the cause which I advocate. It is against that his blows are aimed and he strikes at it through me, because he believes his blows will be the more effectual.

"Having given this direction to his reply, he has imposed on me a double duty to repel his attacks: duty to myself, and to the cause I support. I shall not decline its performance; and when it is discharged, I trust I shall have placed my character as far beyond the darts which he has hurled at it, as my arguments have proved to be above his abilities to reply to them. In doing this, I shall be compelled to speak of myself. No one can be more sensible than I am how odious it is to speak of one's self. I shall endeavor to confine myself within the limits of the strictest propriety; but if any thing should escape me that may wound the most delicate ear, the odium ought in justice to fall not on me, but the senator, who, by his unprovoked and wanton attack, has imposed on me the painful necessity of speaking of myself.

"The leading charge of the senator—that on which all the others depend, and which, being overthrown, they fall to the ground—is that I have gone over; have left his side, and joined the other. By this vague and indefinite expression, I presume he meant to imply that I had either changed my opinion, or abandoned my principle, or deserted my party. If he did not mean one, or all; if I have changed neither opinions, principles, nor party, then the charge meant nothing deserving notice. But if he intended to imply, what I have presumed he did, I take issue on the fact—I meet and repel the charge. It happened, fortunately for me, fortunately for the cause of truth and justice, that it was not the first time that I had offered my sentiments on the question now under consideration. There is scarcely a single point in the present issue on which I did not explicitly express my opinion, four years ago, in my place here, when the removal of the deposits and the questions connected with it were under discussion—so explicitly as to repel effectually the charge of any change on my part; and to make it impossible for me to pursue any other course than I have without involving myself in gross inconsistency. I intend not to leave so important a point to rest on my bare assertion. What I assert stands on record, which I now hold in my possession, and intend, at the proper time, to introduce and read. But, before I do that, it will be proper I should state the questions now at issue, and my course in relation to them; so that, having a clear and distinct perception of them, you may, senators, readily and satisfactorily compare and determine whether my course on the present occasion coincides with the opinions I then expressed.

"There are three questions, as is agreed by all, involved in the present issue: Shall we separate the government from the banks, or shall we revive the league of State banks, or create a national bank? My opinion and course in reference to each are well known. I prefer the separation to either of the others; and, as between the other two, I regard a national bank as a more efficient, and a less corrupting fiscal agent than a league of State banks. It is also well known that I have expressed myself on the present occasion hostile to the banking system, as it exists; and against the constitutional power of making a bank, unless on the assumption that we have the right to receive and treat bank-notes as cash in our fiscal operations, which I, for the first time, have denied on the present occasion. Now, I entertained and expressed all these opinions, on a different occasion, four years ago, except the right of receiving bank-notes, in regard to which I then reserved my opinion; and if all this should be fully and clearly established by the record, from speeches delivered and published at the time, the charge of the senator must, in the opinion of all, however prejudiced, sink to the ground. I am now prepared to introduce, and have the record read. I delivered two speeches in the session of 1833-'34, one on the removal of the deposits, and the other on the question of the renewal of the charter of the late bank. I ask the secretary to turn to the volume lying before him, and read the three paragraphs marked in my speech on the deposits. I will thank him to raise his voice, and read slowly, so that he may be distinctly heard; and I must ask you, senators, to give your attentive hearing; for on the coincidence between my opinions then and my course now, my vindication against this unprovoked and groundless charge rests.

"[The secretary of the Senate read as requested.]

"Such were my sentiments, delivered four years since, on the question of the removal of the deposits, and now standing on record; and I now call your attention senators, while they are fresh in your minds, and before other extracts are read, to the opinions I then entertained and expressed, in order that you may compare them with those that I have expressed, and the course I have pursued on the present occasion. In the first place, I then expressed myself explicitly and decidedly against the banking system, and intimated, in language too strong to be mistaken, that, if the question was then bank or no bank, as it now is, as far as government is concerned, I would not be found on the side of the bank. Now, I ask, I appeal to the candor of all, even the most prejudiced, is there any thing in all this contradictory to my present opinions or course? On the contrary, having entertained and expressed these opinions, could I, at this time, when the issue I then supposed is actually presented, have gone against the separation without gross inconsistency? Again, I then declared myself to be utterly opposed to a combination or league of State banks, as being the most efficient and corrupting fiscal agent the government could select, and more objectionable than a bank of the United States. I again appeal, is there a sentiment or a word in all this contradictory to what I have said, or done, on the present occasion? So far otherwise, is there not a perfect harmony and coincidence throughout, which, considering the distance of time and the difference of the occasion, is truly remarkable; and this extending to all the great and governing questions now at issue?

"To prove all this I again refer to the record. If it shall appear from it that my object was to disconnect the government gradually and cautiously from the banking system, and with that view, and that only, I proposed to use the Bank of the United States for a short time, and that I explicitly expressed the same opinions then as I now have on almost every point connected with the system; I shall not only have vindicated my character from the charge of the senator from Kentucky, but shall do more, much more to show that I did all an individual, standing alone, as I did, could do to avert the present calamities: and, of course, I am free from all responsibility for what has since happened. I have shortened the extracts, as far as was possible to do justice to myself, and have left out much that ought, of right, to be read in my defence, rather than to weary the Senate. I know how difficult it is to command attention to reading of documents; but I trust that this, where justice to a member of the body, whose character has been assailed, without the least provocation, will form an exception. The extracts are numbered, and I will thank the secretary to pause at the end of each, unless otherwise desired.

"[The secretary read as requested.]

"But the removal of the deposits was not the only question discussed at that remarkable and important session. The charter of the United States Bank was then about to expire. The senator from Massachusetts nearest to me [Mr. WEBSTER], then at the head of the committee on finance, suggested, in his place, that he intended to introduce a bill to renew the charter. I clearly perceived that the movement, if made, would fail; and that there was no prospect of doing any thing to arrest the danger approaching, unless the subject was taken up on the broad question of the currency; and that if any connection of the government with the banks could be justified at all, it must be in that relation. I am not among those who believe that the currency was in a sound condition when the deposits were removed in 1834. I then believed, and experience has proved I was correct, that it was deeply and dangerously diseased; and that the most efficient measures were necessary to prevent the catastrophe which has since fallen on the circulation of the country. There was then not more than one dollar in specie, on an average, in the banks, including the United States Bank and all, for six of bank notes in circulation; and not more than one in eleven compared to liabilities of the banks; and this while the United States Bank was in full and active operation; which proves conclusively that its charter ought not to be renewed, if renewed at all, without great modifications. I saw also that the expansion of the circulation, great as it then was, must still farther increase; that the disease lay deep in the system; that the terms on which the charter of the Bank of England was renewed would give a western direction to specie, which, instead of correcting the disorder, by substituting specie for bank notes in our circulation, would become the basis of new banking operations that would greatly increase the swelling tide. Such were my conceptions then, and I honestly and earnestly endeavored to carry them into effect, in order to prevent the approaching catastrophe.

"The political and personal relations between myself and the senator from Massachusetts [Mr. WEBSTER], were then not the kindest. We stood in opposition at the preceding session on the great question growing out of the conflict between the State I represented and the general government, which could not pass away without leaving unfriendly feelings on both sides; but where duty is involved, I am not in the habit of permitting my personal relations to interfere. In my solicitude to avoid coming dangers, I sought an interview, through a common friend, in order to compare opinions as to the proper course to be pursued. We met, and conversed freely and fully, but parted without agreeing. I expressed to him my deep regret at our disagreement, and informed him that, although I could not agree with him, I would throw no embarrassment in his way; but should feel it to be my duty, when he made his motion to introduce a bill to renew the charter of the bank, to express my opinion at large on the state of the currency and the proper course to be pursued; which I accordingly did. On that memorable occasion I stood almost alone. One party supported the league of State banks, and the other the United States Bank, the charter of which the senator from Massachusetts [Mr. WEBSTER.] proposed to renew for six years. Nothing was left me but to place myself distinctly before the country on the ground I occupied, which I did fully and explicitly in the speech I delivered on the occasion. In justice to myself, I ought to have every word of it read on the present occasion. It would of itself be a full vindication of my course. I stated and enlarged on all the points to which I have already referred; objected to the recharter as proposed by the mover; and foretold that what has since happened would follow, unless something effectual was done to prevent it. As a remedy, I proposed to use the Bank of the United States as a temporary expedient, fortified with strong guards, in order to resist and turn back the swelling tide of circulation.

"After having so expressed myself, which clearly shows that my object was to use the bank for a time in such a manner as to break the connection with the system, without a shock to the country or currency, I then proceed and examine the question, whether this could be best accomplished by the renewal of the charter of the United States Bank, or through a league of State banks. After concluding what I had to say on the subject, in my deep solicitude I addressed the three parties in the Senate separately, urging such motives as I thought best calculated to act on them; and pressing them to join me in the measure suggested, in order to avert approaching danger. I began with my friends of the State rights party, and with the administration. I have taken copious extracts from the address to the first, which will clearly prove how exactly my opinions then and now coincide on all questions connected with the banks. I now ask the secretary to read the extract numbered two.

"[The secretary read accordingly.]

"I regret to trespass on the patience of the Senate, but I wish, in justice to myself, to ask their attention to one more, which, though not immediately relating to the question under consideration, is not irrelevant to my vindication. I not only expressed my opinions freely in relation to the currency and the bank, in the speech from which such copious extracts have been read, but had the precaution to define my political position distinctly in reference to the political parties of the day, and the course I would pursue in relation to each. I then, as now, belonged to the party to which it is my glory ever to have been attached exclusively; and avowed, explicitly, that I belonged to neither of the two parties, opposition or administration, then contending for superiority; which of itself ought to go far to repel the charge of the senator from Kentucky, that I have gone over from one party to the other. The secretary will read the last extract.

"[The secretary read.]

"Such, senators, are my recorded sentiments in 1834. They are full and explicit on all the questions involved in the present issue, and prove, beyond the possibility of doubt, that I have changed no opinion, abandoned no principle, nor deserted any party. I stand now on the ground I stood then, and, of course, if my relations to the two opposing parties are changed—if I now act with those I then opposed, and oppose those with whom I then acted, the change is not in me. I, at least, have stood still. In saying this, I accuse none of changing. I leave others to explain their position, now and then, if they deem explanation necessary. But, if I may be permitted to state my opinion, I would say that the change is rather in the questions and the circumstances, than in the opinions or principles of either of the parties. The opposition were then, and are now, national bank men, and the administration, in like manner, were anti-national bank, and in favor of a league of State banks; while I preferred then, as now, the former to the latter, and a divorce from banks to either. When the experiment of the league failed, the administration were reduced to the option between a national bank and a divorce. They chose the latter, and such, I have no reason to doubt, would have been their choice, had the option been the same four years ago. Nor have I any doubt, had the option been then between a league of banks and divorce, the opposition then, as now, would have been in favor of the league. In all this there is more apparent than real change. As to myself, there has been neither. If I acted with the opposition and opposed the administration then, it was because I was openly opposed to the removal of the deposits and the league of banks, as I now am; and if I now act with the latter and oppose the former, it is because I am now, as then, in favor of a divorce, and opposed to either a league of State banks or a national bank, except, indeed, as the means of effecting a divorce gradually and safely. What, then, is my offence? What but refusing to abandon my first choice, the divorce from the banks, because the administration has selected it, and of going with the opposition for a national bank, to which I have been and am still opposed? That is all; and for this I am charged with going over—leaving one party and joining the other.

"Yet, in the face of all this, the senator has not only made the charge, but has said, in his place, that he heard, for the first time in his life, at the extra session, that I was opposed to a national bank! I could place the senator in a dilemma from which there is no possibility of escape. I might say to him, you have either forgot, or not, what I said in 1834. If you have not, how can you justify yourself in making the charge you have? But if you have—if you have forgot what is so recent, and what, from the magnitude of the question and the importance of the occasion, was so well calculated to impress itself on your memory, what possible value can be attached to your recollection or opinions, as to my course on more remote and less memorable occasions, on which you have undertaken to impeach my conduct? He may take his choice.

"Having now established by the record that I have changed no opinion, abandoned no principle, nor deserted any party, the charge of the senator, with all the aspersions with which he accompanied it, falls prostrate to the earth. Here I might leave the subject, and close my vindication. But I choose not. I shall follow the senator up, step by step, in his unprovoked, and I may now add, groundless attack, with blows not less decisive and victorious.

"The senator next proceeded to state, that in a certain document (if he named it, I did not hear him) I assigned as the reason why I could not join in the attack on the administration, that the benefit of the victory would not enure to myself, or my party; or, as he explained himself, because it would not place myself and them in power. I presume he referred to a letter, in answer to an invitation to a public dinner, offered me by my old and faithful friends and constituents of Edgefield, in approbation of my course at the extra session.

"[Mr. CLAY. I do.]

"The pressure of domestic engagements would not permit me to accept their invitation; and, in declining it, I deemed it due to them and myself to explain my course, in its political and party bearing, more fully than I had done in debate. They had a right to know my reasons, and I expressed myself with the frankness due to the long and uninterrupted confidence that had ever existed between us.

"Having made these explanatory remarks, I now proceed to meet the assertion of the senator. I again take issue on the fact. I assigned no such reason as the senator attributes to me. I never dreamed nor thought of such a one; nor can any force of construction extort such from what I said. No; my object was not power or place, either for myself or party. I was far more humble and honest. It was to save ourselves and our principles from being absorbed and lost in a party, more numerous and powerful; but differing from us on almost every principle and question of policy.

"When the suspension of specie payments took place in May last (not unexpected to me), I immediately turned my attention to the event earnestly, considering it as an event pregnant with great and lasting consequences. Reviewing the whole ground, I saw nothing to change in the opinions and principles I had avowed in 1834; and I determined to carry them out, as far as circumstances and my ability would enable me. But I saw that my course must be influenced by the position which the two great contending parties might take in reference to the question. I did not doubt that the opposition would rally either on a national bank, or a combination of State banks, with Mr. Biddle's at the head; but I was wholly uncertain what course the administration would adopt, and remained so until the message of the President was received and read by the secretary at his table. When I saw he went for a divorce, I never hesitated a moment. Not only my opinions and principles long entertained, and, as I have shown, fully expressed years ago, but the highest political motives, left me no alternative. I perceived at once that the object, to accomplish which we had acted in concert with the opposition, had ceased: Executive usurpations had come to an end for the present: and that the struggle with the administration was no longer for power, but to save themselves. I also clearly saw, that if we should unite with the opposition in their attack on the administration, the victory over them, in the position they occupied, would be a victory over us and our principles. It required no sagacity to see that such would be the result. It was as plain as day. The administration had taken position, as I have shown, on the very ground I occupied in 1834; and which the whole State rights party had taken at the same time in the other House, as its journals will prove. The opposition, under the banner of the bank, were moving against them for the very reason that they had taken the ground they did.

"Now, I ask, what would have been the result if we had joined in the attack? No one can now doubt that the victory over those in power would have been certain and decisive, nor would the consequences have been the least doubtful. The first fruit would have been a national bank. The principles of the opposition, and the very object of the attack, would have necessarily led to that. We would have been not only too feeble to resist, but would have been committed by joining in the attack with its avowed object to go for one, while those who support the administration would have been scattered in the winds. We should then have had a bank—that is clear; nor is it less certain, that in its train there would have followed all the consequences which have and ever will follow, when tried—high duties, overflowing revenue, extravagant expenditures, large surpluses; in a word, all those disastrous consequences which have well near overthrown our institutions, and involved the country in its present difficulties. The influence of the institution, the known principles and policy of the opposition, and the utter prostration of the administration party, and the absorption of ours, would have led to these results as certainly as we exist.

"I now appeal, senators, to your candor and justice, and ask, could I, having all these consequences before me, with my known opinions and that of the party to which I belong, and to which only I owe fidelity, have acted differently from what I did? Would not any other course have justly exposed me to the charge of having abandoned my principles and party, with which I am now accused so unjustly? Nay, would it not have been worse than folly—been madness in me, to have taken any other? And yet, the grounds which I have assumed in this exposition are the very *reasons* assigned in my letter, and which the senator has perverted most unfairly and unjustly into the pitiful, personal, and selfish reason, which he has attributed to me. Confirmative of what I say, I again appeal to the record. The secretary will read the paragraph marked in my Edgefield letter, to which, I presume, the senator alluded.

"[The secretary of the Senate reads:]

"As soon as I saw this state of things, I clearly perceived that a very important question was presented for our determination, which we were compelled to decide forthwith—shall we continue our joint attack with the Nationals on those in power, in the new position which they have been compelled to occupy? It was clear, with our joint forces, we could utterly overthrow and demolish them; but it was not less clear that the victory would enure, not to us, but exclusively to the benefit of our allies and their cause. They were the most numerous and powerful, and the point of assault on the position which the party to be assaulted had taken in relation to the banks, would have greatly strengthened the settled principles and policy of the National party, and weakened, in the same degree, ours. They are, and ever have been, the decided advocates of a national bank; and are now in favor of one with a capital so ample as to be sufficient to control the State institutions, and to regulate the currency and exchanges of the country. To join them with their avowed object in the attack to overthrow those in power, on the ground they occupied against a bank, would, of course, not only have placed the government and country in their hands without opposition, but would have committed us, beyond the possibility of extrication, for a bank; and absorbed our party in the ranks of the National Republicans. The first fruits of the victory would have been an overshadowing National Bank, with an immense capital, not less than from fifty to a hundred millions; which would have centralized the currency and exchanges, and with them the commerce and capital of the country, in whatever section the head of the institution might be placed. The next would be the indissoluble union of the political opponents, whose principles and policy are so opposite to ours, and so dangerous to our institutions, as well as oppressive to us.

"I now ask, is there any thing in this extract which will warrant the construction that the senator has attempted to force on it? Is it not manifest that the expression on which he fixes, that the victory would enure, not to us, but exclusively to the benefit of the opposition, alludes not to power or place, but to principle and policy? Can words be more plain? What then becomes of all the aspersions of the senator, his reflections about selfishness and the want of patriotism, and his allusions and illustrations to give them force and effect? They fall to the ground without deserving a notice, with his groundless accusation.

"But, in so premeditated and indiscriminate an attack, it could not be expected that my motives would entirely escape; and we accordingly find the senator very charitably leaving it to time to disclose my motive for going over. Leave it to time to disclose my motive for going over! I who have changed no opinion, abandoned no principle, and deserted no party: I, who have stood still, and maintained my ground against every difficulty, to be told that it is left to time to disclose my motive! The imputation sinks to the earth with the groundless charge on which it rests. I stamp it with scorn in the dust. I pick up the dart, which fell harmless at my feet. I hurl it back. What the senator charges on me unjustly, *he has actually done.* He went over on a memorable occasion, and did not leave it to time to disclose his motive.

"The senator next tells us that I bore a character for stern fidelity; which he accompanied with remarks implying that I had forfeited it by my course on the present occasion. If he means by stern fidelity a devoted attachment to duty and principle, which nothing can overcome, the character is, indeed, a high one; and I trust, not entirely unmerited. I have, at least, the authority of the senator himself for saying that it belonged to me before the present occasion, and it is, of course, incumbent on him to show that I have since forfeited it. He will find the task a Herculean one. It would be by far more easy to show the opposite; that, instead of forfeiting, I have strengthened my title to the character; instead of abandoning any principles, I have firmly adhered to them; and that too, under the most appalling difficulties. If I were to select an instance in the whole course of my life on which, above all others, to rest my claim to the character which the senator attributed to me, it would be this very one, which he has selected to prove that I have forfeited it.

"I acted with the full knowledge of the difficulties I had to encounter, and the responsibility I must incur. I saw a great and powerful party, probably the most powerful in the country, eagerly seizing on the catastrophe which had befallen the currency, and the consequent embarrassments that followed, to displace those in power, against whom they had been long contending. I saw that, to stand between them and their object, I must necessarily incur their deep and lasting displeasure. I also saw that, to maintain the administration in the position they had taken—to separate the government from the banks, I would draw down on me, with the exception of some of the southern banks, the whole weight of that extensive, concentrated, and powerful interest—the most powerful by far of any in the whole community; and thus I would unite against me a combination of political and moneyed influence almost irresistible. Nor was this all. I could not but see that, however pure and disinterested my motives, and however consistent my course with all I had ever said or done, I would be exposed to the very charges and aspersions which I am now repelling. The ease with which they could be made, and the temptation to make them, I saw were too great to be resisted by the party morality of the day—as groundless as I have demonstrated them. But there was another consequence that I could not but foresee, far more painful to me than all others. I but too clearly saw that, in so sudden and complex a juncture, called on as I was to decide on my course instantly, as it were, on the field of battle, without consultation, or explaining my reasons, I would estrange for a time many of my political friends, who had passed through with me so many trials and difficulties, and for whom I feel a brother's love. But I saw before me the path of duty, and, though rugged, and hedged on all sides with these and many other difficulties, I did not hesitate a moment to take it. After I had made up my mind as to my course, in a conversation with a friend about the responsibility I would assume, he remarked that my own State might desert me. I replied that it was not impossible; but the result has proved that I under-estimated the intelligence and patriotism of my virtuous and noble State. I ask her pardon for the distrust implied in my answer; but I ask with assurance it will be granted, on the grounds I shall put it—that, in being prepared to sacrifice her confidence, as dear to me as light and life, rather than disobey on this great question, the dictates of my judgment and conscience, I proved myself worthy of being her representative.

"But if the senator, in attributing to me stern fidelity, meant, not devotion to principle, but to party, and especially the party of which he is so prominent a member, my answer is, that I never belonged to his party, nor owed it any fidelity; and, of course, could forfeit, in reference to it, no character for fidelity. It is true, we acted in concert against what we believed to be the usurpations of the Executive; and it is true that, during the time, I saw much to esteem in those with whom I acted, and contracted friendly relations with many; which I shall not be the first to forget. It is also true that a common party designation was applied to the opposition in the aggregate—not, however, with my approbation; but it is no less true that it was universally known that it consisted of two distinct parties, dissimilar in principle and policy, except in relation to the object for which they had united: the national republican party, and the portion of the State rights party which had separated from the administration, on the ground that it had departed from the true principles of the original party. That I belonged exclusively to that detached portion, and to neither the opposition nor administration party, I prove by my explicit declaration, contained in one of the extracts read from my speech on the currency in 1834. That the party generally, and the State which I represent in part, stood aloof from both of the parties, may be established from the fact that they refused to mingle in the party and political contests of the day. My State withheld her electoral vote in two successive presidential elections; and, rather than to bestow it on either the senator from Kentucky, or the distinguished citizen whom he opposed, in the first of those elections, she threw her vote on a patriotic citizen of Virginia, since deceased, of her own politics; but who was not a candidate; and, in the last, she refused to give it to the worthy senator from Tennessee near me (Judge WHITE), though his principles and views of policy approach so much nearer to hers than that of the party to which the senator from Kentucky belongs.

"And here, Mr. President, I avail myself of the opportunity to declare my present political position, so that there may be no mistake hereafter. I belong to the old Republican State Rights party of '98. To that, and that alone, I owe fidelity, and by that I shall stand through every change, and in spite of every difficulty. Its creed is to be found in the Kentucky resolutions, and Virginia resolutions and report; and its policy is to confine the action of this government within the narrowest limits compatible with the peace and security of these States, and the objects for which the Union was expressly formed. I, as one of that party, shall support all who support its principles and policy, and oppose all who oppose them. I have given, and shall continue to give, the administration a hearty and sincere support on the great question now under discussion, because I regard it as in strict conformity to our creed and policy; and shall do every thing in my power to sustain them under the great responsibility which they have assumed. But let me tell those who are more interested in sustaining them than myself, that the danger which threatens them lies not here, but in another quarter. This measure will tend to uphold them, if they stand fast, and adhere to it with fidelity. But, if they wish to know where the danger is, let them look to the fiscal department of the government. I said, years ago, that we were committing an error the reverse of the great and dangerous one that was committed in 1828, and to which we owe our present difficulties, and all we have since experienced. Then we raised the revenue greatly, when the expenditures were about to be reduced by the discharge of the public debt; and now we have doubled the disbursements, when the revenue is rapidly decreasing; an error, which, although probably not so fatal to the country, will prove, if immediate and vigorous measures be not adopted, far more so to those in power.

"But the senator did not confine his attack to my conduct and motives in reference to the present question. In his eagerness to weaken the cause I support, by destroying confidence in me, he made an indiscriminate attack on my intellectual faculties, which he characterized as metaphysical, eccentric, too much of genius, and too little common sense; and of course wanting a sound and practical judgment.

"Mr. President, according to my opinion, there is nothing of which those who are endowed with superior mental faculties ought to be more cautious, than to reproach those with their deficiency to whom Providence has been less liberal. The faculties of our mind are the immediate gift of our Creator, for which we are no farther responsible than for their proper cultivation, according to our opportunities, and their proper application to control and regulate our actions. Thus thinking, I trust I shall be the last to assume superiority on my part, or reproach any one with inferiority on his; but those who do not regard the rule, when applied to others, cannot expect it to be observed when applied to themselves. The critic must expect to be criticised; and he who points out the faults of others, to have his own pointed out.

"I cannot retort on the senator the charge of being metaphysical. I cannot accuse him of possessing the powers of analysis and generalization, those higher faculties of the mind (called metaphysical by those who do not possess them), which decompose and resolve into their elements the complex masses of ideas that exist in the world of mind—as chemistry does the bodies that surround us in the material world; and without which those deep and hidden causes which are in constant action, and producing such mighty changes in the condition of society, would operate unseen and undetected. The absence of these higher qualities of the mind is conspicuous throughout the whole course of the senator's public life. To this it may be traced that he prefers the specious to the solid, and the plausible to the true. To the same cause, combined with an ardent temperament, it is owing that we ever find him mounted on some popular and favorite measure, which he whips along, cheered by the shouts of the multitude, and never dismounts till he has rode it down. Thus, at one time, we find him mounted on the protective system, which he rode down; at another, on internal improvement; and now he is mounted on a bank, which will surely share the same fate, unless those who are immediately interested shall stop him in his headlong career. It is the fault of his mind to seize on a few prominent and striking advantages, and to pursue them eagerly without looking to consequences. Thus, in the case of the protective system, he was struck with the advantages of manufactures; and, believing that high duties was the proper mode of protecting them, he pushed forward the system, without seeing that he was enriching one portion of the country at the expense of the other; corrupting the one and alienating the other; and, finally, dividing the community into two great hostile interests, which terminated in the overthrow of the system itself. So, now, he looks only to a uniform currency, and a bank as the means of securing it, without once reflecting how far the banking system has progressed, and the difficulties that impede its farther progress; that banking and politics are running together to their mutual destruction; and that the only possible mode of saving his favorite system is to separate it from the government.

"To the defects of understanding, which the senator attributes to me, I make no reply. It is for others, and not me, to determine the portion of understanding which it has pleased the Author of my being to bestow on me. It is, however, fortunate for me, that the standard by which I shall be judged is not the false, prejudiced, and, as I have shown, unfounded opinion which the senator has expressed; but my acts. They furnish materials, neither few nor scant, to form a just estimate of my mental faculties. I have now been more than twenty-six years continuously in the service of this government, in various stations, and have taken part in almost all the great questions which have agitated this country during this long and important period. Throughout the whole I have never followed events, but have taken my stand in advance, openly and freely avowing my opinions on all questions, and leaving it to time and experience to condemn or approve my course. Thus acting, I have often, and on great questions, separated from those with whom I usually acted, and if I am really so defective in sound and practical judgment as the senator represents, the proof, if to be found any where, must be found in such instances, or where I have acted on my sole responsibility. Now, I ask, in which of the many instances of the kind is such proof to be found? It is not my intention to call to the recollection of the Senate all such; but that you, senators, may judge for yourselves, it is due in justice to myself, that I should suggest a few of the most prominent, which at the time were regarded as the senator now considers the present; and then, as now, because where duty is involved, I would not submit to party trammels.

"I go back to the commencement of my public life, the war session, as it was usually called, of 1812, when I first took my seat in the other House, a young man, without experience to guide me, and I shall select, as the first instance, the Navy. At that time the administration and the party to which I was strongly attached were decidedly opposed to this important arm of service. It was considered anti-republican to support it; but acting with my then distinguished colleague, Mr. Cheves, who led the way, I did not hesitate to give it my hearty support, regardless of party ties. Does this instance sustain the charge of the senator?

"The next I shall select is the restrictive system of that day, the embargo, the non-importation and non-intercourse acts. This, too, was a party measure which had been long and warmly contested, and of course the lines of party well drawn. Young and inexperienced as I was, I saw its defects, and resolutely opposed it, almost alone of my party. The second or third speech I made, after I took my seat, was in open denunciation of the system; and I may refer to the grounds I then assumed, the truth of which have been confirmed by time and experience, with pride and confidence. This will scarcely be selected by the senator to make good his charge.

"I pass over other instances, and come to Mr. Dallas's bank of 1814-15. That, too, was a party measure. Banking was then comparatively but little understood, and it may seem astonishing, at this time, that such a project should ever have received any countenance or support. It proposed to create a bank of $50,000,000, to consist almost entirely of what was called then the war stocks; that is, the public debt created in carrying on the then war. It was provided that the bank should not pay specie during the war, and for three years after its termination, for carrying on which it was to lend the government the funds. In plain language, the government was to borrow back its own credit from the bank, and pay to the institution six per cent. for its use. I had scarcely ever before seriously thought of banks or banking, but I clearly saw through the operation, and the danger to the government and country; and, regardless of party ties or denunciations, I opposed and defeated it in the manner I explained at the extra session. I then subjected myself to the very charge which the senator now makes; but time has done me justice, as it will in the present instance.

"Passing the intervening instances, I come down to my administration of the War Department, where I acted on my own judgment and responsibility. It is known to all, that the department, at that time, was perfectly disorganized, with not much less than $50,000,000 of outstanding and unsettled accounts; and the greatest confusion in every branch of service. Though without experience, I prepared, shortly after I went in, the bill for its organization, and on its passage I drew up the body of rules for carrying the act into execution; both of which remain substantially unchanged to this day. After reducing the outstanding accounts to a few millions, and introducing order and accountability in every branch of service, and bringing down the expenditure of the army from four to two and a half millions annually, without subtracting a single comfort from either officer or soldier, I left the department in a condition that might well be compared to the best in any country. If I am deficient in the qualities which the senator attributes to me, here in this mass of details and business it ought to be discovered. Will he look to this to make good his charge?

"From the war department I was transferred to the Chair which you now occupy. How I acquitted myself in the discharge of its duties, I leave it to the body to decide, without adding a word. The station, from its leisure, gave me a good opportunity to study the genius of the prominent measure of the day, called then the American system; of which I profited. I soon perceived where its errors lay, and how it would operate. I clearly saw its desolating effects in one section, and corrupting influence in the other; and when I saw that it could not be arrested here, I fell back on my own State, and a blow was given to a system destined to destroy our institutions, if not overthrown, which brought it to the ground. This brings me down to the present times, and where passions and prejudices are yet too strong to make an appeal, with any prospect of a fair and impartial verdict. I then transfer this, and all my subsequent acts, including the present, to the tribunal of posterity; with a perfect confidence that nothing will be found, in what I have said or done, to impeach my integrity or understanding.

"I have now, senators, repelled the attacks on me. I have settled the account and cancelled the debt between me and my accuser. I have not sought this controversy, nor have I shunned it when forced on me. I have acted on the defensive, and if it is to continue, which rests with the senator, I shall throughout continue so to act. I know too well the advantage of my position to surrender it. The senator commenced the controversy, and it is but right that he should be responsible for the direction it shall hereafter take. Be his determination what it may, I stand prepared to meet him."

CHAPTER XXVIII.

DEBATE BETWEEN MR. CLAY AND MR. CALHOUN REJOINDERS BY EACH.

MR. CLAY:—"As to the personal part of the speech of the senator from South Carolina, I must take the occasion to say that no man is more sincerely anxious to avoid all personal controversy than myself. And I may confidently appeal to the whole course of my life for the confirmation of that disposition. No man cherishes less than I do feelings of resentment; none forgets or forgives an injury sooner than I do. The duty which I had to perform in animadverting upon the public conduct and course of the senator from South Carolina was painful in the extreme; but it was, nevertheless, a public duty; and I shrink from the performance of no duty required at my hands by my country. It was painful, because I had long served in the public councils with the senator from South Carolina, admired his genius, and for a great while had been upon terms of intimacy with him. Throughout my whole acquaintance with him, I have constantly struggled to think well of him, and to ascribe to him public virtues. Even after his famous summerset at the extra session, on more than one occasion I defended his motives when he was assailed; and insisted that it was uncharitable to attribute to him others than those which he himself avowed. This I continued to do, until I read this most extraordinary and exceptionable letter: [Here Mr. Clay held up and exhibited to the Senate the Edgefield letter, dated at Fort Hill, November 3, 1837:] a letter of which I cannot speak in merited terms, without a departure from the respect which I owe to the Senate and to myself. When I read that letter, sir, its unblushing avowals, and its unjust reproaches cast upon my friends and myself, I was most reluctantly compelled to change my opinion of the honorable senator from South Carolina. One so distinguished as he is, cannot expect to be indulged with speaking as he pleases of others, without a reciprocal privilege. He cannot suppose that he may set to the right or the left, cut in and out, and *chasse*, among principles and parties as often as he pleases, without animadversion. I did, indeed, understand the senator to say, in his former speech, that we, the whigs, were unwise and *unpatriotic* in not uniting with him in supporting the bill under consideration. But in that Edgefield letter, among the motives which he assigns for leaving us, I understand him to declare that he could not 'back and sustain those in such opposition, in whose wisdom, firmness, and patriotism, I have no reason to confide.'

"After having written and published to the world such a letter as that, and after what has fallen from the senator, in the progress of this debate, towards my political friends, does he imagine that he can persuade himself and the country that he really occupies, on this occasion, a defensive attitude? In that letter he says:

> "'I clearly saw that our bold and vigorous attacks had made a deep and successful impression. State interposition had overthrown the protective tariff, and with it the American system, and put a stop to the congressional usurpation; and the joint attacks of our party, and that of our old opponents, the national republicans, had effectually brought down the power of the Executive, and arrested its encroachments for the present. It was for that purpose we had united. True to our principle of opposition to the encroachment of power, from whatever quarter it might come, we did not hesitate, after overthrowing the protective system, and arresting legislative usurpation, to join the authors of that system, in order to arrest the encroachments of the Executive, although we differed as widely as the poles on almost every other question, and regarded the usurpation of the Executive but as a necessary consequence of the principles and policy of our new allies.'

"State interposition!—that is as I understand the senator from South Carolina; nullification, he asserts, overthrew the protective tariff and the American system. And can that senator, knowing what he knows, and what I know, deliberately make such an assertion here? I had heard similar boasts before, but did not regard them, until I saw them coupled in this letter with the imputation of a purpose on the part of my friends to disregard the compromise, and revive the high tariff. Nullification, Mr. President, overthrew the protective policy! No, sir. The compromise was not extorted by the terror of nullification. Among other more important motives that influenced its passage, it was a compassionate concession to the imprudence and impotency of nullification! The danger from nullification itself excited no more apprehension than would be felt by seeing a regiment of a thousand boys, of five or six years of age, decorated in brilliant uniforms, with their gaudy plumes and tiny muskets, marching up to assault a corps of 50,000 grenadiers, six feet high. At the commencement of the session of 1832, the senator from South Carolina was in any condition other than that of dictating terms. Those of us who were then here must recollect well his haggard looks and his anxious and depressed countenance. A highly estimable friend of mine, Mr. J. M. Clayton, of Delaware, alluding to the possibility of a rupture with South Carolina, and declarations of President Jackson with respect to certain distinguished individuals whom he had denounced and proscribed, said to me, on more than one occasion, referring to the senator from South Carolina and some of his colleagues, "They are clever fellows, and it will never do to let old Jackson hang them." Sir, this disclosure is extorted from me by the senator.

"So far from nullification having overthrown the protective policy, in assenting to the compromise, it expressly sanctioned the constitutional power which it had so strongly controverted, and perpetuated it. There is protection from one end to the other in the compromise act; modified and limited it is true, but protection nevertheless. There is protection, adequate and abundant protection, until the year 1842; and protection indefinitely beyond it. Until that year, the biennial reduction of duties is slow and moderate, such as was perfectly satisfactory to the manufacturers. Now, if the system were altogether unconstitutional, as had been contended, how could the senator vote for a bill which continued it for nine years? Then, beyond that period, there is the provision for cash duties, home valuations, a long and liberal list of free articles, carefully made out by my friend from Rhode Island (Mr. KNIGHT), expressly for the benefit of the manufacturers; and the power of discrimination, reserved also for their benefit; within the maximum rate of duty fixed in the act. In the consultations between the senator and myself in respect to the compromise act, on every point upon which I insisted he gave way. He was for a shorter term than nine years, and more rapid reduction. I insisted, and he yielded. He was for fifteen instead of twenty per cent. as the maximum duty; but yielded. He was against any discrimination within the limited range of duties for the benefit of the manufacturers; but consented. To the last he protested against home valuation, but finally gave way. Such is the compromise act; and the Senate will see with what propriety the senator can assert that nullification had overthrown the protective tariff and the American system. Nullification! which asserted the extraordinary principle that one of twenty-four members of a confederacy, by its separate action, could subvert and set aside the expressed will of the whole! Nullification! a strange, impracticable, incomprehensible doctrine, that partakes of the character of the metaphysical school of German philosophy, or would be worthy of the puzzling theological controversies of the middle ages.

"No one, Mr. President, in the commencement of the protective policy, ever supposed that it was to be perpetual. We hoped and believed that temporary protection extended to our infant manufactures, would bring them up, and enable them to withstand competition with those of Europe. We thought, as the wise French minister did, who, when urged by a British minister to consent to the equal introduction into the two countries of their respective productions, replied that free trade might be very well for a country whose manufactures had reached perfection, but was not entirely adapted to a country which wished to build up its manufactures. If the protective policy were entirely to cease in 1842, it would have existed twenty-six years from 1816, or 18 from 1824; quite as long as, at either of those periods, its friends supposed might be necessary. But it does not cease then, and I sincerely hope that the provisions contained in the compromise act for its benefit beyond that period, will be found sufficient for the preservation of all our interesting manufactures. For one, I am willing to adhere to, and abide by the compromise in all its provisions, present and prospective, if its fair operation is undisturbed. The Senate well knows that I have been constantly in favor of a strict and faithful adherence to the compromise act. I have watched and defended it on all occasions. I desire to see it faithfully and inviolably maintained. The senator, too, from South Carolina, alleging that the South were the weaker party, has hitherto united with me in sustaining it. Nevertheless, he has left us, as he tells us in his Edgefield letter, because he apprehended that our principles would lead us to the revival of a high tariff.

"The senator from South Carolina proceeds, in his Edgefield letter, to say:

> "'I clearly perceived that a very important question was presented for our determination, which we were compelled to decide forthwith: shall we continue our joint attack with the nationals on those in power, in the new position which they have been compelled to occupy? It was clear that, with our joint forces, we could utterly overthrow and demolish them. But it

was not less clear that *the victory would enure not to us*, but exclusively to the benefit of our allies and their cause.'

"Thus it appears that in a common struggle for the benefit of our whole country, the senator was calculating upon the party advantages which would result from success. He quit us because he apprehended that he and his party would be absorbed by us. Well, what is to be their fate in his new alliance? Is there no absorption there? Is there no danger that the senator and his party will be absorbed by the administration party? Or does he hope to absorb that? Another motive avowed in the letter, for his desertion of us, is, that 'it would also give us the chance of effecting what is still more important to us, the union of the entire South.' What sort of an union of the South does the senator wish? Is not the South already united as a part of the common confederacy? Does he want any other union of it? I wish he would explicitly state. I should be glad, also, if he would define what he means by the South. He sometimes talks of the plantation or staple States. Maryland is partly a staple State. Virginia and North Carolina more so. And Kentucky and Tennessee have also staple productions. Are all these States parts of *his* South? I fear, Mr. President, that the political geography of the senator comprehends a much larger South than that South which is the object of his particular solicitude; and that, to find the latter, we should have to go to South Carolina; and, upon our arrival there, trace him to Fort Hill. This is the disinterested senator from South Carolina!

"But he has left no party, and joined no party! No! None. With the daily evidences before us of his frequent association, counselling and acting with the other party, he would tax our credulity too much to require us to believe that he has formed no connection with it. He may stand upon his reserved rights; but they must be mentally reserved, for they are not obvious to the senses. Abandoned no party? Why this letter proclaims his having quitted us, and assigns his reasons for doing it; one of which is, that we are in favor of that national bank which the senator himself has sustained about twenty-four years of the twenty-seven that he has been in public life. Whatever impression the senator may endeavor to make without the Senate upon the country at large, no man within the Senate, who has eyes to see, or ears to hear, can mistake his present position and party connection. If, in the speech which I addressed to the Senate on a former day, there had been a single fact stated which was not perfectly true, or an inference drawn which was not fully warranted, or any description of his situation which was incorrect, no man would enjoy greater pleasure than I should do in rectifying the error. If, in the picture which I portrayed of the senator and his course, there be any thing which can justly give him dissatisfaction, he must look to the original and not to the painter. The conduct of an eminent public man is a fair subject for exposure and animadversion. When I addressed the Senate before, I had just perused this letter. I recollected all its reproaches and imputations against us, and those which were made or implied in the speech of the honorable senator were also fresh in my memory. Does he expect to be allowed to cast such imputations, and make such reproaches against others without retaliation? Holding myself amenable for my public conduct, I choose to animadvert upon his, and upon that of others, whenever circumstances, in my judgment, render it necessary; and I do it under all just responsibility which belongs to the exercise of such a privilege.

"The senator has thought proper to exercise a corresponding privilege towards myself; and, without being very specific, has taken upon himself to impute to me the charge of going over upon some occasion, and that in a manner which left my motive no matter of conjecture. If the senator mean to allude to the stale and refuted calumny of George Kremer, I assure him I can hear it without the slightest emotion; and if he can find any fragment of that rent banner to cover his own aberrations, he is perfectly at liberty to enjoy all the shelter which it affords. In my case there was no going over about it; I was a member of the House of Representatives, and had to give a vote for one of three candidates for the presidency. Mr. Crawford's unfortunate physical condition placed him out of the question. The choice was, therefore, limited to the venerable gentleman from Massachusetts, or to the distinguished inhabitant of the hermitage. I could give but one vote; and, accordingly, as I stated on a former occasion, I gave the vote which, before I left Kentucky, I communicated to my colleague [Mr. CRITTENDEN], it was my intention to give in the contingency which happened. I have never for one moment regretted the vote I then gave. It is true, that the legislature of Kentucky had requested the representatives from that State to vote for General Jackson; but my own immediate constituents, I knew well, were opposed to his election, and it was their will, and not that of the legislature, according to every principle applicable to the doctrine of instructions, which I was to deposit in the ballot-box. It is their glory and my own never to have concurred in the elevation of General Jackson. They ratified and confirmed my vote, and every representative that they have sent to Congress since, including my friend, the present member, has concurred with me in opposition to the election and administration of General Jackson.

"If my information be not entirely incorrect, and there was any going over in the presidential election which terminated in February, 1825, the senator from South Carolina—and not I—went over. I have understood that the senator, when he ceased to be in favor of himself,—that is, after the memorable movement made in Philadelphia by the present minister to Russia (Mr. DALLAS), withdrawing his name from the canvass, was the known supporter of the election of Mr. Adams. What motives induced him afterwards to unite in the election of General Jackson, I know not. It is not my habit to impute to others uncharitable motives, and I leave the senator to settle that account with his own conscience and his country. No, sir, I have no reproaches to make myself, and feel perfectly invulnerable to any attack from others, on account of any part which I took in the election of 1825. And I look back with entire and conscious satisfaction upon the whole course of the arduous administration which ensued.

"The senator from South Carolina thinks it to be my misfortune to be always riding some hobby, and that I stick to it till I ride it down. I think it is his never to stick to one long enough. He is like a courier who, riding from post to post, with relays of fresh horses, when he changes his steed, seems to forget altogether the last which he had mounted. Now, it is a part of my pride and pleasure to say, that I never in my life changed my deliberate opinion upon any great question of national policy but once, and that was twenty-two years ago, on the question of the power to establish a bank of the United States. The change was wrought by the sad and disastrous experience of the want of such an institution, growing out of the calamities of war. It was a change which I made in common with Mr. Madison, two governors of Virginia, and the great body of the republican party, to which I have ever belonged.

"The distinguished senator sticks long to no hobby. He was once gayly mounted on that of internal improvements. We rode that double—the senator before, and I behind him. He quietly slipped off, leaving me to hold the bridle. He introduced and carried through Congress in 1816, the bill setting apart the large bonus of the Bank of the United States for internal improvements. His speech, delivered on that occasion, does not intimate the smallest question as to the constitutional power of the government, but proceeds upon the assumption of its being incontestable. When he was subsequently in the department of war, he made to Congress a brilliant report, sketching as splendid and magnificent a scheme of internal improvements for the entire nation, as ever was presented to the admiration and wonder of mankind.

"No, sir, the senator from South Carolina is free from all reproach of sticking to hobbies. He was for a bank of the United States in 1816. He proposed, supported, and with his accustomed ability, carried through the charter. He sustained it upon its admitted grounds of constitutionality, of which he never once breathed the expression of a doubt. During the twenty years of its continuance no scruple ever escaped from him as to the power to create it. And in 1834, when it was about to expire, he deliberately advocated the renewal of its term for twelve years more. How profound he may suppose the power of analysis to be, and whatever opinion he may entertain of his own metaphysical faculty,—can he imagine that any plain, practical, common sense man can ever comprehend how it is constitutional to prolong an unconstitutional bank for twelve years? He may have all the speeches he has ever delivered read to us in an audible voice by the secretary, and call upon the Senate attentively to hear them, beginning with his speech in favor of a bank of the United States in 1816, down to his speech *against* a bank of the United States, delivered the other day, and he will have made no progress in his task. I do not speak this in any unkind spirit, but I will tell the honorable senator when he will be consistent. He will be so, when he resolves henceforward, during the residue of his life, never to pronounce the word again. We began our public career nearly together; we remained together throughout the war and down to the peace. We agreed as to a bank of the United States—as to a protective tariff—as to internal improvements—and lately, as to those arbitrary and violent measures which characterized the administration of General Jackson. No two prominent public men ever agreed better together in respect to important measures of national policy. We concur now in nothing. We separate for ever."

Mr. CALHOUN. "The senator from Kentucky says that the sentiments contained in my Edgefield letter then met his view for the first time, and that he read that document with equal pain and amazement. Now it happens that I expressed these self-same sentiments just as strongly in 1834, in a speech which was received with unbounded applause by that gentleman's own party; and of which a vast number of copies were published and circulated throughout the United States.

"But the senator tells us that he is among the most constant men in this world. I am not in the habit of charging others with inconsistency; but one thing I will say, that if the gentleman has not changed *his principles*, he has most certainly changed *his company*; for, though he boasts of setting out in public life a republican of the school of '98, he is now surrounded by some of the most distinguished members of the old federal party. I do not desire to disparage that party. I always respected them as men, though I believed their political principles to be wrong. Now, either the gentleman's associates have changed, or he has; for they are now together, though belonging formerly to different and opposing parties—parties, as every one knows, directly opposed to each other in policy and principles.

"He says I was in favor of the tariff of 1816, and took the lead in its support. He is certainly mistaken again. It was in charge of my colleague and friend, Mr. Lowndes, chairman then of the committee of Ways and Means, as a revenue measure only. I took no other part whatever but to deliver an off-hand speech, at the request of a friend. The question of protection, as a constitutional question, was not touched at all. It was not made, if my memory serves me, for some years after. As to protection, I believe little of it, except what all admit was incidental to revenue, was contained in the act of 1816. As to my views in regard to protection at that early period, I refer to my remarks in 1813, when I opposed a renewal of the non-importation act, expressly on the ground of its giving too much protection to the manufacturers. But while I declared, in my place, that I was opposed to it on that ground, I at the same time stated that I would go as far as I could with propriety, when peace returned, to protect the capital which the war and the extreme policy of the government had turned into that channel. The senator refers to my report on internal improvement, when I was secretary of war; but, as usual with him, forgets to tell that I made it in obedience to a resolution of the House, to which I was bound to answer, and that I expressly stated I did not involve the constitutional question; of which the senator may now satisfy himself, if he will read the latter part of the report. As to the bonus bill, it grew out of the recommendation of Mr. Madison in his last message; and although I proposed that the bonus should be set apart for the purpose of internal improvement, leaving it to be determined thereafter, whether we had the power, or the constitution should be amended, in conformity to Mr. Madison's recommendation. I did not touch the question to what extent Congress might possess the power; and when requested to insert a direct recognition of the power by some of the leading members, I refused, expressly on the ground that, though I believed it existed, I had not made up my mind how far it extended. As to the bill, it was perfectly constitutional in my opinion then, and which still remains unchanged, to set aside the fund proposed, and with the object intended, but which could not be used without specific appropriations thereafter.

"In my opening remarks to-day, I said the senator's speech was remarkable, both for its omissions and mistakes; and the senator infers, with his usual inaccuracy, that I alluded to a difference between his spoken and printed speech, and that I was answering the latter. In this he was mistaken; I hardly ever read a speech, but reply to what is said here in debate. I know no other but the speech delivered here.

"As to the arguments of each of us, I am willing to leave them to the judgment of the country: his speech and arguments, and mine, will be read with the closer attention and deeper interest in consequence of this day's occurrence. It is all I ask."

Mr. CLAY. "It is very true that the senator had on other occasions, besides his Edgefield letter, claimed that the influence arising from the interference of his own State had effected the tariff compromise. Mr. C. had so stated the fact when up before. But in the Edgefield letter the senator took new ground, he denounced those with whom he had been acting, as persons in whom he could have no confidence, and imputed to them the design of renewing a high tariff and patronizing extravagant expenditures, as the natural consequences of the establishment of a bank of the United States, and had presented this as a reason for his recent course. When, said Mr. C., I saw a charge like this, together with an imputation of unworthy motives, and all this deliberately written and published, I could not but feel very differently from what I should have done under a mere casual remark.

"But the senator says, that if I have not changed principles, I have at least got into strange company. Why really, Mr. President, the gentleman has so recently changed his relations that he seems to have forgotten into what company he has fallen himself. He says that some of my friends once belonged to the federal party. Sir, I am ready to go into an examination with the honorable senator at any time, and then we shall see if there are not more members of that same old federal party amongst those whom the senator has so recently joined, than on our side of the house. The plain truth is, that it is the old federal party with whom he is now acting. For all the former grounds of difference which distinguished that party, and were the great subjects of contention between them and the republicans, have ceased from lapse of time and change of circumstances, with the exception of one, and that is the maintenance and increase of executive power. This was a leading policy of the federal party. A strong, powerful, and energetic executive was its favorite tenet. The leading members of that party had come out of the national convention with an impression that under the new constitution the executive arm was too weak. The danger they apprehended was, that the executive would be absorbed by the legislative department of the government; and accordingly the old federal doctrine was that the Executive must be upheld, that its influence must be extended and strengthened; and as a means to this, that its patronage must be multiplied. And what, I pray, is at this hour the leading object of that party, which the senator has joined, but this very thing? It was maintained in the convention by Mr. Madison, that to remove a public officer without valid cause, would rightfully subject a president of the United States to impeachment. But now not only is no reason required, but the principle is maintained that no reason can be asked. A is removed and B is put in his place, because such is the pleasure of the president.

"The senator is fond of the record. I should not myself have gone to it but for the infinite gravity and self-complacency with which he appeals to it in vindication of his own consistency. Let me then read a little from one of the very speeches in 1834, from which he has so liberally quoted, and called upon the secretary to read so loud, and the Senate to listen so attentively:

> "'But there is in my opinion a strong, if not an insuperable objection against resorting to this measure, resulting from the *fact* that an exclusive receipt of specie in the treasury would, to give it efficacy, and to prevent extensive speculation and fraud, require an entire disconnection on the part of the government, with the banking system, in all its forms, and a resort to the strong box, as the means of preserving and guarding its funds—a means, if practicable at all in the present state of things, liable to the objection of being *far less safe, economical, and efficient, than the present.*'"

"Here is a strong denunciation of that very system he is now eulogising to the skies. Here he deprecates a disconnection with all banks as a most disastrous measure; and, as the strongest argument against it, says that it will necessarily lead to the antiquated policy of the strong box. Yet, now the senator thinks the strong box system the wisest thing on earth. As to the acquiescence of the honorable senator in measures deemed by him unconstitutional, I only regret that he suddenly stopped short in his acquiescence. He was, in 1816, at the head of the finance committee, in the other House, having been put there by myself, *acquiescing* all the while in the doctrines of a bank, as perfectly sound, and reporting to that effect. He acquiesced for nearly twenty years, not a doubt escaping from him during the whole time. The year 1834 comes: the deposits are seized, the currency turned up side down, and the senator comes forward and proposes as a remedy a continuation of the Bank of the United States for twelve years—here acquiescing once more; and as he tells us, in order to save the country. But if the salvation of the country would justify his acquiescence in 1816 and in 1834, I can only regret that he did not find it in his heart to acquiesce once more in what would have remedied all our evils.

"In regard to the tariff of 1816, has the senator forgotten the dispute at that time about the protection of the cotton manufacture? The very point of that dispute was, whether we had a right to give protection or not. He admits the truth of what I said, that the constitutional question as to the power of the government to protect our own industry was never raised before 1820 or 1822. It was but first hinted, then controverted, and soon after expanded into nullification, although the senator had supported the tariff of 1816 on the very ground that we had power. I do not now recollect distinctly his whole course in the legislature, but he certainly introduced the bonus bill in 1816, and sustained it by a speech on the subject of internal improvements, which neither expresses nor implies a doubt of the constitutional power. But why set apart a bonus, if the government had no power to make internal improvements? If he wished internal improvements, but conscientiously believed them unconstitutional, why did he not introduce a resolution proposing to amend the constitution? Yet he offered no such thing. When he produced his splendid report from the war department, what did he mean? Why did he tantalize us with that bright and gorgeous picture of canals and roads, and piers and harbors, if it was unconstitutional for us to touch the plan with one of our fingers? The senator says in reply, that this report did not broach the constitutional question. True. But why? Is there any other conclusion than that he did not entertain himself any doubt about it? What a most extraordinary thing would it be, should the head of a department, in his official capacity, present a report to both houses of Congress, proposing a most elaborate plan for the internal improvement of the whole union, accompanied by estimates and statistical tables, when he believed there was no power in either house to adopt any part of it. The senator dwells upon his consistency: I can tell him when he will be consistent—and that is when he shall never pronounce that word again."

Mr. CALHOUN. "As to the tariff of 1816, I never denied that Congress have the power to impose a protective tariff for the purpose of revenue; and beyond that the tariff of 1816 did not go one inch. The question of the constitutionality of the protective tariff was never raised till some time afterwards.

"As to what the senator says of executive power, I, as much as he, am opposed to its augmentation, and I will go as far in preventing it as any man in this House. I maintain that the executive and judicial authorities should have no discretionary power, and as soon as they begin to exercise such power, the matter should be taken up by Congress. These opinions are well grounded in my mind, and I will go as far as any in bringing the Executive to this point. But, I believe, the Executive is now outstripped by the congressional power. He is for restricting the one. I war upon both.

"The senator says I assigned as a reason of my course at the extra session that I suspected that he and the gentleman with whom he acted would revive the tariff. I spoke not of the tariff, but a national bank. I believe that banks naturally and assuredly ally themselves to taxes on the community. The higher the taxes the greater their profits; and so it is with regard to a surplus and the government disbursements. If the banking power is on the side of a national bank, I see in that what may lead to all the consequences which I have described; and I oppose institutions that are likely to lead to such results. When the bank should receive the money of the government, it would ally itself to taxation, and it ought to be resisted on that ground. I am very glad that the question is now fairly met. The fate of the country depends on the point of separation; if there be a separation between the government and banks, the banks will be on the republican side in opposition to taxes; if they unite, they will be in favor of the exercise of the taxing power.

"The senator says I acquiesced in the use of the banks because the banks existed. I did so because the connection existed. The banks were already used as depositories of the government, and it was impossible at once to reverse that state of things. I went on the ground that the banks were a necessary evil. The State banks exist; and would not he be a madman that would annihilate them because their respective bills are uncurrent in distant parts of the country? The work of creating them is done, and cannot be reversed; when once done, it is done for ever.

"I was formerly decided in favor of separating the banks and the government, but it was impossible then to make it, and it would have been followed by nothing but disaster. The senator says the separation already exists; but it is only contingent; whenever the banks resume, the connection will be legally restored. In 1834 I objected to the sub-treasury project, and I thought it not as safe as the system now before us. But it turns out that it was more safe, as appears from the argument of the senator from Delaware, (Mr. Bayard.) I was then under the impression that the banks were more safe but it proves otherwise."

Mr. CLAY. "If the senator would review his speech again, he would see there a plain and explicit denunciation of a sub-treasury system.

"The distinguished senator from South Carolina (I had almost said my friend from South Carolina, so lately and so abruptly has he bursted all amicable relations between us, independent of his habit of change, I think, when he finds into what federal doctrines and federal company he has gotten, he will be disposed soon to feel regret and to return to us,) has not, I am persuaded, weighed sufficiently the import of the unkind imputations contained in his Edgefield letter towards his former allies—imputations that their principles are dangerous to our institutions, and of their want of firmness and patriotism. I have read that singular letter again and again, with inexpressible surprise and regret; more, however, if he will allow me to say so, on his own than on our account.

"Mr. President, I am done; and I sincerely hope that the adjustment of the account between the senator and myself, just made, may be as satisfactory to him as I assure him and the Senate it is perfectly so to me."

Mr. CALHOUN. "I have more to say, but will forbear, as the senator appears desirous of having the last word."

Mr. CLAY. "Not at all."

The personal debate between Mr. Calhoun and Mr. Clay terminated for the day, and with apparent good feeling; but only to break out speedily on a new point, and to lead to further political revelations important to history. Mr. Calhoun, after a long alienation, personal as well as political, from Mr. Van Buren, and bitter warfare upon him, had become reconciled to him in both capacities, and had made a complimentary call upon him, and had expressed to him an approbation of his leading measures. All this was natural and proper after he had become a public supporter of these measures; but a manifestation of respect and confidence so decided, after a seven years' perseverance in a warfare so bitter, could not be expected to pass without the imputation of sinister motives; and, accordingly, a design upon the presidency as successor to Mr. Van Buren was attributed to him. The opposition newspapers abounded with this imputation; and an early occasion was taken in the Senate to make it the subject of a public debate. Mr. Calhoun had brought into the Senate a bill to cede to the several States the public lands within their limits, after a sale of the saleable parts at graduated prices, for the benefit of both parties—the new States and the United States. It was the same bill which he had brought in two years before; but Mr. Clay, taking it up as a new measure, inquired if it was an administration measure? whether he had brought it in with the concurrence of the President? If nothing more had been said Mr. Calhoun could have answered, that it was the same bill which he had brought in two years before, when he was in opposition to the administration; and that his reasons for bringing it in were the same now as then; but Mr. Clay went on to taunt him with his new relations with the chief magistrate, and to connect the bill with the visit to Mr. Van Buren and approval of his measures. Mr. Calhoun saw that the inquiry was only a vehicle for the taunt, and took it up accordingly in that sense: and this led to an exposition of the reasons which induced him to join Mr. Van Buren, and to explanations on other points, which belong to history. Mr. Clay began the debate thus:

> "Whilst up, Mr. Clay would be glad to learn whether the administration is in favor of or against this measure, or stands neutral and uncommitted. This inquiry he should not make, if the recent relations between the senator who introduced this bill and the head of that administration, continued to exist; but rumors, of which the city, the circles, and the press are full, assert that those relations are entirely changed, and have, within a few days, been substituted by others of an intimate, friendly, and confidential nature. And shortly after the time when this new state of things is alleged to have taken place, the senator gave notice of his intention to move to introduce this bill. Whether this motion has or has not any connection with that adjustment of former differences, the public would, he had no doubt, be glad to know. At all events, it is important to know in what relation of support, opposition, or neutrality, the administration actually stands to this momentous measure; and he [Mr. C.] supposed that the senator from South Carolina, or some other senator, could communicate the desired information."

Mr. Calhoun, besides vindicating himself, rebuked the indecorum of making his personal conduct a subject of public remark in the Senate; and threw back the taunt by reminding Mr. Clay of his own change in favor of Mr. Adams.

"He said the senator from Kentucky had introduced other, and extraneous personal matter; and asked whether the bill had the sanction of the Executive; assigning as a reason for his inquiry, that, if rumor was to be credited, a change of personal relation had taken place between the President and myself within the last few days. He [Mr. C.] would appeal to the Senate whether it was decorous or proper that his personal relations should be drawn in question here. Whether he should establish or suspend personal relations with the President, or any other person, is a private and personal concern, which belongs to himself individually to determine on the propriety, without consulting any one, much less the senator. It was none of his concern, and he has no right to question me in relation to it.

"But the senator assumes that a change in my personal relations involves a change of political position; and it is on that he founds his right to make the inquiry. He judges, doubtless, by his own experience; but I would have him to understand, said Mr. C., that what may be true in his own case on a memorable occasion, is not true in mine. His political course may be governed by personal considerations; but mine, I trust, is governed strictly by my principles, and is not at all under the control of my attachments or enmities. Whether the President is personally my friend or enemy, has no influence over me in the discharge of my duties, as, I trust, my course has abundantly proved. Mr. C. concluded by saying, that he felt that these were improper topics to introduce here, and that he had passed over them as briefly as possible."

This retort gave new scope and animation to the debate, and led to further expositions of the famous compromise of 1833, which was a matter of concord between them at the time, and of discord ever since; and which, being much condemned in the first volume of this work, the authors of it are entitled to their own vindications when they choose to make them: and this they found frequent occasion to do. The debate proceeded:

"Mr. Clay contended that his question, as to whether this was an administration measure or not, was a proper one, as it was important for the public information. He again referred to the rumors of Mr. Calhoun's new relations with the President, and supposed from the declarations of the senator, that these rumors were true; and that his support, if not pledged, was at least promised conditionally to the administration. Was it of no importance to the public to learn that these pledges and compromises had been entered into?—that the distinguished senator had made his bow in court, kissed the hand of the monarch, was taken into favor, and agreed henceforth to support his edicts?"

This allusion to rumored pledges and conditions on which Mr. Calhoun had joined Mr. Van Buren, provoked a retaliatory notice of what the same rumor had bruited at the time that Mr. Clay became the supporter of Mr. Adams; and Mr. Calhoun said:

"The senator from Kentucky had spoken much of pledges, understandings, and political compromises, and sudden change of personal relations. He [said Mr. C.] is much more experienced in such things than I am. If my memory serves me, and if rumors are to be trusted, the senator had a great deal to do with such things, in connection with a distinguished citizen; now of the other House; and it is not at all surprising, from his experience then, in his own case, that he should not be indisposed to believe similar rumors of another now. But whether his sudden change of personal relations then, from bitter enmity to the most confidential friendship with that citizen, was preceded by pledges, understandings, and political compromises on the part of one or both, it is not for me to say. The country has long since passed on that."

All this taunt on both sides was mere irritation, having no foundation in fact. It so happened that the writer of this View, on each of these occasions (of sudden conjunctions with former adversaries), stood in a relation to know what took place. In one case he was confidential with Mr. Clay; in the other with Mr. Van Buren. In a former chapter he has given his testimony in favor of Mr. Clay, and against the imputed bargain with Mr. Adams: he can here give it in favor of Mr. Calhoun. He is entirely certain—as much so as it is possible to be in supporting a negative—that no promise, pledge, or condition of any kind, took place between Mr. Calhoun and Mr. Van Buren, in coming together as they did at this juncture. How far Mr. Calhoun might have looked to his own chance of succeeding Mr. Van Buren, is another question, and a fair one. The succession was certainly open in the democratic line. Those who stood nearest the head of the party had no desire for the presidency, but the contrary; and only wished a suitable chief magistrate at the head of the government—giving him a cordial support in all patriotic measures; and preserving their independence by refusing his favors. This allusion refers especially to Mr. Silas Wright; and if it had not been for a calamitous conflagration, there might be proof that it would apply to another. Both Mr. Wright and Mr. Benton refused cabinet appointments from Mr. Van Buren; and repressed every movement in their favor towards the presidency. Under such circumstances, Mr. Calhoun might have indulged in a vision of the democratic succession, after the second term of Mr. Van Buren, without the slippery and ignominious contrivance of attempting to contract for it beforehand. There was certainly a talk about it, and a sounding of public men. Two different friends of Mr. Calhoun, at two different times and places,—one in Missouri (Thomas Hudson, Esq.), and the other in Washington (Gov. William Smith, of Virginia),—inquired of this writer whether he had said that he could not support Mr. Calhoun for the presidency, if nominated by a democratic convention? and were answered that he had, and because Mr. Calhoun was the author of nullification, and of measures tending to the dissolution of the Union. The answer went into the newspapers, without the agency of him who gave it, and without the reasons which he gave: and his opposition was set down to causes equally gratuitous and unfounded—one, personal ill-will to Mr. Calhoun; the other, a hankering after the place himself. But to return to Messrs. Clay and Calhoun. These reciprocal taunts having been indulged in, the debate took a more elevated turn, and entered the region of history. Mr. Calhoun continued:

"I will assure the senator, if there were pledges in his case, there were none in mine. I have terminated my long-suspended personal intercourse with the President, without the slightest pledge, understanding, or compromise, on either side. I would be the last to receive or exact such. The transition from their former to their present personal relation was easy and natural, requiring nothing of the kind. It gives me pleasure to say, thus openly, that I have approved of all the leading measures of the President, since he took the Executive chair, simply because they accord with the principles and policy on which I have long acted, and often openly avowed. The change, then, in our personal relations, had simply followed that of our political. Nor was it made suddenly, as the senator charges. So far from it, more than two years have elapsed since I gave a decided support to the leading measure of the Executive, and on which almost all others since have turned. This long interval was permitted to pass, in order that his acts might give assurance whether there was a coincidence between our political views as to the principles on which the government should be administered, before our personal relations should be changed. I deemed it due to both thus long to delay the change, among other reasons to discountenance such idle rumors as the senator alludes to. That his political course might be judged (said Mr. CALHOUN) by the object he had in view, and not the suspicion and jealousy of his political opponents, he would repeat what he had said, at the last session, was his object. It is, said he, to obliterate all those measures which had originated in the national consolidation school of politics, and especially the senator's famous American system, which he believed to be hostile to the constitution and the genius of our political system, and the real source of all the disorders and dangers to which the country was, or had been, subject. This done, he was for giving the government a fresh departure, in the direction in which Jefferson and his associates would give, were they now alive and at the helm. He stood where he had always stood, on the old State rights ground. His change of personal relation, which gave so much concern to the senator, so far from involving any change in his principles or doctrines, grew out of them."

The latter part of this reply of Mr. Calhoun is worthy of universal acceptance, and perpetual remembrance. The real source of all the disorders to which the country was, or had been subject, was in the system of legislation which encouraged the industry of one part of the Union at the expense of the other—which gave rise to extravagant expenditures, to be expended unequally in the two sections of the Union—and which left the Southern section to pay the expenses of a system which exhausted her. This remarkable declaration of Mr. Calhoun was made in 1839—being four years after the slavery agitation had superseded the tariff agitation,— and which went back to that system of measures, of which protective tariff was the main-spring, to find, and truly find, the real source of all the dangers and disorders of the country—past and present. Mr. Clay replied:

"He had understood the senator as felicitating himself on the opportunity which had been now afforded him by Mr. C. of defining once more his political position; and Mr. C. must say that he had now defined it very clearly, and had apparently given it a new definition. The senator now declared that all the leading measures of the present administration had met his approbation, and should receive his support. It turned out, then, that the rumor to which Mr. C. had alluded was true, and that the senator from South Carolina might be hereafter regarded as a supporter of this administration, since he had declared that all its leading measures were approved by him, and should have his support. As to the allusion which the senator from South Carolina had made in regard to Mr. C.'s support of the head of another administration [Mr. ADAMS], it occasioned Mr. C. no pain whatever. It was an old story, which had long been sunk in oblivion, except when the senator and a few others thought proper to bring it up. But what were the facts of that case? Mr. C. was then a member of the House of Representatives, to whom three persons had been returned, from whom it was the duty of the House to make a selection for the presidency. As to one of those three candidates, he was known to be in an unfortunate condition, in which no one sympathized with him more than did Mr. C. Certainly the senator from South Carolina did not. That gentleman was therefore out of the question as a candidate for the chief magistracy; and Mr. C. had consequently the only alternative of the illustrious individual at the Hermitage, or of the man who was now distinguished in the House of Representatives, and who had held so many public places with honor to himself, and benefit to the country. And if there was any truth in history, the choice which Mr. C. then made was precisely the choice which the senator from South Carolina had urged upon his friends. The senator himself had declared his preference of Adams to Jackson. Mr. C. made the same choice; and his constituents had approved it from that day to this, and would to eternity. History would ratify and approve it. Let the senator from South Carolina make any thing out of that part of Mr. C.'s public career if he could. Mr. C. defied him. The senator had alluded to Mr. C. as the advocate of compromise. Certainly he was. This government itself, to a great extent, was founded and rested on compromise; and to the particular compromise to which allusion had been made, Mr. C. thought no man ought to be more grateful for it than the senator from South Carolina. But for that compromise, Mr. C. was not at all confident that he would have now had the honor to meet that senator face to face in this national capitol."

The allusion in the latter part of this reply was to the President's declared determination to execute the laws upon Mr. Calhoun if an *overt* act of treason should be committed under the nullification ordinance of South Carolina; and the preparations for which (overt act) were too far advanced to admit of another step, either backwards or forwards; and from which most critical condition the compromise relieved those who were too deeply committed, to retreat without ruin, or to advance without personal peril. Mr. Calhoun's reply was chiefly directed to this pregnant allusion.

"The senator from Kentucky has said, Mr. President, that I, of all men, ought to be grateful to him for the compromise act."

[Mr. CLAY. "I did not say 'to me.'"]

"The senator claims to be the author of that measure, and, of course, if there be any gratitude due, it must be to him. I, said Mr. Calhoun, made no allusion to that act; but as the senator has thought proper to refer to it, and claim my gratitude, I, in turn, now tell him I feel not the least gratitude towards him for it. The measure was necessary to save the senator politically: and as he has alluded to the subject, both on this and on a former occasion, I feel bound to explain what might otherwise have been left in oblivion. The senator was then compelled to compromise to save himself. Events had placed him flat on his back, and he had no way to recover himself but by the compromise. This is no after thought. I wrote more than half a dozen of letters home at the time to that effect. I shall now explain. The proclamation and message of General Jackson necessarily rallied around him all the steadfast friends of the senator's system. They withdrew their allegiance at once from him, and transferred it to General Jackson. The senator was thus left in the most hopeless condition, with no more weight with his former partisans than this sheet of paper (raising a sheet from his desk). This is not all. The position which General Jackson had assumed, necessarily attracted towards him a distinguished senator from Massachusetts, not now here [Mr. WEBSTER], who, it is clear, would have reaped all the political honors and advantages of the system, had the contest come to blows. These causes made the political condition of the senator truly forlorn at the time. On him rested all the responsibility, as the author of the system; while all the power and influence it gave, had passed into the hands of others. Compromise was the only means of extrication. He was thus forced by the action of the State, which I in part represent, against his system, by my counsel to compromise, in order to save himself. I had the mastery over him on the occasion."

This is historical, and is an inside view of history. Mr. Webster, in that great contest of nullification, was on the side of President Jackson, and the supreme defender of his great measure—the Proclamation of 1833; and the first and most powerful opponent of the measure out of which it grew. It was a splendid era in his life—both for his intellect, and his patriotism. No longer the advocate of classes, or interests, he appeared the great defender of the Union—of the constitution—of the country—and of the administration, to which he was opposed. Released from the bonds of party, and from the narrow confines of class and corporation advocacy, his colossal intellect expanded to its full proportions in the field of patriotism, luminous with the fires of genius; and commanding the homage, not of party, but of country. His magnificent harangues touched Jackson in his deepest-seated and ruling feeling—love of country! and brought forth the response which always came from him when the country was in peril, and a defender presented himself. He threw out the right hand of fellowship—treated Mr. Webster with marked distinction—commended him with public praise—and placed him on the roll of patriots. And the public mind took the belief, that they were to act together in future; and that a cabinet appointment, or a high mission, would be the reward of his patriotic service. (It was the report of such expected preferment that excited Mr. Randolph (then in no condition to bear excitement) against General Jackson.) It was a crisis in the political life of Mr. Webster. He stood in public opposition to Mr. Clay and Mr. Calhoun. With Mr. Clay he had a public outbreak in the Senate. He was cordial with Jackson. The mass of his party stood by him on the proclamation. He was at a point from which a new departure might be taken:—one at which he could not stand still: from which there must be advance, or recoil. It was a case in which *will*, more than *intellect*, was to rule. He was above Mr. Clay and Mr. Calhoun in intellect—below them in will. And he was soon seen co-operating with them (Mr. Clay in the lead), in the great measure condemning President Jackson. And so passed away the fruits of the golden era of 1833. It was to the perils of this conjunction (of Jackson and Webster) that Mr. Calhoun referred, as the forlorn condition from which the compromise relieved Mr. Clay: and, allowing to each the benefit of his assertion, history avails herself of the declarations of each in giving an inside view of personal motives for a momentous public act. And, without deciding a question of mastery in the disputed victory, History performs her task in recording the fact that, in a brief space, both Mr. Calhoun and Mr. Webster were seen following the lead of Mr. Clay in his great attack upon President Jackson in the session of 1834-'35.

"Mr. Clay, rejoining, said he had made no allusion to the compromise bill till it was done by the senator from South Carolina himself; he made no reference to the events of 1825 until the senator had himself set him the example; and he had not in the slightest and the most distant manner alluded to nullification until after the senator himself had called it up. The senator ought not to have introduced that subject, especially when he had gone over to the authors of the force bill and the proclamation. The senator from South Carolina said that he [Mr. C.] was flat on his back, and that he was my master. Sir, I would not own him as my slave. He my master! and I compelled by him! And, as if it were impossible to go far enough in one paragraph, he refers to certain letters of his own to prove that I was flat on my back! and, that I was not only on my back, but another senator and the President had robbed me! I was flat on my back, and unable to do any thing but what the senator from South Carolina permitted me to do!

"Why, sir, [said Mr. C.] I gloried in my strength, and was compelled to introduce the compromise bill; and compelled, too, by the senator, not in consequence of the weakness, but of the strength, of my position. If it was possible for the senator from South Carolina to introduce one paragraph without showing the egotism of his character, he would not now acknowledge that he wrote letters home to show that he (Mr. C.) was flat on his back, while he was indebted to him for that measure which relieved him from the difficulties in which he was involved. Now, what was the history of the case? Flat as he was on his back, Mr. C. said he was able to produce that compromise, and to carry it through the Senate, in opposition to the most strenuous exertions of the gentleman who, the senator from South Carolina said, had supplanted him, and in spite of his determined and unceasing opposition. There was (said Mr. C.) a sort of necessity operating on me to compel me to introduce that measure. No necessity of a personal character influenced him; but considerations involving the interests, the peace and harmony of the whole country, as well as of the State of South Carolina, directed him in the course he pursued. He saw the condition of the senator from South Carolina and that of his friends; he saw the condition to which he had reduced the gallant little State of South Carolina by his unwise and dangerous measures; he saw, too, that we were on the eve of a civil war; and he wished to save the effusion of blood—the blood of our own fellow-citizens. That was one reason why he introduced the compromise bill. There was another reason that powerfully operated on him. The very interest that the tariff laws were enacted to protect—so great was the power of the then chief magistrate, and so rapidly was that power increasing—was in danger of being sacrificed. He saw that the protective system was in danger of being swept away entirely, and probably at the next session of Congress, by the tremendous power of the individual who then filled the Executive chair; and he felt that the greatest service that he could render it, would be to obtain for it 'a lease for a term of years,' to use an expression that had been heretofore applied to the compromise bill. He saw the necessity that existed to save the protective system from the danger which threatened it. He saw the necessity to advance the great interests of the nation, to avert civil war, and to restore peace and harmony to a distracted and divided country; and it was therefore that he had brought forward this measure. The senator from South Carolina, to betray still further and more strikingly the characteristics which belonged to him, said, that in consequence of his (Mr. C.'s) remarks this very day, all obligations towards him on the part of himself (Mr. CALHOUN), of the State of South Carolina, and the whole South, were cancelled. And what right had the senator to get up and assume to speak of the whole South, or even of South Carolina herself? If he was not mistaken in his judgment of the political signs of the times, and if the information which came to him was to be relied on, a day would come, and that not very distant neither, when the senator would not dare to rise in his place and presume to speak as he had this day done, as the organ of the gallant people of the State he represented."

The concluding remark of Mr. Clay was founded on the belief, countenanced by many signs, that the State of South Carolina would not go with Mr. Calhoun in support of Mr. Van Buren; but he was mistaken. The State stood by her distinguished senator, and even gave her presidential vote for Mr. Van Buren at the ensuing election—being the first time she had voted in a presidential election since 1829. Mr. Grundy, and some other senators, put an end to this episodical and personal debate by turning the Senate to a vote on the bill before it.

CHAPTER XXIX.

INDEPENDENT TREASURY, OR, DIVORCE OF BANK AND STATE: PASSED IN THE SENATE: LOST IN THE HOUSE OF REPRESENTATIVES.

This great measure consisted of two distinct parts: 1. The *keeping* of the public moneys: 2. The hard money currency in which they were to be paid. The two measures together completed the system of financial reform recommended by the President. The adoption of either of them singly would be a step—and a step going half the distance—towards establishing the whole system: and as it was well supposed that some of the democratic party would balk at the hard money payments, it was determined to propose the measures singly. With this view the committee reported a bill for the Independent Treasury—that is to say, for the keeping of the government moneys by its own officers—without designating the currency to be paid to them. But there was to be a loss either way; for unless the hard money payments were made a part of the act in the first instance, Mr. Calhoun and some of his friends could not vote for it. He therefore moved an amendment to that effect; and the hard money friends of the administration supporting his motion, although preferring that it had not been made, and some others voting for it as making the bill obnoxious to some other friends of the administration, it was carried; and became a part of the bill. At the last moment, and when the bill had been perfected as far as possible by its friends, and the final vote on its passage was ready to be taken, a motion was made to strike out that section—and carried—by the helping vote of some of the friends of the administration—as was well remarked by Mr. Calhoun. The vote was, for striking out—*Messrs.* Bayard, Buchanan, Clay of Kentucky, Clayton (Jno. M.), Crittenden, Cuthbert, Davis of Mississippi, Fulton, Grundy, Knight, McKean, Merrick, Morris, Nicholas, Prentiss, Preston, Rives, Robbins, Robinson, Ruggles, Sevier, Smith of Indiana, Southard, Spence, Swift, Talmadge, Tipton, Wall, White, Webster, Williams—31. On the other hand only twenty-one senators voted for retaining the clause. They were—*Messrs.* Allen, of Ohio, Benton, Brown of North Carolina, Calhoun, Clay of Alabama, Hubbard of New Hampshire, King of Alabama, Linn of Missouri, Lumpkin of Georgia, Lyon of Michigan, Mouton of Louisiana, Niles, Norvell, Franklin Pierce, Roane of Virginia, Smith of Connecticut, Strange of North Carolina, Trotter of Mississippi, Robert J. Walker, Silas Wright, Young of Illinois—21.

This section being struck from the bill, Mr. Calhoun could no longer vote for it; and gave his reasons, which justice to him requires to be preserved in his own words:

"On the motion of the senator from Georgia (Mr. CUTHBERT), the 23d section, which provides for the collection of the dues of the government in specie, was struck out, with the aid of a few on this side, and the entire opposition to the divorce on the other. That section provided for the repeal of the joint resolution of 1816, which authorizes the receipt of bank notes as cash in the dues of the public. The effects of this will be, should the bill pass in its present shape, that the government will collect its revenue and make its disbursements exclusively in bank notes; as it did before the suspension took place in May last. Things will stand precisely as they did then, with but a single exception, that the public deposits will be made with the officers of the government instead of the banks, under the provision of the deposit act of 1836. Thus far is certain. All agree that such is the fact; and such the effect of the passage of this bill as it stands. Now, he intended to show conclusively, that the difference between depositing the public money with the public officers, or with the banks themselves, was merely nominal, as far as the operation and profits of the banks were concerned; that they would not make one cent less profit, or issue a single dollar less, if the deposits be kept by the officers of the government instead of themselves; and, of course, that the system would be equally subject to expansions and contractions, and equally exposed to catastrophes like the present, in the one, as the other, mode of keeping.

"But he had other and insuperable objections. In giving the bill originally his support, he was governed by a deep conviction that the total separation of the government and the banks was indispensable. He firmly believed that we had reached a point where the separation was absolutely necessary to save both government and banks. He was under a strong impression that the banking system had reached a point of decrepitude—that great and important changes were necessary to save it and prevent convulsions; and that the first step was a perpetual separation between them and the government. But there could be, in his opinion, no separation—no divorce—without collecting the public dues in the legal and constitutional currency of the country. Without that, all would prove a perfect delusion; as this bill would prove should it pass. We had no constitutional right to treat the notes of mere private corporations as cash; and if we did, nothing would be done.

"These views, and many others similar, he had openly expressed, in which the great body of the gentlemen around him had concurred. We stand openly pledged to them before the country and the world. We had fought the battle manfully and successfully. The cause was good, and having stood the first shock, nothing was necessary, but firmness; standing fast on our position to ensure victory—a great and glorious victory in a noble cause, which was calculated to effect a more important reformation in the condition of society than any in our time—he, for one, could not agree to terminate all those mighty efforts, at this and the extra session, by returning to a complete and perfect reunion with the banks in the worst and most dangerous form. He would not belie all that he had said and done, by voting for the bill as it now stood amended; and to terminate that which was so gloriously begun, in so miserable a farce. He could not but feel deeply disappointed in what he had reason to apprehend would be the result—to have all our efforts and labor thrown away, and the hopes of the country disappointed. All would be lost! No; he expressed himself too strongly. Be the vote what it may, the discussion would stand. Light had gone abroad. The public mind had been aroused, for the first time, and directed to this great subject. The intelligence of the country is every where busy in exploring its depths and intricacies, and would not cease to investigate till all its labyrinths were traced. The seed that has been sown will sprout and grow to maturity; the revolution that has been begun will go through, be our course what it may."

The vote was then taken on the passage of the bill, and it was carried—by the lean majority of two votes, which was only the difference of one voter. The affirmative vote was: Messrs. Allen, Benton, Brown, Clay of Alabama, Cuthbert, Fulton, Hubbard, King, Linn, Lumpkin, Lyon, Morris, Mouton, Niles, Norvell, Pierce, Roane, Robinson, Sevier, Smith of Connecticut, Strange, Trotter, Walker, Wall, Williams, Wright, Young—27. The negatives were: Messrs. Bayard, Buchanan, Calhoun, Clay of Kentucky, Clayton, Crittenden, Davies, Grundy, Knight, McKean, Merrick, Nicholas, Prentiss, Preston, Rives, Robbins, Ruggles, Smith of Indiana, Southard, Spence, Swift, Talmadge, Tipton, Webster, Hugh L. White—25.

The act having passed the Senate by this slender majority was sent to the House of Representatives; where it was lost by a majority of 14. This was a close vote in a house of 236 present; and the bill was only lost by several friends of the administration voting with the entire opposition. But a great point was gained. Full discussion had been had upon the subject, and the public mind was waked up to it.

CHAPTER XXX.

PUBLIC LANDS: GRADUATION OF PRICE: PRE-EMPTION SYSTEM: TAXATION WHEN SOLD.

For all the new States composed territory belonging, or chiefly so to the federal government, the Congress of the United States became the local legislature, that is to say, in the place of a local legislature in all the legislation that relates to the primary disposition of the soil. In the old States this legislation belonged to the State legislatures, and might have belonged to the new States in virtue of their State sovereignty except by the "*compacts*" with the federal government at the time of their admission into the Union, in which they bound themselves, in consideration of land and money grants deemed equivalent to the value of the surrendered rights, not to interfere with the primary disposition of the public lands, nor to tax them while remaining unsold, nor for five years thereafter. These grants, though accepted as equivalents in the infancy of the States, were soon found to be very far from it, even in a mere moneyed point of view, independent of the evils resulting from the administration of domestic local questions by a distant national legislature. The taxes alone for a few years on the public lands would have been equivalent to all the benefits derived from the grants in the compacts. Composed of citizens from the old States where a local legislature administered the public lands according to the local interests—selling lands of different qualities for different prices, according to its quality—granting pre-emptions and donations to first settlers—and subjecting all to taxation as soon as it became public property; it was a national feeling to desire the same advantages; and for this purpose, incessant, and usually vain efforts were made to obtain them from Congress. At this session (1837-'38) a better progress was made, and bills passed for all the purposes through the Senate.

1. The graduation bill. This measure had been proposed for twelve years, and the full system embraced a plan for the speedy and final extinction of the federal title to all the lands within the new States. Periodical reductions of price at the rate of 25 cents per acre until reduced to 25 cents: a preference in the purchase to actual settlers, constituting a pre-emption right: donations to destitute settlers: and the cession of the refuse to States in which they lay:—these were the provisions which constituted the system and which were all contained in the first bills. But finding it impossible to carry all the provisions of the system in any one bill, it became necessary to secure what could be obtained. The graduation-bill was reduced to one feature—reduction of price; and that limited to two reductions, bringing down the price at the first reduction to one dollar per acre: at the next 75 cents per acre. In support of this bill Mr. Benton made a brief speech, from which the following are some passages:

> "The bill comes to us now under more favorable auspices than it has ever done before. The President recommends it, and the Treasury needs the money which it will produce. A gentleman of the opposition [Mr. CLAY], reproaches the President for inconsistency in making this recommendation; he says that he voted against it as senator heretofore, and recommends it as President now. But the gentleman forgets so tell us that Mr. Van Buren, when a member of the Senate, spoke in favor of the general object of the bill from the first day it was presented, and that he voted in favor of one degree of reduction—a reduction of the price of the public lands to one dollar per acre—the last session that he served here. Far from being inconsistent, the President, in this recommendation, has only carried out to their legitimate conclusions the principles which he formerly expressed, and the vote which he formerly gave.

> "The bill, as modified on the motions of the senators from Tennessee and New Hampshire [Messrs. GRUNDY and HUBBARD] stands shorn of half its original provisions. Originally it embraced four degrees of reduction, it now contains but two of those degrees. The two last—the fifty cent, and the twenty-five cent reductions, have been cut off. I made no objection to the motions of those gentlemen. I knew them to be made in a friendly spirit; I knew also that the success of their motions was necessary to the success of any part of the bill. Certainly I would have preferred the whole—would have preferred the four degrees of reduction. But this is a case in which the homely maxim applies, that half a loaf is better than no bread. By giving up half the bill, we may gain the other half; and sure I am that our constituents will

vastly prefer half to nothing. The lands may now be reduced to one dollar for those which have been five years in market, and to seventy-five cents for those which have been ten years in market. The rest of the bill is relinquished for the present, not abandoned for ever. The remaining degrees of reduction will be brought forward hereafter, and with a better prospect of success, after the lands have been picked and culled over under the prices of the present bill. Even if the clauses had remained which have been struck out, on the motions of the gentlemen from Tennessee and New Hampshire, it would have been two years from December next, before any purchases could have been made under them. They were not to take effect until December, 1840. Before that time Congress will twice sit again; and if the present bill passes, and is found to work well, the enactment of the present rejected clauses will be a matter of course.

"This is a measure emphatically for the benefit of the agricultural interest—that great interest, which he declared to be the foundation of all national prosperity, and the backbone, and substratum of every other interest—which was, in the body politic, front rank for service, and rear rank for reward—which bore nearly all the burthens of government while carrying the government on its back—which was the fountain of good production, while it was the pack-horse of burthens, and the broad shoulders which received nearly all losses—especially from broken banks. This bill was for them; and, in voting for it, he had but one regret, and that was, that it did not go far enough—that it was not equal to their merits."

The bill passed by a good majority—27 to 16; but failed to be acted upon in the House of Representatives, though favorably reported upon by its committee on the public lands.

2. The pre-emptive system. The provisions of the bill were simple, being merely to secure the privilege of first purchase to the settler on any lands to which the Indian title had been extinguished; to be paid for at the minimum price of the public lands at the time. A senator from Maryland, Mr. Merrick, moved to amend the bill by confining its benefits to citizens of the United States—excluding unnaturalized foreigners. Mr. Benton opposed this motion, in a brief speech.

"He was entirely opposed to the amendment of the senator from Maryland (Mr. MERRICK). It proposed something new in our legislation. It proposed to make a distinction between aliens and citizens in the acquisition of property. Pre-emption rights had been granted since the formation of the government; and no distinction, until now, had been proposed, between the persons, or classes of persons, to whom they were granted. No law had yet excluded aliens from the acquisition of a pre-emption right, and he was entirely opposed to commencing a system of legislation which was to affect the property rights of the aliens who came to our country to make it their home. Political rights rested on a different basis. They involved the management of the government, and it was right that foreigners should undergo the process of naturalization before they acquired the right of sharing in the government. But the acquisition of property was another affair. It was a private and personal affair. It involved no question but that of the subsistence, the support, and the comfortable living of the alien and his family. Mr. B. would be against the principle of the proposed amendment in any case, but he was particularly opposed to this case. Who were the aliens whom it proposed to affect? Not those who are described as paupers and criminals, infesting the purlieus of the cities, but those who had gone to the remote new States, and to the remote parts of those States, and into the depths of the wilderness, and there commenced the cultivation of the earth. These were the description of aliens to be affected; and if the amendment was adopted, they would be excluded from a pre-emption right in the soil they were cultivating, and made to wait until they were naturalized. The senator from Maryland (Mr. MERRICK), treats this as a case of bounty. He treats the pre-emption right as a bounty from the government, and says that aliens have no right to this bounty. But, is this correct? Is the pre-emption a bounty? Far from it. In point of money, the pre-emptioner pays about as much as any other purchaser. He pays the government price, one dollar and twenty-five cents; and the table of land sales proves that nobody pays any more, or so little more that it is nothing in a national point of view. One dollar twenty-seven and a half cents per acre is the average of all the sales for fifteen years. The twenty millions of acres sold to speculators in the year 1836, all went at one dollar and twenty-five cents per acre. The pre-emption then is not a bounty, but a sale, and a sale for full price, and, what is more, for solid money; for pre-emptioners pay with gold and silver, and not with bank credits. Numerous were the emigrants from Germany, France, Ireland, and other countries, now in the West, and especially in Missouri, and he (Mr. B.) had no idea of imposing any legal disability upon them in the acquisition of property. He wished them all well. If any of them had settled upon the public lands, so much the better. It was an evidence of their intention to become citizens, and their labor upon the soil would add to its product and to the national wealth."

The motion of Mr. Merrick was rejected by a majority of 13. The yeas were: Messrs. Bayard, Clay of Kentucky, Clayton, Crittenden, Davis, Knight, Merrick, Prentiss, Preston, Rives, Robbins, Smith, of Indiana, Southard, Spence, Tallmadge, Tipton, 15. The nays were: Messrs. Allen, Benton, Brown, Buchanan, Calhoun, Clay, of Alabama, Cuthbert, Fulton, Grundy, Hubbard, King, Linn, Lumpkin, Lyon, Mouton, Nicholas, Niles, Nowell, Pierce, Roane, Robinson, Sevier, Walker, Webster, White, Williams, Wright, Young, of Illinois, (28.) The bill being then put to the vote, was passed by a majority of 14.

3. Taxation of public lands when sold. When the United States first instituted their land system, the sales were upon credit, at a minimum price of two dollars, payable in four equal annual payments, with a liability to revert if there should be any failure in the payments. During that time it was considered as public land, nor was the title passed until the patent issued—which might be a year longer. Five years, therefore, was the period fixed, during which the land so sold should be exempt from taxation by the State in which it lay. This continued to be the mode of sale, until the year 1821, when the credit was changed for the cash system, and the minimum price reduced to one dollar twenty-five cents per acre. The reason for the five years exemption from state taxation had then ceased, but the compacts remaining unaltered, the exemption continued. Repeated applications were made to Congress to consent to the modification of the compacts in that article; but always in vain. At this session the application was renewed on the part of the new States; and with success in the Senate, where the bill for that purpose passed nearly unanimously, the negatives being but four, to wit: Messrs. Brown, Clay of Kentucky, Clayton, Southard. Being sent to the H. R. it remained there without action till the end of the session.

CHAPTER XXXI.

SPECIE BASIS FOR BANKS: ONE THIRD OF THE AMOUNT OF LIABILITIES THE LOWEST SAFE PROPORTION: SPEECH OF MR. BENTON ON THE RECHARTER OF THE DISTRICT BANKS.

This is a point of great moment—one on which the public mind has not been sufficiently awakened in this country, though well understood and duly valued in England. The charters of banks in the United States are usually drawn on this principle, that a certain proportion of the capital, and sometimes the whole of it, shall be paid up in gold or silver before the charter shall take effect. This is the usual provision, without any obligation on the bank to retain any part of this specie after it gets into operation; and this provision has too often proved to be illusory and deceptive. In many cases, the banks have borrowed the requisite amount for a day, and then returned it; in many other cases, the proportion of specie, though paid up in good faith, is immediately lent out, or parted with. The result to the public is about the same in both cases; the bank has little or no specie, and its place is supplied by the notes of other banks. The great vice of the banking system in the United States is in banking upon paper—upon the paper of each other—and treating this paper as cash. This may be safe among the banks themselves; it may enable them to settle with one another, and to liquidate reciprocal balances; but to the public it is nothing. In the event of a run upon a bank, or a general run upon all banks, it is specie, and not paper, that is wanted. It is specie, and not paper, which the public want, and must have.

The motion of the senator from Pennsylvania [Mr. BUCHANAN] is intended to remedy this vice in these District banks; it is intended to impose an obligation on these banks to keep in their vaults a quantum of specie bearing a certain proportion to the amount of their immediate liabilities in circulation and deposits. The gentleman's motion is well intended, but it is defective in two particulars: first, in requiring the proportion to be the one-fourth, instead of the one-third, and next, in making it apply to the private deposits only. The true proportion is one-third, and this to apply to all the circulation and deposits, except those which are special. This proportion has been fixed for a hundred years at the Bank of England; and just so often as that bank has fallen below this proportion, mischief has occurred. This is the sworn opinion of the present Governor of the Bank of England, and of the directors of that institution. Before Lord Althorpe's committee in 1832, Mr. Horsley Palmer, the Governor of the Bank, testified in these words:

> "'The average proportion, as already observed, of coin and bullion which the bank thinks it prudent to keep on hand, is at the rate of a third of the total amount of all her liabilities, including deposits as well as issues.' Mr. George Ward Norman, a director of the bank, states the same thing in a different form of words. He says: 'For a full state of the circulation and the deposits, say twenty-one millions of notes and six millions of deposits, making in the whole twenty-seven millions of liabilities, the proper sum in coin and bullion for the bank to retain is nine millions.' Thus, the average proportion of one-third between the specie on hand and the circulation and deposits, must be considered as an established principle at that bank, which is quite the largest, and amongst the oldest—probably, the very oldest bank of circulation in the world."

The Bank of England is not merely required to keep on hand, in bullion, the one-third of its immediate liabilities; it is bound also to let the country see that it has, or has not, that proportion on hand. By an act of the third year of William IV., it is required to make quarterly publications of the average of the weekly liabilities of the bank, that the public may see whenever it descends below the point of safety. Here is the last of these publications, which is a full exemplification of the rule and the policy which now governs that bank:

> Quarterly average of the weekly liabilities and assets of the Bank of England, from the 12th December, 1837, to the 6th of March, 1838, both inclusive, published pursuant to the act 3 and William IV., cap. 98:

Liabilities.		Assets.	
Circulation,	£18,600,000	Securities,	£22,792,900
Deposits,	11,535,000	Bullion,	10,015,000
	£30,135,000		£30,807,000
London, March 12.			

According to this statement, the Bank of England is now safe; and, accordingly, we see that she is acting upon the principle of having bullion enough, for she is shipping gold to the United States.

The proportion in England is one-third. The bank relies upon its debts and other resources for the other two-thirds, in the event of a run upon it. This is the rule in that bank which has more resources than any other bank in the world; which is situated in the moneyed metropolis of the world—the richest merchants its debtors, friends and customers—and the Government of England its debtor and backer, and always ready to sustain it with exchequer bills, and with every exertion of its credit and means. Such a bank, so situated and so aided, still deems it necessary to its safety to keep in hand always the one-third in bullion of the amount of its immediate liabilities. Now, if the proportion of one-third is necessary to the safety of such a bank, with such resources, how is it possible for our banks, with their meagre resources and small array of friends, to be safe with a less proportion?

This is the rule at the Bank of England, and just as often as it has been departed from, the danger of that departure has been proved. It was departed from in 1797, when the proportion sunk to the one-seventh; and what was the result? The stoppage of the banks, and of all the banks in England, and a suspension of specie payments for six-and-twenty years! It was departed from again about a year ago, when the proportion sunk to one-eighth nearly; and what was the result? A death struggle between the paper systems of England and the United States, in which our system was sacrificed to save hers. Her system was saved from explosion! but at what cost?—at what cost to us, and to herself?—to us a general stoppage of all the banks for twelve months; to the English, a general stagnation of business, decline of manufactures, and of commerce, much individual distress, and a loss of two millions sterling of revenue to the Crown. The proportion of one-third may then be assumed as the point of safety in the Bank of England; less than that proportion cannot be safe in the United States. Yet the senator from Pennsylvania proposes less—he proposes the one-fourth; and proposes it, not because he feels it to be the right proportion, but from some feeling of indulgence or forbearance to this poor District. Now, I think that this is a case in which kind feelings can have no place, and that the point in question is one upon which there can be no compromise. A bank is a bank, whether made in a district or a State; and a bank ought to be safe, whether the stockholders be rich or poor. Safety is the point aimed at, and nothing unsafe should be tolerated. There should be no giving and taking below the point of safety. Experienced men fix upon the one-third as the safe proportion; we should not, therefore, take a less proportion. Would the gentleman ask to let the water in the boiler of a steamboat sink one inch lower, when the experienced captain informed him that it had already sunk as low as it was safe to go? Certainly not. So of these banks. One-third is the point of safety; let us not tamper with danger by descending to the one-fourth.

When a bank stops payment, the first thing we see is an exposition of its means, and a declaration of ultimate ability to pay all its debts. This is nothing to the holders of its notes. Immediate ability is the only ability that is of any avail to them. The fright of some, and the necessity of others, compel them to part with their notes. Cool, sagacious capitalists can look to ultimate ability, and buy up the notes from the necessitous and the alarmed. To them ultimate ability is sufficient; to the community it is nothing. It is, therefore, for the benefit of the community that the banks should be required to keep always on hand the one-third of their circulation and deposits; they are then trusted for two-thirds, and this is carrying credit far enough. If pressed by a run, it is as much as a bank can do to make up the other two-thirds out of the debts due to her. Three to one is credit enough, and it is profit enough. If a bank draws interest upon three dollars when it has but one, this is eighteen per cent., and ought to content her. A citizen cannot lend his money for more than six per cent., and cannot the banks be contented with eighteen? Must they insist upon issuing four dollars, or even five, upon one, so as to draw twenty-four or thirty per cent.; and thus, after paying their officers vast salaries, and accommodating friends with loans on easy terms, still make enough out of the business community to cover all expenses and all losses: and then to divide larger profits than can be made at any other business?

The issuing of currency is the prerogative of sovereignty. The real sovereign in this country—the government—can only issue a currency of the actual dollar: can only issue gold and silver—and each piece worth its face. The banks which have the privilege of issuing currency issue paper; and not content with two more dollars out for one that is, they go to five, ten, twenty—failing of course on the first run; and the loss falling upon the holders of its notes—and especially the holders of the small notes.

We now touch a point, said Mr. B., vital to the safety of banking, and I hope it will neither be passed over without decision, nor decided in an erroneous manner. We had up the same question two years ago, in the discussion of the bill to regulate the keeping of the public moneys by the local deposit banks. A senator from Massachusetts (Mr. WEBSTER) moved the question; he (Mr. B.) cordially concurred in it; and the proportion of *one-fourth* was then inserted. He (Mr. B.) had not seen at that time the testimony of the governor and directors of the Bank of England, fixing on the *one-third* as the proper proportion, and he presumed that the senator from Massachusetts (Mr. W.) had not then seen it, as on another occasion he quoted it with approbation, and stated it to be the proportion observed at the Bank of the United States. The proportion of one-fourth was then inserted in the deposit bill; it was an erroneous proportion, but even that proportion was not allowed to stand. After having been inserted in the bill, it was struck out; and it was left to the discretion of the Secretary of the Treasury to fix the proportion. To this I then objected, and gave my reasons for it. I was for fixing the proportion, because I held it vital to the safety of the deposit banks; I was against leaving it to the secretary, because it was a case in which the inflexible rule of law, and not the variable dictate of individual discretion should be exercised; and because I was certain that no secretary could be relied upon to compel the banks to *toe the mark*, when Congress itself had flinched from the task of making them do it. My objections were unavailing. The proportion was struck out of the bill; the discretion of the secretary to fix it was substituted; and that discretion it was impossible to exercise with any effect over the banks. They were, that is to say, many of them were, far beyond the mark then; and at the time of the issuing of the Treasury order in July, 1836, there were deposit banks, whose proportion of specie in hand to their immediate liabilities was as one to twenty, one to thirty, one to forty, and even one to fifty! The explosion of all such banks was inevitable. The issuing of the Treasury order improved them a little: they began to increase their specie, and to diminish their liabilities; but the gap was too wide—the chasm was too vast to be filled: and at the touch of pressure, all these banks fell like nine-pins! They tumbled down in a heap, and lay there, without the power of motion, or scarcely of breathing. Such was the consequence of our error in omitting to fix the proper proportion of specie in hand to the liabilities of our deposit banks: let us avoid that error in the bill now before us.

CHAPTER XXXII.

THE NORTH AND THE SOUTH: COMPARATIVE PROSPERITY: SOUTHERN DISCONTENT: ITS TRUE CAUSE.

To show the working of the federal government is the design of this View—show how things are done under it and their effects; that the good may be approved and pursued, the evil condemned and avoided, and the machine of government be made to work equally for the benefit of the whole Union, according to the wise and beneficent intent of its founders. It thus becomes necessary to show its working in the two great Atlantic sections, originally sole parties to the Union—the North and the South—complained of for many years on one part as unequal and oppressive, and made so by a course of federal legislation at variance with the objects of the confederation and contrary to the intent or the words of the constitution.

The writer of this View sympathized with that complaint; believed it to be, to much extent, well founded; saw with concern the corroding effect it had on the feelings of patriotic men of the South; and often had to lament that a sense of duty to his own constituents required him to give votes which his judgment disapproved and his feelings condemned. This complaint existed when he came into the Senate; it had, in fact, commenced in the first years of the federal government, at the time of the assumption of the State debts, the incorporation of the first national bank, and the adoption of the funding system; all of which drew capital from the South to the North. It continued to increase; and, at the period to which this chapter relates, it had reached the stage of an organized sectional expression in a voluntary convention of the Southern States. It had often been expressed in Congress, and in the State legislatures, and habitually in the discussions of the people; but now it took the more serious form of joint action, and exhibited the spectacle of a part of the States assembling sectionally to complain formally of the unequal, and to them, injurious operation of the common government, established by common consent for the common good, and now frustrating its object by departing from the purposes of its creation. The convention was called commercial, and properly, as the grievance complained of was in its root commercial, and a commercial remedy was proposed.

It met at Augusta, Georgia, and afterwards at Charleston, South Carolina; and the evil complained of and the remedy proposed were strongly set forth in the proceedings of the body, and in addresses to the people of the Southern and Southwestern States. The changed relative condition of the two sections of the country, before and since the Union, was shown in their general relative depression or prosperity since that event, and especially in the reversed condition of their respective foreign import trade. In the colonial condition the comparison was wholly in favor of the South; under the Union wholly against it. Thus, in the year 1760—only sixteen years before the Declaration of Independence—the foreign imports into Virginia were £850,000 sterling, and into South Carolina £555,000; while into New York they were only £189,000, into Pennsylvania £490,000; and into all the New England Colonies collectively only £561,000.

These figures exhibit an immense superiority of commercial prosperity on the side of the South in its colonial state, sadly contrasting with another set of figures exhibited by the convention to show its relative condition within a few years after the Union. Thus, in the year 1821, the imports into New York had risen to $23,000,000—being about seventy times its colonial import at about an equal period before the adoption of the constitution; and those of South Carolina stood at $3,000,000—which, for all practical purposes, may be considered the same that they were in 1760.

Such was the difference—the reversed conditions—of the two sections, worked between them in the brief space of two generations—within the actual lifetime of some who had seen their colonial conditions. The proceedings of the convention did not stop there, but brought down the comparison (under this commercial aspect) to near the period of its own sitting—to the actual period of the highest manifestation of Southern discontent, in 1832—when it produced the enactment of the South Carolina nullifying ordinance. At that time all the disproportions between the foreign commerce of the two sections had inordinately increased. The New York imports (since 1821) had more than doubled; the Virginia had fallen off one-half; South Carolina two-thirds. The actual figures stood: New York fifty-seven millions of dollars, Virginia half a million, South Carolina one million and a quarter.

This was a disheartening view, and rendered more grievous by the certainty of its continuation, the prospect of its aggravation, and the conviction that the South (in its great staples) furnished the basis for these imports; of which it received so small a share. To this loss of its import trade, and its transfer to the North, the convention attributed, as a primary cause, the reversed conditions of the two sections—the great advance of one in wealth and improvements—the slow progress and even comparative decline of the other; and, with some allowance for the operation of natural or inherent causes, referred the effect to a course of federal legislation unwarranted by the grants of the constitution and the objects of the Union, which subtracted capital from one section and accumulated it in the other:—protective tariff, internal improvements, pensions, national debt, two national banks, the funding system and the paper system; the multiplication of offices, profuse and extravagant expenditure, the conversion of a limited into an almost unlimited government; and the substitution of power and splendor for what was intended to be a simple and economical administration of that part of their affairs which required a general head.

These were the points of complaint—abuses—which had led to the collection of an enormous revenue, chiefly levied on the products of one section of the Union and mainly disbursed in another. So far as northern advantages were the result of fair legislation for the accomplishment of the objects of the Union, all discontent or complaint was disclaimed. All knew that the superior advantages of the North for navigation would give it the advantage in foreign commerce; but it was not expected that these facilities would operate a monopoly on one side and an extinction on the other; nor was that consequence allowed to be the effect of these advantages alone, but was charged to a course of legislation not warranted by the objects of the Union, or the terms of the constitution, which created it. To this course of legislation was attributed the accumulation of capital in the North, which had enabled that section to monopolize the foreign commerce which was founded upon southern exports; to cover one part with wealth while the other was impoverished; and to make the South tributary to the North, and suppliant to it for a small part of the fruits of their own labor.

Unhappily there was some foundation for this view of the case; and in this lies the root of the discontent of the South and its dissatisfaction with the Union, although it may break out upon another point. It is in this belief of an incompatibility of interest, from the perverted working of the federal government, that lies the root of southern discontent, and which constitutes the danger to the Union, and which statesmen should confront and grapple with; and not in any danger to slave property, which has continued to aggrandize in value during the whole period of the cry of danger, and is now of greater price than ever was known before; and such as our ancestors would have deemed fabulous. The sagacious Mr. Madison knew this—knew where the danger to the Union lay, when, in the 86th year of his age, and the last of his life, and under the anguish of painful misgivings, he wrote (what is more fully set out in the previous volume of this work) these portentous words:

> "*The visible susceptibility to the contagion of nullification in the Southern States, the sympathy arising from known causes, and the inculcated impression of a permanent incompatibility of interest between the North and the South, may put it in the power of popular leaders, aspiring to the highest stations, to unite the South, on some critical occasion, in some course of action of which nullification may be the first step, secession the second, and a farewell separation the last.*"

So viewed the evil, and in his last days, the great surviving founder of the Union—seeing, as he did, in this inculcated impression of a permanent incompatibility of interest between the two sections, the fulcrum or point of support, on which disunion could rest its lever, and parricidal hands build its schemes. What has been published in the South and adverted to in this View goes to show that an incompatibility of interest between the two sections, though not inherent, has been produced by the working of the government—not its fair and legitimate, but its perverted and unequal working.

This is the evil which statesmen should see and provide against. Separation is no remedy; exclusion of Northern vessels from Southern ports is no remedy; but is disunion itself—and upon the very point which caused the Union to be formed. Regulation of commerce between the States, and with foreign nations, was the cause of the formation of the Union. Break that regulation, and the Union is broken; and the broken parts converted into antagonist nations, with causes enough of dissension to engender perpetual wars, and inflame incessant animosities. The remedy lies in the right working of the constitution; in the cessation of unequal legislation in the reduction of the inordinate expenses of the government; in its return to the simple, limited, and economical machine it was intended to be; and in the revival of fraternal feelings, and respect for each other's rights and just complaints; which would return of themselves when the real cause of discontent was removed.

The conventions of Augusta and Charleston proposed their remedy for the Southern depression, and the comparative decay of which they complained. It was a fair and patriotic remedy—that of becoming their own exporters, and opening a direct trade in their own staples between Southern and foreign ports. It was recommended—attempted—failed. Superior advantages for navigation in the North—greater aptitude of its people for commerce—established course of business—accumulated capital—continued unequal legislation in Congress; and increasing expenditures of the government, chiefly disbursed in the North, and defect of seamen in the South (for mariners cannot be made of slaves), all combined to retain the foreign trade in the channel which had absorbed it; and to increase it there with the increasing wealth and population of the country, and the still faster increasing extravagance and profusion of the government. And now, at this period (1855), the foreign imports at New York are $195,000,000; at Boston $58,000,000; in Virginia $1,250,000; in South Carolina $1,750,000.

This is what the dry and naked figures show. To the memory and imagination it is worse; for it is a tradition of the Colonies that the South had been the seat of wealth and happiness, of power and opulence; that a rich population covered the land, dispensing a baronial hospitality, and diffusing the felicity which themselves enjoyed; that all was life, and joy, and affluence then. And this tradition was not without similitude to the reality, as this writer can testify; for he was old enough to have seen (after the Revolution) the still surviving state of Southern colonial manners, when no traveller was allowed to go to a tavern, but was handed over from family to family through entire States; when holidays were days of festivity and expectation, long prepared for, and celebrated by master and slave with music and feasting, and great concourse of friends and relatives; when gold was kept in desks or chests (after the downfall of continental paper) and weighed in scales, and lent to neighbors for short terms without note, interest, witness, or security; and on bond and land security for long years and lawful usance: and when petty litigation was at so low an ebb that it required a fine of forty pounds of tobacco to make a man serve as constable.

The reverse of all this was now seen and felt,—not to the whole extent which fancy or policy painted—but to extent enough to constitute a reverse, and to make a contrast, and to excite the regrets which the memory of past joys never fails to awaken. A real change had come, and this change, the effect of many causes, was wholly attributed to one—the unequal working of the Federal Government—which gave all the benefits of the Union to the North, and all its burdens to the South. And that was the point on which Southern discontent broke out—on which it openly rested until 1835; when it was shifted to the danger of slave property.

Separation is no remedy for these evils, but the parent of far greater than either just discontent or restless ambition would fly from. To the South the Union is a political blessing; to the North it is both a political and a pecuniary blessing; to both it should be a social blessing. Both sections should cherish it, and the North most. The story of the boy that killed the goose that laid the golden egg every day, that he might get all the eggs at once, was a fable; but the Northern man who could promote separation by any course of wrong to the South would convert that fable into history—his own history—and commit a folly, in a mere profit and loss point of view, of which there is no precedent except in fable.

CHAPTER XXXIII.

PROGRESS OF THE SLAVERY AGITATION: MR. CALHOUN'S APPROVAL OF THE MISSOURI COMPROMISE

This portentous agitation, destined to act so seriously on the harmony, and possibly on the stability of the Union, requires to be noted in its different stages, that responsibility may follow culpability, and the judgment of history fall where it is due, if a deplorable calamity is made to come out of it. In this point of view the movements for and against slavery in the session of 1837-'38 deserve to be noted, as of disturbing effect at the time; and as having acquired new importance from subsequent events. Early in the session a memorial was presented in the Senate from the General Assembly of Vermont, remonstrating against the annexation of Texas to the United States, and praying for the abolition of slavery in the District of Columbia—followed by many petitions from citizens and societies in the Northern States to the same effect; and, further, for the abolition of slavery in the Territories—for the abolition of the slave trade between the States—and for the exclusion of future slave States from the Union.

There was but little in the state of the country at that time to excite an anti-slavery feeling, or to excuse these disturbing applications to Congress. There was no slave territory at that time but that of Florida; and to ask to abolish slavery there, where it had existed from the discovery of the continent, or to make its continuance a cause for the rejection of the State when ready for admission into the Union, and thus form a free State in the rear of all the great slave States, was equivalent to praying for a dissolution of the Union. Texas, if annexed, would be south of 36° 30', and its character, in relation to slavery, would be fixed by the Missouri compromise line of 1820. The slave trade between the States was an affair of the States, with which Congress had nothing to do; and the continuance of slavery in the District of Columbia, so long as it existed in the adjacent States of Virginia and Maryland, was a point of policy in which every Congress, and every administration, had concurred from the formation of the Union; and in which there was never a more decided concurrence than at present.

The petitioners did not live in any Territory, State, or district subject to slavery. They felt none of the evils of which they complained—were answerable for none of the supposed sin which they denounced—were living under a general government which acknowledged property in slaves—and had no right to disturb the rights of the owner: and they committed a cruelty upon the slave by the additional rigors which their pernicious interference brought upon him.

The subject of the petitions was disagreeable in itself; the language in which they were couched was offensive; and the wantonness of their presentation aggravated a proceeding sufficiently provoking in the civilest form in which it could be conducted. Many petitions were in the same words, bearing internal evidence of concert among their signers; many were signed by women, whose proper sphere was far from the field of legislation; all united in a common purpose, which bespoke community of origin, and the superintendence of a general direction. Every presentation gave rise to a question and debate, in which sentiments and feelings were expressed and consequences predicted, which it was painful to hear. While almost every senator condemned these petitions, and the spirit in which they originated, and the language in which they were couched, and considered them as tending to no practical object, and only calculated to make dissension and irritation, there were others who took them in a graver sense, and considered them as leading to the inevitable separation of the States. In this sense Mr. Calhoun said:

> "He had foreseen what this subject would come to. He knew its origin, and that it lay deeper than was supposed. It grew out of a spirit of fanaticism which was daily increasing, and, if not met *in limine*, would by and by dissolve this Union. It was particularly our duty to keep the matter out of the Senate—out of the halls of the National Legislature. These fanatics were interfering with what they had no right. Grant the reception of these petitions, and you will next be asked to act on them. He was for no conciliatory course, no temporizing; instead of yielding one inch, he would rise in opposition; and he hoped every man from the South would stand by him to put down this growing evil. There was but one question that would ever destroy this Union, and that was involved in this principle. Yes; this was potent enough for it,

and must be early arrested if the Union was to be preserved. A man must see little into what is going on if he did not perceive that this spirit was growing, and that the rising generation was becoming more strongly imbued with it. It was not to be stopped by reports on paper, but by action, and very decided action."

The question which occupied the Senate was as to the most judicious mode of treating these memorials, with a view to prevent their evil effects: and that was entirely a question of policy, on which senators disagreed who concurred in the main object. Some deemed it most advisable to receive and consider the petitions—to refer them to a committee—and subject them to the adverse report which they would be sure to receive; as had been done with the Quakers' petitions at the beginning of the government. Others deemed it preferable to refuse to receive them. The objection urged to this latter course was, that it would mix up a new question with the slavery agitation which would enlist the sympathies of many who did not co-operate with the Abolitionists—the question of the right of petition; and that this new question, mixing with the other, might swell the number of petitioners, keep up the applications to Congress, and perpetuate an agitation which would otherwise soon die out. Mr. CLAY, and many others were of this opinion; Mr. CALHOUN and his friends thought otherwise; and the result was, so far as it concerned the petitions of individuals and societies, what it had previously been—a half-way measure between reception and rejection—a motion to lay the question of reception on the table. This motion, precluding all discussion, got rid of the petitions quietly, and kept debate out of the Senate. In the case of the memorial from the State of Vermont, the proceeding was slightly different in form, but the same in substance. As the act of a State, the memorial was received; but after reception was laid on the table. Thus all the memorials and petitions were disposed of by the Senate in a way to accomplish the two-fold object, first, of avoiding discussion; and, next, condemning the object of the petitioners. It was accomplishing all that the South asked; and if the subject had rested at that point, there would have been nothing in the history of this session, on the slavery agitation, to distinguish it from other sessions about that period: but the subject was revived; and in a way to force discussion, and to constitute a point for the retrospect of history.

Every memorial and petition had been disposed of according to the wishes of the senators from the slaveholding States; but Mr. Calhoun deemed it due to those States to go further, and to obtain from the Senate declarations which should cover all the questions of federal power over the institution of slavery: although he had just said that paper reports would do no good. For that purpose, he submitted a series of resolves—six in number—which derive their importance from their comparison, or rather contrast, with others on the same subject presented by him in the Senate ten years later; and which have given birth to doctrines and proceedings which have greatly disturbed the harmony of the Union, and palpably endangered its stability. The six resolutions of this period ('37-'38) undertook to define the whole extent of the power delegated by the States to the federal government on the subject of slavery; to specify the acts which would exceed that power; and to show the consequences of doing any thing not authorized to be done—always ending in a dissolution of the Union. The first four of these related to the States; about which, there being no dispute, there was no debate. The sixth, without naming Texas, was prospective, and looked forward to a case which might include her annexation; and was laid upon the table to make way for an express resolution from Mr. Preston on the same subject. The fifth related to the territories, and to the District of Columbia, and was the only one which excited attention, or has left a surviving interest. It was in these words:

> "*Resolved*, That the intermeddling of any State, or States, or their citizens, to abolish slavery in this District, or any of the territories, on the ground or under the pretext that it is immoral or sinful, or the passage of any act or measure of Congress with that view, would be a direct and dangerous attack on the institutions of all the slaveholding States."

The dogma of "no power in Congress to legislate upon the existence of slavery in territories" had not been invented at that time; and, of course, was not asserted in this resolve, intended by its author to define the extent of the federal legislative power on the subject. The resolve went upon the existence of the power, and deprecated its abuse. It put the District of Columbia and the territories into the same category, both for the exercise of the power and the consequences to result from the intermeddling of States or citizens, or the passage of any act of Congress to abolish slavery in either; and this was admitting the power in the territory, as in the District; where it is an express grant in the grant of all legislative power. The intermeddling and the legislation were deprecated in both solely on the ground of inexpediency. Mr. Clay believed this inexpediency to rest upon different grounds in the District and in the territory of Florida—the only territory in which slavery then existed, and to which Mr. Calhoun's resolution could apply. He was as much opposed as any one to the abolition of slavery in either of these places, but believed that a different reason should be given for each, founded in their respective circumstances; and, therefore, submitted an amendment, consisting of two resolutions—one applicable to the District, the other to the territory. In stating the reasons why slavery should not be abolished in Florida, he quoted the Missouri compromise line of 1820. This was objected to by other senators, on the ground that that line did not apply to Florida, and that her case was complete without it. Of that opinion was the Senate, and the clause was struck out. This gave Mr. Calhoun occasion to speak of that compromise, and of his own course in relation to it; in the course of which he declared himself to have been favorable to that memorable measure at the time it was adopted, but opposed to it now, from having experienced its ill effect in encouraging the spirit of abolitionism:

> "He was glad that the portion of the amendment which referred to the Missouri compromise had been struck out. He was not a member of Congress when that compromise was made, but it is due to candor to state that his impressions were in its favor; but it is equally due to it to say that, with his present experience and knowledge of the spirit which then, for the first time, began to disclose itself, he had entirely changed his opinion. He now believed that it was a dangerous measure, and that it has done much to rouse into action the present spirit. Had it then been met with uncompromising opposition, such as a then distinguished and sagacious member from Virginia [Mr. RANDOLPH], now no more, opposed to it, abolition might have been crushed for ever in its birth. He then thought of Mr. Randolph as, he doubts not, many think of him now who have not fully looked into this subject, that he was too unyielding—too uncompromising—too impracticable; but he had been taught his error, and took pleasure in acknowledging it."

This declaration is explicit. It is made in a spirit of candor, and as due to justice. It is a declaration spontaneously made, not an admission obtained on interrogatories. It shows that Mr. Calhoun was in favor of the compromise at the time it was adopted, and had since changed his opinions—"entirely changed" them, to use his own words—not on constitutional, but expedient grounds. He had changed upon experience, and upon seeing the dangerous effects of the measure. He had been taught his error, and took pleasure in acknowledging it. He blamed Mr. Randolph then for having been too uncompromising; but now thought him sagacious; and believed that if the measure had met with uncompromising opposition at the time, it would have crushed for ever the spirit of abolitionism. All these are reasons of expediency, derived from after-experience, and excludes the idea of any constitutional objection. The establishment of the Missouri compromise line was the highest possible exercise of legislative authority over the subject of slavery in a territory. It abolished it where it legally existed. It for ever forbid it where it had legally existed for one hundred years. Mr. Randolph was the great opponent of the compromise. He gave its friends all their trouble. It was then he applied the phrase, so annoying and destructive to its northern supporters—"dough face,"—a phrase which did them more harm than the best-reasoned speech. All the friends of the compromise blamed his impracticable opposition; and Mr. Calhoun, in joining in that blame, placed himself in the ranks of the cordial friends of the measure. This abolition and prohibition extended over an area large enough to make a dozen States; and of all this Mr. Calhoun had been in favor; and now had nothing but reasons of expediency, and they *ex post facto*, against it. His expressed belief now was, that the measure was dangerous—he does not say unconstitutional, but dangerous—and this corresponds with the terms of his resolution then submitted; which makes the intermeddling to abolish slavery in the District or territories, or any act or measure of Congress to that effect, a "dangerous" attack on the institutions of the slaveholding States. Certainly the idea of the unconstitutionality of such legislation had not then entered his head. The substitute resolve of Mr. Clay differed from that of Mr. Calhoun, in changing the word "intermeddling" to that of "interference;" and confining that word to the conduct of citizens, and making the abolition or attempted abolition of slavery in the District an injury to its own inhabitants as well as to the States; and placing its protection under the faith implied in accepting its cession from Maryland and Virginia. It was in these words:

"That the interference by the citizens of any of the States, with the view to the abolition of slavery in this District, is endangering the rights and security of the people of the District; and that any act or measure of Congress, designed to abolish slavery in this District, would be a violation of the faith implied in the cessions by the States of Virginia and Maryland—a just cause of alarm to the people of the slaveholding States—and have a direct and inevitable tendency to disturb and endanger the Union."

The vote on the final adoption of the resolution was:

"YEAS—Messrs. Allen, Bayard, Benton, Black, Brown, Buchanan, Calhoun, Clay, of Alabama, Clay, of Kentucky, Thomas Clayton, Crittenden, Cuthbert, Fulton, Grundy, Hubbard, King, Lumpkin, Lyon, Nicholas, Niles, Norvell, Franklin Pierce, Preston, Rives, Roane, Robinson, Sevier, Smith, of Connecticut, Strange, Tallmadge, Tipton, Walker, White, Williams, Wright, Young.

"NAYS—Messrs. Davis, Knight, McKean, Morris, Prentiss, Smith, of Indiana, Swift, Webster."

The second resolution of Mr. Clay applied to slavery in a territory where it existed, and deprecated any attempt to abolish it in such territory, as alarming to the slave States, and as violation of faith towards its inhabitants, unless they asked it; and in derogation of its right to decide the question of slavery for itself when erected into a State. This resolution was intended to cover the case of Florida, and ran thus:

"*Resolved*, That any attempt of Congress to abolish slavery in any territory of the United States in which it exists would create serious alarm and just apprehension in the States sustaining that domestic institution, and would be a violation of good faith towards the inhabitants of any such territory who have been permitted to settle with, and hold, slaves therein; because the people of any such territory have not asked for the abolition of slavery therein; and because, when any such territory shall be admitted into the Union as a State, the people thereof shall be entitled to decide that question exclusively for themselves."

And the vote upon it was—

"YEAS—Messrs. Allen, Bayard, Benton, Black, Brown, Buchanan, Calhoun, Clay, of Alabama, Clay, of Kentucky, Crittenden, Cuthbert, Fulton, Grundy, Hubbard, King, Lumpkin, Lyon, Merrick, Nicholas, Niles, Norvell, Franklin Pierce, Preston, Rives, Roane, Robinson, Sevier, Smith, of Connecticut, Strange, Tipton, Walker, White, Williams, Wright, and Young.

"NAYS—Messrs. Thomas Clayton, Davis, Knight, McKean, Prentiss, Robbins, Smith, of Indiana, Swift, and Webster."

The few senators who voted against both resolutions chiefly did so for reasons wholly unconnected with their merits; some because opposed to any declarations on the subject, as abstract and inoperative; others because they dissented from the reasons expressed, and preferred others: and the senators from Delaware (a slave State) because they had a nullification odor about them, as first introduced. Mr. Calhoun voted for both, not in preference to his own, but as agreeing to them after they had been preferred by the Senate; and so gave his recorded assent to the doctrines they contained. Both admit the constitutional power of Congress over the existence of slavery both in the district and the territories, but deprecate its abolition where it existed for reasons of high expediency: and in this view it is believed nearly the entire Senate concurred; and quite the entire Senate on the constitutional point—there being no reference to that point in any part of the debates. Mr. Webster probably spoke the sentiments of most of those voting with him, as well as his own, when he said:

"If the resolutions set forth that all domestic institutions, except so far as the constitution might interfere, and any intermeddling therewith by a State or individual, was contrary to the spirit of the confederacy, and was thereby illegal and unjust, he would give them his hearty and cheerful support; and would do so still if the senator from South Carolina would consent to such an amendment; but in their present form he must give his vote against them."

The general feeling of the Senate was that of entire repugnance to the whole movement—that of the petitions and memorials on the one hand, and Mr. Calhoun's resolutions on the other. The former were quietly got rid of, and in a way to rebuke, as well as to condemn their presentation; that is to say, by motions (sustained by the body) to lay them on the table. The resolutions could not so easily be disposed of, especially as their mover earnestly demanded discussion, spoke at large, and often, himself; "and desired to make the question, on their rejection or adoption, a *test* question." They were abstract, leading to no result, made discussion where silence was desirable, frustrated the design of the Senate in refusing to discuss the abolition petitions, gave them an importance to which they were not entitled, promoted agitation, embarrassed friendly senators from the North, placed some in false positions; and brought animadversions from many. Thus, Mr. Buchanan:

"I cannot believe that the senator from South Carolina has taken the best course to attain these results (quieting agitation). This is the great centre of agitation; from this capital it spreads over the whole Union. I therefore deprecate a protracted discussion of the question here. It can do no good, but may do much harm, both in the North and in the South. The senators from Delaware, although representing a slaveholding State, have voted against these resolutions because, in their opinion, they can detect in them the poison of nullification. Now, I can see no such thing in them, and am ready to avow in the main they contain nothing but correct political principles, to which I am devoted. But what then? These senators are placed in a false position, and are compelled to vote against resolutions the object of which they heartily approve. Again, my friend, the senator from New Jersey (Mr. Wall), votes against them because they are political abstractions of which he thinks the Senate ought not to take cognizance, although he is as much opposed to abolition, and as willing to maintain the constitutional rights of the South as any senator upon this floor. Other senators believe the right of petition has been endangered; and until that has been established they will not vote for any resolutions on the subject. Thus we stand: and those of us in the North who must sustain the brunt of the battle are forced into false positions. Abolition thus acquires force by bringing to its aid the right of petition, and the hostility which exists at the North against the doctrines of nullification. It is in vain to say that these principles are not really involved in the question. This may be, and in my opinion is, true; but why, by our conduct here, should we afford the abolitionists such plausible pretexts? The fact is, and it cannot be disguised, that those of us in the Northern States who have determined to sustain the rights of the slave States at every hazard are placed in a most embarrassing situation. We are almost literally between two fires. Whilst in front we are assailed by the abolitionists, our own friends in the South are constantly driving us into positions where their enemies and our enemies may gain important advantages."

And thus Mr. Crittenden:

"If the object of these resolutions was to produce peace, and allay excitement, it appeared to him that they were not very likely to accomplish such a purpose. More vague and general abstractions could hardly have been brought forward, and they were more calculated to produce agitation and stir up discontent and bad blood than to do any good whatever. Such he knew was the general opinion of Southern men, few of whom, however they assented to the abstractions, approved of this method of agitating the subject. The mover of these resolutions relies mainly on two points to carry the Senate with him: first, he reiterates the cry of danger to the Union; and, next, that if he is not followed in this movement he urges the inevitable consequence of the destruction of the Union. It is possible the gentleman may be mistaken. It possibly might not be exactly true that, to save the Union, it was necessary to follow him. On the contrary, some were of opinion, and he for one was much inclined to be of the same view, that to follow the distinguished mover of these resolutions—to pursue the course of irritation, agitation, and intimidation which he chalked out—would be the very best and surest method that could be chalked out to destroy this great and happy Union."

And thus Mr. Clay:

"The series of resolutions under consideration has been introduced by the senator from South Carolina, after he and other senators from the South had deprecated discussion on the delicate subject to which they relate. They have occasioned much discussion, in which hitherto I have not participated. I hope that the tendency of the resolutions may be to allay the excitement which unhappily prevails in respect to the abolition of slavery; but I confess that, taken altogether, and in connection with other circumstances, and especially considering the manner in which their author has pressed them on the Senate, I fear that they will have the opposite effect; and particularly at the North, that they may increase and exasperate instead of diminishing and assuaging the existing agitation."

And thus Mr. Preston, of South Carolina:

"His objections to the introduction of the resolutions were that they allowed ground for discussion; and that the subject ought never to be allowed to enter the halls of the legislative assembly, was always to be taken for granted by the South; and what would abstract propositions of this nature effect?"

And thus Mr. Strange, of North Carolina:

"What did they set forth but abstract principles, to which the South had again and again certified? What bulwark of defence was needed stronger than the constitution itself? Every movement on the part of the South only gave additional strength to her opponents. The wisest, nay, the only safe, course was to remain quiet, though prepared at the same time to resist all aggression. Questions like this only tended to excite angry feelings. The senator from South Carolina (Mr. CALHOUN) charged him with '*preaching*' to one side. Perhaps he had sermonized too long for the patience of the Senate; but then he had *preached* to all sides. It was the agitation of the question in any form, or shape, that rendered it dangerous. Agitating this question in any shape was ruinous to the South."

And thus Mr. Richard H. Bayard, of Delaware:

"Though he denounced the spirit of abolition as dangerous and wicked in the extreme, yet he did not feel himself authorized to vote for the resolutions. If the doctrines contained in them were correct, then nullification was correct; and if passed might hereafter be appealed to as a precedent in favor of that doctrine; though he acquitted the senator [Mr. CALHOUN] of having the most remote intention of smuggling in any thing in relation to that doctrine under cover of these resolutions."

Mr. Calhoun, annoyed by so much condemnation of his course, and especially from those as determined as himself to protect the slave institution where it legally existed, spoke often and warmly; and justified his course from the greatness of the danger, and the fatal consequences to the Union if it was not arrested.

"I fear (said Mr. C.) that the Senate has not elevated its view sufficiently to comprehend the extent and magnitude of the existing danger. It was perhaps his misfortune to look too much to the future, and to move against dangers at too great a distance, which had involved him in many difficulties and exposed him often to the imputation of unworthy motives. Thus he had long foreseen the immense surplus revenue which a false system of legislation must pour into the Treasury, and the fatal consequences to the morals and institutions of the country which must follow. When nothing else could arrest it he threw himself, with his State, into the breach, to arrest dangers which could not otherwise be arrested; whether wisely or not he left posterity to judge. He now saw with equal clearness—as clear as the noonday sun—the fatal consequences which must follow if the present disease be not timely arrested. He would repeat again what he had so often said on this floor. This was the only question of sufficient magnitude and potency to divide this Union; and divide it it would, or drench the country in blood, if not arrested. He knew how much the sentiment he had uttered would be misconstrued and misrepresented. There were those who saw no danger to the Union in the violation of all its fundamental principles, but who were full of apprehension when danger was foretold or resisted, and who held not the authors of the danger, but those who forewarned or opposed it, responsible for consequences."

"But the cry of disunion by the weak or designing had no terror for him. If his attachment to the Union was less, he might tamper with the deep disease which now afflicts the body politic, and keep silent till the patient was ready to sink under its mortal blows. It is a cheap, and he must say but too certain a mode of acquiring the character of devoted attachment to the Union. But, seeing the danger as he did, he would be a traitor to the Union and those he represented to keep silence. The assaults daily made on the institutions of nearly one half of the States of this Union by the other—institutions interwoven from the beginning with their political and social existence, and which cannot be other than that without their inevitable destruction—will and must, if continued, *make two people of one* by destroying every sympathy between the two great sections—obliterating from their hearts the recollection of their common danger and glory—and implanting in their place a mutual hatred, more deadly than ever existed between two neighboring people since the commencement of the human race. He feared not the circulation of the thousands of incendiary and slanderous publications which were daily issued from an organized and powerful press among those intended to be vilified. They cannot penetrate our section; that was not the danger; it lay in a different direction. Their circulation in the non-slaveholding States was what was to be dreaded. It was infusing a deadly poison into the minds of the rising generation, implanting in them feelings of hatred, the most deadly hatred, instead of affection and love, for one half of this Union, to be returned, on their part, with equal detestation. The fatal, the immutable consequences, if not arrested, and that without delay, were such as he had presented. The first and desirable object is to arrest it in the non-slaveholding States; to meet the disease where it originated and where it exists; and the first step to this is to find some common constitutional ground on which a rally, with that object, can be made. These resolutions present the ground, and the only one, on which it can be made. The only remedy is in the State rights doctrines; and if those who profess them in slaveholding States do not rally on them as their political creed, and organize as a party against the fanatics in order to put them down, the South and West will be compelled to take the remedy into their own hands. They will then stand justified in the sight of God and man; and what in that event will follow no mortal can anticipate. Mr. President (said Mr. C.), we are reposing on a volcano. The Senate seems entirely ignorant of the state of feeling in the South. The mail has just brought us intelligence of a most important step taken by one of the Southern States in connection with this subject, which will give some conception of the tone of feeling which begins to prevail in that quarter."

It was such speaking as this that induced some votes against the resolutions. All the senators were dissatisfied at the constant exhibition of the same remedy (disunion), for all the diseases of the body politic; but the greater part deemed it right, if they voted at all, to vote their real sentiments. Many were disposed to lay the resolutions on the table, as the disturbing petitions had been; but it was concluded that policy made it preferable to vote upon them.

Mr. BENTON did not speak in this debate. He believed, as others did, that discussion was injurious; that it was the way to keep up and extend agitation, and the thing above all others which the abolitionists desired. Discussion upon the floor of the American Senate was to them the concession of an immense advantage—the concession of an elevated and commanding theatre for the display and dissemination of their doctrines. It gave them the point to stand upon from which they could reach every part of the Union; and it gave them the *Register of the Debates*, instead of their local papers, for their organ of communication. Mr. Calhoun was a fortunate customer for them.

The Senate, in laying all their petitions and the memorial of Vermont on the table without debate, signified its desire to yield them no such advantage. The introduction of Mr. Calhoun's resolution frustrated that desire, and induced many to do what they condemned. Mr. Benton took his own sense of the proper course, in abstaining from debate, and confining the expression of his opinions to the delivery of votes: and in that he conformed to the *sense* of the Senate, and the *action* of the House of Representatives. Many hundreds of these petitions were presented in the House, and quietly laid upon the table (after a stormy scene, and the adoption of a new rule), under motions to that effect; and this would have been the case in the Senate, had it not been for the resolutions, the introduction of which was so generally deprecated.

The part of this debate which excited no attention at the time, but has since acquired a momentous importance, is that part in which Mr. Calhoun declared his favorable disposition to the Missouri compromise, and his condemnation of Mr. Randolph (its chief opponent), for opposing it; and his change of opinion since, not for unconstitutionality, but because he believed it to have become dangerous in encouraging the spirit of abolitionism. This compromise was the highest, the most solemn, the most momentous, the most emphatic assertion of Congressional power over slavery in a territory which had ever been made, or could be conceived. It not only abolished slavery where it legally existed; but for ever prohibited it where it had long existed, and that over an extent of territory larger than the area of all the Atlantic slave States put together: and thus yielding to the free States the absolute predominance in the Union.

Mr. Calhoun was for that resolution in 1820,—blamed those who opposed it; and could see no objection to it in 1838 but the encouragement it gave to the spirit of abolitionism. Nine years afterwards (session of 1846-'47) he submitted other resolutions (five in number) on the same power of Congress over slavery legislation in the territories; in which he denied the power, and asserted that any such legislation to the prejudice of the slaveholding emigrants from the States, in preventing them from removing, with their slave property, to such territory, "would be a violation of the constitution and the rights of the States from which such citizens emigrated, and a derogation of that perfect equality which belongs to them as members of this Union; *and would tend directly to subvert the Union itself.*"

These resolutions, so new and startling in their doctrines—so contrary to their antecessors, and to the whole course of the government—were denounced by the writer of this View the instant they were read in the Senate, and, being much discountenanced by other senators, they were never pressed to a vote in that body; but were afterwards adopted by some of the slave State legislatures. One year afterwards, in a debate on the Oregon territorial bill, and on the section which proposed to declare the anti-slavery clause of the ordinance of 1787 to be in force in that territory, Mr. Calhoun denied the power of Congress to make any such declaration, or in any way to legislate upon slavery in a territory. He delivered a most elaborate and thoroughly considered speech on the subject, in the course of which he laid down three propositions:

1. That Congress had no power to legislate upon slavery in a territory, so as to prevent the citizens of slaveholding States from removing into it with their slave property. 2. That Congress had no power to delegate such authority to a territory. 3. That the territory had no such power in itself (thus leaving the subject of slavery in a territory without any legislative power over it at all). He deduced these dogmas from a new insight into the constitution, which, according to this fresh introspection, recognized slavery as a national institution, and carried that part of itself (by its own vigor) into all the territories; and protected slavery there: *ergo*, neither Congress, nor its deputed territorial legislature, nor the people of the territory during their territorial condition, could any way touch the subject—either to affirm, or disaffirm the institution. He endeavored to obtain from Congress a crutch to aid these lame doctrines in limping into the territories by getting the constitution voted into them, as part of their organic law; and, failing in that attempt (repeatedly made), he took position on the ground that the constitution went into these possessions of itself, so far as slavery was concerned, it being a national institution.

These three propositions being in flagrant conflict with the power exercised by Congress in the establishment of the Missouri compromise line (which had become a tradition as a Southern measure, supported by Southern members of Congress, and sanctioned by the cabinet of Mr. Monroe, of which Mr. Calhoun was a member), the fact of that compromise and his concurrence in it was immediately used against him by Senator Dix, of New York, to invalidate his present opinions.

Unfortunately he had forgotten this cabinet consultation, and his own concurrence in its decision—believing fully that no such thing had occurred, and adhering firmly to the new dogma of total denial of all constitutional power in Congress to legislate upon slavery in a territory. This brought up recollections to sustain the tradition which told of the consultation—to show that it took place—that its voice was unanimous in favor of the compromise; and, consequently, that Mr. Calhoun himself was in favor of it. Old writings were produced:

First, a *fac simile* copy of an original paper in Mr. Monroe's handwriting, found among his manuscripts, dated March 4, 1820 (two days before the approval of the Missouri compromise act), and indorsed: "Interrogatories—Missouri—to the Heads of Departments and the Attorney-General;" and containing within two questions: "1. Has Congress a right, under the powers vested in it by the constitution, to make a regulation prohibiting slavery in a territory? 2. Is the 8th section of the act which passed both Houses of Congress on the 3d instant for the admission of Missouri into the Union, consistent with the constitution?" *Secondly*, the draft of an original letter in Mr. Monroe's handwriting, but without signature, date, or address, but believed to have been addressed to General Jackson, in which he says: "The question which lately agitated Congress and the public has been settled, as you have seen, by the passage of an act for the admission of Missouri as a State, unrestricted, and Arkansas, also, when it reaches maturity; and the establishment of the parallel of 36 degrees 30 minutes as a line north of which slavery is prohibited, and permitted south of it. I took the opinion, in writing, of the administration as to the constitutionality of restraining territories, which was explicit in favor of it, and, as it was, that the 8th section of the act was applicable to territories only, and not to States when they should be admitted into the Union." *Thirdly*, an extract from the diary of Mr. John Quincy Adams, under date of the 3d of March, 1820, stating that the President on that day assembled his cabinet to ask their opinions on the two questions mentioned—which the whole cabinet immediately answered unanimously, and affirmatively; that on the 5th he sent the questions in writing to the members of his cabinet, to receive their written answers, to be filed in the department of State; and that on the 6th he took his own answer to the President, to be filed with the rest—all agreeing in the affirmative, and only differing some in assigning, others not assigning reasons for his opinion. The diary states that the President signed his approval of the Missouri act on the 6th (which the act shows he did), and requested Mr. Adams to have all the opinions filed in the department of State.

Upon this evidence it would have rested without question that Mr. Monroe's cabinet had been consulted on the constitutionality of the Missouri compromise line, and that all concurred in it, had it not been for the denial of Mr. Calhoun in the debate on the Oregon territorial bill. His denial brought out this evidence; and, notwithstanding its production and conclusiveness, he adhered tenaciously to his disbelief of the whole occurrence and especially the whole of his own imputed share in it. Two circumstances, specious in themselves, favored this denial: *first*, that no such papers as those described by Mr. Adams were to be found in the department of State; *secondly*, that in the original draft of Mr. Monroe's letter it had first been written that the affirmative answers of his cabinet to his two interrogatories were "*unanimous*" which word had been crossed out and "*explicit*" substituted.

With some these two circumstances weighed nothing against the testimony of two witnesses, and the current corroborating incidents of tradition. In the lapse of twenty-seven years, and in the changes to which our cabinet officers and the clerks of departments are subjected, it was easy to believe that the papers had been mislaid or lost—far easier than to believe that Mr. Adams could have been mistaken in the entry made in his diary at the time. And as to the substitution of "explicit" for "unanimous," that was known to be necessary in order to avoid the violation of the rule which forbid the disclosure of individual opinions in the cabinet consultations. With others, and especially with the political friends of Mr. Calhoun, they were received as full confirmation of his denial, and left them at liberty to accept his present opinions as those of his whole life, uninvalidated by previous personal discrepancy, and uncounteracted by the weight of a cabinet decision under Mr. Monroe: and accordingly the new-born dogma of *no power in Congress to legislate upon the existence of slavery in the territories* became an article of political faith, incorporated in the creed, and that for action, of a large political party. What is now brought to light of the proceedings in the Senate in '37-'38 shows this to have been a mistake—that Mr. Calhoun admitted the power in 1820, when he favored the compromise and blamed Mr. Randolph for opposing it; that he admitted it again in 1838, when he submitted his own resolutions, and voted for those of Mr. Clay. It so happened that no one recollected these proceedings of '37-'38 at the time of the Oregon debate of '47-'48. The writer of this View, though possessing a memory credited as tenacious, did not recollect them, nor remember them at all, until found among the materials collected for this history—a circumstance which he attributes to his repugnance to the whole debate, and taking no part in the proceedings except to vote.

The cabinet consultation of 1820 was not mentioned by Mr. Calhoun in his avowal of 1838, nor is it necessary to the object of this View to pursue his connection with that private executive counselling. The only material inquiry is as to his approval of the Missouri compromise at the time it was adopted; and that is fully established by himself.

It would be a labor unworthy of history to look up the conduct of any public man, and trace him through shifting scenes, with a mere view to personal effect—with a mere view to personal disparagement, by showing him contradictory and inconsistent at some period of his course. Such a labor would be idle, unprofitable, and derogatory; but, when a change takes place in a public man's opinions which leads to a change of conduct, and into a new line of action disastrous to the country, it becomes the duty of history to note the fact, and to expose the contradiction—not for personal disparagement—but to counteract the force of the new and dangerous opinion.

In this sense it becomes an obligatory task to show the change, or rather changes, in Mr. Calhoun's opinions on the constitutional power of Congress over the existence of slavery in the national territories; and these changes have been great—too great to admit of followers if they had been known. *First*, fully admitting the power, and justifying its exercise in the largest and highest possible case. *Next*, admitting the power, but deprecating its exercise in certain limited, specified, qualified cases. *Then*, denying it in a limited and specified case. *Finally*, denying the power any where, and every where, either in Congress, or in the territorial legislature as its delegate, or in the people as sovereign. The last of these mutations, or rather the one before the last (for there are but few who can go the whole length of the three propositions in the Oregon speech), has been adopted by a large political party and acted upon; and with deplorable effect to the country. Holding the Missouri compromise to have been unconstitutional, they have abrogated it as a nullity; and in so doing have done more to disturb the harmony of this Union, to unsettle its foundations, to shake its stability, and to prepare the two halves of the Union for parting, than any act, or all acts put together, since the commencement of the federal government. This lamentable act could not have been done,—could not have found a party to do it,—if Mr. Calhoun had not changed his opinion on the constitutionality of the Missouri compromise line; or if he could have recollected in 1848 that he approved that line in 1820; and further remembered, that he saw nothing unconstitutional in it as late as 1838. The change being now shown, and the imperfection of his memory made manifest by his own testimony, it becomes certain that the new doctrine was an after-thought, disowned by its antecedents—a figment of the brain lately hatched—and which its author would have been estopped from promulgating if these antecedents had been recollected. History now pleads them as an estoppel against his followers.

Mr. Monroe, in his letter to General Jackson, immediately after the establishment of the Missouri compromise, said that that compromise settled the slavery agitation which threatened to break up the Union. Thirty-four years of quiet and harmony under that settlement bear witness to the truth of these words, spoken in the fulness of patriotic gratitude at seeing his country escape from a great danger. The year 1854 has seen the abrogation of that compromise; and with its abrogation the revival of the agitation, and with a force and fury never known before: and now may be seen in fact what was hypothetically foreseen by Mr. Calhoun in 1838, when, as the fruit of this agitation, he saw the destruction of all sympathy between the two sections of the Union—obliteration from the memory of all proud recollections of former common danger and glory—hatred in the hearts of the North and the South, more deadly than ever existed between two neighboring nations. May we not have to witness the remainder of his prophetic vision—"TWO PEOPLE MADE OF ONE!"

P.S.—After this chapter had been written, the author received authentic information that, during the time that John M. Clayton, Esq. of Delaware, was Secretary of State under President Taylor (1849-50), evidence had been found in the Department of State, of the fact, that the opinion of Mr. Calhoun and of the rest of Mr. Monroe's cabinet, had been filed there. In consequence a note of inquiry was addressed to Mr. Clayton, who answered (under date of July 19th, 1855) as follows:

"In reply to your inquiry I have to state that I have no recollection of having ever met with Mr. Calhoun's answer to Mr. Monroe's cabinet queries, as to the constitutionality of the Missouri compromise. It had not been found while I was in the department of state, as I was then informed: but the archives of the department disclose the fact, that Mr. Calhoun, and other members of the cabinet, did answer Mr. Monroe's questions. It appears by an index that these answers were filed among the archives of that department. I was told they had been abstracted from the records, and could not be found; but I did not make a search for them myself. I have never doubted that Mr. Calhoun at least acquiesced in the decision of the cabinet of that day. Since I left the Department of State I have heard it rumored that Mr. Calhoun's answer to Mr. Monroe's queries had been found; but I know not upon what authority the statement was made."

CHAPTER XXXIV.

DEATH OF COMMODORE RODGERS, AND NOTICE OF HIS LIFE AND CHARACTER.

My idea of the perfect naval commander had been formed from history, and from the study of such characters as the Von Tromps and De Ruyters of Holland, the Blakes of England, and the De Tourvilles of France—men modest and virtuous, frank and sincere, brave and patriotic, gentle in peace, terrible in war; formed for high command by nature; and raising themselves to their proper sphere by their own exertions from low beginnings. When I first saw Commodore RODGERS, which was after I had reached senatorial age and station, he recalled to me the idea of those model admirals; and subsequent acquaintance confirmed the impression then made. He was to me the complete impersonation of my idea of the perfect naval commander—person, mind, and manners; with the qualities for command grafted on the groundwork of a good citizen and good father of a family; and all lodged in a frame to bespeak the seaman and the officer.

His very figure and face were those of the naval hero—such as we conceive from naval songs and ballads; and, from the course of life which the sea officer leads—exposed to the double peril of waves and war, and contending with the storms of the elements as well as with the storm of battle. We associate the idea of bodily power with such a life; and when we find them united—the heroic qualities in a frame of powerful muscular development—we experience a gratified feeling of completeness, which fulfils a natural expectation, and leaves nothing to be desired. And when the same great qualities are found, as they often are, in the man of slight and slender frame, it requires some effort of reason to conquer a feeling of surprise at a combination which is a contrast, and which presents so much power in a frame so little promising it; and hence all poets and orators, all painters and sculptors, all the dealers in imaginary perfections, give a corresponding figure of strength and force to the heroes they create.

Commodore Rodgers needed no help from the creative imagination to endow him with the form which naval heroism might require. His person was of the middle height, stout, square, solid, compact; well-proportioned; and combining in the perfect degree the idea of strength and endurance with the reality of manly comeliness—the statue of Mars, in the rough state, before the conscious chisel had lent the last polish. His face, stern in the outline, was relieved by a gentle and benign expression—grave with the overshadowing of an ample and capacious forehead and eyebrows. Courage need not be named among the qualities of Americans; the question would be to find one without it. His skill, enterprise, promptitude and talent for command, were shown in the war of 1812 with Great Britain; in the *quasi* war of 1799 with the French Republic—*quasi* only as it concerned political relations, real as it concerned desperate and brilliant combats at sea; and in the Mediterranean wars with the Barbary States, when those States were formidable in that sea and held Europe under tribute; and which tribute from the United States was relinquished by Tripoli and Tunis at the end of the war with these States—Commodore Rodgers commanding at the time as successor to Barron and Preble. It was at the end of this war, 1804, so valiantly conducted and so triumphantly concluded, that the reigning Pope, Pius the Seventh, publicly declared that America had done more for Christendom against the Barbary States, than all the powers of Europe combined.

He was first lieutenant on the Constellation when that frigate, under Truxton, vanquished and captured the French frigate Insurgent; and great as his merit was in the action, where he showed himself to be the proper second to an able commander, it was greater in what took place after it; and in which steadiness, firmness, humanity, vigilance, endurance, and seamanship, were carried to their highest pitch; and in all which his honors were shared by the then stripling midshipman, afterwards the brilliant Commodore Porter.

The Insurgent having struck, and part of her crew been transferred to the Constellation, Lieut. Rodgers and Midshipman Porter were on board the prize, superintending the transfer, when a tempest arose—the ships parted—and dark night came on. There were still one hundred and seventy-three French prisoners on board. The two young officers had but eleven men—thirteen in all—to guard thirteen times their number; and work a crippled frigate at the same time, and get her into port. And nobly did they do it. For three days and nights did these thirteen (though fresh from a bloody conflict which strained every faculty and brought demands for rest), without sleep or repose, armed to the teeth, watching with eye and ear, stand to the arduous duty—sailing their ship, restraining their prisoners, solacing the wounded—ready to kill, and hurting no one. They did not sail at random, or for the nearest port; but, faithful to the orders of their commander, given under different circumstances, steered for St. Kitts, in the West Indies—arrived there safely—and were received with triumph and admiration.

Such an exploit equalled any fame that could be gained in battle; for it brought into requisition all the qualities for command which high command requires; and foreshadowed the future eminence of these two young officers. What firmness, steadiness, vigilance, endurance, and courage—far above that which the battle-field requires! and one of these young officers, a slight and slender lad, as frail to the look as the other was powerful; and yet each acting his part with the same heroic steadiness and perseverance, coolness and humanity! They had no irons to secure a single man. The one hundred and seventy-three French were loose in the lower hold, a sentinel only at each gangway; and vigilance, and readiness to use their arms, the only resource of the little crew. If history has a parallel to this deed I have not seen it; and to value it in all its extent, it must be remembered that these prisoners were Frenchmen—their inherent courage exalted by the frenzy of the revolution—themselves fresh from a murderous conflict—the decks of the ship still red and slippery with the blood of their comrades; and they with a right, both legal and moral, to recover their liberty if they could. These three days and nights, still more than the victory which preceded them, earned for Rodgers the captaincy, and for Porter the lieutenancy, with which they were soon respectively honored.

American cruisers had gained credit in the war of the Revolution, and in the *quasi* war with the French Republic; and American squadrons had bearded the Barbary Powers in their dens, after chasing their piratical vessels from the seas: but a war with Great Britain, with her one thousand and sixty vessels of war on her naval list, and above seven hundred of these for service, her fleets swelled with the ships of all nations, exalted with the idea of invincibility, and one hundred and twenty guns on the decks of her first-class men-of-war—any naval contest with such a power, with seventeen vessels for the sea, ranging from twelve to forty-four guns (which was the totality which the American naval register could then show), seemed an insanity. And insanity it would have been with even twenty times as many vessels, and double their number of guns, if naval battles with rival fleets had been intended. Fortunately we had naval officers at that time who understood the virtue of cruising, and believed they could do what Paul Jones and others had done during the war of the Revolution.

Political men believed nothing could be done at sea but to lose the few vessels which we had; that even cruising was out of the question. Of our seventeen vessels, the whole were in port but one; and it was determined to keep them there, and the one at sea with them, if it had the luck to get in. I am under no obligation to make the admission, but I am free to acknowledge, that I was one of those who supposed that there was no salvation for our seventeen men-of-war but to run them as far up the creek as possible, place them under the guns of batteries, and collect camps of militia about them, to keep off the British. This was the policy at the day of the declaration of the war; and I have the less concern to admit myself to have been participator in the delusion, because I claim the merit of having profited from experience—happy if I could transmit the lesson to posterity. Two officers came to Washington—Bainbridge and Stewart. They spoke with Mr. Madison, and urged the feasibility of cruising. One-half of the whole number of the British men-of-war were under the class of frigates, consequently no more than matches for some of our seventeen; the whole of her merchant marine (many thousands) were subject to capture. Here was a rich field for cruising; and the two officers, for themselves and brothers, boldly proposed to enter it.

Mr. Madison had seen the efficiency of cruising and privateering, even against Great Britain, and in our then infantile condition, during the war of the Revolution; and besides was a man of sense, and amenable to judgment and reason. He listened to the two experienced and valiant officers; and, without consulting Congress, which perhaps would have been a fatal consultation (for multitude of counsellors is not the council for *bold* decision), reversed the policy which had been resolved upon; and, in his supreme character of constitutional commander of the army and navy, ordered every ship that could cruise to get to sea as soon as possible. This I had from Mr. Monroe, and it is due to Mr. Madison to tell it, who, without pretending to a military character, had the merit of sanctioning this most vital war measure.

Commodore Rodgers was then in New York, in command of the President (44), intended for a part of the harbor defence of that city. Within one hour after he had received his cruising orders, he was under way. This was the 21st of June. That night he got information of the Jamaica fleet (merchantmen), homeward bound; and crowded all sail in the direction they had gone, following the Gulf Stream towards the east of Newfoundland. While on this track, on the 23d, a British frigate was perceived far to the northeast, and getting further off. It was a nobler object than a fleet of merchantmen, and chase was immediately given her, and she gained upon; but not fast enough to get alongside before night.

It was four o'clock in the evening, and the enemy in range of the bow-chasers. Commodore Rodgers determined to cripple her, and diminish her speed; and so come up with her. He pointed the first gun himself, and pointed it well. The shot struck the frigate in her rudder coat, drove through her stern frame, and passed into the gun-room. It was the first gun fired during the war; and was no waste of ammunition. Second Lieutenant Gamble, commander of the battery, pointed and discharged the second—hitting and damaging one of the enemy's stern chasers. Commodore Rodgers fired the third—hitting the stern again, and killing and wounding six men. Mr. Gamble fired again. The gun bursted! killing and wounding sixteen of her own men, blowing up the Commodore—who fell with a broken leg upon the deck. The pause in working the guns on that side, occasioned by this accident, enabled the enemy to bring some stern guns to bear, and to lighten his vessel to increase her speed. He cut away his anchors, stove and threw overboard his boats, and started fourteen tons of water. Thus lightened, he escaped. It was the Belvidera, 36 guns, Captain Byron. The President would have taken her with all ease if she had got alongside; and of that the English captain showed himself duly, and excusably sensible.

The frigate having escaped, the Commodore, regardless of his broken leg, hauled up to its course in pursuit of the Jamaica fleet, and soon got information that it consisted of eighty-five sail, and was under convoy of four men-of-war; one of them a two-decker, another a frigate; and that he was on its track. Passing Newfoundland and finding the sea well sprinkled with the signs of West India fruit—orange peels, cocoanut shells, pine-apple rinds, &c.—the Commodore knew himself to be in the wake of the fleet, and made every exertion to come up with it before it could reach the chops of the channel: but in vain. When almost in sight of the English coast, and no glimpse obtained of the fleet, he was compelled to tack, run south: and, after an extended cruise, return to the United States.

The Commodore had missed the two great objects of his ambition—the fleet and the frigate; but the cruise was not barren either in material or moral results. Seven British merchantmen were captured—one American recaptured—the English coast had been approached. With impunity an American frigate—one of those insultingly styled "fir-built, with a bit of striped bunting at her mast-head,"—had almost looked into that narrow channel which is considered the sanctum of a British ship. An alarm had been spread, and a squadron of seven men-of-war (four of them frigates and one a sixty-four gun ship) were assembled to capture him; one of them the Belvidera, which had escaped at the bursting of the President's gun, and spread the news of her being at sea.

It was a great honor to Commodore Rodgers to send such a squadron to look after him; and became still greater to Captain Hull, in the Constitution, who escaped from it after having been almost surrounded by it. It was evening when this captain began to fall in with that squadron, and at daylight found himself almost encompassed by it—three ahead and four astern. Then began that chase which continued seventy-two hours, in which seven pursued one, and seemed often on the point of closing on their prize; in which every means of progress, from reefed topsails to kedging and towing, was put into requisition by either party—the one to escape, the other to overtake; in which the stern-chasers of one were often replying to the bow-chasers of the other; and the greatest precision of manœuvring required to avoid falling under the guns of some while avoiding those of others; and which ended with putting an escape on a level with a great victory. Captain Hull brought his vessel safe into port, and without the sacrifice of her equipment—not an anchor having been cut away, boat stove, or gun thrown overboard to gain speed by lightening the vessel. It was a brilliant result, with all the moral effects of victory, and a splendid vindication of the policy of cruising—showing that we had seamanship to escape the force which we could not fight.

Commodore Rodgers made another extended cruise during this war, a circuit of eight thousand miles, traversing the high seas, coasting the shores of both continents, searching wherever the cruisers or merchantmen of the enemy were expected to be found; capturing what was within his means, avoiding the rest. A British government packet, with nearly $300,000 in specie, was taken; many merchantmen were taken; and, though an opportunity did not offer to engage a frigate of equal or nearly equal force, and to gain one of those electrifying victories for which our cruisers were so remarkable, yet the moral effect was great—demonstrating the ample capacity of an American frigate to go where she pleased in spite of the "thousand ships of war" of the assumed mistress of the seas; carrying damage and alarm to the foe, and avoiding misfortune to itself.

At the attempt of the British upon Baltimore Commodore Rodgers was in command of the maritime defences of that city, and, having no means of contending with the British fleet in the bay, he assembled all the seamen of the ships-of-war and of the flotilla, and entered judiciously into the combinations for the land defence.

Humane feeling was a characteristic of this brave officer, and was verified in all the relations of his life, and in his constant conduct. Standing on the bank of the Susquehanna river, at Havre de Grace, one cold winter day, the river flooded and filled with floating ice, he saw (with others), at a long distance, a living object—discerned to be a human being—carried down the stream. He ventured in, against all remonstrance, and brought the object safe to shore. It was a colored woman—to him a human being, doomed to a frightful death unless relieved; and heroically relieved at the peril of his own life. He was humane in battle. That was shown in the affair of the Little Belt—chased, hailed, fought (the year before the war), and compelled to answer the hail, and tell who she was, with expense of blood, and largely; but still the smallest possible quantity that would accomplish the purpose. The encounter took place in the night, and because the British captain would not answer the American hail. Judging from the inferiority of her fire that he was engaged with an unequal antagonist, the American Commodore suspended his own fire, while still receiving broadsides from his arrogant little adversary; and only resumed it when indispensable to his own safety, and the enforcement of the question which he had put. An answer was obtained after thirty-one had been killed or wounded on board the British vessel; and this at six leagues from the American coast: and, the doctrine of no right to stop a vessel on the high seas to ascertain her character not having been then invented, no political consequence followed this bloody enforcement of maritime police—exasperated against each other as the two nations were at the time.

At the death of Decatur, killed in that lamentable duel, I have heard Mr. Randolph tell, and he alone could tell it, of the agony of Rodgers as he stood over his dying friend, in bodily contention with his own grief—convulsed within, calm without; and keeping down the struggling anguish of the soul by dint of muscular power.

That feeling heart was doomed to suffer a great agony in the untimely death of a heroic son, emulating the generous devotion of the father, and perishing in the waves, in vain efforts to save comrades more exhausted than himself; and to whom he nobly relinquished the means of his own safety. It was spared another grief of a kindred nature (not having lived to see it), in the death of another heroic son, lost in the sloop-of-war Albany, in one of those calamitous founderings at sea in which the mystery of an unseen fate deepens the shades of death, and darkens the depths of sorrow—leaving the hearts of far distant friends a prey to a long agony of hope and fear—only to be solved in an agony still deeper.

Commodore Rodgers died at the head of the American navy, without having seen the rank of Admiral established in our naval service, for which I voted when senator, and hoped to have seen conferred on him, and on others who have done so much to exalt the name of their country; and which rank I deem essential to the good of the service, even in the cruising system I deem alone suitable to us.

CHAPTER XXXV.

ANTI-DUELLING ACT.

The death of Mr. Jonathan Cilley, a representative in Congress from the State of Maine, killed in a duel with rifles, with Mr. Graves of Kentucky, led to the passage of an act with severe penalties against duelling, in the District of Columbia, or out of it upon agreement within the District. The penalties were—death to all the survivors, when any one was killed: a five years imprisonment in the penitentiary for giving or accepting a challenge. Like all acts passed under a sudden excitement, this act was defective, and more the result of good intentions than of knowledge of human nature. Passions of the mind, like diseases of the body, are liable to break out in a different form when suppressed in the one they had assumed. No physician suppresses an eruption without considering what is to become of the virus which is escaping, if stopped and confined to the body: no legislator should suppress an evil without considering whether a worse one is at the same time planted. I was a young member of the general assembly of Tennessee (1809), when a most worthy member (Mr. Robert C. Foster), took credit to himself for having put down billiard tables in Nashville. Another most worthy member (General Joseph Dixon) asked him how many card tables he had put up in their place? This was a side of the account to which the suppressor of billiard tables had not looked: and which opened up a view of serious consideration to every person intrusted with the responsible business of legislation—a business requiring so much knowledge of human nature, and so seldom invoking the little we possess. It has been on my mind ever since; and I have had constant occasions to witness its disregard—and seldom more lamentably than in the case of this anti-duelling act. It looked to one evil, and saw nothing else. It did not look to the assassinations, under the pretext of self-defence, which were to rise up in place of the regular duel. Certainly it is deplorable to see a young man, the hope of his father and mother—a ripe man, the head of a family—an eminent man, necessary to his country—struck down in the duel; and should be prevented if possible. Still this deplorable practice is not so bad as the bowie knife, and the revolver, and their pretext of self-defence—thirsting for blood. In the duel, there is at least consent on both sides, with a preliminary opportunity for settlement, with a chance for the law to arrest them, and room for the interposition of friends as the affair goes on. There is usually equality of terms; and it would not be called an affair of honor, if honor was not to prevail all round; and if the satisfying a point of honor, and not vengeance, was the end to be attained. Finally, in the regular duel, the principals are in the hands of the seconds (for no man can be made a second without his consent); and as both these are required by the duelling code (for the sake of fairness and humanity), to be free from ill will or grudge towards the adversary principal, they are expected to terminate the affair as soon as the point of honor is satisfied—and, the less the injury, so much the better. The only exception to these rules is, where the principals are in such relations to each other as to admit of no accommodation, and the injury such as to admit of no compromise. In the knife and revolver business, all this is different. There is no preliminary interval for settlement—no chance for officers of justice to intervene—no room for friends to interpose. Instead of equality of terms, every advantage is sought. Instead of consent, the victim is set upon at the most unguarded moment. Instead of satisfying a point of honor, it is vengeance to be glutted. Nor does the difference stop with death. In the duel, the unhurt principal scorns to continue the combat upon his disabled adversary: in the knife and revolver case, the hero of these weapons continues firing and stabbing while the prostrate body of the dying man gives a sign of life. In the duel the survivor never assails the character of the fallen: in the knife and revolver case, the first movement of the victor is to attack the character of his victim—to accuse him of an intent to murder; and to make out a case of self-defence, by making out a case of premeditated attack against the other. And in such false accusation, the French proverb is usually verified—*the dead and the absent are always in the wrong.*

The anti-duelling act did not suppress the passions in which duels originate: it only suppressed one mode, and that the least revolting, in which these passions could manifest themselves. It did not suppress the homicidal intent—but gave it a new form: and now many members of Congress go into their seats with deadly weapons under their garments—ready to insult with foul language, and prepared to kill if the language is resented. The act should have pursued the homicidal intent into whatever form it might assume; and, therefore, should have been made to include all unjustifiable homicides.

The law was also mistaken in the nature of its penalties: they are not of a kind to be enforced, if incurred. It is in vain to attempt to punish more ignominiously, and more severely, a duel than an assassination. The offences, though both great, are of very different degrees; and human nature will recognize the difference though the law may not: and the result will be seen in the conduct of juries, and in the temper of the pardoning power. A species of penalty unknown to the common law, and rejected by it, and only held good when a man was the vassal of his lord—the dogma that the private injury to the family is merged in the public wrong—this species of penalty (amends to the family) is called for by the progress of homicides in our country; and not as a substitute for the death penalty, but cumulative. Under this dogma, a small injury to a man's person brings him a moneyed indemnity; in the greatest of all injuries, that of depriving a family of its support and protector, no compensation is allowed. This is preposterous, and leads to deadly consequences. It is cheaper now to kill a man, than to hurt him; and, accordingly, the preparation is generally to kill, and not to hurt. The frequency, the wantonness, the barbarity, the cold-blooded cruelty, and the demoniac levity with which homicides are committed with us, have become the opprobrium of our country. An incredible number of persons, and in all parts of the country, seem to have taken the code of Draco for their law, and their own will for its execution—kill for every offence. The death penalty, prescribed by divine wisdom, is hardly a scare-crow. Some States have abolished it by statute—some communities, virtually, by a mawkish sentimentality: and every where, the jury being the judge of the law as well as of the fact, find themselves pretty much in a condition to do as they please. And unanimity among twelve being required, as in the English law, instead of a concurrence of three-fifths in fifteen, as in the Scottish law, it is in the power of one or two men to prevent a conviction, even in the most flagrant cases. In this deluge of bloodshed some new remedy is called for in addition to the death penalty; and it may be best found in the principle of compensation to the family of the slain, recoverable in every case where the homicide was not justifiable under the written laws of the land. In this wide-spread custom of carrying deadly weapons, often leading to homicides where there was no previous intent, some check should be put on a practice so indicative of a bad heart—a heart void of social duty, and fatally bent on mischief; and this check may be found in making the fact of having such arms on the person an offence in itself, *prima facie* evidence of malice, and to be punished cumulatively by the judge; and that without regard to the fact whether used or not in the affray.

The anti-duelling act of 1839 was, therefore, defective in not pursuing the homicidal offence into all the new forms it might assume; in not giving damages to a bereaved family—and not punishing the carrying of the weapon, whether used or not—only accommodating the degree of punishment to the more or less use that had been made of it. In the Halls of Congress it should be an offence, in itself, whether drawn or not, subjecting the offender to all the penalties for a high misdemeanor—removal from office—disqualification to hold any office of trust or profit under the United States—and indictment at law besides.

———————————————

CHAPTER XXXVI.

SLAVERY AGITATION IN THE HOUSE OF REPRESENTATIVES, AND RETIRING OF SOUTHERN MEMBERS FROM THE HALL.

The most angry and portentous debate which had yet taken place in Congress, occurred at this time in the House of Representatives. It was brought on by Mr. William Slade, of Vermont, who, besides presenting petitions of the usual abolition character, and moving to refer them to a committee, moved their reference to a select committee, with instructions to report a bill in conformity to their prayer. This motion, inflammatory and irritating in itself, and without practical legislative object, as the great majority of the House was known to be opposed to it, was rendered still more exasperating by the manner of supporting it. The mover entered into a general disquisition on the subject of slavery, all denunciatory, and was proceeding to speak upon it in the State of Virginia, and other States, in the same spirit, when Mr. Legare, of South Carolina, interposed, and—

"Hoped the gentleman from Vermont would allow him to make a few remarks before he proceeded further. He sincerely hoped that gentleman would consider well what he was about before he ventured on such ground, and that he would take time to consider what might be its probable consequences. He solemnly entreated him to reflect on the possible results of such a course, which involved the interests of a nation and a continent. He would warn him, not in the language of defiance, which all brave and wise men despised, but he would warn him in the language of a solemn sense of duty, that if there was 'a spirit aroused in the North in relation to this subject,' that spirit would encounter another spirit in the South full as stubborn. He would tell them that, when this question was forced upon the people of the South, they would be ready to take up the gauntlet. He concluded by urging on the gentleman from Vermont to ponder well on his course before he ventured to proceed."

Mr. Slade continued his remarks when Mr. Dawson of Georgia, asked him for the floor, that he might move an adjournment—evidently to carry off the storm which he saw rising. Mr. Slade refused to yield it; so the motion to adjourn could not be made. Mr. Slade continued, and was proceeding to answer his own inquiry put to himself—*what was Slavery?* when Mr. Dawson again asked for the floor, to make has motion of adjournment. Mr. Slade refused it: a visible commotion began to pervade the House—members rising, clustering together, and talking with animation. Mr. Slade continued, and was about reading a judicial opinion in one of the Southern States which defined a slave to be a chattel—when Mr. Wise called him to order for speaking beside the question—the question being upon the abolition of slavery in the District of Columbia, and Mr. Slade's remarks going to its legal character, as property in a State. The Speaker, Mr. John White, of Kentucky, sustained the call, saying it was not in order to discuss the subject of slavery in any of the States. Mr. Slade denied that he was doing so, and said he was merely quoting a Southern judicial decision as he might quote a legal opinion delivered in Great Britain. Mr. Robertson, of Virginia, moved that the House adjourn. The Speaker pronounced the motion (and correctly), out of order, as the member from Vermont was in possession of the floor and addressing the House. He would, however, suggest to the member from Vermont, who could not but observe the state of the House, to confine himself strictly to the subject of his motion. Mr. Slade went on at great length, when Mr. Petrikin, of Pennsylvania, called him to order; but the Chair did not sustain the call. Mr. Slade went on, quoting from the Declaration of Independence, and the constitutions of the several States, and had got to that of Virginia, when Mr. Wise called him to order for reading papers without the leave of the House. The Speaker decided that no paper, objected to, could be read without the leave of the House. Mr. Wise then said:

"That the gentleman had wantonly discussed the abstract question of slavery, going back to the very first day of the creation, instead of slavery as it existed in the District, and the powers and duties of Congress in relation to it. He was now examining the State constitutions to show that as it existed in the States it was against them, and against the laws of God and man. This was out of order."

Mr. Slade explained, and argued in vindication of his course, and was about to read a memorial of Dr. Franklin, and an opinion of Mr. Madison on the subject of slavery—when the reading was objected to by Mr. Griffin, of South Carolina; and the Speaker decided they could not be read without the permission of the House. Mr. Slade, without asking the permission of the House, which he knew would not be granted, assumed to understand the prohibition as extending only to himself personally, said—"*Then I send them to the clerk: let him read them.*" The Speaker decided that this was equally against the rule. Then Mr. Griffin withdrew the objection, and Mr. Slade proceeded to read the papers, and to comment upon them as he went on, and was about to go back to the State of Virginia, and show what had been the feeling there on the subject of slavery previous to the date of Dr. Franklin's memorial: Mr. Rhett, of South Carolina, inquired of the Chair what the opinions of Virginia fifty years ago had to do with the case? The Speaker was about to reply, when Mr. Wise rose with warmth, and said—"He has discussed the whole abstract question of slavery: of slavery in Virginia: of slavery in my own district: and I now ask all my colleagues to retire with me from this hall." Mr. Slade reminded the Speaker that he had not yielded the floor; but his progress was impeded by the condition of the House, and the many exclamations of members, among whom Mr. Halsey, of Georgia, was heard calling on the Georgia delegation to withdraw with him; and Mr. Rhett was heard proclaiming, that the South Carolina members had already consulted together, and agreed to have a meeting at three o'clock in the committee room of the District of Columbia. Here the Speaker interposed to calm the House, standing up in his place and saying:

> "The gentleman from Vermont had been reminded by the Chair that the discussion of slavery, as existing within the States, was not in order; when he was desirous to read a paper and it was objected to, the Chair had stopped him; but the objection had been withdrawn, and Mr. Slade had been suffered to proceed; he was now about to read another paper, and objection was made; the Chair would, therefore, take the question on permitting it to be read."

Many members rose, all addressing the Chair at the same time, and many members leaving the hall, and a general scene of noise and confusion prevailing. Mr. Rhett succeeded in raising his voice above the roar of the tempest which raged in the House, and invited the entire delegations from all the slave States to retire from the hall forthwith, and meet in the committee room of the District of Columbia. The Speaker again essayed to calm the House, and again standing up in his place, he recapitulated his attempts to preserve order, and vindicated the correctness of his own conduct—seemingly impugned by many. What his personal feelings were on the subject (he was from a slave State), might easily be conjectured. He had endeavored to enforce the rules. Had it been in his power to restrain the discussion, he should promptly have exercised the power; but it was not. Mr. Slade, continuing, said the paper which he wished to read was of the continental Congress of 1774. The Speaker was about to put the question on leave, when Mr. Cost Johnson, of Maryland, inquired whether it would be in order to force the House to vote that the member from Vermont be not permitted to proceed? The Speaker replied it would not. Then Mr. James J. McKay, of North Carolina—a clear, coolheaded, sagacious man—interposed the objection which headed Mr. Slade. There was a rule of the House, that when a member was called to order, he should take his seat; and if decided to be out of order, he should not be allowed to speak again, except on the leave of the House. Mr. McKay judged this to be a proper occasion for the enforcement of that rule; and stood up and said:

> "That the gentleman had been pronounced out of order in discussing slavery in the States; and the rule declared that when a member was so pronounced by the Chair, he should take his seat, and if any one objected to his proceeding again, he should not do so, unless by leave of the House. Mr. McKay did now object to the gentleman from Vermont proceeding any farther."

Redoubled noise and confusion ensued—a crowd of members rising and speaking at once—who eventually yielded to the resounding blows of the Speaker's hammer upon the lid of his desk, and his apparent desire to read something to the House, as he held a book (recognized to be that of the rules) in his hand. Obtaining quiet, so as to enable himself to be heard, he read the rule referred to by Mr. McKay; and said that, as objection had now, for the first time, been made under that rule to the gentleman's resuming his speech, the Chair decided that he could not do so without the leave of the House. Mr. Slade attempted to go on: the Speaker directed him to take his seat until the question of leave should be put. Then, Mr. Slade, still keeping on his feet, asked leave to proceed as in order, saying he would not discuss slavery in Virginia. On that question Mr. Allen, of Vermont, asked the yeas and nays. Mr. Rencher, of North Carolina, moved an adjournment. Mr. Adams, and many others, demanded the yeas and nays on this motion, which were ordered, and resulted in 106 yeas, and 63 nays—some fifty or sixty members having withdrawn. This opposition to adjournment was one of the worst features of that unhappy day's work—the only effect of keeping the House together being to increase irritation, and multiply the chances for an outbreak. From the beginning Southern members had been in favor of it, and essayed to accomplish it, but were prevented by the tenacity with which Mr. Slade kept possession of the floor: and now, at last, when it was time to adjourn any way—when the House was in a condition in which no good could be expected, and great harm might be apprehended, there were sixty-three members—being nearly one-third of the House—willing to continue it in session. They were:

"Messrs. Adams, Alexander, H. Allen, J. W. Allen, Aycrigg, Bell, Biddle, Bond, Borden, Briggs, Wm. B. Calhoun, Coffin, Corwin, Cranston, Curtis, Cushing, Darlington, Davies, Dunn, Evans, Everett, Ewing I. Fletcher, Fillmore, Goode, Grennell, Haley, Hall, Hastings, Henry, Herod, Hoffman, Lincoln, Marvin, S. Mason, Maxwell, McKennan, Milligan, M. Morris, C. Morris, Naylor, Noyes, Ogle, Parmenter, Patterson, Peck, Phillips, Potts, Potter, Rariden, Randolph, Reed, Ridgway, Russel, Sheffer, Sibley, Slade, Stratton, Tillinghast, Toland, A. S. White, J. White, E. Whittlesey—63."

The House then stood adjourned; and as the adjournment was being pronounced, Mr. Campbell of South Carolina, stood up on a chair, and calling for the attention of members, said:

"He had been appointed, as one of the Southern delegation, to announce that all those gentlemen who represented slaveholding States, were invited to attend the meeting now being held in the District committee room."

Members from the slave-holding States had repaired in large numbers to the room in the basement, where they were invited to meet. Various passions agitated them—some violent. Extreme propositions were suggested, of which Mr. Rhett, of South Carolina, in a letter to his constituents, gave a full account of his own—thus:

"In a private and friendly letter to the editor of the Charleston Mercury amongst other events accompanying the memorable secession of the Southern members from the hall of the House of Representatives, I stated to him, that I had prepared two resolutions, drawn as amendments to the motion of the member from Vermont, whilst he was discussing the institution of slavery in the South, 'declaring, that the constitution having failed to protect the South in the peaceable possession and enjoyment of their rights and peculiar institutions, it was expedient that the Union should be dissolved; and the other, appointing a committee of two members from each State, to report upon the best means of peaceably dissolving it.' They were intended as amendments to a motion, to refer with instructions to report a bill, abolishing slavery in the District of Columbia. I expected them to share the fate, which inevitably awaited the original motion, so soon as the floor could have been obtained, viz., to be laid upon the table. My design in presenting them, was, to place before Congress and the people, what, in my opinion, was the true issue upon this great and vital question; and to point out the course of policy by which it should be met by the Southern States."

But extreme counsels did not prevail. There were members present, who well considered that, although the provocation was great, and the number voting for such a firebrand motion was deplorably large, yet it was but little more than the one-fourth of the House, and decidedly less than one half of the members from the free States: so that, even if left to the free State vote alone, the motion would have been rejected. But the motion itself, and the manner in which it was supported, was most reprehensible—necessarily leading to disorder in the House, the destruction of its harmony and capacity for useful legislation, tending to a sectional segregation of the members, the alienation of feeling between the North and the South; and alarm to all the slaveholding States. The evil required a remedy, but not the remedy of breaking up the Union; but one which might prevent the like in future, while administering a rebuke upon the past. That remedy was found in adopting a proposition to be offered to the House, which, if agreed to, would close the door against any discussion upon abolition petitions in future, and assimilate the proceedings of the House, in that particular, to those of the Senate. This proposition was put into the hands of Mr. Patton, of Virginia, to be offered as an amendment to the rules at the opening of the House the next morning. It was in these words:

> "*Resolved*, That all petitions, memorials, and papers, touching the abolition of slavery or the buying, selling, or transferring of slaves, in any State, District, or Territory, of the United States, be laid on the table, without being debated, printed, read, or referred, and that no further action whatever shall be had thereon."

Accordingly, at the opening of the House, Mr. Patton asked leave to submit the resolution—which was read for information. Mr. Adams objected to the grant of leave. Mr. Patton then moved a suspension of the rules—which motion required two-thirds to sustain it; and, unless obtained, this salutary remedy for an alarming evil (which was already in force in the Senate) could not be offered. It was a test motion, and on which the opponents of abolition agitation in the House required all their strength: for unless two to one, they were defeated. Happily the two to one were ready, and on taking the yeas and nays, demanded by an abolition member (to keep his friends to the track, and to hold the free State anti-abolitionists to their responsibility at home), the result stood 135 yeas to 60 nays—the full two-thirds, and fifteen over. The yeas on this important motion, were:

> Messrs. Hugh J. Anderson, John T. Andrews, Charles G. Atherton, William Beatty, Andrew Beirne, John Bell, Bennet Bicknell, Richard Biddle, Samuel Birdsall, Ratliff Boon, James W. Bouldin, John C. Brodhead, Isaac H. Bronson, Andrew D. W. Bruyn, Andrew Buchanan, John Calhoun, C. C. Cambreleng, Wm. B. Campbell, John Campbell, Timothy J. Carter, Wm. B. Carter, Zadok Casey, John Chambers, John Chaney, Reuben Chapman, Richard Cheatham, Jonathan Cilley, John F. H. Claiborne, Jesse F. Cleaveland, Wm. K. Clowney, Walter Coles, Thomas Corwin, Robert Craig, John W. Crocket, Samuel Cushman, Edmund Deberry, John I. De Graff, John Dennis, George C. Dromgoole, John Edwards, James Farrington, John Fairfield, Jacob Fry, jr., James Garland, James Graham, Seaton Grantland, Abr'm P. Grant, William J. Graves. Robert H. Hammond, Thomas L. Hamer, James Harlan, Albert G. Harrison, Richard Hawes, Micajah T. Hawkins, Charles E. Haynes, Hopkins Holsey, Orrin Holt, George W. Hopkins, Benjamin C. Howard, Edward B. Hubley, Jabez Jackson, Joseph Johnson, Wm. Cost Johnson, John W. Jones, Gouverneur Kemble, Daniel Kilgore, John Klingensmith, jr., Joab Lawler, Hugh S. Legare, Henry Logan, Francis S. Lyon, Francis Mallory, James M. Mason, Joshua L. Martin, Abram P. Maury, Wm. L. May, James J. McKay, Robert McClellan, Abraham McClelland, Charles McClure, Isaac McKim, Richard H. Menefee, Charles F. Mercer, Wm. Montgomery, Ely Moore, Wm. S. Morgan, Samuel W. Morris, Henry A. Muhlenberg, John L. Murray, Wm. H. Noble, John Palmer, Amasa J. Parker, John M. Patton, Lemuel Paynter, Isaac S. Pennybacker, David Petrikin, Lancelot Phelps, Arnold Plumer, Zadock Pratt, John H. Prentiss, Luther Reily, Abraham Rencher, John Robertson, Samuel T. Sawyer, Augustine H. Shepperd, Charles Shepard, Ebenezer J. Shields, Matthias Sheplor, Francis O. J. Smith, Adam W. Snyder, Wm. W. Southgate, James B. Spencer, Edward Stanly, Archibald Stuart, Wm. Stone, John Taliaferro, Wm. Taylor, Obadiah Titus, Isaac Toucey, Hopkins L. Turney, Joseph R. Underwood, Henry Vail, David D. Wagener, Taylor Webster, Joseph Weeks, Albert S. White, John White, Thomas T. Whittlesey, Lewis Williams, Sherrod Williams, Jared W. Williams, Joseph L. Williams, Christ'r H. Williams, Henry A. Wise, Archibald Yell.

The nays were:

> Messrs. John Quincy Adams, James Alexander, jr., Heman Allen, John W. Allen, J. Banker Aycrigg, Wm. Key Bond, Nathaniel B. Borden, George N. Briggs, Wm. B. Calhoun, Charles D. Coffin, Robert B. Cranston, Caleb Cushing, Edward Darlington, Thomas Davee, Edward Davies, Alexander Duncan, George H. Dunn, George Evans, Horace Everett, John Ewing, Isaac Fletcher, Millard Filmore, Henry A. Foster, Patrick G. Goode, George Grennell, jr.,

Elisha Haley, Hiland Hall, Alexander Harper, Wm. S. Hastings, Thomas Henry, Wm. Herod, Samuel Ingham, Levi Lincoln, Richard P. Marvin, Samson Mason, John P. B. Maxwell, Thos. M. T. McKennan, Mathias Morris, Calvary Morris, Charles Naylor, Joseph C. Noyes, Charles Ogle, Wm. Parmenter, Wm. Patterson, Luther C. Peck, Stephen C. Phillips, David Potts, jr., James Rariden, Joseph F. Randolph, John Reed, Joseph Ridgway, David Russell, Daniel Sheffer, Mark H. Sibley, Wm. Slade, Charles C. Stratton, Joseph L. Tillinghast, George W. Toland, Elisha Whittlesey, Thomas Jones Yorke.

This was one of the most important votes ever delivered in the House. Upon its issue depended the quiet of the House on one hand, or on the other, the renewal, and perpetuation of the scenes of the day before—ending in breaking up all deliberation, and all national legislation. It was successful, and that critical step being safely over, the passage of the resolution was secured—the free State friendly vote being itself sufficient to carry it: but, although the passage of the resolution was secured, yet resistance to it continued. Mr. Patton rose to recommend his resolution as a peace offering, and to prevent further agitation by demanding the previous question. He said:

"He had offered this resolution in the spirit of peace and harmony. It involves (said Mr. P.), so far as I am concerned, and so far as concerns some portion of the representatives of the slaveholding States, a concession; a concession which we make for the sake of peace, harmony, and union. We offer it in the hope that it may allay, not exasperate excitement; we desire to extinguish, not to kindle a flame in the country. In that spirit, sir, without saying one word in the way of discussion; without giving utterance to any of those emotions which swell in my bosom at the recollection of what took place here yesterday, I shall do what I have never yet done since I have been a member of this House, and which I have very rarely sustained, when done by others: I move the previous question."

Then followed a scene of disorder, which thus appears in the Register of Debates:

"Mr. Adams rose and said. Mr. Speaker, the gentleman precedes his resolution—(Loud cries of 'Order! order!' from all parts of the hall.) Mr. A. He preceded it with remarks—('Order! order!')

"The Chair reminded the gentleman that it was out of order to address the House after the demand for the previous question.

"Mr. Adams. I ask the House—(continued cries of 'Order!' which completely drowned the honorable member's voice.)"

Order having been restored, the next question was—"Is the demand for the previous question seconded?"—which seconding would consist of a majority of the whole House—which, on a division, quickly showed itself. Then came the further question—"*Shall the main question be now put?*"—on which the yeas and nays were demanded, and taken; and ended in a repetition of the vote of the same 63 against it. The main question was then put, and carried; but again, on yeas and nays, to hold free State members to their responsibility; showing the same 63 in the negative, with a few additional votes from free State members, who, having staked themselves on the vital point of suspending the rules, saw no use in giving themselves further trouble at home, by giving an unnecessary vote in favor of stifling abolition debate. In this way, the ranks of the 63 were increased to 74.

Thus was stifled, and in future prevented in the House, the inflammatory debates on these disturbing petitions. It was the great session of their presentation—being offered by hundreds, and signed by hundreds of thousands of persons—many of them women, who forgot their sex and their duties, to mingle in such inflammatory work; some of them clergymen, who forgot their mission of peace, to stir up strife among those who should be brethren. Of the pertinacious 63, who backed Mr. Slade throughout, the most notable were Mr. Adams, who had been President of the United States—Mr. Fillmore, who became so—and Mr. Caleb Cushing, who eventually became as ready to abolish all impediments to the general diffusion of slavery, as he then was to abolish slavery itself in the District of Columbia. It was a portentous contest. The motion of Mr. Slade was, not for an inquiry into the expediency of abolishing slavery in the District of Columbia (a motion in itself sufficiently inflammatory), but to get the command of the House to bring in a bill for that purpose—which would be a decision of the question. His motion failed. The storm subsided; and very few of the free State members who had staked themselves on the issue, lost any thing among their constituents for the devotion which they had shown to the Union.

CHAPTER XXXVII.

ABOLITIONISTS CLASSIFIED BY MR. CLAY ULTRAS DENOUNCED: SLAVERY AGITATORS NORTH AND SOUTH EQUALLY DENOUNCED AS DANGEROUS TO THE UNION.

"It is well known to the Senate, said Mr. Clay, that I have thought that the most judicious course with abolition petitions has not been of late pursued by Congress. I have believed that it would have been wisest to have received and referred them, without opposition, and to have reported against their object in a calm and dispassionate and argumentative appeal to the good sense of the whole community. It has been supposed, however, by a majority of Congress that it was most expedient either not to receive the petitions at all, or, if formally received, not to act definitively upon them. There is no substantial difference between these opposite opinions, since both look to an absolute rejection of the prayer of the petitioners. But there is a great difference in the form of proceeding; and, Mr. President, some experience in the conduct of human affairs has taught me to believe that a neglect to observe established forms is often attended with more mischievous consequences than the infliction of a positive injury. We all know that, even in private life, a violation of the existing usages and ceremonies of society cannot take place without serious prejudice. I fear, sir, that the abolitionists have acquired a considerable apparent force by blending with the object which they have in view a collateral and totally different question arising out of an alleged violation of the right of petition. I know full well, and take great pleasure in testifying, that nothing was remoter from the intention of the majority of the Senate, from which I differed, than to violate the right of petition in any case in which, according to its judgment, that right could be constitutionally exercised, or where the object of the petition could be safely or properly granted. Still, it must be owned that the abolitionists have seized hold of the fact of the treatment which their petitions have received in Congress, and made injurious impressions upon the minds of a large portion of the community. This, I think, might have been avoided by the course which I should have been glad to have seen pursued.

"And I desire now, Mr. President, to advert to some of those topics which I think might have been usefully embodied in a report by a committee of the Senate, and which, I am persuaded, would have checked the progress, if it had not altogether arrested the efforts of abolition. I am sensible, sir, that this work would have been accomplished with much greater ability, and with much happier effect, under the auspices of a committee, than it can be by me. But, anxious as I always am to contribute whatever is in my power to the harmony, concord, and happiness of this great people, I feel myself irresistibly impelled to do whatever is in my power, incompetent as I feel myself to be, to dissuade the public from continuing to agitate a subject fraught with the most direful consequences.

"There are three classes of persons opposed, or apparently opposed, to the continued existence of slavery in the United States. The first are those who, from sentiments of philanthropy and humanity, are conscientiously opposed to the existence of slavery, but who are no less opposed, at the same time, to any disturbance of the peace and tranquillity of the Union, or the infringement of the powers of the States composing the confederacy. In this class may be comprehended that peaceful and exemplary society of 'Friends,' one of whose established maxims is, an abhorrence of war in all its forms, and the cultivation of peace and good-will amongst mankind. The next class consists of apparent abolitionists—that is, those who, having been persuaded that the right of petition has been violated by Congress, co-operate with the abolitionists for the sole purpose of asserting and vindicating that right. And the third class are the real ultra-abolitionists, who are resolved to persevere in the pursuit of their object at all hazards, and without regard to any consequences, however calamitous they may be. With them the rights of property are nothing; the deficiency of the powers of the general government is nothing; the acknowledged and incontestable powers of the States are nothing; civil war, a dissolution of the Union, and the overthrow of a government in which are concentrated the fondest hopes of the civilized world, are nothing. A single idea has taken possession of their minds, and onward they pursue it, overlooking all barriers, reckless and regardless of all consequences. With this class, the immediate abolition of slavery in the District of Columbia, and in the territory of Florida, the prohibition of the removal of slaves from State to State, and the refusal to admit any new State, comprising within its limits the institution of domestic slavery, are but so many means conducing to the accomplishment of the ultimate but perilous end at which they avowedly and boldly aim; are but so many short stages in the long and bloody road to the distant goal at which they would finally arrive. Their purpose is abolition, universal abolition, peaceably if it can, forcibly if it must. Their object is no longer concealed by the thinnest veil; it is avowed and proclaimed. Utterly destitute of constitutional or other rightful power, living in totally distinct communities, as alien to the communities in which the subject on which they would operate resides, so far as concerns political power over that subject, as if they lived in Africa or Asia, they nevertheless promulgate to the world their purpose to be to manumit forthwith, and without compensation, and without moral preparation, three millions of negro slaves, under jurisdictions altogether separated from those under which they live.

"I have said that immediate abolition of slavery in the District of Columbia and in the territory of Florida, and the exclusion of new States, were only means towards the attainment of a much more important end. Unfortunately, they are not the only means. Another, and much more lamentable one is that which this class is endeavoring to employ, of arraying one portion against another portion of the Union. With that view, in all their leading prints and publications, the alleged horrors of slavery are depicted in the most glowing and exaggerated colors, to excite the imaginations and stimulate the rage of the people in the free States against the people in the slave States. The slaveholder is held up and represented as the most atrocious of human beings. Advertisements of fugitive slaves to be sold are carefully collected and blazoned forth, to infuse a spirit of detestation and hatred against one entire and the largest section of the Union. And like a notorious agitator upon another theatre (Mr. Daniel O'Connell), they would hunt down and proscribe from the pale of civilized society the inhabitants of that entire section. Allow me, Mr. President, to say, that whilst I recognize in the justly wounded feelings of the Minister of the United States at the court of St. James much to excuse the notice which he was provoked to take of that agitator, in my humble opinion, he would better have consulted the dignity of his station and of his country in treating him with contemptuous silence. That agitator would exclude us from European society—he who himself can only obtain a contraband admission, and is received with scornful repugnance into it! If he be no more desirous of our society than we are of his, he may rest assured that a state of eternal non-intercourse will exist between us. Yes, sir, I think the American Minister would have best pursued the dictates of true dignity by regarding the language of that member of the British House of Commons as the malignant ravings of the plunderer of his own country, and the libeller of a foreign and kindred people.

"But the means to which I have already adverted are not the only ones which this third class of ultra-Abolitionists are employing to effect their ultimate end. They began their operations by professing to employ only persuasive means in appealing to the humanity, and enlightening the understandings, of the slaveholding portion of the Union. If there were some kindness in this avowed motive, it must be acknowledged that there was rather a presumptuous display also of an assumed superiority in intelligence and knowledge. For some time they continued to make these appeals to our duty and our interest; but impatient with the slow influence of their logic upon our stupid minds, they recently resolved to change their system of action. To the agency of their powers of persuasion, they now propose to substitute the powers of the ballot box; and he must be blind to what is passing before us, who does not perceive that the inevitable tendency of their proceedings is, if these should be found insufficient, to invoke, finally, the more potent powers of the bayonet.

"Mr. President, it is at this alarming stage of the proceedings of the ultra-Abolitionists that I would seriously invite every considerate man in the country solemnly to pause, and deliberately to reflect, not merely on our existing posture, but upon that dreadful precipice down which they would hurry us. It is because these ultra-Abolitionists have ceased to employ the instruments of reason and persuasion, have made their cause political, and have appealed to the ballot box, that I am induced, upon this occasion, to address you.

"There have been three epochs in the history of our country at which the spirit of abolition displayed itself. The first was immediately after the formation of the present federal government. When the constitution was about going into operation, its powers were not well understood by the community at large, and remained to be accurately interpreted and defined. At that period numerous abolition societies were formed, comprising not merely the Society of Friends, but many other good men. Petitions were presented to Congress, praying for the abolition of slavery. They were received without serious opposition, referred, and reported upon by a committee. The report stated that the general government had no power to abolish slavery as it existed in the several States, and that these States themselves had exclusive jurisdiction over the subject. The report was generally acquiesced in, and satisfaction and tranquillity ensued; the abolition societies thereafter limiting their exertions, in respect to the black population, to offices of humanity within the scope of existing laws.

"The next period when the subject of slavery and abolition, incidentally, was brought into notice and discussion, was on the memorable occasion of the admission of the State of Missouri into the Union. The struggle was long, strenuous, and fearful. It is too recent to make it necessary to do more than merely advert to it, and to say, that it was finally composed by one of those compromises characteristic of our institutions, and of which the constitution itself is the most signal instance.

"The third is that in which we now find ourselves, and to which various causes have contributed. The principal one, perhaps, is British emancipation in the islands adjacent to our continent. Confounding the totally different cases of the powers of the British Parliament and those of our Congress, and the totally different conditions of the slaves in the British West India Islands and the slaves in the sovereign and independent States of this confederacy, superficial men have inferred from the undecided British experiment the practicability of the abolition of slavery in these States. All these are different. The powers of the British Parliament are unlimited, and often described to be omnipotent. The powers of the American Congress, on the contrary, are few, cautiously limited, scrupulously excluding all that are not granted, and above all, carefully and absolutely excluding all power over the existence or continuance of slavery in the several States. The slaves, too, upon which British legislation operated, were not in the bosom of the kingdom, but in remote and feeble colonies, having no voice in Parliament. The West India slaveholder was neither representative, or represented in that Parliament. And while I most fervently wish complete success to the British experiment of the West India emancipation, I confess that I have fearful forebodings of a disastrous termination. Whatever it may be, I think it must be admitted that, if the British Parliament treated the West India slaves as freemen, it also treated the West India freemen as slaves. If instead of these slaves being separated by a wide ocean from the parent country, three or four millions of African negro slaves had been dispersed over England, Scotland, Wales and Ireland, and their owners had been members of the British Parliament—a case which would have presented some analogy to our own country—does any one believe that it would have been expedient or practical to have emancipated them, leaving them to remain, with all their embittered feelings, in the United kingdom, boundless as the powers of the British government are?

"Other causes have conspired with the British example to produce the existing excitement from abolition. I say it with profound regret, and with no intention to occasion irritation here or elsewhere, that there are persons in both parts of the Union who have sought to mingle abolition with politics, and to array one portion of the Union against the other. It is the misfortune of free countries that, in high party times, a disposition too often prevails to seize hold of every thing which can strengthen the one side or weaken the other. Prior to the late election of the present President of the United States, he was charged with being an abolitionist, and abolition designs were imputed to many of his supporters. Much as I was opposed to his election, and am to his administration, I neither shared in making or believing the truth of the charge. He was scarcely installed in office before the same charge was directed against those who opposed his election.

"It is not true—I rejoice that it is not true—that either of the two great parties in this country has any design or aim at abolition. I should deeply lament if it were true. I should consider, if it were true, that the danger to the stability of our system would be infinitely greater than any which does, I hope, actually exist. Whilst neither party can be, I think, justly accused of any abolition tendency or purpose, both have profited, and both been injured, in particular localities, by the accession or abstraction of abolition support. If the account were fairly stated, I believe the party to which I am opposed has profited much more, and been injured much less, than that to which I belong. But I am far, for that reason, from being disposed to accuse our adversaries of abolitionism."

CHAPTER XXXVIII.

BANK OF THE UNITED STATES: RESIGNATION OF MR. BIDDLE: FINAL SUSPENSION.

On the first of January of this year this Bank made an exposition of its affairs to the General Assembly of Pennsylvania, as required by its charter, in which its assets aggregated $66,180,396; and its liabilities aggregated $33,180,855: the exposition being verified by the usual oaths required on such occasions.

On the 30th of March following Mr. Biddle resigned his place as president of the Bank, giving as a reason for it that, "*the affairs of the institution were in a state of great prosperity, and no longer needed his services.*"

On the same day the board of directors in accepting the resignation, passed a resolve declaring that the President Biddle had left the institution "*prosperous in all its relations, strong in its ability to promote the interest of the community, cordial with other banks, and secure in the esteem and respect of all connected with it at home or abroad.*"

On the 9th of October the Bank closed her doors upon her creditors, under the mild name of suspension—never to open them again.

In the month of April preceding, when leaving Washington to return to Missouri, I told the President there would be another suspension, headed by the Bank of the United States, before we met again: at my return in November it was his first expression to remind me of that conversation; and to say it was the second time I had foreseen these suspensions, and warned him of them. He then jocularly said, don't predict so any more. I answered I should not; for it was the last time this Bank would suspend.

Still dominating over the moneyed systems of the South and West, this former colossal institution was yet able to carry along with her nearly all the banks of one-half of the Union: and using her irredeemable paper against the solid currency of the New York and other Northern banks, and selling fictitious bills on Europe, she was able to run them hard for specie—curtail their operations—and make panic and distress in the money market. At the same time by making an imposing exhibition of her assets, arranging a reciprocal use of their notes with other suspended banks, keeping up an apparent par value for her notes and stocks by fictitious and collusive sales and purchases, and above all, by her political connection with the powerful opposition—she was enabled to keep the field as a bank, and as a political power: and as such to act an effective part in the ensuing presidential election. She even pretended to have become stronger since the time when Mr. Biddle left her so prosperous; and at the next exposition of her affairs to the Pennsylvania legislature (Jan. 1, 1840), returned her assets at $74,603,142; her liabilities at $36,959,539, and her surplus at $37,643,603. This surplus, after paying all liabilities, showed the stock to be worth a premium of $2,643,603. And all this duly sworn to.

CHAPTER XXXIX.

FIRST SESSION TWENTY-SIXTH CONGRESS: MEMBERS: ORGANIZATION: POLITICAL MAP OF THE HOUSE.

Members of the Senate.

NEW HAMPSHIRE.—Henry Hubbard, Franklin Pierce.

MAINE.—John Ruggles, Reuel Williams.

MASSACHUSETTS.—John Davis. Daniel Webster.

VERMONT.—Sam'l Prentiss, Sam'l S. Phelps.

RHODE ISLAND.—Nehemiah R. Knight, N. F. Dixon.

CONNECTICUT.—Thaddeus Betts, Perry Smith.

NEW YORK.—Silas Wright, N. P. Tallmadge.

NEW JERSEY.—Sam'l L. Southard, Garret D. Wall.

PENNSYLVANIA.—James Buchanan, Daniel Sturgeon.

DELAWARE.—Thomas Clayton.

MARYLAND.—John S. Spence, Wm. D. Merrick.

VIRGINIA.—William H. Roane.

NORTH CAROLINA.—Bedford Brown, R. Strange.

SOUTH CAROLINA.—John C. Calhoun, Wm. Campbell Preston.

GEORGIA.—Wilson Lumpkin, Alfred Cuthbert.

KENTUCKY.—Henry Clay, John J. Crittenden.

TENNESSEE.—Hugh L. White, Alex. Anderson.

OHIO.—William Allen, Benjamin Tappan.

INDIANA.—Oliver H. Smith, Albert S. White.

MISSISSIPPI.—Robert J. Walker, John Henderson.

LOUISIANA.—Robert C. Nicholas, Alexander Mouton.

ILLINOIS.—John M. Robinson, Richard M. Young.

ALABAMA.—Clement C. Clay, Wm. Rufus King.

MISSOURI.—Thomas H. Benton, Lewis F. Linn.

ARKANSAS.—William S. Fulton, Ambrose Sevier.

MICHIGAN.—John Norvell, Augustus S. Porter.

Members of the House of Representatives.

MAINE.—Hugh J. Anderson, Nathan Clifford, Thomas Davee, George Evans, Joshua A. Lowell, Virgil D. Parris, Benjamin Randall, Albert Smith.

NEW HAMPSHIRE.—Charles G. Atherton, Edmund Burke, Ira A. Eastman, Tristram Shaw, Jared W. Williams.

CONNECTICUT.—Joseph Trumbull, William L. Storrs, Thomas W. Williams, Thomas B. Osborne, Truman Smith, John H. Brockway.

VERMONT.—Hiland Hall, William Slade, Horace Everett, John Smith, Isaac Fletcher.

MASSACHUSETTS.—Abbot Lawrence, Leverett Saltonstall, Caleb Cushing, William Parmenter, Levi Lincoln, [Vacancy,] George N. Briggs, William B. Calhoun, William S. Hastings, Henry Williams, John Reed, John Quincy Adams.

RHODE ISLAND.—Chosen by general ticket. Joseph L. Tillinghast, Robert B. Cranston.

NEW YORK.—Thomas B. Jackson, James de la Montayne, Ogden Hoffman, Edward Curtis, Moses H. Grinnell, James Monroe, Gouverneur Kemble, Charles Johnson, Nathaniel Jones, Rufus Palen, Aaron Vanderpoel, John Ely, Hiram P. Hunt, Daniel D. Barnard, Anson Brown, David Russell, Augustus C. Hand, John Fine, Peter J. Wagoner, Andrew W. Doig, John G. Floyd, David P. Brewster, Thomas C. Crittenden, John H. Prentiss, Judson Allen, John C. Clark, S. B. Leonard, Amasa Dana, Edward Rogers, Nehemiah H. Earl, Christopher Morgan, Theron R. Strong, Francis P. Granger, Meredith Mallory, Seth M. Gates, Luther C. Peck, Richard P. Marvin, Millard Fillmore,

Charles F. Mitchell.

NEW JERSEY.—Joseph B. Randolph, Peter
D. Vroom, Philemon Dickerson, William R.
Cooper, Daniel B. Ryall, Joseph Kille.

PENNSYLVANIA.—William Beatty, Richard
Biddle, James Cooper, Edward Davies, John
Davis, John Edwards, Joseph Fornance, John
Galbraith, James Gerry, Robert H. Hammond,
Thomas Henry, Enos Hook, Francis James,
George M. Keim, Isaac Leet, Albert G. Marchand,
Samuel W. Morris, George McCulloch,
Charles Naylor, Peter Newhard, Charles Ogle,
Lemuel Paynter, David Petrikin, William S.
Ramsey, John Sergeant, William Simonton,
George W. Toland, David D. Wagener.

DELAWARE.—Thomas Robinson, jr.

MARYLAND.—James Carroll, John Dennis,
Solomon Hillen, jr., Daniel Jenifer, William
Cost Johnson, Francis Thomas, Philip F.
Thomas, John T. H. Worthington.

VIRGINIA.—Linn Banks, Andrew Beirne,
John M. Botts, Walter Coles, Robert Craig,
George C. Dromgoole, James Garland, William
L. Goggin, John Hill, Joel Holleman, George
W. Hopkins, Robert M. T. Hunter, Joseph
Johnson, John W. Jones, William Lucas,
Charles F. Mercer, Francis E. Rives, Green B.
Samuels, Lewis Steinrod, John Taliaferro, Henry
A. Wise.

NORTH CAROLINA.—Jesse A. Bynum, Henry
W. Connor, Edmund Deberry, Charles Fisher,
James Graham, Micajah T. Hawkins, John
Hill, James J. McKay, William Montgomery,
Kenneth Rayner, Charles Shepard, Edward
Stanly, Lewis Williams.

SOUTH CAROLINA.—Sampson H. Butler, John
Campbell, John K. Griffin, Isaac E. Holmes,
Francis W. Pickens, R. Barnwell Rhett, James
Rogers, Thomas B. Sumter, Waddy Thompson,
jr.

GEORGIA.—Julius C. Alford, Edward J.
Black, Walter T. Colquitt, Mark A. Cooper,
William C. Dawson, Richard W. Habersham,
Thomas B. King, Eugenius A. Nisbet, Lott

Warren.

ALABAMA.—R. H. Chapman, David Hubbard, George W. Crabb, Dixon H. Lewis, James Dillett.

LOUISIANA.—Edward D. White, Edward Chinn, Rice Garland.

MISSISSIPPI.—A. G. Brown, J. Thompson.

MISSOURI.—John Miller, John Jameson.

ARKANSAS.—Edward Cross.

TENNESSEE.—William B. Carter, Abraham McClellan, Joseph L. Williams, Julius W. Blackwell, Hopkins L. Turney, William B. Campbell, John Bell, Meredith P. Gentry, Harvey M. Watterson, Aaron V. Brown, Cave Johnson, John W. Crockett, Christopher H. Williams.

KENTUCKY.—Linn Boyd, Philip Triplett, Joseph Underwood, Sherrod Williams, Simeon W. Anderson, Willis Green, John Pope, William J. Graves, John White, Richard Hawes, L. W. Andrews, Garret Davis, William O. Butler.

OHIO.—Alexander Duncan, John B. Weller, Patrick G. Goode, Thomas Corwin, William Doane, Calvary Morris, William K. Bond, Joseph Ridgway, William Medill, Samson Mason, Isaac Parish, Jonathan Taylor, D. P. Leadbetter, George Sweeny, John W. Allen, Joshua R. Giddings, John Hastings, D. A. Starkweather, Henry Swearingen.

MICHIGAN.—Isaac E. Crary.

INDIANA.—Geo. H. Proffit, John Davis, John Carr, Thomas Smith, James Rariden, Wm. W. Wick, T. A. Howard.

ILLINOIS.—John Reynolds, Zadok Casey, John T. Stuart.

The organization of the House was delayed for many days by a case of closely and earnestly contested election from the State of New Jersey. Five citizens, to wit: John B. Aycrigg, John B. Maxwell, William Halsted, Thomas C. Stratton, Thomas Jones Yorke, had received the governor's certificate as duly elected: five other citizens, to wit: Philemon Dickerson, Peter D. Vroom, Daniel B. Ryall, William R. Cooper, John Kille, claimed to have received a majority of the lawful votes given in the election: and each set demanded admission as representatives. No case of contested election was ever more warmly disputed in the House. The two sets of claimants were of opposite political parties: the House was nearly divided: five from one side and added to the other would make a difference of ten votes: and these ten might determine its character. The first struggle was on the part of the members holding the certificates claiming to be admitted, and to act as members, until the question of *right* should be decided; and as this would give them a right to vote for speaker, it might have had the effect of deciding that important election: and for this point a great struggle was made by the whig party. The democracy could not ask for the immediate admission of the five democratic claimants, as they only presented a case which required to be examined before it could be decided. Their course was to exclude both sets, and send them equally before the committee of contested elections; and in the mean time, a resolution to proceed with the organization of the House was adopted after an arduous and protracted struggle, in which every variety of parliamentary motion was exhausted by each side to accomplish its purpose; and, at the end of three months it was referred to the committee to report which five of the ten contestants had received the greatest number of legal votes. This was putting the issue on the rights of the voters—on the broad and popular ground of choice by the people: and was equivalent to deciding the question in favor of the democratic contestants, who held the certificate of the Secretary of State that the majority of votes returned to his office was in their favor,—counting the votes of some precincts which the governor and council had rejected for illegality in holding the elections. As the constitutional judge of the election, qualifications and returns of its own members, the House disregarded the decision of the governor and council; and, deferring to the representative principle, made the decision turn, not upon the conduct of the officers holding the election, but upon the rights of the voters.

This strenuous contest was not terminated until the 10th of March—nearly one hundred days from the time of its commencement. The five democratic members were then admitted to their seats. In the mean time the election for speaker had been brought on by a vote of 118 to 110—the democracy having succeeded in bringing on the election after a total exhaustion of every parliamentary manœuvre to keep it off. Mr. John W. Jones, of Virginia, was the democratic nominee: Mr. Jno. Bell, of Tennessee, was nominated on the part of the whigs. The whole vote given in was 235, making 118 necessary to a choice. Of these, Mr. Jones received 118: Mr. Bell, 102. Twenty votes were scattered, of which 11, on the whig side, went to Mr. Dawson of Georgia; and 9 on the democratic side were thrown upon three southern members. Had any five of these nine voted for Mr. Jones, it would have elected him: while the eleven given to Mr. Dawson would not have effected the election of Mr. Bell. It was clear the democracy had the majority, for the contested election from New Jersey having been sent to a committee, and neither set of the contestants allowed to vote, the question became purely and simply one of party: but there was a fraction in each party which did not go with the party to which it belonged: and hence, with a majority in the House to bring on the election, and a majority voting in it, the democratic nominee lacked five of the number requisite to elect him. The contest was continued through five successive ballotings without any better result for Mr. Jones, and worse for Mr. Bell; and it became evident that there was a fraction of each party determined to control the election. It became a question with the democratic party what to do? The fraction which did not go with the party were the friends of Mr. Calhoun, and although always professing democratically had long acted with the whigs, and had just returned to the body of the party against which they had been acting. The election was in their hands, and they gave it to be known that if one of their number was taken, they would vote with the body of the party and elect him: and Mr. Dixon H. Lewis, of Alabama, was the person indicated. The extreme importance of having a speaker friendly to the administration induced all the leading friends of Mr. Van Buren to go into this arrangement, and to hold a caucus to carry it into effect. The caucus was held: Mr. Lewis was adopted as the candidate of the party: and, the usual resolves of unanimity having been adopted, it was expected to elect him on the first trial. He was not, however, so elected; nor on the second trial; nor on the third; nor on any one up to the seventh: when, having never got a higher vote than Mr. Jones, and falling off to the one-half of it, he was dropped; and but few knew how the balk came to pass. It was thus: The writer of this View was one of a few who would not capitulate to half a dozen members, known as Mr. Calhoun's friends, long separated from the party, bitterly opposing it, just returning to it, and undertaking to govern it by constituting themselves into a balance wheel between the two nearly balanced parties. He preferred a clean defeat to any victory gained by such capitulation. He was not a member of the House, but had friends there who thought as he did; and these he recommended to avoid the caucus, and remain unbound by its resolves; and when the election came on, vote as they pleased: which they did: and enough of them throwing away their votes upon those who were no candidates, thus prevented the election of Mr. Lewis: and so returned upon the little fraction of pretenders the lesson which they had taught.

It was the same with the whig party. A fraction of its members refused to support the regular candidate of the party; and after many fruitless trials to elect him, he was abandoned—Mr. Robert M. T. Hunter, of Virginia, taken up, and eventually elected. He had voted with the whig party in the New Jersey election case—among the scattering in the votes for speaker; and was finally elected by the full whig vote, and a few of the scattering from the democratic ranks. He was one of the small band of Mr. Calhoun's friends; so that that gentleman succeeded in governing the whig election of speaker, after failing to govern that of the democracy.

In looking over the names of the candidates for speaker it will be seen that the whole were Southern men— no Northern man being at any time put in nomination, or voted for. And this circumstance illustrates a pervading system of action between the two sections from the foundation of the government—the southern going for the honors, the northern for the benefits of the government. And each has succeeded, but with the difference of a success in a solid and in an empty pursuit. The North has become rich upon the benefits of the government: the South has grown lean upon its honors.

This arduous and protracted contest for speaker, and where the issue involved the vital party question of the organization of the House, and where every member classified himself by a deliberate and persevering series of votes, becomes important in a political classification point of view, and is here presented in detail as the political map of the House—taking the first vote as showing the character of the whole.

1. Members voting for Mr. Jones: 113.

Judson Allen, Hugh J. Anderson, Charles G. Atherton, Linn Banks, William Beatty, Andrew Beirne, Julius W. Blackwell, Linn Boyd, David P. Brewster, Aaron V. Brown, Albert G. Brown, Edmund Burke, Sampson H. Butler, William O. Butler, Jesse A. Bynum, John Carr, James Carroll, Zadok Casey, Reuben Chapman, Nathan Clifford, Walter Coles, Henry W. Connor, Robert Craig, Isaac E. Crary, Edward Cross, Amasa Dana, Thomas Davee, John Davis, John W. Davis, William Doan, Andrew W. Doig, George C. Dromgoole, Alexander Duncan, Nehemiah H. Earl, Ira A. Eastman, John Ely, John Fine, Isaac Fletcher, John G. Floyd, Joseph Fornance, John Galbraith, James Gerry, Robert H. Hammond, Augustus C. Hand, John Hastings, Micajah T. Hawkins, John Hill of North Carolina, Solomon Hillen jr., Joel Holleman, Enos Hook, Tilghman A. Howard, David Hubbard, Thomas B. Jackson, John Jameson, Joseph Johnson, Cave Johnson, Nathaniel Jones, George M. Keim, Gouverneur Kemble, Daniel P. Leadbetter, Isaac Leet, Stephen B. Leonard, Dixon H. Lewis, Joshua A. Lowell, William Lucas, Abraham McLellan, George McCulloch, James J. McKay, Meredith Mallory, Albert G. Marchand, William Medill, John Miller, James D. L. Montanya, William Montgomery, Samuel W. Morris, Peter Newhard, Isaac Parrish, William Parmenter, Virgil D. Parris, Lemuel Paynter, David Petrikin, Francis W. Pickens, John H. Prentiss, William S. Ramsey, John Reynolds, R. Barnwell Rhett, Francis E. Rives, Thomas Robinson jr., Edward Rodgers, Green B. Samuels, Tristram Shaw, Charles Shepard, Albert Smith, John Smith, Thomas Smith, David A. Starkweather, Lewis Steenrod, Theron R. Strong, Henry Swearingen, George Sweeny, Jonathan Taylor, Francis Thomas, Philip F. Thomas, Jacob Thompson, Hopkins L. Turney, Aaron Vanderpoel, David D. Wagner, Harvey M. Watterson, John B. Weller, William W. Wick, Jared W. Williams, Henry Williams, John T. H. Worthington.

2. Members voting for Mr. Bell: 102.

John Quincy Adams, John W. Allen, Simeon H. Anderson, Landaff W. Andrews, Daniel D. Barnard, Richard Biddle, William K. Bond, John M. Botts, George N. Briggs, John H. Brockway, Anson Brown, William B. Calhoun, William B. Campbell, William B. Carter, Thomas W. Chinn, Thomas C. Chittenden, John C. Clark, James Cooper, Thomas Corwin, George W. Crabb, Robt. B. Cranston, John W. Crockett, Edward Curtis, Caleb Cushing, Edward Davies, Garret Davis, William C. Dawson, Edmund Deberry, John Dennis, James

Dellet, John Edwards, George Evans, Horace Everett, Millard Fillmore, Rice Garland, Seth M. Gates, Meredith P. Gentry, Joshua R. Giddings, William L. Goggin, Patrick G. Goode, James Graham, Francis Granger, Willis Green, William J. Graves, Moses H. Grinnell, Hiland Hall, William S. Hastings, Richard Hawes, Thomas Henry, John Hill of Virginia, Ogden Hoffman, Hiram P. Hunt, Francis James, Daniel Jenifer, Charles Johnston, William Cost Johnson, Abbott Lawrence, Levi Lincoln, Richard P. Marvin, Samson Mason, Charles F. Mercer, Charles F. Mitchell, James Monroe, Christopher Morgan, Calvary Morris, Charles Naylor, Charles Ogle, Thomas B. Osborne, Rufus Palen, Luther C. Peck, John Pope, George H. Proffit, Benjamin Randall, Joseph F. Randolph, James Rariden, Kenneth Rayner, John Reed, Joseph Ridgway, David Russell, Leverett Saltonstall, John Sergeant, William Simonton, William Slade, Truman Smith, Edward Stanly, William L. Storrs, John T. Stuart, John Taliaferro, Joseph L. Tillinghast, George W. Toland, Philip Triplett, Joseph Trumbull, Joseph R. Underwood, Peter J. Wagner, Edward D. White, John White, Thomas W. Williams, Lewis Williams, Joseph L. Williams, Christopher H. Williams, Sherrod Williams, Henry A. Wise.

3. Scattering: 20.

The following named members voted for William C. Dawson, of Georgia.

Julius C. Alford, John Bell, Edward J. Black, Richard W. Habersham, George W. Hopkins, Hiram P. Hunt, William Cost Johnson, Thomas B. King, Eugenius A. Nisbet, Waddy Thompson, jr., Lott Warren.

The following named members voted for Dixon H. Lewis, of Alabama:

John Campbell, Mark A. Cooper, John K. Griffin, John W. Jones, Walter T. Colquitt.

The following named members voted for Francis W. Pickens, of South Carolina:

Charles Fisher, Isaac E. Holmes, Robert M. T. Hunter, James Rogers, Thomas B. Sumter.

James Garland voted for George W. Hopkins, of Virginia.

Charles Ogle voted for Robert M. T. Hunter, of Virginia.

CHAPTER XL.

FIRST SESSION OF THE TWENTY-SIXTH CONGRESS: PRESIDENT'S MESSAGE.

The President met with firmness the new suspension of the banks of the southern and western half of the Union, headed by the Bank of the United States. Far from yielding to it he persevered in the recommendation of his great measures, found in their conduct new reasons for the divorce of Bank and State, and plainly reminded the delinquent institutions with a total want of the reasons for stopping payment which they had alleged two years before. He said:

"It now appears that there are other motives than a want of public confidence under which the banks seek to justify themselves in a refusal to meet their obligations. Scarcely were the country and government relieved, in a degree, from the difficulties occasioned by the general suspension of 1837, when a partial one, occurring within thirty months of the former, produced new and serious embarrassments, though it had no palliation in such circumstances as were alleged in justification of that which had previously taken place. There was nothing in the condition of the country to endanger a well-managed banking institution; commerce was deranged by no foreign war; every branch of manufacturing industry was crowned with rich rewards; and the more than usual abundance of our harvests, after supplying our domestic wants, had left our granaries and storehouses filled with a surplus for exportation. It is in the midst of this, that an irredeemable and depreciated paper currency is entailed upon the people by a large portion of the banks. They are not driven to it by the exhibition of a loss of public confidence; or of a sudden pressure from their depositors or note-holders, but they excuse themselves by alleging that the current of business, and exchange with foreign countries, which draws the precious metals from their vaults, would require, in order to meet it, a larger curtailment of their loans to a comparatively small portion of the community, than it will be convenient for them to bear, or perhaps safe for the banks to exact. The plea has ceased to be one of necessity. Convenience and policy are now deemed sufficient to warrant these institutions in disregarding their solemn obligations. Such conduct is not merely an injury to individual creditors, but it is a wrong to the whole community, from whose liberality they hold most valuable privileges—whose rights they violate, whose business they derange, and the value of whose property they render unstable and insecure. It must be evident that this new ground for bank suspensions, in reference to which their action is not only disconnected with, but wholly independent of, that of the public, gives a character to their suspensions more alarming than any which they exhibited before, and greatly increases the impropriety of relying on the banks in the transactions of the government."

The President also exposed the dangerous nature of the whole banking system from its chain of connection and mutual dependence of one upon another, so as to make the misfortune or criminality of one the misfortune of all. Our country banks were connected with those of New York and Philadelphia: they again with the Bank of England. So that a financial crisis commencing in London extends immediately to our great Atlantic cities; and thence throughout the States to the most petty institutions of the most remote villages and counties: so that the lever which raised or sunk our country banks was in New York and Philadelphia, while they themselves were worked by a lever in London; thereby subjecting our system to the vicissitudes of English banking, and especially while we had a national bank, which, by a law of its nature, would connect itself with the Bank of England. All this was well shown by the President, and improved into a reason for disconnecting ourselves from a moneyed system, which, in addition to its own inherent vices and fallibilities, was also subject to the vices, fallibilities, and even inimical designs of another, and a foreign system—belonging to a power, always our competitor in trade and manufactures—sometimes our enemy in open war.

"Distant banks may fail, without seriously affecting those in our principal commercial cities; but the failure of the latter is felt at the extremities of the Union. The suspension at New York, in 1837, was every where, with very few exceptions, followed, as soon as it was known; that recently at Philadelphia immediately affected the banks of the South and West in a similar manner. This dependence of our whole banking system on the institutions in a few large cities, is not found in the laws of their organization, but in those of trade and exchange. The banks at that centre to which currency flows, and where it is required in payments for merchandise, hold the power of controlling those in regions whence it comes, while the latter possess no means of restraining them; so that the value of individual property, and the prosperity of trade, through the whole interior of the country, are made to depend on the good or bad management of the banking institutions in the great seats of trade on the seaboard. But this chain of dependence does not stop here. It does not terminate at Philadelphia or New York. It reaches across the ocean, and ends in London, the centre of the credit system. The same laws of trade, which give to the banks in our principal cities power over the whole banking system of the United States, subject the former, in their turn, to the money power in Great Britain. It is not denied that the suspension of the New York banks in 1837, which was followed in quick succession throughout the Union, was partly produced by an application of that power; and it is now alleged, in extenuation of the present condition of so large a portion of our banks, that their embarrassments have arisen from the same cause. From this influence they cannot now entirely escape, for it has its origin in the credit currencies of the two countries; it is strengthened by the current of trade and exchange, which centres in London, and is rendered almost irresistible by the large debts contracted there by our merchants, our banks, and our States. It is thus that an introduction of a new bank into the most distant of our villages, places the business of that village within the influence of the money power in England. It is thus that every new debt which we contract in that country, seriously affects our own currency, and extends over the pursuits of our citizens its powerful influence. We cannot escape from this by making new banks, great or small, State or National. The same chains which bind those now existing to the centre of this system of paper credit, must equally fetter every similar institution we create. It is only by the extent to which this system has been pushed of late, that we have been made fully aware of its irresistible tendency to subject our own banks and currency to a vast controlling power in a foreign land; and it adds a new argument to those which illustrate their precarious situation. Endangered in the first place by their own mismanagement, and again by the conduct of every institution which connects them with the centre of trade in our own country, they are yet subjected, beyond all this, to the effect of whatever measures, policy, necessity, or caprice, may induce those who control the credits of England to resort to. Is an argument required beyond the exposition of these facts, to show the impropriety of using our banking institutions as depositories of the public money? Can we venture not only to encounter the risk of their individual and mutual mismanagement, but, at the same time, to place our foreign and domestic policy entirely under the control of a foreign moneyed interest? To do so is to impair the independence of our government, as the present credit system has already impaired the independence of our banks. It is to submit all its important operations, whether of peace or war, to be controlled or thwarted at first by our own banks, and then by a power abroad greater than themselves. I cannot bring myself to depict the humiliation to which this government and people might be sooner or later reduced, if the means for defending their rights are to be made dependent upon those who may have the most powerful of motives to impair them."

These were sagacious views, clearly and strongly presented, and new to the public. Few had contemplated the evils of our paper system, and the folly and danger of depending upon it for currency, under this extended and comprehensive aspect; but all saw it as soon as it was presented; and this actual dependence of our banks upon that of England became a new reason for the governmental dissolution of all connection with them. Happily they were working that dissolution themselves, and producing that disconnection by their delinquencies which they were able to prevent Congress from decreeing. An existing act of Congress forbid the employment of any non-specie paying bank as a government depository, and equally forbid the use of its paper. They expected to coerce the government to do both: it did neither: and the disconnection became complete, even before Congress enacted it.

The President had recommended, in his first annual message, the passage of a pre-emption act in the settlement of the public lands, and of a graduation act to reduce the price of the lands according to their qualities, governed by the length of time they had been in market. The former of these recommendations had been acted upon, and became law; and the President had now the satisfaction to communicate its beneficial operation.

> "On a former occasion your attention was invited to various considerations in support of a pre-emption law in behalf of the settlers on the public lands; and also of a law graduating the prices for such lands as had long been in the market unsold, in consequence of their inferior quality. The execution of the act which was passed on the first subject has been attended with the happiest consequences, in quieting titles, and securing improvements to the industrious; and it has also, to a very gratifying extent, been exempt from the frauds which were practised under previous pre-emption laws. It has, at the same time, as was anticipated, contributed liberally during the present year to the receipts of the Treasury. The passage of a graduation law, with the guards before recommended, would also, I am persuaded, add considerably to the revenue for several years, and prove in other respects just and beneficial. Your early consideration of the subject is, therefore, once more earnestly requested."

The opposition in Congress, who blamed the administration for the origin and conduct of the war with the Florida Indians, had succeeded in getting through Congress an appropriation for a negotiation with this tribe, and a resolve requesting the President to negotiate. He did so—with no other effect than to give an opportunity for renewed treachery and massacre. The message said:

> "In conformity with the expressed wishes of Congress, an attempt was made in the spring to terminate the Florida war by negotiation. It is to be regretted that these humane intentions should have been frustrated, and that the efforts to bring these unhappy difficulties to a satisfactory conclusion should have failed. But, after entering into solemn engagements with the Commanding General, the Indians, without any provocation, recommenced their acts of treachery and murder. The renewal of hostilities in that Territory renders it necessary that I should recommend to your favorable consideration the measure proposed by the Secretary at War (the armed occupation of the Territory)."

With all foreign powers the message had nothing but what was friendly and desirable to communicate. Nearly every question of dissension and dispute had been settled under the administration of his predecessor. The accumulated wrongs of thirty years to the property and persons of our citizens, had been redressed under President Jackson. He left the foreign world in peace and friendship with his country; and his successor maintained the amicable relations so happily established.

CHAPTER XLI.

DIVORCE OF BANK AND STATE; DIVORCE DECREED.

This measure, so long and earnestly contested, was destined to be carried into effect at this session; but not without an opposition on the part of the whig members in each House, which exhausted both the powers of debate, and the rules and acts of parliamentary warfare. Even after the bill had passed through all its forms—had been engrossed for the third reading, and actually been read a third time and was waiting for the call of the vote, with a fixed majority shown to be in its favor—the warfare continued upon it, with no other view than to excite the people against it: for its passage in the Senate was certain. It was at this last moment that Mr. Clay delivered one of his impassioned and glowing speeches against it.

"Mr. President, it is no less the duty of the statesman than the physician, to ascertain the exact state of the body to which he is to minister before he ventures to prescribe any healing remedy. It is with no pleasure, but with profound regret, that I survey the present condition of our country. I have rarely, I think never, known a period of such universal and intense distress. The general government is in debt, and its existing revenue is inadequate to meet its ordinary expenditure. The States are in debt, some of them largely in debt, insomuch that they have been compelled to resort to the ruinous expedient of contracting new loans to meet the interest upon prior loans; and the people are surrounded with difficulties; greatly embarrassed, and involved in debt. Whilst this is, unfortunately, the general state of the country, the means of extinguishing this vast mass of debt are in constant diminution. Property is falling in value—all the great staples of the country are declining in price, and destined, I fear, to further decline. The certain tendency of this very measure is to reduce prices. The banks are rapidly decreasing the amount of their circulation. About one-half of them, extending from New Jersey to the extreme Southwest, have suspended specie payments, presenting an image of a paralytic, one moiety of whose body is stricken with palsy. The banks are without a head; and, instead of union, concert, and co-operation between them, we behold jealousy, distrust, and enmity. We have no currency whatever possessing uniform value throughout the whole country. That which we have, consisting almost entirely of the issues of banks, is in a state of the utmost disorder, insomuch that it varies, in comparison with the specie standard, from par to fifty per cent. discount. Exchanges, too, are in the greatest possible confusion, not merely between distant parts of the Union, but between cities and places in the same neighborhood. That between our great commercial marts of New York and Philadelphia, within five or six hours of each other, vacillating between seven and ten per cent. The products of our agricultural industry are unable to find their way to market from the want of means in the hands of traders to purchase them, or from the want of confidence in the stability of things. Many of our manufactories stopped or stopping, especially in the important branch of woollens; and a vast accumulation of their fabrics on hand, owing to the destruction of confidence and the wretched state of exchange between different sections of the Union. Such is the unexaggerated picture of our present condition. And amidst the dark and dense cloud that surrounds us, I perceive not one gleam of light. It gives me nothing but pain to sketch the picture. But duty and truth require that existing diseases should be fearlessly examined and probed to the bottom. We shall otherwise be utterly incapable of conceiving or applying appropriate remedies. If the present unhappy state of our country had been brought upon the people by their folly and extravagance, it ought to be borne with fortitude, and without complaint, and without reproach. But it is my deliberate judgment that it has not been—that the people are not to blame—and that the principal causes of existing embarrassments are not to be traced to them. Sir, it is not my purpose to waste the time or excite the feelings of members of the Senate by dwelling long on what I suppose to be those causes. My object is a better, a higher, and I hope a more acceptable one—to consider the remedies proposed for the present exigency. Still, I should not fulfil my whole duty if I did not briefly say that, in my conscience, I believe our pecuniary distresses have mainly sprung from the refusal to recharter the late Bank of the United States; the removal of the public deposits from that institution; the multiplication of State banks in consequence; and the Treasury stimulus given to them to extend their operations; the bungling manner in which the law, depositing the surplus treasure with the States, was executed; the Treasury circular; and although last, perhaps not least, the exercise of the power of the veto on the bill for distributing, among the States, the net proceeds of the sales of the public lands."

This was the opening of the speech—the continuation and conclusion of which was bound to be in harmony with this beginning; and obliged to fill up the picture so pathetically drawn. It did so, and the vote being at last taken, the bill passed by a fair majority—24 to 18. But it had the House of Representatives still to encounter, where it had met its fate before; and to that House it was immediately sent for its concurrence. A majority were known to be for it; but the shortest road was taken to its passage; and that was under the debate-killing pressure of the previous question. That question was freely used; and amendment after amendment cut off; motion after motion stifled; speech after speech suppressed; the bill carried from stage to stage by a sort of silent struggle (chiefly interrupted by the repeated process of calling yeas and nays), until at last it reached the final vote—and was passed—by a majority, not large, but clear—124 to 107. This was the 30th of June, that is to say, within twenty days of the end of a session of near eight months. The previous question, so often abused, now so properly used (for the bill was an old measure, on which not a new word was to be spoken, or a vote to be changed, the only effort being to stave it off until the end of the session), accomplished this good work— and opportunely; for the next Congress was its deadly foe.

The bill was passed, but the bitter spirit which pursued it was not appeased. There is a form to be gone through after the bill has passed all its three readings—the form of agreeing to its title. This is as much a matter of course and form as it is to give a child a name after it is born: and, in both cases, the parents having the natural right of bestowing the name. But in the case of this bill the title becomes a question, which goes to the House, and gives to the enemies of the measure a last chance of showing their temper towards it: for it is a form in which nothing but temper can be shown. This is sometimes done by simply voting against the title, as proposed by its friends—at others, and where the opposition is extreme, it is done by a motion to amend the title by striking it out, and substituting another of odium, and this mode of opposition gives the party opposed to it an opportunity of expressing an opinion on the merits of the bill itself, compressed into an essence, and spread upon the journal for a perpetual remembrance. This was the form adopted on this occasion. The name borne at the head of the bill was inoffensive, and descriptive. It described the bill according to its contents, and did it in appropriate and modest terms. None of the phrases used in debate, such as "Divorce of Bank and State," "Sub-treasury," "Independent Treasury," &c., and which had become annoying to the opposition, were employed, but a plain title of description in these terms: "*An act to provide for the collection, safe-keeping, and disbursing of the public money.*" To this title Mr. James Cooper, of Pennsylvania, moved an amendment, in the shape of a substitute, in these words: "*An act to reduce the value of property, the products of the farmer, and the wages of labor, to destroy the indebted portions of the community, and to place the Treasury of the nation in the hands of the President.*" Before a vote could be taken upon this proposed substitute, Mr. Caleb Cushing, of Massachusetts, proposed to amend it by adding "*to enable the public money to be drawn from the public Treasury without appropriation made by law,*" and having proposed this amendment to Mr. Cooper's amendment, Mr. Cushing began to speak to the contents of the bill. Then followed a scene in which the parliamentary history must be allowed to speak for itself.

> "Mr. CUSHING then resumed, and said he had moved the amendment with a view of making a very limited series of remarks pertinent to the subject. He was then proceeding to show why, in his opinion, the contents of the bill did not agree with its title, when

> "Mr. *Petrikin*, of Pennsylvania, called him to order.

> "The Speaker said the gentleman from Massachusetts had a right to amend the title of the bill, if it were not a proper title. He had, therefore, a right to examine the contents of the bill, to show that the title was improper.

> "Mr. PETRIKIN still objected.

"The Speaker said the gentleman from Pennsylvania would be pleased to reduce his point of order to writing.

"Mr. PROFFIT, of Indiana, called Mr. Petrikin to order; and after some colloquial debate, the objection was withdrawn.

"Mr. CUSHING then resumed, and appeared very indignant at the interruption. He wished to know if the measure was to be forced on the country without affording an opportunity to say a single word. He said they were at the last act in the drama, but the end was not yet. Mr. C. then proceeded to give his reasons why he considered the bill as an unconstitutional measure, as he contended that it gave the Secretary power to draw on the public money without appropriations by law. He concluded by observing that he had witnessed the incubation and hatching of this *cockatrice*, but he hoped the time was not far distant when the people would put their feet on the *reptile* and crush it to the dust.

"Mr. PICKENS, of South Carolina, then rose, and in a very animated manner said he had wished to make a few remarks upon the bill before its passage, but he was now compelled to confine himself in reply to the very extraordinary language and tone assumed by the gentleman from Massachusetts. What right had he to speak of this bill as being forced on the country by "*brutal numbers?*" That gentleman had defined the bill according to *his* conception of it; but he would tell the gentleman, that the bill would, thank God, deliver this government from the hands of those who for so many years had lived by *swindling* the proceeds of honest labor. Yes, said Mr. P., I thank my God that the hour of our deliverance is now so near, from a system which has wrung the hard earnings from productive industry for the benefit of a few irresponsible corporations.

"Sir, I knew the contest would be fierce and bitter. The bill, in its principles, draws the line between the great *laboring and landed interests* of this confederacy, and those who are identified with *capitalists in stocks* and live upon *incorporated credit*. The latter class have lived and fattened upon the fiscal action of this government, from the *funding system* down to the present day—and now they feel like wolves who have been driven back from the warm blood they have been lapping for forty years. Well may the gentleman [Mr. CUSHING], who represents those interests, cry out and exclaim that it is a bill passed in force by fraud and power—it is the power and the spirit of a free people determined to redeem themselves and their government.

"Here the calls to order were again renewed from nearly every member of the opposition, and great confusion prevailed.

"The Speaker with much difficulty succeeded in restoring something like order, and as none of those who had so vociferously called Mr. P. to order, raised any point,

"Mr. PICKENS proceeded with his remarks, and alluding to the words of Mr. Cushing, that "this was the last act of the drama," said this was the first, and not the last act of the drama. There were great questions that lay behind this, connected with the fiscal action of the government, and which we will be called on to decide in the next few years; they were all connected with one great and complicated system. This was the commencement, and only a branch of the system.

"Here the cries of order from the opposition were renewed, and after the storm had somewhat subsided,

"Mr. P. said, rather than produce confusion at that late hour of the day, when this great measure was so near a triumphant consummation, and, in spite of all the exertions of its enemies, was about to become the law of the land, he would not trespass any longer on the attention of the House. But the gentleman had said that because the first section had declared what should constitute the Treasury, and that another section had provided for keeping portions of the Treasury in other places than the safes and vaults in the Treasury building of this place; that, therefore, it was to be inferred that those who were to execute it would draw money from the Treasury without appropriations by law, and thus to perpetrate a fraud upon the constitution. Mr. P. said, let those who are to execute this bill dare to commit this outrage, and use money for purposes not intended in appropriations by law, and they would be visited with the indignation of an outraged and wronged people. It would be too gross and palpable. Such is not the broad meaning and intention of the bill. The construction given by the gentleman was a forced and technical one, and not natural. It was too strained to be seriously entertained by any one for a moment. He raised his protest against it.

"Mr. P. regretted the motion admitted of such narrow and confined debate. He would not delay the passage of the bill upon so small a point. He congratulated the country that we had approached the period when the measure was about to be triumphantly passed into a permanent law of the land. It is a great measure. Considering the lateness of the hour, the confusion in the House, and that the gentleman had had the advantage of an opening speech, he now concluded by demanding the previous question.

"On this motion the disorder among the opposition was renewed with tenfold fury, and some members made use of some very hard words, accompanied by violent gesticulation.

"It was some minutes before any thing approaching order could be restored.

"The Speaker having called on the sergeant-at-arms to clear the aisles,

"The call of the previous question was seconded, and the main question on the amendment to the amendment ordered to be put.

"The motion for the previous question having received a second, the main question was ordered.

"The question was then taken on Mr. Cushing's amendment to the amendment, and disagreed to without a count.

"The question recurring on the substitute of Mr. Cooper, of Pennsylvania, for the original title of the bill,

"Mr. R. GARLAND, of Louisiana, demanded the yeas and nays, which having been ordered, were—yeas 87, nays 128."

Eighty-seven members voted, on yeas and nays, for Mr. Cooper's proposed title, which was a strong way of expressing their opinion of it. For Mr. Cushing's amendment to it, there were too few to obtain a division of the House; and thus the bill became complete by getting a name—but only by the summary, silent, and enforcing process of the previous question. Even the title was obtained by that process. The passage of this act was the distinguishing glory of the Twenty-sixth Congress, and the "crowning mercy" of Mr. Van Buren's administration. Honor and gratitude to the members, and all the remembrance which this book can give them. Their names were:

IN THE SENATE:—Messrs. Allen of Ohio, Benton, Brown of North Carolina, Buchanan, Calhoun, Clay of Alabama, Cuthbert of Georgia, Fulton of Arkansas, Grundy, Hubbard of New Hampshire, King of Alabama, Linn of Missouri, Lumpkin of Georgia, Mouton of Louisiana, Norvell of Michigan, Pierce of New Hampshire, Roane of Virginia, Sevier of Arkansas, Smith of Connecticut, Strange of North Carolina, Tappan of Ohio, Walker of Mississippi, Williams of Maine.

IN THE HOUSE OF REPRESENTATIVES:—Messrs. Judson Allen, Hugh J. Anderson, Charles G. Atherton, William Cost Johnson, Cave Johnson, Nathaniel Jones, John W. Jones, George M. Keim, Gouverneur Kemble, Joseph Kille, Daniel P. Leadbetter, Isaac Leet, Stephen B. Leonard, Dixon H. Lewis, Joshua A. Lowell, William Lucas, Abraham McClellan, George McCulloch, James J. McKay, Meredith Mallory, Albert G. Marchand, William Medill, John

Miller, James D. L. Montanya, Linn Banks, William Beatty, Andrew Beirne, William Montgomery, Samuel W. Morris, Peter Newhard, Isaac Parrish, William Parmenter, Virgil D. Parris, Lemuel Paynter, David Petrikin, Francis W. Pickens, John H. Prentiss, William S. Ramsey, John Reynolds, R. Barnwell Rhett, Francis E. Rives, Thomas Robinson, Jr., Edward Rogers, James Rogers, Daniel B. Ryall, Green B. Samuels, Tristram Shaw, Charles Shepard, Edward J. Black, Julius W. Blackwell, Linn Boyd, John Smith, Thomas Smith, David A. Starkweather, Lewis Steenrod, Theron R. Strong, Thomas D. Sumter, Henry Swearingen, George Sweeney, Jonathan Taylor, Francis Thomas, Philip F. Thomas, Jacob Thompson, Hopkins L. Turney, Aaron Vanderpoel, Peter D. Vroom, David D. Wagener, Harvey M. Watterson, John B. Weller, Jared W. Williams, Henry Williams, John T. H. Worthington.

CHAPTER XLII.

FLORIDA ARMED OCCUPATION BILL: MR. BENTON'S SPEECH: EXTRACTS.

Armed occupation, with land to the occupant, is the true way of settling and holding a conquered country. It is the way which has been followed in all ages, and in all countries, from the time that the children of Israel entered the promised land, with the implements of husbandry in one hand, and the weapons of war in the other. From that day to this, all conquered countries had been settled in that way. Armed[1688] settlement, and a homestead in the soil, was the principle of the Roman military colonies, by which they consolidated their conquests. The northern nations bore down upon the south of Europe in that way: the settlers of the New World—our pilgrim fathers and all—settled these States in that way: the settlement of Kentucky and Tennessee was effected in the same way. The armed settlers went forth to fight, and to cultivate. They lived in stations first—an assemblage of blockhouses (the Roman presidium), and emerged to separate settlements afterwards; and in every instance, an interest in the soil—an inheritance in the land—was the reward of their enterprise, toil, and danger. The peninsula of Florida is now prepared for this armed settlement: the enemy has been driven out of the field. He lurks, an unseen foe, in the swamps and hammocks. He no longer shows himself in force, or ventures a combat; but, dispersed and solitary, commits individual murders and massacres. The country is prepared for armed settlement.

It is the fashion—I am sorry to say it—to depreciate the services of our troops in Florida—to speak of them as having done nothing; as having accomplished no object for the country, and acquired no credit for themselves. This was a great error. The military had done an immensity there; they had done all that arms could do, and a great deal that the axe and the spade could do. They had completely conquered the country; that is to say, they had driven the enemy from the field; they had dispersed the foe; they had reduced them to a roving banditti, whose only warfare was to murder stragglers and families. Let any one compare the present condition of Florida with what it was at the commencement of the war, and see what a change has taken place. Then combats were frequent. The Indians embodied continually, fought our troops, both regulars, militia, and volunteers. Those hard contests cannot be forgotten. It cannot be forgotten how often these Indians met our troops in force, or hung upon the flanks of marching columns, harassing and attacking them at every favorable point. Now all this is done. For two years past, we have heard of no such thing. The Indians, defeated in these encounters, and many of them removed to the West, have now retired from the field, and dispersed in small parties over the whole peninsula of Florida. They are dispersed over a superficies of 45,000 square miles, and that area sprinkled all over with haunts adapted to their shelter, to which they retire for safety like wild beasts, and emerge again for new mischief. Our military have then done much; they have done all that military can do; they have broken, dispersed, and scattered the enemy. They have driven them out of the field; they have prepared the country for settlement, that is to say, for armed settlement. There has been no battle, no action, no skirmish, in Florida, for upwards of two years. The last combats were at Okeechobee and Caloosahatchee, above two years ago. There has been no *war* since that time; nothing but individual massacres. The country has been waiting for settlers for two years; and this bill provides for them, and offers them inducements to settle.

Besides their military labors, our troops have done an immensity of labor of a different kind. They have penetrated and perforated the whole peninsula of Florida; they have gone through the *Serbonian bogs* of that peninsula; they have gone where the white man's foot never before was seen to tread; and where no Indian believed it could ever come. They have gone from the Okeefekonee swamp to the Everglades; they have crossed the peninsula backwards and forwards, from the Gulf of Mexico to the Atlantic Ocean. They have sounded every morass, threaded every hammock, traced every creek, examined every lake, and made the topography of the country as well known as that of the counties of our States. The maps which the topographical officers have constructed, and the last of which is in the Report of the Secretary at War, attest the extent of these explorations, and the accuracy and minuteness of the surveys and examinations. Besides all this, the troops have established some hundreds of posts; they have opened many hundred miles of wagon road; and they have constructed some thousands of feet of causeways and bridges. These are great and meritorious labors. They are labors which prepare the country for settlement; prepare it for the 10,000 armed cultivators which this bill proposes to send there.

Mr. B. said he paid this tribute cheerfully to the merits of our military, and our volunteers and militia employed in Florida; the more cheerfully, because it was the inconsiderate custom of too many to depreciate the labors of these brave men. He took pleasure, here in his place, in the American Senate, to do them justice; and that without drawing invidious comparisons—without attempting to exalt some at the expense of others. He viewed with a favorable eye—with friendly feelings—with prepossessions in their favor—all who were doing their best for their country; and all such—all who did their best for their country—should have his support and applause, whether fortune was more or less kind to them, in crowning their meritorious exertions with success. He took pleasure in doing all this justice; but his tribute would be incomplete, if he did not add what was said by the Secretary at War, in his late report, and also by the immediate commander, General Taylor.

Mr. B. repeated, that the military had done their duty, and deserved well of their country. They had brought the war to that point, when there was no longer an enemy to be fought; when there was nothing left but a banditti to be extirpated. Congress, also, had tried its policy—the policy of peace and conciliation—and the effort only served to show the unparalleled treachery and savageism of the ferocious beasts with which we had to deal. He alluded to the attempts at negotiation and pacification, tried this summer under an intimation from Congress. The House of Representatives, at the last session, voted $5,000 for opening negotiations with these Indians. When the appropriation came to the Senate, it was objected to by himself and some others, from the knowledge they had of the character of these Indians, and their belief that it would end in treachery and misfortune. The House adhered; the appropriation was made; the administration acted upon it, as they felt bound to do; and behold the result of the attempt! The most cruel and perfidious massacres plotted and contrived while making the treaty itself! a particular officer selected, and stipulated to be sent to a particular point, under the pretext of establishing a trading-post, and as a protector, there to be massacred! a horrible massacre in reality perpetrated there; near seventy persons since massacred, including families; the Indians themselves emboldened by our offer of peace, and their success in treachery; and the whole aspect of the war made worse by our injudicious attempt at pacification.

Lt. Col. Harney, with a few soldiers and some citizens, was reposing on the banks of the Caloosahatchee, under the faith of treaty negotiations, and on treaty ground. He was asleep. At the approach of daybreak he was roused by the firing and yells of the Indians, who had got possession of the camp, and killed the sergeant and more than one-half of his men. Eleven soldiers and five citizens were killed; eight soldiers and two citizens escaped. Seven of the soldiers, taking refuge in a small sail-boat, then lying off in the stream, in which the two citizens fortunately had slept that night, as soon as possible weighed anchor, and favored by a light breeze, slipped off unperceived by the Indians. The Colonel himself escaped with great difficulty, and after walking fifteen miles down the river, followed by one soldier, came to a canoe, which he had left there the evening previous, and succeeded, by this means, in getting on board the sail-boat, where he found those who had escaped in her. Before he laid down to sleep, the treacherous Chitto Tustenuggee, partaking his hospitality, lavished proofs of friendship upon him. Here was an instance of treachery of which there was no parallel in Indian warfare. With all their treachery, the treaty-ground is a sacred spot with the Indians; but here, in the very articles of a treaty itself, they plan a murderous destruction of an officer whom they solicited to be sent with them as their protector; and, to gratify all their passions of murder and robbery at once, they stipulate to have their victims sent to a remote point, with settlers and traders, as well as soldiers, and with a supply of goods. All this they arranged; and too successfully did they execute the plan. And this was the beginning of their *execution* of the treaty. Massacres, assassinations, robberies, and house-burnings, have followed it up, until the suburbs of St. Augustine and Tallahasse are stained with blood, and blackened with fire. About seventy murders have since taken place, including the destruction of the shipwrecked crews and passengers on the southern extremity of the peninsula.

The plan of Congress has, then, been tried; the experiment of negotiation has been tried and has ended disastrously and cruelly for us, and with greatly augmenting the confidence and ferocity of the enemy. It puts an end to all idea of finishing the war there by peaceable negotiation. Chastisement is what is due to these Indians, and what they expect. They mean to keep no faith with the government, and henceforth they will expect no faith to be reposed in them. The issue is now made; we have to expel them by force, or give up forty-five thousand square miles of territory—much of it an old settled country—to be ravaged by this banditti.

The plan of Congress has been tried, and has ended in disaster; the military have done all that military can do; the administration have now in the country all the troops which can be spared for the purpose. They have there the one-half of our regular infantry, to wit: four regiments out of eight; they have there the one-half of our dragoons, to wit: one regiment; they even have there a part of our artillery, to wit: one regiment; and they have besides, there, a part of the naval force to scour the coasts and inlets; and, in addition to all this, ten companies of Florida volunteers. Even the marines under their accomplished commander (Col. Henderson), and at his request, have been sent there to perform gallant service, on an element not their own. No more of our troops can be spared for that purpose; the West and the North require the remainder, and more than the remainder. The administration can do no more than it has done with the means at its command. It is laid under the necessity of asking other means; and the armed settlers provided for in this bill are the principal means required. One thousand troops for the war, is all that is asked in addition to the settlers, in this bill.

This then is the point we are at: To choose between granting these means, or doing nothing! Yes, sir, to choose between the recommendations of the administration, and nothing! I say, these, or nothing; for I presume Congress will not prescribe another attempt at negotiation; no one will recommend an increase of ten thousand regular troops; no one will recommend a draft of ten thousand militia. It is, then, the plan of the administration, or nothing; and this brings us to the question, whether the government can now fold its arms, leave the regulars to man their posts, and abandon the country to the Indians? This is now the question; and to this point I will direct the observations which make it impossible for us to abdicate our duty, and abandon the country to the Indians.

I assume it then as a point granted, that Florida cannot be given up—that she cannot be abandoned—that she cannot be left in her present state. What then is to be done? Raise an army of ten thousand men to go there to fight? Why, the men who are there now can find nobody to fight! It is two years since a fight has been had; it is two years since we have heard of a fight. Ten men, who will avoid surprises and ambuscades, can now go from one end of Florida to the other. As warriors, these Indians no longer appear, it is only as assassins, as robbers, as incendiaries, that they lurk about. The country wants settlers, not an army. It has wanted these settlers for two years; and this bill provides for them, and offers them the proper inducements to go. And here I take the three great positions, that this bill is the *appropriate* remedy; that it is the *efficient* remedy; that it is the *cheap* remedy, for the cure of the Florida difficulties. It is the appropriate remedy; for what is now wanted, is not an army to fight, but settlers and cultivators to retain possession of the country, and to defend their possessions. We want people to take possession, and keep possession, and the armed cultivator is the man for that. The blockhouse is the first house to be built in an Indian country; the stockade is the first fence to be put up. Within that blockhouse, and a few of them together—a hollow square of blockhouses, two miles long on each side, two hundred yards apart, and enclosing a good field—safe habitations are found for families. The faithful mastiff, to give notice of the approach of danger, and a few trusty rifles in brave hands, make all safe. Cultivation and defence then goes hand in hand. The heart of the Indian sickens when he hears the crowing of the cock, the barking of the dog, the sound of the axe, and the crack of the rifle. These are the true evidences of the dominion of the white man; these are the proof that the owner has come, and means to stay; and then they feel it to be time for them to go. While soldiers alone are in the country, they feel their presence to be temporary; that they are mere sojourners in the land, and sooner or later must go away. It is the settler alone, the armed settler, whose presence announces the dominion—the permanent dominion—of the white man.

It is the most efficient remedy. On this point we can speak with confidence, for the other remedies have been tried, and have failed. The other remedies are to catch the Indians, and remove them; or, to negotiate with them, and induce them to go off. Both have been tried; both are exhausted. No human being now thinks that our soldiers can catch these Indians; no one now believes in the possibility of removing them by treaty. No other course remains to be tried, but the armed settlement; and that is so obvious, that it is difficult to see how any one that has read history, or has heard how this new world was settled, or how Kentucky and Tennessee were settled, can doubt it.

The peninsula is a desolation. Five counties have been depopulated. The inhabitants of five counties—the survivors of many massacres—have been driven from their homes: this bill is intended to induce them to return, and to induce others to go along with them. Such inducements to settle and defend new countries have been successful in all ages and in all nations; and cannot fail to be effectual with us. *Deliberat Roma, perit Saguntum*, became the watchword of reproach, and of stimulus to action in the Roman Senate when the Senate deliberated while a colony was perishing. *Saguntum perishes while Rome deliberates*: and this is truly the case with ourselves and Florida. That beautiful and unfortunate territory is a prey to plunder, fire, and murder. The savages kill, burn and rob—where they find a man, a house, or an animal in the desolation which they have made. Large part of the territory is the empty and bloody skin of an immolated victim.

CHAPTER XLIII.

ASSUMPTION OF THE STATE DEBTS.

About one-half of the States had contracted debts abroad which they were unable to pay when due, and in many instances were unable to pay the current annual interest. These debts at this time amounted to one hundred and seventy millions of dollars, and were chiefly due in Great Britain. They had been converted into a stock, and held in shares, and had gone into a great number of hands; and from defaults in payments were greatly depreciated. The Reverend Sydney Smith, of witty memory, and amiable withal, was accustomed to lose all his amiability, but no part of his wit, when he spoke of his Pennsylvania bonds—which in fact was very often. But there was another class of these bond-holders who did not exhale their griefs in wit, caustic as it might be, but looked to more substantial relief—to an assumption in some form, disguised or open, virtual or actual, of these debts by the federal government. These British capitalists, connected with capitalists in the United States, possessed a weight on this point which was felt in the halls of Congress. The disguised attempts at this assumption, were in the various modes of conveying federal money to the States in the shape of distributing surplus revenue, of dividing the public land money, and of bestowing money on the States under the fallacious title of a deposit. But a more direct provision in their behalf was wanted by these capitalists, and in the course of the year 1839 a movement to that effect was openly made through the columns of their regular organ—The London Bankers' Circular, emanating from the most respectable and opulent house of the Messrs. Baring, Brothers and Company. At this open procedure on the part of these capitalists, it was deemed expedient to meet the attempt *in limine* by a positive declaration in Congress against the constitutionality, the justice, and the policy of any such measure. With this view Mr. Benton, at the commencement of the first session of Congress after the issuing of the Bankers' Circular, submitted a series of resolutions in the Senate, which, with some modification, and after an earnest debate, were passed in that body. These were the resolutions:

"1. That the assumption of such debts either openly, by a direct promise to pay them, or disguisedly by going security for their payment, or by creating surplus revenue, or applying the national funds to pay them, would be a gross and flagrant violation of the constitution, wholly unwarranted by the letter or spirit of that instrument, and utterly repugnant to all the objects and purposes for which the federal Union was formed.

"2. That the debts of the States being now chiefly held by foreigners, and constituting a stock in foreign markets greatly depreciated, any legislative attempt to obtain the assumption or securityship of the United States for their payment, or to provide for their payment out of the national funds, must have the effect of enhancing the value of that stock to the amount of a great many millions of dollars, to the enormous and undue advantage of foreign capitalists, and of jobbers and gamblers in stocks; thereby holding out inducement to foreigners to interfere in our affairs, and to bring all the influences of a moneyed power to operate upon public opinion, upon our elections, and upon State and federal legislation, to produce a consummation so tempting to their cupidity, and so profitable to their interest.

"3. That foreign interference and foreign influence, in all ages, and in all countries, have been the bane and curse of free governments; and that such interference and influence are far more dangerous, in the insidious intervention of the moneyed power, than in the forcible invasions of fleets and armies.

"4. That to close the door at once against all applications for such assumption, and to arrest at their source the vast tide of evils which would flow from it, it is necessary that the constituted authorities, without delay, shall RESOLVE and DECLARE their utter opposition to the proposal contained in the late London Bankers' Circular in relation to State debts, contracted for local and State purposes, and recommending to the Congress of the United States to assume, or guarantee, or provide for the ultimate payment of said debts."

In the course of the discussion of these resolutions an attempt was made to amend them, and to reverse their import, by obtaining a direct vote of the Senate in favor of distributing the public land revenue among the

States to aid them in the payment of these debts. This proposition was submitted by Mr. Crittenden, of Kentucky; and was in these words: "That it would be just and proper to distribute the proceeds of the sales of the public lands among the several States in fair and ratable proportions; and that the condition of such of the States as have contracted debts is such, at the present moment of pressure and difficulty, as to render such distribution especially expedient and important." This proposition received a considerable support, and was rejected upon yeas and nays—28 to 17. The yeas were Messrs. Betts of Connecticut, Clay of Kentucky, Crittenden, Davis of Massachusetts, Dixon of Rhode Island, Knight of Connecticut, Merrick of Maryland, Phelps of Vermont, Porter of Michigan, Prentiss of Vermont, Ruggles of Maine, Smith of Indiana, Southard of New Jersey, Spence of Maryland, Tallmadge, Webster, White of Indiana. The nays were: Messrs. Allen of Ohio, Anderson of Tennessee, Benton, Bedford Brown, Calhoun, Clay of Alabama, Alfred Cuthbert, Grundy, Henderson of Mississippi, Hubbard, King of Alabama, Linn of Missouri, Lumpkin of Georgia, Mouton, Nicholas of Louisiana, Norvell of Michigan, Pierce, Preston, Roane, Robinson, Sevier, Strange, Sturgeon, Tappan of Ohio, Wall of New Jersey, Williams, Wright. As the mover of the resolutions Mr. Benton supported them in a speech, of which some extracts are given in the next chapter.

CHAPTER XLIV.

ASSUMPTION OF THE STATE DEBTS: MR. BENTON'S SPEECH: EXTRACTS.

The assumption of the State debts contracted for State purposes has been for a long time a measure disguisedly, and now is a measure openly, pressed upon the public mind. The movement in favor of it has been long going on; opposing measures have not yet commenced. The assumption party have the start, and the advantage of conducting the case; and they have been conducting it for a long time, and in a way to avoid the name of assumption while accomplishing the thing itself. All the bills for distributing the public land revenue—all the propositions for dividing surplus revenue—all the refusals to abolish unnecessary taxes—all the refusals to go on with the necessary defences of the country—were so many steps taken in the road to assumption. I know very well that many who supported these measures had no idea of assumption, and would oppose it as soon as discovered; but that does not alter the nature of the measures they supported, and which were so many steps in the road to that assumption, then shrouded in mystery and futurity, now ripened into strength, and emboldened into a public disclosure of itself. Already the State legislatures are occupied with this subject, while we sit here, waiting its approach.

It is time for the enemies of assumption to take the field, and to act. It is a case in which they should give, and not receive, the attack. The President has led the way; he has shown his opinions. He has nobly done his duty. He has shown the evils of diverting the general funds from their proper objects—the mischiefs of our present connection with the paper system of England—and the dangers of foreign influence from any further connection with it. In this he has discharged a constitutional and a patriotic duty. Let the constituted authorities, each in their sphere, follow his example, and declare their opinions also. Let the Senate especially, as part of the legislative power—as the peculiar representative of the States in their sovereign capacity—let this body declare its sentiments, and, by its resolves and discussions, arrest the progress of the measure here, and awaken attention to it elsewhere. As one of the earliest opposers of this measure—as, in fact, the very earliest opposer of the whole family of measures of which it is the natural offspring—as having denounced the assumption in disguise in a letter to my constituents long before the London Bankers' letter revealed it to the public: as such early, steadfast, and first denouncer of this measure, I now come forward to oppose it in form, and to submit the resolves which may arrest it here, and carry its discussion to the forum of the people.

I come at once to the point, and say that disguised assumption, in the shape of land revenue distribution, is the form in which we shall have to meet the danger; and I meet it at once in that disguise. I say there is no authority in the constitution to raise money from any branch of the revenue for distribution among the States, or to distribute that which had been raised for other purposes. The power of Congress to raise money is not unlimited and arbitrary, but restricted, and directed to the national objects named in the constitution. The means, the amount, and the application, are all limited. The means are direct taxes—duties on imports—and the public lands; the objects are the support of the government—the common defence—and the payment of the debts of the Union: the amount to be raised is of course limited to the amount required for the accomplishment of these objects. Consonant to the words and the spirit of the constitution, is the title, the preamble and the tenor of all the early statutes for raising money; they all declare the object for which the money is wanted; they declare the object at the head of the act. Whether it be a loan, a direct tax, or a duty on imports, the object of the loan, the tax, or the duty, is stated in the preamble to the act; Congress thus excusing and justifying themselves for the demand in the very act of making it, and telling the people plainly what they wanted with the money. This was the way in all the early statutes; the books are full of examples; and it was only after money began to be levied for objects not known to the constitution, that this laudable and ancient practice was dropped. Among the enumerated objects for which money can be raised by Congress, is that of paying the debts of the Union; and is it not a manifest absurdity to suppose that, while it requires an express grant of power to enable us to pay the debts of the Union, we can pay those of the States by implication and by indirection? No, sir, no. There is no constitutional way to assume these State debts, or to pay them, or to indorse them, or to smuggle the money to the States for that purpose, under the pretext of dividing land revenue, or surplus revenue, among them. There is no way to do it. The whole thing is constitutionally impossible. It was never thought of by the framers of our constitution. They never dreamed of such a thing.

There is not a word in their work to warrant it, and the whole idea of it is utterly repugnant and offensive to the objects and purposes for which the federal Union was framed.

We have had one assumption in our country and that in a case which was small in amount, and free from the impediment of a constitutional objection; but which was attended by such evils as should deter posterity from imitating the example. It was in the first year of the federal government; and although the assumed debts were only twenty millions, and were alleged to have been contracted for general purposes, yet the assumption was attended by circumstances of intrigue and corruption, which led to the most violent dissension in Congress, suspended the business of the two Houses, drove some of the States to the verge of secession, and menaced the Union with instant dissolution. Mr. Jefferson, who was a witness of the scene, and who was overpowered by General Hamilton, and by the actual dangers of the country, into its temporary support, thus describes it:

"This game was over (funding the soldiers' certificates), and another was on the carpet at the moment of my arrival; and to this I was most ignorantly and innocently made to hold the candle. This fiscal manœuvre is well known by the name of the assumption. Independently of the debts of Congress, the States had, during the war, contracted separate and heavy debts, &c. * * * * This money, whether wisely or foolishly spent, was pretended to have been spent for *general* purposes, and ought therefore to be paid from the *general* purse. But it was objected, that nobody knew what these debts were, what their amount, or what their proofs. No matter; we will guess them to be twenty millions. But of these twenty millions, we do not know how much should be reimbursed to one State or how much to another. No matter; we will guess. And so another scramble was set on foot among the several States, and some got much, some little, some nothing. * * * * This measure produced the most bitter and angry contests ever known in Congress, before or since the union of the States. * * * * The great and trying question, however, was lost in the House of Representatives. So high were the feuds excited by this subject, that on its rejection business was suspended. Congress met and adjourned, from day to day, without doing any thing, the parties being too much out of temper to do business together. The Eastern members particularly, who, with Smith from South Carolina, were the principal gamblers in these scenes, threatened a secession and dissolution. * * * * But it was finally agreed that whatever importance had been attached to the rejection of this proposition, the preservation of the Union, and of concord among the States, was more important; and that, therefore, it would be better that the vote of rejection should be rescinded; to effect which, some members should change their votes. But it was observed that this pill would be peculiarly bitter to the Southern States, and that some concomitant measure should be adopted to sweeten it a little to them. There had before been propositions to fix the seat of government either at Philadelphia, or at Georgetown, on the Potomac; and it was thought that, by giving it to Philadelphia for ten years, and to Georgetown permanently afterwards, this might, as an anodyne, calm in some degree the ferment which might be excited by the other measure alone. So two of the Potomac members (White and Lee, but White with a revulsion of stomach almost convulsive) agreed to change their votes, and Hamilton undertook to carry the other point; and so the assumption was passed, and twenty millions of stock divided among the favored States, and thrown in as a pabulum to the stock-jobbing herd. * * * Still the machine was not complete; the effect of the funding system and of the assumption would be temporary; it would be lost with the loss of the individual members whom it had enriched; and some engine of influence more permanent must be contrived while these myrmidons were yet in place to carry it through. This engine was the Bank of the United States."

What a picture is here presented! Debts assumed in the mass, without knowing what they were in the gross, or what in detail—Congress in a state of disorganization, and all business suspended for many days—secession and disunion openly menaced—compromise of interests—intrigue—buying and selling of votes—conjunction of parties to pass two measures together, neither of which could be passed separately—speculators infesting the halls of legislation, and openly struggling for their spoil—the funding system a second time sanctioned and fastened upon the country—jobbers and gamblers in stocks enriched—twenty millions of additional national debt created—and the establishment of a national bank insured. Such were the evils attending a small assumption of twenty millions of dollars, and that in a case where there was no constitutional impediment to be evaded or surmounted. For in that case the debts assumed had been incurred for the general good—for the general defence during the revolution: in this case they have been incurred for the local benefit of particular States. Half the States have incurred none; and are they to be taxed to pay the debts of the rest?

These stocks are now greatly depreciated. Many of the present holders bought them upon speculation, to take the chance of the rise. A diversion of the national domain to their payment would immediately raise them far above par—would be a present of fifty or sixty cents on the dollar, and of fifty or sixty millions in the gross—to the foreign holders, and, virtually, a present of so much public land to them. It is in vain for the bill to say that the proceeds of the lands are to be divided among the States. The indebted States will deliver their portion to their creditors; they will send it to Europe, they will be nothing but the receivers-general and the sub-treasurers of the bankers and stockjobbers of London, Paris, and of Amsterdam. The proceeds of the sales of the lands will go to them. The hard money, wrung from the hard hand of the western cultivator, will go to these foreigners; and the whole influence of these foreigners will be immediately directed to the enhancement of the price of our public lands, and to the prevention of the passage of all the laws which go to graduate their price, or to grant pre-emptive rights to the settlers.

What more unwise and more unjust than to contract debts on long time, as some of the States have done, thereby invading the rights and mortgaging the resources of posterity, and loading unborn generations with debts not their own? What more unwise than all this, which several of the States have done, and which the effort now is to make all do? Besides the ultimate burden in the shape of final payment, which is intended to fall upon posterity, the present burden is incessant in the shape of annual interest, and falling upon each generation, equals the principal in every periodical return of ten or a dozen years. Few have calculated the devouring effect of annual interest on public debts, and considered how soon it exceeds the principal. Who supposes that we have paid near three hundred millions of interest on our late national debt, the principal of which never rose higher than one hundred and twenty-seven millions, and remained but a year or two at that? Who supposes this? Yet it is a fact that we have paid four hundred and thirty-one millions for principal and interest of that debt; so that near three hundred millions, or near double the maximum amount of the debt itself, must have been paid in interest alone; and this at a moderate interest varying from three to six per cent. and payable at home. The British national debt owes its existence entirely to this policy. It was but a trifle in the beginning of the last century, and might have been easily paid during the reigns of the first and second George; but the policy was to fund it, that is to say, to pay the interest annually, and send down the principal to posterity; and the fruit of that policy is now seen in a debt of four thousand five hundred millions of dollars, two hundred and fifty millions of annual taxes, with some millions of people without bread; while an army, a navy, and a police, sufficient to fight all Europe, is kept under pay, to hold in check and subordination the oppressed and plundered ranks of their own population. And this is the example which the transferrers of the State debt would have us to imitate, and this the end to which they would bring us!

I do not dilate upon the evils of a foreign influence. They are written upon the historical page of every free government, from the most ancient to the most modern: they are among those most deeply dreaded, and most sedulously guarded against by the founders of the American Union. The constitution itself contains a special canon directed against them. To prevent the possibility of this foreign influence, every species of foreign connection, dependence, or employment, is constitutionally forbid to the whole list of our public functionaries. The inhibition is express and fundamental, that "*no person holding any office of profit or trust under the United States shall, without the consent of Congress, accept of any present, emolument, office, or title, of any kind whatever, from any king, prince, or foreign State.*" All this was to prevent any foreign potentate from acquiring partisans or influence in our government—to prevent our own citizens from being seduced into the interests of foreign powers. Yet, to what purpose all these constitutional provisions against petty sovereignties, if we are to invite the moneyed power which is able to subsidize kings, princes, and potentates—if we are to invite this new and master power into the bosom of our councils, give it an interest in controlling public opinion, in directing federal and State legislation, and in filling our cities and seats of government with its insinuating agents, and its munificent and lavish representatives? To what purpose all this wise precaution against the possibility of influence from the most inconsiderable German or Italian prince, if we are to invite the combined bankers of England, France, and Holland, to take a position in our legislative halls, and by a simple enactment of a few words, to convert their hundreds of millions into a thousand millions, and to take a lease of the labor and property of our citizens for generations to come? The largest moneyed operation which we ever had with any foreign power, was that of the purchase of Louisiana from the Great Emperor. That was an affair of fifteen millions. It was insignificant and contemptible, compared to the hundreds of millions for which these bankers are now upon us. And are we, while guarded by the constitution against influence from an emperor and fifteen millions, to throw ourselves open to the machinations of bankers, with their hundreds of millions?

CHAPTER XLV.

DEATH OF GENERAL SAMUEL SMITH, OF MARYLAND; AND NOTICE OF HIS LIFE AND CHARACTER.

He was eighteen years a senator, and nearly as long a member of the House—near forty years in Congress: which speaks the estimation in which his fellow-citizens held him. He was thoroughly a business member, under all the aspects of that character: intelligent, well informed, attentive, upright; a very effective speaker, without pretending to oratory: well read: but all his reading subordinate to common sense and practical views. At the age of more than seventy he was still one of the most laborious members, both in the committee room and the Senate: and punctual in his attendance in either place. He had served in the army of the Revolution, and like most of the men of that school, and of that date, had acquired the habit of punctuality, for which Washington was so remarkable—that habit which denotes a well-ordered mind, a subjection to a sense of duty, and a considerate regard for others. He had been a large merchant in Baltimore, and was particularly skilled in matters of finance and commerce, and was always on committees charged with those subjects—to which his clear head, and practical knowledge, lent light and order in the midst of the most intricate statements. He easily seized the practical points on these subjects, and presented them clearly and intelligibly to the chamber. Patriotism, honor, and integrity were his eminent characteristics; and utilitarian the turn of his mind; and beneficial results the object of his labors. He belonged to that order of members who, without classing with the brilliant, are nevertheless the most useful and meritorious. He was a working member; and worked diligently, judiciously, and honestly, for the public good. In politics he was democratic, and greatly relied upon by the Presidents Jefferson, Madison, and Monroe. He was one of the last of the revolutionary stock that served in the Senate—remaining there until 1833—above fifty years after that Declaration of Independence which he had helped to make good, with his sword. Almost octogenarian, he was fresh and vigorous to the last, and among the most assiduous and deserving members. He had acquired military reputation in the war of the Revolution, and was called by his fellow-citizens to take command of the local troops for the defence of Baltimore, when threatened by the British under General Ross, in 1814—and commanded successfully—with the judgment of age and the fire of youth. At his death, his fellow-citizens of Baltimore erected a monument to his memory—well due to him as one of her longest and most respected inhabitants, as having been one of her eminent merchants, often her representative in Congress, besides being senator; as having defended her both in the war of the Revolution and in that of 1812; and as having made her welfare and prosperity a special object of his care in all the situations of his life, both public and private.

CHAPTER XLVI.

SALT; THE UNIVERSALITY OF ITS SUPPLY; MYSTERY AND INDISPENSABILITY OF ITS USE; TYRANNY AND IMPIETY OF ITS TAXATION; SPEECH OF MR. BENTON: EXTRACTS.

It is probable that salt is the most abundant substance of our globe—that it is more abundant than earth itself. Like other necessaries of life—like air, and water, and food—it is universally diffused, and inexhaustibly supplied. It is found in all climates, and in a great variety of forms. The waters hold it in solution; the earth contains it in solid masses. Every sea contains it. It is found in all the boundless oceans which surround and penetrate the earth, and through all their fathomless depths. Many inland seas, lakes, ponds, and pools are impregnated with it. Streams of saline water, in innumerable places, emerging from the bowels of the earth, approach its surface, and either issue from it in perennial springs, or are easily reached by wells. In the depths of the earth itself it is found in solid masses of interminable extent. Thus inexhaustibly abundant, and universally diffused, the wisdom and goodness of Providence is further manifested in the cheapness and facility of the preparation of this necessary of life, for the use of man. In all the warm latitudes, and especially between the tropics, nature herself performs the work. The beams of the sun evaporate the sea water in all the low and shallow reservoirs, where it is driven by the winds, or admitted by the art of man; and this evaporation leaves behind a deposit of pure salt, ready for use, and costing very little more than the labor of gathering it up. In the interior, and in the colder latitudes, artificial heat is substituted for the beams of the sun: the simplest process of boiling is resorted to; and where fuel is abundant, and especially coal, the preparation of this prime necessary is still cheap and easy; and from six to ten cents the real bushel may be considered as the ordinary cost of production. Such is the bountiful and cheap supply of this article, which a beneficent Providence has provided for us. The Supreme Ruler of the Universe has done every thing to supply his creatures with it. Man, the fleeting shadow of an instant, invested with his little brief authority, has done much to deprive them of it. In all ages of the world, and in all countries, salt has been a subject, at different periods, of heavy taxation, and sometimes of individual or of government monopoly; and precisely, because being an article that no man could do without, the government was sure of its tax, and the monopolizer of his price. Almost all nations, in some period of their history, have suffered the separate or double infliction of a tax, and a monopoly on its salt; and, at some period, all have freed themselves, from one or both. At present, there remain but two countries which suffer both evils, our America, and the British East Indies. All others have got rid of the monopoly; many have got rid of the tax. Among others, the very country from which we copied it, and the one above all others least able to do without the product of the tax. England, though loaded with debt, and taxed in every thing, is now free from the salt tax. Since 1822, it has been totally suppressed; and this necessary of life is now as free there as air and water. She even has a statute to guard its price, and common law to prevent its monopoly.

This act was passed in 1807. The common law of England punishes all monopolizers, forestallers, and regraters. The Parliament, in 1807, took cognizance of a reported combination to raise the price of salt, and examined the manufacturers on oath: and rebuked them.

Mr. B. said that a salt tax was not only politically, but morally wrong: it was a species of impiety. Salt stood alone amidst the productions of nature, without a rival or substitute, and the preserver and purifier of all things. Most nations had regarded it as a mystic and sacred substance. Among the heathen nations of antiquity, and with the Jews, it was used in the religious ceremony of the sacrifices—the head of the victim being sprinkled with salt and water before it was offered. Among the primitive Christians, it was the subject of Divine allusions, and the symbol of purity, of incorruptibility, and of perpetuity. The disciples of Christ were called "the salt of the earth;" and no language, or metaphor, could have been more expressive of their character and mission—pure in themselves, and an antidote to moral, as salt was to material corruption. Among the nations of the East salt always has been, and still is, the symbol of friendship, and the pledge of inviolable fidelity. He that has eaten another's salt, has contracted towards his benefactor a sacred obligation; and cannot betray or injure him thereafter, without drawing upon himself (according to his religious belief) the certain effects of the Divine displeasure. While many nations have religiously regarded this substance, all have abhorred its taxation; and this sentiment, so universal, so profound, so inextinguishable in the human heart, is not to be overlooked by the legislator.

Mr. B. concluded his speech with declaring implacable war against this tax, with all its appurtenant abuses, of monopoly in one quarter of the Union, and of undue advantages in another. He denounced it as a tax upon the entire economy of NATURE and of ART—a tax upon man and upon beast—upon life and upon health—upon comfort and luxury—upon want and superfluity—upon food and upon raiment—on washing, and on cleanliness. He called it a heartless and tyrant tax, as inexorable as it was omnipotent and omnipresent; a tax which no economy could avoid—no poverty could shun—no privation escape—no cunning elude—no force resist—no dexterity avert—no curses repulse—no prayers could deprecate. It was a tax which invaded the entire dominion of human operations, falling with its greatest weight upon the most helpless, and the most meritorious; and depriving the nation of benefits infinitely transcending in value, the amount of its own product. I devote myself, said Mr. B., to the extirpation of this odious tax, and its still more odious progeny— *the salt monopoly of the West.* I war against them while they exist, and while I remain on this floor. Twelve years have passed away—two years more than the siege of Troy lasted—since I began this contest. Nothing disheartened by so many defeats, in so long a time, I prosecute the war with unabated vigor; and, relying upon the goodness of the cause, firmly calculate upon ultimate and final success.

CHAPTER XLVII.

PAIRING OFF.

At this time, and in the House of Representatives, was exhibited for the first time, the spectacle of members "*pairing off*," as the phrase was; that is to say, two members of opposite political parties agreeing to absent themselves from the duties of the House, without the consent of the House, and without deducting their per diem pay during the time of such voluntary absence. Such agreements were a clear breach of the rules of the House, a disregard of the constitution, and a practice open to the grossest abuses. An instance of the kind was avowed on the floor by one of the parties to the agreement, by giving as a reason for not voting that he had "*paired off*" with another member, whose affairs required him to go home. It was a strange annunciation, and called for rebuke; and there was a member present who had the spirit to administer it; and from whom it came with the greatest propriety on account of his age and dignity, and perfect attention to all his duties as a member, both in his attendance in the House and in the committee rooms. That member was Mr. John Quincy Adams, who immediately proposed to the House the adoption of this resolution: "Resolved, that the practice first openly avowed at the present session of Congress, of pairing off, involves, on the part of the members resorting to it, the violation of the constitution of the United States, of an express rule of this House, and of the duties of both parties in the transaction to their immediate constituents, to this House, and to their country." This resolve was placed on the calendar to take its turn, but not being reached during the session, was not voted upon. That was the first instance of this reprehensible practice, fifty years after the government had gone into operation; but since then it has become common, and even inveterate, and is carried to great length. Members pair off, and do as they please—either remain in the city, refusing to attend to any duty, or go off together to neighboring cities; or separate; one staying and one going; and the one that remains sometimes standing up in his place, and telling the Speaker of the House that he had paired off; and so refusing to vote. There is no justification for such conduct, and it becomes a facile way for shirking duty, and evading responsibility. If a member is under a necessity to go away the rules of the House require him to ask leave; and the journals of the early Congresses are full of such applications. If he is compelled to go, it is his misfortune, and should not be communicated to another. This writer had never seen an instance of it in the Senate during his thirty years of service there; but the practice has since penetrated that body; and "pairing off" has become as common in that House as in the other, in proportion to its numbers, and with an aggravation of the evil, as the absence of a senator is a loss to his State of half its weight. As a consequence, the two Houses are habitually found voting with deficient numbers—often to the extent of a third—often with a bare quorum.

In the first age of the government no member absented himself from the service of the House to which he belonged without first asking, and obtaining its leave; or, if called off suddenly, a colleague was engaged to state the circumstance to the House, and ask the leave. In the journals of the two Houses, for the first thirty years of the government, there is, in the index, a regular head for "absent without leave;" and, turning to the indicated page, every such name will be seen. That head in the index has disappeared in later times. I recollect no instance of leave asked since the last of the early members—the Macons, Randolphs, Rufus Kings, Samuel Smiths, and John Taylors of Caroline—disappeared from the halls of Congress.

CHAPTER XLVIII.

TAX ON BANK NOTES: MR. BENTON'S SPEECH: EXTRACTS:

Mr. Benton brought forward his promised motion for leave to bring in a bill to tax the circulation of banks and bankers, and of all corporations, companies or individuals which issued paper currency. He said nothing was more reasonable than to require the moneyed interest which was employed in banking, and especially in that branch of banking which was dedicated to the profitable business of converting lampblack and rags into money, to contribute to the support of the government. It was a large interest, very able, and very proper, to pay taxes, and which paid nothing on their profitable issues—profitable to them—injurious to the country. It was an interest which possessed many privileges over the rest of the community by law; which usurped many others which the laws did not grant; which, in fact, set the laws and the government at defiance whenever it pleased; and which, in addition to all these privileges and advantages, was entirely exempt from federal taxation. While the producing and laboring classes were all taxed; while these meritorious classes, with their small incomes, were taxed in their comforts and necessaries—in their salt, iron, sugar, blankets, hats, coats and shoes, and so many other articles—the banking interest, which dealt in hundreds of millions, which manufactured and monopolized money, which put up and put down prices, and held the whole country subject to its power, and tributary to its wealth, paid nothing. This was wrong in itself, and unjust to the rest of the community. It was an error or mistake in government which he had long intended to bring to the notice of the Senate and the country; and he judged the present conjuncture to be a proper time for doing it. Revenue is wanted. A general revision of the tariff is about to take place. An adjustment of the taxes for a long period is about to be made. This is the time to bring forward the banking interest to bear their share of the public burdens, and the more so, as they are now in the fact of proving themselves to be a great burden on the public, and the public mind is beginning to consider whether there is any way to make them amenable to law and government.

In other countries, Mr. B. said, the banking interest was subject to taxation. He knew of no country in which banking was tolerated, except our own, in which it was not taxed. In Great Britain—that country from which we borrow the banking system—the banking interest pays its fair and full proportion of the public taxes: it pays at present near four millions of dollars. It paid in 1836 the sum of $3,725,400: in 1837 it paid $3,594,300. These were the last years for which he had seen the details of the British taxation, and the amounts he had stated comprehended the bank tax upon the whole united kingdom: upon Scotland and Ireland, as well as upon England and Wales. It was a handsome item in the budget of British taxation, and was levied on two branches of the banking business: on the circulation, and on bills of exchange. In the bill which he intended to bring forward, the circulation alone was proposed to be taxed; and, in that respect, the paper system would still remain more favored here than it was in Great Britain.

In our own country, Mr. B. said, the banking interest had formerly been taxed, and that in all its branches; in its circulation, its discounts, and its bills of exchange. This was during the late war with Great Britain; and though the banking business was then small compared to what it is now, yet the product of the tax was considerable, and well worth the gathering: it was about $500,000 per annum. At the end of the war this tax was abolished; while most of the war taxes, laid at the same time, for the same purpose, and for the same period, were continued in force; among them the tax on salt, and other necessaries of life. By a perversion of every principle of righteous taxation, the tax on banks was abolished, and that on salt was continued. This has remained the case for twenty-five years, and it is time to reverse the proceeding. It is time to make the banks pay and to let salt go free.

Mr. B. next stated the manner of levying the bank tax at present in Great Britain, which he said was done with great facility and simplicity. It was a levy of a fixed sum on the average circulation of the year, which the bank was required to give in for taxation like any other property, and the amount collected by a distress warrant if not paid. This simple and obvious method of making the levy, had been adopted in 1815, and had been followed ever since. Before that time it was effected through the instrumentality of a stamp duty; a stamp being required for each note, but with the privilege of compounding for a gross sum. In 1815 the option of compounding was dropped: a gross amount was fixed by law as the tax upon every million of the circulation; and this change in the mode of collection has operated so beneficially that, though temporary at first, it has been made permanent. The amount fixed was at the rate of £3,500 for every million. This was for the circulation only: a separate, and much heavier tax was laid upon bills of exchange, to be collected by a stamp duty, without the privilege of composition.

Mr. B. here read, from a recent history of the Bank of England, a brief account of the taxation of the circulation of that institution for the last fifty years—from 1790 to the present time. It was at that time that her circulation began to be taxed, because at that time only did she begin to have a circulation which displaced the specie of the country. She then began to issue notes under ten pounds, having been first chartered with the privilege of issuing none less than one hundred pounds. It was a century—from 1694 to 1790—before she got down to £5, and afterwards to £2, and to £1; and from that time the specie basis was displaced, the currency convulsed, and the banks suspending and breaking. The government indemnified itself, in a small degree, for the mischiefs of the pestiferous currency which it had authorized; and the extract which he was about to read was the history of the taxation on the Bank of England notes which, commencing at the small composition of £12,000 per annum, now amounts to a large proportion of the near four millions of dollars which the paper system pays annually to the British Treasury. He read:

> "The Bank, till lately, has always been particularly favored in the composition which they paid for stamp duties. In 1791, they paid composition of £12,000 per annum, in lieu of all stamps, either on bill or notes. In 1799, on an increase of the stamp duty, their composition was advanced to £20,000; and an addition of £4,000 for notes issued under £5, raised the whole to £24,000. In 1804, an addition of not less than fifty per cent. was made to the stamp duty; but, although the Bank circulation of notes under £5 had increased from one and a half to four and a half millions, the whole composition was only raised from £24,000 to £32,000. In 1808, there was a further increase of thirty-three per cent. to the stamp duty, at which time the composition was raised from £32,000 to £42,000. In both these instances, the increase was not in proportion even to the increase of duty; and no allowance whatever was made for the increase in the amount of the bank circulation. It was not till the session of 1815, on a further increase of the stamp duty, that the new principle was established, and the Bank compelled to pay a composition in some proportion to the amount of their circulation. The composition is now fixed as follows: Upon the average circulation of the preceding year, the Bank is to pay at the rate of £3,500 per million, on their aggregate circulation, without reference to the different classes and value of their notes. The establishment of this principle, it is calculated, caused a saving to the public, in the years 1815 and 1816, of £70,000. By the neglect of this principle, which ought to have been adopted in 1799, Mr. Ricardo estimated the public to have been *losers*, and the Bank consequently *gainers*, of no less a sum than *half a million*."

Mr. B. remarked briefly upon the equity of this tax, the simplicity of its levy since 1815, and its large product. He deemed it the proper model to be followed in the United States, unless we should go on the principle of copying all that was evil, and rejecting all that was good in the British paper system. We borrowed the banking system from the English, with all its foreign vices, and then added others of our own to it. England has suppressed the pestilence of notes under £5 (near $25); we retain small notes down to a dollar, and thence to the fractional parts of a dollar. She has taxed all notes; and those under £5 she taxed highest while she had them; we, on the contrary, tax none. The additional tax of £4,000 on the notes under £5 rested on the fair principle of taxing highest that which was most profitable to the owner, and most injurious to the country. The small notes fell within that category, and therefore paid highest.

Having thus shown that bank circulation was now taxed in Great Britain, and had been for fifty years, he proceeded to show that it had also been taxed in the United States. This was in the year 1813. In the month of August of that year, a stamp-act was passed, applicable to banks and to bankers, and taxing them in the three great branches of their business, to wit: the circulation, the discounts, and the bills of exchange. On the circulation, the tax commenced at one cent on a one dollar note, and rose gradually to fifty dollars on notes exceeding one thousand dollars; with the privilege of compounding for a gross sum in lieu of the duty. On the discounts, the tax began at five cents on notes discounted for one hundred dollars, and rose gradually to five dollars on notes of eight thousand dollars and upwards. On bills of exchange, it began at five cents on bills of fifty dollars, and rose to five dollars on those of eight thousand dollars and upwards.

Such was the tax, continued Mr. B., which the moneyed interest, employed in banking, was required to pay in 1813, and which it continued to pay until 1817. In that year the banks were released from taxation, while taxes were continued upon all the comforts and necessaries of life. Taxes are now continued upon articles of prime necessity—upon salt even—and the question will now go before the Senate and country, whether the banking interest, which has now grown so rich and powerful—which monopolizes the money of the country—beards the government—makes distress or prosperity when it pleases—the question is now come whether this interest shall continue to be exempt from tax, while every thing else has to pay.

Mr. B. said he did not know how the banking interest of the present day would relish a proposition to make them contribute to the support of the government. He did not know how they would take it; but he did know how a banker of the old school—one who paid on sight, according to his promise, and never broke a promise to the holder of his notes—he did know how *such* a banker viewed the act of 1813; and he would exhibit his behavior to the Senate; he spoke of the late Stephen Girard of Philadelphia; and he would let him speak for himself by reading some passages from a petition which he presented to Congress the year after the tax on bank notes was laid.

Mr. B. read:

> "That your memorialist has established a bank in the city of Philadelphia, upon the foundation of his own individual fortune and credit, and for his own exclusive emolument, and that he is willing most cheerfully to contribute, in common with his fellow-citizens throughout the United States, a full proportion of the taxes which have been imposed for the support of the national government, according to the profits of his occupation and the value of his estate; but a construction has been given to the acts of Congress laying duties on notes of banks, &c., from which great difficulties have occurred, and great inequalities daily produced to the disadvantage of his bank, that were not, it is confidently believed, within the contemplation of the legislature. And your memorialist having submitted these considerations to the wisdom of Congress, respectfully prays, that the act of Congress may be so amended as to permit the Secretary of the Treasury to enter into a composition for the stamp duty, in the case of private bankers, as well as in the case of corporations and companies, or so as to render the duty equal in its operations upon every denomination of bankers."

Mr. B. had read these passages from Mr. Girard's petition to Congress in 1814, *first*, for the purpose of showing the readiness with which a banker of the old school paid the taxes which the government imposed upon his business; and, next, to show the very considerable amount of that tax, which on the circulation alone amounted to ten thousand dollars on the million. All this, with the additional tax on the discounts, and on the bills of exchange, Mr. Girard was entirely willing to pay, provided all paid alike. All he asked was equality of taxation, and that he might have the benefit of the same composition which was allowed to incorporated banks. This was a reasonable request, and was immediately granted by Congress.

Mr. B. said revenue was one object of his bill: the regulation of the currency by the suppression of small notes and the consequent protection of the constitutional currency, was another: and for that purpose the tax was proposed to be heaviest on notes under twenty dollars, and to be augmented annually until it accomplished its object.

CHAPTER XLIX.

LIBERATION OF SLAVES BELONGING TO AMERICAN CITIZENS IN BRITISH COLONIAL PORTS.

Up to this time, and within a period of ten years, three instances of this kind had occurred. First, that of the schooner Comet. This vessel sailed from the District of Columbia in the year 1830, destined for New Orleans, having, among other things, a number of slaves on board. Her papers were regular, and the voyage in all respects lawful. She was stranded on one of the false keys of the Bahama Islands, opposite to the coast of Florida, and almost in sight of our own shores. The persons on board, including the slaves, were taken by the wreckers, against the remonstrance of the captain and the owners of the slaves, into Nassau, New Providence— one of the Bahama Islands; where the slaves were forcibly seized and detained by the local authorities. The second was the case of the Encomium. She sailed from Charleston in 1834, destined to New Orleans, on a voyage lawful and regular, and was stranded near the same place, and with the same fate with the Comet. She was carried into Nassau, where the slaves were also seized and detained by the local authorities. The slaves belonged to the Messrs. Waddell of North Carolina, among the most respectable inhabitants of the State, and on their way to Louisiana with a view to a permanent settlement in that State. The third case was that of the Enterprize, sailing from the District of Columbia in 1835, destined for Charleston, South Carolina, on a lawful voyage, and with regular papers. She was forced unavoidably, by stress of weather, into Port Hamilton, Bermuda Island, where the slaves on board were forcibly seized and detained by the local authorities. The owners of the slaves, protesting in vain, at the time, and in every instance, against this seizure of their property, afterwards applied to their own government for redress; and after years of negotiation with Great Britain, redress was obtained in the two first cases—the full value of the slaves being delivered to the United States, to be paid to the owners. This was accomplished during Mr. Van Buren's administration, the negotiation having commenced under that of President Jackson. Compensation in the case of the Enterprize had been refused; and the reason given for the distinction in the cases, was, that the two first happened during the time that slavery existed in the British West India colonies—the latter after its abolition there. All these were coasting voyages between one port of the United States and another, and involved practical questions of great interest to all the slave States. Mr. Calhoun brought the question before the Senate in a set of resolutions which he drew up for the occasion; and which were in these words:

> "*Resolved*, That a ship or a vessel on the high seas, in time of peace, engaged in a lawful voyage, is, according to the laws of nations, under the exclusive jurisdiction of the State to which her flag belongs; as much so as if constituting a part of its own domain.

> "*Resolved*, That if such ship or vessel should be forced by stress of weather, or other unavoidable cause, into the port of a friendly power, she would, under the same laws, lose none of the rights appertaining to her on the high seas; but, on the contrary, she and her cargo and persons on board, with their property, and all the rights belonging to their personal relations, as established by the laws of the State to which they belong, would be placed under the protection which the laws of nations extend to the unfortunate under such circumstances.

> "*Resolved*, That the brig Enterprize, which was forced unavoidably by stress of weather into Port Hamilton, Bermuda Island, while on a lawful voyage on the high seas from one port of the Union to another, comes within the principles embraced in the foregoing resolutions; and that the seizure and detention of the negroes on board by the local authority of the island, was an act in violation of the laws of nations, and highly unjust to our own citizens to whom they belong."

It was in this latter case that Mr. Calhoun wished to obtain the judgment of the Senate, and the point he had to argue was, whether a municipal regulation of Great Britain could alter the law of nations? Under that law she made indemnity for the slaves liberated in the two first cases: under her own municipal law she denied it in the latter case. The distinction taken by the British minister was, that in the first cases, slavery existing in this British colony and recognized by law, the persons coming in with their slaves had a property in them which had been divested: in the latter case that slavery being no longer recognized in this colony, there was no property in them after their arrival; and consequently no rights divested. Mr. Calhoun admitted that would be the case if the entrance had been voluntary; but denied it where the entrance was forced; as in this case. His argument was:

> "I object not to the rule. If our citizens had no right to their slaves, at any time after they entered the British territory—that is, if the mere fact of entering extinguished all right to them (for that is the amount of the rule)—they could, of course, have no claim on the British government, for the plain reason that the local authority, in seizing and detaining the negroes, seized and detained what, by supposition, did not belong to them. That is clear enough; but let us see the application: it is given in a few words. He says: 'Now the owners of the slaves on board the Enterprize never were lawfully in possession of those slaves within the British territory;' assigning for reason, 'that before the Enterprize arrived at Bermuda, slavery had been abolished in the British empire'—an assertion which I shall show, in a subsequent part of my remarks, to be erroneous. From that, and that alone, he comes to the conclusion, 'that the negroes on board the Enterprize had, by entering within the British jurisdiction, acquired rights which the local courts were bound to protect.' Such certainly would have been the case if they had been brought in, or entered voluntarily. He who enters voluntarily the territory of another State, tacitly submits himself, with all his rights, to its laws, and is as much bound to submit to them as its citizens or subjects. No one denies that; but that is not the present case. They entered not voluntarily, but from necessity; and the very point at issue is, whether the British municipal laws could divest their owners of property in their slaves on entering British territory, in cases such as the Enterprize, when the vessel has been forced into their territory by necessity, through an act of Providence, to save the lives of those on board. We deny they can, and maintain the opposite ground:—that the law of nations in such cases interposes and protects the vessel and those on board, with their rights, against the municipal laws of the State, to which they have never submitted, and to which it would be cruel and inhuman, as well as unjust, to subject them. Such is clearly the point at issue between the two governments; and it is not less clear, that it is the very point assumed by the British negotiator in the controversy."

This is fair reasoning upon the law of the case, and certainly left the law of nations in full force in favor of the American owners. The equity of the case was also fully stated and the injury shown to be of a practical kind, which self-protection required the United States to prevent for the future. In this sense, Mr. Calhoun argued:

> "To us this is not a mere abstract question, nor one simply relating to the free use of the high seas. It comes nearer home. It is one of free and safe passage from one port to another of our Union; as much so to us, as a question touching the free and safe use of the channels between England and Ireland on the one side, and the opposite coast of the continent on the other, would be to Great Britain. To understand its deep importance to us, it must be borne in mind, that the island of Bermuda lies but a short distance off our coast, and that the channel between the Bahama islands and Florida is not less than two hundred miles in length, and on an average not more than fifty wide; and that through this long, narrow and difficult channel, the immense trade between our ports on the Gulf of Mexico and the Atlantic coast must pass, which, at no distant period, will constitute more than half of the trade of the Union. The principle set up by the British government, if carried out to its full extent, would do much to close this all-important channel, by rendering it too hazardous for use. She has only to give an indefinite extension to the principle applied to the case of the Enterprize, and the work would be done; and why has she not as good a right to apply it to a cargo of sugar or cotton, as to the slaves who produced it."

The resolutions were referred to the committee on foreign relations, which reported them back with some slight alteration, not affecting or impairing their force; and in that form they were unanimously adopted by the

Senate. Although there was no opposition to them, the importance of the occasion justified a record of the vote: and they were accordingly taken by yeas and nays—or rather, by yeas: for there were no nays. This was one of the occasions on which the mind loves to dwell, when, on a question purely sectional and Southern, and wholly in the interest of slave property, there was no division of sentiment in the American Senate.

CHAPTER L.

RESIGNATION OF SENATOR HUGH LAWSON WHITE OF TENNESSEE: HIS DEATH: SOME NOTICE OF HIS LIFE AND CHARACTER.

This resignation took place under circumstances, not frequent, but sometimes occurring in the Senate—that of receiving instructions from the General Assembly of his State, which either operate as a censure upon a senator, or require him to do something which either his conscience, or his honor forbids. Mr. White at this time—the session of 1839-'40—received instructions from the General Assembly of his State which affected him in both ways—condemning past conduct, and prescribing a future course which he could not follow. He had been democratic from his youth—came into the Senate—had grown aged—as such: but of late years had voted generally with the whigs on their leading measures, and classed politically with them in opposition to Mr. Van Buren. In these circumstances he received instructions to reverse his course of voting on these leading measures—naming them; and requiring him to support the administration of Mr. Van Buren. He consulted his self-respect, as well as obeyed a democratic principle; and sent in his resignation. It was the conclusion of a public life which disappointed its whole previous course. From his youth he had been a popular man, and that as the fair reward of conduct, without practising an art to obtain it, or even seeming to know that he was winning it. Bred a lawyer, and coming early to the bar, he was noted for a probity, modesty and gravity—with a learning, ability, assiduity and patience—which marked him for the judicial bench: and he was soon placed upon it—that of the Superior Court. Afterwards, when the judiciary of the State was remodelled, he was placed on the bench of the Supreme Court. It was considered a favor to the public to get him to take the place. That is well known to the writer of this View, then a member of the General Assembly of Tennessee, and the author of the new modelled judiciary. He applied to Judge White, who had at that time returned to the bar to know if he would take the place; and considered the new system accredited with the public on receiving his answer that he would. That was all that he had to do with getting the appointment: he was elected unanimously by the General Assembly, with whom the appointment rested. That is about the way in which he received all his appointments, either from his State, or from the federal government—merely agreeing to take the office if it was offered to him; but not always agreeing to accept: often refusing—as in the case of a cabinet appointment offered him by President Jackson, his political and personal friend of forty years' standing. It was long before he would enter a political career, but finally consented to become senator in the Congress of the United States: always discharging the duties of an office, when accepted, with the assiduity of a man who felt himself to be a machine in the hands of his duty; and with an integrity of purpose which left his name without spot or stain. It is beautiful to contemplate such a career; sad to see it set under a cloud in his advanced years. He became alienated from his old friends, both personally and politically—even from General Jackson; and eventually fell under the censure of his State, as above related—that State which, for more than forty years, had considered it a favor to itself that he should accept the highest offices in her gift. He resigned in January, and died in May—his death accelerated by the chagrin of his spirit; for he was a man of strong feelings, though of such measured and quiet deportment. His death was announced in the Senate by the senator who was his colleague at the time of his resignation—Mr. Alexander Anderson; and the motion for the usual honors to his memory was seconded by Senator Preston, who pronounced on the occasion a eulogium on the deceased as just as it was beautiful.

"I do not know, Mr. President, whether I am entitled to the honor I am about to assume in seconding the resolutions which have just been offered by the senator from Tennessee, in honor of his late distinguished colleague; and yet, sir, I am not aware that any one present is more entitled to this melancholy honor, if it belongs to long acquaintance, to sincere admiration, and to intimate intercourse. If these circumstances do not entitle me to speak, I am sure every senator will feel, in the emotions which swell his own bosom, an apology for my desire to relieve my own, by bearing testimony to the virtues and talents, the long services and great usefulness, of Judge White.

"My infancy and youth were spent in a region contiguous to the sphere of his earlier fame and usefulness. As long as I can remember any thing, I remember the deep confidence he had inspired as a wise and upright judge, in which station no man ever enjoyed a purer reputation, or established a more implicit reliance in his abilities and honesty. There was an antique sternness and justness in his character. By a general consent he was called Cato. Subsequently, at a period of our public affairs very analogous to the present, he occupied a position which placed him at the head of the financial institutions of East Tennessee. He sustained them by his individual character. The name of Hugh L. White was a guarantee that never failed to attract confidence. Institutions were sustained by the credit of an individual, and the only wealth of that individual was his character. From this more limited sphere of usefulness and reputation, he was first brought to this more conspicuous stage as a member of an important commission on the Spanish treaty, in which he was associated with Mr. Tazewell and Mr. King. His learning, his ability, his firmness, and industry, immediately extended the sphere of his reputation to the boundaries of the country. Upon the completion of that duty, he came into this Senate. Of his career here, I need not speak. His grave and venerable form is even now before us—that air of patient attention, of grave deliberation, of unrelaxed firmness. Here his position was of the highest—beloved, respected, honored; always in his place—always prepared for the business in hand—always bringing to it the treasured reflections of a sedate and vigorous understanding. Over one department of our deliberations he exercised a very peculiar control. In the management of our complex and difficult relations with the Indians we all deferred to him, and to this he addressed himself with unsparing labor, and with a wisdom, a patient benevolence, that justified and vindicated the confidence of the Senate.

"In private life he was amiable and ardent. The current of his feelings was warm and strong. His long familiarity with public affairs had not damped the natural ardor of his temperament. We all remember the deep feeling with which he so recently took leave of this body, and how profoundly that feeling was reciprocated. The good will, the love, the respect which we bestowed upon him then, now give depth and energy to the mournful feelings with which we offer a solemn tribute to his memory."

And here this notice would stop if it was the design of this work merely to write on the outside of history—merely to chronicle events; but that is not the design. Inside views are the main design: and this notice of Senator White's life and character would be very imperfect, and vitally deficient, if it did not tell how it happened that a man so favored by his State during a long life should have lost that favor in his last days—received censure from those who had always given praise—and gone to his grave under a cloud after having lived in sunshine. The reason is briefly told. In his advanced age he did the act which, with all old men, is an experiment; and, with most of them, an unlucky one. He married again: and this new wife having made an immense stride from the head of a boarding-house table to the head of a senator's table, could see no reason why she should not take one step more, and that comparatively short, and arrive at the head of the presidential table. This was before the presidential election of 1836. Mr. Van Buren was the generally accepted democratic candidate: he was foremost of all the candidates: and the man who is ahead of all the rest, on such occasions, is pretty sure to have a combination of all the rest against him. Mr. Van Buren was no exception to this rule. The whole whig party wished to defeat him: that was a fair wish. Mr. Calhoun's party wished to defeat him: that was invidious: for they could not elect Mr. Calhoun by it. Many professing democrats wished to defeat him, though for the benefit of a whig: and that was a movement towards the whig camp—where most of them eventually arrived. All these parties combined, and worked in concert; and their line of operations was through the vanity of the victim's wife. They excited her vain hopes. And this modest, unambitious man, who had spent all his life in resisting office pressed upon him by his real friends, lost his power of resistance in his old age, and became a victim to the combination against him—which all saw, and deplored, except himself. As soon as he was committed, and beyond extrication, one of the co-operators against him, a whig member of Congress from Kentucky—a witty, sagacious man of good tact—in the exultation of his feelings wrote the news to a friend in his district, who, in a still higher state of exultation, sent it to the newspapers—thus: "*Judge White is on the track, running gayly, and won't come off; and if he would, his wife won't let him.*" This was the whole story, briefly and cheerily told—and truly. He ran the race! without prejudice to Mr. Van Buren—without benefit to the whig candidates—without support from some who had incited him to the trial: and with great political and social damage to himself.

Long an inhabitant of the same State with Judge White—indebted to him for my law license—moving in the same social and political circle—accustomed to respect and admire him—sincerely friendly to him, and anxious for his peace and honor, I saw with pain the progress of the movement against him, and witnessed with profound grief its calamitous consummation.

CHAPTER LI.

DEATH OF EX-SENATOR HAYNE OF SOUTH CAROLINA: NOTICE OF HIS LIFE AND CHARACTER.

Nature had lavished upon him all the gifts which lead to eminence in public, and to happiness, in private life. Beginning with the person and manners—minor advantages, but never to be overlooked when possessed—he was entirely fortunate in these accessorial advantages. His person was of the middle size, slightly above it in height, well proportioned, flexible and graceful. His face was fine—the features manly, well formed, expressive, and bordering on the handsome: a countenance ordinarily thoughtful and serious, but readily lighting up, when accosted, with an expression of kindness, intelligence, cheerfulness, and an inviting amiability. His face was then the reflex of his head and his heart, and ready for the artist who could seize the moment to paint to the life. His manners were easy, cordial, unaffected, affable; and his address so winning, that the fascinated stranger was taken captive at the first salutation. These personal qualities were backed by those of the mind—all solid, brilliant, practical, and utilitarian: and always employed on useful objects, pursued from high motives, and by fair and open means. His judgment was good, and he exercised it in the serious consideration of whatever business he was engaged upon, with an honest desire to do what was right, and a laudable ambition to achieve an honorable fame. He had a copious and ready elocution, flowing at will in a strong and steady current, and rich in the material which constitutes argument. His talents were various, and shone in different walks of life, not often united: eminent as a lawyer, distinguished as a senator: a writer as well as a speaker: and good at the council table. All these advantages were enforced by exemplary morals; and improved by habits of study, moderation, temperance, self-control, and addiction to business. There was nothing holiday, or empty about him—no lying in to be delivered of a speech of phrases. Practical was the turn of his mind: industry an attribute of his nature: labor an inherent impulsion, and a habit: and during his ten years of senatorial service his name was incessantly connected with the business of the Senate. He was ready for all work—speaking, writing, consulting—in the committee-room as well as in the chamber—drawing bills and reports in private, as well as shining in the public debate, and ready for the social intercourse of the evening when the labors of the day were over. A desire to do service to the country, and to earn just fame for himself, by working at useful objects, brought all these high qualities into constant, active, and brilliant requisition. To do good, by fair means, was the labor of his senatorial life; and I can truly say that, in ten years of close association with him I never saw him actuated by a sinister motive, a selfish calculation, or an unbecoming aspiration.

Thus, having within himself so many qualities and requisites for insuring advancement in life, he also had extrinsic advantages, auxiliary to talent, and which contribute to success in a public career. He was well descended, and bore a name dear to the South—the synonym of honor, courage, and patriotism—memorable for that untimely and cruel death of one of its revolutionary wearers, which filled the country with pity for his fate, and horror for his British executioners. The name of Hayne, pronounced any where in the South, and especially in South Carolina, roused a feeling of love and respect, and stood for a passport to honor, until deeds should win distinction. Powerfully and extensively connected by blood and marriage, he had the generous support which family pride and policy extends to a promising scion of the connection. He had fortune, which gave him the advantage of education, and of social position, and left free to cultivate his talents, and to devote them to the public service. Resident in Charleston, still maintaining its colonial reputation for refined society, and high and various talent, he had every advantage of enlightened and elegant association. Twice happily married in congenial families (Pinckney and Alston), his domestic felicity was kept complete, his connections extended, and fortune augmented. To crown all, and to give effect to every gift with which nature and fortune had endowed him, he had that further advantage, which the Grecian Plutarch never fails to enumerate when the case permits it, and which he considered so auxiliary to the advancement of some of the eminent men whose lives he commemorated—the advantage of being born in a State where native talent was cherished, and where the community made it a policy to advance and sustain a promising young man, as the property of the State, and for the good of the State. Such was, and is, South Carolina; and the young Hayne had the full benefit of the generous sentiment. As fast as years permitted, he was advanced in the State government: as soon as age and the federal constitution permitted, he came direct to the Senate, without passing through the House of Representatives; and to such a Senate as the body then was—Rufus King, John Taylor of Caroline, Mr. Macon,

John Gaillard, Edward Lloyd of Maryland, James Lloyd of Massachusetts, James Barbour of Virginia, General Jackson, Louis McLane of Delaware, Wm. Pinkney of Maryland, Littleton Waller Tazewell, Webster, Nathan Sandford, of New York, M. Van Buren, King of Alabama, Samuel Smith of Maryland, James Brown, and Henry Johnson of Louisiana; and many others, less known to fame, but honorable to the Senate from personal decorum, business talent, and dignity of character. Hayne arrived among them; and was considered by such men, and among such men, as an accession to the talent and character of the chamber. I know the estimate they put upon him, the consideration they had for him, and the future they pictured for him: for they were men to look around, and consider who were to carry on the government after they were gone. But the proceedings of the Senate soon gave the highest evidence of the degree of consideration in which he was held. In the very second year of his service, he was appointed to a high duty—such as would belong to age and long service, as well as to talent and elevated character. He was made chairman of the select committee—and select it was—which brought in the bill for the grants ($200,000 in money, and 24,000 acres of land), to Lafayette; and as such became the organ of the expositions, as delicate as they were responsible, which reconciled such grants to the words and spirit of our constitution, and adjusted them to the merit and modesty of the receiver: a high function, and which he fulfilled to the satisfaction of the chamber, and the country.

Six years afterwards he had the great debate with Mr. Webster—a contest of many days, sustained to the last without losing its interest—(which bespoke fertility of resource, as well as ability in both speakers), and in which his adversary had the advantage of a more ripened intellect, an established national reputation, ample preparation, the choice of attack, and the goodness of the cause. Mr. Webster came into that field upon choice and deliberation, well feeling the grandeur of the occasion; and profoundly studying his part. He had observed during the summer, the signs in South Carolina, and marked the proceedings of some public meetings unfriendly to the Union; and which he ran back to the incubation of Mr. Calhoun. He became the champion of the constitution and the Union, choosing his time and occasion, hanging his speech upon a disputed motion with which it had nothing to do, and which was immediately lost sight of in the blaze and expansion of a great national discussion: himself armed and equipped for the contest, glittering in the panoply of every species of parliamentary and forensic weapon—solid argument, playful wit, biting sarcasm, classic allusion; and striking at a new doctrine of South Carolina origin, in which Hayne was not implicated: but his friends were—and that made him their defender. The speech was *at* Mr. Calhoun, then presiding in the Senate, and without right to reply. Hayne became his sword and buckler, and had much use for the latter to cover his friend—hit by incessant blows—cut by many thrusts: but he understood too well the science of defence in wordy as well as military digladiation to confine himself to fending off. He returned, as well as received blows; but all conducted courteously; and stings when inflicted gently extracted on either side by delicate compliments. Each morning he returned re-invigorated to the contest, like Antæus refreshed, not from a fabulous contact with mother earth, but from a real communion with Mr. Calhoun! the actual subject of Mr. Webster's attack: and from the well-stored arsenal of his powerful and subtle mind, he nightly drew auxiliary supplies. Friends relieved the combatants occasionally; but it was only to relieve; and the two principal figures remained prominent to the last. To speak of the issue would be superfluous; but there was much in the arduous struggle to console the younger senator. To cope with Webster, was a distinction: not to be crushed by him, was almost a victory: to rival him in copious and graceful elocution, was to establish an equality at a point which strikes the masses: and Hayne often had the crowded galleries with him. But, equal argument! that was impossible. The cause forbid it, far more than disparity of force; and reversed positions would have reversed the issue.

I have said elsewhere (Vol. I. of this work), that I deem Mr. Hayne to have been entirely sincere in professing nullification at that time only in the sense of the Virginia resolutions of '98-'99, as expounded by their authors: three years afterwards he left his place in the Senate to become Governor of South Carolina, to enforce the nullification ordinance which the General Assembly of the State had passed, and against which President Jackson put forth his impressive proclamation. Up to this point, in writing this notice, the pen had run on with pride and pleasure—pride in portraying a shining American character: pleasure in recalling recollections of an eminent man, whom I esteemed—who did me the honor to call me friend; and with whom I was intimate. Of all the senators he seemed nearest to me—both young in the Senate, entering it nearly together; born in adjoining States; not wide apart in age; a similarity of political principle: and, I may add, some conformity of tastes and habits. Of all the young generation of statesmen coming on, I considered him the safest—the most like William Lowndes; and best entitled to a future eminent lead. He was democratic, not in the modern sense of the term, as never bolting a caucus nomination, and never thinking differently from the actual administration; but on principle, as founded in a strict, in contradistinction to a latitudinarian construction of the constitution; and as cherishing simplicity and economy in the administration of the federal government, in contradistinction to splendor and extravagance.

With his retiring from the Senate, Mr. Hayne's national history ceases. He does not appear afterwards upon the theatre of national affairs: but his practical utilitarian mind, and ardent industry, found ample and beneficent employment in some noble works of internal improvement. The railroad system of South Carolina, with its extended ramifications, must admit him for its founder, from the zeal he carried into it, and the impulsion he gave it. He died in the meridian of his life, and in the midst of his usefulness, and in the field of his labors—in western North Carolina, on the advancing line of the great iron railway, which is to connect the greatest part of the South Atlantic with the noblest part of the Valley of the Mississippi.

The nullification ordinance, which he became Governor of South Carolina to enforce, was wholly directed against the tariff system of the time—not merely against a protective tariff, but against its fruits—undue levy of revenue, extravagant expenditure; and expenditure in one quarter of the Union of what was levied upon the other. The levy and expenditure were then some twenty-five millions of dollars: they are now seventy-five millions: and the South, while deeply agitated for the safety of slave property—(now as safe, and more valuable than ever, as proved by the witness which makes no mistakes, *the market price*)—is quiet upon the evil which produced the nullification ordinance of 1832: quiet under it, although that evil is three times greater now than then: and without excuse, as the present vast expenditure is the mere effect of mad extravagance. Is this quietude a condemnation of that ordinance? or, is it of the nature of an imaginary danger which inflames the passions, that it should supersede the real evil which affects the pocket? If the Hayne of 1824, and 1832, was now alive, I think his practical and utilitarian mind would be seeking a proper remedy for the real grievance, now so much greater than ever; and that he would leave the fires of an imaginary danger to die out of themselves, for want of fuel.

CHAPTER LII.

ABOLITION OF SPECIFIC DUTIES BY THE COMPROMISE ACT OF 1833: ITS ERROR, AND LOSS TO THE REVENUE, SHOWN BY EXPERIENCE.

The introduction of the universal *ad valorem* system in 1833 was opposed and deprecated by practical men at the time, as one of those refined subtleties which, aiming at an ideal perfection, overlooks the experience of ages, and disregards the warnings of reason. Specific duties had been the rule—ad valorems the exception—from the beginning of the collection of custom-house revenue. The specific duty was a question in the exact sciences, depending upon a mathematical solution by weight, count, or measure: the ad valorem presented a question to the fallible judgment of men, sure to be different at different places; and subject, in addition to the fallibility of judgment, to the chances of ignorance, indifference, negligence and corruption. All this was urged against the act at the time, but in vain. It was a piece of legislation arranged out of doors—christened a compromise, which was to save the Union—brought into the House to be passed without alteration: and was so passed, in defiance of all judgment and reason by the aid of the votes of those—always a considerable per centum in every public body—to whom the name of compromise is an irresistible attraction: amiable men, who would do no wrong of themselves, and without whom the designing could do but little wrong. Objections to this pernicious novelty (of universal ad valorems), were in vain urged then: experience, with her enlightened voice, now came forward to plead against them. The act had been in force seven years: it had had a long, and a fair trial: and that safest of all juries—Time and Experience—now came forward to deliver their verdict. At this session ('39-'40) a message was sent to the House of Representatives by the President, covering reports from the Secretary of the Treasury, and from the Comptroller of the Treasury, with opinions from the late Attorneys-general of the United States (Messrs. Benjamin F. Butler and Felix Grundy), and letters from the collectors of the customs in all the principal Atlantic ports, all relating to the practical operation of the ad valorem system, and showing it to be unequal, uncertain, unsafe—diverse in its construction—injurious to the revenue—open to unfair practices—and greatly expensive from the number of persons required to execute it. The whole document may be profitably studied by all who deprecate unwise and pernicious legislation; but a selection of a few of the cases of injurious operation which it presents will be sufficient to give an idea of the whole. Three classes of goods are selected—silks, linens, and worsted: all staple articles, and so well known as to be the least susceptible of diversity of judgment; and yet on which, in the period of four years, a fraction over five millions of dollars had been lost to the Treasury from diversity of construction between the Treasury officers and the judiciary—with the further prospective loss of one million and three-quarters in the ensuing three years if the act was not amended. The document, at page 44, states the annual ascertained loss during four years' operation of the act on these classes of goods, to be:

"In 1835 -	$624,356	In 1837 -	463,090
1836 -	847,162	1838 -	428,237

"Making in the four years $2,362,845; and the comptroller computes the annual prospective loss during the time the act may remain unaltered, at $800,000. So much for silks; now for linens. The same page, for the same four years, represents the annual loss on this article to be:

In 1835 -	$370,785	In 1837 -	303,241
1836 -	516,988	1838 -	226,375

"Making the sum of $1,411,389 on this article for the four years; to which is to be added the estimated sum of $400,000, for the future annual losses, if the act remains unaltered.

"On worsted goods, for the same time, and on page 45, the report exhibits the losses thus:

In 1835 -	$409,329	In 1837 -	209,391
1836 -	416,832	1838 -	249,590

"Making a total of ascertained loss on this head, in the brief space of four years, amount to the sum of $1,285,142; with a computation of a prospective loss of $500,000 per annum, while the compromise act remains as it is."

Such were the losses from diversity of construction alone on three classes of goods, in the short space of four years; and these classes staple goods, composed of a single material. When it came to articles of mixed material, the diversity became worse. Custom-house officers disagreed: comptrollers and treasurers disagreed: attorneys-general disagreed. Courts were referred to, and their decision overruled all. Many importers stood suits; and the courts and juries overruled all the officers appointed to collect the revenue. The government could only collect what they are allowed. Often, after paying the duty assessed, the party has brought his action and recovered a large part of it back. So that this ad valorem system, besides its great expense, its chance for diversity of opinions among the appraisers, and its openness to corruption, also gave rise to differences among the highest administrative and law officers of the government, with resort to courts of law, in nearly all which the United States was the loser.

CHAPTER LIII.

REFINED SUGAR AND RUM DRAWBACKS: THEIR ABUSE UNDER THE COMPROMISE ACT OF 1833: MR. BENTON'S SPEECH.

Mr. Benton rose to make the motion for which he had given notice on Friday last, for leave to bring in a bill to reduce the drawbacks allowed on the exportation of rum and refined sugars; and the bounties and allowances to fishing vessels, in proportion to the reduction which had been made, and should be made, in the duties upon imported sugars, molasses and salt, upon which these bounties and allowances were respectively granted.

Mr. B. said that the bill, for the bringing in of which he was about to ask leave, proposed some material alteration in the act of 1833, for the modification of the tariff, commonly called the compromise act; and as that act was held by its friends to be sacred and inviolable, and entitled to run its course untouched and unaltered, it became his duty to justify his bill in advance; to give reasons for it before he ventured to submit the question of leave for its introduction; and to show, beforehand, that here was great and just cause for the measure he proposed.

Mr. B. said it would be recollected, by those who were contemporary with the event, and might be seen by all who should now look into our legislative history of that day, that he was thoroughly opposed to the passage of the act of 1833; that he preferred waiting the progress of Mr. Verplanck's bill; that he opposed the compromise act, from beginning to end; made speeches against it, which were not answered; uttered predictions of it, which were disregarded; proposed amendments to it, which were rejected; showed it to be an adjournment, not a settlement, of the tariff question; and voted against it, on its final passage, in a respectable minority of eighteen. It was not his intention at this time to recapitulate all the objections which he then made to the act; but to confine himself to two of those objections, and to those two of them, the truth and evils of which TIME had developed; and for which evils the public good demands an immediate remedy to be applied. He spoke of the drawbacks and allowances founded upon duties, which duties were to undergo periodical reductions, while the drawbacks and allowances remained undiminished; and of the vague and arbitrary tenor of the act, which rendered it incapable of any regular, uniform, or safe execution. He should confine himself to these two objections; and proceed to examine them in the order in which they were mentioned.

At page 208 of the Senate journal, session of 1832-33, is seen this motion: "Moved by Mr. Benton to add to the bill a section in the following words: '*That all drawbacks allowed on the exportation of articles manufactured in the United States from materials imported from foreign countries, and subject to duty, shall be reduced in proportion to the reduction of duties provided for in this act.*'" The particular application of this clause, as explained and enforced at the time, was to sugar and molasses, and the refined sugar, and the rum manufactured from them.

As the laws then stood, and according to the principle of all drawbacks, the exporters of these refined sugars and rum were allowed to draw back from the Treasury precisely as much money as had been paid into the Treasury on the importation of the article out of which the exported article was manufactured. This was the principle, and this was the law; and so rigidly was this insisted upon by the manufacturing and exporting interest, that only four years before the compromise act, namely, in 1829, the drawback on refined sugars exported was raised from four to five cents a pound upon the motion of General Smith, a then senator from Maryland; and this upon an argument and a calculation made by him to show that the quantity of raw sugar contained in every pound of refined sugar, had, in reality, paid five instead of four cents duty. My motion appeared to me self-evidently just, as the new act, in abolishing all specific duties, and reducing every thing to an ad valorem duty of twenty per centum, would reduce the duties on sugar and molasses eventually to the one-third or the one-fourth of their then amount; and, unless the drawback should be proportionately reduced, the exporter of refined sugars and rum, instead of drawing back the exact amount he had paid into the Treasury, would in reality draw back three or four times as much as had been paid in. This would be unjust in itself; and, besides being unjust, would involve a breach of the constitution, for, so much of the drawback as was not founded upon the duty, would be a naked bounty paid for nothing out of the Treasury. I expected my motion to be adopted by a unanimous vote; on the contrary, it was rejected by a vote of 24 to 18;[2] and I had to leave it to Time, that slow, but sure witness, to develope the evils which my arguments had been unable to show, and to enforce the remedies which the vote of the Senate had rejected. That witness has come. Time, with his unerring testimony, has arrived. The act of 1833 has run the greater part of its course, without having reached its ultimate depression of duties, or developed its greatest mischiefs; but it has gone far enough to show that it has done immense injury to the Treasury, and must continue to do it if a remedy is not applied. Always indifferent to my rhetoric, and careful of my facts—always leaving oratory behind, and laboring to establish a battery of facts in front—I have applied at the fountain head of information—the Treasury Department—for all the statistics connected with the subject; and the successive reports which had been received from that department, on the salt duties and the fishing bounties and allowances, and on the sugar and molasses duties, and the drawbacks on exported rum and refined sugar, and which had been printed by the order of the Senate, had supplied the information which constituted the body of facts which must carry conviction to the mind of every hearer.

Mr. B. said he would take up the sugar duties first, and show what had been the operation of the act of 1833, in relation to the revenue from that article, and the drawbacks founded upon it. In document No. 275, laid upon our tables on Friday last, we find four tables in relation to this point, and a letter from the Register of the Treasury, Mr. T. L. Smith, describing their contents.

These tables are all valuable. The whole of the information which they contain is useful, and is applicable to the business of legislation, and goes to enlighten us on the subject under consideration; but it is not in my power, continued Mr. B., to quote them in detail. Results and prominent facts only can be selected; and, proceeding on this plan, I here show to the Senate, from table No. 1, that as early as the year 1837—being only four years after the compromise act—the drawback paid on the exportation of refined sugar actually exceeded the amount of revenue derived from imported sugar, by the sum of $861 71. As the duties continued to diminish, and the drawback remained the same, this excess was increased in 1838 to $12,690; and in 1839 it was increased to $20,154 37. Thus far the results are mathematical; they are copied from the Treasury books; they show the actual operation of the compromise act on this article, down to the end of the last year. These are facts to pause at, and think upon. They imply that the sugar refiners manufactured more sugar than was imported into the United States for each of these three years—that they not only manufactured, but exported, in a refined state, more than was imported into the United States, about 400,000 lbs. more the last of these years—that they paid duty on these quantities, not leaving a pound of imported sugar to have been used or duty paid on it by any other person—and not leaving a pound of their own refined sugar to be used in the United States. In other words, the whole amount of the revenue from brown and clayed sugars was paid over to 29 sugar refiners from 1837: and not only the whole amount, but the respective sums of $861 71, and $12,690, and $20,154 37, in that and the two succeeding years, over and above that amount. This is what the table shows as far as the act has gone; and as we know that the refiners only consumed a small part of the sugar imported, and only exported a part of what they refined, and consequently only paid duty on a small part, it stands to reason that a most enormous abuse has been committed—the fault of the law allowing them to "draw back" out of the Treasury what they had never put into it.

The table then goes on to show the prospective operation of the act for the remainder of the time which it has to run, and which will include the great reductions of duty which are to take place in 1841 and 1842; and here the results become still more striking. Assuming the importation of each succeeding year to be the same that it was in 1839, and the excess of the drawback over the duties will be, for 1840, $37,343 38; for 1841, the same; for 1842, $114,693 94; and for 1843, the sum of $140,477 45. That is to say, these refiners will receive the whole of the revenue from the sugar tax, and these amounts in addition, for these four years; when they would not be entitled, under an honest law, to more than the one fortieth part of the revenue—which, in fact, is more than they received while the law was honest. These will be the bounties payable out of the Treasury in the present, and in the three succeeding years, provided the importation of sugars shall be the same that it was in 1839; but will it be the same? To this question, both reason and experience answer in the negative. They both reply that the importation will increase in proportion to the increased profit which the increasing difference between the duty and the drawback will afford; and this reply is proved by the two first columns in the table under consideration. These columns show that, under the encouragement to importation already afforded by the compromise act, the import of sugar increased in six years from 1,558,971 pounds, costing $72,336, to

11,308,561 pounds, costing $554,119. Here was an enormous increase under a small inducement compared to that which is to follow; so that we have reason to conclude that the importations of the present and ensuing years, unless checked by the passage of the bill which I propose to bring in, will not only increase in the ratio of the past years, but far beyond it; and will in reality be limited only by the capacity of the world to supply the demand: so great will be the inducement to import raw or clayed sugars, and export refined. The effect upon our Treasury must be great. Several hundred thousand dollars per annum must be taken from it for nothing; the whole extracted from the Secretary of the Treasury in hard money; his reports having shown us that, while paper money, and even depreciated paper, is systematically pressed upon the government in payment of duties, nothing but gold and silver will be received back in payment of drawbacks. But it is not the Treasury only that would suffer: the consumers of sugar would come in for their share of the burden: the drawback will keep up the price; and the home consumer must pay the drawback as well as the government; otherwise the refined sugar will seek a foreign market. The consumers of brown sugar will suffer in the same manner; for the manufacturers will monopolize it, and refine it, and have their five cents drawback, either at home or abroad. Add to all this, it will be well if enterprising dealers shall not impose domestic sugars upon the manufacturers, and thus convert the home crop into an article entitled to drawback.

Such are the mischiefs of the act of 1833 in relation to this article; they are great already, and still greater are yet to come. As early as 1837, the whole amount of the sugar revenue, and $861,71 besides, was delivered over to some twenty odd manufacturers of refined sugars! At this day, the whole amount of that revenue goes to these few individuals, and $37,343,38 besides. This is the case this year. Henceforth they are to receive the whole amount of this revenue, with some hundreds of thousands of dollars besides, to be drawn from other branches of revenue, unless this bill is passed which I propose to bring in. This is the effect of the act, dignified with the name of compromise, and hallowed by the imputed character of sacred and inviolable! It turns over a tax levied from seventeen millions of people on an article of essential comfort, and almost a necessary; it turns over this whole tax to a few individuals; and that not being enough to satisfy their demand, they receive the remainder from the National Treasury! It violates the constitution to the whole extent of the excess of the drawback over the duty. It subjects the Treasury to an unforeseen amount of undue demands. It deprives the people of the whole benefit of the reduction of the sugar tax, provided for by the act itself; and subjects them to the mercies of those who may choose to monopolize the article for refinement and exportation. The whole number of persons into whose hands all this money and power is thrown, is, according to a statement derived from Gov. Wolf, the late collector of the customs at Philadelphia, no more than own the 29 sugar refineries; the whole of which, omitting some small ones in the West, and three in New Orleans, are situate on the north side of Mason and Dixon's line. Members from the South and West complain of the unequal working of our revenue system—of the large amounts expended in the northeast—the trifle expended South and West. But, why complain? Their own improvident and negligent legislation makes it so. This bill alone, in only one of its items—the sugar item—will send millions, before 1842, to the north side of that famous line: and this bill was the concoction, and that out of doors, of one member from the South and one more from the West.

Mr. Benton would proceed to the next article to the effect upon which, of the compromise act, he would wish to call their attention; and that article was imported molasses, and its manufacture, in the shape of exported rum. On this article, and its manufacture, the operation of the act was of the same character, though not to the same degree, that it was on sugars; the duties were reduced, while the drawback remained the same. This was constantly giving drawback where no duty had been paid; and in 1842 the whole of the molasses tax will go to these rum distillers—giving the legal implication that they had imported all the molasses that came into the United States, and paid duty on it—and then exported it all in the shape of rum—leaving not a gallon to have been consumed by the rest of the community, nor even a gallon of their own rum to have been drank in the United States. All this is clear from the regular operation of the compromise act, in reducing duties without making a corresponding reduction in the drawbacks founded upon them. But is there not to be cheating in addition to the regular operation of the act? If not, we shall be more fortunate than we have been heretofore, and that under the circumstances of greater temptation. It is well known that whiskey can be converted into New England rum, and exported as such, and receive the drawback of the molasses duty; and that this has been done just as often as the price of whiskey (and the meanest would answer the purpose) was less than the cost of molasses. The process was this. Purchase base whiskey at a low rate—filtrate it through charcoal, to deprive it of smell and taste—then pass it through a rum distillery, in company with a little real rum—and the whiskey would come out rum, very fit to be sold as such at home, or exported as such, with the benefit of drawback. All this has been done, and has been proved to be done; and, therefore, may be done again, and certainly will be done, under the increased temptation which the compromise act now affords, and will continue to afford, if not amended as proposed by the bill I propose to bring in. It was proved before a committee of the House of Representatives in the session of 1827-8. Mr. Jeromus Johnson, then a member of Congress from the city of New York, now a custom-house officer in that city, testified directly to the fact. To the question: "*Are there not large quantities of whiskey used with molasses in the distillation of what is called New England rum?*" He answered: "*There are:*" and that when mixed at the rate of only four gallons to one, and the mixture run through a rum distillery—the whiskey previously deprived of its taste and smell by filtration through charcoal—the best practised rum drinker could not tell the difference—even if appealed to by a custom-house officer. That whiskey is now used for that purpose, is clearly established by the table marked B. That table shows that the importation of foreign molasses for the year 1839 was 392,368 gallons; and the exportation of distilled rum for that quantity was 356,699 gallons; that is to say, nearly as many gallons of rum went out as of molasses came in; and, admitting that a gallon of good molasses will make a gallon of rum, yet the average is below it. Inferior or common molasses falls short of producing gallon for gallon by from 5 to 7½ per cent. Now make an allowance for this deficiency; allow also for the quantity of foreign molasses consumed in the United States in other ways; allow likewise for the quantity of rum made from molasses, and not exported, but consumed at home: allow for these three items, and the conviction becomes irresistible, that whiskey was used in the distillation of rum in the year 1839, and exported with the benefit of drawback! and that such will continue to be the case (if this blunder is not corrected), as the duty gets lower and the temptation to export whiskey, under the disguise of New England rum, becomes greater. After 1842, this must be a great business, and the molasses drawback a good profit on mean whiskey.

Putting these two items together—the sugar and the molasses drawbacks—and some millions must be plundered from the Treasury under the preposterous provisions of this compromise act.

CHAPTER LIV.

FISHING BOUNTIES AND ALLOWANCES, AND THEIR ABUSE: MR. BENTON'S SPEECH: EXTRACTS.

The bill which I am asking leave to introduce, proposes to reduce the fishing bounties and allowances in proportion to the reduction which the salt duty has undergone, and is to undergo; and at the threshold I am met by the question, whether these allowances are founded upon the salt duty, and should rise and fall with it, or are independent of that duty, and can be kept up without it? I hold the affirmative of this question. I hold that the allowances rest upon the duty, and upon nothing else, and that there is neither statute law nor constitution to support them on any other foundation. This is what I hold: but I should not have noticed the question at this time except for the issue joined upon it between the senator from Massachusetts who sits farthest on the other side (Mr. Davis), and myself. He and I have made up an issue on this point; and without going into the argument at this time, I will cite him to the original petition from the Massachusetts legislature, asking for a drawback of the duties, or, as they styled it, "a remission of duties on all the dutiable articles used in the fisheries; and also premiums and bounties:" and having shown this petition, I will point to half a dozen acts of Congress which prove my position—hoping that they may prove sufficient, but promising to come down upon him with an avalanche of authorities if they are not.

The dutiable articles used in the fisheries, and of which a remission duty was asked in the petition, were: salt, rum, tea, sugar, molasses, coarse woollens, lines and hooks, sail-cloth, cordage, iron, tonnage. This petition, presented to Congress in the year 1790, was referred to the Secretary of State (Mr. Jefferson), for a report upon it; and his report was, that a drawback of duties ought to be allowed, and that the fisheries are not to draw support from the Treasury; the words, "drawback of duty," only applying to articles exported, was confined to the salt upon that part of the fish which were shipped to foreign countries: and to this effect was the legislation of Congress. I briefly review the first half dozen of these acts.

1. The act of 1789—the same which imposed a duty of six cents a bushel on salt, and which granted a bounty of five cents a barrel on pickled fish exported, and also on beef and pork exported, and five cents a quintal on dried fish exported—declared these bounties to be "in lieu of a drawback of the duties imposed on the importation of the salt employed and expended thereon." This act is decisive of the whole question. In the first place it declares the bounty to be in lieu of a drawback of the salt duty. In the second place, it conforms to the principle of all drawbacks, and only grants the bounty on the part of the fish which is exported. In the third place, it gives the same bounty, and in the same words, to the exporters of salted beef and pork which is given to the exporters of fish: and certainly mariners were not expected to be created among the raisers of swine and cattle—which negatives the idea of this being an encouragement to the formation of seamen.

2. In 1790 the duty on salt was doubled: it was raised from six to twelve cents a bushel: by the same act the fishing bounties and allowances were also doubled: they were raised from five to ten cents the barrel and the quintal. By this act the bounties and allowances both to fish and provisions, were described to be "in lieu of drawback of the duty on salt used in curing fish and provisions exported."

3. The act of 1792 repeals "the bounty in lieu of drawback on dried fish;" and, "in lieu of that, and as commutation thereof, and as an equivalent therefor," shifts the bounty from the "quintal" of dried fish to the "tonnage" of the fishing vessel; and changes its name from "bounty" to "allowance." This is the key act to the present system of tonnage allowance to the fishing vessel; and was passed upon the petition of the fishermen, and to enable the "crew" of the vessel to draw the bounty instead of letting it fall into the hands of the exporting merchant. It was done upon the fishermen's petition, and for the benefit of the crew, interested in the adventure, and who had paid the duty on the salt which they used. And to exclude all idea of considering this change as a change of policy, and to cut off all inference that the allowance was now to become a bounty from the Treasury as an encouragement for a seaman's nursery, the act went on to make this precise and explicit declaration: "*That the allowance so granted to the fishing vessel was a commutation of, and an equivalent for, the bounty in lieu of drawback of the duties imposed on the importation of the salt used in curing the fish exported.*" This is plain language—the plain language used by legislators of that day—and defies misconception, misunderstanding, or cavil.

4. In 1797 the duty on salt was raised from twelve cents to twenty cents a bushel: by the same act a corresponding increase was made in the bounties both to exported salted provisions and pickled fish, and in the allowance to the fishing vessels. The salt duty was raised one-third and a fraction: and these bounties and allowances were raised one-third. Thirty-three and one-third per cent. was added all round; and the act, to make all sure, was express in again declaring the bounties and allowances to be a commutation in lieu of the drawback of the salt duty.

5. The act of April 12th, 1800, continues the salt duty, and with it all the bounties to salted provisions and pickled fish exported, and all the allowances to fishing vessels, for ten years; and then adds this proviso: "That these allowances shall not be understood to be continued for a longer time than the correspondent duties on salt, respectively, for which the said allowances were granted, shall be payable." Such are the terms of the act of the year 1800. It is a clincher. It nails up, and crushes every thing. It shows that Congress was determined that the salt duty, and the bounties and allowances, should be one and indivisible: that they should come, and go together—should rise and fall together—should live and die together.

6. In 1807, Mr. Jefferson being President, the salt tax was abolished upon his recommendation: and with it all the bounties and allowances to fishing vessels, to pickled fish, and to salted beef and pork were all swept away. The same act abolished the whole. The first section repealed the salt duty: the second repealed the bounties and allowances: and the repeal of both was to take effect on the same day—namely, on the first day of January, 1808: a day which deserves to be nationally commemorated, as the day of the death of an odious, criminal and impious tax. The beneficent and meritorious act was in these words: "*That from and after the first day of January next, so much of any act as allows a bounty on exported salt provisions and pickled fish, in lieu of drawback of the duties on the salt employed in curing the same, and so much of any act as makes allowances to the owners and crews of fishing vessels, in lieu of drawback of the duties paid on the salt used in the same, shall be, and the same hereby is repealed.*" This was the end of the first salt tax in the United States, and of all the bounties and allowances built upon it. It fell, with all its accessories, under the republican administration of Mr. Jefferson—and with the unanimous vote of every republican—and also with the vote of many federalists: so much more favorable were the old federalists than the whigs of this day, to the interests of the people. In fact there were only five votes against the repeal, and not one of these upon the ground that the bounties and allowances were independent of the salt duty.

7. After this, and for six years, there was no salt tax—no fishing bounties or allowances in the United States. The tax, and its progeny lay buried in one common grave, and had no resurrection until the year 1813. The war with Great Britain revived them—the tax and its offspring together; but only as a temporary measure—as a war tax—to cease within one year after the termination of the war. Before that year was out, the tax, and its appendages were continued—not for any determinate period, but until repealed by Congress. They have not been repealed yet! and that was forty years ago! No act could then have been obtained to continue this duty for the short space of three years. The continuance could only be obtained on the argument that Congress could then repeal it at any time; a fallacious reliance, but always seductive to men of easy and temporizing temperaments.

The pretension that these fishing bounties and allowances were granted as encouragement to mariners, is rejected by every word of the acts which grant them, and by the striking fact, that no part of them goes to the whale fisheries. Not a cent of them had ever gone to a whale ship: they had only gone to the cod and mackerel fisheries. The noble whaler of four or five hundred tons, with her ample crew, which sailed twenty thousand miles, doubling a most tempestuous cape before she arrived at the field of her labors—which remained out three years, waging actual war with the monsters of the deep—a war in which a brave heart, a steady eye, and an iron nerve were as much wanted as in any battle with man;—this noble whaler got nothing. It all went to the hook-and-line men—to the cod and mackerel fisheries, which were carried on in diminutive vessels, as small as five tons, and in the rivers, and along the shores, and on the shallow banks of Newfoundland. Meritorious as these hook-and-line fishermen might be, they cannot compare with the whalers: and these whalers receive no bounties and allowances because they pay no duty on imported salt, re-exported by them.

I now come to the clause in my bill which has called forth these preliminary remarks; the third clause, which proposes the reduction of fishing bounties and allowances in proportion to the reduction which the salt tax has undergone, and shall undergo. And here, it is not the compromise act alone that is to be blamed: a previous act shares that censure with it. In 1830 the salt duty was reduced one-half, to take effect in 1830 and 1831; the fishing bounties and allowances should have been reduced one-half at the same time. I made the motion in the Senate to that effect; but it failed of success. When the compromise act was passed in 1833, and provided for a further reduction of the salt duty—a reduction which has now reduced it two-thirds, and in 1841 and '42 will reduce it still lower—when this act was passed, a reduction of the fishing bounties and allowances should have taken place. The two senators who concocted that act in their chambers, and brought it here to be registered as the royal edicts were registered in the times of the old French monarchy; when these two senators concocted this act, they should have inserted a provision in it for the correspondent reduction of the fishing bounties and allowances with the salt tax: they should have placed these allowances, and the refined sugar, and the rum drawbacks, all on the same footing, and reduced them all in proportion to the reduction of the duties on the articles on which they were founded. They did not do this. They omitted the whole; with what mischief you have already seen in the case of rum and refined sugar, and shall presently see in the case of the fishing bounties and allowances. I attempted to supply a part of their omission in making the motion in relation to drawbacks, which was read to you at the commencement of these remarks. Failing in that motion, I made no further attempt, but waited for TIME, the great arbiter of all questions, to show the mischief, and to enforce the remedy. That arbiter is now here, with his proofs in his hand, in the shape of certain reports from the Treasury Department in relation to the salt duty and the fishing bounties and allowances, which have been printed by the order of the Senate, and constitute part of the salt document, No. 196. From that document I now proceed to collect the evidences of one branch of the mischief—the pecuniary branch of it—which the omission to make the proper reductions in these allowances has inflicted upon the country.

The salt duty was reduced one-fourth in the year 1831; the fishing bounties and allowances that year were $313,894; they should have been reduced one-fourth also, which would have made them about $160,000. In 1832 the duty was reduced one-half; the fishing bounties and allowances were paid in full, and amounted to $234,137; they should have been reduced one-half; and then $117,018 would have discharged them. The compromise act was made in 1833, and, under the operation of that act, the salt duty has undergone biennial reductions, until it is now reduced to about one-third of its original amount: if it had provided for the correspondent reduction of the fishing bounties and allowances, there would have been saved from that year to the year 1839—the last to which the returns have been made up—an annual average sum of about $150,000, or a gross sum of about $900,000. The prospective loss can only be estimated; but it is to increase rapidly, owing to the large reductions in the salt duty in the years 1841 and 1842.

The present year, 1840, lacks but a little of exhausting the whole amount of the salt revenue in paying the fishing bounties and allowances; the next year will take more than the whole; and the year after will require about double the amount of the salt revenue of that year to be taken from other branches of the revenue to satisfy the demands of the fishing vessels: thus producing the same result as in the case of the sugar duties—the whole amount of the salt duty, and as much more out of other duties, being paid to the cod and mackerel fishermen, as the whole amount of the sugar tax, and considerably more, is paid to the sugar-refiners. The results for the present year, and the ensuing ones, are of course computed: they are computations founded upon the basis of the last ascertained year's operations. The last year to which all the heads of this branch of business is made up, is the year 1838; and for that year they stand thus: Salt imported, in round numbers, seven millions of bushels; net revenue from it, about $430,000; fishing bounties and allowances, $320,000. Assuming the importation of the present year to be the same, and the bounties and allowances to be the same, the loss to the Treasury will be $206,000; for the salt duty this year will undergo a further reduction. In 1842, when this duty has reached its lowest point, the whole amount of revenue derived from it is computed at about $170,000, while the fishing bounties and allowances continuing the same, namely, about $320,000, the salt revenue in the gross will be little more than half enough to pay it; and, after deducting the weighers' and measurers' fees, which come out of the Treasury, and amount to $52,500 on an importation of seven millions; after deducting this item, there will be a deficiency of about $200,000 in the salt revenue, in meeting the drawbacks, in the shape of bounties and allowances founded upon it. Thus two-thirds of the whole amount of the salt revenue is at this time paid to the fishing vessels. Next year it will all go to them; and after 1842, we shall have to raise money from other sources to the amount of $200,000 per annum, or raise the salt duty itself to produce that amount, in order to satisfy these drawbacks, which were permitted to take the form of bounties and allowances to fishing vessels. Such is the operation of the compromise act! that act which is styled sacred and inviolable!

Of the other mischiefs resulting from this compromise act, which reduced the duties on salt, and the one which preceded it for the same purpose, without reducing the correspondent bounties and allowances to the fishing interest—of these remaining mischiefs, whereof there are many, I mean to mention but one; and merely to mention that, and not to argue it. It is the constitutional objection to the payment of any thing beyond the duty received—the payment of any thing which exceeds the drawback of the duty. Up to that point, I admit the constitutionality of drawbacks, whether passing under that name, or changed to the name of a bounty, or an allowance in lieu of a drawback. I admit the constitutional right of Congress to permit a drawback of the amount paid in: I deny the constitutional right to permit a drawback of any amount beyond what was paid in. This is my position, which I pledge myself to maintain, if any one disputes it; and applying this principle to the fishing bounties and allowances, and also to the drawbacks in the case of refined sugars and rum: and I boldly affirm that the constitution of the United States has been in a state of flagrant violation, under the compromise act, from the day of its passage to the present hour, and will continue so until the bill is passed which I am about to ask leave to bring in.

Sir, I quit this part of my subject with presenting, in a single picture, the condensed view of what I have been detailing. It is, that the whole annual revenue derived from sugar, salt, and molasses, is delivered over gratuitously to a few thousand persons in a particular section of the Union, and is not even sufficient to satisfy their demands! In other words, that a tax upon a nation of seventeen millions of people, upon three articles of universal consumption, articles of necessity, and of comfort, is laid for the benefit of a few dozen rum distillers and sugar refiners, and a few thousand fishermen; and not being sufficient for them, the deficit, amounting to many hundred thousand dollars per annum, is taken from other branches of the revenue, and presented to them! and all this the effect of an act which was made out of doors, which was not permitted to be amended on its passage, and which is now held to be sacred and inviolable! and which will eventually sink under its own iniquities, though sustained now by a cry which was invented by knavery, and is repeated by ignorance, folly, and faction—a cry that that compromise saved the Union. This is the picture I present—which I prove to be true—and the like of which is not to be seen in the legislation, or even in the despotic decrees, of arbitrary monarchs, in any other country upon the face of the earth.

About five millions of dollars have been taken from the Treasury under these bounties and allowances—the greater part of it most unduly and abusefully.[3] The fishermen are only entitled to an amount equal to the duty paid on the imported salt, which is used upon that part of the fish which is exported; and the law requires not only the exportation to be proved, but the landing and remaining of the cargo in a foreign country. They draw back this year $355,000. Do they pay that amount of duty on the salt put on the modicum of fish which they export? Why, it is about the entire amount of the whole salt tax paid by the whole United States! and to justify their right to it, they must consume on the exported part of their fish the whole quantity of foreign salt now imported into the United States—leaving not a handful to be used by the rest of the population, or by themselves on that part of their fish which is consumed at home—and which is so much greater than the exported part. This shows the enormity of the abuse, and that the whole amount of the salt tax now goes to a few thousand fishermen; and if this compromise act is not corrected, that whole amount, after 1842, will not be sufficient to pay this small class—not equal in number to the farmers in a common Kentucky county; and other money must be taken out of the Treasury to make good the deficiency. I have often attempted to get rid of the whole evil, and render a great service to the country, by repealing *in toto* the tax and all the bounties and allowances erected upon it. At present I only propose, and that without the least prospect of success, to correct a part of the abuse, by reducing the payments to the fishermen in proportion to the reduction of the duty on salt: but the true remedy is the one applied under Mr. Jefferson's administration—total repeal of both.

CHAPTER LV.

EXPENDITURES OF THE GOVERNMENT.

At no point does the working of the government more seriously claim the attention of statesmen than at that of its expenses. It is the tendency of all governments to increase their expenses, and it should be the care of all statesmen to restrain them within the limits of a judicious economy. This obligation was felt as a duty in the early periods of our history, and the doctrine of *economy* became a principle in the political faith of the party, which, whether called Republican as formerly, or Democratic as now, is still the same, and was incorporated in its creed. Mr. Jefferson largely rested the character of his administration upon it; and deservedly: for even in the last year of his administration, and after the enlargement of our territory by the acquisition of Louisiana, the expenses of the government were but about three millions and a half of dollars. At the end of Mr. Monroe's administration, sixteen years later, they had risen to about seven millions; and in the last year of Mr. Van Buren's (sixteen years more), they had risen to about thirteen millions. At the same time, at each of these epochs, and in fact, in every year of every administration, there were payments from the Treasury for extraordinary or temporary objects, often far exceeding in amount the regular governmental expenses. Thus, in the last year of Mr. Jefferson, the whole outlay from the Treasury, was about twelve millions and a half; of which eight millions went to the payment of principal and interest on the public debt, and about one million to other extra objects. And in the last year of Mr. Monroe, the whole payments were about thirty-two millions of dollars, of which sixteen millions and a half went to the liquidation of the public debt; and above eight millions more to other extraordinary and temporary objects. Towards the close of Mr. Van Buren's administration, this aggregate of outlay for all objects had risen to about thirty-seven millions, which the opposition called thirty-nine; and presenting this gross sum as the actual expenses of the government, made a great outcry against the extravagance of the administration; and the people, not understanding the subject, were seriously impressed with the force and truth of that accusation, while the real expenses were but about the one-third of that sum. To present this result in a plain and authentic form, the author of this View obtained a call upon the Secretary for the different payments, ordinary and extraordinary, from the Treasury for a series of years, in which the payments would be placed under three heads—the ordinary, the extraordinary, and the public debt—specifying the items of each; and extending from Monroe's time (admitted to be economical), to Mr. Van Buren's charged with extravagance. This return was made by the Secretary, divided into three columns, with specifications, as required; and though obtained for a temporary and transient purpose, it possesses a permanent interest as giving a complete view of the financial working of the government, and fixing points of comparison in the progress of expenditure—very proper to be looked back upon by those who would hold the government to some degree of economy in the use of the public money. There has been no such examination since the year 1840: there would seem to be room for it now (1855), when the aggregate of appropriations exceed seventy millions of dollars. A deduction for extraordinaries would largely reduce that aggregate, but still leave enough behind to astound the lovers of economy. Three branches of expenditure alone, each within itself, exceeds by upwards of four to one, the whole ordinary expenses of the government in the time of Mr. Jefferson; and upwards of double of such expense in the time of Mr. Monroe; and some millions more than the same aggregate in the last year of Mr. Van Buren. These three branches are, 1. The civil, diplomatic, and miscellaneous, $17,265,929 and 50 cents. 2. The naval service (without the pensions and "reserved" list), $15,012,091 and 53 cents. 3. The army, fortifications, military academy (without the pensions), $12,571,496 and 64 cents. These three branches of expenditure alone would amount to about forty-five millions of dollars—to which twenty-six millions more are to be added. The dormant spirit of economy—hoped to be only dormant, not dead—should wake up at this exhibition of the public expenditure: and it is with that view—with the view of engaging the attention of some economical members of Congress, that the exhibit is now made—that this chapter is written—and some regard invoked for the subject of which it treats. The evils of extravagance in the government are great. Besides the burden upon the people, it leads to corruption in the government, and to a janissary horde of office holders to live upon the people while polluting their elections and legislation, and poisoning the fountains of public information in moulding public opinion to their own purposes. More than that. It is the true source of the just discontent of the Southern States, and must aggravate more and more the deep-seated complaint against the unnecessary levy of revenue upon the industry of one half of the Union to be chiefly expended in the other. That complaint was great enough to endanger the Union twenty-five years ago, when the levy and expenditure was thirty odd millions: it is now seventy odd! At the same time it is the opinion of this writer, that a practical man, acquainted with the objects for which the federal government was created, and familiar with its financial working from the time its fathers put it into operation, could take his pen and cross out nearly the one half of these seventy odd millions, and leave the government in full vigor for all its proper objects, and more pure, by reducing the number of those who live upon the substance of the people. To complete the effect of this chapter, some extracts are given in the ensuing one, from the speech made in 1840, upon the expenditures of the government, as presenting practical views upon a subject of permanent interest, and more worthy of examination now than then.

CHAPTER LVI.

EXPENSES OF THE GOVERNMENT, COMPARATIVE AND PROGRESSIVE, AND SEPARATED FROM EXTRAORDINARIES.

Mr. Benton moved to print an extra number of these tabular statements received from the Secretary of the Treasury, and proposed to give his reasons for the motion, and for that purpose, asked that the papers should be sent to him (which was done); and Mr. B. went on to say that his object was to spread before the country, in an authentic form, the full view of all the government expenses for a series of years past, going back as far as Mr. Monroe's administration; and thereby enabling every citizen, in every part of the country, to see the actual, the comparative, and the classified expenditures of the government for the whole period. This proceeding had become necessary, Mr. B. said, from the systematic efforts made for some years past, to impress the country with the belief that the expenditures had increased threefold in the last twelve years—that they had risen from thirteen to thirty-nine millions of dollars; and that this enormous increase was the effect of the extravagance, of the corruption, and of the incompetency of the administrations which had succeeded those of Mr. Adams and Mr. Monroe. These two latter administrations were held up as the models of economy; those of Mr. Van Buren and General Jackson were stigmatized as monsters of extravagance; and tables of figures were so arranged as to give color to the characters attributed to each. These systematic efforts—this reiterated assertion, made on this floor, of *thirteen* millions increased to *thirty-nine*—and the effect which such statements must have upon the minds of those who cannot see the purposes for which the money was expended, appeared to him (Mr. B.), to require some more formal and authentic refutation than any one individual could give—something more imposing than the speech of a solitary member could afford. Familiar with the action of the government for twenty years past—coming into the Senate in the time of Mr. Monroe— remaining in it ever since—a friend to economy in public and in private life—and closely scrutinizing the expenditures of the government during the whole time—he (Mr. B.) felt himself to be very able at any time to have risen in his place, and to have exposed the delusion of this *thirteen* and *thirty-nine* million bugbear; and, if he did not do so, it was because, in the first place, he was disinclined to bandy contradictions on the floor of the Senate; and, in the second place, because he relied upon the intelligence of the country to set all right whenever they obtained a view of the facts. This view he had made himself the instrument of procuring, and the Secretary of the Treasury had now presented it. It was ready for the contemplation of the American people; and he could wish every citizen to have the picture in his own hands, that he might contemplate it at his own fireside, and at his full leisure. He could wish every citizen to possess a copy of this report, now received from the Secretary of the Treasury, under the call of the Senate, and printed by its order; he could wish every citizen to possess one of these authentic copies, bearing the *imprimatur* of the American Senate; but that was impossible; and, limiting his action to what was possible, he would propose to print such number of extra copies as would enable some to reach every quarter of the Union.

Mr. B. then opened the tables, and explained their character and contents. The first one (marked A) consisted of three columns, and exhibited the aggregate, and the classified expenditures of the government from the year 1824 to 1839, inclusive; the second one (marked B) contained the detailed statement of the payments annually made on account of all temporary or extraordinary objects, including the public debt, for the same period. The second table was explanatory of the third column of the first one; and the two, taken together, would enable every citizen to see the actual expenditures, and the comparative expenditures, of the government for the whole period which he had mentioned.

Mr. B. then examined the actual and the comparative expenses of two of the years, taken from the two contrasted periods referred to, and invoked the attention of the Senate to the results which the comparison would exhibit. He took the first and the last of the years mentioned in the tables—the years 1824 and 1839— and began with the first item in the first column. This showed the aggregate expenditures for every object for the year 1824, to have been $31,898,538 47—very near thirty-two millions of dollars, said Mr. B., and if stated alone, and without explanation, very capable of astonishing the public, of imposing upon the ignorant, and of raising a cry against the dreadful extravagance, the corruption, and the wickedness of Mr. Monroe's administration. Taken by itself (and indisputably true it is in itself), and this aggregate of near thirty-two millions is very sufficient to effect all this surprise and indignation in the public mind; but, passing on to the second column to see what were the expenditures, independent of the public debt, and this large aggregate will be found to be reduced more than one half; it sinks to $15,330,144 71. This is a heavy deduction; but it is not all. Passing on to the third column, and it is seen that the actual expenses of the government for permanent and ordinary objects, independent of the temporary and extraordinary ones, for this same year, were only $7,107,892 05; being less than the one-fourth part of the aggregate of near thirty-two millions. This looks quite reasonable, and goes far towards relieving Mr. Monroe's administration from the imputation to which a view of the aggregate expenditure for the year would have subjected it. But, to make it entirely satisfactory, and to enable every citizen to understand the important point of the government expenditures—a point on which the citizens of a free and representative government should be always well informed—to attain this full satisfaction, let us pass on to the second table (marked B), and fix our eyes on its first column, under the year 1824. We shall there find every temporary and extraordinary object, and the amount paid on account of it, the deduction of which reduced an aggregate of near thirty-two millions to a fraction over seven millions. We shall there find the explanation of the difference between the first and third columns. The first item is the sum of $16,568,393 76, paid on account of the principal and interest of the public debt. The second is the sum of $4,891,386 56, paid to merchants for indemnities under the treaty with Spain of 1819, by which we acquired Florida. And so on through nine minor items, amounting in the whole, exclusive of the public debt, to about eight millions and a quarter. This total added to the sum paid on account of the public debt, makes close upon twenty-five millions of dollars; and this, deducted from the aggregate of near thirty-two millions, leaves a fraction over seven millions for the real expenses of the government—the ordinary and permanent expenses—during the last year of Mr. Monroe's administration.

This is certainly a satisfactory result. It exempts the administration of that period from the imputation of extravagance, which the unexplained exhibition of the aggregate expenditures might have drawn upon it in the minds of uninformed persons. It clears that administration from all blame. It must be satisfactory to every candid mind. And now let us apply the test of the same examination to some year of the present administration, now so incontinently charged with ruinous extravagance. Let us see how the same rule will work when applied to the present period; and, for that purpose, let us take the last year in the table, that of 1839. Let others take any year that they please, or as many as they please: I take one, because I only propose to give an example; and I take the last one in the table, because it is the last. Let us proceed with this examination, and see what the results, actual and comparative, will be.

Commencing with the aggregate payments from the Treasury for all objects, Mr. B. said it would be seen at the foot of the first column in the first table, that they amounted to $37,129,396 80; passing to the second column, and it would be seen that this sum was reduced to $25,982,797 75; and passing to the third, and it would be seen that this latter sum was itself reduced to $13,525,800 18; and, referring to the second table, under the year 1839, and it would be seen how this aggregate of thirty-seven millions was reduced to thirteen and a half. It was a great reduction; a reduction of nearly two-thirds from the aggregate amount paid out; and left for the proper expenses of the government—its ordinary and permanent expenses—an inconceivably small sum for a great nation of seventeen millions of souls, covering an immense extent of territory, and acting a part among the great powers of the world. To trace this reduction—to show the reasons of the difference between the first and the third columns, Mr. B. would follow the same process which he had pursued in explaining the expenditures of the year 1824, and ask for nothing in one case which had not been granted in the other.

1. The first item to be deducted from the thirty-seven million aggregate, was the sum of $11,146,599 05, paid on account of the public debt. He repeated, on account of the public debt; for it was paid in redemption of Treasury notes; and these Treasury notes were so much debt incurred to supply the place of the revenue deposited with the States, in 1836, or shut up in banks during the suspension of 1837, or due from merchants, to whom indulgence had been granted. To supply the place of these unattainable funds, the government went in debt by issuing Treasury notes; but faithful to the sentiment which abhorred a national debt, it paid off the debt almost as fast as it contracted it. Above eleven millions of this debt was paid in 1839, amounting to almost the one-third part of the aggregate expenditure of that year; and thus, nearly the one-third part of the sum

which is charged upon the administration as extravagance and corruption, was a mere payment of debt!—a mere payment of Treasury notes which we had issued to supply the place of our misplaced and captured revenue—our three instalments of ten millions cash presented to the States under the false and fraudulent name of a deposit, and our revenue of 1837 captured by the banks when they shut their doors upon their creditors. The glorious administration of President Jackson left the country free from public debt: its worthy successor will do the same.

Removal of Indians from the Southern and Western States, and extinction of their titles, and numerous smaller items, all specified in the third column of the table, amount to about twelve millions and a half more; and these added to the payments on the public debt, the remainder is the expense of the government, and is but about the one-third of the aggregate expenditure—to be precise, about thirteen millions and a half.

With this view of the tabular statements Mr. B. closed the examination of the items of expenditure, and stated the results to be a reduction of the thirty-seven million aggregate in 1839, like that of the thirty-two million aggregate in 1824, to about one-third of its amount. The very first item, that of the payment of public debt in the redemption of Treasury notes, reduced it eleven millions of dollars: it sunk it from thirty-seven millions to twenty-six. The other eighteen items amounted to $12,656,977, and reduced the twenty-six millions to thirteen and a half. Here then is a result which is attained by the same process which applies to the year 1824, and to every other year, and which is right in itself; and which must put to flight and to shame all the attempts to excite the country with this bugbear story of extravagance. In the first place the aggregate expenditures have not increased threefold in fifteen years; they have not risen from thirteen to thirty-nine millions, as incontinently asserted by the opposition; but from thirty-two millions to thirty-seven or thirty-nine. And how have they risen? By paying last year eleven millions for Treasury notes, and more than twelve millions for Indian lands, and wars, removals of Indians, and increase of the army and navy, and other items as enumerated. The result is a residuum of thirteen and a half millions for the real expenses of the government; a sum one and a half millions short of what gentlemen proclaim would be an economical expenditure. They all say that fifteen millions would be an economical expenditure; very well! here is thirteen and a half! which is a million and a half short of that mark.

CHAPTER LVII.

DEATH OF MR. JUSTICE BARBOUR OF THE SUPREME COURT, AND APPOINTMENT OF PETER V. DANIEL, ESQ., IN HIS PLACE.

Mr. Phillip P. Barbour was a representative in Congress from the State of Virginia when I was first elected to the Senate in 1820. I had the advantage—(for advantage I truly deemed it for a young member)—to be in habitual society with such a man—one of the same mess with him the first session of my service. Nor was it accidental, but sought for on my part. It was a talented mess—among others the brilliant orator, William Pinkney of Maryland; and the eloquent James Barbour, of the Senate, brother to the representative: their cousin the representative John S. Barbour, equal to either in the endowments of the mind: Floyd of Virginia: Trimble and Clay of Kentucky. I knew the advantage of such association—and cherished it. From that time I was intimate with Mr. Phillip P. Barbour during the twenty-one winters which his duties, either as representative in Congress, or justice of the Supreme Court, required him to be at Washington. He was a man worthy of the best days of the republic—modest, virtuous, pure: artless as a child: full of domestic affections: patriotic: filially devoted to Virginia as his mother State, and a friend to the Union from conviction and sentiment. He had a clear mind—a close, logical and effective method of speaking—copious without diffusion; and, always speaking to the subject, both with knowledge and sincerity, he was always listened to with favor. He was some time Speaker of the House, and was appointed to the bench of the Supreme Court by President Van Buren in 1837, in place of Mr. Justice Duval, resigned. He had the death which knows no pain, and which, to the body, is sleep without waking. He was in attendance upon the Supreme Court, in good health and spirits, and had done his part the night before in one of the conferences which the labors of the Supreme Bench impose almost nightly on the learned judges. In the morning he was supposed by his servant to be sleeping late, and, finally going to his bedside, found him dead—the face all serene and composed, not a feature or muscle disturbed, the body and limbs in their easy natural posture. It was evident that the machinery of life had stopped of itself, and without a shock. Ossification of the heart was supposed to be the cause. He was succeeded on the Supreme Bench by Peter V. Daniel, Esq., of the same State, also appointed by Mr. Van Buren—one in the first, the other in the last days of his administration.

A beautiful instance in Mr. Barbour of self-denial, and of fidelity to party and to personal friendship, and regard for honor and decorum, occurred while he was a member of the House. Mr. Randolph was in the Senate: the time for his re-election came round: he had some personal enemies in his own party, who, joined to the whig party, could defeat him: and it was a high object with the administration at Washington (that of Mr. Adams), to have him defeated. The disaffected and the opposition combined together, counted their numbers, ascertained their strength, and saw that they could dispose of the election; but only in favor of some one of the same party with Mr. Randolph. They offered the place to Mr. Barbour. It was the natural ascent in the gradation of his appointments; and he desired it; and, it may be said, the place desired him: for he was a man to adorn the chamber of the American Senate. But honor forbid; for with him Burns's line was a law of his nature: *Where you feel your honor grip, let that still be your border.* He was the personal and political friend of Mr. Randolph, and would not be used against him; and sent an answer to the combined parties which put an end to their solicitations. Mr. John Tyler, then governor of the State, and standing in the same relation with Mr. Barbour to Mr. Randolph, was then offered the place: and took it. It was his first step in the road to the whig camp; where he arrived eventually—and lodged, until elected out of it into the vice-presidential chair.

Judge Barbour was a Virginia country gentleman, after the most perfect model of that most respectable class—living on his ample estate, baronially, with his family, his slaves, his flocks and herds—all well cared for by himself, and happy in his care. A farmer by position, a lawyer by profession, a politician of course—dividing his time between his estate, his library, his professional, and his public duties—scrupulously attentive to his duties in all: and strict in that school of politics of which Mr. Jefferson, Mr. Madison, John Taylor of Caroline, Mr. Monroe, Mr. Macon, and others, were the great exemplars. A friend to order and economy in his private life, he carried the same noble qualities into his public stations, and did his part to administer the government with the simplicity and purity which its founders intended for it.

CHAPTER LVIII.

PRESIDENTIAL ELECTION.

Mr. Van Buren was the democratic candidate. His administration had been so acceptable to his party, that his nomination in a convention was a matter of form, gone through according to custom, but the result commanded by the party in the different States in appointing their delegates. Mr. Richard M. Johnson, the actual Vice-President, was also nominated for re-election; and both nominations were made in conformity to the will of the people who sent the delegates. On the part of the whigs the same nominations were made as in the election of 1836—General William Henry Harrison of Ohio, for President; and Mr. John Tyler of Virginia, for Vice-President. The leading statesmen of the whig party were again passed by to make room for a candidate more sure of being elected. The success of General Jackson had turned the attention of those who managed the presidential nominations to military men, and an "odor of gunpowder" was considered a sufficient attraction to rally the masses, without the civil qualifications, or the actual military fame which General Jackson possessed. Availability, to use their own jargon, was the only ability which these managers asked—that is, available for the purposes of the election, and for their own advancement, relying on themselves to administer the government. Mr. Clay, the prominent man, and the undisputed head of the party, was not deemed available; and it was determined to set him aside. How to do it was the question. He was a man of too much power and spirit to be rudely thrust aside. Gentle, and respectful means were necessary to get him out of the way; and for that purpose he was concertedly importuned to withdraw from the canvass. He would not do so, but wrote a letter submitting himself to the will of the convention. When he did so he certainly expected an open decision—a vote in open convention—every delegate acting responsibly, and according to the will of his constituents. Not so the fact. He submitted himself to the convention: the convention delivered him to a committee: the committee disposed of him in a back chamber. It devised a process for getting at a result, which is a curiosity in the chapter of ingenious inventions—which is a study for the complication of its machinery—a model contrivance of the few to govern many—a secure way to produce an intended result without showing the design, and without leaving a trace behind to show what was done: and of which none but itself can be its own delineator: and, therefore, here it is:

> "*Ordered*, That the delegates from each State be requested to assemble as a delegation, and appoint a committee, not exceeding three in number, to receive the views and opinions of such delegation, and communicate the same to the assembled committees of all the delegations, to be by them respectively reported to their principals; and that thereupon the delegates from each State be requested to assemble as a delegation, and ballot for candidates for the offices of President and Vice-President, and having done so, to commit the ballot designating the votes of each candidate, and by whom given, to its committee; and thereupon all the committees shall assemble and compare the several ballots, and report the result of the same to their several delegations, together with such facts as may bear upon the nomination; and said delegation shall forthwith re-assemble and ballot again for candidates for the above offices, and again commit the result to the above committees, and if it shall appear that a majority of the ballots are for any one man for candidate for President, said committee shall report the result to the convention for its consideration; but if there shall be no such majority, then the delegations shall repeat the balloting until such a majority shall be obtained, and then report the same to the convention for its consideration. That the vote of a majority of each delegation shall be reported as the vote of that State; and each State represented here shall vote its full electoral vote by such delegation in the committee."

As this View of the Thirty Years is intended to show the working of our political system, and how things *were* done still more than *what* was done; and as the election of chief magistrate is the highest part of that working; and as the party nomination of a presidential candidate is the election of that candidate so far as the party is concerned: in all these points of view, the device of this resolution becomes historical, and commends itself to the commentators upon our constitution. The people are to elect the President. Here is a process through multiplied filtrations by which the popular sentiment is to be deduced from the masses, collected in little streams, then united in one swelling current, and poured into the hall of the convention—no one seeing the source, or course of any one of the streams. Algebra and alchemy must have been laid under contribution to work out a quotient from such a combination of signs and symbols. But it was done. Those who set the sum could work it: and the quotient was political death to Mr. Clay. The result produced was—for General Scott, 16 votes: for Mr. Clay, 90 votes: for General Harrison, 148 votes. And as the law of these conventions swallows up all minorities in an ascertained majority, so the majority for General Harrison swallowed up the 106 votes given to Mr. Clay and General Scott, made them count for the victor, presenting him as the unanimity candidate of the convention, and the defeated candidate and all their friends bound to join in his support. And in this way the election of 1840 was effected! a process certainly not within the purview of those framers of the constitution, who supposed they were giving to a nation the choice of its own chief magistrate.

From the beginning it had been foreseen that there was to be an embittered contest—the severest ever known in our country. Two powers were in the field against Mr. Van Buren, each strong within itself, and truly formidable when united—the whole whig party, and the large league of suspended banks, headed by the Bank of the United States—now criminal as well as bankrupt, and making its last struggle for a new national charter in the effort to elect a President friendly to it. In elections as in war money is the sinew of the contest, and the broken and suspended banks were in a condition, and a temper, to furnish that sinew without stint. By mutual support they were able to make their notes pass as money; and, not being subject to redemption, it could be furnished without restraint, and with all the good will of a self-interest in putting down the democratic party, whose hard-money policy, and independent treasury scheme, presented it as an enemy to paper money and delinquent banks. The influence of this moneyed power over its debtors, over presses, over travelling agents, was enormous, and exerted to the uttermost, and in amounts of money almost fabulous; and in ways not dreamed of. The mode of operating divided itself into two general classes, one coercive—addressed to the business pursuits and personal interests of the community: the other seductive, and addressed to its passions. The phrases given out in Congress against the financial policy of the administration became texts to speak upon, and hints to act upon. Carrying out the idea that the re-election of Mr. Van Buren would be the signal for the downfall of all prices, the ruin of all industry, and the destruction of all labor, the newspapers in all the trading districts began to abound with such advertisements as these: "*The subscriber will pay six dollars a barrel for flour if Harrison is elected, and three dollars if Van Buren is.*" "*The subscriber will pay five dollars a hundred for pork if Harrison is elected, and two and a half if Van Buren is.*" And so on through the whole catalogue of marketable articles, and through the different kinds of labor: and these advertisements were signed by respectable men, large dealers in the articles mentioned, and well able to fix the market price for them. In this way the result of the election was brought to bear coercively upon the business, the property, and the pecuniary interest of the people. The class of inducements addressed to the passions and imaginations of the people were such as history blushes to record. Log-cabins, coonskins, and hard cider were taken as symbols of the party, and to show its identification with the poorest and humblest of the people: and these cabins were actually raised in the most public parts of the richest cities, ornamented with coonskins after the fashion of frontier huts, and cider drank in them out of gourds in the public meetings which gathered about them: and the virtues of these cabins, these skins, and this cider were celebrated by travelling and stationary orators. The whole country was put into commotion by travelling parties and public gatherings. Steamboats and all public conveyances were crowded with parties singing doggerel ballads made for the occasion, accompanied with the music of drums, fifes, and fiddles; and incited by incessant speaking. A system of public gatherings was got up which pervaded every State, county and town—which took place by day and by night, accompanied by every preparation to excite; and many of which gatherings were truly enormous in their numbers—only to be estimated by the acre; attempts at counting or computing such masses being out of the question. The largest of these gatherings took place at Dayton, in the State of Ohio, the month before the election; and the description of it, as given by its enthusiastic friends, will give a vivid idea of that monster assemblage, and of the myriads of others of which it was only the greatest—differing in degree only, not in kind:

> "Dayton, the whole body there assembled in convention covered *ten acres* by actual measurement! And at no time were there more than two-thirds of the people on the ground. Every house with a flag was a hotel without price—the strings of every door being out, and every latch unfastened! *One hundred thousand!* It were useless to attempt any thing like a detailed

description of this *grand gathering of the people*. We *saw* it all—*felt* it all—and shall bear to our graves, live we yet half a century, the impression it made upon our hearts. But we cannot describe it. No eye that witnessed it, can convey to the mind of another, even a faint semblance of the things it there beheld. The bright and glorious day—the beautiful and hospitable city—the green-clad and heaven-blessed valley—the thousand flags, fluttering in every breeze and waving from every window—the ten thousand banners and badges, with their appropriate devices and patriotic inscriptions—and, more than all, the hundred thousand human hearts beating in that dense and seething mass of people—are things which those alone can properly feel and appreciate, who beheld this grandest spectacle of time. *The number of persons present* was, during the whole of the morning, variously estimated at from seventy-five to ninety thousand. Conjecture, however, was put to rest in the afternoon, at the speakers' stand. Here, while the crowd was compact, as we have elsewhere described it, and during the speech of General Harrison, the ground upon which it stood was measured by three different civil engineers, and allowing to the square yard four persons, the following results were arrived at: the first made it 77,600, the second 75,000, and the third 80,000. During the time of making three measurements, the number of square yards of surface covered was continually changing, by pressure without and resistance from within. Mr. Van Buren and his wiseacre assistants, have so managed currency matters, that we have very little to do business with. We can, therefore, be away from home, a portion of the time, as well as at home. And with respect to our families, *when we leave upon a rally, we take them with us*! Our wives and daughters, we are proud to say, have the blood of their revolutionary mothers and grandmothers coursing through their veins. There is no man among us whose heart is more filled and animated than theirs, by the spirit of seventy-six. Look at the three hundred and fifty at Nashville, who invited Henry Clay, the nation's pride, to be with them and their husbands and brothers on the 15th of August! Look at the four hundred at St. Louis, the nine hundred at the Tippecanoe battle-ground, the five thousand at Dayton! What now, but the spirit of seventy-six, does all this manifest? Ay, and *what tale does it all tell?* Does it not say, that the wicked charlatanry, and mad ambition, and selfish schemings, of the leading members of this administration of the general government, have made themselves felt in the very sanctum sanctorum of domestic life? Does it not speak of the cheerless hearth, where willing hands sit without employment? Does it not speak of the half-recompensed toil of the worn laborer, who finds, now and then, a week's hard work, upon the scant proceeds of which he must subsist himself and his family for a month! Does it not speak of empty larders in the town, while the garners of the country are overflowing? Does it not speak of want here and abundance there, without any medium of exchange to equalize the disparity? Does it not speak of a general disorganization of conventional operations—of embarrassment, stagnation, idleness, and despondency—whose 'malign influences' have penetrated the inner temples of man's home, and aroused, to indignant speech and unusual action, her who is its peace, its gentleness, its love, its all but divinity? The truth is—and it should be told—the women are the very life and soul of these movements of the people. Look at their liberal preparations at Nashville. Look at their boundless hospitality at Dayton. Look at their ardor and activity every where. And last, though far from the least important, look at their presence, in hundreds and by thousands, wherever there is any good to be done, to animate and encourage, and urge on their fathers, husbands and brothers. Whence those six hundred and forty-four flags, whose stars and stripes wave in the morning breeze, from nearly every house-top, as we enter the beautiful little city of Dayton? From the hand of woman. Whence the decorations of these porticoes and balconies, that gleam in the rising sun, as we ride through the broad and crowded streets? From the hand of woman. Whence this handsome and proudly cherished banner, under which the Ohio delegation returned from Nashville, and which now marks the head-quarters of the Cincinnati delegation of one thousand to Dayton? From the hand of woman. Whence yon richly wrought and surpassingly beautiful standard, about which cluster the Tippecanoe hosts, and whose production has cost many weeks of incessant labor? From the hand of woman. And to come down to less poetical but more substantial things, whence all the wholesome viands prepared in the six hundred and forty-four flag-houses around us, for our refreshment, and all the pallets spread for our repose? From the hand of woman."

By arts like these the community was worked up into a delirium, and the election was carried by storm. Out of 294 electoral votes Mr. Van Buren received but 60: out of twenty-six States he received the votes of only seven. He seemed to have been abandoned by the people! On the contrary he had been unprecedentedly supported by them—had received a larger popular vote than ever had been given to any President before! and three hundred and sixty-four thousand votes more than he himself had received at the previous presidential election when he beat the same General Harrison fourteen thousand votes. Here was a startling fact, and one to excite inquiry in the public mind. How could there be such overwhelming defeat with such an enormous increase of strength on the defeated side? This question pressed itself upon every thinking mind; and it was impossible to give it a solution consistent with the honor and purity of the elective franchise. For, after making all allowance for the greater number of voters brought out on this occasion than at the previous election by the extraordinary exertions now made to bring them out, yet there would still be required a great number to make up the five hundred and sixty thousand votes which General Harrison received over and above his vote of four years before. The belief of false and fraudulent votes was deep-seated, and in fact susceptible of proof in many instances. Many thought it right, for the sake of vindicating the purity of elections, to institute a scrutiny into the votes; but nothing of the kind was attempted, and on the second Wednesday in February, 1841, all the electoral votes were counted without objection—General Harrison found to have a majority of the whole number of votes given—and Messrs. Wise and Cushing on the part of the House and Mr. Preston on the part of the Senate, were appointed to give him the formal notification of his election. Mr. Tyler received an equal number of votes with him, and became Vice-president: Mr. Richard M. Johnson fell twelve votes behind Mr. Van Buren, receiving but 48 electoral votes. It was a complete rout of the democratic party, but without a single moral effect of victory. The spirit of the party ran as high as ever, and Mr. Van Buren was immediately, and generally, proclaimed the democratic candidate for the election of 1844.

CHAPTER LIX.

CONCLUSION OF MR. VAN BUREN'S ADMINISTRATION.

The last session of the Twenty-sixth Congress was barren of measures, and necessarily so, as being the last of an administration superseded by the popular voice, and soon to expire; and therefore restricted by a sense of propriety, during the brief remainder of its existence, to the details of business and the routine of service. But his administration had not been barren of measures, nor inauspicious to the harmony of the Union. It had seen great measures adopted, and sectional harmony conciliated. The divorce of Bank and State, and the restoration of the constitutional currency, were illustrious measures, beneficial to the government and the people; and the benefits of which will continue to be felt as long as they shall be kept. One of them dissolved a meretricious connection, disadvantageous to both parties, and most so to the one that should have suffered least, and was made to suffer most. The other carried back the government to what it was intended to be—re-established it as it was in the first year of Washington's administration—made it in fact a hard-money government, giving solidity to the Treasury, and freeing the government and the people from the revulsions and vicissitudes of the paper system. No more complaints about the currency and the exchanges since that time. Unexampled prosperity has attended the people; and the government, besides excess of solid money in time of peace, has carried on a foreign war, three thousand miles from home, with its securities above par during the whole time: a felicitous distinction, never enjoyed by our country before, and seldom by any country of the world. These two measures constitute an era in the working of our government, entitled to a proud place in its history, on which the eye of posterity may look back with gratitude and admiration.

His administration was auspicious to the general harmony, and presents a period of remarkable exemption from the sectional bitterness which had so much afflicted the Union for some years before—and so much more sorely since. Faithful to the sentiments expressed in his inaugural address, he held a firm and even course between sections and parties, and passed through his term without offence to the North or the South on the subject of slavery. He reconciled South Carolina to the Union—received the support of her delegation in Congress—saw his administration receive the approving vote of her general assembly—and counted her vote among those which he received for the presidency—the first presidential vote which she had given in twelve years. No President ever had a more difficult time. Two general suspensions of the banks—one at the beginning, and the other towards the close of his administration—the delinquent institutions in both instances allying themselves with a great political party—were powerful enough to derange and distress the business of the country, and unscrupulous enough to charge upon his administration the mischiefs which themselves created. Meritorious at home, and in his internal policy, his administration was equally so in its foreign relations. The insurrection in Canada, contemporaneous with his accession to the presidency, made a crisis between the United States and Great Britain, in which he discharged his high duties with equal firmness, skill, and success. The border line of the United States, for a thousand miles, was in commotion to join the insurgent Canadians. The laws of neutrality, the duties of good neighborhood, our own peace (liable to be endangered by lawless expeditions from our shores), all required him to repress this commotion. And faithfully he did so, using all the means—judicial and military—which the laws put in his hands; and successfully for the maintenance of neutrality, but with some personal detriment, losing much popular favor in the border States from his strenuous repression of aid to a neighboring people, insurging for liberty, and militarily crushed in the attempt. He did his duty towards Great Britain by preventing succor from going to her revolted subjects; and when the scene was changed, and her authorities did an injury to us by the murder of our citizens, and the destruction of a vessel on our own shore—the case of the Caroline at Schlosser—he did his duty to the United States by demanding redress; and when one of the alleged perpetrators was caught in the State where the outrage had been committed, he did his duty to that State by asserting her right to punish the infraction of her own laws. And although he did not obtain the redress for the outrage at Schlosser, yet it was never *refused* to him, nor the right to redress *denied*, nor the outrage itself *assumed* by the British government as long as his administration lasted. Respected at home, his administration was equally so abroad. Cordially supported by his friends in Congress, he was equally so by his cabinet, and his leading newspaper, the Washington Globe. Messrs. Forsyth, Secretary of State—Woodbury of the Treasury—Poinsett of War—Paulding of the Navy—Kendall and John M. Niles, Postmasters-general—and Butler, Grundy and Gilpin, successive Attorneys-general—were all harmonious and efficient co-operators. With every title to respect, and to public confidence, he was disappointed of a second election, but in a canvass which had had no precedent, and has had no imitation; and in which an increase of 364,000 votes on his previous election, attests an increase of strength which fair means could not have overcome.

ADMINISTRATION OF WILLIAM HENRY HARRISON.

CHAPTER LX.

INAUGURATION OF PRESIDENT HARRISON: HIS CABINET—CALL OF CONGRESS—AND DEATH.

March the 4th, at twelve o'clock, the Senate met in its chamber, as summoned to do by the retiring President, to be ready for the inauguration of the President elect, and the transaction of such executive business as he should bring before it. The body was quite full, and was called to order by the secretary, Mr. Asbury Dickens; and Mr. King, of Alabama, being elected temporary President of the Senate, administered the oath of office to the Vice-president elect, John Tyler, Esq., who immediately took the chair as President of the Senate. The scene in the chamber was simple and impressive. The senators were in their seats: members of the House in chairs. The justices of the Supreme Court, and the foreign diplomatic corps were in the front semicircle of chairs, on the floor of the Senate. Officers of the army and navy were present—many citizens—and some ladies. Every part of the chamber and galleries were crowded, and it required a vigilant police to prevent the entrance of more than the allotted number. After the Vice-president elect had taken his seat, and delivered to the Senate over which he was to preside a well-conceived, well-expressed, and well-delivered address, appropriately brief, a short pause and silence ensued. The President elect entered, and was conducted to the seat prepared for him in front of the secretary's table. The procession was formed and proceeded to the spacious eastern portico, where seats were placed, and the ceremony of the inauguration was to take place. An immense crowd, extending far and wide, stood closely wedged on the pavement and enclosed grounds in front of the portico. The President elect read his inaugural address, with animation and strong voice, and was well heard at a distance. As an inaugural address, it was confined to a declaration of general principles and sentiments; and it breathed a spirit of patriotism which adversaries, as well as friends, admitted to be sincere, and to come from the heart. After the conclusion of the address, the chief justice of the Supreme Court of the United States, Mr. Taney, administered the oath prescribed by the constitution: and the ceremony of inauguration was at an end.

The Senate returned to its chamber, and having received a message from the President with the nominations for his cabinet, immediately proceeded to their consideration; and unanimously confirmed the whole. They were: Daniel Webster, Secretary of State; Thomas Ewing, Secretary of the Treasury; John Bell, Secretary at War; George E. Badger, Secretary of the Navy; Francis Granger, Postmaster-general; John J. Crittenden, Attorney-general.

On the 17th of March, the President issued a proclamation, convoking the Congress in extraordinary session for the 31st day of May ensuing. The proclamation followed the usual form in not specifying the immediate, or direct, cause of the convocation. It merely stated, "That sundry and weighty matters, principally growing out of the condition of the revenue and finances of the country, appear to call for the convocation of Congress at an earlier day than its next annual session, and thus form an extraordinary occasion which, in the judgment of the President, rendered it necessary for the two Houses to convene as soon as practicable."

President Harrison did not live to meet the Congress which he had thus convoked. Short as the time was that he had fixed for its meeting, his own time upon earth was still shorter. In the last days of March he was taken ill: on the fourth day of April he was dead—at the age of 69; being one year under the limit which the psalmist fixed for the term of manly life. There was no failure of health or strength to indicate such an event, or to excite apprehension that he would not go through his term with the vigor with which he commenced it. His attack was sudden, and evidently fatal from the beginning. A public funeral was given him, most numerously attended, and the body deposited in the Congress vault—to wait its removal to his late home at North Bend, Ohio;—whither it was removed in the summer. He was a man of infinite kindness of heart, affectionate to the human race,—of undoubted patriotism, irreproachable integrity both in public and private life; and of a hospitality of disposition which received with equal welcome in his house the humblest and the most exalted of the land.

The public manifestations of respect to the memory of the deceased President, were appropriate and impressive, and co-extensive with the bounds of the Union. But there was another kind of respect which his memory received, more felt than expressed, and more pervading than public ceremonies: it was the regret of the nation, without distinction of party: for it was a case in which the heart could have fair play, and in which political opponents could join with their adversaries in manifestations of respect and sorrow. Both the deceased President, and the Vice-president, were of the same party, elected by the same vote, and their administrations expected to be of the same character. It was a case in which no political calculation could interfere with private feeling; and the national regret was sincere, profound, and pervading. Gratifying was the spectacle to see a national union of feeling in behalf of one who had been so lately the object of so much political division. It was a proof that there can be political opposition without personal animosity.

General Harrison was a native of Virginia, son of a signer of the Declaration of Independence, and a descendant of the "regicide" Harrison who sat on the trial of Charles I.

In the course of the first session of Congress after the death of General Harrison—that session which convened under his call—the opportunity presented itself to the author of this View to express his personal sentiments with respect to him. President Tyler, in his message, recommended a grant of money to the family of the deceased President "in consideration of his expenses in removing to the seat of government, and the limited means which he had left behind;" and a bill had been brought into the Senate accordingly, taking one year's presidential salary ($25,000) as the amount of the grant. Deeming this proceeding entirely out of the limits of the constitution—against the policy of the government—and the commencement of the monarchical system of providing for families, Mr. Benton thus expressed himself at the conclusion of an argument against the grant:

"Personally I was friendly to General Harrison, and that at a time when his friends were not so numerous as in his last days; and if I had needed any fresh evidences of the kindness of his heart, I had them in his twice mentioning to me, during the short period of his presidency, that, which surely I should never have mentioned to him—the circumstance of my friendship to him when his friends were fewer. I would gladly now do what would be kind and respectful to his memory—what would be liberal and beneficial to his most respectable widow; but, to vote for this bill! that I cannot do. High considerations of constitutional law and public policy forbid me to do so, and command me to make this resistance to it, that a mark may be made—a stone set up— at the place where this new violence was done to the constitution—this new page opened in the book of our public expenditures; and this new departure taken, which leads into the bottomless gulf of civil pensions and family gratuities."

The deceased President had been closely preceded, and was rapidly followed, by the deaths of almost all his numerous family of sons and daughters. A worthy son survives (John Scott Harrison, Esq.), a most respectable member of Congress from the State of Ohio.

ADMINISTRATION OF JOHN TYLER.

CHAPTER LXI.

ACCESSION OF THE VICE-PRESIDENT TO THE PRESIDENCY.

The Vice-president was not in Washington when the President died: he was at his residence in lower Virginia: some days would necessarily elapse before he could arrive. President Harrison had not been impressed with the probable fatal termination of his disease, and the consequent propriety of directing the Vice-president to be sent for. His cabinet could not feel themselves justified in taking such a step while the President lived. Mr. Tyler would feel it indelicate to repair to the seat of government, of his own will, on hearing the report of the President's illness. The attending physicians, from the most proper considerations, held out hopes of recovery to near the last; but, for four days before the event, there was a pervading feeling in the city that the President would not survive his attack. His death left the executive government for some days in a state of interregnum. There was no authority, or person present, legally empowered to take any step; and so vital an event as a change in the chief magistrate, required the fact to be formally and publicly verified. In the absence of Congress, and the Vice-president, the members of the late cabinet very properly united in announcing the event to the country, and in despatching a messenger of state to Mr. Tyler, to give him the authentic information which would show the necessity of his presence at the seat of government. He repaired to it immediately, took the oath of office, before the Chief Judge of the Circuit Court of the District of Columbia, William Cranch, Esquire; and appointed the late cabinet for his own. Each was retained in the place held under his predecessor, and with the strongest expressions of regard and confidence.

Four days after his accession to the presidency, Mr. Tyler issued an address, in the nature of an inaugural, to the people of the United States, the first paragraph of which was very appropriately devoted to his predecessor, and to the circumstances of his own elevation to the presidential chair. That paragraph was in these words:

> "Before my arrival at the seat of government, the painful communication was made to you, by the officers presiding over the several departments, of the deeply regretted death of WILLIAM HENRY HARRISON, late President of the United States. Upon him you had conferred your suffrages for the first office in your gift, and had selected him as your chosen instrument to correct and reform all such errors and abuses as had manifested themselves from time to time, in the practical operations of the government. While standing at the threshold of this great work, he has, by the dispensation of an all-wise Providence, been removed from amongst us, and by the provisions of the constitution, the efforts to be directed to the accomplishing of this vitally important task have devolved upon myself. This same occurrence has subjected the wisdom and sufficiency of our institutions to a new test. For the first time in our history, the person elected to the Vice-presidency of the United States, by the happening of a contingency provided for in the constitution, has had devolved upon him the presidential office. The spirit of faction, which is directly opposed to the spirit of a lofty patriotism, may find in this occasion for assaults upon my administration. And in succeeding, under circumstances so sudden and unexpected, and to responsibilities so greatly augmented, to the administration of public affairs, I shall place in the intelligence and patriotism of the people, my only sure reliance.—My earnest prayer shall be constantly addressed to the all-wise and all-powerful Being who made me, and by whose dispensation I am called to the high office of President of this confederacy, understandingly to carry out the principles of that constitution which I have sworn 'to protect, preserve, and defend.'"

Two blemishes were seen in this paragraph, the first being in that sentence which spoke of the "errors and abuses" of the government which his predecessor had been elected to "correct and reform;" and the correction and reformation of which now devolved upon himself. These imputed errors and abuses could only apply to the administrations of General Jackson and Mr. Van Buren, of both which Mr. Tyler had been a zealous opponent; and therefore might not be admitted to be an impartial judge. Leaving that out of view, the bad taste of such a reference was palpable and repulsive. The second blemish was in that sentence in which he contrasted the spirit of "faction" with the spirit of "lofty patriotism," and seemed to refer in advance all the "assaults" which should be made upon his administration, to this factious spirit, warring upon elevated patriotism. Little did he think when he wrote that sentence, that within three short months—within less time than a commercial bill of exchange usually has to run, the great party which had elected him, and the cabinet officers which he had just appointed with such warm expressions of respect and confidence, should be united in that assault! should all be in the lead and van of a public outcry against him! The third paragraph was also felt to be a fling at General Jackson and Mr. Van Buren, and therefore unfit for a place in a President's message, and especially in an inaugural address. It was the very periphrasis of the current party slang against General Jackson, plainly visible through the transparent hypothetical guise which it put on; and was in these words:

> "In view of the fact, well avouched by history, that the tendency of all human institutions is to concentrate power in the hands of a single man, and that their ultimate downfall has proceeded from this cause, I deem it of the most essential importance that a complete separation should take place between the sword and the purse. No matter where or how the public moneys shall be deposited, so long as the President can exert the power of appointing and removing, at his pleasure, the agents selected for their custody, the commander-in-chief of the army and navy is in fact the treasurer. A permanent and radical change should therefore be decreed. The patronage incident to the presidential office, already great, is constantly increasing. Such increase is destined to keep pace with the growth of our population, until, without a figure of speech, an army of officeholders may be spread over the land. The unrestrained power exerted by a selfishly ambitious man, in order either to perpetuate his authority or to hand it over to some favorite as his successor, may lead to the employment of all the means within his control to accomplish his object. The right to remove from office, while subjected to no just restraint, is inevitably destined to produce a spirit of crouching servility with the official corps, which in order to uphold the hand which feeds them, would lead to direct and active interference in the elections, both State and federal, thereby subjecting the course of State legislation to the dictation of the chief executive officer, and making the will of that officer absolute and supreme."

This phrase of "purse and sword," once so appropriately used by Patrick Henry, in describing the powers of the federal government, and since so often applied to General Jackson, for the removal of the deposits, could have no other aim than a fling at him; and the abuse of patronage in removals and appointments to perpetuate power, or hand it over to a favorite, was the mere repetition of the slang of the presidential canvass, in relation to General Jackson and Mr. Van Buren.

Departing from the usual reserve and generalization of an inaugural, this address went into a detail which indicated the establishment of a national bank, or the re-charter of the defunct one, masked and vitalized under a Pennsylvania State charter. That paragraph ran thus:

> "The public interest also demands that, if any war has existed between the government and the currency, it shall cease. Measures of a financial character, now having the sanction of legal enactment, shall be faithfully enforced until repealed by the legislative authority. But I owe it to myself to declare that I regard existing enactments as unwise and impolitic, and in a high degree oppressive. I shall promptly give my sanction to any constitutional measure which, originating in Congress, shall have for its object the restoration of a sound circulating medium, so essentially necessary to give confidence in all the transactions of life, to secure to industry its just and adequate rewards, and to re-establish the public prosperity. In deciding upon the adaptation of any such measure to the end proposed, as well as its conformity to the constitution, I shall resort to the fathers of the great republican school for advice and instruction, to be drawn from their sage views of our system of government, and the light of their ever glorious example."

The concluding part of this paragraph, in which the new President declares that, in looking to the constitutionality and expediency of a national bank, he should look for advice and instruction to the example of the fathers of the Republic, he was understood as declaring that he would not be governed by his own former opinions against a national bank, but by the example of Washington, a signer of the constitution (who signed the charter of the first national bank); and by the example of Mr. Madison, another signer of the constitution, who, yielding to precedent and the authority of judicial decisions, had signed the charter for the second bank, notwithstanding his early constitutional objections to it. In other parts of the paragraph he was considered as declaring in favor of the late United States Bank, as in the previous part of the paragraph where he used the phrases which had become catch-words in the long contest with that bank—"war upon the currency"—"sound circulating medium"—"restoration of national prosperity;" &c., &c. He was understood to express a preference for the re-charter of that institution. And this impression was well confirmed by other circumstances—his zealous report in favor of that bank when acting as volunteer chairman to the Senate's committee which was sent to examine it—his standing a canvass in a presidential election in which the re-charter of that bank, though concertedly blinked in some parts of the Union, was the understood vital issue every where—his publicly avowed preference for its notes over gold, at Wheeling, Virginia—the retention of a cabinet, pledged to that bank, with expressions of confidence in them, and in terms that promised a four years' service together—and his utter condemnation in other parts of his inaugural and in all his public speeches, of every other plan (sub-treasury, state banks, revival of the gold currency), which had been presented as remedies for the financial and currency disorders. All these circumstances and declarations left no doubt that he was not only in favor of a national bank, but of re-chartering the late one; and that he looked to it, and to it alone, for the "sound circulating medium" which he preferred to the constitutional currency—for the keeping of those deposits which he had condemned Jackson for removing from it—and for the restoration of that national prosperity, which the imputed war upon the bank had destroyed.

CHAPTER LXII.

TWENTY-SEVENTH CONGRESS: FIRST SESSION: LIST OF MEMBERS, AND ORGANIZATION OF THE HOUSE.

Members of the Senate.

MAINE.—Reuel Williams, George Evans.

NEW HAMPSHIRE.—Franklin Pierce, Levi Woodbury.

VERMONT.—Samuel Prentis, Samuel Phelps.

MASSACHUSETTS.—Rufus Choate, Isaac C. Bates.

RHODE ISLAND.—Nathan F. Dixon, James F. Simmons.

CONNECTICUT.—Perry Smith, Jaz. W. Huntington.

NEW YORK.—Silas Wright, N. P. Tallmadge.

NEW JERSEY.—Sam. L. Southard, Jacob W. Miller.

PENNSYLVANIA.—James Buchanan, D. W. Sturgeon.

DELAWARE.—Richard H. Bayard, Thomas Clayton.

MARYLAND.—John Leeds Kerr, Wm. D. Merrick.

VIRGINIA.—Wm. C. Rives, Wm. S. Archer.

NORTH CAROLINA.—Wm. A. Graham, Willie P. Mangum.

SOUTH CAROLINA.—Wm. C. Preston, John C. Calhoun.

GEORGIA.—Alfred Cuthbert, John M. Berrien.

ALABAMA.—Clement C. Clay, William R. King.

MISSISSIPPI.—John Henderson, Robert J. Walker.

LOUISIANA.—Alexander Mouton, Alexander Barrow.

TENNESSEE.—A. O. P. Nicholson, Spencer Jarnagin, executive appointment. Ephraim H. Foster.

KENTUCKY.—Henry Clay, J. J. Morehead.

OHIO.—William Allen, Benjamin Tappan.

INDIANA.—Oliver H. Smith, Albert S. White.

ILLINOIS.—Richard M. Young, Sam'l McRoberts.

MISSOURI.—Lewis F. Linn, Thomas H. Benton.

ARKANSAS.—Ambrose H. Sevier, William S. Fulton.

MICHIGAN.—Augustus S. Porter, William Woodbridge.

Members of the House.

MAINE.—Nathaniel Clifford, Wm. P. Fessenden, Benj. Randall, David Bronson, Nathaniel Littlefield, Alfred Marshall, Joshua A. Lowell, Elisha H. Allen.

NEW HAMPSHIRE.—Tristram Shaw, Ira A. Eastman, Charles G. Atherton, Edmund Burke, John R. Reding.

VERMONT.—Hiland Hall, William Slade, Horace Everett, Augustus Young, John Mattocks.

MASSACHUSETTS.—Robert C. Winthrop, Leverett Saltonstall, Caleb Cushing, Wm. Parmenter, Charles Hudson, Osmyn Baker, Geo. N. Briggs, William B. Calhoun, Wm. S. Hastings, Nathaniel B. Borden, Barker Burnell, John Quincy Adams.

RHODE ISLAND.—Joseph L. Tillinghast, William B. Cranston.

CONNECTICUT.—Joseph Trumbull, Wm. W. Boardman, Thomas W. Williams, Thos. B. Osborne, Truman Smith, John H. Brockway.

NEW YORK.—Chas. A. Floyd, Joseph Egbert, John McKeon, James J. Roosevelt, Fernando Wood, Chas. G. Ferris, Aaron Ward, Richard D. Davis, James G. Clinton, John Van Buren, R. McClellan, Jacob Hauck, jr., Hiram P. Hunt, Daniel D. Barnard, Archibald L. Lin, Bernard Blair, Thos. A. Tomlinson, H. Van Rensselaer, John Sanford, Andrew W. Doig, John G. Floyd, David P. Brewster, T. C. Chittenden, Sam. S. Bowne, Samuel Gordon, John C. Clark, Lewis Riggs, Sam. Partridge, Victory Birdseye, A. L. Foster, Christopher Morgan, John Maynard, John Greig, Wm. M. Oliver, Timothy Childs, Seth M. Gates, John Young, Stanley N. Clark, Millard Fillmore, —— Babcock.

NEW JERSEY.—John B. Aycrigg, John P. B. Maxwell, William Halsted, Joseph F. Randolph, Joseph F. Stratton, Thos. Jones Yorke.

PENNSYLVANIA.—Charles Brown, John Sergeant, George W. Tolland, Charles Ingersoll, John Edwards, Jeremiah Brown, Francis James, Joseph Fornance, Robert Ramsay, John Westbrook, Peter Newhard, George M. Keim, Wm. Simonton, James Gerry, James Cooper, Amos Gustine, James Irvine, Benj. Bidlack, John Snyder, Davis Dimock, Albert G. Marchand, Joseph Lawrence, Wm. W. Irwin, William Jack, Thomas Henry, Arnold Plumer.

DELAWARE.—George B. Rodney.

MARYLAND.—Isaac D. Jones, Jas. A. Pearce, James W. Williams, J. P. Kennedy, Alexander Randall, Wm. Cost Johnson, John T. Mason, Augustus R. Sollers.

VIRGINIA.—Henry A. Wise, Francis Mallory, George B. Cary, John M. Botts, R. M. T. Hunter, John Taliaferro, Cuthbert Powell, Linn Banks, Wm. O. Goode, John W. Jones, E. W. Hubbard, Walter Coles, Thomas W. Gilmer, Wm. L. Goggin, R. B. Barton, Wm. A. Harris, A. H. H. Stuart, Geo. W. Hopkins, Geo. W. Summers, S. L. Hays, Lewis Steinrod.

NORTH CAROLINA.—Kenneth Rayner, John R. J. Daniel, Edward Stanly, Wm. H. Washington, James J. McKay, Archibald Arrington, Edmund Deberry, R. M. Saunders, Aug'e H. Shepherd, Abraham Rencher, Green C. Caldwell, James Graham, Lewis Williams.

SOUTH CAROLINA.—Isaac E. Holmes, William Butler, F. W. Pickens, John Campbell, James Rogers, S. H. Butler, Thomas D. Sumter, R. Barnwell Rhett, C. P. Caldwell.

GEORGIA.—Rich'd W. Habersham, Wm. C. Dawson, Julius C. Alvord, Eugenius A. Nisbet, Lott Warren, Thomas Butler King, Roger L. Gamble, Jas. A. Merriwether, Thos. F. Foster.

ALABAMA.—Reuben Chapman, Geo. S. Houston, Dixon H. Lewis, Benj. G. Shields.

MISSISSIPPI.—A. L. Bingaman, W. R. Harley.

LOUISIANA.—Edward D. White, J. B. Dawson, John Moore.

ARKANSAS.—Edward Cross.

TENNESSEE.—Thomas D. Arnold, Abraham McClellan, Joseph L. Williams, Thomas J. Campbell, Hopkins L. Turney, Wm. B. Campbell, Robert L. Caruthers, Meredith P. Gentry, Harvey M. Watterson, Aaron V. Brown, Cave Johnson, Milton Brown, Christopher H. Williams.

KENTUCKY.—Linn Boyd, Philip Triplet, Joseph R. Underwood, Bryan W. Owsley, John B. Thompson, Willis Green, John Pope, James C. Sprigg, John White, Thomas F. Marshall, Landoff W. Andrews, Garret Davis, William O. Butler.

OHIO.—N. G. Pendleton, John B. Weller, Patrick G. Goode, Jeremiah Morrow, William Doane, Calvary Morris, Wm. Russell, Joseph Ridgeway, Wm. Medill, Samson Mason, B. S. Cowan, Joshua Matheot, James Matthews, Geo. Sweeney, S. J. Andrews, Joshua R. Giddings; John Hastings, Ezra Dean, Sam. Stockley.

INDIANA.—George W. Proffit, Richard W. Thompson, Joseph L. White, James H. Cravens, Andrew Kennedy, David Wallace, Henry S. Lane.

MISSOURI.—John Miller, John C. Edwards.

MICHIGAN.—Jacob M. Howard.

Mr. John White of Kentucky (whig), was elected Speaker of the House over Mr. John W. Jones of Virginia, democratic. Mr. Matthew St. Clair Clarke of Pennsylvania (whig), was elected clerk over Mr. Hugh A. Garland of Virginia, democratic. The whigs had a majority of near fifty in the House, and of seven in the Senate; so that all the legislative, and the executive department of the government—the two Houses of Congress and the President and cabinet—were of the same political party, presenting a harmony of aspect frequently wanting during the three previous administrations. Notwithstanding their large majority, the whig party proceeded slowly in the organization of the House in the adoption of rules for its proceeding. A fortnight had been consumed in vain when Mr. Cushing, urgently, and successfully exhorted his whig friends to action:

"I say (continued Mr. Cushing) that it is our fault if this House be disorganized. We are in the majority—we have a majority of forty—and we are responsible to our country, to the constitution, and to our God, for the discharge of our duty here. It is our duty to proceed to the organization of the House, to the transaction of the business for which the country sent us here. And I appeal to the whig party on this floor that they do their duty—that they act manfully and expeditiously, and *that*, howsoever the House may organize, under whatever rules, or under no rules at all; for I am prepared, if this resolution be not adopted, to call upon the Speaker for the second reading of a bill from the Senate, now upon the table, and to move that we proceed with it under the parliamentary law. We can go on under that. We are *a House*, with a speaker, clerk, and officers; and whether we have rules or not is immaterial. We can proceed as the Commons in England do. We can act upon bills by referring them to a Committee of the Whole on the state of the Union, or to select committees, if there are no standing committees. And I am prepared, if the House cannot be organized under the proposition now before us, for the purpose of testing the question and enabling the country to see whose fault it is that we do not go on with its business, to call at once for the action of the House upon that bill under the parliamentary law. Once more I appeal to the whig party, for party lines, I see, are now about to be drawn; I appeal to the whig party, to the friends of the administration—and I recognize but one, and that is the administration of John Tyler— that is the administration, and I recognize no other in the United States at this time; I appeal to the administration party, to the friends of the administration of John Tyler, that at this hour they come to the rescue of their country, and organize the House, under whatever rules: because, if we do not, we shall become, as we are now becoming, the laughing-stock, the scorn, the contempt of the people of these United States."

The bill from the Senate, for action on which Mr. Cushing was so impatient, and so ready to act without rules, was the one for the repeal of the sub-treasury; whilom characterized by him as a serpent hatched of a fowl's egg, (cockatrice); which the people would trample into the dust. Under his urgent exhortation the House soon organized, and made the repeal. Passed so promptly, this repealing bill, with equal celerity, was approved and signed by the President—leaving him in the first quarter of his administration in full possession of that formidable sword and long purse, the imputed union of which in the hands of General Jackson had been his incontinent deprecation, even in his inaugural address. For this repeal of the sub-treasury provided no substitute for keeping the public moneys, and left them without law in the President's hands.

CHAPTER LXIII.

FIRST MESSAGE OF MR. TYLER TO CONGRESS, AND MR. CLAY'S PROGRAMME OF BUSINESS.

The first paragraph in the message related to the death of President Harrison, and after a proper expression of respect and regret, it went on to recommend a grant of money to his family, grounded on the consideration of his expenses in removing to the seat of government, and the limited means of his private fortune:

> "With this public bereavement are connected other considerations which will not escape the attention of Congress. The preparations necessary for his removal to the seat of government, in view of a residence of four years, must have devolved upon the late President heavy expenditures, which, if permitted to burden the limited resources of his private fortune, may tend to the serious embarrassment of his surviving family; and it is therefore respectfully submitted to Congress, whether the ordinary principles of justice would not dictate the propriety of its legislative interposition."

This recommendation was considered by many as being without the pale of the constitution, and of dangerous precedent. With respect to the limited means of which he spoke, the fact was alike true and honorable to the late President. In public employment from early life and during the greatest part of his life, no pecuniary benefit had resulted to him. In situations to afford opportunities for emolument, he availed himself of none. With immense amounts of public money passing through his hands, it all went, not only faithfully to its objects, but without leaving any profit behind from its use. He lived upon his salaries, liberally dispensing hospitality and charities, and with simplicity and economy in all his habits. He used all that he received, and came out of office as he entered it, and died poor. This, among the ancient Romans was a commendable issue of a public career, to be mentioned with honor at the funeral of an illustrious man: and should be so held by all republican people.

The message showed that President Tyler would not have convoked the Congress in extra session had it not been done by his predecessor; but being convoked he would not disturb the arrangement; and was most happy to find himself so soon surrounded by the national representation:

> "In entering upon the duties of this office, I did not feel that it would be becoming in me to disturb what had been ordered by my lamented predecessor. Whatever, therefore, may have been my opinion originally as to the propriety of convening Congress at so early a day from that of its late adjournment, I found a new and controlling inducement not to interfere with the patriotic desires of the late President, in the novelty of the situation in which I was so unexpectedly placed. My first wish, under such circumstances, would necessarily have been to have called to my aid in the administration of public affairs, the combined wisdom of the two Houses of Congress, in order to take their counsel and advice as to the best mode of extricating the government and the country from the embarrassments weighing heavily on both. I am then most happy in finding myself so soon, after my accession to the presidency, surrounded by the immediate representatives of the States and people."

The state of our foreign relations claimed but a brief paragraph. The message stated that no important change had taken place in them since the last session of Congress, and that the President saw nothing to make him doubt the continuance of the peace with which the country was blessed. He passed to home affairs:

> "In order to supply the wants of the government, an intelligent constituency, in view of their best interests, will without hesitation, submit to all necessary burdens. But it is, nevertheless, important so to impose them as to avoid defeating the just expectations of the country growing out of pre-existing laws. The act of the 2d March, 1833, commonly called the compromise act, should not be altered, except under urgent necessities, which are not believed at this time to exist. One year only remains to complete the series of reductions provided for by that law, at which time provisions made by the same, and which law then will be brought

actively in aid of the manufacturing interest of the Union, will not fail to produce the most beneficial results."

This compromise act of 1833, was drawing towards the close of its career, and was proving itself to have been a complete illusion in all the good it had promised, and a sad reality in all the ill that had been predicted of it. It had been framed on the principle of helping manufactures for nine years, and then to be a free trade measure for ever after. The first part succeeded, and so well, in keeping up high duties as to raise far more revenue than the government needed: the second part left the government without revenue for its current uses, and under the necessity of giving up that uniform twenty per centum duty on the value of imports, which was to have been the permanent law of our tariff; and which never became law at all. In the meanwhile, the compromise having provided for periodical reductions in the duties on imported sugars and molasses, made no provision for proportionate reductions of the drawback upon these articles when exported in the changed shape of rum and refined sugars: and enormous sums were drawn from the treasury by this omission in the compromise act—the great refiners and rum distillers driving an immense capital into their business for the mere purpose of getting the gratuitous drawbacks. The author of this View endeavored to supply the omission at the time, and repeatedly afterwards; but these efforts were resisted by the advocates of the compromise until these gratuities becoming enormous, rising from $2,000 per annum, to hundreds of thousands per annum, and finally reaching five hundred thousand, they roused the alarm of the government, and sunk under the enormity of their abuse. Yet it was this compromise which was held too sacred to have its palpable defects corrected, and the inviolability of which was recommended to be preserved, that in addition to its other faults, was making an annual present of some hundreds of thousands of dollars to two classes of manufacturers.

A bank of some kind was recommended, under the name of fiscal agent, as necessary to facilitate the operations of the Treasury, to promote the collection and disbursement of the public revenue, and to supply a currency of uniform value. The message said:

> "In intimate connection with the question of revenue, is that which makes provision for a suitable fiscal agent, capable of adding increased facilities in the collection and disbursement of the public revenues, rendering more secure their custody, and consulting a true economy in the great multiplied and delicate operations of the Treasury department. Upon such an agent depends in an eminent degree, the establishment of a currency of uniform value, which is of so great importance to all the essential interests of society; and on the wisdom to be manifested in its creation, much depends."

These are the reasons which General Hamilton gave for asking the establishment of the first national bank, in 1791, and which have been given ever since, no matter with what variation of phraseology, for the creation of a similar institution. This preference for a bank, under a new name, was confirmed by the rejection of the sub-treasury and hard-money currency, assumed by the message to have been condemned by the people in the result of the presidential election. Speaking of this system, it said: "*If carried through all the stages of its transmutation, from paper and specie to nothing but the precious metals, to say nothing of the insecurity of the public moneys its injurious effects have been anticipated by the country, in its unqualified condemnation.*" The justice and wisdom of this condemnation, thus inferred from the issue of the presidential election, and carried as that election was (and as has been described), has been tested by the experience of many years, without finding that insecurity of the public moneys, and those injurious effects which the message assumed. On the contrary those moneys have been safely kept, and the public prosperity never as great as under the Independent Treasury and the gold and silver currency of the federal government: and long has it been since any politician has allowed himself to be supposed to be against them. Up to the date of that message then—up to the first day of the extra session, 1841—Mr. Tyler may be considered as in favor of a national bank, with its paper currency, and opposed to the gold and silver currency, and the sub-treasury. A distribution of the proceeds of the sales of the public lands was recommended as a means of assisting the States in the payment of their debts, and raising the price of their stocks in foreign markets. Repudiating as unconstitutional, the federal assumption of the State debts, he still recommended a grant of money from the public funds to enable them to meet these debts. In this sense the message said:

"And while I must repudiate, as a measure founded in error, and wanting constitutional sanction, the slightest approach to an assumption by this government of the debts of the States, yet I can see in the distribution adverted to much to recommend it. The compacts between the proprietor States and this government expressly guarantee to the States all the benefits which may arise from the sales. The mode by which this is to be effected addresses itself to the discretion of Congress as the trustee for the States, and its exercise, after the most beneficial manner, is restrained by nothing in the grants or in the constitution so long as Congress shall consult that equality in the distribution which the compacts require. In the present condition of some of the States, the question of distribution may be regarded as substantially a question between direct and indirect taxation. If the distribution be not made in some form or other, the necessity will daily become more urgent with the debtor States for a resort to an oppressive system of direct taxation, or their credit, and necessarily their power and influence, will be greatly diminished. The payment of taxes, often the most inconvenient and oppressive mode, will be exacted in place of contributions for the most part voluntarily made, and therefore comparatively unoppressive. The States are emphatically the constituents of this government, and we should be entirely regardless of the objects held in view by them, in the creation of this government, if we could be indifferent to their good. The happy effects of such a measure upon all the States, would immediately be manifested. With the debtor States it would effect the relief to a great extent of the citizens from a heavy burden of direct taxation, which presses with severity on the laboring classes, and eminently assist in restoring the general prosperity. An immediate advance would take place in the price of the State securities, and the attitudes of the States would become once more, as it should ever be, lofty and erect. Whether such distribution should be made directly to the States in the proceeds of the sales, or in the form of profits by virtue of the operations of any fiscal agency having those proceeds as its basis, should such measure be contemplated by Congress, would well deserve its consideration."

Mr. Tyler, while a member of the democratic party, had been one of the most strict in the construction of the constitution, and one of the most vigilant and inflexible in bringing proposed measures to the test of that instrument—repulsing the most insignificant if they could not stand it. He had been one of the foremost against the constitutionality of a national bank, and voting for a *scire facias* to vacate the charter of the last one soon after it was established. Now, in recommending the grant of money to the family of General Harrison—in recommending a bank under the name of fiscal agent—in preferring a national paper currency—in condemning the currency of the constitution—in proposing a distribution of the land revenue—in providing for the payment of the State debts: in all these recommendations he seemed to have gone far beyond any other President, however latitudinarian. Add to this, he had instituted an inquisition to sit upon the conduct of officers, to hear and adjudge in secret; to the encouragement of informers and debaters, and to the infringement of the liberty of speech, and the freedom of opinion in the subordinates of the government. In view of all this, the author of this work immediately exclaimed:

"What times we have fallen upon! what wonders we witness! how strange are the scenes of the day! We have a President, who has been the foremost in the defence of the constitution, and in support of the rights of the States—whose walk has been on the outward wall of the constitution—his post in the front line of its defenders—his seat on the topmost branches of the democratic tree. I will not disparage the President by saying that he fought side by side with me in defence of the constitution and the States, and against the latitudinarians. It would be to wrong him to place him by my side. His position, as guard of the constitution, was far ahead, and far above mine. He was always in the advance—on the look-out—listening and watching—snuffing danger in the first tainted breeze, and making anticipated battle against the still invisible invader. Hardly any thing was constitutional enough for him. This was but a few brief years ago. Now we see the measures brought forward in the very bud and first blossom of this administration, which leave all former unconstitutional measures far in the rear—which add subterfuge and evasion to open violence, and aim more deadly wounds at the constitution than the fifty previous years of its existence had brought upon it. I know not the sentiment of the President upon these measures, except as disclosed by himself, and say nothing to reach him; but I know the measures themselves—their desperate character, and fatal issues: and I am free to say, if such things can come to pass—if they can survive the double ordeal of the House and the Senate—then there is an end of all that our fathers contended for in the formation of the federal government. To be sure, the machinery of government would still stand. We should still have President, Congress, and a Judiciary—an army, a navy—a taxing power, the tax-payers, the tax-gatherers, and the tax-consumers. But, if such measures as these are to pass—a bill to lavish the public lands on the (indebted) States in order to pay their debts, supply their taxes, and raise the market price of their stock—a contrivance to defraud the constitution, and to smuggle and bribe a bank, though a national bank, through Congress, under the *alius dictus* of fiscal agent—the bill to commence the career of civil pensions and family gratuities—the inquisitorial committee, modelled on the plan of Sir Robert Walpole's committees of secrecy, now sitting in the custom-house of New York, the terror of the honest and the hope of the corrupt—the *ex post facto* edict for the creation of political offences, to be punished on suspicion in *exparte* trials—the schemes for the infringement of the liberty of speech, and for the suppression of freedom of opinion, and for the encouragement and reward of debaters and informers: if such schemes and measures as these are to come to pass, then do I say that all the guards and limitations upon our government are broken down! that our limited government is gone! and a new, wild, and boundless authority, substituted in its place. The new triumvirate—Bank, Congress, and President—will then be supreme. Fraud and corruption, more odious than arms and force, will rule the land. The constitution will be covered with a black veil: and that derided and violated instrument will never be referred to, except for the mock sanction of a fraudulent interpretation, or the insulting ceremony of a derisory adjuration."

Mr. Tyler had delivered a message: Mr. Clay virtually delivered another. In the first week of the session, he submitted a programme of measures, in the form of a resolve, to be adopted by the Senate, enumerating and declaring the particular subjects, to which he thought the attention of Congress should be limited at this extra session. The following was his programme:

> "*Resolved, as the opinion of the Senate*, That at the present session of Congress, no business ought to be transacted, but such as being of an important or urgent nature, may be supposed to have influenced the extraordinary convention of Congress, or such as that the postponement of it might be materially detrimental to the public interest.

> "*Resolved, therefore, as the opinion of the Senate*, That the following subjects ought first, if not exclusively, to engage the deliberation of Congress, at the present session—

> "1st. The repeal of the sub-treasury.

> "2d. The incorporation of a bank adapted to the wants of the people and of the government.

> "3d. The provision of an adequate revenue for the government by the imposition of duties, and including an authority to contract a temporary loan to cover the public debt created by the last administration.

> "4th. The prospective distribution of the proceeds of the public lands.

> "5th. The passage of necessary appropriation bills; and

> "6th. Some modification of the banking system of the District of Columbia, for the benefit of the people of the District.

> "*Resolved*, That it is expedient to distribute the business proper to be done this session, between the Senate and House of Representatives, so as to avoid both Houses acting on the same subject, and at the same time."

It was, probably, to this assumption over the business of Congress—this recommendation of measures which Mr. Clay thought ought to be adopted—that Mr. Cushing alluded in the House, when, in urging the instant repeal of the sub-treasury act, he made occasion to say that he recognized no administration but that of John Tyler. As for the "public debt," here mentioned as being "created by the last administration," it consisted of the treasury notes and loans resorted to to supply the place of the revenue lost under the descending scale of the compromise, and the amount taken from the Treasury to bestow upon the States, under the fraudulent name of a deposit.

CHAPTER LXIV.

REPEAL OF THE INDEPENDENT TREASURY ACT

This was the first measure of the new dominant party, and pursued with a zeal that bespoke a resentment which required gratification, and indicated a criminal which required punishment. It seemed to be considered as a malefactor which had just fallen into the hands of justice, and whose instant death was necessary to expiate his offences. Mr. Clay took the measure into his own charge. It was No. 1, in his list of bills to be passed; and the bill brought in by himself, was No. 1, on the Senate's calendar; and it was rapidly pushed on to immediate decision. The provisions of the bill were as summary as the proceedings upon it were rapid. It provided for instant repeal—to take effect as soon as passed, although it was in full operation all over the United States, and the officers at a distance, charged with its execution, could not know of the repeal until ten or twelve days after the event, and during all which time they would be acting without authority; and, consequently, without official liability for accident or misconduct. No substitute was provided; and when passed, the public moneys were to remain without legal guardianship until a substitute should be provided—intended to be a national bank; but a substitute which would require time to pass it, whether a bank or some other measure. These considerations were presented, but presented in vain to an impatient majority. A respite of a few days, for the act to be known before it took effect, was in vain urged. In vain was it urged that promulgation was part of a law: that no statute was to take effect until it was promulgated; and that time must be allowed for that essential formality. The delay of passing a substitute was urged as certain: the possibility of not passing one at all, was suggested: and then the reality of that alarm of danger to the Treasury—the union of the purse and the sword—which had so haunted the minds of senators at the time of the removal of the deposits; and which alarm, groundless then, was now to have a real foundation. All in vain. The days of the devoted act were numbered: the sun was not to set upon it alive: and late in the evening of a long and hot day in June, the question was called, with a refusal upon yeas and nays by the majority, to allow a postponement until the next day for the purpose of debate. Thus, refused one night's postponement, Mr. Benton, irritated at such unparliamentary haste, and at the unmeasured terms of abuse which were lavished upon the doomed act, rose and delivered the speech, of which some extracts are given in the next chapter.

In the progress of this bill a clause was proposed by Mr. Benton to exclude the Bank of the United States from becoming a depository of public moneys, under the new order of things which the repeal of the Sub-treasury system would bring about; and he gave as a reason, her criminal and corrupt conduct, and her insolvent condition. The clause was rejected by a strict party vote, with the exception of Mr. Archer—who voted for the exclusion. The repeal bill was carried in the Senate by a strict party vote:

> YEAS—Messrs. Archer, Barrow, Bates, Bayard, Berrien, Choate, Clay of Kentucky, Clayton, Dixon, Evans, Graham, Henderson, Huntington, Ker, Mangum, Merrick, Miller, Morehead, Phelps, Porter, Prentiss, Preston, Rives, Simmons, Smith of Indiana, Southard, Tallmadge, White, and Woodbridge—29.

> NAYS—Messrs. Allen, Benton, Calhoun, Clay of Alabama, Fulton, King, McRoberts, Nicholson, Pierce, Sevier, Smith of Connecticut, Sturgeon, Tappan, Walker, Williams, Woodbury, Wright, and Young—18.

In the House the repeal was carried by a decided vote—134 to 87. The negative voters were:

> Messrs. Archibald H. Arrington, Charles G. Atherton, Linn Banks, Henry W. Beeson, Benjamin A. Bidlack, Samuel S. Bowne, Linn Boyd, Aaron V. Brown, Charles Brown, Edmund Burke, Sampson H. Butler, William O. Butler, Green W. Caldwell, Patrick C. Caldwell, George B. Cary, Reuben Chapman, Nathan Clifford, James G. Clinton, Walter Coles, Edward Cross, John R. J. Daniel, Richard D. Davis, John B. Dawson, Ezra Dean, William Doan, Andrew W. Doig, John C. Edwards, Joseph Egbert, Charles G. Ferris, John G. Floyd, Charles A. Floyd, Joseph Fornance, William O. Goode, Samuel Gordon, Amos Gustine, William A. Harris, John Hastings, Samuel L. Hays, Isaac E. Holmes, George W. Hopkins, Jacob Houck, jr., George S. Houston, Edmund W. Hubard, Robert M. T. Hunter,

Charles J. Ingersoll, Wiliam Jack, Cave Johnson, John W. Jones, George M. Keim, Andrew Kennedy, Dixon H. Lewis, Nathaniel S. Littlefied, Joshua A. Lowell, Abraham McClellan, Robert McClellan, James J. McKay, Albert G. Marchand, Alfred Marshall, John Thompson Mason, James Mathews, William Medill, John Miller, William M. Oliver, William Parmenter, Samuel Patridge, William W. Payne, Francis W. Pickens, Arnold Plumer, John R. Reding, Lewis Riggs, James Rogers, James I. Roosevelt, John Sanford, Romulus M. Saunders, Tristram Shaw, Benjamin G. Shields, John Snyder, C. Sprigg, Lewis Steenrod, Hopkins L. Turney, John Van Buren, Aaron Ward, Harvey M. Watterson, John B. Weller, John Westbrook, James W. Williams, Fernando Wood.

CHAPTER LXV.

REPEAL OF THE INDEPENDENT TREASURY ACT: MR. BENTON'S SPEECH.

The lateness of the hour, the heat of the day, the impatience of the majority, and the determination evinced to suffer no delay in gratifying the feeling which demanded the sacrifice of the Independent Treasury system, shall not prevent me from discharging the duty which I owe to the friends and authors of that system, and to the country itself, by defending it from the unjust and odious character which clamor and faction have fastened upon it. A great and systematic effort has been made to cry down the sub-treasury by dint of clamor, and to render it odious by unfounded representations and distorted descriptions. It seems to have been selected as a subject for an experiment at political bamboozling; and nothing is too absurd, too preposterous, too foreign to the truth, to be urged against it, and to find a lodgment, as it is believed, in the minds of the uninformed and credulous part of the community. It is painted with every odious color, endowed with every mischievous attribute, and made the source and origin of every conceivable calamity. Not a vestige of the original appears; and, instead of the old and true system which it revives and enforces, nothing is seen but a new and hideous monster, come to devour the people, and to destroy at once their liberty, happiness and property. In all this the opponents of the system copy the conduct of the French jacobins of the year '89, in attacking the veto power reserved to the king. The enlightened historian, Thiers, has given us an account of these jacobinical experiments upon French credulity; and we are almost tempted to believe he was describing, with the spirit of prophecy, what we have seen taking place among ourselves. He says that, in some parts of the country, the people were taught to believe that the veto was a tax, which ought to be abolished; in others, that it was a criminal, which ought to be hung; in others again, that it was a monster, which ought to be killed; and in others, that it was a power in the king to prevent the people from eating or drinking. As a specimen of this latter species of imposition which was attempted upon the ignorant, the historian gives a dialogue which actually took place between a jacobin politician and a country peasant in one of the remote departments of France, and which ran in about these terms: "*My friend, do you know what the veto is?*" "*I do not.*" "*Then I will tell you what it is. It is this: You have some soup in your porringer; you are going to eat it; the king commands you to empty it on the ground, and you must instantly empty it on the ground: that is the veto!*" This, said Mr. B. is the account which an eminent historian gives us of the means used to bamboozle ignorant peasants and to excite them against a constitutional provision in France, made for their benefit, and which only arrested legislation till the people could speak; and I may say that means little short of such absurdity and nonsense have been used in our country to mislead and deceive the people, and to excite them against the sub-treasury here.

It is my intention, said Mr. B., to expose and to explode these artifices; to show the folly and absurdity of the inventions which were used to delude the people in the country, and which no senator of the opposite party will so far forget himself as to repeat here; and to exhibit the independent treasury as it is—not as a new and hurtful measure just conceived; but as an old and salutary law, fallen into disuse in evil times, and now revived and improved for the safety and advantage of the country.

What is it, Mr. President, which constitutes the system called and known by the name of the sub-treasury, or the independent treasury? It is two features, and two features alone, which constitute the system—all the rest is detail—and these two features are borrowed and taken from the two acts of Congress of September first, and September the second, 1789; the one establishing a revenue system, and the other establishing a treasury department for the United States. By the first of these acts, and by its 30th section, gold and silver coin alone was made receivable in payments to the United States; and by the second of them, section four, the treasurer of the United States is made the receiver, the keeper, and the payer, of the moneys of the United States, to the exclusion of banks, of which only three then existed. By these two laws, the first and the original financial system of the United States was established; and they both now stand upon the statute book, unrepealed, and in full legal force, except in some details. By these laws, made in the first days of the first session of the first Congress, which sat under the constitution, gold and silver coin only was made the currency of the federal treasury, and the treasurer of the United States was made the fiscal agent to receive, to keep, and to pay out that gold and silver coin. This was the system of Washington's administration; and as such it went into effect. All payments to the federal government were made in gold and silver; all such money paid remained in the hands of the treasurer himself, until he paid it out; or in the hands of the collectors of the customs, or the receivers of the land offices, until he drew warrants upon them in favor of those to whom money was due from the government. Thus it was in the beginning—in the first and happy years of Washington's administration. The money of the government was hard money; and nobody touched that money but the treasurer of the United States, and the officers who collected it; and the whole of these were under bonds and penalties for their good behavior, subject to the lawful orders and general superintendence of the Secretary of the Treasury and the President of the United States, who was bound to see the laws faithfully executed. The government was then what it was made to be—a hard-money government. It was made by hard-money men, who had seen enough of the evils of paper money and wished to save their posterity from such evils in future. The money was hard, and it was in the hands of the officers of the government—those who were subject to the orders of the government—and not in the hands of those who were only subject to requisitions—who could refuse to pay, protest a warrant, tell the government to sue, and thus go to law with the government for its own money. The framers of the constitution, and the authors of the two acts of 1789, had seen enough of the evils of the system of requisitions under the confederation to warn them against it under the constitution. They determined that the new government should keep its own hard money, as well as collect it; and thus the constitution, the law, the practice under the law, and the intentions of the hard-money and independent treasury men, were all in harmony, and in full, perfect, and beautiful operation, under the first years of General Washington's administration. All was right, and all was happy and prosperous, at the commencement.

But the spoiler came! General Hamilton was Secretary of the Treasury. He was the advocate of the paper system, the banking system, and the funding system, which were fastened upon England by Sir Robert Walpole, in his long and baneful administration under the first and second George. General Hamilton was the advocate of these systems, and wished to transplant them to our America. He exerted his great abilities, rendered still more potent by his high personal character, and his glorious revolutionary services, to substitute paper money for the federal currency, and banks for the keepers of the public money; and he succeeded to the extent of his wishes. The hard-money currency prescribed by the act of September 1st, 1789, was abolished by construction, and by a Treasury order to receive bank notes; the fiscal agent for the reception, the keeping, and the disbursement of the public moneys, consisting of the treasurer, and his collectors and receivers, was superseded by the creation of a national bank, invested with the privilege of keeping the public moneys, paying them out, and furnishing supplies of paper money for the payment of dues to the government. Thus, the two acts of 1789 were avoided, or superseded; not repealed, but only avoided and superseded by a Treasury order to receive paper, and a bank to keep it and pay it out. From this time paper money became the federal currency, and a bank the keeper of the federal money. It is needless to pursue this departure farther. The bank had its privileges for twenty years—was succeeded in them by local banks—they superseded by a second national bank—it again by local banks—and these finally by the independent treasury system—which was nothing but a return to the fundamental acts of 1789.

This is the brief history—the genealogy rather—of our fiscal agents; and from this it results, that after more than forty years of departure from the system of our forefathers—after more than forty years of wandering in the wilderness of banks, local and national—after more than forty years of wallowing in the slough of paper money, sometimes sound, sometimes rotten—we have returned to the point from which we sat out—hard money for our Federal Treasury; and our own officers to keep it. We returned to the acts of '89, not suddenly and crudely, but by degrees, and with details, to make the return safe and easy. The specie clause was restored, not by a sudden and single step, but gradually and progressively, to be accomplished in four years. The custody of the public moneys was restored to the treasurer and his officers; and as it was impossible for him to take manual possession of the moneys every where, a few receivers-general were given to him to act as his deputies, and the two mints in Philadelphia and New Orleans (proper places to keep money, and their keys in the hands of our officers), were added to his means of receiving and keeping them. This return to the old acts of '89 was accomplished in the summer of 1840. The old system, with a new name, and a little additional organization, has been in force near one year. It has worked well. It has worked both well and easy, and now the question is to repeal it, and to begin again where General Hamilton started us above forty years ago, and which involved us so long in the fate of banks and in the miseries and calamities of paper money. The gentlemen on the other side of the House go for the repeal; we against it; and this defines the position of the two great parties of the day—one standing on ground occupied by General Hamilton and the federalists in the year '91; the other standing on the ground occupied at the same time by Mr. Jefferson and the democracy.

The democracy oppose the repeal, because this system is proved by experience to be the safest, the cheapest, and the best mode of collecting the revenues, and keeping and disbursing the public moneys, which the wisdom of man has yet invented. It is the safest mode of collecting, because it receives nothing but gold and silver, and thereby saves the government from loss by paper money, preserves the standard of value, and causes a supply of specie to be kept in the country for the use of the people and for the support of the sound part of the banks. It is the cheapest mode of keeping the moneys; for the salaries of a few receivers are nothing compared to the cost of employing banks; for banks must be paid either by a per centum, or by a gross sum, or by allowing them the gratuitous use of the public money. This latter method has been tried, and has been found to be the dearest of all possible modes. The sub-treasury is the safest mode of keeping, for the receivers-general are our officers—subject to our orders—removable at our will—punishable criminally—suable civilly—and bound in heavy securities. It is the best mode; for it has no interest in increasing taxes in order to increase the deposits. Banks have this interest. A national bank has an interest in augmenting the revenue, because thereby it augmented the public deposits. The late bank had an average deposit for near twenty years of eleven millions and a half of public money in the name of the treasurer of the United States, and two millions and a half in the names of public officers. It had an annual average deposit of fourteen millions, and was notoriously in favor of all taxes, and of the highest tariffs, and was leagued with the party which promoted these taxes and tariffs. A sub-treasury has no interest of this kind, and in that particular alone presents an immense advantage over any bank depositories, whether a national institution or a selection of local banks. Every public interest requires the independent treasury to be continued. It is the old system of '89. The law for it has been on our statute-book for fifty-two years. Every citizen who is under fifty-two years old has lived all his life under the sub-treasury law, although the law itself has been superseded or avoided during the greater part of the time. Like the country gentleman in Molière's comedy, who had talked prose all his life without knowing it, every citizen who is under fifty-two has lived his life under the sub-treasury law—under the two acts of '89 which constitute it, and which have not been repealed.

We are against the repeal; and although unable to resist it here, we hope to show to the American people that it ought not to be repealed, and that the time will come when its re-establishment will be demanded by the public voice.

Independent of our objections to the merits of this repeal, stands one of a preliminary character, which has been too often mentioned to need elucidation or enforcement, but which cannot be properly omitted in any general examination of the subject. We are about to repeal one system without having provided another, and without even knowing what may be substituted, or whether any substitute whatever shall be agreed upon. Shall we have any, and if any, what? Shall it be a national bank, after the experience we have just had of such institutions? Is it to be a nondescript invention—a fiscality—or fiscal agent—to be planted in this District because we have exclusive jurisdiction here, and which, upon the same argument, may be placed in all the forts and arsenals, in all the dock-yards and navy-yards, in all the lighthouses and powder magazines, and in all the territories which the United States now possess, or may hereafter acquire? We have exclusive jurisdiction over all these; and if, with this argument, we can avoid the constitution in these ten miles square, we can also avoid it in every State, and in every territory of the Union. Is it to be the pet bank system of 1836, which, besides being rejected by all parties, is an impossibility in itself? Is it to be the lawless condition of the public moneys, as gentlemen denounced it, which prevailed from October, 1833, when the deposits were removed from the Bank of the United States, till June, 1836, when the State bank deposit system was adopted; and during all which time we could hear of nothing but the union of the purse and the sword, and the danger to our liberties from the concentration of all power in the hands of one man? Is it to be any one of these, and which? And if neither, then are the two acts of '89, which have never been repealed—which have only been superseded by temporary enactments, which have ceased, or by treasury constructions which no one can now defend—are these two acts to recover their vitality and vigor, and again become the law of the land, as they were in the first years of General Washington's administration, and before General Hamilton overpowered them? If so, we are still to have the identical system which we now repeal, with no earthly difference but the absence of its name, and the want of a few of its details. Be all this as it may—let the substitute be any thing or nothing—we have still accomplished a great point by the objection we have taken to the repeal before the substitute was produced, and by the vote which we took upon that point yesterday. We have gained the advantage of cutting gentlemen off from all plea for adopting their baneful schemes, founded upon the necessity of adopting something, because we have nothing. By their own vote they refuse to produce the new system before they abolish the old one. By their own vote they create the necessity which they deprecate; and having been warned in time, and acting with their eyes open, they cannot make their own conduct a plea for adopting a bad measure rather than none. If Congress adjourns without any system, and the public moneys remain as they did from 1833 to 1836, the country will know whose fault it is; and gentlemen will know what epithets to apply to themselves, by recollecting what they applied to General Jackson from the day the deposits were removed until the deposit act of '36 was passed.

Who demands the repeal of this system? Not the people of the United States; for there is not a solitary petition from the farmers, the mechanics, the productive classes, and the business men, against it. Politicians who want a national bank, to rule the country, and millionary speculators who want a bank to plunder it—these, to be sure, are clamorous for the repeal; and for the obvious reasons that the present system stands in the way of their great plans. But who else demands it? Who else objects to either feature of the sub-treasury—the hard-money feature, or the deposit of our own moneys with our own officers? Make the inquiry—pursue it through its details—examine the community by classes, and see who objects. The hard-money feature is in full force. It took full effect at once in the South and West, because there were no bank-notes in those quarters of the Union of the receivable description: it took full effect in New York and New England, because, having preserved specie payments, specie was just as plenty in that quarter as paper money; and all payments were either actually or virtually in hard money. It was specie, or its equivalent. The hard-money clause then went into operation at once, and who complained of it? The payers of the revenue? No, not one of them. The merchants who pay the duties have not complained; the farmers who buy the public lands have not complained. On the contrary, they rejoice; for hard-money payments keep off the speculator, with his bales of notes borrowed from banks, and enable the farmer to get his land at a fair price. The payers of the revenue then do not complain. How stands it with the next most interested class—the receivers of money from the United States? Are they dissatisfied at being paid in gold and silver? And do they wish to go back to the depreciated paper—the shinplasters—the compound of lampblack and rags—which they received a few years ago? Put this inquiry to the meritorious laborer who is working in stone, in wood, earth, and in iron for you at this moment. Ask him if he is tired of hard-money payments, and wishes the independent treasury system repealed, that he may get a chance to receive his hard-earned wages in broken bank-notes again. Ask the soldier and the mariner the same question. Ask the salaried officer and the contractor the same question. Ask ourselves here if we wish it—we who have seen ourselves paid in gold for years past, after having been for thirty years without a sight of that metal. No, sir, no. Neither the payers of money to the government, nor the receivers of money from the government, object to the hard-money clause in the sub-treasury act. How is it then with the body of the people—the great mass of the productive and business classes? Do they object to the clause? Not at all. They rejoice at it: for they receive, at second-hand, all that comes from the government. No officer, contractor, or laborer, eats the hard money which he receives from the government, but pays it out for the supplies which support his family: it all goes to the business and productive classes: and thus the payments from the government circulate from hand to hand, and go through the whole body of the people. Thus the whole body of the productive classes receive the benefit of the whole amount of the government hard-money payments. Who is it then that objects to it? Broken banks, and their political confederates, are the clamorers against it. Banks which wish to make their paper a public currency: politicians who wish a national bank as a machine to rule the country. These banks, and these politicians, are the sole clamorers against the hard-money clause in the sub-treasury system: they alone clamor for paper money. And how is it with the other clause—the one which gives the custody of the public money to the hands of our own officers, bound to fidelity by character, by official position, by responsibility, by ample securityship—and makes it felony in them to touch it for their own use? Here is a clear case of contention between the banks and the government, or between the clamorers for a national bank and the government. These banks want the custody of the public money. They struggle and strive for it as if it was their own. They fight for it: and if they get it, they will use it as their own—as we all well know; and refuse to render back when they choose to suspend. Thus, the whole struggle for the repeal resolves itself into a contest between the government, and all the productive and business classes on one side, and the federal politicians, the rotten part of the local banks, and the advocates of a national bank on the other.

Sir, the independent treasury has been organized: I say, organized! for the law creating it is fifty-two years old—has been organized in obedience to the will of the people, regularly expressed through their representatives after the question had been carried to them, and a general election had intervened. The sub-treasury system was proposed by President Van Buren in 1837, at the called session: it was adopted in 1840, after the question had been carried to the people, and the elections made to turn upon it. It was established, and clearly established, by the will of the people. Have the people condemned it? Have they expressed dissatisfaction? By no means. The presidential election was no test of this question; nor of any question. The election of General Harrison was effected by the combination of all parties to pull down one party, without any unity among the assailants on the question of measures. A candidate was agreed upon by the opposition for whom all could vote. Suppose a different selection had been made, and an eminent whig candidate taken, and he had been beaten two to one (as would probably have been the case): what then would have been the argument? Why, that the sub-treasury, and every other measure of the democracy, had been approved, two to one. The result of the election admits of no inference against this system; and could not, without imputing a heedless versatility to the people, which they do not possess. Their representatives, in obedience to their will, and on full three years' deliberation, established the system—established it in July, 1840: is it possible that, within four months afterwards—in the month of November following—the same people should condemn their own work?

But the system is to be abolished; and we are to take our chance for something, or nothing, in place of it. The abolition is to take place incontinently—incessantly—upon the instant of the passage of the bill! such is the spirit which pursues it! such the revengeful feeling which burns against it! And the system is still to be going on for a while after its death—for some days in the nearest parts, and some weeks in the remotest parts of the Union. The receiver-general in St. Louis will not know of his official death until ten days after he shall have been killed here. In the mean time, supposing himself to be alive, he is acting under the law; and all he does is without law, and void. So of the rest. Not only must the system be abolished before a substitute is presented, but before the knowledge of the abolition can reach the officers who carry it on; and who must continue to receive, and pay out public moneys for days and weeks after their functions have ceased, and when all their acts have become illegal and void.

Such is the spirit which pursues the measure—such the vengeance against a measure which has taken the money of the people from the moneyed corporations. It is the vengeance of the banking spirit against its enemy—against a system which deprives soulless corporations of their rich prey. Something must rise up in the place of the abolished system until Congress provides a substitute; and that something will be the nest of local banks which the Secretary of the Treasury may choose to select. Among these local banks stands that of the Bank of the United States. The repeal of the sub-treasury has restored that institution to its capacity to become a depository of the public moneys: and well, and largely has she prepared herself to receive them. The Merchants' Bank in New Orleans, her agent there; her branch in New York under the State law; and her branches and agencies in the South and in the West: all these subordinates, already prepared, enable her to take possession of the public moneys in all parts of the Union. That she expected to do so we learn from Mr. Biddle, who considered the attempted resumption in January last as unwise, because, in showing the broken condition of his bank, her claim to the deposits would become endangered. Mr. Biddle shows that the deposits were to have been restored; that, while in a state of suspension, his bank was as good as any. *De noche todas los gatos son pardos.* So says the Spanish proverb. In the dark, all the cats are grey—all of one color: the same of banks in a state of suspension. And in this darkness and assimilation of colors, the Bank of the United States has found her safety and security—her equality with the rest, and her fair claim to recover the keeping of the long-lost deposits. The attempt at resumption exposed her emptiness, and her rottenness—showed her to be the whited sepulchre, filled with dead men's bones. Liquidation was her course—the only honest—the only justifiable course. Instead of that she accepts new terms (just completed) from the Pennsylvania legislatures—affects to continue to exist as a bank: and by treating Mr. Biddle as the Jonas of the ship, when the whole crew were Jonases, expects to save herself by throwing him overboard. That bank is now, on the repeal of the sub-treasury, on a level with the rest for the reception of the public moneys. She is legally in the category of a public depository, under the act of 1836, the moment she resumes: and when her notes are shaved in—a process now in rapid movement—she may assert and enforce her right. She may resume for a week, or a month, to get hold of the public moneys. By the repeal, the public deposits, so far as law is concerned, are restored to the Bank of the United States. When the Senate have this night voted the repeal, they have also voted the restoration of the deposits; and they will have done it wittingly and knowingly, with their eyes open, and with a full perception of what they were doing. When they voted down my proposition of yesterday—a vote in which the whole opposition concurred, except the senator from Virginia who sits nearest me (Mr. Archer)—when they voted down that proposition to exclude the Bank of the United States from the list of future deposit banks, they of course declared that she ought to remain upon the list, with the full right to avail herself of her privilege under the revived act of 1836. In voting down that proposition, they voted up the prostrate bank of Mr. Biddle, and accomplished the great object of the panic of 1833-'34—that of censuring General Jackson, and of restoring the deposits. The act of that great man—one of the most patriotic and noble of his life—the act by which he saved forty millions of dollars to the American people—is reversed. The stockholders and creditors of the institution lose above forty millions, which the people otherwise would have lost. They lose the whole stock, thirty-five millions—for it will not be worth a straw to those who keep it: and the vote of the bank refusing to show their list of debtors—suppressing, hiding and concealing—the rotten list of debts—(in which it is mortifying to see a Southern gentleman concurring)—is to enable the initiated jobbers and gamblers to shove off their stock at some price on ignorant and innocent purchasers. The stockholders lose the thirty-five millions capital: they lose the twenty per centum advance upon that capital, at which many of the later holders purchased it; and which is near seven millions more: they lose the six millions surplus profits which were reported on hand: but which, perhaps, was only a *bank* report: and the holders of the notes lose the twenty to thirty per centum, which is now the depreciation of the notes of the bank—soon to be much more. These losses make some fifty millions of dollars. They now fall on the stockholders, and note-holders: where would they have fallen if the deposits had not been removed? They would have fallen upon the public treasury—upon the people of the United States: for the public is always the goose that is to be first plucked. The public money would have been taken to sustain the bank: taxes would have been laid to uphold her: the high tariff would have been revived for her benefit. Whatever her condition required would have been done by Congress. The bank, with all its crimes and debts—with all its corruptions and plunderings—would have been saddled upon the country—its charter renewed—and the people pillaged of the more than forty millions of dollars which have been lost. Congress would have been enslaved: and a new career of crime, corruption, and plunder commenced. The heroic patriotism of President Jackson saved us from this shame and loss: but we have no Jackson to save us now; and millionary plunderers—devouring harpies—foul birds, and voracious as foul—are again to seize the prey which his brave and undaunted arm snatched from their insatiate throats.

The deposits are restored, so far as the vote of the Senate goes; and if not restored in fact, it will be because policy, and new schemes forbid it. And what new scheme can we have? A nondescript, hermaphrodite, Janus-faced fiscality? or a third edition of General Hamilton's bank of 1791? or a bastard compound, the unclean progeny of both? Which will it be? Hardly the first named. It comes forth with the feeble and rickety symptoms which announce an unripe conception, and an untimely death. Will it be the second? It will be that, or worse. And where will the late flatterers—the present revilers of Mr. Biddle—the authors equally of the bank that is ruined, and of the one that is to be created: where will they find better men to manage the next than they had to manage the last? I remember the time when the vocabulary of praise was exhausted on Mr. Biddle—when in this chamber, and out of it, the censer, heaped with incense, was constantly kept burning under his nose: when to hint reproach of him was to make, if not a thousand chivalrous swords leap from their scabbards, at least to make a thousand tongues, and ten thousand pens, start up to defend him. I remember the time when a senator on this floor, and now on it (Mr. Preston of South Carolina), declared in his place that the bare annunciation of Mr. Biddle's name as Secretary of the Treasury, would raise the value of the people's property one hundred millions of dollars. My friend here on my right (pointing to Senator Woodbury) was the Secretary of the Treasury; and the mere transposition of names and places—the mere substitution of Biddle for Woodbury—was to be worth one hundred millions of dollars to the property of the country! What flattery could rise higher than that? Yet this man, once so lauded—once so followed, flattered, and courted—now lies condemned by all his former friends. They cannot now denounce sufficiently the man who, for ten years past, they could not praise enough: and, after this, what confidence are we to have in their judgments? What confidence are we to place in their new bank, and their new managers, after seeing such mistakes about the former?

Let it not be said that this bank went to ruin since it became a State institution. The State charter made no difference in its character, or in its management: and Mr. Biddle declared it to be stronger and safer without the United States for a partner than with it. The mortal wounds were all given while it was a national institution; and the late report of the stockholders shows not one species of offence, the cotton speculations alone excepted, which was not shown by Mr. Clayton's report of 1832; and being shown, was then defended by the whole power of those who are now cutting loose from the old bank, and clamoring for a new one. Not an act now brought to light, save and except the cotton operation, not even that for which Reuben M. Whitney was crushed to death, and his name constituted the synonyme of perjury and infamy for having told it; not an act now brought to light which was not shown to exist ten years ago, and which was not then defended by the whole federal party; so that the pretension that this institution did well as a national bank, and ill as a State one, is as unfounded in fact, as it is preposterous and absurd in idea. The bank was in the high road to ruin—in the gulf of insolvency—in the slough of crime and corruption—when the patriot Jackson signed the veto, and ordered the removal of the deposits; and nothing but these two great acts saved the people from the loss of the forty millions of dollars which have now fallen upon the stockholders and the note holders, and from the shame of seeing their government the slave and instrument of the bank. Jackson saved the people from this loss, and their government from this degradation; and for this he is now pursued with the undying vengeance of those whose schemes of plunder and ambition were balked by him.

Wise and prudent was the conduct of those who refused to recharter the second Bank of the United States. They profited by the error of their friends who refused to recharter the first one. These latter made no preparations for the event—did nothing to increase the constitutional currency—and did not even act until the last moment. The renewed charter was only refused a few days before the expiration of the existing charter, and the federal government fell back upon the State banks, which immediately sunk under its weight. The men of 1832 acted very differently. They decided the question of the renewal long before the expiration of the existing charter. They revived the gold currency, which had been extinct for thirty years. They increased the silver currency by repealing the act of 1819 against the circulation of foreign silver. They branched the mints. In a word, they raised the specie currency from twenty millions to near one hundred millions of dollars; and thus supplied the country with a constitutional currency to take the place of the United States Bank notes. The supply was adequate, being nearly ten times the average circulation of the national bank. That average circulation was but eleven millions of dollars; the gold and silver was near one hundred millions. The success of our measures was complete. The country was happy and prosperous under it; but the architects of mischief—the political, gambling, and rotten part of the banks, headed by the Bank of the United States, and aided by a political party—set to work to make panic and distress, to make suspensions and revulsions, to destroy trade and business, to degrade and poison the currency; to harass the country until it would give them another national bank: and to charge all the mischief they created upon the democratic administration. This has been their conduct; and having succeeded in the last presidential election, they now come forward to seize the spoils of victory in creating another national bank, to devour the substance of the people, and to rule the government of their country. Sir, the suspension of 1837, on the part of the Bank of the United States and its confederate banks and politicians, was a conspiracy and a revolt against the government. The present suspension is a continuation of the same revolt by the same parties. Many good banks are overpowered by them, and forced into suspension; but with the Bank of the United States, its affiliated banks, and its confederate politicians, it is a revolt and a conspiracy against the government.

Sir, it is now nightfall. We are at the end of a long day when the sun is more than fourteen hours above the horizon, and when a suffocating heat oppresses and overpowers the Senate. My friends have moved adjournments: they have been refused. I have been compelled to speak now, or never, and from this commencement we may see the conclusion. Discussion is to be stifled; measures are to be driven through; and a mutilated Congress, hastily assembled, imperfectly formed, and representing the census of 1830, not of 1840, is to manacle posterity with institutions which are as abhorent to the constitution as they are dangerous to the liberties, the morals, and the property of the people. A national bank is to be established, not even a simple and strong bank like that of General Hamilton, but some monstrous compound, born of hell and chaos, more odious, dangerous, and terrible than any simple bank could be. Posterity is to be manacled, and delivered up in chains to this deformed monster; and by whom? By a rump Congress, representing an expired census of the people, in the absence of members from States which, if they had their members here, would still have but the one-third part of their proper weight in the councils of the Union. The census of 1840 gives many States, and Missouri among the rest, three times their present relative weight; and no permanent measure ought to be discussed until this new relative weight should appear in Congress. Why take the census every ten years, if an expiring representation at the end of the term may reach over, and bind the increased numbers by laws which claim immunity from repeal, and which are rushed through without debate? Am I to submit to such work? No, never! I will war against the bank you may establish, whether a simple or a compound monster; I will war against it by every means known to the constitution and the laws. I will vote for the repeal of its charter as General Harrison and others voted for the repeal of the late bank charter in 1819. I will promote *quo warranto's and sci. fa.'s* against it. I will oppose its friends and support its enemies, and work at its destruction in every legal and constitutional way. I will war upon it while I have breath; and if I incur political extinction in the contest, I shall consider my political life well sold—sold for a high price—when lost in such a cause.

But enough for the present. The question now before us is the death of the sub-treasury. The discussion of the substitute is a fair inquiry in this question. We have a right to see what is to follow, and to compare it with what we have. But gentlemen withhold their schemes, and we strike in the dark. My present purpose is to vindicate the independent treasury system—to free it from a false character—to show it to be what it is, nothing but the revival of the two great acts of September the 1st and September the 2d, 1789, for the collection, safe keeping, and disbursement of the public moneys, under which this government went into operation; and under which it operated safely and successfully until General Hamilton overthrew it to substitute the bank and state system of Sir Robert Walpole, which has been the curse of England, and towards which we are now hurrying again with headlong steps and blindfold eyes.

CHAPTER LXVI.

THE BANKRUPT ACT: WHAT IT WAS: AND HOW IT WAS PASSED.

It has been seen in Mr. Tyler's message that, as a measure of his own administration, he would not have convened Congress in extraordinary session; but this having been done by his predecessor, he would not revoke his act. It was known that the call had been made at the urgent instance of Mr. Clay. That ardent statesman had so long seen his favorite measures baffled by a majority opposition to them in one House or the other, and by the twelve years presidency of General Jackson and Mr. Van Buren, that he was naturally now impatient to avail himself of the advantage of having all the branches of the government in their favor. He did so without delay. Mr. Tyler had delivered his message recommending the measures which he deemed proper for the consideration of Congress: Mr. Clay did the same—that is to say, recommend his list of measures to Congress also, not in the shape of a message, but in the form of a resolve, submitted to the Senate; and which has been given. A bankrupt act was not in his programme, nor in the President's message; and it was well known, and that by evidence less equivocal than its designed exclusion from his list of measures, that Mr. Clay was opposed to such a bill. But parties were so nearly balanced in the Senate, a deduction of two or three from the one side and added to the other would operate the life or death of most important measures, in the event that a few members should make the passage of a favorite measure the indispensable condition of their vote for some others which could not be carried without it. This was the case with the bank bill, and the distribution bill. A bank was the leading measure of Mr. Clay's policy—the corner stone of his legislative edifice. It was number two in his list: it was number one in his affections and in his parliamentary movement. He obtained a select committee on the second day of the session, to take into consideration the part of the President's message which related to the currency and the fiscal agent for the management of the finances; but before that select committee could report a bill, Mr. Henderson, of Mississippi, taking the shortest road to get at his object, asked and obtained leave to bring in a bill to establish a system of bankruptcy. This measure, then, which had no place in the President's message, or in Mr. Clay's schedule, and to which he was averse, took precedence on the calendar of the vital measure for which the extra session was chiefly called; and Mr. Henderson being determinedly supported by his colleague, Mr. Walker, and a few other resolute senators with whom the bankrupt act was an overruling consideration, he was enabled to keep it ahead, and coerce support from as many averse to it as would turn the scale in its favor. It passed the Senate, July 24th, by a close vote, 26 to 23. The yeas were:

> "Messrs. Barrow, Bates, Berrien, Choate, Clay of Kentucky, Clayton, Dixon, Evans, Henderson, Huntington, Kerr, Merrick, Miller, Morehead, Mouton, Phelps, Porter, Simmons, Smith of Indiana, Southard, Tallmadge, Walker, White, Williams, Woodbridge, Young.

> "NAYS—Messrs. Allen, Archer, Bayard, Benton, Buchanan, Calhoun, Clay of Alabama, Cuthbert, Fulton, Graham, King, Linn, McRoberts, Nicholson, Pierce, Prentiss, Rives, Sevier, Smith of Connecticut, Sturgeon, Tappan, Woodbury, Wright."

The distribution bill was a leading measure in Mr. Clay's policy: it ranked next after the national bank. He had also taken it into his own care, and had introduced a bill on leave for the purpose at an early day. A similar bill was also introduced in the House of Representatives. There was no willing majority for the bankrupt bill in either House; but the bank bill and the land bill were made to pass it. The ardent friends of the bankrupt bill embargoed both the others until their favorite measure was secure. They were able to defeat the other two, and determined to do so if they did not get their own measure; and they did get it—presenting the spectacle of a bill, which had no majority in either House, forcing its own passage, and controlling the fate of two others—all of them measures of great national concern.

The bankrupt bill had passed the Senate ahead of the bank bill, and also of the distribution bill, and went to the House of Representatives, where the majority was against it. It seemed doomed in that House. The same bill had originated in that body; but lay upon the table without consideration. The President, beset by a mass of debtors who had repaired to Washington to promote the passage of the bill, sent in a special message in its favor; but without effect. The House bill slept on the table: the Senate bill arrived there, and was soon put to rest upon the same table. Mr. Underwood, of Kentucky, a friend of Mr. Clay, had moved to lay it on the table; and the motion prevailed by a good majority—110 to 97. Information of this vote instantly flew to the Senate. One of the senators, intent upon the passage of the bill, left his seat and went down to the House; and when he returned he informed the writer of this View that the bill would pass—that it would be taken off the table, and put through immediately: and such was the fact. The next day the bill was taken up and passed—the meagre majority of only six for it. The way in which this was done was made known to the writer of this View by the senator who went down to attend to the case when the bill was laid on the table: it was simply to let the friends of the bank and distribution bills know that these measures would be defeated if the bankrupt bill was not passed—that there were enough determined on that point to make sure: and, for the security of the bankrupt bill, it was required to be passed first.

The bill had passed the House with an amendment, postponing the commencement of its operation from November to February; and this amendment required to be communicated to the Senate for its concurrence—which was immediately done. This amendment was a salvo to the consciences of members for their forced votes: it was intended to give Congress an opportunity of repealing the act before it took effect; but the friends of the bill were willing to take it that way—confident that they could baffle the repeal for some months, and until those most interested, had obtained the relief they wanted.

At the time that this amendment was coming up to the Senate that body was engaged on the distribution bill, the debate on the bank veto message having been postponed by the friends of the bank to make way for it. August the 18th had been fixed for that day—12 o'clock the hour. The day and the hour, had come; and with them an immense crowd, and an excited expectation. For it was known that Mr. Clay was to speak—and to speak according to his feelings—which were known to be highly excited against Mr. Tyler. In the midst of this expectation and crowd, and to the disappointment of every body, Mr. Berrien rose and said that—"Under a sense of duty, he was induced to move that the consideration of the executive veto message on the fiscal bank bill be postponed until to-morrow, 12 o'clock."—Mr. Calhoun objected to this postponement. "The day, he said, had been fixed by the friends of the bank bill. The President's message containing his objections to it had now been in possession of the Senate, and on the tables of members for two days. Surely there had been sufficient time to reflect upon it: yet now it was proposed still longer to defer action upon it. He asked the senator from Georgia, who had made the motion, to assign some reason for the proposed delay." The request of Mr. Calhoun for a reason, was entirely parliamentary and proper; and in fact should have been anticipated by giving the reason with the motion—as it was not deferential to the Senate to ask it to do a thing without a reason, especially when the thing to be done was contrary to an expressed resolve of the Senate, and took members by surprise who came prepared to attend to the appointed business, and not prepared to attend to another subject. Mr. Berrien declined to give a reason, and said that—"When the senator from South Carolina expressed his personal conviction that time enough had been allowed for reflection on the message, he expressed what would no doubt regulate his personal conduct; but when he himself stated that, under a sense of duty, he had asked for further time, he had stated his own conviction in regard to the course which ought to be pursued. Senators would decide for themselves which opinion was to prevail."—Mr. Calhoun rejoined in a way to show his belief that there was a secret and sinister cause for this reserve, so novel and extraordinary in legislative proceedings. He said—"Were the motives such as could not be publicly looked at? were they founded on movements external to that chamber? It was certainly due to the Senate that a reason should be given. It was quite novel to refuse it. Some reason was always given for a postponement. He had never known it to be otherwise."—Mr. Berrien remained unmoved by this cogent appeal, and rejoined—"The senator from South Carolina was at liberty to suggest whatever he might think proper; but that he should not conclude him (Mr. Berrien), as having made a motion here for reasons which he could not disclose."—Mr. Calhoun then said that, "this was a very extraordinary motion, the votes of senators upon it ought to be recorded: he would therefore move for the yeas and nays,"—which were ordered, and stood thus: Yeas: Messrs. Archer, Barrow, Bates, Bayard, Berrien, Choate, Clay of Kentucky, Clayton (Thomas of Delaware), Dixon, Evans, Graham, Henderson, Huntingdon, Kerr, Mangum, Merrick, Miller, Morehead, Phelps, Porter, Prentiss, Preston, Rives, Simmons, Smith of Indiana, Southard, Tallmadge, White, and Woodbridge, 29—the supporters of the bank all voting for the postponement, their numbers swelled a little beyond their actual strength by the votes of Mr. Rives, and a few other whigs. The nays were: Messrs. Allen, Benton, Buchanan, Calhoun, Clay of Alabama,

Cuthbert, Fulton, King, Linn, McRoberts, Mouton, A. O. P. Nicholson, Pierce, Sevier, Sturgeon, Tappan, Walker, Williams, Woodbury, Wright, and Young—21. It was now apparent that the postponement of the bank question was a concerted measure of the whig party—that Mr. Berrien was its organ in making the motion—and that the reason for it was a party secret which he was not at liberty to disclose. Events, however, were in progress to make the disclosure.

The distribution bill was next in order, and during its consideration Mr. White, of Indiana, made a remark which attracted the attention of Mr. Benton. Deprecating further debate, as a useless waste of time, Mr. White wished discussion to cease, and the vote be taken—"as he hoped, as well as believed, that the bill would pass, and not alone, but be accompanied by other measures." This remark from Mr. White gave Mr. Benton something to go upon; and he immediately let out what was on his mind.

He thanked the senator from Indiana for his avowal; it was a confirmation of what he well knew before—that measures, at this extraordinary session, were not passed or rejected upon their merits, but made to depend one upon another, and the whole upon a third! It was all bargain and sale. All was conglomerated into one mass, and must go together or fall together. This was the decree out of doors. When the sun dips below the horizon, a private Congress is held, the fate of the measure is decided; a bundle are tied together; and while one goes ahead as a bait, another is held back as a rod.

Mr. Linn, of Missouri, still more frank than his colleague, stigmatized the motive for postponement, and the means that were put in practice to pass momentous bills which could not pass on their own merits; and spoke out without disguise:

> "These artifices grow out of the system adopted for carrying through measures that never could be carried through other than by trick and art. The majority which by force, not by argument, have to carry their measures, must meet in secret—concoct their measures in conclave—and then hold every member of the party bound to support what is thus agreed upon—a master spirit leading all the while. There had been enough of falsehood, misrepresentation and delusion. The presidential election had contained enough of it, without adding to the mass at this session. The country was awake to these impositions, and required only to be informed of the movements of the wire-workers to know how to appreciate their measures. And the people should be informed. As far as it was possible for him and his friends to lay that information before the country, it should be done. Every man in the community must be told how this bank bill, which was intended to rule the country with a moneyed despotism for years to come, had been passed—how a national debt was entailed upon the country—how this bankrupt bill was forced through, as he (Mr. LINN) now understood it was, by a majority of five votes, in the other end of the Capitol, many of its whig opponents dodging behind the columns; and how this land distribution bill was now in the course of being passed, and the tricks resorted to to effect its passage. It was all part and parcel of the same system which was concocted in Harrisburg, wrought with such blind zeal at the presidential election, and perfected by being compressed into a congressional caucus, at an extraordinary called, but uncalled-for, session."

The distribution bill had been under debate for an hour, and Mr. King, of Alabama, was on the floor speaking to it, when the clerk of the House of Representatives appeared at the door of the Senate Chamber with the bankrupt bill, and the amendments made by the House—and asking the concurrence of the Senate. Still standing on his feet, but dropping the line of his argument, Mr. King exclaimed:

> "That, sir, is the bill. There it is sir. That is the bill which is to hurry this land distribution bill to its final passage, without either amendments or debate. Did not the senator know that yesterday, when the bankrupt bill was laid on the table by a decided vote in the other House, the distribution bill could not, by any possibility then existing, be passed in this House? But now the case was altered. A reconsideration of the vote of yesterday had taken place in the other House, and the bankrupt bill was now returned to the Senate for concurrence; after which it would want but the signature of the Executive to become a law. But how had this

change been so suddenly brought about? How, but by putting on the screws? Gentlemen whose States cried aloud for the relief of a bankrupt law, were told they could not have it unless they would pay the price—they must pass the distribution bill, or they should have no bankrupt bill. One part of the bargain was already fulfilled: the bankrupt bill was passed. The other part of the bargain is now to be consummated: the distribution bill can pass now without further delay. He (Mr. KING) had had the honor of a seat in this chamber for many years, but never during that time had he seen legislation so openly and shamefully disgraced by a system of bargain and sale. This extra session of Congress would be long remembered for the open and undisguised extent to which this system had been carried."

Incontinently the distribution bill was laid upon the table, and the bankrupt bill was taken up. This was done upon the motion of Mr. Walker, who gave his reasons, thus:

"He rose not to prolong the debate on the distribution bill, but to ask that it might be laid on the table, that the bill to establish a general bankrupt law, which had just been received from the House, might be taken up, and the amendment, which was unimportant, might be concurred in by the Senate. He expressed his ardent joy at the passage of this bill by this House, which was so imperiously demanded as a measure of great relief to a suffering community, which he desired should not be held in suspense another night; but that they should immediately take up the amendments, and act on them. For this purpose he moved to lay the distribution bill on the table."

Mr. Linn asked for the yeas and nays, that it might be seen how senators voted in this rigadoon legislation, in which movements were so rapid, so complicated, and so perfectly performed. They were ordered, and stood: Yeas—Messrs. Archer, Barrow, Bates, Bayard, Berrien, Choate, Clay of Kentucky, Dixon, Evans, Henderson, Huntington, Kerr, Mangum, Merrick, Miller, Morehead, Phelps, Porter, Preston, Simmons, Smith of Indiana, Southard, Tallmadge, Walker, White, and Woodbridge—26. Nays—Messrs. Allen, Benton, Buchanan, Calhoun, Clay of Alabama, Clayton, Cuthbert, Fulton, Graham, King, Linn, McRoberts, Mouton, Pierce, Sevier, Sturgeon, Tappan, Williams, Woodbury, Wright, and Young—21. So that the whole body of the friends to the distribution bill, voted to lay it down to take up the bankrupt bill, as they had just voted to lay down the bank bill to take up the distribution. The three measures thus travelled in company, but bankrupt in the lead—for the reason, as one of its supporters told Mr. Benton, that they were afraid it would not get through at all if the other measures got through before it. The bankrupt bill having thus superseded the distribution bill, as itself had superseded the bank bill, Mr. Walker moved a concurrence in the amendment. Mr. Buchanan intimated to Mr. Walker that he was taken in—that the postponement was to enable Congress to repeal the bill before it took effect; and, speaking in this sense, said:

"From the tone of the letters he had received from politicians differing with him, he should advise his friend from Mississippi [Mr. WALKER], not to be quite so soft as, in his eagerness to pass this bill, to agree to this amendment, postponing the time for it to take effect to February, as it would be repealed before its operation commenced; although it was now made a price of the passage of the distribution bill. He felt not a particle of doubt but there would be a violent attempt to repeal it next session."

Mr. Walker did not defend the amendment, but took it rather than, by a non-concurrence, to send the bill back to the House, where its friends could not trust it again. He said—"When his friend from Pennsylvania spoke of his being 'soft,' he did not know whether he referred to his head or his heart; but he could assure him he was not soft enough to run the chance of defeating the bill by sending it back to the House."—Mr. Calhoun did not concur with his friend from Pennsylvania, that there would be any effort to repeal this bill. It would be exceedingly popular at its first "go off," and if this bill passed, he hoped that none of his friends would attempt to repeal it. It would, if permitted to work, produce its legitimate effects; and was enough to destroy any administration. He saw that this was a doomed administration. It would not only destroy them, but blow them "sky high."

This was the only instance in which Mr. Calhoun was known to express a willingness that a bad measure should stand because it would be the destruction of its authors; and on this occasion it was merely the ebullition of an excited feeling, as proved when the question of repeal came on at the next session—in which he cordially gave his assistance. The amendment was concurred in without a division, the adversaries of the bill being for the postponement in good faith, and its friends agreeing to it for fear of something worse. There had been an agreement that the three measures were to pass, and upon that agreement the bank bill was allowed to go down to the House before the bankrupt bill was out of it; but the laying that bill on the table raised an alarm, and the friends of the bankrupt required the others to be stopped until their cherished measure was finished: and that was *one* of the reasons for postponing the debate on the bank veto message which could not be disclosed to the Senate. The amendment of the House being agreed to, there was no further vote to be taken on the bill; but a motion was made to suppress it by laying it on the table. That motion brought out a clean vote for and against the bill—23 to 26. The next day it received the approval of the President, and became a law.

The act was not a bankrupt law, but practically an insolvent law for the abolition of debts at the will of the debtor. It applied to all persons in debt—allowed them to commence their proceedings in the district of their own residence, no matter how lately removed to it—allowed constructive notice to creditors in newspapers—declared the abolition of the debt where effects were surrendered and fraud not proved. It broke down the line between the jurisdiction of the federal courts and the State courts in the whole department of debtors and creditors; and bringing all local debts and dealings into the federal courts, at the will of the debtor, to be settled by a federal jurisdiction, with every advantage on the side of the debtor. It took away from the State courts the trials between debtor and creditor in the same State—a thing which under the constitution can only be done between citizens of different States. Jurisdiction over bankruptcies did not include the mass of debtors, but only that class known to legislative and judicial proceedings as bankrupts. To go beyond, and take in all debtors who could not pay their debts, and bring them into the federal courts, was to break down the line between federal and State jurisdictions, and subject all persons—all neighbors—to have their dealings settled in the federal courts. It violated the principle of all bankrupt systems—that of a proceeding on the part of the creditors for their own benefit—and made it entirely a proceeding for the benefit of the debtor, at his own will. It was framed upon the model of the English insolvent debtor's act of George the Fourth; and after closely paraphrasing eighteen provisions out of that act, most flagrantly departed from its remedy in the conclusion, in substituting a release from the *debt* instead of a release from *imprisonment*. In that feature, and in applying to all debts, and in giving the initiative to the debtor, and subjecting the whole proceeding to be carried on at his will, it ceased to be a bankrupt act, and became an insolvent act; but with a remedy which no insolvent act, or bankrupt system, had ever contained before—that of a total abolition of the debt by the act of the debtor alone, unless the creditor could prove fraud; which the sort of trial allowed would render impossible, even where it actually existed. It was the same bill which had been introduced at the previous session, and supported by Mr. Webster in an argument which confounded insolvency with bankruptcy, and assumed every failure to pay a debt to be a bankruptcy. The pressure for the passing of the act was immense. The long disorders of the currency, with the expansions, contractions, suspensions, and breaking of banks had filled the country with men of ruined fortunes, who looked to the extinction of their debts by law as the only means of getting rid of their incumbrances, and commencing business anew. This unfortunate class was estimated by the most moderate observers at an hundred thousand men. They had become a power in the State. Their numbers and zeal gave them weight: their common interest gave them unity: the stake at issue gave them energy. They worked in a body in the presidential election, and on the side of the whigs: and now attended Congress, and looked to that party for the legislative relief for which they had assisted in the election. Nor did they look in vain. They got all they asked—but most unwillingly, and under a moral duresse—and as the price of passing two other momentous bills. Such is legislation in high party times! selfish and sinistrous, when the people believe it to be honest and patriotic! people at home, whose eyes should be opened to the truth, if they wish to preserve the purity of their government. Here was a measure which, of itself, could not have got through either House of Congress: combined with others, it carried itself, and licensed the passing of two more! And all this was done—so nicely were parties balanced—by the zeal and activity (more than the numbers) of a single State, and that a small one, and among the most indebted. In brief, the bankrupt act was passed, and the passage of the bank and distribution bills were licensed by the State of Mississippi, dominated by the condition of its population.

Mr. Buchanan, Mr. Wright, Mr. Woodbury, were the principal speakers against the bill in the Senate. Mr. Benton addressed himself mainly to Mr. Webster's position, confounding insolvency and bankruptcy, as taken at the previous session; and delivered a speech of some research in opposition to that assumption—of which some extracts are given in the next chapter.

CHAPTER LXVII.

BANKRUPT BILL: MR. BENTON'S SPEECH: EXTRACTS.

The great ground which we occupy in relation to the character of this bill (said Mr. B.) is this: that it is not a bankrupt system, but an insolvent law, perverted to a discharge from debts, instead of a discharge from imprisonment. As such, it was denounced from the moment it made its appearance in this chamber, at the last session, and I am now ready to prove it to be such. I have discovered its origin, and hold the evidence in my hand. It is framed upon the English insolvent debtor's act of the 1st of George IV., improved and extended by the act of the 7th of George IV., and by the 1st of Victoria. From these three insolvent acts our famous bankrupt system of 1841 is compiled; and it follows its originals with great fidelity, except in a few particulars, until it arrives at the conclusion, where a vast and terrible alteration is introduced! Instead of discharging the debtor from imprisonment, as the English acts do, our American copy discharges him from his debts! But this is a thing rather to be proved than told; and here is the proof. I have a copy of the British statutes on my table, containing the three acts which I have mentioned, and shall quote from the first one, in the first year of the reign of George IV., and is entitled "*An act for the relief of insolvent debtors in England.*" The preamble recites that it is expedient to make permanent provision for the relief of insolvent debtors in England confined in jail, and who shall be willing to surrender their property to their creditors, and thereby obtain a discharge from imprisonment. For this purpose the act creates a new court, to be called the *insolvent debtor's court*, which was to sit in London, and send commissioners into the counties. The first sections are taken up with the organization of the court. Then come its powers and duties, its modes of proceeding, and the rights of insolvents in it: and in these enactments, as in a mirror, and with a few exceptions (the effect of design, of accident, or of necessity, from the difference of the two forms of government), we perceive the original of our bankrupt act. I quote partly from the body of the statute, but chiefly from the marginal notes, as being a sufficient index to the contents of the sections. (Here the speaker quoted eighteen separate clauses in which the bill followed the English act, constituting the whole essence of the bill, and its mode of proceeding.)

This is the bill which we call bankrupt—a mere parody and perversion of the English insolvent debtor's act. And now, how came such a bill to be introduced? Sir, it grew out of the contentions of party; was brought forward, as a party measure; and was one of the bitter fruits of the election of 1840. The bill was brought forward in the spring of that year, passed in the Senate, and lost in the House. It was contested in both Houses as a party measure, and was taken up as a party topic in the presidential canvass. The debtor class—those irretrievably in debt, and estimated by the most moderate at a hundred thousand men—entered most zealously into the canvass, and on the side of the party which favored the act. The elections were carried by that party—the Congress as well as the presidential. All power is in the hands of that party; and an extra session of the legislature was impatiently called to realize the benefits of the victory. But the opening of the session did not appear to be auspicious to the wishes of the bankrupts. The President's message recommended no bankrupt bill; and the list of subjects enumerated for the action of Congress, and designated in a paper drawn by Mr. Clay, and placed on our journal for our guidance, was equally silent upon that subject. To all appearance, the bankrupt bill was not to come before us at the extra session. It was evidently a deferred subject. The friends and expectants of the measure took the alarm—flocked to Congress—beset the President and the members— obtained from him a special message recommending a bankrupt law; and prevailed on members to bring in the bill. It was brought into the Senate—the same which had been defeated in 1840—and it was soon seen that its passage was not to depend upon its own merits; that its fate was indissolubly connected with another bill; and that one must carry the other.

This is an insolvent bill: it is so proved, and so admitted: and to defend it the argument is, that insolvency and bankruptcy are the same—a mere inability or failure to pay debts. This is the corner stone of the argument for the bill, and has been firmly planted as such, by its ablest supporter (Mr. Webster). He says:

> "Bankruptcies, in the general use and acceptation of the term, mean no more than failures. A bankruptcy is a fact. It is an occurrence in the life and fortunes of an individual. When a man cannot pay his debts, we say that he has become bankrupt, or has failed. Bankruptcy is not merely the condition of a man who is insolvent, and on whom a bankrupt law is already acting.

This would be quite too technical an interpretation. According to this, there never could be bankrupt laws; because every law, if this were the meaning, would suppose the existence of a previous law. Whenever a man's means are insufficient to meet his engagements and pay his debts, the fact of bankruptcy has taken place—a case of bankruptcy has arisen, whether there be a law providing for it or not. A learned judge has said, that a law on the subject of bankruptcies is a law making provision for cases of persons failing to pay their debts. Over the whole subject of these failures, or these bankruptcies, the power of Congress, as it stands on the face of the constitution, is full and complete."

This is an entire mistake. There is no foundation for confounding bankruptcy and insolvency. A debtor may be rich, and yet be a bankrupt. Inability to pay does not even enter as an ingredient into bankruptcy. The whole system is founded on ability and fraud. The bankrupt is defined in Blackstone's commentaries—a work just issued and known to all our statesmen at the time of our Revolution—"*to be a trader, who secretes himself, or does certain other acts to defraud his creditors.*" So far from making insolvency a test of bankruptcy the whole system supposes ability and fraud—ability to pay part or all, and a fraudulent intent to evade payment. And every British act upon the subject directs the surplus to be restored to the debtor if his effects sell for more than pays the debts—a proof that insolvency was no ingredient in the acts.

The eminent advocate of the bill, in confounding insolvency and bankruptcy, has gone to the continent of Europe, and to Scotland, to quote the *cessio bonorum* of the civil law, and to confound it with bankruptcy. He says: "*That bankrupt laws, properly so called, or laws providing for the cessio bonorum, on the continent of Europe and Scotland, were never confined to traders.*" That is true. This *cessio* was never confined to traders: it applied to debtors who could not pay. It was the cession, or surrender of his property by the debtor for the purpose of obtaining freedom for his person—leaving the debt in full force—and all future acquisitions bound for it. I deal in authority, and read from Professor Bell's Commentaries upon the Laws of Scotland—an elegant an instructive work, which has made the reading of Scottish law almost as agreeable to the law reader as the writings of Scott have made Scottish history and manners to the general reader. Mr. Bell treats of the *cessio* and of bankruptcy, and treats of them under distinct heads; and here is what he says of them:

"The law of *cessio bonorum* had its origin in Rome. It was introduced by Julius Cæsar, as a remedy against the severity of the old Roman laws of imprisonment; and his law—which included only Rome and Italy—was, before the time of Diocletian, extended to the provinces. The first law of the code respecting the *cessio bonorum* expresses, in a single sentence, the whole doctrine upon the subject: '*Qui bonis cesserint,*' says the Emperor Alexander Severus, '*nisi solidum creditor receperit, non sunt liberati. In eo enim tantummodo hoc beneficium eis prodest, ne judicati detrahantur in carcerem.*' This institution, having been greatly improved in the civil law, was adopted by those of the European nations who followed that system of jurisprudence. In France, the institution was adopted very nearly as it was received with us. Perhaps, indeed, it was from France that our system received its distinguishing features. The law in that country was, during the seventeenth century, extremely severe—not only against bankrupts (which name they applied to fraudulent debtors alone), but against debtors innocently insolvent. * * * The short digest of the law of *cessio* in Scotland, then, is:

"1. That a debtor who has been a month in prison, for a civil debt, may apply to the court of session—calling all his creditors before that court, by a summons in the king's name; and concluding that he should be freed from prison on surrendering to his creditors all his funds and effects.

"2. That he is entitled to this benefit without any mark of disgrace, if (proving his insolvency) he can satisfy the court, in the face of his creditors, that his insolvency has arisen from innocent misfortune, and is willing to surrender all his property and effects to his creditors.

"3. That, though he may clear himself from any imputation of fraud, still, if he has been extravagant, and guilty of sporting with the money of his creditors, he is, in strict law, not entitled to the *cessio*, but on the condition of wearing the habit (mark of disgrace); but which is now exchanged for a prolongation of his imprisonment.

"4. That, if his creditors can establish a charge of fraud against him, he is not entitled to the *cessio* at all; but must lie in prison, at the mercy of his creditors, till the length of his imprisonment may seem to have sufficiently punished his crime; when, on a petition, the court may admit him to the benefit.

"5. That, if he has not given a fair account of his funds, and shall still be liable to the suspicion of concealment, the court will, in the meanwhile, refuse the benefit of the *cessio*—leaving it to him to apply again, when he is able to present a clearer justification, or willing to make a full discovery."

This is the *cessio*, and its nature and origin are both given. Its nature is that of an insolvent law, precisely as it exists at this day in the United States and in England. Its origin is Roman, dating from the dictatorship of Julius Cæsar. That great man had seen the evils of the severity of the Roman law against debtors. He had seen the iniquity of the law itself, in the cruel condemnation of the helpless debtor to slavery and death at the will of the creditor; and he had seen its impolicy, in the disturbances to which it subjected the republic—the seditions, commotions, and conspiracies, which, from the time of the secession of the people to the *Mons Sacer* to the terrible conspiracy of Catiline, were all built upon the calamities of the debtor class, and had for their object an abolition of debts. Cæsar saw this, and determined to free the commonwealth from a deep-seated cause of commotion, while doing a work of individual justice. He freed the person of the debtor upon the surrender of his property; and this equitable principle, becoming ingrafted in the civil law, spread over all the provinces of the Roman world—has descended to our times, and penetrated the new world—and now forms the principle of the insolvent laws of Europe and America. The English made it permanent by their insolvent law of the first of George the Fourth—that act from which our bankrupt system is compiled; and in two thousand years, and among all nations, there has been no departure from the wise and just principles of Cæsar's edict, until our base act of Congress has undertaken to pervert it into an abolition debt law, by substituting a release from the debt for a release from jail!

This is the *cessio omnium bonorum* of Scotland, to which we are referred as being the same thing with bankruptcy (properly so called), and which is quoted as an example for our act of 1841. And, now, what says Professor Bell of bankruptcy? Does he mention that subject? Does he treat of it under a separate head—as a different thing from the *cessio*—and as requiring a separate consideration? In fact, he does. He happens to do so; and gives it about 300 pages of his second volume, under the title of "System of the Bankrupt Laws;" which system runs on all-fours with that of the English system, and in the main point—that of discharge from his debts—it is identical with the English; requiring the concurrence of four-fifths of the creditors to the discharge; and that bottomed on the judicial attestation of the bankrupt's integrity. Here it is, at page 441 of the second volume:

"The concurrence of the creditors, without which the bankrupt cannot apply to the court for a discharge, must be not that of a mere majority, but a majority of four-fifths in number and value. * * * * The creditors are subject to no control in respect to their concurrence. Against their decision there is no appeal, nor are they bound to account for or explain the grounds of it. They are left to proceed upon the whole train of the bankrupt's conduct, as they may have seen occasion to judge of him; and the refusal of their concurrence is an absolute bar until the opposition be overcome. * * * * The statute requires the concurrence of the trustee, as well as of the creditors. There appears, however, to be this difference between them: that the creditors are entirely uncontrolled in giving or withholding their concurrence; while, on the part of the trustee, it is *debitum justiliæ* either to the bankrupt or to the creditors to give or withhold his concurrence. He acts not as a creditor, but as a judge. To his jurisdiction the bankrupt is subjected by the choice of his creditors; and, on deciding on the bankrupt's conduct, he is not entitled to proceed on the same undisclosed motives or evidence on which a creditor may act, but on the ground of legal objection alone—as fraud, concealment, nonconformity with the statute. In England, the commissioners are public officers—not the mere creatures of the creditors. They are by statute invested with a judicial discretion, which they exercise under the sanction of an oath. Their refusal is taken as if they swore they could not grant the certificate; and no mandamus lies to force them to sign."

So much for bankruptcy and *cessio*—two things very different in their nature, though attempted to be confounded; and each of them still more different from our act, for which they are quoted as precedents. But the author of our act says that bankrupt laws in Scotland are not confined to traders, but take in all persons whatsoever; and he might have added—though, perhaps, it did not suit his purpose at the moment—that those laws, in Scotland, were not confined to natural persons, but also included corporations and corporate bodies. Bell expressly says:

> "Corporate bodies are, in law, considered as persons, when associated by royal authority or act of Parliament. When a community is thus established by public authority, it has a legal existence as a person, with power to hold funds, to sue and to defend. It is, of consequence, subject to diligence; and although personal execution cannot proceed against this ideal-legal person, and so the requisites of imprisonment, &c., cannot be complied with, there seems to be no reason to doubt that a corporation may now be made bankrupt by the means recently provided for those cases in which imprisonment is incompetent."—vol. 2, p. 167.

The gentleman might have quoted this passage from the Scottish law; and then what would have become of his argument against including corporations in the bankrupt act? But he acts the advocate, and quotes what suits him; and which, even if it were applicable, would answer but a small part of his purpose. The Scottish system differs from the English in its application to persons not traders; but agrees with it in the great essentials of perfect security for creditors, by giving them the initiative in the proceedings, discriminating between innocent and culpable bankruptcy, and making the discharge from debt depend upon their consent, bottomed upon an attestation of integrity from the officer that tries the case. It answers no purpose to the gentleman, then, to carry us to Scotland for the meaning of a term in our constitution. It is to no purpose that he suggests that the framers of the constitution might have been looking to Scotland for an example of a bankrupt system. They were no more looking to it in that case, than they were in speaking of juries, and in guarantying the right of jury trials—a jury of twelve, with unanimity, as in England; and not of fifteen, with a majority of eight to give the verdict, as in Scotland. In all its employment of technical, legal, and political phrases, the constitution used them as used in England—the country from which we received our birth, our language, our manners, and customs, and all our systems of law and politics. We got all from England; and, this being the case, there is no use in following the gentleman to the continent of Europe, after dislodging him from Scotland; but as he has quoted the continent for the effect of the *cessio* in abolishing debts, and for its identity with bankruptcy, I must be indulged with giving him a few citations from the Code Napoleon, which embodies the principles of the civil law, and exemplifies the systems of Europe on the subject of bankruptcies and insolvencies. Here they are:

Mr. B. here read copiously from the Code Napoleon, on the subjects of bankruptcies and cession of property; the former contained in the commercial division of the code, the latter in the civil. Bankruptcy was divided into two classes—innocent and fraudulent; both confined to traders (*commerçants*); the former were treated with lenity, the latter with criminal severity. The innocent bankrupt was the *trader* who became unable to pay his debts by the casualties of trade, and who had not lived beyond his means, nor gambled, nor engaged in speculations of pure hazard; who kept fair books, and satisfied his creditors and the judge of his integrity. The fraudulent bankrupt was the *trader* who had lived prodigally, or gambled, or engaged in speculations of pure hazard, or who had not kept books, or not kept them fairly, or misapplied deposits, or violated trusts, or been guilty of any fraudulent practice. He was punished by imprisonment and hard labor for a term of years, and could not be discharged from his debts by any majority of his creditors whatever. Cession of property—in French, *la cession de biens*—was precisely the *cessio omnium bonorum* of the Romans, as established by Julius Cæsar. It applied to all persons, and obtained for them freedom from imprisonment, and from suits, on the surrender of all their present property to their creditors; leaving their future acquisitions liable for the remainder of the debt. It was the insolvent law of the civil law; and thus bankruptcy and insolvency were as distinct on the continent of Europe as in England and Scotland, and governed by the same principles.

Having read these extracts from the civil law, Mr. B. resumed his speech, and went on to say that the gentleman was as unfortunate in his visit to the continent as in his visit to Scotland. In the first place he had no right to go there for exemplification of the terms used in our constitution. The framers of the constitution did not look to other countries for examples. They looked to England alone. In the second place, if we sought them elsewhere, we found precisely the same thing that we found in England: we found bankruptcy and insolvency everywhere distinct and inconvertible. They were, and are, distinct everywhere; here and elsewhere—at home and abroad—in England, Scotland, France, and all over Europe. They have never been confounded anywhere, and cannot be confounded here, without committing a double offence: *first*, violating our own constitution; *secondly*, invading the States. And with this, I dismiss the gentleman's first fundamental position, affirming that he has utterly failed in his attempt to confound bankruptcy with insolvency; and, therefore, has utterly failed to gain jurisdiction for Congress over the general debts of the community, by the pretext of the bankrupt power.

I have said that this so-called bankrupt bill of ours is copied from the insolvent law of the first year of George IV., and its amendments, and so it is, all except section 13 of that act, which is omitted, and for the purpose of keeping out the distinction between bankrupts and insolvents. That section makes the distinction. The act permits all debtors to petition for the benefit of the insolvent law, that is to say, discharge from imprisonment on surrendering their property; yet, in every case in which traders, merchants, &c. petition, the proceedings stop until taken up, and proceeded upon by the creditors. The filing the petition by a person subject to the bankrupt law, is simply held to be an act of bankruptcy, on which the creditors may proceed, or not, as on any other act of bankruptcy, precisely as they please. And thus insolvency and bankruptcy are kept distinct; double provisions on the same subject are prevented; and consistency is preserved in the administration of the laws. Not so under our bill. The omission to copy this 13th section has nullified all that relates to involuntary bankruptcy; puts it into the power of those who are subject to that proceeding to avoid it, at their pleasure, by the simple and obvious process of availing themselves of their absolute right to proceed voluntarily. And now a word upon volunteer bankruptcy. It is an invention and a crudity in our bill, growing out of the confounding of bankruptcy and insolvency. There is no such thing in England, or in any bankrupt system in the world; and cannot be, without reversing all the rules of right, and subjecting the creditor to the mercy of his debtor. The English bankrupt act of the 6th George IV., and the insolvent debtors' act of the 1st of the same reign, admit the bankrupt, as an insolvent, to file his declaration of insolvency, and petition for relief; but there it stops. His voluntary action goes no further than the declaration and petition. Upon that, his creditors, if they please, may proceed against him as a bankrupt, taking the declaration as an act of bankruptcy. If they do not choose to proceed, the case stops. The bankrupt cannot bring his creditors into court, and prosecute his claim to bankruptcy, whether they will or not. This is clear from the 6th section of the bankrupt act of George IV., and the 13th section of the insolvent debtors' act of the 1st year of the same reign; and thus our act of 1841 has the honor of inventing volunteer bankruptcy, and thus putting the abolition of debts in the hands of every person! for these volunteers have a right to be discharged from their debts, without the consent of their creditors!

Mr. Benton then read the two sections of the two acts of George IV. to which he had referred, and commented upon them to sustain his positions. And first the 6th section of the act of George IV. (1826) for the amendment of the bankrupt laws:

> "SEC. 6. That if any such trader shall file in the office of the Lord Chancellor's secretary of bankrupts, a declaration in writing, signed by such trader, and attested by an attorney or solicitor, that he is insolvent or unable to meet his engagements, the said secretary of bankrupts, or his deputy, shall sign a memorandum that such declaration hath been filed; which memorandum shall be authority for the London Gazette to insert an advertisement of such declaration therein; and every such declaration shall, after such advertisement inserted as aforesaid, *be an act of bankruptcy committed by such* TRADER *at the time when such declaration was filed*: but *no* commission shall issue thereupon, *unless* it be sued out within two calendar months next after the insertion of such advertisement, and *unless* such advertisement shall have been inserted in the London Gazette within eight days after such declaration filed. And no docket

shall be struck upon such act of bankruptcy before the expiration of four days next after such insertion of such advertisement, in case such commission is to be executed in London; or before the expiration of eight days next after such insertion, in case such commission is to be executed in the country; and the Gazette containing such advertisement shall be evidence to be received of such declaration having been filed."

Having read this section, Mr. B. said it was explicit, and precluded argument. The voluntary action of the debtor, which it authorized, was limited to the mere filing of the declaration of insolvency. It went no further; and it was confined to traders—to the trading classes—who, alone, were subject to the laws of bankruptcy.

Mr. B. said that the English had, as we all know, an insolvent system, as well as a bankrupt system. They had an insolvent debtors' court, as well as a bankrupt court; and both these were kept separate, although there were no States in England to be trodden under foot by treading down the insolvent laws. Not so with us. Our insolvent laws, though belonging to States called sovereign, are all trampled under foot! There would be a time to go into this. At present, Mr. B. would only say that, in England, bankruptcy and insolvency were still kept distinct; and no insolvent trader was allowed to proceed as a bankrupt. On the contrary, an insolvent, applying in the insolvent debtors' court for the release of his person, could not proceed one step beyond filing his declaration. At that point the creditors took up the declaration, if they pleased, transferred the case to the bankrupt court, and prosecuted the case in that court. This is done by virtue of the 13th section of the insolvent debtors' act of 7th George IV. (1827). Mr. B. read the section, as follows:

"*Insolvent debtors' act of 7th year of George IV. (1827).*

"SEC. 13. *And be it further enacted*, That the filing of the petition of every *person* in actual custody, who shall be subject to the laws concerning bankrupts, and who shall apply by petition to the said court for his or her discharge from custody, according to this act, shall be accounted and adjudged *an act of bankruptcy from the time of filing such petition*; and that any *commission* issuing against such person, and under which he or she shall be declared bankrupt before the time appointed by the said court, and advertised in the *London Gazette*, for hearing the matters of such petition, or at any time within two calendar months from the time of filing such petition, shall have effect to avoid any conveyance and assignment of the estate and effects of such person, which shall have been made in pursuance of the provisions of this act: *Provided, always*, That the filing of such petition shall not be deemed an act of bankruptcy, *unless* such person be so declared bankrupt before the time so advertised as aforesaid, or within such two calendar months as aforesaid; but that every such conveyance and assignment shall be good and valid, notwithstanding any commission of bankruptcy under which such person shall be declared bankrupt after the time so advertised as aforesaid, and after the expiration of such two calendar months as aforesaid."

This (said Mr. B.) accords with the section of the year before in the bankrupt act. The two sections are accordant, and identical in their provisions. They keep up the great distinction between insolvency and bankruptcy, which some of our judges have undertaken to abrogate; they keep up, also, the great distinction between the proper subjects of bankruptcy—to wit: traders, and those who are not traders; and they keep up the distinction between the release of the person (which is the object of insolvent laws) and the extinction of the debt with the consent of creditors, which is the object of bankrupt systems. By this section, if the "*person*" in custody who files a declaration of insolvency shall be a trader, subject to the laws of bankruptcy, it only operates as an act of bankruptcy—upon which the creditors may proceed, or not, as they please. If they proceed, it is done by suing out a commission of bankruptcy; which carries the case to the bankrupt court. If the creditors do not proceed, the petition of the insolvent trader only releases his person. Being subject to bankruptcy, his creditors may call him into the bankrupt court, if they please; if they do not, he cannot take it there, nor claim the benefit of bankruptcy in the insolvent court: he can only get his person released. This is clear from the section; and our bill of 1841 committed something worse than a folly in not copying this section. That bill creates two sorts of bankruptcy—voluntary and involuntary—and, by a singular folly, makes them convertible! so that all may be volunteers, if they please. It makes merchants, traders, bankers, and some others of the *trading* classes, subject to involuntary bankruptcy: then it gives all *persons* whatever the right to proceed voluntarily. Thus the involuntary subjects of bankruptcy may become volunteers; and the distinction becomes ridiculous and null. Our bill, which is compiled from the English Insolvent Debtors' Act, and is itself nothing but an insolvent law perverted to the abolition of debts at the will of the debtor, should have copied the 13th section of the English insolvent law: for want of copying this, it annihilated involuntary bankruptcy—made all persons, traders or not, volunteers who chose to be so—released all debts, at the will of the debtor, without the consent of a single creditor; and committed the most daring legislative outrage upon the rights of property, which the world ever beheld!

CHAPTER LXVIII.

DISTRIBUTION OF THE PUBLIC LAND REVENUE AND ASSUMPTION OF THE STATE DEBTS.

About two hundred millions of dollars were due from States and corporations to creditors in Europe. These debts were in stocks, much depreciated by the failure in many instances to pay the accruing interest—in some instances, failure to provide for the principal. These creditors became uneasy, and wished the federal government to assume their debts. As early as the year 1838 this wish began to be manifested: in the year 1839 it was openly expressed: in the year 1840, it became a regular question, mixing itself up in our presidential election; and openly engaging the active exertions of foreigners. Direct assumption was not urged: indirect, by giving the public land revenue to the States, was the mode pursued, and the one recommended by Mr. Tyler. In his first regular message, he recommended this disposition of the public lands, and with the expressed view of enabling the States to pay their debts, and also to raise the value of the stock. It was a vicious recommendation, and a flagrant and pernicious violation of the constitution. It was the duty of Congress to provide for the payment of the federal debts: that was declared in the constitution. There was no prohibition upon the payment of the State debts: that was a departure from the objects of the Union too gross to require prohibition: and the absence of any authority to do so was a prohibition as absolute as if expressed in the eyes of all those who held to the limitations of the constitution, and considered a power, not granted, as a power denied. Mr. Calhoun spoke with force and clearness, and with more than usual animation, against this proposed breach in the constitution. He said:

> "If the bill should become a law, it would make a wider breach in the constitution, and be followed by changes more disastrous, than any other measure which has ever been adopted. It would, in its violation of the constitution, go far beyond the general welfare doctrine of former days, which stretched the power of the government as far as it was then supposed was possible by construction, however bold. But as wide as were the limits which it assigned to the powers of the government, it admitted by implication that there were limits; while this bill, as I shall show, rests on principles which, if admitted, would supersede all limits. According to the general welfare doctrine, Congress had power to raise money and appropriate it to all objects which might seem calculated to promote the general welfare—that is, the prosperity of the States, regarded in their aggregate character as members of the Union: or, to express it more briefly, and in language once so common, to national objects: thus excluding, by necessary implication, all were not national, as falling within the sphere of the separate States. It takes in what is excluded under the general welfare doctrine, and assumes for Congress the right to raise money, to give by distribution to the States: that is, to be applied by them to those very local State objects to which that doctrine, by necessary implication, denied that Congress had a right to appropriate money; and thus superseding all the limits of the constitution—as far, at least, as the money power is concerned. Such, and so overwhelming, are the constitutional difficulties which beset this measure. No one who can overcome them—who can bring himself to vote for this bill—need trouble himself about constitutional scruples hereafter. He may swallow without hesitation bank, tariff, and every other unconstitutional measure which has ever been adopted or proposed. Yes; it would be easier to make a plausible argument for the constitutionality of the measures proposed by the abolitionists—for abolition itself—than for this detestable bill. And yet we find senators from slaveholding States, the very safety of whose constituents depends upon a strict construction of the constitution, recording their names in favor of a measure from which they have nothing to hope, and every thing to fear. To what is a course so blind to be attributed, but to that fanaticism of party zeal, openly avowed on this floor, which regards the preservation of the power of the whig party as the paramount consideration? It has staked its existence on the passage of this, and the other measures for which this extraordinary session was called; and when it is brought to the alternative of their defeat or success, in their anxiety to avoid the one and secure the other, constituents, constitution, duty, country,—all are forgotten."

Clearly unconstitutional, the measure itself was brought forward at the most inauspicious time—when the Treasury was empty, a loan bill, and a tax bill actually depending; and measures going on to raise money from the customs, not only to support the government, but to supply the place of this very land money proposed to be given to the States. Mr. Benton exposed this aggravation in some pointed remarks:

What a time to choose for squandering this patrimony! We are just in the midst of loans, and taxes, and new and extravagant expenditures, and scraping high and low to find money to support the government. Congress was called together to provide revenue; and we begin with throwing away what we have. We have just passed a bill to borrow twelve millions, which will cost the people sixteen millions to pay. We have a bill on the calendar—the next one in order—to tax every thing now free, and to raise every tax now low, to raise eight or ten millions for the government, at the cost of eighteen or twenty to the people. Sixteen millions of deficit salute the commencement of the ensuing year. A new loan of twelve millions is announced for the next session. All the articles of consumption which escape taxation now, are to be caught and taxed then. Such are the revelations of the chairman of the Finance Committee; and they correspond with our own calculations of their conduct. In addition to all this, we have just commenced the national defences—neglected when we had forty millions of surplus, now obliged to be attended to when we have nothing: these defences are to cost above a hundred millions to create them, and above ten millions annually to sustain them. A new and frightful extravagance has broken out in the Indian Department. Treaties which cannot be named, are to cost millions upon millions. Wild savages, who cannot count a hundred except by counting their fingers ten times over, are to have millions; and the customs to pay all; for the lands are no longer to pay for themselves, or to discharge the heavy annuities which have grown out of their acquisition. The chances of a war ahead: the ordinary expenses of the government, under the new administration, not thirteen millions as was promised, but above thirty, as this session proves. To crown all, the federal party in power! that party whose instinct is debt and tax—whose passion is waste and squander—whose cry is that of the horse-leech, give! give! give!—whose call is that of the grave, more! more! more! In such circumstances, and with such prospects ahead, we are called upon to throw away the land revenue, and turn our whole attention to taxing and borrowing. The custom-house duties—that is to say, foreign commerce, founded upon the labor of the South and West, is to pay all. The farmers and planters of the South and West are to take the chief load, and to carry it. Well may the senator from Kentucky [Mr. CLAY] announce the forthcoming of new loans and taxes—the recapture of the tea and coffee tax, if they escape us now—and the increase and perpetuity of the salt tax. All this must come, and more too, if federalism rules a few years longer. A few years more under federal sway, at the rate things have gone on at this session—this sweet little session called to relieve the people—and our poor America would be ripe for the picture for which England now sits, and which has been so powerfully drawn in the Edinburgh Review. Listen to it, and hear what federalism would soon bring us to, if not stopped in its mad career:

> "Taxes upon every article which enters into the mouth, or covers the back, or is placed under the foot. Taxes upon every thing which it is pleasant to see, hear, feel, smell, or taste. Taxes upon warmth, light, and locomotion. Taxes on every thing on earth, and the waters under the earth; on every thing that comes from abroad, or is grown at home. Taxes on the raw material; taxes on every fresh value that is added to it by the industry of man. Taxes on the sauce which pampers a man's appetite, and the drug that restores him to health; on the ermine which decorates the judge, and the rope which hangs the criminal; on the brass nails of the coffin, and the ribbons of the bride. At bed or board, couchant or levant, we must pay. The schoolboy whips his taxed top; the beardless youth manages his taxed horse with a taxed bridle, on a taxed road. The dying Englishman pours his medicine, which has paid seven per cent., into a spoon that has paid fifteen per cent.; flings himself back upon his chintz bed, which has paid twenty-two per cent.; makes his will on an eight-pound stamp, and expires in the arms of an apothecary, who has paid a license of a hundred pounds for the privilege of putting him to death. His whole property is then immediately taxed from two to ten per cent. Besides the probate, large fees are demanded for burying him in the chancel; his virtues handed down to posterity on taxed marble, and he is then gathered to his fathers, to be taxed no more."

This is the way the English are now taxed, and so it would be with us if the federalists should remain a few years in power.

Execrable as this bill is in itself, and for its objects, and for the consequences which it draws after it, it is still more abominable for the time and manner in which it is driven through Congress, and the contingencies on which its passage is to depend. What is the time?—when the new States are just ready to double their representation, and to present a front which would command respect for their rights, and secure the grant of all their just demands. They are pounced upon in this nick of time, before the arrival of their full representation under the new census, to be manacled and fettered by a law which assumes to be a perpetual settlement of the land question, and to bind their interests for ever. This is the time! what is the manner?—gagged through the House of Representatives by the previous question, and by new rules fabricated from day to day, to stifle discussion, prevent amendments, suppress yeas and nays, and hide the deeds which shunned the light. This was the manner! What was the contingency on which its passage was to depend?—the passage of the bankrupt bill! So that this execrable bill, baited as it was with *douceurs* to old States, and bribes to the new ones, and pressed under the gag, and in the absence of the new representation, was still unable to get through without a bargain for passing the bankrupt bill at the same time. Can such legislation stand? Can God, or man, respect such work?

But a circumstance which distinguished the passage of this bill from all others—which up to that day was without a precedent—was the open exertion of a foreign interest to influence our legislation. This interest had already exerted itself in our presidential election: it now appeared in our legislation. Victorious in the election, they attended Congress to see that their expectations were not disappointed. The lobbies of the House contained them: the boarding-houses of the whig members were their resort: the democracy kept aloof, though under other circumstances they would have been glad to have paid honor to respectable strangers, only avoided now on account of interest and exertions in our elections and legislation. Mr. Fernando Wood of New York brought this scandal to the full notice of the House. "In connection with this point I will add that, at the time this cheat was in preparation—the merchants' petition being drawn up by the brokers and speculators for the congressional market—there were conspicuous bankers in Wall street, anxious observers, if not co-laborers in the movement. Among them might be named Mr. Bates, partner of the celebrated house of Baring, Brothers & Company; Mr. Cryder, of the equally celebrated house of Morrison, Cryder & Company; Mr. Palmer, junior, son of Mr. Horsley Palmer, now, or lately, the governor of the Bank of England. Nor were these 'allies' seen only in Wall street. Their visits were extended to the capitol; and since the commencement of the debate upon this bill in the other House, they have been in the lobbies, attentive, and apparently interested listeners. I make no comment. Comment is unnecessary. I state facts—undeniable facts: and it is with feelings akin to humiliation and shame that I stand up here and state them." These respectable visitors had a twofold object in their attention to our legislation—the getting a national bank established, as well as the State debts provided for. Mr. Benton also pointed out this outrage upon our legislation:

He then took a rapid view of the bill—its origin, character, and effects; and showed it to be federal in its origin, associated with all the federal measures of the present and past sessions; with bank, tariff, assumption of State debts, dependent upon the bankrupt bill for its passage; violative of the constitution and the compacts with the new States; and crowning all its titles to infamy by drawing capitalists from London to attend this extra session of Congress, to promote the passage of this bill for their own benefit. He read a paragraph from the money article in a New York paper, reciting the names and attendance, on account of this bill, of the foreign capitalists at Washington. The passage was in these words:

> "At the commencement of the session, almost every foreign house had a representative here. Wilson, Palmer, Cryder, Bates, Willinck, Hope, Jaudon, and a host of others, came over on various pretences; all were in attendance at Washington, and all seeking to forward the proposed measures. The land bill was to give them three millions per annum from the public Treasury, or thirty millions in ten years, and to raise the value of the stock at least thirty millions more. The revenue bill was to have supplied the deficiency in the Treasury. The loan bill was to have been the basis of an increase of importations and of exchange operations; and the new bank was the instrument of putting the whole in operation."

This Mr. Benton accompanied by an article from a London paper, showing that the capitalists in that city were counting upon the success of their emissaries at Washington, and that the passage of this land bill was the first and most anxious wish of their hearts—that they considered it equivalent to the assumption of the State debts—and that the benefit of the bill would go to themselves. This established the character of the bill, and showed that it had been the means of bringing upon the national legislation the degrading and corrupting influences of a foreign interference. For the first time in the history of our government, foreigners have attended our Congress, to promote the passage of laws for their own benefit. For the first time we have had London capitalists for lobby members; and, mortifying to be told, instead of being repulsed by defeat, they have been encouraged by success; and their future attendance may now be looked for as a matter of course, at our future sessions of Congress, when they have debts to secure, stocks to enhance, or a national bank to establish.

Mr. Benton also denounced the bill for its unconstitutionality, its demagogue character, its demoralizing tendencies, its bid for popularity, and its undaunted attempt to debauch the people with their own money.

The gentleman from Virginia [Mr. ARCHER], to whose speech I am now replying, in allusion to the frequent cry of breach of the constitution, when there is no breach, says he is sick and weary of the cry, wolf! wolf! when there is no wolf. I say so too. The constitution should not be trifled with—should not be invoked on every petty occasion—should not be proclaimed in danger when there is no danger. Granting that this has been done sometimes—that too often, and with too little consideration, the grave question of constitutionality has been pressed into trivial discussions, and violation proclaimed where there was none: granting this, I must yet be permitted to say that such is not the case now. It is not now a cry of wolf! when there is no wolf. It is no false or sham cry now. The boy cries in earnest this time. The wolf has come! Long, lank, gaunt, hungry, voracious, and ferocious, the beast is here! howling, for its prey, and determined to have it at the expense of the life of the shepherd. The political stockjobbers and gamblers raven for the public lands, and tear the constitution to pieces to get at them. They seize, pillage, and plunder the lands. It is not a case of misconstruction, but of violation. It is not a case of misunderstanding the constitution, but of assault and battery—of maim and murder—of homicide and assassination—committed upon it. Never has such a daring outrage been perpetrated—never such a contravention of the object of a confederation—never such a total perversion, and barefaced departure, from all the purposes for which a community of States bound themselves together for the defence, and not for the plunder of each other. No, sir! no! The constitution was not made to divide money. This confederacy was not framed for a distribution among its members of lands, money, property, or effects of any kind. It contains rules and directions for raising money—for levying duties equally, which the new tariff will violate; and for raising direct taxes in proportion to federal population; but it contains no rule for dividing money; and the distributors have to make one as they go, and the rule they make is precisely the one that is necessary to carry the bill; and that varies with the varying strength of the distributing party. In 1836, in the deposit act, it was the federal representation in the two Houses of Congress: in this bill, as it came from the House of Representatives, it was the federal numbers. We have put in representation: it will come back to us with numbers; and numbers will prevail; for it is a mere case of plunder—the plunder of the young States by the old ones—of the weak by the strong. Sir, it is sixteen years since these schemes of distribution were brought into this chamber, and I have viewed them all in the same light, and given them all the same indignant opposition. I have opposed all these schemes as unconstitutional, immoral, fatal to the Union, degrading to the people, debauching to the States; and inevitably tending to centralism on one hand or to disruption on the other. I have opposed the whole, beginning with the first proposition of a senator from New Jersey [Mr. DICKERSON], to divide five millions of the sinking fund, and following the baneful scheme through all its modifications for the distribution of surplus revenue, and finally of land revenue. I have opposed the whole, adhering to the constitution, and to the objects of the confederacy, and scorning the ephemeral popularity which a venal system of plunder could purchase from the victims, or the dupes of a false and sordid policy.

I scorn the bill: I scout its vaunted popularity: I detest it. Nor can I conceive of an object more pitiable and contemptible than that of the demagogue haranguing for votes, and exhibiting his tables of dollars and acres, in order to show each voter, or each State, how much money they will be able to obtain from the Treasury if the land bill passes. Such haranguing, and such exhibition, is the address of impudence and knavery to supposed ignorance, meanness, and folly. It is treating the people as if they were penny wise and pound foolish; and still more mean than foolish. Why, the land revenue, after deducting the expenses, if fairly divided among the people, would not exceed ninepence a head per annum; if fairly divided among the States, and applied to their debts, it would not supersede above ninepence per annum of taxation upon the units of the population. The day for land sales have gone by. The sales of this year do not exceed a million and a half of dollars, which would not leave more than a million for distribution; which, among sixteen millions of people would be exactly fourpence half penny, Virginia money, per head! a *fip* in New York, and a *picaillon* in Louisiana. At two millions, it would be ninepence a head in Virginia, equivalent to a *levy* in New York, and a *bit* in Louisiana! precisely the amount which, in specie times, a gentleman gives to a negro boy for holding his horse a minute at the door. And for this miserable doit—this insignificant subdivision of a shilling—a York shilling—can the demagogue suppose that the people are base enough to violate their constitution, mean enough to surrender the defence of their country, and stupid enough to be taxed in their coffee, tea, salt, sugar, coats, hats, blankets, shoes, shirts; and every article of comfort, decency, or necessity, which they eat, drink, or wear; or on which they stand, sit, sleep, or lie?

The bill was bound to pass. Besides being in the same boat with the other cardinal whig measures—bank, bankrupt, repeal of independent treasury—and all arranged to pass together; and besides being pushed along and supported by the London bankers—it contained within itself the means of success. It was richly freighted with inducements to conciliate every interest. To every new State it made a preliminary distribution of ten per centum (in addition to the five per centum allowed by compact), on the amount of the sales within the State: then it came in for a full share of all the rest in proportion to its population. To the same new States it gave also five hundred thousand acres of land; or a quantity sufficient to make up that amount where less had been granted. To the settlers in the new States, including foreigners who had made the declaration of their intentions to become naturalized citizens, it gave a pre-emption right in the public lands, to the amount of one quarter section: 160 acres. Then it distributed the whole amount of the land revenue, after deduction of the ten and the five per centum to the new States, to all the old States and new States together, in proportion to their population: and included all the States yet to be created in this scheme of distribution. And that no part of the people should go without their share in these largesses, the Territories, though not States, and the District of Columbia, though not a Territory, were also embraced in the plan—each to receive in proportion to its numbers. So many inducements to all sections of the country to desire the bill, and such a chance for popularity to its authors, made sure, not only of its passage, but of its claim to the national gratitude. To the eye of patriotism, it was all a venal proceeding—an attempt to buy up the people with their own money—having the money to borrow first. For it so happened that while the distribution bill was passing in one House, to divide out money among the States and the people, there was a loan bill depending in the other House, to borrow twelve millions of dollars for three years; and also, a tax bill to produce eighteen millions a year to reimburse that loan, and to defray the current expenses of the government. To make a gratuitous distribution of the land revenue (equal to several millions per annum), looked like fatuity; and was so in a financial or governmental point of view. But it was supposed that the distribution scheme would be irresistibly popular—that it would chain the people and the States to the party which passed it—and insure them success in the ensuing presidential elections. Baseless calculation, as it applied to the people! Vain hope, as it applied to themselves! The very men that passed the bill had to repeal it, under the sneaking term of suspension, before their terms of service were out—within less than one year from the time it was passed! to be precise, within eleven calendar months and twelve days, from the day of its passage—counting from the days, inclusive of both, on which John Tyler, President, approved and disapproved it—whereof, hereafter. But it passed! and was obliged to pass. It was a case of mutual assurance with the other whig measures, and passed the Senate by a party vote— Mr. Preston excepted—who "broke ranks," and voted with the democracy, making the negative vote 23. The yeas and nays were:

YEAS—Messrs. Archer, Barrow, Bates, Bayard, Berrien, Choate, Clay of Kentucky, Clayton, Dixon, Evans, Graham, Henderson, Huntington, Kerr, Mangum, Merrick, Miller, Morehead,

Phelps, Porter, Prentiss, Rives, Simmons, Smith of Indiana, Southard, Tallmadge, White, Woodbridge.

NAYS—Messrs. Allen, Benton, Buchanan, Calhoun, Clay of Alabama, Cuthbert, Fulton, King, Linn, McRoberts, Mouton, Nicholson, Pierce, Preston, Sevier, Smith of Connecticut, Sturgeon, Tappan, Walker, Williams, Woodbury, Wright, Young.

In the House the vote was close—almost even—116 to 108. The yeas and nays were:

YEAS—Messrs. John Quincy Adams, Elisha H. Allen, Landaff W. Andrews, Sherlock J. Andrews, Thomas D. Arnold, John B. Aycrigg, Alfred Babcock, Osmyn Baker, Daniel D. Barnard, Victory Birdseye, Henry Black, Bernard Blair, William W. Boardman, Nathaniel B. Borden, John M. Botts, George N. Briggs, John H. Brockway, David Bronson, Jeremiah Brown, Barker Burnell, William B. Calhoun, Thomas J. Campbell, Robert L. Caruthers, Thomas C. Chittenden, John C. Clark, Staley N. Clarke, James Cooper, Benjamin S. Cowen, Robert B. Cranston, James H. Cravens, Caleb Cushing, Edmund Deberry, John Edwards, Horace Everett, William P. Fessenden, Millard Fillmore, A. Lawrence Foster, Seth M. Gates, Meredith P. Gentry, Joshua R. Giddings, William L. Goggin, Patrick G. Goode, Willis Green, John Greig, Hiland Hall, William Halstead, William S. Hastings, Thomas Henry, Charles Hudson, Hiram P. Hunt, James Irvin, William W. Irvin, Francis James, William Cost Johnson, Isaac D. Jones, John P. Kennedy, Henry S. Lane, Joseph Lawrence, Archibald L. Linn, Thomas F. Marshall, Samson Mason, Joshua Mathiot, John Mattocks, John P. B. Maxwell, John Maynard, John Moore, Christopher Morgan, Calvary Morris, Jeremiah Morrow, Thomas B. Osborne, Bryan Y. Owsley, James A. Pearce, Nathaniel G. Pendleton, John Pope, Cuthbert Powell, George H. Proffit, Robert Ramsey, Benjamin Randall, Alexander Randall, Joseph F. Randolph, Kenneth Rayner, Joseph Ridgway, George B. Rodney, William Russel, Leverett Saltonstall, John Sergeant, William Simonton, William Slade, Truman Smith, Augustus R. Sollers, James C. Sprigg, Edward Stanly, Samuel Stokely, Charles C. Stratton, Alexander H. H. Stuart, George W. Summers, John Taliaferro, John B. Thompson, Richard W. Thompson, Joseph L. Tillinghast, George W. Toland, Thomas A. Tomlinson, Philip Triplett, Joseph Trumbull, Joseph R. Underwood, Henry Van Rensselaer, David Wallace, William H. Washington, Edward D. White, Joseph L. White, Thomas W. Williams, Lewis Williams, Joseph L. Williams, Robert C. Winthrop, Thomas Jones Yorke, Augustus Young, John Young.

Those who voted in the negative, are:

NAYS—Messrs. Julius C. Alford, Archibald H. Arrington, Charles G. Atherton, Linn Banks, Henry W. Beeson, Benjamin A. Bidlack, Samuel S. Bowne, Linn Boyd, David P. Brewster, Aaron V. Brown, Milton Brown, Joseph Egbert, Charles G. Ferris, John G. Floyd, Joseph Fornance, Thomas F. Foster, Roger L. Gamble, Thomas W. Gilmer, William O. Goode, Samuel Gordon, James Graham, Amos Gustine, Richard W. Habersham, William A. Harris, John Hastings, Samuel L. Hays, Isaac E. Holmes, George W. Hopkins, Jacob Houck, jr., George S. Houston, Edmund W. Hubard, Robert M. T. Hunter, William Jack, Cave Johnson, John W. Jones, George M. Keim, Edmund Burke, Sampson H. Butler, William Butler, William O. Butler, Green W. Caldwell, Patrick C. Caldwell, John Campbell, William B. Campbell, George B. Cary, Reuben Chapman, Nathan Clifford, Andrew Kennedy, Thomas Butler King, Dixon H. Lewis, Nathaniel S. Littlefield, Joshua A. Lowell, Abraham McClellan, Robert McClellan, James J. McKay, John McKeon, Francis Mallory, Albert G. Marchand, Alfred Marshall, John Thompson Mason, James Mathews, William Medill, James A. Meriwether, John Miller, Peter Newhard, Eugenius A. Nisbet, William M. Oliver, William Parmenter, Samuel Patridge, William W. Payne, Francis W. Pickens, Arnold Plumer, James G. Clinton, Walter Coles, John R. J. Daniel, Richard D. Davis, John B. Dawson, Ezra Dean, Davis Dimock, jr., William Doan, Andrew W. Doig, Ira A. Eastman, John C. Edwards, John R.

Reding, Abraham Rencher, R. Barnwell Rhett, Lewis Riggs, James Rogers, James I. Roosevelt, John Sanford, Romulus M. Saunders, Tristram Shaw, Augustine H. Shepperd, Benjamin G. Shields, John Snyder, Lewis Steenrod, Thomas D. Sumter, George Sweney, Hopkins L. Turney, John Van Buren, Aaron Ward, Lott Warren, Harvey M. Watterson, John B. Weller, John Westbrook, James W. Williams, Henry A. Wise, Fernando Wood.

The progress of the abuse inherent in a measure so vicious, was fully illustrated in the course of these distribution-bills. First, they were merely to relieve the distresses of the people: now they were to make payment of State debts, and to enhance the price of State stocks in the hands of London capitalists. In the beginning they were to divide a surplus on hand, for which the government had no use, and which ought to be returned to the people who had paid it, and who now needed it: afterwards it was to divide the land-money years ahead without knowing whether there would be any surplus or not: now they are for dividing money when there is none to divide—when there is a treasury deficit—and loans and taxes required to supply it. Originally, they were for short and limited terms—first, for one year—afterwards for five years: now for perpetuity. This bill provides for eternity. It is a curiosity in human legislation, and contained a clause which would be ridiculous if it had not been impious—an attempt to manacle future Congresses, and to bind posterity through unborn generations. The clause ran in these words: That if, at any time during the existence of this act, duties on imported goods should be raised above the rate of the twenty per centum on the value as provided in the compromise act of 1833, then the distribution of the land revenue should be suspended, and continue so until reduced to that rate; and then be resumed. Fallacious attempt to bind posterity! It did not even bind those who made it: for the same Congress disregarded it. But it shows to what length the distribution spirit had gone; and that even protective tariff—that former sovereign remedy for all the wants of the people—was sacrificed to it. Mr. Clay undertaking to bind all the Congresses for ever to uniform twenty per centum ad valorem duties. And while the distribution-bill thus undertook to protect and save the compromise of 1833, the new tariff-bill of this session, undertook to return the favor by assuming to protect and save the distribution-bill. Its second section contained this proviso: That if any duty exceeding twenty per centum on the value shall be levied before the 30th day of June, 1842, it should not stop the distribution of the land revenue, as provided for in the distribution act of the present session. Thus, the two acts were made mutual assurers, each stipulating for the life of the other, and connecting things which had no mutual relation except in the coalitions of politicians; but, like other assurers, not able to save the lives they assured. Both acts were gone in a year! And the marvel is how such flimsy absurdities could be put into a statute? And the answer, from the necessity of conciliating some one's vote, without which the bills could not pass. Thus, some Southern anti-tariff men would not vote for the distribution bill unless the compromise of 1833 was protected; and some distribution men of the West would not vote for the anti-tariff act unless the distribution bill was protected. And hence the ridiculous, presumptuous, and idle expedient of mutually insuring each other.

CHAPTER LXIX.

INSTITUTION OF THE HOUR RULE IN DEBATE IN THE HOUSE OF REPRESENTATIVES: ITS ATTEMPT, AND REPULSE IN THE SENATE.

This session is remarkable for the institution of the hour rule in the House of Representatives—the largest limitation upon the freedom of debate which any deliberative assembly ever imposed upon itself, and presents an eminent instance of permanent injury done to free institutions in order to get rid of a temporary annoyance. It was done at a time when the party, called whig, was in full predominance in both Houses of Congress, and in the impatience of delay in the enactment of their measures. It was essentially a whig measure—though with exceptions each way—the body of the whigs going for it; the body of the democracy against it—several eminent whigs voting with them: Mr. John Quincy Adams, William C. Dawson, James A. Pearce, Kenneth Rayner, Edward Stanly, Alexander H. H. Stuart, Edward D. White and others. Mr. Lott Warren moved the rule as an amendment to the body of the rules; and, in the same moment, moved the previous question: which was carried. The vote was immediately taken, and the rule established by a good majority—only seventy-five members voting against it. They were:

> Messrs. John Quincy Adams, Archibald H. Arrington, Charles G. Atherton, Linn Banks, Daniel D. Barnard, John M. Botts, Samuel S. Bowne, Linn Boyd, David P. Brewster, Aaron V. Brown, Edmund Burke, Barker Burnell, Green W. Caldwell, John Campbell, Robert L. Caruthers, George B. Cary, Reuben Chapman, James G. Clinton, Walter Coles, John R. J. Daniel, Wm. C. Dawson, Ezra Dean, Andrew W. Doig, Ira A. Eastman, Horace Everett, Charles G. Ferris, John G. Floyd, Charles A. Floyd, William O. Goode, Samuel Gordon, Samuel L. Hays, George W. Hopkins, Jacob Houck, jr., Edmund W. Hubard, Charles Hudson, Hiram P. Hunt, William W. Irwin, William Jack, Cave Johnson, John W. Jones, George M. Keim, Andrew Kennedy, Thomas Butler King, Dixon H. Lewis, Nathaniel S. Littlefield, Joshua A. Lowell, Abraham McClellan, Robert McClellan, James J. McKay, Francis Mallory, Alfred Marshall, Samson Mason, John Thompson Mason, John Miller, Peter Newhard, William Parmenter, William W. Payne, James A. Pearce, Francis W. Pickens, Kenneth Rayner, John R. Reding, Lewis Riggs, Romulus M. Saunders, William Slade, John Snyder, Augustus R. Sollers, James C. Sprigg, Edward Stanly, Lewis Steenrod, Alexander H. H. Stuart, Hopkins L. Turney, Aaron Ward, John Westbrook, Edward D. White, Joseph L. Williams.

The Roman republic had existed four hundred and fifty years, and was verging towards its fall under the first triumvirate—(Cæsar, Pompey, and Crassus)—before pleadings were limited to two hours before the JUDICES SELECTI. In the Senate the speeches of senators were never limited at all; but even the partial limitation then placed upon judicial pleadings, but which were, in fact, popular orations, drew from Cicero an affecting deprecation of its effect upon the cause of freedom, as well as upon the field of eloquence. The reader of the admired treatise on oratory, and notices of celebrated orators, will remember his lamentation—as wise in its foresight of evil consequences to free institutions, as mournful and affecting in its lamentation over the decline of oratory. Little could he have supposed that a popular assembly should ever exist, and in a country where his writings were read, which would voluntarily impose upon itself a far more rigorous limitation than the one over which he grieved. Certain it is, that with our incessant use of the previous question, which cuts off all debate, and the hour rule which limits a speech to sixty minutes (constantly reduced by interruptions); and the habit of fixing an hour at which the question shall be taken, usually brief, and the intermediate little time not secure for that question: with all these limitations upon the freedom of debate in the House, certain it is that such an anomaly was never seen in a deliberative assembly, and the business of a people never transacted in the midst of such ignorance of what they are about by those who are doing it.

No doubt the license of debate has been greatly abused in our halls of Congress—as in those of the British parliament: but this suppression of debate is not the correction of the abuse, but the destruction of the liberty of speech: and that, not as a personal privilege, but as a representative right, essential to the welfare of the people. For fifty years of our government there was no such suppression: in no other country is there the parallel to it. Yet in all popular assemblies there is an abuse in the liberty of speech, inherent in the right of speech, which gives to faction and folly the same latitude as to wisdom and patriotism. The English have found the best corrective: it is in the House itself—its irregular power: its refusal to hear a member further when they are tired of him. A significant scraping and coughing warns the annoying speaker when he should cease: if the warning is not taken, a tempest drowns his voice: when he appeals to the chair, the chair recommends him to yield to the temper of the House. A few examples reduce the practice to a rule—insures its observance; and works the correction of the abuse without the destruction of debate. No man speaking to the subject, and giving information to the House, was ever scraped and coughed down, in the British House of Commons. No matter how plain his language, how awkward his manner, how confused his delivery, so long as he gives information he is heard attentively; while the practice falls with just, and relentless effect upon the loquacious members, who mistake volubility for eloquence, who delight themselves while annoying the House—who are insensible to the proprieties of time and place, take the subject for a point to stand on: and then speak off from it in all directions, and equally without continuity of ideas or disconnection of words. The practice of the British House of Commons puts an end to all such annoyance, while saving every thing profitable that any member can utter.

The first instance of enforcing this new rule stands thus recorded in the Register of Debates:

"Mr. PICKENS proceeded, in the next place to point out the items of expenditure which might, without the least injury to the interests of the government or to the public service, suffer retrenchment. He quoted the report of the Secretary of the Treasury of December 9, 1840; from it he took the several items, and then stated how much, in his opinion, each might be reduced. The result of the first branch of this reduction of particulars was a sum to be retrenched amounting to $852,000. He next went into the items of pensions, the Florida war, and the expenditures of Congress; on these, with a few minor ones in addition, he estimated that there might, without injury, be a saving of four millions. Mr. P. had gotten thus far in his subject, and was just about to enter into a comparison of the relative advantages of a loan and of Treasury notes, when

"The Chair here reminded Mr. Pickens that his hour had expired.

"Mr. PICKENS. The hour out?

"The CHAIR. Yes, sir.

"Mr. PICKENS. [Looking at his watch.] Bless my soul! Have I run my race?

"Mr. HOLMES asked whether his colleague had not taken ten minutes for explanations?

"Mr. Warren desired that the rule be enforced.

"Mr. PICKENS denied that the House had any constitutional right to pass such a rule.

"The CHAIR again reminded Mr. Pickens that he had spoken an hour.

"Mr. PICKENS would, then, conclude by saying it was the most infamous rule ever passed by any legislative body.

"Mr. J. G. FLOYD of New York, said the gentleman had been frequently interrupted, and had, therefore, a right to continue his remarks.

"The CHAIR delivered a contrary opinion.

"Mr. FLOYD appealed from his decision.

"The CHAIR then rose to put the question, whether the decision of the Chair should stand as the judgment of the House? when

"Mr. FLOYD withdrew his appeal.

"Mr. DAWSON suggested whether the Chair had not possibly made a mistake with respect to the time.

"The CHAIR said there was no mistake.

"Mr. PICKENS then gave notice that he would offer an amendment.

"The CHAIR remarked that the gentleman was not in order.

"Mr. PICKENS said that if the motion to strike out the enacting clause should prevail, he would move to amend the bill by introducing a substitute, giving ample means to the Treasury, but avoiding the evils of which he complained in the bill now under consideration."

The measure having succeeded in the House which made the majority master of the body, and enabled them to pass their bills without resistance or exposure, Mr. Clay undertook to do the same thing in the Senate. He was impatient to pass his bills, annoyed at the resistance they met, and dreadfully harassed by the species of warfare to which they were subjected; and for which he had no turn. The democratic senators acted upon a system, and with a thorough organization, and a perfect understanding. Being a minority, and able to do nothing, they became assailants, and attacked incessantly; not by formal orations against the whole body of a measure, but by sudden, short, and pungent speeches, directed against the vulnerable parts; and pointed by proffered amendments. Amendments were continually offered—a great number being prepared every night, and placed in suitable hands for use the next day—always commendably calculated to expose an evil, and to present a remedy. Near forty propositions of amendment were offered to the first fiscal agent bill alone—the yeas and nays taken upon them seven and thirty times. All the other prominent bills—distribution, bankrupt, fiscal corporation—new tariff act, called revenue—were served the same way. Every proposed amendment made an issue, which fixed public attention, and would work out in our favor—end as it might. If we carried it, which was seldom, there was a good point gained: if we lost it, there was a bad point exposed. In either event we had the advantage of discussion, which placed our adversaries in the wrong; and the speaking fact of the yeas and nays—which told how every man was upon every point. We had in our ranks every variety of speaking talent, from plain and calm up to fiery and brilliant—and all matter-of-fact men—their heads well stored with knowledge. There were but twenty-two of us; but every one a speaker, and effective. We kept their measures upon the anvil, and hammered them continually: we impaled them against the wall, and stabbed them incessantly. The Globe newspaper was a powerful ally (Messrs. Blair and Rives); setting off all we did to the best advantage in strong editorials—and carrying out our speeches, fresh and hot, to the people: and we felt victorious in the midst of unbroken defeats. Mr. Clay's temperament could not stand it, and he was determined to silence the troublesome minority, and got the acquiescence of his party, and the promise of their support: and boldly commenced his operations—avowing his design, at the same time, in open Senate.

It was on the 12th day of July—just four days after the new rule had been enforced in the House, and thereby established (for up to that day, it was doubtful whether it could be enforced)—that Mr. Clay made his first movement towards its introduction in the Senate; and in reply to Mr. Wright of New York—one of the last men in the world to waste time in the Senate, or to speak without edification to those who would listen. It was on the famous fiscal bank bill, and on a motion of Mr. Wright to strike out the large subscription reserved for the government, so as to keep the government unconnected with the business of the bank. The mover made some remarks in favor of his motion—to which Mr. Clay replied: and then went on to say:

"He could not help regarding the opposition to this measure as one eminently calculated to delay the public business, with no other object that he could see than that of protracting to the last moment the measures for which this session had been expressly called to give to the people. This too was at a time when the whole country was crying out in an agony of distress for relief."

These remarks, conveying a general imputation upon the minority senators of factious conduct in delaying the public business, and thwarting the will of the people, justified an answer from any one of them to whom it was applicable: and first received it from Mr. Calhoun.

Mr. Calhoun was not surprised at the impatience of the senator from Kentucky, though he was at his attributing to this side of the chamber the delays and obstacles thrown in the way of his favorite measure. How many days did the senator himself spend in amending his own bill? The bill had been twelve days before the Senate, and eight of those had been occupied by the friends of the bill. That delay did not originate on this side of the House; but now that the time which was cheerfully accorded to him and his friends is to be reciprocated, before half of it is over, the charge of factious delay is raised. Surely the urgency and impatience of the senator and his friends cannot be so very great that the minority must not be allowed to employ as many days in amending their bill as they took themselves to alter it. The senator from Kentucky says he is afraid, if we go on in this way, we will not get through the measures of this session till the last of autumn. Is not the fault in himself, and in the nature of the measures he urges so impatiently? These measures are such as the senators in the minority are wholly opposed to on principle—such as they conscientiously believe are unconstitutional— and is it not then right to resist them, and prevent, if they can, all invasions of the constitution? Why does he build upon such unreasonable expectations as to calculate on carrying measures of this magnitude and importance with a few days of hasty legislation on each? What are the measures proposed by the senator? They comprise the whole federal system, which it took forty years, from 1789 to 1829, to establish—but which are now, happily for the country, prostrate in the dust. And it is these measures, fraught with such important results that are now sought to be hurried through in one extra session; measures which, without consuming one particle of useless time to discuss fully, would require, instead of an extra session of Congress, four or five regular sessions. The senator said the country was in agony, crying for "action," "action." He understood whence that cry came—it came from the holders of State stocks, the men who expected another expansion, to relieve themselves at the expense of government. "Action"—"action," meant nothing but "plunder," "plunder," "plunder;" and he assured the gentleman, that he could not be more anxious in urging on a system of plunder than he (Mr. Calhoun) would be in opposing it. He so understood the senator, and he inquired of him, whether he called this an insidious amendment?

This was a sharp reply, just in its retort, spirited in its tone, judicious in expanding the basis of the new debate that was to come on; and greatly irritated Mr. Clay. He immediately felt that he had no right to impeach the motives of senators, and catching up Mr. Calhoun on that point, and strongly contesting it, brought on a rapid succession of contradictory asseverations: Thus:

"Mr. CLAY. I said no such thing, sir; I did not say any thing about the *motives* of senators.

"Mr. CALHOUN said he understood the senator's meaning to be that the motives of the opposition were factious and frivolous.

"Mr. CLAY. I said no such thing, sir.

"Mr. CALHOUN. It was so understood.

"Mr. CLAY. No, sir; no, sir.

"Mr. CALHOUN. Yes, sir, yes; it could be understood in no other way.

"Mr. CLAY. What I did say, was, that the *effect* of such amendments, and of consuming time in debating them, would be a waste of that time from the business of the session; and, consequently, would produce unnecessary delay and embarrassment. I said nothing of *motives*—I only spoke of the practical *effect* and result.

"Mr. CALHOUN said he understood it had been repeated for the second time that there could be no other motive or object entertained by the senators in the opposition, in making amendments and speeches on this bill, than to embarrass the majority by frivolous and vexatious delay.

"Mr. CLAY insisted that he made use of no assertions as to *motives*.

"Mr. CALHOUN. If the senator means to say that he does not accuse this side of the House of bringing forward propositions for the sake of delay, he wished to understand him.

"Mr. CLAY. I intended that.

"Mr. CALHOUN repeated that he understood the senator to mean that the senators in the opposition were spinning out the time for no other purpose but that of delaying and embarrassing the majority.

"Mr. CLAY admitted that was his meaning, though not thus expressed."

So ended this keen colloquy in which the pertinacity, and clear perceptions of Mr. Calhoun brought out the admission that the impeachment of motives was intended, but not expressed. Having got this admission Mr. Calhoun went on to defy the accusation of faction and frivolity, and to declare a determination in the minority to continue in their course; and put a peremptory question to Mr. Clay.

"Mr. Calhoun observed that to attempt, by such charges of factious and frivolous motives, to silence the opposition, was wholly useless. He and his friends had principles to contend for that were neither new nor frivolous, and they would here now, and at all times, and in all places, maintain them against those measures, in whatever way they thought most efficient. Did the senator from Kentucky mean to apply to the Senate the gag law passed in the other branch of Congress? If he did, it was time he should know that he (Mr. Calhoun), and his friends were ready to meet him on that point."

This question, and the avowed readiness to meet the gagging attempt, were not spoken without warrant. The democratic senators having got wind of what was to come, had consulted together and taken their resolve to defy and to dare it—to resist its introduction, and trample upon the rule, if voted: and in the mean time to gain an advantage with the public by rendering odious their attempt. Mr. Clay answered argumentatively for the rule, and that the people were for it:

"Let those senators go into the country, and they will find the whole body of the people complaining of the delay and interruption of the national business, by their long speeches in Congress; and if they will be but admonished by the people, they will come back with a lesson to cut short their debating, and give their attention more to action than to words. Who ever heard that the people would be dissatisfied with the abridgment of speeches in Congress? He had never heard the shortness of speeches complained of. Indeed, he should not be surprised if the people would got up remonstrances against lengthy speeches in Congress."

With respect to the defiance, Mr. Clay returned it, and declared his determination to bring forward the measure.

"With regard to the intimation of the gentleman from South Carolina [Mr. CALHOUN], he understood him and his course perfectly well, and told him and his friends that, for himself, he knew not how his friends would act; he was ready at any moment to bring forward and support a measure which should give to the majority the control of the business of the Senate of the United States. Let them denounce it as much as they pleased in advance: unmoved by any of their denunciations and threats, standing firm in the support of the interests which he believed the country demands, for one, he was ready for the adoption of a rule which would place the business of the Senate under the control of a majority of the Senate."

Mr. Clay was now committed to bring forward the measure; and was instantly and defyingly invited to do so.

"Mr. CALHOUN said there was no doubt of the senator's predilection for a gag law. Let him bring on that measure as soon as ever he pleases.

"Mr. BENTON. Come on with it."

Without waiting for any thing further from Mr. Clay, Mr. Calhoun proceeded to show him, still further, how little his threat was heeded and taunted him with wishing to revive the spirit of the alien and sedition laws:

"Mr. CALHOUN said it must be admitted that if the senator was not acting on the federal side, he would find it hard to persuade the American people of the fact, by showing them his love of gag laws, and strong disposition to silence both the national councils and the press. Did he not remember something about an alien and sedition law, and can he fail to perceive the relationship with the measure he contemplates to put down debate here? What is the difference, in principle, between his gag law and the alien and sedition law? We are gravely told that the speaking of the representatives of the people, which is to convey to them full information on the subjects of legislation in their councils, is worse than useless, and must be abated. Who consumed the time of last Congress in long speeches, vexatious and frivolous attempts to embarrass and thwart the business of the country, and useless opposition, tending to no end but that out of doors, the presidential election? Who but the senator and his party, then in the minority? But now, when they are in the majority, and the most important measures ever pressed forward together in one session, he is the first to threaten a gag law, to choke off debate, and deprive the minority even of the poor privilege of entering their protest."

Of all the members of the Senate, one of the mildest and most amicable—one of the gentlest language, and firmest purpose—was Dr. Linn, of Missouri. The temper of the minority senators may be judged by the tone and tenor of his remarks.

"He (Mr. LINN) would for his part, make a few remarks here, and in doing so he intended to be as pointed as possible, for he had now, he found, to contend for liberty of speech; and while any of that liberty was left, he would give his remarks the utmost bounds consistent with his own sense of what was due to himself, his constituents, and the country. The whigs, during the late administration, had brought to bear a system of assault against the majority in power, which might justly be characterized as frivolous and vexatious, and nothing else; yet they had always been treated by the majority with courtesy and forbearance; and the utmost latitude of debate had been allowed them without interruption. In a session of six months, they consumed the greater part of the time in speeches for electioneering effect, so that only twenty-eight bills were passed. These electioneering speeches, on all occasions that could be started, whether the presentation of a petition, motion, or a resolution, or discussion of a bill, were uniformly and studiously of the most insulting character to the majority, whose mildest form of designation was "collar men;" and other epithets equally degrading. How often had it been said of the other branch of Congress, "What could be expected from a House so constituted?" Trace back the course of that party, step by step, to 1834, and it may be tracked in blood. The outrages in New York in that year are not forgotten. The fierce and fiendish spirit of strife and usurpation which prompted the seizure of public arms, to turn them against those who were their fellow-citizens, is yet fresh as ever, and ready to win its way to what it aims at. What was done then, under the influence and shadow of the great money power, may be done again. He (Mr. LINN) had marked them, and nothing should restrain him from doing his duty and standing up in the front rank of opposition to keep them from the innovations they meditated. Neither the frown nor menace of any leader of that party—no lofty bearing, or shaking of the mane—would deter him from the fearless and honest discharge of those obligations which were due to his constituents and to the country. He next adverted to the conduct of the whig party when the sub-treasury was under discussion, and reminded the present party in power of the forbearance with which they had been treated, contrasting that treatment with the manifestations now made to the minority. We are now, said Mr. Linn in conclusion, to be checked; but I tell the senator from Kentucky, and any other senator who chooses to tread in his steps, that he is about to deal a double handed game at which two can play. He is welcome to try his skill. But I would expect that some on that side are not prepared to go quite so far; and that there is yet among them sufficient liberality to counterbalance political feeling, and induce them not to object to our right of spending as much time in trying to improve their bill as they have taken themselves to clip and pare and shape it to their own fancies."

Here this irritating point rested for the day—and for three days, when it was revived by the reproaches and threats of Mr. Clay against the minority.

"The House (he said) had been treading on the heels of the Senate, and at last had got the start of it a long way in advance of the business of this session. The reason was obvious. The majority there is for action, and has secured it. Some change was called for in this chamber. The truth is that the minority here control the action of the Senate, and cause all the delay of the public business. They obstruct the majority in the dispatch of all business of importance to the country, and particularly those measures which the majority is bound to give to the country without further delay. Did not this reduce the majority to the necessity of adopting some measure which would place the control of the business of the session in their hands? It was impossible to do without it: it must be resorted to."

To this Mr. Calhoun replied:

"The senator from Kentucky tells the Senate the other House has got before it. How has the other House got before the Senate? By a despotic exercise of the power of a majority. By destroying the liberties of the people in gagging their representatives. By preventing the minority from its free exercise of its right of remonstrance. This is the way the House has got before the Senate. And now there was too much evidence to doubt that the Senate was to be made to keep up with the House by the same means."

Mr. Clay, finding such undaunted opposition to the hour rule, replied in a way to let it be seen that the threat of that rule was given up, and that a measure of a different kind, but equally effective, was to be proposed; and would be certainly adopted. He said:

"If he did not adopt the same means which had proved so beneficial in the other House, he would have something equally efficient to offer. He had no doubt of the cheerful adoption of such a measure when it should come before the Senate. So far from the rule being condemned, he would venture to say that it would be generally approved. It was the means of controlling the business, abridging long and unnecessary speeches, and would be every way hailed as one of the greatest improvements of the age."

This glimpse of another measure, confirmed the minority in the belief of what they had heard—that several whig senators had refused to go with Mr. Clay for the hour rule, and forced him to give it up; but they had agreed to go for the previous question, which he held to be equally effective; and was, in fact, more so—as it cut off debate at any moment. It was just as offensive as the other. Mr. King, of Alabama, was the first to meet the threat, under this new form, and the Register of Debates shows this scene:

"Mr. King said the senator from Kentucky complained of three weeks and a half having been lost in amendments to his bill. Was not the senator aware that it was himself and his friends had consumed most of that time? But now that the minority had to take it up, the Senate is told there must be a gag law. Did he understand that it was the intention of the senator to introduce that measure?

"Mr. CLAY. I will, sir; I will!

"Mr. KING. I tell the senator, then, that he may make his arrangements at his boarding-house for the winter.

"Mr. CLAY. Very well, sir.

"Mr. KING was truly sorry to see the honorable senator so far forgetting what is due to the Senate, as to talk of coercing it by any possible abridgment of its free action. The freedom of debate had never yet been abridged in that body, since the foundation of this government. Was it fit or becoming, after fifty years of unrestrained liberty, to threaten it with a gag law? He could tell the senator that, peaceable a man as he (Mr. KING) was, whenever it was attempted to violate that sanctuary, he, for one, would resist that attempt even unto the death."

The issue was now made up, and the determination on both sides declared—on the part of Mr. Clay, speaking in the name of his party, to introduce the previous question in the Senate, for the purpose of cutting off debate and amendments; on the part of the minority, to resist the rule—not only its establishment, but its execution. This was a delicate step, and required justification before the public, before a scene of resistance to the execution—involving disorder, and possibly violence—should come on. The scheme had been denounced, and defied; but the ample reasons against it had not been fully stated; and it was deemed best that a solid foundation of justification for whatever might happen, should be laid beforehand in a reasoned and considered speech. The author of this View, was required to make that speech; and for that purpose followed Mr. King.

"Mr. Benton would take this opportunity to say a word on this menace, so often thrown out, of a design to stifle debate, and stop amendments to bills in this chamber. He should consider such an attempt as much a violation of the constitution, and of the privileges of the chamber, as it would be for a military usurper to enter upon us, at the head of his soldiery, and expel us from our seats.

"It is not in order, continued Mr. B.—it is not in order, and would be a breach of the privilege of the House of Representatives, to refer to any thing which may have taken place in that House. My business is with our own chamber, and with the threat which has so often been uttered on this floor, during this extra session, of stifling debate, and cutting off amendments, by the introduction of the previous question.

"With respect to debates, senators have a constitutional right to speak; and while they speak to the subject before the House, there is no power any where to stop them. It is a constitutional right. When a member departs from the question, he is to be stopped: it is the duty of the Chair—your duty, Mr. President, to stop him—and it is the duty of the Senate to sustain you in the discharge of this duty. We have rules for conducting the debates, and these rules only require to be enforced in order to make debates decent and instructive in their import, and brief and reasonable in their duration. The government has been in operation above fifty years, and the freedom of debate has been sometimes abused, especially during the last twelve years, when those out of power made the two houses of Congress the arena of political and electioneering combat against the democratic administration in power. The liberty of debate was abused during this time; but the democratic majority would not impose gags and muzzles on the mouths of the minority; they would not stop their speeches; considering, and justly considering, that the privilege of speech was inestimable and inattackable—that some abuse of it was inseparable from its enjoyment—and that it was better to endure a temporary abuse than to incur a total extinction of this great privilege.

"But, sir, debate is one thing, and amendments another. A long speech, wandering off from the bill, is a very different thing from a short amendment, directed to the texture of the bill itself, and intended to increase its beneficial, or to diminish its prejudicial action. These amendments are the point to which I now speak, and to the nature of which I particularly invoke the attention of the Senate.

"By the constitution of the United States, each bill is to receive three readings, and each reading represents a different stage of proceeding, and a different mode of action under it. The first reading is for information only; it is to let the House know what the bill is for, what its contents are; and then neither debate nor amendment is expected, and never occurs, except in extraordinary cases. The second reading is for amendments and debate, and this reading usually takes place in Committee of the Whole in the House of Representatives, and in *quasi* committee in the Senate. The third reading, after the bill is engrossed, is for passage; and then it cannot be amended, and is usually voted upon with little or no debate. Now, it is apparent that the second reading of the bill is the important one—that it is the legislative—the law-making—reading; the one at which the collective wisdom of the House is concentrated upon it, to free it from defects, and to improve it to the utmost—to illustrate its nature, and trace its consequences. The bill is drawn up in a committee; or it is received from a department in the form of a *projet de loi*, and reported by a committee; or it is the work of a single member, and introduced on leave. The bill, before perfected by amendments, is the work of a committee, or of a head of a department, or of a single member; and if amendments are prevented, then the legislative power of the House is annihilated; the edict of a secretary, of a committee, or of a member, becomes the law; and the collected and concentrated wisdom and experience of the House has never been brought to bear upon it.

"The previous question cuts off amendments; and, therefore, neither in England nor in the United States, until now, in the House of Representatives, has that question ever been applied to bills in Committee of the Whole, on the second reading. This question annihilates legislation, sets at nought the wisdom of the House, and expunges the minority. It is always an invidious question, but seldom enforced in England, and but little used in the earlier periods of our own government. It has never been used in the Senate at all, never at any stage of the bill; in the House of Representatives it has never been used on the second reading of a bill, in Committee of the Whole, until the present session—this session, so ominous in its call and commencement, and which gives daily proof of its alarming tendencies, and of its unconstitutional, dangerous, and corrupting measures. The previous question has never yet been applied in this chamber; and to apply it now, at this ominous session, when all the old federal measures of fifty years ago are to be conglomerated into one huge and frightful mass, and rushed through by one convulsive effort; to apply it now, under such circumstances, is to muzzle the mouths, to gag the jaws, and tie up the tongues of those whose speeches would expose the enormities which cannot endure the light, and present to the people these ruinous measures in the colors in which they ought to be seen.

"The opinion of the people is invoked—they are said to be opposed to long speeches, and in favor of action. But, do they want action without deliberation, without consideration, without knowing what we are doing? Do they want bills without amendments—without examination of details—without a knowledge of their effect and operation when they are passed? Certainly the people wish no such thing. They want nothing which will not bear discussion. The people are in favor of discussion, and never read our debates with more avidity than at this ominous and critical extraordinary session. But I can well conceive of those who are against those debates, and want them stifled. Old sedition law federalism is against them: the cormorants who are whetting their bills for the prey which the acts of this session are to give them, are against them: and the advocates of these acts, who cannot answer these arguments, and who shelter weakness under *dignified* silence, they are all weary, sick and tired of a contest which rages on one side only, and which exposes at once the badness of their cause and the defeat of its defenders. Sir, this call for action! action! action! (as it was well said yesterday), comes from those whose cry is, plunder! plunder! plunder!

"The previous question, and the old sedition law, are measures of the same character, and children of the same parents, and intended for the same purposes. They are to hide light—to enable those in power to work in darkness—to enable them to proceed unmolested—and to permit them to establish ruinous measures without stint, and without detection. The introduction of this previous question into this body, I shall resist as I would resist its conversion into a bed of justice—*Lit de Justice*—of the old French monarchy, for the registration of royal edicts. In these beds of justice—the Parliament formed into a bed of justice—the kings before the revolution, caused their edicts to be registered without debate, and without amendment. The king ordered it, and it was done—his word became law. On one occasion, when the Parliament was refractory, Louis XIV. entered the chamber, booted and spurred—a whip in his hand—a horsewhip in his hand—and stood on his feet until the edict was registered. This is what has been done in the way of passing bills without debate or amendment, in France. But, in extenuation of this conduct of Louis the XIV., it must be remembered that he was a very young man when he committed this indiscretion, more derogatory to himself than to the Parliament which was the subject of the indignity. He never repeated it in his riper age, for he was a gentleman as well as a king, and in a fifty years' reign never repeated that indiscretion of his youth. True, no whips may be brought into our legislative halls to enforce the gag and the muzzle, but I go against the things themselves—against the infringement of the right of speech—and against the annihilation of our legislative faculties by annihilating the right of making amendments. I go against these; and say that we shall be nothing but a bed of justice for the registration of presidential, or partisan, or civil chieftain edicts, when debates and amendments are suppressed in this body.

"Sir, when the previous question shall be brought into this chamber—when it shall be applied to our bills in our *quasi* committee—I am ready to see my legislative life terminated. I want no seat here when that shall be the case. As the Romans held their natural lives, so do I hold my political existence. The Roman carried his life on the point of his sword; and when that life ceased to be honorable to himself, or useful to his country, he fell upon his sword, and died. This made of that people the most warlike and heroic nation of the earth. What they did with their natural lives, I am willing to do with my legislative and political existence: I am willing to terminate it, either when it shall cease to be honorable to myself, or useful to my country; and that I feel would be the case when this chamber, stripped of its constitutional freedom, shall receive the gag and muzzle of the previous question."

Mr. Clay again took the floor. He spoke mildly, and coaxingly—reminded the minority of their own course when in power—gave a hint about going into executive business—but still felt it his duty to give the majority the control of the public business, notwithstanding the threatened resistance of the minority.

"He (Mr. CLAY) would, however, say that after all, he thought the gentlemen on the other side would find it was better to go on with the public business harmoniously and good humoredly together, and all would get along better. He would remind the gentlemen of their own course when in power, and the frequent occasions on which the minority then acted with courtesy in allowing their treasury note bills to pass, and on various other occasions. He thought it was understood that they were to go into executive session, and afterwards take up the loan bill. He should feel it his duty to take measures to give the majority the control of the business, maugre all the menaces that had been made."

Here was a great change of tone, and the hint about going into executive business was a sign of hesitation, faintly counterbalanced by the reiteration of his purpose under a sense of duty. It was still the morning hour—the hour for motions, before the calendar was called: the hour for the motion he had been expected to make. That motion was evidently deferred. The intimation of going into executive business, was a surprise. Such business was regularly gone into towards the close of the day's session—after the day's legislative work was done; and this course was never departed from except in emergent cases—cases which would consume a whole day, or could not wait till evening: and no such cases were known to exist at present. This was a pause, and losing a day in the carrying along of those very measures, for hastening which the new rule was wanted. Mr. Calhoun, to take advantage of the hesitation which he perceived, and to increase it, by daring the threatened measure, instantly rose. He was saluted with cries that "the morning hour was out:" "not yet!" said he: "it lacks one minute of it; and I avail myself of that minute:" and then went on for several minutes.

"He thought this business closely analogous to the alien and sedition laws. Here was a palpable attempt to infringe the right of speech. He would tell the senator that the minority had rights under the constitution which they meant to exercise, and let the senator try when he pleased to abridge those rights, he would find it no easy job. When had that (our) side of the Senate ever sought to protract discussion unnecessarily? [Cries of 'never! never!'] Where was there a body that had less abused its privileges? If the gag-law was attempted to be put in force, he would resist it to the last. As judgment had been pronounced, he supposed submission was expected. The unrestrained liberty of speech, and freedom of debate, had been preserved in the Senate for fifty years. But now the warning was given that the yoke was to be put on it which had already been placed on the other branch of Congress. There never had been a body in this or any other country, in which, for such a length of time, so much dignity and decorum of debate had been maintained. It was remarkable for the fact, the range of discussion was less discursive than in any other similar body known. Speeches were uniformly confined to the subject under debate. There could be no pretext for interference. There was none but that of all despotisms. He would give the senator from Kentucky notice to bring on his gag measure as soon as he pleased. He would find it no such easy matter as he seemed to think."

Mr. Linn, of Missouri, rose the instant Mr. Calhoun stopped, and inquired of the Chair if the morning hour was out. The president *pro tempore* answered that it was. Mr. Linn said, he desired to say a few words. The chair referred him to the Senate, in whose discretion it was, to depart from the rule. Mr. Linn appealed to the Senate: it gave him leave: and he stood up and said:

"It was an old Scottish proverb, that threatened people live longest. He hoped the liberties of the Senate would yet outlive the threats of the senator from Kentucky. But, if the lash was to be applied, he would rather it was applied at once, than to be always threatened with it. There is great complaint of delay; but who was causing the delay now growing out of this threat? Had it not been made, there would be no necessity for repelling it. He knew of no disposition on the part of his friends to consume the time that ought to be given to the public business. He had never known his friends, while in the majority, to complain of discussion. He knew very well, and could make allowances, that the senator from Kentucky was placed in a very trying situation. He knew, also, that his political friends felt themselves to be in a very critical condition. If he brought forward measures that were questionable, he had to encounter resistance. But he was in the predicament that he had pledged himself to carry those measures, and, if he did not, it would be his political ruin. He had every thing on the issue, hence his impatience to pronounce judgment against the right of the minority to discuss his measures."

Mr. Clay interrupted Mr. Linn, to say that he had not offered to pronounce judgment. Mr. Linn gave his words "that if the Senate was disposed to do as he thought it ought to do, they would adopt the same rule as the other House." Mr. Clay admitted the words; and Mr. Linn claimed their meaning as pronouncing judgment on the duty of the Senate, and said:

"Very well; if the senator was in such a critical condition as to be obliged to say he cannot get his measures through without cutting off debates, why does he not accept the proposition of taking the vote on his bank bill on Monday? If he brings forward measures that have been battled against successfully for a quarter of a century, is it any wonder that they should be opposed, and time should be demanded to discuss them? The senator is aware that whiggery is dying off in the country, and that there is no time to be lost: unless he and his friends pass these measures they are ruined. All he should say to him was, pass them if he could. If, in order to do it, he is obliged to come on with his gag law, he (Mr. LINN) would say to his friends, let them meet him like men. He was not for threatening, but if he was obliged to meet the crisis, he would do it as became him."

Mr. Berrien, apparently acting on the hint of Mr. Clay, moved to go into the consideration of executive business. A question of order was raised upon that motion by Mr. Calhoun. The Chair decided in its favor. Mr. Calhoun demanded what was the necessity for going into executive business? Mr. Berrien did not think it proper to discuss that point: so the executive session was gone into: and when it was over, the Senate adjourned for the day.

Here, then, was a day lost for such pressing business—the bill, which was so urgent, and the motion, which was intended to expedite it. Neither of them touched: and the omission entirely the fault of the majority. There was evidently a balk. This was the 15th of July. The 16th came, and was occupied with the quiet transaction of business: not a word said about the new rules. The 17th came, and as soon as the Senate met, Mr. Calhoun took the floor; and after presenting some resolutions from a public meeting in Virginia, condemning the call of the extra session, and all its measures, he passed on to correct an erroneous idea that had got into the newspapers, that he himself, in 1812, at the declaration of war against Great Britain, being acting chairman of the committee of foreign relations, who had reported the war bill, had stifled discussion—had hurried the bill through, and virtually gagged the House. He gave a detail of circumstances, which showed the error of this report—that all the causes of war had been discussed before—that there was nothing new to be said, nor desire to speak: and that, for one hour before the vote was taken, there was a pause in the House, waiting for a paper from the department; and no one choosing to occupy any part of it with a speech, for or against the war, or on any subject. He then gave a history of the introduction of the previous question into the House of Representatives.

> "It had been never used before the 11th Congress (1810-12). It was then adopted, as he always understood, in consequence of the abuse of the right of debate by Mr. Gardinier of New York, remarkable for his capacity for making long speeches. He could keep the floor for days. The abuse was considered so great, that the previous question was introduced to prevent it; but so little was it in favor with those who felt themselves forced to adopt it, that he would venture to say without having looked at the journals, that it was not used half a dozen times during the whole war, with a powerful and unscrupulous opposition, and that in a body nearly two-thirds the size of the present House. He believed he might go farther, and assert that it was never used but twice during that eventful period. And now, a measure introduced under such pressing circumstances, and so sparingly used, is to be made the pretext for introducing the gag-law into the Senate, a body so much smaller, and so distinguished for the closeness of its debate and the brevity of its discussion. He would add that from the first introduction of the previous question into the House of Representatives, his impression was that it was not used but four times in seventeen years, that is from 1811 to 1828, the last occasion on the passage of the tariff bill. He now trusted that he had repelled effectually the attempt to prepare the country for the effort to gag the Senate, by a reference to the early history of the previous question in the other House."

Mr. Calhoun then referred to a decision made by Mr. Clay when Speaker of the House, and the benefit of which he claimed argumentatively. Mr. Clay disputed his recollection: Mr. Calhoun reiterated. The senators became heated, Mr. Clay calling out from his seat—"No, sir, No!"—and Mr. Calhoun answering back as he stood—"Yes, sir, yes:" and each giving his own version of the circumstance without convincing the other. He then returned to the point of irritation—the threatened gag;—and said:

> "The senator from Kentucky had endeavored to draw a distinction between the gag law and the old sedition law. He (Mr. Calhoun) admitted there was a distinction—the modern gag law was by far the most odious. The sedition law was an attempt to gag the people in their individual character, but the senator's gag was an attempt to gag the representatives of the people, selected as their agents to deliberate, discuss, and decide on the important subjects intrusted by them to this government."

This was a taunt, and senators looked to see what would follow. Mr. Clay rose, leisurely, and surveying the chamber with a pleasant expression of countenance, said:

> "The morning had been spent so very agreeably, that he hoped the gentlemen were in a good humor to go on with the loan bill, and afford the necessary relief to the Treasury."

The loan bill was then taken up, and proceeded with in a most business style, and quite amicably. And this was the last that was heard of the hour rule, and the previous question in the Senate: and the secret history of their silent abandonment was afterwards fully learnt. Several whig senators had yielded assent to Mr. Clay's desire for the hour rule under the belief that it would only be resisted parliamentarily by the minority; but when they saw its introduction was to produce ill blood, and disagreeable scenes in the chamber, they withdrew their assent; and left him without the votes to carry it: and that put an end to the project of the hour rule. The previous question was then agreed to in its place, supposing the minority would take it as a "compromise;" but when they found this measure was to be resisted like the former, and was deemed still more odious, hurtful and degrading, they withdrew their assent again: and then Mr. Clay, brought to a stand again for want of voters, was compelled to forego his design; and to retreat from it in the manner which has been shown. He affected a pleasantry, but was deeply chagrined, and the more so for having failed in the House where he acted in person, after succeeding in the other where he acted vicariously. Many of his friends were much dissatisfied. One of them said to me: "He gives your party a great deal of trouble, and his own a great deal more." Thus, the firmness of the minority in the Senate—it may be said, their courage, for their intended resistance contemplated any possible extremity—saved the body from degradation—constitutional legislation from suppression—the liberty of speech from extinction, and the honor of republican government from a disgrace to which the people's representatives are not subjected in any monarchy in Europe. The previous question has not been called in the British House of Commons in one hundred years—and never in the House of Peers.

CHAPTER LXX.

BILL FOR THE RELIEF OF MRS. HARRISON, WIDOW OF THE LATE PRESIDENT OF THE UNITED STATES.

Such was the title of the bill which was brought into the House of Representatives for an indemnity, as it was explained to be, to the family of the late President for his expenses in the presidential election, and in removing to the seat of government. The bill itself was in these words: "That the Secretary of the Treasury pay, out of any money in the Treasury not otherwise appropriated, to Mrs. Harrison, widow of William Henry Harrison, late President of the United States, or in the event of her death before payment, to the legal representatives of the said William Henry Harrison, the sum of $25,000." Mr. John Quincy Adams, as reporter of the bill from the select committee to which had been referred that portion of the President's message relating to the family of his predecessor, explained the motives on which the bill had been founded; and said:

> "That this sum ($25,000), as far as he understood, was in correspondence with the prevailing sentiment of the joint committee raised on this subject, and of which the gentleman now in the chair had been a member. There had been some difference of opinion among the members of the committee as to the sum which it would be proper to appropriate, and, also, on the part of one or two gentlemen as to the constitutionality of the act itself in any shape. There had been more objection to the constitutionality than there had been as to the sum proposed. So far as there had been any discussion in the committee, it seemed to be the general sense of those composing it, that some provision ought to be made for the family of the late President, not in the nature of a grant, but as an indemnity for actual expenses incurred by himself first, when a candidate for the presidency. It had been observed in the committee, and it must be known to all members of the House, that, in the situation in which General Harrison had been placed—far from the seat of government, and for eighteen months or two years, while a candidate for the presidency, exposed to a heavy burden of expense which he could not possibly avoid—it was no more than equitable that he should, to a reasonable degree, be indemnified. He had been thus burdened while in circumstances not opulent; but, on the contrary, it had been one ground on which he had received so decided proof of the people's favor, that through a long course of public service he remained poor, which was in itself a demonstrative proof that he had remained pure also. Such had been his condition before leaving home to travel to the seat of government. After his arrival here, he had been exposed to another considerable burden of expense, far beyond any amount he had received from the public purse during the short month he had continued to be President. His decease had left his family in circumstances which would be much improved by this act of justice done to him by the people, through their representatives. The feeling was believed to be very general throughout the country, and without distinction of party, in favor of such a measure."

This bill, on account of its principle, gave rise to a vehement opposition on the part of some members who believed they saw in it a departure from the constitution, and the establishment of a dangerous precedent. Mr. Payne, of Alabama, said:

> "As he intended to vote against this proposition it was due to himself to state the reasons which would actuate him. In doing so he was not called to examine either the merits or demerits of General Harrison. They had nothing to do with the question. The question before the House was, not whether General Harrison was or was not a meritorious individual, but whether that House would make an appropriation to his widow and descendants. That being the question, the first inquiry was, had the House a right to vote this money, and, if they had, was it proper to do so? Mr. P. was one of those who believed that Congress had no constitutional right to appropriate the public money for such an object. He quoted the language of the constitution, and then inquired whether this was an appropriation to pay the debts of the Union, to secure the common defence, or to promote the general welfare? He denied that precedents ever ought to be considered as settling a constitutional question. If

they could, then the people had no remedy. It was not pretended that this money was to be given as a reward for General Harrison's public services, but to reimburse him for the expense of an electioneering campaign. This was infinitely worse."

Mr. Gilmer, of Virginia, said:

"When he had yesterday moved for the rising of the committee, he had not proposed to himself to occupy much of the time of the House in debate, nor was such his purpose at present. With every disposition to vote for this bill, he had then felt, and he still felt, himself unable to give it his sanction, and that for reasons which had been advanced by many of the advocates in its favor. This was not a place to indulge feeling and sympathy: if it were, he presumed there would be but one sentiment throughout that House and throughout the country, and that would be in favor of the bill. If this were an act of generosity, if the object were to vote a bounty, a gratuity, to the widow or relatives of the late President, it seemed to Mr. G. that they ought not to vote it in the representative capacity, out of the public funds, but privately from their own personal resources. They had no right to be generous with the money of the people. Gentlemen might bestow as much out of their own purses as they pleased; but they were here as trustees for the property of others, and no public agent was at liberty to disregard the trust confided to him under the theory of our government. It was quite needless here to attempt an eulogy on the character of the illustrious dead: history has done and would hereafter do ample justice to the civil and military character of William Henry Harrison. The result of the recent election, a result unparalleled in the annals of this country, spoke the sentiment of the nation in regard to his merits, while the drapery of death which shrouded the legislative halls, the general gloom which overspread the nation, spoke that sentiment in accents mournfully impressive. But those rhapsodies in which gentlemen had indulged, might, he thought, better be deferred for some Fourth of July oration, or at least reserved for other theatres than this. They had come up here not to be generous, but to be just. His object now was to inquire whether they could not place this bill on the basis of indisputable justice, so that it might not be carried by a mere partial vote, but might conciliate the support of gentlemen of all parties, and from every quarter of the Union. He wished, if possible, to see the whole House united, so as to give to their act the undivided weight of public sentiment. Mr. G. said he could not bow to the authority of precedent; he should ever act under the light of the circumstances which surrounded him. His wish was, not to furnish an evil precedent to others by his example. He thought the House in some danger of setting one of that character; a precedent which might hereafter be strained and tortured to apply to cases of a very different kind, and objects of a widely different character. He called upon the advocates of the bill to enable all the members of the House, or as nearly all as was practicable (for, after what had transpired yesterday, he confessed his despair of seeing the House entirely united), to agree in voting for the bill."

There was an impatient majority in the House in favor of the passage of the bill, and to that impatience Mr. Gilmer referred as making despair of any unanimity in the House, or of any considerate deliberation. The circumstances were entirely averse to any such deliberation—a victorious party, come into power after a most heated election, seeing their elected candidate dying on the threshold of his administration, poor, and beloved: it was a case for feeling more than of judgment, especially with the political friends of the deceased—but few of whom could follow the counsels of the head against the impulsions of the heart. Amongst these few Mr. Gilmer was one, and Mr. Underwood of Kentucky, another; who said:

"His heart was on one side and his judgment upon the other. If this was a new case, he might be led away by his heart; but as he had heretofore, in his judgment, opposed all such claims he should do so now. He gave his reasons thus at large, because a gentleman from Indiana, on the other side of the House, denounced those who should vote against the bill. He objected, because it was retroactive in its provisions, and because it called into existence legislative discretion, and applied it to past cases—because it provided for the widow of a

President for services rendered by her husband while in office, thus increasing the President's compensation after his death. If it applied to the widow of the President, it applied to the widows of military officers. He considered if this bill passed, that Mr. Jefferson's heirs might with equal propriety claim the same compensation."

If the House had been in any condition for considerate legislation there was an amendment proposed by Mr. Gordon of New York, which might have brought it forth. He proposed an indemnity equal to the amount of one quarter's salary, $6,250. He proposed it, but got but little support for his proposition, the majority calling for the question, and some declaring themselves for $50,000, and some for $100,000. The vote was taken, and showed 66 negatives, comprehending the members who were best known to the country as favorable to a strict construction of the constitution, and an economical administration of the government. The negatives were:

Archibald H. Arrington, Charles G. Atherton, Linn Banks, Henry W. Beeson, Linn Boyd, David P. Brewster, Aaron V. Brown, Charles Brown, Edmund Burke, William O. Butler, Green W. Caldwell, Patrick C. Caldwell, John Campbell, George B. Cary, Reuben Chapman, Nathan Clifford, James G. Clinton, Walter Coles, John R. J. Daniel, Richard D. Davis, William Doan, Andrew W. Doig, Ira A. Eastman, John C. Edwards, Joseph Egbert, John G. Floyd, Charles A. Floyd, James Gerry, William O. Goode, Samuel Gordon, Amos Gustine, William A. Harris, Samuel L. Hays, George W. Hopkins, Jacob Houck, jr., Edmund W. Hubard, Robert M. T. Hunter, Cave Johnson, John W. Jones, George M. Keim, Andrew Kennedy, Joshua A. Lowell, Abraham McClellan, Robert McClellan, James J. McKay, Albert G. Marchand, Alfred Marshall, John Thompson Mason, James Mathews, William Medill, John Miller, Peter Newhard, William W. Payne, Francis W. Pickens, Arnold Plumer, John R. Reding, James Rogers, Romulus M. Saunders, Tristram Shaw, John Snyder, Lewis Steenrod, Hopkins L. Turney, Joseph R. Underwood, Harvey M. Watterson, John B. Weller, James W. Williams.

Carried to the Senate for its concurrence, the bill continued to receive there a determined opposition from a considerable minority. Mr. Calhoun said:

"He believed no government on earth leaned more than ours towards all the corruptions of an enormous pension list. Not even the aristocratic government of Great Britain has a stronger tendency to it than this government. This is no new thing. It was foreseen from the beginning, and the great struggle then was, to keep out the entering wedge. He recollected very well, when he was at the head of the War Department, and the military pension bill passed, that while it was under debate, it was urged as a very small matter—only an appropriation of something like $150,000 to poor and meritorious soldiers of the Revolution, who would not long remain a burden on the Treasury. Small as the sum was, and indisputable as were the merits of the claimants, it was with great difficulty the bill passed. Why was this difficulty—this hesitation on such an apparently irresistible claim? Because it was wisely argued, and with a spirit of prophecy since fulfilled, that it would prove an entering wedge, which, once admitted, would soon rend the pillar of democracy. And what has been the result of that trifling grant? It is to be found in the enormous pension list of this government at the present day.

"He asked to have any part of the Constitution pointed out in which there was authority for making such an appropriation as this. If the authority exists in the Constitution at all, it exists to a much greater extent than has yet been acted upon, and it is time to have the fact known. If the Constitution authorizes Congress to make such an appropriation as this for a President of the United States, it surely authorizes it to make an appropriation of like nature for a doorkeeper of the Senate of the United States, or for any other officer of the government. There can be no distinction drawn. Pass this act, and the precedent is established for the family of every civil officer in the government to be placed on the pension list. Is not this the consummation of the tendency so long combated? But the struggle is in vain—there is not, he would repeat, a government on the face of the earth, in which there is such a tendency to all the corruptions of an aristocratic pension list as there is in this."

Mr. Woodbury said:

"This was the first instance within his (Mr. W.'s) knowledge, of an application to pension a civil officer being likely to succeed; and a dangerous innovation, he felt convinced, it would prove. Any civil officer, by the mere act of taking possession of his office for a month, ought to get his salary for a year, on the reasoning adopted by the senator from Delaware, though only performing a month's service. If that can be shown to be right, he (Mr. W.) would go for this, and all bills of the kind. But it must first be shown satisfactorily. If this lady was really poor, there would be some plea for sympathy, at least. But he could point to hundreds who have that claim, and not on account of civil, but military service, who yet have obtained no such grant, and never will. He could point to others in the civil service, who had gone to great expense in taking possession of office and then died, but no claim of this kind was encouraged, though their widows were left in most abject poverty. All analogy in civil cases was against going beyond the death of the incumbent in allowing either salary or gratuity."

Mr. Pierce said:

"Without any feelings adverse to this claim, political or otherwise, he protested against any legislation based upon our *sympathies*—he protested against the power and dominion of that '*inward arbiter*,' which in private life was almost sure to lead us right; but, as public men, and as the dispensers of other men's means—other men's contributions—was quite as sure to lead us wrong. It made a vast difference whether we paid the money from our own pockets, or drew it from the pockets of our constituents. He knew his weakness on this point, *personally*, but it would be his steady purpose, in spite of taunts and unworthy imputations, to escape from it, as the representative of others. But he was departing from the object which induced him, for a moment, to trespass upon the patience of the Senate. This claim did not come from the family. No gentleman understood on what ground it was placed. The indigence of the family had not even been urged: he believed they were not only in easy circumstances, but affluent. It was not for loss of limb, property, or life, in the military service. If for any thing legitimate, in any sense, or by any construction, it was for the civil services of the husband; and, in this respect, was a broad and dangerous precedent."

In saying that the claim did not come from the family of General Harrison, Mr. Pierce spoke the words which all knew to be true. Where then did it come from? It came, as was well known at the time, from persons who had advanced moneys to the amount of about $22,000, for the purposes mentioned in the bill; and who had a claim upon the estate to that amount.

Mr. Benton moved to recommit the bill with instructions to prefix a preamble, or insert an amendment showing upon what ground the grant was motived. The bill itself showed no grounds for the grant. It was, on its face, a simple legislative donation of money to a lady, describing her as the widow of the late President; but in no way connecting either herself, or her deceased husband, with any act or fact as the alleged ground of the grant. The grant is without consideration: the donee is merely described, to prevent the donation from going to a wrong person. It was to go to Mrs. Harrison. What Mrs. Harrison? Why, the widow of the late President Harrison. This was descriptive, and sufficiently descriptive; for it would carry the money to the right person. But why carry it? That was the question which the bill had not answered; for there is nothing in the mere fact of being the widow of a President which could entitle the widow to a sum of public money. This was felt by the reporter of the bill, and endeavored to be supplied by an explanation, that it was not a "grant" but an "indemnity;" and an indemnity for "actual expenses incurred when he was a candidate for the presidency;" and for expenses incurred after his "arrival at the seat of government;" and as "some provision for his family;" and because he was "poor." Now why not put these reasons into the bill? Was the omission oversight, or design? If oversight, it should be corrected; if design, it should be thwarted. The law should be complete in itself. It cannot be helped out by a member's speech. It was not oversight which caused the omission. The member who reported the bill is not a man to commit oversights. It was design! and because such reasons could not be put on the face of the bill! could not be voted upon by yeas and nays! and therefore must be left blank, that every member may vote upon what reasons he pleases, without being committed to any. This is not the way to legislate; and, therefore, the author of this View moved the re-commitment, with instructions to put a reason on the face of the bill itself, either in the shape of a preamble, or of an amendment—leaving the selection of the reasons to the friends of the bill, who constituted the committee to which it would be sent. Mr. Calhoun supported the motion for re-commitment, and said:

> "Is it an unreasonable request to ask the committee for a specific report of the grounds on which they have recommended this appropriation? No; and the gentlemen know it is not unreasonable; but they will oppose it not on that account; they will oppose it because they know such a report would defeat their bill. It could not be sustained in the face of their own report. Not that there would be no ground assumed, but because those who now support the bill do so on grounds as different as any possibly can be; and, if the committee was fastened down to one ground, those who support the others would desert the standard."

The vote was taken on the question, and negatived. The yeas were: Messrs. Allen, Benton, Calhoun, Clay of Alabama, Fulton, King of Alabama, Linn, McRoberts, Pierce, Sevier Smith of Connecticut, Tappan, Williams of Maine, Woodbury, Wright, Young of Illinois. To the argument founded on the alleged poverty of General Harrison, Mr. Benton replied:

> "Look at the case of Mr. Jefferson, a man than whom no one that ever existed on God's earth were the human family more indebted to. His furniture and his estate were sold to satisfy his creditors. His posterity was driven from house and home, and his bones now lay in soil owned by a stranger. His family are scattered; some of his descendants are married in foreign lands. Look at Monroe—the amiable, the patriotic Monroe, whose services were revolutionary, whose blood was spilt in the war of Independence, whose life was worn out in civil service, and whose estate has been sold for debt, his family scattered, and his daughter buried in a foreign land. Look at Madison, the model of every virtue, public or private, and he would only mention in connection with this subject, his love of order, his economy, and his systematic regularity in all his habits of business. He, when his term of eight years had expired, sent a letter to a gentleman (a son of whom is now upon this floor) [Mr. PRESTON], enclosing a note for five thousand dollars, which he requested him to endorse, and raise the money in Virginia, so as to enable him to leave this city, and return to his modest retreat—his patrimonial inheritance—in that State. General Jackson drew upon the consignee of his cotton crop in New Orleans for six thousand dollars to enable him to leave the seat of government without leaving creditors behind him. These were honored leaders of the republican party. They had all been Presidents. They had made great sacrifices, and left the presidency deeply embarrassed; and yet the republican party who had the power and the strongest disposition to relieve their necessities, felt they had no right to do so by appropriating money from the public Treasury. Democracy would not do this. It was left for the era of federal rule and federal supremacy—who are now rushing the country with steam power into all the abuses and corruptions of a monarchy, with its pensioned aristocracy—and to entail upon the country a civil pension list.

> "To the argument founded on the expense of removing to the seat of government, Mr. Benton replied that there was something in it, and if the bill was limited to indemnity for that expense, and a rule given to go by in all cases, it might find claims to a serious consideration. Such a bill would have principle and reason in it—the same principle and the same reason which allows mileage to a member going to and returning from Congress. The member was supposed during that time to be in the public service (he was certainly out of his own service): he was at expense: and for these reasons he was allowed a compensation for his journeys. But, it was by a uniform rule, applicable to all members, and the same at each session. The same reason and principle with foreign ministers. They received an out-fit before they left home,

and an in-fit to return upon. A quarter's salary, was the in-fit: the out-fit was a year's salary, because it included the expense of setting up a house after the minister arrived at his post. The President finds a furnished house on his arrival at the seat of government, so that the principle and reason of the case would not give to him, as to a minister to a foreign court, a full year's salary. The in-fit would be the proper measure; and that rule applied to the coming of the President elect, and to his going when he retires, would give him $6,250 on each occasion. For such an allowance he felt perfectly clear that he could vote as an act of justice; and nearly as clear that he could do it constitutionally. But it would have to be for a general and permanent act."

The bill was passed by a bare quorum, 28 affirmatives out of 52. The negatives were 16: so that 18 senators—being a greater number than voted against the bill—were either absent, or avoided the vote. The absentees were considered mostly of that class who were willing to see the bill pass, but not able to vote for it themselves. The yeas and nays were:

YEAS—Messrs. Barrow, Bates, Bayard, Berrien, Buchanan, Choate, Clay of Kentucky, Clayton, Dixon, Evans, Graham, Huntington, Mangum, Merrick, Miller, Morehead, Phelps, Porter, Prentiss, Preston, Rives, Simmons, Smith of Indiana, Southard, Tallmadge, Walker, White, Woodbridge.

NAYS—Messrs. Allen, Benton, Calhoun, Clay of Alabama, Fulton, King, Linn, McRoberts, Nicholson, Sevier, Smith of Connecticut, Surgeon, Tappan, Williams, Woodbury, Wright, Young.

It was strenuously opposed by the stanch members of the democratic party, and elaborately resisted in a speech from the writer of this View—of which an extract is given in the next chapter.

CHAPTER LXXI.

MRS. HARRISON'S BILL: SPEECH OF MR. BENTON EXTRACTS.

Mr. Benton said he was opposed to this bill—opposed to it on high constitutional grounds, and upon grounds of high national policy—and could not suffer it to be carried through the Senate without making the resistance to it which ought to be made against a new, dangerous, and unconstitutional measure.

It was a bill to make a grant of money—twenty-five thousand dollars—out of the common Treasury to the widow of a gentleman who had died in a civil office, that of President of the United States; and was the commencement of that system of civil pensions, and support for families, which, in the language of Mr. Jefferson, has divided England, and other European countries into two classes—the tax payers and the tax consumers—and which sends the laboring man supperless to bed.

It is a new case—the first of the kind upon our statute book—and should have been accompanied by a report from a committee, or preceded by a preamble to the bill, or interjected with a declaration, showing the reason for which this grant is made. It is a new case, and should have carried its justification along with it. But nothing of this is done. There is no report from a committee—from the two committees in fact—which sat upon the case. There is no preamble to it, setting forth the reason for the grant. There is no declaration in the body of the bill, showing the reason why this money is voted to this lady. It is simply a bill granting to Mrs. Harrison, widow of William H. Harrison, late President of the United States, the sum of $25,000. Now, all this is wrong, and contrary to parliamentary practice. Reason tells us there should be a report from a committee in such a case. In fact, we have reports every day in every case, no matter how inconsiderable, which even pays a small sum of money to an individual. It is our daily practice, and yet two committees have shrunk from that practice in this new and important case. They would not make a report, though urged to do it. I speak advisedly, for I was of the committee, and know what was done. No report could be obtained; and why? because it was difficult, if not impossible, for any committee to agree upon a reason which would satisfy the constitution, and satisfy public policy, for making this grant. Gentlemen could agree to give the money—they could agree to vote—but they could not agree upon the reason which was to be left upon the record as a justification for the gift and the vote. Being no report, the necessity became apparent for a preamble; but we have none of that. And, worse than all, in the absence of report and preamble, the bill itself is silent on the motive of the grant. It does not contain the usual clause in money bills to individuals, stating, in a few words, for what reason the grant or payment is made. All this is wrong; and I point it out now, both as an argument against the bill, and as a reason for having it recommitted, and returned with a report, or a preamble, or a declaratory clause.

We were told at the last session that a new set of books were to be opened—that the new administration would close up the old books, and open new ones; and truly we find it to be the case. New books of all kinds are opened, as foreign to the constitution and policy of the country, as they are to the former practice of the government, and to the late professions of these new patriots. Many new books are opened, some by executive and some by legislative authority; and among them is this portentous volume of civil pensions, and national recompenses, for the support of families. Military pensions we have always had, and they are founded upon a principle which the mind can understand, the tongue can tell, the constitution can recognize, and public policy can approve. They are founded upon the principle of personal danger and suffering in the cause of the country—upon the loss of life or limb in war. This is reasonable. The man who goes forth, in his country's cause, to be shot at for seven dollars a month, or for forty dollars a month, or even for one or two hundred, and gets his head or his limbs knocked off, is in a very different case from him who serves the same country at a desk or a table, with a quill or a book in his hand, who may quit his place when he sees the enemy coming; and has no occasion to die except in his tranquil and peaceful bed. The case of the two classes is wholly different, and thus far the laws of our country have recognized and maintained the difference. Military pensions have been granted from the foundation of the government—civil pensions, never; and now, for the first time, the attempt is to be made to grant them. A grant of money is to be made to the widow of a gentleman who has not been in the army for near thirty years—who has since that time, been much employed in civil service, and has lately died in a civil office. A pension, or a grant of a gross sum of money, under such circumstances, is a new proceeding under our government, and which finds no warrant in the constitution, and is utterly condemned by high considerations of public policy.

The federal constitution differs in its nature—and differs fundamentally from those of the States. The States, being original sovereignties, may do what they are not prohibited from doing; the federal government, being derivative, and carved out of the States, is like a corporation, the creature of the act which creates it, and can only do what it can show a grant for doing. Now the moneyed power of the federal government is contained in a grant from the States, and that grant authorizes money to be raised either by loans, duties or taxes, for the purpose of paying the debts, supporting the government, and providing for the common defence of the Union. These are the objects to which money may be applied, and this grant to Mrs. Harrison can come within neither of them.

But, gentlemen say this is no pension—it is not an annual payment, but a payment in hand. I say so, too, and that it is so much the more objectionable on that account. A pension must have some rule to go by—so much a month—and generally a small sum, the highest on our pension roll being thirty dollars—and it terminates in a reasonable time, usually five years, and at most for life. A pension granted to Mrs. Harrison on this principle, could amount to no great sum—to a mere fraction, at most, of these twenty-five thousand dollars. It is not a pension, then, but a gift—a gratuity—a large present—a national recompense; and the more objectionable for being so. Neither our constitution, nor the genius of our government, admits of such benefactions. National recompenses are high rewards, and require express powers to grant them in every limited government. The French Consular Constitution of the year 1799, authorized such recompenses; ours does not, and it has not yet been attempted, even in military cases. We have not yet voted a fortune to an officer's or a soldier's family, to lift them from poverty to wealth. These recompenses are worse than pensions: they are equally unfounded in the constitution, more incapable of being governed by any rule, and more susceptible of great and dangerous abuse. We have no rule to go by in fixing the amount. Every one goes by feeling—by his personal or political feeling—or by a cry got up at home, and sent here to act upon him. Hence the diversity of the opinions as to the proper sum to be given. Some gentlemen are for the amount in the bill; some are for double that amount; and some are for nothing. This diversity itself is an argument against the measure. It shows that it has no natural foundation—nothing to rest upon—nothing to go by; no rule, no measure, no standard, by which to compute or compare it. It is all guess-work—the work of the passions or policy—of faction or of party.

By our constitution, the persons who fill offices are to receive a compensation for their services; and, in many cases, this compensation is neither to be increased nor diminished during the period for which the person shall have been elected; and in some there is a prohibition against receiving presents either from foreign States, or from the United States, or from the States of the Union. The office of President comes under all these restrictions, and shows how jealous the framers of the constitution were, of any moneyed influence being brought to bear upon the Chief Magistrate of the Union. All these limitations are for obvious and wise reasons. The President's salary is not to be diminished during the time for which he was elected, lest his enemies, if they get the upper hand of him in Congress, should deprive him of his support, and starve him out of office. It is not to be increased, lest his friends, if they get the upper hand, should enrich him at the public expense; and he is not to receive "*any other emolument*," lest the provision against an increase of salary should be evaded by the grant of gross sums. These are the constitutional provisions; but to what effect are they, if the sums can be granted to the officer's family, which cannot be granted to himself?—if his widow—his wife—his children can receive what he cannot? In this case, the term for which General Harrison was elected, is not out. It has not expired; and Congress cannot touch his salary or bestow upon him or his, any emolument without a breach of the constitution.

It is in vain to look to general clauses of the constitution. Besides the general spirit of the instrument, there is a specific clause upon the subject of the President's salary and emoluments. It forbids him any compensation, except at stated times, for services rendered; it forbids increase or diminution; and it forbids all emolument. To give salary or emolument to his family, is a mere evasion of this clause. His family is himself—so far as property is concerned, a man's family is himself. And many persons would prefer to have money or property conveyed to his family, or some member of it, because it would then receive the destination which his will would give it, and would be free from the claims or contingencies to which his own property—that in his own name—would be subject. There is nothing in the constitution to warrant this proceeding, and there is much in it to condemn it. It is condemned by all the clauses which relate to the levy, and the application of money; and it is specially condemned by the precise clause which regulates the compensation of the President, and which clause would control any other part of the constitution which might come in conflict with it. Condemned upon the constitutional test, how stands this bill on the question of policy and expediency? It is condemned—utterly condemned, and reprobated, upon that test! The view which I have already presented of the difference between military and naval services (and I always include the naval when I speak of the military) shows that the former are proper subjects for pensions—the latter not. The very nature of the service makes the difference. Differing in principle, as the military and civil pensions do, they differ quite as much when you come to details, and undertake to administer the two classes of rewards. The military has something to go by—some limit to it— and provides for classes of individuals—not for families or for individuals—one by one. Though subject to great abuse, yet the military pensions have some limit—some boundary—to their amount placed upon them. They are limited at least to the amount of armies, and the number of wars. Our armies are small, and our wars few and far between. We have had but two with a civilized power in sixty years. Our navy, also, is limited; and compared to the mass of the population, the army and navy must be always small. Confined to their proper subjects, and military and naval pensions have limits and boundaries which confine them within some bounds; and then the law is the same for all persons of the same rank. The military and naval pensioners are not provided for individually, and therefore do not become a subject of favoritism, of party, or of faction. Not so with civil pensions. There is no limit upon them. They may apply to the family of every person civilly employed—that is, to almost every body—and this without intermission of time; for civil services go on in peace and war, and the claims for them will be eternal when once begun. Then again civil pensions and grants of money are given individually, and not by classes, and every case is governed by the feeling of the moment, and the predominance of the party to which the individual belonged. Every case is the sport of party, of faction, of favoritism; and of feelings excited and got up for the occasion. Thus it is in England, and thus it will be here. The English civil pension list is dreadful, both for the amount paid, and the nature of the services rewarded; but it required centuries for England to ripen her system. Are we to begin it in the first half century of our existence? and begin it without rule or principle to go by? Every thing to be left to impulse and favor— by the politics of the individual, his party affinities, and the political complexion of the party in power.

Gentlemen refuse to commit themselves on the record; but they have reasons; and we have heard enough, here and elsewhere, to have a glimpse of what they are. First, poverty: as if that was any reason for voting a fortune to a family, even if it was true! If it was a reason, one half of the community might be packed upon the backs of the other. Most of our public men die poor; many of them use up their patrimonial inheritances in the public service; yet, until now, the reparation of ruined fortune has not been attempted out of the public Treasury. Poverty would not do, if it was true, but here it is not true: the lady in question has a fine estate, and certainly has not applied for this money. No petition of hers is here! No letter, even, that we have heard of! So far as we know, she is ignorant of the proceeding! Certain it is, she has not applied for this grant, either on the score of poverty, or any thing else. Next, election expenses are mentioned; but that would seem to be a burlesque upon the character of our republican institutions. Certainly no candidate for the presidency ought to electioneer for it—spend money for it—and if he did, the public Treasury ought not to indemnify him. Travelling expenses coming on to the seat of government, are next mentioned; but these could be but a trifle, even if the President elect came at his own expense. But we know to the contrary. We know that the contest is for the honor of bringing him; that conveyances and entertainments are prepared; and that friends dispute for precedence in the race of lifting and helping along, and ministering to every want of the man who is so soon to be the dispenser of honor and fortune in the shape of office and contracts. Such a man cannot travel at his own expense. Finally, the fire in the roof of the west wing of the North Bend mansion has been mentioned; but Jackson had the whole Hermitage burnt to the ground when he was President, and would have scorned a gift from the public Treasury to rebuild it. Such are the reasons mentioned in debate, or elsewhere, for this grant. Their futility is apparent on their face, and is proved by the unwillingness of gentlemen to state them in a report, or a preamble, or in the body of the bill itself.

CHAPTER LXXII.

ABUSE OF THE NAVAL PENSION SYSTEM: VAIN ATTEMPT TO CORRECT IT.

The annual bill for these pensions being on its passage, an attempt was made to correct the abuse introduced by the act of 1837. That act had done four things:—1. It had carried back the commencement of invalid naval pensions to the time of receiving the inability, instead of the time of completing the proof. 2. It extended the pensions for death to all cases of death, whether incurred in the line of duty or not. 3. It extended the widows' pensions for life, when five years had been the law both in the army and the navy. 4. It pensioned children until twenty-one years of age, thereby adopting the English pension system. The effects of these changes were to absorb and bankrupt the navy pension fund—a meritorious fund created out of the government share of prize money, relinquished for that purpose;—and to throw the pensions, the previous as well as the future, upon the public treasury—where it was never intended they were to be. This act, so novel in its character—so plundering in its effects—and introducing such fatal principles into the naval pension system, and which it has been found so difficult to get rid of—was one of the deplorable instances of midnight legislation, on the last night of the session; when, in the absence of many, the haste of all, the sleepiness of some, and a pervading inattention, an enterprising member can get almost any thing passed through—and especially as an amendment. It was at a time like this that this pension act was passed, the night of March 3d, 1837—its false and deceptive title ("*An act for the more equitable administration of the Navy Pension Fund*") being probably as much of it as was heard by the few members who heard any thing about it; and the word "equitable," so untruly and deceptiously inserted, probably the only part of it which lodged on their minds. And in that way was passed an act which instantly pillaged a sacred fund of one million two hundred thousand dollars—which has thrown the naval pensioners upon the Treasury, instead of the old navy pension fund, for their support—which introduced the English pension system—which was so hard to repeal; and which has still all its burdens on our finances, and some of its principles in our laws. It is instructive to learn the history of such legislation, and to see its power (a power inherent in the very nature of an abuse, and the greater in proportion to the greatness of the abuse) to resist correction: and with this view the brief debate on an ineffectual attempt in the Senate to repeal the act of this session is here given—Mr. Reuel Williams, of Maine, having the honor to commence the movement.

"The naval pension appropriation bill being under consideration, Mr. WILLIAMS offered an amendment, providing for the repeal of the act of 1837; and went at some length into the reasons in favor of the adoption of the amendment. He said all admitted the injurious tendency of the act of 1837, by which the fund which had been provided by the bravery of our gallant sailors for the relief of the widows and orphans of those who had been killed in battle, or had died from wounds which had been received while in the line of their duty, had been utterly exhausted; and his amendment went to the repeal of that law."

"Mr. MANGUM hoped the amendment would not be adopted—that the system would be allowed to remain as it was until the next session. It was a subject of great complexity, and if this amendment passed it would be equivalent to the repeal of all the naval pension acts."

"Mr. WILLIAMS understood the senator from North Carolina as saying, that if they passed this amendment, and thus repealed the act of 1837, they repeal all acts which grant a pension for disability."

"Mr. MANGUM had said, if they repealed the law of '37, they would cut off every widow and orphan now on the pension list, and leave none except the seamen, officers, and marines, entitled to pensions under the act of 1800."

"Mr. WILLIAMS said the senator was entirely mistaken; and read the law of 1813, which was still in full force, and could not be affected by the repeal of the law of 1837. The law of 1813 gives a pension to the widows and orphans of all who are killed in battle, or who die from wounds received in battle; and also gives pensions to those who are disabled while in the line of their duty. This law was now in force. The additional provisions of the law of 1837 were to carry back the pensions to the time when the disability was incurred, and to extend it to the widows and children of those who died, no matter from what cause, while they were in the naval service. Thus, if an officer or seaman died from intoxication, or even committed suicide, his widow received a pension for life, and his children received pensions until they were twenty-one years of age.

"Again: if officers or seamen received a wound which did not disable them they continued in the service, receiving their full pay for years. When they thought proper they retired from the service, and applied for a pension for disability, which, by the law of 1837, they were authorized to have carried back to the time the disability was incurred, though they had, during the whole series of years subsequent to receiving the disability, and prior to the application for a pension, been receiving their full pay as officers or seamen. It was to prevent the continuance of such abuses, that the amendment was offered."

"Mr. WALKER must vote against this amendment, repealing the act of 1837, because an amendment which had been offered by him and adopted, provided for certain pensions under this very act, and which ought, in justice, to be given."

"Mr. WILLIAMS thought differently, as the specific provision in the amendment of the senator from Mississippi, would except the cases included in it from the operation of the repealing clause."

"Mr. EVANS opposed the amendment, on the ground that it cut off all the amendments adopted, and brought back again the law of 1800."

The proposed amendment of Mr. Williams was then put to the vote—and negatived—only nineteen senators voting for it. The yeas and nays were:

YEAS—Messrs. Allen, Benton, Calhoun, Clay of Alabama, Fulton, King, Linn, McRoberts, Mouton, Nicholson, Pierce, Sevier, Smith of Connecticut, Sturgeon, Tappan, Williams, Woodbury, Wright, Young—19.

NAYS—Messrs. Archer, Barrow, Bates, Bayard, Berrien, Choate, Clay of Kentucky, Clayton, Dixon, Evans, Graham, Huntington, Kerr, Mangum, Merrick, Miller, Morehead, Phelps, Porter, Prentiss, Preston, Simmons, Smith of Indiana, Southard, Tallmadge, Walker, White, Woodbridge—28.

It is remarkable that in this vote upon a palpable and enormous abuse in the navy, there was not a whig vote among the democracy for correcting it, nor a democratic vote, except one, among the negatives. A difference about a navy—on the point of how much, and of what kind—had always been a point of difference between the two great political parties of the Union, which, under whatsoever names, are always the same—each preserving its identity in principles and policy: but here the two parties divided upon an abuse which no one could deny, or defend. The excuse was to put it off to another time, which is the successful way of perpetuating abuses, as there are always in every public assembly, as in every mass of individuals, many worthy men whose easy temperaments delight in temporizations; and who are always willing to put off, temporarily, the repeal of a bad law, or even to adopt temporarily, the enactment of a doubtful one. Mr. Williams' proposed amendment was not one of repeal only, but of enactment also. It repealed the act of 1837, and revived that of 1832, and corrected some injurious principles interjected into the naval pension code—especially the ante-dating of pensions, and the abuse of drawing pay and pension at the same time. This amendment being rejected, and some minor ones adopted, the question came up upon one offered by Mr. Walker—providing that all widows or children of naval officers, seamen, or marines, now deceased, and entitled to pensions under the act of 1837, should receive the same until otherwise directed by law; and excluding all cases from future deaths. Mr. Calhoun proposed to amend this amendment by striking out the substantive part of Mr. Walker's amendment, and after providing for those now on the pension-roll under the act of 1837, confining all future pensioners to the acts of April 23d, 1800—January 24th, 1813—and the second section of the act of the 3d of March, 1814. In support of his motion Mr. Calhoun spoke briefly, and pointedly, and unanswerably; but not quite enough so to save his proposed amendment. It was lost by one vote, and that the vote of the president *pro tempore*, Mr. Southard. The substance of Mr. Calhoun's brief speech is thus preserved in the register of the Congress debates:

"Mr. CALHOUN said that, among the several objections to this, there was one to which he did hope the Senate would apply the correction. The amendment not only kept alive the act of 1837, as to the pensioners now on the list, under that act, but also kept it alive for all future applications which might be made under it, until it should be hereafter repealed, if it ever should be. To this he strongly objected.

"There was one point on which all were agreed, that the act in question was not only inexpedient, but something much worse—that it committed something like a fraud upon the pension fund. It is well known to the Senate that that fund was the result of prize money pledged to the use of meritorious officers and sailors who might be disabled in the service of their country. The whole of this fund, amounting to nearly a million and a half of dollars, was swept away by this iniquitous act, that passed on the third of March—the very last day of the session—introduced and carried through by nobody knows who, and for which nobody seems responsible. He ventured nothing in asserting, that if such an act was now under discussion for the first time, it would not receive a single vote with the present knowledge which the Senate has of the subject, but, on the contrary, would be cast from it with universal scorn and indignation. He went further: it would now be repealed with like unanimity, were it not that many persons had been placed upon the list under the act, which was still in force, which was felt by many to be a sort of a pledge to pay them until the act was formally repealed. But why should we go further? Why should we keep it alive to let in those who are not yet put upon the list? But one answer could be given, and that one stated by the two senators from Massachusetts, that the act partook of the nature of a contract between the government and the officers, sailors and marines, comprehended within its provisions. There might be some semblance of reason for the few cases which have occurred since the passage of the act; but not the slightest as far as it relates to that more numerous class which occurred before its passage. And yet the amendment keeps the act open for the latter as well as the former. As strong as this objection is to the amendment as it stands, there are others not less so.

"It introduces new and extraordinary principles into our pension list. It gives pensions for life—yes, beyond—to children for twenty-one years, as well as the widows of the deceased officer, sailor or marine, who may die while in service. It makes no distinction between the death of the gallant and brave in battle, or him who may die quietly in his hammock or his bed on shore, or even him who commits suicide. Nor does it even distinguish between those who have served a long or a short time. The widows and children of all, however short the service, even for a single day, whatever might be the cause of death, are entitled, under this fraudulent act, to receive pensions, the widow for life, and the children for twenty-one years. To let in this undeserving class, to this unmeasured liberality of public bounty, this act is to be kept alive for an indefinite length of time—till the Congress may hereafter choose to repeal it.

"The object of my amendment, said Mr. C., is to correct this monstrous abuse; and, for this purpose, he proposed so to modify the amendment of the senator from Mississippi, as to exclude all who are not now on the pension roll from receiving pensions under the act of 1837, and also to prevent any one from being put on the navy pension roll hereafter under any act, except those of April 23, 1800, January 20, 1813, and the second section of the act of 30th March, 1814. These acts limit the pensions to the case of officers, sailors and marines, being disabled in the line of their duty, and limit the pensions to their widows and children to five years, even in those meritorious cases. Mr. C. then sent his amendment to the chair. It proposed to strike out all after the word 'now,' and insert, 'the pension roll, under the act of 1837, shall receive their pension till otherwise decided by law, but no one shall hereafter be put on the navy pension roll, under the said act, or any other act, except that of April 23, 1800, and the act of January 24, 1813, and the second section of the act of 3d March, 1814.' The question was then taken on the amendment by a count, and the Chair announced the amendment was lost—ayes 20, noes 21. Mr. Calhoun inquired if the Chair had voted. The Chair said he had voted with the majority. Mr. Buchanan then said he would offer an amendment which he had attempted to get an opportunity of offering in committee. It was to strike out the words 'until otherwise directed by law,' and insert the words 'until the close of the next session of Congress,' so as to limit the operations of the bill to that period. The amendment was adopted, and the amendments to the bill were ordered to be engrossed, and the bill ordered to a third reading."

Mr. Pierce having been long a member of the Pension Committee had seen the abuses to which our pension laws gave rise, and spoke decidedly against their abuse—and especially in the naval branch of the service. He said:

"There were cases of officers receiving pay for full disability, when in command of line-of-battle ships. The law of 1837 gave pay to officers from the time of their disability. He had been long enough connected with the Pension Committee to understand something of it. He had now in his drawer more than fifty letters from officers of the army, neither begging nor imploring, but demanding to be placed on the same footing with the navy in regard to pensions. He thought, on his conscience, that the pension system of this country was the worst on the face of the earth, and that they could never have either an army or a navy until there were reforms of more things than pensions. He pointed to the military academy, appointments to which rested on the influence that could be brought to bear by both Houses of Congress. He had looked on that *scientific institution*, from which no army would ever have a commander while West Point was in the ascendency; and he would tell why. The principles on which Frederick the Great and Napoleon acted were those to make soldiers—where merit was, reward always followed, but had they not witnessed cases of men of character, courage, and capacity, asking, from day to day, in vain for the humble rank of third lieutenant in your army, who would be glad to have such appointments? I know (said Mr. P.) a man who, at the battle of the *Withlacoochie*, had he performed the same service under Napoleon, would have received a *baton*. But in ours what did he get? Three times did that gallant fellow, with his arm broken and hanging at his side, charge the Indians, and drive them from their hammocks, where they were intrenched. The poor sergeant staid in the service until his time expired, and that was all he got for his gallantry and disinterestedness. Such instances of neglect would upset any service, destroy all emulation, and check all proper pride and ambition in subordinates. If ever they were to have a good army or navy, they must promote merit in both branches of service, as every truly great general had done, and every wise government ought to do."

In the House of Representatives an instructive debate took place, chiefly between Mr. Adams, and Mr. Francis Thomas, of Maryland, in which the origin and course of the act was somewhat traced—enough to find out that it was passed in the Senate upon the faith of a committee, without any discussion in the body; and in the House by the previous question, cutting off all debate; and so quietly and rapidly as to escape the knowledge of the most vigilant members—the knowledge of Mr. Adams himself, proverbially diligent. In the course of his remarks he (Mr. Adams) said:

"Upwards of $1,200,000 in the year 1837, constituting that fund, had been accumulating for a number of years. What had become of it, if the fund was exhausted? It was wasted—it was gone. And what was it gone for? Gentlemen would tell the House that it had gone to pay those pensioners not provided for by the 8th and 9th sections of the act which had been read—the act of 1800; but to provide for the payment of others, their wives and children; and their cousins, uncles and aunts, for aught he knew—provided for by the act of 1837. It was gone. Now, he wished gentlemen who were so much attached to the *economies* of the present administration, to make a little comparison between the condition of the fund now and its condition in 1837, when the sum of $1,200,000 had accumulated—from the interest of which all the pensions designated in the act of 1800 were to have been paid. In the space of three little years, this fund of $1,200,000 (carrying an interest of $70,000) was totally gone—absorbed—not a dollar of it left. Yes: there were some State stocks, to be sure; about $18,000 or less; but they were unsaleable; and it was because they were unsaleable that this appropriation, in part, was wanted. How came this act of 1837 to have passed Congress? Because he saw, from the ground taken by the chairman of the committee on naval affairs, that it was Congress that had been guilty of this waste of the public money; the President had nothing to do with it—the administration had nothing to do with it. How, he asked, was this law of 1837 passed? Would the Chairman of the Committee on Naval Affairs tell the House how it had been passed; by whom it had been brought in and supported; and in what manner it had been carried through both Houses of Congress? If he would, we should then hear whether it came from whigs; or from economists, retrenchers, and reformers."

Mr. Francis Thomas, now the Chairman of the Committee on Naval Affairs, in answer to Mr. Adams's inquiry, as to who were the authors of this act of 1837, stated that

"It had been reported to the Senate by the honorable Mr. Robinson, of Illinois, and sent to the Committee on Naval Affairs, of which Mr. Southard was a member, and he had reported the bill to the Senate, by whom it had been passed without a division. The Senate bill coming into the House, had been referred to the Committee on Naval Affairs, in the House. Mr. T. read the names of this committee, among which that of Mr. Wise was one. The bill had been ordered to its third reading without a division, and passed by the House without amendment.

"Mr. Wise explained, stating that, though his name appeared on the naval committee, he was not responsible for the bill. He was at that time but nominally one of the committee—his attention was directed elsewhere—he had other fish to fry—and could no longer attend to the business of that committee [of which he had previously been an active member], being appointed on another, which occupied his time and thoughts."

Mr. Adams, while condemning the act of 1837, would not now refuse to pay the pensioners out of the Treasury. He continued:

"When the act of 1837 was before Congress then was the time to have inquired whether these persons were fairly entitled to such a pension—whether Congress was bound to provide for widows and children, and for relatives in the seventh degree (for aught he knew). But that was not now the inquiry. He thought that, by looking at the journals, gentlemen would see that the bill was passed through under the previous question, or something of that kind. He was in the House, but he could not say how it passed. He was not conscious of it; and the discussion must have been put down in the way in which such things were usually done in this House—by clapping the previous question upon it. No questions were asked; and that was the way in which the bill passed. He did not think he could tell the whole story; but he thought it very probable that there were those in this House who could tell if they would, and who could tell what private interests were provided for in it. He had not been able to look quite far enough behind the curtain to know these things, but he knew that the bill was passed in a way quite common since the reign of reform commenced in squandering away the public treasure. *That* he affirmed, and the Chairman of the Committee on Naval Affairs would not, he thought, undertake to contradict it. So much for that."

Mr. Adams showed that a further loss had been sustained under this pension act of 1837, under the conduct of the House itself, at the previous session, in refusing to consider a message from the President, and in refusing to introduce a resolution to show the loss which was about to be sustained. At that time there was a part of this naval pension fund ($153,000) still on hand, but it was in stocks, greatly depreciated; and the President sent in a report from the Secretary of the Navy, that $50,000 was wanted for the half-yearly payments due the first of July; and, if not appropriated by Congress, the stocks must be sold for what they would bring. On this head, he said:

"Towards the close of the last session of Congress, a message was transmitted by the President, covering a communication from the Secretary of the Navy, suggesting that an appropriation of $50,000 was necessary to meet the payment of pensions coming due on the 1st of July last. The message was sent on the 19th of June, and there was in it a letter from the Secretary of the Navy, stating that the sum of $50,000 was required to pay pensions coming due on the then 1st of July, and that it was found impracticable to effect a sale of the stocks belonging to the fund, even at considerable loss, in time to meet the payment. What did the House do with that message? It had no time to consider it; and then it was that he had offered his resolutions. But the House would not receive them—would not allow them to be read. The time of payment came—and sacrifices of the stocks were made, which were absolutely indispensable so long as the House would not make the payment. And that $50,000 was one of the demonstrations and reductions from the expenditures of 1840, about which the President and the Secretary of the Treasury were congratulating themselves and the country. They called for the $50,000. They told the House that if that sum was not appropriated, it would be necessary to make great sacrifices. Yet the House refused to consider the subject at all.

"He had desired a long time to say this much to the House; and he said it now, although a little *out* of order, because he had never been allowed to say it *in* order. At the last session the House would not hear him upon any thing; and it was that consideration which induced him to offer the resolutions he had read, and which gave something like a sample of these things. He offered them after the very message calling for $50,000 for this very object, had come in. But no, it was not in order, and there was a gentleman here who cried out "*I object!*" He (Mr. A.) was not heard by the House, but he had now been heard; and he hoped that when he should again offer these resolutions, as he wished to do, they might at least be allowed to go on the journal as a record, to show that such propositions had been offered. Those resolutions went utterly and entirely against the system of purchasing State bonds above par, and selling them fifty or sixty per cent. below par."

These debates are instructive, as showing in what manner legislation can be carried on, under the silencing process of the previous question. Here was a bill, slipped through the House, without the knowledge of its vigilant members, by which a fund of one million two hundred thousand dollars was squandered at once, and a charge of about $100,000 per annum put upon the Treasury to supply the place of the squandered fund, to continue during the lives of the pensioners, so far as they were widows or invalids, and until twenty-one years of age, so far as they were children. And it is remarkable that no one took notice of the pregnant insinuation of Mr. Adams, equivalent to an affirmation, that, although he could not tell the whole story of the passage of the act of 1837, there were others in the House who could, if they would; and also could tell what private interests were provided for.

No branch of the public service requires the reforming and retrenching hand of Congress more than the naval, now costing (ocean steam mail lines included) above eighteen millions of dollars: to be precise—$18,586,547, and 41 cents; and exclusive of the coast survey, about $400,000 more; and exclusive of the naval pensions. The civil, diplomatic, and miscellaneous branch is frightful, now amounting to $17,255,929 and 59 cents: and the military, also, now counting $12,571,496 and 64 cents (not including the pensions). Both these branches cry aloud for retrenchment and reform; but not equally with the naval—which stands the least chance to receive it. The navy, being a maritime establishment, has been considered a branch of service with which members from the interior were supposed to have but little acquaintance; and, consequently, but little right of interference. I have seen many eyes open wide, when a member from the interior would presume to speak upon it. By consequence, it has fallen chiefly under the management of members from the sea-coast—the tide-water districts of the Atlantic coast: where there is an interest in its growth, and also in its abuses. Seven navy yards (while Great Britain has but two); the constant building and equally constant repairing and altering vessels;

their renewed equipment; the enlistment and discharge of crews; the schools and hospitals; the dry docks and wet docks; the congregation of officers ashore; and the ample pension list: all these make an expenditure, perennial and enormous, and always increasing, creates a powerful interest in favor of every proposition to spend money on the navy—especially in the north-east, where the bulk of the money goes; and an interest not confined to the members of Congress from those districts, but including a powerful lobby force, supplied with the arguments which deceive many, and the means which seduce more. While this management remains local, reform and retrenchment are not to be expected; nor could any member accomplish any thing without the support and countenance of an administration. Besides a local interest, potential on the subject, against reform, party spirit, or policy, opposes the same obstacle. The navy has been, and still is, to some degree, a party question—one party assuming to be its guardian and protector; and defending abuses to sustain that character. So far as this question goes to the *degree*, and *kind* of a navy—whether fleets to fight battles for the dominion of the seas, or cruisers to protect commerce—it is a fair question, on which parties may differ: but as to abuse and extravagance, there should be no difference. And yet what but abuse—what but headlong, wilful, and irresponsible extravagance, could carry up our naval expenditure to 18 millions of dollars, in time of peace, without a ship of the line afloat! and without vessels enough to perform current service, without hiring and purchasing!

CHAPTER LXXIII.

HOME SQUADRON, AND AID TO PRIVATE STEAM LINES.

Great Britain has a home squadron, and that results from her geographical structure as a cluster of islands, often invaded, more frequently threatened, and always liable to sudden descents upon some part of her coast, resulting from her proximity to continental Europe, and engaged as principal or ally in almost all the wars of that continent. A fleet for home purposes, to cruise continually along her coasts, and to watch the neighboring coasts of her often enemies, was, then, a necessity of her insular position. Not so with the United States. We are not an island, but a continent, geographically remote from Europe, and politically still more so— unconnected with the wars of Europe—having but few of our own; having but little cause to expect descents and invasions, and but little to fear from them, if they came. Piracy had disappeared from the West Indies twenty years before. We had then no need for a home squadron. But Great Britain had one; and therefore we must. That was the true reason, with the desire for a great navy, cherished by the party opposed to the democracy (no matter under what name), and now dominant in all the departments of the government, for the creation of a home squadron at this session. The Secretary of the Navy and the navy board recommended it: Mr. Thomas Butler King, from the Naval Committee of the House, reported a bill for it, elaborately recommended in a most ample report: the two Houses passed it: the President approved it: and thus, at this extra session, was fastened upon the country a supernumerary fleet of two frigates, two sloops, two schooners, and two armed steamers: for the annual subsistence and repairs of which, about nine hundred thousand dollars were appropriated. This was fifteen years ago; and the country has yet to hear of the first want, the first service, rendered by this domestic squadron. In the mean time, it furnishes comfortable pay and subsistence, and commodious living about home, to some considerable number of officers and men.

But the ample report which was drawn up, and of which five thousand extra copies were printed, and the speeches delivered in its favor were bound to produce reasons for this new precaution against the danger of invasion, now to be provided after threescore years of existence without it, and when we had grown too strong, and too well covered our maritime cities with fortresses, to dread the descent of any enemy. Reasons were necessary to be given, and were; in which the British example, of course, was omitted. But reasons were given (in addition to the main object of defence), as that it would be a school for the instruction of the young midshipmen; and that it would give employment to many junior officers then idle in the cities. With respect to the first of these reasons it was believed by some that the merchant service was the best school in which a naval officer was ever trained; and with respect to the idle officers, that the true remedy was not to create so many. The sum appropriated by the bill was in gross—so much for all the different objects named in the bill, without saying how much for each. This was objected to by Mr. McKay of North Carolina, as being contrary to democratic practice, which required specific appropriations; also as being a mere disguise for an increase of the navy; and further that it was not competent for Congress to limit the employment of a navy. He said:

> "That the bill before the committee proposed to appropriate a gross sum to effect the object in view, which he deemed a departure from the wholesome rule heretofore observed in making appropriations. It was known to all that since the political revolution of 1800, which placed the democratic party in power, the doctrine had generally prevailed, that all our appropriations should be specific. Now he would suggest to the chairman whether it would not be better to pursue that course in the present instance. Here Mr. McKay enumerated the different items of expenditure to be provided for in the bill, and named the specific sum for each. This was the form, he said, in which all our naval appropriation bills had heretofore passed. He saw no reason for a departure from this wholesome practice in this instance—a practice which was the best and most effectual means of securing the accountability of our disbursing officers. There was another suggestion he would throw out for the consideration of the chairman, and he thought it possessed some weight. This bill purported to be for the establishment of a home squadron, but he looked upon it as nothing more nor less than for the increase of the navy. Again, could Congress be asked to direct the manner in which this squadron, after it was fitted out, should be employed? It was true that by the constitution,

Congress alone was authorized to build and fit out a navy, but the President was the commander-in-chief, and had alone the power to direct how and where it should be employed. The title of this bill, therefore, should be 'a bill to increase the navy,' for it would not be imperative on the President to employ this squadron on our coasts. Mr. M. said he did not rise to enter into a long discussion, but merely to suggest to the consideration of the chairman of the committee, the propriety of making the appropriations in the bill specific."

"Mr. WISE said that he agreed entirely with the gentleman from North Carolina as to the doctrine of specific appropriations; and if he supposed that this bill violated that salutary principle he should be willing to amend it. But it did not; it declared a specific object, for which the money was given. He did not see the necessity of going into all the items which made up the sum. That Congress had no power to ordain that a portion of the navy should be always retained upon the coast as a home squadron, was to him a new doctrine. The bill did not say that these vessels should never be sent any where else."

"Mr. MCKAY insisted on the ground he had taken, and went into a very handsome eulogy on the principle of specific appropriations of the public money, as giving to the people the only security they had for the proper and the economical use of their money; but this, by the present shape of the bill, they would entirely be deprived of. The bill might be modified with the utmost ease, but he should move no amendments."

Mr. Thomas Butler King, the reporter of the bill, entered largely into its support, and made some comparative statements to show that much money had been expended heretofore on the navy with very inadequate results in getting guns afloat, going as high as eight millions of dollars in a year and floating but five hundred and fifty guns; and claimed an improvement now, as, for seven millions and a third they would float one thousand and seventy guns. Mr. King then said:

"He had heard much about the abuse and misapplication of moneys appropriated for the navy, and he believed it all to be true. To illustrate the truth of the charge, he would refer to the table already quoted, showing on one hand the appropriations made, and on the other the results thereby obtained. In 1800 there had been an appropriation of $2,704,148, and we had then 876 guns afloat; while in 1836, with an appropriation of $7,011,055, we had but 462 guns afloat. In 1841, with an appropriation of a little over *three* millions, we had 836 guns afloat; and in 1838, with an appropriation of over *eight* millions, we had but 554 guns afloat. These facts were sufficient to show how enormous must have been the abuses somewhere."

Mr. King also gave a statement of the French and British navies, and showed their great strength, in order to encourage our own building of a great navy to be able to cope with them on the ocean. He

"Alluded to the change which had manifested itself in the naval policy of Great Britain, in regard to a substitution of steam power for ordinary ships of war. He stated the enumeration of the British fleet, in 1840, to be as follows: ships of the line, 105; vessels of a lower grade, in all, 403; and war steamers, 87. The number of steamers had since then been stated at 300. The French navy, in 1840, consisted of 23 ships of the line, 180 lesser vessels, and 36 steamers; besides which, there had been, at that time, eight more steamers on the stocks. These vessels could be propelled by steam across the Atlantic in twelve or fourteen days. What would be the condition of the lives and property of our people, if encountered by a force of this description, without a gun to defend themselves?"

Lines of railroad, with their steam-cars, had not, at that time, taken such extension and multiplication as to be taken into the account for national defence. Now troops can come from the geographical centre of Missouri in about sixty hours (summoned by the electric telegraph in a few minutes), and arrive at almost any point on the Atlantic coast; and from all the intermediate States in a proportionately less time. The railroad, and the electric telegraph, have opened a new era in defensive war, and especially for the United States, superseding old ideas, and depriving invasion of all alarm. But the bill was passed—almost unanimously—only eight votes against it in the House; namely: Linn Boyd of Kentucky; Walter Coles of Virginia; John G. Floyd of New York; William O. Goode of Virginia; Cave Johnson, Abraham McClelland, and Hopkins L. Turney of Tennessee; and John Thompson Mason of Maryland. It passed the Senate without yeas and nays.

A part of the report in favor of the home squadron was also a recommendation to extend assistance out of the public treasury to the establishment of private lines of ocean steamers, adapted to war purposes; and in conformity to it Mr. King moved this resolution:

> "*Resolved*, That the Secretary of the Navy is hereby directed to inquire into the expediency of aiding individuals or companies in our establishment of lines of armed steamers between some of our principal Northern and Southern ports, and to foreign ports; to advertise for proposals for the establishment of such lines as he may deem most important and practicable; and to report to this House at the next session of Congress."

This resolution was adopted, and laid the foundation for those annual enormous appropriations for private lines of ocean steamers which have subjected many members of Congress to such odious imputations, and which has taken, and is taking, so many millions of the public money to enable individuals to break down competition, and enrich themselves at the public expense. It was a measure worthy to go with the home squadron, and the worst of the two—each a useless waste of money; and each illustrating the difficulty, and almost total impossibility, of getting rid of bad measures when once passed, and an interest created for them.

CHAPTER LXXIV.

RECHARTER OF THE DISTRICT BANKS: MR. BENTON'S SPEECH: EXTRACTS.

Mr. BENTON then proposed the following amendment:

> "*And be it further enacted*, That each and every of said banks be, and they are hereby, expressly prohibited from issuing or paying out, under any pretence whatever, any bill, note, or other paper, designed or intended to be used and circulated as money, of a less denomination than five dollars, or of any denomination between five and ten dollars, after one year from the passage of this bill; or between ten and twenty dollars, after two years from the same time; and for any violation of the provisions of this section, or for issuing or paying out the notes of any bank in a state of suspension, its own inclusive, the offending bank shall incur all the penalties and forfeitures to be provided and directed by the first section of this act for the case of suspension or refusal to pay in specie; to be enforced in like manner as is directed by that section."

Mr. BENTON. The design of the amendment is to suppress two great evils in our banking system: the evil of small notes, and that of banks combining to sustain each other in a state of suspension. Small notes are a curse in themselves to honest, respectable banks, and lead to their embarrassment, whether issued by themselves or others. They go into hands of laboring people, and become greatly diffused, and give rise to panics; and when a panic is raised it cannot be stopped among the holders of these small notes. Their multitudinous holders cannot go into the counting-room to examine assets, and ascertain an ultimate ability. They rush to the counter, and demand pay. They assemble in crowds, and spread alarm. When started, the alarm becomes contagious—makes a run upon all banks; and overturns the good as well as the bad. Small notes are a curse to all good banks. They are the cause of suspensions. When the Bank of England commenced operations, she issued no notes of a less denomination than one hundred pounds sterling; and when the notes were paid into the Bank, they were cancelled and destroyed. But in the course of one hundred and three years, she worked down from one hundred pound notes to one pound notes. And when did they commence reducing the amount of their notes? During the administration of Sir Robert Walpole. When the notes got down to one pound, specie was driven from circulation, and went to France and Holland, and a suspension of six and twenty years followed.

They are a curse to all good banks in another way: they banish gold and silver from the country: and when that is banished the foundation which supports the bank is removed: and the bank itself must come tumbling down. While there is gold and silver in the country—in common circulation—banks will be but little called upon for it: and if pressed can get assistance from their customers. But when it is banished the country, they alone are called upon, and get no help if hard run. All good banks should be against small notes on their own account.

These small notes are a curse to the public. They are the great source of counterfeiting. Look at any price current, and behold the catalogue of the counterfeits. They are almost all on the small denominations—under twenty dollars. And this counterfeiting, besides being a crime in itself, leads to crimes—to a general demoralization in passing them. Holders cannot afford to lose them: they cannot trace out the person from whom they got them. They gave value for them; and pass them to somebody—generally the most meritorious and least able to bear the loss—the day-laborer. Finally, they stop in somebody's hands—generally in the hands of a working man or woman.

Why are banks so fond of issuing these small notes? Why, in the first place, banks of high character are against them: it is only the predatory class that are for them: and, unfortunately, they are a numerous progeny. It is in vain they say they issue them for public accommodation. The public would be much better accommodated with silver dollars, gold dollars—with half, whole, double, and quarter eagles—whereof they would have enough if these predatory notes were suppressed. No! they are issued for profit—for dishonest profit—for the shameful and criminal purpose of getting something for nothing. It is for the wear and tear of these little pilfering messengers! for their loss in the hands of somebody! which loss is the banker's gain! the gain of a day's or a week's work from a poor man, or woman, for nothing. Shame on such a spirit, and criminal punishment on it besides. But although the gains are small individually, and in the petty larceny spirit, yet the aggregate is great; and enters into the regular calculation of profit in these paper money machines; and counts in the end. There is always a large per centum of these notes outstanding—never to come back. When, at the end of twenty-five years, Parliament repealed the privilege granted to the Bank of England to issue notes under five pounds, a large amount were outstanding; and though the repeal took place more than twenty years ago, yet every quarterly return of the Bank now shows that millions of these notes are still outstanding, which are lost or destroyed, and never will be presented. The Bank of England does not now issue any note under five pounds sterling: nor any other bank in England. The large banks repulsed the privilege for themselves, and got it denied to all the small class. To carry the iniquity of these pillaging little notes to the highest point, and to make them open swindlers, is to issue them at one place, redeemable at another. That is to double the cheat— to multiply the chance of losing the little plunderer by sending him abroad, and to get a chance of "*shaving*" him in if he does not go.

The statistics of crime in Great Britain show, that of all the counterfeiting of bank bills and paper securities in that kingdom, more is counterfeited on notes under five pounds than over and it is the same in this country. On whom does the loss of these counterfeit notes fall? On the poor and the ignorant—the laborer and the mechanic. Hence these banks inflict a double injury on the poorer classes; and of all the evils of the banking system, the most revolting is its imposing unequal burdens on that portion of the people the least able to bear them.

Mr. B. then instanced a case in point of an Insurance Company in St. Louis, which, in violation of law, assumed banking privileges, and circulated to a large extent the notes of a suspended bank. Up to Saturday night these notes were paid out from its counter, and the working man and mechanics of St. Louis were paid their week's wages in them. Well, when Monday morning came, the Insurance Company refused to receive one of them, and they fell at once to fifty cents on the dollar. Thus the laborer and the mechanic had three days of their labor annihilated, or had worked three days for the exclusive benefit of those who had swindled them; and all this by a bank having power to receive or refuse what paper they please, and when they please. And the Senate are now called upon to confer the same privilege upon the banks of this district.

Mr. B. said it was against the immutable principles of justice—in opposition to God's most holy canon, to make a thing of value to-day, which will be of none to-morrow. You might as well permit the dry goods merchant to call his yard measure three yards, or the grocer to call his quart three quarts, as to permit the banker to call his dollar three dollars. There is no difference in principle, though more subtle in the manner of doing it. Money is the standard of value, as the yard, and the gallon, and the pound weight, were the standards of measure.

When he proposed the amendment, he considered it a proper opportunity to bring before the people of the United States the great question, whether they should have an exclusive paper currency or not. He wished to call their attention to this war upon the currency of the constitution—a war unremitting and merciless—to establish in this country an exclusive paper currency. This war to subvert the gold and silver currency of the constitution, is waged by that party who vilify your branch mints, ridicule gold, ridicule silver, go for banks at all times and at all places; and go for a paper circulation down to notes of six and a quarter cents. He rejoiced that this question was presented in that body, on a platform so high that every American can see it—the question of a sound or depreciated currency. He was glad to see the advocates of banks, State and national, show their hand on this question.

To hear these paper-money advocates celebrate their idols—for they really seem to worship bank notes—and the smaller and meaner the better—one would be tempted to think that bank notes were the ancient and universal currency of the world, and that gold and silver were a modern invention—an innovation—an experiment—the device of some quack, who deserved no better answer than to be called humbug. To hear them discoursing of "sound banks," and "sound circulating medium," one would suppose that they considered gold and silver unsound, and subject to disease, rottenness, and death. But, why do they apply this phrase "sound" to banks and their currency? It is a phrase never applied to any thing which is not subject to unsoundness—to disease—to rottenness—to death. The very phrase brings up the idea of something subject to unsoundness; and that is true of banks of circulation and their currency: but it is not true of gold and silver:

and the phrase is never applied to them. No one speaks of the gold or silver currency as being sound, and for the reason that no one ever heard of it as rotten.

Young merchants, and some old ones, think there is no living without banks—no transacting business without a paper money currency. Have these persons ever heard of Holland, where there are merchants dealing in tens of millions, and all of it in gold and silver? Have they ever heard of Liverpool and Manchester, where there was no bank of circulation, not even a branch of the Bank of England; and whose immense operations were carried on exclusively upon gold and the commercial bill of exchange? Have they ever heard of France, where the currency amounts to four hundred and fifty millions of dollars, and it all hard money? For, although the Bank of France has notes of one hundred and five hundred, and one thousand francs, they are not used as currency but as convenient bills of exchange, for remittance, or travelling. Have they ever heard of the armies, and merchants, and imperial courts of antiquity? Were the Roman armies paid with paper? did the merchant princes deal in paper? Was Nineveh and Babylon built on paper? Was Solomon's temple so built? And yet, according to these paper-money idolaters, we cannot pay a handful of militia without paper! cannot open a dry goods store in a shanty without paper! cannot build a house without paper! cannot build a village of log houses in the woods, or a street of shanties in a suburb, without a bank in their midst! This is real humbuggery; and for which the industrial classes—the whole working population, have to pay an enormous price. Does any one calculate the cost to the people of banking in our country? how many costly edifices have to be built? what an army of officers have to be maintained? what daily expenses have to be incurred? how many stockholders must get profits? in a word, what a vast sum a bank lays out before it begins to make its half yearly dividend of four or five per centum, leaving a surplus—all to come out of the productive classes of the people? And after that comes the losses by the wear and tear of small notes—by suspensions and breakings—by expansions and contractions—by making money scarce when they want to buy, and plenty when they want to sell. We talk of standing armies in Europe, living on the people: we have an army of bank officers here doing the same. We talk of European taxes; the banks tax us here as much as kings tax their subjects. And this district is crying out for banks. It has six, and wants them rechartered—Congress all the time spending more hard money among them than they can use. They had twelve banks: and what did they have to do? Send to Holland, where there is not a single bank of circulation, to borrow one million of dollars in gold, which they got at five per centum per annum; and then could not pay the interest. At the end of the third year the interest could not be paid; and Congress had to pay it to save the whole corporate effects of the city from being sold—sold to the Dutch, because the Dutch had no banks. And sold it would have been if Congress had not put up the money: for the distress warrant was out, and was to be levied in thirty days. Then what does this city want with banks of circulation? She has no use for them; but I only propose to make them a little safer by suppressing their small notes, and preventing them from dealing in the depreciated notes of suspended, or broken banks.

CHAPTER LXXV.

REVOLT IN CANADA: BORDER SYMPATHY: FIRMNESS OF MR. VAN BUREN: PUBLIC PEACE ENDANGERED—AND PRESERVED:—CASE OF MCLEOD.

The revolt which took place in Canada in the winter of 1837-'8 led to consequences which tried the firmness of the administration, and also tried the action of our duplicate form of government in its relations with foreign powers. The revolt commenced imposingly, with a large show of disjointed forces, gaining advantages at the start; but was soon checked by the regular local troops. The French population, being the majority of the people, were chiefly its promoters, with some emigrants from the United States; and when defeated they took refuge on an island in the Niagara River on the British side, near the Canadian coast, and were collecting men and supplies from the United States to renew the contest. From the beginning an intense feeling in behalf of the insurgents manifested itself all along the United States border, upon a line of a thousand miles—from Vermont to Michigan. As soon as blood began to flow on the Canadian side, this feeling broke out into acts on the American side, and into organization for the assistance of the revolting party—the patriots, as they were called. Men assembled and enrolled, formed themselves into companies and battalions, appointed officers—even generals—issued proclamations—forced the public stores and supplied themselves with arms and ammunition: and were certainly assembling in sufficient numbers to have enabled the insurgents to make successful head against any British forces then in the provinces. The whole border line was in a state of excitement and commotion—many determined to cross over, and assist—many more willing to see the assistance given: the smaller part only discountenanced the proceeding and wished to preserve the relations which the laws of the country, and the duties of good neighborhood, required. To the Canadian authorities these movements on the American side were the cause of the deepest solicitude; and not without reason: for the numbers, the inflamed feeling, and the determined temper of these auxiliaries, presented a force impossible for the Canadian authorities to resist, if dashing upon them, and difficult for their own government to restrain. From the first demonstration, and without waiting for any request from the British minister at Washington (Mr. FOX), the President took the steps which showed his determination to have the laws of neutrality respected. A proclamation was immediately issued, admonishing and commanding all citizens to desist from such illegal proceedings, and threatening the guilty with the utmost penalties of the law. But the President knew full well that it was not a case in which a proclamation, and a threat, were to have efficacy; and he took care to add material means to his words. Instructions were issued to all the federal law officers along the border, the marshals and district attorneys, to be vigilant in making arrests: and many were made, and prosecutions instituted. He called upon the governors of the border States to aid in suppressing the illegal movement: which they did. And to these he added all the military and naval resources which could be collected. Major-general Scott was sent to the line, with every disposable regular soldier, and with authority to call on the governors of New York and Michigan for militia and volunteers: several steamboats were chartered on Lake Erie, placed under the command of naval officers, well manned with regular soldiers, and ordered to watch the lake.

The fidelity, and even sternness with which all these lawless expeditions from the United States, were repressed and rebuked by President Van Buren, were shown by him in his last communication to Congress on the subject; in which he said:

> "Information has been given to me, derived from official and other sources, that many citizens of the United States have associated together to make hostile incursions from our territory into Canada, and to aid and abet insurrection there, in violation of the obligations and laws of the United States, and in open disregard of their own duties as citizens.

> "The results of these criminal assaults upon the peace and order of a neighboring country have been, as was to be expected, fatally destructive to the misguided or deluded persons engaged in them, and highly injurious to those in whose behalf they are professed to have been undertaken. The authorities in Canada, from intelligence received of such intended movements among our citizens, have felt themselves obliged to take precautionary measures against them; have actually embodied the militia, and assumed an attitude to repel the invasion to which they believed the colonies were exposed from the United States. A state of feeling

on both sides of the frontier has thus been produced, which called for prompt and vigorous interference. If an insurrection existed in Canada, the amicable dispositions of the United States towards Great Britain, as well as their duty to themselves, would lead them to maintain a strict neutrality, and to restrain their citizens from all violations of the laws which have been passed for its enforcement. But this government recognizes a still higher obligation to repress all attempts on the part of its citizens to disturb the peace of a country where order prevails, or has been re-established. Depredations by our citizens upon nations at peace with the United States, or combinations for committing them, have at all times been regarded by the American government and people with the greatest abhorrence. Military incursions by our citizens into countries so situated, and the commission of acts of violence on the members thereof, in order to effect a change in its government, or under any pretext whatever, have, from the commencement of our government, been held equally criminal on the part of those engaged in them, and as much deserving of punishment as would be the disturbance of the public peace by the perpetration of similar acts within our own territory."

By these energetic means, invasions from the American side were prevented; and in a contest with the British regulars and the local troops, the disjointed insurgents, though numerous, were overpowered—dispersed—subjected—or driven out of Canada. Mr. Van Buren had discharged the duties of neutrality most faithfully, not merely in obedience to treaties and the law of nations, but from a high conviction of what was right and proper in itself, and necessary to the well-being of his own country as well as that of a neighboring power. Interruption of friendly intercourse with Great Britain, would be an evil itself, even if limited to such interruption: but the peace of the United States might be endangered: and it was not to be tolerated that bands of disorderly citizens should bring on war. He had done all that the laws, and all that a sense of right and justice required—and successfully, to the repression of hostile movements—and to the satisfaction of the British authorities. Faithfully and ably seconded by his Secretary of State (Mr. Forsyth), and by his Attorney-general (Mr. Gilpin), he succeeded in preserving our neutral relations in the most trying circumstances to which they had ever been exposed, and at large cost of personal popularity to himself: for the sympathy of the border States resented his so earnest interference to prevent aid to the insurgents.

The whole affair was over, and happily, when a most unexpected occurrence revived the difficulty—gave it a new turn—and made the soil of the United States itself, the scene of invasion—of bloodshed—of conflagration—and of abduction. Some remnant of the dispersed insurgents had taken refuge on Navy Island, near the Canadian shore; and reinforced by some Americans, were making a stand there, and threatening a descent upon the British colonies. Their whole number has been ascertained to have been no more than some five hundred—but magnified by rumor at the time to as many thousands. A small steamboat from the American side, owned by a citizen of the United States, was in the habit of carrying men and supplies to this assemblage on the island. Her practices became known to the British military authorities, encamped with some thousand men at Chippewa, opposite the island; and it was determined to take her in the fact, and destroy her. It was then the last of December. A night expedition of boats was fitted out to attack this vessel, moored to the island; but not finding her there, the vessel was sought for in her own waters—found moored to the American shore; and there attacked and destroyed. The news of this outrage was immediately communicated to the President, and by him made known to Congress in a special message—accompanied by the evidence on which the information rested, and by a statement of the steps which the President had taken in consequence. The principal evidence was from the master of the boat—her name, the Caroline—and Schlosser, on the American shore, her home and harbor. After admitting that the boat had been employed in carrying men and supplies to the assemblage on Navy Island, his affidavit continues:

"That from this point the Caroline ran to Schlosser, arriving there at three o'clock in the afternoon; that, between this time and dark, the Caroline made two trips to Navy Island, landing as before. That, at about six o'clock in the evening, this deponent caused the said Caroline to be landed at Schlosser, and made fast with chains to the dock at that place. That the crew and officers of the Caroline numbered ten, and that, in the course of the evening, twenty-three individuals, all of whom were citizens of the United States, came on board of the Caroline, and requested this deponent and other officers of the boat to permit them to remain on board during the night, as they were unable to get lodgings at the tavern near by; these requests were acceded to, and the persons thus coming on board retired to rest, as did also all of the crew and officers of the Caroline, except such as were stationed to watch during the night. That, about midnight, this deponent was informed by one of the watch, that several boats filled with men, were making towards the Caroline from the river, and this deponent immediately gave the alarm; and before he was able to reach the deck, the Caroline was boarded by some 70 or 80 men, all of whom were armed. That they immediately commenced a warfare with muskets, swords, and cutlasses, upon the defenceless crew and passengers of the Caroline, under a fierce cry of G—d damn them, give them no quarter; kill every man: fire! fire! That the Caroline was abandoned without resistance, and the only effort made by either the crew or passengers seemed to be to escape slaughter. That this deponent narrowly escaped; having received several wounds, none of which, however, are of a serious character. That immediately after the Caroline fell into the hands of the armed force who boarded her, she was set on fire, cut loose from the dock, was towed into the current of the river, there abandoned, and soon after descended the Niagara Falls: that this deponent has made vigilant search after the individuals, thirty-three in number, who are known to have been on the Caroline at the time she was boarded, and twenty-one only are to be found, one of whom, to wit, Amos Durfee, of Buffalo, was found dead upon the dock, having received a shot from a musket, the ball of which penetrated the back part of the head, and came out at the forehead. James H. King, and Captain C. F. Harding, were seriously, though not mortally, wounded. Several others received slight wounds. The twelve individuals who are missing, this deponent has no doubt, were either murdered upon the steamboat, or found a watery grave in the cataract of the falls. And this deponent further says, that immediately after the Caroline was got into the current of the stream and abandoned, as before stated, beacon lights were discovered upon the Canada shore, near Chippewa; and after sufficient time had elapsed to enable the boats to reach that shore, this deponent distinctly heard loud and vociferous cheering at that point. That this deponent has no doubt that the individuals who boarded the Caroline, were a part of the British forces now stationed at Chippewa."

Ample corroborative testimony confirmed this affidavit—for which, in fact, there was no necessity, as the officer in command of the boats made his official report to his superior (Col. McNab), to the same effect—who published it in general orders; and celebrated the event as an exploit. This report varied but little from the American in any respect, and made it worse in others. After stating that he did not find the Caroline at Navy Island, "as expected," he went in search of her, and found her at Grand Island, and moored to the shore. The report proceeds:

"I then assembled the boats off the point of the Island, and dropped quietly down upon the steamer; we were not discovered until within twenty yards of her, when the sentry upon the gangway hailed us, and asked for the countersign, which I told him we would give when we got on board; he then fired upon us, when we immediately boarded and found from twenty to thirty men upon her decks, who were easily overcome, and in two minutes she was in our possession. As the current was running strong, and our position close to the Falls of Niagara, I deemed it most prudent to burn the vessel; but previously to setting her on fire, we took the precaution to loose her from her moorings, and turn her out into the stream, to prevent the possibility of the destruction of anything like American property. In short, all those on board the steamer who did not resist, were quietly put on shore, as I thought it possible there might be some American citizens on board. Those who assailed us, were of course dealt with according to the usages of war.

"I beg to add, that we brought one prisoner away, a British subject, in consequence of his acknowledging that he had belonged to Duncombe's army, and was on board the steamer to join Mackenzie upon Navy Island. Lieutenant McCormack, of the Royal Navy, and two others were wounded, and I regret to add that five or six of the enemy were killed."

This is the official report of Captain Drew, and it adds the crimes of impressment and abduction to all the other enormities of that midnight crime. The man carried away as a British subject, and because he had belonged to the insurgent forces in Canada, could not (even if these allegations had been proved upon him), been delivered up under any demand upon our government: yet he was carried off by violence in the night.

This outrage on the Caroline, reversed the condition of the parties, and changed the tenor of their communications. It now became the part of the United States to complain, and to demand redress; and it was immediately done in a communication from Mr. Forsyth, the Secretary of State, to Mr. Fox, the British minister, at Washington. Under date of January 5th, 1838, the Secretary wrote to him:

> "The destruction of the property, and assassination of citizens of the United States on the soil of New York, at the moment when, as is well known to you, the President was anxiously endeavoring to allay the excitement, and earnestly seeking to prevent any unfortunate occurrence on the frontier of Canada, has produced upon his mind the most painful emotions of surprise and regret. It will necessarily form the subject of a demand for redress upon her majesty's government. This communication is made to you under the expectation that, through your instrumentality, an early explanation may be obtained from the authorities of Upper Canada, of all the circumstances of the transaction; and that, by your advice to those authorities, such decisive precautions may be used as will render the perpetration of similar acts hereafter impossible. Not doubting the disposition of the government of Upper Canada to do its duty in punishing the aggressors and preventing future outrage, the President, notwithstanding, has deemed it necessary to order a sufficient force on the frontier to repel any attempt of a like character, and to make known to you that if it should occur, he cannot be answerable for the effects of the indignation of the neighboring people of the United States."

In communicating this event to Congress, Mr. Van Buren showed that he had already taken the steps which the peace and honor of the country required. The news of the outrage, spreading through the border States, inflamed the repressed feeling of the people to the highest degree, and formidable retaliatory expeditions were immediately contemplated. The President called all the resources of the frontier into instant requisition to repress these expeditions, and at the same time took measures to obtain redress from the British government. His message to the two Houses said:

> "I regret, however, to inform you that an outrage of a most aggravated character has been committed, accompanied by a hostile, though temporary invasion of our territory, producing the strongest feelings of resentment on the part of our citizens in the neighborhood, and on the whole border line; and that the excitement previously existing, has been alarmingly increased. To guard against the possible recurrence of any similar act, I have thought it indispensable to call out a portion of the militia to be posted on that frontier. The documents herewith presented to Congress show the character of the outrage committed, the measures taken in consequence of its occurrence, and the necessity for resorting to them. It will also be seen that the subject was immediately brought to the notice of the British minister accredited to this country, and the proper steps taken on our part to obtain the fullest information of all the circumstances leading to and attendant upon the transaction, preparatory to a demand for reparation."

The feeling in Congress was hardly less strong than in the border States, on account of this outrage, combining all the crimes of assassination, arson, burglary, and invasion of national territory. An act of Congress was immediately passed, placing large military means, and an appropriation of money in the President's hands, for the protection of our frontier. His demand for redress was unanimously seconded by Congress; and what had been so earnestly deprecated from the beginning, as a consequence of this border trouble—a difficulty between the two nations—had now come to pass; but entirely from the opposite side from which it had been expected.

The British government delayed the answer to the demand for redress—avoided the assumption of the criminal act—excused and justified it—but did not assume it: and in fact could not, without contradicting the official reports of her own officers, all negativing the idea of any intention to violate the territory of the United States. The orders to the officer commanding the boats, was to seek the Caroline at Navy Island, where she had been during the day, and was expected to be at night. In pursuance of this order, the fleet of boats went to the island, near midnight; and not finding the offending vessel there, sought her elsewhere. This is the official report of Capt. Drew, of the Royal Navy, commanding the boats: "I immediately directed five boats to be armed, and manned with forty-five volunteers; and, at about eleven o'clock, P. M., we pushed off from the shore for Navy Island, when not finding her there, as expected, we went in search, and found her moored between the island and the main shore." The island here spoken of as the one between which and the main shore, the Caroline was found, was the American island, called Grand Island, any descent upon which, Colonel McNab had that day officially disclaimed, because it was American territory. The United States Attorney for the District of New York, (Mr. Rodgers), then on the border to enforce the laws against the violators of our neutrality, hearing that there was a design to make a descent upon Grand Island, addressed a note to Col. McNab, commanding on the opposite side of the river, to learn its truth; and received this answer:

> "With respect to the report in the city of Buffalo, that certain forces under my command had landed upon Grand Island—an island within the territory of the United States—I can assure you that it is entirely without foundation; and that so far from my having any intention of the kind, such a proceeding would be in direct opposition to the wishes and intentions of her Britannic majesty's government, in this colony, whose servant I have the honor to be. Entering at once into the feeling which induced you to address me on this subject, I beg leave to call your attention to the following facts: That so far from occupying or intending to occupy, that or any other portion of the American territory, aggressions of a serious and hostile nature have been made upon the forces under my command from that island. Two affidavits are now before me, stating that a volley of musketry from Grand Island was yesterday fired upon a party of unarmed persons, some of whom were females, without the slightest provocation having been offered. That on the same day, one of my boats, unarmed, manned by British subjects, passing along the American shore, and without any cause being given, was fired upon from the American side, near Fort Schlosser, by cannon, the property, I am told, of the United States."

This was written on the 29th day of December, and it was eleven o'clock of the night of that day that the Caroline was destroyed on the American shore. It was Col. McNab, commanding the forces at Chippewa, that gave the order to destroy the Caroline. The letter and the order were both written the same day—probably within the same hour, as both were written in the afternoon: and they were coincident in import as well as in date. The order was to seek the offending vessel at Navy Island, being British territory, and where she was seen at dark: the letter disclaimed both the fact, and the intent, of invading Grand Island, because it was American territory: and besides the disclaimer for himself, Col. McNab superadded another equally positive in behalf of her Majesty's government in Canada, declaring that such a proceeding would be in direct opposition to the wishes and intentions of the colonial government. In the face of these facts the British government found it difficult, and for a long time impossible, to assume this act of destroying the Caroline as a government proceeding. It was never so assumed during the administration of Mr. Van Buren—a period of upwards of three years—to be precise—(and this is a case which requires precision)—three years and two months and seven days: that is to say, from the 29th of December, 1837, to March 3d, 1841.

When this letter of Col. McNab was read in the House of Representatives (which it was within a few days after it was written), Mr. Fillmore (afterwards President of the United States, and then a representative from the State of New York, and, from that part of the State which included the most disturbed portion of the border), stood up in his place, and said:

> "The letter just read by the clerk, at his colleague's request, was written in reply to one from the district attorney as to the reported intention of the British to invade Grand Island; and in it is the declaration that there was no such intention. Now, Mr. F. would call the attention of

the House to the fact that that letter was written on the 29th December, and that it was on the very night succeeding the date of it that this gross outrage was committed on the Caroline. Moreover, he would call the attention of the House to the well-authenticated fact, that, after burning the boat, and sending it over the falls, the assassins were lighted back to McNab's camp, where he was in person, by beacons lighted there for that purpose. Mr. F. certainly deprecated a war with Great Britain as sincerely as any gentleman on that floor could possibly do: and hoped, as earnestly, that these difficulties would be amicably adjusted between the two nations. Yet, he must say, that the letter of McNab, instead of affording grounds for a palliation, was, in reality, a great aggravation of the outrage. It held out to us the assurance that there was nothing of the kind to be apprehended; and yet, a few hours afterwards, this atrocity was perpetrated by an officer sent directly from the camp of that McNab."

At the time that this was spoken the order of Col. McNab to Captain Drew had not been seen, and consequently it was not known that the letter and the order were coincident in their character, and that the perfidy, implied in Mr. Fillmore's remarks, was not justly attributable to Col. McNab: but it is certain he applauded the act when done: and his letter will stand for a condemnation of it, and for the disavowal of authority to do it.

The invasion of New York was the invasion of the United States, and the President had immediately demanded redress, both for the public outrage, and for the loss of property to the owners of the boat. Mr. Van Buren's entire administration went off without obtaining an answer to these demands. As late as January, 1839—a year after the event—Mr. Stevenson, the United States minister in London, wrote: "I regret to say that no answer has yet been given to my note in the case of the Caroline." And towards the end of the same year, Mr. Forsyth, the American Secretary of State, in writing to him, expressed the belief that an answer would soon be given. He says: "I have had frequent conversations with Mr. Fox in regard to this subject—one of very recent date— and from its tone, the President expects the British government will answer your application in the case without much further delay."—Delay, however, continued; and, as late as December, 1840, no answer having yet been received, the President directed the subject again to be brought to the notice of the British government; and Mr. Forsyth accordingly wrote to Mr. Fox:

> "The President deems this to be a proper occasion to remind the government of her Britannic majesty that the case of the "Caroline" has been long since brought to the attention of her Majesty's principal Secretary of State for foreign affairs, who, up to this day, has not communicated its decision thereupon. It is hoped that the government of her Majesty will perceive the importance of no longer leaving the government of the United States uninformed of its views and intentions upon a subject which has naturally produced much exasperation, and which has led to such grave consequences. I avail myself of this occasion to renew to you the assurance of my distinguished consideration."

This was near the close of Mr. Van Buren's administration, and up to that time it must be noted, *first*, that the British government had not assumed the act of Captain Drew in destroying the Caroline; *secondly*, that it had not answered (had not refused redress) for that act. Another circumstance showed that the government, in its own conduct in relation to those engaged in that affair, had not even indirectly assumed it by rewarding those who did it. Three years after the event, in the House of Commons, Lord John Russell, the premier, was asked in his place, whether it was the intention of ministers to recommend to her Majesty to bestow any reward upon Captain Drew, and others engaged in the affair of the Caroline; to which he replied negatively, and on account of the delicate nature of the subject. His answer was: "No reward had been resolved upon, and as the question involved a subject of a very delicate nature, he must decline to answer it further." Col. McNab had been knighted; not for the destruction of the Caroline on United States territory (which his order did not justify, and his letter condemned), but for his services in putting down the revolt.

Thus the affair stood till near the close of Mr. Van Buren's administration, when an event took place which gave it a new turn, and brought on a most serious question between the United States and Great Britain, and changed the relative positions of the two countries—the United States to become the injured party, claiming redress. The circumstances were these: one Alexander McLeod, inhabitant of the opposite border shore, and a British subject, had been in the habit of boasting that he had been one of the destroyers of the Caroline, and that he had himself killed one of the "damned Yankees." There were enough to repeat these boastings on the American side of the line; and as early as the spring of 1838 the Grand Jury for the county in which the outrage had been committed, found a bill of indictment against him for murder and arson. He was then in Canada, and would never have been troubled upon the indictment if he had remained there; but, with a boldness of conduct which bespoke clear innocence, or insolent defiance, he returned to the seat of the outrage—to the county in which the indictment lay—and publicly exhibited himself in the county town. This was three years after the event; but the memory of the scene was fresh, and indignation boiled at his appearance. He was quickly arrested on the indictment, also sued for damages by the owner of the destroyed boat, and committed to jail—to take his trial in the State court of the county of Niagara. This arrest and imprisonment of McLeod immediately drew an application for his release in a note from Mr. Fox to the American Secretary of State. Under date of the 13th December, 1840, he wrote:

"I feel it my duty to call upon the government of the United States to take prompt and effectual steps for the liberation of Mr. McLeod. It is well known that the destruction of the steamboat 'Caroline' was a public act of persons in her Majesty's service, obeying the order of their superior authorities.—That act, therefore, according to the usages of nations, can only be the subject of discussion between the two national governments; it cannot justly be made the ground of legal proceedings in the United States against the individuals concerned, who were bound to obey the authorities appointed by their own government. I may add that I believe it is quite notorious that Mr. McLeod was not one of the party engaged in the destruction of the steamboat 'Caroline,' and that the pretended charge upon which he has been imprisoned rests only upon the perjured testimony of certain Canadian outlaws and their abettors, who, unfortunately for the peace of that neighborhood, are still permitted by the authorities of the State of New York to infest the Canadian frontier. The question, however, of whether Mr. McLeod was or was not concerned in the destruction of the 'Caroline,' is beside the purpose of the present communication. That act was the public act of persons obeying the constituted authorities of her Majesty's province. The national government of the United States thought themselves called upon to remonstrate against it; and a remonstrance which the President did accordingly address to her Majesty's government is still, I believe, a pending subject of diplomatic discussion between her Majesty's government and the United States legation in London. I feel, therefore, justified in expecting that the President's government will see the justice and the necessity of causing the present immediate release of Mr. McLeod, as well as of taking such steps as may be requisite for preventing others of her Majesty's subjects from being persecuted, or molested in the United States in a similar manner for the future."

This note of Mr. Fox is fair and unexceptionable—free from menace—and notable in showing that the demand for redress for the affair of the Caroline was still under diplomatic discussion in London, and that the British government had not then assumed the act of Captain Drew. The answer of Mr. Forsyth was prompt and clear—covering the questions arising out of our duplicate form of government, and the law of nations—and explicit upon the rights of the States, the duties of the federal government, and the principles of national law. It is one of the few answers of the kind which circumstances have arisen to draw from our government, and deserves to be well considered for its luminous and correct expositions of the important questions of which it treats. Under date of the 28th of December, and writing under the instructions of the President, he says:

"The jurisdiction of the several States which constitute the Union is, within its appropriate sphere, perfectly independent of the federal government. The offence with which Mr. McLeod is charged was committed within the territory, and against the laws and citizens of the State of New York, and is one that comes clearly within the competency of her tribunals. It does not, therefore, present an occasion where, under the constitution and laws of the Union, the interposition called for would be proper, or for which a warrant can be found in the powers with which the federal executive is invested. Nor would the circumstances to which you have referred, or the reasons you have urged, justify the exertion of such a power, if it existed. The transaction out of which the question arises, presents the case of a most unjustifiable invasion, in time of peace, of a portion of the territory of the United States, by a band of armed men from the adjacent territory of Canada, the forcible capture by them within our own waters, and the subsequent destruction of a steamboat, the property of a citizen of the United States, and the murder of one or more American citizens. If arrested at the time, the offenders might unquestionably have been brought to justice by the judicial authorities of the State within whose acknowledged territory these crimes were committed; and their subsequent voluntary entrance within that territory, places them in the same situation. The President is not aware of any principle of international law, or, indeed, of reason or justice, which entitles such offenders to impunity before the legal tribunals, when coming voluntarily within their independent and undoubted jurisdiction, because they acted in obedience to their superior authorities, or because their acts have become the subject of diplomatic discussion between the two governments. These methods of redress, the legal prosecution of the offenders, and the application of their government for satisfaction, are independent of each other, and may be separately and simultaneously pursued. The avowal or justification of the outrages by the British authorities might be a ground of complaint with the government of the United States, distinct from the violation of the territory and laws of the State of New York. The application of the government of the Union to that of Great Britain, for the redress of an authorized outrage of the peace, dignity, and rights of the United States, cannot deprive the State of New York of her undoubted right of vindicating, through the exercise of her judicial power, the property and lives of her citizens. You have very properly regarded the alleged absence of Mr. McLeod from the scene of the offence at the time when it was committed, as not material to the decision of the present question. That is a matter to be decided by legal evidence; and the sincere desire of the President is, that it may be satisfactorily established. If the destruction of the Caroline was a public act of persons in her Majesty's service, obeying the order of their superior authorities, this fact has not been communicated to the government of the United States by a person authorized to make the admission; and it will be for the court which has taken cognizance of the offence with which Mr. McLeod is charged, to decide upon its validity when legally established before it."

This answer to Mr. Fox, was read in the two Houses of Congress, on the 5th of January, and was heard with great approbation—apparently unanimous in the Senate. It went to London, and on the 8th and 9th of February, gave rise to some questions and answers, which showed that the British government did not take its stand in approving the burning of the Caroline, until after the presidential election of 1840—until after that election had ensured a change of administration in the United States. On the 8th of February, to inquiries as to what steps had been taken to secure the liberation of McLeod, the answers were general from Lord Palmerston and Lord Melbourne, "*That her Majesty's ministers would take those measures which, in their estimation, would be best calculated to secure the safety of her Majesty's subjects, and to vindicate the honor of the British nation.*" This answer was a key to the instructions actually given to Mr. Fox, showing that they were framed upon a calculation of what would be most effective, and not upon a conviction of what was right. They would do what they thought would accomplish the purpose; and the event showed that the calculation led them to exhibit the war attitude— to assume the offence of McLeod, and to bully the new administration. And here it is to be well noted that the British ministry, up to that time, had done nothing to recognize the act of Captain Drew. Neither to the American minister in London, nor to the Secretary of State here, had they assumed it. More than that: they carefully abstained from indirect, or implied assumption, by withholding pensions to their wounded officers in that affair—one of whom had five severe wounds. This fact was brought out at this time by a question from Mr. Hume in the House of Commons to Lord John Russell, in which—

"He wished to ask the noble lord a question relating to a matter of fact. He believed that, in the expedition which had been formed for the destruction of the Caroline, certain officers, who held commissions in her Majesty's army and navy, were concerned in that affair, and that some of these officers had, in the execution of the orders which were issued, received wounds. The question he wished to ask was, whether or not her Majesty's government had thought proper to award pensions to those officers, corresponding in amount with those which were usually granted for wounds received in the regular service of her Majesty."

This was a pointed question, and carrying an argument along with it. Had the wounded officers received the usual pension? If not, there must be a reason for departing from the usual practice; and the answer showed that the practice had been departed from. Lord John Russell replied:

"That he was not aware of any pensions having been granted to those officers who were wounded in the expedition against the Caroline."

This was sufficiently explicit, and showed that up to the 8th day of February, 1841, the act of Captain Drew had not been even indirectly, or impliedly recognized. But the matter did not stop there. Mr. Hume, a thoroughly business member, not satisfied with an answer which merely implied that the government had not sanctioned the measure, followed it up with a recapitulation of circumstances to show that the government had not answered, one way or the other, during the three years that the United States had been calling for redress; and ending with a plain interrogatory for information on that point.

"He said that the noble lord (Palmerston), had just made a speech in answer to certain questions which had been put to him by the noble lord, the member for North Lancashire; but he (Mr. Hume) wished to ask the House to suspend their opinion upon the subject until they had the whole of the papers laid before the House. He had himself papers in his possession, that would explain many things connected with this question, and which, by-the-bye, were not exactly consistent with the statement which had just been made. It appeared by the papers which he had in his possession, that in January, 1838, a motion was made in the U. S. House of Representatives, calling upon the President to place upon the table of the House, all the papers respecting the Caroline, and all the correspondence which had passed between the government of the United States and the British government on the subject of the destruction of the Caroline. In consequence of that motion, certain papers were laid upon the table, including one from Mr. Stevenson, the present minister here from the U. States. These were accompanied by a long letter, dated the 15th of May, 1838, from that gentleman, and in that letter, the burning of the Caroline was characterized in very strong language. He also stated, that agreeably to the orders of the President, he had laid before the British government the whole of the evidence relating to the subject, which had been taken upon the spot, and Mr. Stevenson *denied he had ever been informed that the expedition against the Caroline was authorized or sanctioned by the British government.* Now, from May, 1838, the time when the letter had been written, up to this hour, no answer had been given to that letter, nor had any satisfaction been given by the British government upon this subject. In a letter dated from London, the 2d of July, Mr. Stevenson stated that he had not received any answer upon the subject, and that he did not wish to press the subject further; but if the government of the United States wished him to do so, he prayed to be informed of it. By the statement which had taken place in the House of Congress, it appeared that the government of the United States had been ignorant of any information that could lead them to suppose that the enterprise against the Caroline had been undertaken by the orders of the British government, or by British authority. That he believed was the ground upon which Mr. Forsyth acted as he had done. He takes his objections, and denies the allegation of Mr. Fox, that neither had he nor her Majesty's government made any communication to him or the authorities of the United States, that the British government had *authorized the destruction of the Caroline.* He (Mr. Hume) therefore hoped that no discussion would take place, until all the papers connected with the matter were laid before the House. He wished to know what the nature of those communications was with Mr. Stevenson and her Majesty's government which had induced him to act as he had done."

Thus the ministry were told to their faces, and in the face of the whole Parliament, that for the space of three years, and under repeated calls, they had never assumed the destruction of the Caroline: and to that assertion the ministry *then* made no answer. On the following day the subject was again taken up, "*and in the course of it Lord Palmerston admitted that the government approved of the burning of the Caroline.*" So says the Parliamentary Register of Debates, and adds: "*The conversation was getting rather warm, when Sir Robert Peel interposed by a motion on the affairs of Persia.*" This was the first knowledge that the British parliament had of the assumption of that act, which undoubtedly had just been resolved upon. It is clear that Lord Palmerston was the presiding spirit of this resolve. He is a bold man, and a man of judgment in his boldness. He probably never would have made such an assumption in dealing with General Jackson: he certainly made no such assumption during the three years he had to deal with the Van Buren administration. The conversation was "getting warm;" and well it might: for this pregnant assumption, so long delayed, and so given, was entirely gratuitous, and unwarranted by the facts. Col. McNab was the commanding officer, and gave all the orders that were given. Captain Drew's report to him shows that his orders were to destroy the vessel at Navy Island: McNab's letter of the same day to the United States District Attorney (Rodgers), shows that he would not authorize an expedition upon United States territory; and his sworn testimony on the trial of McLeod shows that he did not do it in his orders to Captain Drew. That testimony says:

> "I do remember the last time the steamboat Caroline came down previous to her destruction; from the information I received, I had every reason to believe that she came down for the express purpose of assisting the rebels and brigands on Navy Island with arms, men, ammunition, provisions, stores, &c.; to ascertain this fact, I sent two officers with instructions to watch the movements of the boat, to note the same, and report to me; they reported they saw her land a cannon (a six or nine-pounder), several men armed and equipped as soldiers, and that she had dropped her anchor on the east side of Navy Island; on the information I had previously received from highly respectable persons in Buffalo, together with the report of these gentlemen, I determined to destroy her that night. I intrusted the command of the expedition for the purposes aforesaid, to Capt. A. Drew, royal navy; seven boats were equipped, and left the Canadian shore; I do not recollect the number of men in each boat; Captain Drew held the rank of commander in her Majesty's royal navy; I ordered the expedition, and first communicated it to Capt. Andrew Drew, on the beach, where the men embarked a short time previous to their embarkation; Captain Drew was ordered to take and destroy the Caroline wherever he could find her; I gave the order as officer in command of the forces assembled for the purposes aforesaid; they embarked at the mouth of the Chippewa river; in my orders to Captain Drew nothing was said about invading the territory of the United States, but such was their nature that Captain Drew might feel himself justified in destroying the boat wherever he might find her."

From this testimony it is clear that McNab gave no order to invade the territory of the United States; and the whole tenor of his testimony agrees with Captain Drew's report, that it was "expected" to have found the Caroline at Navy Island, where she was in fact immediately before, and where McNab saw her while planning the expedition. No such order was then given by him—nor by any other authority; for the local government in Quebec knew no more of it than the British ministry in London. Besides, Col. McNab was only the military commander to suppress the insurrection. He had no authority, for he disclaimed it, to invade an American possession; and if the British government had given such authority, which they had not, it would have been an outrage to the United States, not to be overlooked. They then assumed an act which they had not done; and assumed it! and took a war attitude! and all upon a calculation that it was the most effectual way to get McLeod released. It was in the evening of the 4th day of March that all Washington city was roused by the rumor of this assumption and demand: and on the 12th day of that month they were all formally communicated to our government. It was to the new administration that this formidable communication was addressed—and addressed at the earliest moment that decency would permit. The effect was to the full extent all that could have been calculated upon; and wholly reversed the stand taken under Mr. Van Buren's administration. The burning of the Caroline was admitted to be an act of war, for which the sovereign, and not the perpetrators, was liable: the invasion of the American soil was also an act of war: the surrender of McLeod could not be effected by an *order* of the federal government, because he was in the hands of a State court, charged with crimes against the laws of that State: but the United States became his defender and protector, with a determination to save him harmless: and all this was immediately communicated to Mr. Fox in unofficial interviews, before the formal communication could be drawn up and delivered. Lord Palmerston's policy was triumphant; and it is necessary to show it in order to show in what manner the Caroline affair was brought to a conclusion; and in its train that of the northeastern boundary, so long disputed; and that of the north-western boundary, never before disputed; and that of the liberated slaves on their way from one United States port to another: and all other questions besides which England wished settled. For, emboldened by the success of the Palmerstonian policy in the case of the Caroline, it was incontinently applied in all other cases of dispute between the countries—and with the same success. But of this hereafter. The point at present is, to show, as has been shown, that the assumption of this outrage was not made until three years after the event, and then upon a calculation of its efficiency, and contrary to the facts of the case; and when made, accompanied by large naval and military demonstrations—troops sent to Canada—ships to Halifax—newspapers to ourselves, the *Times* especially—all odorous of gunpowder and clamorous for war.

This is dry detail, but essential to the scope of this work, more occupied with telling how things were done than what was done: and in pursuing this view it is amazing to see by what arts and contrivances—by what trifles and accidents—the great affairs of nations, as well as the small ones of individuals, are often decided. The finale in this case was truly ridiculous: for, after all this disturbance and commotion—two great nations standing to their arms, exhausting diplomacy, and inflaming the people to the war point—after the formal assumption of McLeod's offence, and war threatened for his release, it turned out that he was not there! and was acquitted by an American jury on ample evidence. He had slept that night in Chippewa, and only heard of the act the next morning at the breakfast table—when he wished he had been there. Which wish afterwards ripened into an assertion that he was there! and, further, had himself killed one of the damned Yankees—by no means the first instance of a man boasting of performing exploits in a fight which he did not see. But what a lesson it teaches to nations! Two great countries brought to angry feelings, to criminative diplomacy, to armed preparation, to war threats—their governments and people in commotion—their authorities all in council, and taxing their skill and courage to the uttermost: and all to settle a national quarrel as despicable in its origin as the causes of tavern brawls; and exceedingly similar to the origin of such brawls. McLeod's false and idle boast was the cause of all this serious difficulty between two great Powers.

Mr. Fox had delivered his formal demand and threat on the 12th day of March: the administration immediately undertook McLeod's release. The assumption of his imputed act had occasioned some warm words in the British House of Commons, where it was known to be gratuitous: its communication created no warmth in our cabinet, but a cold chill rather, where every spring was immediately put in action to release McLeod. Being in the hands of a State court, no order could be given for his liberation; but all the authorities in New York were immediately applied to—governor, legislature, supreme court, local court—all in vain: and then the United States assumed his defence, and sent the Attorney-General, Mr. Crittenden, to manage his defence, and General Scott, of the United States army, to protect him from popular violence; and hastened to lay all their steps before the British minister as fast as they were taken.

The acquittal of McLeod was honorable to the jury that gave it; and his trial was honorable to the judge, who, while asserting the right to try the man, yet took care that the trial should be fair. The judges of the Supreme Court (Bronson, Nelson, and Cowan) refused the *habeas corpus* which would take him out of the State: the Circuit judge gave him a fair trial. It was satisfactory to the British; and put an end to their complaint against us: unhappily it seemed to put an end to our complaint against them. All was postponed for a future general treaty—the invasion of territory, the killing of citizens, the arson of the boat, the impressment and abduction of a supposed British subject—all, all were postponed to the day of general settlement: and when that day came all were given up.

The conduct of the administration in the settlement of the affair became a subject of discussion in both Houses of Congress, and was severely censured by the democracy, and zealously defended by the whigs. Mr. Charles Jared Ingersoll, after a full statement of the extraordinary and successful efforts of the administration of Mr. Van Buren to prevent any aid to the insurgents from the American side, proceeded to say:

"Notwithstanding, however, every exertion that could be and was made, it was impossible altogether to prevent some outbreaks, and among the rest a parcel of some seventy or eighty Canadians, as I have understood, with a very few Americans, took possession of a place near the Canadian shore, called Navy Island, and fortified themselves in defiance of British power. If I have not been misinformed there were not more than eight or ten Americans among them. An American steamboat supplied them with a cannon and perhaps other munitions of war: for I have no disposition to diminish whatever was the full extent of American illegality, but, in this statement of the premises, desire to present the argument with the most unreserved concessions. I am discussing nothing as the member of a party. I consider the Secretary of State as the representative of his government and country. I desire to be understood as not intending to say one word against that gentleman as an individual; as meaning to avoid every thing like personality, and addressing myself to the position he has assumed for the country, without reference to whether he is connected with one administration or another; viewing this as a controversy between the United States and a foreign government, in which all Americans should be of one party, acknowledging no distinction between the acts of Mr. Forsyth and Mr. Webster, but considering the whole affair, under both the successive administrations, as one and indivisible; and on many points, I believe this country is altogether of one and the same sentiment concerning this controversy. It seems to be universally agreed that British *pirates* as they were, as I will show according to the strictest legal definition of the term, in the dead of night, *burglariously invaded* our country, *murdered* at least one of our unoffending fellow-citizens, were guilty of the further crime of *arson* by burning what was at least the temporary dwelling of a number of persons asleep in a steamboat moored to the wharf, and finally cutting her loose, carried her into the middle of the stream, where, by romantic atrocity, unexampled in the annals of crime, they sent her over the Falls of Niagara, with how many persons in her, God only will ever know.

"Now Mr. Speaker, this, in its national aspect, was precisely the same as if perpetrated in your house or mine, and should be resented and punished accordingly. Some time afterwards one of the perpetrators, named McLeod, in a fit of that sort of infatuation with which Providence mostly betrays the guilty, strayed over from Canada to the American shore, like a fool, as he was, and there was soon arrested and imprisoned by that popular police, which is always on the alert to administer justice upon malefactors. First proceeded against, as it appears, for civil redress for the loss of the vessel, he was soon after indicted by the appropriate grand jury, and has remained ever since in custody, awaiting the regular administration of justice. Guilty or innocent, however, there he was, under the ægis of the law of the sovereign State of New York, with the full protection of every branch of the government of that State, when the present administration superseded the last, and the first moment after the late President's inauguration was ungenerously seized by the British minister to present the new Secretary of State with a letter containing the insolent, threatening, and insufferable language which I am about to read from it:

"'The undersigned is instructed to demand from the government of the United States, formally, in the name of the British government, the immediate release of Mr. Alexander McLeod. The transaction in question may have been, as her Majesty's government are of opinion that it was, a justifiable employment of force for the purpose of defending the British territory from the unprovoked attack of a band of British rebels and American pirates, who, having been permitted to arm and organize themselves within the territory of the United States, had actually invaded and occupied a portion of the territory of her Majesty; or it may have been, as alleged by Mr. Forsyth, in his note to the undersigned of the 26th of December, a most unjustifiable invasion in time of peace, of the territory of the United States.'"

"Finally, after a tissue of well elaborated diplomatic contumely, the very absurdity of part of which, in the application of the term pirates to the interfering Americans, is demonstrated by

Mr. Webster—the British minister reiterates, towards the conclusion of his artfully insulting note—that 'be that as it may, her Majesty's government formally demands, upon the grounds already stated, the immediate release of Mr. McLeod; and her Majesty's government entreats the President of the United States—I pray the House to mark the sarcasm of this offensive entreaty—to take into his deliberate consideration the serious nature of the consequences which must ensue from a rejection of this demand.'

"Taken in connection with all the actual circumstances of the case—the tone of the British press, both in England and Canada, the language of members in both Houses of Parliament, and the palpable terms of Mr. Fox's letter itself, it is impossible, I think, not to see we cannot wink so hard as not to perceive that Mr. Fox's is a threatening letter. It surprises me that this should have been a subject of controversy in another part of this building, while I cannot doubt that Mr. Webster was perfectly satisfied of the menacing aspect of the first letter he received from the British minister. Anxious—perhaps laudably anxious—to avoid a quarrel so very unpromising at the very outset of a new administration, he seems to have shut his eyes to what must flash in every American face. And here was his first mistake; for his course was perfectly plain. He had nothing to do but, by an answer in the blandest terms of diplomatic courtesy, to send back the questionable phrases to Mr. Fox, with a respectful suggestion that they looked to him as if conveying a threat; that he hoped not, he believed not; he trusted for the harmony of their personal relations, and the peace of their respective nations, that he was laboring under a mistake; but he could not divest his mind of the impression, that there were in this note of Mr. Fox, certain phrases which, in all controversies among gentlemen as well as nations, inevitably put an end to further negotiation. Mr. Fox must have answered negatively or affirmatively, and the odious indignity which now rankles in the breast of at least a large proportion of the country, interpreting it as the meaning of the British communication, would have been avoided. Mr. Webster had Mr. Fox absolutely in the hollow of his hand. He had an opportunity of enlisting the manly feeling of all his countrymen, the good will of right-minded Englishmen themselves, to a firm and inoffensive stand like this, on the threshold of the correspondence. Why he did not, is not for me to imagine. With no feeling of personal disparagement to that gentleman, I charge this as an obvious, a capital, and a deplorable lapse from the position he should have assumed, in his very first attitude towards the British minister.

"The British argument addressed to him was, that 'the transaction in question was a justifiable employment of public force, with the sanction, or by order of the constituted authorities of a State, engaging individuals in military or naval enterprises in their country's cause, when it would be contrary to the universal practice of civilized nations to fix individual responsibility upon the persons engaged.' This, as I do not hesitate to pronounce it, false assumption of law, is, at once, conceded by Mr. Webster, in the remarkable terms, that the 'government of the United States,' by which he must mean himself, entertains *no doubt* of the asserted British principle. Mr. Webster had just before said, that 'the President is not certain that he understands precisely the meaning intended to be conveyed by her Majesty's government,' 'which doubt,' he adds, 'has occasioned with the President some hesitation.' Thus while the President entertained a doubt, the government entertained no doubt at all; which I cannot understand, otherwise, than that while the President hesitated to concede, the Secretary of State had no hesitation whatever to concede at once the whole British assumption, and surrender at discretion the whole American case. For where is the use of Mr. Webster's posterior, elaborated argument, when told by the British minister that this transaction was *justifiable*, and informed by the public prints that at a very early day, one of the British Secretaries, Lord John Russell, declared in open Parliament that the British government *justified* what is called the *transaction* of McLeod. The matter was ended before Mr. Webster set his powerful mind to produce an argument on the subject. The British crown had taken its position. Mr. Webster knew it had; and he may write the most elegant and pathetic letters till doomsday, with no other effect than to display the purity of his English to admiring fellow-citizens, and the infirmity of his argument to Great Britain and the world. By asserting the legal position which they assume, and justifying the transaction, together with Mr. Webster's concession of their legal position, the transaction is settled. Nothing remains to be done. Mr. Webster may write about it if he will, but Mr. Fox and the British minister hold the written acknowledgment of the American Secretary of State, that the affair is at an end. I call this, sir, a terrible mistake, a fatal blunder, irrecoverable, desperate, leaving us nothing but Mr. Webster's dreadful alternative of cold-blooded, endless, causeless war.

"Our position is false, extremely and lamentably false. The aggrieved party, as we are, and bound to insist upon redress, to require the punishment of McLeod, Drew, and McNab, and the other pirates who destroyed the Caroline, we have been brought to such a reverse of the true state of things, as to be menaced with the wrong-doer's indignation, unless we yield every thing. I care not whose fault it is, whether of this administration or that. In such an affair I consider both the present and the past, as presenting one and the same front to one and the same assailant. I cannot refrain, however, from saying, that whatever may have been our position, it has been greatly deteriorated by Mr. Webster's unfortunate concession.

"Never did man lose a greater occasion than Mr. Webster cast away, for placing himself and his country together, upon a pinnacle of just renown. Great Britain had humbled France, conquered Egypt, subdued vast tracts of India, and invaded the distant empire of China—there was nothing left but our degradation, to fill the measure of her glory, if it consists in such achievements; and she got it by merely demanding, without expecting it. And why have we yielded? Was there any occasion for it? Did she intend to realize her threat? Were the consequences which Mr. Webster was entreated to take into his consideration, the immediate and exterminating warfare, servile war and all, which belligerent newspapers, peers, and other such heralds of hostilities have proclaimed? No such thing. We may rely, I think, with confidence, upon the common good sense of the English nation, not to rush at once upon such extremities, and for such a cause. Mr. Fox took Mr. Webster in the melting mood, and conquered by a threat; that is to say, conquered for the moment; because the results, at some distant day, unless his steps are retraced, will and must be estrangement between kindred nations, and cold-blooded hostilities. I have often thought, Mr. Speaker, that this affair of McLeod is what military men call a demonstration, a feint, a false attack, to divert us from the British design on the State of Maine; of which I trust not one inch will ever be given up. And truly, when we had the best cause in the world, and were the most clearly in the right, it has been contrived, some how or other, to put us in false position, upon the defensive, instead of the offensive, and to perplex the plainest case with vexatious complication and concession."

The latter part of this speech was prophetic—that which related to the designs on the State of Maine. Successful in this experiment of the most efficacious means for the release of McLeod, the British ministry lost no time in making another trial of the same experiment, on the territory of that State—and again successfully: but of this in its proper place. Mr. John Quincy Adams, and Mr. Caleb Cushing, were the prominent defenders of the administration policy in the House of Representatives—resting on the point that the destruction of the Caroline was an act of war. Mr. Adams said:

"I take it that the late affair of the Caroline was in hostile array against the British government, and that the parties concerned in it were employed in acts of war against it: and I do not subscribe to the very learned opinion of the chief justice of the State of New York (not, I hear, the chief justice, but a judge of the Supreme Court of that State), that there was no act of war committed. Nor do I subscribe to it that every nation goes to war only on issuing a declaration or proclamation of war. This is not the fact. Nations often wage war for years, without issuing any declaration of war. The question is not here upon a declaration of war, but acts of war. And I say that in the judgment of all impartial men of other nations, we shall be held as a nation responsible; that the Caroline, there, was in a state of war against Great

Britain; for purposes of war, and the worst kind of war—to sustain an insurrection; I will not say rebellion, because rebellion is a crime, and because I heard them talked of as patriots."

Mr. Cushing said:

"It is strange enough that the friends of Mr. Van Buren should deny that the attack on the Caroline was an act of war. I reply to them not only by exhibiting the reason and the principle of the thing, but by citing the authority of their own President. I hold in my hand a copy of the despatch addressed by Mr. Stevenson to Lord Palmerston, under the direction of Mr. Van Buren, making demand of reparation for the destruction of the Caroline, and in that despatch, which has been published, Mr. Stevenson pursues the only course he could pursue; he proceeds to prove the hostile nature of the act by a full exhibition of facts, and concludes and winds up the whole with declaring in these words: 'The case then is one of open, undisguised, and unwarrantable hostility.' After this, let no one complain of Mr. Webster for having put the case of the Caroline on the same precise ground which Mr. Van Buren had assumed for it, and which, indeed, is the only ground upon which the United States could undertake to hold the British government responsible. And when the gentleman from Pennsylvania is considering the first great negotiation of Mr. Webster, how does he happen to forget the famous, or rather infamous, first great negotiation undertaken by Mr. Van Buren? And is it not an act of mere madness on the part of the friends of Mr. Van Buren, to compel us to compare the two? Here is a despatch before us, addressed in a controversy between the United States and Great Britain, containing one of the ablest vindications of the honor and integrity of the United States that ever was written. Mr. Van Buren began, also, with the discussion of the question between us and Great Britain. And in what spirit?—that of a patriot, a man of honor, and an American? Is not that despatch, on the contrary, a monument of ignominy in the history of the United States? Instead of maintaining the interests of this country, did not Mr. Van Buren, on that occasion, utterly sacrifice them? Did he not dictate in that despatch, a disposition of the great question of the colony trade between the United States and Great Britain, which, from that time to this, has proved most disastrous in its effects on the commercial and navigating interests of the United States? And pernicious as was the object of the despatch, was not the spirit of it infinitely worse? in which, for the first time, party quarrels of the people of the United States were carried into our foreign affairs—in which a preceding administration was impliedly reproached for the zeal with which it had defended our interests—in which it was proclaimed that the new administration started in the world with a set purpose of concession toward Great Britain—in which the honor of the United States was laid prostrate at the foot of the British throne, and the proud name of America, to sustain which our fathers had carried on a first and a second war, as we may have to do a third—that glory which the arms of our enemy could not reach, was, in this truckling despatch, laid low for the first, and, I trust in God, the last time, before the lion of England."

The ground taken by Mr. Adams and Mr. Cushing for the defence of Mr. Webster (for they seemed to consider him, and no doubt truly, as the whole administration in this case) was only shifting the defence from one bad ground to another. The war ground they assumed could only apply between Great Britain and the insurgents: she had no war with the United States: the attack on the Caroline was an invasion of the territory of a neutral power—at peace with the invader. That is a liberty not allowed by the laws of nations—not allowed by the concern which any nation, even the most inconsiderable, feels for its own safety, and its own self-respect. A belligerent party cannot enter the territory of a neutral, even in fresh pursuit of an enemy. No power allows it. That we have seen in our own day, in the case of the Poles, in their last insurrection, driven across the Austrian frontier by the Russians; and the pursuers stopped at the line, and the fugitive Poles protected the instant they had crossed it: and in the case of the late Hungarian revolt, in which the fugitive Hungarians driven across the Turkish frontier, were protected from pursuit. The Turks protected them, Mahometans as they were; and would not give up fugitive Christians to a Christian power; and afterwards assisted the fugitives to escape to Great Britain and the United States. The British then had no right to invade the United States even in fresh pursuit of fugitive belligerents: but the Caroline and crew were not belligerents. She was an American ferry-boat carrying men and supplies to the insurgents, but she was not a combatant. And if she had been—had been a war-vessel belonging to the insurgents, and fighting for them, she could not be attacked in a neutral port. The men on board of her were not Canadian insurgents, but American citizens, amenable to their own country for any infraction of her neutrality laws: and if they had been Canadian insurgents they could not have been seized on American soil; nor even demanded under the extradition clause in the treaty of 1796, even if in force. It did not extend to political offences, either of treason or war. It only applied to the common law offences of murder and forgery. How contradictory and absurd then to claim a right to come and take by violence, what could not be demanded under any treaty or the law of nations. No power gives up a political fugitive. Strong powers protect them openly, while they demean themselves orderly: weak powers get them to go away when not able to protect them. None give them up—not even the weakest. All the countries of Europe—the smallest kingdom, the most petty principality, the feeblest republic, even San Marino—scorn to give up a political fugitive, and though unable to chastise, never fail to resent any violation of its territory to seize them. We alone, and in the case of the Caroline, acknowledge the right of Great Britain to invade our territory, seize and kill American citizens sleeping under the flag of their country, to cut out an American vessel moored in our port, and send her in flames over the Falls of Niagara. We alone do that! but we have done it but once! and history places upon it the stigma of opprobrium.

Mr. William O. Butler of Kentucky, replied to Mr. Cushing, especially to his rehash of the stale imputations, worn out at the time of Mr. Van Buren's senatorial rejection as minister to Great Britain, and said:

"He expected from the gentleman a discussion on national law; but how much was he astonished the next day, on reading his speech in the *Intelligencer*, and finding him making a most virulent attack on the conduct and reputation of Mr. Van Buren. The gentleman referred to the letter of instructions of Mr. Van Buren to our Minister at the Court of St. James, and compared it with the instructions of Mr. Webster to the Attorney-general; speaking of the latter as breathing the statesman and patriot throughout, while he characterizes the former as infamous. Mr. B. said he would not repeat the harsh and offensive terms in which the gentleman had spoken of Mr. Van Buren's letter; he would read what the gentleman said from his printed speech, in order that the House might see the length to which his invectives were carried. [Here Mr. B. read extracts from Mr. Cushing's speech.] The gentleman spoke of comparing the two letters together. But did he think of comparing the thing we complain of with the thing he complains of? No: that would be next to madness. The gentleman shrinks from that comparison, and goes on to compare not the thing we complain of with the letter of Mr. Van Buren, but the beautiful composition of Mr. Webster, written forty days after complying with the British minister's insulting demands, and intended to cover over the instructions to Mr. Crittenden, after which he characterizes Mr. Van Buren's letter as a monument of ignominy. Now Mr. B. said he would make the same reply that a dignified farmer of Kentucky did to a lawyer. The lawyer prosecuted the farmer for a slander, and in the course of the trial took occasion to heap on him all the abuse and invective of which the Billingsgate vocabulary is capable. Yet the jury, without leaving their box, pronounced a verdict of acquittal. The verdict of an honest and intelligent jury, said the farmer, is a sufficient answer to all your abuse. Just so it was with Mr. Van Buren. His letter had made a great noise in the country; had been extensively circulated and read, and had been assailed with the utmost virulence by the opposite party. Yet the highest jury on earth, the American people, had pronounced the acquittal of Mr. Van Buren by electing him to the Chief Magistracy. The gentleman complained that the patriotism of Mr. Webster not only had been assailed, but that the gentleman from Pennsylvania had had the temerity to attack that most beautiful of letters which the patriotic Secretary wrote to Mr. Fox. Now he (Mr. B.) would admit that it was a beautiful piece of composition, and he knew of but one that would compare with it, and that was the proclamation of General Hull, just before surrendering the Northwestern army to the British."

The friends of Mr. Webster had a fashion of extolling his intellect when his acts were in question; and on no occasion was that fashion more largely indulged in than on the present one. His letter, superscribed to Mr. Fox—brought out for home consumption forty days after the satisfactory answer had been given—was exalted to the skies for the harmony of its periods, the beauty of its composition, the cogency of its reasons! without regarding the national honor and interest which it let down into the mud and mire; and without considering that the British imperious demand required in the answer to it, nerve as well as head—and nerve most. It was a case for an iron will, more than for a shining intellect: and iron will was not the strong side of Mr. Webster's character. His intellect was great—his will small. His pursuits were civil and intellectual; and he was not the man, with a goose quill in his hand, to stand up against the British empire in arms. Throughout the debate, in both Houses of Congress, the answer to Mr. Fox was treated by Mr. Webster's friends, as his own; and, no doubt, justly—his supremacy as a jurist being so largely deferred to.

The debate in the House was on the adoption of a resolution offered by Mr. John G. Floyd, of New York, calling on the President for information in relation to the steps taken to aid the liberation of McLeod; and the fate of the resolution was significant of the temper of the House—a desire to get rid of the subject without a direct vote. It was laid upon the table by a good majority—110 to 70. The nays, being those who were for prosecuting the inquiry, were:

> Messrs. Archibald H. Arrington, Charles G. Atherton, Linn Banks, Henry W. Beeson, Benjamin A. Bidlack, Samuel S. Bowne, Linn Boyd, Aaron V. Brown, Charles Brown, Edmund Burke, Reuben Chapman, James G. Clinton, Walter Coles, Edward Cross, John R. J. Daniel, Richard D. Davis, Ezra Dean, William Doan, Andrew W. Doig, Ira A. Eastman, John C. Edwards, Charles G. Ferris, John G. Floyd, Charles A. Floyd, Joseph Fornance, James Gerry, William O. Goode, Samuel Gordon, William A. Harris, John Hastings, Samuel L. Hays, Isaac E. Holmes, Jacob Houck, jr., George S. Houston, Edmund W. Hubard, Charles J. Ingersoll, William Jack, Cave Johnson, John W. Jones, George M. Keim, Abraham McClellan, Robert McClellan, James J. McKay, John McKeon, Albert G. Marchand, Alfred Marshall, John Thompson Mason, James Mathews, William Medill, John Miller, Christopher Morgan, Peter Newhard, William Parmenter, Samuel Patridge, William W. Payne, Arnold Plumer, John Reynolds, Lewis Riggs, Tristram Shaw, John Snyder, Lewis Steenrod, George Sweeny, Thomas A. Tomlinson, Hopkins L. Turney, John Van Buren, Aaron Ward, Harvey M. Watterson, John Westbrook, James W. Williams, Henry A. Wise, Fernando Wood.

The same subject was largely debated in the Senate—among others by Mr. Benton—some extracts from whose speech will constitute the next chapter.

CHAPTER LXXVI.

DESTRUCTION OF THE CAROLINE: ARREST AND TRIAL OF McLEOD: MR. BENTON'S SPEECH: EXTRACTS.

Mr. Benton said the history of our country contained a warning lesson to gentlemen who take the side of a foreign country against their own: he alluded to the case of Arbuthnot and Ambrister, seized among the Seminole Indians in 1818, and hung as outlaws and pirates by the orders of General Jackson. The news of that execution was heard with joy by the American people, who considered these Englishmen as a thousand times more culpable than the wretched savages whom they stimulated to the murder of women and children—men who had abandoned their own country, and the white race to which they belonged, to join savages against a country with which their own government was at peace. The country heard the news of the execution with joy: they approved the act of General Jackson. Not so with the politicians—the politicians of the federal school especially. They condemned it; partisan presses attacked it; and when Congress met, committees of each House of Congress reported against it—loudly condemned it—and were followed by a crowd of speakers. All the phrases now heard in claiming exemption for McLeod, and bewailing his fate, were then heard in deploring the fate of Arbuthnot and Ambrister. Violation of the laws of nations—inhuman—unworthy of the nineteenth century—shocking to humanity—barbarous—uncivilized—subjecting us to reprisals, and even to war from England—drawing upon us the reproaches of Christendom, and even the wrath of Heaven: such were the holiday phrases with which the two Houses of Congress then resounded. To hear what was said, and it would seem that the British lion would be instantly upon us. We were taught to tremble for the return news from England. Well! it came! and what was it? Not one word from the British government against the act of Jackson! Not the scrape of a pen from a minister on the subject! Not a word in Parliament except the unsupported complaint of some solitary members—just enough to show, by the indifference with which it was received, that the British House of Commons had no condemnation to pronounce upon the conduct of General Jackson. Their silence justified him in England, while committees and orators condemned him in his own country: and this justification from abroad, in a case where two Englishmen were actually hanged, should be a warning to gentlemen how they should commit themselves in a case where an Englishman is merely in the hands of justice, and has nothing to fear from "God and the country" if he is as innocent, as he now alleges, and which humanity would wish him to be. General Jackson was right, and the committees and orators who condemned him were wrong. He was right in the law, and in the application of the law. He had no musty volumes of national law to refer to in the swamps of Florida; and he needed none. He had the law of nature, and of nations, in his heart. He had an American heart, and that heart never led him wrong when the rights, the interest, and the honor of his country were at stake. He hung the Englishmen who were inciting savages to the murder of our women and children: and the policy of the measure has become no less apparent than its legality was clear. Before that time Englishmen were habitually in the camp and wigwam of the Indians, stimulating to war upon us: since that time no Englishman has been heard of among them. The example was impressive—its effect salutary— its lesson permanent. It has given us twenty-five years of exemption from British interference in our Indian relations; and if the assassins of the Caroline shall be hung up in like manner it will give us exemption from future British outrage along the extended line which divides the Union from the British Canadian provinces.

It is humiliating to see senators of eminent ability consulting books to find passages to justify an outrage upon their own country. Better far throw away the books, and go by the heart. Then, at least, with American hearts, they would always have the consolation of being on their country's side. Better even to take the rule of the illustrious commodore whose actions have shed so much lustre on the American name (Decatur), and go for their country, right or wrong. Then they would always have their own hearts on their side. Besides, there is no book which fits our case—none which was written for the duplicate form of government which we possess. We have State governments as well as a general government; and those governments have their rights, and are sovereign within their limits. The protection of the lives, liberty, and property of their citizens, is among these rights: the punishment of murder, arson, and burglary, are among these rights. If there was nothing in the law of nations, as written in the books, to recognize these rights, it would be necessary for us to do an act which would cause a new line to be written in these books. But this is not the case. The law of nations as it now stands, is sufficient for us. It has been read from Vattel by several senators; and is conclusive in our favor.

What is it? Why, that if the citizens of one country commit an outrage upon another, you must apply to their sovereign for redress: but if the wrong-doer comes into your country, you may seize and punish him. This is the law of nations, and it fits our case; and we have followed it. The United States, as charged with our foreign relations, have made the demand for redress upon Great Britain: the State of New York, as the wronged local authority, has seized the wrong-doer, when he came upon her territory; and is giving him what he did not give her citizens—a trial for his life: and this she has a right to do: and if the federal government attempts to give up that man, she shrinks from the defence of right, violates the law of nations, and invades the jurisdiction of New York.

This brings us to the case before us. What is it? The facts of the transaction are all spread out in official documents, and sustained upon clear and undeniable testimony. Some Canadian insurgents are on an island, near the Canada shore, entrenching themselves, and receiving aid in men and arms from the American side. An American ferry-boat, the Steamer Caroline, carries that aid. She is seen in the fact—seen by the commanding officer of the British forces, as he stands on the Canadian shore, looking on. He sees her there late in the evening—saw her cast anchor near the island—and determines to destroy her there. Five boats are fitted out in the dark to go and do the work; and if they had done it there, not a word would have been said; for it was a British island, and she was there upon an unlawful business—violating the laws of neutrality, disobeying the laws of her own country, disregarding the proclamation of the President; and doing an act which might bring her own country into trouble. If she had been found there and destroyed, not a word would have been said: but she was not found there, and the captain of the boats, of his own head, contrary to the order which he had received, and which directed him to the British island, and contrary to the letter written by his commanding officer on that very day, abjuring all right and all intent to make a descent upon our coast, because it was ours: this captain, his name Drew, and an officer in the British navy without the knowledge of his commander, determines to cross the line—to steal across the river in the night—oars muffled—all noises silenced—creep upon the unsuspecting vessel, anchored at the shore, sleeping under the flag, and sheltered by the laws of her country, and the law of nations: and stealthily get on board. They run to the berths—cut, stab, slash, and shoot, all that they see—pursue the flying—kill one man on the shore—no distinction of persons— and no quarter the word. Several are killed in the boat: none escape but those whom darkness and confusion favored. Victorious in an attack upon men asleep, the conquerors draw the vessel into the middle of the river— it was just above the falls—set her on fire; and, with all her contents—the dead and the dying, the living and the wounded—send her, luminous in flames, over the frightful cataract of Niagara. One man alone had been spared, and he as a British subject, to be taken home for punishment. These are facts. What do they amount to in law—that of nations, and that of New York, where the deed was done? First, a violation of the law of nations, in invading the soil of the United States—in attacking a vessel (even if it had been a belligerent), in a neutral port—in attacking persons on neutral territory—in impressing and carrying off a man from our territory: then each of these acts was a crime against the municipal laws of New York. McLeod, one of the actors in that cowardly assassination, and conflagration, guilty upon his own boasting, and caught upon the scene of his outrage, now in the hands of justice in the State of New York, while no indemnity is offered for the outrage itself: this perpetrator we are required, and that under a threat, to release from the hands of a State, which has the legal right to try him. All this was years before—near four years before—December, 1837. The news flew upon the wings of the wind. It fired the bosoms of the border inhabitants, upon a line of fifteen hundred miles. Retaliation was in every heart, threats in every mouth, preparation open—war imminent. Mr. Van Buren was then President. To repress the popular risings, proclamations were issued: to prevent acts of retaliation, troops were stationed along the line, and armed steamers floated the river and the lakes: to punish any violation of order, instructions were issued to the district attorneys, and marshals; and the aid of the State authorities was claimed, and obtained. To obtain redress for the outrage to our citizens, and the insults to our national character, immediate application was made to the British government. That government delayed its answer to our just demand—avoided the assumption of the criminal act—excused and justified, without assuming it, either in words, or indirectly, by rewarding the actors, or even giving pensions to those wounded in the attack: for there were several of them in the dark and dastardly attack. Diplomacy was still drawing out its lengthened thread—procrastination the game, and the chapter of accidents the hope—when McLeod, the boaster in Canada of his active share in this triple crime of murder, arson, and robbery, against the State of

New York, and of violated neutrality against the United States, crosses over to the United States, exhibits himself on the very spot of his exploits, and in the sight of those who had often heard of his boasts. Justice then took hold of him. He was arrested on an indictment found against him, immediately after the act; and he was also sued by the owner of the vessel. A trial, of course, in each case, was to take place in the courts of the State whose laws had been violated. Vattel prescribed that. The United States had nothing to do with it. Her business was with his sovereign. To the State it belonged to punish the violation of her own laws, the perpetrator having been caught within her jurisdiction: to the owner of the boat it belonged to sue for damages; and neither the United States, nor the State of New York, had any right to defeat his action, by releasing the defendant. It was a transitory action, and would lay any where where the defendant was caught. McLeod went to jail in both cases—the indictment, and the civil suit; and would seem to have courted that fate by coming over to defy it. The news of these proceedings fly to the British minister in this city (Mr. Henry S. Fox): that minister addresses a note to the Secretary of State (Mr. Forsyth), demanding the release of McLeod: the Secretary answered, by the direction of President Van Buren, that this man, being charged with criminal offences against the State of New York, and sued in a civil action by one of her citizens, the general government had no right to release him: and would not undertake to do so. This answer was read in this chamber on the night of the 5th of January last, when the Senate was composed very nearly as it is now—nearly all the same members—when the present Secretary of State (Mr. Webster), and the present Attorney-general (Mr. Crittenden), were both present: and we all know in what manner that answer of Mr. Forsyth was received. It received the unanimous approbation of this chamber! Mr. B. repeated the expression—unanimous approbation! and said he would pause for correction if he was mistaken. (He paused. Several senators said, yes! yes! No one said the contrary.) Mr. B. continued: I remember that letter well, and the feeling of unanimous approbation which pervaded the chamber when it was read. Every senator that spoke, expressed his approbation. No one signified dissent: and the feeling was then universal that the proper answer had been given by the American government—the answer which the law of nations, our duplicate form of government, the dignity of the Union, the rights of the State of New York, and the rights of the owner of the destroyed vessel—all required to be given. If I am wrong in my recollection, I repeat the request: let me be set right now. (Several voices exclaimed, "right! right!" No one said the contrary.) Mr. B. resumed: a great point—one vital to the case as it concerns our action, and conclusive in this debate, is now established. It is established, that in the month of January last, when the answer of the American Secretary was read in this chamber, we were all of opinion that he had given the correct and proper answer: and among the senators then present were the present Secretary of State, who has undertaken to get McLeod out of the clutches of the law in New York; and also the present attorney-general, who has gone to New York upon that errand. This is enough. Those gentlemen heard the case then, and uttered no dissent. The Senate was then unanimous—including those who dissent now. How was it in the House of Representatives, where the same papers were read at the same time? How was it there, in a body of 220, and the immediate representatives of the people? About the same that it was in the Senate—only more formally expressed. The papers were sent to the Committee of Foreign Affairs. That committee, through Mr. Pickens, its chairman, made an ample report, fully sustaining the answer of the American government: and of that report, five thousand extra copies were printed by the unanimous consent of the House, for distribution among the people.

In the month of January last, it may then be assumed, that the two Houses of Congress approved the decision of President Van Buren; and according to that decision, McLeod was neither to be given up, nor the course of justice in New York interfered with by the federal government. Mr. Fox received the answer of Mr. Forsyth— transmitted it to his government—and received from that government precise instructions to avow and assume the attack on the Caroline as a national act—to make a peremptory demand for the release of McLeod—to threaten us with serious consequences in the event of refusal; and, as the London newspapers said, to demand his passports and leave the country if his demand was not immediately complied with. It was on the evening of the 4th day of March—the day of the inauguration of the new President, so nicely had the British ministry calculated the time—that the news of these instructions arrived in this city; and along with that news came the war-threats, and the war speeches of the press and public men of Great Britain—the threat of many papers to send admirals and war-steamers to batter down our cities; and the diabolical speech of a peer of the realm (Lord Mountcashel) to excite our three millions of slaves to insurrection—to raise all the Indian tribes against us—and to destroy our finances by bursting the paper bubbles on which they floated. Yes! it was on the evening of the 4th day of March that these instructions—these threats—these war annunciations—all arrived together in this city. The new President (General Harrison) had just been inaugurated: his cabinet had just been indicated: the men who were to compose the presidential council were fully known: and I undertook at once to tell what would be done. I said to several—some now in this city if not in this chamber: McLeod will be given up—not directly, but indirectly. Underhanded springs will be set in motion to release him, and a letter will afterwards be cooked up to show to Congress and the people, and to justify what had been done. This is what I said. Persons are now in this city to whom I said it. And now let us resume the succession of events, and see what was done by this new administration which had just been inducted into office in the midst of triumphal processions—under the fire of cannon—the beating of drums—the display of flags; and all the glorious pomp and circumstance of war. Let us see what they did. On the 12th of March—the new administration having been allowed a week to organize—Mr. Fox addresses to Mr. Webster a formal demand, in the name of his government for the release of McLeod, and goes on to say:

> "The grounds upon which the British government made this demand upon the government of the United States are these: that the transaction on account of which Mr. McLeod has been arrested, and is to be put upon his trial, was a transaction of a public character planned and executed by persons duly empowered by her Majesty's colonial authorities to take any steps, and to do any acts which might be necessary for the defence of her Majesty's territories, and for the protection of her Majesty's subjects; and that, consequently, those subjects of her Majesty who engaged in that transaction were performing an act of public duty, for which they cannot be made personally and individually answerable to the laws and tribunals of any foreign country."

And after enforcing this demand, by argument, contesting the answer given by Mr. Forsyth, and suggesting the innocence of McLeod, the letter proceeds to say:

> "But, be that as it may, her Majesty's government formally demands, upon the grounds already stated, the immediate release of Mr. McLeod; and her Majesty's government entreat the President of the United States to take into his most deliberate consideration the serious nature of the consequences which must ensue from a rejection of this demand."

This letter to Mr. Webster bears date on the 12th of March, which was Friday, and will be considered as having been delivered on the same day. On the 15th of the same month, which was Monday, Mr. Webster delivers to the Attorney-general of the United States, a set of instructions, and delivers a copy of the same to Mr. Fox, in which he yields to the demand of this Minister, and despatches the Attorney-general to New York, to effect the discharge of the prisoner. The instructions, among other things, say:

> "You are well aware that the President has no power to arrest the proceeding in the civil and criminal courts of the State of New York. If this indictment were pending in one of the courts of the United States, I am directed to say that the President, upon the receipt of Mr. Fox's last communication, would have immediately directed a *nolle prosequi* to be entered. Whether in this case the Governor of New York have that power, or, if he have, whether he would not feel it his duty to exercise it, are points upon which we are not informed. It is understood that McLeod is holden also on civil process, sued out against him by the owner of the Caroline. We suppose it very clear that the Executive of the State cannot interfere with such process; and, indeed, if such process were pending in the courts of the United States, the President could not arrest it. In such, and many analogous cases, the party prosecuted and sued, must avail himself of his exemption or defence, by judicial proceedings, either in the court into which he is called, or in some other court. But whether the process be criminal or civil, the fact of having acted under public authority, and in obedience to the orders of lawful superiors, must be regarded as a valid defence; otherwise, individuals would be holden responsible for injuries resulting from the acts of government, and even from the operations of public war. You will be furnished with a copy of this instruction, for the use of the Executive of New

York, and the Attorney-general of that State. You will carry with you also authentic evidence of the recognition by the British government of the destruction of the Caroline, as an act of public force, done by national authority. The President is impressed with the propriety of transferring the trial from the scene of the principal excitement to some other and distant county. You will take care that this be suggested to the prisoner's counsel. The President is gratified to learn that the Governor of New York has already directed that the trial take place before the Chief Justice of the State. Having consulted with the Governor you will proceed to Lockport, or wherever else the trial may be holden, and furnish the prisoner's counsel with the evidence of which you will be in possession material to his defence. You will see that he have skilful and eminent counsel, if such be not already retained, and, although you are not desired to act as counsel yourself, you will cause it to be signified to him, and to the gentlemen who may conduct his defence, that it is the wish of this government that, in case his defence be overruled by the court in which he shall be tried, proper steps be taken immediately for removing the cause, by writ of error, to the Supreme Court of the United States. The President hopes that you will use such despatch as to make your arrival at the place of trial sure before the trial comes on; and he trusts you will keep him informed of whatever occurs by means of a correspondence through this Department."

A copy of these instructions, as I have said, was delivered to Mr. Fox at the time they were written. At the same moment they were delivered to the new Attorney-general [Mr. CRITTENDEN], who, thus equipped with written directions for his guide, and accompanied by an officer of high rank in the United States army [Major-general SCOTT], immediately proceeded on the business of his mission to the State of New York, and to the place of the impending trial, at Lockport. About forty days thereafter, namely, on the 24th day of April, Mr. Webster replies to Mr. Fox's letter of the 12th of March; elaborately reviews the case of McLeod—justifies the instructions—absolves the subject—and demands nothing from the sovereign who had assumed his offence. Thus, what I had said on the evening of the 4th of March had come to pass. Underhand springs had been set in motion to release the man; a letter was afterwards cooked up to justify the act. This, sir, is the narrative of the case—the history of it down to the point at which it now stands; and upon this case I propose to make some remarks, and, in the first place, to examine into the legality and the propriety of the mission in which our Attorney-general was employed. I mean this as a preliminary inquiry, unconnected with the general question, and solely relating to the sending of our Attorney-general into any State to interfere in any business in its courts. I believe this mission of Mr. Crittenden to New York was illegal and improper—a violation of our own statutes, and will test it by referring to the law under which the office of Attorney-general was created, and the duties of the officer defined. That law was passed in 1789, and is in these words:

"And there shall also be appointed a meet person, learned in the law, to act as Attorney-general of the United States, who shall be sworn, or affirmed, to a faithful execution of his office; whose duty it shall be to prosecute and conduct all suits in the Supreme Court in which the United States shall be concerned, and to give his advice and opinion upon questions of law, when required by the President of the United States, or when requested by any of the heads of the Departments, touching any matters that may concern their departments; and shall receive such compensation for his services as shall be by law provided."

Here, said Mr. B., are the duties of the Attorney-general. He is subject to no orders whatever from the Secretary of State. That Secretary has nothing to do with him except to request his legal advice on a matter which concerns his department. Advice on a question of municipal law was doubtless what was intended; but no advice of any kind seems to have been asked of the Attorney-general. He seems to have been treated as the official subordinate of the Secretary—as his clerk or messenger—and sent off with "*instructions*" which he was to read and to execute. This was certainly an illegal assumption of authority over the Attorney-general, an assumption which the statute does not recognize. In the next place, this officer is sent into a State court to assist at the defence of a person on trial in that court for a violation of the State laws, and is directed to employ eminent and skilful counsel for him—to furnish him with evidence—to suggest a change of venue—and to take a writ of error to the Supreme Court of the United States, if the defence of the prisoner be overruled by the State court. If brought to the Supreme Court by this writ of error—a novel application of the writ, it must be admitted—then the Attorney-general is to appear in this court for the prisoner, not to prosecute him in the name of the United States, but to dismiss the writ. Now, it is very clear that all this is foreign to the duty of the Attorney-general—foreign to his office—disrespectful and injurious to the State of New York—incompatible with her judicial independence—and tending to bring the general government and the State government into collision. McLeod, a foreigner, is under prosecution in a State court for the murder of its citizens; the importance of the case has induced the Governor of the State, as he has officially informed its legislature, to direct the Attorney-general of the State to repair to the spot, and to prosecute the prisoner in person; and here is the Attorney-general of the United States sent to the same place to defend the same person against the Attorney-general of the State. The admonition to Mr. Crittenden, that he was not desired to act as counsel himself, was an admission that he ought not so to act—that all he was doing was illegal and improper—and that he should not carry the impropriety so far as to make it public by making a speech. He was to oppose the State without publicly appearing to do so; and, as for his duty in the Supreme Court of the United States, he was to violate that outright, by acting for the accused, instead of prosecuting for the United States! From all this, I hold it to be clear, that our Attorney-general has been illegally and improperly employed in this business; that all that he has done, and all the expense that he has incurred, and the fee he may have promised, are not only without law but against law; and that the rights of the State of New York have not only been invaded and infringed in this interference in a criminal trial, but that the rights and interests of the owners of the Caroline, who have brought a civil action against McLeod for damages for the destruction of their property, have been also gratuitously assailed in that part of the Secretary's instructions in which he declares that such civil suit cannot be maintained. I consider the mission as illegal in itself, and involving a triple illegality, *first*, as it concerns the Attorney-general himself, who was sent to a place where he had no right to go; *next*, as it concerns the State of New York, as interfering with her administration of justice; and, *thirdly*, as it concerns the owners of the Caroline, who have sued McLeod for damages, and whose suit is declared to be unmaintainable.

I now proceed, Mr. President, to the main inquiry in this case, the correctness and propriety of the answer given by our Secretary of State to Mr. Fox, and its compatibility with the honor, dignity, and future welfare of this republic.

I look upon the "*instructions*" which were given to Mr. Crittenden, and a copy of which was sent to Mr. Fox, as being THE ANSWER to that Minister; and I deem the letter entitled an answer, and dated forty days afterwards, as being a mere afterpiece—an article for home consumption—a speech for Buncombe, as we say of our addresses to our constituents—a pleading intended for us, and not for the English, and wholly designed to excuse and defend the real answer so long before, and so promptly given. I will give some attention to this, so called, letter, before I quit the case; but for the present my business is with the "*instructions*," a copy of which being delivered to Mr. Fox, was the answer to his demand; and as such was transmitted to the British government, and quoted in the House of Commons as being entirely satisfactory. This quotation took place on the 6th day of May, several days before the, so called, letter of the 24th of April could possibly have reached London. Lord John Russell, in answer to a question from Mr. Hume, referred to these instructions as being satisfactory, and silenced all further inquiry about the affair, by showing that they had all they wanted.

I hold these instructions to have been erroneous, in point of national law, derogatory to us in point of national character, and tending to the future degradation and injury of this republic.

That the Secretary has mistaken the law of the case in consenting to the release of McLeod is persuasively shown by referring to the opinions of the two Houses of Congress in January last. Their opinions were then unanimous in favor of Mr. Forsyth's answer; and that answer was a peremptory refusal either to admit that McLeod ought to be released, or to interfere in his behalf with the courts of New York. The reasons urged by Mr. Fox in his letter to Mr. Forsyth for making the demand, were precisely the same with those subsequently given in the letter to Mr. Webster. The only difference in the two demands was in the formality of the latter, being under instructions from his government, and in the threat which it contained. In other respects the two demands were the same; so that, at the outset of this inquiry, we have the opinions of the Secretary of State, the Attorney-general, and the body of their friends in the two Houses of Congress to plead against themselves. Then we produce against our Secretary the law of nations, as laid down by Vattel. He says:

"However, as it is impossible for the best regulated State, or for the most vigilant and absolute sovereign to model at his pleasure all the actions of his subjects, and to confine them on every occasion to the most exact obedience, it would be unjust to impute to the nation or the sovereign every fault committed by the citizens. We ought not, then, to say, in general, that we have received an injury from a nation, because we have received it from one of its members. But if a nation or its chief approves and ratifies the act of the individual, it then becomes a public concern, and the injured party is then to consider the nation as the real author of the injury, of which the citizen was, perhaps, only the instrument. *If the offended State has in her power the individual who has done the injury, she may, without scruple, bring him to justice, and punish him.* If he has escaped, and returned to his own country, she ought to apply to his sovereign to have justice done in the case."

This is the case before us. The malefactor is taken, and is in the hands of justice. His imputed crime is murder, arson, and robbery. His government, by assuming his crime, cannot absolve his guilt, nor defeat our right to try and punish him according to law. The assumption of his act only adds to the number of the culpable, and gives us an additional offender to deal with them, if we choose. We may proceed against one or both; but to give up the individual when we have him, without redress from the nation, which justifies him, is to throw away the advantage which chance or fortune has put into our hands, and to make a virtual, if not actual surrender, of all claim to redress whatsoever.

The law of nations is clear, and the law of the patriot heart is equally clear. The case needs no book, no more than the hanging of Arbuthnot and Ambrister required the justification of books when General Jackson was in the hommocks and marshes of Florida. A band of foreign volunteers, without knowing what they were going to do, but ready to follow their file leader to the devil, steal across a boundary river in the night, attack unarmed people asleep upon the soil, and under the flag of their country; give no quarter—make no prisoners—distinguish not between young and old—innocent or guilty—kill all—add fire to the sword—send the vessel and its contents over the falls in flames—and run back under cover of the same darkness which has concealed their approach. All this in time of peace. And then to call this an act of war, for which the perpetrators are not amenable, and for which redress must be had by fighting, or negotiating with the nation to which they belong. This is absurd. It is futile and ridiculous. Common sense condemns it. The heart condemns it. Jackson's example in Florida condemns it; and we should render ourselves contemptible if we took any such weak and puerile course.

Mr. Fox nowhere says this act was done by the sovereign's command. He shows, in fact, that it was not so done; and we know that it was not. It was the act of volunteers, unknown to the British government until it was over, and unassumed by them for three years after it occurred. The act occurred in December, 1837; our minister, Mr. Stevenson, demanded redress for it in the spring of 1838. The British government did not then assume it, nor did they assume it at all until McLeod was caught. Then, for the first time, they assume and justify, and evidently for the mere purpose of extricating McLeod. The assumption is void. Governments cannot assume the crimes of individuals. It is only as a military enterprise that this offence can be assumed; and we know this affair was no such enterprise, and is not even represented as such by the British minister. He calls it a "*transaction*." Three times in one paragraph he calls it a "*transaction*;" and whoever heard of a fight, or a battle, being characterized as a transaction? We apply the term to an affair of business, but never to a military operation. How can we have a military operation without war? without the knowledge of the sovereign? without the forms and preliminaries which the laws of nations exact? This was no military enterprise in form, or in substance. It was no attack upon a fort, or a ship of war, or a body of troops. It was no attack of soldiers upon soldiers, but of assassins upon the sleeping and the defenceless. Our American defenders of this act go beyond the British in exalting it into a military enterprise. They take different ground, and higher ground, than the British, in setting up that defence; and are just as wrong now as they were in the case of Arbuthnot and Ambrister.

Incorrect in point of national law, I hold these instructions to have been derogatory to as in point of national character, and given with most precipitate haste when they should not have been given at all. They were given under a formal, deliberate, official threat from the minister; and a thousand unofficial threats from high and respectable sources. The minister says:

> "But, be that as it may, her Majesty's government *formally demands*, upon the grounds already stated, the *immediate* release of Mr. McLeod; and her Majesty's government entreat the President of the United States to take into his most *deliberate consideration* the serious nature of the consequences which must ensue from a rejection of this demand."

Nothing could be more precise and formal than this demand—nothing more significant and palpable than this menace. It is such as should have prevented any answer—such as should have suspended diplomatic intercourse—until it was withdrawn. Instead of that, a most sudden and precipitate answer is given; and one that grants all that the British demanded, and more too; and that without asking any thing from them. It is given with a haste which seems to preclude the possibility of regular deliberation, cabinet council, and official form. The letter of Mr. Fox bears date the 12th of March, which was Friday, and may have been delivered in office hours of that day. The instruction to Mr. Crittenden was delivered on the 15th of March, which was Monday, and a copy delivered to Mr. Fox. This was the answer to the demand and the threat; and thus the answer was given in two days; for Sunday, as the lawyers call it, is *dies non*; that is to say, no day for business; and it is hardly to be presumed that an administration which seems to be returning to the church and state times of Queen Anne, had the office of the Department of State open, and the clerks at their desks on Sunday, instead of being in their pews at church. The answer, then, was given in two days; and this incontinent haste to comply with a threat contrasts wonderfully with the delay—the forty days' delay—before the letter was written which was intended for home consumption; and which, doubtless, was considered as written in good time, if written in time to be shown to Congress at this extra session.

Sir, I hold it to have been derogatory to our national character to have given any answer at all, much less the one that was given, while a threat was hanging over our heads. What must be the effect of yielding to demands under such circumstances? Certainly degradation—national degradation—and an encouragement to Great Britain to continue her aggressive course upon us. That nation is pressing us in the Northeast and Northwest; she is searching our ships on the coast of Africa; she gives liberty to our slaves wrecked on her islands in their transit from one of our ports to another; she nurtures in London the societies which produced the San Domingo insurrection, and which are preparing a similar insurrection for us; and she is the mistress of subjects who hold immense debts against our States, and for the payment of which the national guarantee, or the public lands, are wanted. She has many points of aggressive contact upon us; and what is the effect of this tame submission—this abject surrender of McLeod, without a word of redress for the affair of the Caroline, and under a public threat—what is the effect of this but to encourage her to press us and threaten us on every other point? It must increase her arrogance, and encourage her encroachments, and induce her to go on until submission to further outrage becomes impossible, and war results from the cowardice which courage would have prevented. On this head the history of many nations is full of impressive lessons, and none more so than that of Great Britain. It is a nation of brave people; but they have sometimes had ministers who were not brave, and whose timidity has ended in involving their country in all the calamities of war, after subjecting it to all the disgrace of pusillanimous submission to foreign insult. The administration of Sir Robert Walpole; long, cowardly and corrupt—tyrannical at home and cringing abroad—was a signal instance of this; and, as a warning to ourselves, I will read a passage from English history to show his conduct, and the consequences of it. I read from Smollett, and from his account of the Spanish depredations, and insults upon English subjects, which were continued the whole term of Walpole's administration, and ended in bringing on the universal war which raged throughout Europe, Asia, Africa, and America, and cost the English people so much blood and treasure. The historian says:

> "The merchants of England loudly complained of these outrages; the nation was fired with resentment, and cried for vengeance; but the minister appeared cold, phlegmatic, and timorous. He knew that a war would involve him in such difficulties as must of necessity endanger his administration. The treasure which he now employed for domestic purposes must in that case be expended in military armaments; the wheels of that machine on which he had raised his influence would no longer move; the opposition would of consequence gain

ground, and the imposition of fresh taxes, necessary for the maintenance of the war, would fill up the measure of popular resentment against his person and ministry. Moved by these considerations, he industriously endeavored to avoid a rupture, and to obtain some sort of satisfaction by dint of memorials and negotiations, in which he betrayed his own fears to such a degree as animated the Spaniards to persist in their depredations, and encouraged the court of Madrid to disregard the remonstrances of the British ambassador."

Such is the picture of Walpole's foreign policy; and how close is the copy we are now presenting of it! Under the scourge of Spanish outrage, he was cold, phlegmatic, and timorous; and such is the conduct of our secretary under British outrage. He wanted the public treasure for party purposes, and neglected the public defences: our ministry want the public lands and the public money for *douceurs* to the States, and leave the Union without forts and ships. Walpole sought some sort of satisfaction by dint of negotiation; our minister does the same. The British minister at Madrid was paralyzed by the timidity of the cabinet at home; so is ours paralyzed at London by our submission to Mr. Fox here. The result of the whole was, accumulated outrage, coalitions against England, universal war, the disgrace of the minister, and the elevation of the man to the highest place in his country, and to the highest pinnacle of glory, whom Walpole had dismissed from the lowest place in the British army—that of cornet of horse—for the political offence of voting against him. The elder William Pitt— the dismissed cornet—conducted with glory and success the war which the timidity of Walpole begat; and, that the smallest circumstances might not be wanting to the completeness of the parallel, our prime minister here has commenced his career by issuing an order for treating our military and naval officers as Pitt was treated by Walpole, and for the same identical offence.

Sir, I consider the instructions to Mr. Crittenden as most unfortunate and deplorable. They have sunk the national character in the eyes of England and of Europe. They have lost us the respect which we gained by the late war and by the glorious administration of Jackson. They bring us into contempt, and encourage the haughty British to push us to extremities. We shall feel the effect of this deplorable diplomacy in our impending controversies with that people; and happy and fortunate it will be for us if, by correcting our error, retracing our steps, recovering our manly attitude, discarding our distribution schemes, and preparing for war, we shall be able thereby to prevent war, and to preserve our rights.

I have never believed our English difficulties free from danger. I have not spoken upon the Northeastern question; but the senator from that State who sits on my right (looking at senator WILLIAMS) knows my opinion. He knows that I have long believed that nothing could save the rights of Maine *but the war countenance of our government*. Preparation for war might prevent war, and save the rights of the State. This has been my opinion; and to that point have all my labors tended. I have avoided speeches; I have opposed all distributions of land and money; I have gone for ships, forts and cannon—the *ultima ratio* of Republics as well as kings. I go for them now, and declare it as my opinion that the only way to obtain our rights, and to avoid eventual war with England, is to abandon all schemes of distribution, and to convert our public lands and surplus revenue, when we have it, into cannon, ships and forts.

Hard pressed on the instructions to Mr. Crittenden—prostrate and defenceless there—the gentlemen on the other side take refuge under the letter to Mr. Fox, and celebrate the harmony of its periods, and the beauty of its composition. I grant its merit in these particulars. I admit the beauty of the style, though attenuated into gossamer thinness and lilliputian weakness. I agree that the Secretary writes well. I admit his ability even to compose a prettier letter in less than forty days. But what has all this to do with the question of right and wrong—of honor and shame—of war and peace—with a foreign government? In a contest of rhetoricians, it would indeed be important; but in the contests of nations it dwindles into insignificance. The statesman wants knowledge, firmness, patriotism, and invincible adherence to the rights, honor, and interests of his country. These are the characteristics of the statesman; and tried by these tests, what becomes of this letter, so encomiastically dwelt upon here? Its knowledge is shown by a mistake of the law of nations—its firmness, by yielding to a threat—its patriotism, by taking the part of foreigners—its adherence to the honor, rights and interests of our own country, by surrendering McLeod without receiving, or even demanding, one word of redress or apology for the outrage upon the Caroline!

The letter, besides its fatal concessions, is deficient in manly tone—in American feeling—in nerve—in force—in resentment of injurious imputations—and in enforcement of our just claims to redress for blood spilt, territory invaded, and flag insulted.

The whole spirit of the letter is feeble and deprecatory. It does not repel, but begs off. It does not recriminate, but defends. It does not resent insult—not even the audacious threat—which is never once complained of, nor even alluded to.

This letter is every way an unfortunate production. It does not even show the expense and trouble we took to prevent our citizens from crossing the line and joining the Canadian insurgents. It does not show the expense we were at in raising a new regiment of infantry expressly for that service (several voices said yes, yes, it mentions that). Good, let it be credited accordingly. But it does not mention the appropriation of $650,000 made at one time for that object; it does not mention the numerous calls upon the militia authorities and the civil authorities along the line to assist in restraining our people; it does not mention the arrests of persons, and seizures of arms, which we made; it does not mention the prosecutions which we instituted; it does not show that for two years we were at great expense and trouble to restrain our people; and that this expense and trouble was brought upon us by the excitement produced by the affair of the Caroline. The British brought us an immense expense by that affair, for which they render us no thanks, and the Secretary fails to remind them. The letter does not repel, with the indignant energy which the declaration required, that we had "*permitted*" our citizens to arm and join the insurgents. It repels it, to be sure, but too feebly and gently, and it omits altogether what should never be lost sight of in this case, that the British have taken great vengeance on our people for their rashness in joining this revolt. Great numbers of them were killed in action; many were hanged; and many were transported to the extremities of the world—to Van Diemen's Land, under the antarctic circle—where they pine out a miserable existence, far, far, and for ever removed from kindred, home and friends.

The faults of the letter are fundamental and radical—no beauty of composition, no tropes and figures, no flowers of rhetoric—can balance or gloss over. The objections go to its spirit and substance—to errors of fact and law—to its tameness and timidity—and to its total omission to demand redress from the British government for the outrages on the Caroline, which that government has assumed. She has now assumed that outrage for the first time—assumed it after three years of refusal to speak; and in the assumption offers not one word of apology, or of consolation to our wounded feelings. She claps her arms akimbo, and avows the offence; and our Secretary, in his long and beautiful letter, finds no place to insert a demand for the assumed outrage. He gives up the culprit subject, and demands nothing from the imperious sovereign. He lets go the servant, and does not lay hold of the master. This is a grievous omission. It is tantamount to a surrender of all claim for any redress of any kind. McLeod, the culprit, is given up: he is given up without conditions. The British government assume his offence—demand his release—offer us no satisfaction: and we give him up, and ask no satisfaction. The letter demands nothing—literally nothing: and in that respect again degrades us as much as the surrender upon a threat had already degraded us. This is a most material point, and I mean to make it clear. I mean to show that the Secretary in giving up the alleged instrument, has demanded nothing from the assuming superiors: and this I will do him the justice to show by reading from his own letter. I have examined it carefully, and can find but two places where the slightest approach is made, not even to a demand for redress, but to the suggestion of an intimation of a wish on our side ever to hear the name of the Caroline mentioned again. These two places are on the concluding pages of the letter, as printed by our order. If there are others, let gentlemen point them out, and they shall be read. The two paragraphs I discover, are these:

> "This government, therefore, not only holds itself above reproach in every thing respecting the preservation of neutrality, the observance of the principle of non-intervention, and the strictest conformity, in these respects, to the rules of international law, but it doubts not that the world will do it the justice to acknowledge that it has set an example not unfit to be followed by others, and that, by its steady legislation on this most important subject, it has done something to promote peace and good neighborhood among nations, and to advance the civilization of mankind.

"The President instructs the undersigned to say, in conclusion, that he confidently trusts that this and all other questions of difference between the two governments will be treated by both in the full exercise of such a spirit of candor, justice, and mutual respect, as shall give assurance of the long continuance of peace between the two countries."

This is all I can see that looks to the possible contingency of any future allusion to the case of the Caroline. Certainly there could not be a more effectual abandonment of our claim to redress. The first paragraph goes no further than to "trust" that the grounds may be presented which "justify"—a strange word in such a case—the local authorities in attacking and destroying this vessel; and the second buries it all up by deferring it to the general and peaceful settlement of all other questions and differences between the two countries. Certainly this is a farewell salutation to the whole affair. It is the valedictory to the Caroline. It is the parting word, and is evidently so understood by the British ministry. They have taken no notice of this beautiful letter: they have returned no answer to it; they have not even acknowledged its receipt. The ministry, the parliament, and the press, all acknowledge themselves satisfied—satisfied with the answer which was given to Mr. Fox, on the 12th of March. They cease to speak of the affair; and the miserable Caroline—plunging in flames over the frightful cataract, the dead and the dying both on board—is treated as a gone-by procession, which has lost its interest for ever. Mr. Webster has given it up, by deferring it to general settlement; and in so giving it up, has not only abandoned the rights and honor of his country, but violated the laws of diplomatic intercourse. Outrages and insults are never deferred to a general settlement. They are settled *per se*—and promptly and preliminarily. All other negotiations cease until the insult and outrage is settled. That is the course of Great Britain herself in this case. She assumes the arrest of McLeod to be an offence to the British crown, and dropping all other questions of difference, demands instant reparation for that offence. Mr. Webster should have done the same by the offence to his country. It was prior in time, and should have been prior in settlement—at all events the two offences should have been settled together. Instead of that he hastens to make reparation to the British—does it in person—and without waiting even to draw up a letter in reply to Mr. Fox! and then, of his own head, defers our complaint to a general settlement. This is unheard of, either in national or individual insults. What would we think of a man, who being insulted by an outrage to his family in his house, should say to the perpetrators: "We have some outstanding accounts, and some day or other we may have a general settlement; and then, I trust you will settle this outrage." What would be said of an individual in such a case, must be said of ourselves in this case. In vain do gentlemen point to the paragraph in the letter, so powerfully drawn, which paints the destruction of the Caroline, and the slaughter of the innocent as well as the guilty, asleep on board of her. That paragraph aggravates the demerit of the letter: for, after so well showing the enormity of the wrong, and our just title to redress, it abandons the case without the slightest atonement. But that letter, with all its ample beauties, found no place to rebuke the impressment and abduction of the person claimed as a British subject, because he was a fugitive rebel. Whether so, or not, he could not be seized upon American soil—could not even be given up under the extradition clause in Mr. Jay's treaty, even if in force, which only applied to personal and not to political offences. But that letter, was for Buncombe: it was for home consumption: it was to justify to the American people on the 24th of May, what had been done on the 12th of March. It was superscribed to Mr. Fox, but written for our own people: and so Mr. Fox understood it, and never even acknowledged its receipt.

But gentlemen point to a special phrase in the letter, and quote it with triumph, as showing pluck and fight in our Secretary: it is the phrase, "bloody and exasperated war"—and consider this phrase as a cure for all deficiencies. Alas! it would seem to have been the very thing which did the business for our Secretary. That blood, with war, and exasperation, seems to have hastened his submission to the British demand. But how was it with Mr. Fox? Did it hasten his inclination to pacify us? Did he take it as a thing to quicken him? or, did the British government feel it as an inducement, or stimulus to hasten atonement for the injury they had assumed? Not at all! Far from it! Mr. Fox did not take fright, and answer in two days! nor has he answered yet! nor will he ever while such gentle epistles are written to him. Its effect upon the British ministry is shown by the manner in which they have treated it—the contempt of silence. No, sir! instead of these gentle phrases, there ought to have been two brief words spoken to Mr. Fox—first, your letter contains a threat; and the American government does not negotiate under a threat; *next*, your government has assumed the Caroline outrage to the United States, and now atone for it: and as to McLeod, he is in the hands of justice, and will be tried for his crimes, according to the law of nations. This is the answer which ought to have been given. But not so. Instant submission on our part, was the resolve and the act. Forty days afterwards this fine letter was delivered. Unfortunate as is this boasted letter in so many respects, it has a further sin to answer for, and that is for its place, or order—its collocation and connection—in the printed document which lies before us; and also in its assumption to "enclose" the Crittenden instructions to Mr. Fox—which had been personally delivered to him forty days before. The letter is printed, in the document, before the "instructions," though written forty days after them; and purports to "enclose" what had been long before delivered. Sir, the case of McLeod is not an isolation: it is not a solitary act: it is not an atom lying by itself. But it is a feature in a large picture—a link in a long chain. It connects itself with all the aggressive conduct of Great Britain towards the United States—her encroachments on the State of Maine—her occupation of our territory on the Oregon—her insolence in searching our vessels on the coast of Africa—the liberation of our slaves, wrecked on her islands, when in transition from one part of the Union to another—her hatching in London for the Southern States, what was hatched there above forty years ago for San Domingo: and the ominous unofficial intimation to our aforesaid Secretary, that the federal government is bound for the European debts of the individual States. The McLeod case mixes itself with the whole of these; and the success which has attended British threats in his case, may bring us threats in all the other cases; and blows to back them, if not settled to British liking. Submission invites aggression. The British are a great people—a wonderful people; and can perform as well as threaten. Occupying some islands no larger than two of our States, they have taken possession of the commanding points in the four quarters of the globe, and dominate over an extent of land and water, compared to which the greatest of empires—that of Alexander, of Trajan, of the Caliphs—was a dot upon the map. War is to them a distant occupation—an ex-territorial excursion—something like piracy on a vast scale; in which their fleets go forth to capture and destroy—to circumnavigate the globe; and to return loaded with the spoil of plundered nations. Since the time of William the Conqueror, no foreign hostile foot has trod their soil; and, safe thus far from the ravages of war at home, they are the more ready to engage in ravages abroad. To bully, to terrify, to strike, to crush, to plunder—and then exact indemnities as the price of forbearance—is their policy and their practice: and they look upon us with our rich towns and extended coasts, as a fit subject for these compendious tactics. We all deprecate a war with that people—none deprecate it more than I do—not for its dangers, but for its effects on the business pursuits of the two countries, and its injury to liberal governments: but we shall never prevent war by truckling to threats, and squandering in douceurs to the States what ought to be consecrated to the defence of the country. The result of our first war with this people, when only a fifth of our present numbers, shows what we could do in a seven years' contest: the result of the second shows that, at the end of two years, having repulsed their fleets and armies at all points, we were just ready to light upon Canada with an hundred thousand volunteers, fired by the glories of New Orleans. And in any future war with that nation, woe to the statesman that woos peace at the repulse of the foe. Of all the nations of the earth, we are the people to land upon the coasts of England and Ireland. We are their kin and kith; and the visits of kindred have sympathies and affections, which statutes and proclamations cannot control.

CHAPTER LXXVII.

REFUSAL OF THE HOUSE TO ALLOW RECESS COMMITTEES.

Two propositions submitted at this session to allow committees to sit in the recess, and collect information on industrial subjects—commerce, manufactures, and agriculture—with a view to beneficial legislation, had the effect of bringing out a very full examination into the whole subject—under all its aspects, of constitutionality and expediency. The whole debate was brought on by the principal proposition, submitted by Mr. Winthrop, from the Committee on Commerce, in these words:

> "*Resolved*, That a committee of nine members, not more than one of whom shall be from any one State, be appointed by the Chair, to sit during the recess, for the purpose of taking evidence at the principal ports of entry and elsewhere, as to the operation of the existing system and rates of duties on imports upon the manufacturing, agricultural, and commercial interests of the country, and of procuring, generally, such information as may be useful to Congress in any revision of the revenue laws which may be attempted at the next session."

On this resolution there was but little said. The previous question was soon called, and the resolution carried by a lean majority—106 to 104. A reconsideration was instantly moved by Mr. McKeon of New York, which, after some discussion, was adopted, 106 to 90. The resolution was then laid on the table: from which it was never raised. Afterwards a modification of it was submitted by Mr. Kennedy of Maryland, from the committee on commerce, in these words:

> "*Resolved*, That a select committee of eleven members, not more than one of which shall be from any one State, be appointed by the Chair for the purpose of taking evidence at the principal ports of entry and elsewhere as to the operation of the existing system and rates of duties on imports upon the manufacturing, commercial, and agricultural interests of the country; and of procuring, generally, such information as may be useful to Congress in any revision of the revenue laws which may be attempted at the next session.

> "*Resolved, further*, That said committee be authorized to sit during the recess, and to employ a clerk."

A motion was made by Ingersoll which brought up the question of recess committees on their own merits, stripped of the extraneous considerations which a proposition for such a committee, for a particular purpose, would always introduce. He moved to strike out the words, "*to sit during the recess*." This was the proper isolation of the contested point. In this form the objections to such committees were alone considered, and found to be insuperable. In the first place, no warrant could be found in the constitution for this elongation of itself by the House by means of its committees, and it was inconsistent with that adjournment for which the constitution provides, and with those immunities to members which are limited to the term of service, and the time allowed for travelling to and from Congress. No warrant could be found for them in the constitution, and practical reasons against them presented themselves more forcibly and numerously as the question was examined. The danger of degenerating into faction and favoritism, was seen to be imminent. Committees might be appointed to perambulate the Union—at the short sessions for nine months in the year—spending their time idly, or engaged in political objects—drawing the pay and mileage of members of Congress all the time, with indefinite allowances for contingencies. If one committee might be so appointed, then as many others as the House chose: if by one House, then by both: if to perambulate the United States, then all Europe—constituting a mode of making the tour of Europe at the public expense. All Congress might be so employed: but it was probable that only the dominant party, each in its turn, would so favor its own partisans, and for its own purposes. The practical evils of the measure augmented to the view as more and more examined: and finally, the whole question was put to rest by the decided sense of the House—only sixty-two members voting against the motion to lay it on the table, not to be taken up again: a convenient, and compendious way to get rid of a subject, as it brings on the direct vote, without discussion, and without the process of the previous question to cut off debate.

Such was the decision of the House; and, what has happened in the Senate, goes to confirm the wisdom of their decision. Recess committees have been appointed from that body; and each case of such appointment has become a standing argument against their existence. The first instance was that of a senatorial committee, in the palmy days of the United States Bank, consisting of the friends of that bank, appointed on the motion of its own friends to examine it—spending the whole recess in the work: and concluding with a report lauding the management of the bank, and assailing those who opposed it. Several other senatorial recess committees have since been appointed; but under circumstances which condemn them as an example; and with consequences which exemplify the varieties of abuse to which they are subject; and of which, faction, favoritism, personal objects, ungovernable expense, and little, or no utility, constitute the heads.

CHAPTER LXXVIII.

REDUCTION OF THE EXPENSE OF FOREIGN MISSIONS BY REDUCING THE NUMBER.

A question of permanent and increasing interest was opened at this session, which has become more exigent with time, and deserves to be pursued until its object shall be accomplished. It was the question of reducing the expenses of foreign missions, by reducing the number, and the expediency of returning to the Jeffersonian policy of having no ministers resident, or permanent succession of ministers abroad. The question was brought on by a motion from Mr. Charles Jared Ingersoll to strike from the appropriation bill the salaries of some missions mentioned in it; and this motion brought on the question of, how far the House had a right to interfere in these missions and control them by withholding compensation? and how far it was expedient to diminish their number, and to return to the Jeffersonian policy? Chargés had been appointed to Sardinia and Naples: Mr. Ingersoll thought them unnecessary; as also the mission to Austria, and that the ministers to Spain ought to be reduced to chargéships. Mr. Caleb Cushing considered the appointment of these ministers as giving them "vested rights in their salaries," and that the House was bound to vote. Mr. Ingersoll scouted this idea of "vested rights." Mr. Adams said the office of minister was created by the law of nations, and it belonged to the President and Senate to fill it, and for the Congress to control it, if it judged it necessary, as the British parliament has a right to control the war which the king has a right to declare, namely, by withholding the supplies: but it would require an extreme case to do so after the appointment had been made. He did not think the House ought to lay aside its power to control in a case obviously improper. And he thought the introduction of an appropriation bill, like the present, a fit occasion to inquire into the propriety of every mission; and he thought it expedient to reduce the expenses of our foreign missions, by reducing the number: and with this view he should offer a resolution when it should be in order to do so. Mr. Gilmer, as one of the Committee on Retrenchment, had paid some attention to the subject of our foreign representation; and he believed, with Mr. Adams, that both the grade and the destination of our foreign agents would admit of a beneficial reduction. Mr. Ingersoll rejoined on the different branches of the question, and in favor of Mr. Jefferson's policy, and for following up the inquiry proposed by Mr. Adams; and said:

> "If the stand he had now taken should eventually lead to the retrenchment alluded to in the resolution of the venerable gentleman from Massachusetts, he should be content. He still thought the House might properly exercise its withholding power, not, indeed, so as to stop the wheels of government, but merely to curtail an unnecessary expenditure; and he hoped there would be enough of constitutional feeling, of the *esprit du corps*, to lead them to insist upon their right. He scouted the idea of the President's appointment creating a vested interest in the appointee to his salary as minister. Such a doctrine would be monstrous. The House might be bound by high considerations of policy and propriety, but never by the force of a contract, to appropriate for an appointed minister. This was carrying the principle totally *extra mœnia mundi*. Mr. I. disclaimed opposing these measures on the mere ground of dollars and cents; he alluded to the multiplication of missions to and from this country as introducing examples of lavish expenditure and luxurious living among our own citizens. As to the distinction between temporary and permanent missions, the gentleman from Massachusetts [Mr. CUSHING] perfectly well knew that originally all public missions were temporary; such a thing as a permanent foreign mission was unheard of. This was an invention of modern times; and it had been Mr. Jefferson's opinion that such missions ought not to exist. It was high time that public attention was called to the subject; and he hoped that at the next session Mr. Adams would bring forward and press his resolution of inquiry as to the expediency of reducing the whole system of foreign intercourse."

Mr. Adams afterwards introduced his proposed resolution, which was adopted by the House, and sent to the Committee on Foreign Relations; but which has not yet produced the required reform. This was his resolve:

> "*Resolved*, That the Committee on Foreign Affairs be instructed to inquire into the expediency of reducing the expenditures in the diplomatic department of the government, by diminishing

the number of ministers and other diplomatic agents abroad, and report thereon to the House."

It would be a public benefaction, and a great honor to the member who should do it, for some ardent man to take charge of this subject—revive Mr. Adams' resolution, and pursue the inquiry through all the branches which belong to it: and they are many. First: The full mission of minister plenipotentiary and envoy extraordinary, formerly created only on extraordinary occasions, and with a few great courts, and intrusted to eminent men, are now lavished in profusion; and at secondary courts; and filled with men but little adapted to grace them; and without waiting for an occasion, but rapidly, to accommodate political partisans; and as a mere party policy, recalling a political opponent to make room for an adherent: and so keeping up a perpetual succession, and converting the envoys extraordinary into virtual ministers resident. In the second place, there are no plenipotentiaries now—no ministers with full powers—or in fact with any powers at all, except to copy what is sent to them, and sign what they are told. The Secretaries of State now do the business themselves, either actually making the treaty at home while the minister is idle abroad, or virtually by writing instructions for home effect, often published before they are delivered, and containing every word the minister is to say— with orders to apply for fresh instructions at every new turn the business takes. And communications have now become so rapid and facile that the entire negotiation may be conducted at home—the important minister plenipotentiary and envoy extraordinary being reduced to the functions of a messenger. In the third place, all the missions have become resident, contrary to the policy and interest of our country, which wants no entangling alliances or connections abroad; and to the damage of our treasury, which is heavily taxed to keep up a numerous diplomatic establishment in Europe, not merely useless, but pernicious. In the fourth place, our foreign intercourse has become inordinately expensive, costing above three hundred thousand dollars a year; and for ministers who do not compare with the John Marshalls of Virginia, the John Quincy Adamses, the Pinckneys of South Carolina, the Pinkney of Maryland, the Rufus Kings, Albert Gallatins, James Monroes, the Livingstons, and all that class, the pride of their country, and the admiration of Europe; and which did not cost us one hundred thousand dollars a year, and had something to do, and did it—and represented a nation abroad, and not a party. Prominently among the great subjects demanding reform, is now the diplomatic intercourse of the United States. Reduction of number, no mission without an object to accomplish, no perpetual succession of ministers, no ministers resident, no exclusion of one party by the other from this national representation abroad, no rank higher than a chargé except when a special service is to be performed and then nationally composed: and the expenses inexorably brought back within one hundred thousand dollars a year. Such are the reforms which our diplomatic foreign intercourse has long required—which so loudly called for the hand of correction fifteen years ago, when Mr. Adams submitted his resolution; and all the evils of which have nearly doubled since. It is a case in which the House of Representatives, the immediate representatives of the people, and the sole constitutional originator of taxes upon them, should act as a check upon the President and Senate; and do it as the British House of Commons checks the king, the lords and the ministry—by withholding the supplies.

CHAPTER LXXIX.

INFRINGEMENT OF THE TARIFF COMPROMISE ACT OF 1833: CORRECTION OF ABUSES IN DRAWBACKS

The history, both ostensible and secret, of this act has been given, and its brief existence foretold, although intended for perpetuity, and the fate of the Union, in numerous State legislative resolves, and in inumerable speeches, declared to depend upon its inviolability. It was assumed to have saved the Union: the corollary of that assumption was, that its breach would dissolve the Union. Equally vain and idle were both the assumption and the inference! and equally erroneous was the general voice, which attributed the act to Mr. Clay and Mr. Calhoun. They appeared to the outside observer as the authors of the act: the inside witness saw in Mr. John M. Clayton, of Delaware, and Mr. Robert P. Letcher, of Kentucky, its real architects—the former in commencing the measure and controlling its provisions; the latter as having brought Mr. Calhoun to its acceptance by the communication to him of President Jackson's intentions; and by his exertions in the House of Representatives. It was composed of two parts—one part to last nine years, for the benefit of the manufacturers: the other part to last for ever, for the benefit of the planting and consuming interest. Neither part lived out its allotted time; or, rather, the first part died prematurely, and the second never began to live. It was a *felo de se* from the beginning, and bound to perish of the diseases in it. To Mr. Clay and Mr. Calhoun, it was a political necessity—one to get rid of a stumbling-block (which protective tariff had become); the other to escape a personal peril which his nullifying ordinance had brought upon him: and with both, it was a piece of policy, to enable them to combine against Mr. Van Buren, by postponing their own contention: and a device on the part of Mr. Clayton and Mr. Clay to preserve the protective system, doomed to a correction of its abuses at the ensuing session of Congress. The presidential election was over, and General Jackson elected to his second term, pledged to a revenue tariff and incidental protection: a majority of both Houses of Congress were under the same pledge: the public debt was rapidly verging to extinction: and both the circumstances of the Treasury, and the temper of the government were in harmony with the wishes of the people for a "judicious tariff;" limited to the levy of the revenue required for the economical administration of a plain government, and so levied as to extend encouragement to the home production of articles necessary to our independence and comfort. All this was ready to be done, and the country quieted for ever on the subject of the tariff, when the question was taken out of the hands of the government by a coalition between Mr. Clay and Mr. Calhoun, and a bill concocted, as vicious in principle, as it was selfish and unparliamentary in its conception and execution. The plan was to give the manufacturers their undue protection for nine years, by making annual reductions, so light and trifling during the time, that they would not be felt; and after the nine years, to give the anti-tariff party their millennium, in jumping down, at two leaps, in the two last years, to a uniform *ad valorem* duty of twenty per centum on all duticd articles. All practical men saw at the time how this concoction would work—that it would produce more revenue than the government wanted the first seven years, and leave it deficient afterwards—that the result would be a revulsion of all interests against a system which left the government without revenue—and that, in this revulsion there must be a re-modelling, and an increase in the tariff: all ending in a complete deception to the anti-tariff party, who would see the protective part of the compromise fully enjoyed by the manufacturing interest, and the relief part for themselves wholly lost. All this was seen at the time: but a cry was got up, by folly and knavery, of danger to the Union: this bill was proclaimed as the only means of saving it: ignorance, credulity, timidity and temporizing temperaments united to believe it. And so the bill was accepted as a God-send: the coming of which had saved the Union—the loss of which would destroy it: and the two ostensible architects of the measure (each having worked in his own interest, and one greatly over-reaching the other), were saluted as pacificators, who had sacrificed their ambition upon the altar of patriotism for the good of their country.

The time had come for testing these opinions. We were in the eighth year of the compromise, the first part had nearly run its course: within one year the second part was to begin. The Secretary of the Treasury had declared the necessity of loans and taxes to carry on the government: a loan bill for twelve millions had been passed: a tariff bill to raise fourteen millions more was depending; and the chairman of the Committee of Ways and Means, Mr. Millard Fillmore, thus defended its necessity:

"He took a view of the effects of the compromise act, in the course of which he said that by that act one tenth of the customs over twenty-five per cent. ad valorem was to come off on the 1st January, 1834; and on the 1st January, 1836, another tenth was to be deducted; on the 1st January, 1838, another tenth; and on the 1st January, 1840, another tenth; and on the 1st January, 1842, three tenths more; and on the 1st July, 1842, the remaining three tenths were to be deducted, so that, on that day, what was usually termed the compromise act, was to go fully into effect, and reduce the revenue to 20 per cent. ad valorem on all articles imported into the country. It appeared from a report submitted to this House (he meant the financial report of the Secretary of the Treasury, document No. 2, page 20), showing the amount of imports for the seven years from 1834 to 1840 inclusive, that there were imported into this country one hundred and forty-one million four hundred and seventy-six thousand seven hundred and sixty-nine dollars' worth of goods, of which seventy-one million seven hundred and twenty-eight thousand three hundred and twelve dollars were free of duty, and sixty-nine million seven hundred and forty-eight thousand four hundred and fifty-seven dollars paid duty. Then, having these amounts, and knowing that, by the compromise act, articles paying duty over 20 per cent., and many of them paid more, were to be reduced down to that standard, and all were to pay only 20 per cent., what would be the amount of revenue from that source? Why, its gross amount would only be thirteen million nine hundred and fifty thousand dollars in round numbers—that is, taking the average of goods imported in the last seven years, the whole gross amount of duty that would pass into the Treasury, did all the imported articles pay the highest rate of duty, would only be thirteen million nine hundred and fifty-four thousand dollars—say fourteen millions of dollars in round numbers."

Thus the compromise act, under its second stage, was only to produce about fourteen millions of dollars—little more than half what the exigencies of the government required. Mr. Fillmore passed in review the different modes by which money could be raised. *First*, by loans: and rejected that mode as only to be used temporarily, and until taxes of some kind could be levied. Next, by direct taxation: and rejected that mode as being contrary to the habits and feelings of the people. Thirdly, by duties: and preferred that mode as being the one preferred by the country, and by which the payment of the tax became, in a large degree, voluntary—according to the taste of the payer in purchasing foreign goods. He, therefore, with the Secretary of the Treasury, preferred that mode, although it involved an abrogation of the compromise. His bill proposed twenty per centum additional to the existing duty on certain specified articles—sufficient to make up the amount wanted. This encroachment on a measure so much vaunted when passed, and which had been kept inviolate while operating in favor of one of the parties to it, naturally excited complaint and opposition from the other; and Mr. Gilmer, of Virginia, said:

"In referring to the compromise act, the true characteristics of that act which recommended it strongly to him, were that it contemplated that duties were to be levied for revenue only, and in the next place to the amount only necessary to the supply of the economical wants of the government. He begged leave to call the attention of the committee to the principle recognized in the language of the compromise—a principle which ought to be recognized in all time to come by every department of the government. It is, said he, that duties to be raised for revenue are to be raised to such an amount only as is necessary for an economical administration of the government. Some incidental protection must necessarily be given, and he, for one, coming from an anti-tariff portion of the country, would not object to it. But said he, we were told yesterday by the gentleman from Massachusetts [Mr. ADAMS], that he did not consider the compromise binding, because it was a compact between the South and the West, in which New England was not a party, and it was crammed down her throat by the previous question, he voting against it. The gentleman from Pennsylvania said to-day almost the same thing, for he considered it merely a point of honor which he was willing to concede to the South, and that object gained, there was no longer reason for adhering to it.

"Did the gentleman contend that no law was binding on New England, and on him, unless it is sanctioned by him and the New England delegation? Sir, said Mr. G., I believe that it is binding, whether sanctioned by New England or not. The gentleman said that he would give the public lands to the States, and the compromise act to the dogs. Sir, if the lands are to be given to the States, if upwards of three millions are to be deducted from that source of revenue, and we are then to be told that this furnishes a pretext, first for borrowing, and then for taxing the people, we may well feel cause for insisting on the obligations of the compromise. Sir, said Mr. G., gentlemen know very well that there is some virtue in the compromise act, and that though it may be repudiated by a few of the representatives of the people, yet the people themselves will adhere to it as the means of averting the greatest of evils. But he had seen enough to show him that the power of giving might be construed as the power of taking, and he should not be surprised to see a proposition to assume the debts of the States—for the more that you give, the more that is wanted.

"After some further remarks, Mr. G. said that he was opposed to the hurrying of this important measure through at the present session. Let us wait until sufficient information is obtained to enable us to act judiciously. Let us wait to inquire whether there is any necessity for raising an increased revenue of eight millions of dollars from articles, all of which, under the compromise act, are either free of duty or liable to a duty of less than 20 per cent. Let us not be told that on account of the appropriations for a home squadron, and for fortifications amounting to about three millions of dollars, that it is necessary to raise this large sum. We have already borrowed twelve millions of dollars, and during the remainder of the year, Mr. Ewing tells us that the customs will yield five millions, which together, will make seventeen millions of dollars of available means in the Treasury. Then there was a large sum in the hands of the disbursing officers of the government, and he ventured to assert that there would be more than twenty millions at the disposal of the Treasury before the expiration of the next session of Congress. Are we to be told, said Mr. G., that we are to increase the tariff in order to give to the States this fourth instalment under the deposit act? No sir; let us arrest this course of extravagance at the outset; let us arrest that bill which is now hanging in the other House [the distribution bill], and which I trust will ever hang there. Let us arrest that bill and the proceeds from that source will, in the coming four years, pay this twelve million loan. But these measures are all a part of the same system. Distribution is used as a pretext for a loan, and a loan is used as a pretext for high duties. This was an extraordinary session of Congress, and inasmuch as there would be within a few months a regular session—inasmuch as the Committee on Commerce had reported a resolution contemplating the organization of a select committee, with a view to the collection of information to aid in the revision of the tariff for revenue—and inasmuch as the compromise goes fully into operation in July next— he thought that wisdom, as well as justice, demanded that they should not hurry through so important a measure, when it was not absolutely essential to the wants of the government.

"After some further remarks, Mr. G. said that it was time that he and his whig friends should understand one another. He wanted now to understand what were the cardinal principles of the whig party, of which he was an humble member. He had for six or seven years been a member of that party, and thought he understood their principles, but he much feared that he had been acting under some delusion; and now that they were all here together, he wished to come to a perfect understanding."

The perfect understanding of each other which Mr. Gilmer wished to have with his whig friends, was a sort of an appeal to Mr. Clay to stand by the act of 1833. He represented that party on one side of the compromise, and Mr. Calhoun the other: and now, when it was about to be abrogated, he naturally called on the guaranty of the other side to come to the rescue. Mr. Charles Jared Ingersoll, pleasantly and sarcastically apostrophized the two eminent chiefs, who represented two opposite parties, and gloriously saved the Union (without the participation of the government), at the making of that compromise: and treated it as glory that had passed by:

"I listened with edification to the account of the venerable member from Massachusetts [Mr. ADAMS], of the method of enacting the compromise act—what may be called the perpetration of that memorable measure. Certainly it put an end to fearful strife. Perhaps it saved this glorious Union. I wish to be understood as speaking respectfully of both the distinguished persons who are said to have accomplished it. After all, however, it was rather their individual achievement than an act of Congress. The two chiefs, the towering peaks, of overhanging prohibitory protection and forcible nullification, nodded their summits together, and the work was done, without the active agency of either the executive or legislative branches of government. Its influences on public tranquillity were benignant. But how to be regarded as economical or constitutional lessons, is a different question, which, at this session, I am hardly prepared to unravel. Undiscriminating impost, twenty per cent. flush throughout, on all articles alike, will not answer the purposes of the Union, or of my State. It is not supposed by their advocates that it will. The present bill is to be transient; we are to have more particular, more thorough and permanent laws hereafter. Without giving in my adhesion to the compromise act, or announcing opposition to it, I hope to see such government as will ensure steady employment, at good wages, by which I mean high wages, paid in hard money; no others can be good, high, or adequate, or money at all; for every branch of industry, agricultural, commercial, manufacturing, and navigation, that palmy state of a country, to which this of all others is entitled, *pulcherrimo populi fasligio.*"

Mr. Pickens, of South Carolina, the intimate friend of Mr. Calhoun, also raised his voice against the abrogation of the act which had been kept in good faith by the free-trade party, and the consuming classes while so injurious to them, and was now to be impaired the moment it was to become beneficial:

"All the gentlemen who had spoken denied the binding force of the compromise act. Was this the doctrine of the party in power? Mr. P. had wished to hear from Kentucky, that he might discover whether this had been determined in conclave. The struggle would be severe to bring back the system of 1824, '28, and '32. The fact could no longer be disguised; and gentlemen might prepare themselves for the conflict. He saw plainly that this bill was to be passed by, and that all the great questions of the tariff policy would be again thrown open as though the compromise act had no existence. Was this fair? In 1835-6, when the last administration had taken possession of power, it was determined that the revenue must be reduced; but Mr. P. had at that time insisted that, though there was a surplus, the compromise act was not lightly to be touched, and that it would therefore be better to forbear and let that act run its course. Gentlemen on the other side had then come up and congratulated him on his speech; for they had already received the benefit of that act for four years. Then his doctrine was all right and proper; but now, when the South came to enjoy its share of the benefit, they took the other side, and the compromise was as nothing. One gentleman had said that twenty-eight millions would be needed to carry on the government; another, that twenty-seven; another, that twenty-five; and in this last opinion, the gentleman from Pennsylvania [Mr. INGERSOLL] agreed. And, as this sum could not be raised without duties over 20 per cent. the compromise must be set aside. Until lately Mr. P. had not been prepared for this; he had expected that at least the general spirit of that act would be carried out in the legislation of Congress; but he now saw that the whole tariff question must be met in all its length and breadth."

Very justly did Mr. Pickens say that the bill had been kept inviolate while operating injuriously to the consumers—that no alteration would be allowed in it. That was the course of the Congress to such a degree that a palpable error in relation to drawbacks was not allowed to be rectified, though plundering the Treasury of some hundreds of thousands of dollars per annum. But the new bill was to be passed: it was a necessity: for, in the language of Mr. Adams, the compromise act had beggared the Treasury, and would continue to beggar it—producing only half enough for the support of the government: and the misfortune of the free trade party was, that they did not foresee that consequence at the time, as others did; or seeing it, were obliged to submit to what the high tariff party chose to impose upon them, to release eminent men of South Carolina from the perilous condition in which the nullification ordinance had placed them. It passed the House by a vote of 116 to 101—the vote against it being stronger than the resistance in debate indicated.

The expenses of collecting the duties under the universal *ad valorem* system, in which every thing had to be valued, was enormous, and required an army of revenue officers—many of them mere hack politicians, little acquainted with their business, less attentive to it, giving the most variant and discordant valuations to the same article at different places, and even in the same place at different times; and often corruptly; and more occupied with politics than with custom-house duties. This was one of the evils foreseen when specific duties were abolished to make way for *ad valorems* and home valuations, and will continue until specific duties are restored as formerly, or "*angels*" procured to make the valuations. Mr. Charles Jared Ingersoll exposed this abuse in the debate upon this bill, showing that it cost nearly two millions of dollars to collect thirteen; and that two thousand officers were employed about it, who also employed themselves in the elections. He said:

> "Even the direct tax and internal duties levied during the late war cost but little more than five per cent. for collection; whereas, now, upon an income decreasing under the compromise act in geometrical ratio, the cost of collecting it increases in that ratio; amounting, according to the answer I got from the chairman of the Committee of Ways and Means, to at least twelve per cent.; near two millions of dollars, says the gentleman from Massachusetts [Mr. SALTONSTALL]—one million seven hundred thousand dollars. To manage the customs, government is obliged to employ not less than two thousand officers, heavily paid, and said to be the most active partisans; those who, in this metropolis, are extremely annoying by their importunate contests for office, and elsewhere still more offensive by misconduct, sometimes of a gross kind, as in the instance of one, whom I need not name, in my district. The venerable gentleman from Vermont [Mr. EVERETT] suggested yesterday a tax on auctions as useful to American manufactures. On that, I give no opinion. But this I say, that a stamp tax on bank notes, and a duty on auctions, would not require fifty men to collect them. It is not for us of the minority to determine whether they should be laid. Yet I make bold to suggest to the friends of the great leader, who, next to the President, has the power of legislation at present, that one of three alternatives is inevitable."

The bill went to the Senate where it found its two authors—such to the public; but in relative positions very different from what they were when it was passed—then united, now divided—then concurrent, now antagonistic: and the antagonism, general upon all measures, was to be special on this one. Their connection with the subject made it their function to lead off in its consideration; and their antagonist positions promised sharp encounters—which did not fail to come. From the first word temper was manifest; and especially on the part of Mr. Clay. He proposed to go on with the bill when it was called: Mr. Calhoun wished it put off till Monday. (It was then Friday.) Mr. Clay persevered in his call to go on with the bill, as the way to give general satisfaction. Then ensued a brief and peremptory scene, thus appearing in the Register of Debates:

> "Mr. CALHOUN thought the subject had better lie over. Senators had not an opportunity of examining the amendments; indeed, few had even the bill before them, not expecting it to come up. He agreed with the senator from Kentucky that it was important to give satisfaction, but the best way was to do what was right and proper; and he always found that, in the end, it satisfied more persons than they would by looking about and around to see what particular interest could be conciliated. Whatever touched the revenue touched the pockets of the people, and should be looked to with great caution. Nothing, in his opinion, was so preposterous as to expect, by a high duty on these articles, to increase the revenue. If the duty was placed at 20 per cent. it would be impossible to prevent smuggling. The articles in question would not bear any such duty; indeed, if they were reduced to 5 per cent. more revenue would be realized. He really hoped the senator would let the matter lie over until to-morrow or Monday."

"Mr. CLAY said he always found, when there was a journey to be performed, that it was as well to make the start; if they only got five or six miles on the way, it was so much gained at least."

"Mr. CALHOUN. We ought to have had some notice."

"Mr. CLAY. I give you notice now. Start! start! The amendment was very simple, and easily understood. It was neither more nor less than to exempt the articles named from the list of exceptions in the bill, by which they would be subjected to a duty of 20 per cent. Those who agreed to it could say 'aye,' and those who did not 'no;' and that was all he should say on the subject."

The bill went on. Mr. Calhoun said:

"He was now to be called on to vote for this bill, proposing, as it did, a great increase of taxes on the community, because it was an exigency measure. He should give his votes as if for the permanent settlement of the tariff. The exigency was produced by the gentlemen on the opposite side, and they should be held responsible for it. This necessity had been produced by the present administration—it was of their making, and he should vote for this as if he were settling the taxes, and as if the gentlemen had done their duty, and had not by extravagance and distribution created a deficiency in the Treasury, for which they were responsible. They yesterday passed a bill emptying the Treasury, by giving away the proceeds of the public lands, and to-day we have a bill to supply the deficiency by a resort to a tax which in itself was a violation of the compromise act. The compromise act provides that no duty shall be laid except for the economical support of the government; and he regarded the giving away of the public lands a violation of that act, whether the duty was raised to 20 per cent. or not, because they had not attempted to bring down the expenses of the government to an economical standard. He should proceed with this bill as if he were fixing the tariff; he thought an average of twelve and a half per cent. on our imports would raise an ample revenue for the support of the government, and in his votes on the several classes of articles he should bear this average in mind, imposing higher duties on some, and lower duties on others, as he thought the several cases called for."

"Mr. Benton said the bill came in the right place; and at the right moment: it came to fill up the gap which we had just made in the revenue by voting away the land-money. He should not help to fill that gap. Those who made it may fill it. He knew the government needed money, and must have it, and he did not intend to vote factiously, to stop its wheels, but considerately to compel it to do right. Stop the land-money distribution, and he would vote to supply its place by increased duties on imports; but while that branch of the revenue was lavished on the States in order to purchase popularity for those who squandered it, he would not become accessory to their offence by giving them other money to enable them to do so. The present occasion, he said, was one of high illustration of the vicious and debauching distribution schemes. When those schemes were first broached in this chamber ten years before, it was solely to get rid of a surplus—solely to get rid of money lying idle in the Treasury—merely to return to the people money which they had put into the Treasury and for which there was no public use. Such was the argument for these distributions for the first years they were attempted. Then the distributors advanced a step further, and proposed to divide the land money for a series of years, without knowing whether there would be any surplus or not. Now they have taken the final stride, and propose to borrow money, and divide it: propose to raise money by taxes, and divide it: for that is what the distribution of the land money comes to. It is not a separate fund: it is part of the public revenue: it is in the Treasury: and is as much custom-house revenue, for the customs have to be resorted to to supply its place. It is as much public money as that which is obtained upon loan: for the borrowed money goes to supply its loss. The distribution law is a fraud and a cheat on its face: its object is to debauch the people, and to do it with their own money; and I will neither vote for the act; nor for any tax to supply its place."

It was moved by Mr. Woodbury to include sumach among the dutiable articles, on the ground that it was an article of home growth, and the cultivation of it for domestic manufacturing purposes ought to be encouraged.

Mr. Clay opposed this motion, and fell into a perfect free-trade argument to justify his opposition, and to show that sumach ought to come in free. This gave Mr. Calhoun an opportunity, which was not neglected, to compliment him on his conversion to the right faith; and this compliment led to some interesting remarks on both sides, in which each greeted the other in a very different spirit from what they had done when they were framing that compromise which one of them was now breaking. Thus:

"Mr. CLAY said it was very true that sumach was an article of home growth; but he understood it was abundant where it was not wanted; and where those manufactures exist which would require it, there was none to be found. Under these circumstances, it had not as yet been cultivated for manufacturing purposes, and probably would not be, as long as agricultural labor could be more profitably employed. Imported sumach came from countries where labor was much cheaper than in this country, and he thought it was for the interest of our manufacturers to obtain it upon the cheapest terms they can. Our agricultural labor would be much employed in other channels of industry."

"Mr. CALHOUN was very glad to hear the senator from Kentucky at last coming round in support of this sound doctrine. It was just what he (Mr. Calhoun) had long expected that Mr. Clay would be forced to conform to, that those articles ought to be imported, which can be obtained from abroad on cheaper terms than they can be produced at home."

"Mr. CLAY thought the senator from South Carolina was not entitled to his interpretation of what he (Mr. Clay) had said. The senator converts a few words expressed in favor of continuing the free importation of sumach, under present circumstances, into a general approbation of free trade—a thing wholly out of view in his (Mr. Clay's) mind at the time he made his remarks. It was certainly owing to the peculiar habit of mind in which the senator from South Carolina was so fond of indulging, that he was thus always trying to reduce every thing to his system of abstractions."

These "abstractions," and this "peculiar habit," were a standing resort with Mr. Clay when a little pressed by Mr. Calhoun. They were mere flouts, but authorizing retaliation; and, on the present occasion, when the question was to break up that compromise which (in his part of it, the universal 20 per cent. ad valorems) was the refined essence of Mr. Calhoun's financial system, and which was to be perpetual, and for which he had already paid the consideration in the nine years' further endurance of the protective system: when this was the work in hand, and it aggravated by the imperative manner in which it was brought on—refusal to wait till Monday, and that most extemporaneous notice, accompanied by the command, "start! start!"—all this was a good justification to Mr. Calhoun in the biting spirit which he gave to his replies—getting sharper as he went on, until Mr. Clay pleasantly took refuge under sumach—popularly called shoe-make in the South and West.

"Mr. Calhoun observed that the senator from Kentucky had evidently very strong prejudices against what he calls abstractions. This would be easily understood when we take into consideration what the senator and his friends characterized as abstractions. What he and they called abstractions, was the principle of scrutiny and opposition so powerfully evinced by this side of the Senate, against the low estimates, ruinous projects, and extravagant expenditures which constitute the leading measures of the present administration. As regards the principles of free trade, if these were abstractions, he was happy to know that he was in company with some of the ablest statesmen of Great Britain. He referred to the report recently made in Parliament on this subject—a document of eminent ability."

"Mr. Clay observed that the senator from South Carolina based his abstractions on the theories of books—on English authorities, and on the arguments urged in favor of free trade by a certain party in the British Parliament. Now, he (Mr. Clay), and his friends would not admit of these authorities being entitled to as much weight as the universal practice of nations, which in all parts of the world was found to be in favor of protecting home manufactures to an extent sufficient to keep them in a flourishing condition. This was the whole difference. The senator was in favor of book theory and abstractions: he (Mr. Clay) and his friends were in favor of the universal practice of nations, and the wholesome and necessary protection of domestic manufactures. And what better proof could be given of national decision on this point than that furnished by the recent elections in Great Britain. A report on the subject of free trade, written by the astute and ingenious Scotchman, Mr. Hume, had obtained pretty general circulation in this country. On the principles set forth in that report the British ministry went before the people of England at a general election, and the result proved that they were repudiated."

"Mr. Calhoun had supposed the senator from Kentucky was possessed of more tact than to allude at all to the recent elections in England, and claim them as a triumph of his principles, much less to express himself in such strong terms of approbation at the result. The senator was, however, elated at the favorable result of the late elections to the tory party in England. That was not much to be wondered at, for the interests, objects, and aims of the tory party there and the whig party here, are identical. The identity of the two parties is remarkable. The tory party are the patrons of corporate monopolies; *and are not you?* They are advocates of a high tariff; *and are not you?* They are the supporters of a national bank; *and are not you?* They are for corn-laws—laws oppressive to the mass of the people, and favorable to their own power; *and are not you?* Witness this bill. The tory party in England are not supported by the British people. That party is the representative of the mere aristocracy of the country, which, by the most odious and oppressive system of coercion exercised over the tenantry of the country, has obtained the power of starving the mass of the people, by the continuation of laws exclusively protecting the landed interests, that is, the rent rolls of the aristocracy. These laws that party will uphold, rather than suffer the people to obtain cheap bread. The administration party in England wished to dissipate this odious system of exclusive legislation, and to give the mass of the people cheap bread. This the senator from Kentucky characterizes as ridiculous abstraction. And who are these tories of England? Do not the abolitionists constitute a large portion of that party? Those very abolitionists, who have more sympathy for the negroes of the West India Islands, than for the starving and oppressed white laborers of England. And why? Because it is the interest of the tory party to have high rents at home, and high tariff duties against the sugar of this country, for the protection of the owners of estates in the West India Islands. This is the party, the success of which, at the recent elections in Great Britain, has so elated the senator from Kentucky! The success of that party in England, and of the whig party here, is the success of the great money power, which concentrates the interests of the two parties, and identifies their principles. The struggle of both is a struggle for the ascendency of this great money power. When the whole subject is narrowly looked into, it is seen that the whole question at issue is that of the ascendency of this enormous and dangerous power, or that of popular rights. And this is a struggle which the opposition in this Capitol, to whom alone the people of this country can now look for protection against the measures threatened to be consummated here, will maintain to the last, regardless of the success of the tories abroad or their allies at home."

Mr. Clay did not meet these biting interrogatories. He did not undertake to show any injustice in classifying his modern whig party with the English high tory party, but hauled off, washing his hands of sympathy for that party—a retreat, for which Mr. Calhoun taunted him in his reply. Fact was, the old federal party—and I never refer to them as such in reproach—had become unpopular, and changed name without changing principles. They took that of whig, as having a seductive revolutionary odor, without seeming to perceive that it had not a principle in common with the whigs of the revolution which their adversaries had not also; and that in reality they occupied the precise ground in our political parties which the high tory party did in England. Mr. Calhoun drove this home to Mr. Clay with a point and power, and a closeness of application, which stuck, and required an exculpatory answer, if any could be given. But none such was attempted, either by Mr. Clay, or any of his friends; and the issue has shown the folly of taking a name without corresponding works. The name "whig" has been pretty well given up, without finding a better, and perhaps without saving the commendable principle of conservatism which was in it; and which, in its liberal and enlightened sense, is so essential in all governments. One thing both the disputants seemed to forget, though others did not; and that was, that Mr. Calhoun had acted with this party for ten years against President Jackson.

> "Mr. Clay denied that he had made any boast of the success of the tories in the English elections. He had expressed no sympathy with that party. He cared nothing about their success, though he did hope that the tories would not come into power in this country. He had only adverted to their triumph in England as an evidence of the sense of the English nation on the subject of free trade. His argument was, that no matter what contending politicians said about abstract principles, when it came to the practical action of the whole nation on these principles, that action was found decisive against theories and in favor of the practice of nations all over the globe. As to the success of the tories in England, he had frequently made the remark that this government had more to expect from the justice of a tory minister than a whig ministry, either in England or France, as the latter were afraid of being accused of being swayed by their liberal sentiments."

This was disavowing a fellow-feeling—not showing a difference; and Mr. Calhoun, seeing his advantage, followed it up with clinching vigor, and concluded with a taunt justified by the occasion.

> "Mr. Calhoun said when there was a question at issue between the senator from Kentucky and himself, that senator was not the judge of its accuracy, nor was he; but he would leave it to the Senate, and to all present who had heard the argument, if he had not met it fairly. Did he not quote, in tones of exultation, the triumph of the tory party in England as the triumph of his principles over the principles of free trade? And when he (Mr. Calhoun) had noticed the points of identity in principle between the tory party of England and the whig party of this country, had the senator attempted to reply? Nay more, he had alluded to the striking coincidence between the party affinities in Great Britain and this country, and showed that this victory was not a tory victory only, but an abolitionist victory—the advocates of high taxes on sugar joining the advocates of high taxes on bread, and now the senator wishes to produce the impression that he had not fairly met the question, and tries to make a new issue. There was one trait in the senator's character, which he had often noticed. He makes his onslaughts with great impetuosity, not always thinking where they will carry him; and when he finds himself in difficulty, all his great ingenuity is taxed to make a skilful retreat. Like the French general, Moreau, he is more celebrated for the dexterity of his retreats than the fame of his battles."

Mr. Clay pleasantly terminated this interlude, which was certainly unprofitable to him, by recalling the Senate to the question before them, which was simply in relation to the free, or taxed importation of *sumach*: a word which he pronounced with an air and emphasis, peculiar to himself, and which had the effect of a satiric speech when he wished to make any thing appear contemptible, or ridiculous.

> "Mr. Clay of Kentucky was not going into a dissertation on the political institutions of the British nation. He would merely recapitulate the facts with relation to the question at issue between the administration party in England and the tory party. Here Mr. Clay re-stated the position of both parties at the recent election, and the result; and concluded by declaring, that, after all, it was not a question now before the Senate, whether it was a tory victory in England and a whig victory here, but whether *sumach* was or was not to be admitted free of duty. He thought it would be just as well to revert to that question and let it be decided. For his part, he cared very little whether it was or was not. He would leave it to the Senate to decide the question just as it pleased."

The vote was taken: sumach was taxed: the foreign rival was discouraged—with what benefit to the American farmer, and the domestic grower of the article, the elaborate statistics of the decennial census has yet failed to inform us. But certainly so insignificant a weed has rarely been the occasion of such keen debate, between such eminent men, on a theatre so elevated. The next attempt to amend the bill was at a point of more concern to the American farmer: and appears thus in the Register of Debates:

"Mr. ALLEN had proposed to make salt a free article, which Mr. WALKER had proposed to amend by adding gunny bags.

"Mr. BENTON appealed to the senator from Mississippi to withdraw his amendment, and let the vote be taken on salt.

"Mr. KING also appealed to the senator from Mississippi to withdraw his amendment.

"Mr. WALKER said, at the suggestion of his friends, he should withdraw his amendment for the present, as it was supposed by some it might embarrass the original amendment.

"Mr. HUNTINGTON opposed the amendment as tending to a violation of the compromise act. It would result, also, in the annihilation of the extensive American works engaged in this manufacture, and would give the foreign manufacturers a monopoly in trade, which would tend to greatly increase the price of the article as it entered into the consumption of the country.

"Mr. KING was in favor of the compromise act, so far as it could be maintained. The article of salt entered equally into the consumption of all classes—the poor as well as the rich. He should vote for this amendment. If the senator wished, he would vote to amend the proposition so that it should not take effect till the 30th of June, 1842; and that would prevent its interference with the compromise. He hoped the experiment would be made, and be ascertained whether revenue sufficient for the expenses of government could be raised by taxation on other articles which could better bear it. He should vote for the amendment.

"Mr. BATES said the duty on salt affected two great portions of the community in a very different manner—the interior of the country, which derived their supplies from the domestic manufacture, from salines, and those parts on the seaboard which were supplied with imported salt. The price of salt for the interior of the country, which was supplied with domestic salt, of which there was a great abundance, would not be affected by an imposition of duty, as the price was regulated by the law of nature, and could not be repealed or modified; but the price of salt on the seaboard, which was supplied by imports, and some manufactured from marine water, would, however gentlemen might be disposed to disbelieve it, be increased if the duty were taken off; as the manufactories of salt from marine water would be entirely suspended, since none would continue the investment of their capital in so uncertain a business—the foreign supply being quite irregular. Thus perhaps, a third of the supplies being cut off, a greater demand would arise, and the price be increased on the seaboard, while the interior would not be affected.

"Mr. SEVIER wished to know how much revenue was collected from salt; he had heard it stated that the drawbacks amounted to more than the duty; if so, it would be better to leave it among the free articles.

"Mr. CLAY did not recollect positively; he believed the duty was about $400,000, and the drawbacks near $260,000—the tax greatly exceeded the drawback.

"Mr. CALHOUN said, individually there was, perhaps, no article which he would prefer to have exempted from duty than salt, but he was opposed, by any vote of his, to give a pretext for a violation of the compromise act hereafter. The duty on salt was going off gradually, and full as rapidly as was consistent with safety to commercial interests. No one could regard the bill before them as permanent. It was evident that the whole system would have to be revised under the compromise system.

"Mr. WALKER was warmly in favor of the amendment. He regarded a tax on salt as inhuman and unjust. It was almost as necessary to human life as the air they breathed, and should be exempted from all burdens whatever.

"Mr. ALLEN then modified his amendment so as that it should not take effect until after the 3d of June, 1842.

"Mr. CLAY spoke against the amendment; and said the very circumstance of the universality of its use, was a reason it should come in for its share of taxation. He never talked about the *poor*, but he believed he felt as much, and probably more, than those who did. Who were the poor? Why we were all poor; and any attempt to select certain classes for taxation was absurd, as before the collector came round they might be poor. He expressed the hope that the tax might not be interfered with. This was a subject which Mr. Jefferson and Mr. Macon took under their peculiar care, and other gentlemen had since mounted the hobby, and literally rode it down. He could tell them, if they desired to preserve the compromise, they must leave the salt tax alone.

"The debate was further continued by Messrs. WALKER, BENTON, CALHOUN, and PRESTON, when the question was taken on the adoption of the amendment, and decided in the negative, as follows:

"YEAS—Messrs. Allen, Benton, Buchanan, Clay of Alabama, Cuthbert, Fulton, King, Linn, McRoberts, Mouton, Nicholson, Pierce, Prentiss, Preston, Smith of Connecticut, Tappan, Walker, White, Woodbury, Wright, and Young—21.

"NAYS—Messrs. Archer, Barrow, Bates, Berrien, Calhoun, Choate, Clay of Kentucky, Clayton, Dixon, Evans, Graham, Henderson, Huntington, Ker, Mangum, Merrick, Miller, Porter, Smith of Indiana, Southard, Sturgeon, Tallmadge, and Woodbridge—23.

This odious and impious tax on salt has been kept up by a combination of private and political interests. The cod and mackerel fisheries of New England and the domestic manufacturers of salt on the Kenhawa and in New York, constituting the private interest; and the tariff-protective party constituting the political interest. The duty has been reduced, not abolished; and the injury has become greater to the Treasury in consequence of the reduction; and still remains considerable to the consumers. The salt duty, previous to the full taking effect of the compromise act of 1833, paid the fishing bounties and allowances founded upon it, and left a surplus for the Treasury: now, and since 1842, these bounties and allowances take the whole amount of the salt duty, and a large sum besides, out of the public Treasury. In five years (from 1848 to 1854), the duty produced from about \$210,000, to \$220,000; and the bounties and allowances during the same time, were from about \$240,000, to \$300,000; leaving the Treasury a loser to the amount of the difference: and, without going into figures, the same result may be predicated of every year since 1842. To the consumer the tax still remaining, although only one-fifth of the value, about doubles the cost of the article consumed to the consumer. It sends all the salt to the custom-house, and throws it into the hands of regraters; and they combine, and nearly double the price.

The next attempt to amend the bill was on Mr. Woodbury's motion to exempt tea and coffee from duty, which was successful by a large vote—39 to 10. The nays were: Messrs. Archer, Barrow, Berrien, Clay of Kentucky, Henderson, Leeds, Kerr, Merrick, Preston, Rives, Southard. The bill was then passed by a general vote, only eleven against it, upon the general ground that the government must have revenue: but those who voted against it thought the proper way to stop the land bill was to deny this supply until that was given up.

The compromise act of 1833—by a mere blunder, for it cannot be supposed such an omission could have been intentional—in providing for the reduction of duties on imported sugars, molasses, and salt, made no corresponding provision for the reduction of drawbacks when the sugars underwent refining and exportation; nor upon molasses when converted into rum and exported; nor on the fishing bounties and allowances, when the salt was re-exported on the fish which had been cured by it. This omission was detected at the time by members not parties to the compromise, but not allowed to be corrected by any one unfriendly to the compromise. The author of this View offered an amendment to that effect—which was rejected, by yeas and nays, as follows: Yeas—Messrs. Benton, Buckner, Calhoun, Dallas, Dickerson, Dudley, Forsyth, Johnson, Kane, King, Rives, Robinson, Seymour, Tomlinson, Webster, White, Wilkins, and Wright. Nays—Messrs. Bell,

Bibb, Black, Clay, Clayton, Ewing, Foot, Grundy, Hendricks, Holmes, Knight, Mangum, Miller, Moore, Naudain, Poindexter, Prentiss, Robbins, Silsbee, Smith, Sprague, Tipton, Troup, and Tyler. Of those then voting against this provision, one (Mr. Ewing, as Secretary of the Treasury), now, in 1841, recommended its adoption, so far as it related to refined sugars and rum; another (Mr. Clay), supported his recommendation; a third (Mr. Tyler), approved the act which adopted it: but all this, after the injury had been going on for eight years, and had plundered the Treasury of one and a half millions of dollars. The new tariff act of this extra session made the corresponding reductions, and by a unanimous vote in each House; the writer of this View, besides his motion at the time, having renewed it, and in vain, almost every year afterwards—always rejected on the cry that the compromise was sacred and inviolable—had saved the Union at the time it was made, and would endanger it the day it was broken. Well! it was pretty well broken at this extra session: and the Union was just as much destroyed by its breaking as it had been saved by its making. In one case the reductions of drawback remained untouched—that of the bounties and allowances to the cod and mackerel fisheries, founded on the idea of returning to the fisherman, or the exporter, the amount of duty supposed to have been paid on the imported salt carried back out of the country on that part of the fish which was exported. The fisheries have so long possessed this advantage that they now claim it as a right—no such pretension being set up until it was attacked as an abuse. A committee of the Senate, in the year 1846, of which Mr. Benton was chairman, and Mr. John Davis of Massachusetts, and Mr. Alexander Anderson, were members, made a report which explored this abuse to its source; but without being able to get it corrected. The abuse commenced after the late war with Great Britain, and has taken since that time about six millions of dollars; and is now going at the rate of about three hundred thousand dollars per annum. In the earlier ages of the government, these bounties and allowances were always stated in the annual treasury report, according to their true nature in connection with the salt duties, and as dependent upon those duties: and the sums allowed were always carried out in bushels of salt: which would show how much salt was supposed to have been carried out of the country on the exported fish. A treasury statement of that kind at present, would show about one million three hundred thousand bushels of foreign salt (for it is only on the foreign that the bounties and allowances accrue), so exported, while there is only about one million of bushels imported—nineteen-twentieths of which is employed in other branches of business—beef and pork packing, and bacon curing, for example: and there can be no doubt but that these branches export far more foreign salt on the articles they send abroad, than is done on cod and mackerel exported. In viewing the struggles about these bounties and allowances, I have often had occasion to admire the difference between the legislators of the North and those of the South and West—the former always intent upon the benefits of legislation—the latter upon the honors of the government.

CHAPTER LXXX.

NATIONAL BANK: FIRST BILL.

This was the great measure of the session, and the great object of the whig party, and the one without which all other measures would be deemed to be incomplete, and the victorious election itself little better than a defeat. Though kept out of view as an issue during the canvass, it was known to every member of the party to be the alpha and omega of the contest, and the crowning consummation of ten years labor in favor of a national bank. It was kept in the background for a reason perfectly understood. Both General Harrison and Mr. Tyler had been ultra against a national bank while members of the democratic party: they had both, as members of the House of Representatives voted in a small minority in favor of issuing a writ of *scire facias* against the late Bank of the United States soon after it was chartered; and this could be quoted in the parts of the country where a bank was unpopular. At the same time the party was perfectly satisfied with their present sentiments, and wanted no discussion which might scare off anti-bank men without doing any good on their own side. The bank, then, was the great measure of the session—the great cause of the called session—and as such taken by Mr. Clay into his own care from the first day. He submitted a schedule of measures for the consideration of the body, and for acting on which he said it might be understood the extraordinary session was convoked; he moved for a select committee to report a bill, of which committee he was of course to be chairman: and he moved a call upon the Secretary of the Treasury (Mr. Ewing) for the plan of a bank. It was furnished accordingly, and studiously contrived so as to avoid the President's objections, and save his consistency—a point upon which he was exceedingly sensitive. The bill of the select committee was modelled upon it. Even the title was made ridiculous to please the President, though not as much so as he wished. He objected to the name of bank, either in the title or the body of the charter, and proposed to style it "The Fiscal Institute;" and afterwards the "Fiscal Agent;" and finally the "Fiscal Corporation." Mr. Clay and his friends could not stand these titles; but finding the President tenacious on the title of the bill, and having all the properties of all sorts of banks—discount—deposit—circulation—exchange—all in the plan so studiously contrived, they yielded to the word Fiscal—rejecting each of its proposed addenda—and substituted bank. The title of the instrument then ran thus: "A Bill to incorporate the subscribers to the Fiscal Bank of the United States." Thus entitled, and thus arranged out of doors, it was brought into the Senate, not to be perfected by the collective legislative wisdom of the body, but to be carried through the forms of legislation, without alteration except from its friends, and made into law. The deliberative power of the body had nothing to do with it. Registration of what had been agreed upon was its only office. The democratic members resisted strenuously in order to make the measure odious. Successful resistance was impossible, and a repeal of the act at a subsequent Congress was the only hope—a veto not being then dreamed of. Repeal, therefore, was taken as the watchword, and formal notice of it proclaimed in successive speeches, that all subscribers to the bank should be warned in time, and deprived of the plea of innocence when the repeal should be moved. Mr. Allen, of Ohio, besides an argument in favor of the right of this repeal, produced a resolve from the House Journal of 1819, in which General Harrison, then a member of that body, voted with others for a resolve directing the Judiciary Committee to report a bill to repeal the then United States Bank charter—not to inquire into the expediency of repealing, but to repeal absolutely.

The bill was passed through both Houses—in the Senate by a close vote, 26 to 23—in the House by a better majority, 128 to 98. This was the sixth of August. All was considered finished by the democracy, and a future repeal their only alternative. Suddenly light began to dawn upon them. Rumors came that President Tyler would disapprove the act; which, in fact he did: but with such expressions of readiness to approve another bill which should be free from the objections which he named, as still to keep his party together, and to prevent the explosion of his cabinet. But it made an explosion elsewhere. Mr. Clay was not of a temper to be balked in a measure so dear to his heart without giving expression to his dissatisfaction; and did so in the debate on the veto message; and in terms to assert that Mr. Tyler had violated his faith to the whig party, and had been led off from them by new associations. He said:

> "On the 4th of April last, the lamented Harrison, the President of the United States, paid the
> debt of nature. President Tyler, who, as Vice-President, succeeded to the duties of that office,

arrived in the city of Washington on the 6th of that month. He found the whole metropolis wrapt in gloom, every heart filled with sorrow and sadness, every eye streaming with tears, and the surrounding hills yet flinging back the echo of the bells which were tolled on that melancholy occasion. On entering the Presidential mansion he contemplated the pale body of his predecessor stretched before him, and clothed in the black habiliments of death. At that solemn moment, I have no doubt that the heart of President Tyler was overflowing with mingled emotions of grief, of patriotism and gratitude—above all, of gratitude to that country by a majority of whose suffrages, bestowed at the preceding November, he then stood the most distinguished, the most elevated, the most honored of all living whigs of the United States.

"It was under these circumstances, and in this probable state of mind, that President Tyler, on the 10th day of the same month of April, voluntary promulgated an address to the people of the United States. That address was in the nature of a coronation oath, which the chief of the State, in other countries, and under other forms, takes upon ascending the throne. It referred to the solemn obligations, and the profound sense of duty under which the new President entered upon the high trust which had devolved upon him, by the joint acts of the people and of Providence, and it stated the principles and delineated the policy by which he would be governed in his exalted station. It was emphatically a whig address from beginning to end—every inch of it was whig, and was patriotic.

"In that address the President, in respect to the subject-matter embraced in the present bill, held the following conclusive and emphatic language: 'I shall promptly give my sanction to any constitutional measure which, originating in Congress, shall have for its object the restoration of a sound circulating medium, so essentially necessary to give confidence in all the transactions of life, to secure to industry its just and adequate rewards, and to re-establish the public prosperity. In deciding upon the adaptation of any such measure to the end proposed, as well as its conformity to the Constitution, I shall resort to the fathers of the great republican school for advice and instruction, to be drawn from their sage views of our system of government, and the light of their ever glorious example.'

"To this clause in the address of the President, I believe but one interpretation was given throughout this whole country, by friend and foe, by whig and democrat, and by the presses of both parties. It was by every man with whom I conversed on the subject at the time of its appearance, or of whom I have since inquired, construed to mean that the President intended to occupy the Madison ground, and to regard the question of the power to establish a national bank as immovably settled. And I think I may confidently appeal to the Senate, and to the country, to sustain the fact that this was the contemporaneous and unanimous judgment of the public. Reverting back to the period of the promulgation of the address, could any other construction have been given to its language? What is it? 'I shall promptly give my sanction to any constitutional measure which, originating in Congress,' shall have certain defined objects in view. He concedes the vital importance of a sound circulating medium to industry and to the public prosperity. He concedes that its origin must be in Congress. And, to prevent any inference from the qualification, which he prefixes to the measure, being interpreted to mean that a United States Bank was unconstitutional, he declares that, in deciding on the adaptation of the measure to the end proposed, and its conformity to the constitution, he will resort to the fathers of the great Republican school. And who were they? If the Father of his country is to be excluded, are Madison (the father of the constitution), Jefferson, Monroe, Gerry, Gallatin, and the long list of Republicans who acted with them, not to be regarded as among those fathers? But President Tyler declares not only that he should appeal to them for advice and instruction, but to the light of their ever glorious example. What example? What other meaning could have been possibly applied to the phrase, than that he intended to refer to what had been done during the administrations of Jefferson, Madison, and Monroe?

"Entertaining this opinion of the address, I came to Washington, at the commencement of the session, with the most confident and buoyant hopes that the Whigs would be able to carry all their prominent measures, and especially a Bank of the United States, by far that one of the greatest immediate importance. I anticipated nothing but cordial co-operation between the two departments of government; and I reflected with pleasure that I should find at the head of the Executive branch, a personal and political friend, whom I had long and intimately known, and highly esteemed. It will not be my fault if our amicable relations should unhappily cease, in consequence of any difference of opinion between us on this occasion. The President has been always perfectly familiar with my opinion on this bank question.

"Upon the opening of the session, but especially on the receipt of the plan of a national bank, as proposed by the Secretary of the Treasury, fears were excited that the President had been misunderstood in his address, and that he had not waived but adhered to his constitutional scruples. Under these circumstances it was hoped that, by the indulgence of a mutual spirit of compromise and concession, a bank, competent to fulfil the expectations and satisfy the wants of the people, might be established.

"Under the influence of that spirit, the Senate and the House agreed, 1st, as to the name of the proposed bank. I confess, sir, that there was something exceedingly *outré* and revolting to my ears in the term 'Fiscal Bank;' but I thought, 'What is there in a name? A rose, by any other name, would smell as sweet.' Looking, therefore, rather to the utility of the substantial faculties than to the name of the contemplated institution, we consented to that which was proposed."

In his veto message Mr. Tyler fell back upon his early opinions against the constitutionality of a national bank, so often and so publicly expressed; and recurring to these early opinions he now declared that it would be a crime and an infamy in him to sign the bill which had been presented to him. In this sense he thus expressed himself:

"Entertaining the opinions alluded to, and having taken this oath, the Senate and the country will see that I could not give my sanction to a measure of the character described without surrendering all claim to the respect of honorable men—all confidence on the part of the people—all self-respect—all regard for moral and religious obligations; without an observance of which no government can be prosperous, and no people can be happy. It would be to commit a *crime* which I would not wilfully commit to gain any earthly reward, and which would *justly* subject me to the ridicule and scorn of all virtuous men."

Mr. Clay found these expressions of self-condemnation entirely too strong, showing too much sensibility in a President to personal considerations—laying too much stress upon early opinions—ignoring too completely later opinions—and not sufficiently deferring to those fathers of the government to whom, in his inaugural address, he had promised to look for advice and instruction, both as to the constitutionality of a bank, and its adaptation to the public wants. And he thus animadverted on the passage:

"I must think, and hope I may be allowed to say, with profound deference to the Chief Magistrate, that it appears to me he has viewed with too lively sensibility the personal consequences to himself of his approval of the bill; and that, surrendering himself to a vivid imagination, he has depicted them in much too glowing and exaggerated colors, and that it would have been most happy if he had looked more to the deplorable consequences of a veto upon the hopes, the interests, and the happiness of his country. Does it follow that a magistrate who yields his private judgment to the concurring authority of numerous decisions, repeatedly and deliberately pronounced, after the lapse of long intervals, by all the departments of government, and by all parties, incurs the dreadful penalties described by the President? Can any man be disgraced and dishonored who yields his private opinion to the judgment of the nation? In this case, the country (I mean a majority), Congress, and, according to common fame, an unanimous cabinet, were all united in favor of the bill. Should any man feel himself humbled and degraded in yielding to the conjoint force of such high authority?

Does any man, who at one period of his life shall have expressed a particular opinion, and at a subsequent period shall act upon the opposite opinion, expose himself to the terrible consequences which have been portrayed by the President? How is it with the judge, in the case by no means rare, who bows to the authority of repeated precedents, settling a particular question, whilst in his private judgment the law was otherwise? How is it with that numerous class of public men in this country, and with the two great parties that have divided it, who, at different periods, have maintained and acted on opposite opinions in respect to this very bank question?

"How is it with James Madison, the father of the constitution—that great man whose services to his country placed him only second to Washington—whose virtues and purity in private life—whose patriotism, intelligence, and wisdom in public councils, stand unsurpassed? He was a member of the national convention that formed, and of the Virginia convention that adopted the constitution. No man understood it better than he did. He was opposed in 1791 to the establishment of the Bank of the United States upon constitutional ground; and in 1816 he approved and signed the charter of the late Bank of the United States. It is a part of the secret history connected with the first Bank, that James Madison had, at the instance of General Washington, prepared a veto for him in the contingency of his rejection of the bill. Thus stood James Madison when, in 1815, he applied the veto to a bill to charter a bank upon considerations of expediency, but with a clear and express admission of the existence of a constitutional power in Congress to charter one. In 1816, the bill which was then presented to him being free from the objections applicable to that of the previous year, he sanctioned and signed it. Did James Madison surrender 'all claim to the respect of honorable men—all confidence on the part of the people—all self-respect—all regard for moral and religious obligations?' Did the pure, the virtuous, the gifted James Madison, by his sanction and signature to the charter of the late Bank of the United States, commit a crime which justly subjected him 'to the ridicule and scorn of all virtuous men?'"

But in view of these strong personal consequences to his (Mr. Tyler's) own character in the event of signing the bill, Mr. Clay pointed out a course which the President might have taken which would have saved his consistency—conformed to the constitution—fulfilled his obligations to the party that elected him—and permitted the establishment of that sound currency, and that relief from the public distress, which his inaugural address, and his message to Congress, and his veto message, all so earnestly declared to be necessary. It was to have let the bill lie in his hands without approval or disapproval: in which case it would have become a law without any act of his. The constitution had made provision for the case in that clause in which it declares that—"If any bill shall not be returned by the President within ten days (Sundays excepted) after it shall have been presented to him, the same shall be a law, in like manner as if he had signed it, unless the Congress by their adjournment prevent its return; in which case it shall not be a law." In this case there was no danger of Congress adjourning before the lapse of the ten days; and Mr. Clay adverted to this course as the one, under his embarrassing circumstances the President ought to have adopted, and saved both his consistency and faith to his party. He urged it as a proper course—saying:

"And why should not President Tyler have suffered the bill to become a law without his signature? Without meaning the slightest possible disrespect to him (nothing is further from my heart than the exhibition of any such feeling towards that distinguished citizen, long my personal friend), it cannot be forgotten that he came into his present office under peculiar circumstances. The people did not foresee the contingency which has happened. They voted for him as Vice-President. They did not, therefore, scrutinize his opinions with the care which they probably ought to have done, and would have done, if they could have looked into futurity. If the present state of the fact could have been anticipated—if at Harrisburg, or at the polls, it had been foreseen that General Harrison would die in one short month after the commencement of his administration; that Vice-President Tyler would be elevated to the presidential chair; that a bill, passed by decisive majorities of the first whig Congress, chartering a national bank, would be presented for his sanction; and that he would veto the bill, do I hazard any thing when I express the conviction that he would not have received a solitary vote in the nominating convention, nor one solitary electoral vote in any State in the Union?"

Not having taken this course with the bill, Mr. Clay pointed out a third one, suggested by the conduct of the President himself under analogous circumstances, and which, while preserving his self-respect, would accomplish all the objects in view by the party which elected him, by simply removing the obstacle which stood between them and the object of their hopes; it was to resign the presidency. For this contingency—that of neither President nor Vice-President—the constitution had also made provision in declaring—"In case of the removal of the President from office, or of his death, resignation, or inability to discharge the powers and duties of the said office, the same shall devolve on the Vice-President; and the Congress may by law provide for the case of the removal, death, resignation, or inability both of the President and Vice-President, declaring what officer shall then act as President; and such officer shall act accordingly, until the disability be removed, or a President shall be elected." Congress had acted under this injunction and had devolved the duties of President, first on the president of the Senate *pro tempore*; and if no such temporary president, then on the speaker of the House of Representatives; and requiring a new election to be held on the first Wednesday of the ensuing December if there was time before it for a notification of two months; and if not, then the new election to take place (if the vacant term had not expired on the third day of March after they happened) on the like Wednesday of the next ensuing month of December. Here was provision made for the case, and the new election might have been held in less than four months—the temporary president of the Senate, Mr. Southard, acting as President in the mean time. The legal path was then clear for Mr. Tyler's resignation, and Mr. Clay thus enforced the propriety of that step upon him:

"But, sir, there was still a third alternative, to which I allude not because I mean to intimate that it should be embraced, but because I am reminded of it by a memorable event in the life of President Tyler. It will be recollected that, after the Senate had passed the resolution declaring the removal of the deposits from the Bank of the United States to have been derogatory from the constitution and laws of the United States, for which resolution President (then senator) Tyler had voted, the General Assembly of Virginia instructed the senators from that State to vote for the expunging of that resolution. Senator Tyler declined voting in conformity with that instruction, and resigned his seat in the Senate of the United States. This he did because he could not conform, and did not think it right to go counter to the wishes of those who had placed him in the Senate. If, when the people of Virginia, or the General Assembly of Virginia, were his only constituency, he would not set up his own particular opinion in opposition to theirs, what ought to be the rule of his conduct when the people of twenty-six States—a whole nation—compose his constituency? Is the will of the constituency of one State to be respected, and that of twenty-six to be wholly disregarded? Is obedience due only to the single State of Virginia? The President admits that the Bank question deeply agitated, and continues to agitate, the nation. It is incontestable that it was the great, absorbing, and controlling question, in all our recent divisions and exertions. I am firmly convinced, and it is my deliberate judgment, that an immense majority, not less than two-thirds of the nation, desire such an institution. All doubts in this respect ought to be dispelled by the recent decisions of the two Houses of Congress. I speak of them as evidence of popular opinion. In the House of Representatives, the majority was 131 to 100. If the House had been full, and but for the modification of the 16th fundamental condition, there would have been a probable majority of 47. Is it to be believed that this large majority of the immediate representatives of the people, fresh from amongst them, and to whom the President seemed inclined, in his opening message, to refer this very question, have mistaken the wishes of their constituents?"

The acting President did not feel it to be his duty to resign, although it may be the judgment of history (after seeing the expositions of his secretaries at the resignation of their places consequent upon a second veto to a second bank act), that he ought to have done so. In his veto message he seemed to leave the way open for his approval of a charter free from the exceptions he had taken; and rumor was positive in asserting that he was then engaged in arranging with some friends the details of a bill which he could approve. In allusion to this rumor, Mr. Clay remarked:

"On a former occasion I stated that, in the event of an unfortunate difference of opinion between the legislative and executive departments, the point of difference might be developed, and it would be then seen whether they could be brought to coincide in any measure corresponding with the public hopes and expectations. I regret that the President has not, in this message, favored us with a more clear and explicit exhibition of his views. It is sufficiently manifest that he is decidedly opposed to the establishment of a new Bank of the United States formed after two old models. I think it is fairly to be inferred that the plan of the Secretary of the Treasury could not have received his sanction. He is opposed to the passage of the bill which he has returned; but whether he would give his approbation to any bank, and, if any, what sort of a bank, is not absolutely clear. I think it may be collected from the message, with the aid of information derived through other sources, that the President would concur in the establishment of a bank whose operations should be limited to dealing in bills of exchange to deposits, and to the supply of a circulation, excluding the power of discounting promissory notes. And I understand that some of our friends are now considering the practicability of arranging and passing a bill in conformity with the views of President Tyler. Whilst I regret that I can take no active part in such an experiment, and must reserve to myself the right of determining whether I can or cannot vote for such a bill after I see it in its matured form, I assure my friends that they shall find no obstacle or impediment in me. On the contrary, I say to them, go on: God speed you in any measure which will serve the country, and preserve or restore harmony and concert between the departments of government. An executive veto of a Bank of the United States, after the sad experience of late years, is an event which was not anticipated by the political friends of the President; certainly not by me. But it has come upon us with tremendous weight, and amidst the greatest excitement within and without the metropolis. The question now is, what shall be done? What, under this most embarrassing and unexpected state of things, will our constituents expect of us? What is required by the duty and the dignity of Congress? I repeat that if, after a careful examination of the executive message, a bank can be devised which will afford any remedy to existing evils, and secure the President's approbation, let the project of such a bank be presented. It shall encounter no opposition, if it should receive no support, from me."

The speech of Mr. Clay brought out Mr. Rives in defence of the President, who commenced with saying:

"He came to the Senate that morning to give a silent vote on the bill, and he should have contented himself with doing so but for the observations which had fallen from the senator from Kentucky in respect to the conduct of the President of the United States. Mr. R. had hoped the senator would have confined himself strictly to the merits of the question before the Senate. He told us, said Mr. R., that the question was this: the President having returned the bill for a fiscal bank with his exceptions thereto, the bill was such an one as ought to pass by the constitutional majority of two-thirds; and thus become a law of the land. Now what was the real issue before the Senate? Was it not the naked question between the bill and the objections to it, as compared with each other? I really had hoped that the honorable senator, after announcing to us the issue in this very proper manner, would have confined his observations to it alone; and if he had done so I should not have troubled the Senate with a single word. But what has been the course of the honorable senator? I do not reproach him with it. He, no doubt, felt it necessary, in order to vindicate his own position before the country, to inculpate the course taken by the President: and accordingly about two-thirds of his speech, howsoever qualified by expressions of personal kindness and respect, were taken up in a solemn arraignment of the President of the United States. Most of the allegations put forth by the senator seem to arrange themselves under the general charge of perfidy—of faithlessness to his party, and to the people."

Mr. Rives went on to defend the President at all points, declaring the question of a bank was not an issue in the election—repelling the imputation of perfidy—scouting the suggestions of resignation and of pocketing the bill to let it become law—arguing that General Harrison himself would have disapproved the same bill if he had lived and it had been presented to him. In support of this opinion he referred to the General's early opposition to the national bank of 1816, and to his written answer given during the canvass—"that he would not give his sanction to a Bank of the United States, unless by the failure of all other expedients, it should be demonstrated to be necessary to carry on the operations of government; and unless there should be a general and unequivocal manifestation of the will of the Union in favor of such an institution; and then only as a fiscal, and not as a commercial bank." But this authentic declaration seemed to prove the contrary of that for which it was quoted. It contained two conditions, on the happening of which General Harrison would sign a bank charter—first, the failure of all other plans for carrying on the financial operations of the government; and, secondly, the manifestation of public opinion in favor of it. That the first of these conditions had been fulfilled was well shown by Mr. Rives himself in the concluding passages of his speech where he said: "All previous systems have been rejected and condemned—the sub-treasury—the pet banks—an old-fashioned Bank of the United States—a new-fashioned fiscal agent." The second condition was fulfilled in the presidential election in the success of the whig party, whose first object was a bank; and in the election of members of the House and the Senate, where the majorities were in favor of a bank. The conditions were fulfilled then on which General Harrison was to approve a bank charter; and the writer of this View has no doubt that he would have given his signature to a usual bank charter if he had lived; and from an obligatory sense of duty, and with no more dishonor than Mr. Madison had incurred in signing the act for the second bank charter after having been the great opponent of the first one; and for which signing, as for no act of his life, was dishonor imputed to him. The writer of this View believes that General Harrison would have signed a fair bank charter, and under its proper name; and he believes it, not from words spoken between them, but from public manifestations, seen by every body. 1. His own declaration, stating the conditions on which he would do it; and which conditions were fulfilled. 2. The fact that he was the presidential candidate of the party which was emphatically the bank party. 3. The selection of his cabinet, every member of which was in favor of a national bank. 4. The declaration of Mr. Clay at the head of the list of measures proposed by him for the consideration of Congress at its extra session, in which a national bank was included; and which measures he stated were probably those for which the extraordinary session had been convened by President Harrison—a point on which Mr. Clay must be admitted to be well informed, for he was the well reputed adviser of President Harrison on the occasion.

Mr. Clay rejoined to Mr. Rives, and became more close and pointed in his personal remarks upon Mr. Tyler's conduct, commencing with Mr. Rives' lodgment in the "half-way house," *i.e.* the pet bank system—which was supposed to have been a camping station in the transition from the democratic to the whig camp. He began thus:

> "I have no desire, said he, to prolong this unpleasant discussion, but I must say that I heard with great surprise and regret the closing remark, especially, of the honorable gentleman from Virginia, as, indeed, I did many of those which preceded it. That gentleman stands in a peculiar situation. I found him several years ago in the half-way house, where he seems afraid to remain, and from which he is yet unwilling to go. I had thought, after the thorough riddling which the roof of the house had received in the breaking up of the pet bank system, he would have fled somewhere else for refuge; but, there he still stands, solitary and alone, shivering and pelted by the pitiless storm. The sub-treasury is repealed—the pet bank system is abandoned—the United States Bank bill is vetoed—and now, when there is as complete and perfect a reunion of the purse and the sword in the hands of the executive as ever there was under General Jackson or Mr. Van Buren, the senator is for doing nothing."

There was a whisper at this time that Mr. Tyler had an inner circle of advisers, some democratic and some whig, and most of whom had sojourned in the "half-way house," and who were more confidential and influential with the President than the members of his cabinet. To this Mr. Clay caustically adverted.

"Although the honorable senator professes not to know the opinions of the President, it certainly does turn out in the sequel that there is a most remarkable coincidence between those opinions and his own; and he has, on the present occasion, defended the motives and the course of the President with all the solicitude and all the fervent zeal of a member of his privy council. There is a rumor abroad that a cabal exists—a new sort of kitchen cabinet—whose object is the dissolution of the regular cabinet—the dissolution of the whig party—the dispersion of Congress, without accomplishing any of the great purposes of the extra session—and a total change, in fact, in the whole face of our political affairs. I hope, and I persuade myself, that the honorable senator is not, cannot be, one of the component members of such a cabal; but I must say that there has been displayed by the honorable senator to-day a predisposition, astonishing and inexplicable, to misconceive almost all of what I have said, and a perseverance, after repeated corrections, in misunderstanding—for I will not charge him with wilfully and intentionally misrepresenting—the whole spirit and character of the address which, as a man of honor and as a senator, I felt myself bound in duty to make to this body."

There was also a rumor of a design to make a third party, of which Mr. Tyler was to be the head; and, as part of the scheme, to make a quarrel between Mr. Tyler and Mr. Clay, in which Mr. Clay was to be made the aggressor; and he brought this rumor to the notice of Mr. Rives, repelling the part which inculpated himself, and leaving the rest for Mr. Rives to answer.

"Why, sir, what possible, what conceivable motive can I have to quarrel with the President, or to break up the whig party? What earthly motive can impel me to wish for any other result than that that party shall remain in perfect harmony, undivided, and shall move undismayed, boldly, and unitedly forward to the accomplishment of the all-important public objects which it has avowed to be its aim? What imaginable interest or feeling can I have other than the success, the triumph, the glory of the whig party? But that there may be designs and purposes on the part of certain other individuals to place me in inimical relations with the President, and to represent me as personally opposed to him, I can well imagine—individuals who are beating up for recruits, and endeavoring to form a third party, with materials so scanty as to be wholly insufficient to compose a decent corporal's guard. I fear there are such individuals, though I do not charge the senator as being himself one of them. What a spectacle has been presented to this nation during this entire session of Congress! That of the cherished and confidential friends of John Tyler, persons who boast and claim to be *par excellence*, his exclusive and genuine friends, being the bitter, systematic, determined, uncompromising opponents of every leading measure of John Tyler's administration! Was there ever before such an example presented, in this or any other age, in this or any other country? I have myself known the President too long, and cherished towards him too sincere a friendship, to allow my feelings to be affected or alienated by any thing which has passed here to-day. If the President chooses—which I am sure he cannot, unless falsehood has been whispered into his ears or poison poured into his heart—to detach himself from me, I shall deeply regret it, for the sake of our common friendship and our common country. I now repeat, what I before said, that, of all the measures of relief which the American people have called upon us for, that of a National Bank and a sound and uniform currency has been the most loudly and importunately demanded."

Mr. Clay reiterated his assertion that bank, or no bank, was the great issue of the presidential canvass wherever he was, let what else might have been the issue in Virginia, where Mr. Rives led for General Harrison.

"The senator says that the question of a Bank was not the issue made before the people at the late election. I can say, for one, my own conviction is diametrically the contrary. What may have been the character of the canvass in Virginia, I will not say; probably gentlemen on both sides were, every where, governed in some degree by considerations of local policy. What issues may therefore have been presented to the people of Virginia, either above or below tide water, I am not prepared to say. The great error, however, of the honorable senator, is in thinking that the sentiments of a particular party in Virginia are always a fair exponent of the sentiments of the whole Union. I can tell the senator, that, wherever I was—in the great valley of the Mississippi, in Kentucky, in Tennessee, in Maryland—in all the circles in which I moved, every where, 'Bank or no Bank' was the great, the leading, the vital question."

In conclusion, Mr Clay apostrophized himself in a powerful peroration as not having moral courage enough (though he claimed as much as fell to the share of most men) to make himself an obstacle to the success of a great measure for the public good; in which the allusion to Mr. Tyler and his veto was too palpable to miss the apprehension of any person.

"The senator says that, if placed in like circumstances, I would have been the last man to avoid putting a direct veto upon the bill, had it met my disapprobation; and he does me the honor to attribute to me high qualities of stern and unbending intrepidity. I hope that in all that relates to personal firmness—all that concerns a just appreciation of the insignificance of human life—whatever may be attempted to threaten or alarm a soul not easily swayed by opposition, or awed or intimidated by menace—a stout heart and a steady eye, that can survey, unmoved and undaunted, any mere personal perils that assail this poor transient, perishing frame—I may, without disparagement, compare with other men. But there is a sort of courage which, I frankly confess it, I do not possess—a boldness to which I dare not aspire—a valor which I cannot covet. I cannot lay myself down in the way of the welfare and happiness of my country. That I cannot, I have not the courage to do. I cannot interpose the power with which I may be invested—a power conferred not for my personal benefit, not for my aggrandizement, but for my country's good—to check her onward march to greatness and glory. I have not courage enough, I am too cowardly for that. I would not, I dare not, in the exercise of such a trust, lie down, and place my body across the path that leads my country to prosperity and happiness. This is a sort of courage widely different from that which a man may display in his private conduct and personal relations. Personal or private courage is totally distinct from that higher and nobler courage, which prompts the patriot to offer himself a voluntary sacrifice to his country's good. Apprehensions of the imputation of the want of firmness sometimes impel us to perform rash and inconsiderate acts. It is the greatest courage to be able to bear the imputation of the want of courage. But pride, vanity, egotism, so unamiable and offensive in private life, are vices which partake of the character of crimes in the conduct of public affairs. The unfortunate victim of these passions cannot see beyond the little, petty, contemptible circle of his own personal interests. All his thoughts are withdrawn from his country, and concentrated on his consistency, his firmness, himself. The high, the exalted, the sublime emotions of a patriotism, which, soaring towards Heaven, rises far above all mean, low, or selfish things, and is absorbed by one soul-transporting thought of the good and the glory of one's country, are never felt in his impenetrable bosom. That patriotism which, catching its inspiration from the immortal God, and leaving at an immeasurable distance below, all lesser, grovelling, personal interests and feelings, animates and prompts to deeds of self-sacrifice, of valor, of devotion, and of death itself—that is public virtue—that is the noblest, the sublimest of all public virtues!"

Mr. Rives replied to Mr. Clay, and with respect to the imputed cabal, the privy council, and his own zealous defence of Mr. Tyler, said:

"The senator has indulged his fancy in regard to a certain cabal, which he says it is alleged by rumor (an authority he seems prone to quote of late) has been formed for the wicked purpose of breaking up the regular cabinet, and dissolving the whig party. Though the senator is pleased to acquit me of being a member of the supposed cabal, he says he should infer, from the zeal and promptitude with which I have come forward to defend the motives and conduct of the President, that I was at least a member of his privy council! I thank God, Mr. President, that in his gracious goodness he has been pleased to give me a heart to repel injustice and to defend the innocent, without being laid under any special engagement, as a privy councillor or otherwise, to do justice to my fellow-man; and if there be any gentleman who cannot find in the consciousness of his own bosom a satisfactory explanation of so natural an impulse, I, for one, envy him neither his temperament nor his philosophy. If Mr. Tyler, instead of being a distinguished citizen of my own State, and filling at this moment, a station of the most painful responsibility, which entitles him to a candid interpretation of his official acts at the hands of all his countrymen, had been a total stranger, unknown to me in the relations of private or political friendship, I should yet have felt myself irresistibly impelled by the common sympathies of humanity to undertake his defence, to the best of my poor ability, when I have seen him this day so powerfully assailed for an act, as I verily believe, of conscientious devotion to the constitution of his country and the sacred obligation of his high trust."

With respect to the half-way house, Mr. Rives admitted his sojourn there, and claimed a sometime companionship in it with the senator from Kentucky, just escaped from the lordly mansion, gaudy without, but rotten and rat-eaten within (the Bank of the United States); and glad to shelter in this humble but comfortable stopping place.

"The senator from Kentucky says he found me several years ago in this half-way house, which, after the thorough riddling the roof had received in the breaking up of the pet bank system, he had supposed I would have abandoned. How could I find it in my heart, Mr. President, to abandon it when I found the honorable senator from Kentucky (even after what he calls the riddling of the roof) so anxious to take refuge in it from the ruins of his own condemned and repudiated system, and where he actually took refuge for four long years, as I have already stated. When I first had the honor to meet the honorable senator in this body, I found him not occupying the humble but comfortable half-way house, which has given him shelter from the storm for the last four years, but a more lordly mansion, gaudy to look upon, but altogether unsafe to inhabit; old, decayed, rat-eaten, which has since tumbled to the ground with its own rottenness, devoted to destruction alike by the indignation of man and the wrath of heaven. Yet the honorable senator, unmindful of the past, and heedless of the warnings of the present, which are still ringing in his ears, will hear of nothing but the instant reconstruction of this devoted edifice."

Mr. Rives returned to the imputed cabal, washed his hands of it entirely, and abjured all desire for a cabinet office, or any public station, except a seat in the Senate: thus:

"I owe it to myself, Mr. President, before I close, to say one or two words in regard to this gorgon of a cabal, which the senator tells us, upon the authority of dame Rumor, has been formed to break up the cabinet, to dissolve the whig party, and to form a new or third party. Although the senator was pleased to acquit me of being a member of this supposed cabal, he yet seemed to have some lurking jealousies and suspicions in his mind on the subject. I will tell the honorable senator, then, that I know of no such cabal, and I should really think that I was the last man that ought to be suspected of any wish or design to form a new or third party. I have shown myself at all times restive under mere party influence and control from any quarter. All party, in my humble judgment, tends, in its modern degeneracy, to tyranny, and is attended with serious hazard of sacrificing an honest sense of duty, and the great interests of the country, to an arbitrary lead, directed by other aims. I desire, therefore, to take upon myself no new party bonds, while I am anxious to fulfil, to the fullest extent that a sense of duty to the country will permit, every honorable engagement implied in existing ones. In regard to the breaking up of the cabinet, I had hoped that I was as far above the suspicion of having any personal interest in such an event as any man. I have never sought office, but have often declined it; and will now give the honorable senator from Kentucky a full quit-claim and release of all cabinet pretensions now and for ever. He may rest satisfied that he will never see me in any cabinet, under this or any other administration. During the brief remnant of my public life, the measure of my ambition will be filled by the humble, but honest part I may be permitted to take on this floor in consultations for the common good."

Mr. Rives finished with informing Mr. Clay of a rumor which he had heard—the rumor of a dictatorship installed in the capitol, seeking to govern the country, and to intimidate the President, and to bend every thing to its own will, thus:

"Having disposed of this rumor of a cabal, to the satisfaction, I trust, of the honorable senator, I will tell him of another rumor I have heard, which, I trust, may be equally destitute of foundation. Rumor is busy in alleging that there is an organized dictatorship, in permanent session in this capitol, seeking to control the whole action of the government, in both the legislative and executive branches, and sending deputation after deputation to the President of the United States to teach him his duty, and bring him to terms. I do not vouch for the correctness of this rumor. I humbly hope it may not be true; but if it should unfortunately be so, I will say that it is fraught with far more danger to the regular and salutary action of our balanced constitution, and to the liberties of the people, than any secret cabal that ever has existed or ever will exist."

The allusion, of course, was to Mr. Clay, who promptly disavowed all knowledge of this imputed dictatorship. In this interlude between Mr. Clay and Mr. Rives, both members of the same party, the democratic senators took no part; and the subject was dropped, to be followed by a little conversational debate, of kindred interest, growing out of it, between Mr. Archer of Virginia, and Mr. Clay—which appears thus in the Register of Debates:

"Mr. ARCHER, in rising on the present occasion, did not intend to enter into a discussion on the subject of the President's message. He thought enough had been said on the subject by the two senators who had preceded him, and was disposed, for his part, to let the question be taken without any more debate. His object in rising was to call the attention of the senator from Kentucky to a certain portion of his remarks, in which he hoped the senator, upon reflection, would see that the language used by him had been too harsh. His honorable friend from Kentucky had taken occasion to apply some very harsh observations to the conduct of certain persons who he supposed had instigated the President of the United States in the course he had taken in regard to the bill for chartering the Fiscal Bank of the United States. The honorable senator took occasion to disclaim any allusion to his colleague [Mr. RIVES], and he would say beforehand that he knew the honorable senator would except him also.

"Mr. CLAY said, certainly, sir!"

This was not a parliamentary disclaimer, but a disclaimer from the heart, and was all that Mr. Archer could ask on his own account; but he was a man of generous spirit as well as of high sense of honor, and taking up the case of his colleagues in the House, who seemed to be implicated, and could not appear in the chamber and ask for a disclaimer, Mr. Archer generously did so for them; but without getting what he asked for. The Register says:

"Mr. *Archer.* He would say, however, that the remarks of the senator, harsh as they were, might well be construed as having allusion to his colleagues in the other House. He (Mr. A.) discharged no more than the duty which he knew his honorable colleagues in the other House would discharge towards him were an offensive allusion supposed to be made to him where he could not defend himself, to ask of the honorable senator to make some disclaimer as regarded them.

"Mr. *Clay* here said, no, no.

"Mr. ARCHER. The words of the senator were: 'A low, vulgar, and profligate cabal;' which the senator also designated as a kitchen cabinet, had surrounded the President, and were endeavoring to turn out the present cabinet. Now, who would the public suppose to be that low and infamous cabal? Would the people of the United States suppose it to be composed of any other than those who were sent here by the people to represent them in Congress? He asked the senator from Kentucky to say, in that spirit of candor and frankness which always characterized him, who he meant by that cabal, and to disclaim any allusion to his colleagues in the other House, as he had done for his colleague and himself in this body.

"Mr. CLAY said, if the honorable senator would make an inquiry of him, and stop at the inquiry, without going on to make an argument, he would answer him. He had said this and he would repeat it, and make no disclaimer—that certain gentlemen, professing to be the friends, *par excellence*, of the President of the United States, had put themselves in opposition to all the leading measures of his administration. He said that rumor stated that a cabal was formed, for the purpose of breaking down the present cabinet and forming a new one; and that that cabal did not amount to enough to make a corporal's guard. He did not say who they were; but he spoke of rumor only. Now, he would ask his friend from Virginia [Mr. ARCHER] if he never heard of that rumor? If the gentleman would tell him that he never heard of that rumor, it would give him some claims to an answer.

"Mr. ARCHER confessed that he had heard of such a rumor, but he never heard of any evidence to support it.

"Mr. CLAY. I repeat it here, in the face of the country, that there are persons who call themselves, *par excellence*, the friends of John Tyler, and yet oppose all the leading measures of the administration of John Tyler. I will say that the gentleman himself is not of that cabal, and that his colleague is not. Farther than that, this deponent saith not, and will not say.

"Mr. ARCHER. The gentleman has not adverted to the extreme harshness of the language he employed when he was first up, and he would appeal to gentlemen present for the correctness of the version he (Mr. A.) had given of it. The gentleman said there was a cabal formed—a vile kitchen cabinet—low and infamous, who surrounded the President and instigated him to the course he had taken. That was the language employed by the honorable senator. Now suppose language such as this had been used in the other branch of the national legislature, which might be supposed to refer to him (Mr. A.) where he had not an opportunity of defending himself; what would be the course of his colleagues there? The course of those high-minded and honorable men there toward him, would be similar to that he had taken in regard to them.

"Mr. CLAY. Mr. President, did I say one word about the colleagues of the gentleman? I said there was a cabal formed for the purpose of breaking down the present cabinet, and that that cabal did not number a corporal's guard; but I did not say who that cabal was, and do not mean to be interrogated. Any member on this floor has a right to ask me if I alluded to him; but nobody else has. I spoke of rumor only.

"Mr. ARCHER said a few words, but he was not heard distinctly enough to be reported.

"Mr. CLAY. I said no such thing. I said there was a rumor—that public fame had stated that there was a cabal formed for the purpose of removing the cabinet, and I ask the gentleman if he has not heard of that rumor?

"Mr. ARCHER, after some remarks too low to be heard in the gallery, said it was not the words the gentleman had quoted to which he referred. It was the remark of the gentleman that there was a low and infamous cabal—a vile kitchen cabinet—and the gentleman knew that to his view there could not be a more odious phrase used than kitchen cabinet—and that it was these expressions that he wished an explanation of.

"Mr. BERRIEN said it was the concurrent opinion of all the senators around him, that the senator from Kentucky had spoken of the cabal as a rumor, and as not coming within his own knowledge. He hoped the senator would understand him in rising to make this explanation.

"Mr. ARCHER said he was glad to hear the disclaimer made by the gentleman from Georgia, and he would therefore sit down, under the conviction that the gentleman from Kentucky had made no such blow at his colleagues of the other House, as he had supposed."

Mr. Clay could not disclaim for the Virginia members of the House—that is to say, for all those members. Rumor was too loud with respect to some of them to allow him to do that. He rested upon the rumor; and public opinion justified him in doing so. He named no one, nor was it necessary. They soon named themselves by the virulence with which they attacked him.

The vote was taken on the bill over again, as required by the constitution, and so far from receiving a two-thirds vote, it barely escaped defeat by a simple majority. The vote was 24 to 24; and the yeas and nays were:

"YEAS—Messrs. Barrow, Bates, Bayard, Berrien, Choate, Clay of Kentucky, Dixon, Evans, Graham, Henderson, Huntington, Kerr, Mangum, Merrick, Miller, Morehead, Porter, Prentiss, Preston, Simmons, Smith of Indiana, Southard, Tallmadge, White, Woodbridge.

"NAYS—Messrs. Allen, Archer, Benton, Buchanan, Calhoun, Clay of Alabama, Clayton, Cuthbert, Fulton, King, Linn, McRoberts, Mouton, Nicholson, Pierce, Rives, Sevier, Sturgeon, Tappan, Walker, Williams, Woodbury, Wright, Young."

The rejection of the bank bill gave great vexation to one side, and equal exultation to the other. Hisses resounded from the galleries of the Senate: the President was outraged in his house, in the night, by the language and conduct of a disorderly crowd assembled about it. Mr. Woodbury moved an inquiry into the extent of these two disturbances, and their authors; and a committee was proposed to be charged with the inquiry: but the perpetrators were found to be of too low an order to be pursued, and the proceeding was dropped. Some manifestations of joy or sorrow took place, however, by actors of high order, and went into the parliamentary debates. Some senators deemed it proper to make a complimentary visit to Mr. Tyler, on the night of the reception of the veto message, and to manifest their satisfaction at the service which he had rendered in arresting the bank charter; and it so happened that this complimentary visit took place on the same night on which the President's house had been beset and outraged. It was doubtless a very consolatory compliment to the President, then sorely assailed by his late whig friends; and very proper on the part of those who paid it, though there were senators who declined to join in it—among others, the writer of this View, though sharing the exultation of his party. On the other hand the chagrin of the whig party was profound, and especially that of Mr. Clay, its chief—too frank and impetuous to restrain his feelings, and often giving vent to them— generally bitterly, but sometimes playfully. An occasion for a display of the latter kind was found in the occasion of this complimentary visit of democratic senators to the President, and in the offering of Mr. Woodbury's resolution of inquiry into the disturbances; and he amusingly availed himself of it in a brief speech, of which some extracts are here given:

"An honorable senator from New Hampshire [Mr. WOODBURY] proposed some days ago a resolution of inquiry into certain disturbances which are said to have occurred at the presidential mansion on the night of the memorable 16th of August last. If any such proceedings did occur, they were certainly very wrong and highly culpable. The chief magistrate, whoever he may be, should be treated by every good citizen with all becoming respect, if not for his personal character, on account of the exalted office he holds for and from the people. And I will here say, that I read with great pleasure the acts and resolutions of an early meeting, promptly held by the orderly and respectable citizens of this metropolis, in reference to, and in condemnation of, those disturbances. But, if the resolution had been adopted, I had intended to move for the appointment of a select committee, and that the honorable senator from New Hampshire himself should be placed at the head of it, with a majority of his friends. And will tell you why, Mr. President. I did hear that about eight or nine o'clock on that same night of the famous 16th of August, there was an irruption on the President's house of the whole loco foco party in Congress; and I did not know but that the alleged disorders might have grown out of or had some connection with that fact. I understand that the whole party were there. No spectacle, I am sure, could have been more supremely amusing and ridiculous. If I could have been in a position in which, without being seen, I could have witnessed that most extraordinary reunion, I should have had an enjoyment which no dramatic performance could possibly communicate. I think that I can now see the principal *dramatis personæ* who figured in the scene. There stood the grave and distinguished senator from South Carolina—

["Mr. CALHOUN here instantly rose, and earnestly insisted on explaining; but Mr. CLAY refused to be interrupted or to yield the floor.]

"Mr. CLAY. There, I say, I can imagine stood the senator from South Carolina—tall, careworn, with furrowed brow, haggard, and intensely gazing, looking as if he were dissecting the last and newest abstraction which sprung from metaphysician's brain, and muttering to himself, in half-uttered sounds, 'This is indeed a real crisis!' Then there was the senator from Alabama [Mr. KING], standing upright and gracefully, as if he were ready to settle in the most authoritative manner any question of order, or of etiquette, that might possibly arise between the high assembled parties on that new and unprecedented occasion. Not far off stood the honorable senators from Arkansas and from Missouri [Mr. SEVIER and Mr. BENTON], the latter looking at the senator from South Carolina, with an indignant curl on his lip and scorn in his eye, and pointing his finger with contempt towards that senator [Mr. CALHOUN], whilst he said, or rather seemed to say, 'He call himself a statesman! why, he has never even produced a decent humbug!'

["Mr. BENTON. The senator from Missouri was not there."]

Mr. Clay had doubtless been informed that the senator from Missouri was one of the senatorial procession that night, and the readiness with which he gave his remarks an imaginative turn with respect to him, and the facility with which he went on with his scene, were instances of that versatility of genius, and presence of mind, of which his parliamentary life was so full, and which generally gave him the advantage in sharp encounters. Though refusing to permit explanations from Mr. Calhoun, he readily accepted the correction from Mr. Benton—(probably because neither Mr. Benton, nor his immediate friends, were suspected of any attempt to alienate Mr. Tyler from his whig friends)—and continued his remarks, with great apparent good humor, and certainly to the amusement of all except the immediate objects of his attention.

"Mr. CLAY. I stand corrected; I was only imagining what you would have said if you had been there. Then there stood the senator from Georgia [Mr. CUTHBERT], conning over in his mind on what point he should make his next attack upon the senator from Kentucky. On yonder ottoman reclined the other senator from Missouri on my left [Mr. LINN], indulging, with smiles on his face, in pleasing meditations on the rise, growth, and future power of his new colony of Oregon. The honorable senator from Pennsylvania [Mr. BUCHANAN], I presume, stood forward as spokesman for his whole party; and, although I cannot pretend to imitate his well-known eloquence, I beg leave to make an humble essay towards what I presume to have been the kind of speech delivered by him on that august occasion:

"May it please your Excellency: A number of your present political friends, late your political opponents, in company with myself, have come to deposit at your Excellency's feet the evidences of our loyalty and devotion; and they have done me the honor to make me the organ of their sentiments and feelings. We are here more particularly to present to your Excellency our grateful and most cordial congratulations on your rescue of the country from a flagrant and alarming violation of the constitution, by the creation of a Bank of the United States; and also our profound acknowledgments for the veto, by which you have illustrated the wisdom of your administration, and so greatly honored yourself. And we would dwell particularly on the unanswerable reasons and cogent arguments with which the notification of the act to the legislature had been accompanied. We had been, ourselves, struggling for days and weeks to arrest the passage of the bill, and to prevent the creation of the monster to which it gives birth. We had expended all our logic, exerted all our ability, employed all our eloquence; but in spite of all our utmost efforts, the friends of your Excellency in the Senate and House of Representatives proved too strong for us. And we have now come most heartily to thank your Excellency, that you have accomplished for us that against your friends, which we, with our most strenuous exertions, were unable to achieve."

After this pleasant impersonation of the Pennsylvania senator, Mr. Clay went on with his own remarks.

"I hope the senator will view with indulgence this effort to represent him, although I am but too sensible how far it falls short of the merits of the original. At all events he will feel that there is not a greater error than was committed by the stenographer of the Intelligencer the other day, when he put into my mouth a part of the honorable senator's speech. I hope the honorable senators on the other side of the chamber will pardon me for having conceived it possible that, amidst the popping of champagne, the intoxication of their joy, the ecstasy of their glorification, they might have been the parties who created a disturbance, of which they never could have been guilty had they waited for their '*sober second thoughts*.' I have no doubt the very learned ex-Secretary of the Treasury, who conducted that department with such distinguished ability, and such happy results to the country, and who now has such a profound abhorrence of all the taxes on tea and coffee, though, in his own official reports, he so distinctly recommended them, would, if appointed chairman of the committee, have conducted the investigation with that industry which so eminently distinguishes him; and would have favored the Senate with a report, marked with all his accustomed precision and ability, and with the most perfect lucid clearness."

Mr. Buchanan, who had been made the principal figure in Mr. Clay's imaginary scene, took his satisfaction on the spot, and balanced the account by the description of another night scene, at the east end of the avenue, not entirely imaginary if Dame Rumor may be credited on one side of the question, as well as on the other. He said:

"The honorable senator has, with great power of humor, and much felicity of description, drawn for us a picture of the scene which he supposes to have been presented at the President's house on the ever-memorable evening of the veto. It was a happy effort; but, unfortunately, it was but a fancy sketch—at least so far as I am concerned. I was not there at all upon the occasion. But, I ask, what scenes were enacted on that eventful night at this end of the avenue? The senator would have no cause to complain if I should attempt, in humble imitation of him, to present a picture, true to the life, of the proceedings of himself and his friends. Amidst the dark and lowering clouds of that never-to-be-forgotten night, a caucus assembled in one of the apartments of this gloomy building, and sat in melancholy conclave, deploring the unhappy fate of the whig party. Some rose, and advocated vengeance; 'their voice was still for war.' Others, more moderate, sought to repress the ardent zeal of their fiery compatriots, and advised to peace and prudence. It was finally concluded that, instead of making open war upon Captain Tyler, they should resort to stratagem, and, in the elegant language of one of their number, that they should endeavor 'to head' him. The question was earnestly debated by what means they could best accomplish this purpose; and it was resolved to try the effect of the 'Fiscality' now before us. Unfortunately for the success of the scheme, 'Captain Tyler' was forewarned and forearmed, by means of a private and confidential letter, addressed by mistake to a Virginia coffee-house. It is by means like this that 'enterprises of great pith and moment' often fail. But so desperately intent are the whig party still on the creation of a bank, that one of my friends on this side of the House told me that a bank they would have, though its exchanges should be made in bacon hams, and its currency be small patatoes."

Other senators took the imaginary scene, in which they had been made to act parts, in perfect good temper; and thus the debate on the first Fiscal Bank charter was brought to a conclusion with more amicability than it had been conducted with.

In the course of the consideration of this bill in the Senate, a vote took place which showed to what degree the belief of corrupt practices between the old bank and members of Congress had taken place. A motion was made by Mr. Walker to amend the Fiscal Bank bill so as to prevent any member of Congress from borrowing money from that institution. The motion was resisted by Mr. Clay, and supported by democratic senators on the grounds of the corruptions already practised, and of which repetitions might be expected. Mr. Pierce, of New Hampshire, spoke most fully in favor of the motion, and said:

"It was idle—if it were not offensive, he would say absurd—for gentlemen to discourse here upon the *incorruptibility* of members of Congress. They were like other men—and no better, he believed no worse. They were subject to like passions, influenced by like motives, and capable of being reached by similar *appliances*. History affirmed it. The experience of past years afforded humiliating evidence of the fact. Were we wiser than our fathers? Wiser than the most sagacious and patriotic assemblage of men that the world ever saw? Wiser than the framers of the constitution? What protection did they provide for the country against the *corruptibility* of members of Congress? Why, that no member should hold any office, however humble, which should be created, or the emoluments of which should be increased, during his term of service. How could the influence of a petty office be compared with that of the large *bank accommodations* which had been granted and would be granted again? And yet they were to be told, that in proposing this guard for the whole people, they were fixing an ignominious brand upon themselves and their associates. It seemed to him, that such remarks could hardly be serious; but whether sincere or otherwise, they were not legislating for themselves—not legislating for *individuals*—and he felt no apprehension that the mass, whose rights and interests were involved, would consider themselves aggrieved by such a *brand*.

"The senator from Pennsylvania [Mr. BUCHANAN] while pressing his unanswerable argument in favor of the provision, remarked, that should this bill become a law, no member of Congress 'having a proper sense of delicacy and honor,' with the question of *repeal* before him, could accept a loan from the Bank. That question of 'delicacy and honor' was one to which he (Mr. P.) did not choose now to address himself. He would, however, be guided by the light of experience, and he would take leave to say, that that light made the path before him, upon this proposition, perfectly luminous. By no vote of his should a provision be stricken from this bill, the omission of which would tend to establish a corrupt and corrupting influence— secret and intangible—in the very bosom of the two Houses whose province and duty it would be to pass upon that great question of *repeal*. What had taken place was liable to occur again. Those who were now here and those who would succeed to their places, were not more virtuous, not more secure from the approach of venality, not more elevated above the influence of *certain appliances*, than their predecessors. Well, what did history teach in relation to the course of members of Congress during that most extraordinary struggle between the Bank and the people for supremacy, which convulsed the whole continent from 1831 to 1834?

"He rose chiefly to advert to that page of history, and whether noticed here or not, it would be noticed by his constituents, who, with their children, had an infinitely higher stake in this absorbing question than members of Congress, politicians, or bankers.

"He read from the bank report presented to the Senate in 1834, by the present President of the United States, 'Senate Documents, second session, twenty-third Congress,' p. 320. From that document it appeared that in 1831 there was loaned to fifty-nine members of Congress, the sum of three hundred and twenty-two thousand one hundred and ninety-nine dollars. In 1832, the year when the bank charter was arrested by the veto of that stern old man who occupied the house and hearts of his countrymen, there was loaned to fifty-four members of Congress, the sum of four hundred and seventy-eight thousand and sixty-nine dollars. In 1833, the memorable panic year, there was loaned to fifty-eight members, three hundred and seventy-four thousand seven hundred and sixty-six dollars. In 1834, hope began to decline with the Bank, and so, also, did its line of discounts to members of Congress; but even in that year the loan to fifty-two members amounted to two hundred and thirty-eight thousand five hundred and eighty-six dollars.

"Thus in four years of unparalleled political excitement, growing out of a struggle with the people for the mastery, did that institution grant accommodations to two hundred and twenty-three of the people's representatives, amounting to the vast sum of one million four hundred and thirteen thousand six hundred and twenty dollars. He presented no argument on these facts. He would regard it not merely as supererogation, but an insult to the intelligence of his countrymen. A tribunal of higher authority than the executive and Congress combined, would pass upon the question of 'delicacy and honor,' started by the senator from Pennsylvania, and it would also decide whether in the bank to loan was dangerous or otherwise. He indulged no fears as to the decision of the tribunal in the last resort—the sovereign people."

Mr. Clay remarked that the greater part of these loans were made to members opposed to the bank. Mr. Buchanan answered, no doubt of that. A significant smile went through the chamber, with inquiries whether any one had remained opposed? The yeas and nays were called upon the question—and it was carried; the two Virginia senators, Messrs. Archer and Rives, and Mr. Preston, a Virginian by birth, voting with the democracy, and making the vote 25 yeas to 24 nays. The yeas were: Messrs. Allen, Archer, Benton, Buchanan, Calhoun, Clay of Alabama, Cuthbert, Fulton, King, Linn, McRoberts, Mouton, Nicholson, Pierce, Preston, Rives, Sevier, Smith of Connecticut, Sturgeon, Tappan, Walker, Williams, Woodbury, Wright and Young. The nays were: Messrs. Barrow, Bates, Berrien, Choate, Clay of Kentucky, Clayton, Dixon, Evans, Graham, Henderson, Huntingdon, Leeds Kerr, Mangum, Merrick, Miller, Morehead, Phelps, Porter, Simmons, Smith of Indiana, Southard, Tallmadge, White, Woodbridge. This vote, after the grounds on which the question was put, was considered an explicit senatorial condemnation of the bank for corrupt practices with members of Congress.

CHAPTER LXXXI.

SECOND FISCAL AGENT: BILL PRESENTED: PASSED: DISAPPROVED BY THE PRESIDENT.

This second attempt at a fiscal bill has two histories—one public and ostensible—the other secret and real: and it is proper to write them both, for their own sakes, and also to show in what manner the government is worked. The public history will be given first, and will be given exclusively from a public source—the debates of Congress. We begin with it as it begins there—an extemporaneous graft upon a neglected bill lying on the table of the House of Representatives. Early in the session a bill had been brought in from a select committee on the "currency," which had not been noticed from the time of its introduction. It seemed destined to sleep undisturbed upon the table to the end of the session, and then to expire quietly upon lapse of time. Soon after the rejection of the first fiscal under the qualified veto of the President, Mr. Sergeant of Pennsylvania moved the House (when in that state which is called Committee of the Whole) to take up this bill for consideration: which was done as moved. Mr. Sergeant then stated that, his intention was to move to amend that bill by striking out the whole of it after the enacting clause, and inserting a new bill, which he would move to have printed. Several members asked for the reading of the new bill, or a statement of its provisions; and Mr. Sergeant, in compliance with these requests, stood up and said:

"That, as several inquiries had been made of him with regard to this bill, he would now proceed to make a short statement, to show in what respects it differed from that recently before this House. He would say, first, that there were two or three verbal errors in this bill, and there were words, in two or three places, which he thought had better have been left out, and which were intended to have been omitted by the committee. There were several gentlemen in the present Congress who entertained extreme hostility to the word 'bank,' and, as far as he was concerned, he felt every disposition to indulge their feelings; and he had therefore endeavored throughout this bill to avoid using the word 'bank.' If that word anywhere remained as applicable to the being it was proposed to create by this law, let it go out—let it go out. Now the word 'corporation' sounded well, and he was glad to perceive it gave pleasure to the House. At all events, they had a new *word* to fight against. Now the difference between this bill and that which passed this House some days ago, would be seen by comparison. The present differed from the other principally in three or four particulars, and there were some other parts of the bill which varied, in minor particulars, from that which had been before the House a few days ago. Those differences gentlemen would have no difficulty in discovering and understanding when the bill should have been printed. He would now proceed to answer the inquiries of gentlemen in reference to this bill. Mr. S. then stated the following as the substantial points of difference between the two bills:

"1. The capital in the former bill was thirty millions, with power to extend it to fifty millions. In this bill twenty-one millions, with power to extend it to thirty-five millions. 2. The former bill provided for offices of discount and deposit. In this there are to be agencies only. 3. The dealings of the corporation are to be confined to buying and selling foreign bills of exchange, including bills drawn in one State or territory, and payable in another. There are to be no discounts. 4. The title of the corporation is changed."

This was Friday, the 20th of August. The next day—the bill offered in amendment by Mr. Sergeant having been printed and the House gone into committee—that member moved that all debate upon it in committee of the whole should cease at 4 o'clock that afternoon, and then proceed to vote upon the amendments which might be offered, and report those agreed upon to the House. And having moved this in writing, he immediately moved the previous question upon it. This was sharp practice, and as new as sharp. It was then past 12 o'clock. Such rapidity of proceeding was a mockery upon legislation, and to expose it as such, Mr. Roosevelt of New York moved to amend the time by substituting, instanter, for 4 o'clock, remarking that they might as well have no time for discussion as the time designated. Several members expressing themselves to the same effect, Mr. Sergeant extended the time to 4 o'clock on Monday evening. The brevity of the time was still considered by the minority, and justly, as a mockery upon legislation; and their opinions to that effect were freely expressed. Mr. Cave Johnson asked to be excused from voting on Mr. Sergeant's resolution, giving for the reason that the amendment was a new bill just laid upon the table of members, and that it would be impossible for them to act understandingly upon it in the short time proposed. Mr. Charles Brown of Pennsylvania also asked to be excused from voting, saying that the amendment was a bill of thirty-eight printed pages—that it had only been laid upon their tables ten minutes when the motion to close the debate at 4 o'clock was made—and that it was impossible to act upon it with the care and consideration due to a legislative act, and to one of this momentous importance, and which was to create a great fiscal corporation with vast privileges, and an exclusive charter for twenty years. Mr. Rhett of South Carolina asked to be in like manner excused, reducing his reasons to writing, in the form of a protest. Thus:

"1. Because the rule by which the resolution is proposed is a violation of the spirit of the Constitution of the United States, which declares that the freedom of speech and of the press shall not be abridged by any law of Congress. 2. Because it destroys the character of this body as a deliberative assembly: a *right* to deliberate and discuss measures being no longer in Congress, but with the majority only. 3. Because it is a violation of the rights of the people of the United States, through their representatives, inherited from their ancestors, and enjoyed and practised time immemorial, to speak to the taxes imposed on them, when taxes are imposed. 4. Because by the said rule, a bill may be taken up in Committee of the Whole, be immediately reported to the House, and, by the aid of the previous question, be passed into a law, without one word of debate being permitted or uttered. 5. Because free discussion of the laws by which the people are governed, is not only essential to right legislation, but is necessary to the preservation of the constitution, and the liberties of the people; and to fear or supress it is the characteristic of tyrannies and tyrants only. 6. Because the measure proposed to be forced through the House within less than two days' consideration is one which deeply affects the integrity of the constitution and the liberties of the people; and to pass it with haste, and without due deliberation, would evince a contemptuous disregard of either, and may be a fatal violation of both."

Besides all other objections to this rapid legislation, it was a virtual violation of the rules of the House, made under the constitution, to prevent hasty and inconsiderate, or intemperate action; and which requires a bill to be read three times, each time on a different day, and to be voted upon each time. Technically an amendment, though an entire new bill, is not a bill, and therefore, is not subject to these three readings and votings: substantially and truly, such an amendment is a bill; and the reason of the rule would require it to be treated as such.

Other members asked to be excused from voting; but all being denied that request by an inexorable majority, Mr. Pickens of South Carolina stood up and said: "It is now manifest that the House does not intend to excuse any member from voting. And as enough has been done to call public attention to the odious resolution proposed to be adopted, our object will have been attained: and I respectfully suggest to our friends to go no further in this proceeding!" Cries of "agreed! agreed!" responded to this appeal; and the motion of Mr. Sergeant was adopted. He, himself, then spoke an hour in support of the new bill—one hour of the brief time which was allowed for discussion. Mr. Wise occupied the remainder of the evening against the bill. On Monday, on resuming its consideration, Mr. Turney of Tennessee moved to strike out the enacting clause—which, if done, would put an end to the bill. The motion failed. Some heated discussion took place, which could hardly be called a debate on the bill; but came near enough to it to detect its fraudulent character. It was the old defunct Bank of the United States, in disguise, to come to life again in it. That used-up concern was then in the hands of justice, hourly sued upon its notes, and the contents collected upon execution; and insolvency admitted. It could not be named in any charter: no reference could be made to it by name. But there was a provision in the amended bill to permit it to slip into full life, and take the whole benefit of the new charter. Corporations were to be allowed to subscribe for the stock: under that provision she could take all the stock—and be herself again. This, and other fraudulent provisions were detected: but the clock struck four! and the vote was taken, and the bill passed—125 to 94. The title of the original bill was then amended to conform to its new character;

and, on the motion of Mr. Sergeant was made to read in this wise: "*An act to provide for the better collection, safe keeping, and disbursement of the public revenue, by means of a corporation to be styled the Fiscal Corporation of the United States.*" Peals of laughter saluted the annunciation of this title; and when it was carried to the Senate, as it immediately was, for the concurrence of that body, and its strange title was read out, ridicule was already lying in wait for it; and, under the mask of ridicule, an attack was made upon its real character, as the resuscitation of Mr. Biddle's bank: and Mr. Benton exclaimed—

"Heavens what a name! long as the moral law—half sub-treasury, and half national bank—and all fraudulent and deceptive, to conceal what it is; and entirely too long. The name is too long. People will never stand it. They cannot go through all that. We must have something shorter—something that will do for every day use. Corporosity! that would be a great abridgment; but it is still too long. It is five syllables, and people will not go above two syllables, or three at most, and often hang at one, in names which have to be incontinently repeated. They are all economical at that, let them be as extravagant as they may be in spending their money. They will not spend their breath upon long names which have to be repeated every day. They must have something short and pointed; and, if you don't give it to them, they will make it for themselves. The defunct Fiscal Bank was rapidly taking the title of fiscality; and, by alliteration, rascality; and if it had lived, would soon have been compendiously and emphatically designated by some brief and significant title. The Fiscal Corporation cannot expect to have better luck. It must undergo the fate of all great men and of all great measures, overburdened with titles—it must submit to a short name. There is much virtue in a name; and the poets tell us there are many on whose conception Phœbus never smiled, and at whose birth no muse, or grace, was present. In that predicament would seem to be this intrusive corporosity, which we have received from the other House, and sent to our young committee, and which has mutation of title without alteration of substance, and without accession of euphony, or addition of sense. Some say a name is nothing—that a rose by any other name would smell as sweet. So it will; and a thorn by any other name would stick as deep. And so of these fiscals, whether to be called banks or corporations. They will still be the same thing—a thorn in our side—but a short name they must have. This corporosity must retrench its extravagance of title.

"I go for short names, and will give reasons for it. The people will have short names, although they may spoil a fine one; and I will give you an instance. There was a most beautiful young lady in New Orleans some years ago, as there always has been, and still are many such. She was a *Creole*, that is to say, born in this country, of parents from Europe. A gentleman who was building a superb steamboat, took it into his head to honor this young lady, by connecting her name with his vessel; so he bestowed upon it the captivating designation of LA BELLE CREOLE. This fine name was painted in golden letters on the sides of his vessel; and away she went, with three hundred horse power, to Kentucky and Ohio. The vessel was beautiful, and the name was beautiful, and the lady was beautiful; but all the beauty on earth could not save the name from the catastrophe to which all long titles are subjected. It was immediately abbreviated, and, in the abbreviation, sadly deteriorated. At first, they called her the *bell*—not the French *belle*, which signifies fine or beautiful—but the plain English *bell*, which in the Holy Scriptures, was defined to be a tinkling cymbal. This was bad enough; but worse was coming. It so happens that the vernacular pronunciation of *creole*, in the Kentucky waters, is cre-owl; so they began to call this beautiful boat the *cre-owl* but things did not stop here. It was too extravagant to employ two syllables when one would answer as well, and be so much more economical; so the first half of the name was dropped, and the last retained; and thus *La Belle Creole*—the beautiful creole—sailed up and down the Mississippi all her life by the name, style, title, and description of, THE OWL! (Roars of laughing in the Senate, with exclamations from several, that it was a good name for a bank—that there was an Owl-Creek Bank in Ohio once, now dead and insolvent, but, in its day, as good as the best.)

"Mr. B. continued. I do not know whether owl will do for this child of long name, and many fathers; but we must have a name, and must continue trying till we get one. Let us hunt far and wide. Let us have recourse to the most renowned Æsop and his fables, and to that one of his fables which teaches us how an old black cat succeeded in getting at the rats again after having eaten up too many of them, and become too well known, under her proper form, to catch any more. She rolled herself over in a meal tub—converted her black skin into white—and walked forth among the rats as a new and innocent animal that they had never seen before. All were charmed to see her! but a quick application of teeth and claws to the throats and bellies of the rats, let them see that it was their old acquaintance, the black cat; and that whitening the skin did not alter the instincts of the animal, nor blunt the points of its teeth and claws. The rats, after that, called her the meal-tub cat, and the mealy cat. May we not call this corporosity the meal-tub bank? A cattish name would certainly suit it in one particular; for, like a cat, it has many lives, and a cat, you know, must be killed nine times before it will die; so say the traditions of the nursery; and of all histories the traditions of children are the most veracious. They teach us that cats have nine lives. So of this bank. It has been killed several times, but here it is still, scratching, biting, and clawing. Jackson killed it in 1832; Tyler killed it last week. But this is only a beginning. Seven times more the *Fates* must cut the thread of its hydra life before it will yield up the ghost.

"The meal tub! No insignificant, or vulgar name. It lives in history, and connects its fame with kings and statesmen. We all know the Stuarts of England—an honest and bigoted race in the beginning, but always unfortunate in the end. The second Charles was beset by plots and cabals. There were many attempts, or supposed attempts to kill him; many plots against him, and some very ridiculous; among the rest one which goes by the name of the meal-tub plot; because the papers which discovered it were found in the meal-tub where the conspirators, or their enemies, had hid them.

"Sir, I have given you a good deal of meal this morning; but you must take more yet. It is a *fruitful* theme, and may give us a good name before we are done with it. I have a reminiscence, as the novel writers say, and I will tell it. When a small boy, I went to school in a Scotch Irish neighborhood, and learnt many words and phrases which I have not met with since, but which were words of great pith and power; among the rest shake-poke. (Mr. ARCHER: I never heard that before.) Mr. BENTON: but you have heard of poke. You know the adage: do not buy a pig in the poke; that is to say, in the bag; for poke signifies bag, or wallet, and is a phrase much used in the north of England, and among the Scotch Irish in America. A pig is carried to market in a poke, and if you buy it without taking it out first, you may be 'taken in.' So corn is carried to a mill in a poke, and when brought home, ground into meal, the meal remains in the poke, in the houses of poor families, until it is used up. When the bag is nearly empty, it is turned upside down, and shaken; and the meal that comes out is called the shake-poke, that is to say, the last shake of the bag. By an easy and natural metaphor, this term is also applied to the last child that is born in a family; especially if it is puny or a rickety concern. The last child, like the last meal, is called a shake-poke; and may we not call this *fiscalous corporation* a shake-poke also, and for the same reason? It is the last—the last at all events for the session! it is the last meal in their bag—their shake-poke! and it is certainly a rickety concern.

"I do not pretend to impose a name upon this bantling; that is a privilege of paternity, or of sponsorship, and I stand in neither relation to this babe. But a name of brevity—of brevity and significance—it must have; and, if the fathers and sponsors do not bestow it, the people will: for a long name is abhorred and eschewed in all countries. Remember the fate of John Barebone, the canting hypocrite in Cromwell's time. He had a very good name, John Barebone; but the knave composed a long verse, like Scripture, to sanctify himself with it, and intituled himself thus:—'Praise God, Barebone, for if Christ had not died for you, you would be damned, Barebone.' Now, this was very sanctimonious; but it was too long—too much of a good thing—and so the people cut it all off but the last two words, and called the fellow *'damned Barebone,'* and nothing else but damned Barebone, all his life after. So let this corporosity beware: it may get itself damned before it is done with us, and Tyler too."

The first proceeding in the Senate was to refer this bill to a committee, and Mr. Clay's select committee would naturally present itself as the one to which it would go: but he was too much disgusted at the manner in which his own bill had been treated to be willing to take any lead with respect to this second one; and, in fact, had so expressed himself in the debate on the veto message. A motion was made to refer it to another select committee, the appointing of which would be in the President of the Senate—Mr. Southard, of New Jersey. Mr. Southard, like Mr. Sergeant, was the fast friend of the United States Bank, to be revived under this bill; and like him conducted the bill to the best advantage for that institution. Mr. Sergeant had sprung the bill, and rushed it through, backed by the old bank majority, with a velocity which distanced shame in the disregard of all parliamentary propriety and all fair legislation. He had been the attorney of the bank for many years, and seemed only intent upon its revivification—no matter by what means. Mr. Southard, bound by the same friendship to the bank, seemed to be animated by the same spirit, and determined to use his power in the same way. He appointed exclusively the friends of the bank, and mostly of young senators, freshly arrived in the chamber. Mr. King, of Alabama, the often President of the Senate *pro tempore*, and the approved expounder of the rules, was the first—and very properly the first—to remark upon the formation of this one-sided committee; and to bring it to the attention of the Senate. He exposed it in pointed terms.

"Mr. KING observed, that in the organization of committees by Congress, the practice had been heretofore invariable—the usage uniform. The first business, on the meeting of each House, after the selection of officers and organizing, was to appoint the various standing committees. In designating those to whom the various subjects to which it is proposed to call the attention of Congress shall be referred, the practice always has been to place a majority of the friends of the administration on each committee. This is strictly correct, in order to insure a favorable consideration of the various measures which the administration may propose to submit to their examination and decision. A majority, however, of the friends of the administration, is all that has heretofore been considered either necessary or proper to be placed on those committees; and in every instance a minority of each committee consists of members supposed to be adverse to the measures of the dominant party. The propriety of such an arrangement cannot fail to strike the mind of every senator. All measures should be carefully examined; objections suggested; amendments proposed; and every proposition rendered as perfect as practicable before it is reported to the House for its action. This neither can, nor will, be controverted. In the whole of his [Mr. KING's] congressional experience, he did not know of a single instance in which this rule had been departed from, until now. But there has been a departure from this usage, sanctioned by justice and undeviating practice, which had given to it the force and obligation of law; and he [Mr. KING] felt it to be his duty to call the attention of the Senate to this most objectionable innovation. Yesterday a bill was reported from the House of Representatives for the chartering of a fiscal corporation. It was immediately taken up, read twice on the same day, and, on the motion of the senator from Georgia, ordered to be referred to a select committee. This bill embraced a subject of the greatest importance, one more disputed upon constitutional grounds, as well as upon the grounds of expediency, than any other which has ever agitated this country. This bill, of such vast importance, fraught with results of the greatest magnitude, in which the whole country takes the liveliest interest, either for or against its adoption, has been hurried through the other House in a few days, almost without discussion, and, as he [Mr. K.], conceived, in violation of the principles of parliamentary law, following as it did, immediately on the heels of a similar bill, which had, most fortunately for the country, received the veto of the President, and ultimately rejected by the Senate. The rules of the Senate forbade him to speak of the action of the other House on this subject as he could wish. He regretted that he was not at liberty to present their conduct plainly to the people, to show to the country what it has to expect from the dominant party here, and what kind of measures may be expected from the mode of legislation which has been adopted. The fiscal corporation bill has, however, come to us, and he [Mr. KING] and his friends, much as they were opposed to its introduction or passage, determined to give it a fair and open opposition. No objection was made to the motion of the senator from Georgia to send it to a select committee, and that that committee should be appointed by the presiding officer. The President of the Senate made the selection; but, to his [Mr. K.'s] great surprise, on reading the names this morning in one of the public papers, he found they were all members of the dominant party: not one selected for this most important committee belongs to the minority in this body opposed to the bill. Why was it, he [Mr. KING] must be permitted to ask, that the presiding officer had departed from a rule which, in all the fluctuations of party, and in the highest times of party excitement, had never before been departed from?

"There must have been a motive in thus departing from a course sanctioned by time, and by every principle of propriety. It will be for the presiding officer to state what that motive was. Mr. King must be permitted to repeat, the more to impress it on the minds of senators, that during more than twenty years he had been in Congress, he had never known important committees to be appointed, either standing or select, in which some member of the then minority did not constitute a portion, until this most extraordinary selection of a committee, to report on this most important bill. Would it not [said Mr. KING] have been prudent, as well as just, to have given to the minority a fair opportunity of suggesting their objections in committee? The friends of the measure would then be apprised of those objections, and could prepare themselves to meet them. He [Mr. KING] had not risen to make a motion, but merely to present this extraordinary proceeding to the view of the Senate, and leave it there; but, he believed, in justice to his friends, and to stamp this proceeding with condemnation, he would move that two additional members be added to the committee."

The President of the Senate, in answer to the remarks of Mr. King, read a rule from Jefferson's Manual in which it is said that, a bill must be committed to its friends to improve and perfect it, and not to its enemies who would destroy it. And under this rule Mr. Southard said he had appointed the committee. Mr. Benton then stood up, and said:

"That is the *Lex Parliamentaria* of England from which you read, Mr. President, and is no part of our rules. It is English authority—very good in the British Parliament, but not valid in the American Senate. It is not in our rules—neither in the rules of the House nor in those of the Senate; and is contrary to the practice of both Houses—their settled practice for fifty years. From the beginning of our government we have disregarded it, and followed a rule much more consonant to decency and justice, to public satisfaction, and to the results of fair legislation, and that was, to commit our business to mixed committees—committees consisting of friends and foes of the measure, and of both political parties—always taking care that the friends of the measure should be the majority; and, if it was a political question, that the political party in power should have the majority. This is our practice; and a wise and good practice it is, containing all the good that there is in the British rule, avoiding its harshness, and giving both sides a chance to perfect or to understand a measure. The nature of our government—its harmonious and successful action—requires both parties to have a hand in conducting the public business, both in the committees and the legislative halls; and this is the first session at which committee business, or legislative business, has been confined, or attempted to be confined, to one political party. The clause which you read, Mr. President, I have often read myself; not for the purpose of sending a measure to a committee of exclusive friends, but to prevent it from going to a committee of exclusive enemies—in fact to obtain for it a mixed committee—such as the democracy has always given when in power—such as it will again give when in power—and such as is due to fair, decent, satisfactory, and harmonious legislation."

Mr. Benton, after sustaining Mr. King in his view of the rules and the practice, told him that he was deceived in his memory in supposing there had never been a one-sided committee in the Senate before: and remarked:

"That senator is very correct at all times; but he will not take it amiss if I shall suggest to him that he is in error now—that there has been one other occasion in which a one-sided committee was employed—and that in a very important case—concerning no less a power than Mr. Biddle's bank, and even Mr. Biddle himself. I speak of the committee which was sent by this Senate to examine the Bank of the United States in the summer of 1834, when charged with insolvency and criminality by General Jackson—charges which time have proved to be true—and when the whole committee were of one party, and that party opposed to General Jackson, and friendly to the bank. And what became then of the rule of British parliamentary law, which has just been read? It had no application then, though it would have cut off every member of the committee; for not one of them was favorable to the inquiry, but the contrary; and the thing ended as all expected. I mention this as an instance of a one-sided committee, which the senator from Alabama has overlooked, and which deserves to be particularly remembered on this occasion, for a reason which I will mention; and which is, that both these committees were appointed in the same case—for the same Bank of the United States—one to whitewash it—which it did; the other to smuggle it into existence under a charter in which it cannot be named. And thus, whenever that bank is concerned, we have to look out for tricks and frauds (to say no more), even on the high floors of national legislation."

Mr. Buchanan animadverted with justice and severity upon the tyranny with which the majority in the House of Representatives had forced the bill through, and marked the fact that not a single democratic member had succeeded in getting an opportunity to speak against it. This was an unprecedented event in the history of parties in America, or in England, and shows the length to which a bank party would go in stifling the right of speech. In all great measures, before or since, and in all countries possessing free institutions, the majority has always allowed to the adversary the privilege of speaking to the measures which were to be put upon them: here for the first time it was denied; and the denial was marked at the time, and carried at once into parliamentary history to receive the reprobation due to it. This was the animadversion of Mr. Buchanan:

"The present bill to establish a fiscal corporation was hurried through the House of Representatives with the celerity, and, so far as the democracy was concerned, with the silence of despotism. No democratic member had an opportunity of raising his voice against it. Under new rules in existence there, the majority had predetermined that it should pass that body within two days from the commencement of the discussion. At first, indeed, the determination was that it should pass the first day; but this was felt to be too great an outrage; and the mover was graciously pleased to extend the time one day longer. Whilst the bill was in Committee of the Whole, it so happened that, in the struggle for the floor, no democratic member succeeded in obtaining it; and at the destined hour of four in the afternoon of the second day, the committee rose, and all further debate was arrested by the previous question. The voice of that great party in this country to which I am proud to belong, was, therefore, never heard through any of its representatives in the House against this odious measure. Not even one brief hour, the limit prescribed by the majority to each speaker, was granted to any democratic member."

The bill went to the committee which had been appointed, without the additional two members which Mr. King had suggested; and which suggestion, not being taken up by the majority, was no further pressed. Mr. Berrien, chairman of that committee, soon reported it back to the Senate—without alteration; as had been foreseen. He spoke two hours in its favor—concluding with the expression that the President would give it his approval—founding that opinion on the President's message at the commencement of the session—on his veto message of the first fiscal bill—on the report of the Secretary of the Treasury—and on this Secretary's subsequent plan for a bank framed with the view to avoid his constitutional objections. Mr. Clay declared his intention to vote for the bill, not that it went as far as he could wish, but that it would go a good distance—would furnish a sound national currency, and regulate exchanges. Mr. Archer, who had voted against the first bank, and who was constitutionally opposed to a national bank, made a speech chiefly to justify his vote in favor of the present bill. It was well known that no alteration would be permitted in the bill—that it had been arranged out of doors, and was to stand as agreed upon: but some senators determined to offer amendments, merely to expose the character of the measure, to make attacks upon the most vulnerable points; and to develope the spirit which conducted it. In this sense Mr. Benton acted in presenting several amendments, deemed proper in themselves, and which a foreknowledge of their fate would not prevent him from offering. The whole idea of the institution was, that it was to be a treasury bank; and hence the pertinacity with which "fiscal," synonymous with treasury, was retained in all the titles, and conformed to in all its provisions: and upon this idea the offered amendments turned.

"Mr. BENTON said he had an amendment to offer, which the Senate would presently see was of great importance. It was, to strike out from the ninth line of the first section the word 'States.' It was in that provision assigning seventy thousand shares to individual companies, corporations, or *States*. This was a new kind of stockholders: a new description of co-partners with stockjobbers in a banking corporation. States had no right to be seduced into such company; he would therefore move to have them struck out: let the word "States" be taken out of that line. To comprehend the full force and bearing of this amendment it would be necessary to keep in view that the sixteenth section of this charter designates the Fiscal Corporation the Treasury of the United States. It expressly says that—

"'All public moneys in deposit in said corporation, or standing on its books to the credit of the *Treasurer*, shall be taken and deemed to be *in the Treasury of the United States*, and all payments made by the Treasurer shall be in checks drawn on said corporation.'

"Yes, sir! this *Fisc* is to be the Treasury of the United States; and the Treasury of the United States is to be converted into a corporation, and not only forced into partnership with individuals, companies, and corporations, but into joint stock co-partnership with the States. The general government is to appoint three directors, and the rest of the partners will have the appointment of the other six. The corporators will be two to one against the general government, and they will of course have the control of the Treasury of this Union in their hands. Now he was for sticking to the constitution, not only in spirit and meaning, but to the letter; and the constitution gives no authority to individuals, companies, corporations, and States, to take the public Treasury of the Union out of the hands of the general government. The general government alone, and acting independently of any such control, is required by the constitution to manage its own fiscal affairs. Here it is proposed to retain only one-third of the control of this Treasury in the hands of the general government—the other two-thirds may fall exclusively into the hands of the States, and thus the Treasury of the whole Union may be at the disposal of such States as can contrive to possess themselves of the two-thirds of the stock they are authorized to take. If it is the object to let those States have the funds of the Treasury to apply to their own use, the scheme is well contrived to attain that end. He, however, was determined not to let that plan be carried without letting the people know who were its supporters; he should, therefore, demand the yeas and nays on his amendment."

"Mr. BERRIEN explained that the objection raised against the sixteenth section was merely technical. The words did not convert the bank into the United States Treasury; they merely provided for a conformity with laws regulating the lodgment and withdrawal of Treasury funds. The question was then taken on the amendment, which was rejected as follows: Yeas— Messrs. Allen, Benton, Buchanan, Clay of Alabama, King, Linn, McRoberts, Mouton, Nicholson, Pierce, Sevier, Smith of Connecticut, Sturgeon, Tappan, Walker, Woodbury, Wright, and Young—18. Nays—Messrs. Archer, Barrow, Bates, Berrien, Choate, Clay of Kentucky, Clayton, Dixon, Evans, Graham, Henderson, Huntington, Kerr, Mangum, Merrick, Miller, Morehead, Phelps, Porter, Prentiss, Preston, Rives, Simmons, Smith of Indiana, Southard, Tallmadge, White, and Woodbridge—28."

Mr. Benton then moved to strike out "corporations" from the enumeration of persons and powers which should possess the faculty of becoming stockholders in this institution, with the special view of keeping out the Pennsylvania Bank of the United States, and whose name could not be presented openly for a charter, or re-charter:

> "The late United States Bank had means yet to keep a cohort of lawyers, agents, cashiers, and directors, who would not lose sight of the hint, and who were panting to plunge their hands into Uncle Sam's pocket. There was nothing to prevent the corporators of the late United States Bank becoming the sole owners of these two-thirds of the stock in the new Fiscality. The sixteenth fundamental rule of the eleventh section is the point where we are to find the constitutionality of this Fiscality. The little pet banks of every State may be employed as agents. This is a tempting bait for every insolvent institution in want of Treasury funds to strain every nerve and resort to every possible scheme for possessing themselves of the control of the funds of the United States. This object was to defeat such machinations. On this amendment he would demand the yeas and nays. The question was then taken on the amendment, and decided in the negative as follows: Yeas—Messrs. Allen, Benton, Buchanan, Calhoun, Clay of Alabama, Fulton, King, Linn, McRoberts, Mouton, Nicholson, Pierce, Rives, Sevier, Smith of Connecticut, Sturgeon, Tappan, Walker, Woodbury, Wright, and Young—21. Nays—Messrs. Archer, Barrow, Bates, Berrien, Choate, Clay of Kentucky, Clayton, Dixon, Evans, Graham, Henderson, Huntington, Kerr, Mangum, Merrick, Miller, Morehead, Phelps, Porter, Prentiss, Preston, Simmons, Smith of Indiana, Tallmadge, White, and Woodbridge—26."

Mr. Rives objected to the exchange dealings which this fiscal corporation was to engage in, as being discounts when the exchange had some time to run. He referred to his former opinions, and corrected a misapprehension of Mr. Berrien. He was opposed to discounts in every form; while this bill authorizes discounts to any amount on bills of exchange. He offered no amendment, but wished to correct the misunderstanding of Mr. Berrien, who held that this bill, in this particular, was identical with the amendment offered to the first bill by Mr. Rives, and that it was in strict conformity with the President's message.

> "Mr. BENTON fully concurred with the senator from Virginia [Mr. RIVES], that cashing bills of exchange was just as much a discounting operation as discounting promissory notes; it was, in fact, infinitely worse. It was the greatest absurdity in the world, to suppose that the flimsy humbug of calling the discounting of bills of exchange—gamblers' kites, and race-horse bills of exchange—a 'dealing in exchanges' within the meaning of the terms used in the President's veto message. As if the President could be bamboozled by such a shallow artifice. Only look at the operation under this bill. A needy adventurer goes to one of these agencies, and offers his promissory note with securities, in the old-fashioned way, but is told it cannot be discounted—the law is against it. The law, however, may be evaded if he put his note into another shape, making one of his sureties the drawer, and making the other, who lives beyond the State line, his drawee, in favor of himself, as endorser; and in that shape the kite will be *cashed*, deducting the interest and a per centage besides in the shape of exchange. Here is discount added to usury; and is not that worse than discounting promissory notes?"

The President had dwelt much upon "local discounts," confining the meaning of that phrase to loans obtained on promissory notes. He did not consider money obtained upon a bill of exchange as coming under that idea—nor did it when it was an exchange of money—when it was the giving of money in one place for money in another place. But that true idea of a bill of exchange was greatly departed from when the drawer of the bill had no money at the place drawn on, and drew upon time, and depended upon getting funds there in time; or taking up the bill with damages when it returned protested. Money obtained that way was a discount obtained, and on far worse terms for the borrower, and better for the bank, than on a fair promissory note: and the rapacious banks forced their loans, as much as possible into this channel. So that this fiscal bank was limited to do the very thing it wished to do, and which was so profitable to itself and so oppressive to the borrower. This, Mr. Tappan, of Ohio, showed in a concise speech.

"Mr. TAPPAN said, when senators on the other side declare that this bank bill is intended to withhold from the corporation created by it the power of making loans and discounts, he felt himself bound to believe that such was their honest construction of it. He was, however, surprised that any man, in the slightest degree acquainted with the banking business of the country, who had read this bill, should suppose that, under its provisions, the company incorporated by it would not have unlimited power to loan their paper and to discount the paper of their customers. The ninth fundamental article says, that 'the said corporation shall not, directly or indirectly, deal or trade in any thing except foreign bills of exchange, *including bills or drafts drawn in one State or Territory and payable in another.'* This bill, in this last clause, sanctioned a mode of discounting paper, and making loans common in the Western country. He spoke of a mode of doing business which he had full knowledge of, and he asked senators, therefore, to look at it. A man who wants a loan from a bank applies to the directors, and is told, we can lend you the money, but we do not take notes for our loans—you must give us a draft; but, says the applicant, I have no funds any where to draw upon; no matter, say the bankers, if your draft is not met, or expected to be met, because you have no funds, that need make no difference; you may pay it here, *with the exchange*, when the time it has to run is out; so the borrower signs a draft or bill of exchange on somebody in New York, Philadelphia, or Baltimore, and pays the discount for the time it has to run; when that time comes round, the borrower pays into the bank the amount of his draft, with two, four, six, or ten per cent., whatever the rate of exchange may be, and the affair is settled, and he gets a renewal for sixty days, by further paying the discount on the sum borrowed; and if it is an accommodation loan, it it renewed from time to time by paying the discount and exchange. Very few of the Western banks, he believed, discounted notes; they found it much more profitable to deal in exchange, as it is called; but this dealing in exchange enables the banks to discount as much paper, and to loan as much of their own notes, as the old-fashioned mode of discounting; it is a difference in form merely, with this advantage to the banks, that it enables them to get from their customers ten or twelve per cent. on their loans, instead of six, to which, in discounting notes, they are usually restricted. How then, he asked, could senators say that this bill did not give the power to make loans and discounts? He had shown them how, under this law, both loans and discounts will be made without limitation."

Mr. Benton then went on with offering his amendments, and offered one requiring all the stockholders in this corporation Fisc (which was to be the Treasury of the United States), to be citizens of the United States, for the obvious reason of preventing the national treasury from falling under the control of foreigners. M. Berrien considered the amendment unnecessary, as there was already a provision that none but citizens of the United States should take the original stock; and the only effect of the provision would be to lessen the value of the stock. Mr. Benton considered this provision as a fraudulent contrivance to have the appearance of excluding foreigners from being stockholders while not doing so. The prohibition upon them as original subscribers was nothing, when they were allowed to become stockholders by purchase. His amendment was intended to make the charter what it fraudulently pretended to be—a bank owned by American citizens. The word "original" would be a fraud unless the prohibition was extended to assignees. And he argued that the senator from Georgia (Mr. Berrien), had admitted the design of selling to foreigners by saying that the value of the stock would be diminished by excluding foreigners from its purchase. He considered the answer of the senator double, inconsistent, and contradictory. He first considered the amendment unnecessary, as the charter already confined original subscriptions to our own citizens; and then considered it would injure the price of the stock to be so limited. That was a contradiction. The fact was, he said, that this bill was to resurrect, by smuggling, the old United States Bank, which was a British concern; and that the effect would be to make the British the governors and masters of our treasury: and he asked the yeas and nays on his motion, which was granted, and they stood—19 to 26, and were: YEAS—Messrs. Allen, Benton, Buchanan, Clay of Alabama, Cuthbert, Fulton, King, Linn, McRoberts, Mouton, Nicholson, Pierce, Sevier, Sturgeon, Tappan, Walker, Woodbury, Wright, and Young—19. NAYS—Messrs. Archer, Barrow, Bates, Berrien, Clay of Kentucky, Clayton, Dixon, Evans, Graham, Henderson, Huntington, Kerr, Mangum, Merrick, Miller, Morehead, Phelps, Porter, Prentiss,

Preston, Rives, Simmons, Smith of Indiana, Tallmadge, White, and Woodbridge—26. Considering this a vital question, and one on which no room should be left for the majority to escape the responsibility of putting the United States Treasury in the hands of foreigners—even alien enemies in time of war, as well as rival commercial competitors in time of peace—Mr. Benton moved the same prohibition in a different form. It was to affix it to the eleventh fundamental rule of the eleventh section of the bill, which clothes the corporation with power to make rules to govern the assignment of stock: his amendment was to limit these assignments to American citizens. That was different from his first proposed amendment, which included both original subscribers and assignees. The senator from Georgia objected to that amendment as unnecessary, because it included a class already prohibited as well as one that was not. Certainly it was unnecessary with respect to one class, but necessary with respect to the other—necessary in the estimation of all who were not willing to see the United States Treasury owned and managed by foreigners. He wished now to hear what the senator from Georgia could say against the proposed amendment in this form. Mr. Berrien answered: "He hoped the amendment would not prevail. The original subscribers would be citizens of the United States. To debar them from transferring their stock, would be to lessen the value of the stock, which they rendered valuable by becoming the purchasers of it." Mr. Benton rejoined, that his amendment did not propose to prevent the original subscribers from selling their stock, or any assignee from selling; the only design of the amendment was to limit all these sales to American citizens; and that would be its only effect if adopted. And as to the second objection, a second time given, that it would injure the value of the stock, he said it was a strange argument, that the paltry difference of value in shares to the stockholders should outweigh the danger of confiding the Treasury of the United States to foreigners—subjects of foreign potentates. He asked the yeas, which were granted—and stood—21 to 27: the same as before, with the addition of some senators who had come in. These several proposed amendments, and the manner in which they were rejected, completed the exposure of the design to resuscitate the defunct Bank of the United States, just as it had been, with its foreign stockholders, and extraordinary privileges. It was to be the old bank revived, disguised, and smuggled in. It was to have the same capital as the old one—thirty-five millions: for while it said the capital was to be twenty-one millions, there was a clause enabling Congress to add on fourteen millions—which it would do as soon as the bill passed. Like the old bank, it was to have the United States for a partner, owning seven millions of the stock. The stock was all to go to the old Bank of the United States; for the subscriptions were to be made with commissioners appointed by the Secretary of the Treasury—who, it was known, would appoint the friends of the old bank; so that the whole subscription would be in her hands; and a charter for her fraudulently and deceptiously obtained. The title of the bill was fraudulent, being limited to the management of the "*public*" moneys, while the body of it conferred all the privileges known to the three distinct kinds of banks:—1. Circulation. 2. Exchange. 3. Discount and deposit—the discount being in the most oppressive and usurious form on inland and mere neighborhood bills of exchange, declared by the charter to be foreign bills for the mere purpose of covering these local loans.

> "Mr. WALKER moved an amendment, requiring that the bills in which the Bank should deal should be drawn at short dates, and on goods already actually shipped. It was negatived by yeas and nays, as follows:—YEAS—Messrs. Allen, Benton, Buchanan, Calhoun, Clay of Alabama, Fulton, King, Linn, McRoberts, Mouton, Nicholson, Pierce, Rives, Sevier, Smith of Connecticut, Sturgeon, Tappan, Walker, Woodbury, Wright, and Young—21. NAYS— Messrs. Archer, Barrow, Bates, Berrien, Choate, Clay of Kentucky, Clayton, Dixon, Evans, Graham, Henderson, Huntington, Kerr, Mangum, Merrick, Miller, Morehead, Phelps, Porter, Prentiss, Preston, Simmons, Smith of Indiana, Southard, Tallmadge, White, and Woodbridge—27. Mr. ALLEN moved an amendment to make the directors, in case of suspension, personally liable for the debts of the bank. This was negatived as follows: YEAS— Messrs. Allen, Benton, Buchanan, Clay of Alabama, Cuthbert, Fulton, King, Linn, McRoberts, Mouton, Nicholson, Pierce, Sevier, Smith of Connecticut, Sturgeon, Tappan, Walker, Woodbury, Wright, and Young—20. NAYS—Messrs. Archer, Barrow, Bates, Berrien, Choate, Clay of Kentucky, Clayton, Dixon, Evans, Graham, Henderson, Huntington, Kerr, Mangum, Merrick, Miller, Morehead, Phelps, Porter, Prentiss, Preston, Rives, Simmons, Smith of Indiana, Southard, Tallmadge, White, and Woodbridge—28."

The character of the bill having been shown by the amendments offered and rejected, there was no need to offer any more, and the democratic senators ceased opposition, that the vote might be taken on the bill: it was so; and the bill was passed by the standing majority. Concurred in by the Senate without alteration, it was returned to the House, and thence referred to the President for his approval, or disapproval. It was disapproved, and returned to the House, with a message stating his objections to it; where it gave rise to some violent speaking, more directed to the personal conduct of the President than to the objections to the bill stated in his message. In this debate Mr. Botts, of Virginia, was the chief speaker on one side, inculpating the President: Mr. Gilmer of Virginia, and Mr. Proffit of Indiana, on the other were the chief respondents in his favor. The vote being taken there appeared 103 for the bill, 80 against it—which not being a majority of two-thirds, the bill was rejected: and so ends the public and ostensible history of the second attempt to establish a national bank at this brief session under the guise, and disguise, of a misnomer: and a long one at that.

The negative votes, when rejected on the final vote for want of two-thirds of the House, were:

"Messrs. Archibald H. Arrington, Charles G. Atherton, Linn Banks, Benjamin A. Bidlack, Linn Boyd, David P. Brewster, Aaron V. Brown, Charles Brown, William O. Butler, Patrick C. Caldwell, John Campbell, Reuben Chapman, James G. Clinton, Walter Coles, Richard D. Davis, John B. Dawson, Ezra Dean, Andrew W. Doig, Ira A. Eastman, John C. Edwards, Joseph Egbert, Charles G. Ferris, John G. Floyd, Charles A. Floyd, Joseph Fornance, James Gerry, Thomas W. Gilmer, William O. Goode, Amos Gustine, William A. Harris, John Hastings, Samuel L. Hays, Isaac E. Holmes, George W. Hopkins, Jacob Houck, jr., George S. Houston, Edmund W. Hubard, Robert M. T. Hunter, Charles J. Ingersoll, William W. Irwin, William Jack, Cave Johnson, John W. Jones, George M. Keim, Andrew Kennedy, Dixon H. Lewis, Abraham McClellan, Robert McClellan, James J. McKay, John McKeon, Francis Mallory, Albert G. Marchand, John Thompson Mason, James Mathews, William Medill, John Miller, Peter Newhard, William Parmenter, Samuel Patridge, Wm. W. Payne, Arnold Plumer, George H. Proffit, John Reynolds, R. Barnwell Rhett, Lewis Riggs, James Rogers, Tristram Shaw, Benjamin G. Shields, John Snyder, Lewis Steenrod, George Sweney, Hopkins L. Turney, John Van Buren, Aaron Ward, Harvey M. Watterson, John B. Weller, John Westbrook, James W. Williams, Henry A. Wise, Fernando Wood."

CHAPTER LXXXII.

SECRET HISTORY OF THE SECOND BILL FOR A FISCAL AGENT, CALLED FISCAL CORPORATION: ITS ORIGIN WITH MR. TYLER: ITS PROGRESS THROUGH CONGRESS UNDER HIS LEAD: ITS REJECTION UNDER HIS VETO.

Soon after the meeting of Congress in this extra session—in the course of the first week of it—Mr. Gilmer, of Virginia, held a conversation with a whig member of the House, in which he suggested to him that "a couple of gentlemen of about their size," might become important men in this country—leading men—and get the control of the government. An explanation was requested—and given. It was to withdraw Mr. Tyler from the whig party, and make him the head of a third party, in which those who did it would become chiefs, and have control in the administration. This was the explanation; and the scheme was based, not upon any particular circumstances, but upon a knowledge of Mr. Tyler's character and antecedents: and upon a calculation that he would be dazzled with the idea of being the head of a party, and let the government fall into the hands of those who pleased him—his indolence, and want of business habits disqualifying him for the labors of administration. Democratic doctrines were to be the basis of the new party, especially opposition to a national bank: but recruits from all parties received. The whig member to whom this suggestion for the third party was made, declined to have any thing to do with it: nor was he further consulted. But his eyes were opened, and he had to see; and he saw other whigs do what he would not. And he had received a clue which led to the comprehension of things which he did not see, and had got an insight that would make him observant. But his lips were sealed under an injunction; and remained so, as far as the public was concerned. I never heard him quoted for a word on the subject; but either himself, or some one equally well informed, must have given Mr. Clay exact information; otherwise he could not have hit the nail on the head at every lick, as he did in his replies to Mr. Rives and Mr. Archer in the debate on the first veto message: as shown in the preceding chapter.

The movement went on: Mr. Tyler fell into it: the new party germinated, microscopically small; but potent in the President's veto power. A national bank was the touchstone; and that involved a courtship with the democracy—a breach with the whigs. The democracy rejoiced, and patted Mr. Tyler on the shoulder—even those who despised the new party: for they deemed it fair to avail themselves of a treachery of which they were not the authors; and felt it to be a retributive justice to deprive the whigs of the fruits of a victory which they had won by log-cabin, coonskin, and hard cider tactics; and especially to effect the deprivation in the person of one whom they had taken from the democratic camp, and set up against his old friends—the more annoying to them because he could tell of their supposed misdeeds when he was one of them. To break their heads with such a stick had retribution in it, as well as gratification: and Mr. Tyler was greatly extolled. To the whigs, it was a galling and mortifying desertion, and ruinous besides. A national bank was their life—the vital principle—without which they could not live as a party—the power which was to give them power: which was to beat down their adversaries—uphold themselves—and give them the political and the financial control of the Union. To lose it, was to lose the fruits of the election, with the prospect of losing the party itself. Indignation was their pervading feeling; but the stake was too great to be given up in a passion; and policy required the temporizing expedient of conciliation—the proud spirit of Mr. Clay finding it hard to bend to it; but yielding a little at first. The breach with the whigs was resolved on: how to effect it without too much rudeness—without a violence which would show him an aggressor as well as a deserter—was the difficulty; and indirect methods were taken to effect it. Newspapers in his interest—the *Madisonian* at Washington and *Herald* at New York—vituperated the whig party, and even his cabinet ministers. Slights and neglects were put upon those ministers: the bank question was to complete the breach; but only after a long management which should have the appearance of keeping faith with the whigs, and throwing the blame of the breach upon them. This brings us to the point of commencing the history of the second fiscal bank bill, ending with a second veto, and an open rupture between the President and the whigs.

The beginning of the second bill was laid in the death of the first one; as the seed of a separation from his cabinet was planted in the same place. The first veto message, in rejecting one bill, gave promise to accept another, and even defined the kind of bill which the President could approve: this was encouraging to the whigs. But that first veto was resolved upon, and the message for it drawn, without consultation with his cabinet—without reference to them; and without their knowledge—except from hearsay and accident. They first got wind of it in street rumor, and in paragraphs in the *Madisonian*, and in letters to the *New York Herald*: and got the first knowledge of it from coming in upon the President while he was drawing it. This was a great slight to his cabinet, and very unaccountable to ministers who, only two short months before, had been solicited to remain in their places—had been saluted with expressions of confidence; and cheered with the declaration that their advice and counsel would be often wanted. They felt the slight of the neglected consultation, as well as the disappointment in the rejected bill; but the President consoled them for the disappointment (saying nothing about the slight) by showing himself ready, and even impatient for another bill. This readiness for another bill is thus related by Mr. Ewing, the Secretary of the Treasury, in his letter of resignation of his office addressed to the President; dated Sept. 11th, 1841:

> "On the morning of the 16th of August I called at your chamber, and found you preparing the first veto message, to be despatched to the Senate. The Secretary of War came in also, and you read a portion of the message to us. He observed that though the veto would create a great sensation in Congress, yet he thought the minds of our friends better prepared for it than they were some days ago, and he hoped it would be calmly received, especially as it did not shut out all hope of a bank. To this you replied, that you really thought that there ought to be no difficulty about it; that you had sufficiently indicated the kind of a bank you would approve, and that Congress might, if they saw fit, pass such a bill in three days."

Mr. Bell, the Secretary of War, referred to in the foregoing statement of Mr. Ewing, thus gives his account of the same interview:

> "I called on the President on official business on the morning of Monday the 16th of August, before the first veto message was sent in. I found him reading the message to the Secretary of the Treasury. He did me the honor to read the material passages to me. Upon reading that part of it which treats of the superior importance and value of the business done by the late Bank of the United States in furnishing exchanges between different States and sections of the Union, I was so strongly impressed with the idea that he meant to intimate that he would have no objection to a bank which should be restricted to dealing in exchanges, that I interrupted him in the reading, and asked if I was to understand (by what he had just read) that he was prepared to give his assent to a bank in the District of Columbia, with offices or agencies in the States, having the privilege, without their assent, to deal in exchanges between them, and in foreign bills. He promptly replied that he thought experience had shown the necessity of such a power in the government. And (after some further remarks favorable to such a bill) expressed the opinion that nothing could be more easy than to pass a bill which would answer all necessary purposes—that it could be done in three days."

Such are the concurrent statements of two of the cabinet; and Mr. Alexander A. Stuart, a member of the House of Representatives from Virginia, thus gives his statement to the same effect in his account of the readiness of the President, amounting to anxiety, for the introduction and passage of a second bill.

> "After the adjournment of the House (on the 16th of August), Mr. Pearce of Maryland (then a representative in Congress, now a senator) called at my boarding-house, and informed me that he was induced to believe that there was still some hope of compromising the difficulties between Congress and the President, by adopting a bank bill on the basis of a proposition which had been submitted by Mr. Bayard (Richard H.) in the Senate, modified so as to leave out the last clause which authorized the conversion of the agencies into offices of discount and deposit on certain contingencies. He produced to me a portion of the Senate journal, containing that proposition, with the obnoxious clause crossed out with ink; and requested me to visit the President and see if we could not adjust the difficulty. At first I declined, but at length yielded to his desire, and promised to do so. About 5 o'clock, I drove to the President's house, but found him engaged with a distinguished *democratic* senator. This I thought rather a bad omen; but I made known my wish for a private audience; which in a few

minutes was granted. This was the first occasion on which I had ventured to approach the President on the subject. I made known to him at once the object of my visit, and expressed the hope that some measure might be adopted to heal the division between himself and the whig party in Congress. I informed him of the existence of the committee to which I referred, and mentioned the names of those who composed it, and relied on their age and known character for prudence and moderation, as the best guarantees of the conciliatory spirit of the whig party in Congress. He seemed to meet me in the proper temper, and expressed the belief that a fair ground of compromise might yet be agreed upon. I then made known what I had heard of his opinions in regard to Mr. Bayard's proposition. He asked me if I had it with me? I replied in the affirmative, and produced the paper, which had been given to me by Mr. Pearce with the clause struck out, as above stated. He read it over carefully, and said it would do, making no objection whatever to the clause in regard to the establishment of agencies in the several States without their assent. But he said the capital was too large, and referred to Mr. Appleton and Mr. Jaudon as authority to prove that ten or fifteen millions would be enough. I objected that it might hereafter be found insufficient; and as the charter had twenty years to run, it might be as well to provide against a contingency which would leave the government dependent on the bank for permission to enlarge the capital; and to obviate the difficulty I suggested the propriety of giving to Congress the power to increase it as the public exigencies should require. To this he assented; and by his direction I made the note on the margin of the paper; 'capital to be 15 millions of dollars—to be increased at the option of Congress when public interests require.' The President then said: 'Now if you will send me this bill I will sign it in twenty-four hours.' (After informing the President that there was a statute in Virginia against establishing agencies of foreign banks in the State, he said), 'This must be provided for:' and he then took the paper and wrote on the margin the following words, which were to come in after the word 'or,' and before the word 'bank' in the first line of the proposition of Mr. Bayard, (the blank line in this paper), 'In case such agencies are forbidden by the laws of the State.' I remonstrated against this addition as unnecessary, and not meeting the objection; but he said: 'Let it stand for the present; I will think about it.'— The President then instructed me to go to Mr. Webster, and have the bill prepared at once; and as I rose to leave him, after cautioning me not to expose him to the charge of dictating to Congress, he held my right hand in his left, and raising his right hand upwards, exclaimed with much feeling: 'Stuart! if you can be instrumental in passing this bill through Congress, I will esteem you the best friend I have on earth.'"

The original paper of Mr. Bayard, here referred to, with the President's autographic emendations upon it, were in the possession of Mr. Benton, and burnt in the conflagration of his house, books and papers, in February, 1855.

These statements from Messrs. Ewing, Bell, and Stuart are enough (though others might be added) to show that Mr. Tyler, at the time that he sent in the first veto message, was in favor of a second bill—open and earnest in his professions for it—impatient for its advent—and ready to sign it within twenty-four hours. The only question is whether these professions were sincere, or only phrases to deceive the whigs—to calm the commotion which raged in their camp—and of which he was well informed—and to avert the storm which was ready to burst upon him; trusting all the while to the chapter of contingencies to swamp the bill in one of the two Houses, or to furnish pretexts for a second veto if it should come back to his hands. The progress of the narrative must solve the problem; and, therefore, let it proceed.

The 18th of August—the day on which Mr. Clay was to have spoken in the Senate on the first veto message, and which subject was then postponed on the motion of Mr. Berrien for reasons which he declined to state— Mr. Tyler had a meeting with his cabinet, in which the provisions of the new bill were discussed, and agreed upon—the two members picked out (one in each House—Mr. Sergeant and Mr. Berrien) to conduct it—the cabinet invited to stand by him (the President) and see that the bill passed. Mr. Ewing gives this account, of this days' work, in his letter of resignation addressed to the President.

"I then said to you, 'I have no doubt that the House having ascertained your views will pass a bill in conformity to them, provided they can be satisfied that it would answer the purposes of the Treasury, and relieve the country.' You then said, 'cannot my cabinet see that this is brought about? You must stand by me in this emergency. Cannot you see that a bill passes Congress such as I can approve without inconsistency?' I declared again my belief that such a bill might be passed. And you then said to me, 'what do you understand to be my opinions? State them: so that I may see that there is no misapprehension about them.' I then said that I understood you to be of opinion that Congress might charter a bank in the District of Columbia, giving it its location here. To this you assented. That they might authorize such bank to establish offices of discount and deposit in the several States, with the assent of the States. To this you replied, 'don't name discounts: they have been the source of the most abominable corruptions, and are wholly unnecessary to enable the bank to discharge its duties to the country and the government.' I observed in reply that I was proposing nothing, but simply endeavoring to state what I had understood to be your opinion as to the powers which Congress might constitutionally confer on a bank; that on that point I stood corrected. I then proceeded to say that I understood you to be of opinion that Congress might authorize such bank to establish agencies in the several States, with power to deal in bills of exchange, without the assent of the States, to which you replied, 'yes, if they be foreign bills, or bills drawn in one State and payable in another. That is all the power necessary for transmitting the public funds and regulating exchanges and the currency.' Mr. Webster then expressed, in strong terms, his opinion that such a charter would answer all just purposes of government and be satisfactory to the people; and declared his preference for it over any which had been proposed, especially as it dispensed with the assent of the States to the creation of an institution necessary for carrying on the fiscal operations of government. He examined it at some length, both as to its constitutionality and its influence on the currency and exchanges, in all which views you expressed your concurrence, desired that such a bill should be introduced, and especially that it should go into the hands of some of your *friends*. To my inquiry whether Mr. Sergeant would be agreeable to you, you replied that he would. You especially requested Mr. Webster and myself to communicate with Messrs. Berrien and Sergeant on the subject, to whom you said you had promised to address a note, but you doubted not that this personal communication would be equally satisfactory. You desired us, also, in communicating with those gentlemen, not to commit you personally, lest, this being recognized as your measure, it might be made a subject of comparison to your prejudice in the course of discussion. You and Mr. Webster then conversed about the particular wording of the 16th fundamental article, containing the grant of power to deal in exchanges, and of the connection in which that grant should be introduced; you also spoke of the name of the institution, desiring that *that* should be changed. To this I objected, as it would probably be made a subject of ridicule, but you insisted that there was much in a name, and this institution ought not to be called a bank. Mr. Webster undertook to adapt it in this particular to your wishes. Mr. Bell then observed to Mr. Webster and myself that we had no time to lose; that if this were not immediately attended to, another bill, less acceptable, might be got up and reported. We replied that we would lose no time. Mr. Webster accordingly called on Messrs. Berrien and Sergeant immediately, and I waited on them by his appointment at 5 o'clock on the same day, and agreed upon the principles of the bill in accordance with your expressed wishes. And I am apprised of the fact, though it did not occur in my presence, that after the bill was drawn up, and before it was reported, it was seen and examined by yourself; that your attention was specially called to the 16th fundamental article: that on full examination you concurred in its provisions: that at the same time its name was so modified as to meet your approbation: and the bill was reported and passed, in all essential particulars, as it was when it came through your hands."

The sixteenth fundamental article, here declared to have been especially examined and approved by the President, was the part of the bill on which he afterwards rested his objections to its approval, and the one that had been previously adjusted to suit him in the interview with Mr. Stuart: Mr. Sergeant, and Mr. Berrien (mentioned as the President's choice to conduct the bill through the two Houses), were the two members that actually did it; and they did it with a celerity which subjected themselves to great censure; but which corresponded with the President's expressed desire to have it back in three days. Every part of the bill was made to suit him. The title, about which he was so solicitous to preserve his consistency, and about which his cabinet was so fearful of incurring ridicule, was also adjusted to his desire. Mr. Bell says of this ticklish point: "A name, he (the President) said, was important. What should it be? Fiscal Institute would do." It was objected to by a member of the cabinet, and Fiscal Bank preferred. He replied, "there was a great deal in a name, and he did not want the word bank to appear in the bill." Finally, Fiscal Corporation was agreed upon. Other members of the cabinet, in their letters of resignation, who were present on the 18th, when the bill was agreed upon, corroborated the statement of Mr. Ewing, in all particulars. Mr. Badger said, "It was then distinctly stated and understood that such an institution (the plan before the cabinet) met the approbation of the President, and was deemed by him free from constitutional objections; that he desired (if Congress should deem it necessary to act upon the subject during the session) that such an institution should be adopted by that body, and that the members of his cabinet should aid in bringing about that result: and Messrs. Webster and Ewing were specially requested by the President to have a communication on the subject with certain members of Congress. In consequence of what passed at this meeting I saw such friends in Congress as I deemed it proper to approach, and urged upon them the passage of a bill to establish such an institution (the one agreed upon), assuring them that I did not doubt it would receive the approbation of the President. Mr. Bell is full and particular in his statement, and especially on the point of constitutionality in the 16th fundamental article—the reference to Mr. Webster on that point—his affirmative opinion, and the concurrence of the President in it. A part of the statement is here given—enough for the purpose."

> "The President then gave the outline of such a bank, or fiscal institution, as he thought he could sanction. It was to be in the District of Columbia, to have the privilege of issuing its own notes, receive moneys on deposit, and to deal in bills of exchange between the States, and between the United States and foreign states. But he wished to have the opinion of his cabinet upon it. His own consistency and reputation must be looked to. He considered his cabinet his friends, who must stand by and defend whatever he did upon the subject. He appealed particularly to Mr. Webster, for his opinion on the point of consistency; and whether there was not a clear distinction between the old bank of the United States—a bank of discount and deposit—and the one he now thought of proposing; and whether the constitutional question was not different. He reminded us that in all his former speeches and reports, he had taken the ground that Congress had no constitutional power to charter a bank which had the power of local discount. Mr. Webster pointed out the distinction between the two plans, which appeared to be satisfactory to him."

On the point of having himself understood, and all chance for misunderstanding obviated, the President was very particular, and requested Mr. Ewing to repeat what he (the President) had said. Mr. Ewing did so; and having at one point deviated from the President's understanding, he was stopped—corrected—set right; and then allowed to go on to the end. Mr. Bell's own words must tell the rest.

> "The President said he was then understood. He requested Mr. Webster particularly to communicate with the gentlemen (Messrs. Sergeant and Berrien), who had waited upon him that morning, and to let them know the conclusions to which he had come. He also requested Mr. Ewing to aid in getting the subject properly before Congress. He requested that they would take care not to commit him by what they said to members of Congress, to any intention to dictate to Congress. They might express their confidence and belief that such a bill as had just been agreed upon would receive his sanction; but it should be as matter of inference from his veto message and his general views. He thought he might request that the measure should be put into the hands of some friend of his own upon whom he could rely.

Mr. Sergeant was named, and he expressed himself satisfied that he should have charge of it. He also expressed a wish to see the bill before it was presented to the House, if it could be so managed."

Thus instructed and equipped, the members of the cabinet went forth as requested, and had such success in preparing a majority of the members of each House for the reception of this Fiscal Corporation bill, and for its acceptance also that it was taken up to the exclusion of all business, hurried along, and passed incontinently—as shown in the public history of the bill in the preceding chapter; and with such disregard of decent appearances, as drew upon the President's two conductors of the bill (Messrs. Sergeant and Berrien) much censure at the time—to be vetoed, like the first; and upon objections to that 16th fundamental rule, which had been the subject of such careful consideration—of autographic correction—clear understanding—and solemn ratification. And here the opportunity occurs, and the occasion requires, the correction of a misapprehension into which senators fell (and to the prejudice of Mr. Berrien), the day he disappointed the public and the Senate in putting off the debate on the first veto message, and taking up the bankrupt bill. He declined to give a reason for that motion, and suspicion assigned it to an imperious requisition on the part of the senators who had taken the bankrupt act to their bosoms, and who held the fate of Mr. Clay's leading measures in their hands. It was afterwards known that this was a mistake, and that this postponement, as well as the similar one the day before, were both yielded to conciliate Mr. Tyler—to save him from irritation (for he had a nervous terror of Mr. Clay's impending speech) while the new bill was in process of concoction. This process was commenced on the 16th of August, continued on the 17th, and concluded on the 18th. Mr. Clay consented to the postponement of his anti-veto speech both on the 17th and on the 18th, not to disturb this concoction; and spoke on the 19th—being the day after the prepared bill had been completed, and confided to its sponsors in the House and the Senate. All this is derived from Mr. Alexander A. Stuart's subsequent publication, to comprehend which fully, his account of his connection with the subject must be taken up from the moment of his leaving the President's house, that night of the 16th; and premising, that the whig joint committee of which he speaks, was a standing little body of eminent whigs, whose business it was to fix up measures for the action of the whole party in Congress. With this preliminary view, the important statement of Mr. Stuart will be given.

"Upon leaving the President, I took a hack, and drove immediately to Mr. Webster's lodgings, which were at the opposite end of the city; but, unfortunately he was not at home. I then returned to my boarding-house, where I told what had transpired to my messmates, Mr. Summers, and others. After tea I went to the meeting of the joint committee, of which I have already spoken. I there communicated to Mr. Sergeant, before the committee was called to order, what had occurred between the President and myself. When the committee was first organized there was a good deal of excitement, and difference of opinion; and an animated debate ensued on various propositions which were submitted. Finally I was invited by Mr. Sergeant to state to the committee what had passed between the President and myself; which I did, accompanied by such remarks as I thought would have a tendency to allay excitement, and lead to wise and dispassionate conclusions. After much deliberation, the committee concluded to recommend to the whig party, in both Houses of Congress, to accede to the President's views. A difficulty was then suggested, that the veto message had been made the order of the day at noon, and Mr. Clay had the floor; and it was supposed that the debate might possibly assume such a character as to defeat our purposes of conciliation. Mr. Mangum at once pledged himself that Mr. Clay should offer no obstacle to the adjustment of our difficulties; and engaged to obtain his assent to the postponement of the orders of the day, until we should have an opportunity of reporting to a general meeting of the whig party, and ascertaining whether they would be willing to accept a bank on the basis agreed on by Mr. Tyler and myself—with this understanding the committee adjourned. On the next day (17th of August) Mr. Mangum, with Mr. Clay's assent, moved the postponement of the discussion of the veto, and it was agreed to (see Senate Journal, p. 170): and on the 18th of August the subject was again, with Mr. Clay's concurrence, postponed, on the motion of Mr. Berrien. (Senate Journal, p. 173.) During this time the whigs held their general meeting, and agreed to adopt a bill on the President's plan; and Mr. Sergeant and Mr. Berrien were requested to see that it was properly drawn; and, if necessary, to seek an interview with the President to be certain that there was no misunderstanding as to his opinions. From this statement, confirmed by the journals of the Senate, it will be seen with how much truth Mr. Tyler has charged Mr. Clay with an intolerant and dictatorial spirit, and a settled purpose to embarrass his administration. So far from such being the fact, I state upon my own personal knowledge, that Mr. Clay made every sacrifice consistent with honor and patriotism, to avoid a rupture with Mr. Tyler. The result of the labors of Messrs. Sergeant and Berrien, was the second bank bill, which these distinguished jurists supposed to be in conformity with the President's views."

From this array of testimony it would seem certain that the President was sincerely in favor of passing this second bill: but this account has a *per contra* side to it; and it is necessary to give the signs and facts on the other side which show him against it from the beginning. These items are:—1. The letters in the *New York Herald*, which, from the accuracy with which they told beforehand what the President was to do, had acquired a credit not to be despised; and which foreshadowed the veto, lauding the President and vituperating his cabinet. 2. A sinister rumor to that effect circulating in the city, and countenanced by the new friends who were intimate with the President. 3. The concourse of these at his house. 4. The bitter opposition to it from the same persons in the House and the Senate; a circumstance on which Mr. Clay often remarked in debate, with a significant implication. 5. What happened to Mr. Bell; and which was this: on the 17th day of August Mr. Tyler requested him to make up a statement from the operations of the war department (its receipts and disbursements) to show the advantage of such a bank as they had agreed upon, and to be used as an argument for it. Mr. Bell complied with alacrity, and carried the statement to the President himself the same evening—expecting to be thanked for his zeal and activity. Quite the contrary. "He received the statements which I gave him (writes Mr. Bell) with manifest indifference, and alarmed me by remarking that he began to doubt whether he would give his assent (as I understood him) to any bill." 6. What happened to Mr. Webster and Mr. Ewing, and which is thus related by the latter in his letter of resignation to the President: "You asked Mr. Webster and myself each to prepare and present you an argument touching the constitutionality of the bill (as agreed upon); and before those arguments could be prepared and read by you, you declared, as I heard and believe, to gentlemen, members of the House, that you would cut off your right hand rather than approve it." 7. What passed between Mr. Wise and Mr. Thompson of Indiana in the debate on the veto of this bill, and which thus appears on the Congress Register: "Mr. Wise rose and said, that he had *always* felt perfectly assured that the President would not sign a bank: that if he had been waked up at any hour of the night he would have declared his opposition to a bank." To which Mr. Thompson: "Then why not tell us so at once? Why all this subterfuge and prevarication—this disingenuous and almost criminal concealment? What labor, care, and anxiety he would have saved us." 8. Rumors that Mr. Tyler was endeavoring to defeat the bill while on its passage. 9. Proof *point blanc* to that effect. As this is a most responsible allegation, it requires a clear statement and exact proof; and they shall both be given. On the 25th of August, after the bill had passed the House and was still before the Senate, Mr. Webster wrote a letter to Messrs. Choate and Bates (the two senators from Massachusetts) in which, speaking in the interest of the President, and of his personal knowledge, he informed them that the President had seen the rapid progress of the bill in the House with regret, and wished it might have been postponed;—and advised the whigs to press it no further; and justified this change in the President on Mr. Botts' letter, which had just appeared. This is the allegation, and here is the proof in the letter itself—afterwards furnished for publication by Mr. Webster to the editors of the *Madisonian*:

"GENTLEMEN:—As you spoke last evening of the general policy of the whigs, under the present posture of affairs, relative to the bank bill, I am willing to place you in full possession of my opinion on that subject.

"It is not necessary to go further back, into the history of the past, than the introduction of the present measure into the House of Representatives.

"That introduction took place, within two or three days, after the President's disapproval of the former bill; and I have not the slightest doubt that it was honestly and fairly intended as a measure likely to meet the President's approbation. I do not believe that one in fifty of the whigs had any sinister design whatever, if there was an individual who had such design.

"But I know that the President had been greatly troubled, in regard to the former bill, being desirous, on one hand, to meet the wishes of his friends, if he could, and on the other, to do justice to his own opinions.

"Having returned this first bill with objections, a new one was presented in the House, and appeared to be making rapid progress.

"*I know the President regretted this, and wished the whole subject might have been postponed.* At the same time, I believed he was disposed to consider calmly and conscientiously whatever other measure might be presented to him. But in the mean time Mr. Botts' very extraordinary letter made its appearance. Mr. Botts is a whig of eminence and influence in our ranks. I need not recall to your mind the contents of the letter. It is enough to say, that it purported that the whigs designed to circumvent their own President, to 'head him' as the expression was and to place him in a condition of embarrassment. From that moment, I felt that it was the duty of the whigs to forbear from pressing the bank bill further, at the present time. I thought it was but just in them to give decisive proof that they entertained no such purpose, as seemed to be imputed to them. And since there was reason to believe, that the President would be glad of time, for information and reflection, before being called on to form an opinion on another plan for a bank—a plan somewhat new to the country—I thought his known wishes ought to be complied with. I think so still. I think this is a course, just to the President, and wise on behalf of the whig party. *A decisive rebuke ought, in my judgment, to be given to the intimation, from whatever quarter, of a disposition among the whigs to embarrass the President.* This is the main ground of my opinion; and such a rebuke, I think, would be found in the general resolution of the party to postpone further proceedings on the subject to the next session, now only a little more than three months off.

"The session has been fruitful of important acts.—The wants of the Treasury have been supplied; provisions have been made for fortifications, and for the navy; the repeal of the sub-treasury has passed; the bankrupt bill, that great measure of justice and benevolence, has been carried through; and the land bill seems about to receive the sanction of Congress.

"In all these measures, forming a mass of legislation, more important, I will venture to say, than all the proceedings of Congress for many years past, the President has cordially concurred.

"I agree, that the currency question is, nevertheless, the great question before the country; but considering what has already been accomplished, in regard to other things; considering the difference of opinion which exists upon this remaining one; and, considering, especially, that it is the duty of the whigs effectually to repel and put down any supposition, that they are endeavoring to put the President in a condition, in which he must act under restraint or embarrassment, I am fully and entirely persuaded, that the bank subject should be postponed to the next session. I am gentlemen, your friend and obedient servant. (Signed, Daniel Webster, and addressed to Messrs. Choate and Bates, senators from Massachusetts, and dated, August 25th, 1841.)"

This is the proof, and leaves it indisputable that the President undertook to defeat his own bill. No more can be said on that point. The only point open to remark, and subject to examination, is the reason given by Mr. Webster for this conduct in the President; and this reason is found in Mr. Botts' letter—which had just made its appearance. That letter might be annoyance—might be offensive—might excite resentment: but it could not change a constitutional opinion, or reverse a state policy, or justify a President in breaking his word to his cabinet and to the party that had elected him. It required a deeper reason to work such results; and the key to that reason is found in the tack taken in the first eight or nine days of the session to form a third party, breaking with the whigs, settling back on the democracy, and making the bank veto the point of rupture with one, the cement with the other, the rallying points of the recruits, and the corner-stone of the infant Tyler party. That was the reason: and all the temporizing and double-dealing—pushing the bill forward with one hand, and pulling back with the other—were nothing but expedients to avert or appease the storm that was brewing, and to get through the tempest of his own raising with as little damage to himself as possible. The only quotable part of this letter was the phrase, "*Head Captain Tyler, or die:*" a phrase quoted by the public to be laughed at—by Mr. Webster, to justify Mr. Tyler's attempt to defeat his own bill, so solemnly prepared and sent to the whigs, with a promise to sign it in twenty-four hours if they would pass it. The phrase was fair though it presented a ridiculous image. This "heading," applied to a person signifies to check, or restrain; applied to animals (which is its common use in the South and the West) is, to turn one round which is running the wrong way, and make it go back to the right place. Taken in either sense, the phrase is justifiable, and could only mean checking Mr. Tyler in his progress to the new party, and turning him back to the party that elected him Vice-president. As for the "dying," that could imply no killing of persons, nor any death of any kind to "Captain Tyler," but only the political death of the whigs if their President left them. All this Mr. Webster knew very well, for he was a good philologist, and knew the meaning of words. He was also a good lawyer, and knew that an odious meaning must be given to an innocent word when it is intended to make it offensive. The phrase was, therefore, made to signify a design to circumvent the President with a view to embarrass him—Mr. Clay being the person intended at the back of Mr. Botts in this supposed circumvention and embarrassment. But circumvent was not the word of the letter, nor its synonyme; and is a word always used in an evil sense—implying imposition, stratagem, cheat, deceit, fraud. The word "heading" has no such meaning: and thus the imputed offence, gratuitously assumed, makes its exit for want of verity. Embarrassment is the next part of the offence, and its crowning part, and fails like the other. Mr. Clay had no such design. That is proved by Mr. Stuart, and by his own conduct—twice putting off his speech—holding in his proud spirit until chafed by Mr. Rives—then mollifying indignant language with some expressions of former regard to Mr. Tyler. He had no design or object in embarrassing him. No whig had. And they all had a life and death interest (political) in conciliating him, and getting him to sign: and did their best to do so. The only design was to get him to sign his own bill—the fiscal corporation bill—which he had fixed up himself, title and all—sent out his cabinet to press upon Congress—and desired to have it back in three days, that he might sign it in twenty-four hours. The only solution is, that he did not expect it to come back—that he counted on getting some whigs turned against it, as tried without avail on Messrs. Choate and Bates; and that he could appease the whig storm by sending in the bill, and escape the performance of his promise by getting it defeated. This is the only solution; and the fact is that he would have signed no bank bill, under any name, after the eighth or ninth day of the session—from the day that he gave into the scheme for the third party, himself its head, and settling back upon his *ci-devant* democratic character. From that day a national bank of any kind was the Jonas of his political ship—to be thrown overboard to save the vessel and crew.

And this is the secret history of the birth, life and death of the second fiscal bank, called fiscal corporation—doomed from the first to be vetoed—brought forward to appease a whig storm—sometimes to be postponed—commended to the nursing care of some—consigned to the strangling arts of others: but doomed to be vetoed when it came to the point as being the corner-stone in the edifice of the new party, and the democratic baptismal regeneration of Mr. Tyler himself.

CHAPTER LXXXIII.

THE VETO MESSAGE HISSED IN THE SENATE GALLERIES.

The Senate chamber, and its galleries, were crowded to their utmost capacity to hear the reading of the veto message, and to witness the proceedings to which it would give rise. The moment the reading was finished hisses broke forth, followed by applauses. Both were breaches of order, and contempts of the Senate; but the hisses most so, as being contemptuous in themselves, independent of the rule which forbids them, and as being also the causes of the applauses, which are only contemptuous by virtue of the rule which forbids manifestations of satisfaction as well as of dissatisfaction at any thing done in the Senate: and because a right to applaud would involve a right to judge; and, by implication, to condemn as well as to approve. The President of the Senate heard a disturbance, and gave the raps on the table to restore order: but Mr. Benton, who was on the look-out for the outrage, was determined that it should not go off with raps upon the table: he thought there ought to be raps on the offenders, and immediately stood up and addressed the Chair.

> "Mr. President, there were hisses here, at the reading of the presidential message. I heard them, sir, and I feel indignant that the American President shall be insulted. I have been insulted by the hisses of ruffians in this gallery, when opposing the old Bank of the United States. While I am here, the President shall never be insulted by hisses in this hall. I ask for no such thing as clearing the galleries, but let those who have made the disturbance be pointed out to the sergeant-at-arms, and be turned out from the galleries. Those who have dared to insult our form of government—for in insulting this message they have insulted the President and our form of government—those ruffians who would not have dared to insult the King, surrounded by his guard, have dared to insult the American President in the American Senate; and I move that the sergeant-at-arms be directed to take them into custody."

This motion of Mr. Benton was opposed by several senators, some because they did not hear the disturbance, some because it was balanced, being as much clapping as hissing; some because they were in doubt about the power to punish for a contempt; and some from an amiable indisposition to disturb the people who had disturbed the Senate, and who had only yielded to an ebullition of feeling. This sort of temporizing with an outrage to the Senate only stimulated Mr. Benton to persevere in his motion; which he did until the object was accomplished. The Register of Debates shows the following remarks and replies; which are given here to show the value of perseverance in such a case, and to do justice to the Senate which protected itself:

> "Mr. RIVES regretted that any disturbance had taken place. He doubted not but the senator thought he heard it, but must say, in all sincerity, he did not hear the hiss. At all events, it was so slight and of short duration, that the majority of the Senate scarcely heard it. He hoped that no proceedings of this kind would take place, and that this manifestation of disturbance, when so deep an interest was felt, and which was so immediately quieted, would be passed over. The general opinion of the senators around him was, that the honorable senator was mistaken.

> "Mr. BENTON. I am not mistaken— I am not.

> "Mr. RIVES. He hoped they would pass it by, as one of those little ebullitions of excitement which were unavoidable, and which was not offered to insult this body, or the President of the United States.

> "Mr. BENTON heard the hisses, and heard them distinctly; if a doubt was raised on it, he would bring the matter to a question of fact, 'true or not true.' No man should doubt whether he heard them or not. He came here this day prepared to see the American President insulted by bank bullies; and he told his friends that it had been done, and that they never could proceed in action on a bank, when the American Senate would not be insulted, either by hissing on one side, or clapping on the other. He told them, if it was done, as sure as the American President should be insulted this day, by bank ruffians, just so sure he should rise

in his place and move to have those disturbers of the honor and dignity of the Senate brought to the bar of the Senate. He would not move to clear the galleries, for a thousand orderly people were there, who were not to be turned out for the disturbance of a few ruffians. He would tell the senator from Virginia that he (the senator) should hang no doubt on his declaration; and if it were doubted, he would appeal to senators near him. [Mr. WALKER. I will answer, most directly, that I heard it, and I believe the same bully is going on now.] A national bank (continued Mr. B.) is not, as yet, our master, and shall not be; and he would undertake to vindicate the honor of the Senate, from the outrages perpetrated on it by the myrmidons of a national bank. Were the slaves of a national bank to have the privilege of insulting the Senate, just as often as a vote passed contrary to their wishes? It was an audacity that must be checked—and checked before they went with arms in their hands to fire on those who gave votes contrary to their wishes, or assassinate them on their way home. He put the whole at defiance—the entire bank, and its myrmidons.

"Mr. PRESTON said if any thing had occurred in the gallery out of order, it should be strictly inquired into and punished. He himself did not hear the manifestations of disapprobation, alluded to by the senators on the other side; but it was sufficient for him that the senators heard it, or supposed that they heard it. [Mr. BENTON. We did not *suppose* we heard it; we knew it.] In this case (continued Mr. P.), a formal investigation should take place. It was a contempt of the Senate, and, as a member of the Senate, he desired to see an investigation— to see the charge fixed on some person, and if properly sustained, to see punishment awarded. Manifestations of praise or censure were eminently wrong, and eminently dangerous; and it was due to every member of the Senate that they should preserve the dignity of the body by checking it. He hoped, therefore, if a formal motion was made, it would be discovered who had caused the disturbance, and that they would be properly punished.

"Mr. BUCHANAN said this was a very solemn and momentous occasion, which would form a crisis, perhaps, in the politics of the country; and he should hope, as he believed that every American citizen present in the galleries would feel the importance of this crisis, and feel deeply sensible of the high character to which every man, blessed with birth in this free country, should aim. He heard, distinctly heard, the hiss referred to by the senator from Missouri [Mr. BENTON], but he was bound to say it was not loud and prolonged, but was arrested in a moment, he believed partly from the senator rising, and partly from the good sense and good feeling of the people in the galleries. Under these circumstances, as it only commenced and did not proceed, if he had the power of persuasion, he would ask the senator from Missouri to withdraw his motion.

"[Mr. BENTON. I never will, so help me God.]

"He thought it better, far better, that they proceed to the important business before them, under the consideration that they should not be disturbed hereafter; and if they were, he would go as far as the senator from Missouri in immediately arresting it. He would much rather go on with the business in hand.

"Mr. LINN reminded the Senate that when the bank bill had passed the Senate there was a loud manifestation of approbation in the gallery, of which no notice was taken. He believed on the present occasion there was approbation as well as hisses; but both were instantly suppressed. He had distinctly heard both. No doubt it was the promptness with which his colleague had got up to check the disturbance, which had prevented it from going further. He had no doubt some law ought to be passed making it punishable to commit any outrage of this kind on either House of Congress.

"Mr. MERRICK thought with the senator from Pennsylvania, that this was a very solemn occasion. There had been tokens of assent and dissent. The President of the Senate at the moment rapped very hard till order was restored. The disorder was but momentary. He trusted some allowance would be made for the excitement so natural on the occasion.

"Mr. KING suggested the difficulty that might arise out of pursuing the matter further. He had witnessed something of the kind once before, and when the offender was brought to the bar, great embarrassment was created by not knowing how to get rid of him. He thought it would be better to pass over the matter and proceed to the consideration of the message, or to the appointment of a time for its consideration.

"The CHAIR explained that having heard some noise, without considering whether it was approbation or disapprobation, he had called the Senate to order; but could not say that he had or had not heard hisses.

"Mr. RIVES explained that he did not mean to say the senator from Missouri did not hear the hisses, but that he himself did not hear them, and he believed many gentlemen around him did not hear any. But as the senator from Missouri had avowedly come prepared to hear them, no doubt he did, more sensitively than others. He would ask the senator to be satisfied with the crush which the mother of monsters had got, and not to bear too hard on the solitary bank ruffian, to use his own expression, who had disapproved of the monster's fate. He hoped the senator would withdraw the motion.

"Mr. LINN observed that the senator from Virginia, by his own remarks, doubting that there were any hisses, had forced the senator from Missouri to persist in having the proof. However, he now understood that point was settled; and the object being accomplished, he hoped his colleague would withdraw the motion.

"Mr. PRESTON again expressed his concurrence in the propriety of the motion, and hoped effectual steps would be taken to prevent the recurrence of such a scene.

"Mr. ALLEN made some appropriate remarks, and concluded by stating that he understood the offender was in custody, and expressed his sorrow for having done what he was not at the time aware was an offence; as, therefore, all the ends had been accomplished which his friend had in view when he refused to withdraw his motion, he hoped he would now withdraw it.

"Mr. WALKER said, when the senator from Missouri [Mr. BENTON] pledged himself not to withdraw his motion to arrest the individual who had insulted the Senate and the country by hissing the message of the President of the United States, that pledge arose from the doubt expressed by the senator from Virginia [Mr. RIVES] whether the hissing had taken place. That doubt was now solved. When the senator from Missouri appealed to his friends as to the truth of the fact stated by him, he [Mr. WALKER] had risen, and pointed to that portion of the gallery from which the hissing proceeded. Our assistant Sergeant-at-Arms had proceeded to that quarter of the gallery designated by him [Mr. W.], and this officer had now in his possession one of the offenders, who acknowledged his indecent conduct, and who was prepared to point out many of those who had joined him. The object of the senator was, therefore, now accomplished; the fact of the indecorum was established, and the offender, as moved by the senator from Missouri, was now in custody. This, Mr. W. hoped, would be sufficient punishment, especially as Mr. W. understood the offender expressed his penitence for the act, as one of sudden impulse. As, then, the formal trial of this individual would occupy much time, Mr. W. hoped the matter would be dropped here, and let us proceed, as required by the Constitution, to consider the message of the President returning the bank bill, with his objections. This message, Mr. W. said, he regarded as the most important which ever emanated from an American President, and under circumstances the most solemn and imposing. The President, in perfect and glorious consistency with a long life of usefulness and honor, has placed his veto upon the charter of a National Bank, and, Mr. W. said, his heart was too full of gratitude to the Giver of all good for this salvation of the country, and rescue of the Constitution, to engage in the business of inflicting punishment upon an individual, said to be respectable, and who had in part atoned for his offence by the expression of his repentance. Let him go, then, and sin no more, and let us proceed to the consideration of that Veto Message, which he, Mr. W. had confidently predicted at the very commencement of this session, and recorded that opinion at its date in the journals of the day. Many then doubted the correctness of this prediction, but, he, Mr. W. whilst he stated at the time that he was not authorized to speak for the President of the United States, based his conviction upon his knowledge of Mr. TYLER as a man and a senator, and upon his long and consistent opposition to the creation of any such bank, as was now proposed to be established.

"Mr. BENTON said he had been informed by one of the officers of the Senate [Mr. BEALE] that one of the persons who made the disorder in the gallery had been seized by him, and was now in custody and in the room of the Sergeant-at-Arms. This the officers had very properly done of their own motion, and without waiting for the Senate's order. They had done their duty, and his motion had thus been executed. His motion was to seize the disorderly, and bring them to the bar of the Senate. One had been seized; he was in custody in an adjoining room; and if he was still acting contemptuously to the Senate, he should move to bring him to the bar; but that was not the case. He was penitent and contrite. He expressed his sorrow for what he had done, and said he had acted without ill design, and from no feelings of contempt to the President or Senate. Under these circumstances, all was accomplished that his motion intended. The man is in custody and repentant. This is sufficient. Let him be discharged, and there is an end of the affair. His motion now was that the President direct him to be discharged. Mr. B. said he had acted from reflection, and not from impulse, in this whole affair. He expected the President to be insulted: it was incident to the legislation on national bank charters. When they were on the carpet, the Senate, the President, and the American people must all be insulted if the bank myrmidons are disappointed. He told his family before he left home, that the Senate and the President would be insulted by hisses in the gallery this day, and that he would not let it pass—that it would be an insult, not merely to the President and Senate, but to the whole American people, and to their form of government—and that it should not pass. He came here determined to nip this business in the bud—and to prevent an insult to the President in this chamber from being made a precedent for it elsewhere. We all know the insolence of the national bank party—we know the insolence of their myrmidons—we know that President Tyler, who has signed this veto message, is subject to their insults—beginning here, and following him wherever he goes. He [Mr. B.] was determined to protect him here, and, in doing so, to set the example which would be elsewhere followed. He repeated: an insult to the President for an official act, was not an insult to the man, but to the whole American people, and to their form of government. Would these bank myrmidons insult a king, surrounded by his guards? Not at all. Then they should not insult an American President with impunity whenever he was present. In the Senate or out of it, he would defend the President from personal outrage and indignity. As to the numerous and respectable auditory now present, his motion did not reach them. He had not moved to clear the galleries; for that would send out the respectable audience, who had conducted themselves with propriety. The rule of order was "*to clear the galleries*;" but he had purposely avoided that motion, because the disorder came from a few, and the respectable part of the audience ought not to suffer for an offence in which they had no share. Mr. B. said the man being in custody, his motion was executed and superseded; its object was accomplished, and, he being contrite, he would move to discharge him.

"The President of the Senate ordered him to be discharged."

CHAPTER LXXXIV.

RESIGNATION OF MR. TYLER'S CABINET.

This event, with the exception of Mr. Webster who was prevailed upon to remain, took place on the 11th day of September—being two days after the second veto message—the one on the fiscal corporation bill—had been sent to the House of Representatives. It was a thing to take place in consequence of the President's conduct in relation to that bill; but the immediate cause, or rather, the circumstance which gave impulse to the other causes, was the appearance of a letter from Washington city in the New York Herald in which the cabinet was much vituperated—accused of remaining in their places contrary to the will of the President, and in spite of the neglects and slights which he put upon them with a view to make them resign. Appearing in that paper, which had come to be considered as the familiar of the President, and the part in relation to the slights and neglects being felt to be true, it could not escape the serious attention of those to whom it referred. But there was something else in it which seemed to carry its origin directly to the President himself. There was an account of a cabinet meeting in it, in which things were told which were strictly confidential between the President and his ministers—which had actually occurred; and which no one but themselves or the President could have communicated. They conferred together: the conviction was unanimous that the President had licensed this communication: and this circumstance authorized them to consider the whole letter as his, of course by subaltern hand. To this letter Mr. Ewing alluded in his letter of resignation when he said to the President: "The very secrets of our cabinet councils made their appearance in an infamous paper, printed in a neighboring city, the columns of which were daily charged with flattery of yourself and foul abuse of your cabinet." There was no exception in the letter in favor of any one. All were equally included: all took their resolutions together (Mr. Granger excepted who was not present), and determined to resign at once, and in a body, and to publish their reasons—the circumstances under which they acted justifying, in their opinion, this abrupt and unceremonious separation from their chief. All carried this resolve into effect, except Mr. Webster, who was induced to reconsider his determination, and to remain. The reasons for this act should be given, so far as they are essential, in the words of the retiring ministers themselves: and, accordingly here they are; and first from Mr. Ewing:

> "This bill, framed and fashioned according to your own suggestions, in the initiation of which I and another member of your cabinet were made by you the agents and negotiators, was passed by large majorities through the two Houses of Congress, and sent to you, and you rejected it. Important as was the part which I had taken, at your request, in the origination of this bill, and deeply as I was committed for your action upon it, you never consulted me on the subject of the veto message. You did not even refer to it in conversation, and the first notice I had of its contents was derived from rumor. And to me, at least, you have done nothing to wipe away the personal indignity arising out of the act. I gathered, it is true, from your conversation, shortly after the bill had passed the House, that you had a strong purpose to reject it; but nothing was said like softening or apology to me, either in reference to myself or to those with whom I had communicated at your request, and who had acted themselves and induced the two Houses to act upon the faith of that communication. And, strange as it may seem, the veto message attacks in an especial manner the very provisions which were inserted at your request; and even the name of the corporation, which was not only agreed to by you, but especially changed to meet your expressed wishes, is made the subject of your criticism. Different men might view this transaction in different points of light, but, under these circumstances, as a matter of personal honor, it would be hard for me to remain of your counsel, to seal my lips and leave unexplained and undisclosed where lies in this transaction the departure from straightforwardness and candor. So far indeed from admitting the encouragement which you gave to this bill in its inception, and explaining and excusing your sudden and violent hostility towards it, you throw into your veto message an interrogatory equivalent to an assertion that it was such a bill as you had already declared could not receive your sanction. Such is the obvious effect of the first interrogatory clause on the second page. It has all the force of an assertion without its open fairness. I have met and refuted this, the

necessary inference from your language, in my preceding statement, the correctness of which you I am sure will not call in question."

Of the cause assigned for the President's change in relation to the bill, namely Mr. Botts' letter, Mr. Ewing thus expresses himself:

"And no doubt was thrown out on the subject (veto of the fiscal corporation bill) by you, in my hearing, or within my knowledge, until the letter of Mr. Botts came to your hands. Soon after the reading of that letter, you threw out strong intimations that you would veto the bill if it were not postponed. That letter I did and do most unequivocally condemn, but it did not effect the constitutionality of the bill, or justify you in rejecting it on that ground; it could affect only the expediency of your action; and, whatever you may now believe as to the scruples existing in your mind, in this and in a kindred source there is strong ground to believe they have their origin."

Mr. Badger, Secretary of the Navy:

"At the cabinet meeting held on the 18th of August last (the attorney-general and the postmaster-general being absent), the subject of an exchange bank, or institution, was brought forward by the President himself, and was fully considered. Into the particulars of what passed I do not propose now to enter. It will be sufficient to say that it was then distinctly stated and understood that such an institution met the approbation of the President, and was deemed by him free of constitutional objections; that he desired (if Congress should deem it necessary to act upon the subject during the session) that such an institution should be adopted by that body, and that the members of his cabinet would aid in bringing about that result; and Messrs. Webster and Ewing were specially requested by the President to have a communication upon the subject with certain members of Congress. In consequence of what passed at this meeting, I saw such friends in Congress as I deemed it proper to approach, and urged upon them the passage of a bill to establish such an institution, assuring them that I did not doubt it would receive the approbation of the President. The bill was passed, as the public know, and was met by the veto. Now, if the President, after the meeting of the 18th August, had changed his mind as to the constitutional power of Congress, and had come to doubt or deny what he had admitted in that meeting (which is the most favorable interpretation that can be put upon his conduct), it was, in my opinion, a plain duty on his part to have made known to the gentlemen concerned this change of sentiment—to have offered them an apology for the unpleasant situation in which they were placed by his agency—or, at least, to have softened, by a full explanation of his motives, his intended veto of a measure in promoting the success of which they, at his request, had rendered their assistance. But this the President did not do. Never, from the moment of my leaving his house on the 18th, did he open his lips to me on the subject. It was only from the newspapers, from rumor, from hearsay, I learned that he had denied the constitutionality of the proposed institution, and had made the most solemn asseverations that he would never approve a measure which I knew was suggested by himself, and which had been, at his own instance, introduced into Congress. It is scarcely necessary to say that I have not supposed, and do not now suppose, that a difference merely between the President and his cabinet, either as to the constitutionality or the expediency of a bank, necessarily interposes any obstacles to a full and cordial co-operation between them in the general conduct of his administration; and therefore deeply as I regretted the veto of the first bill, I did not feel myself at liberty to retire on that account from my situation. But the facts attending the initiation and disapproval of the last bill made a case totally different from that— one it is believed without a parallel in the history of our cabinets; presenting, to say nothing more, a measure embraced and then repudiated—efforts prompted and then disowned— services rendered and then treated with scorn or neglect. Such a case required, in my judgment, upon considerations, private and public, that the official relations subsisting between the President and myself should be immediately dissolved."

Mr. BELL, Secretary at War.

"I called to see the President on official business on the morning (Monday, 16th August) before the first veto message was sent in. I found him reading the message to the Secretary of the Treasury. He did me the honor to read the material passages to me. Upon reading that part of it which treats of the superior importance and value of the business done by the late bank of the United States in furnishing exchanges between the different States and sections of the Union, I was so strongly impressed with the idea that he meant to intimate that he would have no objection to a bank which should be restricted in dealing in exchanges, that I interrupted him in the reading, and asked if I was to understand, by what he had just read, that he was prepared to give his assent to a bank in the District of Columbia, with offices or agencies in the States, having the privilege, without their assent, to deal in exchanges between them, and in foreign bills. He promptly replied that he thought experience had shown the necessity of such a power in the government. I could not restrain the immediate expression of my gratification upon hearing this avowal. I said to the President at once, that what I had feared would lead to fatal dissension among our friends, I now regarded as rather fortunate than otherwise; that his veto of the bill then before him (the first one), would lead to the adoption of a much better one. I also congratulated him upon the happy circumstance of the delay which had taken place in sending in his veto message. The heat and violence which might have been expected if the veto had been sent in immediately upon the passage of the bill, would now be avoided. Time had been given for cool reflection, and as the message did not exclude the idea of a bank in some form, no unpleasant consequences would be likely to follow. He expressed his great surprise that there should be so much excitement upon the subject; said that he had had his mind made up on the bill before him from the first, but had delayed his message that there should be time for the excitement to wear off; that nothing could be more easy than to pass a bill which would answer all necessary purposes; that it could be done in three days. The next day, having occasion to see the President again, he requested me to furnish him with such information as the war department afforded of the embarrassments attending the transfer and disbursement of the public revenue to distant points on the frontier, in Florida, &c. He at the same time requested me to draw up a brief statement of my views upon the subject, showing the practical advantages and necessity of such a fiscal institution as he had thought of proposing. Such information as I could hastily collect from the heads of the principal disbursing bureaus of the department I handed to him on the evening of the same day, knowing that time was of the utmost importance in the state in which the question then was. He received the statements I gave him with manifest indifference, and alarmed me by remarking that he began to doubt whether he would give his assent (as I understood him) to any bank."

This was Mr. Bell's first knowledge of the second bill—all got from the President himself, and while he was under nervous apprehension of the storm which was to burst upon him. He goes on to detail the subsequent consultations with his cabinet, and especially with Mr. Webster, as heretofore given; and concludes with expressing the impossibility of his remaining longer in the cabinet.

Mr. CRITTENDEN, the attorney-general, resigned in a brief and general letter, only stating that circumstances chiefly connected with the fiscal agent bills, made it his duty to do so. His reserve was supposed to be induced by the close friendly relation in which he stood with respect to Mr. Clay. Palliation for Mr. Tyler's conduct was attempted to be found by some of his friends in the alleged hostility of Mr. Clay to him, and desire to brow-beat him, and embarrass him. No doubt Mr. Clay was indignant, and justly so, at the first veto, well knowing the cause of it as he showed in his replies to Mr. Rives and Mr. Archer: but that was after the veto. But even then the expression of his indignation was greatly restrained, and he yielded to his friends in twice putting off his speech on that first veto, that he might not disturb Mr. Tyler in his preparation of the second bill. The interest at stake was too great—no less than the loss of the main fruits of the presidential election—for him to break voluntarily with Mr. Tyler. He restrained himself, and only ceased his self-restraint, when temporizing would no longer answer any purpose; and only denounced Mr. Tyler when he knew that he had gone into the embraces of a third party—taken his stand against any national bank as a means of reconciling himself to the democracy—and substituted "*a secret cabal*" (which he stigmatized as "*a kitchen cabinet*") in place of his constitutional advisers.

Two days after the appearance of those letters of resignation, the whole of which came out in the National Intelligencer, Mr. Webster published his reasons for not joining in that act with his colleagues: and justice to him requires this paper to be given in his own words. It is dated September 13th, and addressed to Messrs. Gales and Seaton, the well reliable whig editors in Washington.

> "Lest any misapprehension should exist, as to the reasons which have led me to differ from the course pursued by my late colleagues, I wish to say that I remain in my place, first, because I have seen no sufficient reasons for the dissolution of the late cabinet, by the voluntary act of its own members. I am perfectly persuaded of the absolute necessity of an institution, under the authority of Congress, to aid revenue and financial operations, and to give the country the blessings of a good currency and cheap exchanges. Notwithstanding what has passed, I have confidence that the President will co-operate with the legislature in overcoming all difficulties in the attainment of these objects; and it is to the union of the whig party—by which I mean the whole party, the whig President, the whig Congress, and the whig people—that I look for a realization of our wishes. I can look nowhere else. In the second place, if I had seen reasons to resign my office, I should not have done so, without giving the President reasonable notice, and affording him time to select the hands to which he should confide the delicate and important affairs now pending in this department."

Notwithstanding the tone of this letter, it is entirely certain that Mr. Webster had agreed to go out with his colleagues, and was expected to have done so at the time they sent in their resignations; but, in the mean while, means had been found to effect a change in his determination, probably by disavowing the application of any part of the New York Herald letter to him—certainly (as it appears from his letter) by promising a co-operation in the establishment of a national bank (for that is what was intended by the blessings of a sound currency and cheap exchanges): and also equally certain, from the same letter, that he was made to expect that he would be able to keep all whiggery together—whig President Tyler, whig members of Congress, and whig people, throughout the Union. The belief of these things shows that Mr. Webster was entirely ignorant of the formation of a third party, resting on a democratic basis; and that the President himself was in regular march to the democratic camp. But of all this hereafter.

The reconstruction of his cabinet became the immediate care of the President, and in the course of a month it was accomplished. Mr. Walter Forward, of Pennsylvania, was appointed Secretary of the Treasury; the department of War was offered to Mr. Justice McLean of the Supreme Court of the United States, and upon his refusal to accept the place, it was conferred upon John C. Spencer, Esq., of New York; Mr. Abel P. Upshur, of Virginia, was appointed Secretary of the Navy—Hugh S. Legare, Esq., of South Carolina, Attorney-General—Charles A. Wickliffe, Esq., of Kentucky, Postmaster-General. This cabinet was not of uniform political complexion. Mr. Webster had been permanently of that party which, under whatsoever name, had remained antagonistic to the democracy. Mr. Forward came into public life democratic, and afterwards acted with its antagonists: the same of Mr. Wickliffe and Mr. Spencer: Mr. Upshur a whig, classed with Mr. Calhoun's political friends—Mr. Legare the contrary, and democratic, and distinguished for opposition to nullification, secession, and disunion.

CHAPTER LXXXV.

REPUDIATION OF MR. TYLER BY THE WHIG PARTY: THEIR MANIFESTO: COUNTER MANIFESTO BY MR. CALEB CUSHING.

The conduct of Mr. Tyler in relation to a national bank produced its natural effect upon the party which had elected him—disgust and revolt. In both Houses of Congress individual members boldly denounced and renounced him. He seemed to be crushed there, for his assailants were many and fierce—his defenders few, and feeble. But a more formal act of condemnation, and separation was wanted—and had. On the 11th day of September—the day of the cabinet resignations, and two days after the transmission of the second veto message—the whigs of the two Houses had a formal meeting to consider what they should do in the new, anomalous, and acephalous condition in which they found themselves. The deliberations were conducted with all form. Mr. Senator Dixon of Rhode Island and Mr. Jeremiah Morrow of Ohio—both of them men venerable for age and character—were appointed presidents; and Messrs. Kenneth Rayner of North Carolina, Mr. Christopher Morgan of New York, and Richard W. Thompson of Indiana—all members of the House—were appointed secretaries. Mr. Mangum of North Carolina, then offered two resolutions:

> "1. That it is expedient for the whigs of the Senate and House of Representatives of the United States to publish an address to the people of the United States, containing a succinct exposition of the prominent proceedings of the extra session of Congress, of the measures that have been adopted, and those in which they have failed, and the causes of such failure; together with such other matters as may exhibit truly the condition of the whig party and whig prospects.

> "2. That a committee of three on the part of the Senate, and five on the part of the House, be appointed to prepare such address, and submit it to a meeting of the whigs on Monday morning next, the 13th inst., at half past 8 o'clock."

Both resolutions were unanimously adopted, and Messrs. Berrien of Georgia, Tallmadge of New York, and Smith of Indiana were appointed on the part of the Senate; and Messrs. Everett of Vermont, Mason of Ohio, Kennedy of Maryland, John C. Clark of New York, and Rayner of North Carolina, on the part of the House.

At the appointed time the meeting reassembled, and the committee made their report. Much of it was taken up with views and recommendations in relation to the general policy of the party: it is only of what relates to the repudiation of Mr. Tyler that this history intends to speak: for government with us is a struggle of parties: and it is necessary to know how parties are put up, and put down, in order to understand how the government is managed. An opening paragraph of the address set forth that, for twelve years the whigs had carried on a contest for the regulation of the currency, the equalization of exchanges, the economical administration of the finances, and the advancement of industry—all to be accomplished by means of a national bank—declaring these objects to be misunderstood by no one—and the bank itself held to be secured in the presidential election, and its establishment the main object of the extra session. The address then goes on to tell how these cherished hopes were frustrated:

> "It is with profound and poignant regret that we find ourselves called upon to invoke your attention to this point. Upon the great and leading measure touching this question, our anxious endeavors to respond to the earnest prayer of the nation have been frustrated by an act as unlooked for as it is to be lamented. We grieve to say to you that by the exercise of that power in the constitution which has ever been regarded with suspicion, and often with odium, by the people—a power which we had hoped was never to be exhibited on this subject, by a whig President—we have been defeated in two attempts to create a fiscal agent, which the wants of the country had demonstrated to us, in the most absolute form of proof, to be eminently necessary and proper in the present emergency. Twice have we, with the utmost diligence and deliberation, matured a plan for the collection, safe-keeping and disbursing of the public moneys through the agency of a corporation adapted to that end, and twice has it been our fate to encounter the opposition of the President, through the application of the

veto power. The character of that veto in each case, the circumstances in which it was administered, and the grounds upon which it has met the decided disapprobation of your friends in Congress, are sufficiently apparent in the public documents and the debates relating to it. This subject has acquired a painful interest with us, and will doubtless acquire it with you, from the unhappy developments with which it is accompanied. We are constrained to say, that we find no ground to justify us in the conviction that the veto of the President has been interposed on this question solely upon conscientious and well-considered opinions of constitutional scruple as to his duty in the case presented. On the contrary, too many proofs have been forced upon our observation to leave us free from the apprehension, that the President has permitted himself to be beguiled into an opinion that, by this exhibition of his prerogative, he might be able to divert the policy of his administration into a channel which should lead to new political combinations, and accomplish results which must overthrow the present divisions of party in the country; and finally produce a state of things which those who elected him, at least, have never contemplated. We have seen from an early period of the session, that the whig party did not enjoy the confidence of the President. With mortification we have observed that his associations more sedulously aimed at a free communion with those who have been busy to prostrate our purposes, rather than those whose principles seemed to be most identified with the power by which he was elected. We have reason to believe that he has permitted himself to be approached, counselled and influenced by those who have manifested least interest in the success of whig measures. What were represented to be his opinions and designs have been freely and even insolently put forth in certain portions, and those not the most reputable, of the public press, in a manner that ought to be deemed offensive to his honor, as it certainly was to the feelings of those who were believed to be his friends. In the earnest endeavor manifested by the members of the whig party in Congress to ascertain specifically the President's notions in reference to the details of such a bill relating to a fiscal agent as would be likely to meet his approbation, the frequent changes of his opinion, and the singular want of consistency in his views, have baffled his best friends, and rendered the hope of adjustment with him impossible."

"The plan of an exchange bank, such as was reported after the first veto, the President is understood by more than one member of Congress to whom he expressed his opinion, to have regarded as a favorite measure. It was in view of this opinion, suggested as it is in his first veto, and after using every proper effort to ascertain his precise views upon it, that the committee of the House of Representatives reported their second bill. It made provision for a bank without the privilege of local discounting, and was adapted as closely as possible to that class of mercantile operations which the first veto message describes with approbation, and which that paper specifically illustrates by reference to the 'dealings in the exchanges' of the Bank of the United States in 1833, which the President affirms 'amounted to upwards of one hundred millions of dollars.' Yet this plan, when it was submitted to him, was objected to on a new ground. The last veto has narrowed the question of a bank down to the basis of the sub-treasury scheme, and it is obvious from the opinions of that message that the country is not to expect any thing better than the exploded sub-treasury, or some measure of the same character, from Mr. TYLER. In the midst of all these varieties of opinion, an impenetrable mystery seemed to hang over the whole question. There was no such frank interchange of sentiment as ought to characterize the intercourse of a President and his friends, and the last persons in the government who would seem to have been intrusted with his confidence on those embarrassing topics were the constitutional advisers which the laws had provided for him. In this review of the position into which the late events have thrown the whig party, it is with profound sorrow we look to the course pursued by the President. He has wrested from us one of the best fruits of a long and painful struggle, and the consummation of a glorious victory; he has even perhaps thrown us once more upon the field of political strife, not weakened in numbers, nor shorn of the support of the country, but stripped of the arms which success had placed in our hands, and left again to rely upon that high patriotism which for twelve years sustained us in a conflict of unequalled asperity, and which finally brought us to the fulfilment of those brilliant hopes which he has done so much to destroy."

Having thus shown the loss, by the conduct of the President, of all the main fruits of a great victory after a twelve years' contest, the address goes on to look to the future, and to inquire what is to be the conduct of the party in such unexpected and disastrous circumstances? and the first answer to that inquiry is, to establish a permanent separation of the whig party from Mr. Tyler, and to wash their hands of all accountability for his acts.

"In this state of things, the whigs will naturally look with anxiety to the future, and inquire what are the actual relations between the President and those who brought him into power; and what, in the opinion of their friends in Congress, should be their course hereafter. On both of these questions we feel it to be our duty to address you in perfect frankness and without reserve, but, at the same time, with due respect to others. In regard to the first, we are constrained to say that the President, by the course he has adopted in respect to the application of the veto power to two successive bank charters, each of which there was just reason to believe would meet his approbation; by his withdrawal of confidence from his real friends in Congress and from the members of his cabinet; by his bestowal of it upon others notwithstanding their notorious opposition to leading measures of his administration, has voluntarily separated himself from those by whose exertions and suffrages he was elevated to that office through which he reached his present exalted station. The existence of this unnatural relation is as extraordinary as the annunciation of it is painful and mortifying. What are the consequences and duties which grow out of it? The first consequence is, that those who brought the President into power can be no longer, in any manner or degree, justly held responsible or blamed for the administration of the executive branch of the government; and that the President and his advisers should be exclusively hereafter deemed accountable."

Then comes the consideration of what they are to do? and after inculcating, in the ancient form, the laudable policy of supporting their obnoxious President when he was '*right*,' and opposing him when he was '*wrong*'— phrases repeated by all parties, to be complied with by none—they go on to recommend courage and unity to their discomfited ranks—to promise a new victory at the next election; and with it the establishment of all their measures, crowned by a national bank.

"The conduct of the President has occasioned bitter mortification and deep regret. Shall the party, therefore, yielding to sentiments of despair, abandon its duty, and submit to defeat and disgrace? Far from suffering such dishonorable consequences, the very disappointment which it has unfortunately experienced should serve only to redouble its exertions, and to inspire it with fresh courage to persevere with a spirit unsubdued and a resolution unshaken, until the prosperity of the country is fully re-established, and its liberties firmly secured against all danger from the abuses, encroachments or usurpations of the executive department of the government."

This was the manifesto, so far as it concerns the repudiation of Mr. Tyler, which the whig members of Congress put forth: it was answered (under the name of an address to his constituents) by Mr. Cushing, in what may be called a counter manifesto: for it was on the same subject as the other, and counter to it at all points—especially on the fundamental point of, *which party the President was to belong to!* the manifesto of the whig members assigning him to the democracy—the counter manifesto claiming him for the whigs! In this, Mr. Cushing followed the lead of Mr. Webster in his letter of resignation: and, in fact, the whole of his pleading (for such it was) was an amplification of Mr. Webster's letter to the editors of the National Intelligencer, and of the one to Messrs. Bates and Choate, and of another to Mr. Ketchum, of New York. The first part of the address of Mr. Cushing, is to justify the President for changing his course on the fiscal corporation bill; and this attempted in a thrust at Mr Clay thus:

"A caucus dictatorship has been set up in Congress, which, not satisfied with ruling that body to the extinguishment of individual freedom of opinion, seeks to control the President in his proper sphere of duty, denounces him before you for refusing to surrender his independence and his conscience to its decree, and proposes, through subversion of the fundamental provisions and principles of the constitution, to usurp the command of the government. It is a question, therefore, in fact, not of legislative measures, but of revolution. What is the visible, and the only professed, origin of these extraordinary movements? The whig party in Congress have been extremely desirous to cause a law to be enacted at the late session, incorporating a national bank. Encountering, in the veto of the President, a constitutional obstacle to the enactment of such a law at the late session, a certain portion of the whig party, represented by the caucus dictatorship, proceeds then, in the beginning, to denounce the President. Will you concur in this denunciation of the President?"

This was the accusation, first hinted at by Mr. Rives in the Senate, afterwards obscurely intimated in Mr. Webster's letter to the two Massachusetts senators; and now broadly stated by Mr. Cushing; without, however, naming the imputed dictator; which was, in fact, unnecessary. Every body knew that Mr. Clay was the person intended; with what justice, not to repeat proofs already given, let the single fact answer, that these caucus meetings (for such there were) were all subsequent to Mr. Tyler's change on the bank question! and in consequence of it! and solely with a view to get him back! and that by conciliation until after the second veto. In this thrust at Mr. Clay Mr. Cushing was acting in the interest of Mr. Webster's feelings as well as those of Tyler; for since 1832 Mr. Clay and Mr. Webster had not been amicable, and barely kept in civil relations by friends, who had frequently to interpose to prevent, or compose outbreaks; and even to make in the Senate formal annunciation of reconciliation effected between them. But the design required Mr. Clay to be made the cause of the rejection of the bank bills; and also required him to be crippled as the leader of the anti-administration whigs. In this view Mr. Cushing resumes:

"When Lord Grenville broke up the whig party of England, in 1807, by the unseasonable pressure of some great question, and its consequent loss, 'Why,' said Sheridan, 'did they not put it off as Fox did? I have heard of men running their heads against a wall; but this is the first time I ever heard of men building a wall, and squaring it, and clamping it, for the express purpose of knocking out their brains against it.' This *bon mot* of Sheridan's will apply to the whig party in Congress, if, on account of the failure of the bank bill at the late session, they secede from the administration, and set up as a *Tertium Quid* in the government, neither administration nor opposition."

Having presented this spectacle of their brains beaten out against a wall of their own raising, if the whig party should follow Mr. Clay into opposition to the Tyler-Webster administration, Mr. Cushing took the party on another tack—that of the bird in the hand, which is worth two in the bush; and softly commences with them on the profit of using the presidential power while they had it:

"Is it wise for the whig party to throw away the actuality of power for the current four years? If so, for what object? For some contingent *possibility* four years hence? If so, what one? Is the contingent possibility of advancing to power four years hence any one particular man in its ranks, whoever he may be, and however eminently deserving, a sufficient object to induce the whig party to abdicate the power which itself as a body possesses now?"

And changing again, and from seduction to terror, he presents to them, as the most appalling of all calamities, the possible election of a democratic President at the next election through the deplorable divisions of the whig party.

"If so, will its abdication of power now tend to promote that object? Is it not, on the contrary, the very means to make sure the success of some candidate of the democratic party?"

Proceeding to the direct defence of the President, he then boldly absolves him from any violation of faith in rejecting the two bank bills. Thus:

"In refusing to sign those bills, then, he violated no engagement, and committed no act of perfidy in the sense of a forfeited pledge."

And advancing from exculpation to applause, he makes it an act of conscience in Mr. Tyler in refusing to sign them, and places him under the imperious command of a triple power—conscience, constitution, oath; without the faculty of doing otherwise than he did.

"But, in this particular, the President, as an upright man, could do no otherwise than he did. He conscientiously *disapproved* those bills. And the constitution, which he was sworn to obey, *commands* him, expressly and peremptorily commands him, if he do not approve of any bill presented to him for his signature, to return it to the House of Congress in which it originated. 'If he approve he shall sign it: *if not*, he SHALL return it,' are the words of the constitution. Would you as conscientious men yourselves, forbid the President of the United States to have a conscience?"

Acquittal of the President of all hand in the initiation of the second bill, is the next task of Mr. Cushing, and he boldly essays it.

"The President, it is charged, trifled with one or more of the retiring secretaries. Of what occurred at cabinet meetings, the public knows and can know nothing. But, as to the main point, whether he initiated the fiscal corporation bill. This idea is incompatible with the dates and facts above stated, which show that the consideration of a new bill was forced on the President by members of Congress. It is, also, incompatible with the fact that, on Tuesday, the 17th of August, as it is said by the Secretary of War, the President expressed to him doubt as to any bill."

Now what happened in these cabinet meetings is well known to the public from the concurrent statement of three of the secretaries, and from presidential declarations to members of Congress, and these statements cover the main point of the initiation of the second bill by the President himself; and that not on the 18th, but the 16th of August, and not only to his cabinet but to Mr. Stuart of Virginia the same evening; and that it was two days afterwards that the two members of Congress called upon him (Messrs. Sergeant and Berrien), not to force him to take a bill, but to be forced by him to run his own bill through in three days. Demurring to the idea that the President could be forced by members of Congress to adopt an obnoxious bill, the brief statement is, that it is not true. The same is to be said of the quoted remark of the Secretary at War, Mr. Bell, that the President expressed to him a doubt whether he would sign any bank bill—leaving out the astonishment of the Secretary at that declaration, who had been requested by the President the day before to furnish facts in favor of the bill; and who came to deliver a statement of these facts thus prepared, and in great haste, upon request; and when brought, received with indifference! and a doubt expressed whether he would sign any bill. Far from proving that the President had a consistent doubt upon the subject, which is the object of the mutilated quotation from Mr. Bell—it proves just the contrary! proves that the President was for the bill, and began it himself, on the 16th; and was laying an anchor to windward for its rejection on the 17th! having changed during the night.

The retirement of all the cabinet ministers but one, and that for such reasons as they gave, is treated by Mr. Cushing as a thing of no signification, and of no consequence to any body but themselves. He calls it a common fact which has happened under many administrations, and of no permanent consequence, provided good successors are appointed. All that is right enough where secretaries retire for personal reasons, such as are often seen; but when they retire because they impeach the President of great moral delinquency, and refuse to remain with him on that account, the state of the case is altered. He and they are public officers; and officers at the head of the government; and their public conduct is matter of national concern; and the people have a right to inquire and to know the public conduct of public men. The fact that Mr. Webster remained is considered as overbalancing the withdrawal of all the others; and is thus noticed by Mr. Cushing:

"And that, whilst those gentlemen have retired, yet the Secretary of State, in whose patriotism and ability you have more immediate cause to confide, has declared that he knows no sufficient cause for such separation, and continues to co-operate cordially with the President in the discharge of the duties of that station which he fills with so much honor to himself and advantage to the country."

Certainly it was a circumstance of high moment to Mr. Tyler that one of his cabinet remained with him. It was something in such a general withdrawing, and for such reasons as were given, and was considered a great sacrifice on the part of Mr. Webster at the time. As such it was well remembered a short time afterwards, when Mr. Webster, having answered the purposes for which he was retained, was compelled to follow the example of his old colleagues. The address of Mr. Cushing goes on to show itself, in terms, to be an answer to the address of the whig party—saying:

"Yet an address has gone forth from a portion of the members of Congress, purporting to be the *unanimous* act of a meeting of THE whigs of Congress, which, besides arraigning the President on various allegations of fact and surmises not fact, recommends such radical changes of the constitution."

The address itself of the whig party is treated as the work of Mr. Clay—as an emanation of that caucus dictatorship in Congress of which he was always the embodied idea. He says:

"Those changes, if effected, would concentrate the chief powers of government in the hands of that of which this document (the whig address) itself is an emanation, namely a caucus dictatorship of Congress."

This defence by Mr. Cushing, the letters of Mr. Webster, and all the writers in the interests of Mr. Tyler himself, signified nothing against the concurrent statements of the retiring senators, and the confirmatory statements of many members of Congress. The whig party recoiled from him. Instead of that "whig President, whig Congress, and whig people," formed into a unit, with the vision of which Mr. Webster had been induced to remain when his colleagues retired—instead of this unity, there was soon found diversity enough. The whig party remained with Mr. Clay; the whig Secretary of State returned to Massachusetts, inquiring, "*where am I to go?*" The whig defender of Mr. Tyler went to China, clothed with a mission; and returning, found that greatest calamity, the election of a democratic President, to be a fixed fact; and being so fixed, he joined it, and got another commission thereby: while Mr. Tyler himself, who was to have been the Roman cement of this whig unity, continued his march to the democratic camp—arrived there   knocked at the gate—asked to be let in: and was refused. The national democratic Baltimore convention would not recognize him.

CHAPTER LXXXVI.

THE DANISH SOUND DUES.

This subject was brought to the attention of the President at this extra session of Congress by a report from the Secretary of State, and by the President communicated to Congress along with his message. He did not seem to call for legislative action, as the subject was diplomatic, and relations were established between the countries, and the remedy proposed for the evil stated was simply one of negotiation. The origin and history of these dues, and the claims and acquiescences on which they rest, are so clearly and concisely set forth by Mr. Webster, and the amelioration he proposed so natural and easy for the United States, and the subject now acquiring an increasing interest with us, that I draw upon his report for nearly all that is necessary to be said of it in this chapter; and which is enough for the general reader. The report says:

"The right of Denmark to levy these dues is asserted on the ground of ancient usage, coming down from the period when that power had possession of both shores of the Belt and Sound. However questionable the right or uncertain its origin, it has been recognised by European governments, in several treaties with Denmark, some of whom entered into it at as early a period as the fourteenth century; and inasmuch as our treaty with that power contains a clause putting us on the same footing in this respect as other the most favored nations, it has been acquiesced in, or rather has not been denied by us. The treaty of 1645, between Denmark and Holland, to which a tariff of the principal articles then known in commerce, with a rule of measurement and a fixed rate of duty, was appended, together with a subsequent one between the same parties in 1701, amendatory and explanatory of the former, has been generally considered as the basis of all subsequent treaties, and among them of our own, concluded in 1826, and limited to continue ten years from its date, and further until the end of one year, after notice by either party of an intention to terminate it, and which is still in force.

"Treaties have also been concluded with Denmark, by Great Britain, France, Spain, Portugal, Russia, Prussia and Brazil, by which, with one or two exceptions in their favor, they are placed on the same footing as the United States. There has recently been a general movement on the part of the northern powers of Europe, with regard to the subject of these Sound dues, and which seems to afford to this government a favorable opportunity, in conjunction with them, for exerting itself to obtain some such alteration or modification of existing regulations as shall conduce to the freedom and extension of our commerce, or at least to relieve it from some of the burdens now imposed, which, owing to the nature of our trade, operate, in many instances, very unequally and unjustly on it in comparison with that of other nations.

"The ancient tariff of 1645, by which the payment of these dues was regulated, has never been revised, and by means of the various changes which have taken place in commerce since that period, and of the alteration in price in many articles therein included, chiefly in consequence of the settlement of America, and the introduction of her products, into general commerce, it has become quite inapplicable. It is presumed to have been the intention of the framers of that tariff to fix a duty of about one per centum ad valorem upon the articles therein enumerated, but the change in value of many of those commodities, and the absence of any corresponding change in the duty, has, in many instances, increased the ad valorem from one per centum to three, four, and even seven; and this, generally, upon those articles which form the chief exports of the United States, of South America, and the West India Islands: such as the articles of cotton, rice, raw sugar, tobacco, rum, Campeachy wood, &c. On all articles not enumerated in this ancient tariff it is stipulated by the treaty of 1701 that the 'privileged nations,' or those who have treaties with Denmark, shall pay an ad valorem of one per cent.; but the value of these articles being fixed by some rules known only to the Danish government, or at least unknown to us, this duty appears uncertain and fluctuating, and its estimate is very much left to the arbitrary discretion of the custom house officers at Elsinore.

"It has been, by some of the public writers in Denmark, contended that goods of privileged nations, carried in the vessels of unprivileged nations, should not be entitled to the limitation of one per centum ad valorem, but should be taxed one and a quarter per centum, the amount levied on the goods of unprivileged nations; and, also, that this limitation should be confined to the direct trade, so that vessels coming from or bound to the ports of a nation not in treaty with Denmark should pay on their cargoes the additional quarter per cent.

"These questions, although the former is not of so much consequence to us, who are our own carriers, are still in connection with each other, of sufficient importance to render a decision upon them, and a final understanding, extremely desirable. These Sound dues are, moreover, in addition to the port charges of light money, pass-money, &c., which are quite equal to the rates charged at other places, and the payment of which, together with the Sound dues, often causes to vessels considerable delay at Elsinore.

"The port charges, which are usual among all nations to whose ports vessels resort, are unobjectionable, except that, as in this case, they are mere consequences of the imposition of the Sound dues, following, necessarily, upon the compulsory delay at Elsinore of vessels bound up and down the Sound with cargoes, with no intention of making any importation into any port of Denmark, and having no other occasion for delay at Elsinore than that which arises from the necessity of paying the Sound dues, and, in so doing, involuntarily subjecting themselves to these other demands. These port duties would appear to have some reason in them, because of the equivalent; while, in fact, they are made requisite, with the exception, perhaps, of the expense of lights, by the delay necessary for the payment of the Sound dues.

"The amount of our commerce with Denmark, direct, is inconsiderable, compared with that of our transactions with Russia, Sweden, and the ports of Prussia, and the Germanic association on the Baltic; but the sum annually paid to that government in Sound dues, and the consequent port charges by our vessels alone, is estimated at something over one hundred thousand dollars. The greater proportion of this amount is paid by the articles of cotton, sugar, tobacco, and rice; the first and last of these paying a duty of about three per cent. ad valorem, reckoning their value at the places whence they come.

"By a list published at Elsinore, in 1840, it appears that between April and November of that year, seventy-two American vessels, comparatively a small number, lowered their topsails before the castle of Cronberg. These were all bound up the Sound to ports on the Baltic, with cargoes composed in part of the above-named products, upon which alone, according to the tariff, was paid a sum exceeding forty thousand dollars for these dues. Having disposed of these cargoes, they returned laden with the usual productions of the countries on the Baltic, on which, in like manner, were paid duties on going out through the Sound, again acknowledging the tribute by an inconvenient and sometimes hazardous ceremony. The whole amount thus paid within a period of eight months on inward and outward bound cargoes, by vessels of the United States, none of which were bound for, or intended to stop at, any port in Denmark, except compulsorily at Elsinore, for the purpose of complying with these exactions, must have exceeded the large sum above named."

This is the burden, and the history of it which Mr. Webster so succinctly presents. The peaceful means of negotiation are recommended to obtain the benefit of all the reductions in these dues which should be granted to other nations; and this natural and simple course is brought before the President in terms of brief and persuasive propriety.

"I have, therefore, thought proper to bring this subject before you at this time, and to go into these general statements in relation to it, which might be carried more into detail, and substantiated by documents now at the department, to the end that, if you should deem it expedient, instructions may be given to the representative of the United States at Denmark to enter into friendly negotiations with that government, with a view of securing to the commerce of the United States a full participation in any reduction of these duties, or the benefits resulting from any new arrangements respecting them which may be granted to the commerce of other states."

This is the view of an American statesman. No quarrelling, or wrangling with Denmark, always our friend: no resistance to duties which all Europe pays, and were paying not only before we had existence as a nation, but before the continent on which we live had been discovered: no setting ourselves up for the liberators of the Baltic Sea: no putting ourselves in the front of a contest in which other nations have more interest than ourselves. It is not even recommended that we should join a congress of European ministers to solicit, or to force, a reduction or abolition of these duties; and the policy of engaging in no entangling alliances, is well maintained in that abstinence from associated negotiation. The Baltic is a European sea. Great powers live upon its shores: other great powers near its entrance: and all Europe nearer to it than ourselves. The dues collected at Elsinore present a European question which should be settled by European powers, all that we can ask being (what Denmark has always accorded) the advantage of being placed on the footing of the most favored nation. We might solicit a further reduction of the dues on the articles of which we are the chief carriers to that sea—cotton, rice, tobacco, raw sugar; but solicit separately without becoming parties to a general arrangement, and thereby making ourselves one of its guarantees. Negotiate separately, asking at the same time to be continued on the footing of the most favored nation. This report and recommendation of Mr. Webster is a gem in our State papers—the statement of the case condensed to its essence, the recommendation such as becomes our geographical position and our policy; the style perspicuous, and even elegant in its simplicity.

I borrow from the *Boston Daily Advertiser* (Mr. Hale the writer) a condensed and clear account of the success of Mr. Webster's just and wise recommendations on this subject:

"He recommended that 'friendly negotiations' be instituted with the Danish government, 'with a view to securing to the United States a full participation in any reduction of these duties, or the benefits resulting from any new arrangements respecting them, which may be granted to the commerce of other states.'

"This recommendation was doubtless adopted; for the concluding papers of the negotiation appear among the documents communicated to Congress. The Danish government made a complete revision of the ancient tariff, establishing new specific duties on all articles of commerce, with one or two exceptions, in which the one per cent. ad valorem duty was retained.

"The duties were not increased in any instance, and on many of the articles they were largely reduced; on some of them as large a discount as 83 per cent. was made, and a great number were reduced 50 per cent. Of the articles particularly mentioned by Mr. Webster as forming the bulk of the American commerce paying these duties, the duty on raw sugar was reduced from 9 stivers on 100 pounds to 5 stivers; on rice (in paddy) the duty was reduced from 15 stivers to 6 stivers. On some other articles of importance to American commerce the duties were reduced in a larger proportion; on some dyewoods the reduction was from 30 stivers to 8, and on others from 36 to 12, per thousand pounds; and on coffee the reduction was from 24 to 6 stivers per 100 pounds, thereby making it profitable to ship this article directly up the Baltic, instead of to Hamburgh, and thence by land across to Lubec, which had previously been done to avoid the Sound dues.

"It was also provided that no unnecessary formalities should be required from the vessels passing through the Sound. The lowering of top-sails, complained of by Mr. Webster, was dispensed with. We mention this circumstance because a recent article in the *New York Tribune* speaks of this formality as still required. It was abolished thirteen years ago. A number of other accommodations were also granted on the part of Denmark in modification of the harshness of former regulations. The time for the functionaries to attend at their offices was prolonged, and an evident disposition was manifested to make great abatements in the rigor of enforcing as well as in the amount of the tax.

"These concessions were regarded as eminently favorable, and as satisfactory to the United States. Mr. Webster cordially expressed this sentiment in a letter to Mr. Isaac Rand Jackson, then our Chargé d'Affaires for Denmark, bearing date June 25, 1842, and also in another letter, two days later, to Mr. Steen Billé, the Danish Chargé d'Affaires in the United States. In the former letter Mr. Webster praised Mr. Jackson's 'diligence and fidelity in discharging his duties in regard to this subject.'"

Greatly subordinate as the United States are geographically in this question, they are equally, and in fact, duly and proportionably so in interest. Their interest is in the ratio of their distance from the scene of the imposition; that is to say, as units are to hundreds, and hundreds to thousands. Taking a modern, and an average year for the number of vessels of different powers which passed this Sound and paid these duties—the year 1850—and the respective proportions stand thus: English, 5,448 vessels; Norwegian, 2,553; Swedish, 1,982; Dutch, 1,900; Prussian, 2,391; Russian, 1,138; American, 106—being about the one-fiftieth part of the English number, and about the one-twentieth part of the other powers. But that is not the way to measure the American interest. The European powers aggregately present one interest: the United States sole another: and in this point of view the proportion of vessels is as two hundred to one. The whole number of European vessels in a series of five years—1849 to 1853—varied from 17,563 to 21,586; the American vessels during the same years varying from 76 to 135. These figures show the small comparative interest of the United States in the reduction, or abolition of these dues—large enough to make the United States desirous of reduction or abolition—entirely too small to induce her to become the champion of Europe against Denmark: and, taken in connection with our geographical position, and our policy to avoid European entanglement, should be sufficient to stamp as Quixotic, and to qualify as mad, any such attempt.

CHAPTER LXXXVII.

LAST NOTICE OF THE BANK OF THE UNITED STATES.

For ten long years the name of this bank had resounded in the two Halls of Congress. For twenty successive sessions it had engrossed the national legislature—lauded, defended, supported—treated as a power in the State: and vaunted as the sovereign remedy for all the diseases to which the finances, the currency, and the industry of the country could be heir. Now, for the first time in that long period, a session passed by—one specially called to make a bank—in which the name of that institution was not once mentioned: never named by its friends! seldom by its foes. Whence this silence? Whence this avoidance of a name so long, so lately, and so loudly invoked? Alas! the great bank had run its career of audacity, crime, oppression, and corruption. It was in the hands of justice, for its crimes and its debts—was taken out of the hands of its late insolvent directory—placed in the custody of assignees—and passed into a state of insolvent liquidation. Goaded by public reproaches, and left alone in a state of suspension by other banks, she essayed the perilous effort of a resumption. Her credit was gone. It was only for payment that any one approached her doors. In twenty days she was eviscerated of six millions of solid dollars, accumulated by extraordinary means, to enable her to bid for a re-charter at the extra session. This was the last hope, and which had been resolved upon from the moment of General Harrison's election. She was empty. The seventy-six millions of assets, sworn to the month before, were either undiscoverable, or unavailable. The shortest month in the year had been too long for her brief resources. Early in the month of February, her directory issued a new decree of suspension—the third one in four years; but it was in vain to undertake to pass off this stoppage for a suspension. It was felt by all to be an insolvency, though bolstered by the usual protestations of entire ability, and firm determination to resume briefly. An avalanche of suits fell upon the helpless institution, with judgments carrying twelve per cent. damages, and executions to be levied on whatever could be found. Alarmed at last, the stockholders assembled in general meeting, and verified the condition of their property. It was a wreck! nothing but fragments to be found, and officers of the bank feeding on these crumbs though already gorged with the spoils of the monster.

A report of the affairs of the institution was made by a committee of the stockholders: it was such an exhibition of waste and destruction, and of downright plundering, and criminal misconduct, as was never seen before in the annals of banking. Fifty-six millions and three quarters of capital out of sixty-two millions and one quarter (including its own of thirty-five) were sunk in the limits of Philadelphia alone: for the great monster, in going down, had carried many others along with her; and, like the strong man in Scripture, slew more in her death than in her life. Vast was her field of destruction—extending all over the United States—and reaching to Europe, where four millions sterling of her stock was held, and large loans had been contracted. Universally on classes the ruin fell—foreigners as well as citizens—peers and peeresses, as well as the ploughman and the wash-woman—merchants, tradesmen, lawyers, divines: widows and orphans, wards and guardians: confiding friends who came to the rescue: deceived stockholders who held on to their stock, or purchased more: the credulous masses who believed in the safety of their deposits, and in the security of the notes they held—all—all saw themselves the victims of indiscriminate ruin. An hundred millions of dollars was the lowest at which the destruction was estimated; and how such ruin could be worked, and such blind confidence kept up for so long a time, is the instructive lesson for history: and that lesson the report of the stockholders' committee enables history to give.

From this authentic report it appears that from the year 1830 to 1836—the period of its struggles for a re-charter—the loans and discounts of the bank were about doubled—its expenses trebled. Near thirty millions of these loans were not of a mercantile character—neither made to persons in trade or business, nor governed by the rules of safe endorsement and punctual payment which the by-laws of the institution, and the very safety of the bank, required; nor even made by the board of directors, as the charter required; but illegally and clandestinely, by the exchange committee—a small derivation of three from the body of the committee, of which the President of the bank was *ex officio* a member, and the others as good as nominated by him. It follows then that these, near thirty millions of loans, were virtually made by Mr. Biddle himself; and in violation of the charter, the by-laws and the principles of banking. To whom were they made? To members of Congress, to editors of newspapers, to brawling politicians, to brokers and jobbers, to favorites and connections: and all with a view to purchase a re-charter, or to enrich connections, and exalt himself—having the puerile vanity to delight in being called the "Emperor Nicholas." Of course these loans were, in many instances, not expected to be returned—in few so secured as to compel return: and, consequently, near all a dead loss to the stockholders, whose money was thus disposed of.

The manner in which these loans were made to members of Congress, was told to me by one of these members who had gone through this process of bank accommodation; and who, voting against the bank, after getting the loan, felt himself free from shame in telling what had been done. He needed $4,000, and could not get it at home: he went to Philadelphia—to the bank—inquired for Mr. Biddle—was shown into an ante-room, supplied with newspapers and periodicals; and asked to sit, and amuse himself—the president being engaged for the moment. Presently a side door opened. He was ushered into the presence—graciously received—stated his business—was smilingly answered that he could have it, and more if he wished it: that he could leave his note with the exchange committee, and check at once for the proceeds: and if inconvenient to give an indorser before he went home, he could do it afterwards: and, whoever he said was good, would be accepted. And in telling me this, the member said he could read "bribery" in his eyes.

The loans to brokers to extort usury upon—to jobbers, to put up and down the price of stocks—to favorites, connections, and bank officers, were enormous in amount, indefinite in time, on loose security, or none: and when paid, if at all, chiefly in stocks at above their value. The report of the committee thus states this abuse:

> "These loans were generally in large amounts. In the list of debtors on 'bills receivable' of the first of January 1837, twenty-one individuals, firms and companies, stand charged, each with an amount of one hundred thousand dollars and upwards. One firm of this city received accommodations of this kind between August 1835, and November 1837, to the extent of 4,213,878 dollars 30 cents—more than half of which was obtained in 1837. The officers of the bank themselves received in this way, loans to a large amount. In March 1836, when the bank went into operation, under its new charter, Mr. Samuel Jaudon, then elected its principal cashier, was indebted to it, 100,500 dollars. When he resigned the situation of cashier, and was appointed foreign agent, he was in debt 408,389 dollars 25 cents; and on the first of March 1841, he still stood charged with an indebtedness of 117,500 dollars. Mr. John Andrews, first assistant cashier, was indebted to the bank in March 1836, 104,000 dollars. By subsequent loans and advances made during the next three years, he received in all, the sum of 426,930 dollars 67 cents. Mr. Joseph Cowperthwaite, then second assistant cashier, was in debt to the bank in March 1836, 115,000 dollars; when he was appointed cashier in September, 1837, 326,382 dollars 50 cents: when he resigned, and was elected a director by the board, in June 1840, 72,860 dollars, and he stands charged March 3, 1841, on the books with the sum of 55,081 dollars 95 cents. It appears on the books of the bank, that these three gentlemen were engaged in making investments on their joint accounts, in the stock and loan of the Camden and Woodbury railroad company Philadelphia, Wilmington, and Baltimore railroad company, Dauphin and Lycoming coal lands, and Grand Gulf railroad and banking company."

These enormous loans were chiefly in the year 1837, at the time when the bank stopped payment on account of the "specie circular," the "removal of the deposits," and other alleged misdoings of the democratic administrations: and this is only a sample of the way that the institution went on during that period of fictitious distress, and real oppression—millions to brokers and favorites, not a dollar to the man of business.

Two agencies were established in London—one for the bank, under Mr. Jaudon, to borrow money; the other for a private firm, of which Mr. Biddle was partner, and his young son the London head—its business being to sell cotton, bought with the dead notes of the old bank. Of the expenses and doings of these agencies, all bottomed upon the money of the stockholders (so far as it was left), the committee gave this account:

> "When Mr. Jaudon was elected to the place of foreign agent, he was the principal cashier, at a salary of 7,000 dollars per annum. The bank paid the loss on the sale of his furniture, 5,074 dollars, and the passage of himself and family to London, a further sum of 1,015 dollars. He was to devote himself exclusively to the business of the bank, to negotiate an uncovered credit

in England, to provide for the then existing debt in Europe, to receive its funds, to pay its bills and dividends, to effect sales of stocks, and generally to protect the interests of the bank and 'the country at large.' For these services he was to receive the commission theretofore charged and allowed to Baring Brothers & Company, equal to about 28,000 dollars per annum. In addition to which, the expenses of the agency were allowed him, including a salary of 1,000 pounds sterling to his brother, Mr. Charles B. Jaudon, as his principal clerk. From the increase of money operations, arising from facilities afforded by the agency, the amount upon which commissions were charged was greatly augmented, so that the sums paid him for his country services up to January, 1841, amounted at nine per cent. exchange to 178,044 dollars 47 cents, and the expenses of the agency to 35,166 dollars 99 cents. In addition to these sums, he was allowed by the exchange committee, an extra commission of one per cent. upon a loan effected in October, 1839, of 800,000 pounds, say $38,755 56; and upon his claim for a similar commission, upon subsequent loans in France and Holland, to the amount of $8,337,141 90, the board of directors, under the sanction of a legal opinion, from counsel of high standing, and the views of the former president, by whom the agreement with Mr. Jaudon was made, that the case of extraordinary loans was not anticipated, nor meant to be included in the original arrangement, allowed the further charge of $83,970 37. These several sums amount to $335,937, 39, as before stated."

A pretty expensive agency, although the agent was to devote himself exclusively to the business of the bank, protecting its interests, and those of "the country at large"—an addition to his mission, this protection of the country at large, which illustrates the insolent pretensions of this imperious corporation. Protect the country at large! while plundering its own stockholders of their last dollar. And that furniture of this bank clerk! the loss on the sale of which was $5,074! and which loss the stockholders made up: while but few of them had that much in their houses. The whole amount of loans effected by this agency was twenty-three millions of dollars; of which a considerable part was raised upon fictitious bills, drawn in Philadelphia without funds to meet them, and to raise money to make runs upon the New York banks, compel them to close again: and so cover her own insolvency in another general suspension: for all these operations took place after the suspension of 1837. The committee thus report upon these loans, and the gambling in stock speculations at home:

"Such were some of the results of the resolution of March, 1835, though it cannot be questioned, that much may be fairly attributed to the unhappy situation of the business and exchanges of the country, concurring with the unfortunate policy pursued by the administration of the bank. Thus the institution has gone on to increase its indebtedness abroad, until it has now more money borrowed in Europe, than it has on loan on its list of active debt in America. To this has been superadded, extensive dealing in stocks, and a continuation of the policy of loaning upon stock securities, though it was evidently proper upon the recharter, that such a policy should be at once and entirely abandoned. Such indeed was its avowed purpose, yet one year afterwards, in March, 1837, its loans on stocks and other than personal security had increased $7,821,541, while the bills discounted on personal security, and domestic exchange had suffered a diminution of $9,516,463 78. It seems to have been sufficient, to obtain money on loan, to pledge the stock of an 'incorporated company,' however remote its operation or uncertain its prospects. Many large loans originally made on a pledge of stocks, were paid for in the same kind of property, and that too at par, when in many instances they had become depreciated in value. It is very evident to the committee, that several of the officers of the bank were themselves engaged in large operations in stocks and speculations, of a similar character, with funds obtained of the bank, and at the same time loans were made to the companies in which they were interested, and to others engaged in the same kind of operations, in amounts greatly disproportionate to the means of the parties, or to their proper and legitimate wants and dealings. The effect of this system, was to monopolize the active means of the institution, and disable it from aiding and accommodating men engaged in business really productive and useful to the community; and as might have been anticipated, a large part of the sums thus loaned were ultimately lost, or the bank compelled, on disadvantageous terms as to price, to take in payment stocks, back lands and other fragments of the estates of great speculators."

The cotton agency seemed to be an ambidextrous concern—both individual and corporation—its American office in the Bank of the United States—the purchases made upon ten millions of its defunct notes—the profits going to the private firm—the losses to the bank. The committee give this history:

"In the course of the investigation the attention of the committee has been directed to certain accounts, which appear on the books as 'advances on merchandise,' but which were, in fact, payments for cotton, tobacco and other produce, purchased by the direction of the then President, Mr. Nicholas Biddle, and shipped to Europe on account of himself and others. These accounts were kept by a clerk in the foreign exchange department, this department being under the charge of Mr. Cowperthwaite, until September 22, 1837, when he was elected cashier, and of Mr. Thomas Dunlap, until March 20, 1840, when he was chosen president. The original documents, necessary to enable the committee to arrive at all the facts in relation to these transactions, were not accessible, having been retained, as was supposed, by the parties interested, as private papers. A succinct view of the whole matter, sufficient to convey to the stockholders a general idea of its character, may be drawn from the report of a committee of the board of directors, appointed on the 21st of July, 1840, for the purpose of adjusting and settling these accounts, and who reported on the 21st of December, 1840, which report with the accompanying accounts, is spread at large upon the minutes. The first transactions were in July, 1837, and appear as advances, to A. G. Jaudon, to purchase cotton for shipment to Baring Brothers & Co. of Liverpool, the proceeds to be remitted to their house in London, then acting as the agents of the bank. The amount of these shipments was 2,182,998 dollars 28 cents. The proceeds were passed to the credit of the bank, and the account appears to be balanced. The results, as to the profit and loss, do not appear, and the committee had no means of ascertaining them, nor the names of the parties interested. In the autumn of 1837, when the second of these transactions commenced, it will be recollected, that Mr. Samuel Jaudon had been appointed the agent of the bank to reside in London. About the same time, a co-partnership was formed between Mr. May Humphreys, then a director of the bank, and a son of Mr. Nicholas Biddle, under the firm of Biddle & Humphreys. This house was established at Liverpool, and thenceforward acted as agents for the sale of the produce shipped to that place which comprised a large proportion of the whole amount. In explanation of these proceedings, the committee annex to their report a copy of a letter dated Philadelphia, December 28, 1840, to the president and directors of the bank, from Mr. Joseph Cabot, one of the firm of Bevan & Humphreys, and who became a director at the election in January, 1838. This letter was read to the board, December 29, 1840, but was not inserted on the minutes.

"This arrangement continued during the years 1837, 1838 and 1839, the transactions of which amounted to 8,969,450 dollars 95 cents. The shipments were made principally to Biddle and Humphreys, were paid for by drafts on Bevan and Humphreys—the funds advanced by the bank, and the proceeds remitted to Mr. Samuel Jaudon, agent of the bank in London. It appears that there was paid to Messrs. Bevan and Humphreys by the bank in Philadelphia during the months of March, April, and May, 1839, the sum of eight hundred thousand dollars, and the account was thus balanced. The committee have reason to believe, that this sum constituted a part or perhaps the whole of the profits derived from the second series of shipments. How, and among whom, it was distributed, they have not been informed, but from the terms of the final settlement, to be adverted to presently, each one will be at liberty to make his own inferences. The third and last account, amounting to 3,241,042 dollars 83 cents, appears on the books, as 'bills on London, advances S. V. S. W.' These letters stand for the name of S. V. S. Wilder, of New York.—Messrs. Humphreys and Biddle, to whom these consignments were made, continued their accounts in the name of Bevan and Humphreys, but without the knowledge of that firm, as appears by Mr. Cabot's letter of December 28, 1840. The result of these last shipments, was a loss of 962,524 dollars 13 cents. Of this amount the sum of 553,908 dollars 57 cents was for excess of payments by Messrs. Humphreys and Biddle to the London agency, beyond the proceeds of sale, with interest thereon. The parties interested, claimed and were allowed a deduction for loss on 526,000 dollars of southern funds, used in the purchase of cotton, when at a discount, the sum of 310,071 dollars 30 cents; and also this sum, being banker's commission to Messrs. Humphreys and Biddle on advances to Samuel Jaudon, agent, 21,061 dollars 86 cents, making 331,133 dollars 16 cents, and leaving to be settled by the parties the sum of 631,390 dollars 97 cents."

Thus, the profit of eight hundred thousand dollars on the first shipments of cotton went to this private firm, though not shown on the books to whom; and the loss of nine hundred and sixty-two thousand five hundred and twenty-four dollars and thirteen cents on the last shipments went to the bank; but this being objected to by some of the directors, it was settled by Mr. Biddle and the rest—the bank taking from them stocks, chiefly of Texas, at par—the sales of the same being slow at a tithe of their face. The bank had also a way of guaranteeing the individual contracts of Mr. Biddle for millions; of which the report gives this account:

"Upon the eighteenth day of August, 1838, the bank guaranteed a contract made by Mr. Nicholas Biddle in his individual capacity, for the purchase of two thousand five hundred bonds of the State of Mississippi, of two thousand dollars each, amounting in the whole to 5,000,000 dollars. The signature of Mr. Thomas Dunlap, then second assistant cashier, was affixed to the guarantee, in behalf of the bank, upon the verbal authority of the president. Upon the 29th of January, 1839, the bank guaranteed to the State of Michigan, the punctual fulfilment of the obligations of the Morris canal and banking company, for the purchase of bonds of that state, to the extent of 3,145,687 dollars 50 cents. for 2,700,000 taken at par, and including interest on the instalments payable every three months up to January, 1843. On the 29th of April, 1839, the bank guaranteed a contract entered into by Mr. Thomas Dunlap in his individual capacity for the purchase of one million of dollars of the 'Illinois and Michigan canal stock.' In regard to these transactions, the committee can find no authority on the minutes of the board, and have been referred to none, by the president, upon whom they called for information."

Unintelligible accounts of large amounts appeared in the profit and loss side of the bank ledger; which, not explaining themselves, the parties named as receiving the money, were called upon for explanations—which they refused to give. Thus:

"In this last account there is a charge under date of June 30, 1840, of $400,000 to 'parent bank notes account,' which has not been explained to the satisfaction of the committee. It must be also mentioned, that among the expenditures of the bank, there is entered, at various dates, commencing May 5, 1836, sums amounting in all to 618,640 dollars 15 cents, as paid on the 'receipts of Mr. N. Biddle,' of 'Mr. N. Biddle and J. Cowperthwaite,' and 'cashier's vouchers.' As the committee were unable to obtain satisfactory information upon the subject of these expenses from the books or officers of the bank, application was made by letter to Mr. N. Biddle and Mr. J. Cowperthwaite, from whom no reply has been received."

These enormous transactions generally without the knowledge of the directory, usually upon the initials of a member of the exchange committee; and frequently upon a deposit of stock in the cash drawer. Besides direct loans to members of Congress, and immense fees, there was a process of entertainment for them at immense expense—nightly dinners at hotels—covers for fifty: and the most costly wines and viands: and this all the time. Besides direct applications of money in elections, the bank became a fountain of supply in raising an election fund where needed, taking the loss on itself. Thus, in 1833, in the presidential election in Kentucky, some politicians went into the branch bank at Lexington, assessed the party in each county for the amount wanted in that county—drew drafts for the amount of the assessment on some ardent friends in the county, received the cash for the drafts from the bank, and applied it to the election—themselves not liable if the assessment was not paid, but the same to go to the profit and loss account of the bank. In such operations as all these, and these are not all, it was easy for the bank to be swallowed up: and swallowed up it was totally.

The losses to the stockholders were deplorable, and in many instances attended with circumstances which aggravated the loss. Many were widows and children, their *all* invested where it was believed to be safe; and an ascertained income relied on as certain, with eventual return of the capital. Many were unfortunately deceived into the purchase or retention of stock, by the delusive bank reports. The makers of these reports themselves held no quantity of the stock—only the few shares necessary to qualify them for the direction. Foreign holders were numerous, attracted by the, heretofore, high credit of American securities, and by the implications of the name—Bank of the United States; implying a national ownership, which guaranteed national care in its management, and national liability on its winding up. Holland, England, France suffered, but the English most of all the foreigners. The London Banker's Circular thus described their loss:

> "The proportion of its capital held by British subjects is nearly four millions sterling; it may be described as an entire loss. And the loss we venture, upon some consideration, to say is greater than the aggregate of all the losses sustained by the inhabitants of the British Islands, from failure of banks in this country, since Mr. Patterson established the banks of England and Scotland at the close of the seventeenth century. The small population of Guernsey and Jersey hold £200,000 of the stock of this U. States Bank. Call it an entire loss, and it is equal to a levy of three or four pounds on every man, woman, and child in the whole community of those islands—a sum greater than was ever raised by taxation in a single year on any people in the whole world. Are these important facts? if facts they be. Then let statesmen meditate upon them, for by their errors and reckless confidence in delusive theories they have been produced."

The credit of the bank, and the price of stock was kept up by delusive statements of profits, and fictitious exhibition of assets and false declarations of surpluses. Thus, declaring a half-yearly dividend of four per centum, January 1st, 1839, with a surplus of more than four millions; on the first of July of the same year, another half-yearly dividend of four per centum, with a surplus of more than four millions; on the 15th of January, the same year, announcing a surplus of three millions; and six weeks thereafter, on the first of January, announcing a surplus of five millions; while the assets of the bank were carried up to seventy-six millions. In this way credit was kept up. The creating of suspensions—that of 1837, and subsequent—cost immense sums, and involved the most enormous villainy; and the last of these attempts—the run upon the New York banks to stop them again before she herself stopped for the last time—was gigantically criminal, and ruinous to itself. Mr. Joseph Cowperthwaite (perfectly familiar with the operation) describes it to the life, and with the indifference of a common business transaction. Premising that a second suspension was coming on, it was deemed best (as in the first one of 1837) to make it begin in New York; and the operation for that purpose is thus narrated:

> "After the feverish excitement consequent on this too speedy effort to return to cash payments had in a good degree subsided, another crisis was anticipated, and it was feared that the banks generally would be obliged again to suspend. This was, unhappily, too soon to be realized, for the storm was then ready to burst, but, instead of meeting its full force at once, it was deemed best to make it fall first upon the banks of New York. To effect this purpose, large means were necessary, and to procure these, resort was had to the sale of foreign exchange. The state of the accounts of the bank with its agents abroad did not warrant any large drafts upon them, especially that of the Messrs. Hottinguer in Paris. This difficulty, however, it was thought might be avoided, by shipping the coin to be drawn from the New York banks immediately to meet the bills. Accordingly, large masses of exchange, particularly bills on Paris, which were then in great demand, were sent to New York to be sold without limit. Indeed, the bills were signed in blank, and so sent to New York; and although a large book was thus forwarded, it was soon exhausted, and application was made to the agent of the Paris house in New York for a further supply, who drew a considerable amount besides. The proceeds of these immense sales of exchange created very heavy balances against the

New York banks, which, after all, signally failed in producing the contemplated effect. The bills not being provided for, nor even regularly advised, as had uniformly been the custom of the bank, were dishonored; and although the agent in London did every thing which skill and judgment could accomplish, the credit of the bank was gone, and from that day to the present its effects upon the institution have been more and more disastrous."

"Deemed best to make the storm fall first upon the banks of New York;" and for that purpose to draw bills without limit, without funds to meet them, in such rapid succession as to preclude the possibility of giving notice—relying upon sending the gold which they drew out of the New York banks to Paris, to meet the same bills (all the while laying that exportation of gold to the wickedness of the specie circular), and failing to get the money there as fast as these "race-horse" bills went—they returned dishonored—came rolling back by millions, protested in Paris, to be again protested in Philadelphia. Then the bubble burst. The credit which sustained the monster was gone. Ruin fell upon itself, and upon all who put their trust in it; and certainly this last act, for the criminality of its intent and the audacity of its means, was worthy to cap and crown the career of such an institution.

It was the largest ruin, and the most criminal that has been seen since the South Sea and Mississippi schemes; yet no one was punished, or made to refund. Bills of indictment were found by the grand jury of the county of Philadelphia against Nicholas Biddle, Samuel Jaudon, and John Andrews, for a conspiracy to defraud the stockholders in the bank; and they were arrested, and held to bail for trial. But they surrendered themselves into custody, procured writs of *habeas corpus* for their release; and were discharged in vacation by judges before whom they were brought. It has been found difficult in the United States to punish great offenders—much more so than in England or France. In the cases of the South Sea and Mississippi frauds, the principal actors, though men of high position, were criminally punished, and made to pay damages. While these delinquencies were going on in the Bank of the United States, an eminent banker of London—Mr. Fauntleroy—was hanged at Tyburn, like a common felon—for his bank misdeeds: and while some plundered stockholders are now (autumn of 1855) assembled in Philadelphia, searching in vain for a shilling of their stock, three of the greatest bankers in London are receiving sentence of transportation for fourteen years for offences, neither in money nor morals, the hundredth part of the ruin and crime perpetrated by our American bank—bearing the name of the United States. The case presents too strong a contrast, and teaches too great a lesson to criminal justice to be omitted; and here it is:

"The firm had been in existence for nearly two centuries. The two elder partners of the firm had been distinguished for munificent charities, for an advocacy of great moral reforms, and an active participation in the religious or philanthropic measures of the day. They had always been liberal givers, had presided at Exeter Hall meetings, built chapels, and generally acted the part of liberal and useful members of society; and one of them, Sir John Dean Paul, was a baronet by descent, and allied to some of the highest nobility of England. He was first cousin to the present Lord Ravensworth, the honorable Augustus and Adolphus Liddell, the rector of St. Paul's, Knightsbridge, the Countess of Hardwicke, Viscountess Barrington, Lady Bloomfield; and, above all, the honorable Mrs. Villiers, sister-in-law to the Earl of Clarendon. These connections, however, in a country where rank and social position have peculiar influence, did not save them from a criminal trial and utter disgrace. One of their customers, in obedience to what he believed to be a duty to society, having personally inquired into the affairs of the firm, proceeded to lay a criminal information against Messrs. Strahan, Paul, and Bates, which led to their indictment and subsequent trial before the criminal court. This gentleman was the Rev. Dr. Griffith, Prebendary of Rochester, a wealthy ecclesiastic and a personal friend of all the partners of the firm, with which he had been a large depositor for many years. On the twenty-fifth of October the trial came on before Mr. Baron Alderson, assisted by Baron Martin and Justice Willes. The defendants appeared in court, attended by Sir Frederick Thesiger, Mr. Ballantyne, Sergeant Byles, and other almost equally eminent counsel. The Attorney-general appeared for the prosecution, and the evidence adduced at the trial, disclosed the following facts: Dr. Griffith, the prosecutor in the proceedings, and who, at the time of the failure of the defendants, had money and securities on deposit with them to the amount of £22,000, about five years ago empowered them to purchase for him on three different occasions, Danish five per cent. bonds to the value of £5,000. The defendants purchased the bonds, upon which they regularly received the dividends, and credited Dr. Griffith with the same on their books. This continued until March, 1854, when Sir John D. Paul, to relieve the embarrassments under which the firm were laboring, sold these securities, together with others with which they were entrusted, and appropriated the proceeds, amounting to over £12,000, to the use of the firm. This, as we have stated, was no offence at common law, and the indictment was preferred upon a statutory provision found in the 7th and 8th of George IV., cap. 29. The rigid severity of the penal law in England on this subject will be better appreciated when we add, that the bonds were replaced by others of equal value, in the June following their misappropriation, just one year previous to the failure of the firm; and that the indictment only charged the defendants with misappropriating them in this single instance, although it was shown that the second set of bonds were again sold for the use of the firm in April, 1855; Dr. Griffith having, in the interval, regularly received his dividends; so that, although the firm might be perfectly solvent at this moment, the fact that they had sold the bonds in March, 1851, even if they had replaced them in June, 1854, and had credited Dr. Griffith with the dividends on them between those dates, would still render them liable to an indictment. The case, therefore, overlooking the final misappropriation of the bonds, and the failure of the firm in 1855, was narrowed down to the single issue—whether they had been sold in 1854 without the consent of Dr. Griffith."

For misappropriating sixty thousand dollars of one of their customers—using it without his consent—these three great London bankers were sentenced to fourteen years' transportation: for misappropriating thirty-five millions, and sinking twenty-one millions more in other institutions, the wrong-doers go free in the United States—giving some countenance among us to the sarcasm of the Scythian philosopher, that laws are cobwebs which catch the weak flies, and let the strong ones break through. The Judge (Mr. Baron Alderson) who tried this case (that of the three London bankers), had as much heart and feeling as any judge, or man ought to have; but he also had a sense of his own duty, and of his obligations to the laws, and to the country; and in sentencing men of such high position, and with whom he had been intimate and social, he combined in the highest degree the feelings of a man with the duties of the judge. He said to the prisoners:

"William Strahan, Sir John Dean Paul, and Robert Makin Bates, the jury have now found you guilty of the offence charged upon you in the indictment—the offence of disposing of securities which were entrusted by your customers to you as bankers, for the purpose of being kept safe for their use, and which you appropriated, under circumstances of temptation, to your own. A greater and more serious offence can hardly be imagined in a great commercial city like this. It tends to shake confidence in all persons in the position you occupied, and it has shaken the public confidence in establishments like that you for a long period honorably conducted. I do very, very much regret that it falls to my lot to pass any sentence on persons in your situation; but yet the public interest and public justice require it; and it is not for me to shrink from the discharge of any duty, however painful, which properly belongs to my office. I should have been very glad, if it had pleased God that some one else now had to discharge that duty. I have seen (continued the learned judge, with deep emotion) at least one of you under very different circumstances, sitting at my side in high office, instead of being where you now are, and I could scarcely then have fancied to myself that it would ever come to me to pass sentence on you. But so it is, and this is a proof, therefore, that we all ought to pray not to be led into temptation. You have been well educated, and held a high position in life, and the punishment which must fall on you will consequently be the more seriously and severely felt by you, and will also greatly affect those connected with you, who will most sensitively feel the disgrace of your position. All that I have to say is, that I cannot conceive any worse case of the sort arising under the act of Parliament, applicable to your offence. Therefore, as I cannot conceive any worse case under the act, I can do nothing else but impose the sentence therein provided for the worst case, namely, the most severe punishment, which is, that you be severally transported for fourteen years."

For the admiration of all in our America—for the imitation of those who may be called to act in the like cases—with the sad conviction that the administration of criminal justice is not equal in our Republic to what it is in the monarchies of Europe: for the benefit of all such, this brief notice of judicial action in an English court against eminent, but culpable bankers, is here given—contrasting so strikingly with the vain attempts to prosecute those so much more culpable in our own country.

CHAPTER LXXXVIII.

END AND RESULTS OF THE EXTRA SESSION.

This extraordinary session, called by President Harrison, held under Mr. Tyler, dominated by Mr. Clay, was commenced on the 31st of May and ended the 13th of September: seventy-five days' session—and replete with disappointed calculations, and nearly barren of permanent results. The whigs expected from it an easy and victorious course of legislation, and the consolidation of their power by the inauguration of their cherished measures for acting on the people—national bank—paper money national currency—union of bank and state—distribution of public money—bankrupt act—monopoly of office. The democracy saw no means of preventing these measures; but relied upon the goodness of their cause, the badness of the measures to be adopted by the whigs, and the blunders they would commit, to give them eventual victory, and soon to restore parties to their usual relative positions. The defection of Mr. Tyler was not foreseen: his veto of a national bank was not counted upon: the establishment of that institution was considered certain: and the only remedy thought of was in the repeal of the law establishing it. As a public political corporation, that repealability came within the decision of the Supreme Court of the United States in the Dartmouth College case; and being established for the good of the state, it became amenable to the judgment of the State upon the question of good, or evil—to be decided by the political power. Repealability was then the reliance against a national bank; and that ground was immediately taken, and systematically urged—both for the purpose of familiarizing the people with the idea of repeal, and of deterring capitalists from taking its stock. The true service that Mr. Tyler did the democratic party was in rejecting the bank charters (for such they both were, though disguised with ridiculous names). Numerically he weakened the whig ranks but little: potentially not at all—as those who joined him, took office: and became both useless to him, and a reproach. That *beau ideal*, of a whig unity—"whig President, whig Congress, and whig people"—which Mr. Webster and Mr. Cushing were to realize, vanished: and they with it—leaving Mr. Tyler without whig, and without democratic adherents; but with a small party of his own as long as he was in a condition to dispense office. The legislation of the session was a wreck. The measures passed, had no duration. The bankrupt act, and the distribution act, were repealed by the same Congress that passed them—under the demand of the people. The new tariff act, called revenue—was changed within a year. The sub-treasury system, believed to have been put to death, came to life again. Gold and silver, intended to have been ignored as a national currency, had become that currency—both for the national coffers, and the people's pockets. Of all the measures of that extraordinary session, opening with so much hope, nothing now remains to recall the idea of its existence, but, *first*—THE HOME SQUADRON! keeping idle watch on our safe coasts, at the cost of a million per annum. *Next*, THE OCEAN LINE STEAMERS! plundering the country of two millions annually, oppressing fair competition and damaging the character of Congress. And last, not least, THAT ONE HOUR RULE! which has silenced the representatives of the people in the House of Representatives, reduced the national legislation to blind dictation, suppressed opposition to evil measures, and deprived the people of the means of knowing the evil that Congress is doing.

To the democracy it was a triumphant session—triumphant in every thing that constitutes moral and durable triumph. They had broken down the whig party before the session was over—crushed it upon its own measures; and were ready for the elections which were to reverse the party positions. The Senate had done it. The House, oppressed by the hour rule, and the tyrannical abuse of the previous question, had been able to make but little show. The two-and-twenty in the Senate did the work; and never did I see a body of men more effective or brilliant—show a higher spirit or a more determined persistence. To name the speakers, would be to enumerate all—except Mr. Mouton, who not having the English language perfect was limited to his vote—always in place, and always faithful. The Globe newspaper was a powerful assistant, both as an ally working in its own columns, and as a vehicle of communication for our daily debates. Before the session was over we felt ourselves victorious, and only waiting for the day when the elections were to show it. Of all our successes, that of keeping the hour rule, and the previous question out of the American Senate, was the most brilliant, and durably beneficent—rising above party—entering the high region of free government—preserving the liberty of speech—preserving to republican government its distinctive and vital feature, that of free debate; and saving national legislation from unresisted party dictation.

CHAPTER LXXXIX.

FIRST ANNUAL MESSAGE OF PRESIDENT TYLER.

This message coming in so soon after the termination of the extra session—only two months after it—was necessarily brief and meagre of topics, and presents but few points worthy of historical remembrance. The first subject mentioned was the acquittal of McLeod, which had taken place in the recess: and with which result the British government was content. The next subject was, the kindred matter of the Caroline; on which the President had nothing satisfactory to communicate, but expressed a high sense of the indignity which had been offered to the United States, and evinced a becoming spirit to obtain redress for it. He said:

"I regret that it is not in my power to make known to you an equally satisfactory conclusion in the case of the Caroline steamer, with the circumstances connected with the destruction of which, in December, 1837, by an armed force fitted out in the Province of Upper Canada, you are already made acquainted. No such atonement as was due for the public wrong done to the United Stares by this invasion of her territory, so wholly irreconcilable with her rights as an independent power, has yet been made. In the view taken by this government, the inquiry whether the vessel was in the employment of those who were prosecuting an unauthorized war against that Province, or was engaged by the owner in the business of transporting passengers to and from Navy Island in hopes of private gain, which was most probably the case, in no degree alters the real question at issue between the two governments. This government can never concede to any foreign government the power, except in a case of the most urgent and extreme necessity, of invading its territory, either to arrest the persons or destroy the property of those who may have violated the municipal laws of such foreign government, or have disregarded their obligations arising under the law of nations. The territory of the United States must be regarded as sacredly secure against all such invasions, until they shall voluntarily acknowledge their inability to aquit themselves of their duties to others. And in announcing this sentiment, I do but affirm a principle which no nation on earth would be more ready to vindicate, at all hazards, than the people and government of Great Britain."

The finances were in a bad condition, and the President chiefly referred to the report of the Secretary of the Treasury upon them. Of the loan of twelve millions authorized at the previous session, only five millions and a half had been taken—being the first instance, and the last in our financial history in which, in time of peace, our government was unable to borrow money. A deficiency existed in the revenues of the year, and for the ensuing year that deficiency was estimated, would amount to a fraction over fourteen millions of dollars. To meet this large deficit the secretary recommended—*first*, an extension of the term for the redeemability of the remainder of the authorized loan, amounting to $6,500,000. *Secondly*, the re-issue of the five millions of treasury notes authorized at the previous session. *Thirdly*, the remainder ($2,718,570) to be made up by additional duties on imported articles. While recommending these fourteen millions and a quarter to be raised by loans, treasury notes, and duties, the President recommended the land revenue should still remain as a fund for distribution to the States, and was solicitous that, in the imposition of new duties, care should be taken not to impair the mutual assurance for each other's life which the land distribution bill, and the compromise clause contained in the tariff bill of the extra session provided for each other—saying: "It might be esteemed desirable that no such augmentation of the duties should take place as would have the effect of annulling the land proceeds distribution act of the last session, which act it declared to be inoperative the moment the duties are increased beyond 20 per centum—the maximum rate established by the compromise act." This recommendation, so far as it applied to the compromise act, was homage to the dead; and so far as it related to continuing the distribution of the land revenue was, probably, the first instance in the annals of nations in which the chief magistrate of a country has recommended the diversion and gratuitous distribution of a large branch of its revenues, recommending at the same time, money to be raised by loans, taxes, and government notes to supply the place of that given away. The largeness of the deficiency was a point to be accounted for; and that was done by showing the great additional expenses to be incurred—and especially in the navy, for which the new secretary (Mr. Upshur) estimated enormously, and gave rise to much searching discussion in Congress: of which, in its place. But the chief item in the message was another modification of the fiscalities of the extra session, with a new name, and an old countenance upon it, except where it was altered for the worse. This new plan was thus introduced by the President:

"In pursuance of a pledge given to you in my last message to Congress, which pledge I urge as an apology for adventuring to present you the details of any plan, the Secretary of the Treasury will be ready to submit to you, should you require it, a plan of finance which, while it throws around the public treasure reasonable guards for its protection, and rests on powers acknowledged in practice to exist from the origin of the government, will, at the same time, furnish to the country a sound paper medium, and afford all reasonable facilities for regulating the exchanges. When submitted, you will perceive in it a plan amendatory of the existing laws in relation to the Treasury department—subordinate in all respects to the will of Congress directly, and the will of the people indirectly—self-sustaining should it be found in practice to realize its promises in theory, and repealable at the pleasure of Congress. It proposes by effectual restraints, and by invoking the true spirit of our institutions, to separate the purse from the sword; or more properly to speak, denies any other control to the President over the agents who may be selected to carry it into execution, but what may be indispensably necessary to secure the fidelity of such agents; and, by wise regulations, keeps plainly apart from each other private and public funds. It contemplates the establishment of a Board of Control at the seat of government, with agencies at prominent commercial points, or wherever else Congress shall direct, for the safe-keeping and disbursement of the public moneys, and a substitution, at the option of the public creditor, of treasury notes, in lieu of gold and silver. It proposes to limit the issues to an amount not to exceed $15,000,000—without the express sanction of the legislative power. It also authorizes the receipt of individual deposits of gold and silver to a limited amount, and the granting certificates of deposit, divided into such sums as may be called for by the depositors. It proceeds a step further, and authorizes the purchase and sale of domestic bills and drafts, resting on a real and substantial basis, payable at sight, or having but a short time to run, and drawn on places not less than one hundred miles apart—which authority, except in so far as may be necessary for government purposes exclusively, is only to be exerted upon the express condition, that its exercise shall not be prohibited by the State in which the agency is situated."

This was the prominent feature of the message, and appeared to Mr. Benton to be so monstrous and dangerous that it ought not to be allowed to get out of the Senate without a mark of reprobation should be first set upon it. The moment the reading was finished, the usual resolve was offered to print extra copies, when he rose and inveighed against the new fiscality with great vehemence, saying:

"He could not reconcile it to himself to let the resolution pass without making a few remarks on that part of the message which related to the new fiscal agent. Looking at that feature of it, as read, he perceived that the President gave an outline of his plan, leaving it to the Secretary of the Treasury to furnish the details in his report. He (Mr. BENTON) apprehended that nothing in those details could reconcile him to the project, or in any manner meet his approbation. There were two main points presented in the plan, to which he never could agree—both being wholly unconstitutional and dangerous. One was that of emitting bills of credit, or issuing a treasury currency. Congress had no constitutional authority to issue paper money, or emit federal bills of credit; and the other feature is to authorize this government to deal in exchanges. The proposition to issue bills of credit, when under consideration at the formation of the constitution, was struck out with the express view of making this government a hard money government—not capable of recognizing any other than a specie currency—a currency of gold and silver—a currency known and valued, and equally understood by every one. But here is a proposition to do what is expressly refused to be allowed by the framers of the constitution—to exercise a power not only not granted to Congress, but a power expressly denied. The next proposition is to authorize the federal government to deal in and regulate exchanges, and to furnish exchange to merchants. This is a new invention—a modern idea of the power of this government, invented by Mr. Biddle, to help out a national bank. Much as General Hamilton was in favor of paper money, he never went the length of recommending government bills of credit, or dealings in exchange by the United States Treasury. The fathers of the church, Macon, and John Randolph, and others, called this a hard money government: they objected to bank paper; but here is government paper; and that goes beyond Hamilton, much as he was in favor of the paper system. The whole scheme making this government a regulator of exchange—a dealer in exchange—a furnisher of exchange—is absurd, unconstitutional, and pernicious, and is a new thing under the sun.

"Now he (Mr. BENTON) objected to this government becoming a seller of exchange to the country (which is transportation of money), for which there is no more authority than there is for its furnishing transportation of goods or country produce. There is not a word in the constitution to authorize it—not a word to be found justifying the assumption. The word exchange is not in the constitution. What does this message propose? Congress is called upon to establish a board with agencies, for the purpose of furnishing the country with exchanges. Why should not Congress be also called on to furnish that portion of the community engaged in commerce with facilities for transporting merchandise? The proposition is one of the most pernicious nature, and such as must lead to the most dangerous consequences if adopted.

"The British debt began in the time of Sir Robert Walpole, on issues of exchequer bills—by which system the British nation has been cheated, and plunged irretrievably in debt to the amount of nine hundred millions of pounds. The proposition that the government should become the issuer of exchequer notes, is one borrowed from the system introduced in England by Sir Robert Walpole, whose whig administration was nothing but a high tory administration of Queen Anne: and infinitely worse; for Walpole's exchequer bills were for large sums, for investment: this scheme goes down to five dollar notes for common and petty circulation. He (Mr. BENTON) had much to say on this subject, but this was not the time for entering at large into it. This perhaps was not the proper occasion to say more; nor would it, he considered, be treating the President of the United States with proper respect to enter upon a premature discussion. He could not, however, in justice to himself, allow this resolution to pass without stating his objections to two such obnoxious features of the proposed fiscality, looking, as he did, upon the whole thing as one calculated to destroy the whole structure of the government, to change it from the hard money it was intended to be, to the paper money government it was intended not to be, and to mix it up with trade, which no one ever dreamed of. He (Mr. BENTON) had on another occasion stated that this administration would go back not only to the federal times of '98, but to the times of Sir Robert Walpole and Queen Anne, and the evidence is now before us.

"He (Mr. BENTON) had only said a few words on this occasion, because he could not let the proposition to sanction bills of credit go without taking the very earliest opportunity of expressing his disapprobation, and denouncing a system calculated to produce the same results which had raised the funded debt of Great Britain from twenty-one millions to nine hundred millions of pounds. He should avail himself of the first appropriate opportunity to maintain the ground he had assumed as to the identity of this policy with that of Walpole, by argument and references, that this plan of the President's was utterly unconstitutional and dangerous—part borrowed from the system of English exchequer issues, and part from Mr. Biddle's scheme of making the federal government an exchange dealer—though Mr. Biddle made the government act indirectly through a board of bank directors, and this makes it act directly through a board of treasury directors and their agents.

"This is the first time that a formal proposition has been made to change our hard money government (as it was intended to be) into a paper money machine; and it is the first time that there has been a proposal to mix it up with trade and commerce, by making it a furnisher of exchanges, a bank of deposit, a furnisher of paper currency, and an imitator of the old confederation in its continental bills and a copyist of the English exchequer system. Being the first time these unconstitutional and pernicious schemes were formally presented to Congress, he felt it to be his duty to disclose his opposition to them at once. He would soon speak more fully."

The President in his message referred to the accompanying report of the Secretary of the Treasury (Mr. Walter Forward), for the details of his plan; and in looking at these they were found to comprise all the features of a bank of circulation, a bank of deposit, and a bank of discount upon bills of exchange—all in the hands of the government, and they to become the collectors and keepers of the public moneys, and the furnishers of a national paper money currency, in sums adapted to common dealings, both to the people and the federal government. It was a revolting scheme, and fit for instant condemnation, but in great danger of being adopted from the present predominance of that party in all the departments of the government which was so greatly addicted to the paper system.

CHAPTER XC.

THIRD PLAN FOR A FISCAL AGENT, CALLED EXCHEQUER BOARD: MR. BENTON'S SPEECH AGAINST IT: EXTRACTS.

MR. PRESIDENT:—I have said on several occasions since the present administration was formed, that we had gone back not merely to the federal times of General Hamilton, but far beyond them—to the whig times of Sir Robert Walpole, and the tory times of Queen Anne. When I have said this I did not mean it for sarcasm, or for insult, or to annoy the feelings of those who had just gotten into power. My aim was far higher and nobler—that of showing the retrograde movement which our government was making, and waking up the country to a sense of its dangers before it was too late; and to the conviction of the necessity of arresting that movement, and recovering the ground which we have lost. When I had said that we had gone back to the Walpole and Queen Anne times of the British government, I knew full well the extent of the declaration which I had made, and the obligation which I had imposed on myself to sustain my assertion, and I knew that history would bear me out in it. I knew all this; and I felt that if I could show to the American people that we had retrograded to the most calamitous period of British history—the period from which her present calamities all date—and that we were about to adopt the systems of policy which she then adopted, and which has led to her present condition; I felt that if I could do this, I might succeed in rousing up the country to a sense of its danger before it was too late to avoid the perils which are spread before us. The administration of Sir Robert Walpole was the fountain-head of British woes. All the measures which have led to the present condition of the British empire, and have given it more debt and taxes, more paupers, and more human misery than ever before was collected under the sway of one sceptre: all these date from the reigns of the first and second George; when this minister, for twenty-five years, was the ruler of parliament by means of the moneyed interest, and the ruler of kings by beating the tories at their own game of non-resistance and passive obedience to the royal will. The tories ruled under Queen Anne: they went for church and state, and rested for support on the landed interest. The whigs came into power with the accession of George the First: they went for bank and state; and rested for support on the moneyed interest. Sir Robert Walpole was the head of the whig party; and immediately became the favorite of that monarch, and afterwards of his successor; and, availing himself during that long period of power of all the resources of genius, unimpeded by the obstacle of principles, he succeeded in impressing his own image upon the age in which he lived, and giving to the government policy the direction which it has followed ever since. Morals, politics, public and private pursuits, all received the impress of the minister's genius; and what that genius produced I will now proceed to show: I read from Smollet's continuation of Hume:

> "This was the age of interested projects, inspired by a venal spirit of adventure, the natural consequence of that avarice, fraud, and profligacy which the MONEYED CORPORATIONS had introduced. The vice, luxury, and prostitution of the age—the almost total extinction of sentiment, honor, and public spirit—had prepared the minds of men for slavery and corruption. The means were in the hands of the ministry: the public treasure was at their devotion: they multiplied places and pensions, to increase the number of their dependents: they squandered away the national treasure without taste, discernment, decency, or remorse: they enlisted an army of the most abandoned emissaries, whom they employed to vindicate the worst measures in the face of truth, common sense, and common honesty; and they did not fail to stigmatize as Jacobites, and enemies to the government, all those who presumed to question the merit of their administration. The interior government of Great Britain was chiefly managed by Sir Robert Walpole, a man of extraordinary talents, who had from low beginnings raised himself to the head of the ministry. Having obtained a seat in the House of Commons, he declared himself one of the most forward partisans of the whig faction. He was endued with a species of eloquence which, though neither nervous nor elegant, flowed with great facility, and was so plausible on all subjects, that even when he misrepresented the truth, whether from ignorance or design, he seldom failed to persuade that part of his audience for whose hearing his harangue was chiefly intended. He was well acquainted with the nature of the public funds, and understood the whole mystery of

stockjobbing. This knowledge produced a connection between him and the MONEY CORPORATIONS, which served to enhance his importance."

Such was the picture of Great Britain in the time of Sir Robert Walpole, and such was the natural fruit of a stockjobbing government, composed of bank and state, resting for support on heartless corporations, and lending the wealth and credit of the country to the interested schemes of projectors and adventurers. Such was the picture of Great Britain during this period; and who would not mistake it (leaving out names and dates) for a description of our own times, in our own America, during the existence of the Bank of the United States and the thousand affiliated institutions which grew up under its protection during its long reign of power and corruption? But, to proceed, with English history:

Among the corporations brought into existence by Sir Robert Walpole, or moulded by him into the form which they have since worn, were the South Sea Company, the East India Company, the Bank of England, the Royal Insurance Company, the London Insurance Company, the Charitable Corporation, and a multitude of others, besides the exchequer and funding systems, which were the machines for smuggling debts and taxes upon the people and saddling them on posterity. All these schemes were brought forward under the pretext of paying the debts of the nation, relieving the distresses of the people, assisting the poor, encouraging agriculture, commerce, and manufactures; and saving the nation from the burden of loans and taxes. Such were the pretexts for all the schemes. They were generally conceived by low and crafty adventurers, adopted by the minister, carried through parliament by bribery and corruption, flourished their day; and ended in ruin and disgrace. A brief notice of the origin and pretensions of the South Sea scheme, may serve for a sample of all the rest, and be an instructive lesson upon the wisdom of all government projects for the relief of the people. I say, a notice of its origin and pretensions; for the progress and termination of the scheme are known to everybody, while few know (what the philosophy of history should be most forward to teach) that this renowned scheme of fraud, disgrace, and ruin, was the invention of a London scrivener, adopted by the king and his minister, passed through parliament by bribes to the amount of £574,000; and that its vaunted object was to pay the debts of the nation, to ease the burdens of the subject, to encourage the industry of the country, and to enrich all orders of men. These are the things which should be known; these are the things which philosophy, teaching by the example of history, proposes to tell, in order that the follies of one age or nation may be a warning to others; and this is what I now want to show. I read again from the same historian:

> "The king (George I.) having recommended to the Commons the consideration of proper means for lessening the national debt, was a prelude to the famous South Sea act, which became productive of so much mischief and infatuation. The scheme was projected by Sir John Blunt, who had been bred a scrivener, and was possessed of all the cunning, plausibility and boldness requisite for such an undertaking. He communicated his plan to the Chancellor of the Exchequer, as well as to one of the Secretaries of State. He answered all their objections, and the plan was adopted. They foresaw their own private advantage in the execution of the design. The pretence for the scheme was to discharge the national debt, by reducing all the funds into one. The Bank and the South Sea Company outbid each other. The South Sea Company altered their original plan, and offered such high terms to government that the proposals of the Bank were rejected: and a bill was ordered to be brought into the House of Commons, formed on the plan presented by the South Sea Company. The bill passed without amendment or division; and on the 7th day of April, 1720, received the royal assent. Before any subscription could be made, a fictitious stock of £574,000 had been disposed of by the directors to facilitate the passing of the bill. Great part of this was distributed among the Earl Sunderland, Mr. Craggs, Secretary of State, the Chancellor of the Exchequer, the Duchess of Kendall, the Countess of Platen, and her two nieces" (mistresses of the king, &c.)

This is a sample of the origin and pretensions of nearly all the great corporations which were chartered and patronized by the Walpole whigs: all of them brought forward under the pretext of relieving the people and the government—nearly all of them founded in fraud or folly—carried through by corruption—and ending in disgrace and calamity. Leaving out names, and who would not suppose that I had been reading the history of our own country in our own times? The picture suits the United States in 1840 as well as it suited England in

1720: but at one point, the comparison, if pushed a step further, would entirely fail; all these corporation plunderers were punished in England! Though favored by the king and ministry, they were detested by the people, and pursued to the extremity of law and justice. The South Sea swindlers were fined and imprisoned—their property confiscated—their names attainted—and themselves declared incapable of holding any office of honor or profit in the kingdom. The president and cashier of the *charitable corporation*—(which was chartered to relieve the distresses of the poor, and which swindled the said poor out of £600,000 sterling)—this president and this cashier were pursued into Holland—captured—brought back—criminally punished—and made to disgorge their plunder. Others, authors and managers of various criminal corporations, were also punished: and in this the parallel ceases between the English times and our own. With us, the swindling corporations are triumphant over law and government. Their managers are in high places—give the tone to society—and riot in wealth. Those who led, or counselled the greatest ruin which this, or any country ever beheld—the Bank of the United States—these leaders, their counsellors and abettors, are now potential with the federal government—furnish plans for new systems of relief—and are as bold and persevering as ever in seizing upon government money and government credit to accomplish their own views. In all this, the parallel ceases; and our America sinks in the comparison.

Corporation credit was ruined in Great Britain, by the explosions of banks and companies—by the bursting of bubbles—by the detection of their crimes—and by the crowning catastrophe of the South Sea scheme: it is equally ruined with us, and by the same means, and by the crowning villany of the Bank of the United States. Bank and state can no longer go together in our America: the government can no longer repose upon corporations. This is the case with us in 1841; and it was the case with Great Britain in 1720. The South Sea explosion dissolved (for a long time) the connection there; the explosion of the Bank of the United States has dissolved it here. New schemes become indispensable: and in both countries the same alternative is adopted. Having exhausted corporation credit in England, the Walpole whigs had recourse to government credit, and established a Board of Exchequer, to strike government paper. In like manner, the new whigs, having exhausted corporation credit with us, have recourse to government credit to supply its place; and send us a plan for a federal exchequer, copied with such fidelity of imitation from the British original that the description of one seems to be the description of the other. Of course I speak of the exchequer feature of the plan alone. For as to all the rest of our cabinet scheme—its banking and brokerage conceptions—its exchange and deposit operations—its three dollar issues in paper for one dollar specie in hand—its miserable one-half of one per centum on its Change-alley transactions—its Cheapside under-biddings of rival bankers and brokers:—as to all these follies (for they do not amount to the dignity of errors) they are not copied from any part of the British exchequer system, or any other system that I ever heard of, but are the uncontested and unrivalled production of our own American genius. I repeat it: our administration stands to-day where the British government stood one hundred and twenty years ago. Corporation credit exhausted, public credit is resorted to; and the machinery of an exchequer of issues becomes the instrument of cheating and plundering the people in both countries. The British invent: we copy: and the copy proves the scholar to be worthy of the master. Here is the British act. Let us read some parts of it: and recognize in its design, its structure, its object, its provisions, and its machinery, the true original of this plan (the exchequer part) which the united wisdom of our administration has sent down to us for our acceptance and ratification. I read, not from the separate and detached acts of the first and second George, but from the revised and perfected system as corrected and perpetuated in the reign of George the Third. (Here Mr. Benton compared the two systems through the twenty sections which compose the British act, and the same number which compose the exchequer bill of this administration.)

Here, resumed Mr. B. is the original of our exchequer scheme! here is the original of which our united administration has unanimously sent us down a faithful copy. In all that relates to the exchequer—its design—operation—and mode of action—they are one and the same thing! identically the same. The design of both is to substitute government credit for corporation credit—to strike paper money for the use of the government—to make this paper a currency, as well as a means of raising loans—to cover up and hide national debt—to avoid present taxes in order to increase them an hundred fold in future—to throw the burdens of the present day upon a future day; and to load posterity with our debts in addition to their own. The design of both is the same, and the structure of both is the same. The English board consists of the lord treasurer for the time being, and three commissioners to be appointed by the king; our board is to consist of the Secretary of the Treasury and the Treasurer for the time being, and three commissioners to be appointed by the President and Senate. The English board is to superintend and direct the form and mode of preparing and issuing the exchequer bills; our board is to do the same by our treasury notes. The English bills are to be receivable in all payments to the public; our treasury notes are to be received in like manner in all federal payments. The English board appoints paymasters, clerks and officers to assist them in the work of the exchequer; ours is to appoint agents in the States, with officers and clerks to assist them in the same work. The English paymasters are to give bonds, and be subject to inspection; our agents are to do and submit to the same. The English exchequer bills are to serve for a currency; and for that purpose the board may contract with persons, bodies politic and corporate, to take and circulate them; our board is to do the same thing through its agencies in the States and territories. The English exchequer bills are to be exchanged for ready money; ours are to be exchanged in the same manner. In short, the plans are the same, one copied from the other, identical in design, in structure, and in mode of operation; and wherein they differ (as they do in some details), the advantage is on the side of the British. For example: 1. The British pay interest on their bills, and raise the interest when necessary to sustain them in the market. Ours are to pay no interest, and will depreciate from the day they issue. 2. The British cancel and destroy their bills when once paid: we are to reissue ours, like common bank notes, until worn out with use. 3. The British make no small bills; none less than £100 sterling ($500), we begin with five dollars, like the old continentals; and, like them, will soon be down to one dollar, and to a shilling. 4. The British board could issue no bill except as specially authorized from time to time by act of Parliament: ours is to keep out a perpetual issue of fifteen millions; thus creating a perpetual debt to that amount. 5. The British board was to have no deposit of government stocks: ours are to have a deposit of five millions, to be converted into money when needed, and to constitute another permanent debt to that amount. 6. The British gave a true title to their exchequer act: we give a false one to ours. They entitled theirs, "*An act for regulating the issuing and paying off, of exchequer bills:*" we entitle ours, "*A bill amendatory of the several acts establishing the Treasury department.*" In these and a few other particulars the two exchequers differ; but in all the essential features—design—structure—operation—they are the same.

Having shown that our proposed exchequer was a copy of the British system, and that we are having recourse to it under the same circumstances: that in both countries it is a transit from corporation credit deceased, to government credit which is to bear the brunt of new follies and new extravagances: having shown this, I next propose to show the manner in which this exchequer system has worked in England, that, from its workings there, we may judge of its workings here. This is readily done. Some dates and figures will accomplish the task, and enlighten our understandings on a point so important. I say some dates and figures will do it. Thus: at the commencement of this system in England the annual taxes were 5 millions sterling: they are now 50 millions. The public debt was then 40 millions: it is now 900 millions, the unfunded items included. The interest and management of the debt were then 1½ millions: they are now 30 millions.

Here Mr. B. exhibited a book—the index to the British Statutes at large—containing a reference to all the issues of exchequer bills from the last year of the reign of George I. (1727) to the fourth year of the reign of her present Majesty (1840). He showed the amounts issued under each reign, and the parallel growth of the national debt, until these issues exceeded a thousand millions, and the debt, after all payments made upon it, is still near one thousand millions. Mr. B. here pointed out the annual issues under each reign, and then the totals for each reign, showing that the issues were small and far between in the beginning—large and close together in the conclusion—and that it was now going on faster than ever.

The following was the table of the issues under each reign:

Geo. I. in 1727 (one year),	£370,000
Geo. II. from 1727 to 1760 (33 years),	11,500,000
Geo. III. from 1760 to 1820 (60 years),	542,500,000
Geo. IV. from 1820 to 1831 (11 years),	320,000,000

Will. IV. from 1831 to 1837 (6 years),	160,000,000
Victoria I. from 1837 to 1840 (4 years),	160,000,000
	£1 140,370,000

Near twelve hundred millions of pounds sterling in less than a century and a quarter—we may say three-quarters of a century, for the great mass of the issues have taken place since the beginning of the reign of George III. The first issue was the third of a million; under George II., the average annual issue was the third of a million; under George III., the annual average was nine millions; under George IV. it was thirty millions; under William IV. twenty-three millions; and under Victoria, it is twenty-one millions. Such is the progress of the system—such the danger of commencing the issue of paper money to supply the wants of a government.

This, continued Mr. B., is the fruit of the exchequer issues in England, and it shows both the rapid growth and dangerous perversion of such issues. The first bills of this kind ever issued in that country were under William III., commonly called the Prince of Orange, in the year 1696. They were issued to supply the place temporarily of the coin, which was all called in to be recoined under the superintendence of Sir Isaac Newton. The first bills were put out by King William only for this temporary purpose, and were issued as low as ten pounds and five pounds sterling. It was not until more than thirty years afterwards, and when corporation credit had failed, that Sir Robert Walpole revived the idea of these bills, and perverted them into a currency, and into instruments for raising money for the service of the government. His practice was to issue these bills to supply present wants, instead of laying taxes or making a fair and open loan. When due, a new issue took up the old issue; and when the quantity would become great, the whole were funded; that is to say saddled upon posterity. The fruit of the system is seen in the 900,000,000 of debt which Great Britain still owes, after all the payments made upon it. The amount is enormous, overwhelming, appalling; such as never could have been created under any system of taxes or loans. In the nature of things government expenditure has its limits when it has to proceed upon taxation or borrowing. Taxes have their limit in the capacity of the people to pay: loans have their limit in the capacity of men to lend; and both have their restraints in the responsibility and publicity of the operation. Taxes cannot be laid without exciting the inquiry of the people. Loans cannot be made without their demanding wherefore. Money, i. e. gold and silver, cannot be obtained, but in limited and reasonable amounts, and all these restraints impose limits upon the amount of government expenditure and government debt. Not so with the noiseless, insidious, boundless progress of debt and expenditure upon the issue of government paper! The silent working of the press is unheard heard by the people. Whether it is one million or twenty millions that is struck, is all one to them. When the time comes for payment, the silent operation of the funding system succeeds to the silent operation of the printing press; and thus extravagant expenditures go on—a mountain of debt grows up—devouring interest accrues—and the whole is thrown upon posterity, to crush succeeding ages, after demoralizing the age which contracted it.

The British debt is the fruit of the exchequer system in Great Britain, the same that we are now urged to adopt, and under the same circumstances; and frightful as is its amount, that is only one branch—one part of the fruit—of the iniquitous and nefarious system. Other parts remain to be stated, and the first that I name is, that a large part of this enormous debt is wholly false and factitious! McCulloch states two-fifths to be fictitious; other writers say more; but his authority is the highest, and I prefer to go by it. In his commercial dictionary, now on my table, under the word "*funds*," he shows the means by which a stock for £100 would be granted when only £60 or £70 were paid for it; and goes on to say:

> "In consequence of this practice, the principal of the debt now existing amounts to nearly two-fifths more than the amount actually advanced by the lender."

So that the English people are bound for two-fifths more of capital, and pay two-fifths more of annual interest, on account of their debt than they ever received. Two-fifths of 900,000,000 is 360,000,000; and two-fifths of 30,000,000 is 12,000,000; so that here is fictitious debt to the amount of $1,600,000,000 of our money, drawing $60,000,000 of interest, for which the people of England never received a cent; and into which they were juggled and cheated by the frauds and villanies of the exchequer and funding systems! those systems which we are now unanimously invited by our administration to adopt. The next fruit of this system is that of the kind of money, as it was called, which was considered lent, and which goes to make up the three-fifths of the debt admitted to have been received; about the one-half of it was received in depreciated paper during the long bank suspension which took place from 1797 to 1823, and during which time the depreciation sunk as low as 30 per centum. Here, then, is another deduction of near one-third to be taken off the one-half of[32] the three-fifths which is counted as having been advanced by the lenders. Finally, another bitter drop is found in this cup of indebtedness, that the lenders were mostly jobbers and gamblers in stocks, without a shilling of their own to go upon, and who by the tricks of the system became the creditors of the government for millions. These gentry would puff the stocks which they had received—sell them at some advance—and then lend the government a part of its own money. These are the lenders—these the receivers of thirty millions sterling of taxes—these the scrip nobility who cast the hereditary nobles into the shade, and who hold tributary to themselves all the property and all the productive industry of the British empire. And this is the state of things which our administration now proposes for our imitation.

This is the way the exchequer and funding system have worked in England; and let no one say they will not work in the same manner in our own country. The system is the same in all countries, and will work alike every where. Go into it, and we shall have every fruit of the system which the English people now have; and of this most of our young States, and of our cities, and corporations, which have gone into the borrowing business upon their bonds, are now living examples. Their bonds were their exchequer bills. They used them profusely, extravagantly, madly, as all paper credit is used. Their bonds were sold under par, though the discount was usually hid by a trick: pay was often received in depreciated paper. Sharpers frequently made the purchase, who had nothing to pay but a part of the proceeds of the same bonds when sold. And thus the States and cities are bound for debts which are in a great degree fictitious, and are bound to lenders who had nothing to lend; and such are the frauds of the system which is presented to us, and must be our fate, if we go into the exchequer system.

I have shown the effect of an exchequer of issues in Great Britain to strike paper money for a currency, and as a substitute for loans and taxes. I have shown that this system, adopted by Sir Robert Walpole upon the failure of corporation credit, has been the means of smuggling a mountain load of debt upon the British people, two-fifths of which is fraudulent and fictitious; that it has made the great body of the people tributaries to a handful of fundholders, most of whom, without owning a shilling, were enabled by the frauds of the paper system and the funding system, to lend millions to the government. I have shown that this system, thus ruinous in England, was the resort of a crafty minister to substitute government credit for the exhausted credit of the moneyed corporations, and the exploded bubbles; and I have shown that the exchequer plan now presented to us by our administration, is a faithful copy of the English original. I have shown all this; and now the question is, shall we adopt this copy? This is the question; and the consideration of it implies the humiliating conclusion, that we have forgot that we have a constitution, and we have gone back to the worst era of English history— to times of the South Sea bubble, to take lessons in the science of political economy. Sir, we have a Constitution! and if there was any thing better established than another, at the time of its adoption, it was that the new government was a hard-money government, made by hard-money men, who had seen and felt the evils of government paper, and who intended for ever to cut off the new government from the use of that dangerous expedient. The question was made in the Convention (for there was a small paper money party in that body), and solemnly decided that the government should not emit paper money, bills of credit, or paper currency of any kind. It appears from the history of the Convention, that the first draft of the constitution contained a paper clause, and that it stood in connection with the power to raise money; thus: "*To borrow money, and emit bills, on the credit of the United States.*" When this clause came up for consideration, Mr. Gouverneur Morris moved to strike out the words, "*and emit bills,*" and was seconded by Mr. Pierce Butler. "Mr. Madison thought it sufficient to prevent them from being made a tender." "Mr. Ellsworth thought this a favorable moment to shut and bar the door against paper money. The mischief of the various experiments which had been made, were now fresh in the public mind, and had excited the disgust of all the respectable part of America. By withholding the power from the new government, more friends of influence would be gained to it than by almost any thing else. Paper money can in no case be necessary. Give the government credit, and other resources will offer. The power may do harm, never good." Mr. Wilson said: "It will have a most salutary influence on the credit of the United States, to remove the possibility of paper money. This expedient can never succeed while its mischiefs are remembered; and as long as it can be resorted to, it will be a bar to other resources." "Mr. Butler remarked that paper was a legal tender in no country in Europe. He was urgent for disarming the government of such a power." "Mr. Read thought the words, if not struck out, would be as alarming as the mark of the beast in Revelations." "Mr. Langdon had rather reject the whole plan than retain the three words, 'and emit bills.'" A few members spoke in favor of retaining the clause; but, on taking the vote, the sense of the convention was almost unanimously against it. Nine States voted for striking out: two for retaining.

If there were a thousand constitutional provisions in favor of paper money, I should still be against it—against the thing itself, *per se* and *propter se*—on account of its own inherent baseness and vice. But the Constitution is against it—clearly so upon its face; upon its history; upon its early practice; upon its uniform interpretation. The universal expression at the time of its adoption was, that the new government was a hard money government, made by hard money men, and that it was to save the country from the curse of paper money. This was the universal language—this the universal sentiment; and this hard money character of the new government was one of the great recommendations in its favor, and one of the chief inducements to its adoption. All the early action of the government conformed to this idea—all its early legislation was as true to hard money as the needle is to the pole. The very first act of Congress for the collection of duties on imports, passed in the first year of the new government's existence, and enacted by the very men who had framed the Constitution—this first act required those duties to be paid "*in gold and silver coin only;*" the word *only*, which is a contraction for the old English *onely*, being added to cut off the possibility of an intrusion, or an injection of a particle of paper money into the Treasury of the United States. The first act for the sale of public lands required them to be paid for in "*specie*"—the specie circular of 1836 was only the enforcement of that act; and the hard money clause in the independent treasury was a revival of these two original and fundamental revenue laws. Such were the early legislative interpretations of the Constitution by the men who made it; and corresponding with these for a long time after the commencement of the government, were the interpretations of all public men, and of no one more emphatically than of him who is now the prominent member of this administration, and to whose hand public opinion attributes the elaborate defence of the Cabinet Exchequer plan which has been sent down to us. In two speeches, delivered by that gentleman in the House of Representatives in the year 1816, he thus expressed himself on the hard money character of our government, and on the folly and danger of the paper system:

> "No nation had a better currency than the United States. There was no nation which had guarded its currency with more care: for the framers of the Constitution and those who had enacted the early statutes on the subject, were hard money men. They had felt and duly appreciated the evils of a paper medium: they, therefore, sedulously guarded the currency of the United States from debasement. The legal currency of the United States was gold and silver coin: this was a subject in regard to which Congress had run into no folly. Gold and silver currency was the law of the land at home, and the law of the world abroad: there could, in the present condition of the world, be no other currency."

So spake the present Secretary of State in February, 1816; and speaking so, he spoke the language of the Constitution, of the statesman, and of the enlightened age in which we live. He was right in saying that Congress, up to that time, had run into no folly in relation to the currency; that is to say, had not attempted to supersede the hard money of the Constitution by a national currency of paper. I can say the same for Congress up to the present day. Can the Secretary answer in like manner for the cabinet of which he is a member? Can he say of *it*, that *it* has run into no folly in relation to the currency? The secretary is right again in saying that, in the present condition of the world, there can be no other currency than gold and silver. Certainly he is right. Gold and silver is the measure of values. The actual condition of the world requires that measure to be uniform and universal. The whole world is now in a state of incessant intercommunication. Commercial, social, political relations are universal. Dealings and transactions are immense. All nations, civilized and barbarian, acknowledge the validity of the gold and silver standard; and the nation that should attempt to establish another, would derange its connections with the world, and put itself without the pale of its monetary system. The Secretary was right in saying that, in the present condition of the world, in the present state of the universal intercommunications of all mankind, there could be no measure of values but that which was universally acknowledged, and that all must conform to that measure. In this he showed a grasp of mind—a comprehension and profundity of intellect—which merits encomium, and which casts far into the shade the lawyer-like argument, in the shape of a report, which has been sent down to us.

The senator from Virginia [Mr. Rives] felicitates himself upon the character of these proposed exchequer bills, because they are not to be declared by law to be a legal tender: as if there was any necessity for such a declaration! Far above the law of the land is the law of necessity! far above the legal tender, which the statute enacts, is the forced tender which necessity compels. There is no occasion for the statutory enactment: the paper will soon enact the law for itself—that law which no power can resist, no weakness can shun, no art elude, no cunning escape. It is the prerogative of all paper money to expel all hard money; and then to force itself into every man's hand, because there is nothing else for any hand to receive. It is the prerogative of all paper money to do this, and of government paper above all other. Let this government go into the business of paper issues: let it begin to stamp paper for a currency, and it will quickly find itself with nothing but paper on its hands;—paper to pay out—paper to receive in;—the specie basis soon gone—and the vile trash depreciating from day to day until it sinks into nothing, and perishes on the hands of the ignorant, the credulous, and the helpless part of the community.

The same senator [Mr. RIVES] consoles himself with the small amount of these exchequer bills which are to be issued—only fifteen millions of dollars. Alas! sir, does he recollect that that sum is seven times the amount of our first emission of continental bills? that it is fifteen times the amount of Sir Robert Walpole's first emission of exchequer bills? and double the amount of the first emission of the French assignats? Does he consider these things, and recollect that it is the first step only which costs the difficulty? and that, in the case of government paper money, the subsequent progress is rapid in exact proportion to the difficulty of the first step? Does he not know that the first emission of our continental bills was two millions of dollars, and that in three years they amounted to two hundred millions? that the first issue of Sir Robert Walpole's exchequer bills was the third of a million, and that they have since exceeded a thousand millions? that the first emission of assignats was the third of a milliard of francs, and that in seven years they amounted to forty-five thousand milliards? Thus it has been, and thus it will be. The first issues of government paper are small, and with difficulty obtained, and upon plausible pretexts of necessity and relief. The subsequent issues are large, and obtained without opposition, and put out without the formality of an excuse. This is the course, and thus it will be with us if we once begin. We propose fifteen millions for the start: grant it: it will soon be fifteen hundred millions! and those who go to that excess will be far less blamable than those who made the first step.

I have said that the present administration have gone back far beyond the times of General Hamilton—that they have gone to the times of Sir Robert Walpole; and I prove it by showing how faithfully they copy his policy in pursuing the most fatal of his measures. Yes, sir, they have gone back not merely far beyond where General Hamilton actually stood, but to the point to which he refused to go. He refused to go to government paper money. That great man, though a friend to bank paper, was an enemy to government paper. He condemned and deprecated the whole system of government issues. He has left his own sentiments on record on this point, and they deserve in this period of the retrogression of our government to be remembered, and to be cited on this floor. In his report on a national bank in 1791, he ran a parallel between the dangers of bank paper and government paper, assigning to the latter the character of far greatest danger and mischief—an opinion in which I fully concur with him. In that report, he thus expressed himself on the dangers of government paper:

> "The emitting of paper money by the authority of the government is wisely prohibited to the individual States by the National Constitution: and the spirit of the prohibition should not be disregarded by the government of the United States. Though paper emissions, under a general authority, might have some advantages not applicable, and be free from disadvantages which are applicable, to the like emissions by the States separately, yet they are of a nature so liable to abuse—and, it may even be affirmed, so certain of being abused—that the wisdom of the government will be shown in never trusting itself with the use of so seducing and dangerous an expedient. The stamping of paper is an operation so much easier than the laying of taxes, that a government in the practice of paper emissions would rarely fail, in any such emergency,

to indulge itself too far in the employment of that resource, to avoid, as much as possible, one less auspicious to present popularity. If it should not even be carried so far as to be rendered an absolute bubble, it would at least be likely to be extended to a degree which would occasion an inflated and artificial state of things, incompatible with the regular and prosperous course of the political economy."

A division has taken place in the great whig party on this point. It has split into two wings—a great, and a small wing. The body of the party stand fast on the Hamiltonian ground of 1791: a fraction of the party have slid back to the Walpole ground of 1720. The point of difference between them is a government bank and government paper on one hand, and a banking company under a national charter, issuing bank notes, on the other. This is the point of difference, and it is a large one, very visible to every eye; and I am free to say that, with all my objections to the national bank and its paper, I am far more opposed to government banking, and to government issues of paper money.

The Tyler-Webster whigs are for government banking—for making the transit from corporation credit, no longer available, to government credit, which is to stand the brunt of new follies and new extravagances. They go for the British exchequer system, with all the folly and degradation of modern banking superadded and engrafted upon it. And what are the pretexts for this flagrant attempt? The same that were urged by the scrivener, John Blunt, in favor of his South Sea bubble—and by the gambler, John Law, in favor of the Mississippi scheme. To relieve the public distress—to aid the government and the people—to make money plenty, and to raise the price of property and wages: these are the pretexts which usher in our exchequer scheme, and which have ushered in all the paper money bubbles and projects which have ever afflicted and disgraced mankind. Relief to the people has been the pretext for the whole; and they have all ended in the same way—in the enrichment of sharpers—the plunder of nations—and the shame of governments. All these schemes have been brought forward in the same way, and although base upon their face, and clearly big with shame and ruin, and opposed by the wise and good of the times, yet there seem to be seasons of national delusion when the voice of judgment, reason, and honor is drowned under the clamor of knaves and dupes; and when the highest recommendation of a new plan is its absolute folly, knavery, and audacity. Thus it was in England during the reign of the moneyed corporations under the protection of Walpole. Wise men opposed all the mad schemes of that day, and exposed in advance all their disastrous and disgraceful issues. Mr. Shippen, Sir Joseph Jekyll, Mr. Barnard, Sir William Wyndham, Mr. Pulteney, Lord Morpeth (that Howard blood which has not yet degenerated), all these and many others opposed the South Sea, exchequer issues, and other mad schemes of their day—to be overpowered then, but to be remembered, and quoted with honor now. The chancellor of France, the wise and virtuous D'Aguesseau, was exiled from Paris by the Regent Duke of Orleans for opposing and exposing the Mississippi scheme of the gambler, John Law; but his name lives in the pantheon of history; and I take a pleasure in citing it here, in the American Senate, as well in honor to him, as to encourage others to sacrifice themselves in the noble task of resisting the mad delusions of the day. Every nation has its seasons of delusion. They seem to come, like periodical epidemics, once in so many ages or centuries; and while they rage, neither morals nor reason can make head against them. The have to run out. We have just had our season of this delusion, when every folly, from a national bank whose notes were to circulate in China, to the *morus multicaulis* whose leaves were to breed fortunes to the envied possessors; when every such folly had its day of triumph and exultation over reason, judgment, morals and common sense. Happily this season is passing away—the delusion is wearing off—before this cabinet plan of a government bank, with its central board, its fifty-two branches, its national engine to strike paper, its brokerage and exchange dealings, its Cheapside and Change-Alley operations in real business transactions, its one-half of one per centum profits, its three dollars in paper money to any one who was fool enough to deposit one dollar in the hard: happily our season of delusion is passing off before this monstrous scheme was presented. Otherwise, its adoption would have been inevitable. Its very monstrosity would have made it irresistibly captivating to the diseased public appetite if presented while still in its morbid state.

But the senator from Virginia who sits over the way [Mr. RIVES], who has spoken in this debate, and who appears as a *quasi* defender of this cabinet plan of relief, he demands if the senator from Missouri (my poor self) will do nothing to relieve the distress of the people and of the government? He puts the question to me, and I answer it readily; yes! I will do my part towards relieving this distress, but not exactly in the mode which he seems to prefer—not by applying a cataplasm of lamp-black and rags to the public wounds! whether that cataplasm should be administered by a league of coon-box banks in the States, or by a Biddle king bank in Philadelphia, or by a Walpole exchequer bank in Washington city. I would relieve the distress by the application of appropriate remedies to notorious diseases—a bankrupt act to bankrupt banks—taxation to bank issues—restoration of the land revenue to its proper destination—the imposition of economy upon this taxing, borrowing, squandering, gold-hating, paper-loving administration; and by restoring, as soon as possible, the reign of democracy, economy, and hard money.

The distress! still the distress. Distress, still the staple of all the whig speeches made here, and of all the cabinet reports which come down to us. Distress is the staple of the whole. "Motley is their only wear." Why, sir, I have heard about that distress before; and I am almost tempted to interrupt gentlemen in the midst of their pathetic rehearsals as the Vicar of Wakefield interrupted Jenkinson in the prison, when he began again the same learned dissertation upon the cosmogony or creation of the world; and gave him the same quotations from Sanconiathan, Manetho, Berosus, and Lucanus Ocellus, with which he entertained the good old Vicar at the fair, while cheating him out of Blackberry, after having cheated Moses out of the colt. You know the incident, said Mr. B. (addressing himself to Mr. Archer, who was nodding recognition), you remember the incident, and know the Vicar begged pardon for interrupting so much learning, with the declaration of his belief that he had had the honor to hear it all before. In like manner, I am almost tempted to stop gentlemen with a beg-pardon for interrupting so much distress, and declaring my belief that I have heard it all before. Certain it is, that for ten years past I have been accustomed to hear the distress orations on this floor; and for twenty-two years I have been accustomed to see distress in our country; but never have I seen it, or heard of it, that it did not issue from the same notorious fountain—the MONEYED CORPORATIONS—headed and conducted by the Juggernaut of federal adoration, the Biddle King Bank of the United States! I have seen this distress for two and twenty years; first, from 1819 to 1826; then again in 1832—'33—'34—'37—'39; and I see something of it now. The Bank of the United States commenced the distress in 1819, and gave a season of calamity which lasted as long as one of the seven years' plagues of Egypt. It was a seven years' agony; but at that time distress was not the object, but only the effect of her crimes and follies. In 1832 she renewed the distress as an object *per se* and *propter se* to force a renewal of her charter. In 1833-'34 she entered upon it with new vigor—with vast preparation—upon an immense scale—and all her forces—to coerce a restoration of the deposits, which the patriot President had saved by taking from her. In 1837 she headed the conspiracy for the general suspension (and accomplished it by the aid of the deposit distribution act) for the purpose of covering up and hiding her own insolvency in a general catastrophe, and making the final, agonizing death-struggle, to clutch the re-charter. In 1839 she forced the second suspension (which took place all south and west of New York) and endeavored to force it all north and east of that place, and make it universal, in order to conceal her own impending bankruptcy. She failed in the universality of this second suspension only for want of the means and power which the government deposits would have given her. She succeeded with her limited means, and in her crippled condition, over three-fourths of the Union; and now the only distress felt is in the places which have felt her power;—in the parts of the country which she has regulated—and arises from the institutions which have followed her lead—obeyed her impulse—imitated her example—and now keep up, for their own profit, and on their own account, the distress of which they were nothing but the vicarious agents in the beginning. Sir, there has been no distress since 1819 which did not come from the moneyed corporations; and since 1832, all the distress which we have seen has been factitious and factious—contrived of purpose, made to order, promulgated upon edict—and spread over the people, in order to excite discontents against the administration, to overturn the democracy, to re-establish federalism, to unite bank and state—and to deliver up the credit and revenue of the Union, and the property and industry of the people, to the pillage and plunder of the muckworm nobility which the crimes of the paper system have made the lords of the land. This is the only distress we have seen; and had it not been that God had given our country a Jackson, their daring schemes would all have succeeded; and we and our children, and all the property and labor of our country, would have been as completely tributary to the moneyed corporations of America, as the people of Great Britain are to the Change-alley lords who hold the certificates of their immense national debt.

Distress!—what, sir, are not the whigs in power, and was not all distress to cease when the democracy was turned out? Did they not carry the elections? Has Mr. Van Buren not gone to Kinderhook? Is General Jackson not in the Hermitage? Are democrats not in the minority in Congress, and expelled from office every where? Were not "*Tippecanoe* and *Tyler too*" both elected? Is not whiggery in entire possession of the government? Have they not had their extra session, called to relieve the country, and passed all the relief measures, save one?—all save one!—all except their national bank, of which this fine exchequer bank is to be the metempsychosis.

The cry is distress! and the remedy a national poultice of lamp-black and rags! This is the disease, and this the medicine. But let us look before we act. Let us analyze the case—examine the pathology of the disease—that is the word, I believe (looking at Dr. LINN, who nodded assent), and see its cause and effect, the habits and constitution of the patient, and the injuries he may have suffered. The complaint is, distress: the specifications are, depreciated currency, and deranged exchanges. The question is, where? all over the Union? not at all— only in the South and West. All north and east of New York is free from distress—the exchanges fair—the currency at par: all south and west of that city the distress prevails—the exchanges (as they are called) being deranged and the currency depreciated. Why? Because, in one quarter—the happy quarter—the banks pay their debts: in the other—the distressed quarter—they refuse to pay. Here then is the cause, and the effect. This is the analysis of the case—the discovery of the nature and locality of the disease—and the key to its cure. Make the refractory banks comply with their promises; and there is an end of depreciated paper and deranged exchanges, and of all the distress which they create; and that without a national bank, or its base substitute, an exchequer bank; or a national institution of any kind to strike paper money. Make the delinquent banks pay up, or wind up. And why not? Why should not the insolvent wind up, and the solvent pay up? Why should not the community know the good from the bad? Suspension puts all on a level, and the community cannot distinguish between them. Our friend Sancho (looking at Mr. MOUTON) has a proverb that suits the case: "*De noche todos los gatos son pardos.*"

"M. MOUTON: '*De nuit tous les chats sont gris.*'"

"Mr. BUCHANAN: What is all that?"

"Mr. BENTON: It is this: Our friend, Sancho Panza, says that, in the dark all the cats are of one color. [A laugh.] So of these banks. In a state of suspension they are all of one credit; but as the light of a candle soon discriminates the black cats from the white ones, so would the touch of a bankrupt act speedily show the difference between a rotten bank and a solvent one.

But currency—currency—a national currency of uniform value, and universal circulation: this is what modern whigs demand, and call upon Congress to give it; meaning all the while a national currency of paper money. I deny the power of Congress to give it, and aver its folly if it had. The word currency is not in the constitution, nor any word which can be made to signify paper money. Coin is the only thing mentioned in that instrument; and the only power of Congress over it is to regulate its value. It is an interpolation, and a violation of truth to say that the constitution authorizes Congress to regulate the value of paper money, or to create paper money. It is a calumny upon the constitution to say any such thing; and I defy the whole phalanx of the paper money party to produce one word in that instrument to justify their imputation. Coin, and not paper, is the thing to be regulated; coin, and not paper, is the currency mentioned and intended; and this coin it is the duty of Congress to preserve, instead of banishing it from circulation. Paper banishes coin; and by creating, or encouraging paper, Congress commits a double violation of the constitution; *first*, by favoring a thing which the constitution condemns; and, *secondly*, by destroying the thing which it meant to preserve. But the paper money party say there is not gold and silver enough in the world to answer the purposes of a currency; and, therefore, they must have paper. I answer, if this was true, we must first alter our constitution before we can create, or adopt paper money. But it is not true! the assertion is unfounded and erroneous to the last degree, and implies the most lamentable ignorance of the specie resources of commercial and agricultural countries. The world happens to contain more specie than such countries can use; and it depends upon each one to have its share when it pleases. This is an assertion as easily proved as made; and I proceed to the proof of it, because it is a point on which there is much misunderstanding; and on which the public good requires authentic information. I will speak first of our own country, and of our own times—literally, my own times.

I have some tabular statements on hand, Mr. President, made at the Treasury, on my motion, and which show our specie acquisitions during the time that I have sat in this chair: I say, sat in *this* chair, for I always sit in the same place. I never change my position, and therefore never have to find it or define it. These tables show our imports of gold and silver during this time—a period of twenty-one years—to have been on the custom-house books, 182 millions of dollars: making an allowance for the amounts brought by passengers, and not entered on the books, and the total importation cannot be less than 200 millions. The coinage at our Mint during the same period, is 66 millions of dollars. The product of our gold mines during that period has been several millions; and many millions of gold have been dragged from their hiding places and restored to circulation by the gold bill of 1834. Putting all together, and our specie acquisitions must have amounted to 220 or 230 millions of dollars in these twenty-one years; being at the average rate of ten or eleven millions per annum.

Not specie enough in the world to do the business of the country! What an insane idea! Do people who talk in that way know any thing about the quantity of specie that there is in the world, or even in Europe and America, and the amount that different nations, according to their pursuits, can employ in their business? If they do not, let them listen to what Gallatin and Gouge say upon the subject, and let them learn something which a man should know before he ventures an opinion upon currency. Mr. Gallatin, in 1831, thus speaks of the quantity of gold and silver in Europe and America:

> "The total amount of gold and silver produced by the mines of America, to the year 1803, inclusively, and remaining there or exported to Europe, has been estimated by Humboldt at about five thousand six hundred millions of dollars; and the product of the years 1804-1830, may be estimated at seven hundred and fifty millions. If to this we add one hundred millions, the nearly ascertained product, to this time, of the mines of Siberia, about four hundred and fifty millions for the African gold dust, and for the product of the mines of Europe (which yielded about three millions a year, in the beginning of this century), from the discovery of America to this day, and three hundred millions for the amount existing in Europe prior to the discovery of America, we find a total not widely differing from the fact, of seven thousand two hundred millions of dollars. It is much more difficult to ascertain the amount which now remains in Europe and America together. The loss by friction and accidents might be estimated, and researches made respecting the total amount which has been exported to countries beyond the Cape of Good Hope; but that which has been actually consumed in gilding, plated ware, and other manufactures of the same character, cannot be correctly ascertained. From the imperfect data within our reach, it may, we think, be affirmed, that the amount still existing in Europe and America certainly exceeds four thousand, and most probably falls short of five thousand millions of dollars. Of the medium, or four thousand five hundred millions, which we have assumed, it appears that from one-third to two-fifths is used as currency, and that the residue consists of plate, jewels, and other manufactured articles. It is known, that of the gross amount of seven thousand two hundred millions of dollars, about eighteen hundred millions, or one-fourth of the whole in value, and one-forty-eighth in weight, consisted of gold. Of the four thousand five hundred millions, the presumed remaining amount in gold and silver, the proportion of gold is probably greater, on account of the exportation to India and China having been exclusively in silver, and of the greater care in preventing every possible waste in an article so valuable as gold."

Upon this statement, Mr. Gouge, in his Journal of Banking, makes the following remarks:

> "We begin to-day with Mr. Gallatin's estimate of the quantity of gold and silver in Europe and America. In a work published by him in 1831, entitled 'Considerations on the Currency and Banking system of the United States,' he estimates the amount of precious metals in these two quarters of the world at between four thousand and five thousand million dollars. This, it will be recollected, was ten years ago. The amount has since been considerably increased, as the mines have annually produced millions, and the demand for the China trade has been greatly diminished.

"Taking the medium, however, of the two sums stated by Mr. Gallatin—four thousand five hundred million dollars—and supposing the population of Europe and America to be two hundred and seventy-seven millions, it will amount to sixteen dollars and upwards for every man, woman, and child, on the two continents. The same gentleman estimates the whole amount of currency in the United States in 1829, paper and specie together at only six dollars a head.

"It is not too much to say, that if the natural laws of supply and demand had not been interfered with, the United States would have, in proportion to population, four, five, six, seven, yea, eight times as much gold and silver as many of the countries of Europe. Take it at only the double of the average for the population of the two continents, and it will amount to thirty-two dollars a head, or to five hundred and fourteen millions. This would give us one-ninth part of the stock of gold and silver of Europe and America, while our population is but one-sixteenth: but for the reasons already stated, under a natural order of things, we should have, man for man, a much larger portion of the precious metals, than falls to the lot of most countries of Europe.

"Suppose, however, we had but the average of sixteen dollars a head. This would amount to two hundred and fifty-seven millions.

"On two points do people (that is, some people) capitally err. First, in regard to the quantity of gold and silver in the world: this is much greater than they imagine it to be. Next, in regard to the amount of money required for commercial purposes: this is much smaller than they suppose it to be. Under a sound money, sound credit, and sound banking system, ten dollars a head would probably be amply sufficient in the United States."

The points on which the statesman's attention should be fixed in these statements are: 1. The quantity of gold and silver in Europe and America, to wit, $4,500,000,000. 2. Our fair proportion of that quantity, to wit, $257,000,000, or $16 per head. 3. Our inability to use more than $10 a head. 4. The actual amount of our whole currency, paper and specie, in 1830 (when the Bank of the United States was in all its glory), and which was only $6 a head. 5. The ease with which the United States can supply itself with its full proportion of the whole quantity if it pleased, and have $16 per head (if it could use it, which it cannot) for every human being in the Union.

These are the facts which demand our attention, and it is only at a single point that I now propose to illustrate, or to enforce them; and that is, as to the quantity of money per head which any nation can use. This differs among different nations according to their pursuits, the commercial and manufacturing people requiring most, because their payments are daily or weekly for every thing they use: food, raiment, labor and raw materials. With agricultural people it is less, because they produce most of what they consume, and their large payments are made annually from the proceeds of the crops. Thus, England and France (both highly manufacturing and commercial) are ascertained to employ fourteen dollars per head (specie and paper combined) for their whole population: Russia, an agricultural country, is ascertained to employ only four dollars per head; and the United States, which is chiefly agricultural, but with some considerable admixture of commerce and manufactures, ten dollars are believed to be the maximum which they could employ. In this opinion I concur. I think ten dollars per head, an ample average circulation for the Union; and it is four dollars more than we had in 1830, when the Bank of the United States was at the zenith of its glory. The manufacturing and commercial districts might require more—all the agricultural States less;—and perhaps an agricultural State without a commercial town, or manufactures, like Mississippi, could not employ five dollars per head. Here then are the results: Our proportion of the gold and silver in Europe and America is two hundred and fifty-seven millions of dollars: we had but twenty millions in 1830: we have ninety millions now; and would require but eighty millions more (one hundred and seventy millions in the whole) in the present state of our population, slaves included (for their labor is to be represented by money and themselves supported), to furnish as much currency, and that in gold and silver, as the country could possibly use; consequently sustaining the prices of labor and property at their maximum amount. Of that sum, we now have about the one-half in the country, to wit, ninety millions;

making five dollars per head; and as that sum was gained in seven years of Jacksonian policy, it follows of course, that another seven years of the same policy, would give us the maximum supply that we could use of the precious metals; and that gold, silver, and the commercial bill of exchange, could then constitute the safe, solid, constitutional, moral, and never-failing currency of the Union.

The facility with which any industrious country can supply itself with a hard-money currency—can lift itself out of the mud and mire of depreciated paper, and mount the high and clean road of gold and silver; the ease with which any industrious people can do this, has been sufficiently proved in our own country, and in many others. We saw it in the ease with which the Jackson policy gained us ninety millions of dollars in seven years. We saw it at the close of the Revolution, when the paper money sunk to nothing, ceased to circulate, and specie re-appeared, as by magic. I have asked the venerable Mr. MACON how long it was after paper stopped, before specie re-appeared at that period of our history? his answer was: No time at all. As soon as one stopped, the other came. We have seen it in England at the end of the long bank suspension, which terminated in 1823. Parliament allowed the bank four years to prepare for resumption: at the end of two years—half the time— she reported herself ready—having in that short space accumulated a mass of twenty millions sterling (one hundred millions of dollars) in gold; and, above all, we have seen it in France, where the great Emperor restored the currency in the short space of six years, from the lowest degree of debasement to the highest point of brilliancy. On becoming First Consul, in 1800, he found nothing but depreciated assignats in the county:—in six years his immortal campaigns—Austerlitz, Jena, Friedland—all the expenses of his imperial court, surpassing in splendor that of the Romans, and rivalling the almost fabulous magnificence of the Caliphs of Bagdad—all his internal improvements—all his docks, forts, and ships—all the commerce of his forty millions of subjects—all these were carried on by gold and silver alone; and from having the basest currency in the world, France, in six years, had near the best; and still retains it. These instances show how easy it is for any country that pleases to supply itself with an ample currency of gold and silver—how easy it will be for us to complete our supplies—that in six or seven years we could saturate the land with specie! and yet we have a formal cabinet proposition to set up a manufactory of paper money!

The senator from Mississippi [Mr. WALKER] who sits on my right, has just visited the island of Cuba, and has told us what he has seen there—a pure metallic currency of gold—twelve millions of dollars of it to a population of one million of souls, half slaves—not a particle of paper money—prices of labor and property higher than in the United States—industry active—commerce flourishing: a foreign trade of twenty-four millions of dollars, which, compared to population and territory, is so much greater than ours that it would require ours to be four hundred and twenty-five millions to be equal to it! This is what the senator from Mississippi tells us that he has seen; and would to God that we had all seen it. Would to God that the whole American Congress had seen it. Devoutly do I wish that it was the custom now, as in ancient times, for legislators to examine the institutions of older countries before they altered those of their own country. The Solons and Lycurguses of antiquity would visit Egypt, and Crete, and other renowned places in the East, before they would touch the laws of Sparta or Athens; in like manner I should rejoice to see our legislators visit the hard money countries—Holland, France, Cuba—before they went further with paper money schemes in our own country. The cabinet, I think, should be actually put upon such a voyage. After what they have done, I think they should be shipped on a visit to the lands of hard money. And although it might seem strange, under our form of government, thus to travel our President and cabinet, yet I must be permitted to say that I can find constitutional authority for doing so, just as soon as they can find constitutional authority for sending such a scheme of finance and currency as they have spread before us.

Holland and Cuba have the best currencies in the world: it is gold and the commercial bill of exchange, with small silver for change, and not a particle of bank paper. France has the next best: it is gold, with the commercial bill of exchange, much silver, and not a bank note below five hundred francs (say one hundred dollars). And here let me do justice to the wisdom and firmness of the present king of the French. The Bank of France lately resolved to reduce the minimum size of its notes to two hundred francs (say forty dollars). The king gave them notice that if they did it, the government would consider it an injury to the currency, and would take steps to correct the movement. The Bank rescinded its resolution; and Louis Philippe, in that single act (to say nothing of others) showed himself to be a patriot king, worthy of every good man's praise, and of every legislator's imitation. The United States have the basest currency in the world: it is paper, down to cents; and that paper supplied by irresponsible corporations, which exercise the privilege of paying, or not, just as it suits their interest or politics. We have the basest currency upon the face of the earth; but it will not remain so. Reform is at hand; probably from the mild operation of law; if not, certainly from the strong arm of ruin. God has prescribed morality, law, order, government, for the conduct of human affairs; and he will not permit these to be too long outraged and trampled under foot. The day of vindicating the outraged law and order of our country, is at hand; and its dawn is now visible. The excess of bank enormity will cure itself under the decrees of Providence; and the cure will be more complete and perfect, than any that could come from the hands of man.

It may seem paradoxical, but it is true, that there is no abundant currency, low interest, and facility of loans, except in hard money countries: paper makes scarcity, high interest, usury, extortion, and difficulty of borrowing. Ignorance supposes that to make money plenty, you must have paper: this is pure nonsense. Paper drives away all specie, and then dies itself for want of specie; and leaves the country penniless until it can recruit.

The Roman historians, Mr. President, inform us of a strange species of madness which afflicted the soldiers of Mark Antony on their retreat from the Parthian war. Pressed by hunger they ate of unknown roots and herbs which they found along the base of the Armenian mountains, and among the rest, of one which had the effect of depriving the unfortunate man of memory and judgment. Those who ate of this root forgot that they were Romans—that they had arms—a general—a camp, and their lives, to defend. And wholly possessed of a single idea, which became fixed, they neglected all their duties and went about turning over all the stones they could find, under the firm conviction that there was a great treasure under it which would make them rich and happy. Nothing could be more deplorable, say the historians, than to see these heroic veterans, the pride of a thousand fields, wholly given up to this visionary pursuit, their bodies prone to the earth, day after day, and turning over stones in search of this treasure, until death from famine, or the Parthian arrow, put an end at once to their folly and their misery. Such is the account which historians give us of this strange madness amongst Antony's soldiers; and it does seem to me that something like it has happened to a great number of our Americans, and even to our cabinet council—that they have forgotten that we have such a thing as a constitution—that there are such things as gold and silver—that there are limitations upon government power—and that man is to get his living by toil and labor, and the sweat of his brow, and not by government contrivances; that they have forgot all this, and have become possessed of a fixed idea, that paper money is the *summum bonum* of human life; that lamp-black and rags, perfumed with the odor of nationality, is a treasure which is to make everybody rich and happy; and, thereupon incontinently pursue this visionary treasure—this figment of the brain—this disease of the mind. Possessed of this idea, they direct all their thoughts to the erection of a national institution—no matter what—to strike paper money, and circulate it upon the faith of the credit and revenues of the Union: and no argument, no reason, no experience of our own, or of other nations, can have the least effect in dislodging that fixed and sovereign conception. To this we are indebted for the cabinet plan of the federal exchequer and its appurtenances, which has been sent down to us. To this we are indebted for the crowds who look for relief from the government, instead of looking for it in their own labor, their own industry, and their own economy. To this we are indebted for all the paper bubbles and projects which are daily presented to the public mind: and how it all is to end, is yet in the womb of time; though I greatly suspect that the catastrophe of the federal exchequer and its appurtenances will do much towards curing the delusion and turning the public mind from the vain pursuit of visionary government remedies, to the solid relief of hard money, hard work, and instant compulsion of bank resumption.

The proposition which has been made by our President and cabinet, to commence a national issue of paper money, has had a very natural effect upon the public mind, that of making people believe that the old continental bills are to be revived, and restored to circulation by the federal government. This belief, so naturally growing out of the cabinet movement, has taken very wide and general root in the public mind; and my position in the Senate and connection with the currency questions, have made me the centre of many communications on the point. Daily I receive applications for my opinion, as to the revival of this long deceased and venerable currency. The very little boys at the school have begged my little boy to ask their father about it, and let them know, that they may hunt up the one hundred dollar bills which their mothers had given them for thumb papers, and which they had thrown by on account of their black and greasy looks. I receive letters from all parts of the Union, bringing specimens of these venerable relics, and demanding my opinion of the probability of their resuscitation. These letters contain various propositions—some of despair—some of hope—some of generous patriotism—and all evidently sincere. Some desire me to exhibit the bundle they enclose to the Senate, to show how the holders have been cheated by paper money; some want them paid; and if the government cannot pay at present, they wish them funded, and converted into a national stock, as part of the new national debt. Some wish me to look at them, on my own account; and from this sample, to derive new hatred to paper money, and to stand up to the fight with the greater courage, now that the danger of swamping us in lamp-black and rags is becoming so much greater than ever. Others, again, rising above the degeneracy of the times, and still feeling a remnant of that patriotism for which our ancestors were so distinguished, and which led them to make so many sacrifices for their country, and hearing of the distress of the government and its intention to have recourse to an emission of new continental bills, propose at once to furnish it with a supply of the old bills. Of this number is a gentleman whose letter I received last night, and which, being neither confidential in its nature, nor marked so, and being, besides, honorable to the writer, I will, with the leave of the Senate, here read:

> "EAST WEYMOUTH, MASSACHUSETTS, January 8, 1842.

> "DEAR SIR:—Within you have a few continentals, or promises to pay in gold or silver, which may now be serviceable to the Treasury, which the whigs have bankrupted in the first year of their reign, and left members without pay for their landlords. They may serve to start the new fiscality upon; and, if they should answer the purpose, and any more are wanted, please let me know, and another batch will come on from your friend and servant,

> "LOWELL BICKNELL.

> "Hon. THOMAS H. BENTON, United States Senate,
> Washington city."

This is the letter, resumed Mr. B., and these the contents (holding up a bundle of old continentals). This is an assortment of them, beginning at nine dollars, and descending regularly through eight, seven, six, five, four, three, two, one, and the fractional parts of a dollar, down to the one-sixth part of a dollar. I will read the highest and lowest in the bundle, as a sample of the whole. The highest runs thus:

> "This bill entitles the bearer to receive nine Spanish milled dollars, or the value thereof in gold or silver, according to the resolves of the Congress held at Philadelphia, the 10th day of May, 1775.

> "Signed,

> WILLIAM CRAIG."

The margins are covered with the names of the States, and with the words *continental currency*, in glaring capitals, and the Latin motto, *Sustine vel abstine* (Sustain it, or let it alone). The lowest runs thus:

> "One-sixth of a dollar, according to a resolve of Congress passed at Philadelphia, February 17th, 1776.

> "Signed,

> B. BRANNAN."

The device on this note is a sun shining through a glass, with the word *fugio* (I fly) for the motto—a motto sufficiently appropriate, whether emblematic of the fugitive nature of time, or of paper money.

These are a sample of the bills sent me in the letter which I have just read; and now the mind naturally reverts to the patriotic proposition to supply the administration with these old bills instead of putting out a new emission. For myself I incline to the proposition. If the question is once decided in favor of a paper emission, I am decidedly in favor of the old continental currency in preference to any new edition—as much so as I prefer the old Revolutionary whigs to the new whigs of this day. I prefer the old bills; and that for many and cogent reasons. I will enumerate a few of these reasons:—1. They are ready made to our hand, and will save all the expense and time which the preparations of new bills would require. The expense would probably be no objection with this administration; but, in the present condition of the Treasury, the other consideration, that of time, must have great weight. 2. They cannot be counterfeited. Age protects them from that. The wear and tear of seventy long years cannot be impressed on the face of the counterfeits, cunning as their makers may be. 3. Being limited in quantity, and therefore incapable of contraction or inflation at the will of jobbers in stocks or politics, they will answer better for a measure of values. 4. They are better promises than any that will be made at this day; for they are payable in Spanish milled dollars, which are at a premium of three per cent, in our market over other dollars; and they are payable in gold *or* silver, disjunctively, so as to give the holder his option of the metals. 5. They are made by better men than will make the bills of the present day— men better known to Europe and America—of higher credit and renown—whose names are connected with the foundation of the republic, and with all the glorious recollections of the revolution. Without offence to any, I can well say that no Congress of the present day can rank with our Revolutionary assemblies who signed the Declaration of Independence with ropes round their necks, staked life, honor, and fortune in a contest where all the chances were against them; and nobly sustained what they had dared to proclaim. We cannot rank with them, nor our paper ever have the credit of theirs. 6. They are of all sizes, and therefore ready for the catastrophe of the immediate flight, dispersion, absconding, and inhumation of all the specie in the country, for which the issue of a government paper would be the instant and imperative signal. Our cabinet plan comes no lower than five dollars, whereby great difficulty in making change at the Treasury would accrue until a supplementary act could be passed, and the small notes and change tickets be prepared. The adoption of the old continental would prevent this balk, as the notes from one to ten dollars inclusive would be ready for all payments which ended in even dollars; and the fractional notes would be ready for all that ended in shillings or sixpences. 7. And, finally, because it is right in itself that we should take up the old continentals before we begin to make new ones. For these, and other reasons, I am bold to declare that if we must have a Congress paper-money, I prefer the paper of the Congress of 1776 to that of 1842.

Sir, the Senate must pardon me. It is not my custom to speak irreverently of official matters; but there are some things too light for argument—too grave for ridicule—and which it is difficult to treat in a becoming manner. This cabinet plan of a federal exchequer is one of those subjects; and to its strange and novel character, part tragic and part farcical, must be attributed my more than usually defective mode of speaking. I plead the subject itself for the imperfection of my mode of treating it.

CHAPTER XCI.

THE THIRD FISCAL AGENT, ENTITLED A BOARD OF EXCHEQUER.

This measure, recommended by the President, was immediately taken up in each branch of Congress. In the House of Representatives a committee of a novel character—one without precedent, and without imitation—was created for it: "*A select committee on the finances and the currency,*" composed of nine members, and Mr. Caleb Cushing its chairman. Through its chairman this committee, with the exception of two of its members (Mr. Garret Davis of Kentucky, and Mr. John P. Kennedy, of Maryland), made a most elaborate report, recommending the measure, and accompanied by a bill to carry it into effect. The ruling feature of the whole plan was a national currency of paper-money, to be issued by the federal government, and to be got into circulation through payments made by it, and by its character of receivability in payment of public dues. To clear the ground for the erection of this new species of national currency, all other kinds of currency were reviewed and examined—their good and their bad qualities stated—and this government currency pronounced to combine the good qualities, and to avoid the bad of all other kinds. National bank-notes were condemned for one set of reasons: local bank-notes for another: and as for gold and silver, the reporter found so many defects in such a currency, and detailed them with such precision, that it looked like drawing up a bill of indictment against such vicious substitutes for money. In this view the report said

> "But the precious metals themselves, in addition to their uses for coin, are likewise, whether coined or uncoined, a commodity, or article of production, consumption, and merchandise. Themselves are a part of that general property of the community, of all the rest of which they are the measure; and they are of actual value different in different places, according to the contingencies of government or commerce. Their aggregate quantity is subject to be diminished by casual destruction or absorption in the arts of manufacture, or to be diminished or augmented by the greater or less number or productiveness of mines; and thus their aggregate value relatively to other commodities is liable to perpetual change. The influence of these facts upon prices, upon public affairs, and upon commerce, is visible in all the financial history of modern times. Besides which, coin is subject to debasement, or to be made a legal tender, at a rate exceeding its actual value, by the arbitrary act of the government, which controls its coinage and prescribes its legal value. In times when the uses of a paper currency and of public stocks were not understood or not practised, and communities had not begun to resort to a paper symbol or nominal representative of money, capable of being fabricated at will, the adulteration of coin, instead of it, was, it is well known, the frequent expedient of public necessity or public cupidity to obtain relief from some pressing pecuniary embarrassment. Moreover, the precious metals, though of less bulk in proportion to their value than most other commodities, yet cannot be transported from place to place without cost and risk; coin is subject to be stolen or lost, and in that case cannot be easily identified, so as to be reclaimed; the continual counting of it in large sums is inconvenient; it would be unsafe, and would cause much money to remain idle and unfruitful, if every merchant kept constantly on hand a sum of coin for all his transactions; and the displacement of large amounts of coin, its transfer from one community or one country to another, is liable to occasion fluctuations in the value of property or labor, and to embarrass commercial operations."

Having thus shown the demerit of all other sorts of currency, and cleared the way for this new species, the report proceeds to recommend it to the adoption of the legislature, with an encomium upon the President, and on the select committee on the finances and the currency, who had so well discharged their duty in proposing it; thus:

> "The President of the United States, in presenting this plan to Congress, has obeyed the injunction of the constitution, which requires him to recommend to their consideration such measures as he shall judge necessary and expedient; he has fully redeemed the engagements in this respect which he had previously made to Congress: and thus he has faithfully

discharged his whole duty to the constitution and the Union. The committee, while animated by the highest respect for his views, have yet deemed it due to him, to themselves, to the occasion, and to the country, to give to those views a free and unbiassed examination. They have done so; and in so doing, they have also discharged their duty. They respectfully submit the result to the House in the bill herewith reported. They believe this measure to contain the elements of usefulness and public good; and, as such, they recommend it to the House. But they feel no pride of opinion concerning it; and, if in error, they are ready to follow the lead of better lights, if better there be, from other quarters; being anxious only to minister to the welfare of the people whom they represent. It remains now for Congress to act in the matter; the country demands that in some way we shall act; and the times appeal to us to act with decision, with moderation, with impartiality, with independence. Long enough, the question of the national finances has been the sport of passion and the battle-cry of party. Foremost of all things, the country, in order to recover itself, needs repose and order for its material interest, and a settled purpose in that respect (what it shall be is of less moment, but at any rate *some* settled purpose) on the part of the federal government. If, careless of names and solicitous only for things, aiming beyond all intermediate objects to the visible mark of the practicable and attainable good—if Congress shall in its wisdom concur at length in some equitable adjustment of the currency question, it cannot fail to deserve and secure the lasting gratitude of the people of the United States."

After reading this elaborate report, Mr. Cushing also read the equally elaborate bill which accompanied it: and that was the last of the bill ever heard of in the House. It was never called up for consideration, but died a natural death on the calendar on which it was placed. In the Senate the fate of the measure was still more compendiously decided. The President's recommendation, the ample report of the Secretary of the Treasury, and the bill drawn up at the Treasury itself, were all sent to the Committee of Finance; which committee, deeming it unworthy of consideration, through its chairman, Mr. Evans, of Maine, prayed to be discharged from the consideration of it: and were so discharged accordingly. But, though so lightly disposed of, the measure did not escape ample denunciation. Deeming the proposition an outrage upon the constitution, an insult to gold and silver, and infinitely demoralizing to the government and dangerous to the people, Mr. Benton struck another blow at it as it went out of the Senate to the committee. It was on the motion to refer the subject to the Finance Committee, that he delivered a speech of three hours against it: of which some extracts were given in Chapter XC.

CHAPTER XCII.

ATTEMPTED REPEAL OF THE BANKRUPT ACT.

As soon as Congress met in the session 1841-'2 the House of Representatives commenced the repeal of this measure. The period for the act to take effect had been deferred by an amendment in the House from the month of November, which would be before the beginning of the regular session, to the month of February— for the well-known purpose of giving Congress an opportunity to repeal it before it went into operation. The act was odious in itself, and the more so from the manner in which it was passed—coercively, and by the help of votes from those who condemned it, but who voted for it to prevent its friends from defeating the bank bill, and the land distribution bill. Those two measures were now passed, and many of the coerced members took their revenge upon the hated bill to which they had temporarily bowed. The repeal commenced in the House, and had a rapid progress through that body. A motion was made to instruct the Judiciary Committee to bring in a bill for the repeal; and that motion succeeded by a good majority. The bill was brought in, and, under the pressure of the previous question, was quickly brought to a vote. The yeas were 124—the nays 96. It then went to the Senate, where it was closely contested, and lost by one vote—22 for the repeal: 23 against it. Thus a most iniquitous act got into operation, by the open joining of measures which could not pass alone; and by the weak calculation of some members of the House, who expected to undo a bad vote before it worked its mischief. The act was saved by one vote; but met its fate at the next session—having but a short run; while the two acts which it passed were equally, and one of them still more short lived. The fiscal bank bill, which was one that it carried, never became a law at all: the land distribution bill, which was the other, became a law only to be repealed before it had effect. The three confederate criminal bills which had mutually purchased existence from each other, all perished prematurely, fruitless and odious—inculcating in their history and their fate, an impressive moral against vicious and foul legislation.

CHAPTER XCIII.

DEATH OF LEWIS WILLIAMS, OF NORTH CAROLINA, AND NOTICE OF HIS LIFE AND CHARACTER.

He was one of those meritorious and exemplary members whose labors are among the most useful to their country: diligent, modest, attentive, patriotic, inflexibly honest—a friend to simplicity and economy in the working of the government, and an enemy to all selfish, personal, and indirect legislation. He had the distinction to have his merits and virtues commemorated in the two Houses of Congress by two of the most eminent men of the age—Mr. Clay and Mr. Adams—who respectively seconded in the House to which each belonged, the customary motion for funeral honors to his memory. Mr. Adams said:

"Mr. Speaker, I second the motion, and ask the indulgence of the House for the utterance of a few words, from a heart full to overflowing with anguish which no words can express. Sir, my acquaintance with Mr. Williams commenced with the second Congress of his service in this House. Twenty-five years have since elapsed, during all which he has been always here at his post, always true to his trust, always adhering faithfully to his constituents and to his country—always, and through every political vicissitude and revolution, adhered to faithfully by them. I have often thought that this steadfastness of mutual attachment between the representative and the constituent was characteristic of both; and, concurring with the idea just expressed with such touching eloquence by his colleague (Mr. Rayner), I have habitually looked upon Lewis Williams as the true portraiture and personification of the people of North Carolina. Sir, the loss of such a man at any time, to his country, would be great. To this House, at this juncture, it is irreparable. His wisdom, his experience, his unsullied integrity, his ardent patriotism, his cool and deliberate judgment, his conciliatory temper, his firm adherence to principle—where shall we find a substitute for them? In the distracted state of our public counsels, with the wormwood and the gall of personal animosities adding tenfold bitterness to the conflict of rival interests and discordant opinions, how shall we have to deplore the bereavement of *his* presence, the very light of whose countenance, the very sound of whose voice, could recall us, like a talisman, from the tempest of hostile passions to the calm composure of harmony and peace.

"Mr. Williams was, and had long been, in the official language which we have adopted from the British House of Commons, the *Father* of the House; and though my junior by nearly twenty years, I have looked up to him in this House, with the reverence of filial affection, as if he was the father of us all. The seriousness and gravity of his character, tempered as it was with habitual cheerfulness and equanimity, peculiarly fitted him for that relation to the other members of the House, while the unassuming courtesy of his deportment and the benevolence of his disposition invited every one to consider him as a brother. Sir, he is gone! The places that have known him shall know him no more; but his memory shall be treasured up by the wise and the good of his contemporaries, as eminent among the patriots and statesmen of this our native land; and were it possible for any Northern bosom, within this hall, ever to harbor for one moment a wish for the dissolution of our National Union, may the spirit of our departed friend, pervading every particle of the atmosphere around us, dispel the delusion of his soul, by reminding him that, in that event, he would no longer be the countryman of Lewis Williams."

Mr. Clay, in the Senate, who was speaker of the House when the then young Lewis Williams first entered it, bore his ample testimony from intimate personal knowledge, to the merits of the deceased; and, like Mr. Adams, professed a warm personal friendship for the individual, as well as exalted admiration for the public man.

"Prompted by a friendship which existed between the deceased and myself, of upwards of a quarter of a century's duration, and by the feelings and sympathies which this melancholy occasion excites, will the Senate allow me to add a few words to those which have been so well and so appropriately expressed by my friend near me [Mr. Graham], in seconding the motion he has just made? Already, during the present session, has Congress, and each House, paid the annual instalment of the great debt of Nature. We could not have lost two more worthy and estimable men than those who have been taken from us. My acquaintance with the lamented Lewis Williams commenced in the fall of 1815, when he first took his seat as a member of the House of Representatives from the State of North Carolina, and I re-entered that House after my return from Europe. From that period until his death, a cordial and unbroken friendship has subsisted between us; and similar ties were subsequently created with almost every member of his highly respectable family. When a vacancy arose in the responsible and laborious office of chairman of the Committee of Claims, which had been previously filled by another distinguished and lamented son of North Carolina (the late Mr. Yancy), in virtue of authority vested in me, as the presiding officer of the House, I appointed Mr. Williams to fill it. Always full of labor, and requiring unremitting industry, it was then, in consequence of claims originating in the late war, more than ever toilsome. He discharged his complicated duties with the greatest diligence, ability, impartiality, and uprightness, and continued in the office until I left the House in the year 1825. He occasionally took part in the debates which sprung up on great measures brought for the advancement of the interests of the country, and was always heard with profound attention, and, I believe, with a thorough conviction of his perfect integrity. Inflexibly adhering always to what he believed to be right, if he ever displayed warmth or impatience, it was excited by what he thought was insincere, or base, or ignoble. In short, Lewis Williams was a true and faithful image of the respectable State which he so long and so ably served in the national councils—intelligent, quiet, unambitious, loyal to the Union, and uniformly patriotic. We all feel and deplore, with the greatest sensibility, the heavy loss we have so suddenly sustained. May it impress us with a just sense of the frailty and uncertainty of human life! And, profiting by his example, may we all be fully prepared for that which is soon to follow."

Mr. Williams reflected the character of his State; and that was a distinction so obvious and so honorable that both speakers mentioned it, and in doing so did honor both to the State and the citizen. And she illustrated her character by the manner in which she cherished him. Elected into the General Assembly as soon as age would permit, and continued there until riper age would admit him into the Federal Congress, he was elected into that body amongst the youngest of its members; and continued there by successive elections until he was the longest sitting member, and became entitled to the Parliamentary appellation of Father of the House. Exemplary in all the relations of public and private life, he crowned a meritorious existence by an exemplary piety, and was as remarkable for the close observance of all his christian obligations as he was for the discharge of his public duties.

CHAPTER XCIV.

THE CIVIL LIST EXPENSES: THE CONTINGENT EXPENSES OF CONGRESS: AND THE REVENUE COLLECTION EXPENSE.

Pursuing the instructive political lesson to be found in the study of the progressive increased expenditures of the government, we take up, in this chapter, the civil list in the gross, and two of its items in detail—the contingent expenses of Congress, and the expense of collecting the revenue—premising that the civil list, besides the salaries of civil officers, includes the foreign diplomatic intercourse, and a variety of miscellanies. To obtain the proper comparative data, recourse is again had to Mr. Calhoun's speech of this year (1842) on the naval appropriation.

"The expenditures under the first head have increased since 1823, when they were $2,022,093, to $5,492,030 98, the amount in 1840; showing an increase, in seventeen years, of 2 7-10 to 1, while the population has increased only about ¾ to 1, that is, about 75 per cent.—making the increase of expenditures, compared to the increase of population, about 3 6-10 to 1. This enormous increase has taken place although a large portion of the expenditures under this head, consisting of salaries to officers, and the pay of members of Congress, has remained unchanged. The next year, in 1841, the expenditure rose to $6,196,560. I am, however, happy to perceive a considerable reduction in the estimates for this year, compared with the last and several preceding years; but still leaving room for great additional reduction to bring the increase of expenditures to the same ratio with the increase of population, as liberal as that standard of increase would be.

"That the Senate may form some conception, in detail, of this enormous increase, I propose to go more into particulars in reference to two items: the contingent expenses of the two Houses of Congress, and that of collecting the duties on imports. The latter, though of a character belonging to the civil list, is not included in it, or either of the other heads; as the expenses incident to collecting the customs, are deducted from the receipts, before the money is paid into the Treasury.

"The contingent expenses (they exclude the pay and mileage of members) of the Senate in 1823 were $12,841 07, of which the printing cost $6,349 56, and stationery $1,631 51; and that of the House, $37,848 95, of which the printing cost $22,314 41, and the stationery $3,877 71. In 1840, the contingent expenses of the Senate were $77,447 22, of which the printing cost $31,285 32, and the stationery $7,061 77; and that of the House $199,219 57, of which the printing cost $65,086 46, and the stationery $36,352 99. The aggregate expenses of the two Houses together rose from $50,690 02 to $276,666; being an actual increase of 5 4-10 to 1, and an increase, in proportion to population, of about 7 2-10 to one. But as enormous as this increase is, the fact that the number of members had increased not more than about ten per cent. from 1823 to 1840, is calculated to make it still more strikingly so. Had the increase kept pace with the increase of members (and there is no good reason why it should greatly exceed it), the expenditures would have risen from $50,690 to $55,759, only making an increase of but $5,069; but, instead of that, it rose to $276,666, making an increase of $225,970. To place the subject in a still more striking view, the contingent expenses in 1823 were at the rate of $144 per member, which one would suppose was ample, and in 1840, $942. This vast increase took place under the immediate eyes of Congress; and yet we were told at the extra session, by the present chairman of the Finance Committee, that there was no room for economy, and that no reduction could be made; and even in this discussion he has intimated that little can be done. As enormous as are the contingent expenses of the two Houses, I infer from the very great increase of expenditures under the head of civil list generally, when so large a portion is for fixed salaries, which have not been materially increased for the last seventeen years, that they are not much less so throughout the whole range of this branch of the public service.

"I shall now proceed to the other item, which I have selected for more particular examination, the increased expenses of collecting the duties on imports. In 1823 it was $766,699, equal to 3 86-100 per cent. on the amount collected, and 98-100 on the aggregate amount of imports; and in 1840 it had increased to $1,542,319 24, equal to 14 13-100 per cent. on the amount collected, and to 1 58-100 on the aggregate amount of the imports, being an actual increase of nearly a million, and considerably more than double the amount of 1823. In 1839 it rose to $1,714,515.

"From these facts, there can be little doubt that more than a million annually may be saved under the two items of contingent expenses of Congress, and the collection of the customs, without touching the other great items comprised under the civil list, the executive and judicial departments, the foreign intercourse, light-houses, and miscellaneous. It would be safe to put down a saving of at least a half million for them."

The striking facts to be gleaned from these statements are—That the civil list in 1821 was about two millions of dollars; in 1839, four and a half millions; and in 1841, six millions and a fraction. That the contingent expenses of Congress during the same periods respectively, were, $50,000, and $276,000. And the collection of the custom house revenue at the same periods, the respective sums of $766,000, and $1,542,000. These several sums were each considered extravagant, and unjustifiable, at the time Mr. Calhoun was speaking; and each was expected to feel the pruning knife of retrenchment. On the contrary, all have risen higher— inordinately so—and still rising: the civil and diplomatic appropriation having attained 17 millions: the contingent expenses of Congress 4 to 510,000: and the collection of the customs to above two millions.

CHAPTER XCV.

RESIGNATION AND VALEDICTORY OF MR. CLAY

In the month of March, of this year, Mr. Clay resigned his place in the Senate, and delivered a valedictory address to the body, in the course of which he disclosed his reasons. Neither age, nor infirmities, nor disinclination for public service were alleged as the reasons. Disgust, profound and inextinguishable, was the ruling cause—more inferrible than alleged in his carefully considered address. Supercession at the presidential convention of his party to make room for an "available" in the person of General Harrison—the defection of Mr. Tyler—the loss of his leading measures—the criminal catastrophe of the national bank for which he had so often pledged himself—and the insolent attacks of the petty adherents of the administration in the two Houses, (too annoying for his equanimity, and too contemptible for his reply): all these causes of disgust, acting upon a proud and lofty spirit, induced this withdrawal from a splendid theatre for which, it was evident, he had not yet lost his taste. The address opened with a retrospect of his early entrance into the Senate, and a grand encomium upon its powers and dignity as he had found it, and left it. Memory went back to that early year, 1806, when just arrived at senatorial age, he entered the American Senate, and commenced his high career—a wide and luminous horizon before him, and will and talent to fill it. After some little exordium, he proceeded:

"And now, allow me, Mr. President, to announce, formally and officially, my retirement from the Senate of the United States, and to present the last motion which I shall ever make within this body; but, before making that motion, I trust I shall be pardoned for availing myself of this occasion to make a few observations. At the time of my entry into this body, which took place in December, 1806, I regarded it, and still regard it, as a body which may be compared, without disadvantage, to any of a similar character which has existed in ancient or modern times; whether we look at it in reference to its dignity, its powers, or the mode of its constitution; and I will also add, whether it be regarded in reference to the amount of ability which I shall leave behind me when I retire from this chamber. In instituting a comparison between the Senate of the United States and similar political institutions, of other countries, of France and England, for example, he was sure the comparison might be made without disadvantage to the American Senate. In respect to the constitution of these bodies: in England, with only the exception of the peers from Ireland and Scotland, and in France with no exception, the component parts, the members of these bodies, hold their places by virtue of no delegated authority, but derive their powers from the crown, either by ancient creation of nobility transmitted by force of hereditary descent, or by new patents as occasion required an increase of their numbers. But here, Mr. President, we have the proud title of being the representatives of sovereign States or commonwealths. If we look at the powers of these bodies in France and England, and the powers of this Senate, we shall find that the latter are far greater than the former. In both those countries they have the legislative power, in both the judicial with some modifications, and in both perhaps a more extensive judicial power than is possessed by this Senate; but then the last and undefined and undefinable power, the treaty-making power, or at least a participation in the conclusions of treaties with foreign powers, is possessed by this Senate, and is possessed by neither of the others. Another power, too, and one of infinite magnitude, that of distributing the patronage of a great nation, which is shared by this Senate with the executive magistrate. In both these respects we stand upon ground different from that occupied by the Houses of Peers of England and of France. And I repeat, that with respect to the dignity which ordinarily prevails in this body, and with respect to the ability of its members during the long period of my acquaintance with it, without arrogance or presumption, we may say, in proportion to its numbers, the comparison would not be disadvantageous to us compared with any Senate either of ancient or modern times."

He then gave the date of the period at which he had formed the design to retire, and the motive for it—the date referring to the late presidential election, and the motive to find repose in the bosom of his family.

"Sir, I have long—full of attraction as public service in the Senate of the United States is—a service which might fill the aspirations of the most ambitious heart—I have nevertheless long desired to seek that repose which is only to be found in the bosom of one's family—in private life—in one's home. It was my purpose to have terminated my senatorial career in November, 1840, after the conclusion of the political struggle which characterized that year."

The termination of the presidential election in November, was the period at which Mr. Clay intended to retire: the determination was formed before that time—formed from the moment that he found himself superseded at the head of his party by a process of intricate and trackless filtration of public opinion which left himself a dreg where he had been for so many years the head. It was a mistake, the effect of calculation, which ended more disastrously for the party than for himself. Mr. Clay could have been elected at that time. The same power which elected General Harrison could have elected him. The banks enabled the party to do it. In a state of suspension, they could furnish, without detriment to themselves, the funds for the campaign. Affecting to be ruined by the government, they could create distress: and thus act upon the community with the double battery of terror and seduction. Lending all their energies and resources to a political party, they elected General Harrison in a hurrah! and could have done the same by Mr. Clay. With him the election would have been a reality—a victory bearing fruit: with General Harrison and Mr. Tyler—through Providence with one, and defection in the other—the triumph, achieved at so great expense, became ashes in the mouths of the victors. He then gave his reasons for not resigning, as he had intended, at the termination of the election: it was the hope of carrying his measures at the extra session, which he foresaw was to take place.

"But I learned very soon, what my own reflections indeed prompted me to suppose would take place, that there would be an extra session; and being desirous, prior to my retirement, to co-operate with my friends in the Senate in restoring, by the adoption of measures best calculated to accomplish that purpose, that degree of prosperity to the country, which had been, for a time, destroyed, I determined upon attending the extra session, which was called, as was well known, by the lamented Harrison. His death, and the succession which took place in consequence of it, produced a new aspect in the affairs of the country. Had he lived, I do not entertain a particle of doubt that those measures which, it was hoped, might be accomplished at that session, would have been consummated by a candid co-operation between the executive branch of the government and Congress; and, sir, allow me to say (and it is only with respect to the extra session), that I believe if there be any one free from party feelings, and free from bias and from prejudice, who will look at its transactions in a spirit of candor and of justice, but must come to the conclusion to which, I think, the country generally will come, that if there be any thing to complain of in connection with that session, it is not as to what was done and concluded, but as to that which was left unfinished and unaccomplished."

Disappointed in his expectations from the extra session, by means which he did not feel it necessary to recapitulate, Mr. Clay proceeds to give the reasons why he still deferred his proposed resignation, and appeared in the Senate again at its ensuing regular session.

"After the termination of that session, had Harrison lived, and had the measures which it appeared to me it was desirable to have accomplished, been carried, it was my intention to have retired; but I reconsidered that determination, with the vain hope that, at the regular session of Congress, what had been unaccomplished at the extra session, might then be effected, either upon the terms proposed or in some manner which would be equivalent. But events were announced after the extra session—events resulting, I believe, in the failure to accomplish certain objects at the extra session—events which seemed to throw upon our friends every where present defeat—this hope, and the occurrence of these events, induced me to attend the regular session, and whether in adversity or in prosperity, to share in the fortunes of my friends. But I came here with the purpose, which I am now about to effectuate, of retiring as soon as I thought I could retire with propriety and decency, from the public councils."

Events after the extra session, as well as the events of the session, determined him to return to the regular one. He does not say what those subsequent events were. They were principally two—the formation of a new cabinet wholly hostile to him, and the attempt of Messrs. Tyler, Webster and Cushing to take the whig party from him. The hostility of the cabinet was nothing to him personally; but it indicated a fixed design to thwart him on the part of the President, and augured an indisposition to promote any of his measures. This augury was fulfilled as soon as Congress met. The administration came forward with a plan of a government bank, to issue a national currency of government paper—a thing which he despised as much as the democracy did; and which, howsoever impossible to succeed itself, was quite sufficient, by the diversion it created, to mar the success of any plan for a national bank. Instead of carrying new measures, it became clear that he was to lose many already adopted. The bankrupt act, though forced upon him, had become one of his measures; and that was visibly doomed to repeal. The distribution of the land revenue had become a political monstrosity in the midst of loans, taxes and treasury notes resorted to to supply its loss: and the public mind was in revolt against it. The compromise act of 1833, for which he was so much lauded at the time, and the paternity of which he had so much contested at the time, had run its career of folly and delusion—had left the Treasury without revenue, and the manufacturers without protection; and, crippled at the extra session, it was bound to die at this regular one—and that in defiance of the mutual assurance for continued existence put into the land bill; and which, so far from being able to assure the life of another bill, was becoming unable to save its own. Losing his own measures, he saw those becoming established which he had most labored to oppose. The specie circular was taking effect of itself, from the abundance of gold and the baseness of paper. The divorce of Bank and State was becoming absolute, from the delinquency of the banks. There was no prospect ahead either to carry new measures, or to save old ones, or to oppose the hated ones. All was gloomy ahead. The only drop of consolation which sweetened the cup of so much bitterness was the failure of his enemies to take the whig party from him. That parricidal design (for these enemies owed their elevation to him) exploded in its formation—aborted in its conception; and left those to abjure whiggism, and fly from its touch, who had lately combined to consolidate Congress, President and people into one solid whig mass. With this comfort he determined to carry into effect his determination to resign, although it was not yet the middle of the session, and that all-important business was still on the anvil of legislation—to say nothing of the general diplomatic settlement, to embrace questions from the peace of 1783, which it was then known Great Britain was sending out a special mission to effect. But, to proceed with the valedictory. Having got to the point at which he was to retire, the veteran orator naturally threw a look back upon his past public course.

> "From the year 1806, the period of my entering upon this noble theatre of my public service, with but short intervals, down to the present time, I have been engaged in the service of my country. Of the nature and value of those services which I may have rendered during my long career of public life, it does not become me to speak. History, if she deigns to notice me, and posterity—if a recollection of any humble service which I may have rendered shall be transmitted to posterity—will be the best, truest, and most impartial judges; and to them I defer for a decision upon their value. But, upon one subject, I may be allowed to speak. As to my public acts and public conduct, they are subjects for the judgment of my fellow-citizens; but my private motives of action—that which prompted me to take the part which I may have done, upon great measures during their progress in the national councils, can be known only to the Great Searcher of the human heart and myself; and I trust I shall be pardoned for repeating again a declaration which I made thirty years ago: that whatever error I may have committed—and doubtless I have committed many during my public service—I may appeal to the Divine Searcher of hearts for the truth of the declaration which I now make, with pride and confidence, that I have been actuated by no personal motives—that I have sought no personal aggrandizement—no promotion from the advocacy of those various measures on which I have been called to act—that I have had an eye, a single eye, a heart, a single heart, ever devoted to what appeared to be the best interests of the country."

With this retrospection of his own course was readily associated the recollection of the friends who had supported him in his long and eventful, and sometimes, stormy career.

"But I have not been unsustained during this long course of public service. Every where on this widespread continent have I enjoyed the benefit of possessing warm-hearted, and enthusiastic, and devoted friends—friends who knew me, and appreciated justly the motives by which I have been actuated. To them, if I had language to make suitable acknowledgments, I would now take leave to present them, as being all the offering that I can make for their long continued, persevering and devoted friendship."

These were general thanks to the whole body of his friends, and to the whole extent of his country; but there were special thanks due to nearer friends, and the home State, which had then stood by him for forty-five years (and which still stood by him ten years more, and until death), and fervidly and impressively he acknowledged this domestic debt of gratitude and affection.

"But, sir, if I have a difficulty in giving utterance to an expression of the feelings of gratitude which fill my heart towards my friends, dispersed throughout this continent, what shall I say— what can I say—at all commensurate with my feelings of gratitude towards that State whose humble servitor I am? I migrated to the State of Kentucky nearly forty-five years ago. I went there as an orphan, who had not yet attained his majority—who had never recognized a father's smile—poor, penniless, without the favor of the great—with an imperfect and inadequate education, limited to the means applicable to such a boy;—but scarcely had I set foot upon that generous soil, before I was caressed with parental fondness—patronized with bountiful munificence—and I may add to this, that her choicest honors, often unsolicited, have been freely showered upon me; and when I stood, as it were, in the darkest moments of human existence—abandoned by the world, calumniated by a large portion of my own countrymen, she threw around me her impenetrable shield, and bore me aloft, and repelled the attacks of malignity and calumny, by which I was assailed. Sir, it is to me an unspeakable pleasure that I am shortly to return to her friendly limits; and that I shall finally deposit (and it will not be long before that day arrives) my last remains under her generous soil, with the remains of her gallant and patriotic sons who have preceded me."

After this grateful overflow of feelings to faithful friends and country, came some notice of foes, whom he might forgive, but not forget.

"Yet, sir, during this long period, I have not escaped the fate of other public men, in this and other countries. I have been often, Mr. President, the object of bitter and unmeasured detraction and calumny. I have borne it, I will not say always with composure, but I have borne it without creating any disturbance. I have borne it, waiting in unshaken and undoubting confidence, that the triumphs of truth and justice would ultimately prevail; and that time would settle all things as they ought to be settled. I have borne them under the conviction, of which no injustice, no wrong, no injury could deprive me, that I did not deserve them, and that He to whom we are all to be finally and ultimately responsible, would acquit me, whatever injustice I might experience at the hands of my fellow-men."

This was a general reference to the attacks and misrepresentations with which, in common with all eminent public men of decided character, he had been assailed; but there was a recent and offensive imputation upon him which galled him exceedingly—as much so for the source from which it came as for the offence itself: it was the imputation of the dictatorship, lavished upon him during the extra session; and having its origin with Mr. Tyler and his friends. This stung him, coming from that source—Mr. Tyler having attained his highest honors through his friendship: elected senator by his friends over Mr. Randolph, and taken up for Vice-President in the whig convention (whereby he became both the second and the first magistrate of the republic) on account of the excessive affection which he displayed for Mr. Clay. To this recent, and most offensive imputation, he replied specially:

"Mr. President, a recent epithet (I do not know whether for the purpose of honor or of degradation) has been applied to me; and I have been held up to the country as a dictator! Dictator! The idea of dictatorship is drawn from Roman institutions; and there, when it was created, the person who was invested with this tremendous authority, concentrated in his own person the whole power of the state. He exercised unlimited control over the property and lives of the citizens of the commonwealth. He had the power of raising armies, and of raising revenue by taxing the people. If I have been a dictator, what have been the powers with which I have been clothed? Have I possessed an army, a navy, revenue? Have I had the distribution of the patronage of the government? Have I, in short, possessed any power whatever? Sir, if I have been a dictator, I think those who apply the epithet to me must at least admit two things: in the first place, that my dictatorship has been distinguished by no cruel executions, stained by no deeds of blood, soiled by no act of dishonor. And they must no less acknowledge, in the second place (though I do not know when its commencement bears date, but I suppose, however, that it is intended to be averred, from the commencement of the extra session), that if I have been invested with, or have usurped the dictatorship, I have at least voluntarily surrendered the power within a shorter period than was assigned by the Roman laws for its continuance."

Mr. Clay led a great party, and for a long time, whether he dictated to it or not, and kept it well bound together, without the usual means of forming and leading parties. It was a marvel that, without power and patronage (for the greater part of his career was passed in opposition as a mere member of Congress), he was able so long and so undividedly to keep so great a party together, and lead it so unresistingly. The marvel was solved on a close inspection of his character. He had great talents, but not equal to some whom he led. He had eloquence—superior in popular effect, but not equal in high oratory to that of some others. But his temperament was fervid, his will strong, and his courage daring; and these qualities, added to his talents, gave him the lead and supremacy in his party—where he was always dominant, but twice set aside by the politicians. It was a galling thing to the President Tyler, with all the power and patronage of office, to see himself without a party, and a mere opposition member at the head of a great one—the solid body of the whigs standing firm around Mr. Clay, while only some flankers and followers came to him; and they importunate for reward until they got it. Dictatorship was a natural expression of resentment under such circumstances; and accordingly it was applied—and lavishly—and in all places: in the Senate, in the House, in the public press, in conversation, and in the manifesto which Mr. Cushing put out to detach the whigs from him. But they all forgot to tell that this imputed dictatorship at the extra session, took place after the defection of Mr. Tyler from the whig party, and as a consequence of that defection—some leader being necessary to keep the party together after losing the two chiefs they had elected—one lost by Providence, the other by treachery. This account settled, he turned to a more genial topic—that of friendship; and to make atonement, reconciliation and peace with all the senators, and they were not a few, with whom he had had some rough encounters in the fierce debate. Unaffectedly acknowledging some imperfection of temper, he implored forgiveness from all whom he had ever offended, and extended the hand of friendship to every brother member.

"Mr. President, that my nature is warm, my temper ardent, my disposition in the public service enthusiastic, I am ready to own. But those who suppose they may have seen any proof of dictation in my conduct, have only mistaken that ardor for what I at least supposed to be patriotic exertions for fulfilling the wishes and expectations by which I hold this seat; they have only mistaken the one for the other. Mr. President, during my long and arduous services in the public councils, and especially during the last eleven years, in the Senate, the same ardor of temperament has characterized my actions, and has no doubt led me, in the heat of debate, in endeavoring to maintain my opinions in reference to the best course to be pursued in the conduct of public affairs, to use language offensive, and susceptible of ungracious interpretation, towards my brother senators. If there be any who entertain a feeling of dissatisfaction resulting from any circumstance of this kind, I beg to assure them that I now make the amplest apology. And, on the other hand, I assure the Senate, one and all, without exception and without reserve, that I leave the Senate chamber without carrying with me to my retirement a single feeling of dissatisfaction towards the Senate itself or any one of its members. I go from it under the hope that we shall mutually consign to perpetual oblivion whatever of personal animosities or jealousies may have arisen between us during the repeated collisions of mind with mind."

This moving appeal was strongly responded to in spontaneous advances at the proper time—deferred for a moment by a glowing and merited tribute to his successor (Mr. Crittenden), and his own solemn farewell to the Senate.

"And now, allow me to submit the motion which is the object that induced me to arise upon this occasion. It is to present the credentials of my friend and successor, who is present to take my place. If, Mr. President, any void could be created by my withdrawal from the Senate of the United States, it will be filled to overflowing by my worthy successor, whose urbanity, gallant bearing, steady adherence to principle, rare and uncommon powers of debate, are well known already in advance to the whole Senate. I move that the credentials be received, and at the proper moment that the oath required be administered. And now, in retiring as I am about to do from the Senate, I beg leave to deposit with it my fervent wishes, that all the great and patriotic objects for which it was instituted, may be accomplished—that the destiny designed for it by the framers of the constitution may be fulfilled—that the deliberations, now and hereafter, in which it may engage for the good of our common country, may eventuate in the restoration of its prosperity, and in the preservation and maintenance of her honor abroad, and her best interests at home. I retire from you, Mr. President, I know, at a period of infinite distress and embarrassment. I wish I could have taken leave of the public councils under more favorable auspices: but without meaning to say at this time, upon whom reproaches should fall on account of that unfortunate condition, I think I may appeal to the Senate and to the country for the truth of what I say, when I declare that at least no blame on account of these embarrassments and distresses can justly rest at my door. May the blessings of Heaven rest upon the heads of the whole Senate, and every member of it; and may every member of it advance still more in fame, and when they shall retire to the bosoms of their respective constituencies, may they all meet there that most joyous and grateful of all human rewards, the exclamation of their countrymen, 'well done, thou good and faithful servant.' Mr. President, and Messieurs Senators, I bid you, one and all, a long, a last, a friendly farewell."

Mr. Preston concluded the ceremony by a motion to adjourn. He said he had well observed from the deep sensation which had been sympathetically manifested, that there could be but little inclination to go on with business in the Senate, and that he could not help participating in the feeling which he was sure universally prevailed, that something was due to the occasion. The resignation which had just taken place was an epoch in the annals of the country. It would undoubtedly be so considered in history. And he did not know that he could better consult the feelings of the Senate than by moving an adjournment: which motion was made and agreed to. Senators, and especially those who had had their hot words with the retiring statesman, now released from official restraint, went up, and made return of all the kind expressions which had been addressed to them. But the valedictory, though well performed, did not escape the criticism of senators, as being out of keeping with the usages of the body. It was the first occasion of the kind; and, thus far, has been the last; and it might not be recommendable for any one, except another Henry Clay—if another should ever appear—to attempt its imitation.

CHAPTER XCVI.

MILITARY DEPARTMENT: PROGRESS OF ITS EXPENSE.

There is no part of the working of the government, at which that part of the citizens who live upon their own industry should look more closely, than into its expenditures. The progress of expense in every branch of the public service should be their constant care; and for that purpose retrospective views are necessary, and comparisons between different periods. A preceding chapter has given some view of this progress and comparison in the Navy Department: the present one will make the same retrospect with respect to the army, and on the same principles—that of taking the aggregate expense of the department, and then seeing the effective force produced, and the detailed cost of such force. Such comparative view was well brought up by Mr. Calhoun for a period of twenty years—1822 to 1842—in the debate on the naval appropriations; and it furnishes instructive data for this examination. He said:

"I shall now pass to the military, with which I am more familiar. I propose to confine my remarks almost entirely to the army proper, including the Military Academy, in reference to which the information is more full and minute. I exclude the expenses incident to the Florida war, and the expenditures for the ordnance, the engineer, the topographical, the Indian, and the pension bureaus. Instead of 1823, for which there is no official and exact statement of the expenses of the army, I shall take 1821, for which there is one made by myself, as Secretary of War, and for the minute correctness of which, I can vouch. It is contained in a report made under a call of the House of Representatives, and comprises a comparative statement of the expenses of the army proper, for the years 1818, '19, '20, and '21, respectively, and an estimate of the expense of 1823. It may be proper to add, which I can with confidence, that the comparative expense of 1823, if it could be ascertained, would be found to be not less favorable than 1821. It would probably be something more so.

"With these remarks, I shall begin with a comparison, in the first place, between 1821 and the estimate for the army proper for this year. The average aggregate strength of the army in the year 1821, including officers, professors, cadets, and soldiers, was 8,109, and the proportion of officers, including the professors of the Military Academy, to the soldiers, including cadets, was 1 to 12 18-100, and the expenditure $2,180,093 53, equal to $263 91 for each individual. The estimate for the army proper for 1842, including the Military Academy, is $4,453,370 16. The actual strength of the army, according to the return accompanying the message at the opening of the session, was 11,169. Assuming this to be the average strength for this year, and adding for the average number of the Academy, professors and cadets, 300, it will give within a very small fraction $390 for each individual, making a difference of $136 in favor of 1821. How far the increase of pay, and the additional expense of two regiments of dragoons, compared to other descriptions of troops, would justify this increase, I am not prepared to say. In other respects, I should suppose, there ought to be a decrease rather than an increase, as the prices of clothing, provisions, forage, and other articles of supply, as well as transportation, are, I presume, cheaper than in 1821. The proportion of officers to soldiers I would suppose to be less in 1842, than in 1821, and of course, as far as that has influence, the expense of the former ought to be less per man than the latter. With this brief and imperfect comparison between the expense of 1821 and the estimates for this year, I shall proceed to a more minute and full comparison between the former and the year 1837. I select that year, because the strength of the army, and the proportion of officers to men (a very material point as it relates to the expenditure) are almost exactly the same.

"On turning to document 165 (H. R., 2d sess., 26th Con.), a letter will be found from the then Secretary of War (Mr. Poinsett) giving a comparative statement, in detail, of the expense of the army proper, including the Military Academy, for the years 1837, '38, '39 and '40. The strength of the army for the first of these years, including officers, professors, cadets, and soldiers, was 8,107, being two less than in 1821. The proportion of officers and professors, to the cadets and soldiers, 11 46-100, being 72-100 more than 1821. The expenditure for 1837, $3,308,011, being $1,127,918 more than 1821. The cost per man, including officers, professors, cadets, and soldiers, was in 1837 $408 03, exceeding that of 1821 by $144 12 per man. It appears by the letter of the Secretary, that the expense per man rose in 1838 to $464 35; but it is due to the head of the department, at the time, to say, that it declined under his administration, the next year, to $381 65; and in the subsequent, to $380 63. There is no statement for the year 1841; but as there has been a falling off in prices, there ought to be a proportionate reduction in the cost, especially during the present year, when there is a prospect of so great a decline in almost every article which enters into the consumption of the army. Assuming that the average strength of the army will be kept equal to the return accompanying the President's message, and that the expenditure of the year should be reduced to the standard of 1821, the expense of the army would not exceed $2,895,686, making a difference, compared with the estimates, of $1,557,684; but that, from the increase of pay, and the greater expense of the dragoons, cannot be expected. Having no certain information how much the expenses are necessarily increased from those causes, I am not prepared to say what ought to be the actual reductions; but, unless the increase of pay, and the increased cost because of the dragoons are very great, it ought to be very considerable.

"I found the expense of the army in 1818, including the Military Academy, to be $3,702,495, at a cost of $451 57 per man, including officers, professors, cadets, and soldiers, and reduced it in 1821 to $2,180,098, at a cost of $263 91; and making a difference between the two years, in the aggregate expenses of the army, of $1,522,397, and $185 66 per man. There was, it is true, a great fall in prices in the interval; but allowing for that, by adding to the price of every article entering into the supplies of the army, a sum sufficient to raise it to the price of 1818, there was still a difference in the cost per man of $163 95. This great reduction was effected without stinting the service or diminishing the supplies, either in quantity or quality. They were, on the contrary, increased in both, especially the latter. It was effected through an efficient organization of the staff, and the co-operation of the able officers placed at the head of each of its divisions. The cause of the great expense at the former period, was found to be principally in the neglect of public property, and the application of it to uses not warranted by law. There is less scope, doubtless, for reformation in the army now. I cannot doubt, however, but that the universal extravagance which pervaded the country for so many years, and which increased so greatly the expenses both of government and individuals, has left much room for reform in this, as well as other branches of the service."

This is an instructive period at which to look. In the year 1821, when Mr. Calhoun was Secretary at War, the cost of each man in the military service (officers and cadets included) was, in round numbers, 264 dollars per man: in the year 1839, when Mr. Poinsett was Secretary, and the Florida war on hand, the cost per man was 380 dollars: in the year 1842, the second year of Mr. Tyler's administration, the Florida war still continuing, it was 390 dollars per man: now, in 1855, it is about 1,000 dollars a man. Thus, the cost of each man in the army has increased near three fold in the short space of about one dozen years. The same result will be shown by taking the view of these increased expenses in a different form—that of aggregates of men and of cost. Thus, the aggregate of the army in 1821 was 8,109 men, and the expense was $2,180,093: in 1839 the aggregate of the army was about 8,000 men—the cost $3,308,000: in 1842 the return of the army was 11,169—the appropriation asked for, and obtained $4,453,370. Now, 1854, the aggregate of the army is 10,342—the appropriations ten millions and three quarters! that is to say, with nearly one thousand men less than in 1842, the cost is upwards of six millions more. Such is the progress of waste and extravagance in the army—fully keeping up with that in the navy.

In a debate upon retrenchment at this session, Mr. Adams proposed to apply the pruning knife at the right place—the army and navy: he did not include the civil and diplomatic, which gave no sign at that time of attaining its present enormous proportions, and confined himself to the naval and military expenditure. After ridiculing the picayune attempts at retrenchment by piddling at stationery and tape, and messengers' pay, he pointed to the army and navy; and said:

"There you may retrench millions! in the expenses of Congress, you retrench picayunes. You never will retrench for the benefit of the people of this country, till you retrench the army and navy twenty millions. And yet he had heard of bringing down the expenditures of the government to twenty millions. Was this great retrenchment to be effected by cutting off the paper of members, by reducing the number of pages, and cutting down the salaries of the door-keepers? How much could be retrenched in that way? If there was to be any real retrenchment, it must be in the army and navy. A sincere and honest determination to reduce the expenses of the government, was the spirit of a very large portion of the two parties in the House; and that was a spirit in which the democracy had more merit than the other party. He came here as an humble follower of those who went for retrenchment; and, so help him God, so long as he kept his seat here, he would continue to urge retrenchment in the expenditures of the military and naval force. Well, what was the corresponding action of the Executive on this subject? It was a recommendation to increase the expenditures both for the army and navy. They had estimates from the War and Navy Departments of twenty millions. The additions proposed to the armed force, as he observed yesterday, fifteen millions would not provide for. Where was the spirit of retrenchment on the part of the Executive, which Congress had a right to expect? How had he met the spirit manifested by Congress for retrenchment of the expenditures of the government? By words—words—and nothing else but words."

A retrenchment, to be effectual, requires the President to take the lead, as Mr. Jefferson did at the commencement of his administration. A solitary member, or even several members acting together, could do but little: but they should not on that account forbear to "*cry aloud and spare not.*" Their voice may wake up the people, and lead to the election of a President who will be on the side of republican economy, instead of royal extravagance. This writer is not certain that 20 millions, on these two heads, could have been retrenched at the time Mr. Adams spoke; but he is sure of it now.

CHAPTER XCVII.

PAPER MONEY PAYMENTS: ATTEMPTED BY THE FEDERAL GOVERNMENT: RESISTED: MR. BENTON'S SPEECH.

The long continued struggle between paper money and gold was now verging to a crisis. The gold bill, rectifying the erroneous valuation of that metal, had passed in 1834: an influx of gold coin followed. In seven years the specie currency had gone up from twenty millions to one hundred. There was five times as much specie in the country as there was in 1832, when the currency was boasted to be solid under the regulation of the Bank of the United States. There was as much as the current business of the country and of the federal government could use: for these 100 millions, if allowed to circulate and to pass from hand to hand, in every ten hands that they passed through, would do the business of one thousand millions. Still the administration was persistent in its attempts to obtain a paper money currency: and the national bank having failed, and all the efforts to get up paper money machines (under the names of fiscal agent, fiscal corporation, and exchequer board) having proved abortive, recourse was had to treasury notes, with the quality of re-issuability attached to them. Previous issues had been upon the footing of any other promissory note: when once paid at the treasury, it was extinguished and cancelled. Now they were made re-issuable, like common bank notes; and a limited issue of five millions of dollars became unlimited from its faculty of successive emission. The new administration converted these notes into currency, to be offered to the creditors of the government in the proportion of two-thirds paper, and one-third specie; and, from the difficulty of making head against the government, the mass of the creditors were constrained to take their dues in this compound of paper and specie. Mr. Benton determined to resist it, and to make a case for the consideration and judgment of Congress and the country, with the view of exposing a forced unconstitutional tender, and inciting the country to a general resistance. For this purpose he had a check drawn for a few days' compensation as senator, and placed it in the hands of a messenger for collection, inscribed, "the hard, or a protest." The hard was not delivered: the protest followed: and Mr. Benton then brought the case before the Senate, and the people, in a way which appears thus in the register of the Congress debates (and which were sufficient for their objects as the forced tender of the paper money was immediately stopped):

Mr. Benton rose to offer a resolution, and to precede it with some remarks, bottomed upon a paper which he held in his hand, and which he would read. He then read as follows:

[COMPENSATION NO. 149.]
OFFICE OF SECRETARY OF THE SENATE OF THE U. S. A.

WASHINGTON, *31st January, 1842.*

Cashier of the Bank of Washington,

Pay to Hon. THOMAS H. BENTON, or order one hundred and forty-two dollars. $142 (Signed)

ASBURY DICKENS,
Secretary of the Senate.

(Endorsed). ☞ *"The hard, or a protest.*

"THOMAS H. BENTON."

DISTRICT OF COLUMBIA,
    Washington County, Set:

Be it known, That on the thirty-first day of January, 1842, I, George Sweeny, Notary Public, by lawful authority duly commissioned and sworn, dwelling in the County and District aforesaid, at the request of the honorable Thomas H. Benton, presented at the bank of Washington, the original check whereof the above is a true copy, and demanded there payment of the sum of money in the said check specified, whereunto the cashier of said bank answered: "The whole amount cannot be paid in specie, as treasury notes alone have been deposited here to meet the Secretary of the Senate's checks; but I am ready to pay this check in one treasury note for one hundred dollars, bearing six per cent. interest, and the residue in specie."

Therefore I, the said notary, at the request aforesaid, have protested, and by these presents do solemnly protest, against the drawer and endorser of this said check, and all others whom it doth or may concern, for all costs, exchange, or re-exchange, charges, damages, and interests, suffered and to be suffered for want of payment thereof.

[SEAL]

In testimony whereof, I have hereunto set my hand and affixed my Seal Notarial, this first day of February, 1842.

GEORGE SWEENY,
Notary Public.

Protesting, $1 75.

Recorded in Protest Book, G. S. No. 4, page 315.

Mr. B. said this paper explained itself. It was a check and a protest. The check was headed "*compensation*," and was drawn by the Secretary of the Senate for so much pay due to him (Mr. B.) for his per diem attendance in Congress. It had been presented at the proper place for payment, and it would be seen by the protest that payment was refused, unless he (Mr. B.) would consent to receive two-thirds paper and about one-third specie. He objected to this, and endorsed upon the check, as an instruction to the messenger who carried it, these words: "*The hard, or a protest.*" Under instructions the protest came, and with it notarial fees to the amount of $1,75, which were paid in the hard. Mr. B. said this was what had happened to himself, here at the seat of government; and he presumed the same thing was happening to others, and all over the Union. He presumed the time had arrived when paper money payments, and forced tenders of treasury notes, were to be universal, and when every citizen would have to decide for himself whether he would submit to the imposition upon his rights, and to the outrage upon the Constitution, which such a state of things involved. Some might not be in a situation to submit. Necessity, stronger than any law, might compel many to submit; but there were others who were in a situation to resist; and, though attended with some loss and inconvenience, it was their duty to do so. Tyranny must be resisted; oppression must be resisted; violation of the Constitution must be resisted; folly or wickedness must be resisted; otherwise there is an end of law, of liberty, and of right. The government becomes omnipotent, and rides and rules over a prostrate country, as it pleases. Resistance to the tyranny or folly of a government becomes a sacred duty, which somebody must perform, and the performance of which is always disagreeable, and sometimes expensive and hazardous. Mr. Hampden resisted the payment of ship money in England: and his resistance cost him money, time, labor, losses of every kind, and eventually the loss of his life. His share of the ship money was only twenty shillings, and a suggestion of self-interest would have required him to submit to the imposition, and put up with the injury. But a feeling of patriotism prompted him to resist for others, not for himself—to resist for the benefit of those who could not resist for themselves; and, above all, to resist for the sake of the Constitution of the country, trampled under foot by a weak king and a profligate minister. Mr. Hampden resisted the payment of ship money to save the people of England from oppression, and the constitution from violation. Some person must resist the payment of paper money here, to save the people from oppression, and the Constitution from violation; and if persons in station, and at the seat of government will not do it, who shall? Sir, resistance must be made; the safety of the country, and of the Constitution demands it. It must be made here: for here is the source and presence of the tyranny. It must be made by some one in station: for the voice of those in private life could not be heard. Some one must resist, and for want of a more suitable person, I find myself under the necessity of doing it—and I do it with the less reluctance because it is in my line, as a hard-money man; and because I do not deem it quite as dangerous to resist our paper money administration as Hampden found it to resist Charles the First and the Duke of Buckingham.

There is no dispute about the fact, and the case which I present is neither a first one, nor a solitary one. The whig administration, in the first year of its existence, is without money, and without credit, and with no other means of keeping up but by forced payments of paper money, which it strikes from day to day to force into the hands, and to stop the mouths of its importunate creditors. This is its condition; and it is the natural result of the folly which threw away the land revenue—which repealed the hard money clause of the independent treasury—which repealed the prohibition against the use of small notes by the federal government—which has made war upon gold, and protected paper—and which now demands the establishment of a national manufactory of paper money for the general and permanent use of the federal government. Its present condition is the natural result of these measures; and bad as it is, it must be far worse if the people do not soon compel a return to the hard money and economy of the democratic administrations. This administration came into power upon a promise to carry on the government upon thirteen millions per annum; the first year is not yet out; it has already had a revenue of twenty odd millions, a loan bill for twelve millions, a tax bill for eight or ten millions, a treasury note bill for five millions: and with all this, it declares a *deficit*, and shows its insolvency, by denying money to its creditors, and forcing them to receive paper, or to go without pay. In a season of profound peace, and in the first year of the whig administration, this is the condition of the country! a condition which must fill the bosom of every friend to our form of government with grief and shame.

Sir, a war upon the currency of the constitution has been going on for many years; and the heroes of that war are now in power. They have ridiculed gold, and persecuted it in every way, and exhausted their wits in sarcasms upon it and its friends. The humbug gold bill was their favorite phrase; and among other exhibitions in contempt of this bill and its authors, were a couple of public displays—one in May, 1837, the other in the autumn of 1840—at Wheeling, in Virginia, by two gentlemen (Mr. Tyler and Mr. Webster), now high functionaries in this government, in which empty purses were held up to the contemplation of the crowd, in derision of the gold bill and its authors. Sir, that bill was passed in June, 1834; and from that day down to a few weeks ago, we were paid in gold. Every one of us had gold that chose it. Now the scene is reversed. Gold is gone; paper has come. Forced payments, and forced tenders of paper, is the law of the whig administration! and empty purses may now be held up with truth, and with sorrow, as the emblem both of the administration and its creditors.

The cause of this disgraceful state of things, Mr. B. said, he would not further investigate at present. The remedy was the point now to be attended to. The government creditor was suffering; the constitution was bleeding; the character of the country was sinking into disgrace; and it was the duty of Congress to apply a remedy to so many disasters. He, Mr. B. saw the remedy; but he had not the power to apply it. The power was in other hands; and to them he would wish to commit the inquiry which the present condition of things imperiously required of Congress to make.

Mr. B. said here was a forced payment of paper money—a forced tender of paper money—and forced loans from the citizens. The loan to be forced out of him was $100, at 6 per cent.; but he had not the money to lend, and should resist the loan. Those who have money will not lend it, and wisely refuse to lend it to an administration which throws away its rich pearl—the land revenue. The senator from North Carolina [Mr. MANGUM] proposes a reduction of the pay of the members by way of relief to the Treasury, but Mr. B. had no notion of submitting to it: he had no notion of submitting to a deduction of his pay to enable an administration to riot in extravagance, and to expend in a single illegal commission in New York (the Poindexter custom house inquisition), more than the whole proposed saving from the members' pay would amount to. He had no notion of submitting to such curtailments, and would prefer the true remedy, that of restoring the land revenue to its proper destination; and also restoring economy, democracy, and hard money to power.

Mr. Benton then offered the following resolution, which was adopted:

> "*Resolved*, That the Committee on Finance be instructed to inquire into the nature of the payments now made, or offered to be made, by the federal government to its creditors. Whether the same are made in hard money or in paper money? Whether the creditors have

their option? Whether the government paper is at a discount? And what remedy, if any, is necessary to enable the government to keep its faith with its creditors, so as to save them from loss, the Constitution from violation, and the country from disgrace?"

CHAPTER XCVIII.

CASE OF THE AMERICAN BRIG CREOLE, WITH SLAVES FOR NEW ORLEANS, CARRIED BY MUTINY INTO NASSAU, AND THE SLAVES LIBERATED.

At this time took place one of those liberations of slaves in voyages between our own ports, of which there had already been four instances; but no one under circumstances of such crime and outrage. Mutiny, piracy, and bloodshed accompanied this fifth instance of slaves liberated by British authorities while on the voyage from one American port to another. The brig Creole, of Richmond, Virginia, had sailed from Norfolk for New Orleans, among other cargo, having 135 slaves on board. When out a week, and near the Bahama Islands, a mutiny broke out among the slaves, or rather nineteen of them, in the night, manifesting itself instantly and unexpectedly upon the officers and crew of the brig, and the passengers. The mutineers, armed with knives and handspikes, rushed to the cabin, where the officers not on duty, the wife and children of the captain, and passengers were asleep. They were knocked down, stabbed and killed, except as they could save themselves in the dark. In a few minutes the mutineers were masters of the vessel, and proceeded to arrange things according to their mind. All the slaves except the 19 were confined in the hold, and great apprehensions entertained of them, as they had refused to join in the mutiny, many of them weeping and praying—some endeavoring to save their masters, and others hiding to save themselves. The living, among the officers, crew and passengers were hunted up, and their lives spared to work the ship. They first demanded that they should be carried to Liberia—a design which was relinquished upon representations that there was not water and provisions for a quarter of the voyage. They then demanded to go to a British island, and placing the muzzle of a musket against the breast of the severely wounded captain, menaced him with instant death if he did not comply with their demand. Of course he complied, and steered for Nassau, in the island of Providence. The lives of his wife and children were spared, and they, with other surviving whites, were ordered into the forward hold. Masters of the ship, the 19 mutineers took possession of the cabin—ate there—and had their consultations in that place. All the other slaves were rigorously confined in the hold, and fears expressed that they would rise on the mutineers. Not one joined them. The affidavits of the master and crew taken at Nassau, say:

> "None but the 19 went into the cabin. They ate in the cabin, and others ate on deck as they had done the whole voyage. The 19 were frequently closely engaged in secret conversation, but the others took no part in it, and appeared not to share in their confidence. The others were quiet and did not associate with the mutineers. The only words that passed between the others and the 19, were when the others asked them for water *or grub*, or something of the kind. The others were kept under as much as the whites were. The 19 drank liquor in the cabin and invited the whites to join them, but not the other negroes. Madison, the ring-leader, gave orders that the cooking for all but the 19 should be as it was before, and appointed the same cook for them. The nineteen said that all they had done was for their freedom. The others said nothing about it. They were much afraid of the nineteen. They remained forward of the mainmast. The nineteen took possession of the after part of the brig, and stayed there the whole time or were on watch. The only knives found after the affray, were two sheath knives belonging to the sailors. The captain's bowie knife and the jack knife. None of the other negroes had any other knives. Madison sometimes had the bowie knife, and sometimes Ben had it. No other negro was seen with that knife. On Monday afternoon Madison got the pistol from one of the nineteen, and said he did not wish them to have any arms when they reached Nassau. The nineteen paraded the deck armed, while the other negroes behaved precisely as they had done before the mutiny. About 10 o'clock, P. M., on the 8th day of November, 1841, they made the light of Abaco. Ben had the gun. About 10 o'clock P. M. he fired at Stevens, who came on deck as already stated. Merritt and Gifford (officers of the vessel) alternately kept watch. Ben, Madison, Ruffin and Morris (four principal mutineers) kept watch by turns, the whole time up to their arrival at Nassau, with knives drawn. So close was the watch, that it was impossible to rescue the brig. Neither passengers, officers or sailors were allowed to communicate with each other. The sailors performed their usual duties."

Arrived at Nassau, a pilot came on board—all the men in his boat being negroes. He and his men on coming on board, mingled with the slaves, and told them they were free men—that they should go on shore, and never be carried away from there. The regular quarantine officer then came on board, to whom Gifford, first mate of the vessel, related all the circumstances of the mutiny. Going ashore with the quarantine officer, Gifford related all the same circumstances to the Governor of the island, and to the American Consul at Nassau. The consul, in behalf of the vessel and all interested, requested that a guard should be sent on board to protect the vessel and cargo, and keep the slaves on board until it could be known what was to be done. The Governor did so—sending a guard of twenty-four negro soldiers in British uniform, with loaded muskets and fixed bayonets. The affidavits then say:

"From Tuesday the 10th, till Friday the 12th day of November, they tied Ben Blacksmith, Addison, Ruffin, and Morris, put them in the long boat, placed a sentry over them, and fed them there. They mingled with the negroes, and told the women they were free, and persuaded them to remain in the island. Capt. Fitzgerald, commanding the company, told many of the slaves owned by Thomas McCargo, in presence of many other of the slaves, how foolish they were, that they had not, when they rose, killed all the whites on board, and run the vessel ashore, and then they would have been free, and there would have been no more trouble about it. This was on Wednesday. Every day the officers and soldiers were changed at 9 o'clock, A.M. There are 500 regular soldiers on the island, divided into four equal companies, commanded by four officers, called captains. There was a regular sentry stationed every night, and they put all the men slaves below, except the four which were tied, and placed a guard over the hatchway. They put them in the hold at sunset, and let them out at sunrise. There were apparently from twelve to thirteen thousand negroes in the town of Nassau and vicinity, and about three or four thousand whites."

The next day the Queen's attorney-general for this part of her West Indian possessions, came on board the brig, attended by three magistrates and the United States consul, and took the depositions of all the white persons on board in relation to the mutiny. That being done, the attorney-general placed the 19 mutineers in the custody of the captain and his guard of 24 negro soldiers, and ordered them upon the quarter-deck. The affidavits then continue:

"There were about fifty boats lying round the brig, all filled with men from the shore, armed with clubs, and subject to the order of the attorney-general, and awaiting a signal from one of the civil magistrates; a sloop was towed from the shore by some of our boats, and anchored near the brig—this sloop was also filled with men armed with clubs; all the men in the boats were negroes. The fleet of boats was under the immediate command of the pilot who piloted the brig into the harbor. This pilot, partly before the signal was given by one of the magistrates, said that he wished they would get through the business; that they had their time and he wanted his.

"The attorney-general here stepped on the quarter-deck, and addressing himself to all the persons except the nineteen who were in custody, said, 'My friends, you have been detained a short time on board the Creole for the purpose of ascertaining the individuals who were concerned in this mutiny and murder. They have been identified, and will be detained, and the rest of you are free, and at liberty to go on shore, and wherever you please.' Then addressing the prisoners he said: 'Men, there are nineteen of you who have been identified as having been engaged in the murder of Mr. Hewell, and in an attempt to kill the captain and others. You will be detained and lodged in prison for a time, in order that we may communicate with the English government, and ascertain whether your trial shall take place here or elsewhere.' At this time Mr. Gifford, the mate of the vessel, then in command, the captain being on shore, under the care of a physician, addressed the attorney-general in the presence of the magistrates, protested against the boats being permitted to come alongside of the vessel, or that the negroes other than the mutineers should be put on shore. The attorney-general replied that Mr. Gifford had better make no objection, but let them go quietly on shore, for if he did, there might be bloodshed. At this moment one of the magistrates ordered Mr. Merritt, Mr. McCargo, and the other passengers, to look to their money and effects, as he apprehended that the cabin of the Creole would be sacked and robbed.

"The attorney-general with one of the magistrates, stepped into his boat and withdrew into the stream, a short distance from the brig, when they stopped. A magistrate on the deck of the Creole gave the signal for the boats to approach instantly. With a hurrah and a shout, a fleet of boats came alongside of the brig, and the magistrates directed the men to remain on board of their own boats, and commanded the slaves to leave the brig and go on board the boats. They obeyed his orders, and passing from the Creole into the boats, were assisted, many of them, by this magistrate. During this proceeding, the soldiers and officers were on the quarter-deck of the Creole, armed with loaded muskets and bayonets fixed, and the attorney-general with one of the magistrates in his boat, lay at a convenient distance, looking on. After the negroes had embarked in the boats, the attorney-general and magistrate pushed out their boat, and mingled with the fleet, congratulating the slaves on their escape, and shaking hands with them. Three cheers were then given, and the boats went to the shore, where thousands were waiting to receive them."

The 19 mutineers were then taken on shore, and lodged in prison, while many of the slaves—the greater part of them—who were proclaimed to be liberated, begged to be allowed to proceed with their masters to New Orleans, but were silenced by threats, and the captain told that his vessel should be forfeited if he attempted to carry any of them away. Only four, by hiding themselves, succeeded in getting off with their masters. The next day a proceeding took place in relation to what was called "the baggage of the passengers;" which is thus stated in the affidavits:

"On Monday following these events, being the 15th day of November, the attorney-general wrote a letter to Captain Ensor, informing him that the *passengers* of the Creole, as he called the slaves, had applied to him for assistance in obtaining their baggage which was still on board the brig, and that he should assist them in getting it on shore. To this letter, Gifford, the officer in command of the vessel, replied that there was no baggage on board belonging to the slaves that he was aware of, as he considered them cargo, and the property of their owners, and that if they had left any thing on board the brig, it was the property also of their masters; and besides he could not land any thing without a permit from the custom house, and an order from the American consul. The attorney-general immediately got a permit from the custom-house, but no order from the American consul, and put an officer of the customs on board the brig, and demanded the delivery of the baggage of the slaves aforesaid to be landed in the brig's boat. The master of the Creole, not feeling himself at liberty to refuse, permitted the officer with his men to come on board and take such baggage and property as they chose to consider as belonging to the slaves. They went into the hold of the vessel, and took all the wearing apparel, blankets, and other articles, as also one bale of blankets, belonging to Mr. Lockett, which had not been opened. These things were put on board of the boat of the officer of the customs, and carried on shore."

The officers of the American brig earnestly demanded that the mutineers should be left with them to be carried into a port of the United States to be tried for their mutiny and murder; but this demand was positively refused—the attorney-general saying that they would take the orders of the British government as to the place. This was tantamount to an acquittal, and even justification of all they had done, as according to the British judicial decisions a slave has a right to kill his master to obtain his freedom. This outrage (the forcible liberation of the slaves, refusal to permit the mutineers to be brought to their own country for trial, and the abstraction of articles from the brig belonging to the captain and crew), produced much exasperation in the slave States. Coming so soon after four others of kindred character, and while the outrage on the Caroline was still unatoned for, it bespoke a contempt for the United States which was galling to the feelings of many besides the inhabitants of the States immediately interested. It was a subject for the attention both of the Executive government and the Congress; and accordingly received the notice of both. Early in the session of '41-'42, Mr.

Calhoun submitted a call in the Senate, in which the President was requested to give information of what he had heard of the outrage, and what steps he had taken to obtain redress. He answered through the Secretary of State (Mr. Webster), showing that all the facts had been regularly communicated, and that he (the Secretary) had received instructions to draw up a despatch on the subject to the American minister in London (Mr. Edward Everett); which would be done without unnecessary delay. On receiving this message, Mr. Calhoun moved to refer it to the Committee on Foreign Relations—prefacing his motion with some remarks, and premising that the Secretary had answered well as to the facts of the case.

"As to the remaining portion of the resolution, that which asked for information as to what steps had been taken to bring the guilty in this bloody transaction to justice, and to redress the wrong done to our citizens, and the indignity offered to our flag, he regretted to say, the report of the Secretary is very unsatisfactory. He, Mr. C., had supposed, in a case of such gross outrage, that prompt measures for redress would have been adopted. He had not doubted, but that a vessel had been despatched, or some early opportunity seized for transmitting directions to our minister at the court of St. James, to demand that the criminals should be delivered to our government for trial; more especially, as they were detained with the view of abiding the decision of the government at home. But in all this he had been in a mistake. Not a step has been yet taken—no demand made for the surrender of the murderers, though the Executive must have been in full possession of the facts for more than a month. The only reply is, that he (the Secretary) had received the orders of the President to prepare a despatch for our minister in London, which would be 'prepared without unnecessary delay.' He (Mr. Calhoun) spoke not in the spirit of censure; he had no wish to find fault; but he thought it due to the country, and more especially, of the portion that has so profound an interest in this subject, that he should fearlessly state the facts as they existed. He believed our right to demand the surrender of the murderers clear, beyond doubt, and that, if the case was fairly stated, the British government would be compelled, from a sense of justice, to yield to our demand; and hence his deep regret that there should have been such long delay in making any demand. The apparent indifference which it indicates on the part of the government, and the want of our views on the subject, it is to be feared, would prompt to an opposite decision, before any despatch can now be received by our minister.

"He repeated that the case was clear. He knew that an effort had been made, and he regretted to say, even in the South, and through a newspaper in this District, but a morning or two since, to confound the case with the ordinary one of a criminal fleeing from the country where the crime was perpetrated, to another. He admitted that it is a doubtful question whether, by the laws of nations, in such a case, the nation to which he fled, was bound to surrender him on the demand of the one where the crime was committed. But that was not this case, nor was there any analogy between them. This was mutiny and murder, committed on the ocean, on board of one of our vessels, sailing from one port to another on our own coast, in a regular voyage, committed by slaves, who constituted a part of the cargo, and forcing the officers and crew to steer the vessel into a port of a friendly power. Now there was nothing more clear, than that, according to the laws of nations, a vessel on the ocean is regarded as a portion of the territory of the State to which she belongs, and more emphatically so, if possible, in a coasting voyage; and that if forced into a friendly port by an unavoidable necessity, she loses none of the rights that belong to her on the ocean. Contrary to these admitted principles, the British authorities entered on board of the Creole, took the criminals under their own jurisdiction, and that after they had ascertained them to be guilty of mutiny and murder, instead (as they ought to have done) of aiding the officers and crew in confining them, to be conveyed to one of our ports, where they would be amenable to our laws. The outrage would not have been greater, nor more clearly contrary to the laws of nations, if, instead of taking them from the Creole, they had entered our territory, and forcibly taken them from one of our jails; and such, he could scarcely doubt, would be the decision of the British government itself, if the facts and reasons of the case be fairly presented before its decision is made. It would be clearly the course she would have adopted had the mutiny and murder been perpetrated by a portion of the crew, and it can scarcely be that she will regard it less criminal, or less imperiously her duty, to surrender the criminals, because the act was perpetrated by slaves. If so, it is time we should know it."

The Secretary soon had his despatch ready and as soon as it was ready, it was called for at the instance of a friend of the Secretary, communicated to the Senate and published for general information, clearly to counteract the impressions which Mr. Calhoun's remarks had made. It gave great satisfaction in its mode of treating the subject, and in the intent it declared to demand redress:

"The British government cannot but see that this case, as presented in these papers, is one calling loudly for redress. The 'Creole' was passing from one port of the United States to another, in a voyage perfectly lawful, with merchandise on board, and also with slaves, or persons bound to service, natives of America, and belonging to American citizens, and which are recognized as property by the constitution of the United States in those States in which slavery exists. In the course of the voyage some of the slaves rose upon the master and crew, subdued them, murdered one man, and caused the vessel to be carried into Nassau. The vessel was thus taken to a British port, not voluntarily, by those who had the lawful authority over her, but forcibly and violently, against the master's will, and with the consent of nobody but the mutineers and murderers: for there is no evidence that these outrages were committed with the concurrence of any of the slaves, except those actually engaged in them. Under these circumstances, it would seem to have been the plain and obvious duty of the authorities at Nassau, the port of a friendly power, to assist the American consul in putting an end to the captivity of the master and crew, restoring to them the control of the vessel, and enabling them to resume their voyage, and to take the mutineers and murderers to their own country to answer for their crimes before the proper tribunal. One cannot conceive how any other course could justly be adopted, or how the duties imposed by that part of the code regulating the intercourse of friendly states, which is generally called the comity of nations, could otherwise be fulfilled. Here was no violation of British law attempted or intended on the part of the master of the 'Creole,' nor any infringement of the principles of the law of nations. The vessel was lawfully engaged in passing from port to port, in the United States. By violence and crime she was carried, against the master's will, out of her course, into the port of a friendly power. All was the result of force. Certainly, ordinary comity and hospitality entitled him to such assistance from the authorities of the place as should enable him to resume and prosecute his voyage and bring the offenders to justice. But, instead of this, if the facts be as represented in these papers, not only did the authorities give no aid for any such purpose, but they did actually interfere to set free the slaves, and to enable them to disperse themselves beyond the reach of the master of the vessel or their owners. A proceeding like this cannot but cause deep feeling in the United States."

Mr. Calhoun was so well satisfied with this despatch that, as soon as it was read, he stood up, and said:

"The letter which had been read was drawn up with great ability, and covered the ground which had been assumed on this subject by all parties in the Senate. He hoped that it would have a beneficial effect, not only upon the United States, but Great Britain. Coming from the quarter it did, this document would do more good than in coming from any other quarter."

This was well said of the letter, but there was a paragraph in it which damped the expectations of some senators—a paragraph which referred to the known intention to send out a special minister (Lord Ashburton) to negotiate a general settlement of differences with Great Britain—and which expressed a wish that this special minister should be clothed with power to settle this case of the Creole. That looked like deferring it to a general settlement, which, in the opinion of some, was tantamount to giving it up.

CHAPTER XCIX.

DISTRESS OF THE TREASURY: THREE TARIFF BILLS, AND TWO VETOES: END OF THE COMPROMISE ACT.

Never were the coffers and the credit of the Treasury—not even in the last year of the war with Great Britain (1814)—at a lower ebb, or more pitiable point, than at present. A deficit of fourteen millions in the Treasury—a total inability to borrow, either at home or abroad, the amount of the loan of twelve millions authorized the year before—treasury-notes below par—a million and a half of protested demands—a revenue from imports inadequate and decreasing: such was the condition of the Treasury, and all the result of three measures forced upon the previous administration by the united power of the opposition, and the aid of temporizing friends, too prone to take alarm in transient difficulties, and too ready to join the schemes of the opposition for temporary relief, though more injurious than the evils they were intended to remedy. These three measures were: 1. Compromise act of 1833. 2. The distribution of surplus revenue in 1837. 3. The surrender of the land revenue to the States. The compromise act, by its slow and imperceptible reductions of revenue during its first seven years, created a large surplus: by its abrupt and precipitous falling off the last two, made a deficit. The distribution of this surplus, to the amount of near thirty millions, took away the sum which would have met this deficiency. And the surrender of the land revenue diverted from its course the second largest stream of revenue that came into the Treasury: and the effect of the whole was to leave it without money and without credit: and with a deficit which was ostentatiously styled, "*the debt of the late administration.*" Personally considered, there was retributive justice in this calamitous visitation. So far as individuals were concerned it fell upon those who had created it. Mr. Tyler had been the zealous promoter of all these measures: the whig party, whose ranks he had joined, had been their author: some obliging democrats were the auxiliaries, without which they could not have been carried. The administration of President Tyler now needed the money: his former whig friends had the power to grant, or withhold it: and they chose, either to withhold, or to grant upon terms which Mr. Tyler repulsed. They gave him two tariff revenue bills in a month, which he returned with vetoes, and had to look chiefly to that democracy whom he had left to join the whigs (and of whom he had become the zealous opponent), for the means of keeping his administration alive.

A bill called a "*provisional tariff*" was first sent to him: he returned it with the objections which made it impossible for him to approve it: and of which these objections were the chief:

> "It suspends, in other words, abrogates for the time, the provision of the act of 1833, commonly called the 'compromise act.' The only ground on which this departure from the solemn adjustment of a great and agitating question seems to have been regarded as expedient is, the alleged necessity of establishing, by legislative enactments, rules and regulations for assessing the duties to be levied on imports, after the 30th June, according to the home valuation; and yet the bill expressly provides that 'if before the 1st of August there be no further legislation upon the subject, the laws for laying and collecting duties shall be the same as though this act had not been passed.' In other words, that the act of 1833, imperfect as it is considered, shall in that case continue to be, and to be executed under such rules and regulations as previous statutes had prescribed, or had enabled the executive department to prescribe for that purpose, leaving the supposed chasm in the revenue laws just as it was before.

> "The bill assumes that a distribution of the proceeds of the public lands is, by existing laws, to be made on the first day of July, 1842, notwithstanding there has been an imposition of duties on imports exceeding twenty per cent. up to that day, and directs it to be made on the 1st of August next. It seems to me very clear that this conclusion is equally erroneous and dangerous; as it would divert from the Treasury a fund sacredly pledged for the general purposes of the government, in the event of a rate of duty above twenty per cent. being found necessary for an economical administration of the government. The act of September last, which provides for the distribution, couples it inseparably with the condition that it shall cease—first, in case of war; second, as soon and so long as the rate of duties shall, for any

reason whatever, be raised above twenty per cent. Nothing can be more clear, express, or imperative, than this language. It is in vain to allege that a deficit in the Treasury was known to exist, and that means were taken to supply this deficit by loan when the act was passed."

These reasons show the vice and folly of the acts which a pride of consistency still made him adhere to. That compromise act of 1833 assumed to fix the tariff to eternity, *first*, by making existing duties decline through nine years to a uniform ad valorem of twenty per centum on all dutied articles; *next*, by fixing it there for ever, giving Congress leave to work under it on articles then free; but never to go above it: and the mutual assurance entered into between this act and the land distribution act of the extra session, was intended to make sure of both objects—the perpetual twenty per centum, and the land distribution. One hardly knows which to admire most, the arrogance, or the folly, of such presumptuous legislation: and to add to its complication there was a clear division of opinion whether any duty at all, for want of a law appointing appraisers, could be collected after the 30th of June. Between the impracticability, and the unintelligibility of the acts, and his consistency, he having sanctioned all these complicated and dependent measures, it was clear that Mr. Tyler's administration was in a deplorable condition. The low credit of the government, in the impossibility of getting a small loan, was thus depicted:

> "Who at the time foresaw or imagined the possibility of the present real state of things, when a nation that has paid off her whole debt since the last peace, while all the other great powers have been increasing theirs, and whose resources already so great, are yet but in the infancy of their development, should be compelled to haggle in the money market for a paltry sum, not equal to one year's revenue upon her economical system."

Not able to borrow, even in time of peace, a few millions for three years! This was in the the time of paper money. Since gold became the federal currency, any amount, and in time of war, has been at the call of the government; and its credit so high, and its stock so much above par, that twenty per centum premium is now paid for the privilege of paying, before they are due, the amounts borrowed during the Mexican war:

> "This connection (the mutual assurance between the compromise act and the land distribution) thus meant to be inseparable, is severed by the bill presented to me. The bill violates the principle of the acts of 1833, and September, 1841, by suspending the first, and rendering, for a time, the last inoperative. Duties above twenty per cent. are proposed to be levied, and yet the *proviso* in the distribution act is disregarded. The proceeds of the sales are to be distributed on the 1st of August; so that, while the duties proposed to be enacted exceed twenty per cent. no suspension of the distribution to the States is permitted to take place. To abandon the principle for a month is to open the way for its total abandonment. If such is not meant, why postpone at all? Why not let the distribution take place on the 1st of July, if the law so directs? (which, however, is regarded as questionable.) But why not have limited the provision to that effect? Is it for the accommodation of the Treasury? I see no reason to believe that the Treasury will be in better condition to meet the payment on the 1st of August, than on the 1st of July."

Here Mr. Tyler was right in endeavoring to get back, even temporarily, the land revenue; but slight as was this relaxation of their policy, it brought upon him keen reproaches from his old friends. Mr. Fillmore said:

> "On what principle was this veto based? The President could not consent that the distribution of the proceeds of the public lands should cease for a single day. Now, although that was the profession, yet it appeared to have been but a pretence. Mr. F. wished to speak with all respect to the chief magistrate, but of his message he must speak with plainness. What was the law which that message vetoed? It authorized the collection of duties for a single month as they were levied on the first of January last, to allow time for the consideration of a permanent revenue for the country; it postponed the distribution of the proceeds of the public lands till the month should expire, and Congress could provide the necessary supplies for the exhausted Treasury. But what would be the effect of the veto now on the table? Did it prevent the distribution? By no means; it reduced the duties, in effect, to twenty per cent., and authorized

the distribution of the land fund among the States; and that distribution would, in fact, take place the day after to-morrow. That would be the practical operation of this paper. When Congress had postponed the distribution for a month, did it not appear like pretence in the chief magistrate to say that he was forced to veto the bill from Congress, to prevent the distribution, which his veto, and that alone, would cause to take place? Congress had been willing to prevent the distribution, but the President, by one and the same blow, cut down the revenue at a moment when his Secretary could scarce obtain a loan on any terms, and in addition to this distributed the income from the public domain! In two days the distribution must take place. Mr. F. said he was not at all surprised at the joy with which the veto had been hailed on the other side of the house, or at the joyful countenances which were arrayed there; probably this act was but the consummation of a treaty which had been long understood as in process of negotiation. If this was the ratification of such treaty, Mr. F. gave gentlemen much joy on the happy event. He should shed no tears that the administration had passed into its appropriate place. This, however, was a matter he should not discuss now; he should desire the message might be laid on the table till to-morrow and be printed. Mr. F. said he was free to confess that we were now in a crisis which would shake this Union to its centre. Time would determine who would yield and who was right; whether the President would or would not allow the representatives of the people to provide a revenue in the way they might think best for the country, provided they were guilty of no violation of the constitution. The President had now told them, in substance, that he had taken the power into his own hands; and although the highest financial officer of the government declared it as his opinion, that it was doubtful whether the duties could be collected which Congress had provided by law, the President told the House that any further law was unnecessary; that he had power enough in his own hands, and he should use it; that he had authorized the revenue officers to do all that was necessary. This then would be in fact the question before the country: whether Congress should legislate for the people of this country or the Executive?"

Mr. Alexander H. H. Stuart, of Virginia, took issue with the President on the character of the land distribution bill, and averred it to have been an intended part of the compromise from the beginning. He said:

"That the President has rested his veto upon the grounds of expediency alone, and not upon any conscientious or constitutional scruples. He withholds his assent because of its supposed conflict with the compromise act of 1833. I take issue with the President in regard to this matter of fact, and maintain that there is no such conflict. The President's particular point of objection to the temporary tariff bill is that it contemplates a prospective distribution of the land proceeds. Now, conceding that the President has put a correct construction on our bill, I aver that it is no violation of the compromise act to withdraw the land proceeds from the ordinary purposes of the government, and distribute them among the States. On the contrary, I maintain that that act distinctly contemplates the distribution of the land proceeds, that the *distribution was one of the essential elements of the compromise*, and that the *failure to distribute* the land fund now *would of itself be a violation of the* true understanding of those who adopted the *compromise*, and a palpable fraud upon the rights of one of the parties to it."

Mr. Caruthers, of Tennessee, was still more pointed to the same effect, referring to Mr. Tyler's conduct in the Virginia General Assembly to show that he was in favor of the land revenue distribution, and considered its cessation as a breach of the compromise. He referred to his,

"Oft-quoted resolutions in the legislature of Virginia, in 1839, urging the distribution, and conveying the whole proceeds of the lands, not only ceded but acquired by purchase and by treaty. Mr. C. also referred to the adroit manner in which Mr. Tyler had at that time met the charge of his opponents (that he desired to violate the compromise act) by the introduction of the well known proviso, that the General Assembly did not mean to infringe or disturb the provisions of the compromise act."

The vote was taken upon the returned bill, as required by the constitution; and falling far short of the required two-thirds, it was rejected. But the exigencies of the Treasury were so great that a further effort to pass a revenue bill was indispensable; and one was accordingly immediately introduced into the House. It differed but little from the first one, and nothing on the land revenue distribution clause, which it retained in full. That clause had been the main cause of the first veto: it was a challenge for a second! and under circumstances which carried embarrassment to the President either way. He had been from the beginning of the policy, a supporter of the distribution; and at the extra session had solemnly recommended it in his regular message. On the other hand, he had just disapproved it in his message returning the tariff bill. He adhered to this latter view; and said:

> "On the subject of distributing the proceeds of the sales of the public lands, in the existing state of the finances, it has been my duty to make known my settled convictions on various occasions during the present session of Congress. At the opening of the extra session, upwards of twelve mouths ago, sharing fully in the general hope of returning prosperity and credit, I recommended such a distribution; but that recommendation was even then expressly coupled with the condition that the duties on imports should not exceed the rate of twenty per cent, provided by the compromise act of 1833. The bill which is now before me proposes, in its 27th section, the total repeal of one of the provisos in the act of September; and, while it increases the duties above twenty per cent., directs an unconditional distribution of the land proceeds. I am therefore subjected a second time, in the period of a few days, to the necessity of either giving my approval to a measure which, in my deliberate judgment, is in conflict with great public interests; or of returning it to the House in which it originated, with my objections. With all my anxiety for the passage of a law which would replenish an exhausted Treasury, and furnish a sound and healthy encouragement to mechanical industry, I cannot consent to do so at the sacrifice of the peace and harmony of the country, and the clearest convictions of public duty."

The reasons were good, and ought to have prevented Congress from retaining the clause; but party spirit was predominant, and in each House the motion to strike out the clause had been determined by a strict party vote. An unusual course was taken with this second veto message: it was referred to a select committee of thirteen members, on the motion of Mr. Adams; and from that committee emanated three reports upon it—one against it, and two for it; the committee dividing politically in making them. The report against it was signed by ten members; the other two by the remaining three members; but they divided, so as to present two signatures to one report, and a single one to the other. Mr. Adams, as the chairman, was the writer of the majority report, and made out a strong case against Mr. Tyler personally, but no case at all in favor of the distribution clause. The report said:

> "Who could imagine that, after this most emphatic *coupling* of the revenue from duties of impost, with revenue from the proceeds of the sales of the public lands, the first and paramount objection of the President to this bill should be, that it unites two subjects which, so far from having any affinity to one another, are wholly incongruous in their character; which two subjects are identically the same with those which *he* had coupled together in his recommendation to Congress at the extra session? If there was no affinity between the parties, why did he join them together? If the union was illegitimate, who was the administering priest of the unhallowed rites? It is objected to this bill, that it is both a revenue and an appropriation bill? What then? Is not the act of September 4, 1841, approved and signed by the President himself, both a revenue and an appropriation bill? Does it not enact that, in the event of an insufficiency of impost duties, not exceeding twenty per centum ad valorem, to defray the current expenses of the government, the proceeds of the sales of the lands shall be levied as part of the same revenue, and appropriated to the same purposes?"

The report concluded with a strong denunciation of, what it considered, an abuse of the veto power, and a contradiction of the President's official recommendation and conduct:

"The power of the present Congress to enact laws essential to the welfare of the people has been struck with apoplexy by the Executive hand. Submission to his will, is the only condition upon which he will permit them to act. For the enactment of a measure earnestly recommended by himself, he forbids their action, unless *coupled* with a *condition* declared by himself to be on a subject so totally different, that he will not suffer them to be coupled in the same law. With that condition, Congress cannot comply. In this state of things, he has assumed, as the committee fully believe, the exercise of the whole legislative power to himself, and is levying millions of money upon the people, without any authority of law. But the final decision of this question depends neither upon legislative nor executive, but upon judicial authority; nor can the final decision of the Supreme Court upon it be pronounced before the close of the present Congress."

The returned bill being put to the vote, was found to lack as much as the first of the two-thirds majority, and was rejected. But revenue was indispensable. Daily demands upon the government were undergoing protest. The President in his last message had given in $1,400,000 of such dishonored demands. The existing revenue from imports, deficient as it was, was subjected to a new embarrassment, that of questioned legality for want of a law of appraisement under the compromise, and merchants paid their duties under protest, and with notices of action against the collector to recover them back. It was now near the end of August. Congress had been in session nine months—an unprecedentedly long session, and that following immediately on the heels of an extra session of three months and a half. Adjournment could not be deferred, and could not take place without providing for the Treasury. The compromise and the land distribution were the stumbling-blocks: it was determined to sacrifice them together, but without seeming to do so. A contrivance was fallen upon: duties were raised above twenty per centum: and that breach of the mutual assurance in relation to the compromise, immediately in terms of the assurance, suspended the land revenue distribution—to continue it suspended while duties above the compromise limit continued to be levied. And as that has been the case ever since, the distribution of the revenue has been suspended ever since. Such were the contrivances, ridiculous inventions, and absurd circumlocutions which Congress had recourse to to get rid of that land distribution which was to gain popularity for its authors; and to get rid of that compromise which was celebrated at the time as having saved the Union, and the breach of which was deprecated in numerous legislative resolves as the end of the Union, and which all the while was nothing but an arrogant piece of monstrosity, patched up between two aspiring politicians, to get rid of a stumbling-block in each other's paths for the period of two presidential elections. In other respects one of the worst features of that personal and pestiferous legislation has remained— the universal ad valorems—involving its army of appraisers, their diversity of appraisement from all the imperfections to which the human mind is subject—to say nothing of the chances for ignorance, indifference, negligence, favoritism, bribery and corruption. The act was approved the 30th day of August; and Congress forthwith adjourned.

CHAPTER C.

MR. TYLER AND THE WHIG PARTY: CONFIRMED SEPARATION.

At the close of the extra session, a vigorous effort was made to detach the whig party from Mr. Clay. Mr. Webster in his published letter, in justification of his course in remaining in the cabinet when his colleagues left it, gave as a reason the expected unity of the party under a new administration. "A whig president, a whig Congress, and a whig people," was the vision that dazzled and seduced him. Mr. Cushing published his address, convoking the whigs to the support of Mr. Tyler. Mr. Clay was stigmatized as a dictator, setting himself up against the real President. Inducements as well as arguments were addressed to the whig ranks to obtain recruits: all that came received high reward. The arrival of the regular session was to show the fruit of these efforts, and whether the whig party was to become a unity under Mr. Tyler, Mr. Webster, and Mr. Cushing, or to remain embodied under Mr. Clay. It remained so embodied. Only a few, and they chiefly who had served an apprenticeship to party mutation in previous changes, were seen to join him: the body of the party remained firm, and militant—angry and armed; and giving to President Tyler incessant proofs of their resentment. His legislative recommendations were thwarted, as most of them deserved to be: his name was habitually vituperated or ridiculed. Even reports of committees, and legislative votes, went the length of grave censure and sharp rebuke. The select committee of thirteen, to whom the consideration of the second tariff, in a report signed by nine of its members, Mr. Adams at their head, suggested impeachment as due to him:

> "The majority of the committee believe that the case has occurred, in the annals of our Union, contemplated by the founders of the constitution by the grant to the House of Representatives of the power to impeach the President of the United States; but they are aware that the resort to that expedient might, in the present condition of public affairs, prove abortive. They see that the irreconcilable difference of opinion and of action between the legislative and executive departments of the government is but sympathetic with the same discordant views and feelings among the people."

A rebuking resolve, and of a retributive nature, was adopted by the House. It has been related (Vol. I.) that when President Jackson sent to the Senate a protest against the senatorial condemnation pronounced upon him in 1835, the Senate refused to receive it, and adopted resolutions declaring the protest to be a breach of the privileges of the body in interfering with the discharge of their duties. The resolves so adopted were untrue, and the reverse of the truth—the whole point of the protest being that the condemnation was extra-judicial and void, coming under no division of power which belonged to the Senate: not legislative, for it proposed no act of legislation: not executive, for it applied to no treaty or nomination: not judicial, for it was founded in no articles of impeachment from the House, and without forming the Senate into a court of impeachment. The protest considered the condemnatory sentence, and justly, as the act of a town meeting, done in the Senate-chamber, and by senators; but of no higher character than if done by the same number of citizens in a voluntary town meeting. This was the point, and whole complaint of the protest; but the Senate, avoiding to meet it in that form, put a different face upon it, as an interference with the constitutional action of the Senate, attacking its independence; and, therefore, a breach of its privileges. Irritated by the conduct of the House in its reports upon his tariff-veto messages, Mr. Tyler sent in a protest also, as President Jackson had done, but without attending to the difference of the cases, and that, in its action upon the veto messages, the House was clearly acting within its sphere—within its constitutional legislative capacity; and, consequently, however disagreeable to him this action might be, it was still legislative and constitutional, and such as the House had a legal *right* to adopt, whether just or unjust. Overlooking this difference, Mr. Tyler sent in his protest also: but the House took the distinction; and applied legitimately to the conduct of Mr. Tyler what had been illegally applied to General Jackson, with the aggravation of turning against himself his own votes on that occasion—Mr. Tyler being one of the senators who voted in favor of the three resolves against President Jackson's protest. When this protest of Mr. Tyler was read in the House, Mr. Adams stood up, and said:

> "There seemed to be an expectation on the part of some gentlemen that he should propose to the House some measure suitable to be adopted on the present occasion. Mr. A. knew of no reason for such an expectation, but the fact that he had been the mover of the resolution

for the appointment of the committee which had made the report referred to in the message; had been appointed by the Speaker, chairman of the committee; and that the report against which the President of the United States had sent to the House such a multitude of protests, was written by him. So far as it had been so written, Mr. A. held himself responsible to the House, to the country, to the world, and to posterity; and, so far as he was the author of the report, he held himself responsible to the President also. The President should hear from him elsewhere than here on that subject. Mr. A. went on to say that it was because the report had been adopted by the House, and not because it had been written by him, that the President had sent such a bundle of protests; and therefore Mr. A. felt no necessity or obligation upon himself to propose what measures the House ought to adopt for the vindication of its own dignity and honor; and perhaps, from considerations of delicacy, he was indeed the very last man in the House who should propose any measure, under the circumstances."

Mr. Botts, of Virginia, a member of the committee which had made the report, after some introductory remarks, went on to say:

"In 1834 the Senate had adopted certain resolutions, condemning the course of President Jackson in the removal of the deposits from the Bank of the United States to the State banks. In consequence of this movement on the part of the Senate, President Jackson sent to that body a *protest* against the right of the Senate to express any opinion censuring his public course; and, what made the case then stronger than the present case, was, that the Senate constituted the jury by whom he was to be tried, should any impeachment be brought against him. The Senate, after a long, elaborate discussion of the whole matter, and the most eloquent and overpowering torrent of debate that ever was listened to in this country, adopted the three following resolutions:

'1. *Resolved*, That, while the Senate is, and ever will be, ready to receive from the President all such messages and communications as the constitution and laws, and the usual course of business, authorize him to transmit to it; yet it cannot recognize any right in him to make a formal protest against votes and proceedings of the Senate, declaring such votes and proceedings to be illegal and unconstitutional, and requesting the Senate to enter such protests on its journal.'

"On this resolution the yeas and nays were taken; and it was adopted, by a vote of 27 to 16: and, among the recorded votes in its favor, stood the names of John Tyler, now acting President of the United States, and Daniel Webster, now his prime minister.

"The second resolution was as follows:

'2. *Resolved*, That the aforesaid protest is a breach of the privileges of the Senate, and that it be not entered on the journal.'

"The same vote, numerically, was given in favor of this resolution; and among the yeas stood the names of John Tyler, now acting President of the United States, and of Daniel Webster, now his prime minister.

"The third resolutions read as follows:

'3. *Resolved*, That the President of the United States has no right to send a protest to the Senate against any of its proceedings.'

"And in sanction of this resolution also, the record shows the names of the same John Tyler and Daniel Webster."

Mr. Botts forbore to make any remarks of his own in support of the adoption of these resolutions, but read copious extracts from the speech of Mr. Webster in support of the same resolutions when offered in the Senate; and, adopting them as his own, called for the previous question; which call was sustained; and the main question being put, and the vote taken on the resolutions separately, they were all carried by large majorities. The yeas and nays on the first resolve, were:

"YEAS—Messrs. Adams, Landaff W. Andrews, Arnold, Babcock, Barnard, Birdseye, Blair, Boardman, Borden, Botts, Brockway, Jeremiah Brown, Calhoun, William B. Campbell, Thomas J. Campbell, Caruthers, Chittenden, John C. Clark, Cowen, Garrett Davis, John Edwards, Everett, Fillmore, Gamble, Gentry, Graham, Granger, Green, Habersham, Hall, Halsted, Howard, Hudson, Joseph R. Ingersoll, Isaac D. Jones, John P. Kennedy, King, Linn, McKennan, S. Mason, Mathiot, Mattocks, Maxwell, Maynard, Mitchell, Moore, Morrow, Osborne, Owsley, Pope, Powell, Ramsey, Benj. Randall, A. Randall, Randolph, Rayner, Ridgway, Rodney, William Russell, James M. Russell, Saltonstall, Shepperd, Simonton, Slade, Truman Smith, Sprigg, Stanly, Stratton, Summers, Taliaferro, John B. Thompson, Richard W. Thompson, Tillinghast, Toland, Tomlinson, Triplett, Trumbull, Underwood, Van Rensselaer, Wallace, Warren, Washington, Thomas W. Williams, Joseph L. Williams, Yorke, and Augustus Young—87.

"NAYS—Messrs. Arrington, Atherton, Black, Boyd, Aaron V. Brown, Burke, Wm. O. Butler, P. C. Caldwell, Casey, Coles, Cross, Cushing, Richard D. Davis, Dawson, Gordon, Harris, Hastings, Hays, Hopkins, Hubbard, William W. Irwin, Cave Johnson, John W. Jones, Abraham McClellan, Mallory, Medill, Newhard, Oliver, Parmenter, Payne, Proffit, Read, Reding, Reynolds, Riggs, Rogers, Shaw, Shields, Steenrod, Jacob Thompson, Van Buren, Ward, Weller, James W. Williams, Wise, and Wood—46."

The other two resolves were adopted by, substantially, the same vote—the whole body of the whigs voting for the adoption. And this may be considered, so far as Congress was concerned, as the authoritative answer to that idea of whig unity which had induced Mr. Webster to remain in the cabinet. General Jackson was then alive, and it must have looked to him like retributive justice to see two of those (Mr. Tyler and Mr. Webster) who had voted his protest to be a breach of privilege, when it was not, now receiving the same vote from their own party; and that in a case where the breach of privilege was real.

CHAPTER CI.

LORD ASHBURTON'S MISSION, AND THE BRITISH TREATY.

Sixty years had elapsed since the treaty of peace between the United States and Great Britain which terminated the war of the revolution, and established the boundaries between the revolted colonies, now independent States, and the remaining British possessions in North America. A part of these boundaries, agreed upon in the treaty of peace, remained without acknowledgment and without sanction on the part of the British government: it was the part that divided the (now) State of Maine from Lower Canada, and was fixed by the words of the treaty, "*along the highlands which divide the waters which empty themselves into the river St. Lawrence from those which fall into the Atlantic Ocean.*" Nothing could be more simple, or of more easy ascertainment than this line. Any man that knew his right hand from his left, and who could follow a ridge, and not get off of it to cross any water flowing to the right or the left, could trace the boundary, and establish it in the very words of the treaty. In fact there was no tangible dispute about it. The British government had agreed to it under a misapprehension as to the course of these highlands; and as soon as their true course was found out, that government refused to carry that part of the treaty into effect, and for a reason which was very frankly told, *after the treaty of 1842*, by a British civil engineer who had been employed by his government to search out the course of the boundary along those highlands. He said:

> "The treaty of 1783 proposed to establish the boundary between the two countries along certain highlands. The Americans claimed these highlands to run in a northeasterly direction from the head of the Connecticut River, in a course which would have brought the boundary within the distance of twenty miles from the river St. Lawrence, and which, besides cutting off the posts and military routes leading from the province of New Brunswick to Quebec, would have given them various military positions to command and overawe that river and the fortress of Quebec."

This was the objection to the highland boundary. It brought the United States frontier within twenty miles of Quebec, and went one degree and a half north of Quebec! skirting and overlooking Lower Canada all the way, and cutting off all communication between that inland province and the two Atlantic provinces of Nova Scotia and New Brunswick, and between Quebec and Halifax. It was a boundary which commanded the capital of British North America, and which flanked and dominated the principal British province for one hundred and fifty miles. Military considerations rendered such a boundary just as repugnant to the British as the same considerations rendered it acceptable to us; and from the moment it was seen that the State of Maine was projected far north of Quebec and brought up to the long line of heights which looked down upon that capital, the resolution was not to abide that boundary. Negotiation began immediately, and continued, without fruit, for thirty years. That brought the parties to the Ghent Treaty, at the end of the war of 1812, where all attempts to settle the boundary ended in making provision for referring the question to the arbitrament of a friendly sovereign. This was done, the king of the Netherlands being agreed upon as the arbiter. He accepted the trust— executed it—and made an award nearly satisfactory to the British government because it cut off a part of the northern projection of Maine, and so admitted a communication, although circuitous, between Halifax and Quebec; but still leaving the highland boundary opposite that capital. The United States rejected the award because it gave up a part of the boundary of 1783; and thus the question remained for near thirty years longer— until the treaty of 1842—Great Britain demanding the execution of the award—the United States refusing it. And thus the question stood when the special mission arrived in the United States. That mission was well constituted for its purposes. Lord Ashburton, as Mr. Alexander Baring, and head of the great banking house of Baring and Brothers, had been known for more than a generation for his friendly sentiments towards the United States, and business connection with the people and the government; and was, besides, married to an American lady. The affability of his manners was a further help to his mission, the whole of which was so composed (Mr. Mildmay, Mr. Bruce and Mr. Stepping, all gentlemen of mind, tact, and pleasing deportment) as to be real auxiliaries in accomplishing the object of his mission. It was a special mission, sent to settle questions, and return; and so confined to its character of special, that Mr. Fox, the resident minister, although entirely agreeable to the United States and his own government, was not joined in it. It was the first time the

United States had been so honored by Great Britain, and the mission took the character of beneficent, in professing to come to settle all questions between the two governments; but ended in only settling such as suited Great Britain, and in the way that suited her. At the head of those questions was the northeastern boundary, which was settled by giving up the line of 1783, retiring the whole line from the heights which flanked Lower Canada, cutting off as much of Maine as admitted of a pretty direct communication between Halifax and Quebec; and thus granting to Great Britain far more than the award gave her, and with which she had been content. The treaty also made a new boundary in the northwest, from Lake Superior to the Lake of the Woods, also to the prejudice of the United States, retiring the line to the south, and depriving the United States' fur traders of the great line of transportation between these two lakes, which the treaty of 1783 gave to them. The treaty also bound the United States to pay for Rouse's Point, at the outlet of Lake Champlain, which the treaty of '83 and the award of the king of the Netherlands gave to us as a matter of right. It also bound the United States to keep up a squadron, in conjunction with the British, on the coast of Africa for the suppression of the slave trade—nominally for five years, but in reality indefinitely, by the addition of that clause (so seductive and insidious, and so potent in saddling an onerous measure permanently upon a people) which is always resorted to when perpetuity is intended, and cannot be stipulated—the clause which continues the provision in force, after its limited term, until one of the parties give notice to the contrary. An extradition clause was also wanted by Great Britain, and she got it—broad enough to cover the recapture of her subjects whether innocent or guilty, and to include political offenders while professing to take only common felons. These were the points Great Britain wished settled; and she got them all arranged according to her own wishes: others which the United States wished settled, were omitted, and indefinitely adjourned. At the head of these was the boundary beyond the Rocky Mountains. Oregon was in dispute. The United States wished it settled: Great Britain wished that question to remain as it was, as she had the possession, and every day was ripening her title. Oregon was adjourned. The same of the Caroline, the Schlosser outrage—the liberation of slaves at Bermuda and Nassau—the refusal to shelter fugitive slaves in Canada: all were laid over, and for ever. Every thing that the United States wished settled was left unsettled, especially Oregon—a question afterwards pregnant with "inevitable war." Besides obtaining all she wished by treaty, Great Britain also made a great acquisition by statute law. An act of Congress was passed to fit the case of McLeod (in future), and to take such offenders out of the hands of the States.

Notwithstanding its manifold objections the treaty was so framed as to secure its ratification, and to command acquiescence in the United States while crowned with the greatest applause in Great Britain. Lord Ashburton received the formal thanks of parliament for his meritorious labors. Ministers and orators united in declaring that he had accomplished every object that Great Britain desired, and in the way she desired it—and left undone every thing which she wished to remain as it was. The northeastern boundary being altered to suit her, they made a laugh, even in parliament, of the manner in which they had served us. It had so happened, immediately after the peace of '83, that the king's geographer made a map of the United States and the Canadas, to show their respective boundaries; and on that map the line of '83 was laid down correctly, along the highlands, overlooking and going beyond Quebec; and had marked it with a broad red line. He made it for the king, George the Third, who wrote upon it with his own hand—*This is Oswald's line.* (Mr. Richard Oswald being the British negotiator of the provisional treaty of peace of '82 which established that boundary, and which was adopted in the definitive treaty of peace in '83.) This map disappeared from its accustomed place about the time Lord Ashburton's mission was resolved upon, not to be brought over to America by him to assist in finding the true line, but to be hid until the negotiation was over. Some member of parliament hinted at this removal and hiding, during the discussion on the motion of thanks, with an intimation that he thought British honor would have been better consulted by showing this map to the American negotiator: Lord Brougham, the mover of the motion, amused himself at this conception, and thought it would have been carrying frankness a little too far, in such a negotiation, for the British negotiator to have set out with showing, "*that he had no case*"—"*that he had not a leg to stand on.*" His lordship's speech on the occasion, which was more amusing to himself and the parliament than it can be to an American, nevertheless deserves a place in this history of the British treaty of 1842; and, accordingly, here it is:

> "It does so happen that there was a map published by the King's geographer in this country
> in the reign of his Majesty George III., and here I could appeal to an illustrious Duke whom

I now see, whether that monarch was not as little likely to err from any fulness of attachment towards America, as any one of his faithful subjects? [The Duke of *Cambridge*.] Because he well knows that there was no one thing which his reverend parent had so much at heart as the separation from America, and there was nothing he deplored so much as that separation having taken place. The King's geographer, Mr. Faden, published his map 1783, which contains, not the British, but the American line. Why did not my noble friend take over a copy of that map? My noble friend opposite (Lord Aberdeen) is a candid man; he is an experienced diplomatist, both abroad and at home; he is not unlettered, but thoroughly conversant in all the craft of diplomacy and statesmanship. Why did he conceal this map? We have a right to complain of that; and I, on the part of America, complain of that. You ought to have sent out the map of Mr. Faden, and said, 'this is George the Third's map.' But it never occurred to my noble friend to do so. Then, two years after Mr. Faden published that map, another was published, and that took the British line. This, however, came out after the boundary had become matter of controversy *post litem motam*. But, at all events, my noble friend had to contend with the force of the argument against Mr. Webster, and America had a right to the benefit of both maps. My noble friend opposite never sent it over, and nobody ever blamed him for it. But that was not all. What if there was another map containing the American line, and never corrected at all by any subsequent chart coming from the same custody? And what if that map came out of the custody of a person high in office in this country—nay, what if it came out of the custody of the highest functionary of all—of George III. himself? I know that map—I know a map which I can trace to the custody of George III., and on which there is the American line and not the English line, and upon which there is a note, that from the handwriting, as it has been described to me, makes me think it was the note of George III. himself: 'This is the line of Mr. Oswald's treaty in 1783,' written three or four times upon the face of it. Now, suppose this should occur—I do not say that it has happened—but it may occur to a Secretary of State for Foreign Affairs,—either to my noble friend or Lord Palmerston, who, I understand by common report, takes a great interest in the question; and though he may not altogether approve of the treaty, he may peradventure envy the success which attended it, for it was a success which did not attend any of his own American negotiations. But it is possible that my noble friend, or Lord Palmerston, may have discovered that there was this map, because George III.'s library by the munificence of George IV. was given to the British Museum, and this map must have been there; but it is a curious circumstance that it is no longer there. I suppose it must have been taken out of the British Museum for the purpose of being sent over to my noble friend in America; and that, according to the new doctrines of diplomacy, he was bound to have used it when there, in order to show that he had no case—that he had not a leg to stand upon. Why did he not take it over with him? Probably he did not know of its existence. I am told that it is not now in the British Museum, but that it is in the Foreign Office. Probably it was known to exist; but somehow or other that map, which entirely destroys our contention and gives all to the Americans, has been removed from the British Museum, and is now to be found at the Foreign Office. Explain it as you will, that is the simple fact, that this important map was removed from the Museum to the Office, and not in the time of my noble friend (Lord Aberdeen)."

Thus did our simplicity, and their own dexterity, or ambi-dexterity, as the case may be, furnish sport for the British parliament: and thus, "*without a case*," and, "*without a leg to stand upon*," was Lord Ashburton an overmatch for our Secretary-negotiator, with a good case to show, and two good legs to rest on. This map with its red line, and the King's autographic inscription upon it, was afterwards shown to Mr. Everett, upon his request, by Lord Aberdeen; and the fact communicated by him to the Department of State. But the effect of the altered line was graphically stated at a public dinner in honor of it by the same gentleman (Mr. Featherstonhaugh), whose view of the old boundary has already been given.

"Now, gentlemen, if you will divert your attention for a moment from the conflicting statements you may have read in regard to the merits of the compromise which has been made, I will explain them to you in a few words. The American claim, instead of being maintained, has been altogether withdrawn and abandoned; the territory has been divided into equal moieties, as nearly as possible; we have retained that moiety which secures to us every object that was essential to the welfare of our colonies; all our communications, military and civil, are for ever placed beyond hostile reach; and all the military positions on the highlands claimed by America are, without exception, secured for ever to Great Britain."

So spoke a person who had searched the country under the orders of the British government—who knew what he said—and who says there was a compromise, in which our territory (for that is the English of it) was divided into two equal parts, and the part that contained every thing that gave value to the whole, was retained by Great Britain for her share. But there were some members of the American Senate, as will be seen in the sequel, who had no occasion to wait for parliamentary revelations, or dinner-table exultations, in order to understand the merits of this treaty of 1842; and who put their opinions in a form and place, while the treaty was undergoing ratification, to speak for themselves in after time.

Many anomalies attended the conducting of the negotiations which ended in the production of the treaty. As far as could be seen there was no negotiation—none in the diplomatic sense of the term. There were no protocols, minutes, or record to show the progress of things—to show what was demanded, what was offered, and what was agreed upon. Articles came forth ripe and complete, without a trace of their progression; and when thus produced a letter would be drawn up to recommend it—not to the British government, who needed no recommendation of any part of it—but to the American people, who otherwise might not have perceived its advantages. In the next place the treaty was made by a single negotiator on each side, Mr. Fox the resident minister not having been joined with Lord Ashburton, and no one on the American side joined with Mr. Webster, and he left without instructions from the President. On this point Mr. Benton remarked in the debate on the treaty:

"In this case the employment of a single negotiator was unjustifiable. The occasion was great, and required several, both for safety and for satisfaction. The negotiation was here. Our country is full of able men. Two other negotiators might have been joined without delay, without trouble, and almost without expense. The British also had another negotiator here (Mr. Fox); a minister of whom I can say without disparagement to any other, that, in the two and twenty years which I have sat in this Senate, and had occasion to know the foreign ministers, I have never known his superior for intelligence, dignity, attention to his business, fidelity to his own Government, and decorum to ours. Why not add Mr. Fox to Lord Ashburton, unless to prevent an associate from being given to Mr. Webster? Was it arranged in London that the whole negotiation should be between two, and that these two should act without a witness, and without notes or minutes of their conferences? Be this as it may, the effect is the same; and all must condemn this solitary business between two ministers, when the occasion so imperiously demanded several."

The want of instructions was also animadverted upon by Mr. Benton, as a departure from the constitutional action of the government, and injurious in this case, as the three great sections of the Union had each its peculiar question to get settled, and the Secretary-negotiator belonged to one only of these sections, and the only one whose questions had been settled.

"By the theory of our government, the President is the head of the Executive Department, and must treat, through his agents and ministers, with foreign powers. He must tell them what to do, and should tell that in unequivocal language, that there may be no mistake about it. He must command and direct the negotiation; he must order what is done. This is the theory of our government, and this has been its practice from the beginning of Washington's to the end of Mr. Van Buren's administration; and never was it more necessary than now. Being but one negotiator, and he not approved by the Senate for that purpose, and being from an interested State, it was the bounden duty of the President to have guided and directed every thing. He is the head of the Union, and should have attended to the interest of the whole Union; on the contrary, he abandons every thing to his Secretary, and this Secretary takes care of one section of the Union, and of his own State, and of Great Britain; and leaves the other two sections of the Union out of the treaty. The Northern States, coterminous with Canada, get their boundaries adjusted; Massachusetts gets money, which her sister States are to pay; and Great Britain takes two slices, and all her military frontiers, from the State of Maine! the Southern and Western States are left as they were."

It was known that certain senators were consulted as the treaty went along, not publicly, but privately, visiting the negotiators upon request for that purpose, agreeing to it in these conferences; and thus forestalling their official action. This anomaly Mr. Benton thus exposed:

"The irregular manner in which the ratification of this treaty has been sought, by consultations with individual members, before it was submitted to the Senate. Here I tread upon delicate ground; and if I am wrong, this is the time and the place to correct me. I speak in the hearing of those who must know whether I am mistaken. I have reason to believe that the treaty has been privately submitted to senators—their opinions obtained—the judgment of the body forestalled; and then sent here for the forms of ratification. [One senator said he had not been consulted.] Mr. B. in continuation: Certainly not, as the senator says so; and so of any other gentleman who will say the same. I interrogate no one. I have no right to interrogate any one. I do not pretend to say that all were consulted; that would have been unnecessary; and besides, I know I was not consulted myself; and I know many others who were not. All that I intend to say is, that I have reason to think that this treaty has been ratified out of doors! and that this is a great irregularity, and bespeaks an undue solicitude for it on the part of its authors, arising from a consciousness of its indefensible character."

The war argument was also pressed into the service of the ratification, and vehemently relied upon as one of the most cogent arguments in its favor. The treaty, or war! was the constant alternative presented, and not without effect upon all persons of gentle and temporizing spirit. Mr. Benton also exposed the folly and mischief of yielding to such a threat—declaring it to be groundless, and not to be yielded to if it was not.

"The fear of war. This Walpole argument is heavily pressed upon us, and we are constantly told that the alternatives lie between this treaty—the whole of it, just as it is—or war! This is a degrading argument, if true; and infamous, if false! and false it is: and more than that, it is as shameless as it is unfounded! What! the *peace* mission come to make war! It is no such thing. It comes to take advantage of our deplorable condition—to take what it pleases, and to repulse the rest. Great Britain is in no condition to go to war with us, and every child knows it. But I do not limit myself to argument, and general considerations, to disprove this war argument. I refer to the fact which stamps it with untruth. Look to the notes of Sir Charles Vaughan and Mr. Bankhead, demanding the execution of the award, and declaring that *its execution would remove every impediment to the harmony of the two countries*. After that, and while holding these authentic declarations in our hands, are we to be told that the peace mission requires more than the award? requires one hundred and ten miles more of boundary? requires $500,000 for Rouse's Point, which the award gave us without money? requires a naval and diplomatic alliance, which she dared not mention in the time of Jackson or Van Buren? requires the surrender of '*rebels*' under the name of criminals? and puts the South and West at defiance, while conciliating the non-slaveholding States? and gives us war, if we do not consent to all this degradation, insult, and outrage? Are we to be told this? No, sir, no! There is no danger of war; but this treaty may make a war, if it is ratified. It gives up all advantages; leaves us with great questions unsettled; increases the audacity of the British; weakens and degrades us; and leaves us no alternative but war to save the Columbia, to prevent impressment, to resist search, to repel Schlosser invasions, and to avoid a San Domingo insurrection in the South, excited from London, from Canada, and from Nassau."

The mission had been heralded as one of peace—as a beneficent overture for a universal settlement of all difficulties—and as a plan to establish the two countries on a footing of friendship and cordiality, which was to leave each without a grievance, and to launch both into a career of mutual felicity. On the contrary only a few were settled, and those few the only ones which concerned Great Britain and the northern States: the rest which peculiarly concerned the South and the West, were adjourned to London—that is to say, to the Greek calends. On this point Mr. Benton said:

"We were led to believe, on the arrival of the special minister, that he came as a messenger of peace, and clothed with full powers to settle every thing; and believing this, his arrival was hailed with universal joy. But here is a disappointment—a great disappointment. On receiving the treaty and the papers which accompany it, we find that *all* the subjects in dispute have not been settled; that, in fact, only three out of seven are settled; and that the minister has returned to his country, leaving four of the contested subjects unadjusted. This is a disappointment; and the greater, because the papers communicated confirm the report that the minister came with full powers to settle every thing. The very first note of the American negotiator—and that in its very first sentence, confirms this belief, and leaves us to wonder how a mission that promised so much, has performed so little. Mr. Webster's first note runs thus: 'Lord Ashburton having been charged by the Queen's government with full powers to negotiate and settle all matters in discussion between the United States and England, and having on his arrival at Washington announced,' &c., &c. Here is a declaration of full power to settle every thing; and yet, after this, only part is settled, and the minister has returned home. This is unexpected, and inconsistent. It contradicts the character of the mission, balks our hopes, and frustrates our policy. As a confederacy of States, our policy is to settle every thing or nothing; and having received the minister for that purpose, this complete and universal settlement, or nothing, should have been the *sine qua non* of the American negotiator.

"From the message of the President which accompanies the treaty, we learn that the questions in discussion between the two countries were: 1. The Northern boundary. 2. The right of search in the African seas, and the suppression of the African slave trade. 3. The surrender of fugitives from justice. 4. The title to the Columbia River. 5. Impressment. 6. The attack on the Caroline. 7. The case of the Creole, and of other American vessels which had shared the same fate. These are the subjects (seven in number) which the President enumerates, and which he informs us occupied the attention of the negotiators. He does not say whether these were all the subjects which occupied their attention. He does not tell us whether they discussed any others. He does not say whether the British negotiator opened the question of the State debts, and their assumption or guarantee by the Federal government! or whether the American negotiator mentioned the point of the Canadian asylum for fugitive slaves (of which twelve thousand have already gone there) seduced by the honors and rewards which they receive, and by the protection which is extended to them. The message is silent upon these further subjects of difference if not of discussion, between the two countries; and, following the lead of the President, and confining ourselves (for the present) to the seven subjects of dispute named by him, and we find three of them provided for in the treaty—four of them not: and this constitutes a great objection to the treaty—an objection which is aggravated by the nature of the subjects settled, or not settled. For it so happens that, of the subjects in discussion, some were general, and affected the whole Union; others were local, and affected sections. Of these general subjects, those which Great Britain had most at heart are provided for; those which most concerned the United States are omitted: and of the three sections of the Union which had each its peculiar grievance, one section is quieted, and two are left as they were. This gives Great Britain an advantage over us as a nation: it gives one section of the Union an advantage over the two others, sectionally. This is all wrong, unjust, unwise, and impolitic. It is wrong to give a foreign power an advantage over us: it is wrong to give one section of the Union an advantage over the others. In their differences with foreign powers, the States should be kept united: their peculiar grievances should not be separately settled, so as to disunite their several complaints. This is a view of the objection which commends itself most gravely to the Senate. We are a confederacy of States, and a confederacy in which States classify themselves sectionally, and in which each section has its local feelings and its peculiar interests. We are classed in three sections; and each of these sections had a peculiar grievance against Great Britain; and here is a treaty to adjust the grievances of one, and but one, of these three sections. To all intents and purposes, we have a separate treaty—a treaty between the Northern States and Great Britain; for it is a treaty in which the North is provided for, and the South and West left out. Virtually, it is a separate treaty with a part of the States; and this forms a grave objection to it in my eyes.

"Of the nine Northern States whose territories are coterminous with the dominions of her Britannic Majesty, six of them had questions of boundary or of territory, to adjust; and all of these are adjusted. The twelve Southern slaveholding States had a question in which they were all interested—that of the protection and liberation of fugitive or criminal slaves in Canada and the West Indies: this great question finds no place in the treaty, and is put off with phrases in an arranged correspondence. The whole great West takes a deep interest in the fate of the Columbia River, and demands the withdrawal of the British from it: this large subject finds no place in the treaty, nor even in the correspondence which took place between the negotiators. The South and West must go to London with their complaints: the North has been accommodated here. The mission of peace has found its benevolence circumscribed by the metes and boundaries of the sectional divisions in the Union. The peace-treaty is for one section: for the other two sections there is no peace. The non-slaveholding States, coterminous with the British dominions are pacified and satisfied: the slaveholding and the Western States, remote from the British dominions, are to suffer and complain as heretofore. As a friend to the Union—a friend to justice—and as an inhabitant of the section which is both slaveholding and Western, I object to the treaty which makes this injurious distinction amongst the States."

The merits of the different stipulations in the treaty were fully spoken to by several senators—among others, by Mr. Benton—some extracts from whose speech will constitute some ensuing chapters.

CHAPTER CII.

BRITISH TREATY: THE PRETERMITTED SUBJECTS: MR. BENTON'S SPEECH: EXTRACTS.

I. The Columbia River and its Valley.

The omitted or pretermitted subjects are four: the Columbia River—impressment—the outrage on the Caroline—and the liberation of American slaves, carried by violence or misfortune into the British West India islands, or enticed into Canada. Of these, I begin with the Columbia, because equal in importance to any, and, from position, more particularly demanding my attention. The country on this great river is ours: diplomacy has endangered its title: the British have the possession and have repulsed us from the whole extent of its northern shore, and from all the fur region on both sides of the river, and up into all the valleys and gorges of the Rocky Mountains. Our citizens are beginning to go there; and the seeds of national contestation between the British and Americans are deeply and thickly sown in that quarter. From the moment that we discovered it, Great Britain has claimed this country; and for thirty years past this claim has been a point of contested and deferred diplomacy, in which every step taken has been a step for the benefit of her claim, and for the injury of ours. The germ of a war lies there; and this mission of peace should have eradicated that germ. On the contrary, it does not notice it! Neither the treaty nor the correspondence names or notices it! and if it were not for a meagre and stinted paragraph in the President's message, communicating and recommending the treaty, we should not know that the name of the Oregon had occurred to the negotiators. That paragraph is in these words:

> "After sundry informal communications with the British minister upon the subject of the claims of the two countries to territory west of the Rocky Mountains, so little probability was found to exist of coming to any agreement on that subject at present, that it was not thought expedient to make it one of the subjects of formal negotiation, to be entered upon between this government and the British minister, as part of his duties under his special mission."

This is all that appears in relation to a disputed country, equal in extent to the Atlantic portion of the old thirteen United States; superior to them in climate, soil, and configuration; adjacent to the valley of the Mississippi; fronting Asia; holding the key to the North Pacific Ocean; the only country fit for colonization on the extended coast of Northwest America; a country which belongs to the United States by a title as clear as their title to the District of Columbia; which a resolve of Congress, during Mr. Monroe's administration, declared to be occluded against European colonization; which Great Britain is now colonizing; and the title to which has been a subject of diplomatic discussion for thirty years. This is all that is heard of such a country, and such a dispute, in this mission of peace, which was to settle every thing. To supply this omission, and to erect some barrier against the dangers of improvident, indifferent, ignorant, or treacherous diplomacy in future negotiations in relation to this great country, it is my purpose at present to state our title to it; and, in doing so, to expose the fallacy of the British pretensions; and thus to leave in the bosom of the Senate, and on the page of our legislative history, the faithful evidences of our right, and which shall attest our title to all succeeding generations.

(Here Mr. Benton went into a full derivation of the American title to the Columbia River and its valley, between the parallels of 42 and 49 degrees of north latitude—taking the latter boundary from the tenth article of the treaty of Utrecht, and the former from the second article of the Florida treaty of 1819, with Spain.)

The treaty of Utrecht between France and England, as all the world knows, was the treaty which put an end to the wars of Queen Anne and Louis XIV., and settled their differences in America as well as in Europe. Both England and France were at that time large territorial possessors in North America—the English holding Hudson's Bay and New Britain, beyond Canada, and her Atlantic colonies on this side of it; and France holding Canada and Louisiana. These were vast possessions, with unfixed boundaries. The tenth article of the treaty of Utrecht provided for fixing these boundaries. Under this article, British and French commissioners were appointed to define the possessions of the two nations; and by these commissioners two great points were fixed (not to speak of others), which have become landmarks in the definition of boundaries in North America, namely: the Lake of the Woods, and the 49th parallel of north latitude west of that lake. These two points were established above a century and a quarter ago, as dividing the French and British dominions in that quarter. As successful rebels, we acquired one of these points at the end of the Revolution. The treaty of Independence of 1783 gave us the Lake of the Woods as a landmark in the (then) north-west corner of the Union. As successors to the French in the ownership of Louisiana, we acquired the other; the treaty of 1803 having given us that province as France and Spain had held it; and that was, on the north, by the parallel of 49 degrees. Beginning in the Lake of the Woods, our northern Louisiana boundary followed the 49th parallel to the west. How far? is now the important question; and I repeat the words of the report of the commissioners, accepted by their respective nations, when I answer—"INDEFINITELY!" I quote the words of the report when I answer (omitting all the previous parts of the line), "*to the latitude of 49 degrees north of the equator, and along that parallel indefinitely to the west.*" [A senator asked where all this was found.] Mr. BENTON. I find it in the state papers of France and England above an hundred years ago, and in those of the United States since the acquisition of Louisiana. I quote now from Mr. Madison's instructions, when Secretary of State under Mr. Jefferson in 1804, to Mr. Monroe, then our minister in London; and given to him to fortify him in his defence of our new acquisition. The cardinal word in this report of the commissioners is the word "*indefinitely;*" and that word it was the object of the British to expunge, from the moment that we discovered the Columbia, and acquired Louisiana—events which were of the same era in our history, and almost contemporaneous. In the negotiations with Mr. Monroe (which ended in a treaty, rejected by Mr. Jefferson without communication to the Senate), the effort was to limit the line, and to terminate it at the Rocky Mountains; well knowing that if this line was suffered to continue *indefinitely* to the west, it would deprive them of all they wanted; for it would strike the ocean three degrees north of the mouth of the Columbia. Without giving us what we were entitled to by right of discoveries, and as successors to Spain, it would still take from Great Britain all that she wanted—which was the mouth of the river, its harbor, the position which commanded it, and its right bank, in the rich and timbered region of tide-water. The line on the 49th parallel would cut her off from all these advantages; and, therefore, to mutilate that line, and stop it at the Rocky Mountains, immediately became her inexorable policy. At Ghent, in 1814, the effort was renewed. The commissioners of the United States and those of Great Britain could not agree; and nothing was done. At London, in 1818, the effort was successful; and in the convention then signed in that city, the line of the treaty of Utrecht was stopped at the Rocky Mountains. The country on the Columbia was laid open for ten years to the joint occupation of the citizens and subjects of both powers; and, afterwards, by a renewed convention at London, this joint occupation was renewed indefinitely, and until one of the parties should give notice for its termination. It is under this privilege of joint occupation that Great Britain has taken exclusive possession of the right bank of the river, from its head to its mouth, and also exclusive possession of the fur trade on both sides of the river, into the heart of the Rocky Mountains. My friend and colleague [Mr. LINN] has submitted a motion to require the President to give the stipulated notice for the termination of this convention—a convention so unequal in its operation, from the inequality of title between the two parties, and from the organized power of the British in that quarter under the powerful direction of the Hudson's Bay Fur Company. Thus our title as far as latitude 49, so valid under the single guarantee of the treaty of Utrecht, without looking to other sources, has been jeoparded by this improvident convention; and the longer it stands, the worse it is for us.

A great fault of the treaty of 1818 was in admitting an organized and powerful portion of the British people to come into possession of our territories jointly with individual and disconnected possessors on our part. The Hudson's Bay Company held dominion there on the north of our territories. They were powerful in themselves, perfectly organized, protected by their government, united with it in policy, and controlling all the Indians from Canada and the Rocky Mountains out to the Pacific Ocean, and north to Baffin's Bay. This company was admitted, by the convention of 1818, to a joint possession with us of all our territories on the Columbia River. The effect was soon seen. Their joint possession immediately became exclusive on the north bank of the river. Our fur-traders were all driven from beyond the Rocky Mountains; then driven out of the mountains; more than a thousand of them killed: forts were built; a chain of posts established to communicate with Canada and Hudson's Bay; settlers introduced; a colony planted; firm possession acquired; and, at the end of the ten years when the *joint* possession was to cease, the intrusive possessors, protected by their government, refused to go—began to set up title—and obtained a renewal of the convention, without limit of time, and until they shall receive notice to quit. This renewed convention was made in 1828; and, instead of joint possession with us for ten years, while we should have joint possession with them of their rivers, bays, creeks and harbors, for the same time—instead of this, they have had exclusive possession of our territory, our river, our harbor, and our creeks and inlets, for above a quarter of a century. They are establishing themselves as in a permanent possession—making the fort Vancouver, at the confluence of the Multnomah and Columbia, in tide-water, the seat of their power and operations. The notice required never will be given while the present administration is in power; nor obeyed when given, unless men are in power who will protect the rights and the honor of their country. The fate of Maine has doubled the dangers of the Columbia, and nearly placed us in a position to choose between war and INFAMY, in relation to that river.

Another great fault in the convention was, in admitting a *claim* on the part of Great Britain to any portion of these territories. Before that convention, she stated no claim; but asked a favor—the favor of joint possession for ten years: now she sets up title. That title is backed by possession. Possession among nations, as well as among individuals, is eleven points out of twelve; and the bold policy of Great Britain well knows how to avail itself of these eleven points. The Madawaska settlement has read us a lesson on that head; and the success there must lead to still greater boldness elsewhere. The London convention of 1818 is to the Columbia, what the Ghent treaty of 1814 was to Maine; that is to say, the first false step in a game in which we furnish the whole stake, and then play for it. In Maine the game is up. The bold hand of Great Britain has clutched the stake; and nothing but the courage of our people will save the Columbia from the same catastrophe.

I proceed with more satisfaction to our title under the Nootka Sound treaty, and can state it in a few words. All the world knows the commotion which was excited in 1790 by the Nootka Sound controversy between Great Britain and Spain. It was a case in which the bullying of England and the courage of Spain were both tried to the *ne plus ultra* point, and in which Spanish courage gained the victory. Of course, the British writers relate the story in their own way; but the debates of the Parliament, and the terms of the treaty in which all ended, show things as they were. The British, presuming on the voyages of Captain Cook, took possession of Nootka; the Spanish Viceroy of Mexico sent a force to fetch the English away, and placed them in the fortress of Acapulco. Pitt demanded the release of his English, their restoration to Nootka, and an apology for the insult to the British Crown, in the violation of its territory and the persons of its subjects; the Spaniard refused to release, refused the restoration, and the apology, on the ground that Nootka was Spanish territory, and declared that they would fight for its possession. Then both parties prepared for war. The preparations fixed the attention of all Europe. Great Britain bullied to the point of holding the match over the touch-hole of the cannon; but the Spaniards remaining firm, she relaxed, and entered into a convention which abnegated her claim. She accepted from the Spaniards the privilege of landing and building huts on the unoccupied parts of the coast, for the purpose of fishing and trading; and while this acceptance nullified her claim, yet she took nothing under it—not even temporary use—never having built a hut, erected a tent, or commenced any sort of settlement on any part of the coast. Mr. Fox keenly reproached Mr. Pitt with the terms of this convention, being, as he showed, a limitation instead of an acquisition of rights.

Our title is clear: that of the British is null. She sets up none—that is, she states no derivation of title. There is not a paper upon the face of the earth, in which a British minister has stated a title, or even a claim. They have endeavored to obtain the country by the arts of diplomacy; but never have stated a title, and never can state one. The fur-trader, Sir Alexander McKenzie, prompted the acquisition, gave the reason for it, and never pretended a title. His own discoveries gave no title. They were subsequent to the discovery of Captain Gray, and far to the north of the Columbia. He never saw that river. He missed the head sources of it, fell upon the *Tacouche Tesse*, and struck the Pacific in a latitude 500 miles (by the coast) to the north of the Columbia. His subsequent discoveries were all north of that point. He was looking for a communication with the sea—for a river, a harbor, and a place for a colony—within the dominions of Great Britain; and, not finding any, he boldly recommended his government to seize the Columbia River, to hold it, and to expel the Americans from the whole country west of the Rocky Mountains. And upon these pretensions the British claim has rested, until possession has made them bold enough to exclude it from the subjects of formal negotiation between the two countries. The peace-mission refused us peace on that point. The President tells us that there is "*no probability of coming to any agreement at present!*" Then when can the agreement be made? If refused now, when is it to come? Never, until we show that we prefer war to ignominious peace.

This is the British title to the Columbia, and the only one that she wants for any thing. It suits her to have that river: it is her interest to have it: it strengthens her, and weakens others, for her to have it; and, therefore, have it she will. This is her title, and this her argument. Upon this title and argument, she gets a slice from Maine, and gains the mountain barrier which covers Quebec; and, upon this title and argument, she means to have the Columbia River. The events of the late war, and the application of steam power to ocean navigation, begat her title to the country between Halifax and Quebec: the suggestions of McKenzie begat her title to the Columbia. Improvident diplomacy on our part, a war countenance on her part, and this strange treaty, have given success to her pretensions in Maine: the same diplomacy, and the same countenance, have given her a foothold on the Columbia. It is for the Great West to see that no traitorous treaty shall abandon it to her. The President, in his message, says that there was no chance for any "*agreement*" about it at present; that it would not be made the subject of a "*formal negotiation*" at present; that it could not be included in the duties of the "*special mission.*" Why so? The mission was one of peace, and to settle every thing; and why omit this pregnant question? Was this a war question, and therefore not to be settled by the peace mission? Why not come to an agreement now, if agreement is ever intended? The answer is evident. No agreement is ever intended. Contented with her possession, Great Britain wants delay, that *time* may ripen *possession* into *title*, and fortunate events facilitate her designs. My colleague and myself were sounded on this point: our answers forbade the belief that we would compromise or sacrifice the rights and interests of our country; and this may have been the reason why there were no "*formal*" negotiations in relation to it. Had we been "*soft enough,*" there might have been an agreement to divide our country by the river, or, to refer the whole title to the decision of a friendly sovereign! We were not *soft enough* for that; and if such a paper, marked B, and identified with the initials of our Secretary, had been sent to the Missouri delegation, as was sent to the Maine commissioners, instead of subduing us to the purposes of Great Britain, it would have received from the whole delegation the answer due to treason, to cowardice, and to insolence.

But, it is demanded, what do we want with this country, so far off from us? I answer by asking, in my turn, what do the British want with it, who are so much further off? They want it for the fur trade; for a colony; for an outlet to the sea; for the communication across the continent; for a road to Asia; for the command of one hundred and forty thousand Indians against us; for the port and naval station which is to command the commerce and navigation of the North Pacific Ocean, and open new channels of trade with China, Japan, Polynesia, and the great East. They want it for these reasons; and we want it for the same; and because it adjoins us, and belongs to us, and should be possessed by our descendants, who will be our friends; and not by aliens, who will be our enemies.

Forty years ago, it was written by Humboldt that the valley of the Columbia invited Europeans to found a fine colony there; and, twenty years ago, the American Congress adopted a resolve, *that no part of this continent was open to European colonization.* The remark of Humboldt was that of a sagacious European; the resolve of Congress was the work of patriotic Americans. It remains to be seen which will prevail. The convention of 1818 has done us the mischief; it put the European power in possession: and possession with nations, still more than with individuals, is the main point in the contest. It will require the western pioneers to recover the lost ground; and they must be encouraged in the enterprise by liberal grants of lands, by military protection, and by governmental authority. It is time for the bill of my colleague to pass. The first session of the first Congress under the new census should pass it. The majority will be democratic, and the democracy will demand that great work at their hands. I put no faith in negotiation. I expect nothing but loss and shame from any negotiation in London. Our safety is in the energy of our people; in their prompt occupation of the country; and in their invincible determination to maintain their rights.

I do not dilate upon the value and extent of this great country. A word suffices to display both. In extent, it is larger than the Atlantic portion of the old thirteen United States; in climate, softer; in fertility, greater; in salubrity, superior; in position, better, because fronting Asia, and washed by a tranquil sea. In all these particulars, the western slope of our continent is far more happy than the eastern. In configuration, it is inexpressibly fine and grand—a vast oblong square, with natural boundaries, and a single gateway into the sea.

The snow-capped Rocky Mountains enclose it to the east, an iron-bound coast on the west: a frozen desert on the north, and sandy plains on the south. All its rivers, rising on the segment of a vast circumference, run to meet each other in the centre; and then flow together into the ocean, through a gap in the mountain, where the heats of summer and the colds of winter are never felt; and where southern and northern diseases are equally unknown. This is the valley of the Columbia—a country whose every advantage is crowned by the advantages of position and configuration: by the unity of all its parts—the inaccessibility of its borders—and its single introgression to the sea. Such a country is formed for union, wealth, and strength. It can have but one capital, and that will be a Thebes; but one commercial emporium, and that will be Tyre, queen of cities. Such a country can have but one people, one interest, one government: and that people should be American— that interest ours—and that government republican. Great Britain plays for the whole valley: failing in that, she is willing to divide by the river. Accursed and infamous be the man that divides or alienates it!

II.—IMPRESSMENT.

Impressment is another of the omitted subjects. This having been a cause of war in 1812, and being now declared, by the American negotiator, to be a sufficient cause for future wars, it would naturally, to my mind, have been included in the labors of a special mission, dedicated to peace, and extolled for its benevolent conception. We would have expected to find such a subject, after such a declaration, included in the labors of such a mission. Not so the fact. The treaty does not mention impressment. A brief paragraph in the President's message informs us that there was a correspondence on this point; and, on turning to this correspondence, we actually find two letters on the subject: one from Mr. Webster to Lord Ashburton—one from Lord Ashburton to Mr. Webster: both showing, from their dates, that they were written after the treaty was signed; and, from their character, that they were written for the public, and not for the negotiators. The treaty was signed on the 9th of August; the letters were written on the 8th and 9th of the same month. They are a plea, and a reply; and they leave the subject precisely where they found it. From their date and character, they seem to be what the lawyers call the *postea*—that is to say, the *afterwards*; and are very properly postponed to the end of the document containing the correspondence, where they find place on the 120th page. They look *ex post facto* there; and, putting all things together, it would seem as if the American negotiator had said to the British lord (after the negotiation was over): 'My Lord, here is impressment—a pretty subject for a composition; the people will love to read something about it; so let us compose.' To which, it would seem, his lordship had answered: 'You may compose as much as you please for your people; I leave that field to you: and when you are done, I will write three lines for my own government, to let it know that I stick to impressment.' In about this manner, it would seem to me that the two letters were got up; and that the American negotiator in this little business has committed a couple of the largest faults: *first*, in naming the subject of impressment at all! *next*, in ever signing a treaty, after having named it, without an unqualified renunciation of the pretension!

Sir, the same thing is not always equally proper. Time and circumstances qualify the proprieties of international, as well as of individual intercourse; and what was proper and commendable at one time, may become improper, reprehensible, and derogatory at another. When George the Third, in the first article of his first treaty with the United States, at the end of a seven years' war, acknowledged them to be free, sovereign, and independent States, and renounced all dominion over them, this was a proud and glorious consummation for us, and the crowning mercy of a victorious rebellion. The same acknowledgment and renunciation from Queen Victoria, at present, would be an insult for her to offer—a degradation for us to accept. So of this question of impressment. It was right in all the administrations previous to the late war, to negotiate for its renunciation. But after having gone to war for this cause; after having suppressed the practice by war; after near thirty years' exemption from it—after all this, for our negotiator to put the question in discussion, was to compromise our rights! To sign a treaty without its renunciation, after having proposed to treat about it, was to relinquish them! Our negotiator should not have mentioned the subject. If mentioned to him by the British negotiator, he should have replied, that the answer to that pretension was in the cannon's mouth!

But to name it himself, and then sign without renunciation, and to be invited to London to treat about it—to do this, was to descend from our position; to lose the benefit of the late war; to revive the question; to invite the renewal of the practice, by admitting it to be an unsettled question—and to degrade the present generation, by admitting that they would negotiate where their ancestors had fought. These are fair inferences; and inferences not counteracted by the euphonious declaration that the American government is "*prepared to say*" that the practice of impressment cannot hereafter be allowed to take place!—as if, after great study, we had just arrived at that conclusion! and as if we had not declared much more courageously in the case of the Maine boundary, the Schlosser massacre, and the Creole mutiny and murder! The British, after the experience they have had, will know how to value our courageous declaration, and must pay due respect to our flag! For one, I never liked these declarations, and never made a speech in favor of any one of them; and now I like them less than ever, and am *prepared* to put no further faith in the declarations of gentlemen who were for going to war for the smallest part of the Maine boundary in 1838, and now surrender three hundred miles of that boundary for fear of war, when there is no danger of war. I am *prepared to say* that I care not a straw for the heroic declarations of such gentlemen. I want actions, not phrases. I want Mr. Jefferson's act in 1806—*rejection of any treaty with Great Britain that does not renounce impressment!* And after having declared, by law, black impressment on the coast of Africa to be piracy; after stipulating to send a fleet there, to enforce our law against that impressment—after this, I am ready to do the same thing against white impressment on our own coasts, and on the high seas. I am ready to enact that the impressment of my white fellow-citizens out of an American ship is an act of piracy; and then to follow out that enactment in its every consequence.

The correspondence between our Secretary negotiator and Lord Ashburton on this subject, has been read to you—that correspondence which was drawn up after the treaty was finished, and intended for the American public: and what a correspondence it is! What an exchange of phrases! One denies the right of impressment: the other affirms it. Both wish for an amicable agreement; but neither attempts to agree. Both declare the season of peace to be the proper time to settle this question; and both agree that the present season of peace is not the convenient one. Our Secretary rises so high as to declare that the administration "*is now prepared*" to put its veto on the practice: the *British negotiator* shows that his Government is still prepared to resume the practice whenever her interest requires it. Our negotiator hopes that his communication will be received in the spirit of peace: the British minister replies, that it will. Our secretary then persuades himself that the British minister will communicate his sentiments in this respect, to his own government: his Lordship promises it faithfully. And, thereupon, they shake hands and part.

How different this holiday scene from the firm and virile language of Mr. Jefferson: "*No treaty to be signed without a provision against impressment*;" and this language backed by the fact of the instant rejection of a treaty so signed! Lord Chatham said of *Magna Charta* that it was homely Latin, but worth all the classics. So say I of this reply of Mr. Jefferson: it is plain English, but worth all the phrases which rhetoric could ever expend upon the subject. It is the only answer which our secretary negotiator should have given, after committing the fault of broaching the subject. Instead of that, he commences rhetorician, new vamps old arguments, writes largely and prettily; and loses the question by making it debatable. His adversary sees his advantage, and seizes it. He abandons the field of rhetoric to the lawyer negotiator; puts in a fresh claim to impressment; saves the question from being lost by a non-user; re-establishes the debate, and adjourns it to London. He keeps alive the pretension of impressment against us, the white race, while binding us to go to Africa to fight it down for the black race; and has actually left us on lower ground in relation to this question, than we stood upon before the late war. If this treaty is ratified, we must begin where we were in 1806, when Mr. Monroe and Mr. Pinckney went to London to negotiate against impressment; we must begin where they did, with the disadvantage of having yielded to Great Britain all that she wanted, and having lost all our vantage-ground in the negotiation. We must go to London, engage in a humiliating negotiation, become the spectacle of nations, and the sport of diplomacy; and wear out years in begging to be spared from British seizure, when sitting under our own flag, and sailing in our own ship: we must submit to all this degradation, shame and outrage, unless Congress redeems us from the condition into which we have fallen, and provides for the liberty of our people on the seas, by placing American impressment where African impressment has already been placed—piracy by law! For one, I am ready to vote the act—to execute it—and to abide its every consequence.

III.—THE LIBERATED SLAVES.

The case of the Creole, as it is called, is another of the omitted subjects. It is only one of a number of cases (differing in degree, but the same in character) which have occurred within a few years, and are becoming more frequent and violent. It is the case of American vessels, having American slaves on board, and pursuing a lawful voyage, and being driven by storms or carried by violence into a British port, and their slaves liberated by British law. This is the nature of the wrong. It is a general outrage liable to occur in any part of the British dominions, but happens most usually in the British West India islands, which line the passage round the Florida reefs in a voyage between New Orleans and the Atlantic ports. I do not speak of the 12,000 slaves (worth at a moderate computation, considering they must be all grown, and in youth or middle life, at least $6,000,000) enticed into Canada, and received with the honors and advantages due to the first class of emigrants. I do not speak of these, nor of the liberation of slaves carried voluntarily by their owners into British ports: the man who exposes his property wilfully to the operation of a known law, should abide the consequences to which he has subjected it. I confine myself to cases of the class mentioned—such as the Encomium, the Comet, the Enterprise, the Creole, and the Hermosa—cases in which wreck, tempest, violence, mutiny and murder were the means of carrying the vessel into the interdicted port; and in which the slave property, after being saved to the owners from revolt and tempests, became the victim and the prey of British law. It is of such cases that I complain, and of which I say that they furnish no subject for the operation of injurious laws, and that each of these vessels should have been received with the hospitality due to misfortune, and allowed to depart with all convenient despatch, and with all her contents of persons and property. This is the law of nations: it is what the civilization of the age requires. And it is not to be tolerated in this nineteenth century that an American citizen, passing from one port to another of his own country, with property protected by the laws of his country, should encounter the perils of an unfortunate navigator in the dark ages, shipwrecked on a rude and barbarian coast. This is not to be tolerated in this age, and by such a power as the United States, and after sending a fleet to Africa to protect the negroes. Justice, like charity, should begin at home; and protection should be given where allegiance is exacted. We cannot tolerate the spoil and pillage of our own citizens, within sight of our own coasts, after sending 4,000 miles to redress the wrongs of the black race. But if this treaty is ratified it seems that we shall have to endure it, or seek redress by other means than negotiation. The previous cases were at least ameliorated by compensation to their owners for the liberation of the slaves; but in the more recent and most atrocious case of the Creole, there is no indemnity of any kind—neither compensation to the owners whose property has been taken; nor apology to the Government, whose flag has been insulted; nor security for the future, by giving up the practice. A treaty is signed without a stipulation of any kind on the subject; and as it would seem, to the satisfaction of those who made it, and of the President, who sends it to us. A correspondence has been had; the negotiators have exchanged diplomatic notes on the subject; and these notes are expected to be as satisfactory to the country as to those who now have the rule of it. The President in his message says:

> "On the subject of the interference of the British authorities in the West Indies, a confident hope is entertained that the correspondence which has taken place, showing the *grounds* taken by this government, and the *engagements* entered into by the British minister, will be found such as to satisfy the just expectation of the people of the United States."—*Message, August 9.*

This is a short paragraph for so large a subject; but it is all the message contains. But let us see what it amounts to, and what it is that is expected to satisfy the just expectations of the country. It is the *grounds* taken in the correspondence, and the *engagements* entered into by the British minister, which are to work out this agreeable effect.

And it is of the *grounds* stated in the Secretary's two letters, and the *engagement*, entered into in Lord Ashburton's note, that the President predicates his belief of the public satisfaction in relation to this growing and most sensitive question. This brings us to these grounds, and this engagement, that we may see the nature and solidity of the one, and the extent and validity of the other. The grounds for the public satisfaction are in the Secretary's letters; the engagement is in Lord Ashburton's letter; and what do they amount to? On the part of the Secretary, I am free to say that he has laid down the law of nations correctly; that he has well stated the principles of public law which save from hazard or loss, or penalty of any kind, the vessel engaged in a lawful trade, and driven or carried against her will, into a prohibited port. He has well shown that, under such circumstances, no advantage is to be taken of the distressed vessel; that she is to be received with the hospitality due to misfortune, and allowed to depart, after receiving the succors of humanity, with all her contents of persons and things. All this is well laid down by our Secretary. Thus far his grounds are solid. But, alas, this is all talk! and the very next paragraph, after a handsome vindication of our rights under the law of nations, is to abandon them! I refer to the paragraph commencing: "*If your Lordship has no authority to enter into a stipulation by treaty for the prevention of such occurrences hereafter,*" &c. This whole paragraph is fatal to the Secretary's grounds, and pregnant with strange and ominous meanings. In the first place, it is an admission, in the very first line, that no treaty stipulation to prevent future occurrences of the same kind can be obtained here! that the special mission, which came to settle every thing, and to establish peace, will not settle this thing; which the Secretary, in numerous paragraphs, alleges to be a dangerous source of future war! This is a strange contradiction, and most easily got over by our Secretary. In default of a treaty stipulation (which he takes for granted, and evidently makes no effort to obtain), he goes on to solicit a personal engagement from his Lordship; and an engagement of what? That the law of nations shall be observed? No! but that instructions shall be given to the British local authorities in the islands, which shall lead them to regulate their conduct in conformity with the rights of citizens of the United States, and the just expectations of their government, and in such manner as shall, in future, take away all reasonable ground of complaint. This is the extent of the engagement which was so solicited, and which was to supply the place of a treaty stipulation! If the engagement had been given in the words proposed, it would not have been worth a straw. But it is not given in those words, but with glaring and killing additions and differences. His Lordship follows the commencement of the formula with sufficient accuracy; but, lest any possible consequence might be derived from it, he takes care to add, that when these slaves do reach them "*no matter by what means,*" there is no alternative! Hospitality, good wishes, friendly feeling, the duties of good neighborhood—all give way! The British law governs! and that law is too well known to require repetition. This is the sum and substance of Lord Ashburton's qualifications of the *engagement*; and they show him to be a man of honor, that would not leave the Secretary negotiator the slightest room for raising a doubt as to the nature of the instructions which he engaged to have given. These instructions go only to the mode of executing the law. His Lordship engages only for the civility and gentleness of the manner—*the suaviter in modo*; while the firm execution of the law itself remains as it was—*fortiter in re.*

Lord Ashburton proposes London as the best place to consider this subject. Mr. Webster accepts London, and hopes that her Majesty's government will give us treaty stipulations to remove all further cause for complaint on this subject. This is his last hope, contained in the last sentence of his last note. And now, why a treaty stipulation hereafter, if this engagement is such (as the President says it is) as to satisfy the just expectations of the people of the United States? Why any thing more, if that is enough? And if treaty stipulations are wanting (as in fact they are), why go to London for them—the head-quarters of abolitionism, the seat of the World's Convention for the abolition of slavery, and the laboratory in which the insurrection of San Domingo was fabricated? Why go to London? Why go any where? Why delay? Why not do it here? Why not include it among the beatitudes of the vaunted peace mission? The excuse that the minister had not powers, is contradictory and absurd. The Secretary negotiator tells us, in his first letter, that the minister came with full powers to settle every subject in discussion. This was a subject in discussion; and had been since the time of the Comet, the Encomium, and the Enterprise—years ago. If instructions were forgotten, why not send for them? What are the steamers for, that, in the six months that the peace mission was here, they could not have brought these instructions a dozen times? No! the truth is, the British government would do nothing upon this subject when she found she could accomplish all her own objects without granting any thing.

IV.—BURNING OF THE CAROLINE.

The Caroline is the last of the seven subjects in the arrangement which I make of them. I reserve it for the last; the extreme ignominy of its termination making it, in my opinion, the natural conclusion of a disgraceful negotiation. It is a case in which all the sources of national degradation seem to have been put in requisition—diplomacy; legislation; the judiciary; and even the military. To volunteer propitiations to Great Britain, and to deprecate her wrath, seem to have been the sole concern of the administration, when signal reparation was due from her to us. And here again we have to lament the absence of all the customary disclosures in the progress of negotiations. No protocol, no minutes, no memorandums: nothing to show how a subject began, went on, and reached its consummation. Every thing was informal in this anomalous negotiation. Wat Tyler never hated the ink-horn worse than our Secretary-negotiator hated it upon this occasion. It was only after a thing was finished, that the pen was resorted to; and then merely to record the agreement, and put a face upon it for the public eye. In this way many things may have been discussed, which leave no written trace behind them; and it would be a curious circumstance if so large a subject, and one so delicate as the State debts, should find itself in that predicament.

The case of the Caroline is now near four years old. It occurred in December of the year 1838, under Mr. Van Buren's administration; but it was not until March, 1841, and until the new administration was in power, that the question assumed its high character of a quarrel between the United States and Great Britain. Before that time, the outrage upon the Caroline was only the act of the individuals engaged in it. The arrest of one of these individuals brought out the British government. She assumed the offence; alleged the outrage to have been perpetrated by her authority; and demanded the release of McLeod, under the clear implication of a national threat if he was not surrendered. The release was demanded unconditionally—not the slightest apology or atonement being offered for the outrage on the Caroline, out of which the arrest of McLeod grew. The arrogant demand of the British was delivered to the new Secretary of State on the 12th day of March. Instead of refusing to answer under a threat, he answered the sooner; and, in his answer went far beyond what the minister [Mr. Fox] had demanded. He despatched the Attorney-general of the United States to New York, to act as counsel for McLeod; he sent a Major-general of the United States army along with him, to give emphasis to his presence; and he gave a false version to the law of nations, which would not only cover the McLeod case, but all succeeding cases of the same kind. I consider all this the work of the State Department; for General Harrison was too new in his office, too much overwhelmed by the army of applicants who besieged him and soon destroyed his life, to have the time to study the questions to which the arrest of McLeod, and the demand for his release, and the assumption of his crime by the British government gave rise. The Romans had a noble maxim—grand in itself, and worthy of them, because they acted upon it. PARCERE SUBJECTIS, DEBELLARE SUPERBOS: Spare the humble—humble the proud. Our administration has invoked this maxim to cover its own conduct. In giving up McLeod they say it is to lay hold of the sovereign—that the poor servant is spared while the proud master is to be held to account. Fine phrases these, which deceive no one: for both master and servant are let go. Our people were not deceived by these grave professions. They believed it was all a pretext to get out of a difficulty; that, what between love and fear of the British, the federal party was unwilling to punish McLeod, or to see him punished by the State of New York; that the design was to get rid of responsibility, by getting rid of the man; and, that when he was gone, we should hear no more of these new Romans calling his sovereign to account. This was the opinion of the democracy, very freely expressed at the time; and so it has all turned out to be. McLeod was acquitted, and got off; the British government became responsible, on the administration's own principles; they have not been held to that responsibility; no atonement or apology has been made for the national outrage at Schlosser; and the President informs us that no further complaint, on account of this aggression on the soil and sovereignty of the Union, and the lives of its citizens, is to be made!

A note has been obtained from Lord Ashburton, and sent to us by the President, declaring three things—first, that the burning of the Caroline, and killing the people, was a serious fact; secondly, that no disrespect was intended to the United States in doing it; thirdly, that the British government unfeignedly hopes there will be no necessity for doing it again. This is the extent, and the whole extent, to which the special minister, with all his politeness and good nature, and with all his desire to furnish the administration with something to satisfy the public, could possibly go. The only thing which I see him instructed by his government to say, or which in itself amounts to a positive declaration, is the averment that her Majesty's government "*considers it a most serious fact*" that, in the hurried execution of this *necessary* service, a violation of the United States territory was committed. This is admitted to be a fact!—a serious fact!—and a most serious fact! But as for any sorrow for it, or apology for it, or promise not to commit such serious facts again, or even not to be so hurried the next time—this is what the minister nowhere says, or insinuates. On the contrary, just the reverse is declared; for the justification of this "*most serious fact*" as being the result of a hurried execution of a "*necessary service*," is an explicit averment that the aforesaid "*most serious fact*" will be repeated just so often as her Majesty's government shall deem it necessary to her service. As to the polite declaration, that no disrespect was intended to the United States while invading its territory, killing its citizens, setting a steamboat on fire, and sending her in flames over the falls of Niagara—such a declaration is about equivalent to telling a man that you mean him no disrespect while cudgelling him with both hands over the head and shoulders.

The celebrated Dr. Johnson was accustomed to say that there was a certain amount of gullibility in the public mind, which must be provided for. It would seem that our Secretary-negotiator had possessed himself of this idea, and charged himself with the duties under it, and had determined to make full provision for all the gullibility now extant. He has certainly provided *quantum suffcit* of humbuggery in this treaty, and in his correspondence in defence of it, to gorge the stomachs of all the gulls of the present generation, both in Europe and America.

Our Secretary is full of regret that McLeod was so long imprisoned, makes excuses for the New York court's decisions against him, and promises to call the attention of Congress to the necessity of providing against such detention in future. He says, in his last letter to Lord Ashburton:

> "It was a subject of *regret* that the release of McLeod was so long delayed. A State court—and that not of the highest jurisdiction—decided that, on summary application, embarrassed, as it would appear, by technical difficulties, he could not be released by that court. His discharge, shortly afterward, by a jury, to whom he preferred to submit his case, rendered unnecessary the further prosecution of the legal question. It is for the Congress of the United States, whose attention has been *called* to the subject to say what further provision ought to be made to expedite proceedings in such cases."

Such is the valedictory of our Secretary—his sorrows over the fate of McLeod. That individual had been released for a year past. His arrest continued but for a few months, with little personal inconvenience to himself; with no danger to his life, if innocent; and with the gratification of a notoriety flattering to his pride, and beneficial to his interest. He is probably highly delighted with the honors of the occurrence, and no way injured by his brief and comfortable imprisonment. Yet the sorrow of our Secretary continues to flow. At the end of a year, he is still in mourning, and renews the expression of his regret for the poor man's detention, and gives assurances against such delays in future;—this in the same letter in which he closes the door upon the fate of his own countrymen burnt and murdered in the Caroline, and promises never to disturb the British government about them again. McLeod and all Canadians are encouraged to repeat their *most serious facts upon us*, by the perfect immunity which both themselves and their government have experienced. And to expedite their release, if hereafter arrested for such *facts*, they are informed that Congress had been "*called*" upon to pass the appropriate law—and passed it was! The *habeas corpus* act against the States, which had slept for many months in the Senate, and seemed to have sunk under the public execration—this bill was "*called*" up, and passed contemporaneously with the date of this letter. And thus the special minister was enabled to carry home with him an act of Congress to lay at the footstool of his Queen, and to show that the measure of atonement to McLeod was complete: that the executive, the military, the legislative, and the judicial departments had all been put in requisition, and faithfully exerted themselves to protect her Majesty's subjects from being harmed for a past invasion, conflagration, and murder; and to secure them from being called to account by the State courts for such trifles in future.

And so ends the case of the Caroline and McLeod. The humiliation of this conclusion, and the contempt and future danger which it brings upon the country, demand a pause, and a moment's reflection upon the catastrophe of this episode in the negotiation. The whole negotiation has been one of shame and injury; but this catastrophe of the McLeod and Caroline affair puts the finishing hand to our disgrace. I do not speak of the individuals who have done this work, but of the national honor which has been tarnished in their hands. Up to the end of Mr. Van Buren's administration, all was safe for the honor of the country. Redress for the outrage at Schlosser had been demanded; interference to release McLeod had been refused; the false application of the laws of war to a state of peace had been scouted. On the 4th day of March, 1841, the national honor was safe; but on that day its degradation commenced. Timing their movements with a calculated precision, the British government transmitted their assumption of the Schlosser outrage, their formal demand for the release of McLeod, and their threat in the event of refusal, so as to arrive here on the evening of the day on which the new administration received the reins of government. Their assumption, demand, and threat, arrived in Washington on the evening of the 4th day of March, a few hours after the inauguration of the new powers was over. It seemed as if the British had said to themselves: This is the time—our friends are in power—we helped to elect them—now is the time to begin. And begin they did. On the 8th day of March, Mr. Fox delivered to

Mr. Webster the formal notification of the assumption, made the demand, and delivered the threat. Then the disgraceful scene began. They reverse the decision of Mr. Van Buren's administration, and determine to interfere in behalf of McLeod, and to extricate him by all means from the New York courts. To mask the ignominy of this interference, they pretend it is to get at a nobler antagonist; and that they are going to act the Romans, in sparing the humble and subduing the proud. It is with Queen Victoria with whom they will deal! McLeod is too humble game for them. McLeod released, the next thing is to get out of the scrape with the Queen; and for that purpose they invent a false reading of the law of nations, and apply the laws of war to a state of peace. The *jus belli*, and not the *jus gentium*, then becomes their resort. And here ends their grand imitation of the Roman character. To assume the laws of war in time of peace, in order to cover a craven retreat, is the nearest approach which they make to war. Then the special minister comes. They accept from him private and verbal explanations, in full satisfaction to themselves of all the outrage at Schlosser: but beg the minister to write them a little apology, which they can show to the people. The minister refuses; and thereupon they assume that they have received it, and proclaim the apology to the world. To finish this scene, to complete the propitiation of the Queen, and to send her minister home with legal and parchment evidence in his hand of our humiliation, the expression of regret for the arrest and detention of McLeod is officiously and gratuitously renewed; the prospect of a like detention of any of her Majesty's subjects in future is pathetically deplored; and, to expedite their delivery from State courts when they again invade our soil, murder our citizens, and burn our vessels, the minister is informed that Congress has been "*called*" upon to pass a law to protect them from these courts. And here "*a most serious fact*" presents itself. Congress has actually obeyed the "*call*"—passed the act—secured her Majesty's subjects in future—and given the legal parchment evidence of his success to her minister before he departs for his home. The infamous act—the habeas corpus against the States—squeamishly called the "*remedial justice act*"—is now on the statute-book; the original polluting our code of law, the copy lying at the footstool of the British Queen. And this is the point we have reached. In the short space of a year and a half, the national character has been run down, from the pinnacle of honor to the abyss of disgrace. I limit myself now to the affair of McLeod and the Caroline alone; and say that, in this business, exclusive of other disgraces, the national character has been brought to the lowest point of contempt. It required the Walpole administration five-and-twenty long years of cowardly submission to France and Spain to complete the degradation of Great Britain: our present rulers have completed the same work for their own country in the short space of eighteen months. And this is the state of our America! that America which Jackson and Van Buren left so proud! that America which, with three millions of people fought and worsted the British empire—with seven millions fought it, and worsted it again—and now, with eighteen millions, truckles to the British Queen, and invents all sorts of propitiatory apologies for her, when the most ample atonement is due to itself. Are we the people of the Revolution?—of the war of 1812?—of the year 1834, when Jackson electrified Europe by threatening the King of France with reprisals!

McLeod is given up because he is too weak; the Queen is excused, because she is too strong; propitiation is lavished where atonement is due; an apology accepted where none was offered; the statute of limitations pleaded against an insult, by the party which received it! And the miserable performers in all this drama of national degradation expect to be applauded for magnanimity, when the laws of honor and the code of nations, stamp their conduct with the brand of cowardice.

CHAPTER CIII.

BRITISH TREATY: NORTHEASTERN BOUNDARY ARTICLE: MR. BENTON'S SPEECH: EXTRACT.

The establishment of the low-land boundary in place of the mountain boundary, and parallel to it. This new line is 110 miles long. It is on this side of the awarded line—not a continuation of it, but a deflection from it; and evidently contrived for the purpose of weakening our boundary, and retiring it further from Quebec. It will be called in history the Webster line. It begins on the awarded line, at a lake in the St. Francis River; breaks off at right angles to the south, passes over the valley of the St. John in a straight line, and equidistant from that river and the mountain, until it reaches the north-west branch of the St. John, when approaching within forbidden distance of Quebec, it deflects to the east; and then holds on its course to the gorge in the mountain at the head of Metjarmette creek. A view of the map will show the character of this new line; the words of the treaty show how cautiously it was guarded; and the want of protocols hides its paternity from our view. The character of the line is apparent; and it requires no military man, or military woman, or military child, to say to whose benefit it enures. A man of any sort—a woman of any kind—a child of any age—can tell that! It is a British line, made for the security of Quebec. Follow its calls on the map, and every eye will see this design.

The surrender of the mountain boundary between the United States and Great Britain on the frontiers of Maine. This is a distinct question from the surrender of territory. The latter belonged to Maine: the former to the United States. They were national, and not State boundaries—established by the war of the Revolution, and not by a State law or an act of Congress; and involving all the considerations which apply to the attack and defence of nations. So far as a State boundary is coterminous with another State, it is a State question, and may be left to the discretion of the States interested: so far as it is coterminous with a foreign power, it is a national question, and belongs to the national authority. A State cannot be permitted to weaken and endanger the nation by dismembering herself in favor of a foreigner; by demolishing a strong frontier, delivering the gates and keys of a country into the hands of a neighboring nation, and giving them roads and passes into the country. The boundaries in question were national, not State; and the consent of Maine, even if given, availed nothing. Her defence belongs to the Union; is to be made by the blood and treasure of the Union; and it was not for her, even if she had been willing, to make this defence more difficult, more costly, and more bloody, by giving up the strong, and substituting the weak line of defence. Near three hundred miles of this strong national frontier have been surrendered by this treaty—being double as much as was given up by the rejected award. The King of the Netherlands, although on the list of British generals, and in the pay of the British Crown, was a man of too much honor to deprive us of the commanding mountain frontier opposite to Quebec; and besides, Jackson would have scouted the award if he had attempted it. The King only gave up the old line to the north of the head of the St. Francis River; and for this he had some reason, as the mountain there subsided into a plain, and the ridge of the highlands (in that part) was difficult to follow: our negotiator gives up the boundary for one hundred and fifty miles on this side the head of the St. Francis, and without pretext; for the mountain ridge was there three thousand feet high. The new part given up, from the head of the St. Francis to Metjarmette portage, is invaluable to Great Britain. It covers her new road to Quebec, removes us further from that city, places a mountain between us, and brings her into Maine. To comprehend the value of this new boundary to Great Britain, and its injury to us, it is only necessary to follow it on a map—to see its form—know its height, the depth of its gorges, and its rough and rocky sides. The report of Capt. Talcott will show its character— three thousand feet high: any map will show its form. The gorge at the head of the Metjarmette creek—a water of the St. Lawrence—is made the *terminus ad quem* of the new conventional lowland line: beyond that gorge, the mountain barrier is yielded to Great Britain. Now take up a map. Begin at the head of the Metjarmette creek, within a degree and a half of the New Hampshire line—follow the mountain north—see how it bears in upon Quebec—approaching within two marches of that great city, and skirting the St. Lawrence for some hundred miles. All this is given up. One hundred and fifty miles of this boundary is given up on this side the awarded line; and the country left to guess and wonder at the enormity and fatuity of the sacrifice. Look at the new military road from Halifax to Quebec—that part of it which approaches Quebec and lies between the mountain and the St. Lawrence. Even by the awarded line, this road was forced to cross the mountain at or beyond the head of the St. Francis, and then to follow the base of the mountain for near one hundred miles;

with all the disadvantages of crossing the spurs and gorges of the mountain, and the creeks and ravines, and commanded in its whole extent by the power on the mountain. See how this is changed by the new boundary! the road permitted to take either side of the mountain—to cross where it pleases—and covered and protected in its whole extent by the mountain heights, now exclusively British. Why this new way, and this security for the road, unless to give the British still greater advantages over us than the awarded boundary gave? A palliation is attempted for it. It is said that the mountain is unfit for cultivation; and the line along it could not be ascertained; and that Maine consented. These are the palliations—insignificant if true, but not true in their essential parts. And, first, as to the poverty of the mountain, and the slip along its base, constituting this area of 893 square miles surrendered on this side the awarded line: Captain Talcott certifies it to be poor, and unfit for cultivation. I say so much the better for a frontier. As to the height of the mountains, and the difficulty of finding the dividing ridge, and the necessity of adopting a conventional line: I say all this has no application to the surrendered boundary on this side the awarded line at the head of the St. Francis. On this side of that point, the mountain ridge is lofty, the heights attain three thousand feet; and navigable rivers rise in them, and flow to the east and to the west—to the St. Lawrence and the Atlantic. Hear Captain Talcott, in his letter to Mr. Webster: (The letter read.)

This letter was evidently obtained for the purpose of depreciating the lost boundary, by showing it to be unfit for cultivation. The note of the Secretary-negotiator which drew it forth is not given, but the answer of Captain Talcott shows its character; and its date (that of the 14th of July) classes it with the testimony which was hunted up to justify a foregone conclusion. The letter of Captain Talcott is good for the Secretary's purpose, and for a great deal more. It is good for the overthrow of all the arguments on which the plea for a conventional boundary stood. What was that plea? Simply, that the highlands in the neighborhood of the north-west corner of Nova Scotia could not be traced; and that it was necessary to substitute a conventional line in their place. And it is the one on which the award of the King of the Netherlands turned, and was, to the extent of a part of his award, a valid one. But it was no reason for the American Secretary to give one hundred and fifty miles of mountain line on this side the awarded line, where the highlands attained three thousand feet of elevation, and turned navigable rivers to the right and left. Lord Ashburton, in his letter of the 13th of June, commences with this idea: that the highlands described in the treaty could not be found, and had been so admitted by American statesmen; and quotes a part of a despatch from Mr. Secretary Madison in 1802 to Mr. Rufus King, then U. S. Minister in London. I quote the whole despatch, and from this it appears—1. That the part at which the treaty could not be executed, for want of finding the highlands, was the *point* to be constituted by the intersection of the due north line from the head of the St. Croix with the *line* drawn along the highlands. 2. That this *point* might be substituted by a conventional one agreed upon by the three commissioners. 3. That from this *point*, so agreed upon, the *line* was to go to the *highlands*, and to follow them wherever they could be ascertained, to the head of the Connecticut River. This is the clear sense of Mr. Madison's letter and Mr. Jefferson's message; and it is to be very careless to confound this *point* (which they admitted to be dubious, for want of highlands at that place) with the *line* itself, which was to run near 300 miles on the elevations of a mountain reaching 3,000 feet high. The King of the Netherlands took a great liberty with this *point* when he brought it to the St. John's River: our Secretary-negotiator took a far greater liberty with it when he brought it to the head of the Metjarmette creek; for it is only at the head of this creek that our *line* under the new treaty begins to climb the highlands. The King of the Netherlands had some apology for his conventional *point* and conventional *line* to the head of the St. Francis—for the highlands were sunk into table-land where the *point* ought to be, and which was the *terminus a quo* of his conventional line: but our negotiator had no apology at all for turning this conventional line south, and extending it 110 miles through the level lands of Maine, where the mountain highlands were all along in sight to the west. It is impossible to plead the difficulty of finding the highlands for this substitution of the lowland boundary, in the whole distance from the head of the St. Francis, where the King of the Netherlands fixed the commencement of our mountain line, to the head of the Metjarmette, where our Secretary fixed its commencement. Lord Ashburton's quotation from Mr. Madison's letter is partial and incomplete: he quotes what answers his purpose, and is justifiable in so doing. But what must we think of our Secretary-negotiator, who neglected to quote the remainder of that letter, and show that it was a conventional *point*, and not a conventional *line*, that Mr. Jefferson and Mr. Madison proposed? and that this conventional *point* was merely to fix the north-west angle of Nova Scotia, where, in fact, there were no highlands; after which, the line was to proceed to the elevated ground dividing the waters, &c., and then follow the highlands to the head of the Connecticut? Why did our Secretary omit this correction of the British minister's quotation, and thus enable him to use American names against us?

To mitigate the enormity of this barefaced sacrifice, our Secretary-negotiator enters into a description of the soil, and avers it to be unfit for cultivation. What if it were so? It is still rich enough to bear cannon, and to carry the smuggler's cart; and that is the crop Great Britain wishes to plant upon it. Gibraltar and Malta are rocks; yet Great Britain would not exchange them for the deltas of the Nile and of the Ganges. It is not for growing potatoes and cabbages that she has fixed her eye, since the late war, on this slice of Maine; but for trade and war—to consolidate her power on our north-eastern border, and to realize all the advantages which steam power gives to her new military and naval, and commercial station, in Passamaquoddy Bay; and her new route for trade and war through Halifax and Maine to Quebec. She wants it for great military and commercial purposes; and it is pitiful and contemptible in our negotiator to depreciate the sacrifice as being poor land, unfit for cultivation, when power and dominion, not potatoes and cabbages, is the object at stake. But the fact is, that much of this land is good; so that the excuse for surrendering it without compensation is unfounded as well as absurd.

I do not argue the question of title to the territory and boundaries surrendered. That work has been done in the masterly report of the senator from Pennsylvania [Mr. BUCHANAN], and in the resolve of the Senate, unanimously adopted, which sanctioned it. That report and that resolve were made and adopted in the year 1838—seven years after the award of the King of the Netherlands—and vindicated our title to the whole extent of the disputed territory. After this vindication, it is not for me to argue the question of title. I remit that task to abler and more appropriate hands—to the author of the report of 1838. It will be for him to show the clearness of our title under the treaty of 1783—how it was submitted to in Mr. Jay's treaty of 1794, in Mr. Liston's correspondence of 1798, in Mr. King's treaty of 1803, in Mr. Monroe's treaty of 1807, and in the conferences at Ghent—where, after the late war had shown the value of a military communication between Quebec and Halifax, a variation of the line was solicited as a favor, by the British commissioners, to establish that communication. It will be for him also to show the progress of the British claim, from the solicited favor of a road, to the assertion of title to half the territory, and all the mountain frontier of Maine; and it will further be for him to show how he is deserted now by those who stood by him then. It will be for him to expose the fatal blunder at Ghent, in leaving our question of title to the arbitration of a European sovereign, instead of confiding the marking of the line to three commissioners, as proposed in all the previous treaties, and agreed to in several of them. To him, also, it will belong to expose the contradiction between rejecting the award for adopting a conventional line, and giving up part of the territory of Maine; and now negotiating a treaty which adopts two conventional lines, gives up all that the award did, and more too, and a mountain frontier besides; and then pays money for Rouse's Point, which came to us without money under the award. It will be for him to do these things. For what purpose? some one will say. I answer, for the purpose of vindicating our honor, our intelligence, and our good faith, in all this affair with Great Britain; for the purpose of showing how we are wronged in character and in rights by this treaty; and for the purpose of preventing similar wrongs and blunders in time to come. Maine may be dismembered, and her boundaries lost, and a great military power established on three sides of her; but the Columbia is yet to be saved? There we have a repetition of the Northeastern comedy of errors on our part, and of groundless pretension on the British part, growing up from a petition for joint possession for fishing and hunting, to an assertion of title and threat of war; this groundless pretension dignified into a claim by the lamentable blunder of the convention of London in 1818. We may save the Columbia by showing the folly, or worse, which has dismembered Maine.

The award of the King of the Netherlands was acceptable to the British, and that award was infinitely better for us; and it was not only accepted by the British, but insisted upon; and its non-execution on our part was made a subject of remonstrance and complaint against us. After this, can any one believe that the "*peace mission*" was sent out to make war upon us if we did not yield up near double as much as she then demanded? No, sir! there is no truth in this cry of war. It is only a phantom conjured up for the occasion. From Jackson and Van Buren the British would gladly have accepted the awarded boundary: the federalists prevented it, and even refused a new negotiation. Now, the same federalists have yielded double as much, and are thanking God that the British condescend to accept it. Such is federalism: and the British well knew their time, and their men, when they selected the present moment to send their special mission; to double their demands; and to use arguments successfully, which would have been indignantly repelled when a Jackson or a Van Buren was at the head of the government—or, rather, would never have been used to such Presidents. The conduct of our Secretary-negotiator is inexplicable. He rejects the award, because it dismembers Maine; votes against new negotiations with England; and announces himself ready to shoulder a musket and march to the highland boundary, and there fight his death for it. This was under Jackson's administration. He now becomes negotiator himself; gives up the highland boundary in the first note; gives up all that was awarded by the King of the Netherlands; gives up 110 miles on this side of that award; gives up the mountain barrier which covered Maine, and commanded the Halifax road to Quebec; gives $500,000 for Rouse's Point, which the King of the Netherland's allotted us as our right.

CHAPTER CIV.

BRITISH TREATY: NORTHWESTERN BOUNDARY: MR. BENTON'S SPEECH: EXTRACTS.

The line from Lake Superior to the Lake of the Woods never was susceptible of a dispute. That from the Lake of the Woods to the head of the Mississippi was disputable, and long disputed; and it will not do to confound these two lines, so different in themselves, and in their political history. The line from Lake Superior was fixed by landmarks as permanent and notorious as the great features of nature herself—the Isle Royale, in the northwest of Lake Superior, and the chain of small lakes and rivers which led from the north of that isle to the Lake of the Woods. Such were the precise calls of the treaty of 1783, and no room for dispute existed about it. The Isle Royale was a landmark in the calls of the treaty, and a great and distinguished one it was—a large rocky island in Lake Superior, far to the northwest, a hundred miles from the southern shore; uninhabitable, and almost inaccessible to the Indians in their canoes; and for that reason believed by them to be the residence of the Great Spirit, and called in their language, *Menong*. This isle was as notorious as the lake itself, and was made a landmark in the treaty of 1783, and the boundary line directed to go to the north of it, and then to follow the chain of small lakes and rivers called "Long Lake," which constituted the line of water communication between Lake Superior and the Lake of the Woods, a communication which the Indians had followed beyond the reach of tradition, which was the highway of nations, and which all travellers and traders have followed since its existence became known to our first discoverers. A line through the Lake Superior, from its eastern outlet to the northward of the Isle Royale, leads direct to this communication; and the line described was evidently so described for the purpose of going to that precise communication. The terms of the call are peculiar. Through every lake and every water-course, from Lake Ontario to the Lake Huron, the language of the treaty is the same: the line is to follow the *middle* of the lake. Through every river it is the same: the *middle* of the main channel is to be followed. On entering Lake Superior, this language changes. It is no longer the *middle* of the lake that is to constitute the boundary, but a line through the lake to the "northward" of Isle Royale—a boundary which, so far from dividing the lake equally, leaves almost two-thirds of it on the American side. The words of the treaty are these:

> "Thence through Lake Superior, northward of the isles Royale and Philippeaux, to the Long Lake; thence through the middle of said Long Lake, and the water communication between it and the Lake of the Woods, to the Lake of the Woods," &c.

These are the words of the call; and this variation of language, and this different mode of dividing the lake, were for the obvious purpose of taking the shortest course to the Long Lake, or Pigeon River, which led to the Lake of the Woods. The communication through these little lakes and rivers was evidently the object aimed at; and the call to the north of Isle Royale was for the purpose of getting to that object. The island itself was nothing, except as a landmark. Though large (for it is near one hundred miles in circumference), it has no value, neither for agriculture, commerce, nor war. It is sterile, inaccessible, remote from shore; and fit for nothing but the use to which the Indians consigned it—the fabulous residence of a fabulous deity. Nobody wants it— neither Indians nor white people. It was assigned to the United States in the treaty of 1783, not as a possession, but as a landmark, and because the shortest line through the lake, to the well-known route which led to the Lake of the Woods, passed to the north of that isle. All this is evident from the maps, and all the maps are here the same; for these features of nature are so well defined that there has never been the least dispute about them. The commissioners under the Ghent treaty (Gen. Porter for the United States, and Mr. Barclay for Great Britain), though disagreeing about several things, had no disagreement about Isle Royale, and the passage of the line to the north of that isle. In their separate reports, they agreed upon this; and this settled the whole question. After going to the north of Isle Royale, to get out of the lake at a known place, it would be absurd to turn two hundred miles south, to get out of it at an unknown place. The agreement upon Isle Royale settled the line to the Lake of the Woods, as it was, and as it is: but it so happened that, in the year 1790, the English traveller and fur-trader Mr. (afterwards Sir Alexander) McKenzie, in his voyage to the Northwest, travelled up this line of water communication, saw the advantages of its exclusive possession by the British; and proposed in his "History of the Fur Trade," to obtain it by turning the line down from Isle Royale, near two hundred miles, to St. Louis River in the southwest corner of the lake. The Earl of Selkirk, at the head of the Hudson's Bay Company, repeated the suggestion; and the British government, for ever attentive to the interests of its subjects, set up a claim, through the Ghent commissioners, to the St. Louis River as the boundary. Mr. Barclay made the question, but too faintly to obtain even a reference to the arbitrator; and Lord Ashburton had too much candor and honor to revive it. He set up no pretension to the St. Louis River, as claimed by the Ghent commissioners: he presented the Pigeon River as the "long lake" of the treaty of 1783, and only asked for a point six miles south of that river; and he obtained all he asked. His letter of the 17th of July is explicit on this point. He says:

> "In considering the second point, it really appears of little importance to either party how the line be determined through the wild country between Lake Superior and the Lake of the Woods, but it is important that some line should be fixed and known. I would propose that the line be taken from a point about six miles south of Pigeon River, where the Grand Portage commences on the lake, and continued along the line of the said portage, alternately by land and water, to Lac la Pluie—the existing route by land and by water remaining common by both parties. This line has the advantage of being known, and attended with no doubt or uncertainty in running it."

These are his Lordship's words: Pigeon River, instead of St. Louis River! making no pretension to the four millions of acres of fine mineral land supposed to have been saved between these two rivers; and not even alluding to the absurd pretension of the Ghent commissioner! After this, what are we to think of the candor and veracity of an official paper, which would make a merit of having saved four millions of acres of fine mineral land, "northward of the claim set up by the British commissioner under the Ghent treaty?" What must we think of the candor of a paper which boasts of having "included this within the United States," when it was never out of the United States? If there is any merit in the case, it is in Lord Ashburton—in his not having claimed the 200 miles between Pigeon River and St. Louis River. What he claimed, he got; and that was the southern line, commencing six miles south of Pigeon River, and running south of the true line to Rainy Lake. He got this; making a difference of some hundreds of thousands of acres, and giving to the British the exclusive possession of the best route; and a joint possession of the one which is made the boundary. To understand the value of this concession, it must be known that there are two lines of communication from the Lake Superior to the Lake of the Woods, both beginning at or near the mouth of Pigeon River; that these lines are the channels of trade and travelling, both for Indians, and the fur-traders; that they are water communications; and that it was a great point with the British, in their trade and intercourse with the Indians, to have the exclusive dominion of the best communication, and a joint possession with us of the other. This is what Lord Ashburton claimed—what the treaty gave him—and what our Secretary-negotiator became his agent and solicitor to obtain for him. I quote the Secretary's letter of the 25th of July to Mr. James Ferguson, and the answers of Mr. Ferguson of the same date, and also the letter of Mr. Joseph Delafield, of the 20th of July, for the truth of what I say. From these letters, it will be seen that our Secretary put himself to the trouble to hunt testimony to justify his surrender of the northern route to the British; that he put leading questions to his witnesses, to get the information which he wanted; and that he sought to cover the sacrifice, by depreciating the agricultural value of the land, and treating the difference between the lines as a thing of no importance. Here is the letter. I read an extract from it:

> "What is the general nature of the country between the mouth of Pigeon River and the Rainy Lake? Of what formation is it, and how is its surface? and will any considerable part of its area be fit for cultivation? Are its waters active and running streams, as in other parts of the United States? Or are they dead lakes, swamps, and morasses? If the latter be their general character, at what point, as you proceed westward, do the waters receive a more decided character as running streams?

> "There are said to be two lines of communication, each partly by water and partly by portages, from the neighborhood of Pigeon River to the Rainy Lake: one by way of Fowl Lake, the Saganaga Lake, and the Cypress Lake; the other by way of Arrow River and Lake; then by way of Saganaga Lake, and through the river Maligne, meeting the other route at Lake la Croix,

and through the river Namekan to the Rainy Lake. Do you know any reason for attaching great preference to either of these two lines? Or do you consider it of no importance, in any point of view, which may be agreed to? Please be full and particular on these several points."

Here are leading questions, such as the rules of evidence forbid to be put to any witness, and the answers to which would be suppressed by the order of any court in England or America. They are called "leading," because they *lead* the witness to the answer which the lawyer wants; and thereby tend to the perversion of justice. The witnesses are here led to two points: first, that the country between the two routes or lines is worth nothing for agriculture; secondly, that it is of no importance to the United States which of the two lines is established for the boundary. Thus led to the desired points, the witnesses answer. Mr. Ferguson says:

"As an agricultural district, this region will always be valueless. The pine timber is of high growth, equal for spars, perhaps, to the Norway pine, and may, perhaps, in time, find a market; but there are no alluvions, no arable lands, and the whole country may be described as one waste of rock and water.

"You have desired me also to express an opinion as to any preference which I may know to exist between the several lines claimed as boundaries through this country, between the United States and Great Britain.

"Considering that Great Britain abandons her claim by the Fond du Lac and the St. Louis River; cedes also Sugar Island (otherwise called St. George's Island) in the St. Marie River; and agrees, generally, to a boundary following the old commercial route, commencing at the Pigeon River, I do not think that any reasonable ground exists to prevent a final determination of this part of the boundary."

And Mr. Delafield adds:

"As an agricultural district, it has no value or interest, even prospectively, in my opinion. If the climate were suitable (which it is not), I can only say that I never saw, in my explorations there, tillable land enough to sustain any permanent population sufficiently numerous to justify other settlements than those of the fur-traders; and, I might add, fishermen. The fur-traders there occupied nearly all those places; and the opinion now expressed is the only one I ever heard entertained by those most experienced in these northwestern regions.

"There is, nevertheless, much interest felt by the fur-traders on this subject of boundary. To them, it is of much importance, as they conceive; and it is, in fact, of national importance. Had the British commissioner consented to proceed by the Pigeon River (which is the Long Lake of Mitchell's map), it is probable there would have been an agreement. There were several reasons for his pertinacity, and for this disagreement; which belong, however, to the private history of the commission, and can be stated when required. The Pigeon River is a continuous water-course. The St. George's Island, in the St. Marie River, is a valuable island, and worth as much, perhaps, as most of the country between the Pigeon River and Dog River route, claimed for the United States, in an agricultural sense."

These are the answers; and while they are conclusive upon the agricultural character of the country between the two routes, and present it as of no value; yet, on the relative importance of the routes as boundaries, they refuse to follow the *lead* which the question held out to them, and show that, as commercial routes, and, consequently, as commanding the Indians and their trade, a question of national importance is involved. Mr. Delafield says the fur-traders feel much interest in this boundary: to them, it is of much importance; and it is, in fact, of national importance. These are the words of Mr. Delafield; and they show the reason why Lord Ashburton was so tenacious of this change in the boundary. He wanted it for the benefit of the fur-trade, and for the consequent command which it would give the British over the Indians in time of war. All this is apparent; yet our Secretary would only look at it as a corn and potato region! And finding it not good for that purpose, he surrenders it to the British! Both the witnesses look upon it as a sacrifice on the part of the United

States, and suppose some equivalent in other parts of the boundary was received for it. There was no such equivalent: and thus this surrender becomes a gratuitous sacrifice on the part of the United States, aggravated by the condescension of the American Secretary to act as the attorney of the British minister, and seeking testimony by unfair and illegal questions; and then disregarding the part of the answers which made against his design.

CHAPTER CV.

BRITISH TREATY: EXTRADITION ARTICLE: MR. BENTON'S SPEECH: EXTRACT.

I proceed to the third subject and last article in the treaty—the article which stipulates for the mutual surrender of fugitive criminals. And here again we are at fault for these same protocols. Not one word is found in the correspondence upon this subject, the brief note excepted of Lord Ashburton of the 9th of August—the day of the signature of the treaty—to say that its ratification would require the consent of the British parliament, and would necessarily be delayed until the parliament met. Except this note, not a word is found upon the subject; and this gives no light upon its origin, progress, and formation—nothing to show with whom it originated—what necessity for it in this advanced age of civilization, when the comity of nations delivers up fugitive offenders upon all proper occasions—and when explanations upon each head of offences, and each class of fugitives, is so indispensable to the right understanding and the safe execution of the treaty. Total and black darkness on all these points. Nor is any ray of light found in the President's brief paragraphs in relation to it. Those paragraphs (the work of his Secretary, of course) are limited to the commendation of the article, and are insidiously deceptive, as I shall show at the proper time. It tells us nothing that we want to know upon the origin and design of the article, and how far it applies to the largest class of fugitive offenders from the United States—the slaves who escape with their master's property, or after taking his life—into Canada and the British West Indies. The message is as silent as the correspondence on all these points; and it is only from looking into past history, and contemporaneous circumstances, that we can search for the origin and design of this stipulation, so unnecessary in the present state of international courtesy, and so useless, unless something unusual and extraordinary is intended. Looking into these sources, and we are authorized to refer the origin and design of the stipulation to the British minister, and to consider it as one of the objects of the special mission with which we have been honored. Be this as it may, I do not like the article. Though fair upon its face, it is difficult of execution. As a general proposition, atrocious offenders, and especially between neighboring nations, ought to be given up; but that is better done as an affair of consent and discretion, than under the constraints and embarrassments of a treaty obligation. Political offenders ought not to be given up; but under the stern requisitions of a treaty obligation, and the benefit of an *ex parte* accusation, political offenders may be given up for murder, or other crimes, real or pretended; and then dealt with as their government pleases. Innocent persons should not be harassed with groundless accusations; and there is no limit to these vexations, if all emigrants are placed at the mercy of malevolent informers, subjected to arrest in a new and strange land, examined upon *ex parte* testimony, and sent back for trial if a probable case is made out against them.

This is a subject long since considered in our country, and on which we have the benefit both of wise opinions and of some experience. Mr. Jefferson explored the whole subject when he was Secretary of State under President Washington, and came to the conclusion that these surrenders could only be made under three limitations:—1. Between coterminous countries. 2. For high offences. 3. A special provision against political offenders. Under these limitations, as far back as the year 1793, Mr. Jefferson proposed to Great Britain and Spain (the only countries with which we held coterminous dominions, and only for their adjacent provinces) a mutual delivery of fugitive criminals. His proposition was in these words:

> "Any person having committed murder of malice prepense, not of the nature of treason, or
> forgery, within the United States or the Spanish provinces *adjoining* thereto, and fleeing from
> the justice of the country, shall be delivered up by the government where he shall be found,
> to that from which he fled, whenever demanded by the same."

This was the proposition of that great statesman: and how different from those which we find in this treaty! Instead of being confined to coterminous dominions, the jurisdiction of the country is taken for the theatre of the crime; and that includes, on the part of Great Britain, possessions all over the world, and every ship on every sea that sails under her flag. Instead of being confined to two offences of high degree—murder and forgery—one against life, the other against property—this article extends to seven offences; some of which may be incurred for a shilling's worth of property, and another of them without touching or injuring a human being. Instead of a special provision in favor of political offenders, the insurgent or rebel may be given up for murder, and then hanged and quartered for treason; and in the long catalogue of seven offences, a charge may be made, and an *ex parte* case established, against any political offender which the British government shall choose to pursue.

To palliate this article, and render it more acceptable to us, we are informed that it is copied from the 27th article of Mr. Jay's treaty. That apology for it, even if exactly true, would be but a poor recommendation of it to the people of the United States. Mr. Jay's treaty was no favorite with the American people, and especially with that part of the people which constituted the republican party. Least of all was this 27th article a favorite with them. It was under that article that the famous Jonathan Robbins, alias Thomas Nash, was surrendered—a surrender which contributed largely to the defeat of Mr. Adams, and the overthrow of the federal party, in 1800. The apology would be poor, if true: but it happens to be not exactly true. The article in the Webster treaty differs widely from the one in Jay's treaty—and all for the worse. The imitation is far worse than the original—about as much worse as modern whiggery is worse than ancient federalism. Here are the two articles; let us compare them:

MR. WEBSTER'S TREATY.

> "*Article 10.*—It is agreed that the United States and her Britannic Majesty shall, upon mutual requisitions by them, or their ministers, officers, or authorities, respectively made, deliver up to justice all persons who, being charged with the crime of murder, or assault with intent to commit murder, or piracy, or arson, or robbery, or forgery, or the utterance of forged papers committed within the jurisdiction of either, shall seek an asylum, or shall be found, within the territories of the other: provided, that this shall only be done, upon such evidence of criminality as, according to the laws of the place where the fugitive or person so charged shall be found, would justify his apprehension and commitment for trial, if the crime or offence had there been committed; and the respective judges and other magistrates shall have power, jurisdiction, and authority, upon complaint made under oath, to issue a warrant for the apprehension of the fugitive or person so charged, that he may be brought before such judges, or other magistrates, respectively, to the end that the evidence of criminality may be heard and considered; and if, on such hearing, the evidence be deemed sufficient to sustain the charge, it shall be the duty of the examining judge, or magistrate, to certify the same to the proper executive authority, that a warrant may issue for the surrender of such fugitive. The expense of such apprehension and delivery shall be borne and defrayed by the party who makes the requisition, and receives the fugitive."

MR. JAY'S TREATY.

> "*Article 27.*—It is further agreed that his Majesty and the United States, on mutual requisitions by them, respectively, or by their respective ministers, or officers, authorized to make the same, will deliver up to justice all persons who, being charged with murder, or forgery, committed within the jurisdiction of either, shall seek an asylum within any of the countries of the other: provided, that this shall only be done on such evidence of criminality as, according to the laws of the place where the fugitive or person so charged shall be found, would justify his apprehension and commitment for trial if the offence had there been committed. The expense of such apprehension and delivery shall be borne and defrayed by those who make the requisition, and receive the fugitive."

These are the two articles, and the difference between them is great and striking. First, the number of offences for which delivery of the offender is to be made, is much greater in the present treaty. Mr. Jay's article is limited to two offences—murder and forgery: the two proposed by Mr. Jefferson; but without his qualification to exclude political offences, and to confine the deliveries to offenders from coterminous dominions. The present treaty embraces these two, and five others, making seven in the whole. The five added offences are—assault, with intent to commit murder; piracy; robbery; arson; and the utterance of forged paper. These additional five offences, though high in name, might be very small in degree. Assault, with intent to murder, might be without touching or hurting any person; for, to lift a weapon at a person within striking distance, without striking, is an assault: to level a fire-arm at a person within carrying distance, and without firing, is an assault; and the offence being in the intent, is difficult of proof. Mr. Jefferson excluded it, and so did Jay's treaty; because the offence was too small and too equivocal to be made a matter of international arrangement. Piracy was excluded, because it was absurd to speak of a pirate's country. He has no country. He is *hostis humani generis*—the enemy of the human race; and is hung wherever he is caught. The robbery might be of a shilling's worth of bread; the arson, of burning a straw shed; the utterance of forged paper, might be the emission or passing of a counterfeit sixpence. All these were excluded from Jay's treaty, because of their possible insignificance, and the door they opened to abuse in harassing the innocent, and in multiplying the chances for getting hold of a political offender for some other offence, and then punishing him for his politics.

Striking as these differences are between the present article and that of Mr. Jay's treaty, there is a still more essential difference in another part; and a difference which nullifies the article in its only material bearing in our favor. It is this: Mr. Jay's treaty referred the delivery of the fugitive to the executive power. This treaty intervenes the judiciary, and requires two decisions from a judge or magistrate before the governor can act. This nullifies the treaty in all that relates to fugitive slaves guilty of crimes against their masters. In the eye of the British law, they have no master, and can commit no offence against such a person in asserting their liberty against him, even unto death. A slave may kill his master, if necessary to his escape. This is legal under British law; and, in the present state of abolition feeling throughout the British dominions, such killing would not only be considered fair, but in the highest degree meritorious and laudable. What chance for the recovery of such a slave under this treaty? Read it—the concluding part—after the word "committed," and see what is the process to be gone through. Complaint is to be made to a British judge or justice. The fugitive is brought before this judge or justice, that the evidence of the criminality may be heard and considered—such evidence as would justify the apprehension, commitment, and trial of the party, if the offence had been committed there. If, upon this hearing, the evidence be deemed sufficient to sustain the charge, the judge or magistrate is to certify the fact to the executive authority; and then, and not until then, the surrender can be made. This is the process; and in all this the new treaty differs from Jay's. Under his treaty the delivery was a ministerial act, referring itself to the authority of the governor: under this treaty, it becomes a judicial act, referring itself to the discretion of the judge, who must twice decide against the slave (first, in issuing the warrant; and next, in trying it) before the governor can order the surrender. Twice judicial discretion interposes a barrier, which cannot be forced; and behind which the slave, who has robbed or killed his master, may repose in safety. What evidence of criminality will satisfy the judge, when the act itself is no crime in his eyes, or under his laws, and when all his sympathies are on the side of the slave? What chance would there be for the judicial surrender of offending slaves in the British dominions, under this treaty, when the provisions of our own constitution, within the States of our own Union, in relation to fugitive slaves, cannot be executed? We all know that a judicial trial is immunity to a slave pursued by his owner, in many of our own States. Can such trials be expected to result better for the owner in the British dominions, where the relation of master and slave is not admitted, and where abolitionism is the policy of the government, the voice of the law, and the spirit of the people? Killing his master in defence of his liberty, is no offence in the eye of British law or British people; and no slave will ever be given up for it.

(Mr. WRIGHT here said, that counterfeiting American securities, or bank notes, was no offence in Canada; and the same question might arise there in relation to forgers.)

Mr. BENTON resumed. Better far to leave things as they are. Forgers are now given up in Canada, by executive authority, when they fly to that province. This is done in the spirit of good neighborhood; and because all honest governments have an interest in suppressing crimes, and repelling criminals. The governor acts from a sense of propriety, and the dictates of decency and justice. Not so with the judge. He must go by the law; and when there is no law against the offence, he has nothing to justify him in delivering the offender.

Conventions for the mutual surrender of large offenders, where dominions are coterminous, might be proper. Limited, as proposed by Mr. Jefferson in 1793, and they might be beneficial in suppression of border crimes and the preservation of order and justice. But extended as this is to a long list of offenders—unrestricted as it is in the case of murder—applying to dominions in all parts of the world, and to ships in every sea—it can be nothing but the source of individual annoyance and national recrimination. Besides, if we surrender to Great

Britain, why not to Russia, Prussia, Austria, France, and all the countries of the world? If we give up the Irishman to England, why not the Pole to Russia, the Italian to Austria, the German to his prince; and so on throughout the catalogue of nations? Sir, the article is a pestiferous one; and as it is determinable upon notice, it will become the duty of the American people to elect a President who will give the notice, and so put an end to its existence.

Addressing itself to the natural feelings of the country, against high crimes and border offenders, and in favor of political liberty, the message of the President communicating and recommending this treaty to us, carefully presents this article as conforming to our feelings in all these particulars. It is represented as applicable only to high crimes—to border offenders; and to offences not political. In all this, the message is disingenuous and deceptive, and calculated to ravish from the ignorant and the thoughtless an applause to which the treaty is not entitled. It says:

> "The surrender to justice of persons who, having committed high crimes, seek an asylum in the territories of a *neighboring* nation, would seem to be an act due to the cause of general justice, and properly belonging to the present state of civilization and intercourse. The *British provinces* of North America are separated from the States of the Union by a line of several thousand miles; and, along portions of this line, the amount of population on either side is quite considerable, *while the passage of the boundary is always easy.*

> "Offenders against the law *on the one side transfer themselves to the other*. Sometimes, with great difficulty they are brought to justice; but very often they wholly escape. A consciousness of immunity, from the power of avoiding justice in this way, instigates the unprincipled and reckless to the commission of offences; *and the peace and good neighborhood of the border are consequently often disturbed.*

> "In the case of offenders fleeing from Canada into the United States, the governors of States are often applied to for their surrender; and questions of a very embarrassing nature arise from these applications. It has been thought highly important, therefore, to provide for the whole case by a proper treaty stipulation. The article on the subject, in the proposed treaty, is carefully confined to such offences as all mankind agree to regard as heinous and destructive of the security of life and of property. In this careful and specific enumeration of crimes, the object has been to exclude all political offences, or criminal charges arising from wars or intestine commotions. Treason, misprision of treason, libels, desertion from military service, and other offences of a similar character, are excluded."

In these phrases the message recommends the article to the Senate and the country; and yet nothing could be more fallacious and deceptive than such a recommendation. It confines the surrender to border offenders—Canadian fugitives: yet the treaty extends it to all persons committing offences under the "*jurisdiction*" of Great Britain—a term which includes all her territory throughout the world, and every ship or fort over which her flag waves. The message confines the surrender to high crimes: yet we have seen that the treaty includes crimes which may be of low degree—low indeed! A hare or a partridge from a preserve; a loaf of bread to sustain life; a sixpenny counterfeit note passed; a shed burnt; a weapon lifted, without striking! The message says all political crimes, all treasons, misprision of treason, libels, and desertions are excluded. The treaty shows that these offences are not excluded—that the limitations proposed by Mr. Jefferson are not inserted; and, consequently, under the head of murder, the insurgent, the rebel, and the traitor who has shed blood, may be given up; and so of other offences. When once surrendered, he may be tried for any thing. The fate of Jonathan Robbins, alias Nash, is a good illustration of all this. He was a British sailor—was guilty of mutiny, murder, and piracy on the frigate Hermione—deserted to the United States—was demanded by the British minister as a murderer under Jay's treaty—given up as a murderer—then tried by a court-martial on board a man-of-war for mutiny, murder, desertion, and piracy—found guilty—executed—and his body hung in chains from the yard-arm of a man-of-war. And so it would be again. The man given up for one offence, would be tried for another; and in the number and insignificance of the offences for which he might be surrendered, there would be no difficulty in reaching any victim that a foreign government chose to pursue. If this article had been in force in the time of the Irish rebellion, and Lord Edward Fitzgerald had escaped to the United States after wounding, as he did, several of the myrmidons who arrested him, he might have been demanded as a fugitive from justice, for the assault with intent to kill; and then tried for treason, and hanged and quartered; and such will be the operation of the article if it continues.

CHAPTER CVI.

BRITISH TREATY; AFRICAN SQUADRON FOR THE SUPPRESSION OF THE SLAVE TRADE; MR. BENTON'S SPEECH; EXTRACT.

The suppression of the African slave-trade is the second subject included in the treaty; and here the regret renews itself at the absence of all the customary lights upon the origin and progress of treaty stipulations. No minutes of conference; no protocols; no draughts or counterdraughts; no diplomatic notes; not a word of any kind from one negotiator to the other. Nothing in relation to the subject, in the shape of negotiation, is communicated to us. Even the section of the correspondence entitled "*Suppression of the slave-trade*"—even this section professedly devoted to the subject, contains not a syllable upon it from the negotiators to each other, or to their Governments; but opens and closes with communications from American naval officers, evidently extracted from them by the American negotiator, to justify the forthcoming of preconceived and foregone conclusions. Never since the art of writing was invented could there have been a treaty of such magnitude negotiated with such total absence of necessary light upon the history of its formation. Lamentable as is this defect of light upon the formation of the treaty generally, it becomes particularly so at this point, where a stipulation new, delicate, and embarrassing, has been unexpectedly introduced, and falls upon us as abruptly as if it fell from the clouds. In the absence of all appropriate information from the negotiators themselves, I am driven to glean among the scanty paragraphs of the President's message, and in the answers of the naval officers to the Secretary's inquiries. Though silent as to the origin and progress of the proposition for this novel alliance, they still show the important particular of the motives which caused it.

Passing from the political consequences of this entanglement—consequences which no human foresight can reach—I come to the immediate and practical effects which lie within our view, and which display the enormous inexpediency of the measure. First: the expense in money—an item which would seem to be entitled to some regard in the present deplorable state of the treasury—in the present cry for retrenchment—and in the present heavy taxation upon the comforts and necessaries of life. This expense for 80 guns will be about $750,000 per annum, exclusive of repairs and loss of lives. I speak of the whole expense, as part of the naval establishment of the United States, and not of the mere expense of working the ships after they have gone to sea. Nine thousand dollars per gun is about the expense of the establishment; 80 guns would be $720,000 per annum, which is $3,600,000 for five years. But the squadron is not limited to a maximum of 80 guns; that is the minimum limit: it is to be 80 guns "at the least." And if the party which granted these 80 shall continue in power, Great Britain may find it as easy to double the number, as it was to obtain the first eighty. Nor is the time limited to five years; it is only determinable after that period by giving notice; a notice not to be expected from those who made the treaty. At the least, then, the moneyed expense is to be $3,600,000; if the present party continues in power, it may double or treble that amount; and this, besides the cost of the ships. Such is the moneyed expense. In ships, the wear and tear of vessels must be great. We are to prepare, equip, and maintain in service, on a coast 4,000 miles from home, the adequate number of vessels to carry these 80 guns. It is not sufficient to send the number there; they must be kept up and maintained in service there; and this will require constant expenses to repair injuries, supply losses and cover casualties. In the employment of men, and the waste of life and health, the expenditure must be large. Ten men and two officers to the gun, is the smallest estimate that can be admitted. This would require a complement of 960 men. Including all the necessary equipage of the ship, and above 1,000 persons will be constantly required. These are to be employed at a vast distance from home; on a savage coast; in a perilous service; on both sides of the equator; and in a climate which is death to the white race. This waste of men—this wear and tear of life and constitution—should stand for something in a Christian land, and in this age of roaming philanthropy; unless, indeed, in excessive love for the blacks, it is deemed meritorious to destroy the whites. The field of operations for this squadron is great; the term "coast of Africa" having an immense application in the vocabulary of the slave-trade. On the western coast of Africa, according to the replies of the naval officers Bell and Paine, the trade is carried on from Senegal to Cape Frio—a distance of 3,600 miles, following its windings as the watching squadrons would have to go. But the track of the slavers between Africa and America has to be watched, as well as the immediate coast; and this embraces a space in the ocean of 35 degrees on each side of the equator (say four thousand miles), and covering the American coast from Cuba to Rio Janeiro; so that the coast of

Africa—the western coast alone—embraces a diagram of the ocean of near 4,000 miles every way, having the equator in the centre, and bounded east and west by the New and the Old World. This is for the western coast only: the eastern is nearly as large. The same naval officers say that a large trade in negroes is carried on in the Mahometan countries bordering on the Red Sea and the Persian Gulf, and in the Portuguese East India colonies; and, what is worthy to be told, it is also carried on in the British presidency of Bombay, and other British Asiatic possessions. It is true, the officers say the American slavers are not yet there; but go there they will, according to all the laws of trading and hunting, the moment they are disturbed, or the trade fails on the western coast. Wherever the trade exists, the combined powers must follow it: for good is not to be done by halves, and philanthropy is not to be circumscribed by coasts and latitudes. Among all the strange features in the comedy of errors which has ended in this treaty that of sending American ministers abroad, to close the markets of the world against the slave-trade, is the most striking. Not content with the expenses, loss of life, and political entanglement of this alliance, we must electioneer for insults, and send ministers abroad to receive, pocket, and bring them home.

In what circumstances do we undertake all this fine work? What is our condition at home, while thus going abroad in search of employment? We raise 1,000 men for foreign service, while reducing our little army at home! We send ships to the coast of Africa, while dismounting our dragoons on the frontiers of Missouri and Arkansas! We protect Africa from slave-dealers, and abandon Florida to savage butchery! We send cannon, shot, shells, powder, lead, bombs, and balls, to Africa, while denying arms and ammunition to the young men who go to Florida! We give food, clothes, pay, to the men who go to Africa, and deny rations even to those who go to Florida! We cry out for retrenchment, and scatter $3,600,000 at one broad cast of the hand! We tax tea and coffee, and send the money to Africa! We are borrowing and taxing, and striking paper money, and reducing expenses at home, when engaging in this new and vast expense for the defence of Africa! What madness and folly! Has Don Quixote come to life, and placed himself at the head of our Government, and taken the negroes of Africa, instead of the damsels of Spain, for the objects of his chivalrous protection?

The slave-trade is diabolical and infamous; but Great Britain is not the country to read us a lesson upon its atrocity, or to stimulate our exertions to suppress it. The nation which, at the peace of Utrecht, made the *asiento*—the slave contract—a condition of peace, fighting on till she obtained it; the nation which entailed African slavery upon us—which rejected our colonial statutes for its suppression[4]—which has many, many ten millions, of white subjects in Europe and in Asia in greater slavery of body and mind, in more bodily misery and mental darkness, than any black slaves in the United States;—such a nation has no right to cajole or to dragoon us into alliances and expenses for the suppression of slavery on the coast of Africa. We have done our part on that subject. Considering the example and instruction we had from Great Britain, we have done a wonderful part. The constitution of the United States, mainly made by slaveholding States, authorized Congress to put an end to the importation of slaves by a given day. Anticipating the limited day by legislative action, the Congress had the law ready to take effect on the day permitted by the constitution. On the 1st day of January, 1808, Thomas Jefferson being President of the United States, the importation of slaves became unlawful and criminal. A subsequent act of Congress following up the idea of Mr. Jefferson in his first draught of the Declaration of Independence, qualified the crime as piratical, and delivered up its pursuers to the sword of the law, and to the vengeance of the world, as the enemies of the human race. Vessels of war cruising on the coast of Africa, under our act of 1819, have been directed to search our own vessels—to arrest the violators of the law, and bring them in—the ships for confiscation, and the men for punishment. This was doing enough— enough for a young country, far remote in the New World, and whose policy is to avoid foreign connections and entangling alliances. We did this voluntarily, without instigation, and without supervision from abroad; and now there can be no necessity for Great Britain to assume a superiority over us in this particular, and bind us in treaty stipulations, which destroy all the merit of a voluntary action. We have done enough; and it is no part of our business to exalt still higher the fanatical spirit of abolition, which is now become the stalking-horse of nations and of political powers. Our country contains many slaves, derived from Africa; and, while holding these, it is neither politic nor decent to join the crusade of European powers to put down the African slave-trade. From combinations of powers against the present slave-takers, there is but a step to the combination of the same powers against the present slaveholders; and it is not for the United States to join in the first movement, which leads to the second. "No entangling alliances" should be her motto! And as for her part in preventing the foreign slave-trade, it is sufficient that she prevents her own citizens, in her own way, from engaging in it; and that she takes care to become neither the instrument, nor the victim, of European combinations for its suppression.

The eighth and ninth articles of the treaty bind us to this naval alliance with Great Britain. By these articles we stipulate to keep a squadron of at least 80 guns on the coast of Africa for five years for the suppression of this trade—with a further stipulation to keep it up until one or the other party shall give notice of a design to retire from it. This is the insidious way of getting an onerous measure saddled upon the country. Short-sighted people are fascinated with the idea of being able to get rid of the burden when they please; but such burdens are always found to be the most interminable. In this case Great Britain will never give the notice: our government will not without a congressional recommendation, and it will be found difficult to unite the two Houses in a request. The stipulation may be considered permanent under the delusion of a five years' limit, and an optional continuance.

The papers communicated do not show at whose instance these articles were inserted; and the absence of all minutes of conferences leaves us at a loss to trace their origin and progress in the hands of the negotiators. The little that is seen would indicate its origin to be wholly American; evidence *aliunde* proves it to be wholly British; and that our Secretary-negotiator was only doing the work of the British minister in assuming the ostensible paternity of the articles. In the papers communicated, there is not a syllable upon the subject from Lord Ashburton. His finger is not seen in the affair. Mr. Webster appears as sole mover and conductor of the proposition. In his letter of the 30th of April to Captains Bell and Paine of the United States navy, he first approaches the subject, and opens it with a series of questions on the African slave-trade. This draws forth the answers which I have already shown. This is the commencement of the business. And here we are struck with the curious fact, that this letter of inquiry, laying the foundation for a novel and extraordinary article in the treaty, bears date 44 days before the first written communication from the British to the American negotiator! and 47 days before the first written communication from Mr. Webster to Lord Ashburton! It would seem that much was done by word of mouth before pen was put to paper; and that in this most essential part of the negotiations, pen was not put to paper at all, from one negotiator to the other, throughout the whole affair. Lord Ashburton's name is never found in connection with the subject! Mr. Webster's only in the notes of inquiry to the American naval officers. Even in these he does not mention the treaty, nor allude to the negotiation, nor indicate the purpose for which information was sought! So that this most extraordinary article is without a clew to its history, and stands in the treaty as if it had fallen from the clouds, and chanced to lodge there! Even the President's message, which undertakes to account for the article, and to justify it, is silent on the point, though laboring through a mass of ambiguities and obscurities, evidently calculated to raise the inference that it originated with us. From the papers communicated, it is an American proposition, of which the British negotiator knew nothing until he signed the treaty. That is the first place where his name is seen in conjunction with it, or seen in a place to authorize the belief that he knew of it. Yet, it is certainly a British proposition; it is certainly a British article. Since the year 1806 Great Britain has been endeavoring to get the United States into some sort of arrangement for co-operation in the suppression of the African slave-trade. It was slightly attempted in Mr. Jefferson's time—again at Ghent; but the warning-voice of the Father of his country—*no entangling alliances*—saved us on each occasion. Now we are yoked—yoked in with the British on the coast of Africa; and when we can get free from it, no mortal can foresee.

CHAPTER CVII.

EXPENSE OF THE NAVY: WASTE OF MONEY NECESSITY OF A NAVAL PEACE ESTABLISHMENT, AND OF A NAVAL POLICY.

The naval policy of the United States was a question of party division from the origin of parties in the early years of the government—the federal party favoring a strong and splendid navy, the republican a moderate establishment, adapted to the purposes of defence more than of offence: and this line of division between the parties (under whatsoever names they have since worn), continues more or less perceptible to the present time. In this time (the administration of Mr. Tyler) all the branches being of the same political party, and retaining the early principles of the party under the name of whig, the policy for a great navy developed itself with great vigor. The new Secretary, Mr. Upshur, recommended a large increase of ships, seamen, and officers, involving an additional expense of about two millions and a half in the naval branch of the service; and that at a time when a deficit of fourteen millions was announced, and a resort to taxes, loans and treasury notes recommended to make it up; and when no emergency required increase in that branch of the public service. Such a recommendation brought on a debate in which the policy of a great navy was discussed—the necessity of a naval peace establishment was urged—the cost of our establishment examined—and the waste of money in the naval department severely exposed. Mr. Calhoun, always attentive to the economical working of the government, opened the discussion on this interesting point.

"The aggregate expense of the British navy in the year 1840 amounted to 4,980,353 pounds sterling, deducting the expense of transport for troops and convicts, which does not properly belong to the navy. That sum, at $4 80 to the pound sterling, is equal to $23,905,694 46. The navy was composed of 392 vessels of war of all descriptions, leaving out 36 steam vessels in the packet service, and 23 sloops fitted for foreign packets. Of the 392, 98 were line of battle ships, of which 19 were building; 116 frigates, of which 14 were building; 68 sloops, of which 13 were building; 44 steam vessels, of which 16 were building; and 66 gun brigs, schooners, and cutters, of which 12 were building.

"The effective force of the year—that which was in actual service, consisted of 3,400 officers, 3,998 petty officers, 12,846 seamen, and 9,000 marines, making an aggregate of 29,244. The number of vessels in actual service were 175, of which 24 were line of battle ships, 31 frigates, 30 steam vessels, and 45 gun brigs, schooners, and cutters, not including the 30 steamers and 24 sloops in the packet service, at an average expenditure of $573 for each individual, including officers, petty officers, seamen, and marines.

"Our navy is composed, at present, according to the report of the Secretary accompanying the President's message, of 67 vessels—of which 11 are line of battle ships, 17 frigates, 18 sloops of war, 2 brigs, 4 schooners, 4 steamers, 3 store ships, 3 receiving vessels, and 5 small schooners. The estimates for the year are made on the assumption, that there will be in service during the year, 2 ships of the line, 1 razee, 6 frigates, 20 sloops, 11 brigs and schooners, 3 steamers, 3 store ships and 8 small vessels; making in the aggregate, 53 vessels. The estimates for the year, for the navy and marine corps, as has been stated, is $8,705,579 83, considerably exceeding one-third of the entire expenditures of the British navy for 1840.

"Mr. C. contended there should be no difference in the expenses of the two navies. We should build as cheap and employ men as cheap, or we should not be able to compete with the British navy. If our navy should prove vastly more expensive than the British navy, we might as well give up, and he recommended this matter to the consideration of the Senate.

"Among the objects of retrenchment, I place at the head the great increase that is proposed to be made to the expenditures of the navy, compared with that of last year. It is no less than $2,508,032 13, taking the expenditures of last year from the annual report of the Secretary. I see no sufficient reason, at this time, and in the present embarrassed condition of the Treasury, for this great increase. I have looked over the report of the Secretary hastily, and find none assigned, except general reasons, for an increased navy, which I am not disposed to controvert. But I am decidedly of the opinion, that the commencement ought to be postponed till some systematic plan is matured, both as to the ratio of increase and the description of force of which the addition should consist, and till the department is properly organized, and in a condition to enforce exact responsibility and economy in its disbursements. That the department is not now properly organized, and in that condition, we have the authority of the Secretary himself, in which I concur. I am satisfied that its administration cannot be made effective under the present organization, particularly as it regards its expenditures."

"The expenses of this government were of three classes: the civil list, the army and the navy; and all of these had been increased enormously since 1823. The remedy now was to compare the present with the past, mark the difference, and compel the difference to be accounted for. He cited 1823, and intended to make that the standard, because that was the standard for him, the government being then economically administered. He selected 1823, also, because in 1824 we commenced a new system, and that of protection, which had done so much evil. We had made two tariffs since then, the origin of all evils. The civil list rose in seventeen years from about $2,000,000 to $6,000,000—nearly a threefold proportion compared with the increase of population. In Congress the increase had been enormous. The increase of contingent expenses had been fivefold, and compared with population, sixfold. The aggregate expenses of the two Houses now amounted to more than $250,000. The expense of collecting revenue had also been enormously increased. From 1823 it had gone up from $700,000 to $1,700,000—an increase of one million of dollars. The expense on collection in 1823 was but one per cent., now one per cent. and 5-100. Under the tariff these increases were made from 1824 to 1828. Estimating the expenses of collection at $800,000, about $1,000,000 would be saved. The judiciary had increased in this proportion, and the light-house department also. In the war department, in 1822 (the only year for which he had estimates), the expenses per man were but $264; now the increase had gone up to $400 for each individual. At one time it had been as much as $480 for each individual—$1,400,000 could be saved here in the army proper, including the military academy alone. It might be said that one was a cheap and the other a dear year. Far otherwise; meat was never cheaper, clothing never as cheap as now. All this resulted from the expansive force of a surplus revenue. In 1822 he had reduced the expenses of every man in the army.

"It had been proposed to increase the expenditures of the navy two and a half millions of dollars over the past year, and he was not ready for this. Deduct two millions from this recommendation, and it would be two millions saved. These appropriations, at least, might go over to the next session. The expenses of the marine corps amounted to nearly six hundred thousand dollars, nearly six hundred dollars a head—two hundred dollars a head higher than the army, cadets and all. He hoped the other expenses of the navy department were not in proportion so high as this. Between the reductions which might be made in the marine corps and the navy, two millions and a half might be saved.

"The Secretary of the Treasury estimates for 32 millions of dollars for the expenses of the current year. I am satisfied that $17,000,000 were sufficient to meet the per annum expenses of the government, and that this sum would have been according to the ratio of population. This sum, by economy, could be brought down to fifteen millions, and thus save nine millions over the present estimates. This could be done in three or four years—the Executive leading the way, and Congress co-operating and following the Executive."

This was spoken in the year 1842. Mr. Calhoun was then confident that the ordinary expenses of the government should not exceed 17 millions of dollars, and that, with good economy that sum might be further reduced two millions, making the expenses but 15 millions per annum. The navy was one of the great points to which he looked for retrenchment and reduction; and on that point he required that the annual appropriation for the navy should be decreased instead of being augmented; and that the money appropriated should be more judiciously and economically applied. The President should lead the way in economy and retrenchment. Organization as well as economy was wanted in the navy—a properly organized peace establishment. The peace establishment of the British navy in 1840, was 24 millions—there being 173 vessels in commission. Instead of reduction, the expense of our navy, also in time of peace, is gaining largely upon hers. It is nearly doubled since Mr. Calhoun spoke—15 millions in 1855.

Mr. Woodbury, who had been Secretary of the Navy under President Jackson, spoke decidedly against the proposed increase, and against the large expenditure in the department, and its unfavorable comparison with the expenses of the British navy in time of peace. He said:

"There are twenty-nine or thirty post-captains now on leave or waiting orders, and from thirty to forty commanders. Many of them are impatient to be called into active service—hating a life of indolence—an idle loafing life—and who are anxious to be performing some public service for the pay they receive. It was, generally, not their fault that they were not on duty; but ours, in making them so numerous that they could not be employed. He dwelt on the peace establishment of England—for her navy averaged £18,000,000 in time of war, before the year 1820—but her peace establishment was now only £5,000,000 to 6,000,000. Gentlemen talk of 103 post-captains being necessary, for employment in commission; while England has only 70 post-captains employed in vessels in commission. She had fewer commanders so employed than our whole number of the same grade.

"The host of English navy officers was on retired and half-pay—less in amount than ours by one-third when full, and not one-half of full pay often, when retired; and her seamen only half. Her vessels afloat, also, were mostly small ones—63 of them being steamers, with only one or two guns on an average.

"That the navy ought to be regulated by law, every gentleman admits. Without any express law, was there not a manifest propriety in any proviso which should prevent the number of appointments from being carried half up, or quite up to the standard of the British navy, on full pay? It would be a great relief to the Executive, and the head of the Navy Department, to fix some limitation on appointments, by which the importunities with which they are beset shall not be the occasion of overloading the Government with a greater number of officers in any grade than the exigencies of the service actually demand. A clerk in any public office, a lieutenant in the army, a judge could not be appointed without authority of law; and why should there not be a similar check with regard to officers in the navy?

"It was urged heretofore, in official communications by himself, that it would be proper to limit Executive discretion in this; and a benefit to the Executive and the departments would also accrue by passing laws regulating the peace establishment. He had submitted a resolution for that purpose, in December last, which had not been acted on; though he hoped it yet would be acted upon before our adjournment. It was better to bring this matter forward in an appropriation bill, than that there should be no check at all. It is the only way in which the House now finds it practicable to effect any control on this question. It could only be done in an appropriation bill, which gives that House the power of control as to navy officers. There should be no reflection on the House on this account; for there is no reflection on the Executive or the Senate. It is their right and duty in the present exigency. He considered the introduction of it into this bill under all the circumstances, not only highly excusable, but justifiable. He did not mean to say that a separate law would not, in itself, if prepared early and seasonably, be more desirable; but he contended this check was better than none at all. When acting on this proviso the Senate is acting on the whole bill. It was not put in without some meaning. It was not merely to strip the Executive and the Senate of the appointing power, now unlimited: its object was to reduce the expenses of the navy, from the Secretary of the Navy's estimate of eight and a half millions of dollars, to about $6,293,000. That was the whole effect of the whole measure, and of all the changes in the bill.

"The difference between both sides of the Senate on this subject seemed to be, that one believed the navy ought to be kept upon a *quasi* war establishment; and the other, in peace and not expecting war, believed it ought to be on a peace establishment;—not cut down below that, but left liberally for peace.

"During the administration of the younger Adams, there was a peace establishment of the navy; and was it not then perfectly efficient and prosperous for all peace purposes? Yet the average expenditure then was only from three to four millions. It was so under General Jackson. Under Mr. Adams, piracy was extirpated in the West Indies. Under his successor, the Malays in the farthest India were chastised; and a semi-banditti broken up at the Falkland Islands. It was not till 1836 '37 that a large increase commenced. But why? Because there was an overflowing treasury. We were embarrassed with money, rather than for money. An exploring expedition was then decided upon. But even with that expedition—so noble and glorious in some respects—six millions and a fraction were the whole expenses. But why should it now at once be raised to eight and a half millions?"

The British have a peace as well as a war establishment for their navy; and the former was usually about one-third of the latter. We have no naval peace establishment. It is all on the war footing, and is now (1855) nearly double the expense of what it was in the war with Great Britain. A perpetual war establishment, when there is no war. This is an anomaly which no other country presents, and which no country can stand, and arises from the act of 1806, which authorizes the President "*to keep in actual service, in time of peace, so many of the frigates and other armed public vessels of the United States as in his judgment the nature of the service might require, and to cause the residue thereof to be laid up in ordinary in convenient ports.*" This is the discretion which the act of 1806 gives to the President—unlimited so far as that clause goes; but limited by two subsequent clauses limiting the number of officers to be employed to 94, and the whole number of seamen and boys to 925; and placing the unemployed officers on half pay without rations—a degree of reduction which made them anxious to be at sea instead of remaining unemployed at home. Under Mr. Jefferson, then, the act of 1806 made a naval peace establishment; but doing away all the limitations of that act, and leaving nothing of it in force but the presidential discretion to employ as many vessels as the service might require, the whole navy is thrown into the hands of the President: and the manner in which he might exercise that discretion might depend entirely upon the view which he would take of the naval policy which ought to be pursued—whether great fleets for offence, or cruisers for defence. All the limitations of the act of 1806 have been thrown down—even the limitation to half pay; and unemployed pay has been placed so high as to make it an object with officers to be unemployed. Mr. Reuel Williams, of Maine, exposed this solecism in a few pertinent remarks. He said:

"Half of the navy officers are now ashore, and there can be no necessity for such a number of officers as to admit of half being at sea, and the other half on land. Such was not the case heretofore. It was in 1835 that such increase of shore pay was made, as caused it to be the interest of the officers to be off duty. The only cure for this evil was, either to reduce the pay when off duty, or to limit the time of relaxation, and to adjust the number to the actual requirements of the service."

The vote was taken upon the increase proposed by the Secretary of the Navy, and recommended by the President, and it was carried by one vote—the yeas and nays being well defined by the party line.

"YEAS—Messrs. Archer, Barrow, Bates, Berrien, Choate, Clayton, Conrad, Crittenden, Evans, Graham, Henderson, Huntington, Kerr, Mangum, Merrick, Miller, Morehead, Porter, Preston, Rives, Simmons, Tallmadge, and Woodbridge—23."

"NAYS—Messrs. Allen, Bagby, Benton, Buchanan, Crafts, Cuthbert, Fulton, King, Linn, McRoberts, Sevier, Smith of Connecticut, Smith of Indiana, Sturgeon, Tappan, Walker, White, Wilcox, Williams, Woodbury, Wright and Young—22."

Mr. Benton spoke chiefly to the necessity of having a naval policy—a policy which would determine what was to be relied on—a great navy for offence, or a moderate one for defence; and a peace establishment in time of peace, or a war establishment in peace as well as war. Some extracts from his speech are given in the next chapter.

CHAPTER CVIII.

EXPENSES OF THE NAVY: MR. BENTON'S SPEECH: EXTRACTS.

I propose to recall to the recollection of the Senate the attempt which was made in 1822—being seven years after the war—to limit and fix a naval peace establishment; and to fix it at about one-fourth of what is now proposed, and that that establishment was rejected because it was too large. Going upon the plan of Mr. Jefferson's act of 1806, it took the number of men and officers for the limitation, discouraged absence on shore by reducing the pay one-half and withholding rations; collected timber for future building of vessels; and directed all to remain in port which the public service did not require to go abroad. It provided for one rear-admiral; five commodores; twenty-five captains; thirty masters commandant; one hundred and ninety lieutenants; four hundred midshipmen; thirty-five surgeons; forty-five surgeon's mates: six chaplains; forty pursers; and three thousand five hundred men and boys—in all a little over four thousand men. Yet Congress refused to adopt this number. This shows what Congress then thought of the size of a naval peace establishment. Mr. B. was contemporary with that bill—supported it—knows the reason why it was rejected— and that was, because Congress would not sanction so large an establishment. To this decision there was a close adherence for many years. In the year 1833—eleven years after that time, and when the present senator from New Hampshire [Mr. WOODBURY] was Secretary of the Navy, the naval establishment was but little above the bill of 1822. It was about five thousand men, and cost about four millions of dollars, and was proposed by that Secretary to be kept at about that size. Here Mr. B. read several extracts from Mr. Woodbury's report of 1833—the last which he made as Secretary of the Navy—which verified these statements. Mr. B. then looked to the naval establishment on the 1st of January, 1841, and showed that the establishment had largely increased since Mr. Woodbury's report, and was far beyond my calculation in 1822. The total number of men, of all grades, in the service in 1841, was a little over eight thousand; the total cost about six millions of dollars—being double the amount and cost of the proposed peace establishment of the United States in the year 1822, and nearly double the actual establishment of 1833. Mr. B. then showed the additions made by executive authority in 1841, and that the number of men was carried up to upwards of eleven thousand, and the expense for 1842 was to exceed eight millions of dollars! This (he said) was considered an excessive increase; and the design now was to correct it, and carry things back to what they were a year before. This was the design; and this, so far from being destructive to the navy, was doing far more for it than its most ardent friends proposed or hoped for a few years before.

Mr. B. here exhibited a table showing the actual state of the navy, in point of numbers, at the commencement of the years 1841 and 1842; and showed that the increase in one year was nearly as great as it had been in the previous twenty years; and that its totality at the latter of these periods was between eleven and twelve thousand men, all told. This is what the present administration has done in one year—the first year of its existence: and it is only the commencement of their plan—the first step in a long succession of long steps. The further increases, still contemplated were great, and were officially made known to the Congress, and the estimates increased accordingly. To say nothing of what was in the Senate in its executive capacity, Mr. B. would read a clause from the report of the Senate's Committee on Naval Affairs, which showed the number of vessels which the Secretary of the Navy proposed to have in commission, and the consequent vast increase of men and money which would be required. (The following is the extract from Mr. Bayard's report):

> "The second section of the act of Congress of the 21st April, 1806, expressly authorizes the President 'to keep in actual service, in time of peace, so many of the frigates and other public armed vessels of the United States, as in his judgment the nature of the service may require.' In the exercise of this discretion, the committee are informed by the Secretary of the Navy that he proposes to employ a squadron in the Mediterranean, consisting of two ships of the line, four frigates, and four sloops and brigs—in all, ten vessels; another squadron on the Brazil station, consisting, also, of two ships-of-the-line, four frigates, and four sloops and brigs; which two squadrons will be made from time to time to exchange their stations, and thus to traverse the intermediate portion of the Atlantic. He proposes, further, to employ a squadron in the Pacific, consisting of one ship-of-the-line, two frigates, and four sloops; and

a similar squadron of one ship of the line, two frigates, and four sloops in the East Indies; which squadrons, in like manner, exchanging from time to time their stations, will traverse the intermediate portion of the Pacific, giving countenance and protection to the whale fishery in that ocean. He proposes, further, to employ a fifth squadron, to be called the home squadron, consisting of one ship-of-the-line, three frigates, and three sloops, which, besides the duties which its name indicates, will have devolved upon it the duties of the West India squadron, whose cruising ground extended to the mouth of the Amazon, and as far as the 30th degree of west longitude from London. He proposes, additionally, to employ on the African coast one frigate and four sloops and brigs—in all, five vessels; four steamers in the Gulf of Mexico, and four steamers on the lakes. There will thus be in commission seven ships-of-the-line, sixteen frigates, twenty-three sloops and brigs, and eight steamers—in all, fifty-four vessels."

This is the report of the committee. This is what we are further to expect. Five great squadrons, headed by ships of the line; and one of them that famous home squadron hatched into existence at the extra session one year ago, and which is the ridicule of all except those who live at home upon it, enjoying the emoluments of service without any service to perform. Look at it. Examine the plan in its parts, and see the enormity of its proportions. Two ships-of-the-line, four frigates, and four sloops and brigs for the Mediterranean—a sea as free from danger to our commerce as is the Chesapeake Bay. Why, sir, our Secretary is from the land of Decatur, and must have heard of that commander, and how with three little frigates, one sloop, and a few brigs and schooners, he humbled Algiers, Tripoli, and Tunis, and put an end to their depredations on American ships and commerce. He must have heard of Lord Exmouth, who, with less force than he proposes to send to the Mediterranean, went there and crushed the fortifications of Algiers, and took the bond of the pirates never to trouble a Christian again. And he must have heard of the French, who, since 1830, are the owners of Algiers. Certainly the Mediterranean is as free from danger to-day as is the Chesapeake Bay; and yet our Secretary proposes to send two ships-of-the-line, four frigates, and four sloops to that safe sea, to keep holiday there for three years. Another squadron of the same magnitude is to go to Brazil, where a frigate and a sloop would be the extent that any emergency could require, and more than has ever been required yet. The same of the Pacific Ocean, where Porter sailed in triumph during the war with one little frigate; and a squadron to the East Indies, where no power has any navy, and where our sloops and brigs would dominate without impediment. In all fifty-four men-of-war! Seven ships-of-the-line, sixteen frigates, twenty-three sloops and brigs, and eight steamers. And all this under Jefferson's act of 1806, when there was not a ship-of-the-line, nor a large frigate, nor twenty vessels of all sorts, and part of them to remain in port—only the number going forth that would require nine hundred and twenty-five men to man them! just about the complement of one of these seven ships-of-the-line. Does not presidential discretion want regulating when such things as these can be done under the act of 1806? Has any one calculated the amount of this increase, and counted up the amount of men and money which it will cost? The report does not, and, in that respect, is essentially deficient. It ought to be counted, and Mr. B. would attempt it. He acknowledged the difficulty of such an undertaking; how easy it was for a speaker—and especially such a speaker as he was—to get into a fog when he got into masses of millions, and so bewilder others as well as himself. To avoid this, details must be avoided, and results made plain by simplifying the elements of calculation. He would endeavor to do so, by taking a few plain data, in this case—the data correct in themselves, and the results, therefore, mathematically demonstrated.

He would take the guns and the men—show what we had now, and what we proposed to have; and what was the cost of each gun afloat, and the number of men to work it. The number of guns we now have afloat is nine hundred and thirty-seven; the number of men between eleven and twelve thousand; and the estimated cost for the whole, a fraction over eight millions of dollars. This would give about twelve men and about nine thousand dollars to each gun. [Mr. BAYARD asked how could these nine thousand dollars a gun be made out?] Mr. BENTON replied. By counting every thing that was necessary to give you the use of the gun—every thing incident to its use—every thing belonging to the whole naval establishment. The end, design, and effect of the whole establishment, was to give you the use of the gun. That was all that was wanted. But, to get it, an establishment had to be kept up of vast extent and variety—of shops and yards on land, as well as ships at sea—of salaries and pensions, as well as powder and balls. Every expense is counted, and that gives the cost per gun. Mr. B. said he would now analyze the gentleman's report, and see what addition these five squadrons would make to the expense of the naval establishment. The first point was, to find the number of guns which they were to bear, and which was the element in the calculation that would lead to the results sought for. Recurring to the gentleman's report, and taking the number of each class of vessels, and the number of guns which each would carry, and the results would be:

7 ships-of-the-line, rating 74, but carrying 80 guns,	560
16 frigates, 44 guns each,	704
13 sloops, 20 guns each,	260
10 brigs, 10 guns each,	100
8 steamers, 10 guns each,	80
	1,704

Here (said Mr. B.) is an aggregate of 1,704 guns, which, at $9,000 each gun, would give $15,336,000, as the sum which the Treasury would have to pay for a naval establishment which would give us the use of that number. Deduct the difference between the 937, the present number of guns, and this 1,704, and you have 767 for the increased number of guns, which, at $9,000 each, will give $6,903,000 for the increased cost in money. This was the moneyed result of the increase. Now take the personal increase—that is to say, the increased number of men which the five squadrons would require. Taking ten men and two officers to the gun—in all, twelve—and the increased number of men and officers required for 767 guns would be 8,204. Add these to the 11,000 or 12,000 now in service, and you have close upon 20,000 men for the naval peace establishment of 1843, costing about fifteen millions and a half of dollars.

But I am asked, and in a way to question my computation, how I get at these nine thousand dollars cost for each gun afloat? I answer—by a simple and obvious process. I take the whole annual cost of the navy department, and then see how many guns we have afloat. The object is to get guns afloat, and the whole establishment is subordinate and incidental to that object. Not only the gun itself, the ship which carries it, and the men who work it, are to be taken into the account, but the docks and navy-yards at home, the hospitals and pensions, the marines and guards—every thing, in fact, which constituted the expense of the naval establishment. The whole is employed, or incurred, to produce the result—which is, so many guns at sea to be fired upon the enemy. The whole is incurred for the sake of the guns, and therefore all must be counted. Going by this rule (said Mr. B.), it would be easily shown that his statement of yesterday was about correct—rather under than over; and this could be seen by making a brief and plain sum in arithmetic. We have the number of guns afloat, and the estimated expense for the year: the guns 936; the estimate for the year is $8,705,579. Now, divide this amount by the number of guns, and the result is a little upwards of $9,200 to each one. This proves the correctness of the statement made yesterday; it proves it for the present year, which is the one in controversy. The result will be about the same for several previous years. Mr. B. said he had looked over the years 1841 and 1838, and found this to be the result: in 1841, the guns were 747, and the expense of the naval establishment $6,196,516. Divide the money by the guns, and you have a little upwards of $8,300. In 1838, the guns were 670, and the expense $5,980,971. This will give a little upwards of $8,900 to the gun. The average of the whole three years will be just about $9,000.

Thus, the senator from New Hampshire [Mr. WOODBURY] and himself were correct in their statement, and the figures proved it. At the same time, the senator from Delaware [Mr. BAYARD] is undoubtedly correct in taking a small number of guns, and saying they may be added without incurring an expense of more than three or four thousand dollars. Small additions may be made, without incurring any thing but the expense of the gun itself, and the men who work it. But that is not the question here. The question is to almost double the number; it is to carry up 937 to 1,700. Here is an increase intended by the Secretary of the Navy of near 800 guns—perhaps quite 800, if the seventy-fours carry ninety guns, as intimated by the senator [Mr. BAYARD] this day. These seven or eight hundred guns could not be added without ships to carry them, and all the expense on land which is incident to the construction of these ships. These seven or eight hundred additional guns would require seven or eight thousand men, and a great many officers. Ten men and two officers to the gun is the estimate. The present establishment is near that rate, and the increase must be in the same proportion. The present number of men in the navy, exclusive of officers, is 9,784: which is a fraction over ten to the gun. The number of officers now in service (midshipmen, surgeons, &c., included) is near 1,300, besides the list of nominations not yet confirmed. This is in the proportion of nearly one and a half to a gun. Apply the whole to the intended increase—the increase which the report of the committee discloses to us—and you will have close upon 17,000 men and 2,000 officers for the peace establishment of the navy—in all, near 20,000 men! and this, independent of those employed on land, and the 2,000 mechanics and laborers who are usually at our navy-yards. Now, these men and officers cost money: two hundred and twenty-six dollars per annum per man, and eight hundred and fifty dollars per annum per officer, was the average cost in 1833, as stated in the report of the then Secretary of the Navy, the present senator from New Hampshire [Mr. WOODBURY]. What it is now, Mr. B. did not know, but knew it was greater for the officers now, than it was then. But one thing he did know—and that was, that a naval peace establishment of the magnitude disclosed in the committee's report (six squadrons, 54 vessels, 1,700 guns, 17,000 men, and 2,000 or 3,000 officers) would break down the whole navy of the United States.

Mr. B. said we had just had a presidential election carried on a *hue-and-cry* against extravagance, and a *hurrah* for a change, and a promise to carry on the government for thirteen millions of dollars; and here were fifteen and a half millions for one branch of the service! and those who oppose it are to be stigmatized as architects of ruin, and enemies of the navy; and a *hue-and-cry* raised against them for the opposition. He said we had just voted a set of resolutions [Mr. CLAY'S] to limit the expenses of the government to twenty-two millions; and yet here are two-thirds of that sum proposed for one branch of the service—a branch which, under General Jackson's administration, cost about four millions, and was intended to be limited to about that amount. This was the economy—the retrenchment—the saving of the people's money, which was promised before the election!

Mr. B. would not go into points so well stated by the senator from New Hampshire [Mr. WOODBURY] on yesterday, that our present peace naval establishment exceeds the cost of the war establishment during the late war; that we pay far more money, and get much fewer guns and men than the British do for the same money. He would omit the tables which he had on hand to prove these important points, and would go on to say that it was an obligation of imperious duty on Congress to arrest the present state of things; to turn back the establishment to what it was a year ago; and to go to work at the next session of Congress to regulate the United States naval peace establishment by law. When that bill came up, a great question would have to be decided—the question of a navy for defence, or for offence! When that question came on, he would give his opinion upon it, and his reasons for that opinion. A navy of some degree, and of some kind, all seemed to be agreed upon; but what it is to be—whether to defend our homes, or carry war abroad—is a question yet to be decided, and on which the wisdom and the patriotism of the country would be called into requisition. He would only say, at present, that coasts and cities could be defended without great fleets at sea. The history of continental Europe was full of the proofs. England, with her thousand ships, could do nothing after Europe was ready for her, during the late wars of the French revolution. He did not speak of attacks in time of peace, like Copenhagen, but of Cadiz and Teneriffe in 1797, and Boulogne and Flushing in 1804, where Nelson, with all his skill and personal daring, and with vast fleets, was able to make no impression.

Mr. B. said the navy was popular, and had many friends and champions; but there was such a thing as killing by kindness. He had watched the progress of events for some time, and said to his friends (for he made no speeches about it) that the navy was in danger—that the expense of it was growing too fast—that there would be reaction and revulsion. And he now said that, unless things were checked, and moderate counsels prevailed, and law substituted for executive discretion (or indiscretion, as the case might be), the time might not be distant when this brilliant arm of our defence should become as unpopular as it was in the time of the elder Mr. Adams.

CHAPTER CIX.

MESSAGE OF THE PRESIDENT AT THE OPENING OF THE REGULAR SESSION OF 1842-3.

The treaty with Great Britain, and its commendation, was the prominent topic in the forepart of the message. The President repeated, in a more condensed form, the encomiums which had been passed upon it by its authors, but without altering the public opinion of its character—which was that it was really a *British* treaty, Great Britain getting every thing settled which she wished, and all to her own satisfaction; while all the subjects of interest to the United States were adjourned to an indefinite future time, as well known then as now never to occur. One of these deferred subjects was a matter of too much moment, and pregnant with too grave consequences, to escape general reprobation in the United States: it was that of the Columbia River, exclusively possessed by the British under a joint-occupation treaty: and which possession only required time to ripen it into a valid title. The indefinite adjournment of that question was giving Great Britain the time she wanted; and the danger of losing the country was turning the attention of the Western people towards saving it by sending emigrants to occupy it. Many emigrants had gone: more were going: a tide was setting in that direction. In fact the condition of this great American territory was becoming a topic of political discussion, and entering into the contests of party; and the President found it necessary to make further excuses for omitting to settle it in the Ashburton treaty, and a necessity to attempt to do something to soothe the public mind. He did so in this message:

> "It would have furnished additional cause for congratulation, if the treaty could have embraced all subjects calculated in future to lead to a misunderstanding between the two governments. The territory of the United States, commonly called the Oregon Territory, lying on the Pacific Ocean, north of the forty-second degree of latitude, to a portion of which Great Britain lays claim, begins to attract the attention of our fellow-citizens; and the tide of population, which has reclaimed what was so lately an unbroken wilderness in more contiguous regions, is preparing to flow over those vast districts which stretch from the Rocky Mountains to the Pacific Ocean. In advance of the acquirement of individual rights to these lands, sound policy dictates that every effort should be resorted to by the two governments to settle their respective claims. It became manifest, at an early hour of the late negotiations, that any attempt, for the time being, satisfactorily to determine those rights, would lead to a protracted discussion which might embrace, in its failure, other more pressing matters; and the Executive did not regard it as proper to waive all the advantages of an honorable adjustment of other difficulties of great magnitude and importance, because this, not so immediately pressing, stood in the way. Although the difficulty referred to may not, for several years to come, involve the peace of the two countries, yet I shall not delay to urge on Great Britain the importance of its early settlement."

The excuse given for the omission of this subject in the Ashburton negotiations is lame and insufficient. Protracted discussion is incident to all negotiations, and as to losing other matters of more pressing importance, all that were of importance to the United States were given up any way, and without getting any equivalents for them. The promise to urge an early settlement could promise but little fruit after Great Britain had got all she wanted; and the discouragement of settlement, by denying land titles to the emigrants until an adjustment could be made, was the effectual way to abandon the country to Great Britain. But this subject will have an appropriate chapter in the history of the proceedings of Congress to encourage that emigration which the President would repress.

The termination of the Florida war was a subject of just congratulation with the President, and was appropriately communicated to Congress.

> "The vexatious, harassing, and expensive war which so long prevailed with the Indian tribes inhabiting the peninsula of Florida, has happily been terminated; whereby our army has been relieved from a service of the most disagreeable character, and the Treasury from a large

expenditure. Some casual outbreaks may occur, such as are incident to the close proximity of border settlers and the Indians; but these, as in all other cases, may be left to the care of the local authorities, aided, when occasion may require, by the forces of the United States."

The President does not tell by what treaty of peace this war was terminated, nor by what great battle it was brought to a conclusion: and there were none such to be told—either of treaty negotiated, or of battle fought. The war had died out of itself under the arrival of settlers attracted to its theatre by the Florida armed occupation act. No sooner did the act pass, giving land to each settler who should remain in the disturbed part of the territory five years, than thousands repaired to the spot. They went with their arms and ploughs—the weapons of war in one hand and the implements of husbandry in the other—their families, flocks and herds, established themselves in blockhouses, commenced cultivation, and showed that they came to stay, and intended to stay. Bred to the rifle and the frontier, they were an overmatch for the Indians in their own mode of warfare; and, interested in the peace of the country, they soon succeeded in obtaining it. The war died out under their presence, and no person could tell when, nor how; for there was no great treaty held, or great battle fought, to signalize its conclusion. And this is the way to settle all Indian wars—the cheap, effectual and speedy way to do it: land to the armed settler, and rangers, when any additional force is wanted—rangers, not regulars.

But a government bank, under the name of exchequer, was the prominent and engrossing feature of the message. It was the same paper-money machine, borrowed from the times of Sir Robert Walpole, which had been recommended to Congress at the previous session and had been so unanimously repulsed by all parties. Like its predecessor it ignored a gold and silver currency, and promised paper. The phrases "sound currency"—"sound circulating medium"—"safe bills convertible at will into specie," figured throughout the scheme; and to make this government paper a local as well as a national currency, the denomination of its notes was to be carried down at the start to the low figure of five dollars—involving the necessity of reducing it to one dollar as soon as the banishment of specie which it would create should raise the usual demand for smaller paper. To do him justice, his condensed argument in favor of this government paper, and against the gold and silver currency of the constitution, is here given:

"There can be but three kinds of public currency: 1st. Gold and silver; 2d. The paper of State institutions; or, 3d. A representative of the precious metals, provided by the general government, or under its authority. The sub-treasury system rejected the last, in any form; and, as it was believed that no reliance could be placed on the issues of local institutions, for the purposes of general circulation, it necessarily and unavoidably adopted specie as the exclusive currency for its own use. And this must ever be the case, unless one of the other kinds be used. The choice, in the present state of public sentiment, lies between an exclusive specie currency on the one hand, and government issues of some kind on the other. That these issues cannot be made by a chartered institution, is supposed to be conclusively settled. They must be made, then, directly by government agents. For several years past, they have been thus made in the form of treasury notes, and have answered a valuable purpose. Their usefulness has been limited by their being transient and temporary; their ceasing to bear interest at given periods, necessarily causes their speedy return, and thus restricts their range of circulation; and being used only in the disbursements of government, they cannot reach those points where they are most required. By rendering their use permanent, to the moderate extent already mentioned, by offering no inducement for their return, and by exchanging them for coin and other values, they will constitute, to a certain extent, the general currency so much needed to maintain the internal trade of the country. And this is the exchequer plan, so far as it may operate in furnishing a currency."

It would seem impossible to carry a passion for paper money, and of the worst kind, that of government paper, farther than President Tyler did; but he found it impossible to communicate his passion to Congress, which repulsed all the exchequer schemes with the promptitude which was due to an unconstitutional, pernicious, and gratuitous novelty. The low state of the public credit, the impossibility of making a loan, and the empty state of the Treasury, were the next topics in the message.

"I cannot forego the occasion to urge its importance to the credit of the government in a financial point of view. The great necessity of resorting to every proper and becoming expedient, in order to place the Treasury on a footing of the highest respectability, is entirely obvious. The credit of the government may be regarded as the very soul of the government itself—a principle of vitality, without which all its movements are languid, and all its operations embarrassed. In this spirit the Executive felt itself bound, by the most imperative sense of duty, to submit to Congress, at its last session, the propriety of making a specific pledge of the land fund, as the basis for the negotiation of the loans authorized to be contracted. I then thought that such an application of the public domain would, without doubt, have placed at the command of the government ample funds to relieve the Treasury from the temporary embarrassments under which it labored. American credit had suffered a considerable shock in Europe, from the large indebtedness of the States, and the temporary inability of some of them to meet the interest on their debts. The utter and disastrous prostration of the United States Bank of Pennsylvania had contributed largely to increase the sentiment of distrust, by reason of the loss and ruin sustained by the holders of its stock—a large portion of whom were foreigners, and many of whom were alike ignorant of our political organization, and of our actual responsibilities. It was the anxious desire of the Executive that, in the effort to negotiate the loan abroad, the American negotiator might be able to point the money-lender to the fund mortgaged for the redemption of the principal and interest of any loan he might contract, and thereby vindicate the government from all suspicion of bad faith, or inability to meet its engagements. Congress differed from the Executive in this view of the subject. It became, nevertheless, the duty of the Executive to resort to every expedient in its power to negotiate the authorized loan. After a failure to do so in the American market, a citizen of high character and talent was sent to Europe—with no better success; and thus the mortifying spectacle has been presented, of the inability of this government to obtain a loan so small as not in the whole to amount to more than one-fourth of its ordinary annual income; at a time when the governments of Europe, although involved in debt, and with their subjects heavily burdened with taxation, readily obtain loans of any amount at a greatly reduced rate of interest. It would be unprofitable to look further into this anomalous state of things; but I cannot conclude without adding, that, for a government which has paid off its debts of two wars with the largest maritime power of Europe, and now owing a debt which is almost next to nothing, when compared with its boundless resources—a government the strongest in the world, because emanating from the popular will, and firmly rooted in the affections of a great and free people—and whose fidelity to its engagements has never been questioned—for such a government to have tendered to the capitalists of other countries an opportunity for a small investment of its stock, and yet to have failed, implies either the most unfounded distrust in its good faith, or a purpose, to obtain which, the course pursued is the most fatal which could have been adopted. It has now become obvious to all men that the government must look to its own means for supplying its wants; and it is consoling to know that these means are altogether adequate for the object. The exchequer, if adopted, will greatly aid in bringing about this result. Upon what I regard as a well-founded supposition, that its bills would be readily sought for by the public creditors, and that the issue would, in a short time, reach the maximum of \$15,000,000, it is obvious that \$10,000,000 would thereby be added to the available means of the treasury, without cost or charge. Nor can I fail to urge the great and beneficial effects which would be produced in aid of all the active pursuits of life. Its effects upon the solvent State banks, while it would force into liquidation those of an opposite character, through its weekly settlements, would be highly beneficial; and, with the advantages of a sound currency, the restoration of confidence and credit would follow, with a numerous train of blessings. My convictions are most strong that these benefits would flow from the adoption of this measure; but, if the result should be adverse, there is this security in connection with it—that the law creating it may be repealed at the pleasure of the legislature, without the slightest implication of its good faith."

It is impossible to read this paragraph without a feeling of profound mortification at seeing the low and miserable condition to which the public credit had sunk, both at home and abroad; and equally mortifying to see the wretched expedients which were relied upon to restore it: a government bank, issuing paper founded on its credit and revenues, and a hypothecation of the lands, their proceeds to help to bolster up the slippery and frail edifice of governmental paper: the United States unable to make a loan to the amount of one-fourth of its revenues! unable to borrow five millions of dollars! unable to borrow any thing, while the overloaded governments of Europe could borrow as much as they pleased. It was indeed a low point of depressed credit—the lowest that the United States had ever seen since the declaration of Independence. It was a state of humiliation and disgrace which could not be named without offering some reason for its existence; and that reason was given: it was the "disastrous prostration," as it was called—the crimes and bankruptcy, as should have been called, of the Pennsylvania Bank of the United States! that bank which, in adding Pennsylvania to its name, did not change its identity, or its nature; and which for ten long years had been the cherished idol of the President, his Secretary of State, and his exchequer orator on the floor of the House—for which General Jackson had been condemned and vituperated—and on the continued existence of which the whole prosperity of the government and the people, and their salvation from poverty and misery, was made to depend. That bank was now given as the cause of the woful plight into which the public credit was fallen—and truly so given! for while its plunderings were enormous, its crimes were still greater: and the two put together—an hundred millions plundered, and a mass of crimes committed—the effect upon the American name was such as to drive it with disgrace from every exchange in Europe. And the former champions of the bank, uninstructed by experience, unabashed by previous appalling mistakes, now lavish the same encomiums on an exchequer bank which they formerly did on a national bank; and challenge the same faith for one which they had invoked for the other. The exchequer is now, according to them, the sole hope of the country: the independent treasury and hard money, its only danger. Yet the exchequer was repulsed—the independent treasury and gold was established: and the effect, that that same country which was unable to borrow five millions of dollars, has since borrowed many ten millions, and is now paying a premium of 20 per centum—actually paying twenty dollars on the hundred—to purchase the privilege of paying loans before they are due.

CHAPTER CX.

REPEAL OF THE BANKRUPT ACT: MR. BENTON'S SPEECH; EXTRACTS.

The spectacle was witnessed in relation to the repeal of this act which has rarely been seen before—a repeal of a great act of national legislation by the same Congress that passed it—by the same members sitting in the same seats—and the repeal approved by the same President who had approved the enactment. It was a homage to the will of the people, and the result of the general condemnation which the act received from the community. It had been passed as a party measure: its condemnation was general without regard to party: and the universality of the sentiment against it was honorable to the virtue and intelligence of the people. In the commencement of the session 1842-'43, motions were made in both Houses to repeal the act; and in the Senate the practical bad working of the act, and of the previous act, was shown as an evidence of the unfruitfulness of the whole system, and of the justice and wisdom of leaving the whole relation of debtor and creditor in relation to insolvency, or bankruptcy, to the insolvent laws of the States. In offering a petition in the Senate for the repeal of the act from the State of Vermont, Mr. Benton said:

"He would take the opportunity which the presentation of this petition offered, to declare that, holding the bankrupt act to be unconstitutional at six different points (the extinction of the debt without the consent of a given majority of the creditors being at the head of these points), he would vote for no repeal which would permit the act to continue in force for the trial of depending cases, unless with provisions which would bring the action of the law within the constitution. To say nothing, at present, of other points of unconstitutionality, he limited himself to the abolition of debts without the consent of a given majority of the creditors. This, he held, no power in our country can do. Congress can only go as far as the bankrupt systems of England and other countries go; and that is, to require the consent of a given majority of the creditors (four-fifths in number and value in England and Scotland), and that founded upon a judicial certificate of integrity by the commissioners who examined the case, and approved afterwards by the Lord Chancellor. Upon these principles only could Congress act: upon these principles the Congress of 1800 acted, in making a bankrupt act: and to these principles he would endeavor to conform the action of the present act so long as it might run. He held all the certificates granted by the courts to be null and void; and that the question of the validity would be carried before the courts, and before the tribunal of public opinion. The federal judges decided the alien and sedition law to be constitutional. The people reversed that decision, and put down the men who held it. This bankrupt act was much more glaringly unconstitutional—much more immoral—and called more loudly upon the people to rise against it. If he was a United States judge, he would decide the act to be unconstitutional. If he was a State court, and one of these certificates of discharge from debts should be pleaded in bar before him, on an action brought for the recovery of the old debt, he would treat the certificate as a nullity, and throw it out of court. If commanded by the Supreme Court, he would resign first. The English law held all bankrupts, whose certificates were not signed by the given majority of the creditors, to be *uncertificated*; and, as such, he held all these to be who had received certificates under our law. They had no certificate of discharge from a given majority of the creditors; and were, therefore, what the English law called '*uncertificated bankrupts.*' He said the bankrupt systems formed the creditors into a partnership for the management of the debtor's estate, and his discharge from debt; and, in this partnership, a given majority acted for the whole, all having the same interest in what was lost or saved; and, therefore, to be governed by a given majority, doing what was best for the whole. But even to this there were limitations. The four-fifths could not release the debt of the remaining fifth, except upon a certificate of integrity from the commissioners who tried the case, and a final approval by the Lord Chancellor. The law made itself party to the discharge, as it does in a case of divorce, and for the sake of good morals; and required the judicial certificate of integrity, without which the release of four-fifths of the creditors would not extinguish the debt of the other fifth. It is only in this way that Congress can act. It can only act according to the established principles of the bankrupt systems. It had no inherent or supreme authority over debts. It could not abolish debts as it pleased. It could not confound bankruptcy and insolvency, and so get hold of all debts, and sweep them off as it pleased. All this was despotism, such as only could be looked for in a government which had no limits, either on its moral or political powers. The attempt to confound insolvency and bankruptcy, and to make Congress supreme over both, was the most daring attack on the constitution, on the State laws, on the rights of property, and on public morals, which the history of Europe or America exhibited. There was no parallel to it in Europe or America. It was repudiation—universal repudiation of all debts—at the will of the debtor. The law was subversive of civil society; and he called upon Congress, the State legislatures, the federal and State judiciaries—and, above all, the people—to brand it for unconstitutionality and immorality, and put it down.

"Mr. B. said he had laid down the law, but he would refer to the *forms* which the wisdom of the law provided for executing itself. These *forms* were the highest evidences of the law. They were framed by men learned in the law—approved by the courts—and studied by the apprentices to the law. They should also be studied by the journeymen—by the professors—and by the ermined judges. In this case, especially, they should be so studied. Bankruptcy was a branch of the law but little studied in our country. The mass of the community were uninformed upon it; and the latitudinarians, who could find no limits to the power of our government were daringly presuming upon the general ignorance, by undertaking to confound bankruptcy and insolvency, and claiming for Congress a despotic power over both. This daring attempt must be chastised. Congress must be driven back within the pale of the constitution; and for that purpose, the principles of the bankrupt systems must be made known to the people. The *forms* are one of the best modes of doing this: and here are the *forms* of a bankrupt's certificate in Great Britain—the country from which our constitution borrowed the system. [Mr. B. then read from Jacob's Law Dictionary, title *Bankruptcy*, at the end of the title, the *three* forms of the certificates which were necessary to release a debtor from his debts.] The first form was that of the commissioners who examined the case, and who certified to the integrity of the bankrupt, and that he had conformed in all particulars to the act. The second form was that of the certificate of four-fifths of his creditors, '*allowing him to be discharged from his debts.*' The third was the certificate of the Lord Chancellor, certifying that notice of these two certificates having been published for twenty-one days in the London Gazette, and no cause being shown to the contrary, the certificates granted by the commissioners and by the creditors were '*confirmed.*' Then, and not till then, could the debtor be discharged from his debts; and with all this, the act of 1800 in the United States perfectly agreed, only taking two-thirds instead of four-fifths of the creditors. Congress could only absolve debts in this way, and that among the proper subjects of a bankrupt law: and the moral sense of the community must revolt against any attempt to do it in any other form. The present act was repudiation—criminal repudiation, as far as any one chose to repudiate—and must be put down by the community."

On the question for the repeal of the act, Mr. Benton took occasion to show it to be an invasion of the rights of the States, over the ordinary relations of debtor and creditor within their own limits, and a means of eating up estates to the loss of both debtor and creditor, and the enrichment of assignees, who make the settlement of the estate a life-long business, and often a legacy to his children.

"A question cannot arise between two neighbors about a dozen of eggs, without being liable to be taken from the custody of the laws of the States, and brought up to the federal courts. And now, when this doctrine that insolvency and bankruptcy are the same, if a continuance of the law is to be contrived, it must be done in conformity with such a fallacy. The law has proved to be nothing but a great insolvent law, for the abolition of debts, for the benefit of debtors; and would it be maintained that a permanent system ought to be built up on such a foundation as that?

"Some months ago, he read in a Philadelphia paper a notice to creditors to come forward for a dividend of half a cent in the dollar, in a case of bankruptcy pending under the old law of 1800, since the year 1801. And, three or four days ago, he read a notice in a London paper, calling on creditors to come in for a dividend of five-sixths of a penny in the pound, in a case of bankruptcy pending since the year 1793. Here has been a case where the waste of property has been going on for fifty years in England, and another case where it has been going on in this country forty-one or forty-two years. He had been himself twenty-three years in the Senate, and, during that time, various efforts were made to revive the old law of 1800 in some shape or other; but never, till last session, in the shape in which the present law passed. And how could this law be expected to stand, when even the law of 1800 (which was in reality a bankrupt law) could not stand; but was, in the first year of its operation, condemned by the whole country?"

The passage of the act had been a reproach to Congress: its repeal should do them honor, and still more the people, under whose manifest and determined will it was to be done. The repeal bill readily passed the Senate, and then went to the House, where it was quickly passed, and under pressure of the previous question, by a vote 128 to 98. The history of the passage of these two measures (bankrupt and distribution) each of which came to an untimely end, is one of those legislative arcana which should be known, that such legislation may receive the reprobation which it deserves. The public only sees the outside proceeding, and imagines a wise and patriotic motive for the enactment of important laws. Too often there is neither wisdom nor patriotism in such enactment, but bargain, and selfishness, and duresse of circumstances. So it was in this case. The misconduct and misfortunes of the banks and the vices inherent in paper money, which had so long been the currency of the country, had filled the Union with pecuniary distress, and created an immense body of insolvent debtors, estimated by some at five hundred thousand: and all these were clamorous for a bankrupt act. The State of Mississippi was one of those most sorely afflicted with this state of things, and most earnest for the act. Her condition governed the conduct of her senators, and their votes made the bankrupt act, and passed the fiscal bank through the Senate. Such are the mysteries of legislation.

A bankrupt act, though expressly authorized by the constitution, had never been favored by the American people. It was tried fifty years ago, and condemned upon a two years' experience. Persevering efforts had since been made for a period of twenty years to obtain another act, but in vain. It was the opinion of Mr. Lowndes, expressed at the last session that he served, that no act framed upon the principles of the British system would ever be suitable to our country—that the complex and expensive machinery of the system, so objectionable in England, where debtors and creditors were comparatively near together, would be intolerable in the United States, where they were so widely separated, and the courts so sparsely scattered over the land, and so inconvenient to the majority of parties and witnesses. He believed a simple system might be adopted, reducing the process to a transaction between the debtor and his creditors, in which courts would have but little to do except to give effect to their agreement. The principle of his plan was that there should be a meeting of the creditors, either on the invitation of the failing debtor, or the summons of a given number of creditors; and when together, and invested with power to examine into the debtor's affairs, and to examine books and take testimony, that they themselves, by a given majority of two-thirds or three-fourths in value, should decide every question, make a *pro rata* division of the effects, and grant a certificate of release: the release to be of right if the effects were taken. This simple process would dispense with the vexatious question, of what constitutes an act of bankruptcy? And substitute for it the broad inquiry of failing circumstances—in the solution of which, those most interested would be the judges. It would also save the devouring expenses of costs and fees, and delays equally devouring, and the commissioners that must be paid, and the assignees who frequently become the beneficiaries of the debtor's effects—taking what he collects for his own fees, and often making a life estate of it. The estate of a bankrupt, in the hands of an assignee, Mr. Randolph was accustomed to call, "a lump of butter in a dog's mouth;" a designation which it might sometimes bear from the rapidity with which it was swallowed; but more frequently it was a bone to gnaw, and to be long gnawed before it was gnawed up. As an evidence of this, Mr. Benton read a notice from a Philadelphia paper, published while this debate was going on, inviting creditors to come forward and receive from the assignee a dividend of half a cent in the dollar, in a case of bankruptcy under the old act of 1800; also a notice in a London paper for the creditors to come in and receive a dividend of five-sixths of a penny in the pound in a case depending since 1793—the assignees respectively having been administering, one of them forty-one years, and the other fifty-two years, the estate of the debtor; and probably collecting each year about as much as paid his own fees.

The system has become nearly intolerable in England. As far back as the year 1817, the British Parliament, moved by the pervading belief of the injustice and abuses under their bankrupt laws, appointed a commissioner to examine into the subject, and to report the result of their investigation. It was done; and such a mass of iniquity revealed, as to induce the Lord Chancellor to say that the system was a disgrace to the country—that the assignees had no mercy either upon the debtor or his creditors—and that it would be better to repeal every law on the subject. The system, however, was too much interwoven with the business of the country to be abandoned. The report of the commissioners only led to a revision of the laws and attempted ameliorations; the whole of which were disregarded by our Congress of 1841, as were the principles of all previous bankrupt acts either in Great Britain, on the European Continent, or in the United States. That Congress abandoned the fundamental principle of all bankrupt systems—that of a proceeding of the creditors for their own benefit, and made it practically an insolvent law at the will of the debtor, for the abolition of his debt at his own pleasure. Iniquitous in itself, vicious in its mode of being passed, detested by the community, the life of the act was short and ignominious. Mr. Buchanan said it would be repealed in two years: and it was. Yet it was ardently contended for. Crowds attended Congress to demand it. Hundreds of thousands sent up their petitions. The whole number of bankrupts was stated by the most moderate at one hundred thousand: and Mr. Walker declared in his place that, if the act was not passed, thousands of unfortunate debtors would have to wear the chains of slavery, or be exiled from their native land.

CHAPTER CXI.

MILITARY ACADEMY AND ARMY EXPENSES.

The instincts of the people have been against this academy from the time it took its present form under the act of 1812, and those subsequent and subsidiary to it: many efforts have been made to abolish or to modify it: and all unsuccessful—partly from the intrinsic difficulty of correcting any abuse—partly from the great number interested in the Academy as an eleemosynary institution of which they have the benefit—and partly from the wrong way in which the reformers go to work. They generally move to abolish the whole system, and are instantly met by Washington's recommendation in favor of it. In the mean time Washington never saw such an institution as now shelters behind his name; and possibly would never have been in the army, except as a private soldier, if it had existed when he was a young man. He never recommended such an academy as we have: he never dreamed of such a thing: he recommended just the reverse of it, in recommending that cadets, serving in the field with the companies to which they were attached, and receiving the pay, clothing, and ration of a sergeant, should be sent—such of them as showed a stomach for the hardships, as well as a taste for the pleasures and honors of the service, and who also showed a capacity for the two higher branches of the profession (engineering and artillery)—to West Point, to take instruction from officers in these two branches of the military art: and no more. At this session one of the usual movements was made against it—an attack upon the institution in its annual appropriation bill, by moving to strike out the appropriation for its support, and substitute a bill for its abolition. Mr. Hale made the motion, and was supported in it by several members. Mr. McKay, chairman of the committee, which had the appropriation bill in charge, felt himself bound to defend it, but in doing so to exclude the conclusion that he was favorable to the academy. Begging gentlemen, therefore, to withdraw their motion, he went on to say:

"He was now, and always had been, in favor of a very material alteration in the organization of this institution. He did not think that the government should educate more young men than were necessary to fill the annual vacancies in the army. It was beyond dispute, that the number now educated was more than the average annual vacancies in the army required; and hence the number of supernumerary second lieutenants—which he believed was now something like seventy; and would be probably thirty more the next year. This, however, did not present the true state of the question. In a single year, in consequence of an order issued from the war department, that all the officers who were in the civil service of the railroad and canal companies, &c., should join their respective regiments, there were upwards of one hundred resignations. Now, if these resignations had not taken place, the army would have been overloaded with supernumerary second lieutenants. He was for reducing the number of cadets, but at the same time would make a provision by which parents and guardians should have the privilege of sending their sons and wards there to be educated, at their own expense. This (Mr. M. said) was the system adopted in Great Britain; and it appeared, by a document he had in his hand, that there were three hundred and twenty gentlemen cadets, and fifteen officers educated at the English Military Academy, at a much less expense than it required to educate two hundred and twenty cadets at West Point. He agreed with much of what had been said by the gentleman from Connecticut, Mr. Seymour, that it would be an amelioration of our military service, to open the door of promotion to meritorious non-commissioned officers and privates. Under the present system, no man who was a non-commissioned officer or private, however meritorious, had the least chance of promotion. It was true that there were instances of such men getting commissions, but they were very rare; and the consequence was, that the ranks of the army were filled with some of the worst men in the country, and desertions had prevailed to an enormous extent. Mr. McK. here gave from the documents, the number of annual desertions, from the year 1830 to 1836, showing an average of one thousand. He would not now, however, enlarge on this subject, but would reserve his remarks till the bill for reorganizing the academy, which he understood was to be reported by the Military Committee, should come in."

Mr. McKay was not counted among the orators of the House: he made no pretension to fine speaking: but he was one of those business, sensible, upright men, who always spoke sense and reason, and to the point, and generally gave more information to the House in a few sentences than could often be found in one of the most pretentious speeches. Of this character were the remarks which he made on this occasion; and in the four statements that he made, *first*, that upwards of one hundred West Point officers had resigned their commissions in one year when ordered to quit civil service and join their corps; *secondly*, that there was a surplus of seventy graduates at that time for whom there was no place in the army; *thirdly*, that at the English Military Academy, three hundred and thirty-five cadets and officers were instructed at much less expense than two hundred and twenty with us; *fourthly*, that the annual desertions from the rank and file of the army had averaged one thousand men per annum for six years together, these desertions resulting from want of promotion and disgust at a service which was purely necessary. Mr. McKay was followed by another speaker of the same class with himself—Mr. Cave Johnson, of Tennessee; who stood up and said:

> "That there was no certainty that the bill to be reported by the Military Committee, which the gentleman referred to, would be reached this session; and he was therefore for effecting a reform now that the subject was before them. He would, therefore, suggest to the gentleman from New Hampshire to withdraw his amendment, and submit another, to the following effect: That no money appropriated in this bill, or hereafter to be appropriated, shall be applied to the payment of any cadet hereafter to be appointed; and the terms of service of those who have warrants now in the academy shall be held to cease from and after four years from the time of their respective appointments. The limitation of this appropriation now, would put an end to the academy, unless the House would act on the propositions which would be hereafter made. He was satisfied it ought to be abolished, and he would at once abolish it, but for the remarks of his friend from North Carolina; he therefore hoped his friend from New Hampshire would adopt the suggestions which had been made."

Mr. Harralson, of Georgia, chairman of the Committee on Military Affairs, felt himself called upon by his position to come to the defence of the institution, which he did in a way to show that it was indefensible. He

> "Intimated that that committee would propose some reductions in the number of cadets; and when that proposition came before the House, these amendments could be appropriately offered. The proposition would be made to reduce the number of the cadets to the wants of the army. But this appropriation should now be made; and if, by any reductions hereafter made, it should be found more than adequate to the wants of the institution, the balance would remain in the Treasury, and would not be lost to the country. He explained the circumstances under which, in 1836, some persons educated as cadets at West Point became civil engineers, and accepted employment on projected lines of railroad; and asserted that no class of our countrymen were more ready to obey the call of their country, in any exigency which might arise."

Mr. Orlando Ficklin, of Illinois, not satisfied with the explanations made by the chairman on military affairs, returned to the charge of the one hundred resignations in one year; and said:

> "He had listened to the apology or excuse rendered by the chairman of the Committee on Military Affairs, for the cadets who resigned in 1836. And what was that excuse? Why, forsooth, though they had been educated at the government expense, yet, because they could get better pay by embarking in other pursuits, they deserted the service of the country which had educated them, and prepared them for her service. He did not intend to detain the committee at present, but he must be permitted to say to those who were in favor of winding up the concern, that they ought not to vote an appropriation of a single dollar to that institution, unless the same bill contained a provision, in language as emphatic as it could be made, declaring that this odious, detestable, and aristocratic institution, shall be brought to a close. If it did not cost this government a single dollar, he would still be unwilling that it should be kept up. He was not willing that the door of promotion should be shut against the

honest and deserving soldier, and that a few dandies and band-box heroes, educated at that institution, should enjoy the monopoly of all the offices. Mr. F. adverted to the present condition of the army. It was filled up, he said, by foreigners. Native Americans, to whom they should naturally look as the defenders of the country, were deterred from entering it. It would be well, he thought, to have a committee of investigation, that the secrets of the prison-house might be disclosed, and its abuses brought to light."

Mr. Black, of Georgia, proposed an amendment, compelling the cadets to serve ten years, and keeping up the number: upon which Mr. Hale remarked:

"The amendment of the gentleman from Georgia would seem to imply that there were not officers enough: whereas the truth was there were more than enough. The difficulty was, there were already too many. The Army Register showed a list already of seventy supernumeraries; and more were being turned out upon us every year. The gentleman from New York had made a most unhappy illustration of the necessity for educating cadets for the army, by comparing them with the midshipmen in the navy. What was the service rendered by midshipmen on board our national vessels? Absolutely none. They were of no sort of use; and precisely so was it with these cadets. He denied that General Washington ever recommended a military academy like the present institution; and, if he had done so, he would, instead of proclaiming it, have endeavored to shield his great name from such a reproach."

The movement ended as usual, in showing necessity for a reform, and in failing to get it.

CHAPTER CXII.

EMIGRATION TO THE COLUMBIA RIVER, AND FOUNDATION OF ITS SETTLEMENT BY AMERICAN CITIZENS: FREMONT'S FIRST EXPEDITION.

The great event of carrying the Anglo-Saxon race to the shore of the Pacific Ocean, and planting that race firmly on that sea, took place at this time, beginning in 1842, and largely increasing in 1843. It was not an act of the government, leading the people and protecting them; but, like all the other great emigrations and settlements of that race on our continent, it was the act of the people, going forward without government aid or countenance, establishing their possession, and compelling the government to follow with its shield, and spread it over them. So far as the action of the government was concerned, it operated to endanger our title to the Columbia, to prevent emigration, and to incur the loss of the country. The first great step in this unfortunate direction was the treaty of joint occupation, as it was called, of 1818; by which the British, under the fallacious idea of mutuality, where there was nothing mutual, were admitted to a delusive joint occupation, with ourselves, intended to be equal—but which quickly became exclusive on their part: and was obliged to become so, from the power and organization of their Hudson Bay Company, already flanking the country and ready to cross over and cover it. It is due to the memory of President Monroe, under whose administration this unfortunate treaty was made, to say that, since the publication of the first volume of this View, the author has been informed by General Jesup (who had the fact from Mr. Monroe himself at the time), that his instructions had not authorized this arrangement (which in fact the commissioners intimated in their correspondence), and only after much hesitation prevailed on himself to send it to the Senate. That treaty was for ten years, and the second false step was in its indefinite extension by another of 1828, until one or the other of the parties should give notice for its discontinuance—the most insidious and pernicious of all agreements, being so easy to be adopted, and so hard to be got rid of. The third great blunder was in not settling the Oregon question in the Ashburton negotiation, when we had a strong hold upon the British government in its earnest desire to induce us to withdraw our northeastern boundary from the neighborhood of Lower Canada, and to surrender a part of Maine for the road from Halifax to Quebec. The fourth step in this series of governmental blunders, was the recommendation of President Tyler to discountenance emigration to Oregon, by withholding land from the emigrants, until the two governments had settled the title—a contingency too remote to be counted upon within any given period, and which every year's delay would make more difficult. The title to the country being thus endangered by the acts of the government, the saving of it devolved upon the people—and they saved it. In 1842, incited by numerous newspaper publications, upwards of a thousand American emigrants went to the country, making their long pilgrimage overland from the frontiers of Missouri, with their wives and children, their flocks and herds, their implements of husbandry and weapons of defence—traversing the vast inclined plane to the base of the Rocky Mountains, crossing that barrier (deemed impassable by Europeans), and descending the wide slope which declines from the mountains to the Pacific. Six months would be consumed in this journey, filled with hardships, beset by dangers from savage hostility, and only to be prosecuted in caravans of strength and determination. The Burnets and Applegates from Missouri were among the first leaders, and in 1843, some two thousand more joined the first emigration. To check these bold adventurers was the object of the government: to encourage them, was the object of some Western members of Congress, on whom (in conjunction with the people) the task of saving the Columbia evidently devolved. These members were ready for their work, and promptly began. Early in the session, Mr. Linn, a senator from Missouri, introduced a bill for the purpose, of which these were the leading provisions:

> "That the President of the United States is hereby authorized and required to cause to be erected, at suitable places and distances, a line of stockade and blockhouse forts, not exceeding five in number, from some point on the Missouri and Arkansas rivers into the best pass for entering the valley of the Oregon; and, also, at or near the mouth of the Columbia River.

> "That provision hereafter shall be made by law to secure and grant six hundred and forty acres, or one section of land, to every white male inhabitant of the territory of Oregon, of the age of eighteen years and upward, who shall cultivate and use the same for five consecutive years; or to his heir or heirs-at-law, if such there be, in case of his decease. And to every such

inhabitant or cultivator (being a married man) there shall be granted, in addition, one hundred and sixty acres to the wife of said husband, and the like quantity of one hundred and sixty acres to the father for each child under the age of eighteen years he may have, or which may be born within the five years aforesaid.

"That no sale, alienation, or contract of any kind, shall be valid, of such lands, before the patent is issued therefor; nor shall the same be liable to be taken in execution, or bound by any judgment, mortgage, or lien, of any kind, before the patent is so issued; and all pretended alienations or contracts for alienating such lands, made before the issuing of the patents, shall be null and void against the settler himself, his wife, or widow, or against his heirs-at-law, or against purchasers, after the issuing of the patent.

"That the President is hereby authorized and required to appoint two additional Indian agents, with a salary of two thousand dollars each, whose duty it shall be (under his direction and control) to superintend the interests of the United States with any or every Indian tribe west of any agency now established by law.

"That the sum of one hundred thousand dollars be appropriated, out of any money in the Treasury not otherwise appropriated, to carry into effect the provisions of this act.

"SEC. 2. *And be it further enacted,* That the civil and criminal jurisdiction of the supreme court and district courts of the territory of Iowa, be, and the same is hereby, extended over that part of the Indian territories lying west of the present limits of the said territory of Iowa, and south of the forty-ninth degree of north latitude, and west of the Rocky Mountains, and north of the boundary line between the United States and the Republic of Texas, not included within the limits of any State; and also, over the Indian territories comprising the Rocky Mountains and the country between them and the Pacific Ocean, south of fifty-four degrees and forty minutes of north latitude, and north of the forty-second degree of north latitude; and justices of the peace may be appointed for the said territory, in the same manner and with the same powers as now provided by law in relation to the territory of Iowa: *Provided,* That any subject of the government of Great Britain, who shall have been arrested under the provisions of this act for any crime alleged to have been committed within the territory westward of the Stony or Rocky Mountains, while the same remains free and open to the vessels, citizens, and subjects of the United States and of Great Britain, pursuant to stipulations between the two powers, shall be delivered up, on proof of his being such British subject, to the nearest or most convenient authorities having cognizance of such offence by the laws of Great Britain, for the purpose of being prosecuted and tried according to such laws.

"SEC. 3. *And be it further enacted,* That one associate judge of the supreme court of the territory of Iowa, in addition to the number now authorized by law, may, in the discretion of the President, be appointed, to hold his office by the same tenure and for the same time, receive the same compensation, and possess all the powers and authority conferred by law upon the associate judges of the said territory; and one judicial district shall be organized by the said supreme court, in addition to the existing number, in reference to the jurisdiction conferred by this act; and a district court shall be held in the said district by the judge of the supreme court, at such times and places as the said court shall direct; and the said district court shall possess all the powers and authority vested in the present district courts of the said territory, and may, in like manner, appoint its own clerk.

"SEC. 4. *And be it further enacted,* That any justice of the peace, appointed in and for the territories described in the second section of this act, shall have power to cause all offenders against the laws of the United States to be arrested by such persons as they shall appoint for that purpose, and to commit such offenders to safe custody for trial, in the same cases and in the manner provided by law in relation to the Territory of Iowa; and to cause the offenders so committed to be conveyed to the place appointed for the holding of a district court for the said Territory of Iowa, nearest and most convenient to the place of such commitment, there to be detained for trial, by such persons as shall be authorized for that purpose by any judge of the supreme court, or any justice of the peace of the said Territory; or where such offenders are British subjects, to cause them to be delivered to the nearest and most convenient British authorities, as hereinbefore provided; and the expenses of such commitment, removal, and detention, shall be paid in the same manner as provided by law in respect to the fees of the marshal of the said territory."

These provisions are all just and necessary for the accomplishment of their object, and carefully framed to promote emigration, and to avoid collisions with the British, or hostilities with the Indians. The land grants were the grand attractive feature to the emigrants: the provision for leaving British offenders to British jurisdiction was to avoid a clash of jurisdictions, and to be on an equality with the British settlers over whom the British Parliament had already extended the laws of Canada; and the boundaries within which our settlers were to be protected, were precisely those agreed upon three years later in a treaty between the two powers. The provisions were all necessary for their object, and carefully framed to avoid infraction of any part of the unfortunate treaty of 1818; but the bill encountered a strenuous, and for a long time a nearly balanced, opposition in the Senate—some opposed to the whole object of settling the country at any time—some to its present settlement, many to the fear of collision with the British subjects already there, or infraction of the treaty of 1818. Mr. McDuffie took broad ground against it.

"For whose benefit are we bound to pass this bill? Who are to go there, along the line of military posts, and take possession of the only part of the territory fit to occupy—that part lying upon the sea-coast, a strip less than one hundred miles in width; for, as I have already stated, the rest of the territory consists of mountains almost inaccessible, and low lands which are covered with stone and volcanic remains, where rain never falls, except during the spring; and even on the coast no rain falls, from April to October, and for the remainder of the year there is nothing but rain. Why, sir, of what use will this be for agricultural purposes? I would not for that purpose give a pinch of snuff for the whole territory. I wish to God we did not own it. I wish it was an impassable barrier to secure us against the intrusion of others. This is the character of the country. Who are we to send there? Do you think your honest farmers in Pennsylvania, New York, or even Ohio or Missouri, will abandon their farms to go upon any such enterprise as this? God forbid! if any man who is to go to that country, under the temptations of this bill, was my child—if he was an honest industrious man, I would say to him, for God's sake do not go there. You will not better your condition. You will exchange the comforts of home, and the happiness of civilized life, for the pains and perils of a precarious existence. But if I had a son whose conduct was such as made him a fit subject for Botany Bay, I would say in the name of God, go. This is my estimate of the importance of the settlement. Now, what are we to gain by making the settlement? In what shape are our expenditures there to be returned? When are we to get any revenue from the citizens of ours who go to that distant territory—3,300 miles from the seat of government, as I have it from the senator from Missouri? What return are they going to make us for protecting them with military posts, at the expense at the outset of $200,000, and swelling hereafter God knows how much—probably equalling the annual expenses of the Florida war. What will they return us for this enormous expense, after we have tempted them, by this bill, to leave their pursuits of honest industry, to go upon this wild and gambling adventure, in which their blood is to be staked?"

Besides repulsing the country as worthless, Mr. McDuffie argued that there was danger in taking possession of it—that the provisions of the bill conflicted with the stipulations of the treaty of 1818—and that Great Britain, though desirous of peace with the United States, would be forced into war in defence of her rights and honor. Mr. Calhoun was equally opposed as his colleague to the passage of the bill, but not for the same reasons. He deemed the country well worth having, and presenting great commercial advantages in communicating with China and Japan, which should not be lost.

"I do not agree with my eloquent and able colleague that the country is worthless. He has underrated it, both as to soil and climate. It contains a vast deal of land, it is true, that is barren and worthless; but not a little that is highly productive. To that may be added its commercial advantages, which will, in time, prove to be great. We must not overlook the important events to which I have alluded as having recently occurred in the Eastern portion of Asia. As great as they are, they are but the beginning of a series of a similar character, which must follow at no distant day. What has taken place in China, will, in a few years, be followed in Japan, and all the eastern portions of that continent. Their ports, like the Chinese, will be opened, and the whole of that large portion of Asia, containing nearly half of the population and wealth of the globe, will be thrown open to the commerce of the world, and be placed within the pales of European and American intercourse and civilization. A vast market will be created, and a mighty impulse will be given to commerce. No small portion of the share that would fall to us with this populous and industrious portion of the globe, is destined to pass through the ports of the Oregon Territory to the valley of the Mississippi, instead of taking the circuitous and long voyage round Cape Horn; or the still longer, round the Cape of Good Hope. It is mainly because I place this high estimate on its prospective value, that I am so solicitous to preserve it, and so adverse to this bill, or any other precipitate measure which might terminate in its loss. If I thought less of its value, or if I regarded our title less clear, my opposition would be less decided."

Infraction of the treaty and danger of war—the difficulty and expense of defending a possession so remote—the present empty condition of the treasury—were further reasons urged by Mr. Calhoun in favor of rejecting the bill; but having avowed himself in favor of saving our title to the country, it became necessary to show his mode of doing so, and fell upon the same plan to ripen and secure our title, which others believed was wholly relied upon by Great Britain to ripen and secure hers—Time! an element which only worked in favor of the possessor; and that possessor was now Great Britain. On this head he said:

"The question presents itself, how shall we preserve this country? There is only one means by which it can be; but that, fortunately, is the most powerful of all—*time. Time* is acting for us; and, if we shall have the wisdom to trust its operation, it will assert and maintain our right with resistless force, without costing a cent of money, or a drop of blood. There is often in the affairs of government, more efficiency and wisdom in non-action, than in action. All we want to effect our object in this case, is 'a wise and masterly inactivity.' Our population is rolling towards the shores of the Pacific, with an impetus greater than what we realize. It is one of those forward movements which leaves anticipation behind. In the period of thirty-two years which have elapsed since I took my seat in the other House, the Indian frontier has receded a thousand miles to the West. At that time, our population was much less than half what it is now. It was then increasing at the rate of about a quarter of a million annually; it is now not less than six hundred thousand; and still increasing at the rate of something more than three per cent. compound annually. At that rate, it will soon reach the yearly increase of a million. If to this be added, that the region west of Arkansas and the State of Missouri, and south of the Missouri River, is occupied by half civilized tribes, who have their lands secured to them by treaty (and which will prevent the spread of population in that direction), and that this great and increasing tide will be forced to take the comparatively narrow channel to the north of that river and south of our northern boundary, some conception may be formed of the strength with which the current will run in that direction, and how soon it will reach the eastern gorges of the Rocky Mountains. It will soon—far sooner than anticipated—reach the Rocky Mountains, and be ready to pour into the Oregon Territory, when it will come into our possession without resistance or struggle—or, if there should be resistance, it would be feeble and ineffectual. We would then be as much stronger there, comparatively, than Great Britain, as she is now stronger than we are; and it would then be as idle in her to attempt to assert and maintain her exclusive claim to the territory against us, as it would now be in us to attempt it against her. Let us be wise, and abide our time, and it will accomplish all that we desire, with far more certainty and with infinitely less sacrifice, than we can without it."

Mr. Calhoun averred and very truly, that his opposition to the bill did not grow out of any opposition to the growth of the West—declared himself always friendly to the interests of that great section of our country, and referred to his course when he was Secretary at war to prove it.

"I go back to the time when I was at the head of the War Department. At that early period I turned my attention particularly to the interest of the West. I saw that it required increased security to its long line of frontier, and greater facility of carrying on intercourse with the Indian tribes in that quarter, and to enable it to develope its resources—especially that of its fur-trade. To give the required security, I ordered a much larger portion of the army to that frontier; and to afford facility and protection for carrying on the fur-trade, the military posts were moved much higher up the Mississippi and Missouri rivers. Under the increased security and facility which these measures afforded, the fur-trade received a great impulse. It extended across the continent in a short time, to the Pacific, and north and south to the British and Mexican frontiers; yielding in a few years, as stated by the Senator from Missouri [Mr. Linn], half a million of dollars annually. But I stopped not there. I saw that individual enterprise on our part, however great, could not successfully compete with the powerful incorporated Canadian and Hudson Bay Companies, and that additional measures were necessary to secure permanently our fur-trade. For that purpose I proposed to establish a post still higher up the Missouri, at the mouth of the Yellow Stone River, and to give such unity and efficiency to our intercourse and trade with the Indian tribes between our Western frontier and the Pacific ocean, as would enable our citizens engaged in the fur-trade to compete successfully with the British traders. Had the measures proposed been adopted, we would not now have to listen to the complaint, so frequently uttered in this discussion, of the loss of that trade."

The inconsistent argument of Mr. McDuffie, that the country was worthless, and yet that Great Britain would go to war for it, was thus answered by Mr. Linn:

"The senator from South Carolina somewhat inconsistently urges that the country is bleak, barren, volcanic, rocky, a waste always flooded when it is not parched; and insists that, worthless as it is, Great Britain will go at once to war for it. Strange that she should in 1818 have held so tenaciously to what is so worthless! Stranger still, that she should have stuck yet closer to it in 1827, when she had had still ampler time to learn the bootlessness of the possession! And strangest of all, that she should still cling to it with the grasp of death! Sir, I cannot for my life help thinking that she and the senator have formed a very different estimate of the territory, and that she is (as she ought to be) a good deal the better informed. She knows well its soil climate, and physical resources, and perfectly comprehends its commercial and geographical importance. And knowing all this, she was ready to sink all sense of justice, stifle all respect for our clear title, and hasten to root her interests in the soil, so as to secure the strong, even when most wrongful, title of possession."

The danger of waiting for Great Britain to strengthen her claim was illustrated by Mr. Linn, by what had happened in Maine. In 1814 she proposed to purchase the part she wanted. She afterwards endeavored to negotiate for a right of way across the State. Failing in that attempted negotiation, as in the offer to purchase, she boldly set up a claim to all she wanted—demanded it as matter of right—and obtained it by the Ashburton treaty—the United States paying Massachusetts and Maine for the dismembered part. Deprecating a like result from temporizing measures with respect to Oregon, Mr. Linn said:

"So little before 1813 or 1814 did Great Britain ever doubt your claim to the lately contested territory in Maine, that in 1814 she proposed to *purchase* that part of it which she desired. She next treated for a right of way. It was refused; and she then set up a claim to the soil. This method has sped no ill with her; for she has got what she wanted, AND MADE YOU PAY FOR IT. Her Oregon game is the same. She has set her heart upon a strip of territory north of the Oregon, and seems determined to pluck it from us, either by circumvention or force. Aware of the political as well as legal advantages of possession, she is strengthening hers in every way not too directly responsible. She is selecting and occupying the best lands, the most favorable sites. These she secures to the settlers under contracts. For any counteraction of yours, she may take, and is taking, possession of the whole territory. She has appropriated sites for mills, manufactories, and farms. If one of these has been abandoned for a better, she reverts to it, if a citizen of yours occupies it, and ejects him. She tells her people she will protect them in whatever they have laid, or may lay, their hands upon. If she can legitimately do this, why may not we? Is this a joint occupation of which she is to have the sole benefit? Had you as many citizens there as she, you would be compelled to protect them; and if you have not, why is it but because she keeps them off, and you refuse to offer them the inducements which she holds out? Give them a prospective grant of lands, and insure them the shelter of your laws, and they will soon congregate there in force enough to secure your rights and their own."

The losses already sustained by our citizens from the ravages of Indians, incited against them by the British Hudson Bay company, were stated by Mr. Linn upon good authority, to be five hundred men in lives taken in the first ten years of the joint occupation treaty, and half a million of dollars in property robbed or destroyed, besides getting exclusive possession of our soil, and the command of our own Indians within our own limits: and he then contrasted this backwardness to protect our own citizens on their own soil with the readiness to expend untold amounts on the protection of our citizens engaged in foreign commerce; and even in going to the coast of Africa to guard the freedom of the negro race.

"Wherever your sails whiten the sea, in no matter what clime, against no matter whom, the national arm stretches out its protection. Every where but in this unhappy territory, the persons and the pursuits of your citizens are watched over. You count no cost when other interests are concerned, when other rights are assailed; but you recoil here from a trifling appropriation to an object of the highest national importance, because it enlists no sectional influence. Contrast, for instance, your supineness about the Oregon Territory, with your alacrity to establish, for guarding the slave coast and Liberia, a squadron costing $600,000 annually, and which you have bound yourself by treaty to keep up for five years, with great exposure of lives and vessels. By stipulation, eighty guns (one-twelfth of your force afloat) is kept upon this service; and, as your naval expenditure amounts to about seven millions a year, this (its twelfth part) will make, in five years, three millions bestowed in watching the coast of Africa, and guarding the freedom of the negro race! For this you lavish millions; and you grudge $100,000 to the great American and national object of asserting your territorial rights and settling your soil. You grant at once what furthers the slave policy of a rival power, and deny the means of rescuing from its grasp your own property and soil."

This African squadron has now been kept up more than twice five years, and promises to be perpetual; for there was that delusive clause in the article, so tempting to all temporizing spirits, that after the lapse of the five years, the squadron was still to be kept up until the United States should give notice to terminate the article. This idea of notice to terminate a treaty, so easy to put in it, and so difficult to be given when entanglement and use combine to keep things as they are, was shown to be almost impossible in this treaty of joint occupation of the Columbia. Mr. Calhoun had demanded of Mr. Linn, why not give the notice to terminate the treaty before proceeding to settle the country? to which he answered:

"The senator from South Carolina [Mr. CALHOUN], has urged that we should, first of all, give the twelve months' notice of our renunciation of the treaty. He [Mr. LINN] could only answer that he had repeatedly, by resolutions, urged that course in former years; but always in vain. He had ever been met with the answer: 'This is not the proper time—wait.' Meanwhile, the adverse possession was going on, fortifying from year to year the British claim and the British resources, to make it good. Mr. Madison had encouraged the bold and well-arranged scheme of Astor to fortify and colonize. He was dispossessed; and the nucleus of empire which his establishments formed, passed into the hands of the Hudson Bay Company, now the great instrument of English aggrandizement in that quarter. The senator insists that, by the treaty, there should be a joint possession. Be it so, if you will. But where is our part of this joint possession? In what does it consist, or has it consisted? We have no posts there, no agent, no military power to protect traders. Nay, indeed, no traders! For they have disappeared before foreign competition; or fallen a sacrifice to the rifle, the tomahawk, or the scalping knife of those savages whom the Hudson Bay Company can always make the instruments of systematic massacre of adventurous rivals."

Mr. Benton spoke at large in defence of the bill, and first of the clause in it allotting land to the settlers, saying:

"The objections to this bill grew out of the clause granting land to the settlers, not so much on account of the grants themselves, as on account of the exclusive jurisdiction over the country, which the grants would seem to imply. This was the objection; for no one defended the title of the British to one inch square of the valley of Oregon. The senator from Arkansas [Mr. SEVIER], who has just spoken, had well said that this was an objection to the whole bill; for the rest would be worth nothing, without these grants to the settlers. Nobody would go there without the inducement of land. The British had planted a power there—the Hudson Bay Fur Company—in which the old Northwest Company was merged; and this power was to them in the New World what the East India company was to them in the Old World: it was an arm of the government, and did every thing for the government which policy, or treaties prevented it from doing for itself. This company was settling and colonizing the Columbia for the British government, and we wish American citizens to settle and colonize it for us. The British government gives inducement to this company. It gives them trade, commerce, an exclusive charter, laws, and national protection. We must give inducement also; and our inducement must be land and protection. Grants of land will carry settlers there; and the senator from Ohio [Mr. TAPPAN] was treading in the tracks of Mr. Jefferson (perhaps without having read his recommendation, although he has read much) when he proposed, in his speech of yesterday, to plant 50,000 settlers, with their 50,000 rifles, on the banks of the Oregon. Mr. Jefferson had proposed the same thing in regard to Louisiana. He proposed that we should settle that vast domain when we acquired it; and for that purpose, that donations of land should be made to the first 30,000 settlers who should go there. This was the right doctrine, and the old doctrine. The white race were a land-loving people, and had a right to possess it, because they used it according to the intentions of the Creator. The white race went for land, and they will continue to go for it, and will go where they can get it. Europe, Asia, and America, have been settled by them in this way. All the States of this Union have been so settled. The principle is founded in their nature and in God's command; and it will continue to be obeyed. The valley of the Columbia is a vast field open to the settler. It is ours, and our people are beginning to go upon it. They go under the expectation of getting land; and that expectation must be confirmed to them. This bill proposes to confirm it; and if it fails in this particular, it fails in all. There is nothing left to induce emigration; and emigration is the only thing which can save the country from the British, acting through their powerful agent—the Hudson Bay Company."

Mr. Benton then showed from a report of Major Pilcher, Superintendent of Indian Affairs, and who had visited the Columbia River, that actual colonization was going on there, attended by every circumstance that indicated ownership and the design of a permanent settlement. Fort Vancouver, the principal of these British establishments, for there are many of them within our boundaries, is thus described by Major Pilcher:

"This fort is on the north side of the Columbia, nearly opposite the mouth of the Multnomah, in the region of tide-water, and near the head of ship navigation. It is a grand position, both in a military and commercial point of view, and formed to command the whole region watered by the Columbia and its tributaries. The surrounding country, both in climate and soil, is capable of sustaining a large population; and its resources in timber give ample facilities for ship-building. This post is fortified with cannon; and, having been selected as the principal or master position, no pains have been spared to strengthen or improve it. For this purpose, the old post near the mouth of the river has been abandoned. About one hundred and twenty acres of ground are in cultivation; and the product in wheat, barley, oats, corn, potatoes, and other vegetables, is equal to what is known in the best parts of the United States. Domestic animals are numerous—the horned cattle having been stated to me at three hundred; hogs, horses, sheep, and goats, in proportion; also, the usual domestic fowls: every thing, in fact, indicating a permanent establishment. Ship-building has commenced at this place. One vessel has been built and rigged, sent to sea, and employed in the trade of the Pacific Ocean. I also met a gentleman, on my way to Lake Winnipec, at the portage between the Columbia and Athabasca, who was on his way from Hudson's Bay to Fort Colville, with a master ship-carpenter, and who was destined for Fort Vancouver, for the purpose of building a ship of considerable burden. Both grist and saw-mills have been built at Fort Vancouver: with the latter, they saw the timber which is needed for their own use, and also for exportation to the Sandwich Islands; upon the former, their wheat is manufactured into flour. And, from all that I could learn, this important post is silently growing up into a colony; and is, perhaps, intended as a future military and naval station, which was not expected to be delivered up at the expiration of the treaty which granted them a temporary and joint possession."

Mr. Benton made a brief deduction of our title to the Columbia to the 49th parallel under the treaty of Utrecht, and rapidly traced the various British attempts to encroach upon that line, the whole of which, though earnestly made and perseveringly continued, failed to follow that great line from the Lake of the Woods to the shores of the Pacific. He thus made this deduction of title:

"Louisiana was acquired in 1803. In the very instant of signing the treaty which brought us that province, another treaty was signed in London (without a knowledge of what was done in Paris), fixing, among other things, the line from the Lake of the Woods to the Mississippi. This treaty, signed by Mr. Rufus King and Lord Hawkesbury, was rejected by Mr. Jefferson, without reference to the Senate, on account of the fifth article (which related to the line between the Lake of the Woods and the head of the Mississippi), for fear it might compromise the northern boundary of Louisiana and the line of 49 degrees. In this negotiation of 1803, the British made no attempt on the line of the 49th degree, because it was not then known to them that we had acquired Louisiana; but Mr. Jefferson, having a knowledge of this acquisition, was determined that nothing should be done to compromise our rights, or to unsettle the boundaries established under the treaty of Utrecht.

"Another treaty was negotiated with Great Britain in 1807, between Messrs. Monroe and William Pinckney on one side, and Lords Holland and Auckland on the other. The English were now fully possessed of the fact that we had acquired Louisiana, and become a party to the line of 49 degrees; and they set themselves openly to work to destroy that line. The correspondence of the ministers shows the pertinacity of these attempts; and the instructions of Mr. Adams, in 1818 (when Secretary of State, under Mr. Monroe), to Messrs. Rush and Gallatin, then in London, charged with negotiating a convention on points left unsettled at Ghent, condense the history of the mutual propositions then made. Finally, an article was agreed upon, in which the British succeeded in mutilating the line, and stopping it at the Rocky Mountains. This treaty of 1807 shared the fate of that of 1803, but for a different reason. It was rejected by Mr. Jefferson, without reference to the Senate, because it did not contain an explicit renunciation of the pretension of impressment!

"At Ghent the attempt was renewed: the arrest of the line at the Rocky Mountains was agreed upon, but the British coupled with their proposition a demand for the free navigation of the Mississippi, and access to it through the territories of the United States; and this demand occasioned the whole article to be omitted. The Ghent treaty was signed without any stipulation on the subject of the line along the 49th degree, and that point became a principal object of the ministers charged with completing at London, in 1818, the subjects unfinished at Ghent in 1814. Thus the British were again foiled; but, true to their design, they persevered and accomplished it in the convention signed at London in 1818. That convention arrested the line at the mountains, and opened the Columbia to the joint occupation of the British; and, being ratified by the United States, it has become binding and obligatory on the country. But it is a point not to be overlooked, or undervalued, in this case, that it was in the year 1818 that this arrestation of the line took place; that up to that period it was in full force in all its extent, and, consequently, in full force to the Pacific Ocean; and a complete bar (leaving out all other barriers) to any British acquisition, by discovery, south of 49 degrees in North America."

The President in his message had said that "informal conferences" had taken place between Mr. Webster and Lord Ashburton on the subject of the Columbia, but he had not communicated them. Mr. Benton obtained a call of the Senate for them: the President answered it was incompatible with the public interest to make them public. That was a strange answer, seeing that all claims by either party, and all negotiations on the subjects between them, whether concluded or not, and whether successful or not should be communicated.

"The President, in his message recommending the peace treaty, informs us that the Columbia was the subject of "*informal conferences*" between the negotiators of that treaty; but that it could not then be included among the subjects of formal negotiation. This was an ominous annunciation, and should have opened the eyes of the President to a great danger. If the peace mission, which came here to settle every thing, and which had so much to gain in the Maine boundary and the African alliance;—if this mission could not agree with us about the Columbia, what mission ever can? To an inquiry from the Senate to know the nature and extent of these "*informal conferences*" between Mr. Webster and Lord Ashburton, and to learn the reason why the Columbia question could not have been included among the subjects of formal negotiation—to these inquiries, the President answers, that it is incompatible with the public interest to communicate these things. This is a strange answer, and most unexpected. We have no political secrets in our country, neither among ourselves nor with foreigners. On this subject of the Columbia, especially, we have no secrets. Every thing in relation to it has been published. All the conferences heretofore have been made public. The protocols, the minutes, the conversations, on both sides, have all been published. The British have published their claim, such as it is: we have published ours. The public documents are full of them, and there can be nothing in the question itself to require secrecy. The negotiator, and not the subject, may require secrecy. Propositions may have been made, and listened to, which no previous administration would tolerate, and which it may be deemed prudent to conceal until it has taken the form of a stipulation, and the cry of war can be raised to ravish its ratification from us. All previous administrations, while claiming the whole valley of the Columbia, have refused to admit a particle of British claim *south* of 49 degrees. Mr. Adams, under Mr. Monroe, peremptorily refused to submit any such claim even to arbitration. The Maine boundary, settled by the treaty of 1783, had been submitted to arbitration; but this boundary of 49 was refused. And now, if, after all this, any proposition has been made by our government to give up the north bank of the river, I, for one, shall not fail to brand such a proposition with the name of treason."

This paragraph was not without point, and even inuendo. The north bank of the Columbia with equal rights of navigation in the river, and to the harbor at its mouth, had been the object of the British from the time that the fur-trader, and explorer, Sir Alexander McKenzie, had shown that there was no river and harbor suitable to commerce and settlement north of that stream. They had openly proposed it in negotiations: they had even gone so far as to tell our commissioners of 1818, that no treaty of boundaries could be made unless that river became the line, and its waters and the harbor at the mouth made common to both nations—a declaration which should have utterly forbid the idea of a joint occupation, as such occupation was admitting an equality of title and laying a foundation for a division of the territory. This cherished idea of dividing by the river had pervaded every British negotiation since 1818. It was no secret: the British begged it: we refused it. Lord Ashburton, there is reason to know, brought out the same proposition. In his first diplomatic note he stated that he came prepared to settle all the questions of difference between the two countries; and this affair of the Columbia was too large, and of too long standing, and of too much previous negotiation to have been overlooked. It was not overlooked. The President says that there were conferences about it, qualified as informal: which is evidence there would have been formal negotiation if the informal had promised success. The informal did not so promise; and the reason was, that the two senators from Missouri being sounded on the subject of a conventional divisional line, repulsed the suggestion with an earnestness which put an end to it; and this knowledge of a proposition for a conventional line induced the indignant language which those two senators used on the subject in all their speeches. If they had yielded, the valley of the Columbia would have been divided; for that is the way the whole Ashburton treaty was made. Senators were sounded by the American negotiator, each on the point which lay nearest to him; and whatever they agreed to was put into the treaty. Thus the cases of the liberated slaves at Nassau and Bermuda were given up—the leading southern senators agreeing to it beforehand, and voting for the treaty afterwards. The writer of this View had this fact from Mr. Bagby, who refused to go with them, and voted against the ratification of the treaty.

"This pretension to the Columbia is an encroachment upon our rights and possession. It is a continuation of the encroachments which Great Britain systematically practises upon us. Diplomacy and audacity carry her through, and gain her position after position upon our borders. It is in vain that the treaty of 1783 gave us a safe military frontier. We have been losing it ever since the late war, and are still losing it. The commission under the treaty of Ghent took from us the islands of Grand Menan, Campo Bello, and Indian Island, on the coast of Maine, and which command the bays of Fundy and Passamaquoddy. Those islands belonged to us by the treaty of peace, and by the laws of God and nature; for they are on our coast, and within wading distance of it. Can we not wade to these islands? [Looking at senator WILLIAMS, who answered, 'We can wade to one of them.'] Yes, wade to it! And yet the British worked them out of us; and now can wade to us, and command our land, as well as our water. By these acquisitions, and those of the late treaty, the Bay of Fundy will become a great naval station to overawe and scourge our whole coast, from Maine to Florida. Under the same commission of the Ghent treaty, she got from us the island of Boisblanc, in the mouth of the Detroit River, and which commands that river and the entrance into Lake Erie. It was ours under the treaty of 1783; it was taken from us by diplomacy. And now an American ship must pass between the mouths of two sets of British batteries—one on Boisblanc; the other directly opposite, at Malden; and the two batteries within three or four hundred yards of each other. Am I right as to the distance? [Looking at Senator WOODBRIDGE, who answered, 'The distance is three hundred yards.'] Then comes the late treaty, which takes from us (for I will say nothing of what the award gave up beyond the St. John) the mountain frontier, 3,000 feet in height, 150 miles long, approaching Quebec and the St. Lawrence, and, in the language of Mr. Featherstonhaugh, 'commanding all their communications, and commanding and overawing Quebec itself.' This we have given up; and, in doing so, have given up our military advantages in that quarter, and placed them in the hands of Great Britain, to be used against ourselves in future wars. The boundary between the Lake Superior and the Lake of the Woods has been altered by the late treaty, and subjected us to another encroachment, and to the loss of a military advantage, which Great Britain gains. To say nothing about Pigeon River as being or not being the '*long lake*' of the treaty of 1783; to say nothing of that, there are yet two routes commencing in that stream—one bearing far to the south, and forming the large island called 'Hunter's.' By the old boundary the line went the northern route; by the new, it goes to the south; giving to the British a large scope of our territory (which is of no great value), but giving them, also, the exclusive possession of the old route, the best route, and the one commanding the Indians, which is of great importance. The encroachment now attempted upon the Columbia, is but a continuation of this system of encroachments which is kept up against us, and which, until 1818, labored even to get the navigation of the Mississippi, by laboring to make the line from the Lake of the Woods reach its head spring. If Great Britain had succeeded in getting this line to touch the Mississippi, she was then to claim the navigation of the river, under the law of nations, contrary to her doctrine in the case of the people of Maine and the river St. John. The line of the 49th parallel of north latitude is another instance of her encroaching policy; it has been mutilated by the persevering efforts of British diplomacy; and the breaking of that line was immediately followed by the most daring of all her encroachments—that of the Columbia River."

The strength of the bill was tested by a motion to strike out the land-donation clause, which failed by a vote of 24 to 22. The bill was then passed by the same vote—the yeas and nays being:

"YEAS.—Messrs. Allen, Benton, Buchanan, Clayton, Fulton, Henderson, King, Linn, McRoberts, Mangum, Merrick, Phelps, Sevier, Smith of Connecticut, Smith of Indiana, Sturgeon, Tappan, Walker, White, Wilcox, Williams, Woodbury, Wright, Young."

"NAYS.—Messrs. Archer, Bagby, Barrow, Bates, Bayard, Berrien, Calhoun, Choate, Conrad, Crafts, Dayton, Evans, Graham, Huntington, McDuffie, Miller, Porter, Rives, Simmons, Sprague, Tallmadge, Woodbridge."

The bill went to the House, where it remained unacted upon during the session; but the effect intended by it was fully produced. The vote of the Senate was sufficient encouragement to the enterprising people of the West. Emigration increased. An American settlement grew up at the mouth of the Columbia. Conventional agreements among themselves answered the purpose of laws. A colony was planted—had planted itself—and did not intend to retire from its position—and did not. It remained and grew; and that colony of self-impulsion, without the aid of government, and in spite of all its blunders, saved the Territory of Oregon to the United States: one of the many events which show how little the wisdom of government has to do with great events which fix the fate of countries.

Connected with this emigration, and auxiliary to it, was the first expedition of Lieutenant Frémont to the Rocky Mountains, and undertaken and completed in the summer of 1842—upon its outside view the conception of the government, but in fact conceived without its knowledge, and executed upon solicited orders, of which the design was unknown. Lieutenant Frémont was a young officer, appointed in the topographical corps from the class of citizens by President Jackson upon the recommendation of Mr. Poinsett, Secretary at War. He did not enter the army through the gate of West Point, and was considered an intrusive officer by the graduates of that institution. Having, before his appointment, assisted for two years the learned astronomer, Mr. Nicollet, in his great survey of the country between the Missouri and Mississippi, his mind was trained to such labor; and instead of hunting comfortable berths about the towns and villages, he solicited employment in the vast regions beyond the Mississippi. Col. Abert, the chief of the corps, gave him an order to go to the frontier beyond the Mississippi. That order did not come up to his views. After receiving it he carried it back, and got it altered, and the Rocky Mountains inserted as an object of his exploration, and the South Pass in those mountains named as a particular point to be examined, and its position fixed by him. It was through this Pass that the Oregon emigration crossed the mountains, and the exploration of Lieutenant Frémont had the double effect of fixing an important point in the line of the emigrants' travel, and giving them encouragement from the apparent interest which the government took in their enterprise. At the same time the government, that is, the executive administration, knew nothing about it. The design was conceived by the young lieutenant: the order for its execution was obtained, upon solicitation, from his immediate chief—importing, of course, to be done by his order, but an order which had its conception elsewhere.

CHAPTER CXIII.

LIEUTENANT FREMONT'S FIRST EXPEDITION: SPEECH, AND MOTION OF SENATOR LINN.

A communication was received from the War Department, in answer to a call heretofore made for the report of Lieutenant Frémont's expedition to the Rocky Mountains. Mr. Linn moved that it be printed for the use of the Senate; and also that one thousand extra copies be printed.

"In support of his motion," Mr. L. said, "that in the course of the last summer a very interesting expedition had been undertaken to the Rocky Mountains, ordered by Col. Abert, chief of the Topographical Bureau, with the sanction of the Secretary at War, and executed by Lieutenant Frémont of the topographical engineers. The object of the expedition was to examine and report upon the rivers and country between the frontiers of Missouri and the base of the Rocky Mountains; and especially to examine the character, and ascertain the latitude and longitude of the South Pass, the great crossing place to these mountains on the way to the Oregon. All the objects of the expedition have been accomplished, and in a way to be beneficial to science, and instructive to the general reader, as well as useful to the government.

"Supplied with the best astronomical and barometrical instruments, well qualified to use them, and accompanied by twenty-five *voyageurs*, enlisted for the purpose at St. Louis, and trained to all the hardships and dangers of the prairies and the mountains, Mr. Frémont left the mouth of the Kansas, on the frontiers of Missouri, on the 10th of June; and, in the almost incredibly short space of four months returned to the same point, without an accident to a man, and with a vast mass of useful observations, and many hundred specimens in botany and geology.

"In executing his instructions, Mr. Frémont proceeded up the Kansas River far enough to ascertain its character, and then crossed over to the Great Platte, and pursued that river to its source in the mountains, where the Sweet Water (a head branch of the Platte) issues from the neighborhood of the South Pass. He reached the Pass on the 8th of August, and describes it as a wide and low depression of the mountains, where the ascent is as easy as that of the hill on which this Capitol stands, and where a plainly beaten wagon road leads to the Oregon through the valley of Lewis's River, a fork of the Columbia. He went through the Pass, and saw the head-waters of the Colorado, of the Gulf of California; and, leaving the valleys to indulge a laudable curiosity and to make some useful observations, and attended by four of his men, he climbed the loftiest peak of the Rocky Mountains, until then untrodden by any known human being; and, on the 15th of August, looked down upon ice and snow some thousand feet below, and traced in the distance the valleys of the rivers which, taking their rise in the same elevated ridge, flow in opposite directions to the Pacific Ocean and to the Mississippi. From that ultimate point he returned by the valley of the Great Platte, following the stream in its whole course, and solving all questions in relation to its navigability, and the character of the country through which it flows.

"Over the whole course of this extended route, barometrical observations were made by Mr. Frémont, to ascertain elevations both of the plains and of the mountains; astronomical observations were taken, to ascertain latitudes and longitudes; the face of the country was marked as arable or sterile; the facility of travelling, and the practicability of routes, noted; the grand features of nature described, and some presented in drawings; military positions indicated; and a large contribution to geology and botany was made in the varieties of plants, flowers, shrubs, trees, and grasses, and rocks and earths, which were enumerated. Drawings of some grand and striking points, and a map of the whole route, illustrate the report, and facilitate the understanding of its details. Eight carts, drawn by two mules each, accompanied the expedition; a fact which attests the facility of travelling in this vast region. Herds of buffaloes furnished subsistence to the men; a short, nutritious grass, sustained the horses and mules. Two boys (one of twelve years of age, the other of eighteen), besides the enlisted men, accompanied the expedition, and took their share of its hardships; which proves that boys, as well as men, are able to traverse the country to the Rocky Mountains.

"The result of all his observations Mr. Frémont had condensed into a brief report—enough to make a document of ninety or one hundred pages; and believing that this document would be of general interest to the whole country, and beneficial to science, as well as useful to the government, I move the printing of the extra number which has been named.

"In making this motion, and in bringing this report to the notice of the Senate, I take a great pleasure in noticing the activity and importance of the Topographical Bureau. Under its skilful and vigilant head [Colonel Abert], numerous valuable and incessant surveys are made; and a mass of information collected of the highest importance to the country generally, as well as to the military branch of the public service. This report proves conclusively that the country, for several hundred miles from the frontier of Missouri, is exceedingly beautiful and fertile; alternate woodland and prairie, and certain portions well supplied with water. It also proves that the valley of the river Platte has a very rich soil, affording great facilities for emigrants to the west of the Rocky Mountains.

"The printing was ordered."

CHAPTER CXIV.

OREGON COLONIZATION ACT: MR. BENTON'S SPEECH.

MR. BENTON said: On one point there is unanimity on this floor; and that is, as to the title to the country in question. All agree that the title is in the United States. On another point there is division; and that is, on the point of giving offence to England, by granting the land to our settlers which the bill proposes. On this point we divide. Some think it will offend her—some think it will not. For my part, I think she will take offence, do what we may in relation to this territory. She wants it herself, and means to quarrel for it, if she does not fight for it. I think she will take offence at our bill, and even at our discussion of it. The nation that could revive the question of impressment in 1842—which could direct a peace mission to revive that question—the nation that can insist upon the right of search, and which was ready to go to war with us for what gentlemen call a few acres of barren ground in a frozen region—the nation that could do these things, and which has set up a claim to our territory on the western coast of our own continent, must be ripe and ready to take offence at any thing that we may do. I grant that she will take offence; but that is not the question with me. Has she a *right* to take offence? That is my question! and this being decided in the negative, I neither fear nor calculate consequences. I take for my rule of action the maxim of President Jackson in his controversy with France—ask nothing but what is right, submit to nothing wrong and leave the consequences to God and the country. That maxim brought us safely and honorably out of our little difficulty with France, notwithstanding the fears which so many then entertained; and it will do the same with Great Britain, in spite of our present apprehensions. Courage will keep her off, fear will bring her upon us. The assertion of our rights will command her respect; the fear to assert them will bring us her contempt. The question, then, with me, is the question of right, and not of fear! Is it right for us to make these grants on the Columbia? Has Great Britain just cause to be offended at it? These are my questions; and these being answered to my satisfaction, I go forward with the grants, and leave the consequences to follow at their pleasure.

The fear of Great Britain is pressed upon us; at the same time her pacific disposition is enforced and insisted upon. And here it seems to me, that gentlemen fall into a grievous inconsistency. While they dwell on the peaceable disposition of Great Britain, they show her ready to go to war with us for nothing, or even for our own! The northeastern boundary is called a dispute for a few acres of barren land in a frozen region, worth nothing; yet we are called upon to thank God Almighty and Daniel Webster for saving us from a war about these few frozen and barren acres. Would Great Britain have gone to war with us for these few acres? and is that a sign of her pacific temper? The Columbia is admitted on all hands to be ours; yet gentlemen fear war with Great Britain if we touch it—worthless as it is in their eyes. Is this a sign of peace? Is it a pacific disposition to go to war with us, for what is our own; and which is besides, according to their opinion, not worth a straw? Is this peaceful? If it is, I should like to know what is hostile. The late special minister is said to have come here, bearing the olive branch of peace in his hand. Granting that the olive branch was in one hand, what was in the other? Was not the war question of impressment in the other? also, the war question of search, on the coast of Africa? also, the war question of the Columbia, which he refused to include in the peace treaty? Were not these three war questions in the other hand?—to say nothing of the Caroline; for which he refused atonement; and the Creole, which he says would have occasioned the rejection of the treaty, if named in it. All these war questions were in the other hand; and the special mission, having accomplished its peace object in getting possession of the military frontiers of Maine, has adjourned all the war questions to London, where we may follow them if we please. But there is one of these subjects for which we need not go to London—the Creole, and its kindred cases. The conference of Lord Ashburton with the abolition committee of New York shows that that question need not go to London—that England means to maintain all her grounds on the subject of slaves, and that any treaty inconsistent with these grounds would be rejected. This is what he says:

> "Lord Ashburton said that, when the delegation came to read his correspondence with Mr. Webster, they would see that he had taken all possible care to prevent any injury being done to the people of color; that, if he had been willing to introduce an article including cases similar to that of the Creole, his government would never have ratified it, as they will adhere to the great principles they have so long avowed and maintained; and that the friends of the slave in

England would be very watchful to see that no wrong practice took place under the tenth article."

This is what his lordship said in New York, and which shows that it was not want of instructions to act on the Creole case, as alleged in Mr. Webster's correspondence, but want of inclination in the British government to settle the case. The treaty would have been rejected, if the Creole case had been named in it; and if we had had a protocol showing that fact, I presume the important note of Lord Ashburton would have stood for as little in the eyes of other senators as it did in mine, and that the treaty would have found but few supporters. The Creole case would not be admitted into the treaty; and what was put in it, is to give the friends of the slaves in England a right to watch us, and to correct our wrong practices under the treaty! This is what the protocol after the treaty informs us; and if we had had a protocol before it, it is probable that there would have been no occasion for this conference with the New York abolitionists. Be that as it may, the peace mission, with its olive branch in one hand, brought a budget of war questions in the other, and has carried them all back to London, to become the subject of future negotiations. All these subjects are pregnant with danger. One of them will force itself upon us in five years—the search question—which we have purchased off for a time; and when the purchase is out we must purchase again, or submit to be searched, or resist with arms. I repeat it: the pacific England has a budget of war questions now in reserve for us, and that we cannot escape them by fearing war. Neither nations nor individuals ever escaped danger by fearing it. They must face it, and defy it. An abandonment of a right, for fear of bringing on an attack, instead of keeping it off, will inevitably bring on the outrage that is dreaded.

Other objections are urged to this bill, to which I cannot agree. The distance is objected to it. It is said to be eighteen thousand miles by water (around Cape Horn), and above three thousand miles by land and water, through the continent. Granted. The very distance, by Cape Horn, was urged by me, twenty years ago, as a reason for occupying and fortifying the mouth of the Columbia. My argument was, that we had merchant ships and ships of war in the North Pacific Ocean; that these vessels were twenty thousand miles from an Atlantic port; that a port on the western coast of America was indispensable to their safety; and that it would be suicidal in us to abandon the port we have there to any power, and especially to the most formidable and domineering naval power which the world ever saw. And I instanced the case of Commodore Porter, his prizes lost, and his own ship eventually captured in a neutral port, because we had no port of our own to receive and shelter him. The twenty thousand miles distance, and dangerous and tempestuous cape to be doubled, were with me arguments in favor of a port on the western coast of America, and, as such, urged on this floor near twenty years ago. The distance through the continent is also objected to. It is said to exceed three thousand miles. Granted. But it is further than that to Africa, where we propose to build up a colony of negroes out of our recaptured Africans. Our eighty-gun fleet is to carry her intercepted slaves to Liberia: so says the correspondence of the naval captains (Bell and Paine) with Mr. Webster. Hunting in couples with the British, at an expense of money (to say nothing of the loss of lives and ships) of six hundred thousand dollars per annum, to recapture kidnapped negroes, we are to carry them to Liberia, and build up a black colony there, four thousand miles from us, while the Columbia is too far off for a white colony! The English are to carry their redeemed captives to Jamaica, and make apprentices of them for life. We are to carry ours to Liberia; and then we must go to Liberia to protect and defend them. Liberia is four thousand miles distant, and not objected to on account of the distance; the Columbia is not so far, and distance becomes a formidable objection.

The expense is brought forward as another objection, and repeated, notwithstanding the decisive answer it has received from my colleague. He has shown that it is but a fraction of the expense of the African squadron; that this squadron is the one-twelfth part of our whole naval establishment, which is to cost us seven millions of dollars per annum, and that the annual cost of the squadron must be near six hundred thousand dollars, and its expense for five years three millions. For the forts in the Oregon—forts which are only to be stockades and block-houses, for security against the Indians—for these forts, only one hundred thousand dollars is appropriated; being the sixth part of the annual expense, and the thirtieth part of the whole expense, of the African fleet. Thus the objection of expense becomes futile and ridiculous. But why this everlasting objection of expense to every thing western? Our dragoons dismounted, because, they say, horses are too expensive. The western rivers unimproved, on account of the expense. No western armory, because of the expense. Yet hundreds of thousands, and millions, for the African squadron!

Another great objection to the bill is the land clause—the grants of land to the settler, his wife, and his children. Gentlemen say they will vote for the bill if that clause is stricken out; and I say, I will vote against it if that clause is stricken out. It is, in fact, the whole strength and essence of the bill. Without these grants, the bill will be worth nothing. Nobody will go three thousand miles to settle a new country, unless he gets land by it. The whole power of the bill is in this clause; and if it is stricken out, the friends of the bill will give it up. They will give it up now, and wait for the next Congress, when the full representation of the people, under the new census, will be in power, and when a more auspicious result might be expected.

Time is invoked, as the agent that is to help us. Gentlemen object to the present time, refer us to the future, and beg us to wait, and rely upon TIME and NEGOTIATIONS to accomplish all our wishes. Alas! *time* and *negotiation* have been fatal agents to us, in all our discussions with Great Britain. Time has been constantly working for her, and against us. She now has the exclusive possession of the Columbia; and all she wants is *time*, to ripen her possession into title. For above twenty years—from the time of Dr. Floyd's bill, in 1820, down to the present moment—the present time, for vindicating our rights on the Columbia, has been constantly objected to; and we were bidden to wait. Well, we have waited: and what have we got by it? Insult and defiance!—a declaration from the British ministers that large British interests have grown up on the Columbia during this time, which they will protect!—and a flat refusal from the olive-branch minister to include this question among those which his peaceful mission was to settle! No, sir; time and negotiation have been bad agents for us, in our controversies with Great Britain. They have just lost us the military frontiers of Maine, which we had held for sixty years; and the trading frontier of the Northwest, which we had held for the same time. Sixty years' possession, and eight treaties, secured these ancient and valuable boundaries: one negotiation, and a few days of time, have taken them from us! And so it may be again. The Webster treaty of 1842 has obliterated the great boundaries of 1783—placed the British, their fur company and their Indians, within our ancient limits: and I, for one, want no more treaties from the hand which is always seen on the side of the British. I go now for vindicating our rights on the Columbia; and, as the first step towards it, passing this bill, and making these grants of land, which will soon place the thirty or forty thousand rifles beyond the Rocky Mountains, which will be our effective negotiators.

CHAPTER CXV.

NAVY PAY AND EXPENSES: PROPOSED REDUCTION: SPEECH OF MR. MERIWETHER, OF GEORGIA: EXTRACTS.

Mr. Meriwether said "that it was from no hostility to the service that he desired to reduce the pay of the navy. It had been increased in 1835 to meet the increase of labor elsewhere, &c.; and a decline having taken place there, he thought a corresponding decline should take place in the price of labor in the navy. At the last session of Congress, this House called on the Secretary of the Navy for a statement of the pay allowed each officer previous to the act of 1835. From the answer to that resolution, Mr. M. derived the facts which he should state to the House. He was desirous of getting the exact amount received by each grade of officers, to show the precise increase by the act of 1835. Aided by that report, the Biennial Register of 1822, and the Report of the Secretary of the Navy for 1822, furnishing the estimates for the 'full pay and full rations' of each grade of officers, he was enabled to present the entire facts accurately. Previous to that time, the classification of officers was different from what it has been since; but, as far as like services have been rendered under each classification, the comparative pay is presented under each. Previous to 1835, the pay of the 'commanding officer of the navy' was $100 per month, and sixteen rations per day, valued at 25 cents each ration; which amounted, 'full pay and full rations,' to $2,660 per annum. The same officer as senior captain in service receives now $4,500; while 'on leave,' he receives $3,500 per annum. Before 1835, a 'captain commanding a squadron' received the same pay as the commanding officer of the navy, and the same rations; amounting, in all, to $2,660; that same officer, exercising the same command, receives now $4,000. Before 1835, a captain commanding a vessel of 32 guns and upwards, received $100 per month and eight rations per day—being a total of $1,930 per annum; a captain commanding a vessel of 20 and under 32 guns, received $75 per month and six rations per day—amounting to $1,447 50 per annum. Since 1835, these same captains, when performing these same duties, receive $3,500; and when at home, by their firesides, 'waiting orders,' receive $2,500 per annum. Before 1835, a 'master commanding' received $60 per month and five rations per day—amounting to $1,176 per annum. Since that time, the same officer, in sea service, receives $2,500 per annum; at other duty, $2,100 per annum; and 'waiting orders,' $1,800 per annum. Before 1835, a 'lieutenant commanding' received $50 per month and four rations per day; which amounted to $965 per annum. Since that time, the same officer receives, for similar services, $1,800 per annum. Before 1835, a lieutenant on other duty received $40 per month, and three rations per day—amounting to $761 per annum. Since that time, for the same services, that same officer has received $1,500 per annum; and when 'waiting orders,' $1,200 per annum. Before 1835, a midshipman received $19 per month and one ration per day—making $319 25 per annum. Since that time, a passed midshipman on duty received $750 per annum; if 'waiting orders,' $600; a midshipman received, in sea service, $400; on other duty, $350; and 'waiting orders,' $300 per annum. Surgeons, before 1835, received $50 per month and two rations per day—amounting to $787 50; they now receive from $1,000 to $2,700 per annum. Before 1835, a 'schoolmaster' received $25 per month and two rations per day; now, under the name of a professor, he receives $1,200 per annum.

"Before 1835, a carpenter, boatswain, and gunner received $20 per month and two rations per day—making $427 50 each per annum; they now receive, if employed on a ship-of-the-line, $750, on a frigate $600, on other duty $500, and 'waiting orders' $360 per annum. A similar increase has been made in the pay of all other officers. The pay of seamen has not been enlarged, and it is proposed to leave it as it is. In several instances, an officer idle, 'waiting orders,' receives more pay now than one of similar grade received during the late war, when he exposed his life in battle in defence of his country. At the navy-yards the pay of officers was greater than at sea. Before 1835, a captain commandant received for pay, rations, candles, and servants' hire, $3,013 per annum, besides fuel; the same officer, for the same services, receives now $3,500 per annum. A master commandant received $1,408 per annum, with fuel; the same officer now receives $2,100 per annum. A lieutenant received $877, with fuel; the same officer receives now $1,500. At naval stations, before the act of 1835, a captain received $2,660 per annum; he now receives $3,500 per annum. A lieutenant received $761 per annum, and he now receives $1,500 per annum. Before and since the act of 1835, quarters were furnished the officers at navy yards and stations. Before that time, the pay and emoluments were estimated for in dollars and cents, and appropriated for as pay; and the foregoing statements are taken from the actual 'estimates' of the navy department, and, as such, show the whole pay and emoluments received by each officer.

"The effect of this increase of pay has been realized prejudicially in more ways than one. In the year 1824, there were afloat in the navy, 404 guns; in 1843, 946 guns. The cost of the item of pay alone for each gun, then, was $2,360; now the cost is $3,500.

"The naval service has become, to a great extent, one of ease and of idleness. The high pay has rendered its offices mostly sinecures; hence the great effort to increase the number of officers. Every argument has been used, every entreaty resorted to, to augment that corps. We have seen the effect of this, that in one year (1841) there were added 13 captains, 41 commanders, 42 lieutenants, and 163 midshipmen, without any possibly conceivable cause for the increase; and when, at the same time, these appointments were made, there were 20 captains 'waiting orders,' and 6 'on leave;' 26 commanders 'waiting orders,' and 3 'on leave;' 103 lieutenants 'on leave and waiting orders,' and 16 midshipmen 'on leave and waiting orders.' The pay of officers 'waiting orders' amounted, during the year 1841, to $261,000; and now the amount required for the pay of that same idle corps, increased by a useless and unnecessary increase of the navy, is $395,000! It is a fact worthy of notice that, under the old pay in 1824, there were 28 captains, 4 of whom were 'waiting orders,' of 30 commanders, only 7 were 'waiting orders.' Under the new pay, in 1843, there are 68 captains, of whom 38 are 'waiting orders;' 97 commanders, of whom 57 are 'waiting orders and on leave.' The item of pay, in 1841, amounted to $2,335,000, and we are asked to appropriate for the next twelve months $3,333,139. To give employment to as many officers as possible, it is proposed to extend greatly our naval force; increasing the number of our vessels in commission largely, and upon every station, notwithstanding our commerce is reduced, and we are at peace with all the world, and have actually purchased our peace from the only nation from which we apprehended difficulty.

"It was stated somewhere, in some of the reports, that the appropriation necessary to defray the expenses of courts-martial in the navy would be, this year $50,000. This was a very large amount, when contrasted with the service. The disorderly conduct of the navy was notorious—no one could defend it. The country was losing confidence in it daily, and becoming more unwilling to bear the burdens of taxation to foster or sustain it. A few years since, its expenditures did not exceed four millions and a half: they are now up to near eight millions of dollars. Its expense is greater now than during the late war with England. Notwithstanding the unequivocal declarations of Congress, at the last session, against the increase of the navy, and in favor of its reduction, the Secretary passes all unheeded, and moves on in his bold career of folly and extravagance, without abiding for a moment any will but his own. Nothing more can be hoped for, so long as the navy has such a host of backers, urging its increase and extravagance—from motives of personal interest too often. The axe should be laid at once to the root of the evil: cut down the pay, and it will not then be sought after so much as a convenient resort for idlers, who seek the offices for pay, expecting and intending that but little service shall be rendered in return, because but very little is needed. The salaries are far beyond any compensation paid to any other officer of government, either State or Federal, for corresponding services. A lieutenant receives higher pay than a very large majority of the judges of the highest judicatories known to the States; a commander far surpasses them, and equals the salaries of a majority of the Governors of the States. Remove the temptation which high pay and no labor present, and you will obviate the evil. Put down the salaries to where they were before the year 1835, and you will have no greater effort after its offices than you had before. So long as the salaries are higher than similar talents can command in civil life, so long will applicants flock to the navy for admission, and the constant tendency will be to increase its expenses. The policy of our government is to keep a very small army and navy during time of peace, and to insure light taxes, and to induce the preponderance of the civil over the military authorities. In time of peace we shall meet with no difficulty in sustaining an efficient navy, as we always have done. In time of war, patriotism will call forth our people to the service. Those who would not heed this call are not wanted; for those who fight for pay will, under all circumstances, fight for those who will pay the best. The navy cannot complain of this proposed reduction; for its pay was increased in view of the increasing value of labor and property throughout the whole country. No other pay was increased; and why should not this be reduced?—not the whole amount actually increased, but only a small portion of the increase? It is due to the country; and no one should object. We are now supporting the government on borrowed money. The revenues will not be sufficient to support it hereafter; and reduction has to take place sooner or later, and upon some one or all of the departments. Upon which ought it to fall more properly than on that which has been defended against the prejudices resulting from the high prices which have recently fallen upon every department of labor and property?

"By the adoption of the amendment proposed, there will be a permanent and annual saving of about $400,000 in the single item of pay. And from the embarrassed condition of the treasury, so large a sum of money might, with the greatest propriety, be saved; more especially since by the late British treaty concluded at this place, an annual increase is to be made to the navy expenditures of some $600,000, as it is stated, to keep a useless squadron on the coast of Africa. The estimates for pay for the present year greatly exceed those of the last year. We appropriated for the last year's service for pay, &c., $2,335,000. The sum asked for the same service this year is $2,953,139. Besides, there is the sum of $380,000 asked for clothing—a new appropriation, never asked for before. The clothing for seamen being paid for by themselves, so much of the item of pay as was necessary had hitherto been expended in clothing for them, which was received by them in lieu of money. Now a separate fund is asked, which is to be used as pay, and will increase that item so much, making a sum-total of $3,333,139; which is an excess of $998,139 over and above that appropriated for the like purpose last session.

"The Secretary of the Navy says that his plan of keeping the ships sailing over the ocean (where possibly no vessel can or will see them, and where the people with whom we trade can never learn any thing of our greatness, on account of the absence of our ships from their ports, being kept constantly sailing from station to station) will 'require larger squadrons than we have heretofore employed.' He then states that his estimates are prepared for squadrons upon this large and expensive scale. 'This,' he says, 'it is my duty to do, submitting to Congress to determine whether, under the circumstances, so large a force can properly be put in commission or not. If the condition of the treasury will warrant it (of which they are the judges), I have no hesitation in recommending the largest force estimated for.' It is well known that the condition of the treasury will not warrant this force. We must fall back upon the force of last year, as the *ultimatum* that can be sustained. Our appropriations for pay last year were $1,000,000 less than those now asked for. This can be cut off without prejudice to the service; and with the reduction proposed in the salaries, $1,400,000 can be saved from waste, and applied to sustain a depleted treasury. Increase is now unreasonable and impracticable.

"A portion of the home squadron, authorized in September, 1841, has not yet gone to sea for the want of seamen. While our commerce is failing, and our sailors are idle, they will not enter the service. The flag-ship of that squadron is yet in port without her complement of men. Why then only increase officers and build ships, when you cannot get men to man them?

"From 1829 to 1841, the sums paid to officers 'waiting orders,' were, 1829, $197,684; in 1830, $156,025; in 1831, $231,378; in 1832, $204,290; in 1833, $205,233; in 1834, $202,914; in 1835, $219,036; in 1836, $212,362; in 1837, $250,930; in 1838, $297,000; in 1839, $265,043; in 1840, $265,000; in 1841, $252,856.

"The honorable member also showed from the report of the chief of the medical department, that, out of the appropriation for medicine there had been purchased in one year 31 blue cloth frock coats with navy buttons and a silver star on them, 31 pairs of blue cassimere pantaloons, and 31 blue cassimere vests with navy buttons—all for pensioners. He also shows that under the head of medicine there had been purchased out of the same fund, whiskey, coal, clothing, spirits, harness, stationery, hay, corn, oats, stoves, beef, mutton, fish, bread, charcoal, &c., to the amount of some $4,000; and, in general, that purchases of all articles were generally made from particular persons, and double prices paid. Many examples of this were given, among them the purchase of certain surgical instruments in Philadelphia from the favored sellers for the sum of $1,224 and 54 cents, which it was proved had been purchased by them from the maker, in the same city, for $669 and 81 cents: and in the same proportion in the purchases generally."

CHAPTER CXVI.

EULOGY ON SENATOR LINN: SPEECHES OF MR. BENTON AND MR. CRITTENDEN.

IN SENATE: *Tuesday, December 12, 1843.—*

The death of Senator LINN.

The journal having been read, Mr. Benton rose and said:

"Mr. PRESIDENT:—I rise to make to the Senate the formal communication of an event which has occurred during the recess, and has been heard by all with the deepest regret. My colleague and friend, the late Senator Linn, departed this life on Tuesday, the 3d day of October last, at the early age of forty-eight years, and without the warnings or the sufferings which usually precede our departure from this world. He had laid him down to sleep, and awoke no more. It was to him the sleep of death! and the only drop of consolation in this sudden and calamitous visitation was, that it took place in his own house, and that his unconscious remains were immediately surrounded by his family and friends, and received all the care and aid which love and skill could give.

"I discharge a mournful duty, Mr. President, in bringing this deplorable event to the formal notice of the Senate; in offering the feeble tribute of my applause to the many virtues of my deceased colleague, and in asking for his memory the last honors which the respect and affection of the Senate bestow upon the name of a deceased brother.

"LEWIS FIELD LINN, the subject of this annunciation, was born in the State of Kentucky, in the year 1795, in the immediate vicinity of Louisville. His grandfather was Colonel William Linn, one of the favorite officers of General George Rodgers Clark, and well known for his courage and enterprise in the early settlement of the Great West. At the age of eleven he had fought in the ranks of men, in the defence of a station in western Pennsylvania, and was seen to deliver a deliberate and effective fire. He was one of the first to navigate the Ohio and Mississippi from Pittsburg to New Orleans, and back again—a daring achievement, which himself and some others accomplished for the public service, and amidst every species of danger, in the year 1776. He was killed by the Indians at an early period; leaving a family of young children, of whom the worthy Colonel William Pope (father of Governor Pope, and head of the numerous and respectable family of that name in the West) became the guardian. The father of Senator LINN was among these children; and, at an early age, skating upon the ice near Louisville, with three other boys, he was taken prisoner by the Shawanee Indians, carried off, and detained captive for three years, when all four made their escape and returned home, by killing their guard, traversing some hundred miles of wilderness, and swimming the Ohio River. The mother of Senator LINN was a Pennsylvanian by birth; her maiden name Hunter; born at Carlisle; and also had heroic blood in her veins. Tradition, if not history, preserves the recollection of her courage and conduct at Fort Jefferson, at the Iron Banks, in 1781, when the Indians attacked and were repulsed from that post. Women and boys were men in those days.

"The father of Senator LINN died young, leaving this son but eleven years of age. The cares of an elder brother[5] supplied (as far as such a loss could be supplied) the loss of a father; and under his auspices the education of the orphan was conducted. He was intended for the medical profession, and received his education, scholastic and professional, in the State of his nativity. At an early age he was qualified for the practice of medicine, and commenced it in the then territory, now State, of Missouri; and was immediately amongst the foremost of his profession. Intuitive sagacity supplied in him the place of long experience; and boundless benevolence conciliated universal esteem. To all his patients he was the same; flying with alacrity to every call, attending upon the poor and humble as zealously as on the rich and powerful, on the stranger as readily as on the neighbor, discharging to all the duties of nurse and friend as well as of physician, and wholly regardless of his own interest, or even of his own health, in his zeal to serve and to save others.

"The highest professional honors and rewards were before him. Though commencing on a provincial theatre, there was not a capital in Europe or America in which he would not have attained the front rank in physic or surgery. But his fellow-citizens perceived in his varied abilities, capacity and aptitude for service in a different walk. He was called into the political field by an election to the Senate of his adopted State. Thence he was called to the performance of judicial duties, by a federal appointment to investigate land titles. Thence he was called to the high station of senator in the Congress of the United States—first by an executive appointment, then by three successive almost unanimous elections. The last of those elections he received but one year ago, and had not commenced his duties under it—had not sworn in under the certificate which attested it—when a sudden and premature death put an end to his earthly career. He entered this body in the year 1833; death dissolved his connection with it in 1843. For ten years he was a beloved and distinguished member of this body; and surely a nobler or a finer character never adorned the chamber of the American Senate.

"He was my friend; but I speak not the language of friendship when I speak his praise. A debt of justice is all that I can attempt to discharge: an imperfect copy of the *true man* is all that I can attempt to paint.

"A sagacious head, and a feeling heart, were the great characteristics of Dr. LINN. He had a judgment which penetrated both men and things, and gave him near and clear views of far distant events. He saw at once the bearing—the remote bearing of great measures, either for good or for evil; and brought instantly to their support, or opposition, the logic of a prompt and natural eloquence, more beautiful in its delivery, and more effective in its application, than any that art can bestow. He had great fertility of mind, and was himself the author and mover of many great measures—some for the benefit of the whole Union—some for the benefit of the Great West—some for the benefit of his own State—many for the benefit of private individuals. The pages of our legislative history will bear the evidences of these meritorious labors to a remote and grateful posterity.

"Brilliant as were the qualities of his head, the qualities of his heart still eclipse them. It is to the heart we look for the character of the man; and what a heart had LEWIS LINN! The kindest, the gentlest, the most feeling, and the most generous that ever beat in the bosom of bearded man! And yet, when the occasion required it, the bravest and the most daring also. He never beheld a case of human woe without melting before it; he never encountered an apparition of earthly danger without giving it defiance. Where is the friend, or even the stranger, in danger, or distress, to whose succor he did not fly, and whose sorrowful or perilous case he did not make his own? When—where—was he ever called upon for a service, or a sacrifice, and rendered not, upon the instant, the one or the other, as the occasion required?

"The senatorial service of this rare man fell upon trying times—high party times—when the collisions of party too often embittered the ardent feelings of generous natures; but who ever knew bitterness, or party animosities in him? He was, indeed, a party man—as true to his party as to his friend and his country; but beyond the line of duty and of principle—beyond the debate and the vote—he knew no party, and saw no opponent. Who among us all, even after the fiercest debate, ever met him without meeting the benignant smile and the kind salutation? Who of us all ever needed a friend without finding one in him? Who of us all was ever stretched upon the bed of sickness without finding him at its side? Who of us all ever knew of a personal difficulty of which he was not, as far as possible, the kind composer?

"Such was Senator Linn, in high party times, here among us. And what he was here, among us, he was every where, and with every body. At home among his friends and neighbors; on the high road among casual acquaintances; in foreign lands among strangers; in all, and in every of these situations, he was the same thing. He had kindness and sympathy for every human being; and the whole voyage of his life was one continued and benign circumnavigation of all the virtues which adorn and exalt the character of man. Piety, charity, benevolence, generosity, courage, patriotism, fidelity, all shone conspicuously in him, and might extort from the beholder the impressive interrogatory, '*For what place was this man made?*' Was it for the Senate, or the camp? For public or for private life? For the bar or the bench? For the art which heals the diseases of the body, or that which cures the infirmities of the State? For which of all these was he born? And the answer is, 'For all!' He was born to fill the largest and most varied circle of human excellence; and to crown all these advantages, Nature had given him what the great Lord Bacon calls a perpetual letter of recommendation—a countenance, not only good, but sweet and winning—radiant with the virtues of his soul—captivating universal confidence; and such as no stranger could behold—no traveller, even in the desert, could meet, without stopping to reverence, and saying 'Here is a man in whose hands I could deposit life, liberty, fortune, honor!' Alas! that so much excellence should have perished so soon! that such a man should have been snatched away at the early age of forty-eight, and while all his faculties were still ripening and developing!

"In the life and character of such a man, so exuberant in all that is grand and beautiful in human nature, it is difficult to particularize excellences or to pick out any one quality, or circumstance, which could claim pre-eminence over all others. If I should attempt it, I should point, among his measures for the benefit of the whole Union, to the Oregon Bill; among his measures for the benefit of his own State, to the acquisition of the Platte Country; among his private virtues, to the love and affection which he bore to that brother—the half-brother only—who, only thirteen years older than himself had been to him the tenderest of fathers. For twenty-nine years I had known the depth of that affection, and never saw it burn more brightly than in our last interview, only three weeks before his death. He had just travelled a thousand miles out of his way to see that brother; and his name was still the dearest theme of his conversation—a conversation, strange to tell! which turned, not upon the empty and fleeting subjects of the day, but upon things solid and eternal—upon friendship, and upon death, and upon the duties of the living to the dead. He spoke of two friends whom it was natural to believe that he should survive, and to whose memories he intended to pay the debt of friendship. Vain calculation! Vain impulsion of generosity and friendship! One of these two friends now discharges that mournful debt to him: the other[6] has written me a letter, expressing his '*deep sorrow for the untimely death of our friend*, Dr. LINN.'"

Mr. BENTON then offered the following resolutions:

"*Resolved unanimously*, That the members of the Senate, from sincere desire of showing every mark of respect due to the memory of the Hon. LEWIS F. LINN, deceased, late a member thereof, will go into mourning, by wearing crape on the left arm for thirty days.

"*Resolved unanimously*, That, as an additional mark of respect for the memory of the Hon. LEWIS F. LINN, the Senate do now adjourn."

"Mr. CRITTENDEN said: I rise, Mr. President, to second the motion of the honorable senator from Missouri, and to express my cordial concurrence in the resolutions he has offered.

"The highest tribute of our respect is justly due to the honored name and memory of Senator Linn, and there is not a heart here that does not pay it freely and plenteously. These resolutions are but responsive to the general feeling that prevails throughout the land, and will afford to his widow and his orphans the consolatory evidence that their *country* shares their grief, and mourns for their bereavement.

"I am very sensible, Mr. President, that the very appropriate, interesting, and eloquent remarks of the senator from Missouri [Mr. BENTON] have made it difficult to add any thing that will not impair the effect of what he has said; but I must beg the indulgence of the Senate for a few moments. Senator Linn was by birth a Kentuckian, and my countryman. I do not dispute the claims of Missouri, his adopted State; but I wish it to be remembered, that I claim for Kentucky the honor of his nativity; and by the great law that regulates such precious inheritances, a portion, at least, of his fame must descend to his native land. It is the just ambition and right of Kentucky to gather together the bright names of her children, no matter in what lands their bodies may be buried, and to preserve them as her jewels and her crown. The name of Linn is one of her jewels; and its pure and unsullied lustre shall long remain as one of her richest ornaments.

"The death of such a man is a national calamity. Long a distinguished member of this body, he was continually rewarded with the increasing confidence of the great State he so honorably represented; and his reputation and usefulness increased at every step of his progress.

"In the Senate his death is most sensibly felt. We have lost a colleague and friend, whose noble and amiable qualities bound us to him as with 'hooks of steel.' Who of us that knew him can forget his open, frank, and manly bearing—that smile, that seemed to be the pure, warm sunshine of the heart, and the thousand courtesies and kindnesses that gave a 'daily beauty to his life?'

"He possessed a high order of intellect; was resolute, courageous, and ardent in all his pursuits. A decided party man, he participated largely and conspicuously in the business of the Senate and the conflicts of its debates; but there was a kindliness and benignity about him, that, like polished armor, turned aside all feelings of ill-will or animosity. He had political opponents in the Senate, but not one enemy.

"The good and generous qualities of our nature were blended in his character;

'——and the elements So mixed in him, that Nature might stand up And say to all the world—*This was a man.*'

The resolutions were then adopted, and the Senate adjourned.

CHAPTER CXVII.

THE COAST SURVEY: ATTEMPT TO DIMINISH ITS EXPENSE, AND TO EXPEDITE ITS COMPLETION, BY RESTORING THE WORK TO NAVAL AND MILITARY OFFICERS.

Under the British government, not remarkable for its economy, the survey of the coasts is exclusively made by naval officers, and the whole service presided by an admiral, of some degree—usually among the lowest; and these officers survey not only the British coasts throughout all their maritime possessions, but the coasts of other countries where they trade, when it has not been done by the local authority. The survey of the United States began in the same way, being confined to army and navy officers; and costing but little: now it is a civil establishment, and the office which conducts it has almost grown up into a department, under a civil head, and civil assistance costing a great annual sum. From time to time efforts have been made to restore the naval superintendence of this work, as it was when it was commenced under Mr. Jefferson: and as it now is, and always has been, in Great Britain. At the session 1842-'3, this effort was renewed; but with the usual fate of all attempts to put an end to any unnecessary establishment, or expenditure. A committee of the House had been sitting on the subject for two sessions, and not being able to agree upon any plan, proposed an amendment to the civil and diplomatic appropriation bill, by which the legislation, which they could not agree upon, was to be referred to a board of officers; and their report, when accepted by the President, was to become law, and to be carried into effect by him. Their proposition was in these words:

> "That the sum of one hundred thousand dollars be appropriated, out of any money in the Treasury not otherwise appropriated, for continuing the survey of the coast of the United States: *Provided*, That this, and all other appropriations hereafter to be made for this work, shall, until otherwise provided by law, be expended in accordance with a plan of re-organizing the mode of executing the survey, to be submitted to the President of the United States by a board of officers which shall be organized by him, to consist of the present superintendent, his two principal assistants, and the two naval officers now in charge of the hydrographical parties, and four from among the principal officers of the corps of topographical engineers; none of whom shall receive any additional compensation whatever for this service, and who shall sit as soon as organized. And the President of the United States shall adopt and carry into effect the plan of said board, as agreed upon by a majority of its members; and the plan of said board shall cause to be employed as many officers of the army and navy of the United States as will be compatible with the successful prosecution of the work; the officers of the navy to be employed on the hydrographical parts, and the officers of the army on the topographical parts of the work. And no officer of the army or navy shall hereafter receive any extra pay, out of this or any future appropriations, for surveys."

In support of this proposition, Mr. Mallory, the mover of it, under the direction of the committee, said:

> "It would be perceived by the House, that this amendment proposed a total re-organization of the work; and if it should be carried out in the spirit of that amendment, it would correct many of the abuses which some of them believed to exist and would effect a saving of some $20,000 or $30,000, by dispensing with the services of numerous civil officers, believed not to be necessary, and substituting for them officers of the topographical corps and officers of the navy. The committee had left the plan of the survey to be decided on by a board of officers, and submitted to the President for his approval, as they had not been able to agree among themselves on any detailed plan. He had, to be sure, his own views as to how the work should be carried on; but as they did not meet the concurrence of a majority of the committee, he could not bring them before the House in the form of a report."

This was the explanation of the proposition. Not being able to agree to any act of legislation themselves, they refer it to the President, and a board, to do what they could not, but with an expectation that abuses in the work would be corrected, expense diminished, and naval and military officers substituted, as far as compatible with the successful prosecution of the work. This was a lame way of getting a reform accomplished. To say nothing of the right to delegate legislative authority to a board and the President, that mode of proceeding was the most objectionable that could have been devised. It is a proverb that these boards are a machine in the hands of the President, in which he and they equally escape responsibility—they sheltering themselves under his approval—he, under their recommendation and, to make sure of his approval, it is usually obtained before the recommendation is made. This proposed method of effecting a reform was not satisfactory to those who wished to see this branch of the service subjected to an economical administration, and brought to a conclusion within some reasonable time. With that view, Mr. Charles Brown, of Pennsylvania, moved a reduction of the appropriation of more than one half, and a transference of the work from the Treasury department (where it then was) to the navy department where it properly belonged; and proposed the work to be done by army and naval officers. In support of his proposal, he said:

"The amendment offered under the instructions of the committee, did not look to the practical reform which the House expected when this subject was last under discussion. He believed, that there was a decided disposition manifested in the House to get clear of the present head of the survey; yet the amendment of the gentleman brought him forward as the most prominent member of it. He thought the House decided, when the subject was up before, that the survey should be carried on by the officers of the general government; and he wished it to be carried on in that way now. He did not wish to pay some hundred thousand dollars as extra pay for officers taken from private life, when there were so many in the navy and army perfectly competent to perform this service. This work had cost nearly a million of dollars ($720,000) by the employment of Mr. Hassler and his civil assistants alone, without taking into consideration the pay of the officers of the navy and army who were engaged in it."

The work had then been in hand for thirty years, and the average expense of each year would be $22,000; but it was now increased to a hundred thousand; and Mr. Brown wished it carried back more than half—a saving to be effected by transferring the work to the Navy Department, where there were so many officers without employment—receiving pay, and nothing to do. In support of his proposal, Mr. Brown went into an examination of the laws on the subject, to show that this work was begun under a law to have it done as he proposed; and he agreed that the army and navy officers (so many of whom were without commands), were competent to it; and that it was absurd to put it under the Treasury Department.

"The law of February 10, 1807, created the coast survey, put it in the hands of the President, and authorized him to use army and navy officers, navy vessels, astronomers, and other persons. In August, 1816 Mr. Hassler was appointed superintendent. His agreement was to "make the principal triangulation and consequent calculations himself; to instruct the engineer and naval officers employed under him; and he wanted two officers of engineers, topographical or others, and some cadets of said corps, in number according to circumstances. April 14, 1818, that part of the law of 1807 was repealed which authorized the employment of other persons than those belonging to the army and navy. Up to this time over $55,000 were expended in beginning the work and buying instruments, for which purpose Mr. Hassler was in England from August 1811, to 1815.

"June 10, 1832, the law of 1807 was revived, and Mr. Hassler was again appointed superintendent. The work has been going on ever since. The coast has been triangulated from Point Judith to Cape Henlopen (say about 300 miles); but only a part of the off-shore soundings have been taken. There are about 3,000 miles of seaboard to the United States. $720,000 have been expended already. It is stated, in Captain Swift's pamphlet, that the survey of the coast was under the Treasury Department, because Mr. Hassler was already engaged under that department, making weights and measures. These are all made now. When the coast survey was begun, the topographical corps existed but in name. In 1838, it was organized and enlarged, and is now an able and useful corps. Last year Congress established a hydrographical bureau in the Navy Department. There are numbers of naval officers capable of doing hydrographical duties under this bureau. The coast survey is the most important topographical and hydrographical work in the country. We have a topographical and a hydrographical bureau, yet neither of them has any connection with this great national work. Mr. Hassler has just published from the opinion of the Marquis de La Place (Chamber of Peers, session of 1816-'17), upon the French survey, this valuable suggestion, viz: 'Perhaps even the great number of geographical engineers which our present state of peace allows to employ in this work, to which it is painful to see them strangers, would render an execution more prompt, and less expensive.'

"The Florida war is now over; many works of internal improvement are suspended; there must be topographical officers enough for the coast survey. The Russian government has employed an able American engineer to perform an important scientific work; but that wise government requires that all the assistants shall come from its corps of engineers, which is composed of army and navy officers. If the coast survey is to be a useful public work, let the officers conduct it under their bureaus. The officers would then take a pride in this duty, and do it well, and do it cheap. The supervision of the bureaus would occasion *system*, fidelity, and entire responsibility. More than $30,000 are now paid annually to citizens, for salary out of the coast survey appropriation. This could be saved by employing officers. Make exclusive use of them, and half the present annual appropriation would suffice. Can the treasury department manage the survey understandingly? The Secretary of the Treasury has already enough to do in the line of his duty; and, as far as the survey is concerned, a clerk in the Treasury Department is the secretary. Can a citizen superintendent, of closet and scientific habits; or can a clerk in the Treasury Department, manage, with efficiency and economy, so many land and water parties, officers, men, vessels, and boats? The Navy Department pays out of the navy appropriation the officers and men now lent to the Treasury for the survey. The Secretary of the Navy appears to have no control over the expenditures of this part of the naval appropriation. He does not even select the officers detailed for this duty, though he knows his own material best, and those who are most suitable. This navy duty has become treasury patronage, with commands, extra pay, &c.

"The Treasury Department has charge of the vessels; they are bought by the coast-survey appropriation; the off-shore soundings are only in part taken. There arc not vessels enough, and of the right sort, to take these soundings, and in the right way. Steamers are wanted. The survey appropriation cannot bear the expense, but if the Navy Department had charge of the hydrography, it could put suitable vessels on the coast squadron, and employ them on the coast survey, agreeably to the law of 1807. Last year the vessels did no soundings until about the 1st of June, although the spring opened early. The Treasury had not the means to equip the vessels until the appropriation bill passed Congress. But if the navy had charge of vessels, the few naval stores they wanted might have been furnished from the navy stores, or given from second-hand articles not on charge at the yards. Had good arrangements been made, the Delaware Bay might readily have been finished last fall, and the chart of it got out at once. Now, the topographical corps makes surveys for defences; the navy officers make charts along the coast; and the coast survey goes over the same place a third time. If the officers did this work, the army might get the military information, and the navy the hydrographical knowledge, which the interest of the country requires that each of these branches of the public defence should have; and this, at the expense of but one survey; for, at places where defences might be required, the survey could be done with the utmost minuteness. The officers of the army and navy need not clash. The topographical corps (aided by junior navy officers willing to serve under that bureau—and the recent Florida war and the present coast survey system, show that navy officers are willing to serve, for the public good, under other departments than their own) would do the topography and furnish the shore line. The hydrographical officers would receive the shore line, take the soundings, and make the chart. The same principle is now at work, and works well. The navy officers now get the shore line from the citizens in the shore parties. The President could direct the War and Navy Secretaries to make such rules, through the bureaus, as would obviate every difficulty. Employing officers would secure for the public, system, economy, and despatch. The information obtained would be got by the right persons and kept in the right hands. Government would have complete command of the persons employed; and should the work ever be suspended, might, at pleasure, set them to work again on the same duty. The survey he wished to be prosecuted without delay; and all he wanted was to have it under the most efficient management. If it was found that the officers of the navy and army were not competent, it could be remedied hereafter; but it was due to them to give them a fair trial, before they were condemned. Certainly they ought not to be disgraced and condemned in advance. It was an insult to them to suppose that Mr. Hassler was the only man in the country capable of superintending this work; and that they could not carry on the survey of our coast by triangulation. They had been for some time, and were now, surveying the lakes; and he believed their surveys would be equally correct with Mr. Hassler's. We had a bureau of hydrography of the navy, and a corps of topographical engineers, which were expressly created to perform this kind of service; while there was the military academy at West Point, which qualified the officers to perform it. The people would hardly believe that these officers (educated at the expense of the government) were not capable of performing the services for which they were educated; and if they thought so, they would be for abolishing that institution. They would say that these officers should be dismissed, and others appointed in their places, who were qualified.

"He never could acknowledge that there was no other man but Mr. Hassler in the country capable of carrying on the work. This might have been the case when he was first appointed, thirty years ago; but since that time they had a number of officers educated at the military academy, while many others in the civil walks of life had qualified themselves for scientific employments. He was sure that the officers of the army and navy were competent to perform this work. There was but little now for the topographical engineers to do; and he had no doubt that many of them, as well as officers of the navy, would be glad to be employed on the coast survey. Indeed, several officers of the navy had told him that they would like such employment, rather than be idle, as they then were. From the rate the coast survey had thus far proceeded, it would take more than a hundred years to complete it. Certainly this was too slow. He hoped, therefore, a change would be made. In the language of the report of Mr. Aycrigg: 'We should then have the survey conducted on a system of practical utility, and moving *right* end foremost.'"

These were wise suggestions, and unanswerable; but although they could not be answered they could be prevented from becoming law. Instead of reform of abuses, reduction of expense, and speedy termination of the work, all the evils intended to be reformed went on and became greater than ever, and all are still kept up upon the same arguments that sustained the former. It is worthy of note to hear the same reason now given for continuing the civilian, Mr. Bache, at the head of this work, which was given for thirty years for retaining Mr. Hassler in the same place, namely, that there is no other man in the country that can conduct the work. But that is a tribute which servility and interest will pay to any man who is at the head of a great establishment; and is always paid more punctually where the establishment ought to be abolished than where it ought to be preserved; and for the obvious reason, that the better one can stand on its own merits, while the worse needs the support of incessant adulation. Mr. Brown's proposal was rejected—the other adopted; and the coast survey now costs above five hundred thousand dollars a year in direct appropriations, besides an immense amount indirectly in the employment of government vessels and officers: and no prospect of its termination. But the friends of this great reform did not abandon their cause with the defeat of Mr. Brown's proposition. Another was offered by Mr. Aycrigg of New Jersey, who moved to discontinue the survey until a report could be made upon it at the next session; and for this motion there were 75 yeas—a respectable proportion of the House, but not a majority. The yeas were:

"Messrs. Landaff W. Andrews, Sherlock J. Andrews, Thomas D. Arnold, John B. Aycrigg, Alfred Babcock, Henry W. Beeson, Benjamin A. Bidlack, David Bronson, Aaron V. Brown,

Milton Brown, Edmund Burke, William B. Campbell, Thomas J. Campbell, Robert L. Caruthers, Zadok Casey, Reuben Chapman, Thomas C. Chittenden, James Cooper, Mark A. Cooper, Benjamin S. Cowen, James H. Cravens, John R. J. Daniel, Garrett Davis, Ezra Dean, Edmund Deberry, Andrew W. Doig, John Edwards, John C. Edwards, Joseph Egbert, William P. Fessenden, Roger L. Gamble, Thomas W. Gilmer, Willis Green, William Halsted, Jacob Houck, jr., Francis James, Cave Johnson, Nathaniel S. Littlefield, Abraham McClellan, James J. McKay, Alfred Marshall, John Mattocks, John P. B. Maxwell, John Maynard, William Medill, Christopher Morgan, William M. Oliver, Bryan Y. Owsley, William W. Payne, Nathaniel G. Pendleton, Francis W. Pickens, John Pope, Joseph F. Randolph, Kenneth Rayner, Abraham Rencher, John Reynolds, Romulus M. Saunders, Tristram Shaw, Augustine H. Shepperd, Benjamin G. Shields, William Slade, Samuel Stokely, Charles C. Stratton, John T. Stuart, John B. Thompson, Philip Triplett. Hopkins L. Turney, David Wallace, Aaron Ward, Edward D. White, Joseph L. White, Joseph L. Williams, Thomas Jones Yorke, John Young."

The friends of economy in Congress, when once more strong enough to form a party, will have a sacred duty to perform to the country—that of diminishing, by nearly one-half, the present mad expenditures of the government: and the abolition of the present coast-survey establishment should be among the primary objects of retrenchment. It is a reproach to our naval and military officers, and besides untrue in point of fact, to assume them to be incapable of conducting and of performing this work: it is a reproach to Congress to vote annually an immense sum on the civil superintendence and conduct of this work, when there are more idle officers on the pay-roll than could be employed upon it.

CHAPTER CXVIII.

DEATH OF COMMODORE PORTER, AND NOTICE OF HIS LIFE AND CHARACTER.

The naval career of Commodore Porter illustrates in the highest degree that which almost the whole of our naval officers, each according to his opportunity, illustrated more or less—the benefits of the cruising system in our naval warfare. It was the system followed in the war of the Revolution, in the *quasi* war with France, and in the war of 1812—imposed upon us by necessity in each case, not adopted through choice. In neither of these wars did we possess ships-of-the-line and fleets to fight battles for the dominion of the seas; fortunately, we had not the means to engage in that expensive and fatal folly; but we had smaller vessels (frigates the largest) to penetrate every sea, attack every thing not too much over size, to capture merchantmen, and take shelter when pressed where ships-of-the-line and fleets could not follow. We had the enterprising officers which a system of separate commands so favorably developes, and the ardent seamen who looked to the honors of the service for their greatest reward. Wages were low; but reward was high when the man before the mast, or the boy in the cabin, could look upon his officer, and see in his past condition what he himself was, and in his present rank what he himself might be. Merit had raised one and might raise the other.

The ardor for the service was then great; the service itself heroic. A crew for a frigate has been raised in three hours. Instant sailing followed the reception of the order. Distant and dangerous ground was sought, fierce and desperate combat engaged; and woe to the enemy that was not too much over size! Five, ten, twenty minutes would make her a wreck and a prize. Almost every officer that obtained a command showed himself an able commander. Every crew was heroic; every cruise daring: every combat a victory, where proximate equality rendered it possible. Never did any service, in any age or country, exhibit so large a proportion of skilful, daring, victorious commanders, mainly developed by the system of warfare which gave so many a chance to show what they were. Necessity imposed that system; judgment should continue it. Economy, efficiency, utility, the impossibility of building a navy to cope with the navies of the great maritime Powers, and the insanity of doing it if we could, all combine to recommend to the United States the system of naval warfare which does the most damage to the enemy with the least expense to ourselves, which avoids the expensive establishments which oppress the finances of other nations, and which renders useless, for want of an antagonist, the great fleets which they support at so much cost.

Universally illustrated as the advantages of this system were by almost all our officers in the wars of the Revolution, of '98, and 1812, it was the fortune of Commodore Porter, in the late war with Great Britain, to carry that illustration to its highest point, and to show, in the most brilliant manner, what an American cruiser could do. Of course we speak of his cruise in the Pacific Ocean, prefaced by a little preliminary run to the Grand Banks, which may be considered as part of it—a cruise which the boy at school would read for its romance, the mature man for its history, the statesman for the lesson which it teaches.

The Essex, a small frigate of thirty-two guns, chiefly carronades, and but little superior to a first-class sloop-of-war of the present day, with a crew of some three hundred men, had the honor to make this illustrious cruise. Leaving New York in June, soon after the declaration of war, and making some small captures, she ran up towards the Grand Banks, and in the night discovered a fleet steering north, all under easy sail and in open order, wide spaces being between the ships. From their numbers and the course they steered Captain Porter judged them to be enemies, and wished to know more about them.

Approaching the sternmost vessel and entering into conversation with her, he learnt that the fleet was under the convoy of a frigate, the Minerva, thirty-six guns, and a bomb-vessel, both then ahead; and that the vessels of the fleet transported one thousand soldiers. He could have cut off this vessel easily, but the information he had received opened a more brilliant prospect. He determined to pass along through the fleet, the Essex being a good sailer, speaking the different vessels as he quietly passed them, get alongside of the frigate, and carry her by an energetic attack. In execution of this plan he passed on without exciting the least suspicion, and came up with the next vessel; but this second one was more cautious than the first, and, on the Essex's ranging up alongside of her, she took alarm and announced her intention to give the signal of a stranger having joined the fleet. This put an end to disguise and brought on prompt action. The vessel, under penalty of being fired into, was instantly ordered to surrender and haul out of the convoy. This was so quietly done as to be unnoticed by the other ships. On taking possession of her she was found to be filled with soldiers, one hundred and fifty of them, and all made prisoners of war.

A few days afterwards the Essex fell in with the man-of-war Alert, of twenty guns and a full crew. The Alert began the action. In eight minutes it was finished, and the British ship only saved from sinking by the help of her captors. It was the first British man-of-war taken in this contest, and so easily, that not the slightest injury was done to the Essex, either to the vessel or her crew. Crowded now with prisoners (for the crew of the Alert had to be taken on board, in addition to the one hundred and fifty soldiers and the previous captures), all chafing in their bondage, and ready to embrace the opportunity of the first action to rise, Captain Porter agreed with the commander of the Alert to convert her into a cartel, and send her into port at St. John's, with the prisoners, to await their exchange. Continuing her cruise, the Essex twice fell in with the enemy's frigates having other vessels of war in company, so that a fair engagement was impossible. The Essex then returned to the Delaware to replenish her stores, and, sailing thence in October, 1812, she fairly commenced her great cruise.

Captain Porter was under orders to proceed to the coast of Brazil, and join Commodore Bainbridge at a given rendezvous, cruising as he went. It was not until after he had run the greater part of the distance, crossing the equator, that he got sight of the first British vessel, a small man-of-war brig, discovered in the afternoon, chased, and come up with in the night, having previously boldly shown her national colors. The two vessels were then within musket shot. Not willing to hurt a foe too weak to fight him, Captain Porter hailed and required the brig to surrender. Instead of complying, the arrogant little man-of-war turned upon its pursuer, attempting to cross the stern of the Essex, with the probable design to give her a raking fire and escape in the dark. Still the captain would not open his guns upon so diminutive a foe until he had tried the effect of musketry upon her. A volley was fired into her, killing one man, when she struck. It was the British government packet Nocton, ten guns, thirty-one men, and having fifty-five thousand silver dollars on board.

Pursuing his cruise south to the point of rendezvous, an English merchant vessel was captured, one of a convoy of six which had left Rio the evening before in charge of a man-of-war schooner. The rest of the convoy was out of sight, but, taking its track, a long and fruitless chase was given; and the Essex repaired to the point of rendezvous, without meeting with further incident. Commodore Bainbridge had been there, and had left; and, being now under discretionary orders, Captain Porter determined to use the discretion with which he was invested, and took the bold resolution to double Cape Horn, enter the Pacific Ocean, put twenty thousand miles between his vessel and an American port, and try his fortune among British whalers, merchantmen, and ships-of-war in that vast and remote sea.

It was a bold enterprise, such as few governments would have ordered, which many would have forbid, and which the undaunted resolution of a bold commander alone could take. He had every thing against him: no depots, no means of repairing or refitting; only one chart; the Spanish American States subservient to the British, and unreliable for the impartiality of neutrals, much less for the sympathy of neighbors. He was deficient both in provisions and naval stores, but expected to furnish himself from the enemy, whose vessels in that capacious and distant sea, were always well supplied; and the silver taken from the British government packet would be a means towards paying wages.

In the middle of January, after a most tempestuous passage, he had doubled the Cape, entered the Pacific, his characteristic motto, FREE TRADE AND SAILORS' RIGHTS, at the mast-head, and ran for Valparaiso—the great point of maritime resort in the South Pacific. He had expected to find it a Spanish town, as it was when he left the United States: he found it Chilian, for Chili, in the mean time, had declared her independence: and this change he had a right to deem favorable, as, in addition to the advantages of conventional neutrality, it was fair to count upon the good feeling of a young and neighboring republic. In this he was not disappointed, being well received, meeting good treatment, obtaining supplies, and acquiring valuable information. He learnt that the American whalers were in great danger, most of them ignorant of the war, cruisers in pursuit of them, and one already taken. He learnt also that the Viceroy of Peru had sent out corsairs against American shipping—a piece of information of the highest moment, as it showed him an enemy where he expected a neutral, and enabled him to know how to deal with Peruvian ships when he should meet them. This criminality on the part of the viceroy was the result of a conclusion of his own, that as Spain and Great Britain were allies against France, so they would soon be allies against the United States, and that he, as a good Spanish viceroy should begin without waiting for the orders. This let Captain Porter see that he had two enemies instead of one to contend with in the Pacific; and this information, as it showed increase of danger to American interests, increased his ardor to go to their protection; which he promptly did.

Barely taking time to hurry on board the supplies, which six months already at sea rendered indispensable, he was again in pursuit of the enemy, and soon had the good fortune to fall in with an American whale-ship, which gave the important intelligence that a Peruvian corsair had just captured two American whalers off Coquimbo and was making for that place, with a British vessel in company. This was exciting information, and presented a three-fold enterprise to the chivalrous spirit of Porter—to rescue the American, punish the Peruvian, and capture the Englishman. Instantly all sail was set for Coquimbo, the American whaler which had given the information in company, and all hearts beating high with expectation, and with the prospect of performing some generous and gallant deed.

In a few hours a strange sail was descried in the distance, with a smaller vessel in company; and soon the sail was suspected to be a cruiser, disguised as a whaler. Then some pretty play took place, allowable in maritime war, although entirely a game of deception. The stranger showed Spanish colors; the Essex showed English, and then fired a gun to leeward. The whaler in company with the Essex hoisted the American flag *beneath* the English jack. All these false indications are allowable to gain advantages before fighting, but not to fight under, when true colors must be shown by the attacking ship under the penalty of piracy.

Gun signals were then resorted to. The stranger fired a shot ahead of the Essex, as much as to say *stop and talk*; the Essex fired a shot over him, signifying *come nearer*. She came, for the implication was that the next shot would be into her. When nearer, the stranger sent an armed boat to board the Essex; but the boat was directed to return with an order to the stranger to pass under the frigate's lee (*i. e.* under her guns), and to send an officer on board to apologise for the shots he had fired at an *English* man-of-war. The order was promptly complied with. The stranger came under the lee of the Essex and sent her lieutenant on board, who, not suspecting where he was, readily told him that his ship was the Nereyda, Peruvian privateer, of fifteen guns and a full crew; that they were cruising for Americans, and had already taken two (the same mentioned by the whaler); and that the smaller vessel in company was one of these.

After giving this information he made the apology for the shot, which was that, having put one of their American prizes in charge of a small crew, the English letter-of-marque Nimrod had fallen in with it and taken it from the crew, and that they were cruising for this Nimrod with a view to obtain redress, and had mistaken this frigate for her, and hence the shot ahead of her; and hoped the explanation would constitute a sufficient apology. It did so; Capt. Porter was perfectly satisfied with it, and still more so, with the information which accompanied it. It placed the accomplishment of one of his three objects immediately in his hands, and the one perhaps dearest to his heart—that of catching the Peruvian corsair which was preying upon American commerce. So, civilly dismissing the lieutenant, he waited until he had got aboard of the Nereyda, then run up the American flag, fired a shot over the corsair, and stood ready to fire into her. The caution was sufficient: the Peruvian surrendered immediately, with her prize. Thus was the piratical capture of two American whalers promptly chastised, and one of them released, and the Peruvian informed that he and his countrymen were cruising against Americans in mistake, and would be treated as pirates if they continued the practice. This admonition put an end to Peruvian seizure of American vessels.

Believing that the other American whaler captured by the Nereyda, and taken from her prize-crew by the Nimrod would be carried to Lima, Captain Porter immediately bore away for its port (Callao), approached it, hauled off to watch, saw three vessels standing in, prepared to cut them off, and especially the foremost, which he judged to be an American. She was so, and was cut off—the very whaler he was in search of. It was the Barclay; and the master, crew and all, so rejoiced at their release that they immediately joined their deliverer. The Barclay became the consort of the Essex; her crew enlisted under Porter; the master became (what he greatly needed) a pilot for him in the vast and unknown sea he was traversing. There was now a good opportunity to look into this most frequented of Peruvian ports, which Captain Porter did, showing English colors; and, seeing nothing within that he would have a right to catch when it came out, nor gaining any special information, and finding that nothing had occurred there to make known his arrival in the Pacific, he immediately sailed again, to make the most of his time before the fact of his presence should be known and the alarm spread.

He stood across the main towards Chatham Island and Charles Island, approaching which three sail were discovered in the same moment—two in company, the other apart and in a different direction. The one apart was attended to first, pursued, summoned, captured, and proved to be the fine British whaler Montezuma, with fourteen hundred barrels of oil on board. A crew was put on board of her, and chase given to the other two. They had taken the alarm, seeing what was happening to the Montezuma, and were doing their best to escape. The Essex gained upon them; but when within eight miles it fell calm, dead still—one of those atmospheric stagnations frequent in the South Sea. Sailing ceased; boats were hoisted out; the first lieutenant, Downes, worthy second to Porter, was put in command. Approached within a quarter of a mile, the two ships showed English colors and fired several guns. Economizing powder and time, the boats only replied with their oars, pulling hard to board quick; seeing which the two ships struck, each in succession, as the boarders were closing. They proved to be the Georgiana and the Policy, both whalers, the former built for the East India service, pierced for eighteen guns, and having six mounted when taken. Having the reputation of a fast vessel, the captain determined to equip her as a cruiser, which was done with her own guns and those of the Policy—this latter, like the Georgiana, pierced for eighteen guns, but mounting ten.

A very proper compliment was paid to Lieut. Downes in giving him the command of this British ship, thus added to the American navy with his good exertions. An armament of 16 guns, and a crew of 41 men, and her approved commander, it was believed would make her an over-match for any English letters of marque, supposed to be cruising among these islands, and justify occasional separate expeditions.

By these three captures Capt. Porter was enabled to consummate the second part of his plan—that of living upon the enemy. He got out of them ample supplies of beef, bread, pork, water, and Gallipagos tortoises. Besides food for the men, many articles were obtained for repairing his own ship: and accordingly the rigging was overhauled and tarred down, many new spars were fitted, new cordage supplied, the Essex repainted—all in the middle of the Pacific, and at the expense of a Power boasting great fleets, formidable against other fleets, but useless against a daring little cruiser.

Getting into his field of operation in the month of April, Capt. Porter had already five vessels under his command—the Montezuma, the Georgiana, the Barclay, and the Policy, in addition to the Essex. All cruising together towards the middle of that month, and near sunset in the evening, a sail was perceived in the distant horizon. A night-chase might permit her to escape; a judicious distribution of his little squadron, without alarming, might keep her in view till morning. It was distributed accordingly. At daylight the sail was still in sight, and, being chased, she was soon overtaken and captured. It was the British whaler Atlantic, 355 tons, 24 men, pierced for 20 guns, and carrying 8 18-pounder carronades. While engaged in this chase another sail was discovered, pursued, and taken. It was the Greenwich, of 338 tons, 18 guns, and 25 men; and like the other was an English letter of marque.

In the meanwhile the now little man-of-war the Georgiana, under Lieut. Downes, made a brief excursion of her own among the islands, apart from the Essex, and with brilliant success. He took, without resistance, the British whale ships Catherine, of 270 tons, 8 guns, and 29 men, and Rose, of 220 tons, 8 guns and 21 men; and, after a sharp combat, a third whaler, the Hector, 270 tons, 25 men, pierced for 20 guns and 11 mounted. In this action the lieutenant, after having manned his two prizes, had but 21 men and boys left to manage his ship, fight the Hector, and keep down fifty prisoners. After manning the Hector and taking her crew on board his own vessel, he had but ten men to perform the double duty of working the vessel and guarding seventy-three prisoners; yet he brought all safe to his captain, who then had a little fleet of nine sail under his command, all of his own creation, and created out of the enemy.

The class of some of his prizes enabled the captain to increase the efficiency of his force by some judicious changes. The Atlantic, being nearly one hundred tons larger than the Georgiana, a faster ship, and every way a better cruiser, was converted into a sloop-of-war, armed with twenty guns, manned by sixty men, named the

Essex Junior; and the intrepid Downes put in command of her. The Greenwich, also armed with guns, but only a crew to work her (for so many prizes to man left their cruisers with their lowest number,) was converted into a store-ship, and received all the spare stores of the other ships. A few days afterwards the Sir Andrew Hammond was captured, believed to be about the last of the British whalers in those parts, and among the finest. She was a ship of three hundred and ten tons, twelve guns, and thirty-one men; and had a large supply of beef, pork, bread, wood, and water—adding sensibly to the supplies of the little fleet.

The fourth of July arrived, and was gaily kept, and with the triumph of victorious feelings, firing salutes with British guns, charged with British powder. It was a proud celebration, and must have looked like an illusion of the senses to the British prisoners, accustomed to extol their country as the mistress of the seas, and to consider American ships as the impressment ground of the British navy. The celebration over, the little fleet divided; Essex Junior bound to Valparaiso, with the Hector, Catherine, Policy, and Montezuma, prizes, and the Barclay, re-captured ship, under convoy. The Essex, with the Greenwich and Georgiana, steered for the Gallipagos Islands, and fell in with three sail at once, the whole of which were eventually captured: one, the English whaler Charlton, of 274 tons, ten guns, and 21 men; another, the largest of the three, the Seringapatam, of 357 tons, 14 guns, and 40 men; the smallest of the three, the New Zealander, 260 tons, 8 guns, and 23 men. Here were 900 tons of shipping, 32 guns, and 75 men all taken at once, and, as it were, at a single glance at the sea.

The Seringapatam had been built for a cruiser, and, of all the ships in the Pacific, was the most dangerous to American commerce. It had just come out, and had already made a prize. Finding that the master had no commission, and that he had commenced cruising in anticipation of one, and thereby subjected himself to be treated as a pirate, Captain Porter had him put in irons, and sent to the United States to be tried for his life. While finding himself encumbered with prisoners, and his active strength impaired by the guards they required, he released a number on parole, and gave them up one of the captured ships (the Charlton) to proceed to Rio Janeiro. The Georgiana and the New Zealander were despatched to the United States, each laden with the oil taken from the British whalers. Encumbered with prizes, as well as with prisoners, and no American port in which to place them (for the mouth of the Columbia, though claimed by the United States since 1804, and settled under Mr. John Jacob Astor since 1811, had not then been nationally occupied), Captain Porter undertook to provide a place of his own. Repairing to the wild and retired island of Nooaheevah, he selected a sequestered inlet, built a little fort upon it, warped three of his prizes under its guns, left a little garrison of twenty-one men under Lieutenant Gamble to man it, and then went upon another cruise.

The story of the remainder of his cruise is briefly told. He had learnt that the British government, thoroughly aroused by his operations in the Pacific, had sent out a superior force to capture him. Taking the Essex Junior with him, he sailed for Valparaiso, entered the harbor, and soon a superior British frigate and a sloop of war entered also. Captain Hillyar, for that was the British captain's name, saluted the American frigate courteously, inquiring for the health of Captain Porter; but the British frigate (the Phœbe) came so near that a collision seemed inevitable, and looked as if intended, her men being at quarters and ready for action. In a moment Captain Porter was equally ready, and that either for boarding or raking, for the vessels had got so close that the Phœbe, in hauling off, passed her jib-boom (that spar which runs out from the bowsprit) over the deck of the Essex, and lay with her bow to the broadside of the American. It was a fatal position, and would have subjected her to immediate capture or destruction, justifiable by the undue intimacy of an enemy. Captain Porter might have fired into her; but, reluctant to attack in a neutral port, he listened to the protestations of the British captain, accepted his declaration of innocent intentions and accidental contact, and permitted him to haul off from a situation in which he could have been destroyed in a few minutes. Could he have foreseen what was to happen to himself soon after in the same port, he could not have been so forbearing to the foe nor so respectful to the Chilian authorities.

For six weeks the hostile vessels watched each other, the British vessel sometimes lying off and on outside of the harbor, and when so at sea the Essex going out and offering to fight her single handed; for the Essex Junior was too light to be of any service in a frigate fight. Other British ships of war being expected at Valparaiso, and no combat to be had with the Phœbe without her attendant sloop, Captain Porter determined to take his opportunity to escape from the harbor—which the superior sailing of the Essex would enable him to do when the British ships were a few miles off, as they often were—Essex Junior escaping at the same time by parting company, as it was certain that both the British ships would follow the American frigate.

March 28th, 1813, was a favorable day for the attempt—the wind right, the enemy far enough out, and the Essex in perfect order for fighting or sailing. The attempt was made, and with success, until, doubling a headland which formed part of the harbor, a squall carried away the maintopmast, crippling the ship and greatly disabling her. Capt. Porter put back for the harbor, and though getting within it, and within pistol shot of the shore, and within half a mile from a detached battery, could not reach the usual anchoring ground before the approach of the enemy compelled him to clear for action. A desperate but most unequal combat raged for near three hours—an inferior crippled frigate contending with a frigate and a sloop in perfect order. The crippled mast of the Essex allowed the enemy to choose his distance, which he always did with good regard to his own safety, using his long eighteens at long distances—keeping out of the reach of Porter's carronades, out of the reach of boarding, and only within range of six long twelves which played with such effect that at the end of half an hour both British ships hauled off to repair damages. Having repaired, both returned, and got such a position that not a gun of the crippled Essex could bear upon them. An attempt was made to close upon them and get near enough to cripple the sloop and drive her out of the fight for the remainder of the action; but the frigate edged away, choosing her distance, and using her long guns with terrible effect upon the Essex, which could not send back a single shot.

The brave and faithful Downes pulled through the fire of the enemy in an open boat to take the orders of his captain; but his light guns could be of no service, and he was directed to look to his own ship. Twice more the Essex endeavored to close upon the British frigate, but she edged away each time, keeping the distance which was safe to himself and destructive to the Essex. By this time half the whole crew were killed or wounded, and the ship on fire. Capt. Porter then attempted to run her on shore; but the wind failed when within musket shot of the land. Leave was then given to the crew to save themselves by swimming, which but few would do. At last the surrender became imperative. The Essex struck, and her heroic commander and surviving men and officers became prisoners of war. Thousands of persons—all Valparaiso—witnessed the combat. The American consul, Mr. Poinsett, witnessed it and claimed the protection of the fort, only to receive evasive answers, as the authorities were now favorable to the British. It was a clear case of violated neutrality, tried by any rule. First, the Essex was within the harbor, though not at the usual anchoring place, which she could not reach; secondly, she was under the guns of the detached fort, only half a mile distant; thirdly, she was within the territorial jurisdiction of Chili, whether measured by the league or by the range of cannon, and no dispute about either, as the shore was at hand, and the British balls which missed the Essex hit the land.

After the surrender some arrangements were made with Capt. Hillyar. Some prisoners were exchanged upon the spot, part of those made by Capt. Porter being available for an equal number of his own people. Essex Junior became a cartel to carry home himself and officers and others of his men on parole; but this man of daring deeds was not allowed to reach home without another proof of his determined spirit. When within thirty miles of New York, Essex Junior was brought to by the British razee Saturn, Capt. Nash, who denied the right of Capt. Hillyar to allow the cartel, and ordered her to lie by him during the night. Capt. Porter put off in a whale-boat, and, though long chased, saved himself by the chance of a fog coming to the aid of hard rowing.

And thus ended this unparalleled cruise—ending with a disaster. But the end could not efface the past; could not undo the captures which had been made; could not obscure the glory which had been acquired; cannot impair the lesson which its results impress on the minds of statesmen. It had lasted eighteen months, and during that time the little frigate had done every thing for itself and the country. It had lived and flourished upon the enemy. Not a dollar had been drawn from the public Treasury, either for pay or supplies; all came from the foe. Money, provisions, munitions, additional arms, spars, cordage, rigging, and vessels to constitute a little fleet, all came from the British. Far more than enough for all purposes was taken and much destroyed; for damage as well as protection was an object of the expedition—damage to the British, protection to Americans; and nobly were both objects accomplished. Surpluses, as far as possible, were sent home; and, though in part recaptured, these accidents did not diminish the merit of the original capture. The great whale trade of the British in the Pacific was broken up, the supply of oil was stopped, the London lamps were in the condition of those of the "foolish virgins," and a member of Parliament declared in his place that the city had burnt dark for a year.

The personal history of Commodore Porter, for such he became, was full of incident and adventure, all in keeping with his generous and heroic character. Twice while a lad and serving in merchant vessels in the West Indies, he was impressed by the British, and, by his courage and conduct made his escape, each time. A third attempt at impressment was repulsed by the bloody defeat of the press-gang. The same attempt, renewed with increased numbers, was again repulsed with loss to the British party—young Porter, only sixteen, among the most courageous defenders of the vessel. He was upwards of a year a prisoner at Tripoli, being first lieutenant on board the Philadelphia when she grounded before that city and was captured. He was midshipman with the then Lieutenant Rodgers, when the two young officers and eleven men performed that marvel of endurance, firmness, steadiness, and seamanship, in working for three days and nights, without sleep or rest, on the French frigate Insurgent, guarding all the time their 173 prisoners, and conducting the prize safe into port—as related in the notice of Commodore Rodgers.

After his return from the Pacific, he was employed in suppressing piracy in the West Indies, which he speedily accomplished; but for punishing an insult to the flag in the island of Porto Rico, he incurred the displeasure of his government, and the censure of a court martial. His proud spirit would not brook a censure which he deemed undeserved; and he resigned his commission in the navy, of which he was so brilliant an ornament. The writer of this View was a close observer of that trial, and believed the Commodore to have been hardly dealt by, and considered the result a confirmation of his general view of courts martial where the government interferes—an interference (when it happens) generally for a purpose, either to convict or acquit; and rarely failing of its object in either case, as the court is appointed by the government, dependent upon it for future honor and favor, acts in secret, and subject to the approval of the Executive.

Stung to the quick by such requital of his services, the brave officer resigned his commission, and left the country which he had served so faithfully, and loved so well, and took service in the Republic of Mexico, then lately become independent and desirous to create a navy. But he was not allowed to live and mourn an exile in a foreign land. President Jackson proposed to restore him to his place in the navy, but he refused the restoration upon the same ground that he had resigned upon—would not remain in a service under an unreversed sentence of unjust censure. President Jackson then gave him the place of Consul General at Algiers; and, upon the reduction of that place by the French, appointed him the United States Charge d'Affaires to the Sublime Porte—a mission afterwards raised to Minister Resident by act of Congress for his special benefit. The Sultan Mahmoud—he who suppressed the Janissaries, introduced European reforms, and so greatly favored Christians and strangers—was then on the throne, and greatly attached to the Commodore, whose conversation and opinions he often sought. He died in this post, and was brought home to be buried in the country which gave him birth, and which no personal wrong could make him cease to love. A national ship of war, the Truxton, brought him home—a delicate compliment in the selection of the vessel bearing the name of the commander under whom he first served.

Humanity was a ruling feature in his character, and of this he gave constant proof—humane to the enemy as well as to his own people. Of his numerous captures he never made one by bloodshed when milder means could prevail; always preferring, by his superior seamanship, to place them in predicaments which coerced surrender. Patriotism was a part of his soul. He was modest and unpretentious; never seeming to know that he had done things of which the world talked, and of which posterity would hear. He was a "lion" nowhere but on the quarter-deck, and in battle with the enemies of his country. He was affectionate to his friends and family, just and kind to his men and officers, attaching all to him for life and for death. His crew remaining with him when their terms were expiring in the Pacific, and refusing to quit their commander when authorized to do so at Valparaiso, were proofs of their devotion and affection.

Detailed history is not the object of this notice, but character and instruction—the deeds which show character, and the actions which instruct posterity; and in this view his career is a lesson for statesmen to study—to study in its humble commencement as well as in its dazzling and splendid culmination. Schools do not form such commanders; and, if they did, the wisdom of government would not detect the future illustrious captain in the man before the mast, or in the boy in the cabin. Born in Boston, the young Porter came to man's estate in Baltimore, and went to sea at sixteen in the merchant ship commanded by his father—the worthy father of such a son—making many voyages to the West Indies. There he *earned* his midshipman's warrant, and there he learned the seamanship which made him the worthy second of Rodgers in that marvellous management of the Insurgent, which faithful history will love to commemorate. Self-made in the beginning, he was self-acting through life, and will continue to act upon posterity, if amenable to the lesson taught by his life: the merchant service, the naval school, cruisers, the naval force, separate commands for young men. With a little 32 gun frigate, all carronades except a half-dozen stern chasers, and they only twelve-pounders, he dominated for a year in the vast Pacific Ocean; with a 44 and her attendant sloop-of-war, brig, and schooner, he would have dominated there to the end of the war. He was the Paul Jones of the "second war of Independence," with a more capacious and better regulated mind, and had the felicity to transmit as well as to inherit the qualities of a commander. The name of Porter is yet borne with honorable promise on the roll of the American navy.

CHAPTER CXIX.

REFUNDING OF GENERAL JACKSON'S FINE.

During his defence of New Orleans in the winter of 1814-'15, General Jackson was adjudged to have committed a contempt of court, in not producing the body of a citizen in obedience to a writ of *habeas corpus*, whom he had arrested under martial law which he had proclaimed and enforced for the defence of the city. He was fined for the contempt, and paid it himself, refusing to permit his friends, and even the ladies of New Orleans who presented the money ($1,000), to pay it for him. He submitted to the judgment of the court, paying the amount before he left the court room, but protesting against it as an illegal exaction, and as involving the imputation of illegality on his conduct. This conveyed a reproach under which he was always sensitive, but to relieve himself from which he would countenance no proceeding while he was still on the theatre of public action, and especially while he was President. His retirement to private life removed the obstacle to the action of his friends and soon thereafter Mr. Linn, a senator from the State of Missouri, brought in a bill for refunding the fine. This was a quarter of a century after it had been imposed. On getting notice of this proceeding General Jackson wrote a letter to Senator Linn, of which the leading paragraphs are here given.

"Having observed in the newspapers that you had given notice of your intention to introduce a bill to refund to me the fine (principal and interest) imposed by Judge Hall, for the declaration of martial law at New Orleans, it was my determination to address you on the subject; but the feeble state of my health has heretofore prevented it. I felt that it was my duty to thank you for this disinterested and voluntary act of justice to my character, and to assure you that it places me under obligations which I shall always acknowledge with gratitude.

"It is not the amount of the fine that is important to me: but it is the fact that it was imposed for reasons which were not well founded; and for the exercise of an authority which was necessary to the successful defence of New Orleans; and without which, it must be now obvious to all the world, the British would have been in possession, at the close of the war, of that great emporium of the West. In this point of view it seems to me that the country is interested in the passage of the bill; for exigencies like those which existed at New Orleans may again arise; and a commanding-general ought not to be deterred from taking the necessary responsibility by the reflection that it is in the power of a vindictive judge to impair his private fortune, and place a stain upon his character which cannot be removed. I would be the last man on earth to do any act which would invalidate the principle that the military should always be subjected to the civil power; but I contend, that at New Orleans no measure was taken by me which was at war with this principle, or which, if properly understood, was not necessary to preserve it.

"When I declared martial law, Judge Hall was in the city; and he visited me often, when the propriety of its declaration was discussed, and was recommended by the leading and patriotic citizens. Judging from his actions, he appeared to approve it. The morning the order was issued he was in my office; and when it was read, he was heard to exclaim: '*Now the country may be saved: without it, it was lost.*' How he came afterwards to unite with the treacherous and disaffected, and, by the exercise of his power, endeavored to paralyze my exertions, it is not necessary here to explain. It was enough for me to know, that if I was excusable in the declaration of martial law in order to defend the city when the enemy were besieging it, it was right to continue it until all danger was over. For full information on this part of the subject, I refer you to my defence under Judge Hall's rule for me to appear and show cause why an attachment should not issue for a contempt of court. This defence is in the appendix to 'Eaton's Life of Jackson.'

"There is no truth in the rumor which you notice, that the fine he imposed was paid by others. Every cent of it was paid by myself. When the sentence was pronounced, Mr. Abner L. Duncan (who had been one of my aides-de-camp, and was one of my counsel), hearing me request Major Reed to repair to my quarters and bring the sum—not intending to leave the room until the fine was paid—asked the clerk if he would take his check. The clerk replied in the affirmative, and Mr. Duncan gave the check. I then directed my aide to proceed forthwith, get the money, and meet Mr. Duncan's check at the bank and take it up; which was done. These are the facts; and Major Davezac, now in the Assembly of New York, can verify them.

"It is true, as I was informed, that the ladies did raise the amount to pay the fine and costs; but when I heard of it, I advised them to apply it to the relief of the widows and orphans that had been made so by those who had fallen in the defence of the country. It was so applied, as I had every reason to believe; but Major Davezac can tell you more particularly what was done with it."

The refunding of the fine in the sense of a pecuniary retribution, was altogether refused and repulsed both by General Jackson and his friends. He would only have it upon the ground of an illegal exaction—as a wrongful exercise of authority—and as operating a declaration that, in declaring martial law, and imprisoning the citizen under it, and in refusing to produce his body upon a writ of *habeas corpus*, and sending the judge himself out of the city, he was justified by the laws of the land in all that he did. Congress was quite ready, by a general vote, to refund the fine in a way that would not commit members on the point of legality. It was a thing constantly done in the case of officers sued for official acts, and without strict inquiry into the legality of the act where the officer was acting in good faith for the public service. In all such cases Congress readily assumed the pecuniary consequences of the act, either paying the fine, or damages awarded, or restoring it after it had been paid. General Jackson might have had his fine refunded in the same way without opposition; but it was not the money, but release from the imputation of illegal conduct that he desired; and with a view to imply that release the bill was drawn: and that made it the subject of an earnestly contested debate in both Houses. In the Senate, where the bill originated, Mr. Tappan of Ohio, vindicated the recourse to martial law, and as being necessary for the safety of the city.

"I ask you to consider the position in which he was placed; the city of New Orleans was, from the necessity of the case, his camp; the British, in superior force, had landed, and were eight or nine miles below the city; within three hours' march; in his camp were many over whom he had no control, whom he could not prevent (or punish by any process of civil law) from conveying intelligence to the enemy of his numbers, means of defence or offence, as well as of his intended or probable movements; was not the entire command of his own camp necessary to any efficient action? It seems to me that this cannot be doubted. In time of war, when the enemy's force is near, and a battle is impending, if your general is obliged, by the necessities of his position, and the propriety of his operations, to occupy a city as his camp, he must have the entire command of such city, for the plain reason that it is impossible, without such command, to conduct his operations with that secrecy which is necessary to his success. The neglect, therefore, to take such command, would be to neglect the duty which his country had imposed upon him. I perceive but two ways in which General Jackson could have obtained the command of his own camp; one was by driving all the inhabitants out of the city, the other by declaring martial law. He wisely and humanely chose the latter, and by so doing, saved the city from being sacked and plundered, and its inhabitants from being outraged or destroyed by the enemy."

But this arrest of a citizen, and refusal to obey a writ of habeas corpus, was after the British had been repulsed, and after a rumor of peace had arrived at the city, but a rumor coming through a British commander, and therefore not to be trusted by the American general. He thought the peace a probable, but by no means a certain event: and he could not upon a probability relax the measures which a sense of danger had dictated. The reasons for this were given by the General himself in his answer to show cause why the rule which had been granted should not be made absolute.

"The enemy had retired from their position, it is true; but they were still on the coast, and within a few hours' sail of the city. They had been defeated, and with loss; but that loss was to be repaired by expected reinforcements. Their numbers much more than quadrupled all the regular forces which the respondent could command; and the term of service of his most efficient militia force was about to expire. Defeat, to a powerful and active enemy, was more likely to operate as an incentive to renewed and increased exertion, than to inspire them with despondency, or to paralyze their efforts. A treaty, it is true, had been probably signed, but yet it might not be ratified. Its contents even had not transpired; so that no reasonable conjecture could be formed whether it would be acceptable; and the influence which the account of the signature had on the army was deleterious in the extreme, and showed a necessity for increased energy, instead of relaxation of discipline. Men who had shown themselves zealous in the preceding part of the campaign, became lukewarm in the service. Wicked and weak men, who, from their situation in life, ought to have furnished a better example, secretly encouraged the spirit of insubordination. They affected to pity the hardships of those who were kept in the field; they fomented discontent, by insinuating that the merits of those to whom they addressed themselves, had not been sufficiently noticed or applauded; and disorder rose to such an alarming height, that at one period only fifteen men and one officer were found out of a whole regiment, stationed to guard the very avenue through which the enemy had penetrated into the country. At another point, equally important, a whole corps, on which the greatest reliance had been placed, operated upon by the acts of a foreign agent, suddenly deserted their post. If, trusting to an uncertain peace, the respondent had revoked his proclamation, or ceased to act under it, the fatal security by which they were lulled, would have destroyed all discipline, dissolved all his force, and left him without any means of defending the country against an enemy instructed by the traitors within our bosom, of the time and place at which he might safely make his attack. In such an event, his life, which would certainly have been offered up, would have been but a feeble expiation for the disgrace and misery into which his criminal negligence would have plunged the country."

A newspaper in the city published an inflammatory article, assuming the peace to be certain, though not communicated by our government, inveighed against the conduct of the General in keeping up martial law as illegal and tyrannical, incited people to disregard it, and plead the right of volunteers to disband who had engaged to serve during the war. Louallier, a member of the General Assembly, was given up as the author of the article: the General had him arrested and confined. Judge Hall issued a writ of habeas corpus to release his body: General Jackson ordered the Judge out of the city, and sent a guard to conduct him out. All this took place on the 10th and 11th of March: on the 13th authentic news of the peace arrived, and the martial law ceased to exist. Judge Hall returned to the city, and Mr. Tappan thus relates what took place:

"Instead of uniting with the whole population, headed by their venerable bishop, in joy and thankfulness for a deliverance almost miraculous, achieved by the wisdom and energy of the General and the gallantry of his army, he was brooding over his own imaginary wrongs, and planning some method to repair his wounded dignity. On this day, twenty-seven years ago, he caused a rule of the district court to be served on General Jackson, to appear before him and show cause why an attachment should not issue against him for:—1st. Refusing to obey a writ issued by Judge Hall. 2d. Detaining an original paper belonging to the court. And 3d, for imprisoning the Judge. The first cause was for the General refusing to obey a writ of *habeas corpus* in the case of Louallier; the second for detaining the writ. The whole of these three causes assigned are founded on the hypothesis, that instead of General Jackson having command of his camp, he exercised a limited authority under the control of the civil magistracy. I trust I have satisfied you that martial law did in fact exist, and of necessary consequence, that Judge Hall's authority was suspended. If he was injured by it, surely he was not the proper person to try General Jackson for that injury. The principal complaint against General Jackson was for imprisoning the Judge. The imprisonment consisted in sending an officer to escort him out of camp; and for this, instead of taking the regular legal remedy, by an action for assault and false imprisonment, in the State court, which was open to him as well as every other citizen, he called the General to answer before himself. He went before the Judge and proffered to show cause; the Judge would not permit him to do this, nor would he allow him to assign his reasons in writing for his conduct, but, without trial, without a hearing of his defence, he fined him one thousand dollars. You all know the conduct of the General on that occasion; he saved the Judge from the rising indignation of the people and paid his fine to the United States marshal. These proceedings of Judge Hall were not only exceedingly outrageous, but they were wholly illegal and void; for, as says an eminent English jurist, 'even an act of parliament cannot make a man a judge in his own cause.' This was truly and wholly the cause of the Judge himself. If a law of Congress had existed which authorized him to sit in judgment upon any man for an injury inflicted upon himself, such a law would have been a mere dead letter, and the Judge would have been bound to disregard it. It was the violation of this principle of jurisprudence which aroused the indignation of the people and endangered the life of his contemptible judge. I am aware of the law of contempt; it is the power of self-preservation given to the courts; it results from necessity alone, and extends no further than necessity strictly requires; it has no power to avenge the wrongs and injuries done to the judge, unless those wrongs obstruct the regular course of justice. I am aware also of the manner in which the law of contempt has been administered in our courts where no statute law regulated it, and it was left to the discretion of the judges to determine what was or was not a contempt. In one case a man was fined for contempt for reviewing the opinion of a judge in a newspaper. This judge was impeached before this body and acquitted, because not quite two-thirds of the Senate voted him guilty. Some senators, thinking probably that as Congress had neglected to pass a law on the subject of contempt, the judge had nothing to govern his discretion in the matter, and therefore ought not to be convicted. Congress immediately passed such a law, and no contempts have occurred since in the United States courts."

The speech of Judge Tappan covered the facts of the case, upon which, and other speeches delivered, the Senate made up its mind, and the bill was passed, though upon a good division, and a visible development of party lines. The yeas were:

"Messrs. Allen, Bagby, Benton, Buchanan, Calhoun, Cuthbert, Fulton, Graham, Henderson, King, Linn, McDuffie, McRoberts, Mangum, Rives, Sevier, Smith of Connecticut, Smith of Indiana, Sprague, Sturgeon, Tallmadge, Tappan, Walker, Wilcox, Williams, Woodbury, Wright, Young—28."

The nays were:

"Messrs. Archer, Barrow, Bates, Bayard, Berrien, Choate, Clayton, Conrad, Crafts, Crittenden, Dayton, Evans, Huntington, Kerr, Merrick, Miller, Morehead, Phelps, White, Woodbridge—20."

In the House it was well supported by Mr. Charles Jared Ingersoll, and others, and passed at the ensuing session by a large majority—158 to 28. This gratifying result took place before the death of General Jackson, so that he had the consolation of seeing the only two acts which impugned the legality of any part of his conduct—the senatorial condemnation for the removal of the deposits, and the proceedings in New Orleans under martial law—both condemned by the national representation, and the judicial record as well as the Senate journal, left free from imputation upon him.

CHAPTER CXX.

REPEAL OF THE BANKRUPT ACT: ATTACK OF MR. CUSHING ON MR. CLAY: ITS REBUKE.

This measure was immediately commenced in the House of Representatives, and pressed with vigor to its conclusion. Mr. Everett, of Vermont, brought in the repeal bill on leave, and after a strenuous contest from a tenacious minority, it was passed by the unexpected vote of two to one—to be precise—140 to 72. In the Senate it had the same success, and greater, being passed by nearly three to one—34 to 13: and the repealing act being carried to Mr. Tyler, he signed it as promptly as he had signed the bankrupt act itself. This was a splendid victory for the minority who had resisted the passage of the bill, and for the people who had condemned it. The same members, sitting in the same chairs, who a year and a half before, passed the act, now repealed it. The same President who had recommended it in a message, and signed the act as soon as it passed, now signed the act which put an end to its existence. A vicious and criminal law, corruptly passed, and made the means of passing two other odious measures, was itself now brought to judgment, condemned, and struck from the statute-book; and this great result was the work of the people. All the authorities—legislative, executive, and judicial—had sustained the act. Only one judge in the whole United States (R. W. Wells, Esq., United States district judge for Missouri), condemned it as unconstitutional. All the rest sustained it, and he was overruled. But the intuitive sense of honor and justice in the people revolted at it. They rose against it in masses, and condemned it in every form—in public meetings, in legislative resolves, in the press, in memorials to Congress, and in elections. The tables of the two Houses were loaded with petitions and remonstrances, demanding the repeal, and the members were simply the organs of the people in pronouncing it. Never had the popular voice been more effective—never more meritoriously raised. The odious act was not only repealed, but its authors rebuked, and compelled to pronounce the rebuke upon themselves. It was a proud and triumphant instance of the innate, upright sentiment of the people, rising above all the learning and wisdom of the constituted authorities. Nor was it the only instance. The bankrupt act of forty years before, though strictly a bankrupt act as known to the legislation of all commercial countries, was repealed within two years after its passage—and that by the democratic administration of Mr. Jefferson: this of 1841, a bankrupt act only in name—an act for the abolition of debts at the will of the debtor in reality—had a still shorter course, and a still more ignominious death. Two such condemnations of acts for getting rid of debts, are honorable to the people, and bespeak a high degree of reverence for the sacred obligations between debtor and creditor; and while credit is due to many of the party discriminated as federal in 1800, and as whig in 1840 (but always the same), for their assistance in condemning these acts, yet as party measures, the honor of resisting their passage and conducting their repeal, in both instances, belongs to the democracy.

The repeal of this act, though carried by such large majorities, and so fully in accordance with the will of the people, was a bitter mortification to the administration. It was their measure, and one of their measures of "relief" to the country. Mr. Webster had drawn the bill, and made the main speech for it in the Senate, before he went into the cabinet. Mr. Tyler had recommended it in a special message, and promptly gave it his approving signature. To have to sign a repeal bill, so soon, condemning what he had recommended and approved, was most unpalatable: to see a measure intended for the "relief" of the people repulsed by those it was intended to relieve, was a most unwelcome vision. From the beginning the repeal was resisted, and by a species of argument, not addressed to the merits of the measure, but to the state of parties, the conduct of men, and the means of getting the government carried on. Mr. Caleb Cushing was the organ of the President, and of the Secretary of State in the House; and, identifying himself with these two in his attacks and defences, he presented a sort of triumvirate in which he became the spokesman of the others. In this character he spoke often, and with a zeal which outran discretion, and brought him into much collision with the House, and kept him much occupied in defending himself, and the two eminent personages who were not in a position to speak for themselves. A few passages from these speeches, from both sides, will be given to show the state of men and parties at that time, and how much personal considerations had to do with transacting the business of Congress. Thus:

"Mr. Cushing, who was entitled to the floor, addressed the House at length, in reply to the remarks made by various gentlemen, during the last three weeks, in relation to the present administration. He commenced by remarking that the President of the United States was accused of obstructing the passage of whig measures of relief, and was charged with uncertainty and vacillation of purpose. As these charges had been made against the President, he felt it to be his duty to ask the country who was chargeable with vacillation and uncertainty of purpose, and the destruction of measures of relief? Who were they who, with sacrilegious hands, were seeking to expunge the last measure of the 'ill-starred' extra session from the statute-books? Forty-seven whigs, he answered, associated with the democratic party in the House, and formed a coalition to blot out that measure. He repeated it: forty-seven whigs formed a coalition with the democrats to expunge all the remains of the extra session which existed. For three weeks past, there had been constantly poured forth the most eloquent denunciations of the President, of the Secretary of State, and of himself. He might imagine, as was said by Warren Hastings when such torrents of denunciation were poured out upon him, that there was some foundation for the imputation of the orators. He should inquire into the merits of the political questions, and into the accusations made against him. He was told that he had thrown a firebrand into the House—that he had brought a tomahawk here. He denied it. He had done no such thing. It was not true that he commenced the debate which was carried on; and when gentlemen said that he had volunteered remarks out of the regular order, in reply to the gentleman from Tennessee [Mr. ARNOLD], he told them that they were not judges. His mode of defence was counter-attack, and it was for him to judge of the argument. If he carried the war into the enemy's camp, the responsibility was with those who commenced the attack."

Mr. Clay, though retiring from Congress, and not a member of the House of Representatives, was brought into the debate, and accused of setting up a dictatorship, and baffling or controlling the constitutional administration:

"The position of the two great parties, and those few who stood here to defend the acts of the administration, was peculiar. Our government was now undergoing a test in a new particular. This was the first time that the administration of the government had ever devolved upon the Vice-President. Now, he had called upon the people and the House to adapt themselves to that contingency, and support the constitution; for with the 'constitutional fact' was associated the party fact; and whilst the President was not a party chief, there was a party chief of the party in power. The question was, whether there could be two administrations—one, a constitutional administration, by the President; and the other a party administration, exercised by a party chief in the capitol? With this issue before him—whether the President, or the party leader—the chief in the White House, or the chief in the capitol—should carry on the administration—he felt it to be a duty which he owed to the government of his country to give his aid to the constitutional chief. That was the real question which had pervaded all our contests thus far."

Such an unparliamentary reference to Mr. Clay, a member of a different House, could not pass without reply in a place where he could not speak for himself, but where his friends were abundant. Mr. Garret Davis, of Kentucky, performed that office, and found in the fifteen years' support of Mr. Clay by Mr. Cushing (previous to his sudden adhesion to Mr. Tyler at the extra session), matter of personal recrimination:

"Mr. Garret Davis replied to the portion of the speech of the gentleman from Massachusetts [Mr. CUSHING] relating to the alleged dictation of the ex-senator from Kentucky [Mr. CLAY]. The gentleman from Massachusetts declared that there were but two alternatives—one, a constitutional administration, under the lead of the President; and the other, a faction, under the lead of the senator from Kentucky. Such remarks were no more nor less than calumnies on that distinguished man; and he would ask the gentleman what principle Mr. Clay had changed, by which he had obtained the ill-will of the gentleman, after having had his support for fifteen years previous to the extra session? He asked, Did the senator from Kentucky bring forward any new measure at the extra session? Did he enter upon any untrodden path, in order to embarrass the path of John Tyler? No, was the answer."

Reverting to the attacks on the administration, Mr. Cushing considered them as the impotent blows of a faction, beating its brains out against the immovable rock of the Tyler government:

"It was now nearly two years since, in accordance with a vote of the people, a change took place in the administration of the government. Since that time, an internecine war had arisen in the dominant party. The war had now been pursued for about one year and a half; but, in the midst of it, the federal government, with its fixed constitution, had stood, like the god Terminus, defying the progress of those who were rushing against it. The country had seen one party throw itself against the immovable rock of the constitution. What had been the consequence? The party thus hurling itself against the constitutional rock was dashed to atoms."

Mr. Cushing did not confine his attempts to gain adherents to Mr. Tyler, to the terrors of denunciations and anathemas: he superadded the seductive arguments of persuasion and enticement, and carried his overtures so far as to be charged with putting up the administration favor to auction, and soliciting bidders. He had said:

"Now he would suppose a man called to be President of the United States. It mattered not whether he was elected, or whether the office devolved upon him by contingencies contemplated in the constitution. He was President. What, then, was his first duty? To consider how to discharge his functions. He (Mr. C.) thought the President was bound to look around at the facts, and see by what circumstances he was supported. Gentlemen might talk of treason; much had been said on that subject; but the question for the individual who might happen to be President to consider was, How is the government to be carried out? By whose aid? He (Mr. Cushing) would say to that party now having the majority (and whom, on account of that circumstance, it was more important he should address), that if they gave him no aid, it was his duty to seek aid from their adversaries. If the whigs continue to blockade the wheels of the government, he trusted that the democrats would be patriotic enough to carry it on."

Up to this point Mr. Cushing had addressed himself to the whigs to come to the support of Mr. Tyler: despairing of success there he now turned to the democracy. This open attempt to turn from one party to the other, and to take whichever he could get, turned upon him a storm of ridicule and reproach. Mr. Thompson, of Indiana, said:

"The gentleman seemed to have assumed the character of auctioneer for this bankrupt administration, and he took it that the gentleman would be entitled to a good part of its effects. This was the first time in the history of any civilized country that a government had, through the person of its acknowledged leader—a man doing most of its speaking, and much of its thinking—stalked into a representative assembly, and openly put up the administration in the common market to the highest bidder."

But Mr. Cushing did not limit himself to seductive appliances in turning to the democracy for support to Mr. Tyler: he dealt out denunciation to them also, and menaced them with the fate of the shattered whig party if they did not come to the rescue. On this Mr. Thompson remarked:

"The gentleman also told the minority that they would be dashed to pieces, like their predecessors, unless they came into the measures of the President; but it yet remained to be seen whether he would get a bid. Judging from the expression of opinion by the leading organ of the democratic party, he (Mr. T.) was inclined to think that no bid would be offered by a portion of that party. He thought, from givings-out, in various quarters, that the President would ultimately have to resort to this 'constitutional fact,' to defend himself against a large portion even of that party. Indeed, it was doubtful whether there would be bidders from either side."

Mr. Cushing had said that there were persons connected with the administration who would yet be heard of for the Presidency, and seemed to present that contingency also as a reason why support should be given it. To this intimation Mr. Thompson made an indignant reply:

"He recollected well—though he was very young at the time, and not prepared to take part in the political discussions of the day—that, during the administration of the distinguished and venerable gentleman from Massachusetts [Mr. ADAMS] there arose in this country a party, who, upon the bare supposition (which was dispelled on an examination of the facts)—upon the bare suspicion that there was what was called a bargain, intrigue, and management between the then head of the administration, and another distinguished citizen who was a member of his cabinet, made it a subject of the most bitter and vindictive denunciation. Yet, notwithstanding that this part of our history was still fresh in the recollection of the gentleman from Massachusetts—when we see, in this age of republican liberty, a gentleman descended from a line of illustrious Revolutionary ancestry—coming, too, almost from the very Cradle of Liberty, and acting as the organ of the administration on this floor—boldly, shamelessly, and unblushingly offering the spoils of office as a consideration for party support, we may well have cause for alarm. How many clerkships were there in Philadelphia to be disposed of in this manner? From the collector down to the lowest tide-waiter, the power of appointment was to be directed for the purpose of operating on the coming presidential contest. Who, now, would charge the whig party with shaping their measures with a view to the elevation of a particular individual, after hearing the bold and open avowal from the gentleman that the present administration would shape their measures for the purpose of operating on the coming contest? But (said Mr. T.) there was something exceedingly ridiculous in the idea of the administration party—and such a party, too!—coming into the Representative hall, and telling its members that it had the power to dispose of the various candidates for the Presidency at its pleasure, and controlling the votes of nearly three millions of freemen by means of its veto power, and the power of appointment and removal."

Mr. Cushing had belonged to the federal party, since called whig, up to the time that he joined Mr. Tyler, and had been all that time a fierce assailant of the democratic party: the energy with which he now attacked that party, and the warmth with which he wooed the other, brought on him many reproaches, some rough and cutting—some tender and deprecatory; as this from Mr. Thompson:

"The gentleman exulted in the fate of the whig party, and told them with much satisfaction that their party was destroyed. Now, let him ask the gentleman, in the utmost sincerity of his heart, whether he did not feel some little mortification and regret when he saw the banner under which he had so often rallied trailing in the dust, and trampled under the feet of those against whom he had fought for so many years?"

Foremost of the whigs in zeal and activity, Mr. Cushing, as one of the most prominent men of the party, was appointed when the presidential vote of 1840 was counted in the House, as one of the committee of two to wait upon General Harrison and formally make known to him his election. In two months afterwards General Harrison died—Mr. Tyler became President and quit the whigs: Mr. Cushing quit at the same time; and not content with quitting, threw all the obloquy upon them which, for fifteen years, he had lavished upon the democracy; and in quitting the whigs he reversed his conduct in all the measures of his life, and without giving a reason for the change in a single instance. Mr. Garret Davis summed up these changes in a scathing peroration, from which some extracts are here given:

"The gentleman occupies a strange position and puts forth extraordinary notions, considering the measures and principles which he always, until the commencement of this administration, advocated with so much zeal and ability I had read many of his speeches before I knew him. I admired his talents and attainments; I approved of the soundness of his views, and was instructed and fortified in my own. But he is wonderfully metamorphosed; and I think if he will examine the matter deliberately, he will find it to be quite as true, that he has broken his neck politically in jumping his somersets, as that 'the whig party has knocked out its brains against the fixed fact.' He tells us that party is nothing but an association of men struggling for power; and that he contemns measures—that measures are not principles. The gentleman must have been reading the celebrated treatise, 'The Prince,' for such dicta are of the school of Machiavelli; and his sudden and total abandonment of all the principles as well as measures, to which he was as strongly pledged as any whig, good and true, proves that he had studied his lesson to some purpose. At the extra session of 1837, he opposed the sub-treasury in a very elaborate speech, in which we find these passages: 'We are to have a government paper currency, recognizable by the government of the United States, and employed in its dealings; but it is to be irredeemable government paper? 'If the scheme were not too laughingly absurd to spend time in arguing about it seriously; if the mischiefs of a government paper currency had not had an out-and-out trial both in Europe and America, I might discuss it as a question of political economy. But I will not occupy the committee in this way. I am astounded at the fatuity of any set of men who can think of any such project.' This is what he said of the sub-treasury. Now, he is the unscrupulous advocate of the exchequer, a measure embodying both the sub-treasury and a great organized government bank, and fraught with more frightful dangers than his own excited imagination had pictured in the whole three years.

"He was one of the stanchest supporters of a United States bank. He characterized 'the refusal of the late President (Jackson) to sign the bill re-chartering the bank, like the removal of the deposits, to be in defiance and violation of the popular will,' and characterized as felicitous the periods of time when we possessed a national bank, and as calamitous the periods that we were without them, saying—'Twice for long periods of time, have we tried a national bank, and in each period it has fulfilled its appointed purpose of supplying a safe and equal currency, and of regulating and controlling the issues of the State banks. Twice have we tried for a few years to drag on without a national bank, and each of these experiments has been a season of disaster and confusion.' And yet, sir, he has denied that he was ever the supporter of a bank of the United States, and is now one of the most rabid revilers of such an institution.

"He was for Mr. Clay's land bill; and he has abandoned, and now contemns it. No man has been more frequent and unsparing in his denunciations of General Jackson; and now he is the sycophantic eulogist of the old hero. He was the unflinching defender of the constitutional rights and powers of Congress. This administration has not only resorted to the most flagitious abuse of the veto power, but has renewed every other assault, open or insidious, of Presidents Jackson and Van Buren upon Congress, which he, at the time, so indignantly rebuked; and he now justifies them all. He has gone far ahead of the extremest parasites of executive power. John Tyler vetoed four acts of Congress which the gentleman had voted for, and strange, by his subtle sophistry, he defended each of the vetoes; and most strange, when the House, in conformity to the provisions of the constitution, voted again upon the measures, his vote was recorded in their favor, and to overrule the very vetoes of which he had just been the venal advocate."

This versatility of Mr. Cushing, in the support of vetoes, was one of the striking qualities developed in his present change of parties. He had condemned the exercise of that power in General Jackson in the case of the Bank of the United States, and dealt out upon him unmeasured denunciation for that act: now he became the supporter of all the vetoes of Mr. Tyler, even when those vetoes condemned his own votes, and when they condemned the fiscal bank charter which Mr. Tyler himself had devised and arranged for Congress. He became the champion, unrivalled, of Mr. Webster and Mr. Clay, defending them in all things; but now in attacking Mr. Clay whom he had so long, and until so recently, so closely, followed and loudly applauded, he became obnoxious to the severe denunciations of that gentleman's friends.

CHAPTER CXXI.

NAVAL EXPENDITURES, AND ADMINISTRATION ATTEMPTS AT REFORM: ABORTIVE.

The annual appropriation for this branch of the service being under consideration, Mr. Parmenter, the chairman of the naval committee, proposed to limit the whole number of petty officers, seamen, ordinary seamen, landsmen and boys in the service to 7,500; and Mr. Slidell moved an amendment to get rid of some 50 or 60 masters' mates who had been illegally appointed by Mr. Secretary Henshaw, during his brief administration of the naval department in the interval between his nomination by Mr. Tyler and his rejection by the Senate. These motions brought on a debate of much interest on the condition of the navy itself, the necessity of a peace establishment, and the reformation of abuses. Mr. Cave Johnson, of Tennessee—

"Expressed himself gratified to see the limitation proposed by the chairman of the Committee on Naval Affairs; that he had long believed that we should have a peace establishment for the navy, as well as the army; and that the number of officers and men in each should be limited to the necessities of the public service. Heretofore the navy had been left to the discretion of the Secretary, only limited by the appropriation bills. He urged upon the chairman of the Naval Committee the propriety of reducing still further. If he did not misunderstand the amendment, it proposed to man the number of vessels required for the next year in the same way that we would do in time of war, as we have heretofore done. He thought there should be a difference in the complement of men required for each ship in war and in peace. He read a table, showing that in the British service, first class men-of-war of 120 guns, in time of peace had on board (officers, men, and marines) 886 men, whilst the same class in our service had on board 1,200, officers, men, and marines—near one-third more officers and men in the American service than were employed in the British. The table showed about the same difference in vessels of inferior size. He thought the number of men and officers should be regulated for a peace, and not a war establishment. He expressed the hope that the chairman of the Naval Committee would so shape his amendment as to fix the number of officers and men for a peace establishment. He was desirous of having a peace establishment, and the expenditures properly regulated. This branch of the service, together with the army, were the great sources of expenditure. He read a table, showing the expenditures of these branches of the public service from 1821 to 1842, as follows: ($235,000,000.) He said the country would be astonished to see the immense sums expended on the army and navy; and, as he thought, without any adequate return to the country. He could see no advantage to the country from this immense expenditure—no adequate return. He was aware of the excuse made for it—the protection of our commerce. This was a mere pretext—an excuse for throwing upon the public treasury an immense number of men, who might be much more profitably to the country employed in other occupations. He alluded to the Mediterranean squadron and the expenditures for the protection of our commerce on that sea; and expressed the opinion that our expenditures at that station equalled the whole of the commerce east of the Straits of Gibraltar—that it would be better for the country to pay for the commerce than protect it; that there was no more need to protect our commerce in the Mediterranean than there was in the Chesapeake Bay. Such a thing as pirates in that sea had been scarcely heard of in the last twenty years. He expressed his determination to vote for the amendment, but hoped the chairman would so shape it as to make a regular peace establishment."

The member from Tennessee was entirely right in his desire for a naval peace establishment, but the principle on which such an establishment should be formed, was nowhere developed. It was generally treated as a naval question, dependent upon the number of naval marine—others a commercial question, dependent upon our amount of commerce; while, in fact, it is a political question, dependent upon the state of the world. Protection of commerce is the reason always alleged: that reason, pursued into its constituent parts, would always involve two inquiries, and both of them to be answered in reference to the amount of commerce, and its dangers in any sea. To measure the amount of a naval peace establishment, and its distribution in different seas, the amount of danger must be considered: and that is constantly varying with the changing state of the world. The great seat of danger was formerly in the Mediterranean Sea; and squadrons proportioned to the amount of that danger were sent there: since the extirpation of the piratical powers on the coast of the sea, there is no danger to commerce there, and no need for any protection; yet larger squadrons are sent there than ever. Formerly there was piracy in the West Indies, and protection was needed there: now there is no piracy, and no protection needed, and yet a home squadron must watch those islands. So of other places. There is no danger in many places now in which there was much formerly; and where we have most commerce there is no danger at all. This protection, the object of a naval peace establishment, is only required against lawless or barbarian powers: such powers require the presence of some ships of war to restrain their piratical disposition. The great powers which recognize the laws of nations, need no such negotiators as men-of-war. They do not commit depredations to be redressed by a broadside into a town: if they do injury to commerce it is either accidental, or in pursuance to some supposed right: and in either case friendly ministers are to negotiate, and the political power to resolve, before cannon are fired. Here then is the measure of a peace establishment: it is in the number and power of the barbarian or half-barbarian powers which are not amenable to the laws of nations, and whose lawless propensities can only be restrained by the fear of immediate punishment. There are but few of these powers at present—much fewer than there were fifty years ago, and can only be found by going to the extremities of the globe—and are of no force when found, and can be kept in perfect order by cruisers. As for the squadrons kept up in the Mediterranean, the Pacific coast, Brazil, and East Indies, they are there without a reason, and against all reason—have nothing to do but stay abroad three years, and then come home—to be replaced by another for another three years: and so on, until there shall be reform. Better far, if all these squadrons are to be kept up, that they should remain at home, spending their money at home instead of abroad, and just as serviceable to commerce. As for the home squadron, that was established by law, without reason, and should be suppressed without delay: and as for the African squadron, that was established by treaty to please Great Britain, and ought, in the first place, not to have been established at all; and in the second place, should have been suppressed as soon as the five years' obligation to keep it up had expired.

Mr. Hamlin, of Maine, spoke to the body of the case, and with knowledge of the subject, and a friendly feeling to the navy—but not such feeling as could wink at its abuses. He said:

> "He trusted he was the very last person who would detract from the well-merited fame of the navy; but he had another rule of action: he would endeavor so to vote in relation to this subject, as to check, if possible, what he believed the gross and extravagant expenditure of public money: and he referred gentlemen, in corroboration of this assertion that there was extravagance in the expenditures, to the report of the Committee on Naval Affairs. The facts which stared them in the face from every quarter justified him in the assertion that there was gross extravagance. Mr. H. referred to various items of expenditure, in proof of the existence of extravagance."

'Mr. Hamlin pointed to the enormous increase in the number of officers in the navy, constantly augmenting in a time of peace, instead of being diminished as the public good required:

> "He produced tables, taken from official returns, to show that the greater number of these officers were necessarily unemployed, and were spending their time at home in idleness. He had nothing to urge against any officer of the navy; they could not be blamed for receiving the allowance which the law gave them, whether employed or not;—but he asked gentlemen to examine the great disparity between the number of naval officers, as regulated by statute, and the number now in existence."

This was said before the naval school was created: since the establishment of that school, enough are legally appointed to officer a great navy. Two hundred and fifty midshipmen constantly there, coming off by annual deliveries, and demanding more ships and commissions than the public service and the public Treasury can bear. Illegal appointments have ceased, but the evil of excessive appointments is greater than ever.

Mr. Hamlin produced some items of extravagance, one of which he summed up, showing as the result that $2,142 97 was expended at one hospital in liquors for the "sick," and $10,288 53 for provisions: and then went on to say:

> "The amount expended within a period of one year on the coast of Florida by the commander of this little squadron, was five hundred and four thousand five hundred and eighty dollars; and yet the gentleman from South Carolina found in this nothing to induce the House to restrict the appropriations. Mr. H. said he would go for the amendment. He would go for any thing to stop the drafts these leeches were making on the Treasury. His principal object, however, in rising, was to call on the members to redeem the pledges of economy that they made at the beginning of the session, and he trusted that now that they had the opportunity they would redeem them. He was from a commercial State, and would be the last man to do any act that would be injurious to commerce; but he did not understand how commerce could be benefited or protected by suffering this enormous and profligate waste of public money to be continued. By introducing a proper system of economy and accountability, the navy would be more efficient, and the government would be able to employ more ships and more guns to protect commerce than they now did."

Mr. Hale replied to several members, and went on to speak of abuses in the navy expenditures, and the irresponsibility of officers:

> "There was an old maxim in the navy, that there was no law for a post-captain, and really the adage seemed now to be verified. The navy (said Mr. H.) is utterly without law, and the document just read by the gentleman from Maine [Mr. HAMLIN] showing the expenditures of the Florida squadron, proved it. Such conduct as was described in that document ought to make every American blush; but what was the result of it? Why, the officer came forward and demanded of the Secretary of the Navy (Mr. Henshaw) extra compensation as commander of a foreign squadron, and the Secretary paid him from five to seven thousand dollars more. It was to correct a thousand such abuses as this, that had crept into the navy, that he would offer the amendment which had been read for the information of the committee. Mr. H. went on to comment on the large amount of money unnecessarily expended for the navy. We have, said he, twice as many officers as there is any use for, and they receive higher pay than the officers of any navy in the world."

Mr. Hale believed we had too many navy-yards, and mentioned the condition of the one nearest his own home, as an exemplification of his opinion, Portsmouth, New Hampshire—

> "Where were stationed twenty-six officers, at an expense of $30,000 a year, and all to command six seamen and twelve ordinary seamen. This yard was commanded by a post-captain; and what duties had he to perform? Why, just nothing. What had the commander to do? Why, to help the captain; and as for the lieutenants, they had nothing to do but to give orders to the midshipmen."

The movement ended without results, and so of all desultory efforts at reform at any time. Abuses in the expenditure of public money are not of a nature to surrender at the first summons, nor to yield to any thing but persevering and powerful efforts. A solitary member, or a few members, can rarely accomplish any thing. The ready and efficient remedy lies with the administration, but for that purpose a Jefferson is wanted at the head of the government—a man not merely of the right principles, but of administrative talent, to know how to apply his economical doctrines. Such a President would now find a great field for economy and retrenchment in reducing our present expenditures about the one-half—from seventy odd millions to thirty odd. Next after an administration should come some high-spirited and persevering young men, who would lay hold, each of some great abuse, and pursue it without truce or mercy—year in, and year out—until it was extirpated. Some such may arise—one to take hold of the navy, one of the army, one of the civil and diplomatic—and gain honor for themselves and good for their country at the same time.

CHAPTER CXXII.

CHINESE MISSION: MR. CUSHING'S APPOINTMENT AND NEGOTIATION.

Ten days before the end of the session 1842-'3, there was taken up in the House of Representatives a bill reported from the Committee of Foreign Relations, to provide the means of opening future intercourse between the United States and China. The bill was unusually worded, and gave rise to criticism and objection. It ran thus:

> "That the sum of forty thousand dollars be, and the same is hereby, appropriated and placed at the disposal of the President of the United States, to enable him to establish the future commercial relations between the United States and the Chinese Empire on terms of national equal reciprocity; the said sum to be accounted for by the President, under the restrictions and in the manner prescribed by the act of first of July, one thousand seven hundred and ninety, entitled 'An act providing the means of intercourse between the United States and foreign nations.'"

This bill was unusual, and objectionable in all its features. It appropriated a gross sum to be disposed of for its object as the President pleased, being the first instance in a public act of a departure from the rule of specific appropriations which Mr. Jefferson introduced as one of the great reforms of the republican or democratic party. It withdrew the settlement of the expenditure of this money from the Treasury officers, governed by law, to the President himself, governed by his discretion. It was copied from the act of July 1st, 1790, but under circumstances wholly dissimilar, and in violation of the rule which condemned gross, and required specific, appropriations. That act was made in the infancy of our government, and when preliminary, informal, and private steps were necessary to be taken before public negotiations could be ventured. It was under that act that Mr. Gouverneur Morris was privately authorized by President Washington to have the unofficial interviews with the British ministry which opened the way for the public mission which ended in the commercial treaty of 1794. Private advances were necessary with several powers, in order to avoid rebuff in a public refusal to treat with us. Great latitude of discretion was, therefore, entrusted to the President; and that President was Washington. A gross sum was put into his hands, to be disposed of as he should deem proper for its object, that of intercourse between the United States and foreign nations, and to account for such part of the expenditure of the sum as, in his judgment, might be made public, and he was limited in the sums he might allow to $9,000 outfit, and $9,000 salary to a full minister—to $4,500 per annum to a chargé de affaires—and to $1,350 to a secretary of legation. This bill for the Chinese mission was framed upon that early act of 1790, and even adopted its mode of accounting for the money by leaving it to the President to suppress the items of the expenditure, when he should judge it proper. The bill was loose and latitudinous enough to shock the democratic side of the House; but not enough so to satisfy its friends; and accordingly the first movement was to enlarge the President's discretion, by striking from the bill the word "restrictions" which applied to his application of the money. Mr. Adams made the motion, and as he informed the House in the course of the discussion, at the instance and according to the wish of the Secretary of State (Mr. Webster). This motion gave rise to much objection. Mr. Meriwether, a member of the committee which had reported the bill, spoke first; and said:

> "He opposed the amendment. If he understood its effect, it would be to leave the mission without any restriction. The bill, as it came from the Committee on Foreign Affairs, placed this mission on the same footing as other missions. The Secretary of State, however, wished the whole sum placed at his own disposal and control—wished it left to him to pay as much as he pleased. He (Mr. M.) did not consider this mission to China as a matter of so much importance as had been claimed for it. He thought it would be difficult to persuade the people of that country to change their polity, give up their aversion to foreigners, and enter into commercial intercourse with other nations. He wished, at any rate, to have this mission placed on the same footing as other missions. He knew not how the whole of this sum of $40,000 was to be expended, although he was a member of the Committee on Foreign Affairs. Our ministers generally receive $9,000 a year salary, and $9,000 outfit. Now, if the amendment of

the gentleman from Massachusetts [Mr. ADAMS] should be adopted, it would be in the power of the President to pay the minister who might be sent to China $20,000 outfit, and $20,000 more salary. The minister would be subject to no expense, would go out in a national vessel, and would not be compelled to land until it suited his pleasure. Why make a difference in the case of China? Was that mission of greater importance than the French? Look at Turkey—a semi-barbarous country—where our minister received $6,000 a year. He thought if $6,000 was enough for the services of Commodore Porter at Constantinople, that sum would be sufficient for any minister that might be sent out to China. When the amendment now before the committee should have been disposed of, he should move to place the mission to China upon the same footing with that to Turkey."

In these remarks Mr. Meriwether shows it was the sense of the committee to make the appropriation in the usual specific form, leaving the accountability to the usual Treasury settlement; but that the bill was changed to its present shape at the instance of the Secretary of State. Some members placed their objections on the ground of no confidence in the administration that was to expend the money: thus, Mr. J. C. Clark, of New York:

"In the British Parliament, it is a legitimate ground of objection to a supply bill, that the objector has no confidence in the ministry. This bill proposes to vest in the President and Secretary of State a large discretion in the expenditure of forty thousand dollars; and I agree with my friend from Georgia [Mr. MERIWETHER], that there is good reason to doubt the propriety of giving to these men the disbursement of any money not imperiously called for by the exigencies of the public service. I place my opposition to this bill solely on the ground of an utter want of confidence in the political integrity of the President and some of his official advisers."

Mr. Adams replied to these objections:

"He did not think it necessary to waste the time of the House in arguing the propriety of a mission to China. The message of the President was sufficient on that point.

"He then replied to the objections urged against the bill, on the ground that it placed too much confidence in the President, and that the appropriation was to be made without restriction. The motion which he had submitted, to strike out the restrictions of law, which were applicable to other diplomatic appropriations, was made after a consultation with the Secretary of State, who thought that to impose restrictions might embarrass the progress of the negotiations."

Mr. McKeon, of New York, opposed the whole scheme of the mission to China, believing it to be unnecessary, and to be conducted with too much pomp and expense, and to lay the foundation for a permanent mission. He said:

"There was nothing so very peculiar in the case of China, that Congress should depart from the usual restrictions of law, which applied to diplomatic appropriations generally. He thought it would be better to take the matter quietly, and go about it in a quiet business manner. Should the bill pass as reported by the committee, it would authorize a minister at a salary of $9,000 and $9,000 outfit. Pass it according to the amendment of the gentleman from Massachusetts [Mr. ADAMS], and $40,000 would thereby be placed at the disposal of the Executive—more than he (Mr. McK.) was willing to see placed in the hands of any President. He should be as liberal as any man in fixing the salaries of the minister and secretary. But the appropriation was only a beginning. The largest ship in this country (the Pennsylvania) would no doubt be selected to carry out whomsoever should be selected as minister, in order to give as much *eclat* as possible to our country. Then other vessels would have to be sent to accompany this ship, and to sail where her size would not allow her to go. These, and other paraphernalia, would have to be provided for the minister; and this $40,000 would be but a beginning of the expense. He concluded by expressing the hope that the motion to strike out the restrictions contained in the bill, and thereby place the whole appropriation at the disposal of the President, would not prevail."

Mr. Bronson, of Maine, expressed it as his conviction, that we should possess more information before such a measure as that of sending a minister plenipotentiary to China should be adopted. He should prefer having a commercial agent for the present. The question was then taken on Mr. Adams's proposed amendment, and resulted in its adoption—80 votes for it; 55 against it. The previous question being called, the bill was then passed without further debate or amendment—yeas 96: nays 59. The nays were:

"Messrs.—Thomas D. Arnold, Archibald H. Arrington, Charles G. Atherton, Benjamin A. Bidlack, John M. Botts, David Bronson, Milton Brown, Charles Brown, Edmund Burke, William O. Butler, Patrick C. Caldwell, William B. Campbell, Zadock Casey, John C. Clark, Nathan Clifford, Walter Coles, Benjamin S. Cowen, James H. Cravens, George W. Crawford, Garrett Davis, Andrew W. Doig, William P. Fessenden, Charles A. Floyd, A. Lawrence Foster, Roger L. Gamble, James Gerry, William L. Goggin, William O. Goode, Willis Green, William A. Harris, John Hastings, Samuel L. Hays, Jacob Houck, jr., Robert M. T. Hunter, John W. Jones, George M. Keim, Nathaniel S. Littlefield, Abraham McClellan, James J. McKay, John McKeon, Albert G. Marchand, Alfred Marshall, John Maynard, James A. Meriwether, John Moore, Bryan Y. Owsley, Kenneth Rayner, John R. Reding, John Reynolds, R. Barnwell Rhett, James Rogers, William Smith, John Snyder, James C. Sprigg, Edward Stanley, Lewis Steenrod, Charles C. Stratton, John T. Stuart, Samuel W. Trotti."

It was observed that Mr. Cushing, though a member of the committee which reported the bill, and a close friend to the administration, took no part in the proceedings upon this bill—neither speaking nor voting for or against it: a circumstance which strengthened the belief that he was to be the beneficiary of it.

It was midnight on the last day of the session when the bill was called up in the Senate. Mr. Wright of New York, desired to know the reason for so large an appropriation in this case. He was answered by Mr. Archer, the senatorial reporter of the bill, who said it was not intended that the salary of the minister, or agent, together with his outfit, should exceed $18,000 per annum—the amount usually appropriated for such missions. Supposing the mission to occupy two years, and the sum is not too much, and the remoteness of the country to be negotiated with, justifies the full appropriation in advance. Mr. Wright replied that the explanation was not at all satisfactory to him: the compensation to an agent in China could be voted annually, and applied annually, as conveniently as any other. Mr. Benton objected to any mission at all, and especially to such a one as the bill provided for. He argued that—

"There was no necessity for a treaty with China, was proved by the fact that our trade with that country had been going on well without one for a century or two, and was now growing and increasing constantly. It was a trade conducted on the simple and elementary principle of 'here is one,' and 'there is the other'—all ready-money, and hard money, or good products—no credit system, no paper money. For a long time this trade took nothing but silver dollars. At present it is taking some other articles, and especially a goodly quantity of Missouri lead. This has taken place without a treaty, and without an agent at $40,000 expense. All things are going on well between us and the Chinese. Our relations are purely commercial, conducted on the simplest principles of trade, and unconnected with political views. China has no political connection with us. She is not within the system, or circle, of American policy. She can have no designs upon us, or views in relation to us; and we have no need of a minister to watch and observe her conduct. Politically and commercially the mission is useless. By the Constitution, all the ministers are to be appointed by the Senate; but this minister to China is to be called an agent, and sent out by the President without the consent of the Senate; and thus, by imposing a false name upon the minister, defraud the Senate of their control over the appointment. The enormity of the sum shows that the mission is to be more expensive than any one ever sent from the United States; and that it is to be one of the first grade, or of a higher grade than any known in our country. Nine thousand dollars per annum, and the same for an outfit, is the highest compensation known to our service; yet this $40,000 mission may double that amount, and still the minister be only called an agent, for the purpose of cheating the Senate out of its control over the appointment. The bill is fraudulent in relation to the compensation to be given to this ambassadorial agent. No sum is fixed, but he is to take what he pleases for himself and his suite. He and they are to help themselves; and, from the amount allowed, they may help themselves liberally. In all other cases, salaries and compensations are fixed by law, and graduated by time; here there is no limit of either money or time. This mission goes by the job—$40,000 for the job—without regard to time or cost. A summer's work, or a year's work, it is all the same thing: it is a job, and is evidently intended to enable a gentleman, who loves to travel in Europe and Asia, to extend his travels to the Celestial Empire at the expense of the United States, and to write a book. The settlement of the accounts is a fraud upon the Treasury. In all cases of foreign missions, except where secret services are to be performed, and spies and informers to be dealt with, the accounts are settled at the Treasury Department, by the proper accounting officers; when secret services are to be covered, the fund out of which they are paid is then called the contingent foreign intercourse fund; and are settled at the State Department, upon a simple certificate from the President, that the money has been applied according to its intention. It was in this way that the notorious John Henry obtained his $50,000 during the late war; and that various other sums have been paid out to secret agents at different times. To this I do not object. Every government, in its foreign intercourse, must have recourse to agents, and have the benefit of some services, which would be defeated if made public; and which must, therefore, be veiled in secrecy, and paid for privately. This must happen in all governments; but not so in this case of the Chinese mission. Here, secrecy is intended for what our own minister, his secretary, and his whole suite, are to receive. Not only what they may give in bribes to Chinese, but what they may take in pay to themselves, is to be a secret. All is secret and irresponsible! And it will not do to assimilate this mission to the oldest government in the world, to the anomalous and anonymous missions to revolutionary countries. Such an analogy has been attempted in defence of this mission, and South American examples cited; but the cases are not analogous. Informal agencies, with secret objects, are proper to revolutionary governments; but here is to be a public mission, and an imposing one—the grandest ever sent out from the United States.—To attempt to assimilate such a mission to a John Henry case, or to a South American agency, is absurd and impudent; and is a fraud upon the system of accountability to which all our missions are subjected.

"The sum proposed is the same that is in the act of 1790, upon which the bill is framed. That act appropriated $40,000: but for what? For one mission? one man? one agent? one by himself, one? No. Not at all. That appropriation of 1790 was for all the missions of the year—all of every kind—public as well as secret: the forty thousand dollars in this bill is for one man. The whole diplomatic appropriation in the time of Washington is now to be given to one man: and it is known pretty well who it is to be. Forty thousand dollars to enable one of our citizens to get to Peking, and to bump his head nineteen times on the ground, to get the privilege of standing up in the presence of his majesty of the celestial empire. And this is our work in the last night of this Congress. It is now midnight: and, like the midnight which preceded the departure of the elder Adams from the government, the whole time is spent in making and filling offices. Providing for favorites, and feeding out of the public crib, is the only work of those whose brief reign is drawing to a close, and who have been already compelled by public sentiment to undo a part of their work. The bankrupt act is repealed by the Congress that made it; the distribution act has shared the same fate; and if they had another session to sit, the mandamus act against the States, the habeas corpus against the States, this Chinese mission, and all the other acts, would be undone. It would be the true realization of the story of the queen who unravelled at night the web that she wove during the day. As it is, enough has been done, and undone, to characterize this Congress—to entitle it to the name of Ulysses' wife—not because (like the virtuous Penelope) it resisted seduction—but because, like her, its own hands unravelled its own work."

Mr. Archer replied that the ignominious prostrations heretofore required of foreign ministers in the Imperial Chinese presence, were all abolished by the treaty with Great Britain, and that the Chinese government had expressed a desire to extend to the United States all the benefits of that treaty, and this mission was to conclude the treaty which she wished to make. Mr. Benton replied, so much the less reason for sending this expensive mission. We now have the benefits of the British treaty, and we have traded for generations with China without a treaty, and without a quarrel, and can continue to do so. She extends to us and to all nations the benefits of the British treaty: the consul at Canton, Dr. Parker, or any respectable merchant there, can have that treaty copied, and sign it for the United States; and deem himself well paid to receive the fortieth part of this appropriation. Mr. Woodbury wished to see a limitation placed upon the amount of the annual compensation, and moved an amendment, that not more than nine thousand dollars, exclusive of outfit, be allowed to any one person for his annual compensation. Mr. Archer concurred in the limitation, and it was adopted. Mr. Benton then returned to one of his original objections—the design of the bill to cheat the Senate out of its constitutional control over the appointment. He said the language of the bill was studiously ambiguous. Whether the person was to be a minister, a chargé, or an agent, was not expressed. He now desired to know whether it was to be understood that the person intended for this mission was to be appointed by the President alone, without asking the advice and consent of the Senate? Mr. Archer replied that he had no information on the subject. Mr. Conrad of Louisiana, said that he would move an amendment that might obviate the difficulty; he would move that no agent be appointed without the consent of the Senate. This amendment was proposed, and adopted—31 yeas; 9 nays. These amendments were agreed to by the House; and, thus limited and qualified, the bill became a law.

The expected name did not come. The Senate adjourned, and no appointment could be made until the next session. It was not a vacancy happening in the recess which the President could fill by a temporary appointment, to continue to the end of the next session. It was an original office created during the session, and must be filled at the session, or wait until the next one. The President did neither. There were two constitutional ways open to him—and he took neither. There was one unconstitutional way—and he took it. In brief, he made the appointment in the recess; and not only so made it, but sent off the appointee (Mr. Caleb Cushing) also in the recess. Scarcely had the Senate adjourned when it was known that Mr. Cushing was to go upon this mission as soon as the ships could be got ready to convey him: and in the month of May he departed. This was palpably to avoid the action of the Senate, where the nomination of Mr. Cushing would have been certain of rejection. He had already been three times rejected in one day upon a nomination for Secretary of the Treasury—receiving but two votes on the last trial. All the objections which applied to him for the Treasury appointment, were equally in force for the Chinese mission; and others besides. It was an original vacancy, and could not be filled during the recess by a temporary appointment. It was not a vacancy "happening" in the recess of the Senate, and therefore to be temporarily filled without the Senate's previous consent, lest the public interest in the meanwhile should suffer. It was an office created, and the emolument fixed, during the time that Mr. Cushing was a member of Congress: consequently he was constitutionally interdicted from receiving it during the continuance of that term. His term expired on the third of March: he was constitutionally ineligible up to the end of that day: and this upon the words of the constitution. Upon the reasons and motives of the constitution, he was ineligible for ever. The reason was, to prevent corrupt and subservient legislation—to prevent members of Congress from conniving or assisting at the enactment of laws for their own benefit, and to prevent Presidents from rewarding legislative subservience. Tested upon these reasons Mr. Cushing was ineligible after, as well as before, the expiration of his congressional term: and such had been the practice of all the previous Presidents. Even in the most innocent cases, and where no connivance could possibly be supposed of the member, would any previous President appoint a member to a place after his term expired, which he could not receive before it: as shown in Chapter XXX of the first volume of this View. In the case of Mr. Cushing all the reasons, founded in the motives of the constitutional prohibition, existed to forbid his appointment. He had deserted his party to join Mr. Tyler. He worked for him in and out of the House, and even deserted himself to support him—as in the two tariff bills of the current session; for both of which he voted, and then voted against them when vetoed: for which he was taunted by Mr. Granger, of New York.[7] There was besides a special provision in the law under which he was appointed to prevent the appointment from being made without the concurrence of the Senate. (The notice of the proceedings in the Senate when the bill which ripened into that law, have shown the terms of that provision, and the reasons of its adoption.) It is no answer to that pregnant amendment to say that the nomination would be sent in at the next session. That session would not come until six months after Mr. Cushing had sailed! not until he had arrived at his post! not until he had placed the entire diameter of the terraqueous globe between himself and the Senate! and a still greater distance between the Treasury and the $40,000 which he had drawn out of it!

Two squadrons of ships-of-war were put in requisition to attend this minister. The Pacific squadron, then on the coast of South America, was directed to proceed to China, to meet him: a squadron was collected at Norfolk to convey him. This squadron consisted of the new steam frigate, Missouri—the frigate Brandywine, the sloop-of-war Saint Louis, and the brig Perry—carrying altogether near two hundred guns; a formidable accompaniment for a peace mission, seeking a commercial treaty. Mr. Cushing had a craving to embark at Washington, under a national salute, and the administration gratified him: the magnificent steam frigate, Missouri, was ordered up to receive him. Threading the narrow and crooked channel of the Potomac River, the noble ship ran on an oyster bank, and fifteen of her crew, with a promising young officer, were drowned in getting her off. The minister had a desire to sail down the Mediterranean, seeing its coasts, and landing in the ancient kingdom of the Pharaohs: the administration deferred to his wishes. The Missouri was ordered to proceed to the Mediterranean, which the ill-fated vessel was destined never to enter; for, arriving at Gibraltar, she took fire and burned up—baptizing the anomalous mission in fire and blood, as well as in enormous expense. The minister proceeded in a British steamer to Egypt, and then by British conveyance to Bombay, where the Norfolk squadron had been ordered to meet him. The Brandywine alone was there, but the minister entered her, and proceeded to the nearest port to Canton, where, reporting his arrival and object, a series of diplomatic contentions immediately commenced between himself and "Ching, of the celestial dynasty, Governor-general of that part of the Central Flowery Kingdom." Mr. Cushing informed this governor that he was on his way to Peking, to deliver a letter from the President of the United States to the Emperor, and to negotiate a treaty of commerce; and, in the mean time, to take the earliest opportunity to inquire after the health of the august Emperor. To this inquiry Ching answered readily that, "At the present moment the great Emperor is in the enjoyment of happy old age and quiet health, and is at peace with all, both far and near:" but with respect to the intended progress to Peking, he demurs, and informs the minister that the imperial permission must first be obtained. "I have examined," he says, "and find that every nation's envoy which has come to the Central Flowery Kingdom with a view of proceeding to Peking, there to be presented to the august Emperor, has ever been required to wait outside of the nearest port on the frontier till the chief magistrate of the province clearly memorialize the Emperor, and request the imperial will, pointing out whether the interview may be permitted." With respect to the treaty of friendship and commerce, the governor declares there is no necessity for it—that China and America have traded together two hundred years in peace and friendship without a treaty—that all nations now had the benefit of the treaty made with Great Britain, which treaty was necessary to establish relations after a war; and that the United States, having had no war with China, had no need for a treaty. He supposes that, having heard of the British treaty, the United States began to want one also, and admits the idea is excellent, but unnecessary, and urges against it:

> "As to what is stated, of publicly deliberating upon the particulars of perpetual peace, inasmuch as it relates to discoursing of good faith, peace, and harmony, the idea is excellent; and it may seem right, because he has heard that England has settled all the particulars of a treaty with China, he may desire to do and manage in the same manner. But the circumstances of the two nations are not the same, for England had taken up arms against China for several years, and, in beginning to deliberate upon a treaty, these two nations could not avoid suspicion; therefore, they settled the details of a treaty, in order to confirm their good faith; but since your honorable nation, from the commencement of commercial intercourse with China, during a period of two hundred years, all the merchants who have come to Canton, on the one hand, have observed the laws of China without any disagreement, and on the other, there has been no failure of treating them with courtesy, so that there has not been the slightest

room for discord; and, since the two nations are at peace, what is the necessity of negotiating a treaty? In the commencement, England was not at peace with China; and when afterwards these two nations began to revert to a state of peace, it was indispensable to establish and settle details of a treaty, in order to oppose a barrier to future difficulties. I have now discussed this subject, and desire the honorable plenipotentiary maturely to consider it. Your honorable nation, with France and England, are the three great foreign nations that come to the south of China to trade. But the trade of America and England with China is very great. Now, the law regulating the tariff has changed the old established duties, many of which have been essentially diminished, and the customary expenditures (exactions?) have been abolished. Your honorable nation is treated in the same manner as England; and, from the time of this change in the tariff, all kinds of merchandise have flowed through the channels of free trade, among the people, and already has your nation been bedewed with its advantages. The honorable plenipotentiary ought certainly to look at and consider that the Great Emperor, in his leniency to men from afar, has issued edicts commanding the merchants and people peaceably to trade, which cannot but be beneficial to the nations. It is useless, with lofty, polished, and empty words, to alter these unlimited advantages."

In all this alleged extension of the benefits of the British treaty to all nations, Ching was right in what he said. The Emperor had already done it, and the British government had so determined it from the beginning. It was a treaty for the commercial world as well as for themselves, and had been so declared by the young Queen Victoria in her speech communicating the treaty to Parliament. "Throughout the whole course of my negotiations with the government of China, I have uniformly disclaimed the wish for any exclusive advantages. It has been my desire that equal favor should be shown to the industry and commercial enterprise of all nations." There was really no necessity for a treaty, which as often begets dissensions as prevents them; and if one was desirable, it might have been had through Dr. Parker, long a resident of China, and now commissioner there, and who was Secretary of Legation and interpreter in Mr. Cushing's mission, and the medium of his communications with the Chinese; and actually the man of business who did the business in conducting the negotiations. But Mr. Cushing perseveres in his design to go to Peking, alleging that, "He deems himself bound by the instructions of his government to do so." Ching replies that he has received the imperial order "to stop and soothe him." Ching also informs him that the treaty with Great Britain was negotiated, not at Peking but at Canton, and also its duplicate with Portugal, and that a copy of it was in the hands of the American consul at Canton, for the information and benefit of American merchants. In his anxiety to prevent a foreign ship-of-war from approaching Peking, the Chinese governor intimated that, if a treaty was indispensable, a commissioner might come to Canton for that purpose; and on inquiry from Mr. Cushing how long it would take to send to Peking and get a return, Ching answered, three months—the distance being so great. Mr. Cushing objects to that delay—declares he cannot wait so long, as the season for favorable navigation to approach Peking may elapse; and announces his determination to proceed at once in the Brandywine, without waiting for any permission; and declares that a refusal to receive him would be a national insult, and a just cause of war. Here is the extract from his letter:

"Under these circumstances, inasmuch as your Excellency does not propose to open to me the inland road to Peking, in the event of my waiting here until the favorable monsoon for proceeding to the north by sea shall have passed away, and as I cannot, without disregard of the commands of my government, permit the season to elapse without pursuing the objects of my mission, I shall immediately leave Macao in the Brandywine. I feel the less hesitation in pursuing this course, in consideration of the tenor of the several communications which I have received from your Excellency. It is obvious, that if the court had entertained any very particular desire that I should remain here, it would have caused an imperial commissioner to be on the spot, ready to receive me on my arrival, or, at any rate, instructions would have been forwarded to your Excellency for the reception of the legation; since, in order that no proper act of courtesy towards the Chinese government should be left unobserved, notice was duly given last autumn, by the consul of the United States, that my government had appointed a minister to China. The omission of the court to take either of these steps seems to indicate expectation, on its part, that I should probably land at some port in the north."

That is to say, at some port in the Yellow Sea, or its river nearest to Peking. This must have been a mode of reasoning new to Governor Ching, that an omission to provide for Mr. Cushing at the port where foreigners were received, should imply a license for him to land where they were not, except on express, imperial permission. Much as Ching must have been astonished at this American logic, he must have been still more so at the penalty announced for disregarding it! nothing less than "national insult," and "just cause of war." For the letter continues:

> "Besides which, your Excellency is well aware, that it is neither the custom in China, nor consistent with the high character of its Sovereign, to decline to receive the embassies of friendly states. To do so, indeed, would among Western States be considered an act of national insult, and a just cause of war."

This sentence, as all that relates to Mr. Cushing's Chinese mission, is copied from his own official despatches; so that, what would be incredible on the relation of others, becomes undeniable on his own. National insult and just cause of war, for not allowing him to go to Peking!

Mr. Cushing justifies his refusal to negotiate at Canton as the British envoy had done, and not being governed by the ceremony observed in his case, on the ground that the circumstances were not analogous—that Great Britain had chastised the Chinese, and taken possession of one of their islands—and that it would be necessary for the United States to do the same to bring him within the rules which were observed with Sir Henry Pottinger, the British minister. This intimation, as impertinent as unfeeling, and as offensive as unfounded, was thus expressed:

> "In regard to the mode and place of deliberating upon all things relative to the perpetual peace and friendship of China and the United States, your Excellency refers to the precedent of the late negotiations with the plenipotentiary of Great Britain. The rules of politeness and ceremony observed by Sir Henry Pottinger, were doubtless just and proper in the particular circumstances of the case. But, to render them fully applicable to the United States, it would be necessary for my government, in the first instance, to subject the people of China to all the calamities of war, and especially to take possession of some island on the coast of China as a place of residence for its minister. I cannot suppose that the imperial government wishes the United States to do this. Certainly no such wish is entertained at present by the United States, which, animated with the most amicable sentiments towards China, feels assured of being met with corresponding deportment on the part of China."

The Brandywine during this time was still at Macao, the port outside of the harbor, where foreign men-of-war are only allowed to come; but Mr. Cushing, following up the course he had marked out for himself, directed that vessel to enter the inner port, and sail up to Whampoa; and also to require a salute of twenty-one guns to be fired. Against this entrance the Chinese government remonstrated, as being against the laws and customs of the empire, contrary to what the British had done when they negotiated their treaty, and contrary to an article in that treaty which only permitted that entrance to a small vessel with few men and one petty officer: and if the Brandywine had not entered, he forbids her to come; and if she had, requires her to depart: and as for the salute, he declares he has no means of firing it; and, besides, it was against their laws. The governor expressed himself with animation and feeling on this subject, at the indignity of violating their laws, and under the pretext of paying him a compliment—for that was the only alleged cause of the intrusive entrance of the Brandywine. He wrote:

> "But it is highly necessary that I should also remark, concerning the man-of-war Brandywine coming up to Whampoa. The Bogue makes an outer portal of Kwang Tung, where an admiral is stationed to control and guard. Heretofore, the men-of-war of foreign nations have only been allowed to cast anchor in the seas without the mouth of the river, and have not been permitted to enter within. This is a settled law of the land, made a long time past. Whampoa

is the place where merchant ships collect together, not one where men-of-war can anchor. Now, since the whole design of merchantmen is to trade, and men-of-war are prepared to fight, if they enter the river, fright and suspicion will easily arise among the populace, thus causing an obstacle in the way of trade. Furthermore, the two countries are just about deliberating upon peace and good will, and suddenly to have a man-of-war enter the river, while we are speaking of good faith and cultivating good feeling, has not a little the aspect of distrust. Among the articles of the commercial regulations it is provided, that an English government vessel shall be allowed to remain at anchor at Whampoa, and that a deputy shall be appointed to control the seamen. The design of this, it was evident, was to put an end to strife, and quell disputes. But this vessel is a small one, containing but few troops, and moreover brings a petty officer, so that it is a matter of but little consequence, one way or another. If your country's man-of-war Brandywine contains five hundred and more troops, she has also a proportionately large number of guns in her, and brings a commodore in her; she is in truth far different from the government vessel of the British, and it is inexpedient for her to enter the river; and there are, in the aspect of the affair, many things not agreeable."

Nevertheless Mr. Cushing required the ship to enter the inner port, to demand a return-salute of twenty-one guns, and permission to the American commodore to make his compliments in person to the Chinese governor. This governor then addressed a remonstrance to the American commodore, which runs thus:

"When your Excellency first arrived in the Central Flowery Land, you were unacquainted with her laws and prohibitions—that it was against the laws for men-of-war to enter the river. Having previously received the public officer's (Cushing's) communication, I, the acting governor, have fully and clearly stated to him that the ship should be detained outside. Your Excellency's present coming up to Blenheim reach is therefore, no doubt, because the despatch sent previously to his Excellency Cushing had not been made known to you—whence the mistake. Respecting the salute of twenty-one guns, as it is a salute among western nations, it does [not] tally with the customs of China. Your Excellency being now in China, and, moreover, entered the river, it is not the same as if you were in your own country; and, consequently, it will be inexpedient to have the salute performed here; also, China has no such salute as firing twenty-one guns; and how can we imitate your country's custom in the number, and make a corresponding ceremony in return? It will, indeed, not be easy to act according to it. When the English admirals Parker and Saltoun came up to Canton, they were both in a passage vessel, not in a man-of-war, when they entered the river; nor was there any salute. This is evidence plain on this matter.

"Concerning what is said regarding a personal visit to this officer to pay respects, it is certainly indicative of good intention; but the laws of the land direct that whenever officers from other countries arrive upon the frontier, the governor and other high officers, not having received his Majesty's commands, cannot hold any private intercourse with them; nor can a deputy, not having received a special commission from the superior officers, have any private intercourse with foreign functionaries. It will consequently be inexpedient that your Excellency (whose sentiments are so polite and cordial) and I, the acting governor, should have an interview; for it is against the settled laws of the land."

Having thus violated the laws and customs of China in sending the Brandywine, Mr. Cushing follows it up with threats and menaces—assumes the attitude of an injured and insulted minister of peace—and, for the sake of China, regrets what may happen. In this vein he writes:

"It is customary, among all the nations of the West, for the ships of war of one country to visit the ports of another in time of peace, and, in doing so, for the commodore to exchange salutes with the local authorities, and to pay his compliments in person to the principal public functionary. To omit these testimonies of good will is considered as evidence of a hostile, or at least of an unfriendly feeling. But your Excellency says the provincial government has no authority to exchange salutes with Commodore Parker, or to receive a visit of ceremony from him. And I deeply regret, for the sake of China, that such is the fact. China will find it very difficult to remain in peace with any of the great States of the West, so long as her provincial governors are prohibited either to give or to receive manifestations of that peace, in the exchange of the ordinary courtesies of national intercourse. And I cannot forbear to express my surprise, that, in the great and powerful province of Kwang Tung, the presence of a single ship of war should be cause of apprehension to the local government. Least of all, should such apprehension be entertained in reference to any ships of war belonging to the United States, which now feels, and (unless ill-treatment of our public agents should produce a change of sentiments) will continue to feel, the most hearty and sincere good will towards China. Coming here, in behalf of my government, to tender to China the friendship of the greatest of the Powers of America, it is my duty, in the outset, not to omit any of the tokens of respect customary among western nations. If these demonstrations are not met in a correspondent manner, it will be the misfortune of China, but it will not be the fault of the United States."

In these sentences China is threatened with a war with the United States on account of her ill-treatment of the United States' public agents, meaning himself—the ill-treatment consisting in not permitting him to trample, without restraint, upon the laws and customs of the country. In this sense, Ching the governor, understood it, and answered:

"Regarding what is said of the settled usages of western nations—that not to receive a high commissioner from another state is an insult to that state—this certainly, with men, has a warlike bearing. But during the two hundred years of commercial intercourse between China and your country, there has not been the least animosity nor the slightest insult. It is for harmony and good will your Excellency has come; and your request to proceed to the capital, and to have an audience with the Emperor, is wholly of the same good mind. If, then, in the outset, such pressing language is used, it will destroy the admirable relations."

To this Mr. Cushing rejoins, following up the menace of war for the "*ill-treatment*" he was receiving—justifying it if it comes—reminds China of the five years' hostilities of Great Britain upon her—points to her antiquated customs as having already brought disasters upon her; and suggests a dismemberment of her empire as a consequence of war with the United States, provoked by ill-treatment of her public agents. Thus:

"I can only assure your Excellency, that this is not the way for China to cultivate good will and maintain peace. The late war with England was caused by the conduct of the authorities at Canton, in disregarding the rights of public officers who represented the English government. If, in the face of the experience of the last five years, the Chinese government now reverts to antiquated customs, which have already brought such disasters upon her, it can be regarded in no other light than as evidence that she invites and desires [war with] the other great western Powers. The United States would sincerely regret such a result. We have no desire whatever to dismember the territory of the empire. Our citizens have at all times deported themselves here in a just and respectful manner. The position and policy of the United States enable us to be the most disinterested and the most valuable of the friends of China. I have flattered myself, therefore, and cannot yet abandon the hope, that the imperial government will see the wisdom of promptly welcoming and of cordially responding to the amicable assurances of the government of the United States."

Quickly following this despatch was another, in which Mr. Cushing rises still higher in his complaints of molestation and ill-treatment—refers to the dissatisfaction which the American people will experience—thought they would have done better, having just been whipped by the British—confesses that his exalted opinion of China is undergoing a decline—hopes they will do better—postpones for a while his measures of redress—suspends his resentment—and by this forbearance will feel himself the better justified for what he may do if forced to act. But let his own words speak:

"I must not conceal from your Excellency the extreme dissatisfaction and disappointment which the people of America will experience when they learn that their Envoy, instead of being promptly and cordially welcomed by the Chinese government, is thus molested and delayed, on the very threshold of the province of Yuh. The people of America have been accustomed to consider China the most refined and the most enlightened of the nations of the East; and they will demand, how it is possible, if China be thus refined, she should allow herself to be wanting in courtesy to their Envoy; and, if China be thus enlightened, how it is possible that, having just emerged from a war with England, and being in the daily expectation of the arrival of the Envoy of the French, she should suffer herself to slight and repel the good will of the United States. And the people of America will be disposed indignantly to draw back the proffered hand of friendship, when they learn how imperfectly the favor is appreciated by the Chinese government. In consenting, therefore, to postpone, for a short time longer, my departure for the North (Peking), and in omitting, for however brief a period, to consider the action of the Chinese government as one of open disrespect to the United States, and to take due measures of redress, I incur the hazard of the disapprobation and censure of my government; for the American government is peculiarly sensitive to any act of foreign governments injurious to the honor of the United States. It is the custom of American citizens to demean themselves respectfully towards the people and authorities of any foreign nation in which they may, for the time being, happen to reside. Your Excellency has frankly and truly borne witness to the just and respectful deportment which both scholars and merchants of the United States have at all times manifested in China. But I left America as a messenger of peace. I came into China full of sentiments of respect and friendship towards its sovereign and its people. And notwithstanding what has occurred, since my arrival here, to chill the warmth of my previous good will towards China, and to bring down the high conceptions I had previously been led to form in regard to the courtesy of its government, I am loth to give these up entirely, and in so doing put an end perhaps to the existing harmonious relations between the United States and China. I have therefore to say to your Excellency, that I accept, for the present, your assurances of the sincerity and friendship of the Chinese government. I suspend all the resentment which I have just cause to feel on account of the obstructions thrown in the way of the progress of the legation, and other particulars of the action of the Imperial and Provincial governments, in the hope that suitable reparation will be made for these acts in due time. I commit myself, in all this, to the integrity and honor of the Chinese government; and if, in the sequel, I shall prove to have done this in vain, I shall then consider myself the more amply justified, in the sight of all men, for any determination which, out of regard for the honor of the United States, it may be my duty to adopt under such circumstances."

It was now the middle of May, 1844: the correspondence with Ching had commenced the last of February: the three months had nearly elapsed, within which a return answer was to be had from Peking: and by extraordinary speed the answer arrived. It contained the Emperor's positive refusal to suffer Mr. Cushing to come to Peking—enjoined him to remain where he was—cautioned him not to "agitate disorder"—and informing him that an Imperial commissioner would proceed immediately to Canton, travelling with the greatest celerity, and under orders to make one hundred and thirty-three miles a day, there to draw up the treaty with him. This information took away the excuse for the intrusive journey, or voyage, to Peking, and also showed that a commercial treaty might be had with China, without inflicting upon her the calamities of war, or breeding national dissensions out of diplomatic contentions. It made a further suspension of his resentment, and postponement of the measures which the honor of the United States required him to take for the molestations and ill treatment which the federal government had received in his person. These formidable measures, well known to be belligerent, were postponed, not abandoned; and the visit to Peking, forestalled by the arrival of an imperial commissioner to sign a treaty, was also postponed, not given up—its pretext now diminished, and reduced to the errand of delivering Mr. Tyler's letter to the Emperor. He consents to treat at Canton, but makes an excuse for it in the want of a steamer, and the non-arrival of the other ships of the squadron, which would have enabled him to approach Canton, intimidate the government, and obtain from their fears the concessions which their manners and customs forbid. All this he wrote himself to his government, and he is entitled to the benefit of his own words:

> "So far as regards the objects of adjusting in a proper manner the commercial relations of the United States and China, nothing could be more advantageous than to negotiate with Tsiyeng at Canton, instead of running the risk of compromising this great object by having it mixed up at Tien Tsin, or elsewhere at the north, with questions of reception at Court. Add to which the fact that, with the Brandywine alone, without any steamer, and without even the St. Louis and the Perry, it would be idle to repair to the neighborhood of the Pih-ho, in any expectation of acting upon the Chinese by intimidation, and obtaining from their fears concessions contrary to the feeling and settled wishes of the Imperial government. To remain here, therefore, and meet Tsiyeng, if not the most desirable thing, is at present the only possible thing. It is understood that Tsiyeng will reach Canton from the 5th to the 10th of June."

This commissioner, Tsiyeng, arrived at the time appointed, and fortunately for the peace and honor of the country, as the St. Louis sloop-of-war, and the man-of-war brig Perry, arrived two days after, and put Mr. Cushing in possession of the force necessary to carry out his designs upon China. In the joy of receiving this accession to his force, he thus writes home to his government:

> "It is with great pleasure I inform you that the St. Louis arrived here on the 6th instant, under the command of Lieutenant Keith, Captain Cocke (for what cause I know not, and cannot conceive), after detaining the ship at the Cape of Good Hope three months, having at length relinquished the command to Mr. Keith. And on the same day arrived also the Perry, commanded by Lieutenant Tilton. The arrival of these vessels relieves me from a load of solicitude in regard to the public business; for if matters do not go smoothly with Tsiyeng, the legation has now the means of proceeding to and acting at the North."

"If matters do not go smoothly with Tsiyeng!" and the very first step of Mr. Cushing was an attempt to ruffle that smoothness. The Chinese commissioner announced his arrival at Canton, and made known his readiness to draw up the treaty instantly. In this communication, the name of the United States, as according to Chinese custom with all foreign nations, was written in a lower column than that of the Chinese government—in the language of Mr. Cushing, "the name of the Chinese government stood higher in column by one character than that of the United States." At this collocation of the name of his country, Mr. Cushing took fire, and instantly returned the communication to the Imperial commissioner, "even at the hazard (as he informed his government) of at once cutting off all negotiation." Fortunately Tsiyeng was a man of sense, and of elevation of character, and immediately directed his clerk to elevate the name of the United States to the level of the column which contained that of China. By this condescension on the part of the Chinese commissioner, the negotiation was saved for the time, and the cannon and ammunition of our three ships of war prevented from being substituted for goose-quills and ink. The commissioner showed the greatest readiness, amounting to impatience, to draw up and execute the treaty; which was done in as little time as the forms could be gone through: and the next day the commissioner, taking his formal leave of the American legation, departed for Peking—a hint that, the business being finished, Mr. Cushing might depart also for his home. But he was not in such a hurry to return. "His pride and his feelings (to use his own words) had been mortified" at not being permitted to go to Peking—at being in fact stopped at a little island off the coast, where he had to transact all his business; and his mind still reverted to the cherished idea of going to Peking, though his business would be now limited to the errand of carrying Mr. Tyler's letter to the Emperor. In his despatch, immediately after the conclusion of this treaty, he justifies himself for not having gone before the Chinese commissioner arrived, placing the blame on the slow arrival of the St. Louis and the Perry, the non-arrival at all of the Pacific squadron, and the want of a steamer.

> "With these reflections present to my mind, it only needed to consider further whether I should endeavor to force my way to Peking, or at least, by demonstration of force at the mouth of the Pih-ho, attempt to intimidate the Imperial government into conceding to me

free access to the Court. In regard to this it is to be observed, that owing to the extraordinary delays of the St. Louis on her way here, I had no means of making any serious demonstration of force at the north, prior to the time when Tsiyeng arrived at Canton, on his way to Macao, there to meet me and negotiate a treaty. And with an Imperial commissioner near at hand, ready and willing to treat, would it have been expedient, or even justifiable, to enter upon acts of hostility with China, in order, if possible, to make Peking the place of negotiation?"

The correspondence does not show what was the opinion of the then administration upon this problem of commencing hostilities upon China after the commissioner had arrived to make the treaty; and especially to commit these hostilities to force a negotiation at Peking, where no treaty with any power had ever been negotiated, and where he expected serious difficulties in his presentation at court, as Mr. Cushing was determined not to make the prostrations (i. e. bumping his head nineteen times against the floor), which the Chinese ceremonial required.

"I have never disguised from myself the serious difficulties which I might have to encounter in forcing my way to Peking; and, if voluntarily admitted there, the difficulties almost equally serious connected with the question of presentation at court; for I had firmly resolved not to perform the acts of prostration to the Emperor. I struggled with the objections until intelligence was officially communicated to me of the appointment of Tsiyeng as imperial commissioner, and of his being actually on his way to Canton. To have left Macao after receiving this intelligence would have subjected me to the imputation of fleeing from, and, as it were, evading a meeting with Tsiyeng; and such an imputation would have constituted a serious difficulty (if not an insuperable one) in the way of successful negotiation at the North."

The despatch continues:

"On the other hand, I did not well see how the United States could make war on China to change the ceremonial of the court. And for this reason, it had always been with me an object of great solicitude to dispose of all the commercial questions by treaty, before venturing on Peking."

"Did not well see how the United States could make war on China to change the ceremonial of the court." This is very cool language, and implies that Mr. Cushing was ready to make the war—(assuming himself to be the United States, and invested with the war power)—but could not well discover any pretext on which to found it. He then excuses himself for not having done better, and gone on to Peking without stopping at the outer port of Canton, and so giving the Chinese time to send down a negotiator there, and so cutting off the best pretext for forcing the way to China: and this excuse resolves itself into the one so often given—the want of a sufficient squadron to force the way. Thus:

"If it should be suggested that it would have been better for me to have proceeded at once to the North (Peking), without stopping at Macao, I reply, that this was impracticable at the time of my arrival, with the Brandywine alone, before the southerly monsoon had set in, and without any steamer; that if at any time I had gone to the North in the view of negotiating there, I should have been wholly dependent on the Chinese for the means of lodging and subsisting on shore, and even for the means of landing at the mouth of the Pih-ho; that only at Macao could I treat independently, and that here, of necessity, must all the pecuniary and other arrangements of the mission be made, and the supplies obtained for the squadron. Such are the considerations and the circumstances which induced me to consent to forego proceeding to Peking."

So that, after all, it was only the fear of being whipt and starved that prevented Mr. Cushing from fighting his way to the foot-stool of power in the Tartar half of the Chinese Empire. The delay of the two smaller vessels, the non-arrival of the Pacific squadron, and the want of a steamer, were fortunate accidents for the peace and honor of the United States; and even the conflagration of the magnificent steam frigate, Missouri, with all her equipments, was a blessing, compared to the use to which she would have been put if Mr. Cushing's desire to see the coasts of the Mediterranean and the banks of the Nile had not induced him to take her to Gibraltar, instead of doubling the Cape of Good Hope in company with the Brandywine. Finally, he gives the reason for all this craving desire to get to Peking, which was nothing more nor less (and less it could not be) than the gratification of his own feelings of pride and curiosity. Hear him:

> "And in regard to Peking itself, I have obtained the means of direct correspondence between the two governments immediately, and an express engagement, that if hereafter a minister of the French, or any other power, should be admitted to the court, the same privilege shall be accorded to the United States. If the conclusion of the whole matter be one less agreeable to my own feelings of pride or curiosity, it is, at any rate, the most important and useful to my country, and will therefore, I trust, prove satisfactory to the President."

It does not appear from any published instructions of the administration (then consisting of Mr. Tyler and his new cabinet after the resignation of all the whig members except Mr. Webster), how far Mr. Cushing was warranted in his belligerent designs upon China; but the great naval force which was assigned to him, the frankness with which he communicated all his bellicose intentions, the excuses which he made for not having proceeded to hostilities and the dismemberment of the Empire, and the encomiums with which his treaty was communicated to the Senate—all bespeak a consciousness of approbation on the part of the administration, and the existence of an expectation which might experience disappointment in his failing to make war upon the Chinese. In justice to Mr. Webster, it must be told that, although still in the cabinet when Mr. Cushing went to China, yet his day of influence was over: he was then in the process of being forced to resign: and Mr. Upshur, then Secretary of the Navy, was then virtually, as he was afterwards actually, Secretary of State, when the negotiations were carried on.

The publication of Mr. Cushing's correspondence, which was ordered by the Senate, excited astonishment, and attracted the general reprobation of the country. Their contents were revolting, and would have been incredible except for his own revelations. Narrated by himself they coerced belief, and bespoke an organization void of the moral sense, and without the knowledge that any body else possessed it. The conduct of the negotiator was condemned, his treaty was ratified, and the proceedings on his nomination remain a senatorial secret—the injunction of secrecy having never been removed from them.

CHAPTER CXXIII.

THE ALLEGED MUTINY, AND THE EXECUTIONS (AS THEY WERE CALLED) ON BOARD THE UNITED STATES MAN-OF-WAR, SOMERS.

In the beginning of this year the public mind was suddenly astounded and horrified, at the news of a mutiny on board a national ship-of-war, with a view to convert it into a pirate, and at the same time excited to admiration and gratitude at the terrible energy with which the commander of the ship had suppressed it—hanging three of the ringleaders on the spot without trial, bringing home twelve others in irons—and restraining the rest by the undaunted front which the officers assumed, and the complete readiness in which they held themselves to face a revolt. It was a season of profound peace, and the astounding news was like claps of thunder in a clear sky. It was an unprecedented event in our navy, where it had been the pride and glory of the seamen to stand by their captain and their ship to the last man, and to die exultingly to save either. Unlike almost all mutinies, it was not a revolt against oppression, real or imagined, and limited to the seizure of the ship and the death or expulsion of the officers, but a vast scheme of maritime depredation, in which the man-of-war, converted into a piratical cruiser, was to roam the seas in quest of blood and plunder, preying upon the commerce of all nations—robbing property, slaughtering men, and violating women. A son of a cabinet minister, and himself an officer, was at the head of the appalling design; and his name and rank lent it a new aspect of danger. Every aggravation seemed to attend it, and the horrifying intelligence came out in a way to magnify its terrors, and to startle the imagination as well as to overpower the judgment. The vessel was the bearer of her own news, and arriving on the coast, took a reserve and mystery which lent a terrific force to what leaked out. She stopped off the harbor of New York, and remained outside two days, severely interdicting all communication with the shore. A simple notice of her return was all that was made public. An officer from the vessel, related to the commander, proceeded to Washington city—giving out fearful intimations as he went along—and bearing a sealed report to the Secretary of the Navy. The contents of that report went direct into the government official paper, and thence flew resounding through the land. It was the official and authentic report of the fearful mutiny. The news being spread from the official source, and the public mind prepared for his reception, the commander brought his vessel into port—landed: and landed in such a way as to increase the awe and terror inspired by his narrative. He went direct, in solemn procession, at the head of his crew to the nearest church, and returned thanks to God for a great deliverance. Taken by surprise, the public mind delivered itself up to joy and gratitude for a marvellous escape, applauding the energy which had saved a national ship from mutiny, and the commerce of nations from piratical depredation. The current was all on one side. Nothing appeared to weaken its force, or stop its course. The dead who had been hanged, and sent to the bottom of the sea, could send up no voice: the twelve ironed prisoners on the deck of the vessel, were silent as the dead: the officers and men at large actors in what had taken place, could only confirm the commander's official report. That report, not one word of which would be heard in a court of justice, was received as full evidence at the great tribunal of public opinion. The reported confessions which it contained (though the weakest of all testimony in the eye of the law, and utterly repulsed when obtained by force, terror or seduction), were received by the masses as incontestable evidence of guilt.

The vessel on which all this took place was the United States man-of-war, Somers—her commander Alexander Slidell Mackenzie, Esq., with a crew of 120 all told, 96 of which were apprentice boys under age. She had gone out on one of those holiday excursions which are now the resource of schools to make seamen. She had crossed the Atlantic and was returning to the United States by way of the West Indies, when this fearful mutiny was discovered. It was communicated by the purser's steward to the purser—by him to the first lieutenant—by him to the commander: and the incredulous manner in which he received it is established by two competent witnesses—the lieutenant who gave it to him, and the commander himself: and it is due to each to give the account of this reception in his own words: and first the lieutenant shall speak:

> "I reported the thing (the intended mutiny) to the commander immediately. He took it very coolly, said the vessel was in a good state of discipline, and expressed his doubts as to the truth of the report."

This is the testimony of the lieutenant before the court-martial which afterwards sat upon the case, and two points are to be noted in it—*first*, that the commander did not believe it; and, *secondly*, that he declared the vessel to be in a good state of discipline: which was equivalent to saying, there was no danger, even if the information was true. Now for the commander's account of the same scene, taken from his official report:

> "Such was the purport of the information laid before me by Lieut. Gansevoort, and although he was evidently impressed with the reality of the project, yet it seemed to me so monstrous, so improbable, that I could not forbear treating it with ridicule. I was under the impression that Mr. Spencer had been reading piratical stories, and had amused himself with Mr. Wales"—(the informer).

Ridicule was the only answer which the commander deemed due to the information, and in that he was justified by the nature of the information itself. A purser's steward (his name Wales) had told the lieutenant that midshipman Spencer had called him into a safe place the night before, and asked him right off—"Do you fear death? do you fear a dead man? are you afraid to kill a man?"—and getting satisfactory answers to these questions, he immediately unfolded to him his plan of capturing the ship, with a list of four certain and ten doubtful associates, and eighteen *nolens volens* assistants to be forced into the business; and then roaming the sea with her as a pirate, first calling at the Isle of Pines (Cuba) for confederates. It was a ridiculous scheme, both as to the force which was to take the ship, and her employment as a buccaneer—the state of the ocean and of navigation being such at that time as to leave a sea-rover, pursued as he would be by the fleets of all nations, without a sea to sail in, without a coast to land on, without a rock or corner to hide in. The whole conception was an impossibility, and the abruptness of its communication to Wales was evidence of the design to joke him. As such it appeared to the commander at the time. It was at 10 o'clock in the morning of the 26th of November, 1842, approaching the West Indies from the coast of Africa, that this information was given by the lieutenant to the commander. Both agree in their account of the ridicule with which it was received; but the commander, after the deaths of the implicated, and when making out his official report to the Secretary of the Navy, forgot to add what he said to the lieutenant—that the vessel was in a good state of discipline—equivalent to saying it could not be taken. Further, he not only forgot to add what he said, but remembered to say the contrary: and on his trial undertook to prove that the state of the ship was bad, and had been so for weeks; and even since they left the coast of Africa. In this omission to report to the Secretary a fact so material, as he had remarked it to his lieutenant, and afterwards proving the contrary on his trial, there is room for a pregnant reflection which will suggest itself to every thinking mind—still more when the silence of the log-book upon this "bad" state of the crew, corresponds with the commander's account that it was good. But, take the two accounts in what they agree, and it is seen that at 10 o'clock in the morning Lieutenant Gansevoort's whole report of the conspiracy and mutiny, as derived from the purser's steward (Wales) was received with ridicule—as the romance of a boy who had been reading piratical stories, and was amusing himself with the steward—a landsman, of whom the commander gives a bad account as having bought a double quantity of brandy—twice as much as his orders justified, before leaving New York;—and afterwards stealing it on the voyage. By five o'clock in the evening of the same day, and without hearing any thing additional, the commander became fully impressed with the truth of the whole story, awfully impressed with the danger of the vessel, and fully resolved upon a course of terrible energy to prevent the success of the impending mutiny. Of this great and sudden change in his convictions it becomes the right of the commander to give his own account of its inducing causes: and here they are, taken from his official report:

> "In the course of the day, Lieut. Gansevoort informed me that Mr. Spencer had been in the wardroom examining a chart of the West Indies, and had asked the assistant surgeon some questions about the Isle of Pines, and the latter had informed him that it was a place much frequented by pirates, and drily asked if he had any acquaintances there.—He passed the day rather sullenly in one corner of the steerage, as was his usual custom, engaged in examining a small piece of paper, and writing upon it with his pencil, and occasionally finding relaxation in working with a penknife at the tail of a devilfish, one of which he had formed into a sliding ring for his cravat. Lieut. Gansevoort also made an excuse of duty to follow him to the foretop, where he found him engaged in having some love device tattooed on his arm by

Benjamin F. Green, ordinary seaman, and apprentice. Lieut. Gansevoort also learned that he had been endeavoring for some days to ascertain the rate of the chronometer, by applying to Mid. Rodgers, to whom it was unknown, and who referred him to the master. He had been seen in secret and nightly conferences with the boatswain's mate, S. Cromwell, and seaman Elisha Small. I also heard that he had given money to several of the crew; to Elisha Small on the twelfth of September, the day before our departure from New York; the same day on which, in reply to Commodore Perry's injunctions to reformation, he had made the most solemn promises of amendment; to Samuel Cromwell on the passage to Madeira; that he had been in the habit of distributing tobacco extensively among the apprentices, in defiance of the orders of the navy department, and of my own often reiterated; that he had corrupted the ward-room steward, caused him to steal brandy from the ward-room mess, which he, Mr. Spencer, had drunk himself, occasionally getting drunk when removed from observation, and had also administered to several of the crew; that, finally, he was in the habit of amusing the crew by making music with his jaw. He had the faculty of throwing his jaw out of joint, and by contact of the bones, playing with accuracy and elegance a variety of airs. Servile in his intercourse with me, when among the crew he loaded me with blasphemous vituperation, and proclaimed that it would be a pleasing task to roll me overboard off the round-house. He had some time before drawn a brig with a black flag, and asked one of the midshipmen what he thought of it; he had repeatedly asserted in the early part of the cruise, that the brig might easily be taken; he had quite recently examined the hand of midshipman Rodgers, told his fortune, and predicted for him a speedy and violent death."

Surely the historian, as well as the poet may say: To the jealous mind, trifles light as air are confirmations strong as proofs from holy writ. Here are fourteen causes of suspected mutiny enumerated, part of which causes are eminently meritorious in a young naval officer, as those of studying the chart of the West Indies (whither the vessel was going), and that of learning the rate of the chronometer; another part of which is insignificant, as giving tobacco to the apprentice boys, and giving money to two of the seamen; others again would show a different passion from that of piracy, as having love devices tattooed on his arm; others again would bespeak the lassitude of idleness, as whittling at the tail of a devilfish, and making a ring for his cravat, and drawing a brig with a black flag; others again would indicate playfulness and humor, as examining the palm of young Rodgers' hand, and telling his fortune, which fortune, of course, was to be startling, as a sudden and violent death, albeit this young Rodgers was his favorite, and the only one he asked to see when he was about to be hung up—(a favor which was denied him); others again are contradicted by previous statements, as, that Spencer corrupted the purser's steward and made him steal brandy, the commander having before reported that steward for the offence of purchasing a double quantity of brandy before he left New York—a circumstance which implied a sufficient inclination to use the extra supply he had laid in (of which he had the custody), without being corrupted by Spencer to steal it; others of these causes again were natural, and incidental to Spencer's social condition in the vessel, as that of talking with the seamen, he being objected to by his four roommates (who were the commander's relations and connections), and considered one too many in their room, and as such attempted to be removed to another ship by the commander himself; another, that occasionally he got drunk when removed from observation, a fault rather too common (even when in the presence of observation) to stand for evidence of a design to commit mutiny on board a man-of-war; another, that blasphemous vituperation of the commander which, although it might be abusive, could neither be blasphemous (which only applies to the abuse of God), nor a sign of a design upon the vessel, but only of contempt for the commander; finally, as in that marvellous fine music with the jaw out of joint, playing with skill and accuracy a variety of elegant airs by the contaction of the luxated ends of the bones. Taken as true, and this musical habit might indicate an innocency of disposition. But it is ridiculously false, and impossible, and as such ridiculous impossibility it was spared the mention even of contempt during the whole court-martial proceedings. Still it was one of the facts gravely communicated to the Secretary of the Navy as one of the means used by Spencer to seduce the crew. While ridicule, contempt and scorn are the only proper replies to such absurd presumptions of guilt, there were two of them presented in such a way as to admit of an inquiry into their truth, namely, the fortune-telling and the chronometer: Midshipman Rodgers testified before the court that this fortune-telling was a steerage amusement, and that he was to die, not only suddenly and violently, but also a gambler; and that as for the examination of the chronometer, it was with a view to a bet between himself and Rodgers as to the time that the vessel would get to St. Thomas—the bet on Spencer's side, being on eight days. Yet, the diseased mind of the commander could see nothing in those little incidents, but proof of a design to kill Rodgers (with the rest) before the ship got to St. Thomas, and afterwards to run to the Isle of Pines. Preposterous as these fourteen reasons were, they were conclusive with the commander, who forthwith acted upon them, and made the arrest of Spencer.

> "At evening quarters I ordered through my clerk, O. H. Perry, doing the duty also of midshipman and aid, all the officers to lay aft on the quarter deck, excepting the midshipman stationed on the forecastle. The master was ordered to take the wheel, and those of the crew stationed abaft sent to the mainmast. I approached Mr. Spencer, and said to him, 'I learn, Mr. Spencer, that you aspire to the command of the Somers.' With a deferential, but unmoved and gently smiling expression, he replied, 'Oh no, sir.' 'Did you not tell Mr. Wales, sir, that you had a project to kill the commander, the officers, and a considerable portion of the crew of this vessel, and to convert her into a pirate?' 'I may have told him so, sir, but it was in a joke.' 'You admit then that you told him so?' 'Yes, sir, but in joke!' 'This, sir, is joking on a forbidden subject—this joke may cost you your life!'"

This was the answer of innocence: guilt would have denied every thing. Here all the words are admitted, with a promptitude and frankness that shows they were felt to be what they purported—the mere admission of a joke. The captain's reply shows that the life of the young man was already determined upon. It was certainly a punishable joke—a joke upon a forbidden subject: but how punishable? certainly among the minor offences in the navy, offences prejudicial to discipline; and to be expiated by arrest, trial, condemnation for breach of discipline, and sentence to reprimand, suspension; or some such punishment for inconsiderate offences. But, no. The commander replies upon the spot, '*this joke may cost you your life*.' and in that he was prophetic, being the fulfiller of his own prophecy. The informer Wales had reported a criminal paper to be in the neckcloth of the young man: the next movement of the commander was to get possession of that paper: and of that attempt he gives this account:

> "'Be pleased to remove your neckhandkerchief.' It was removed and opened, but nothing was found in it. I asked him what he had done with a paper containing an account of his project which he had told Mr. Wales was in the back of his neckhandkerchief. 'It is a paper containing my day's work; and I have destroyed it.' 'It is a singular place to keep day's work in.' 'It is a convenient one,' he replied, with an air of deference and blandness."

Balked in finding this confirmation of guilt, the commander yet proceeded with his design, and thus describes the arrest:

> "I said to him, 'You must have been aware that you could only have compassed your designs by passing over my dead body, and after that the bodies of all the officers. You had given yourself a great deal to do. It will be necessary for me to confine you.' I turned to Lieutenant Gansevoort and said, 'Arrest Mr. Spencer, and put him in double irons.' Mr. Gansevoort stepped forward, and took his sword; he was ordered to sit down in the stern port, double ironed, and as an additional security handcuffed. I directed Lieut. Gansevoort to watch over his security, to order him to be put to instant death if he was detected speaking to, or holding intelligence in any way, with any of the crew. He was himself made aware of the nature of these orders. I also directed Lieut. Gansevoort to see that he had every comfort which his safe keeping would admit of. In confiding this task to Lieut. Gansevoort, his kindness and humanity gave me the assurance that it would be zealously attended to; and throughout the period of Mr. Spencer's confinement, Lieut. Gansevoort, whilst watching his person with an eagle eye, and ready at any moment to take his life should he forfeit that condition of silence on which his safety depended, attended to all his wants, covered him with his own grego when

squalls of rain were passing over, and ministered in every way to his comfort with the tenderness of a woman."

Double-ironed—handcuffed—bagged (for he was also tied up in a bag), lying under the sun in a tropical clime, and drenched with squalls of rain—silent—instant death for a word or a sign—Lieutenant Gansevoort, armed to the teeth, standing over him, and watching, with "eagle eye," for the sound or motion which was to be the forfeit of life: for six days and nights, his irons examined every half hour to see that all were tight and safe, was this boy (of less than nineteen) thus confined; only to be roused from it in a way that will be told. But the lieutenant could not stand to his arduous watch during the whole of that time. His eagle eye could not resist winking and shutting during all that time. He needed relief—and had it—and in the person of one who showed that he had a stomach for the business—Wales, the informer: who, finding himself elevated from the care of pea-jackets, molasses, and tobacco, to the rank of sentinel over a United States officer, improved upon the lessons which his superiors had taught him, and stood ready, a cocked revolver in hand, to shoot, not only the prisoners (for by this time there were three), for a thoughtless word or motion, but also to shoot any of the crew that should make a suspicious sign:—such as putting the hand to the chin, or touching a handspike within forty feet of the said Mr. Wales. Hear him, as he swears before the court-martial:

> "I was officer in charge of the prisoners: we were holy-stoning the decks. I noticed those men who missed their muster kept congregating round the stern of the launch, and kept talking in a secret manner. I noticed them making signs to the prisoners by putting their hands up to their chins: Cromwell was lying on the starboard arm-chest: he rose up in his bed. I told him if I saw any more *signs* passing between them *I should put him to death: my orders were to that effect.* He laid down in his bed. I then went to the stern of the launch, found Wilson, and a number of small holy-stones collected there, and was endeavoring to pull a gun handspike from the stern of the launch: *what his intentions were I don't know.* I cocked a pistol, and ordered him to the lee-gangway to draw water. I told him if I saw him pulling at the handspike I should blow his brains out."

This comes from Mr. Wales himself, not from the commander's report, where this handspike-incident is made to play a great part; thus:

> "Several times during the night there were symptoms of an intention to strike some blow. Mr. Wales detected Charles A. Wilson attempting to draw out a handspike from under the launch, with an evident purpose of felling him; and when Mr. Wales cocked his pistol and approached, he could only offer some lame excuse for his presence there. I felt more anxious than I had yet done, and remained continually on deck."

Here is a discrepancy. Wales swears before the court that he did not know what Wilson's intentions were in pulling at the handspike: the captain, who did not see the pulling, reports to the Secretary of the Navy that it was done with the evident intent of felling Wales! while Wales himself, before the court-martial, not only testified to his ignorance of any motive for that act, but admitted upon cross-examination, that the handspike was not drawn at all—only attempted! and that he himself was forty feet from Wilson at the time! (but, more of this handspike hereafter.) Still the impression upon the commander's mind was awful. He felt more anxious than ever: he could not rest: he kept continually on deck. Armed to the teeth he watched, listened, interrogated, and patrolled incessantly. Surely the man's crazy terrors would excite compassion were it not for the deeds he committed under their influence.—But the paper that was to have been found in Spencer's cravat, and was not found there: it was found elsewhere, and the commander in his report gives this account of it:

> "On searching the locker of Mr. Spencer, a small razor-case was found, which he had recently drawn, with a razor in it, from the purser. Instead of the razor, the case was found to contain a small paper, rolled in another; on the inner one were strange characters, which proved to be Greek, with which Mr. Spencer was familiar. It fortunately happened that there was another midshipman on board the Somers who knew Greek—one whose Greek, and every thing else that he possessed, was wholly devoted to his country. The Greek characters, converted by midshipman Henry Rodgers into our own, exhibited well known names among the crew. The

certain—the doubtful—those who were to be kept whether they would or not—arranged in separate rows; those who were to do the work of murder in the various apartments, to take the wheel, to open the arm-chests."

The paper had about thirty names upon it: four under the head of "certain:" ten under that of doubtful, and the remainder under the head of *nolens volens*—which was construed by the Latinists on board to signify men who were to be made to join in the mutiny whether they would or not: and these *nolens volens* who were to be forced were more numerous than those who were to force them. Eighteen unwilling men to be forced into mutiny and piracy by four willing and ten uncertain; and of the four willing, one of them the informer himself! and another not in the ship! and a third Spencer! leaving but one under Spencer to do the work. The names of all were spelt with the Greek alphabet. Of course these *nolens volens* men could not have been counted in any way among the mutineers; yet they were always counted to make up the thirty, as, of less than that number it would not have been seemly for a man-of-war to have been afraid; yet some of these were brought home in irons. The ten marked doubtful should not have been held to be guilty upon any principle of human justice— the humanity of the law always giving the benefit of the doubt to the suspected criminal. This brings the inquiry to the four "certain:" and of these four, it turned out that one of them (Andrews) was a personage not in the vessel! Another was the veritable Mr. Wales himself! who was the informer, and the most determined opposer of the mutiny—leaving but two (Spencer and McKinley) to do the work of murder in the various departments: and of this McKinley it will eventually be seen with what justice his name was there. The names of Small and Cromwell, both of whom were hung with Spencer, were neither of them in this certain list—nor that of Cromwell in any: in fact, there was nothing against him, and Small was only included in Wales's information. So that the "certain" mutineers were reduced to two, both of whom were in irons, and bagged, and five others out of the doubtful and *nolens volens* classes. There was no evidence to show that this was Spencer's razor-case: it was new, and like the rest obtained from the purser. There was no evidence how it got into Spencer's locker: Wales and Gansevoort were the finders. There was no evidence that a single man whose name was in the list, knew it to be there. Justice would have required these points to have been proven; but with respect to the writing upon this paper it was readily avowed by Spencer to be his—an avowal accompanied by a declaration of its joking character, which the law would require to go with it always, but which was disregarded.

Small and Cromwell were not arrested with Spencer, but afterwards, and not upon accusations, but upon their looks and attitudes, and accident to the sky-sail-mast, which will be noted at the proper time. The first point is to show the arrestation upon looks and motions; and of that the commander gave this account in the official report:

> "The following day being Sunday, the crew were inspected at quarters, ten o'clock. I took my station abaft with the intention of particularly observing Cromwell and Small. The third, or master's division, to which they both belonged, always mustered at morning quarters upon the after part of the quarter deck, in continuation of the line formed by the crews of the guns. The persons of both were faultlessly clean. They were determined that their appearance in this respect should provoke no reproof. Cromwell stood up to his full stature, his muscles braced, his battle-axe grasped resolutely, his cheek pale, but his eye fixed as if indifferently at the other side. He had a determined and dangerous air. Small made a very different figure. His appearance was ghastly; he shifted his weight from side to side, and his battle-axe passed from one hand to the other; his eye wandered irresolutely, but never towards mine. I attributed his conduct to fear; I have since been led to believe that the business upon which he had entered was repugnant to his nature, though the love of money and of rum had been too strong for his fidelity."

Here were two men adjudged guilty of mutiny and piracy upon their looks, and attitude, and these diametrically opposed in each case. One had a dangerous air—the other a ghastly air. One looked resolute—the other irresolute. One held his battle-axe firmly griped—the other shifted his from hand to hand. One stood up steadily on both legs—the other shifted his weight uneasily from leg to leg. In one point only did they agree— in that of faultless cleanliness: a coincidence which the commander's judgment converted into evidence of guilt, as being proof of a determination that, so far as clean clothes went, there should be no cause for judging them pirates: a conclusion to the benefit of which the whole crew would be entitled, as they were proved on the court-martial to be all "faultlessly clean" at this Sunday inspection—as they always were at such inspection—as the regulations required them to be—and for a fault in which any one of them would have been punished. Yet upon these looks, and attitudes, suspicions were excited, which, added to the incident of a mast broken by the blundering order of the commander's nephew, caused the arrest and death of two citizens.

After the crew had been inspected, divine service was performed, the crew attending before the time, and behaving well; and the commander again availed himself of the occasion to examine the countenances of the men; and, happily, without finding any thing to give him distrust. He thus describes the scene:

> "After quarters the church was rigged. The crew mustered up with their prayer-books, and took their seats without waiting for all hands to be called, and considerably before five bells, or half-past ten—the usual time of divine service. The first lieutenant reported all ready, and asked me if he should call all hands to muster. I told him to wait for the accustomed hour. Five bells were at length struck, and all hands called to muster. The crew were unusually attentive, and the responses more than commonly audible. The muster succeeded, and I examined very carefully the countenances of the crew, without discovering any thing that gave me distrust."

This Sunday then (Nov. 27th) being the first Sunday, and the first day after the arrest of Spencer, had passed half by without any thing discoverable to excite distrust, except the cleanliness, the looks, and the attitudes of Small and Cromwell at the morning inspection. At the second ordeal, that of the church service, the whole crew came out well, and all seemed to be safe and right up to this time—being twenty-four hours after the arrest of Spencer—the event which was expected to rouse his accomplices to some outbreak for his rescue. But that critical day was not destined to pass away without an event which confirmed all the suspicions of the commander, and even indicated the particular criminals. Before the sun had gone down, this event occurred; and as it became the turning point in the case, and the point of departure in the subsequent tragic work, the commander shall have the benefit of telling it himself:

> "In the afternoon, the wind having moderated, skysails and royal studding-sails were set. In going large I had always been very particular to have no strain upon the light braces leading forward, as the tendency of such a strain was to carry away the light yards and masts. Whilst Ward M. Gagely, one of the best and most skilful of our apprentices, was yet on the main royal yard, after setting the main skysail, a sudden jerk of the weather main royal brace given by Small and another, whose name I have not discovered, carried the topgallant-mast away in the sheeve hole, sending forward the royal mast with royal skysail, royal studding sail, main-topgallant staysail, and the head of the gaff topsail. Gagely was on the royal yard. I scarcely dared to look on the booms or in the larboard gangways where he should have fallen. For a minute I was in intense agony: in the next I saw the shadow of the boy through the topgallant sail, rising rapidly towards the topgallant yard, which still remained at the mast head. Presently he rose to view, descended on the after side to the topgallant-mast cap, and began to examine with coolness to see what was first to be done to clear the wreck. I did not dream at the time that the carrying away of this mast was the work of treachery—but I knew that it was an occasion of this sort, the loss of a boy overboard, or an accident to a spar, creating confusion and interrupting the regularity of duty, which was likely to be taken advantage of by the conspirators were they still bent on the prosecution of their enterprise."

The commander did not dream at the time of treachery: did not dream of it when he saw the mast fall: and well he might not, for he had given the order himself to set the skysails, the ship running "large" at the time, i. e. with a favorable wind, and when a slight press of sail might carry away the elevated, light, and unsupported mast which carried the skysail. He did not dream of treachery when he saw it fall under an order which himself had given: but quickly he had that dream, and he must tell himself how it came to him; thus:

> "To my astonishment, all those who were most conspicuously named in the programme of Mr. Spencer, no matter in what part of the vessel they might be stationed, mustered at the

main-top masthead—whether animated by some new-born zeal in the service of their country, or collected there for the purpose of conspiring, it was not easy to decide. The coincidence confirmed the existence of a dangerous conspiracy, suspended, yet perhaps not abandoned."

This is the way the dream began, in astonishment at seeing all those most conspicuously nominated in the razor-case paper, rush to the scene of the disaster. Now, for the misfortune of this paragraph, it came to be proved before the court-martial, and after the men were dead, that the majority of those who ran forward were not named in the paper at all! and especially that one of the two was not upon it who were presently seized as guilty, and whose haste to perform a duty was the passport to death. The crew ran to the place. This would seem to be the most natural conduct imaginable. They ran to the place where the mast and boy were expected to fall. They flew to the place at which the commander, in his intense agony, did not dare to look. This haste to such a place was proof of guilt, take it either way, either as animated by some new-born zeal to hide past defection, or to collect for a conspiracy. The commander finds it hard to decide between these two purposes; but take which he might, it was confirmation of a dangerous conspiracy, and of its suspension, not abandonment. The sudden running to the place was the proof of the conspiracy: the jerk which Small, and another whose name has never yet been discovered, gave to the weather main royal brace, pointed out the two eminently guilty. What put the seal upon the confirmation of all this guilt was the strange and stealthy glances which Spencer, in his irons, and his head then out of the bag (for the heads were left out in the day time) cast at it. Hear him:

"The eye of Mr. Spencer travelled perpetually to the masthead, and cast thither many of those strange and stealthy glances which I had before noticed."

The commander nowhere tells when and how he had previously seen these sinister glances—certainly not before the revelations of Wales, as, up to that time, he was anxious before the court-martial to show that Spencer was kindly regarded by him. But the glances. What more natural than for Spencer to look at such a startling scene! a boy falling in the wreck of a broken mast, and tumbling shrouds, from fifty feet high: and look he did—a fair and honest look, his eyes steadfastly fixed upon it, as proved by the commander's own witnesses on the court-martial—especially midshipman Hays—who testified to the fixed and steady look; and this in answer to a question from the commander tending to get a confirmation of his own report. Nor did any one whatever see those strange and furtive glances which the commander beheld. Now to the breaking of the mast. This incident was reviewed at the time by two competent judges—Mr. Fenimore Cooper, the naval historian, and himself an ex-naval officer, and Captain William Sturgis of Boston, one of the best navigators that Boston ever bred (and she has bred as good as the world ever saw). They deemed the breaking of that slender, elevated, unbraced mast the natural result of the order which the commander gave to set the skysail, going as the vessel then was. She was in the trade-winds, running into West Indies from the coast of Africa, and running "large," as the mariners express it; that is to say, with the wind so crossing her course as to come strong upon her beam or quarter, and send her well before it. With such a wind, these experienced seamen say that the order which the commander gave might well break that mast. It would increase the press of sail on that delicate and exposed mast, able to bear but little at the best, and often breaking without a perceptible increase of pressure upon it. But the order which he gave was not the one given to the men. He gave his order to his relation, Mr. O. H. Perry, to have a small pull on one brace; instead of that the order given to the men was, to haul, that is, pull hard, on another; which was directly contrary to the order he had received—one slacking, the other increasing the press of sail. Under that order the men with alacrity threw their whole weight on the wrong brace; and the mast cracked, reeled, and fell immediately. The commander himself saw all this— saw the fault his nephew had committed—sent for him—reproved him in the face of the crew—told him it was his fault—the effect of his inattention. All this was fully proved before the court-martial. Perry's own testimony admitted it. Thus—questioned by the judge advocate: "After the mast was carried away were you sent for by the commander?" Answer: "Yes, sir." "Who came for you?" A. "I don't recollect the person." "Was it not McKee?" A. "I don't recollect." "What then occurred between you and the commander?" A. "He asked me why I did not attend to my duties better? and said I must do it better in future." "What was the commander alluding to?" A. "To my not attending to the brace at the time they were hauling on it." "Did he say to you, *'this is all your fault, sir?'* or words to that effect?" A. "I don't recollect." "What reply did you make the commander?"

A. "I did not make any. I said, I think, that I understood the order to haul on the brace." There was also something else proved there, which, like the other, was not reported in the commander's account of that portentous event, which was the immediate cause of a new and terrible line of conduct. First, there is no mention on the log-book of this rush of the men aft: secondly, there is no mention in it of any suspected design to carry away this topgallant mast. The commander was seeing when he wrote his report what the keeper of the log-book did not see at the time it should have happened. And this point is here dismissed with the remark that, in this case (the men coming fast to the work) was the sign of guilt: in other cases, coming slow was the same sign: so that, fast or slow, from the time Wales made his revelation, to the time of hanging, all motions, however opposite to each other, were equally signs of the same guilt. The account of this incident being given, the report proceeds:

> "The wreck being cleared, supper was piped down before sending up the new mast. After supper the same persons mustered again at the mast head, and the topgallant mast was fidded, the light yards crossed, and the sails set. By this time it was dark, and quarters had been unavoidably dispensed with: still I thought, under all the circumstances, that it was scarcely safe to leave Cromwell at large during the night. The night was the season of danger. After consulting Lieutenant Gansevoort, I determined to arrest Cromwell. The moment he reached the deck, an officer was sent to leeward to guard the lee-rigging; and the main stays were also thought of, though not watched. As his voice was heard in the top, descending the rigging, I met him at the foot of Jacob's ladder, surrounded by the officers, guided him aft to the quarter-deck, and caused him to sit down. On questioning him as to the secret conversation he had held the night before with Mr. Spencer, he denied its being he. He said; 'It was not me, sir, it was Small!' Cromwell was the tallest man on board, and Small the shortest. Cromwell was immediately ironed; and Small, then pointed out by an associate to increased suspicion, was also sent for, interrogated, and ironed. Increased vigilance was now enjoined upon all the officers; henceforward, all were perpetually armed. Either myself, or the first lieutenant was always on deck; and, generally, both of us were."

Two more were now arrested, and in giving an account of these arrests, as of all others (fifteen in the whole), the commander forgets to tell that the arrested persons were bagged, as well as double-ironed and handcuffed, and their irons ordered to be examined every half hour day and night—a ceremony which much interfered with sleep and rest. And now for the circumstances which occasioned these arrests: and first of Cromwell. There are but two points mentioned; first, "under all the circumstances." These have been mentioned, and comprise his looks and attitudes at the morning inspection, and his haste in getting to the scene of the wreck when the mast fell. The next was his answer to the question upon his secret conversation with Spencer the night before. This "night before," seems to be a sad blunder in point of time. Spencer was in irons on the larboard arm-chest at that time, a guard over him, and holding his life from minute to minute by the tenure of silence, the absence of signs, and the absence of understanding looks with any person. It does not seem possible that he could have held a conversation, secret or public, with any person during that night, or after his arrest until his death; nor is any such any where else averred: and it is a stupid contradiction in itself. If it was secret, it could not be known: if it was open, both the parties would have been shot instantly. Upon its stupid contradiction, as well as upon time, the story is falsified. Besides this blunder and extreme improbability, there is other evidence from the commander himself, to make it quite sure that nobody could have talked with Spencer that night. The men were in the hammocks, and the ship doubly guarded, and the officers patrolling the deck with pistols and cutlasses. Of this, the report says: "That night the officers of the watch were armed with cutlasses and pistols, and the rounds of both decks made frequently, to see that the crew were in their hammocks, and that there were no suspicious collections of individuals about the deck." Under these circumstances, it would seem impossible that the previous night's conversation could have been held by any person with Mr. Spencer. Next, supposing there was a secret conversation. It might have been innocent or idle; for its subject is not intimated; and its secret nature precludes all knowledge of it. So much for Cromwell: now for Small. His case stands thus: "Pointed out by an associate to increased suspicion." Here association in guilt is assumed; a mode of getting at the facts he wanted, almost invariable with the commander, Mackenzie. Well, the answer of Cromwell, "It was not me, it was Small!" would prove no guilt if it was true; but it is impossible to have been true. But this was only cause of "increased" suspicion: so that there was suspicion before; and all the causes of this had been detailed in the official report. First, there were the causes arising at inspection that morning—faultless cleanliness, shifting his battle-axe from one hand to the other, resting alternately on the legs, and a ghastly look—to wit: a ghostly look. He was interrogated: the report does not say about what: nor does it intimate the character of the answers. But there were persons present who heard the questions and the answers, and who told both to the court-martial. The questions were as to the conversation with Spencer, which Wales reported; and the answers were, yes—that he had foolish conversations with Spencer, but no mutiny. Still there was a stumbling block in the way of arresting Small. His name was nowhere made out as certain by Spencer. This was a balk: but there was the name of a man in the list who was not in the vessel: and this circumstance of a man too few, suggested an idea that there should be a transaction between these names; and the man on the list who had no place in the ship, should give place to him who had a place in the ship, and no place on the list: so Small was assumed to be Andrews; and by that he was arrested, though proved to be Small by all testimony—that of his mother inclusive.

The three prisoners were bagged, and how that process was performed upon them, they did not live to tell: but others who had undergone the same investment, did: and from them the operation will be learnt. With the arrest of these two, the business of Sunday closed; and Monday opened with much flogging of boys, and a speech from the commander, of which he gives an abstract, and also displays its capital effects:

> "The effect of this (speech of the 28th) upon the crew was various: it filled many with horror at the idea of what they had escaped from: it inspired others with terror at dangers awaiting them from their connection with the conspiracy. The thoughts of returning to that home, and those friends from whom it had been intended to cut them off for ever, caused many of them to weep. I now considered the crew tranquillized and the vessel safe."

Now, whether this description of the emotions excited by the captain's oratory, be reality or fancy, it is still good for one thing: it is good for evidence against himself! good evidence, at the bar of all courts, and at the high tribunal of public opinion. It shows that the captain, only two days before the hanging, was perfect master of his ship—that the crew was tranquillized, and the vessel safe! and all by the effect of his oratory: and consequently, that he had a power within himself by which he could control the men, and mould them into the emotions which he pleased. The 28th day came. The commander had much flogging done, and again made a speech, but not of such potency as the other. He stopped Spencer's tobacco, and reports that, "the day after it was stopped, his spirits gave way entirely. He remained the whole day with his face buried in the gregoe and when it was raised, it was bathed in tears." So passed the 28th. "On the 29th (continues the report) all hands were again called to witness punishment," and the commander made another speech. But the whole crew was far from being tranquillized. During the night seditious cries were heard. Signs of disaffection multiplied. The commander felt more uneasy than he had ever done before. The most seriously implicated collected in knots. They conferred together in low tones, hushing up, or changing the subject when an officer approached. Some of the petty officers had been sounded by the first lieutenant, and found to be true to their colors: they were under the impression that the vessel was yet far from being safe—that there were many still at liberty that ought to be confined—that an outbreak, having for its object the rescue of the prisoners, was seriously contemplated. Several times during the night there were symptoms of an intention to strike some blow. Such are a specimen of the circumstances grouped together under vague and intangible generalities with which the day of the 29th is ushered in, all tending to one point, the danger of a rescue, and the necessity for more arrests. Of these generalities, only one was of a character to be got hold of before the court-martial, and it will take a face, under the process of judicial examination of witnesses, very different from that which it wore in the report. After these generalities, applying to the mass of the crew, come special accusations against four seamen—Wilson, Green, McKee, McKinley: and of these special accusations, a few were got hold of by the judge advocate on the court-martial. Thus:

> 1. *The handspike sign.*—"Mr. Wales detected Charles A. Wilson attempting to draw out a handspike from under the launch, with an evident purpose of felling him; and when Wales cocked his pistol, and approached, he could only offer some lame excuse for his presence there."

This is the amount of the handspike portent, as reported to the Secretary of the Navy among the signs which indicated the immediate danger of the rising and the rescue. This Wales, of course, was a witness for the commander, and on being put on the stand, delivered his testimony in a continued narrative, covering the whole case. In that narrative, he thus introduces the handspike incident:

> "I then went to the stern of the launch, found Wilson had a number of small holystones collected there, and was endeavoring to pull a gun handspike from the stern of the launch: what his intentions were I don't know. I cocked a pistol, and ordered him in the gangway to draw water. I told him if I saw him pulling on the handspike, I should blow his brains out."

"I then went to the stern," &c. This period of time of going to the stern of the launch, was immediately after this Wales had detected persons making signs to the prisoners by putting their hands to their chins, and when he told Cromwell if he saw any more signs between them he should put him to death. It was instantly after this detection and threat, and of course at a time when this purser's steward was in a good mood to see signs and kill, that he had this vision of the handspike: but he happens to swear that he does not know with what intent the attempt to pull it out was made. Far from seeing, as the commander did when he wrote the report, that the design to fell him was evident, he does not know what the design was at all; but he gives us a glimpse at the inside of his own heart, when he swears that he would blow out the brains of Wilson if he saw him again attempting to pull out the handspike, when he did not know what it was for. Here is a murderous design attributed to Wilson on an incident with Wales, in which Wales himself saw no design of any kind; and thus, upon his direct examination, and in the narrative of his testimony, he convicts the commander of a cruel and groundless misstatement. But proceed to the cross-examination: the judge advocate required him to tell the distance between himself and Wilson when the handspike was being pulled by Wilson? He answered forty feet, more or less! and so this witness who had gone to the stern of the launch, was forty feet from that stern when he got there.

> 2. *Missing their muster.*—"McKinley, Green, and others, missed their musters. Others of the implicated also missed their musters. I could not contemplate this growth of disaffection without serious uneasiness. Where was this thing to end? Each new arrest of prisoners seemed to bring a fresh set of conspirators forward to occupy the first place."

The point of this is the missing the musters; and of these the men themselves give this account, in reply to questions from the judge advocate:

> "It was after the arrest (of Spencer), me and McKee (it is McKinley speaks) turned in and out with one another when the watch was called: we made a bargain in the first of the cruise to wake one another up when the watches were called. I came up on deck, awaked by the noise of relieving guards, 15 minutes too late, and asked McKee why he did not call me? He told me that the officer would not let him stir: that they were ordered to lie down on the deck, and when he lay down he fell asleep, and did not wake up: that was why I missed my muster, being used to be waked up by one another."

Such is the natural account, veracious upon its face, which McKinley gives for missing, by 15 minutes, his midnight muster, and which the commander characterized as a lame excuse, followed by immediate punishment, and a confirmed suspicion of mutiny and piracy. All the others who missed musters had their excuses, true on their face, good in their nature, and only varying as arising from the different conditions of the men at the time.

> 3. *The African knife sign.*—"In his sail-bag (Wilson's) was found an African knife of an extraordinary shape—short, and gradually expanding in breadth, sharp on both sides. It was of no use for any honest purpose. It was only fit to kill. It had been secretly sharpened, by his own confession, the day before with a file to a perfect edge."

The history of this knife, as brought out before the court-martial was this (McKinley, the witness):

> "I was ashore on the coast of Africa—I believe it was at Monrovia that I went ashore, I having no knife at the time. I went ashore there, and saw one of the natives with a knife. I spoke to

Mr. Heiskill (the purser) about buying it for me. He sent me aboard the brig (Somers) with some things in the second cutter. When I came back Warner had bought the knife I looked at, and Mr. Heiskill bought an African dirk instead of that, and gave it to me. I came on board with the knife, and wore it for two or three days. Wilson saw it, and said he wanted to buy it as a curiosity to take to New York. I would not let him have it then. I went up on the topgallant yard, and it nearly threw me off. It caught in some of the rigging. When I came down, I told Wilson he might have it for one dollar. He promised to give a dollar out of the first grog money, or the first dollar he could get."

So much for this secret and formidable weapon in the history of its introduction to the ship—coming through the purser Heiskill, one of the supporters of Commander Mackenzie in all the affairs of these hangings—given as a present to McKinley, a cot-boy, *i. e.* who made up the cots for the officers, who had been a waiter at Howard's Hotel (N. Y.), and who was a favorite in the ship's crew. As for the uses to which it could only be put—no honest use, and only fit to kill—it was proved to be in current use as a knife, cutting holes in hammocks, shifting their numbers, &c.

4. *The battle-axe alarm.*—"He had begun also to sharpen his battle-axe with the same assistant (the file): one part of it he had brought to an edge."

The proof was the knife and the battle-axe were publicly sharpened as often as needed, and that battle-axes, like all other arms, were required to be kept in perfect order; and that, sharp and shining was their desired condition. Every specified sign of guilt was cleared up before the court-martial—one only excepted; and the mention of that was equally eschewed by each party. It was the sign of music from the luxated jaw! Both parties refrained from alluding to that sign on the trial—one side from shame, the other from pity. Yet it was gravely reported to the Secretary of the Navy as fact, and as a means of seducing the crew. Returning to generalities, the informer Wales, presents himself prominently on this day—this 29th of November, memorable for its resolves; and groups a picture which was to justify all that was to be done in two days more, and of which the initiation and preliminary steps were then taken.

"The crew still continued very much dissatisfied, grumbling the whole time. The master-at-arms was sick at the time, and I attended to his duties, and had charge of the berth deck. Their manner was so insulting that I had to bring three or four up for punishment (with the cat-and-nine-tails.) The dissatisfaction continued to increase (this was the 30th I think), and continued till the execution took place, when I noticed a marked change in their manner: those who were the most unruly and insolent were the first to run and obey an order: they seemed to anticipate an order."—"Before that, an order had to be given two or three times before it was executed, and when they did execute it, they would go growling along, as though they did not care whether it was done or not. They went slow."

This swearing of Wales tallies with the report of the commander in bringing the mutiny up to the bursting point on the 29th of November. That was a point necessary to be reached, as it will be seen hereafter, and to be reached on that day. There was one other point necessary to be made out, and that was, the mutiny was to break forth before they arrived at the island of St. Thomas, as at that place the mutineers could be landed, or transhipped, and so the whole thing evaporate. They were now within less than four days of that island. Spencer had bet just before they would be there in eight days—a bet which seemed to say that he had no thought of preventing her from arriving there. But it was now necessary to have the mutiny to take place before they got to that island: and this essential point was established by Wales, by an addition to his previous testimony fixing that point. This addition to his testimony caused an inquiry to be put to him by the judge advocate before the court: "When did you first swear that Mr. Spencer told you that the mutiny would break out shortly before your arrival at St. Thomas?" Answer: "At the examination of officers, and of men by the officers. I forget what day, but I think it was on the 30th of November." This was corroborated in the view of the commander by the fortune-telling of the young Rodgers' fate—to die suddenly, i.e. in the mutiny before they got to St. Thomas, without adding the remainder of the prediction, that he was to die a gambler; and without adding the essential fact, that Spencer had a bet that she would arrive there by a given day.

On the 30th day of November, at nine o'clock in the morning, a letter was delivered by the commander to Lieutenant Gansevoort, Surgeon Leecock and Purser Heiskill, and four midshipmen, stating the dangers of the ship, and calling upon them to enlighten the commander with their opinion as to what should be done with Spencer, Small and Cromwell. The letter was not addressed to any of the acting midshipmen, the reason why being thus stated: "Though they had done men's duty in the late transaction, they were still boys: their opinion could add but little force to that of the other officers: it would have been hard, at their early age, to call upon them to say whether three of their fellow-creatures should live or die." So reasoned the commander with respect to the acting midshipmen. It would seem that the same reasoning should have excused the four midshipmen on whom this hard task was imposed. The letter was delivered at 9 o'clock in the morning: the nominated officers met in (what was called) a council: and proceeded immediately to take, what they called testimony, to be able to give the required opinion. Thirteen seamen were examined, under oath—an extra-judicial oath of no validity in law, and themselves punishable at common law for administering it: and this testimony written down in pencil on loose and separate slips of paper—the three persons whose lives were to be passed upon, having no knowledge of what was going on. Purser Heiskill being asked on the court-martial, why, on so important occasion pen and ink was not used, answered, he did not know—"that there were no lawyers there:" as if lawyers were necessary to have pen and ink used. The whole thirteen, headed by Wales, swore to a pattern: and such swearing was certainly never heard before, not even in the smallest magistrate's court, and where the value of a cow and calf was at stake: hearsays, beliefs, opinions; preposterous conclusions from innocent or frivolous actions: gratuitous assumptions of any fact wanted: and total disregard of every maxim which would govern the admissibility of evidence. Thus:

> HENRY KING: "Believed the vessel was in danger of being taken by them: thinks Cromwell the head man: thinks they have been engaged in it ever since they left New York: thinks if they could get adrift, there would be danger of the vessel being taken: thinks Spencer, Small, Cromwell and Wilson were the leaders: thinks if Golderman and Sullivan could get a party among the crew now that they would release the prisoners and take the vessel, and that they are not to be trusted."—CHARLES STEWART: "Have seen Cromwell and Spencer talking together often—talking low: don't think the vessel safe with these prisoners on board: this is my deliberate opinion from what I've heard King, the gunner's mate, say (that is) that he had heard the boys say that there were spies about: I think the prisoners have friends on board who would release them if they got a chance. I can't give my opinion as to Cromwell's character: I have seen him at the galley getting a cup of coffee now and then."—CHARLES ROGERS: "I believe Spencer gave Cromwell 15 dollars on the passage to Madeira—Cromwell showed it to me and said Spencer had given it to him. If we get into hard weather I think it will be hard to look out for all the prisoners: I believe if there are any concerned in the plot, it would not be safe to go on our coast in cold or bad weather with the prisoners: I think they would rise and take the vessel: I think if Cromwell, Small, and Spencer were disposed of, our lives would be much safer. Cromwell and Small understand navigation: these two are the only ones among the prisoners capable of taking charge of the vessel."—ANDREW ANDERSON: "Have seen Spencer and Cromwell often speaking together on the forecastle, in a private way: never took much notice: I think it's plain proof they were plotting to take this vessel out of the hands of her officers: from the first night Spencer was confined, and from what I heard from my shipmates, I suspected that they were plotting to take the vessel: I think they are safe from here to Saint Thomas (West Indies), but from thence home I think there is great danger on account of the kind of weather on the coast, and squalls."—OLIVER B. BROWNING: "I would not like to be on board the brig if he (Cromwell) was at large: I do not bear him any ill will: I do not know that he bears me any ill will: I do not think it safe to have Cromwell, Spencer and Small on board: I believe that if the men were at their stations taking care of the vessel in bad weather, or any other time when they could get a chance, they would try and capture the vessel if they could get a chance: to tell you God Almighty's truth, I believe some of the cooks about the galley, I think they are the main backers."—H. M. GARTY: "Believes Spencer, Small and Cromwell were determined on taking the brig: he supposes to turn pirates

or retake slavers: on or about the 11th of October heard Spencer say the brig could be taken with six men: I think there are some persons at large who would voluntarily assist the prisoners if they had an opportunity: thinks if the prisoners were at large the brig would certainly be in great danger: thinks there are persons adrift yet who would, if any opportunity offered, rescue the prisoners: thinks the vessel would be safer if Cromwell, Spencer, and Small were put to death."—GEORGE W. WARNER: "Have seen Cromwell and Spencer sitting together frequently: have heard Spencer ask Cromwell what sort of a slaver this vessel would make? he replied, he thought she would make a nice slaver: have no doubt he had joined Spencer in the project of taking this vessel: thinks Cromwell would have taken the vessel to the north west coast: Cromwell was in a slaver and taken a year since at Cuba: has seen Spencer give Cromwell cigars: thinks Cromwell deserves to be hung: thinks he is the most dangerous man in the ship: if I had my way I would hang him."—VAN VELSON: "A good while since Spencer said he would like to have a ship to go to the north-west coast: Cromwell and him was thick: should think Cromwell meant to join Spencer to take this vessel: Spencer thought he could raise money to get a ship. My reason for thinking that Cromwell meant to join Spencer in taking this vessel, is because I have frequently seen them in close conversation."

The drift of all this swearing was to show that the men ought not only to be put to death, but immediately, to prevent a rescue, and before they got to St. Thomas, and to make an excuse for not bringing them to the United States, pleading the difficulty to guard them in bad weather on the coast of the United States. (Among the persons examined, and one of those who "thinks the vessel would be safer if Cromwell, Spencer, and Small were put to death," was one Garty—Sergeant Michael H. Garty—who will be especially noticed hereafter.) The examination of these persons, though commenced immediately on receiving the commander's letter, was not finished until nine o'clock of the next morning, December the first; and then upon the pressing application of Gansevoort (who was absent much of the time), and telling the council that the commander was waiting for it. The answer was soon prepared, and delivered, declaring Spencer, Cromwell, and Small to be guilty of mutiny according to the evidence which had come to their knowledge, and that they were leagued with others still at large; and then goes on to say—"We are convinced that it would be impossible to carry them to the United States, and that the safety of the public property, the lives of ourselves, and of those committed to our charge, require that (giving them sufficient time to prepare) they should be put to death in a manner best calculated to make a beneficial impression upon the disaffected." And this recommendation was signed by the whole seven to whom the commander's letter had been addressed—among them two names illustrious in the annals of our navy. The heart grieves over that view, but draws a veil over the names, and absolves the boys from the guilt of the transaction. We know the power of the quarter deck. The midshipman must be born a Cato, or a Macon (and such men are only born once in ages) to be able to stand up against the irresistible will of that deck. History refuses to see these boys as agents in the transaction. Mackenzie, Gansevoort, Leecock and Heiskill, are the persons with whom she deals.

The narrative, thus far following the commander's report, is here suspended for the purpose of bringing in some circumstances not related in that report, and which came out before the court-martial; and the relation of which is due to the truth of history. 1. That the three persons whose lives were thus passed upon were, during this whole time, lying on the deck in their multiplied irons, and tied up in strong tarpaulin bags, wholly unconscious of any proceeding against them, and free from fear of death, as they had been made to understand by the commander that they were to be brought home to the United States for trial; and who reported that to have been his first intention. 2. While this examination was going on, and during the first day of it, Gansevoort (the head of the council) went to Spencer (telling him nothing of his object), for the purpose of getting proofs of his guilt, to be used against him whereof he got none; and thus tells his errand in answer to a question before the court-martial: "I am under the impression it was the 30th (of November), for the purpose of his proving more clearly his guilt. I took him the paper (razor-case paper), that he might translate it so I could understand it. My object was to obtain from him an acknowledgment of his guilt." 3. That it had been agreed among the upper officers two days before that, if any more prisoners were made, the three first taken should suffer immediate death on account of the impossibility of guarding more than they had. This dire conclusion came out upon question and answer, from one of the midshipmen who was in the council. "Had you any discussion on the 28th of November, as to putting the three prisoners to death?" Answer: "I don't recollect what day Gansevoort asked me my opinion, if it became necessary to make more prisoners, if we should be able to guard them? I told him no." "Did you *then* give it as your opinion that Cromwell, Small, and Spencer should be put to death?" Answer: "Yes, sir." Four more officers of the council were ascertained to have been similarly consulted at the same time, and to have answered in the same way: so that the deaths of the three men were resolved upon two days before the council was established to examine witnesses, and enlighten the commander with their opinions. 4. That it had been resolved that, if more prisoners were taken, the three already in the bags must be put to death; and, accordingly, while the council was sitting, and in the evening of their session, and before they had reported an opinion, four more arrests were made: so that the condition became absolute upon which the three were to die before the council had finished their examination.

This is, perhaps, the first instance in the annals of military or naval courts, in which the commander fixed a condition on which prisoners were to be put to death—which condition was to be an act of his own, unknown to the prisoners, but known to the court, and agreed to be acted upon before it was done: and which was done and acted upon!

These are four essential circumstances, overlooked by the commander in his report, but brought out upon interrogatories before the court. The new arrests are duly reported by the commander. They were: Wilson, Green, McKinley, McKee. The commander tells how the arrests were made. "These individuals were made to sit down as they were taken, and when they were ironed, I walked deliberately round the battery, followed by the first lieutenant; and we made together a very careful inspection of the crew. Those who (though known to be very guilty) were considered to be the least dangerous, were called out and interrogated: care was taken not to awaken the suspicions of such as from courage and energy were really formidable, unless it were intended to arrest them. Our prisoners now amounted to seven, filling up the quarter deck, and rendering it very difficult to keep them from communicating with each other, interfering essentially with the management of the vessel." This is the commander's account of the new arrests, but he omits to add that he bagged them as fast as taken and ironed; and as that bagging was an investment which all the prisoners underwent, and an unusual and picturesque (though ugly) feature in the transaction, an account will be given of it in the person of one of the four, which will stand for all. It is McKinley who gives it, and who was bagged quite home to New York, and became qualified, to give his experience of these tarpaulin sacks, both in the hot region of the tropics and the cold blasts of the New York latitude in the dead of winter. Question by the judge advocate: "When were you put in the bags?" Answer: "After the examination and before we got to St. Thomas." "How were the bags put on you?" Answer: "They were laid on deck, and we got into them as well as we could, feet foremost." "Was your bag ever put over your head?" Answer: "Yes, sir. The first night it was tied over my head." "Who was the person who superintended, and did it?" Answer; "*Sergeant Garty was always there when we were put into the bags.* I could not see. I could not say who tied it over my head. He (Garty) was there then." "Did you complain of it?" Answer: "After a while the bag got very hot. Whoever was the officer I don't know. I told him I was smothering. I could not breathe. He came back with the order that I could not have it untied. I turned myself round as well as I could, and got my mouth to the opening of the bag, and staid so till morning." Question by a member of the court: "Did you find the bag comfortable when not tied over your head?" Answer: "No, sir. It was warm weather: it was uncomfortable. On the coast (of the United States in December) they would get full of rain water, nearly up to my knees." Catching at this idea of comfort in irons and a bag, Commander Mackenzie undertook to prove them so; and put a leading question, to get an affirmative answer to his own assertion that this bagging was done for the "comfort" of the prisoners—a new conception, for which he seemed to be entirely indebted to this hint from one of the court. The mode of McKinley's arrest, also gives an insight into the manner in which that act was performed on board a United States man-of-war; and is thus described by McKinley himself. To the question, when he was arrested, and how, he answers: "On the 30th of November, at morning quarters I was arrested. The commander put Wilson into irons. When he was put in irons the commander cried, 'Send McKinley aft.' I went aft. The commander and Gansevoort held pistols at my head, and told me to sit down. Mr. Gansevoort told King, the gunner, to stand by to knock out their brains if they should make a false motion. I was put in irons then. He ordered Green and McKee aft: he put them in irons also. Mr. Gansevoort ordered me to get on all fours, and creep round to the larboard side, as I could not walk." And that is the way it was done!

The three men were thus doomed to death, without trial, without hearing, without knowledge of what was going on against them; and without a hint of what had been done. One of the officiating officers who had sat in the council, being asked before the court if any suggestion, or motion, was made to apprise the prisoners of what was going on, and give them a hearing, answered that there was not. When Governor Wall was on trial at the Old Bailey for causing the death of a soldier twenty years before at Goree, in Africa, for imputed mutiny, he plead the sentence of a drum-head court-martial for his justification. The evidence proved that the men so tried (and there were just three of them) were not before that court, and had no knowledge of its proceedings, though on the ground some forty feet distant—about as far off as were the three prisoners on board the Somers, with the difference that the British soldiers could see the court (which was only a little council of officers); while the American prisoners could not see their judges. This sort of a court which tried people without hearing them, struck the British judges; and when the witness (a foot soldier) told how he saw the Governor speaking to the officers, and saw them speaking to one another for a minute or two, and then turning to the Governor, who ordered the man to be called out of the ranks to be tied on a cannon for punishment: when the witness told that, the Lord Chief Baron McDonald called out—"Repeat that." The witness repeated it. Then the Chief Baron inquired into the constitution of these drum-head courts, and to know if it was their course to try soldiers without hearing them: and put a question to that effect to the witness. Surprised at the question, the soldier, instead of answering it direct, yes or no, looked up at the judge, and said: "My Lord, I thought an Englishman had that privilege every where." And so thought the judge, who charged the jury, accordingly, and that even if there was a mutiny; and so thought the jury, who immediately brought in a verdict for murder; and so thought the King (George III.), who refused to pardon the Governor, or to respite him for longer than eight days, or to remit the anatomization of his dead body. There was law then in England against the oppressors of the humble, and judges to execute it, and a king to back them.

The narrative will now be resumed at the point at which it was suspended, and Commander Mackenzie's official report will still be followed for the order of the incidents, and his account of them.

It was nine o'clock on the morning of the first of December, that Gansevoort went into the ward-room to hurry the completion of the letter which the council of officers was drawing up, and which, under the stimulating remark that the commander was waiting for it, was soon ready. Purser Heiskill, who had been the pencil scribe of the proceedings, carried the letter, and read it to the commander. In what manner he received it, himself will tell:

> "I at once concurred in the justice of their opinion, and in the necessity of carrying its recommendation into immediate effect. There were two others of the conspirators almost as guilty, so far as the intention was concerned, as the three ringleaders who had been first confined, and to whose cases the attention of the officers had been invited. But they could be kept in confinement without extreme danger to the ultimate safety of the vessel. The three chief conspirators alone were capable of navigating and sailing her. By their removal the motive to a rescue, a capture, and a carrying out of their original design of piracy was at once taken away. Their lives were justly forfeited to the country which they had betrayed; and the interests of that country and the honor and security of its flag required that the sacrifice, however painful, should be made. In the necessities of my position I found my law, and in them also I must trust to find my justification."

The promptitude of this concurrence precludes the possibility of deliberation, for which there was no necessity, as the deaths had been resolved upon two days before the council met, and as Gansevoort communicated with the commander the whole time. There was no need for deliberation, and there was none; and the rapidity of the advancing events proves there was no time for it. And in this haste one of the true reasons for hanging Small and Cromwell broke forth. They were the only two of all the accused (Spencer excepted) who could sail or navigate a vessel! and a mutiny to take a ship, and run her as a roving pirate, without any one but the chief to sail and navigate her, would have been a solecism too gross even for the silliest apprehension. Mr. M. C. Perry admitted upon his cross-examination that this knowledge was "one of the small reasons" for hanging them—meaning among the lesser reasons. Besides, three at least, may have been deemed necessary to make a mutiny. Governor Wall took that number; and riots, routs, and unlawful assemblies require it: so that in having three for a mutiny, the commander was taking the lowest number which parity of cases, though of infinitely lower degree, would allow. The report goes on to show the commander's preparations for the sacrifice; which preparations, from his own showing, took place before the assembling of the council, and in which he showed his skill and acumen.

"I had for a day or two been disposed to arm the petty officers. On this subject alone the first lieutenant differed from me in opinion, influenced in some degree by the opinions of some of the petty officers themselves, who thought that in the peculiar state of the vessel the commander and officers could not tell whom to trust, and therefore had better trust no one. I had made up my own mind, reasoning more from the probabilities of the case than from my knowledge of their characters, which was necessarily less intimate than that of the first lieutenant, that they could be trusted, and determined to arm them. I directed the first lieutenant to muster them on the quarter deck, to issue to each a cutlass, pistol and cartridge-box, and to report to me when they were armed. I then addressed them as follows: 'My lads! you are to look to me—to obey my orders, and to see my orders obeyed! Go forward!'"

This paragraph shows that the arming of the petty officers for the crisis of the hangings had been meditated for a day or two—that it had been the subject of consultation with the lieutenant, and also of him with some of the petty officers; and it was doubtless on this occasion that he took the opinions of the officers (as proved on the court-martial trial) on the subject of hanging the three prisoners immediately if any more arrests were made. The commander and his lieutenant differed on the question of arming these petty officers—the only instance of a difference of opinion between them: but the commander's calculation of probabilities led him to overrule the lieutenant—to make up his own mind in favor of arming: and to have it done. The command at the conclusion is eminently concise, and precise, and entirely military; and the ending words remind us of the French infantry charging command: "En avant, mes enfans!" in English—"Forward, my children."

The reception of the council recommendation, and the order for carrying it into effect, were simultaneous: and carried into effect it was with horrible rapidity, and to the utmost letter—all except in one particular—which forms a dreadful exception. The council had given the recommendation with the Christian reservation of allowing the doomed and helpless victims "sufficient time to prepare"—meaning, of course, preparation for appearance at the throne of God. That reservation was disregarded. Immediate execution was the word! and the annunciation of the death decree, and the order for putting it in force, were both made known to the prisoners in the same moment, and in the midst of the awful preparations for death.

"I gave orders to make immediate preparation for hanging the three principal criminals at the mainyard arms. All hands were now called to witness the punishment. The afterguard and idlers of both watches were mustered on the quarterdeck at the whip (the halter) intended for Mr. Spencer: forecastle-men and foretop-men at that of Cromwell, to whose corruption they had been chiefly exposed. The maintop of both watches, at that intended for Small who, for a month, had filled the situation of captain of the maintop. The officers were stationed about the decks, *according to the watch bill I had made out the night before*, and the petty officers were similarly distributed, with orders to cut down whoever should let go the whip (the rope) with even one hand; or fail to haul on (pull at the rope) when ordered."

Here it is unwittingly told that the guard stations at the hangings were all made out the night before.

For the information of the unlearned in nautical language, it may be told that what is called the whip at sea, is not an instrument of flagellation, but of elevation—a small tackle with a single rope, used to hoist light bodies; and so called from one of the meanings of the word whip, used as a verb, then signifying to snatch up suddenly. It is to be hoped that the sailors appointed to haul on this tackle had been made acquainted (though the commander's report does not say so) with the penalty which awaited them if they failed to pull at the word, or let go, even with one hand. The considerate arrangement for hanging each one at the spot of his imputed worst conduct, and under an appropriate watch, shows there had been deliberation on that part of the subject— deliberation which requires time—and for which there was no time after the reception of the council's answer;

and which the report itself, so far as the watch is concerned, shows was made out the night before. The report continues:

> "The ensign and pennant being bent on, and ready for hoisting, I now put on my full uniform, and proceeded to execute the most painful duty that has ever devolved on an American commander—*that of announcing to the criminals their fate.*"

It has been before seen that these victims had no knowledge of the proceedings against them, while the seven officers were examining, in a room below, the thirteen seamen whose answers to questions (or rather, whose thoughts) were to justify the fate which was now to be announced to them. They had no knowledge of it at the time, nor afterwards, until standing in the midst of the completed arrangements for their immediate death. They were brought into the presence of death before they knew that any proceedings had been had against them, and while under the belief, authorized by the commander himself, that they were to be brought home for trial. Their fate was staring them in the face before they knew it had been doomed. The full uniform of a commander in the American navy had been put on for the occasion, with what view is not expressed; and, in this imposing costume,—feathers and chapeau, gold lace and embroidery, sword and epaulettes—the commander proceeded to announce their fate to men in irons—double irons on the legs, and iron cuffs on the hands—and surrounded by guards to cut them down on the least attempt to avoid the gallows which stood before them. In what terms this annunciation, or rather, these annunciations (for there was a separate address to each victim, and each address adapted to its subject) were made, the captain himself will tell.

> "I informed Mr. Spencer that when he had been about to take my life, and to dishonor me as an officer when in the execution of my rightful duty, without cause of offence to him, on speculation, it had been his intention to remove me suddenly from the world, in the darkness of the night, without a moment to utter one murmur of affection to my wife and children—one prayer for their welfare. His life was now forfeited to his country; and the necessities of the case growing out of his corruption of the crew, compelled me to take it. I would not, however, imitate his intended example. If there yet remained one feeling true to nature, it should be gratified. *If he had any word to send to his parents, it should be recorded, and faithfully delivered.* Ten minutes should be granted him for this purpose; and Midshipman Egbert Thompson was called to note the time, and inform me when the ten minutes had elapsed."

Subsequent events require this appeal to Spencer, and promise to him, to be noted. He is invoked, in the name of Nature, to speak to his parents, and his words promised delivery. History will have to deal with that invocation, and promise.

This is the autographic account of the annunciation to Spencer; and if there is a parallel to it in Christendom, this writer has yet to learn the instance. The vilest malefactors, convicts of the greatest crimes, are allowed an interval for themselves when standing between time and eternity; and during that time they are left, undisturbed, to their own thoughts. Even pirates allow that much to vanquished and subdued men. The ship had religious exercises upon it, and had multiplied their performance since the mutiny had been discovered. The commander was a devout attendant at these exercises, and harangued the crew morally and piously daily, and in this crisis twice or thrice a day. He might have been of some consolation to the desolate youth in this supreme moment. He might have spoken to him some words of pity and of hope: he might at least have refrained from reproaches: he might have omitted the comparison in which he assumed to himself such a superiority over Spencer in the manner of taking life. It was the Pharisee that thanked God he was not like other men, nor like that Publican. But the Pharisee did not take the Publican's life, nor charge him with crimes. Besides, the comparison was not true, admitting that Spencer intended to kill him in his sleep. There is no difference of time between one minute and ten minutes in the business of killing; and the most sudden death— a bullet through the heart in sleep—would be mercy compared to the ten minutes' reprieve allowed Spencer: and that time taken up (as the event proved) in harassing the mind, enraging the feelings, and in destroying the character of the young man before he destroyed his body. It is to be hoped that the greater part of what the commander says he said to Spencer, was not said: it would be less discreditable to make a false report in such cases than to have said what was alleged; and there were so many errors in the commander's report that disbelief of it becomes easy, and even obligatory. It is often variant or improbable in itself, and sometimes impossible; and almost entirely contradicted by the testimony. In the vital—really vital—case of holding the watch, he is contradicted. He says Midshipman Thompson was called to note the time, and to report its expiration. Mr. O. H. Perry swore in the court that the order was given to him—that he reported it—and that the commander said, "very well." This was clear and positive: but Mr. Thompson was examined to the same point, and testified thus: That he heard him (the commander) say something about ten minutes—that he told Mr. Perry, he thinks, to note the time—that Perry and himself both noted it—thinks he reported it—don't recollect what the commander said—is under an impression he said "very good." So that Mr. Perry was called to note the time, and did it, and reported it, and did not know that Thompson had done it. To the question, "What did Mr. Thompson say when he came back from reporting the time?" the answer is: "I did not know that he reported it." At best, Mr. Thompson was a volunteer in the business, and too indifferent to it to know what he did. Mr. O. H. Perry is the one that had the order, and did the duty. Now it is quite immaterial which had the order: but it is very material that the commander should remember the true man.—The manner in which the young man received this dreadful intelligence, is thus reported:

> "This intimation quite overpowered him. He fell upon his knees, and said he was not fit to
> die."

"Was not fit to die!" that is to say, was not in a condition to appear before his God. The quick perishing of the body was not the thought that came to his mind, but the perishing of his soul, and his sudden appearance before his Maker, unpurged of the sins of this life. Virtue was not dead in the heart which could forget itself and the world in that dread moment, and only think of his fitness to appear at the throne of Heaven. Deeply affecting as this expression was—am not fit to die—it was still more so as actually spoken, and truly stated by competent witnesses before the court. "When he told him he was to die in ten minutes, Spencer told him he was not fit to die—that he wished to live longer to get ready. The commander said, I know you are not, but I cannot help it."—A remark which was wicked in telling him he knew he was not fit to die, and false, in saying he could not help it. So far from not being able to help it, he was the only man that could prevent the preparation for fitness. The answer then was, an exclamation of unfitness to die, and a wish to live longer to get ready. But what can be thought of the heart which was dead to such an appeal? and which, in return, could occupy itself with reproaches to the desolate sinner; and could deliver exhortations to the trembling fleeting shadow that was before him, to study looks and attitudes, and set an example of decorous dying to his two companions in death? for that was the conduct of Mackenzie: and here is his account of it:

> "I repeated to him his own catechism, and begged him at least to let the *officer* set to the men
> he had corrupted and seduced, the example of dying with decorum."

"The men whom he had corrupted and seduced,"—outrageous words, and which the commander says, "immediately restored him to entire self-possession." But they did not turn away his heart from the only thing that occupied his mind—that of fitting himself, as well as he could, to appear before his God. He commenced praying with great fervor, and begging from Heaven that mercy for his soul which was denied on earth to his body.

The commander then went off to make the same annunciation to the other two victims, and returning when the ten minutes was about half out—when the boy had but five minutes to live, as he was made to believe—he soon made apparent the true reason which all this sudden announcement of death in ten minutes was in reality intended for. It was to get confessions! it was to make up a record against him! to excite him against Small and Cromwell! to take advantage of terror and resentment to get something from him for justification in taking his life! and in that work he spent near two hours, making up a record against himself of revolting atrocity, aggravated and made still worse by the evidence before the court. The first movement was to make him believe that Cromwell and Small had informed upon him, and thus induce him to break out upon them, or to confess, or to throw the blame upon the others. He says:

> "I returned to Mr. Spencer. I explained to him how Cromwell had made use of him. I told
> him that remarks had been made about the two, and not very flattering to him, and which he

might not care to hear; and which showed the relative share ascribed to each of them in the contemplated transaction. He expressed great anxiety to hear what was said."

It is to be borne in mind that Spencer was in prayer, with but five minutes to go upon, when Mackenzie interrupts him with an intimation of what Small and Cromwell had said of him, and piques his curiosity to learn it by adding, "which he might not care to hear"—artfully exciting his curiosity to know what it was. The desire thus excited, he goes on to tell him that one had called him a damn fool, and the other had considered him Cromwell's tool: thus:

> "One had told the first lieutenant: 'In my opinion, sir, you have the damned fool on the larboard arm-chest, and the damned villain on the starboard.' And another had remarked, that after the vessel should have been captured by Spencer, Cromwell might allow him to live, provided he made himself useful; he would probably make him his secretary."

Spencer was on the larboard arm-chest; Cromwell on the starboard: so that Small was the speaker, and the damned fool applied to Spencer, and the damned villain to Cromwell: and Spencer, who had all along been the chief, was now to be treated as an instrument, only escaping with his life if successful in taking the vessel, and, that upon condition of making himself useful; and then to have no higher post on the pirate than that of Cromwell's secretary. This was a hint to Spencer to turn States' evidence against Cromwell, and throw the whole blame on him. The commander continues, still addressing himself to Spencer—

> "*I think this would not have suited your temper.*"

This remark, inquisitively made, and evidently to draw out something against Cromwell, failed of its object. It drew no remark from Spencer; it merely acted upon his looks and spirit, according to the commander—who proceeds in this strain:

> "This effectually aroused him, and his countenance assumed a demoniacal expression. He said no more of the innocence of Cromwell. Subsequent circumstances too surely confirmed his admission of his guilt. He might perhaps have wished to save him, in fulfilment of some mutual oath."

This passage requires some explanation. Spencer had always declared his total ignorance of Cromwell, and of his visionary schemes: he repeated it earnestly as Mackenzie turned off to go and announce his fate to him. Having enraged him against the man, he says he now said no more about Cromwell's innocence; and catching up that silence as an admission of his guilt, he quotes it as such; but remembering how often Spencer had absolved him from all knowledge even of his foolish joking, he supposes he wished to save him—in fulfilment of some mutual oath. This imagined cause for saving him is shamefully gratuitous, unwarranted by a word from any delator, not inferrible from any premises, and atrociously wicked. In fact this whole story after the commander returned from Small and Cromwell, is without warrant from any thing tangible. Mackenzie got it from Gansevoort; and Gansevoort got one half from one, and the other half from another, without telling which, or when—and it was provably not then; and considering the atrocity of such a communication to Spencer at such time, it is certainly less infamous to the captain and lieutenant to consider it a falsehood of their own invention, to accomplish their own design. Mackenzie's telling it, however, was infernal. The commander then goes on with a batch of gratuitous assumptions, which shows he had no limit in such assumptions but in his capacity at invention. Hear them!

> "He (Spencer) more probably hoped that he might yet get possession of the vessel, and carry out the scheme of murder and outrage matured between them. It was in Cromwell that he had apparently trusted, in fulfilment of some agreement for a rescue; and he eloquently plead to Lieutenant Gansevoort when Cromwell was ironed, for his release, as altogether ignorant of his designs, and innocent. He had endeavored to make of Elisha Andrews appearing on the list of the "certain," an *alias* for Small, though his name as Small appeared also in the list of those to effect the murder in the cabin, by falsely asserting that Small was a feigned name, when he had evidence in a letter addressed by Small's mother to him that Small was her name as well as his."

Assumptions without foundations, inferences without premises, beliefs without knowledge, thoughts without knowing why, suspicions without reasons—are all a species of *inventions* but little removed from direct falsehood, and leaves the person who indulges in them without credit for any thing he may say. This was pre-eminently the case with the commander Slidell Mackenzie, and with all his informers; and here is a fine specimen of it in himself. First: the presumed probability that Spencer yet hoped to get possession of the vessel, and carry out the scheme of murder and piracy which he had matured. What a presumption in such a case! the case of men, ironed, bagged and helpless,—standing under the gallows in the midst of armed men to shoot and stab for a motion or a sign—and a presumption, not only without a shadow to rest upon, but contradicted by the entire current of all that was sworn—even by Garty and Wales. "Fulfilment of secret agreement for rescue." Secret! Yes! very secret indeed! There was not a man on board the vessel that ever heard such a word as rescue pronounced until after the arrests! The crazy misgivings of a terrified imagination could alone have invented such a scheme of rescue. The name of Small was a sad stumbling block in the road to his sacrifice, as that of Andrews to the truth of the razor case paper. One was not in the list, and the other was not in the ship: and all these forced assumptions were to reconcile these contradictions; and so the idea of an *alias dictus* was fallen upon, though no one had ever heard Small called Edward Andrews, and his mother, in her letter, gave her own name as her son's, as Small. Having now succeeded in getting Spencer enraged against his two companions in death, the commander takes himself to his real work—that of getting confessions—or getting up something which could be recorded as confessions, under the pretext of writing to his father and mother: and to obtain which all this refined aggravation of the terrors of death had been contrived. But here recourse must be had to the testimony before the court to supply details on which the report is silent, or erroneous, and in which what was omitted must be brought forward to be able to get at the truth. McKinley swears that he was six or eight feet from Spencer when the commander asked him if he wished to write. Spencer answered that he did. An apprentice named Dunn was then ordered to fetch paper and campstool out of the cabin. Spencer took the pen in his hand, and said—"I cannot write." "The commander spoke to him in a low tone. I do not know what he then said. I saw the commander writing. Whether Mr. Spencer asked him to write for him or not, I can't say."—Mr. Oliver H. Perry swears: "Saw the commander order Dunn to bring him paper and ink: saw the commander write: was four or five feet from him while writing: heard no part of the conversation between the commander and Spencer: was writing ten or fifteen minutes."—Other witnesses guess at the time as high as half an hour. The essential parts of this testimony, are—*first*, That Spencer's hands were ironed, and that he could not write: *secondly*, that the commander, instead of releasing his hands, took the pen and wrote himself: *thirdly*, that he carried on all his conversation with Spencer in so low a voice that those within four or five feet of him (and in the deathlike stillness which then prevailed, and the breathless anxiety of every one) *heard not a word of what passed between them!* neither what Mackenzie said to Spencer, nor Spencer said to him. Now the report of the commander is silent upon this lowness of tone which could not be heard four or five feet—silent upon the handcuffs of Spencer—silent upon the answer of Spencer that he could not write; and for which he substituted on the court-martial the answer that he "declined to write"—a substitution which gave rise to a conversation between the judge advocate and Mackenzie, which the judge advocate reported to the court in writing; and which all felt to be a false substitution both upon the testimony, and the facts of the case. A man in iron handcuffs cannot write! but it was necessary to show him "declining" in order to give him a recording secretary! And it is silent upon the great fact that he sat on the arm-chest with Spencer, and whispering so low that not a human being could hear what passed: and, consequently, that Mackenzie chose that he himself should be the recording secretary on that occasion, and that no one could know whether the record was true or false. The declaration in the report that Spencer read what was written down, and agreed to it, will be attended to hereafter. The point at present is the secrecy, and the fact that the man the most interested in the world in getting confessions from Spencer, was the recorder of these confessions, without a witness! without even Wales, Gansevoort, Garty; or any one of his familiars. For the rest, it becomes a fair question, which every person can solve for themselves, whether it is possible for two persons to talk so low to one another for, from a quarter to half an hour, in such profound stillness, and amidst so much excited expectation, and no one in arm's length able to hear one word. If this is deemed impossible, it may be a reasonable belief that nothing material was said between them—that Mackenzie wrote without dictation from Spencer; and wrote what the necessity of his condition required—confessions to supply the place of total want of proof—admissions of guilt—acknowledgments that he deserved to die—begging forgiveness. And so large a part of what he reported was proved to be false, that this reasonable belief of a fabricated dialogue becomes almost a certainty.

The commander, now become sole witness of Spencer's last words—words spoken if at all—after his time on earth was out—after the announcement in his presence that the ten minutes were out—and hearing the commander's response to the notification, "Very well:" this commander thus proceeds with his report: "I asked him if he had no message to send to his friends? He answered none that they would wish to receive. When urged still further to send some words of consolation in so great an affliction, he said, 'Tell them I die wishing them every blessing and happiness. I deserve death for this and many other crimes—there are few crimes I have not committed. I feel sincerely penitent, and my only fear of death is that my repentance may come too late.'"—This is what the commander reports to the Secretary of the Navy, and which no human witness could gainsay, because no human being was allowed to witness what was said at the time; but there is another kind of testimony, independent of human eyes and ears, and furnished by the evil-doer himself, often in the very effort to conceal his guilt, and more convincing than the oath of any witness, and which fate, or accident, often brings to light for the relief of the innocent and the confusion of the guilty. And so it was in this case with Commander Alexander Slidell Mackenzie. That original record made out upon inaudible whispers on the camp-stool! It still existed—and was produced in court—and here is the part which corresponds (should correspond) with this quoted part of the report; and constituting the first part of the confession: "When asked if he had any message to send: none that they would wish to receive. Afterwards, that you die wishing them every blessing and happiness; deserved death for this and other sins; that you felt sincerely penitent, and only fear of death was that your repentance might *be too late*."—Compared together, and it is seen that the words "other sins," in the third sentence, is changed into "*many other crimes*,"—words of revoltingly different import—going beyond what the occasion required—and evidently substituted as an introduction to the further gratuitous confession: "*There are few crimes which I have not committed*." Great consolation in this for those parents for whom the record was made, and who never saw it except as promulgated through the public press. In any court of justice the entire report would be discredited upon this view of flagrant and wicked falsifications. For the rest, there is proof that the first sentence is a fabrication. It is to be recollected that this inquiry as to Spencer's wishes to communicate with his parents was made publicly, and before the pen, ink and paper was sent for, and that the answer was the inducement to send for those writing materials. That public answer was heard by those around, and was thus proved before the court-martial—McKinley the witness: "*The commander asked him if he wished to write?* Mr. Spencer said he did. The commander ordered Dunn to fetch paper and campstool out of the cabin. Spencer took the pen in his hand—he said, 'I cannot write.' The commander spoke to him in a low tone: I do not know what he then said. I saw the commander writing." This testimony contradicts the made-up report, in showing that Spencer was asked to write himself, instead of sending a message: that the declaration, "*nothing that they would wish to hear*," is a fabricated addition to what he did say—and that he was prevented from writing, not from disinclination and declining, as the commander attempted to make out, but because upon trial—after taking the pen in his hand—he could not with his handcuffs on. Certainly this was understood beforehand. Men do not write in iron handcuffs. They were left on to permit the commander to become his secretary, and to send a message for him: which message he never sent! the promise to do so being a mere contrivance to get a chance of writing for the Secretary of the Navy, and the public.

The official report continues: "I asked him if there was any one he had injured, to whom he could yet make reparation—any one suffering obloquy for crimes which he had committed. He made no answer; but soon after continued: 'I have wronged many persons, but chiefly my parents.' He said 'this will kill my poor mother.' I was not before aware that he had a mother." The corresponding sentences in the original, run thus: "Many that he had wronged, but did not know how reparation could be made to them. Your parents most wronged ... himself by saying he had entertained same idea in John Adams and Potomac, but had not ripened into.... Do you not think that such a mania should ... certainly. Objected to manner of death." The dots in place of words indicate the places where the writing was illegible. The remarkable variations between the report and the original in these sentences is, that the original leaves out all those crimes which he had committed, and which were bringing obloquy upon others, and to which he made no answer, but shows that he did make answer as to having wronged persons, and that answer was, that he did not know how reparation could be made. There is no mention of mother in this part of the original—it comes in long after. Then the John Adams and the

Potomac, which are here mentioned in the twelfth line of the original, only appear in the fifty-sixth in the report—and the long gap filled up with things not in the original—and the word "idea," as attributed to Spencer, substituted by "mania."

The report continues (and here it is told once for all, that the quotations both from the report and the original, of which it should be a copy, follow each in its place in consecutive order, leaving no gap between each quoted part and what preceded it): "*when recovered from the pain of this announcement (the effect upon his mother)*, I asked him if it would not have been still more dreadful had he succeeded in his attempt, murdered the officers and the greater part of the crew of the vessel, and run that career of crime which, with so much satisfaction he had marked out for himself: he replied after a pause; 'I do not know what would have become of me if I had succeeded.' I told him Cromwell would soon have made way with him, and McKinley would probably have cleared the whole of them from his path." The corresponding part of the original runs thus: "Objected to manner of death: requested to be shot. Could not make any distinction between him and those he had seduced. Justifiable desire at first to.... The last words he had to say, and hoped they would be believed, that Cromwell was innocent ... Cromwell. Admitted it was just that no distinction should be made."—This is the consecutive part in the original, beginning in utter variance with what should be its counterpart—hardly touching the same points—leaving out all the cruel reproaches which the official report heaps upon Spencer—ending with the introduction of Cromwell, but without the innocence which the original contains, with the substitution of Cromwell's destruction of him, and with the addition of McKinley's destruction of them all, and ultimate attainment of the chief place in that long career of piracy which was to be ran—and ran in that state of the world in which no pirate could live at all. What was actually said about Cromwell's innocence by Spencer and by McKinley as coming from Cromwell "to stir up the devil between them," as the historian Cooper remarked, was said before this writing commenced! said when Mackenzie returned from announcing the ten minutes lease of life to him and Small! which Mackenzie himself had reported in a previous part of his report, before the writing materials were sent for: and now, strange enough, introduced again in an after place, but with such alterations and additions as barely to leave their identity discoverable.

The official report proceeds: "'I fear,' said he, 'this may injure my father.' I told him it was too late to think of that—that had he succeeded in his wishes it would have injured his father much more—that had it been possible to have taken him home as I intended to do, it was not in nature that his father should not have interfered to save him—*that for those who have friends or money in America there was no punishment for the worst of crimes*—that though this had nothing to do with my determination, which had been forced upon me in spite of every effort I had made to avert it, I, on this account the less regretted the dilemma in which I was placed: it would injure his father a great deal more if he got home alive, should he be condemned and yet escape. The best and only service which he could do his father was to die."—Now from the original, beginning at the end of the last quotation: "Asked that his face might be covered. Granted. When he found that his repentance might not be in season, I referred him to the story of the penitent thief. Tried to find it. Could not. Read the Bible, the prayer-book. Did not know what would have become of him if he had succeeded. Makes no objection to death, but objects to time. Reasons—God would understand of him offences ... many crimes. Dies, praying God to bless and preserve.... I am afraid this will injure my father."—The quotation from the report opens with apprehended fear of injury to his father: it concludes with commending him to die, as the only service he could render that parent: and the whole is taken up with that topic, and crowned with the assertion that, for those who have friends or money in America there is no punishment for the worst of crimes—a sweeping reproach upon the American judiciary; and, however unfounded in his broad denunciation, may he not himself have counted on the benefit of the laxity of justice which he denounced? and—more—did he not receive it? The rest of the paragraph is only remarkable for the declaration of the intention to have brought his prisoners home, and of the change, of which intention they had no notice until placed in the presence of the completed preparations for death, and told they had but ten minutes, by the watch, to live.—Turning to the original of this paragraph, and it will be seen that it opens with preparations for death—goes on in the same spirit—barely mentions his father—and ends with his death—"*dies praying God to bless and preserve*".... This is evidently the termination of the whole scene. It carries him through the last preparations, and ends his life—sees him die praying to God. Now does the report give any of these circumstances? None. Does the report stop there? It does not. Does it go on? Yes: two hundred and thirty lines further. And the original record go on further? Yes:

sixty lines further—which was just double the distance it had come. Here was a puzzle. The man to be talking double as much after his death as before it. This solecism required a solution—and received it before the court-martial: and the solution was that this double quantity was written after hanging—how long, not stated—but after it. Before the court Mackenzie delivered in a written and sworn statement, that his record embracing what was taken down from the lips of Spencer finished at the sentence—"*I am afraid this will injure my father.*" and that the remainder was written shortly afterwards. Now the part written before the death was thirty-three lines: the part written shortly after it, is above fifty. This solecism explained, another difficulty immediately arises. The commander reported that, "he (Spencer) *read over what he (Mackenzie) had written down,*" and agreed to it all, with one exception—which was corrected. Now he could not have read the fifty odd lines which were written after his death. (All the lines here mentioned are the short ones in the double column pages of the published, "Official Proceedings of the Naval Court Martial.)" These fifty odd lines could not have been read by Spencer. That is certain. The previous thirty-three it is morally certain he never read. They are in some places illegible—in others unintelligible; and are printed in the official report with blanks because there were parts which could not be read. No witness says they were read by Spencer.

The additional fifty odd lines, expanded by additions and variations into about two hundred in the official report, requires but a brief notice, parts of it being amplifications and aggravations of what had been previously noted, and additional insults to Spencer; with an accumulation of acknowledgments of guilt, of willingness to die, of obligations to the commander, and entreaties for his forgiveness. One part of the reported scene was even more than usually inhuman. Spencer said to him: "But are you not going too far? are you not too fast? does the law entirely justify you?" To this the commander represents himself as replying: "That he (Spencer) had not consulted him in his arrangements—that his opinion could not be an unprejudiced one—that I had consulted all his brother officers, his messmates included, except the boys; and I placed before him their opinion. He stated that it was just—that he deserved death," For the honor of human nature it is to be hoped that Mackenzie reports himself falsely here—which is probable, both on its face, and because it is not in the original record. The commander says that he begged for one hour to prepare himself for death, saying the time is so short, asking if there was time for repentance, and if he could be changed so soon (from sin to grace). To the request for the hour, the commander says no answer was given: to the other parts he reminded him of the *thief* on the cross, who was pardoned by our Saviour, and that for the rest, God would understand the difficulties of his situation and be merciful. The commander also represents himself as recapitulating to Spencer the arts he had used to seduce the crew. The commander says upwards of an hour elapsed before the hanging: he might have said two hours: for the doom of the prisoners was announced at about eleven, and they were hung at one. But no part of this delay was for their benefit, as he would make believe, but for his own, to get confessions under the agonies of terror. No part of it—not even the whole ten minutes—was allowed to Spencer to make his peace with God; but continually interrupted, questioned, outraged, inflamed against his companions in death, he had his devotions broken in upon, and himself deprived of one peaceful moment to commune with God.

The report of the confessions is false upon its face: it is also invalidated by other matter within itself, showing that Mackenzie had two opposite ways of speaking of the same person, and of the same incident, before and after the design upon Spencer's life. I speak of the attempt, and of the reasons given for it, to get the young man transferred to another vessel before sailing from New York. According to the account given first of these reasons, and at the time, the desire to get him out of the Somers was entirely occasioned by the crowded state of the midshipmen's room—seven, where only five could be accommodated. Thus:

> "When we were on the eve of sailing, two midshipmen who had been with me before, and in whom I had confidence, joined the vessel. This carried to seven, the number to occupy a space capable of accommodating only five. I had heard that Mr. Spencer had expressed a willingness to be transferred from the Somers to the Grampus. I directed Lieut. Gansevoort to say to him that if he would apply to Commodore Perry to detach him (there was no time to communicate with the Navy Department), I would second the application. He made the application; I seconded it, earnestly urging that it should be granted on the score of the comfort of the young officers. The commodore declined detaching Mr. Spencer, but offered

to detach midshipman Henry Rodgers, who had been last ordered. I could not consent to part with Midshipman Rodgers, whom I knew to be a seaman, an officer, a gentleman; a young man of high attainments within his profession and beyond it. The Somers sailed with seven in her steerage. They could not all sit together round the table. The two oldest and most useful had no lockers to put their clothes in, and have slept during the cruise on the steerage deck, the camp-stools, the booms, in the tops, or in the quarter boats."

Nothing can be clearer than this statement. It was to relieve the steerage room where the young midshipmen congregated, that the transfer of Spencer was requested; and this was after Captain Mackenzie had been informed that the young man had been dismissed from the Brazilian squadron, for drunkenness. "And this fact," he said, "made me very desirous of his removal from the vessel, chiefly on account of the young men who were to mess and be associated with him, the rather that two of them were connected with me by blood and two by marriage; and all four intrusted to my especial care." After the deaths he wrote of the same incident in these words:

"The circumstance of Mr. Spencer's being the son of a high officer of the government, by enhancing his baseness in my estimation, made me more desirous to be rid of him. On this point I beg that I may not be misunderstood. I revere authority. I recognize, in the exercise of its higher functions in this free country, the evidences of genius, intelligence, and virtue; but I have no respect for the base son of an honored father; on the contrary, I consider that he who, by misconduct sullies the lustre of an honorable name, is more culpable than the unfriended individual whose disgrace falls only on himself. I wish, however, to have nothing to do with baseness in any shape; the navy is not the place for it. On these accounts I readily sought the first opportunity of getting rid of Mr. Spencer."

Here the word base, as applicable to the young Spencer, occurs three times in a brief paragraph, and this baseness is given as the reason for wishing to get the young man, not out of the ship, but out of the navy! And this sentiment was so strong, that reverence for Spencer's father could not control it. He could have nothing to do with baseness. The navy is not the place for it. Now all this was written after the young man was dead, and when it was necessary to make out a case of justification for putting him, not out of the ship, nor even out of the navy, but out of the world. This was an altered state of the case, and the captain's report accommodated itself to this alteration. The reasons now given go to the baseness of the young man: those which existed at the time, went to the comfort of the four midshipmen, connected by blood and alliance with the captain, and committed to his special care:—as if all in the ship were not committed to his special care, and that by the laws of the land—and without preference to relations. The captain even goes into an account of his own high moral feelings at the time, and disregard of persons high in power, in showing that he then acted upon a sense of Spencer's baseness, maugre the reverence he had for his father and his cabinet position. Every body sees that these are contradictions—that all this talk about baseness is after-talk—that all these fine sentiments are of subsequent conception: in fact, that the first reasons were those of the time, before he expected to put the young man to death, and the next after he had done it! and when the deed exacted a justification, and that at any cost of invention and fabrication. The two accounts are sufficient to establish one of those errors of fact which the law considers as discrediting a witness in all that he says. But it is not all the proof of erroneous statement which the double relation of this incident affords: there is another, equally flagrant. The captain, in his after account, repulses association with baseness, that is with Spencer, in any shape: his elaborate report superabounds with expressions of the regard with which he had treated him during the voyage, and even exacts acknowledgment of his kindness while endeavoring to torture out of him confessions of guilt.

The case of Spencer was now over: the cases of Small and Cromwell were briefly despatched. The commander contrived to make the three victims meet in a narrow way going to the sacrifice, all manacled and hobbling along, helped along, for they could not walk, by persons appointed to that duty. Gansevoort helped Spencer— a place to which he had entitled himself by the zeal with which he had pursued him. The object of the meeting was seen in the use that was made of it. It was to have a scene of crimination and recrimination between the prisoners, in which mutual accusations were to help out the miserable testimony and the imputed confessions. They are all made to stop together. Spencer is made to ask the pardon of Small for having seduced him: Small is made to answer, and with a look of horror—"*No, by God!*" an answer very little in keeping with the lowly and Christian character of Small, and rebutted by ample negative testimony: for this took place after the secret whispering was over, and in the presence of many. Even Gansevoort, in giving a minute account of this interview, reports nothing like it, nor any thing on which it could be founded. Small really seems to have been a gentle and mild man, imbued with kind and pious feelings, and no part of his conduct corresponds with the brutal answer to Spencer attributed to him. When asked if he had any message to send, he answered, "I have nobody to care for me but a poor old mother, and I had rather she did not know how I died." In his Bible was found a letter from his mother, filled with affectionate expressions. In that letter the mother had rejoiced that her son was contented and happy, as he had informed her; upon which the commander maliciously remarked, in his report, "that was before his acquaintance with Spencer." There was nothing against him, but in the story of the informer, Wales. He instantly admitted his "foolish conversations" with Spencer when arrested, but said it was no mutiny. When standing under the ship gallows (yard-arm) he began a speech to his shipmates, declaring his innocence, saying "I am no pirate: I never murdered any body!" At these words Mackenzie sung out to Gansevoort, "Is that right?" meaning, ought he to be allowed to speak so? He was soon stopped, and Gansevoort swears he said "he deserved his punishment." Cromwell protested his innocence to the last, and with evident truth. When arrested, he declared he knew nothing about the mutiny, and the commander told him he was to be carried home with Spencer to be tried; to which he answered, "I assure you I know nothing about it." His name was not on the razor-case paper. Spencer had declared his ignorance of all his talk, when the commander commenced his efforts, under the ten minutes' reprieve, to get confessions, and when Spencer said to him, as he turned off to go to Small and Cromwell with the ten minutes' news—the first they heard of it: "As these are the last words I have to say, I trust they will be believed: Cromwell is innocent." When told his doom, he (Cromwell) exclaimed, "God of the Universe look down upon me; I am innocent! Tell my wife—tell Lieutenant Morris I die innocent!" The last time that Mackenzie had spoken to him before was to tell him he would be carried to the United States for trial. The meeting of the three victims was crowned by reporting them, not only as confessing, and admitting the justice of their deaths, but even praising it, as to the honor of the flag, and—penitently begging pardon and forgiveness from the commander and his lieutenant!—and they mercifully granting the pardon and forgiveness! The original record says there were no "hangmen" on board the ship: but that made no balk. The death signal, and command, were given by the commander and his lieutenant—the former firing the signal gun himself—the other singing out "whip!" at which word the three wretched men went up with a violent jerk to the yard-arm. There is something unintelligible about Cromwell in the last words of this original "record." It says: "S. Small stept up. Cromwell overboard, rose dipping to yard-arm." Upon which the editor remarks: "The above paper of Commander Mackenzie is so illegible, as not to be correctly written" (copied). Yet it was this paper that Spencer is officially reported to have read while waiting to be jerked up, and to have agreed to its correctness—and near two-thirds of which were not written until after his death!

The men were dead, and died innocent, as history will tell and show. Why such conduct towards them—not only the killing, but the cruel aggravations? The historian Cooper, in solving this question, says that such was the obliquity of intellect shown by Mackenzie in the whole affair, that no analysis of his motives can be made on any consistent principle of human action. This writer looks upon personal resentment as having been the cause of the deaths, and terror, and a desire to create terror, the cause of the aggravations. Both Spencer and Cromwell had indulged in language which must have been peculiarly offensive to a man of the commander's temperament, and opinion of himself—an author, an orator, a fine officer. They habitually spoke of him before the crew, as "the old humbug—the old fool;" graceless epithets, plentifully garnished with the prefix of "damned;" and which were so reported to the captain (after the discovery of the mutiny—never before) as to appear to him to be "blasphemous vituperation." This is the only tangible cause for hanging Spencer and Cromwell, and as for poor Small, it would seem that his knowledge of navigation, and the necessity of having three mutineers, decided his fate: for his name is on neither of the three lists (though on the distribution list), and he frankly told the commander of Spencer's foolish conversations—always adding, it was no mutiny. These are the only tangible, or visible causes for putting the men to death. The reason for doing it at the time it was done, was for fear of losing the excuse to do it. The vessel was within a day and a half of St. Thomas, where she was ordered to go—within less time of many other islands to which she might go—in a place to meet vessels at any time, one of which she saw nearly in her course, and would not go to it. The excuse for not going to these near islands, or joining the vessel seen, was that it was disgraceful to a man-of-war to seek protection from foreigners! as if it was more honorable to murder than to take such protection. But the excuse was proved to be false; for it was admitted the vessel seen was too far off to know her national character: therefore, she was not avoided as a foreigner, but for fear she might be American. The same of the islands: American vessels were sure to be at them, and therefore these islands were not gone to. It was therefore indispensable to do the work before they got to St. Thomas, and all the machinery of new arrests, and rescue was to justify that consummation. And as for not being able to carry the ship to St. Thomas, with an obedient crew of 100 men, it was a story not to be told in a service where Lieutenant John Rodgers and Midshipman Porter, with 11 men, conducted a French frigate with 173 French prisoners, three days and nights, into safe port.

The three men having hung until they ceased to give signs of life, and still hanging up, the crew were piped down to dinner, and to hear a speech from the commander, and to celebrate divine service—of which several performances the commander gives this account in his official report:

> "The crew were now piped down from witnessing punishment, and all hands called to cheer ship. I gave the order, 'stand by to give three hearty cheers for the flag of our country!' Never were three heartier cheers given. In that electric moment I do not doubt that the patriotism of even the worst of the conspirators for an instant broke forth. I felt that I was once more completely commander of the vessel which had been entrusted to me; equal to do with her whatever the honor of my country might require. The crew were now piped down and piped to dinner. I noticed with pain that many of the boys, as they looked to the yard-arm, indulged in laughter and derision."

He also gives an impressive account of the religious service which was performed, the punctuality and devotion with which it was attended, and the appropriate prayer—that of thanks to God for deliverance from a great danger—with which it was concluded.

> "The service was then read, the responses audibly and devoutly made by the officers and crew, and the bodies consigned to the deep. This service was closed with that prayer so appropriate to our situation, appointed to be read in our ships of war, 'Preserve us from the dangers of the sea, and from the violence of enemies; that we may be a safeguard to the United States of America, and a security for such as pass on the seas upon their lawful occasions; that the inhabitants of our land may in peace and quietude serve thee our God; and that we may return in safety to enjoy the blessings of our land, with the fruits of our labor, with a thankful remembrance of thy mercies, to praise and glorify thy holy name through Jesus Christ our Lord.'"

This religious celebration concluded, and the prayer read, the commander indulges in a remark upon their escape from a danger plotted before the ship left the United States, as unfeeling, inhuman and impious at the time, as it was afterwards proved to be false and wicked. After the arrest of Spencer, the delators discovered that he had meditated these crimes before he left the United States, and had let his intention become known at a house in the Bowery at New York. In reference to that early inception of the plot, now just found out by the commander, he thus remarks:

> "In reading this (prayer) and in recollecting the uses to which the Somers had been destined, as I now find, before she quitted the waters of the United States, I could not but humbly hope that divine sanction would not be wanting to the deed of that day."

Here it is assumed for certain that piratical uses were intended for the vessel by Spencer before he left New York; and upon that assumption the favor of Heaven was humbly hoped for in looking down upon the deed of that day. Now what should be the look of Heaven if all this early plotting should be a false imputation—a mere invention—as it was proved to be. Before the court-martial it was proved that the sailor boarding-house remark about this danger to the Somers, was made by another person, and before Spencer joined the vessel—and from which vessel the commander knew he had endeavored to get transferred to the Grampus, after he had come into her—the commander himself being the organ of his wishes. Foiled before the court in attaching this boarding-house remark to Spencer, the delators before the court undertook to fasten it upon Cromwell: there again the same fate befell them: the remark was proved to have been made by a man of the name of Phelps, and before Cromwell had joined the vessel: and so ended this last false and foul insinuation in his report.

The commander then made a speech, whereof he incorporates a synopsis in his report; and of which, with its capital effects upon the crew, he gives this account:

> "The crew were now ordered aft, and I addressed them from the trunk, on which I was standing. I called their attention first to the fate of the unfortunate young man, whose ill-regulated ambition, directed to the most infamous ends, had been the exciting cause of the tragedy they had just witnessed. I spoke of his honored parents, of his distinguished father, whose talents and character had raised him to one of the highest stations in the land, to be one of the six appointed counsellors of the representative of our national sovereignty. I spoke of the distinguished social position to which this young man had been born; of the advantages of every sort that attended the outset of his career, and of the professional honors to which a long, steady, and faithful perseverance in the course of duty might ultimately have raised him. After a few months' service at sea, most wretchedly employed, so for as the acquisition of professional knowledge was concerned, he had aspired to supplant me in a command which I had only reached after nearly 30 years of faithful servitude; and for what object I had already explained to them. I told them that their future fortunes were in their own control: they had advantages of every sort and in an eminent degree for the attainment of professional knowledge. The situations of warrant officers and of masters in the navy were open to them. They might rise to commands in the merchant service, to respectability, to competence, and to fortune; but they must advance regularly, and step by step; every step to be sure, must be guided by truth, honor, and fidelity. I called their attention to Cromwell's case. He must have received an excellent education, his handwriting was even elegant. But he had also fallen through brutish sensuality and the greedy thirst for gold."

But there was another speech on the Sunday following, of which the commander furnishes no report, but of which some parts were remembered by hearers—as thus by McKee:—(the judge advocate having put the question to him whether he had heard the commander's addresses to the crew after the execution). Answer: "I heard him on the Sunday after the execution: he read Mr. Spencer's letters: he said he was satisfied the young man had been lying to him for half an hour before his death." Another witness swore to the same words, with the addition, "that he died with a lie in his mouth." Another witness (Green) gives a further view into this letter-reading, and affords a glimpse of the object of such a piece of brutality. In answer to the same question, if he heard the commander's speech the Sunday after the execution? He answered, "Yes, sir. I heard him read over Mr. Spencer's letter, and pass a good many remarks on it. He said that Cromwell had been very cruel to the boys: that he had called him aft, and spoke to him about it several times. To the question, Did he say any thing of Mr. Spencer? he answered—"Yes, sir. He said he left his friends, lost all his clothes, and shipped in a whaling vessel." To the question whether any thing was said about Mr. Spencer's truth or falsehood? he answered: "I heard the commander say, this young man died with a lie in his mouth; but do not know whether he meant Mr. Spencer, or some one else." It is certain the commander was making a base use of these letters, as he makes no mention of them any where, and they seem to have been used solely to excite the crew against Cromwell and Spencer.

In finding the mother's letter in Small's bible, the captain finds occasion to make two innuendos against the dead Spencer, then still hanging up. He says:

> "She expressed the joy with which she had learned from him that he was so happy on board the Somers (at that time Mr. Spencer had not joined her); that no grog was served on board of her. Within the folds of this sacred volume he had preserved a copy of verses taken from

the Sailor's Magazine, enforcing the value of the bible to seamen. I read these verses to the crew. Small had evidently valued his bible, but could not resist temptation."

This happiness of Small is discriminated from his acquaintance with Spencer: it was before the time that Spencer joined the ship! as if his misery began from that time! when it only commenced from the time he was seized and ironed for mutiny. Then the temptation which he could not resist, *innuendo*, tempted by Spencer— of which there was not even a tangible hearsay, and no temptation necessary. Poor Small was an habitual drunkard, and drank all that he could get—his only fault, as it seems. But this bible of Small's gave occasion to another speech, and moral and religious harangue, of which the captain gave a report, too long to be noticed here except for its characteristics, and which go to elucidate the temper and state of mind in which things were done:

> "I urged upon the youthful sailors to cherish their bibles with a more entire love than Small had done; to value their prayer books also; they would find in them a prayer for every necessity, however great; a medicine for every ailment of the mind. I endeavored to call to their recollection the terror with which the three malefactors had found themselves suddenly called to enter the presence of an offended God. No one who had witnessed that scene could for a moment believe even in the existence of such a feeling as honest Atheism: a disbelief in the existence of a God. They should also remember that scene. They should also remember that Mr. Spencer, in his last moments, had said that 'he had wronged many people, but chiefly his parents.' From these two circumstances they might draw two useful lessons: a lesson of filial piety, and of piety toward God. With these two principles for their guides they could never go astray."

This speech was concluded with giving cheers to God, not by actual shouting, but by singing the hundredth psalm, and cheering again—all for deliverance from the hands of the pirates. Thus:

> "In conclusion, I told them that they had shown that they could give cheers for their country; they should now give cheers to their God, for they would do this when they sung praises to his name. The colors were now hoisted, and above the American ensign, the only banner to which it may give place, the banner of the cross. The hundredth psalm was now sung by all the officers and crew. After which, the usual service followed; when it was over, I could not avoid contrasting the spectacle presented on that day by the Somers, with what it would have been in pirates' hands."

During all this time the four other men in irons sat manacled behind the captain, and he exults in telling the fine effects of his speaking on these "deeply guilty," as well as upon all the rest of the ship's crew.

> "But on this subject I forbear to enlarge. I would not have described the scene at all, so different from the ordinary topics of an official communication, but for the unwonted circumstances in which we were placed, and the marked effect which it produced on the ship's company, even on those deeply guilty members of it who sat manacled behind me, and that it was considered to have done much towards restoring the allegiance of the crew."

Of these deeply guilty, swelled to twelve before the ship got home, three appeared before the court-martial, and gave in their experience of that day's work. McKee, the first one, testifies that he had so little suspicion of what was going on, that, when he saw the commander come upon deck in full uniform, he supposed that some ship was seen, and that it was the intention to visit or speak her. To the question, what passed between yourself and the commander, after the execution? he answered: "He said he could find nothing against any of the four that were then in irons—if he had found any proof our fate would have been the same; and if he could find any excuse for not taking them home in irons, he would do so. I understood him to mean he would release them from their irons." Green, another of them, in answer to the question whether the commander spoke to him after hanging, answered—"Yes, sir. He said he could not find any thing against us; if he could, our fate would have been the same as the other three. He asked me if I was satisfied with it?" McKinley was the third, and to the same question, whether the commander spoke to him on the day of the executions? he answered—

"He did while the men were hanging at the yard arm, but not before. He came to me, and said, 'McKinley, did you hear what I said to those other young men?' I told him, 'No, sir.' 'Well,' said he, 'it is the general opinion of the officers that you are a pretty good boy, but I shall have to take you home in irons, to see what the Secretary of the Navy can do for you.' He said: 'In risking your life for other persons (or something to that effect) is all that saves you.' He left me then, and I spoke to Mr. Gansevoort—I asked him if he thought the commander thought I was guilty of any thing of the kind. He said: 'No, I assure you if he did, he would have strung you up.'" Wilson, the fourth of the arrested, was not examined before the court; but the evidence of three of them, with McKenzie's refusal to proceed against them in New York, and the attempt to tamper with one of them, is proof enough that he had no accusation against these four men: that they were arrested to fulfil the condition on which the first three were to be hanged, and to be brought home in irons with eight others, to keep up the idea of mutiny.

The report having finished the history of the mutiny—its detection, suppression, execution of the ringleaders, and seizure of the rest (twelve in all) to be brought home in bags and irons—goes on, like a military report after a great victory, to point out for the notice and favor of the government, the different officers and men who had distinguished themselves in the affair, and to demand suitable rewards for each one according to his station and merits. This concluding part opened thus:

> "In closing this report, a pleasing, yet solemn duty devolves upon me, which I feel unable adequately to fulfil—to do justice to the noble conduct of every one of the officers of the Somers, from the first lieutenant to the commander's clerk, who has also, since her equipment, performed the duty of midshipman. Throughout the whole duration of the difficulties in which we have been involved, their conduct has been courageous, determined, calm, self-possessed—animated and upheld always by a lofty and chivalrous patriotism, perpetually armed by day and by night, waking and sleeping, with pistols often cocked for hours together."

The commander, after this general encomium, brings forward the distinguished, one by one, beginning of course with his first lieutenant:

> "I cannot forbear to speak particularly of Lieutenant Gansevoort. Next to me in rank on board the Somers, he was my equal in every respect to protect and defend her. The perfect harmony of our opinions, and of our views of what should be done, on each new development of the dangers which menaced the integrity of command, gave us a unity of action that added materially to our strength. Never since the existence of our navy has a commanding officer been more ably and zealously seconded by his lieutenant."

Leaving out every thing minor, and dependent upon the oaths of others, there are some things sworn to by Gansevoort himself which derogate from his chivalrous patriotism. *First*, going round to the officers who were to sit in council upon the three prisoners, and taking their agreement to execute the three on hand if more arrests were made. *Secondly*, encouraging and making those arrests on which the lives of the three depended. *Thirdly*, going out of the council to obtain from Spencer further proofs of his guilt—Spencer not knowing for what purpose he was thus interrogated. *Fourthly*, his calmness and self-possession were shown in the fire of his pistol while assisting to arrest Cromwell, and in that consternation inspired in him at the running towards where he was of a cluster of the apprentice boys, scampering on to avoid the boatswain's colt—a slender cord to whip them over the clothes, like a switch. Midshipman Rodgers had gone aft, or forward, as the case may be, to drive a parcel of these boys to their duty, taking the boatswain along to apply his colt to all the hindmost. Of course the boys scampered briskly to escape the colt. The lieutenant heard them coming—thought they were the mutineers—sung out, God! they are coming—levelled his revolver, and was only prevented from giving them the contents of the six barrels, had they not sung out "It is me—it is me;" for that is what the witnesses stated. But the richness of the scene can only be fully seen from the lieutenant's own account of it, which he gave before the court with evident self-satisfaction: "The commander and myself were standing on the larboard side of the quarter deck, at the after end of the trunk: we were in conversation: it was dark at the time. I heard an unusual noise—a rushing aft toward the quarter deck; I said to the commander, 'God! I believe they are coming.' I had one of Colt's pistols, which I immediately drew and cocked: the commander said his pistols were below. I jumped on the trunk, and ran forward to meet them. As I was going along I sung out to them not to come aft. I told them I would blow the first man's brains out who would put his foot on the quarter deck. I held my pistol pointed at the tallest man that I saw in the starboard gangway, and I think Mr. Rodgers sung out to me, that he was sending the men aft to the mast rope. I then told them they must have no such unusual movements on board the vessel: what they did, they must do in their usual manner: they knew the state of the vessel, and might get their brains blown out before they were aware of it. Some other short remarks, I do not recollect at this time what they were, and ordered them to come aft and man the mast rope: to move quietly." To finish this view of Mr. Gansevoort's self-possession, and the value of his "beliefs," it is only necessary to know that, besides letting off his pistol when Cromwell was arrested, he swore before the court that, "I had an idea that he (Cromwell) meant to take me overboard with him," when they shook hands under the gallows yard arm, and under that idea, "turned my arm to get clear of his grasp."

The two non-combatants, purser Heiskill and assistant surgeon Leecock, come in for high applause, although for the low business of watching the crew and guarding the prisoners. The report thus brings them forward:

> "Where all, without exception, have behaved admirably, it might seem invidious to particularize: yet I cannot refrain calling your attention to the noble conduct of purser H. W. Heiskill, and passed assistant surgeon Leecock, for the services which they so freely yielded beyond the sphere of their immediate duties."

The only specification of this noble conduct, and of these services beyond their proper sphere, which is given in the report, is contained in this sentence:

> "Both he and Mr. Heiskill cheerfully obeyed my orders to go perpetually armed, to keep a regular watch, to guard the prisoners: the worst weather could not drive them from their posts, or draw from their lips a murmur."

To these specifications of noble conduct, and extra service, might have been added those of eaves-dropping and delation—capacity to find the same symptoms of guilt in opposite words and acts—sitting in council to judge three men whom they had agreed with Gansevoort two days before to hang if necessary to make more arrests, and which arrests, four in number, were made with their concurrence and full approbation. Finally, he might have told that this Heiskill was a link in the chain of the revelation of the mutinous and piratical plot. He was the purser of whom Wales was the steward, and to whom Wales revealed the plot—he then revealing to Gansevoort—and Gansevoort to Mackenzie. It was, then, through his subordinate (and who was then stealing his liquor) and himself that the plot was detected.

A general presentation of government thanks to all the officers, is next requested by the lieutenant:

> "I respectfully request that the thanks of the Navy Department may be presented to all the officers of the Somers, for their exertions in the critical situation in which she has been placed. It is true they have but performed their duty, but they have performed it with fidelity and zeal."

The purser's steward, Wales, is then specially and encomiastically presented, and a specific high reward solicited for him:

> "I respectfully submit, that Mr. J. W. Wales, by his coolness, his presence of mind, and his fidelity, has rendered to the American navy a memorable service. I had a trifling difficulty with him, not discreditable to his character, on the previous cruise to Porto Rico—on that account he was sought out, and tampered with. But he was honest, patriotic, humane; he resisted temptation, was faithful to his flag, and was instrumental in saving it from dishonor. A pursership in the navy, or a handsome pecuniary reward, would after all be an inconsiderable recompense, compared with the magnitude of his services."

Of this individual the commander had previously reported a contrivance to make a mistake in doubling the allowed quantity of brandy carried out on the cruise, saying: "By accident, as it was thought at the time, but subsequent developments would rather go to prove by design, he (Wales) had contrived to make a mistake, and the supply of brandy was ordered from two different groceries; thus doubling the quantity intended to be taken." Of this double supply of brandy thus contrived to be taken out, the commander reports Wales for continual "*stealing*" of it—always adding that he was seduced into these "thefts" by Spencer. Being a temperance man, the commander eschews the use of this brandy on board, except furtively for the corruption of the crew by Spencer through the seduction of the steward: thus: "None of the brandy was used in the mess, and all of it is still on board except what was stolen by the steward at the request of Mr. Spencer, and drank by him, and those he endeavored to corrupt." By his own story this Wales comes under the terms of Lord Hale's idea of a "desperate villain"—a fellow who joins in a crime, gets the confidence of accomplices, then informs upon them, gets them hanged, and receives a reward. This was the conduct of Wales upon his own showing: and of such informers the pious and mild Lord Hale judicially declared his abhorrence—held their swearing unworthy of credit unless corroborated—said that they had done more mischief in getting innocent people punished than they had ever done good in bringing criminals to justice. Upon this view of his conduct, then, this Wales comes under the legal idea of a desperate villain. Legal presumptions would leave him in this category but the steward and the commander have not left it there. They have lifted a corner of the curtain which conceals an unmentionable transaction, to which these two persons were parties—which was heard of, but not understood by the crew—which was hugger-muggered into a settlement between them about the time of Spencer's arrest, though originating the preceding cruise—which neither would explain—which no one could name—and of which Heiskill, the intermediate between his steward and the commander, could know nothing except that it was of a "delicate nature," and that it had been settled between them. The first hint of this mysterious transaction was in the commander's report—in his proud commendation of this steward for a pursership in the United States Navy—and evidently to rehabilitate his witness, and to get a new lick at Spencer. The hint runs thus: "I had a trifling difficulty, not discreditable to his character, on the previous cruise to Porto Rico." On the trial the purser Heiskill was interrogated as to the nature of this difficulty between his subordinate and his superior. To the question—"Did he know any thing, and what, about a misunderstanding between the steward and the commander at Porto Rico?" he answered, "he knew there was a misunderstanding, which Wales told him was explained to the satisfaction of the commander." To the further question, "Was it of a delicate nature?" the answer was, "yes, sir." To the further question, as to the time when this misunderstanding was settled? the purser answered: "I do not know—some time since, I believe." Asked if it was before the arrest? he answers: "I think Mr. Wales spoke of this matter before the arrest." Pressed to tell, if it was shortly before the arrest, the purser would neither give a long nor a short time, but ignored the inquiry with the declaration, "I won't pretend to fix upon a time." Wales himself interrogated before the court, as to the fact of this misunderstanding, and also as to what it was? admitted the fact, but refused its disclosure. His answer, as it stands in the official report of the trial is: "I had a difficulty, but decline to explain it." And the obliging court submitted to the contempt of this answer.

Left without information in a case so mysterious, and denied explanation from those who could give it, history can only deal with the facts as known, and with the inferences fairly resulting from them; and, therefore, can only say, that there was an old affair between the commander and the purser's steward, originating in a previous voyage, and settled in this one, and settled before the arrest of midshipman Spencer; and secondly, that the affair was of so delicate a nature as to avoid explanation from either party. Now the word "delicate" in this connection, implies something which cannot be discussed without danger—something which will not bear handling, or exposure—and in which silence and reserve are the only escapes from a detection worse than any suspicion. And thus stands before history the informer upon the young Spencer—the thief of brandies, the desperate villain according to Lord Hale's classification, and the culprit of unmentionable crime, according to his own implied admission. Yet this man is recommended for a pursership in the United States navy, or a handsome pecuniary reward; while any court in Christendom would have committed him for perjury, on his own showing, in his swearing before the court-martial.

Sergeant Michael H. Garty is then brought forward; thus:

> "Of the conduct of Sergeant Michael H. Garty (of the marines) I will only say it was worthy of the noble corps to which he has the honor to belong. Confined to his hammock by a malady which threatened to be dangerous, at the moment when the conspiracy was

discovered, he rose upon his feet a well man. Throughout the whole period, from the day of Mr. Spencer's arrest to the day after our arrival, and until the removal of the mutineers, his conduct was calm, steady, and soldierlike. But when his duty was done, and health was no longer indispensable to its performance, his malady returned upon him, and he is still in his hammock. In view of this fine conduct, I respectfully recommend that Sergeant Garty be promoted to a second lieutenancy in the marine corps. Should I pass without dishonor through the ordeal which probably awaits me, and attain in due time to the command of a vessel entitled to a marine officer, I ask no better fortune than to have the services of Sergeant Garty in that capacity."

Now here is something like a miracle. A bedridden man to rise up a well man the moment his country needed his services, and to remain a well man to the last moment those services required, and then to fall down a bedridden man again. Such a miracle implies a divine interposition which could only be bottomed on a full knowledge of the intended crime, and a special care to prevent it. It is quite improbable in itself, and its verity entirely marred by answers of this sergeant to certain questions before the court-martial. Thus: "When were you on the sick list in the last cruise?" Answer: "I was twice on the list: the last time about two days." Now these two days must be that hammock confinement from the return of the malady which immediately ensued on the removal of the mutineers (the twelve from the Somers to the North Carolina guardship at New York), and which seemed as chronic and permanent as it was before the arrest. Questioned further, whether he "remained in his hammock the evening of Spencer's arrest?" the answer is, "Yes, sir: I was in and out of it all that night." So that the rising up a well man does not seem to have been so instantaneous as the commander's report would imply. The sergeant gives no account of this malady which confined him to his hammock in the marvellous way the commander reports. He never mentioned it until it was dragged out of him on cross-examination. He was on the sick list. That does not imply bedridden. Men are put on the sick list for a slight indisposition: in fact, to save them from sickness. Truth is, this Garty seems to have been one of the class of which every service contains some specimens—scamps who have a pain, and get on the sick list when duty runs hard; and who have no pain, and get on the well list, as soon as there is something pleasant to do. In this case the sergeant seems to have had a pleasant occupation from the alacrity with which he fulfilled it, and from the happy relief which it procured him from his malady as long as it lasted. That occupation was superintendent of the bagging business. It was he who attended to the wearing and fitting of the bags—seeing that they were punctually put on when a prisoner was made, tightly tied over the head of nights, and snugly drawn round the neck during the day. To this was added eavesdropping and delating, and swearing before all the courts, and in this style before the council of officers: "Thinks there are some persons at large that would voluntarily assist the prisoners if they had an opportunity."—"Thinks if the prisoners were at large the brig would certainly be in great danger."—"Thinks there are persons adrift yet, who, if opportunity offered, would rescue the prisoners."—"Thinks the vessel would be safer if Cromwell, Spencer, and Small were put to death."—"Thinks Cromwell a desperate fellow."—"Thinks their object (that of Cromwell and Spencer), in taking slavers, would be to convert them to their own use, and not to suppress the slave trade." All this was swearing like a sensible witness, who knew what was wanted, and would furnish it. It covered all the desired points. More arrests were wanted at that time to justify the hanging of the prisoners on hand: he thinks more arrests ought to be made. The fear of a rescue was wanted: he thinks there will be a rescue attempted. The execution of the prisoners is wanted: he thinks the vessel would be safer if they were all three put to death. And it was for these noble services—bagging prisoners, eavesdropping, delating, swearing to what was wanted—that this sergeant had his marvellous rise-up from a hammock, and was now recommended for an officer of marines. History repulses the marvel which the commander reports. A kind Providence may interpose for the safety of men and ships, but not through an agent who is to bag and suffocate innocent men—to eaves-drop and delate—to swear in all places, and just what was wanted—all by thoughts, and without any thing to bottom a thought upon. Certainly this Sergeant Garty, from his stomach for swearing, must have something in common, besides nativity, with Mr. Jemmy O'Brien; and, from his alacrity and diligence in taking care of prisoners, would seem to have come from the school of the famous Major Sirr, of Irish rebellion memory.

Mr. O. H. Perry, the commander's clerk and nephew, the same whose blunder in giving the order about the mast, occasioned it to break; and, in breaking, to become a sign of the plotting, mutiny, and piracy; and the same that held the watch to mark the ten minutes that Spencer was to live: this young gentleman was not forgotten, but came in liberally for praise and spoil—the spoil of the young man whose messmate he had been, against whom he had testified, and whose minutes he had counted, and proclaimed when out:

> "If I shall be deemed by the Navy Department to have had any merit in preserving the Somers from those treasonable toils by which she had been surrounded since and before her departure from the United States, I respectfully request that it may accrue without reservation for my nephew O. H. Perry, now clerk on board the Somers, and that his name may be placed on the register in the name left vacant by the treason of Mr. Spencer. I think, under the peculiar circumstances of the case, an act of Congress, if necessary, might be obtained to authorize the appointment."

All these recommendations for reward and promotion, bespeak an obliquity of mental vision, equivalent to an aberration of the mind; and this last one, obliquitous as any, superadds an extinction of the moral sense in demanding the spoil of the slain for the reward of a nephew who had promoted the death of which he was claiming the benefit. The request was revolting! and, what is equally revolting, it was granted. But worse still. An act of Congress at that time forbid the appointment of more midshipmen, of which there were then too many, unless to fill vacancies: hence the request of the commander, that his nephew's name may take the place in the Navy Register of the name left vacant by the "*treason*" of Mr. Spencer!

The commander, through all his witnesses, had multiplied proofs on the attempts of Spencer to corrupt the crew by largesses lavished upon them—such as tobacco, segars, nuts, sixpences thrown among the boys, and two bank-notes given to Cromwell on the coast of Africa to send home to his wife before the bank failed. Now what were the temptations on the other side? What the inducements to the witnesses and actors in this foul business to swear up to the mark which Mackenzie's acquittal and their promotion required? The remarks of Mr. Fenimore Cooper, the historian, here present themselves as those of an experienced man speaking with knowledge of the subject, and acquaintance with human nature:

> "While on this point we will show the extent of the temptations that were thus inconsiderately placed before the minds of these men—what preferment they had reason to hope would be accorded to them should Mackenzie's conduct be approved, *viz*.: Garty, from the ranks, to be an officer, with twenty-five dollars per month, and fifty cents per diem rations: and the prospect of promotion. Wales, from purser's steward, at eighteen dollars a month, to quarter-deck rank, and fifteen hundred dollars per annum. Browning, Collins, and Stewart, petty officers, at nineteen dollars a month, to be boatswains, with seven hundred dollars per annum. King, Anderson, and Rogers, petty officers, at nineteen dollars a month, to be gunners, at seven hundred dollars per annum. Dickinson, petty officer, at nineteen dollars a month, to be carpenter, with seven hundred dollars per annum."

Such was the list of temptations placed before the witnesses by Commander Mackenzie, and which it is not in human nature to suppose were without their influence on most of the persons to whom they were addressed.

The commander could not close his list of recommendations for reward without saying something of himself. He asked for nothing specifically, but expected approbation, and looked forward to regular promotion, while gratified at the promotions which his subordinates should receive, and which would redound to his own honor. He did not ask for a court of inquiry, or a court-martial, but seemed to apprehend, and to deprecate them. The Secretary of the Navy immediately ordered a court of inquiry—a court of three officers to report upon the facts of the case, and to give their opinion. There was no propriety in this proceeding. The facts were admitted, and the law fixed their character. Three prisoners had been hanged without trial, and the law holds that to be murder until reduced by a judicial trial to a lower degree of offence—to manslaughter, excusable, or justifiable homicide. The finding of the court was strongly in favor of the commander; and unless this finding and opinion were disapproved by the President, no further military proceeding should be had—no court-martial ordered—the object of the inquiry being to ascertain whether there was necessity for one. The necessity being negatived, and that opinion approved by the President, there was no military rule of action which could go on to a court-martial: to the general astonishment such a court was immediately ordered—and assembled with such precipitation that the judge advocate was in no condition to go on with the trial; and, up to the third day of its sitting, was without the means of proceeding with the prosecution; and for his justification in not being able to go on, and in asking some delay, the judge advocate, Wm. H. Norris, Esq., of Baltimore, submitted to the court this statement in writing:

> "The judge advocate states to the court that he has not been furnished by the department, as yet, with any list of witnesses on the part of the government: that he has had no opportunity of conversing with any of the witnesses, of whose names he is even entirely ignorant except by rumor in respect to a few of them; and that, therefore, he would need time to prepare the case by conversation with the officers and crew of the brig Somers, before he can commence the case on the part of the government. The judge advocate has issued two subpœnas, *duces tecum*, for the record in the case of the court of inquiry into the alleged mutiny, which have not yet been returned, and by which record he could have been notified of the witnesses and facts to constitute the case of the government."

The judge advocate then begged a delay, which was granted, until eleven o'clock the next day. Here then was a precipitation, unheard of in judicial proceedings, and wholly incompatible with the idea of any real prosecution. The cause of this precipitancy becomes a matter of public inquiry, as the public interest requires the administration of justice to be fair and impartial. The cause of it then was this: The widow of Cromwell, to whom he had sent his last dying message, that he was innocent, undertook to have Mackenzie prosecuted before the civil tribunals for the murder of her husband. She made three attempts, all in vain. One judge, to whom an application for a warrant was made, declined to grant it, on the ground that he was too much occupied with other matters to attend to that case—giving a written answer to that effect. A commissioner of the United States, appointed to issue warrants in all criminal cases, refused one in this case, because, as he alleged, he had no authority to act in a military case. The attempt was then made in the United States district court, New York, to get the Grand Jury to find an indictment: the court instructed the jury that it was not competent for a civil tribunal to interfere with matters which were depending before a naval tribunal: in consequence of which instruction the bill was ignored. Upon this instruction of the court the historian, Cooper, well remarks: "That after examining the subject at some length, we are of opinion that the case belonged exclusively to the civil tribunals." Here, then, is the reason why Mackenzie was run so precipitately before the court-martial. It was to shelter him by an acquittal there: and so apprehensive was he of being got hold of by some civil tribunal, before the court-martial could be organized, that he passed the intervening days between the two courts "in a bailiwick where the ordinary criminal process could not reach him."—(Cooper's Review of the Trial.) When the trial actually came on, the judge advocate was about as bad off as he was the first day. He had a list of witnesses. They were Mackenzie's officers—and refused to converse with him on the nature of their testimony. He stated their refusal to the court—declared himself without knowledge to conduct the case—and likened himself to a new comer in a house, having a bunch of keys given to him, without information of the lock to which each belonged—so that he must try every lock with every key before he could find out the right one.

The hurried assemblage of the court being shown, its composition becomes a fair subject of inquiry. The record shows that three officers were excused from serving on their own application after being detailed as members of the court; and the information of the day made known that another was excused before he was officially detailed. The same history of the day informs that these four avoided the service because they had opinions against the accused. That was all right in them. Mackenzie was entitled to an impartial trial, although he allowed his victims no trial at all. But how was it on the other side? any one excused there for opinions in favor of the accused? None! and history said there were members on the court strongly in favor of him—as the proceedings on the trial too visibly prove. Engaged in the case without a knowledge of it, the judge advocate confined himself to the testimony of one witness, merely proving the hanging without trial; and then left the field to the accused. It was occupied in great force—a great number of witnesses, all the reports of Mackenzie himself, all the statements before the council of officers—all sorts of illegal, irrelevant, impertinent or frivolous testimony—every thing that could be found against the dead since their death, in addition to all before—assumption or assertion of any fact or inference wanted—questions put not only leading to the answer wanted, but affirming the fact wanted—all the persons served as witnesses who had been agents or instruments in the murders—Mackenzie himself submitting his own statements before the court: such was the trial! and the issue was conformable to such a farrago of illegalities, absurdities, frivolities, impertinences and wickednesses. He was acquitted; but in the lowest form of acquittal known to court-martial proceedings. "Not proven," was the equivocal mode of saying "not guilty:" three members of the court were in favor of conviction for murder. The finding was barely permitted to stand by the President. To approve, or disprove court-martial proceedings is the regular course: the President did neither. The official promulgation of the proceedings wound up with this unusual and equivocal sanction: "As these charges involved the life of the accused, and as the finding is in his favor, he is entitled to the benefit of it, as in the analogous case of a verdict of not guilty before a civil court, and there is no power which can constitutionally deprive him of that benefit. The finding, therefore, is simply *confirmed*, and carried into effect without any expression of approbation or disapprobation on the part of the President: no such expression being necessary." No acquittal could be of lower order, or less honorable. The trial continued two months; and that long time was chiefly monopolized by the defence, which became in fact a trial of the dead—who, having no trial while alive, had an ample one of sixty days after their deaths. Of course they were convicted—the dead and the absent being always in the wrong. At the commencement of the trial, two eminent counsel of New York—Messrs. Benjamin F. Butler and Charles O'Connor, Esqs.,—applied to the court at the instance of the father of the young Spencer to be allowed to sit by, and put questions approved by the court; and offer suggestions and comments on the testimony when it was concluded. This request was entered on the minutes, and refused. So that at the long *post mortem* trial which was given to the boy after his death, the father was not allowed to ask one question in favor of his son.

And here two remarks require to be made—first, as to that faithful promise of the Commander Mackenzie to send to his parents the dying message of the young Spencer: not a word was ever sent! all was sent to the Navy Department and the newspapers! and the "faithful promise," and the moving appeal to the "feelings of nature," turn out to have been a mere device to get a chance to make a report to the Secretary of the Navy of confessions to justify the previous condemnation and the pre-determined hanging. Secondly: That the Secretary despatched a man-of-war immediately on the return of Mackenzie to the Isle of Pines, to capture the confederate pirates (according to Wales's testimony), who were waiting there for the young Spencer and the Somers. A bootless errand. The island was found, and the pines; but no pirates! nor news of any for near twenty years! Thus failed the indispensable point in the whole piratical plot: but without balking in the least degree the raging current of universal belief.

The trial of Mackenzie being over, and he acquitted, the trial of the rest of the implicated crew—the twelve mutineers in irons—would naturally come on; and the court remained in session for that purpose. The Secretary of the Navy had written to the judge advocate to proceed against such of them as he thought proper: the judge advocate referred that question to Mackenzie, giving him the option to choose any one he pleased to carry on the prosecutions. He chose Theodore Sedgwick, Esq., who had been his own counsel on his trial. Mackenzie was acquitted on the 28th of March: the court remained in session until the 1st of April: the judge advocate heard nothing from Mackenzie with respect to the prosecutions. On that day Mackenzie not being present, he was sent for. He was not to be found! and the provost marshal ascertained that he had gone to his residence in the country, thirty miles off. This was an abandonment of the prosecutions, and in a very unmilitary way—by running away from them, and saying nothing to any body. The court was then dissolved—the prisoners released—and the innocence of the twelve stood confessed by the recreancy of their fugitive prosecutor. It was a confession of the innocence of Spencer, Small, and Cromwell; for he was tried for the three murders together. The trial of Mackenzie had been their acquittal in the eyes of persons accustomed to analyze evidence, and to detect perjuries in made-up stories. But the masses could form no such analysis. With them the confessions were conclusive, though invalidated by contradictions, and obtained, if obtained at all, under a refinement of terror and oppression which has no parallel on the deck of a pirate. When has such a machinery of terror been contrived to shock and torture a helpless victim? Sudden annunciation of death in the midst of preparations to take life: ten minutes allowed to live, and these ten minutes taken up with interruptions. An imp of darkness in the shape of a naval officer in full uniform, squat down at his side, writing and whispering; and evidently making out a tale which was to murder the character in order to justify the murder of the body. Commander Mackenzie had once lived a year in Spain, and wrote a book upon its manners and customs, as a "Young American." He must have read of the manner in which confessions were obtained in the dungeons of the Inquisition. If he had, he showed himself an apt scholar; if not, he showed a genius for the business from which the familiars of the Holy Office might have taken instruction.

Spencer's real design was clearly deducible even from the tenors of the vile swearing against him. He meant to quit the navy when he returned to New York, obtain a vessel in some way, and go to the northwest coast of America—to lead some wild life there; but not piratical, as there is neither prey nor shelter for pirates in that quarter. This he was often saying to the crew, and to this his list of names referred—mixed up with foolish and even vicious talk about piracy. His first and his last answer was the same—that it was all a joke. The answer of Small was the same when he was arrested; and it was well brought out by the judge advocate in incessant questions during the two months' trial, that there was not a single soul of the crew, except Wales, that ever heard Spencer mention one word about mutiny! and not one, inclusive of Wales, that ever heard one man of the vessel speak of a rescue of the prisoners. Remaining long in command of the vessel as Mackenzie did, and with all his power to punish or reward, and allowed as he was to bring forward all that he was able to find since the deaths of the men, yet he could not find one man to swear to these essential points; so that in a crew steeped in mutiny, there was not a soul that had heard of it! in a crew determined upon a rescue of prisoners, there was not one that ever heard the word pronounced. The state of the brig, after the arrests, was that of crazy cowardice and insane suspicion on the part of the officers—of alarm and consternation on the part of the crew. Armed with revolvers, cutlasses and swords, the officers prowled through the vessel, ready to shoot any one that gave them a fright—the weapon generally cocked for instant work. Besides the officers, low wretches, as Wales and Garty, were armed in the same way, with the same summary power over the lives and deaths of the crew. The vessel was turned into a laboratory of spies, informers, eavesdroppers and delators. Every word, look, sign, movement, on the part of the crew, was equally a proof of guilt. If the men were quick about their duty, it was to cover up their guilt: if slow, it was to defy the officers. If they talked loud, it was insolence: if low, it was plotting. If collected in knots, it was to be ready to make a rush at the vessel: if keeping single and silent, it was because, knowing their guilt, they feigned aversion to escape suspicion. Belief was all that was wanted from any delator. Belief, without a circumstance to found it upon, and even contrary to circumstances, was accepted as full legal evidence. Arrests were multiplied, to excite terror, and to justify murder. The awe-stricken crew, consisting four-fifths of apprentice boys, was paralyzed into dead silence and abject submission. Every arrest was made without a murmur. The prisoners were ironed and bagged as mere animals. No one could show pity, much less friendship. No one could extend a comfort, much less give assistance. Armed sentries stood over them, day and night, to shoot both parties for the slightest sign of intelligence—and always to shoot the prisoner first. What Paris was in the last days of the Reign of Terror, the United States brig Somers was during the terrible week from the arrest to the hanging of Spencer.

Analogous to the case of Commander Mackenzie was that of Lieutenant Colonel Wall, of the British service, Governor of Goree on the coast of Africa—the circumstances quite parallel, and where they differ, the difference in favor of Wall—but the conclusion widely different. Governor Wall fancied there was a mutiny in the garrison, the one half (of 150) engaged in it, and one Armstrong and two others, leaders in it. He ordered the "long roll" to be beat—which brings the men, without arms, into line on the parade. He conversed a few minutes with the officers, out of hearing of the men, then ordered the line to form circle, a cannon to be placed in the middle of it, the three men tied upon it, and receive 800 blows each with an inch thick rope. It was not his intent to kill them, and the surgeon of the garrison, as in all cases of severe punishment, was ordered to attend, and observe it: which he did, saying nothing: the three men died within a week. This was in the year 1782. Wall came home—was arrested (by the civil authority), broke custody and fled—was gone twenty years, and seized again by the civil authority on his return to England. The trial took place at the Old Bailey, and the prisoner easily proved up a complete case of mutiny, seventy or eighty men, assembled in open day before the governor's quarters, defying authority, clamoring for supposed rights, and cursing and damning. The full case was sworn up, and by many witnesses; but the attorney-general, Sir Edward Law (afterwards Lord Ellenborough), and the solicitor-general, Mr. Percival (afterwards First Lord of the Treasury and Chancellor of the Exchequer), easily took the made-up stories to pieces, and left the governor nakedly exposed, a false accuser of the dead, after having been the foul murderer of the innocent. It was to no purpose that he plead, that the punishment was not intended to kill: it was answered that it was sufficient that it was likely to kill, and did kill. To no purpose that he proved by the surgeon that he stood by, as the regulations required, to judge the punishment, and said nothing: the eminent counsel proved upon him, out of his own mouth, that he was a young booby, too silly to know the difference between a cat-o'-nine-tails, which cut the skin, and an inch rope, which bruised to the vitals. The Lord Chief Baron McDonald, charged the jury that if there was no mutiny, it was murder; and if there was mutiny, and no trial, it was murder. On this latter point, he said to the jury: "*If you are of opinion that there was a mutiny, you are then to consider the degree of it, and whether there was as much attention paid to the interest of the person accused as the circumstances of the case would admit, by properly advising him, and giving him an opportunity of justifying himself if he could.*" The governor was only tried in one case, found guilty, hanged within eight days, and his body, like that of any other murderer, delivered up to the surgeons for dissection—the King on application, first for pardon, then for longer respite, and last for remission of the anatomization, refusing any favor, upon the ground that it was worse than any common murder—being done by a man in authority, far from the eye of the government, on helpless people subject to his power, and whom he was bound to protect, and to defend from oppression. It is a case—a common one in England since the judges became independent of the crown—which does honor to British administration of justice: and, if any one wishes to view the extremes of judicial exhibitions—legality, regularity, impartiality, knowledge of the law, promptitude on one hand, and the reverse of it all on the other—let them look at the proceedings of the one-day trial of Governor Wall before a British civil court, and the two months' trial of Commander Mackenzie before an American naval court-martial. But the comparison would not be entirely fair. Courts-martial, both of army and navy, since the trial of Admiral Byng in England to Commodore Porter, Commander Mackenzie, and Lieutenant-colonel Frémont in the United States, have been machines in the hands of the government (where it took an interest in the event), to acquit, or convict: and has rarely disappointed the intention. Cooper proposes, in view of the unfitness of the military courts for judicial investigation, that they be stripped of all jurisdiction in such cases: and his opinion strongly addresses itself to the legislative authority.

Commander Mackenzie had been acquitted by the authorities: he had been complimented by a body of eminent merchants: he had been applauded by the press: he had been encomiastically reviewed in a high literary periodical. The loud public voice was for him: but there was a small inward monitor, whose still and sinister whisperings went cutting through the soul. The acquitted and applauded man withdrew to a lonely retreat, oppressed with gloom and melancholly, visible only to a few, and was only roused from his depression to give signs of a diseased mind. It was five years after the event, and during the war with Mexico. The administration had conceived the idea of procuring peace through the instrumentality of Santa Anna—then an exile at Havana; and who was to be returned to his country upon some arrangement of the American government. This writer going to see the President (Mr. Polk) some day about this time, mentioned to him a visit from Commander Slidell Mackenzie to this exiled chief. The President was startled, and asked how this came to be known to me. I told him I read it in the Spanish newspapers. He said it was all a profound secret, confined to his cabinet. The case was this: a secret mission to Santa Anna was resolved upon: and the facile Mr. Buchanan, Secretary of State, dominated by the representative Slidell (brother to the commander), accepted this brother for the place. Now the views of the two parties were diametrically opposite. One wanted secrecy—the other notoriety. Restoration of Santa Anna to his country, upon an agreement, and without being seen in the transaction, was the object of the government; and that required secrecy: removal from under a cloud, restoration to public view, rehabilitation by some mark of public distinction, was the object of the Slidells; and that required notoriety: and the game being in their hands, they played it accordingly. Arriving at Havana, the secret minister put on the full uniform of an American naval officer, entered an open *volante*, and driving through the principal streets at high noon, proceeded to the suburban residence of the exiled dictator. Admitted to a private interview (for he spoke Spanish, learnt in Spain), the plumed and decorated officer made known his secret business. Santa Anna was amazed, but not disconcerted. He saw the folly and the danger of the proceeding, eschewed blunt overture, and got rid of his queer visitor in the shortest time, and the civilest phrases which Spanish decorum would admit. The repelled minister gone, Santa Anna called back his secretary, exclaiming as he entered—"*Porque el Presidente me ha enviado este tonto?*" (Why has the President sent me this fool?) It was not until afterwards, and through the instrumentality of a sounder head, that the mode of the dictator's return was arranged: and the folly which Mackenzie exhibited on this occasion was of a piece with his crazy and preposterous conceptions on board the Somers.

Fourteen years have elapsed since this tragedy of the Somers. The chief in that black and bloody drama (unless Wales is to be considered the master-spirit, and the commander and lieutenant only his instruments) has gone to his long account. Some others, concerned with him, have passed away. The vessel itself, bearing a name illustrious in the navy annals, has gone to the bottom of the sea—foundering—and going down with all on board; the circling waves closing over the heads of the doomed mass, and hiding all from the light of Heaven before they were dead. And the mind of seamen, prone to belief in portents, prodigies, signs and judgments, refer the hapless fate of the vessel to the innocent blood which had been shed upon her.

History feels it to be a debt of duty to examine this transaction to the bottom, and to judge it closely—not with a view to affect individuals, but to relieve national character from a foul imputation. It was the crime of individuals: it was made national. The protection of the government, the lenity of the court, the evasions of the judiciary, and the general approving voice, made a nation's offence out of the conduct of some individuals, and brought reproach upon the American name. All Christendom recoiled with horror from the atrocious deed: all friends to America beheld with grief and amazement the national assumption of such a crime. Cotemporary with the event, and its close observer, the writer of this View finds confirmed now, upon the fullest examination, the severe judgment which he formed upon it at the time.

The naval historian, Fenimore Cooper (who himself had been a naval officer), wrote a clear exposure of all the delusion, falsehood, and wickedness of this imputed mutiny, and of the mockery of the court-martial trial of Mackenzie: but unavailing in the then condition of the public mind, and impotent against the vast machinery of the public press which was brought to bear on the dead. From that publication, and the official record of the trial, this view of the transaction is made up.

CHAPTER CXXIV.

RETIREMENT OF MR. WEBSTER FROM MR. TYLER'S CABINET.

Mr. Tyler's cabinet, as adopted from President Harrison, in April 1841, had broken up, as before related, in September of the same year—Mr. Webster having been prevailed upon to remain, although he had agreed to go out with the rest, and his friends thought he should have done so. His remaining was an object of the greatest importance with Mr. Tyler, abandoned by all the rest, and for such reasons as they published. He had remained with Mr. Tyler until the spring of the year 1843, when the progress of the Texas annexation scheme, carried on privately, not to say clandestinely, had reached a point to take an official form, and to become the subject of government negotiation, though still secret. Mr. Webster, Secretary of State, was an obstacle to that negotiation. He could not even be trusted with the secret, much less with the conduct of the negotiations. How to get rid of him was a question of some delicacy. Abrupt dismission would have revolted his friends. Voluntary resignation was not to be expected, for he liked the place of Secretary of State, and had remained in it against the wishes of his friends. Still he must be got rid of. A middle course was fallen upon—the same which had been practised with others in 1841—that of compelling a resignation. Mr. Tyler became reserved and indifferent to him. Mr. Gilmer and Mr. Upshur, with whom he had but few affinities, took but little pains to conceal their distaste to him. It was evident to him when the cabinet met, that he was one too many; and reserve and distrust was visible both in the President and the Virginia part of his cabinet. Mr. Webster felt it, and named it to some friends. They said, resign! He did so; and the resignation was accepted with an alacrity which showed that it was waited for. Mr. Upshur took his place, and quickly the Texas negotiation became official, though still private; and in this appointment, and immediate opening of the Texas negotiation, stood confessed, the true reason for getting rid of Mr. Webster.

CHAPTER CXXV.

DEATH OF WILLIAM H. CRAWFORD.

He was among the few men of fame that I have seen, that aggrandized on the approach—that having the reputation of a great man, became greater, as he was more closely examined. There was every thing about him to impress the beholder favorably and grandly—in stature "a head and shoulders" above the common race of men, justly proportioned, open countenance, manly features, ready and impressive conversation, frank and cordial manners. I saw him for the first time in 1820, when he was a member of Mr. Monroe's cabinet—when the array of eminent men was thick—when historic names of the expiring generation were still on the public theatre, and many of the new generation (to become historic) were entering upon it: and he seemed to compare favorably with the foremost. And that was the judgment of others. For a long time he was deferred to generally, by public opinion, as the first of the new men who were to become President. Mr. Monroe, the last of the revolutionary stock, was passing off: Mr. Crawford was his assumed successor. Had the election come on one term sooner, he would have been the selected man: but his very eminence became fatal to him. He was formidable to all the candidates, and all combined against him. He was pulled down in 1824; but at an age, with an energy, a will, a talent and force of character, which would have brought him up within a few years, if a foe more potent than political combinations had not fallen upon him: he was struck with paralysis before the canvass was over, but still received an honorable vote, and among such competitors as Jackson, Adams, and Clay. But his career was closed as a national man, and State appointments only attended him during the remaining years of his life.

Mr. Crawford served in the Senate during Mr. Madison's administration, and was the conspicuous mark in that body, then pre-eminent for its able men. He had a copious, ready and powerful elocution—spoke forcibly and to the point—was the Ajax of the administration, and as such, had constantly on his hands the splendid array of federal gentlemen who then held divided empire in the Senate chamber. Senatorial debate was of high order then—a rivalship of courtesy, as well as of talent: and the feeling of respect for him was not less in the embattled phalanx of opposition, than in the admiring ranks of his own party. He was invaluable in the Senate, but the state of Europe—then convulsed with the approaching downfall of the Great Emperor—our own war with Great Britain, and the uncertainty of the new combinations which might be formed—all required a man of head and nerve—of mind and will, to represent the United States at the French Court: and Mr. Crawford was selected for the arduous post. He told Mr. Madison that the Senate would be lost if he left it (and it was); but a proper representative in France in that critical juncture of Europe, was an overpowering consideration—and he went. Great events took place while he was there. The Great Emperor fell: the Bourbons came up, and fell. The Emperor reappeared, and fell again. But the interests of the United States were kept unentangled in European politics; and the American minister was the only one that could remain at his post in all these sudden changes. At the marvellous return from Elba, he was the sole foreign representative remaining in Paris. Personating the neutrality of his country with decorum and firmness, he succeeded in commanding the respect of all, giving offence to none. From this high critical post he was called by Mr. Monroe, at his first election, to be Secretary of the Treasury; and, by public expectation, was marked for the presidency. There was a desire to take him up at the close of Mr. Monroe's first term; but a generous and honorable feeling would not allow him to become the competitor of his friend; and before the second term was out, the combinations had become too strong for him. He was the last candidate nominated by a Congress caucus, then fallen into great disrepute, but immeasurably preferable, as an organ of public opinion, to the conventions of the present day. He was the dauntless foe of nullification; and, while he lived, that heresy could not root in the patriotic soil of Georgia.

CHAPTER CXXVI.

FIRST SESSION OF THE TWENTY-EIGHTH CONGRESS: LIST OF MEMBERS: ORGANIZATION OF THE HOUSE OF REPRESENTATIVES.

Senate.

MAINE.—John Fairfield, George Evans.

NEW HAMPSHIRE.—Levi Woodbury, Charles G. Atherton.

VERMONT.—Samuel Phelps, William C. Upham.

MASSACHUSETTS.—Rufus Choate, Isaac C. Bates.

RHODE ISLAND.—William Sprague, James F. Simmons.

CONNECTICUT.—J. W. Huntington, John M. Niles.

NEW YORK.—N. P. Tallmadge, Silas Wright.

NEW JERSEY.—W. L. Dayton, Jacob W. Miller.

PENNSYLVANIA.—D. W. Sturgeon, James Buchanan.

DELAWARE.—R. H. Bayard, Thomas Clayton.

MARYLAND.—William D. Merrick, Reverdy Johnson.

VIRGINIA.—Wm. C. Rives, Wm. S. Archer.

NORTH CAROLINA.—Willie P. Mangum, Wm. H. Haywood, jr.

SOUTH CAROLINA.—Daniel E. Hugér, George McDuffie.

GEORGIA.—John M. Berrien, Walter T. Colquitt.

ALABAMA.—William R. King, Arthur P. Bagby.

MISSISSIPPI.—John Henderson, Robert J. Walker.

LOUISIANA.—Alexander Barrow, Alexander Porter.

TENNESSEE.—E. H. Foster, Spencer Jarnagan.

KENTUCKY.—John T. Morehead, John J. Crittenden.

OHIO.—Benjamin Tappan, William Allen.

INDIANA.—Albert S. White, Ed. A. Hannegan.

ILLINOIS.—James Semple, Sidney Breese.

MISSOURI.—T. H. Benton, D. R. Atchison.

ARKANSAS.—Wm. S. Fulton, A. H. Sevier.

MICHIGAN.—A. S. Porter, W. Woodbridge.

House of Representatives.

MAINE.—Joshua Herrick, Robert P. Dunlap, Luther Severance, Hannibal Hamlin.

MASSACHUSETTS.—Robert C. Winthrop, Daniel P. King, William Parmenter, Charles Hudson, (Vacancy), John Quincy Adams, Henry Williams, Joseph Grinnel.

NEW HAMPSHIRE.—Edmund Burke, John R. Reding, John P. Hale, Moses Norris, jr.

RHODE ISLAND.—Henry Y. Cranston, Elisha R. Potter.

CONNECTICUT.—Thomas H. Seymour, John Stewart, George S. Catlin, Samuel Simons.

VERMONT.—Solomon Foot, Jacob Collamer, George P. Marsh, Paul Dillingham, jr.

NEW YORK.—Selah B. Strong, Henry C. Murphy, J. Philips Phœnix, William B. Maclay, Moses G. Leonard, Hamilton Fish, Jos. H. Anderson, R. D. Davis, Jas. G. Clinton, Jeremiah Russell, Zadoc Pratt, David L. Seymour, Daniel D. Barnard, Wm. G. Hunter, Lemuel Stetson, Chesselden Ellis, Charles S. Benton, Preston King, Orville Hungerford, Samuel Beardsley, J. E. Cary, S. M. Purdy, Orville Robinson, Horace Wheaton, George Rathbun, Amasa Dana, Byram Green, Thos. J. Patterson, Charles H. Carroll, Wm. S. Hubbell, Asher Tyler, Wm. A. Moseley, Albert Smith, Washington Hunt.

NEW JERSEY.—Lucius Q. C. Elmer, George Sykes, Isaac G. Farlee, Littleton Kirkpatrick, Wm. Wright.

PENNSYLVANIA.—Edward J. Morris, Joseph R. Ingersoll, John T. Smith, Charles J. Ingersoll, Jacob S. Yost, Michael H. Jenks, Abrah. R. McIlvaine, Henry Nes, James Black, James Irvin, Andrew Stewart, Henry D. Foster, Jeremiah Brown, John Ritter, Rich. Brodhead, jr., Benj. A. Bidlack, Almond H. Read, Henry Frick, Alexander Ramsey, John Dickey, William Wilkins, Samuel Hays, Charles M. Read, Joseph Buffington.

DELAWARE.—George B. Rodney.

MARYLAND.—J. M. S. Causin, F. Brengle, J. Withered, J. P. Kennedy, Dr. Preston, Thomas A. Spence.

VIRGINIA.—Archibald Atkinson, Geo. C. Dromgoole, Walter Coles, Edmund Hubard, Thomas W. Gilmer, John W. Jones, Henry A. Wise, Willoughby Newton, Samuel Chilton, William F. Lucas, William Taylor, A. A. Chapman, Geo. W. Hopkins, Geo. W. Summers, Lewis Steenrod.

NORTH CAROLINA.—Thomas J. Clingman, D. M. Barringer, David S. Reid, Edmund Deberry, R. M. Saunders, James J. McKay, J. R. Daniel, A. H. Arrington, Kenneth Rayner.

SOUTH CAROLINA.—James A. Black, Richard F. Simpson, Joseph A. Woodward, John Campbell, Artemas Burt, Isaac E. Holmes, R. Barnwell Rhett.

GEORGIA.—E. J. Black, H. A. Haralson, J. H. Lumpkin, Howell Cobb, Wm. H. Stiles, Alexander H. Stevens, A. H. Chappell.

KENTUCKY.—Linn Boyd, Willis Green, Henry Grider, George A. Caldwell, James Stone, John White, William P. Thompson, Garrett Davis, Richard French, J. W. Tibbatts.

TENNESSEE.—Andrew Johnson, William T. Senter, Julius W. Blackwell, Alvan Cullom, George W. Jones, Aaron V. Brown, David W. Dickinson, James H. Peyton, Cave Johnson, John B. Ashe, Milton Brown.

OHIO.—Alexander Duncan, John B. Weller, Robt. C. Schenck, Joseph Vance, Emery D. Potter, Joseph J. McDowell, John I. Vanmeter, Elias Florence, Heman A. Moore, Jacob Brinkerhoff, Samuel F. Vinton, Perley B. Johnson, Alexander Harper, Joseph Morris, James Mathews, Wm. C. McCauslin, Ezra Dean, Daniel R. Tilden, Joshua R. Giddings, H. R. Brinkerhoff.

LOUISIANA.—John Slidell, Alcée Labranche, John B. Dawson, P. E. Bossier.

INDIANA.—Robt. Dale Owen, Thomas J. Henley, Thomas Smith, Caleb B. Smith, Wm. J. Brown, John W. Davis, Joseph A. Wright, John Pettit, Samuel C. Sample, Andrew Kennedy.

ILLINOIS.—Robert Smith, John A. McClernand, Orlando B. Ficklin, John Wentworth, Stephen A. Douglass, Joseph P. Hoge, J. J. Hardin.

ALABAMA.—James Dellet, James E. Belser, Dixon H. Lewis, William W. Payne, George S. Houston, Reuben Chapman, Felix McConnell.

MISSISSIPPI.—Wm. H. Hammett, Robert W. Roberts, Jacob Thompson, Tilghman M. Tucker.

MISSOURI.—James M. Hughes, James H. Relfe, Gustavus B. Bower, James B. Bowlin, John Jameson.

[5665]ARKANSAS.—Edward Cross.

MICHIGAN.—Robert McClelland, Lucius Lyon, James B. Hunt.

Territorial Delegates.

FLORIDA.—David Levy.

WISCONSIN.—Henry Dodge.

IOWA.—Augustus C. Dodge.

The election of Speaker was the first business on the assembling of the Congress, and its result was the authentic exposition of the state of parties. Mr. John W. Jones, of Virginia, the democratic candidate, received 128 votes on the first ballot, and was elected—the whig candidate (Mr. John White, late Speaker) receiving 59. An adverse majority of more than two to one was the result to the whig party at the first election after the extra session of 1841—at the first election after that "log-cabin, hard-cider and coon-skin" campaign in which the whigs had carried the presidential election by 234 electoral votes against 60: so truly had the democratic senators foreseen the destruction of the party in the contests of the extra session of 1841. The Tyler party was "no where"—Mr. Wise alone being classified as such—the rest, so few in number as to have been called the "corporal's guard," had been left out of Congress by their constituents, or had received office from Mr. Tyler, and gone off. Mr. Caleb McNulty, of Ohio, also democratic, was elected clerk of the House, and by a vote of two to one, thus ousting an experienced and capable whig officer, in the person of Mr. Matthew St. Clair Clarke—a change which turned out to be unfortunate for the friends of the House, and mortifying to those who did it—the new clerk becoming a subject of indictment for embezzlement before his service was over.

CHAPTER CXXVII.

MR. TYLER'S SECOND ANNUAL MESSAGE.

The prominent topics of the message were the state of our affairs with Great Britain and Mexico—with the former in relation to Oregon, the latter in relation to Texas. In the same breath in which the President announced the happy results of the Ashburton treaty, he was forced to go on and show the improvidence of that treaty on our part, in not exacting a settlement of the questions which concerned the interests of the United States, while settling those which lay near to the interests of Great Britain. The Oregon territorial boundary was one of these omitted American subjects; but though passed over by the government in the negotiations, it was forced upon its attention by the people. A stream of emigration was pouring into that territory, and their presence on the banks of the Columbia caused the attention of both governments to be drawn to the question of titles and boundaries; and Mr. Tyler introduced it accordingly to Congress.

"A question of much importance still remains to be adjusted between them. The territorial limits of the two countries in relation to what is commonly known as the Oregon Territory, still remains in dispute. The United States would be at all times indisposed to aggrandize themselves at the expense of any other nation; but while they would be restrained by principles of honor, which should govern the conduct of nations as well as that of individuals, from setting up a demand for territory which does not belong to them, they would as unwillingly consent to a surrender of their rights. After the most rigid, and, as far as practicable, unbiassed examination of the subject, the United States have always contended that their rights appertain to the entire region of country lying on the Pacific, and embraced within 42° and 54° 40' of north latitude. This claim being controverted by Great Britain, those who have preceded the present Executive—actuated, no doubt, by an earnest desire to adjust the matter upon terms mutually satisfactory to both countries—have caused to be submitted to the British Government propositions for settlement and final adjustment, which, however, have not proved heretofore acceptable to it. Our Minister at London has, under instructions, again brought the subject to the consideration of that Government; and while nothing will be done to compromit the rights or honor of the United States, every proper expedient will be resorted to, in order to bring the negotiation now in the progress of resumption to a speedy and happy termination."

This passage, while letting it be seen that we were already engaged in a serious controversy with Great Britain—engaged in it almost before the ink was dry which had celebrated the peace mission which was to settle all questions—also committed a serious mistake in point of fact, and which being taken up as a party watchword, became a difficult and delicate point of management at home: it was the line of 54 degrees 40 minutes north for our northern boundary on the Pacific. The message says that the United States have always contended for that line. That is an error. From the beginning of the dispute, the United States government had proposed the parallel of 49 degrees, as being the continuation of the dividing line on this side of the Rocky Mountains, and governed by the same law—the decision of the commissaries appointed by the British and French under the tenth article of the treaty of Utrecht to establish boundaries between them on the continent of North America. President Jefferson offered that line in 1807—which was immediately after the return of Messrs. Lewis and Clark from their meritorious expedition, and as soon as it was seen that a question of boundary was to arise in that quarter with Great Britain. President Monroe made the same offer in 1818, and also in 1824. Mr. Adams renewed it in 1826: so that, so far from having always claimed to 54-40, the United States had always offered the parallel of 49. As to 54-40, no American statesman had ever thought of originating a title there. It was a Russian point of demarcation on the coast and islands—not a continental line at all—first assigned to the Russian Fur Company by the Emperor Paul, and afterwards yielded to Russia by the United States and Great Britain, separately, in separating their respective claims on the north-west of America. She was allowed to come south to that point on the coast and islands, not penetrating the interior of the continent—leaving the rest for Great Britain and the United States to settle as they could. It was proposed at the time that the three powers should settle together—in a tripartite treaty: but the Emperor Alexander, like a wise man, contented himself with settling his own boundary, without mixing himself in the dispute between the United States and Great Britain. This he did about the year 1820: and it was long afterwards, and by those who knew but little of this establishment of a southern limit for the Russian Fur Company, that this point established in their charter, and afterwards agreed to by the United States and Great Britain, was taken up as the northern boundary for the United States. It was a great error in Mr. Tyler to put this Russian limit in his message for our line; and, being taken up by party spirit, and put into one of those mushroom political creeds, called "platforms" (wherewith this latter generation has been so plentifully cursed), it came near involving the United States in war.

The prospective war with Mexico on the subject of Texas was thus shadowed forth:

"I communicate herewith certain despatches received from our Minister at Mexico, and also a correspondence which has recently occurred between the envoy from that republic and the Secretary of State. It must be regarded as not a little extraordinary that the government of Mexico, in anticipation of a public discussion, which it has been pleased to infer, from newspaper publications, as likely to take place in Congress, relating to the annexation of Texas to the United States, should have so far anticipated the result of such discussion as to have announced its determination to visit any such anticipated decision by a formal declaration of war against the United States. If designed to prevent Congress from introducing that question as a fit subject for its calm deliberation and final judgment, the Executive has no reason to doubt that it will entirely fail of its object. The representatives of a brave and patriotic people will suffer no apprehension of future consequences to embarrass them in the course of their proposed deliberations. Nor will the Executive Department of the government fail, for any such cause, to discharge its whole duty to the country."

At the time of communicating this information to Congress, the President was far advanced in a treaty with Texas for her annexation to the United States—an event which would be war itself with Mexico, without any declaration on her part, or our part—she being then at war with Texas as a revolted province, and endeavoring to reclaim her to her former subjection. Still prepossessed with his idea of a national currency of paper money, in preference to gold and silver, the President recurs to his previous recommendation for an Exchequer bank—regrets its rejection by Congress,—vaunts its utility—and thinks that it would still aid, in a modified form, in restoring the currency to a sound and healthy state.

"In view of the disordered condition of the currency at the time, and the high rates of exchange between different parts of the country, I felt it to be incumbent on me to present to the consideration of your predecessors a proposition conflicting in no degree with the constitution or the rights of the States, and having the sanction—not in detail, but in principle—of some of the eminent men who had preceded me in the executive office. That proposition contemplated the issuing of treasury notes of denominations not less than five, nor more than one hundred dollars, to be employed in payment of the obligations of the government in lieu of gold and silver, at the option of the public creditor, and to an amount not exceeding $15,000,000. It was proposed to make them receivable every where, and to establish at various points depositories of gold and silver, to be held in trust for the redemption of such notes, so as to insure their convertibility into specie. No doubt was entertained that such notes would have maintained a par value with gold and silver—thus furnishing a paper currency of equal value over the Union, thereby meeting the just expectations of the people, and fulfilling the duties of a parental government. Whether the depositories should be permitted to sell or purchase bills under very limited restrictions, together with all its other details, was submitted to the wisdom of Congress, and was regarded as of secondary importance. I thought then, and think now, that such an arrangement would have been attended with the happiest results. The whole matter of the currency would have been placed where, by the constitution, it was designed to be placed—under the immediate supervision and control of Congress. The action of the government would have been independent of all corporations; and the same eye which rests unceasingly on the specie currency, and guards it against adulteration, would also have rested on the paper currency, to control and regulate its issues, and protect it against depreciation. Under all the responsibilities attached to the station which I occupy, and in redemption of a pledge given to the last Congress, at the close of its first session, I submitted the suggestion to its consideration at two consecutive sessions. The recommendation, however, met with no favor at its hands. While I am free to admit that the necessities of the times have since become greatly ameliorated, and that there is good reason to hope that the country is safely and rapidly emerging from the difficulties and embarrassments which every where surrounded it in 1841, yet I cannot but think that its restoration to a sound and healthy condition would be greatly expedited by a resort to the expedient in a modified form."

Such were still the sighings and longings of Mr. Tyler for a national currency of paper money. They were his valedictory to that delusive cheat. Before he had an opportunity to present another annual message, the Independent Treasury System, and the revived gold currency had done their office—had given ease and safety to the government finances, had restored prosperity and confidence to the community, and placed the country in a condition to dispense with all small money paper currency—all under twenty dollars—if it only had the wisdom to do so.

CHAPTER CXXVIII.

EXPLOSION OF THE GREAT GUN ON BOARD THE PRINCETON MAN-OF-WAR: THE KILLED AND WOUNDED.

On the morning of the 28th of February, a company of some hundred guests, invited by Commodore Stockton, including the President of the United States, his cabinet, members of both Houses of Congress, citizens and strangers, with a great number of ladies, headed by Mrs. Madison, ex-presidentess, repaired on board the steamer man-of-war Princeton, then lying in the river below the city, to witness the working of her machinery (a screw propeller), and to observe the fire of her two great guns—throwing balls of 225 pounds each. The vessel was the pride and pet of the commodore, and having undergone all the trials necessary to prove her machinery and her guns, was brought round to Washington for exhibition to the public authorities. The day was pleasant—the company numerous and gay. On the way down to the vessel a person whispered in my ear that Nicholas Biddle was dead. It was my first information of that event, and heard not without reflections on the instability and shadowy fleetingness of the pursuits and contests of this life. Mr. Biddle had been a Power in the State, and for years had baffled or balanced the power of the government. He had now vanished, and the news of his death came in a whisper, not announced in a tumult of voices; and those who had contended with him might see their own sudden and silent evanescence in his. It was a lesson upon human instability, and felt as such; but without a thought or presentiment that, before the sun should go down, many of that high and gay company should vanish from earth—and the one so seriously impressed barely fail to be of the number.

The vessel had proceeded down the river below the grave of Washington—below Mount Vernon—and was on her return, the machinery working beautifully, the guns firing well, and the exhibition of the day happily over. It was four-o'clock in the evening, and a sumptuous collation had refreshed and enlivened the guests. They were still at the table, when word was brought down that one of the guns was to be fired again; and immediately the company rose to go on deck and observe the fire—the long and vacant stretch in the river giving full room for the utmost range of the ball. The President and his cabinet went foremost, this writer among them, conversing with Mr. Gilmer, Secretary of the Navy. The President was called back: the others went on, and took their places on the left of the gun—pointing down the river. The commodore was with this group, which made a cluster near the gun, with a crowd behind, and many all around. I had continued my place by the side of Mr. Gilmer, and of course was in the front of the mass which crowded up to the gun. The lieutenant of the vessel, Mr. Hunt, came and whispered in my ear that I would see the range of the ball better from the breech; and proposed to change my place. It was a tribute to my business habits, being indebted for this attention to the interest which I had taken all day in the working of the ship, and the firing of her great guns. The lieutenant placed me on a carronade carriage, some six feet in the rear of the gun, and in the line of her range. Senator Phelps had stopped on my left, with a young lady of Maryland (Miss Sommerville) on his arm. I asked them to get on the carriage to my right (not choosing to lose my point of observation): which they did—the young lady between us, and supported by us both, with the usual civil phrases, that we would take care of her. The lieutenant caused the gun to be worked, to show the ease and precision with which her direction could be changed and then pointed down the river to make the fire—himself and the gunners standing near the breech on the right. I opened my mouth wide to receive the concussion on the inside as well as on the outside of the head and ears, so as to lessen the force of the external shock. I saw the hammer pulled back—heard a tap—saw a flash—felt a blast in the face, and knew that my hat was gone: and that was the last that I knew of the world, or of myself, for a time, of which I can give no account. The first that I knew of myself, or of any thing afterwards, was rising up at the breech of the gun, seeing the gun itself split open—two seamen, the blood oozing from their ears and nostrils, rising and reeling near me—Commodore Stockton, hat gone, and face blackened, standing bolt upright, staring fixedly upon the shattered gun. I had heard no noise— no more than the dead. I only knew that the gun had bursted from seeing its fragments. I felt no injury, and put my arm under the head of a seaman, endeavoring to rise, and falling back. By that time friends had ran up, and led me to the bow—telling me afterwards that there was a supernatural whiteness in the face and hands— all the blood in fact having been driven from the surface. I saw none of the killed: they had been removed before consciousness returned. All that were on the left had been killed, the gun bursting on that side, and throwing a large fragment, some tons weight, on the cluster from which I had been removed, crushing the front rank with its force and weight. Mr. Upshur, Secretary of State; Mr. Gilmer, Secretary of the Navy; Commodore Kennon, of the navy; Mr. Virgil Maxey, late United States chargé at the Hague; Mr. Gardiner of New York, father-in-law that would have been to Mr. Tyler—were the dead. Eleven seamen were injured—two mortally. Commodore Stockton was scorched by the burning powder, and stunned by the concussion; but not further injured. I had the tympanum of the left ear bursted through, the warm air from the lungs issuing from it at every breathing. Senator Phelps and the young lady on my right, had fallen inwards towards the gun, but got up without injury. We all three had fallen inwards, as into a vacuum. The President's servant who was next me on the left was killed. Twenty feet of the vessels bulwark immediately behind me was blown away. Several of the killed had members of their family on board—to be deluded for a little while, by the care of friends, with the belief that those so dear to them were only hurt. Several were prevented from being in the crushed cluster by the merest accidents—Mr. Tyler being called back—Mr. Seaton not finding his hat in time—myself taken out of it the moment before the catastrophe. Fortunately there were physicians on board to do what was right for the injured, and to prevent blood-letting, so ready to be called for by the uninformed, and so fatal when the powers of life were all on the retreat. Gloomily and sad the gay company of the morning returned to the city, and the calamitous intelligence flew over the land. For myself, I had gone through the experience of a sudden death, as if from lightning, which extinguishes knowledge and sensation, and takes one out of the world without thought or feeling. I think I know what it is to die without knowing it—and that such a death is nothing to him that revives. The rapid and lucid working of the mind to the instant of extinction, is the marvel that still astonishes me. I heard the tap—saw the flash—felt the blast—and knew nothing of the explosion. I was cut off in that inappreciable point of time which intervened between the flash and the fire—between the burning of the powder in the touch-hole, and the burning of it in the barrel of the gun. No mind can seize that point of time—no thought can measure it; yet to me it was distinctly marked, divided life from death—the life that sees, and feels, and knows—from death (for such it was for the time), which annihilates self and the world. And now is credible to me, or rather comprehensible, what persons have told me of the rapid and clear working of the mind in sudden and dreadful catastrophes—as in steamboat explosions, and being blown into the air, and have the events of their lives pass in review before them, and even speculate upon the chances of falling on the deck, and being crushed, or falling on the water and swimming: and persons recovered from drowning, and running their whole lives over in the interval between losing hope and losing consciousness.

CHAPTER CXXIX.

RECONSTRUCTION OF MR. TYLER'S CABINET.

This was the second event of the kind during the administration of Mr. Tyler—the first induced by the resignation of *Messrs*. Ewing, Crittenden, Bell, and Badger, in 1841; the second, by the deaths of *Messrs*. Upshur and Gilmer by the explosion of the Princeton gun. Mr. Calhoun was appointed Secretary of State; John C. Spencer of New York, Secretary of the Treasury; William Wilkins of Pennsylvania, Secretary at War; John Y. Mason, of Virginia, Secretary of the Navy; Charles A. Wickliffe, of Kentucky, Postmaster General; John Nelson, of Maryland, Attorney General. The resignation of Mr. Spencer in a short time made a vacancy in the Treasury, which was filled by the appointment of George M. Bibb, of Kentucky.

CHAPTER CXXX.

DEATH OF SENATOR PORTER, OF LOUISIANA: EULOGIUM OF MR. BENTON.

MR BENTON. I rise to second the motion which has been made to render the last honors of this chamber to our deceased brother senator, whose death has been so feelingly announced; and in doing so, I comply with an obligation of friendship, as well as conform to the usage of the Senate. I am the oldest personal friend which the illustrious deceased could have upon this floor, and amongst the oldest which he could have in the United States. It is now, sir, more than the period of a generation—more than the third of a century—since the then emigrant Irish boy, Alexander Porter, and myself, met on the banks of the Cumberland River, at Nashville, in the State of Tennessee; when commenced a friendship which death only dissolved on his part. We belonged to a circle of young lawyers and students at law, who had the world before them, and nothing but their exertions to depend upon. First a clerk in his uncle's store, then a student at law, and always a lover of books, the young Porter was one of that circle, and it was the custom of all that belonged to it to spend their leisure hours in the delightful occupation of reading. History, poetry, elocution, biography, the ennobling speeches of the living and the dead, were our social recreation; and the youngest member of the circle was one of our favorite readers. He read well, because he comprehended clearly, felt strongly, remarked beautifully upon striking passages, and gave a new charm to the whole with his rich, mellifluous Irish accent. It was then that I became acquainted with Ireland and her children, read the ample story of her wrongs, learnt the long list of her martyred patriots' names, sympathized in their fate, and imbibed the feelings for a noble and oppressed people which the extinction of my own life can alone extinguish.

Time and events dispersed that circle. The young Porter, his law license signed, went to the Lower Mississippi; I to the Upper. And, years afterwards, we met on this floor, senators from different parts of that vast Louisiana which was not even a part of the American Union at the time that he and I were born. We met here in the session of 1833-'34—high party times, and on opposite sides of the great party line; but we met as we had parted years before. We met as friends; and, though often our part to reply to each other in the ardent debate, yet never did we do it with other feelings than those with which we were wont to discuss our subjects of recreation on the banks of the Cumberland.

I mention these circumstances, Mr. President, because, while they are honorable to the deceased, they are also justificatory to myself for appearing as the second to the motion which has been made. A personal friendship of almost forty years gives me a right to appear as a friend to the deceased on this occasion, and to perform the office which the rules and the usage of the Senate permit, and which so many other senators would so cordially and so faithfully perform.

In performing this office, I have, literally, but little less to do but to second the motion of the senator from Louisiana (Mr. Barrow). The mover has done ample justice to his great subject. He also had the advantage of long acquaintance and intimate personal friendship with the deceased. He also knew him on the banks of the Cumberland, though too young to belong to the circle of young lawyers and law students, of which the junior member—the young Alexander Porter—was the chief ornament and delight. But he knew him—long and intimately—and has given evidence of that knowledge in the just, the feeling, the cordial, and impressive eulogium which he has just delivered on the life and character of his deceased friend and colleague. He has presented to you the matured *man*, as developed in his ripe and meridian age: he has presented to you the finished scholar—the eminent lawyer—the profound judge—the distinguished senator—the firm patriot—the constant friend—the honorable man—the brilliant converser—the social, cheerful, witty companion. He has presented to you the ripe fruit, of which I saw the early blossom, and of which I felt the assurance more than thirty years ago, that it would ripen into the golden fruit which we have all beheld.

Mr. President, this is no vain or empty ceremonial in which the Senate is now engaged. Honors to the illustrious dead go beyond the discharge of a debt of justice to them, and the rendition of consolation to their friends: they become lessons and examples for the living. The story of their humble beginning and noble conclusion, is an example to be followed, and an excitement to be felt. And where shall we find an example more worthy of imitation, or more full of encouragement, than in the life and character of Alexander Porter?—a lad of tender age—an orphan with a widowed mother and younger children—the father martyred in the cause of freedom—an exile before he was ten years old—an ocean to be crossed, and a strange land to be seen, and a wilderness of a thousand miles to be penetrated before he could find a resting-place for the sole of his foot: then education to be acquired, support to be earned, and even citizenship to be gained, before he could make his own talents available to his support: conquering all these difficulties by his own exertions, and the aid of an affectionate uncle—(I will name him, for the benefactor of youth deserves to be named, and named with honor in the highest places)—with no other aid but that of an uncle's kindness, Mr. Alexander Porter, sen., merchant of Nashville, also an emigrant from Ireland, and full of the generous qualities which belong to the children of that soil: this lad, an exile and an orphan from the Old World, thus starting in the New World, with every thing to gain before it could be enjoyed, soon attained every earthly object, either brilliant or substantial, for which we live and struggle in this life—honors, fortune, friends; the highest professional and political distinction; long a supreme judge in his adopted State; twice a senator in the Congress of the United States—wearing all his honors fresh and glowing to the last moment of his life—and the announcement of his death followed by the adjournment of the two Houses of the American Congress! What a noble and crowning conclusion to a beginning so humble, and so apparently hopeless! Honors to such a life—the honors which we now pay to the memory of Senator Porter—are not mere offerings to the dead, or mere consolations to the feelings of surviving friends and relations; they go further, and become incentives and inducements to the ingenuous youth of the present and succeeding generations, encouraging their hopes, and firing their spirits with a generous emulation.

Nor do the benefits of these honors stop with individuals, nor even with masses, or generations of men. They are not confined to *persons*, but rise to *institutions*—to the noble republican institutions under which such things can be! Republican government itself—that government which holds man together in the proud state of equality and liberty—this government is benefited by the exhibition of the examples such as we now celebrate, and by the rendition of the honors such as we now pay. Our deceased brother senator has honored and benefited our free republican institutions by the manner in which he has advanced himself under them; and we make manifest that benefit by the honors which we pay him. He has given a practical illustration of the working of our free, and equal, and elective form of government; and our honors proclaim the nature of that working. What is done in this chamber is not done in a corner, but on a lofty eminence, seen of all people. Europe, as well as America, will see how our form of government has worked in the person of an orphan exiled boy, seeking refuge in the land which gives to virtue and talent all that they will ever ask—the free use of their own exertions for their own advancement.

Our deceased brother was not an American citizen by accident of birth; he became so by the choice of his own will, and by the operation of our laws. The events of his life, and the business of this day, shows this title to citizenship to be as valid in our America as it was in the great republic of antiquity. I borrow the thought, not the language of Cicero, in his pleading for the poet Archias, when I place the citizen who becomes so by law and choice on an equal footing with the citizen who becomes so by chance. And, in the instance before us, we may say that our adopted citizen has repaid us for the liberality of our laws; that he has added to the stock of our national character by the contributions which he has brought to it in the purity of his private life, the eminence of his public services, the ardor of his patriotism, and the elegant productions of his mind.

And here let me say—and I say it with pride and satisfaction—our deceased brother senator loved and admired his adopted country, with a love and admiration increasing with his age, and with his better knowledge of the countries of the Old World. A few years ago, and after he had obtained great honor and fortune in this country, he returned on a visit to his native land, and to the continent of Europe. It was an occasion of honest exultation for the orphan emigrant boy to return to the land of his fathers, rich in the goods of this life, and clothed with the honors of the American Senate. But the visit was a melancholy one to him. His soul sickened at the state of his fellow man in the Old World (I had it from his own lips), and he returned from that visit with stronger feelings than ever in favor of his adopted country. New honor awaited him here—that of a second election to the American Senate. But of this he was not permitted to taste; and the proceedings of this day announce his second brief elevation to this body, and his departure from it through the gloomy portals of death, and the radiant temple of enduring fame.

CHAPTER CXXXI.

NAVAL ACADEMY, AND NAVAL POLICY OF THE UNITED STATES.

By scraps of laws, regulations, and departmental instructions, a Naval Academy has grown up, and a naval policy become established for the United States, without the legislative wisdom of the country having passed upon that policy, and contrary to its previous policy, and against its interest and welfare. A Naval Academy, with 250 pupils, and annually coming off in scores, makes perpetual demand for ships and commissions; and these must be furnished, whether required by the public service or not; and thus the idea of a limited navy, or of a naval peace establishment, is extinguished; and a perpetual war establishment in time of peace is growing up upon our hands. Prone to imitate every thing that was English, there was a party among us from the beginning which wished to make the Union, like Great Britain, a great naval power, without considering that England was an island, with foreign possessions; which made a navy a necessity of her position and her policy, while we were a continent, without foreign possessions, to whom a navy would be an expensive and idle encumbrance; without considering that England is often by her policy required to be aggressive, the United States never; without considering that England is a part of the European system, and subject to wars (to her always maritime) in which she has no interest, while the United States, in the isolation of their geographical position, and the independence of their policy, can have no wars but her own; and those defensive. On the other hand, there was a large party, and dominant after the presidential election of 1800, which saw great evil in emulating Great Britain as a naval power, and made head against that emulation in all the modes of acting on the public mind: speeches and votes in Congress, essays, legislative declarations. The most authoritative, and best considered declaration of the principles of this party, was made some fifty years ago, in the General Assembly of Virginia, in the era of her greatest men; and when the minds of these men, themselves fathers of the State, was most profoundly turned to the nature, policy, and working of our government. All have heard of the Virginia resolutions of 1798-'99, to restrain the unconstitutional and unwise action of the federal government: there were certain other cotemporaneous resolutions from the same source in relation to a navy, of which but little has been known; and which, for forty years, and now, are of more practical importance than the former. In the session of her legislature, 1799-1800, in their "Instructions to Senators," that General Assembly said:

> "With respect to the navy, it may be proper to remind you, that whatever may be the proposed object of its establishment, or whatever may be the prospect of temporary advantages resulting therefrom, it is demonstrated by the experience of all nations, which have ventured far into naval policy, that such prospect is ultimately delusive; and that a navy has ever, in practice, been known more as an instrument of power, a source of expense, and an occasion of collisions and of wars with other nations, than as an instrument of defence, of economy, or of protection to commerce. Nor is there any nation, in the judgment of this General Assembly, to whose circumstances these remarks are more applicable than to the United States."

Such was the voice of the great men of Virginia, some fifty years ago—the voice of reason and judgment then; and more just, judicious, and applicable, now, than then. Since that time the electro-magnetic telegraph, and the steam-car, have been invented—realizing for defensive war, the idea of the whole art of war, as conceived and expressed by the greatest of generals—DIFFUSION FOR SUBSISTENCE: CONCENTRATION FOR ACTION. That was the language of the Great Emperor: and none but himself could have so conceived and expressed that idea. And now the ordinary commander can practise that whole art of war, and without ever having read a book upon war. He would know what to have done, and the country would do it. Play the telegraph at the approach of an invader, and summon the volunteer citizens to meet him at the water's edge. They would be found at home, diffused for subsistence: they would concentrate for action, and at the rate of 500 miles a day, or more if need be. In two days they would come from the Mississippi to the Atlantic. It would be the mere business of the accumulation of masses upon a given point, augmenting continually, and attacking incessantly. Grand tactics, and the "nineteen manœuvres," would be unheard of: plain and direct killing would be the only work. No amount of invading force could sustain itself a fortnight on any part of our coast. If hundreds of thousands were not enough to cut them up, millions would come—arms, munitions, provisions, arriving at the same time. With this defence—cheap, ready, omnipotent—who, outside of an insane hospital, would think of building and keeping up eternal fleets to meet the invader and fight him at sea? The idea would be senseless, if practicable; but it would be impracticable. There will never be another naval action fought for the command of the seas. There has been none such fought since the French and British fleets met off Ouessant, in 1793. That is the last instance of a naval action fought upon consent: all the rest have been mere catching and whipping: and there will never be another. Fleets must approach equality before they can fight; and with her five hundred men-of-war on hand, Great Britain is too far ahead to be overtaken by any nation, even if any one was senseless enough to incur her debt and taxes for the purpose. Look at Russia: building ships from the time of Peter the Great; and the first day they were wanted, all useless and a burden! only to be saved by the strongest fortifications in the world, filled with the strongest armies of the world! and all burnt, or sunk, that could not be so protected. Great Britain is compelled by the necessities of her position, to keep up great fleets: the only way to make head against them is to avoid swelling their numbers with the fleets of other nations—avoid the Trafalgars, Aboukirs, Copenhagens, St. Vincents—and prey upon her with cruisers and privateers. It is the profound observation of Alison, the English historian of the wars of the French revolution that the American cruisers did the British more mischief in their two years' war of 1812, than all the fleets of France did during their twenty years' war. What a blessing to our country, if American statesmen could only learn that one little sentence in Alison.

The war of 1812 taught American statesmen a great lesson; but they read it backwards, and understood it the reverse of its teaching. It taught the efficacy of cruising—the inefficacy of fleets. American cruisers, and privateers, did immense mischief to British commerce and shipping: British fleets did no mischief to America. Their cruisers did some mischief—their fleets none. And that is the way to read the lesson taught by the naval operations of the war of 1812. Cruisers, to be built when they are needed for use: not fleets to rot down in peace, while waiting for war. Yet, for forty years we have been building great ships—frigates equal to ships of the line: liners, nearly double the old size—120 guns instead of seventy-fours. Eleven of these great liners have been built, merely to rot! at enormous cost in the building, and great continual cost to delay the rotting; which, nevertheless, goes on with the regularity and certainty of time. A judicious administrative economy would have them all broken up (to say nothing of others), and the serviceable parts all preserved, to be built into smaller vessels when there shall be need for them. It is forty years since this system of building vessels for which there was no use, took its commencement, and the cry for more is greater now than it was in the beginning; and must continue. A history of each ship built in that time—what the building cost? what the repairs? what the alterations? what the equipment? what the crew? and how many shot she fired at an enemy? would be a history which ought to be instructive; for it would show an incredible amount of money as effectually wasted as if it had been thrown into the sea. Great as this building and rotting has been for forty years past, it must continue to become greater. The Naval Academy is a fruitful mother, bearing 250 embryo officers in her womb at a time, and all the time; and most of them powerfully connected: and they must have ships and commissions, when they leave the mother's breast. They are the children of the country, and must be provided for—they and their children after them. This academy commits the government to a great navy, as the Military Academy commits it to a great army. It is no longer the wants of the country, but of the *eleves* of the institution which must be provided for; and routine officers are to take all the places. Officers are now to be made in schools, whether they have any vocation for the profession or not; and slender is the chance of the government to get one that would ever have gained a commission by his own exertions. This writer was not a senator for thirty years, and the channel of incessant applications for cadet and midshipman places, without knowing the motives on which such applications were made; and these motives may be found in three classes. First, and most honorable would be the case of a father, who would say—"I have a son, a bright boy, that I have been educating for a profession, but his soul is on fire for the army, or navy, and I have yielded to his wishes, though against my own, and believe if he gets the place, that he will not dishonor his country's flag." One of the next class would say—"I have a son, and he is not a bright boy (meaning that he is a booby), and cannot take a profession, but he would do very well in the army or navy." Of the third class, an unhappy father would say—"I have a son, a smart boy, but wild (meaning he was vicious), and I want to get him in the army or navy, where he could be disciplined." These, and the hereditary class (those whose fathers and grandfathers have been in the service) are the descriptions of applicants for these appointments; so that, it may be seen, the chances are three or four to one against getting a suitable subject for an officer; and of those who are suitable, many resign soon after they have got educated at public expense, and go into civil life. Routine officers are, therefore, what may be expected from these schools—officers whom nature has not licensed, and who keep out of the service those whom she has. The finest naval officers that the world ever saw, were bred in the merchant service; and of that England, Holland, France, Genoa, and Venice, are proofs; and none more so than our own country. The world never saw a larger proportion of able commanders than our little navy of the Revolution, and of the Algerine and Tripolitan wars, and the war of 1812, produced. They all came (but few exceptions) from the merchant service; and showed an ability and zeal which no school-house officers will ever equal.

Great Britain keeps up squadrons in time of peace, and which is a necessity of her insular position, and of her remote possessions: we must have squadrons also, though no use for them abroad, and infinitely better to remain in our own ports, and spend the millions at home which are now spent abroad. There is not a sea in which our commerce is subject to any danger of a kind which a man-of-war would prevent, or punish, in which a cruiser would not be sufficient. All our squadrons are anomalies, and the squadron system should be broken up. The Home should never have existed, and owes its origin to the least commendable period of our existence; the same of the African, conceived at the same time, put upon us by treaty, under the insidious clause that we could get rid of it in five years, and which has already continued near three times five; and which timidity and conservatism will combine to perpetuate—that timidity which is the child of temporization, and sees danger in every change. As for the Mediterranean, the Brazil, the Pacific, the East India squadron, they are mere British imitations without a reason for the copy, and a pretext for saying the ships are at sea. The fact is, they are in comfortable stations, doing nothing, and had far better be at home, and in ordinary. One hundred and forty court-martials, many dismissions without courts, and two hundred eliminations at a single dash, proclaim the fact that our navy is idle! and that this idleness gives rise to dissipation, to dissensions, to insubordination, to quarrels, to accusations, to court-martials. The body of naval officers are as good as any other citizens, but idleness is a destroyer which no body of men can stand. We have no use for a navy, and never shall have; yet we continue building ships and breeding officers—the ships to rot—the officers to become "the cankers of a calm world and a long peace."

The Virginia resolves of 1799-1800 on the subject of a navy, contain the right doctrine for the United States, even if the state of the world had remained what it was—even if the telegraph and the steam-car had not introduced a new era in the art of defensive war. It is the most expensive and inefficient of all modes of warfare. Its cost is enormous: its results nothing. A naval victory decides nothing but which shall have the other's ships.

In the twenty years of the wars of the French revolution, Great Britain whipped all the inimical fleets she could catch. She got all their ships; and nothing but their ships. Not one of her naval victories had the least effect upon the fate of the wars: land battles alone decided the fate of countries, and commanded the issues of peace or war. Concluding no war, they are one of the fruitful sources of beginning wars. Only employed (by those who possess them) at long intervals, they must be kept up the whole time. Enormously expensive, the expense is eternal. Armies can be disbanded—navies must be kept up. Long lists of officers must be receiving pay when doing nothing. Pensions are inseparable from the system. Going to sea in time of peace is nothing but visiting foreign countries at the expense of the government. The annual expense of our navy now (all the heads of expense incident to the establishment included) is some fifteen millions of dollars: the number of men employed, is some 10,000—being at a cost of $1,500 a man, and they nothing to do. The whole number of guns afloat is some 2,000—which is at the rate of some $9,000 a gun; and they nothing in the world to shoot at. The expense of a navy is enormous. The protection of commerce is a phrase incessantly repeated, and of no application. Commerce wants no protection from men-of-war except against piratical nations; and they are fewer now than they were fifty years ago; and some cruisers were then sufficient. The Mediterranean, which was then the great seat of piracy, is now as free from it as the Chesapeake Bay is. We have no naval policy— no system adapted by the legislative wisdom—no peace establishment—no understood principle of action in relation to a navy. All goes by fits and starts. A rumor of war is started: more ships are demanded: a combined interest supports the demand—officers, contractors, politicians. The war does not come, but the ships are built, and rot: and so on in a circle without end.

CHAPTER CXXXII.

THE HOME SQUADRON: ITS INUTILITY AND EXPENSE.

Early in the session of '43-'44, Mr. Hale, of New Hampshire, brought into the House a resolution of inquiry into the origin, use, and expense of the home squadron: to which Mr. Hamlin, of Maine, proposed the further inquiry to know what service that squadron had performed since it had been created. In support of his proposition, Mr. Hale said:

"He believed they were indebted to this administration for the home squadron. The whole sixteen vessels which composed that squadron were said to be necessary to protect the coasting trade; and though the portion of the country from which he came was deeply concerned in the coasting trade, yet he himself was convinced that many of those vessels might be dispensed with. If this information were laid before the House, they would have something tangible on which to lay their hands, in the way of retrenchment and reform. He wanted this information for the purpose of pointing out to the House where an enormous expense might be cut down, without endangering any of the interests of the country. Gentlemen had talked about being prepared with a sufficient navy to meet and contend with the naval power of Great Britain; but had they any idea of the outlay which was required to support such a navy? The expense of the navy of Great Britain amounted to between eighty and a hundred millions of dollars annually. We were not in want of such a great naval establishment to make ourselves respected at home or abroad. General Jackson alone had produced an impression upon one of the oldest nations of Europe, which it would be impossible for this administration to do with the assistance of all the navies in the world."

Mr. Jared Ingersoll was in favor of retrenchment and economy, but thought the process ought to begin in the civil and diplomatic department—in the Congress itself, and in the expenses it allowed for multiplied missions abroad and incessant changes in the incumbents. With respect to abuses in the naval expenditures, he said:—

"He had no knowledge of his own on this subject; but he had learned from a distinguished officer of the navy, that in the navy-yards, in the equipment of ships, by the waste and extravagance caused by allowing officers to rebuild ships when they pleased, and the loss on the provisions of ships just returned from sea, which have been taken or thrown away, the greatest abuses have been practised, which have assisted in swelling up the naval expenditures to their present enormous amount."

Mr. Adams differed from Mr. Ingersoll in the scheme of beginning retrenchment on the civil list, and presented the army and the navy as the two great objects of wasteful expenditure, and the points at which reform ought to begin, and especially with retrenching this home squadron, for which he had voted in 1841, but now condemned. He said:

"The gentleman gave the House, undoubtedly, a great deal of instruction as to the manner in which it should carry out retrenchment and reform, and finally elect a President; but his remarks did not happen to apply to the motion of the gentleman from New Hampshire; for he led them away from that motion, and told them, in substance, that it was not the nine million of dollars asked for by the Secretary of the Navy—and he did not know how much asked for the army—that was to be retrenched. Oh, no! The army and the navy were not the great expenses of this nation; it was not by curtailing the military and naval expenditures that economy was to be obtained; but by beginning with the two Houses of Congress. And what was the comparison, to come to dollars and cents, between the expenses of that House and the Navy Department? Why, the gentleman, with all his exaggerating eloquence, had made the executive, legislative, and judicial powers of the country, to cost at least two millions of dollars; while the estimates for the navy were nine millions, to enable our ships to go abroad and display the stripes and stars. And for what purpose was it necessary to have this home squadron? Was the great maritime power of the earth in such a position towards us as to authorize us to expect a hostile British squadron on our coasts? No; he believed not. Then what was this nine millions of dollars wanted for? There was a statement, two years ago, in the report of the Secretary of the Navy, in which they were told that our present navy, in comparison with that of Great Britain, was only as one to eight—that is, that the British navy was eight times as large as ours. Now, in that year eight millions of dollars was asked for for the navy; the report of the present year asks for nine millions. This report contained the principle that we must go on to increase our navy until it is at least one-half as large as that of Great Britain; and what, then, was the proportion of additional expense we must incur to arrive at that result? Why, four times eight are thirty-two; so that it will take an annual expenditure of thirty-two millions to give us a navy half as large as that of Great Britain. If, however, gentlemen were to go on in this way, $32,000,000—nay, $50,000,000 would not be enough to pay the expense of their navy. He expressed his approval of the resolution of the gentleman from New Hampshire, and his gratification that it had come from such a quarter— a quarter which was so deeply interested in having a due protection for their mercantile navy and their coasting trade, by the establishment of a home squadron. At the time the home squadron was first proposed, he was, himself, in favor of it, and it was adopted with but very little opposition; and the reason was, because the House did not understand it at that time. It looked to a war with Great Britain. It looked more particularly to a war with Great Britain (the honorable gentleman was understood to say), provided she took the island of Cuba. He saw no necessity for a large navy, unless it was to insult other nations, by taking possession of their territory in time of peace. What was the good, he asked, of a navy which cost the country $9,000,000 a year, compared with what was done there in the legislative department of the nation? He expressed his ardent hope that the gentleman from Tennessee [Mr. Cave Johnson], and the gentleman from North Carolina [Mr. McKay]—now the chairman of the Committee of Ways and Means—would persevere in the same spirit that marked their conduct during the last Congress, and still advocate reductions in the army and the navy."

Mr. Hale replied to the several gentlemen who, without offering a word in favor of the utility of this domestic squadron, were endeavoring to keep it up; and who, without denying the great abuse and extravagance in the naval disbursements, were endeavoring to prevent their correction by starting smaller game—and that smaller game not to be pursued, and bagged, but merely started to prevent the pursuit of the great monster which was ravaging the fields. Thus:—

"He believed that the greatest abuses existed in every department of the government, and that the extravagances of all required correction. Look at the army of 8,000 men only, kept up at an expense to the nation of $1,000 for each man. Was not this a crying abuse that ought to be corrected? Why, if the proposition had succeeded to increase the army to 20,000 men, the expenditure at this rate would have been twenty millions annually. If any gentleman knew of the existence of abuses, let him bring them to the notice of the House, and he would vote not only for the proper inquiry into them, but to apply the remedy. In regard to this home squadron, he begged leave to disclaim any of the suspicions entertained by the gentleman from Massachusetts. In offering his resolution he had no reference to Cuba, or any thing else suggested by the gentleman. He wanted the House and the country to look at it as the Secretary of the Navy presented it to their view. As to the pretence that it was intended for the protection of the coasting trade, it was a most idle one. He wished the gentlemen from Maine (the State most largely interested in that trade) to say whether they needed any such protection. He would answer for them, and say that they did not. He himself lived among those who were extensively engaged in the coasting trade, and part of his property was invested in it. He could, therefore, speak with some knowledge on the subject; and he hesitated not to say, that the idea of keeping up this squadron for its protection was a most preposterous and idle one. Sir, said he, the navy has been the pet child of the nation, and, like all other pet children, has run away with the whole patrimonial estate. If it were found that the best interest of the country required the maintenance of the home squadron, then he would go for it; but if it were found to be utterly useless, as he believed, then he was decidedly against it. But he would give this further notice; that he did not mean to stop here; that when the appropriations should come up, he intended to propose to limit those appropriations to a sum sufficient only to support the squadron stationed in the Mediterranean. It was entirely useless for this country to endeavor to contend with monarchies in keeping up the pageantry of a naval establishment."

The proposed inquiry produced no result, only ending in demonstrating what was well known to the older members, namely, the difficulty, and almost impossibility of introducing any reform, or economy into the administration of any department of the government unless the Executive takes the lead. And of this truth a striking instance occurred at this session and upon this subject. The executive government, that is to say, the President and his Secretary of the Navy had made a lawless expenditure of about $700,000 during the recess of Congress; and Congress under a moral duress, was compelled to adopt that expenditure as its own, and make it good. When the clause in the naval appropriation bill for covering this item, was under consideration, Mr. Ezra Dean, of Ohio, stood up and said:

"It was nothing less than a bill making appropriations to the amount of $750,000 which had been expended by the department in virtue of its own will and pleasure, and without the sanction of any law whatever; and the House was called on to approve this proceeding. He had supposed that any department which took upon itself the power of expending the public money, without authority of law, would have been subjected to the severest rebuke of Congress. He had supposed that this would have been a reform Congress, and that all the abuses of this administration would be ferreted out and corrected; but in this he had been grievously disappointed. He had endeavored to get the consent of the House to take up the navy retrenchment bill, which would correct all these abuses, but he had been mistaken; and so far from being able to get the bill before the House, he had been unable even to get the yeas and nays on the question of taking it up. There was great reason for this. This Navy Department had been for the last two years the great vortex which had swallowed up two-thirds of the revenues of the government. In 1840, a law was passed that no money should be expended for the building of ships without the express sanction of Congress; and yet, in defiance of this law, the Navy Department had gone on to build an iron steamship at Pittsburg, and six sloops-of-war; and he was told that part of the appropriations in this bill were to complete these vessels. Mr. D. then spoke of the utter uselessness of these steamships on the western waters, and referred to the number of ships that were now rotting for want of use, both on the stocks and laid up in ordinary; and particularly referred to the magnificent ship Delaware, which had just returned from a cruise, and was dismantled, and laid up to rot at Norfolk, while the department was clamorous for building more ships. There were not only more ships now built and building than could be used, but there were three times as many officers as could be employed. There were 96 commanders, with salaries of $3,500 a-year, while there was only employment for 38 of them; and there were 68 captains, while there was only employment for but 18. He then referred to the number of officers waiting orders, and on leave of absence, and said that the country would be astonished to learn, that for such officers, the country was now paying $283,700 a year; and that, by referring to the records of the Navy Department, it would be found that for the last twenty years, more than half of the officers of the navy were drawing their pay and emoluments while at home, on leave of absence, or waiting orders. Mr. D. spoke of many other abuses in the navy, which he said required correction, and expressed his great regret that he had not been able to get the House to act on his navy retrenchment bill."

Mr. McKay, of North Carolina, who was the chairman of the Committee of Ways and Means, whose duty it became to present this item in the appropriation bill, fully admitted its illegality and wastefulness; but plead the necessity of providing for its payment, as the money had been earned by work and labor done on the faith of the government, and to withhold payment would be a wrong to laborers, and no punishment to the officers who had occasioned the illegal expenditure. A high officer had done this wrong. He was ready to join in a vote of censure upon him: but to repudiate the debt, and leave laboring people without pay for their work and materials was what he could not do. And thus ended the session with sanctioning an abuse of $700,000 in one item in the navy, which session had opened with a manly attempt to correct some of its extravagances. And thus have ended all similar attempts since. A powerful combined interest pushes forward an augmented navy, without regard to any object but their own interest in it. First, the politicians who raise a clamor of war at the return of each presidential canvass, and a cry for ships to carry it on. Next, the naval officers, who are always in favor of more ships to give more commands. And, thirdly, the contractors who are to build these ships, and get rich upon their contracts. These three parties combine to build ships, and Congress becomes a helpless instrument in their hands. The friends of economy, and of a wise national policy, which prefers cruisers and privateers to ships of the line, may deliver their complaints in vain. Ship building, and ship rotting, goes on unchecked, and even with accelerated speed; and must continue to so go on until the enormity of the abuse produces a revulsion which, in curing the abuse may nearly kill the navy itself.

CHAPTER CXXXIII.

PROFESSOR MORSE: HIS ELECTRO-MAGNETIC TELEGRAPH.

Communication of intelligence by concerted signals is as old as the human race, and by all, except the white race, remains where it was six thousand years ago. The smokes raised on successive hills to give warning of the approach of strangers, or enemies, were found to be the same by Frémont in his western explorations which were described by Herodotus as used for the same purpose by the barbarian nations of his time: the white race alone has made advances upon that rude and imperfect mode of communication, and brought the art to a marvellous perfection, but only after the intervention of thousands of years. It was not until the siege of Vienna by the Turks, that the very limited intelligence between the besieged in a city and their friends outside, was established by the telegraph: and it was not until the breaking out of the French revolution that that mode of intelligence was applied to the centre and to the circumference of a country: and at that point it was stationary for fifty years. It was reserved for our own day, and our own country to make the improvement which annihilates distance, which disregards weather and darkness, and which rivals the tongue and the pen in the precision and infinitude of its messages. Dr. Franklin first broached the idea of using electricity for communicating intelligence: Professor Morse gave practical application to his idea. This gentleman was a portrait painter by profession, and had been to Europe to perfect himself in his art. Returning in the autumn of 1832, and while making the voyage, the recent discoveries and experiments in electro-magnetism, and the affinity of electricity to magnetism, or rather their probable identity, became a subject of casual conversation between himself and a few of the passengers. It had recently been discovered that an electric spark could be obtained from a magnet, and this discovery had introduced a new branch of science, to wit: magneto-electricity. Dr. Franklin's experiments on the velocity of electricity, exceeding that of light, and exceeding 180,000 miles in a moment, the feasibility of making electricity the means of telegraphic intercourse, that is to say of writing at a distance, struck him with great force, and became the absorbing subject of his meditations. The idea of telegraphing by electricity was new to him. Fortunately he did not know that some eminent philosophers had before conceived the same idea, but without inventing a plan by which the thought could be realized. Knowing nothing of their ideas, he was not embarrassed or impeded by the false lights of their mistakes. As the idea was original with him, so was his plan. All previous modes of telegraphing had been by evanescent signs: the distinctive feature of Morse's plan was the self-recording property of the apparatus, with its ordinarily inseparable characteristic of audible clicks, answering the purposes of speech; for, in impressing the characters, the sounds emitted by the machinery gave notice of each that was struck, as well understood by the practised ear as the recorded language was by the eye. In this he became the inventor of a new art—the art of telegraphic recording, or imprinting characters telegraphically.

Mr. Morse then had his invention complete in his head, and his labor then begun to construct the machinery and types to reduce it to practice, in which having succeeded to the entire satisfaction of a limited number of observers in the years 1836 and '37, he laid it before Congress in the year 1838, made an exhibit of its working before a committee, and received a favorable report. Much time was then lost in vain efforts to procure patents in England and France, and returning to Congress in 1842, an appropriation of $30,000 was asked for to enable the inventor to test his discovery on a line of forty miles, between Washington and Baltimore. The appropriation was granted—the preparations completed by the spring of 1844, and messages exchanged instantaneously between the two points. The line was soon extended to New York, and since so multiplied, that the Morse electro-magnetic telegraph now works over 80,000 miles in America and 50,000 in Europe. It is one of the marvellous results of science, putting people who are thousands of miles apart in instant communication with the accuracy of a face to face conversation. Its wonderful advantages are felt in social, political, commercial and military communications, and, in conjunction with the steam car, is destined to work a total revolution in the art of defensive warfare. It puts an end to defensive war on the ocean, to the necessity of fortifications, except to delay for a few days the bombardment of a city. The approach of invaders upon any point, telegraphed through the country, brings down in the flying cars myriads of citizen soldiers, arms in hand and provisions in abundance, to overwhelm with numbers any possible invading force. It will dispense with fleets and standing armies, and all the vast, cumbrous, and expensive machinery of a modern army. Far from dreading an invasion, the telegraph and the car may defy and dare it—may invite any number of foreign troops to land—and assure the whole of them of death or captivity, from myriads of volunteers launched upon them hourly from the first moment of landing until the last invader is a corpse or a prisoner.

CHAPTER CXXXIV.

FREMONT'S SECOND EXPEDITION.

"The government deserves credit for the zeal with which it has pursued geographical discovery." Such is the remark which a leading paper made upon the discoveries of Frémont, on his return from his second expedition to the Great West; and such is the remark which all writers will make upon all his discoveries who write history from public documents and outside views. With all such writers the expeditions of Frémont will be credited to the zeal of the government for the promotion of science; as if the government under which he acted had conceived and planned these expeditions, as Mr. Jefferson did that of Lewis and Clark, and then selected this young officer to carry into effect the instructions delivered to him. How far such history would be true in relation to the first expedition, which terminated in the Rocky Mountains, has been seen in the account which has been given of the origin of that undertaking, and which leaves the government innocent of its conception; and, therefore, not entitled to the credit of its authorship, but only to the merit of permitting it. In the second, and greater expedition, from which great political as well as scientific results have flowed, their merit is still less; for, while equally innocent of its conception, they were not equally passive to its performance—countermanding the expedition after it had begun; and lavishing censure upon the adventurous young explorer for his manner of undertaking it. The fact was, that his first expedition barely finished, Mr. Frémont sought and obtained orders for a second one, and was on the frontier of Missouri with his command when orders arrived at St. Louis to stop him, on the ground that he had made a military equipment which the peaceful nature of his geographical pursuit did not require! as if Indians did not kill and rob scientific men as well as others if not in a condition to defend themselves. The particular point of complaint was that he had taken a small mountain howitzer, in addition to his rifles: and which, he was informed, was charged to him, although it had been furnished upon a regular requisition on the commandant of the Arsenal at St. Louis, approved by the commander of the military department (Colonel, afterwards General Kearney). Mr. Frémont had left St. Louis, and was at the frontier, Mrs. Frémont being requested to examine the letters that came after him, and forward those which he ought to receive. She read the countermanding orders, and detained them! and Frémont knew nothing of their existence until after he had returned from one of the most marvellous and eventful expeditions of modern times—one to which the United States are indebted (among other things) for the present ownership of California, instead of seeing it a British possession. The writer of this View, who was then in St. Louis, approved of the course which his daughter had taken (for she had stopped the orders before he knew of it); and he wrote a letter to the department condemning the recall, repulsing the reprimand which had been lavished upon Frémont, and demanding a court-martial for him when he should return. The Secretary at War was then Mr. James Madison Porter, of Pennsylvania; the chief of the Topographical corps the same as now (Colonel Aberts), himself an office man, surrounded by West Point officers, to whose pursuit of easy service Frémont's adventurous expeditions was a reproach; and in conformity to whose opinions the secretary seemed to have acted. On Frémont's return, upwards of a year afterwards, Mr. William Wilkins, of Pennsylvania, was Secretary at War, and received the young explorer with all honor and friendship, and obtained for him the brevet of captain from President Tyler. And such is the inside view of this piece of history—very different from what documentary evidence would make it.

To complete his survey across the continent, on the line of travel between the State of Missouri and the tide-water region of the Columbia, was Frémont's object in this expedition; and it was all that he had obtained orders for doing; but only a small part, and to his mind, an insignificant part, of what he proposed doing. People had been to the mouth of the Columbia before, and his ambition was not limited to making tracks where others had made them before him. There was a vast region beyond the Rocky Mountains—the whole western slope of our continent—of which but little was known; and of that little, nothing with the accuracy of science. All that vast region, more than seven hundred miles square—equal to a great kingdom in Europe—was an unknown land—a sealed book, which he longed to open, and to read. Leaving the frontier of Missouri in May, 1843, and often diverging from his route for the sake of expanding his field of observation, he had arrived in the tide-water region of Columbia in the month of November; and had then completed the whole service which his orders embraced. He might then have returned upon his tracks, or been brought home by sea, or hunted the most pleasant path for getting back; and if he had been a routine officer, satisfied with fulfilling an order, he would have done so. Not so the young explorer who held his diploma from Nature, and not from the United States' Military Academy. He was at Fort Vancouver, guest of the hospitable Dr. McLaughlin, Governor of the British Hudson Bay Fur Company; and obtained from him all possible information upon his intended line of return—faithfully given, but which proved to be disastrously erroneous in its leading and governing feature. A southeast route to cross the great unknown region diagonally through its heart (making a line from the Lower Columbia to the Upper Colorado of the Gulf of California), was his line of return: twenty-five men (the same who had come with him from the United States) and a hundred horses, were his equipment; and the commencement of winter the time of starting—all with out a guide, relying upon their guns for support; and, in the last resort, upon their horses—such as should give out! for one that could carry a man, or a pack, could not be spared for food.

All the maps up to that time had shown this region traversed from east to west—from the base of the Rocky Mountains to the Bay of San Francisco—by a great river called the *Buena Ventura*: which may be translated, the *Good Chance*. Governor McLaughlin believed in the existence of this river, and made out a conjectural manuscript map to show its place and course. Frémont believed in it, and his plan was to reach it before the dead of winter, and then hybernate upon it. As a great river, he knew that it must have some rich bottoms; covered with wood and grass, where the wild animals would collect and shelter, when the snows and freezing winds drove them from the plains: and with these animals to live on, and grass for the horses, and wood for fires, he expected to avoid suffering, if not to enjoy comfort, during his solitary sojourn in that remote and profound wilderness. He proceeded—soon encountered deep snows which impeded progress upon the high lands—descended into a low country to the left (afterwards known to be the Great Basin, from which no water issues to any sea)—skirted an enormous chain of mountain on the right, luminous with glittering white snow— saw strange Indians, who mostly fled—found a desert—no Buena Ventura: and death from cold and famine staring him in the face. The failure to find the river, or tidings of it, and the possibility of its existence seeming to be forbid by the structure of the country, and hybernation in the inhospitable desert being impossible, and the question being that of life and death, some new plan of conduct became indispensable. His celestial observations told him that he was in the latitude of the Bay of San Francisco, and only seventy miles from it. But what miles! up and down that snowy mountain which the Indians told him no men could cross in the winter—which would have snow upon it as deep as the trees, and places where people would slip off, and fall half a mile at a time;—a fate which actually befell a mule, packed with the precious burden of botanical specimens, collected along a travel of two thousand miles. No reward could induce an Indian to become a guide in the perilous adventure of crossing this mountain. All recoiled and fled from the adventure. It was attempted without a guide—in the dead of winter—accomplished in forty days—the men and surviving horses—a woful procession, crawling along one by one: skeleton men leading skeleton horses—and arriving at Suter's Settlement in the beautiful valley of the Sacramento; and where a genial warmth, and budding flowers, and trees in foliage, and grassy ground, and flowing streams, and comfortable food, made a fairy contrast with the famine and freezing they had encountered, and the lofty *Sierra Nevada* which they had climbed. Here he rested and recruited; and from this point, and by way of Monterey, the first tidings were heard of the party since leaving Fort Vancouver.

Another long progress to the south, skirting the western base of the Sierra Nevada, made him acquainted with the noble valley of the San Joaquin, counterpart to that of the Sacramento; when crossing through a gap and turning to the left, he skirted the Great Basin; and, by many deviations from the right line home, levied incessant contributions to science from expanded lands, not described before. In this eventful exploration all the great features of the western slope of our continent were brought to light—the Great Salt Lake, the Utah Lake, the Little Salt Lake; at all which places, then desert, the Mormons now are; the Sierra Nevada, then solitary in the snow, now crowded with Americans, digging gold from its flanks; the beautiful valleys of the Sacramento and San Joaquin, then alive with wild horses, elk, deer, and wild fowls, now smiling with American cultivation; the Great Basin itself, and its contents; the Three Parks; the approximation of the great rivers which, rising together in the central region of the Rocky Mountains, go off east and west, towards the rising and the setting sun:—all these, and other strange features of a new region, more Asiatic than American, were brought to light, and revealed to public view in the results of this exploration. Eleven months he was never out of sight of snow; and sometimes, freezing with cold, would look down upon a sunny valley, warm with genial heat;—sometimes panting with the summer's heat, would look up at the eternal snows which crowned the neighboring mountain. But it was not then that California was secured to the Union—to the greatest power of the New World—to which it of right belonged: but it was the first step towards the acquisition, and the one that led to it. That second expedition led to a third, just in time to snatch the golden California from the hands of the British, ready to clutch it. But of this hereafter. Frémont's second expedition was now over. He had left the United States a fugitive from his government, and returned with a name that went over Europe and America, and with discoveries bearing fruit which the civilized world is now enjoying.

CHAPTER CXXXV.

TEXAS ANNEXATION: SECRET ORIGIN; BOLD INTRIGUE FOR THE PRESIDENCY.

In the winter of 1842-'3, nearly two years before the presidential election, there appeared in a Baltimore newspaper an elaborately composed letter on the annexation of Texas, written by Mr. Gilmer, a member of Congress from Virginia, urging the immediate annexation, as necessary to forestall the designs of Great Britain upon that young country. These designs, it was alleged, aimed at a political and military domination on our south-western border, with a view to abolition and hostile movements against us; and the practical part of the letter was an earnest appeal to the American people to annex the Texas republic immediately, as the only means of preventing such great calamities. This letter was a clap of thunder in a clear sky. There was nothing in the political horizon to announce or portend it. Great Britain had given no symptom of any disposition to war upon us, or to excite insurrection among our slaves. Texas and Mexico were at war, and to annex the country was to adopt the war: far from hastening annexation, an event desirable in itself when it could be honestly done, a premature and ill-judged attempt, upon groundless pretexts, could only clog and delay it. There was nothing in the position of Mr. Gilmer to make him a prime mover in the annexation scheme; and there was much in his connections with Mr. Calhoun to make him the reflector of that gentleman's opinions. The letter itself was a counterpart of the movement made by Mr. Calhoun in the Senate, in 1836, to bring the Texas question into the presidential election of that year; its arguments were the amplification of the seminal ideas then presented by that gentleman: and it was his known habit to operate through others. Mr. Gilmer was a close political friend, and known as a promulgator of his doctrines—having been the first to advocate nullification in Virginia.

Putting all these circumstances together, I believed, the moment I saw it, that I discerned the finger of Mr. Calhoun in that letter, and that an enterprise of some kind was on foot for the next presidential election— though still so far off. I therefore put an eye on the movement, and by observing the progress of the letter, the papers in which it was republished, their comments, the encomiums which it received, and the public meetings in which it was commended, I became satisfied that there was no mistake in referring its origin to that gentleman; and became convinced that this movement was the resumption of the premature and abortive attempt of 1836. In the course of the summer of 1843, it had been taken up generally in the circle of Mr. Calhoun's friends, and with the zeal and pertinacity which betrayed the spirit of a presidential canvass. Coincident with these symptoms, and indicative of a determined movement on the Texas question, was a pregnant circumstance in the executive branch of the government. Mr. Webster, who had been prevailed upon to remain in Mr. Tyler's cabinet when all his colleagues of 1841 left their places, now resigned his place, also— induced, as it was well known, by the altered deportment of the President towards him; and was succeeded first by Mr. Legare, of South Carolina, and, on his early death, by Mr. Upshur, of Virginia.

Mr. Webster was inflexibly opposed to the Texas annexation, and also to the presidential elevation of Mr. Calhoun; the two gentlemen, his successors, were both favorable to annexation, and one (Mr. Upshur) extremely so to Mr. Calhoun; so that, here were two steps taken in the suspected direction—an obstacle removed and a facility substituted. This change in the head of the State Department, upon whatever motive produced, was indispensable to the success of the Texas movement, and could only have been made for some great cause never yet explained, seeing the service which Mr. Webster did Mr. Tyler in remaining with him when the other ministers withdrew. Another sign appeared in the conduct of the President himself. He was undergoing another change. Long a democrat, and successful in getting office at that, he had become a whig, and with still greater success. Democracy had carried him to the Senate; whiggism elevated him to the vice-presidency; and, with the help of an accident, to the presidency. He was now settling back, as shown in a previous chapter, towards his original party, but that wing of it which had gone off with Mr. Calhoun in the nullification war—a natural line of retrogression on his part, as he had travelled it in his transit from the democratic to the whig camp. The papers in his interest became rampant for Texas; and in the course of the autumn, the rumor became current and steady that negotiations were in progress for the annexation, and that success was certain.

Arriving at Washington at the commencement of the session of 1843-'44, and descending the steps of the Capitol in a throng of members on the evening of the first day's sitting, I was accosted by Mr. Aaron V. Brown, a representative from Tennessee, with expressions of great gratification at meeting with me so soon; and who immediately showed the cause of his gratification to be the opportunity it afforded him to speak to me on the subject of the Texas annexation. He spoke of it as an impending and probable event—complimented me on my early opposition to the relinquishment of that country, and my subsequent efforts to get it back, and did me the honor to say that, as such original enemy to its loss and early advocate of its recovery, I was a proper person to take a prominent part in now getting it back. All this was very civil and quite reasonable, and, at another time and under other circumstances, would have been entirely agreeable to me; but preoccupied as my mind was with the idea of an intrigue for the presidency, and a land and scrip speculation which I saw mixing itself up with it, and feeling as if I was to be made an instrument in these schemes, I took fire at his words, and answered abruptly and hotly: *That it was, on the part of some, an intrigue for the presidency and a plot to dissolve the Union—on the part of others, a Texas scrip and land speculation; and that I was against it.*

This answer went into the newspapers, and was much noticed at the time, and immediately set up a high wall between me and the annexation party. I had no thought at the time that Mr. Brown had been moved by anybody to sound me, and presently regretted the warmth with which I had replied to him—especially as no part of what I said was intended to apply to him. The occurrence gave rise to some sharp words at one another afterwards, which, so far as they were sharp on my part, I have since condemned, and do not now repeat.

Some three months afterwards there appeared in the *Richmond Enquirer* a letter from General Jackson to Mr. Brown, in answer to one from Mr. Brown to the general, covering a copy of Mr. Gilmer's Texas letter, and asking the favor of his (the general's) opinion upon it: which he promptly and decidedly gave, and fully in favor of its object. Here was a revelation and a coincidence which struck me, and put my mind to thinking, and opened up a new vein of exploration, into which I went to work, and worked on until I obtained the secret history of the famous "Jackson Texas letter" (as it came to be called), and which played so large a part in the Texas annexation question, and in the presidential election of 1844; and which drew so much applause upon the general from many who had so lately and so bitterly condemned him. This history I now propose to give, confining the narrative to the intrigue for the presidential nomination, leaving the history of the attempted annexation (treaty of 1844) for a separate chapter, or rather chapters; for it was an enterprise of many aspects, according to the taste of different actors—presidential, disunion, speculation.

The outline of this history—that of the letter—is brief and authentic; and, although well covered up at the time, was known to too many to remain covered up long. It was partly made known to me at the time, and fully since. It runs thus:

Mr. Calhoun, in 1841-'2, had resumed his design (intermitted in 1840) to stand for the presidency, and determined to make the annexation of Texas—immediate annexation—the controlling issue in the election. The death of President Harrison in 1841, and the retreat of his whig ministers, and the accession of his friends to power in the person of Mr. Tyler (then settling back to his old love), and in the persons of some of his cabinet, opened up to his view the prospect of a successful enterprise in that direction; and he fully embraced it, and without discouragement from the similar budding hopes of Mr. Tyler himself, which it was known would be without fruit, except what Mr. Calhoun would gather—the ascendant of his genius assuring him the mastery when he should choose to assume it. His real competitors (foreseen to be Mr. Van Buren and Mr. Clay) were sure to be against it—immediate annexation—and they would have a heavy current to encounter, all the South and West being for the annexation, and a strong interest, also, in other parts of the Union. There was a basis to build upon in the honest feelings of the people, and inflammatory arguments to excite them; and if the opinion of General Jackson could be obtained in its favor, the election of the annexation candidate was deemed certain.

With this view the Gilmer letter was composed and published, and sent to him—and was admirably conceived for his purpose. It took the veteran patriot on the side of his strong feelings—love of country and the Union—distrust of Great Britain—and a southern susceptibility to the dangers of a servile insurrection. It carried him back to the theatre of his glory—the Lower Mississippi—and awakened his apprehensions for the safety of that most vulnerable point of our frontier. Justly and truly, but with a refinement of artifice in this case, it presented annexation as a strengthening plaster to the Union, while really intended to sectionalize it, and to effect disunion if the annexation failed. This idea of strengthening the Union had, and in itself deserved to have, an invincible charm for the veteran patriot. Besides, the recovery of Texas was in the line of his policy, pursued by him as a favorite object during his administration; and this desire to get back that country, patriotic in itself, was entirely compatible with his acquiescence in its relinquishment as a temporary sacrifice in 1819; an acquiescence induced by the "*domestic*" reason communicated to him by Mr. Monroe.

The great point in sending the Gilmer letter to him, with its portents of danger from British designs, was to obtain from him the expression of an opinion in favor of "immediate" annexation. No other opinion would do any good. A future annexation, no matter how soon after 1844, would carry the question beyond the presidential election, and would fall in with the known opinions of Mr. Van Buren and Mr. Clay, and most other American statesmen, the common sentiment being for annexation, when it could be honestly accomplished. Such annexation would make no issue at all. It would throw Texas out of the canvass. Immediate was, therefore, the game; and to bring General Jackson to that point was the object. To do that, the danger of British occupation was presented as being so imminent as to admit of no delay, and so disastrous in its consequences as to preclude all consideration of present objections. It was a bold conception, and of critical execution. Jackson was one of the last men in the world to be tampered with—one of the last to be used against a friend or for a foe—the very last to be willing to see Mr. Calhoun President—and the very first in favor of Mr. Van Buren. To turn him against his nature and his feelings in all these particulars was a perilous enterprise: but it was attempted—and accomplished.

It has already been shown that the letter of Mr. Gilmer was skilfully composed for its purpose: all the accessories of its publication and transmission to General Jackson were equally skilfully contrived. It was addressed to a friend in Maryland, which was in the opposite direction from the *locus* of its origin. It was drawn out upon the call of a friend: that is the technical way of getting a private letter before the public. It was published in Baltimore—a city where its writer did not live. The name of the friend in Maryland who drew it out, was concealed; and that was necessary to the success of the scheme, as the name of this suspected friend (Mr. Duff Green) would have fastened its origin on Mr. Calhoun. And thus the accessories of the publication were complete, and left the mind without suspicion that the letter had germinated in a warm southern latitude. It was then ready to start on its mission to General Jackson; but how to get it there, without exciting suspicion, was the question. Certainly Mr. Gilmer would have been the natural agent for the transmission of his own letter; but he stood too close to Mr. Calhoun—was too much his friend and intimate—to make that a safe adventure. A medium was wanted, which would be a conductor of the letter and a non-conductor of suspicion; and it was found in the person of Mr. Aaron V. Brown. But he was the friend of Mr. Van Buren, and it was necessary to approach him through a medium also, and one was found in one of Mr. Gilmer's colleagues— believed to be Mr. Hopkins, of the House, who came from near the Tennessee line; and through him the letter reached Mr. Brown.

And thus, conceived by one, written by another, published by a third, and transmitted through two successive mediums, the missive went upon its destination, and arrived safely in the hands of General Jackson. It had a complete success. He answered it promptly, warmly, decidedly, affirmatively. So fully did it put him up to the point of "immediate" annexation, that his impatience outstripped expectation. He counselled haste— considered the present the accepted time—and urged the seizure of the "golden opportunity" which, if lost now, might never return. The answer was dated at the Hermitage, March 12th, 1843, and was received at Washington as soon as the mail could fetch it. Of course it came to Mr. Brown, to whom it belonged, and to whom it was addressed; but I did not hear of it in his hands. My first information of it was in the hands of Mr. Gilmer, in the hall of the House, immediately after its arrival—he, crossing the hall with the letter in his hand, greatly elated, and showing it to a confidential friend, with many expressions of now confident triumph over Mr. Van Buren. The friend was permitted to read the letter, but with the understanding that nothing was to be said about it at that time.

Mr. Gilmer then explained to his friend the purpose for which this letter had been written and sent to General Jackson, and the use that was intended to be made of his answer (if favorable to the design of the authors), which use was this: It was to be produced in the nominating convention, to overthrow Mr. Van Buren, and give Mr. Calhoun the nomination, both of whom were to be interrogated beforehand; and as it was well known what the answers would be—Calhoun for and Van Buren against immediate annexation—and Jackson's answer coinciding with Calhoun's, would turn the scale in his favor, "and blow Van Buren sky high."

This was the plan, and this the state of the game, at the end of February, 1843; but a great deal remained to be done to perfect the scheme. The sentiment of the democratic party was nearly unanimous for Mr. Van Buren, and time was wanted to undermine that sentiment. Public opinion was not yet ripe for immediate annexation, and time was wanted to cultivate that opinion. There was no evidence of any British domination or abolition plot in Texas, and time was wanted to import one from London. All these operations required time—more of it than intervened before the customary period for the meeting of the convention. That period had been the month of December preceding the year of the election, and Baltimore the place for these assemblages since Congress presidential caucuses had been broken down—that near position to Washington being chosen for the convenient attendance of that part of the members of Congress who charged themselves with these elections. If December remained the period for the meeting, there would be no time for the large operations which required to be performed; for, to get the delegates there in time, they must be elected beforehand, during the summer—so that the working season of the intriguers would be reduced to a few months, when upwards of a year was required. To gain that time was the first object, and a squad of members, some in the interest of Mr. Calhoun, some professing friendship to Mr. Van Buren, but secretly hostile to him, sat privately in the Capitol, almost nightly, corresponding with all parts of the country, to get the convention postponed. All sorts of patriotic motives were assigned for this desired postponement, as that it would be more convenient for the delegates to attend—nearer to the time of election—more time for public opinion to mature; and most favorable to deliberate decision. But another device was fallen upon to obtain delay, the secret of which was not put into the letters, nor confided to the body of the nightly committee. It had so happened that the opposite party—the whigs—since the rout of the Congress presidential caucuses, had also taken the same time and place for their conventions—December, and Baltimore—and doubtless for the same reason, that of the more convenient attending of the President-making members of Congress; and this led to an intrigue with the whigs, the knowledge of which was confined to a very few. It was believed that the democratic convention could be the more readily put off if the whigs would do the like—and do it first.

There was a committee within the committee—a little nest of head managers—who undertook this collusive arrangement with the whigs. They proposed it to them, professing to act in the interest of Mr. Calhoun, though in fact against him, as well as against Mr. Van Buren. The whigs readily agreed to this proposal, because, being themselves then unanimous for Mr. Clay, it made no difference at what time he should be nominated; and believing they could more easily defeat Mr. Calhoun than Mr. Van Buren, they preferred him for an antagonist. They therefore agreed to the delay, and both conventions were put off (and the whigs first, to enable the democrats to plead it) from December, 1843, to May, 1844. Time for operating having now been gained, the night squad in the Capitol redoubled their activity to work upon the people. Letter writers and newspapers were secured. Good, easy members, were plied with specious reasons—slippery ones were directly approached. Visitors from the States were beset and indoctrinated. Men were picked out to operate on the selfish, and the calculating; and myriads of letters were sent to the States, to editors, and politicians. All these agents worked to a pattern, the primary object being to undo public sentiment in favor of Mr. Van Buren, and to manufacture one, ostensibly in favor of Mr. Calhoun, but in reality without being for him—they being for any one of four (Mr. Cass, Mr. Buchanan, Colonel Johnson, Mr. Tyler), in preference to either of them. They were for neither, and the only difference was that Mr. Calhoun believed they were for him: Mr. Van Buren knew they were against him. They professed friendship for him; and that was necessary to enable them to undermine him. The stress of the argument against him was that he could not be elected, and the effort was to make good that assertion. Now, or never, was the word with respect to Texas. Some of the squad sympathized with the speculators in Texas land and scrip; and to these Mr. Calhoun was no more palatable than Mr. Van Buren. They were both above plunder. Some wanted office, and knew that neither of these gentlemen would give it to them. They had a difficult as well as tortuous part to play. Professing democracy, they colluded with whigs. Professing friendship to Mr. Van Buren, they co-operated with Mr. Calhoun's friends to defeat him. Co-operating with Mr. Calhoun's friends, they were against his election. They were for any body in preference to either, and especially for men of easy temperaments, whose principles were not entrenched behind strong wills. To undo public sentiment in favor of Mr. Van Buren was their labor; to get unpledged and uninstructed delegates into convention, and to get those released who had been appointed under instructions, was the consummation of their policy. A convention untrammelled by instructions, independent of the people, and open to the machinations of a few politicians, was what was wanted. The efforts to accomplish these purposes were prodigious, and constituted the absorbing night and day work of the members engaged in it. After all, they had but indifferent success—more with politicians and editors than with the people. Mr. Van Buren was almost universally preferred. Delegates were generally instructed to support his nomination. Even in the Southern States, in direct question between himself and Mr. Calhoun, he was preferred—as in Alabama and Mississippi. No delegates were released from their instructions by any competent authority, and only a few in any, by clusters of local politicians, convenient to the machinations of the committee in the Capitol—as at Shockoe Hill, Richmond, Virginia, where Mr. Ritchie, editor of the *Enquirer* (whose proclivity to be deceived in a crisis was generally equivalent in its effects to positive treachery), led the way—himself impelled by others.

The labors of the committee, though intended to be secret, and confined to a small circle, and chiefly carried on in the night, were subject to be discovered; and were so; and the discovery led to some public denunciations. The two senators from Ohio, Messrs. William Allen, and Tappan, and ten of the representatives from that State, published a card in the *Globe* newspaper, denouncing it as a conspiracy to defeat the will of the people. The whole delegation from South Carolina (Messrs. McDuffie and Huger, senators, and the seven representatives), fearing that they might be suspected on account of their friendship for Mr. Calhoun, published a card denying all connection with the committee; an unnecessary precaution, as their characters were above that suspicion. Many other members published cards, denying their participation in these meetings; and some, admitting the participation, denied the intrigue, and truly, as it concerned themselves; for all the disreputable part was kept secret from them—especially the collusion with the whigs, and all the mysteries of the Gilmer letter. Many of them were sincere friends of Mr. Van Buren, but deceived and cheated themselves, while made the instrument of deceiving and cheating others. It was probably one of the most elaborate pieces of political cheatery that has ever been performed in a free country, and well worthy to be studied by all who would wish to extend their knowledge of the manner in which presidential elections may be managed, and who would wish to see the purity of elections preserved and vindicated.

About this time came an occurrence well calculated to make a pause, if any thing could make a pause, in the working of political ambition. The explosion of the great gun on board the Princeton steamer took place, killing, among others, two of Mr. Tyler's cabinet (Mr. Upshur and Mr. Gilmer), both deeply engaged in the Texas project—barely failing to kill Mr. Tyler, who was called back in the critical moment, and who had embraced the Texas scheme with more than vicarious zeal; and also barely failing to kill the writer of this View, who was standing at the breech of the gun, closely observing its working, as well as that of the Texas game, and who fell among the killed and stunned, fortunately to rise again. Commodore Kennon, Mr. Virgil Maxcy, Mr. Gardiner, of New York, father-in-law (that was to be) of the President, were also killed; a dozen seamen were wounded, and Commodore Stockton burnt and scorched as he stood at the side of the gun. Such an occurrence was well calculated to impress upon the survivors the truth of the divine admonition: "What shadows we are—what shadows we pursue." But it had no effect upon the pursuit of the presidential shadow. Instantly Mr. Calhoun was invited to take Mr. Upshur's place in the Department of State, and took it with an alacrity, and with a patronizing declaration, which showed his zeal for the Texas movement, and as good as avowed its paternity. He declared he took the place for the Texas negotiation alone, and would quit it as soon as that negotiation should be finished. In brief, the negotiation, instead of pausing in the presence of so awful a catastrophe, seemed to derive new life from it, and to go forward with accelerated impetuosity. Mr. Calhoun put his eager activity into it: politicians became more vehement—newspapers more clamorous: the interested classes (land and scrip speculators) swarmed at Washington; and Mr. Tyler embraced the scheme with a fervor which induced the suspicion that he had adopted the game for his own, and intended to stand a cast of the presidential die upon it.

The machinations of the committee, though greatly successful with individuals, and with the politicians with whom they could communicate, did not reach the masses, who remained firm to Mr. Van Buren; and it became necessary to fall upon some new means of acting upon them. This led to a different use of the Jackson Texas letter from what had been intended. It was intended to have been kept in the background, a secret in the hands of its possessors, until the meeting of the convention—then suddenly produced to turn the scale between Mr. Calhoun and Mr. Van Buren; and this design had been adhered to for about the space of a year, and the letter kept close: it was then recurred to as a means of rousing the masses.

Jackson's name was potential with the people, and it was deemed indispensable to bring it to bear upon them. The publication of the letter was resolved upon, and the *Globe* newspaper selected for the purpose, and Mr. Aaron V. Brown to have it done. All this was judicious and regular. The *Globe* had been the organ of General Jackson, and was therefore the most proper paper to bring his sentiments before the public. It was the advocate of Mr. Van Buren's election, and therefore would prevent the suspicion of sinistrous design upon him. Mr. Brown was the legal owner of the letter, and a professing friend of Mr. Van Buren, and, therefore, the proper person to carry it for publication.

He did so; but the editor, Mr. Blair, seeing no good that it could do Mr. Van Buren, but, on the contrary, harm, and being sincerely his friend, declined to publish it; and, after examination, delivered it back to Mr. Brown. Shortly thereafter, to wit, on the 22d of March, 1844, it appeared in the Richmond *Enquirer*, post-dated, that is to say, the date of 1843 changed into 1844—whether by design or accident is not known; but the post-date gave the letter a fresher appearance, and a more vigorous application to the Texas question. The fact that this letter had got back to Mr. Brown, after having been given up to Mr. Gilmer, proved that the letter travelled in a circle while kept secret, and went from hand to hand among the initiated, as needed for use.

The time had now come for the interrogation of the candidates, and it was done with all the tact which the delicate function required. The choice of the interrogator was the first point. He must be a friend, ostensible if not real, to the party interrogated. If real, he must himself be deceived, and made to believe that he was performing a kindly service; if not, he must still have the appearance. And for Mr. Van Buren's benefit a suitable performer was found in the person of Mr. Hamett, a representative in Congress from Mississippi, whose letter was a model for the occasion, and, in fact has been pretty well followed since. It abounded in professions of friendship to Mr. Van Buren—approached him for his own good—sought his opinion from the best of motives; and urged a categorical reply, for or against, immediate annexation. The sagacious Mr. Van Buren was no dupe of this contrivance, but took counsel from what was due to himself; and answered with candor, decorum and dignity. He was against immediate annexation, because it was war with Mexico, but for it when it could be done peaceably and honorably: and he was able to present a very fair record, having been in favor of getting back the country (in a way to avoid difficulties with Mexico) when Secretary of State, under President Jackson. His letter was sent to a small circle of friends at Washington before it was delivered to its address; but to be delivered immediately; which was done, and soon went into the papers.

Mr. Calhoun had superseded the necessity of interrogation in his letter of acceptance of the State Department: he was a hot annexationist, although there was an ugly record to be exhibited against him. In his almost thirty years of public life he had never touched Texas, except for his own purposes. In 1819, as one of Mr. Monroe's cabinet, he had concurred in giving it away, in order to conciliate the anti-slavery interest in the Northeast by curtailing slave territory in the Southwest. In 1836 he moved her immature annexation, in order to bring the question into the presidential election of that year, to the prejudice of Mr. Van Buren; and urged instant action, because delay was dangerous. Having joined Mr. Van Buren after his election, and expecting to become his successor, he dropped the annexation for which he had been so impatient, and let the election of 1840 pass by without bringing it into the canvass; and now revived it for the overthrow of Mr. Van Buren, and for the excitement of a sectional controversy, by placing the annexation on strong sectional grounds. And now, at the approach of the election in 1844, after years of silence, he becomes the head advocate of annexation; and with all this forbidding record against him, by help of General Jackson's letter, and the general sentiment in favor of annexation, and the fictitious alarm of British abolition and hostile designs, he was able to appear as a champion of Texas annexation, baffling the old and consistent friends of the measure with the new form which had been given to the question. Mr. Clay was of this class. Of all the public men he was able to present the best and fairest Texas record. He was opposed to the loss of the province in 1819, and offered resolutions in the House of Representatives, supported by an ardent speech, in which he condemned the treaty which gave it away. As Secretary of State, under Mr. Adams, he had advised the recovery of the province, and opened negotiations to that effect, and wrote the instructions under which Mr. Poinsett, the United States minister, made the attempt. As a western man, he was the natural champion of a great western interest—pre-eminently western, while also national. He was interrogated according to the programme, and answered with firmness that, although an ancient and steadfast friend to the recovery of the country, he was opposed to immediate annexation, as adopting the war with Mexico, and making that war by treaty, when the war-making power belonged to Congress. There were several other democratic candidates, the whole of whom were interrogated, and answered promptly in favor of immediate annexation—some of them improving their letters, as advised, before publication. Mr. Tyler, also, now appeared above the horizon as a presidential candidate, and needed no interrogatories to bring out his declaration for immediate annexation, although he had voted against Mr. Clay's resolution condemning the sacrifice of the province. In a word, the Texas hobby was multitudinously mounted, and violently ridden, and most violently by those who had been most indifferent to it before. Mr. Clay and Mr. Calhoun were the only candidates that answered like statesmen, and they were both distanced.

The time was approaching for the convention to meet, and, consequently, for the conclusion of the treaty of annexation, which was to be a touchstone in it. It was signed the 12th of April, and was to have been sent to the Senate immediately, but was delayed by a circumstance which created alarm—made a balk—and required a new turn to be taken. Mr. Van Buren had not yet answered the interrogatories put to him through Mr. Hamett, or rather his answer had not yet been published. Uneasiness began to be felt, lest, like so many others, he should fall into the current, and answer in a way that would enable him to swim with it. To relieve this uncertainty, Mr. Blair was applied to by Mr. Robert J. Walker to write to him, and get his answer. This was a very proper channel to apply through. Mr. Blair, as the fast friend of Mr. Van Buren, had the privilege to solicit him. Mr. Calhoun, as the political adversary of Mr. Van Buren, could not ask Mr. Blair to do it. Mr. Walker stood in a relation to be ready for the work all round; as a professing friend of Mr. Van Buren, though co-operating with Mr. Calhoun and all the rest against him, he could speak with Mr. Blair on a point which seemed to be for Mr. Van Buren's benefit. As co-operating with Mr. Calhoun, he could help him against an adversary, though intending to give him the go-by in the end. As being in all the Texas mysteries, he was a natural person to ferret out information on every side. He it was, then, to whose part it fell to hasten the desired answer from Mr. Van Buren, and through the instrumentality of Mr. Blair. Mr. Blair wrote as solicited, not seeing any trap in it; but had received no answer up to the time that the treaty was to go to the Senate. Ardent for Texas, and believing in the danger of delay, he wrote and published in the *Globe* a glowing article in favor of immediate annexation. That article was a poser and a dumbfounder to the confederates. It threw the treaty all aback. Considering Mr. Blair's friendship for Mr. Van Buren, and their confidential relations, it was concluded that this article could not have been published without his consent—that it spoke his sentiments—and was in fact his answer to the letter which had been sent to him. Here was an ugly balk. It seemed as if the long intrigue had miscarried—as if the plot was going to work out the contrary way, and elevate the man it was intended to put down. In this unexpected conjuncture a new turn became indispensable—and was promptly taken.

Mention has been made in the forepart of this chapter, of the necessity which was felt to obtain something from London to bolster up the accusation of that formidable abolition plot which Great Britain was hatching in Texas, and on the alleged existence of which the whole argument for immediate annexation reposed. The desired testimony had been got, and oracularly given to the public, as being derived from a "*private letter from a citizen of Maryland, then in London.*" The name of this Maryland citizen was not given, but his respectability and reliability were fully vouched; and the testimony passed for true. It was to the point in charging upon the British government, with names and circumstances, all that had been alleged; and adding that her abolition machinations were then in full progress. This went back to London, immediately transmitted there by the British minister at Washington, Sir Richard Pakenham; and being known to be false, and felt to be scandalous, drew from the British Secretary of State (Lord Aberdeen) an indignant, prompt, and peremptory contradiction. This contradiction was given in a despatch, dated December 26th, 1843. It was communicated by Sir Richard Pakenham to Mr. Upshur, the United States Secretary of State, on the 26th day of February, 1844—a few days before the lamentable death of that gentleman by the bursting of the Princeton gun. This despatch, having no object but to contradict an unfounded imputation, required no answer—and received none. It lay in the Department of State unacknowledged until after the treaty had been signed, and until the day of the appearance of that redoubtable article in the *Globe*, which had been supposed to be Mr. Van Buren's answer to the problem of immediate annexation. Then it was taken up, and, on the 18th day of April, was elaborately answered by Mr. Calhoun in a despatch to the British minister—not to argue the point of the truth of the Maryland citizen's private letter—but to argue quite off upon a new text. It so happened that Lord Aberdeen—after the fullest contradiction of the imputed design, and the strongest assurances of non-interference with any slavery policy either of the United States or of Texas—did not stop there; but, like many able men who are not fully aware of the virtue of stopping when they are done, went on to add something more, of no necessary connection or practical application to the subject—a mere general abstract declaration on the subject of slavery; on which Mr. Calhoun took position, and erected a superstructure of alarm which did more to embarrass the opponents of the treaty and to inflame the country, than all other matters put together. This cause for this new alarm was found in the superfluous declaration, "*That Great Britain desires, and is constantly exerting herself to procure the general abolition of slavery throughout the world.*" This general declaration, although preceded and followed by reiterated assurances of non-interference with slavery in the United States, and no desire for any dominant influence in Texas, were seized upon as an open avowal of a design to abolish slavery every where. These assurances were all disregarded. Our secretary established himself upon the naked declaration, stripped of all qualifications and denials. He saw in them the means of making to a northern man (Mr. Van Buren) just as perilous the support as the opposition of immediate annexation. So, making the declaration of Lord Aberdeen the text of a most elaborate reply, he took up the opposite ground (support and propagation of slavery), arguing it generally in relation to the world, and specially in relation to the United States and Texas; and placing the annexation so fully upon that ground, that all its supporters must be committed to it. Here was a new turn, induced by Mr. Blair's article in the *Globe*, and by which the support of the treaty would be as obnoxious in the North as opposition to it would be in the South.

It must have been a strange despatch for a British minister to receive—an argument in favor of slavery propagandism—supported by comparative statements taken from the United States census, between the numbers of deaf, dumb, blind, idiotic, insane, criminal, and paupers among the free and the slave negroes—showing a large disproportion against the free negroes; and thence deducing a conclusion in favor of slavery. It was a strange diplomatic despatch, and incomprehensible except with a knowledge of the circumstances in which it was written. It must have been complete mystification to Lord Aberdeen; but it was not written for him, though addressed to him, and was sent to those for whom it was intended long before he saw it. The use that was made of it showed for whom it was written. Two days after its date, and before it had commenced its maritime voyage to London, it was in the American Senate—sent in with the treaty, with the negotiation of which it had no connection, being written a week after its signature, and after the time that the treaty would have been sent in had it not been for the appearance of the article (supposed to speak Mr. Van Buren's sentiments) in the *Globe*. It was no embarrassment to Mr. Van Buren, whose letter in answer to the interrogatories had been written, and was soon after published. It was an embarrassment to others. It made the annexation a sectional and a slavery question, and insured the rejection of the treaty. It disgusted northern senators; and that was one of the objects with which it had been written. For the whole annexation business had been conducted with a double aspect—one looking to the presidency, the other to disunion; and the latter the alternative, to the furtherance of which the rejection of the treaty by northern votes was an auxiliary step.

And while the whole negotiation bore that for one of its aspects from the beginning, this *ex post facto* despatch, written after the treaty was signed, and given to the American public before it got to the British Secretary of State, became the distinct revelation of what had been before dimly shadowed forth. All hope of the presidency from the Texas intrigue had now failed—the alternative aspect had become the absolute one; and a separate republic, consisting of Texas and some Southern States, had become the object. Neither the exposure of this object nor the history of the attempted annexation belong to this chapter. A separate chapter is required for each. And this incident of the Maryland citizen's private letter from London, Lord Aberdeen's contradiction, and the strange despatch of Mr. Calhoun to him, are only mentioned here as links in the chain of the presidential intrigue; and will be dismissed with the remark that the Maryland citizen was afterwards found out, and was discovered to be a citizen better known as an inhabitant of Washington than of Maryland; and that the private letter was intended to be for public use and paid for out of the contingent fund of the State Department; and the writer, a person whose name was the synonym of subserviency to Mr. Calhoun; namely, Mr. Duff Green.

All this was afterwards brought out under a call from the United States Senate, moved by the writer of this View, who had been put upon the track by some really private information: and when the Presidential Message was read in the Senate, disclosing all these facts, he used an expression taken from a Spanish proverb which had some currency at the time: "*At last the devil is pulled from under the blanket.*"

The time was approaching for the meeting of the democratic presidential convention, postponed by collusion with the whigs (the managers in each party), from the month of December to the month of May—the 27th day of it. It was now May, and every sign was not only auspicious to Mr. Van Buren, but ominous to his opponents. The delegates almost universally remained under instructions to support him. General Jackson, seeing how his letter to Mr. Brown had been used, though ignorant of the artifice by which it had been got from him, and justly indignant at finding himself used for a foe and against a friend, and especially when he deemed that foe dangerous to the Union—wrote a second Texas letter, addressed to the public, in which, while still adhering to his immediate annexation opinions, also adhered to Mr. Van Buren as his candidate for the presidency; and this second letter was a wet blanket upon the fires of the first one. The friends of Mr. Calhoun, seeing that he would have no chance in the Baltimore convention, had started a project to hold a third one in New York; a project which expired as soon as it got to the air; and in connection with which Mr. Cass deemed it necessary to make an authoritative contradiction of a statement made by Mr. Duff Green, who undertook to convince him, in spite of his denials, that he had agreed to it. In proportion as Mr. Calhoun was disappearing from this presidential canvass, Mr. Tyler was appearing in it; and eventually became fully developed as a candidate, intrusively on the democratic side; but his friends, seeing no chance for him in the democratic national convention, he got up an individual or collateral one for himself—to meet at the same time and place; but of this hereafter. This chapter belongs to the intrigue against Mr. Van Buren.

CHAPTER CXXXVI.

DEMOCRATIC CONVENTION FOR THE NOMINATION OF PRESIDENTIAL CANDIDATES.

The Convention met—a motley assemblage, called democratic—many self-appointed, or appointed upon management or solicitation—many alternative substitutes—many members of Congress, in violation of the principle which condemned the Congress presidential caucuses in 1824—some nullifiers; and an immense outside concourse. Texas land and scrip speculators were largely in it, and more largely on the outside. A considerable number were in favor of no particular candidate, but in pursuit of office for themselves— inflexible against any one from whom they thought they would not get it, and ready to go for any one from whom they thought they could. Almost all were under instructions for Mr. Van Buren, and could not have been appointed where such instructions were given, except in the belief that they would be obeyed. The business of undoing instructions had been attended with but poor success—in no instance having been done by the instructing body, or its equivalent. Two hundred and sixty-six delegates were present—South Carolina absent; and it was immediately seen that after all the packing and intriguing, the majority was still for Mr. Van Buren. It was seen that he would be nominated on the first ballot, if the majority was to govern. To prevent that, a movement was necessary, and was made. In the morning of the first day, before the verification of the authority of the delegates—before organization—before prayers—and with only a temporary chairman—a motion was made to adopt the two-thirds rule, that is to say, the rule which required a concurrence of two-thirds to effect a nomination. That rule had been used in the two previous nominating conventions—not to thwart a majority, but to strengthen it; the argument being that the result would be the same, the convention being nearly unanimous; that the two-thirds would be cumulative, and give more weight to the nomination. The precedent was claimed, though the reason had failed; and the effect might now be to defeat the majority instead of adding to its voice.

Men of reflection and foresight objected to this rule when previously used, as being in violation of a fundamental principle—opening the door for the minority to rule—encouraging intrigue and combination— and leading to corrupt practices whenever there should be a design to defeat the popular will. These objections were urged in 1832 and in 1836, and answered by the reply that the rule was only adopted by each convention for itself, and made no odds in the result: and now they were answered with "precedents." A strenuous contest took place over the adoption of this rule—all seeing that the fate of the nomination depended upon it. Mr. Romulus M. Saunders of North Carolina, was its mover. Messrs. Robert J. Walker, and Hopkins of Virginia, its most active supporters: and precedent the stress of their argument. Messrs. Morton of Massachusetts, Clifford of Maine, Dickinson and Butler of New York, Medary of Ohio, and Alexander Kayser of Missouri, were its principal opponents: their arguments were those of principle, and the inapplicability of precedents founded on cases where the two-thirds vote did not defeat, but strengthened the majority. Mr. Morton of Massachusetts, spoke the democratic sentiment when he said:

> "He was in the habit of advancing his opinions in strong and plain language, and he hoped that no exception would be taken to any thing that he might say. He thought the majority principle was the true one of the democratic party. The views which had been advanced on the other side of the question were mainly based upon precedent. He did not think that they properly applied here. We were in danger of relying too much upon precedent—let us go upon principle. He had endeavored, when at school, to understand the true principles of republicanism. He well recollected the nominations of Jefferson and others, and the majority principle had always ruled. In fact it was recognized in all the different ramifications of society. The State, county and township conventions were all governed by this rule."

Mr. Benjamin F. Butler, of New York, enforced the majority principle as the one which lay at the foundation of our government—which prevailed at the adoption of every clause in the Declaration of Independence— every clause in the constitution—all the legislation, and all the elections, both State and federal; and he totally denied the applicability of the precedents cited. He then went on to expose the tricks of a caucus within a caucus—a sub and secret caucus—plotting and combining to betray their instructions through the instrumentality and under the cover of the two-thirds rule. Thus:

> "He made allusion to certain caucusing and contriving, by which it was hoped to avert the well-ascertained disposition of the majority of the democracy. He had been appointed a delegate to the convention, and accepted his credentials, as did his colleagues, with instructions to support and do all in their power to secure the nomination of a certain person (V.B.). By consenting to the adoption of the two-thirds rule, he, with them, would prove unfaithful to their trust and their honor. He knew well that in voting by simple majority, the friend he was pledged to support would receive ten to fifteen majority, and, consequently, the nomination. If two-thirds should be required to make a choice, that friend must inevitably be defeated, and that defeat caused by the action of States which could not be claimed as democratic."

This last remark of Mr. Butler should sink deep into the mind of every friend to the elective system. These conventions admitted delegations from anti-democratic States—States which could not give a democratic vote in the election, and yet could control the nomination. This is one of the most unfair features in the convention system.

The rule was adopted, and by the help of delegates instructed to vote for Mr. Van Buren, and who took that method of betraying their trust while affecting to fulfil it. The body then organized and the balloting commenced, all the States present except South Carolina, who stood off, although she had come into it at the preceding convention, and cast her vote for Mr. Van Buren. Two hundred and sixty-six electoral votes were represented, of which 134 would be the majority, and 177 the two-thirds. Mr. Van Buren received 151 on the first ballot, gradually decreasing at each successive vote until the seventh, when it stood at 99; probably about the true number that remained faithful to their constituents and their pledges. Of those who fell off it was seen that they chiefly consisted of those professing friends who had supported the two-thirds rule, and who now got an excuse for their intended desertion and premeditated violation of instructions in being able to allege the impossibility of electing the man to whom they were pledged.

At this stage of the voting, a member from Ohio (Mr. Miller) moved a resolve, *that Mr. Van Buren, having received a majority of the votes on the first ballot, was duly nominated, and should be so declared.* This motion was an unexpected step, and put delegates under the necessity of voting direct on the majority principle, which lies at the foundation of all popular elections, and at the foundation of the presidential election itself, as prescribed by the constitution. That instrument only requires a majority of the electoral votes to make an election of President; this intriguing rule requires him to get two-thirds before he is competent to receive that majority. The motion raised a storm. It gave rise to a violent, disorderly, furious and tumultuary discussion—a faint idea of which may be formed from some brief extracts from the speeches:

> Mr. Brewster, of Pennsylvania.—"They (the delegation from this State) had then been solemnly instructed to vote for Martin Van Buren first, and to remain firm to that vote as long as there was any hope of his success. He had been asked by gentlemen of the convention why the delegation of Pennsylvania were so divided in their vote. He would answer that it was because some gentlemen of the delegation did not think proper to abide by the solemn instructions given them, but rather chose to violate those instructions. Pennsylvania had come there to vote for Martin Van Buren, and she would not desert him until New York had abandoned him. The delegation had entered into a solemn pledge to do so; and he warned gentlemen that if they persisted in violating that pledge, they would be held to a strict account by their constituency, before whom, on their return home, they would have to hang their heads with shame. Sorry would he be to see them return, after having violated their pledge."

> Mr. Hickman, of Pennsylvania.—"He charged that the delegation from the 'Keystone State' had violated the solemn pledge taken before they were entitled to seats on the floor. He asserted on the floor of this convention, and would assert it every where, that the delegation from Pennsylvania came to the convention instructed to vote for, and to use every means to

obtain the nomination of Martin Van Buren for President, and Richard M. Johnson for Vice President; and yet a portion of the delegation, among whom was his colleague who had just preceded him, had voted against the very proposition upon which the fate of Martin Van Buren hung. He continued his remarks in favor of the inviolability of instructions and in rebuke of those of the Pennsylvania delegation, who had voted for the two-thirds rule, knowing, as they did, that it would defeat Mr. Van Buren's nomination."

Mr. Bredon, of Pennsylvania.—"He had voted against the two-thirds rule. He had been instructed, he said, and he believed had fulfilled those instructions, although he differed from some of his colleagues. His opinion was, that they were bound by instructions only so long as they were likely to be available, and then every member was at liberty to consult his own judgment. He had stood by Mr. Van Buren, and would continue to do so until the New York and Ohio delegates flew the track."

Mr. Frazer, of Pennsylvania, "replied to the remarks of his colleagues, and amidst much and constantly increasing confusion, explained his motives for having deserted Mr. Van Buren. On the last ballot he had voted for James K. Polk, and would do so on the next, despite the threat that had been thrown out, that those who had not voted for Mr. Van Buren would be ashamed to show their faces before their constituents. He threw back the imputation with indignation. He denied that he had violated his pledge; that he had voted for Mr. Van Buren on three ballots, but finding that Mr. Van Buren was not the choice of the convention, he had voted for Mr. Buchanan. Finding that Mr. Buchanan could not succeed, he had cast his vote for James K. Polk, the bosom friend of General Jackson, and a pure, whole-hogged democrat, the known enemy of banks, distribution, &c. He had carried out his instructions as he understood them, and others would do the same."

Mr. Young, of New York, "said it had been intimated that New York desired pertinaciously to force a candidate upon the convention. This he denied. Mr. Van Buren had been recommended by sixteen States to this convention for their suffrages before New York had spoken on the subject, and when she did speak it was with a unanimous voice, and, if an expression of opinion on the part of these people could now be had, it would be found that they had not changed. (As Mr. Y proceeded the noise and confusion increased.) It was true, he said, that a firebrand had been thrown into their camp by the 'Mongrel administration at Washington,' and this was the motive seized upon as a pretext for a change on the part of some gentlemen. That firebrand was the abominable Texas question, but that question, like a fever, would wear itself out or kill the patient. It was one that should have no effect; and some of those who were now laboring to get up an excitement on a subject foreign to the political contest before them, would be surprised, six months hence, that they had permitted their equanimity to be disturbed by it. Nero had fiddled while Rome was burning, and he believed that this question had been put in agitation for the especial purpose of advancing the aspiring ambition of a man, who, he doubted not, like Nero, 'was probably fiddling while Rome was falling.'"

The crimination and recrimination in the Pennsylvania delegation, arose from division among the delegates: in some other delegations the disregard of instructions was unanimous, and there was no one to censure another, as in Mississippi. The Pennsylvania delegation, may be said to have decided the nomination. They were instructed to vote for Mr. Van Buren, and did so, but they divided on the two-thirds rule, and gave a majority of their votes for it, that is to say, 13 votes; but as 13 was not a majority of 26, one delegate was got to stand aside: and then the vote stood 13 to 12. The Virginia delegation, headed by the most respectable William H. Roane (with a few exceptions), remained faithful—disregarding the attempt to release them at Shockoe Hill, and voting steadily for Mr. Van Buren, as well on all the ballotings as on the two-thirds question—which was the real one. Some members of the Capitol nocturnal committee were in the convention, and among its most active managers—and the most zealous against Mr. Van Buren. In that profusion of letters with which they covered the country to undermine him, they placed the objection on the ground of the impossibility of electing him: now it was seen that the impossibility was on the other side—that it was impossible to defeat him, except by betraying trusts, violating instructions, combining the odds and ends of all factions; and then getting a rule adopted by which a minority was to govern.

The motion of Mr. Miller was not voted upon. It was summarily disposed of, without the responsibility of a direct vote. The enemies of Mr. Van Buren having secured the presiding officer at the start, all motions were decided against them; and after a long session of storm and rage, intermitted during the night for sleep and intrigue, and resumed in the morning, an eighth ballot was taken: and without hope for Mr. Van Buren. As his vote went down, that for Messrs. Cass, Buchanan, and R. M. Johnson rose; but without ever carrying either of them to a majority, much less two-thirds. Seeing the combination against him, the friends of Mr. Van Buren withdrew his name, and the party was then without a candidate known to the people. Having killed off the one chosen by the people, the convention remained masters of the field, and ready to supply one of its own. The intrigue, commenced in 1842, in the Gilmer letter, had succeeded one-half. It had put down one man, but another was to be put up; and there were enough of Mr. Van Buren's friends to defeat that part of the scheme. They determined to render their country that service, and therefore withdrew Mr. Van Buren, that they might go in a body for a new man. Among the candidates for the vice-presidency was Mr. James K. Polk, of Tennessee. His interest as a vice-presidential candidate lay with Mr. Van Buren, and they had been much associated in the minds of each other's friends. It was an easy step for them to support for the first office, on the loss of their first choice, the citizen whom they intended for the second. Without public announcements, he was slightly developed as a presidential candidate on the eighth ballot; on the ninth he was unanimously nominated, all the president-makers who had been voting for others—for Cass, Buchanan, Johnson—taking the current the instant they saw which way it was going, in order that they might claim the merit of conducting it. "You bring but seven captives to my tent, but thousands of you took them," was the sarcastic remark of a king of antiquity at seeing the multitude that came to claim honors and rewards for taking a few prisoners. Mr. Polk might have made the same exclamation in relation to the multitude that assumed to have nominated him. Their name was legion: for, besides the unanimous convention, there was a host of outside operators, each of whom claimed the merit of having governed the vote of some delegate. Never was such a multitude seen claiming the merit, and demanding the reward, for having done what had been done before they heard of it.

The nomination was a surprise and a marvel to the country. No voice in favor of it had been heard; no visible sign in the political horizon had announced it. Two small symptoms—small in themselves and equivocal in their import, and which would never have been remembered except for the event—doubtfully foreshadowed it. One was a paragraph in a Nashville newspaper, hypothetically suggesting that Mr. Polk should be taken up if Mr. Van Buren should be abandoned; the other, the ominous circumstance that the Tennessee State nominating convention made a recommendation (Mr. Polk) for the second office, and none for the first; and Tennessee being considered a Van Buren State, this omission was significant, seeming to leave open the door for his ejection, and for the admission of some other person. And so the delegates from that State seemed to understand it, voting steadily against him, until he was withdrawn.

The ostensible objection to the last against Mr. Van Buren, was his opposition to immediate annexation. The shallowness of that objection was immediately shown in the unanimous nomination of his bosom friend, Mr. Silas Wright, identified with him in all that related to the Texas negotiation, for Vice-President. He was nominated upon the proposition of Mr. Robert J. Walker—a main-spring in all the movements against Mr. Van Buren, whose most indefatigable opponents sympathized with the Texas scrip and land speculators. Mr. Wright instantly declined the nomination; and Mr. George M. Dallas, of Pennsylvania, was taken in his place.

The Calhoun New York convention expired in the conception. It never met. The Tyler Baltimore convention was carried the length of an actual meeting, and went through the forms of a nomination, without the distraction of a rival candidate. It met the same day and place with the democratic convention, as if to officiate with it, and to be ready to offer a *pis aller*, but to no purpose. It made its own nomination—received an elaborate letter of thanks and acceptance from Mr. Tyler, who took it quite seriously; and two months afterwards joined the democracy for Polk and Dallas, against Clay and Frelinghuysen—his old whig friends. He had co-operated in all the schemes against Mr. Van Buren, in the hope of being taken up in his place; and there was an interest, calling itself democratic, which was willing to oblige him. But all the sound heart of the democracy recoiled from the idea of touching a man who, after having been raised high by the democracy, had gone over to the whigs, to be raised still higher, and now came back to the democracy to obtain the highest office they could give.

And here ends the history of this long intrigue—one of the most elaborate, complex and daring, ever practised in an intelligent country; and with too much success in putting down some, and just disappointment in putting up others: for no one of those who engaged in this intrigue ever reached the office for which they strived. My opinion of it was expressed, warmly but sincerely, from the first moment it was broached to me on the steps of the Capitol, when accosted by Mr. Brown, down to the rejection of the treaty in the Senate, and the defeat of Mr. Van Buren in the convention. Of this latter event, the author of this View thus wrote in a public letter to Missouri:

> "Neither Mr. Polk nor Mr. Dallas has any thing to do with the intrigue which has nullified the choice of the people, and the rights of the people, and the principles of our government, in the person of Mr. Van Buren; and neither of them should be injured or prejudiced by it. Those who hatched that intrigue, have become its victims. They who dug a pit for the innocent have fallen into it; and there let them lie, for the present, while all hands attend to the election, and give us our full majority of ten thousand in Missouri. For the rest, the time will come; and people now, as twenty years ago (when their choice was nullified in the person of General Jackson), will teach the Congress intriguers to attend to law-making and let President-making and un-making alone in future. The Texas treaty, which consummated this intrigue, was nothing but the final act in a long conspiracy, in which the sacrifice of Mr. Van Buren had been previously agreed upon; and the nomination of Mr. Wright for Vice-President proves it; for his opinions and those of Mr. Van Buren, on the Texas question, were identical, and if fatal to one should have been fatal to the other. Besides, Mr. Van Buren was right, and whenever Texas is admitted, it will have to be done in the way pointed out by him. Having mentioned Mr. Wright, I will say that recent events have made him known to the public, as he has long been to his friends, *the Cato of America, and a star of the first magnitude in our political firmament.*"

And now, why tell these things which may be quoted to the prejudice of democratic institutions? I answer: To prevent that prejudice! and to prevent the repetition of such practices. Democracy is not to be prejudiced by it, for it was the work of politicians; and as far as depended upon the people, they rebuked it. The intrigue did not succeed in elevating any of its authors to the presidency; and the annexation treaty, the fruit of so much machination, was rejected by the Senate; and the annexation afterwards effected by the legislative concurrence of the two powers. From the first inception, with the Gilmer letter, down to the Baltimore conclusion in the convention, the intrigue was carried on; and was only successful in the convention by the help of the rule which made the minority its master. That convention is an era in our political history, to be looked back upon as the starting point in a course of usurpation which has taken the choice of President out of the hands of the people, and vested it in the hands of a self-constituted and irresponsible assemblage. The wrong to Mr. Van Buren was personal and temporary, and died with the occasion, and constitutes no part of the object in writing this chapter: the wrong to the people, and the injury to republican institutions, and to our frame of government, was deep and abiding, and calls for the grave and correctional judgment of history. It was the first instance in which a body of men, unknown to the laws and the constitution, and many of them (as being members of Congress, or holding offices of honor or profit) constitutionally disqualified to serve even as electors, assumed to treat the American presidency as their private property, to be disposed at their own will and pleasure; and, it may be added, for their own profit: for many of them demanded, and received reward. It was the first instance of such a disposal of the presidency—for these nominations are the election, so far as the party is concerned; but not the last. It has become the rule since, and has been improved upon. These assemblages now perpetuate themselves, through a committee of their own, ramified into each State, sitting permanently from four years to four years; and working incessantly to govern the election that is to come, after having governed the one that is past. The man they choose must always be a character of no force, that they may rule him: and they rule always for their own advantage—"constituting a power behind the throne greater than the throne." The reader of English history is familiar with the term, "cabal," and its origin—taking its spelling from the initial letters of the names of the five combined intriguing ministers of Charles II.—and taking its meaning from the conduct and characters of these five ministers. What that meaning was, one of the five wrote to another for his better instruction, not suspecting that the indefatigable curiosity of a subsequent generation would ever ferret out the little missive. Thus: "*The principal spring of our actions was to have the government in our own hands; that our principal views were the conservation of this power—great employments to ourselves—and great opportunities of rewarding those who have helped to raise us, and of harming those who stood in opposition to us.*" Such was the government which the "cabal" gave England; and such is the one which the convention system gives us: and until this system is abolished, and the people resume their rights, the elective principle of our government is suppressed: and the people have no more control over the selection of the man who is to be their President, than the subjects of kings have over the birth of the child who is to be their ruler.

CHAPTER CXXXVII.

PRESIDENTIAL: DEMOCRATIC NATIONAL CONVENTION: MR. CALHOUN'S REFUSAL TO SUBMIT HIS NAME TO IT: HIS REASONS.

Before the meeting of this convention Mr. Calhoun, in a public address to his political friends, made known his determination not to suffer his name to go before that assemblage as a candidate for the presidency, and stated his reasons for that determination. Many of those reasons were of a nature to rise above personal considerations—to look deep into the nature and working of our government—and to show objections to the convention system (as practised), which have grown stronger with time. His first objection was as to the mode of choosing delegates, and the manner of their giving in their votes—he contending for district elections, and the delegates to vote individually, and condemning all other modes of electing and voting:

> "I hold, then, that the convention should be so constituted, as to utter fully and clearly the voice of the people, and not that of political managers, or office holders and office seekers, and for that purpose, I hold it indispensable that the delegates should be appointed directly by the people, or to use the language of General Jackson, should be 'fresh from the people.' I also hold, that the only possible mode to effect this, is for the people to choose the delegates by districts, and that they should vote *per capita*. Every other mode of appointing would be controlled by political machinery, and place the appointments in the hands of the few, who work it."

This was written ten years ago: there have been three of these conventions since that time by each political party: and each have verified the character here given of them. Veteran office holders, and undaunted office seekers, collusively or furtively appointed, have had the control of these nominations—the office holders all being forbid by the constitution to be even electors, and the office seekers forbid by shame and honor (if amenable to such sensations), to take part in nominating a President from whom they would demand pay for their vote. Mr. Calhoun continues:

> "I object, then, to the proposed convention, because it will not be constituted in conformity with the fundamental articles of the republican creed. The delegates to it will be appointed from some of the States, not by the people in districts, but, as has been stated, by State conventions en masse, composed of delegates appointed in all cases, as far as I am informed, by county or district conventions, and in some cases, if not misinformed, these again composed of delegates appointed by still smaller divisions, or a few interested individuals. Instead then of being directly, or fresh from the people, the delegates to the Baltimore convention will be the delegates of delegates; and of course removed, in all cases, at least three, if not four degrees from the people. At each successive remove, the voice of the people will become less full and distinct, until, at last, it will be so faint and imperfect, as not to be audible. To drop metaphor, I hold it impossible to form a scheme more perfectly calculated to annihilate the control of the people over the presidential election, and vest it in those who make politics a trade, and who live or expect to live on the government."

Mr. Calhoun proceeds to take a view of the working of the constitution in a fair election by the people and by the States, and considered the plan adopted as a compromise between the large and the small States. In the popular election through electors, the large States had the advantage, as presenting masses of population which would govern the choice: in the election by States in the House of Representatives, the small States had the advantage, as the whole voted equally. This, then, was considered a compromise. The large States making the election when they were united: when not united, making the nomination of three (five as the constitution first stood), out of which the States chose one. This was a compromise; and all compromises should be kept when founded in the structure of the government, and made by its founders. Total defeat of the will of the people, and total frustration of the intent of the constitution, both in the electoral nomination and the House choice of a President, was seen in the exercise of this power over presidential nominations by Congress caucuses, before their corruption required a resort to conventions, intended to be the absolute reflex of the popular will. Of this Mr. Calhoun says:

> "The danger was early foreseen, and to avoid it, some of the wisest and most experienced statesmen of former days so strongly objected to congressional caucuses to nominate candidates for the presidency, that they never could be induced to attend them; among these it will be sufficient to name Mr. Macon and Mr. Lowndes. Others, believing that this provision of the constitution was too refined for practice, were solicitous to amend it, but without impairing the influence of the smaller States in the election. Among these, I rank myself. With that object, resolutions were introduced, in 1828, in the Senate by Colonel Benton, and in the House by Mr. McDuffie, providing for districting the State, and for referring the election back to the people, in case there should be no choice, to elect one from the two highest candidates. The principle which governed in the amendment proposed, was to give a fair compensation to the smaller States for the surrender of their advantage in the eventual choice, by the House, and at the same time to make the mode of electing the President more strictly in conformity with the principles of our popular institutions, and to be less liable to corruption, than the existing. They (the resolutions of McDuffie and Benton) received the general support of the party, but were objected to by a few, as not being a full equivalent to the smaller States."

The Congress presidential caucuses were put down by the will of the people, and in both parties at the same time. They were put down for not conforming to the will of the people, for incompatibility between the legislative and the elective functions, for being in office at the same time, for following their own will, instead of representing that of their constituents. Mr. Calhoun concurred in putting them down, but preferred them a hundred times over to the intriguing, juggling, corrupt and packed machinery into which the conventions had so rapidly degenerated.

> "And here let me add, that as objectionable as I think a congressional caucus for nominating a President, it is, in my opinion, far less so than a convention constituted as is proposed. The former had indeed many things to recommend it. Its members consisting of senators and representatives, were the immediate organs of the State legislatures, or the people; were responsible to them, respectively, and were for the most part, of higher character, standing, and talents. They voted per capita, and what is very important, they represented fairly the relative strength of the party in their respective States. In all these important particulars, it was all that could be desired for a nominating body, and formed a striking contrast to the proposed convention; and yet, it could not be borne by the people in the then purer days of the republic. I, acting with General Jackson and most of the leaders of the party at that time, contributed to put it down, because we believed it to be liable to be acted on and influenced by the patronage of the government—an objection far more applicable to a convention constituted as the one proposed, than to a congressional caucus. Far however was it from my intention, in aiding to put that down, to substitute in its place what I regard as a hundred times more objectionable in every point of view. Indeed, if there must be an intermediate body between the people and the election, unknown to the constitution, it may be well questioned whether a better than the old plan of a congressional caucus can be devised."

Mr. Calhoun considered the convention system, degenerated to the point it was in 1844, to have been a hundred times more objectionable than the Congress caucuses which had been repudiated by the people: measured by the same scale, and they are a thousand times worse at present—having succeeded to every objection that was made against the Congress caucuses, and superadded a multitude of others going directly to scandalous corruption, open intrigue, direct bargain and sale, and flagrant disregard of the popular will. One respect in which they had degenerated from the Congress caucus was in admitting a State to give its full vote in nominating a President, which could either give no vote at all, or a divided one, to the nominated candidate. In the Congress caucus that anomaly could not happen. The members of the party only voted: and if there were no members of a party from a State, there was no vote from that State in the caucus: if a divided representation, then a vote according to the division. This was fair, and prevented a nomination being made by those who could do nothing in the election. This objection to the convention system, and a grievous one it is as practised, he sets forth in a clear and forcible point of view. He says:

"I have laid down the principle, on which I rest the objection in question, with the limitation, that the relative weight of the States should be maintained, making due allowance for their relative party strength. The propriety of the limitation is so apparent, that but a few words, in illustration, will be required. The convention is a party convention, and professedly intended to take the sense of the party, which cannot be done fairly, if States having but little party strength, are put on equality with those which have much. If that were done, the result might be, that a small portion of the party from States the least sound, politically, and which could give but little support in Congress, might select the candidate, and make the President, against a great majority of the soundest, and on which the President and his administration would have to rely for support. All this is clearly too unfair and improper to be denied. There may be a great difficulty in applying a remedy in a convention, but I do not feel myself called upon to say how it can be done, or by what standard the relative party strength of the respective States should be determined; perhaps the best would be their relative strength in Congress at the time. In laying down the principle, I added the limitation for the sake of accuracy, and to show how imperfectly the party must be represented, when it is overlooked. I see no provision in the proposed convention to meet it."

The objection is clearly and irresistibly shown: the remedy is not so clear. The Congress representation for the time being is suggested for the rule of the convention: it is not always the true rule. A safer one is, the general character of the State—its general party vote—and its probable present party strength. Even that rule may not attain exact precision; but, between a rule which may admit of a slight error, and no rule at all to keep out notorious unfounded votes—votes representing no constituency, unable to choose an elector, having no existence when the election comes on, yet potential at the nomination, and perhaps governing it: between these two extremes there is no room for hesitation, or choice: the adoption of some rule which would exclude notoriously impotent votes, becomes essential to the rights and safety of the party, and is peremptorily demanded by the principle of popular representation. The danger of centralizing the nomination—(which, so far as the party is concerned, is the election)—in the hands of a few States, by the present convention mode of nomination, is next shown by Mr. Calhoun.

"But, in order to realize how the convention will operate, it will be necessary to view the combined effects of the objections which I have made. Thus viewed, it will be found, that a convention so constituted, tends irresistibly to centralization—centralization of the control over the presidential election in the hands of a few of the central, large States, at first, and finally, in political managers, office-holders, and office-seekers; or to express it differently, in that portion of the community, who live, or expect to live on the government, in contradistinction to the great mass, who expect to live on their own means or their honest industry; and who maintain the government; and politically speaking, emphatically the people. That such would be the case, may be inferred from the fact, that it would afford the means to some six or seven States lying contiguous and not far from the centre of the Union, to control the nomination, and through that the election, by concentrating their united votes in the convention. Give them the power of doing so, and it would not long lie dormant. What may be done by combination, where the temptation is so great, will be sure ere long to be done. To combine and conquer, is not less true as a maxim, where power is concerned, than 'divide and conquer.' Nothing is better established, than that the desire for power can bring together and unite the most discordant materials."

After showing the danger of centralizing the nomination in the hands of a few great contiguous States, Mr. Calhoun goes on to show the danger of a still more fatal and corrupt centralization—that of throwing the nomination into the meshes of a train-band of office-holders and office-seekers—professional President-makers, who live by the trade, having no object but their own reward, preferring a weak to a strong man because they can manage him easiest: and accomplishing their purposes by corrupt combinations, fraudulent contrivances, and direct bribery. Of these train-bands, Mr. Calhoun says:

> "But the tendency to centralization will not stop there. The appointment of delegates en masse by State convention, would tend at the same time, and even with great force, to neutralize the control in the hands of the few, who make politics a trade. The farther the convention is removed from the people, the more certainly the control over it will be placed in the hands of the interested few, and when removed three or four degrees, as has been shown it will be, where the appointment is by State conventions, the power of the people will cease, and the seekers of Executive favor will become supreme. At that stage, an active, trained and combined corps will be formed in the party, whose whole time and attention will be directed to politics. Into their hands the appointments of delegates in all the stages will fall, and they will take special care that none but themselves or their humble and obedient dependents shall be appointed. The central and State conventions will be filled by the most experienced and cunning, and after nominating the President, they will take good care to divide the patronage and offices, both of the general and State governments, among themselves and their dependents. But why say *will*? Is it not *already the case*? Have there not been many instances of State conventions being filled by office holders and office seekers, who, after making the nomination, have divided the offices in the State among themselves and their partisans, and joined in recommending to the candidate whom they have just nominated to appoint them to the offices to which they have been respectively allotted? If such be the case in the infancy of the system, it must end, if such conventions should become the established usage, in the President nominating his successor. When it comes to that, it will not be long before the sword will take the place of the constitution."

And it has come to that. Mr. Tyler set the example in 1844—immediately after this address of Mr. Calhoun was written—and had a presidential convention of his own, composed of office holders and office seekers. Since then the example has been pretty well followed; and now any President that pleases may nominate his successor by having the convention filled with the mercenaries in office, or trying to get in. The evil has now reached a pass that must be corrected, or the elective franchise abandoned. Conventions must be reformed—that is to say, purged of office holders and office seekers—purged of impotent votes—purged of all delegates forbid by the constitution to be electors—purged of intrigue, corruption and jugglery—and brought to reflect the will of the people; or, they must suffer the fate of the Congress caucuses, and be put down. Far better—a thousand times better—to let the constitution work its course; as many candidates offer for President as please; and if no one gets a majority of the whole, then the House of Representatives to choose one from the three highest on the list. In that event, the people would be the nominating body: they would present the three, out of which their representatives would be obliged to take one. This would be a nomination by the *People*, and an election by the States.

One other objection to these degenerate conventions Mr. Calhoun did not mention, but it became since he made his address a prominent one, and an abuse in itself, which insures success to the train-band mercenaries whose profligate practices he so well describes. This is the two-thirds rule, as it is called; the rule that requires a vote of two-thirds of the convention to make a nomination. This puts it in the power of the minority to govern the majority, and enables a few veteran intriguers to manage as they please. And when it is remembered that many are allowed—even the delegates of whole States—to vote in the convention, which can give no vote to the party at the election, it might actually happen that the whole nomination might be contrived and made by straw-delegates, whose constituency could not give a single electoral vote.

CHAPTER CXXXVIII.

ANNEXATION OF TEXAS: SECRET NEGOTIATION PRESIDENTIAL INTRIGUE: SCHEMES OF SPECULATION AND DISUNION.

The President's annual message at the commencement of the session 1843-'44, contained an elaborated paragraph on the subject of Texas and Mexico, which, to those not in the secret, was a complete mystification: to others, and especially to those who had been observant of signs, it foreshadowed a design to interfere in the war between those parties, and to take Texas under the protection of the Union, and to make her cause our own. A scheme of annexation was visible in the studied picture presented of homogeniality between that country and the United States, geographically and otherwise; and which homogeniality was now sufficient to risk a war with Great Britain and Mexico (for the message squinted at war with both), to get Texas back, although it had not been sufficient when the country was ceded to Spain to prevent Mr. Tyler from sanctioning the cession—as he did as a member of the House in 1820 in voting against Mr. Clay's resolution, disapproving and condemning that cession. This enigmatical paragraph was, in fact, intended to break the way for the production of a treaty of annexation, covertly conceived and carried on with all the features of an intrigue, and in flagrant violation of the principles and usages of the government. Acquisitions of territory had previously been made by legislation, and by treaty, as in the case of Louisiana in 1803, and of Florida in 1819; but these treaties were founded upon legislative acts—upon the consent of Congress previously obtained—and in which the treaty-making power was but the instrument of the legislative will. This previous consent and authorization of Congress had not been obtained—on the contrary, had been eschewed and ignored by the secrecy with which the negotiation had been conducted; and was intended to be kept secret until the treaty was concluded, and then to force its adoption for the purpose of increasing the area of slave territory, or to make its rejection a cause for the secession of the Southern States; and in either event, and in all cases, to make the question of annexation a controlling one in the nomination of presidential candidates, and also in the election itself.

The complication of this vast scheme, leading to a consummation so direful as foreign war and domestic disunion, and having its root in personal ambition, and in scrip and land speculation, and spoliation claims— the way it was carried on, and the way it was defeated—altogether present one of the most instructive lessons which the working of our government exhibits; and the more so as the two prominent actors in the scheme had reversed their positions since Texas had been retroceded to Spain. Mr. Calhoun was then in favor of curtailing the area of slave territory, and as a member of Mr. Monroe's cabinet, counselled the establishment of the Missouri compromise line, which abolished slavery in all the upper half of the great province of Louisiana; and, as a member of the same cabinet, counselled the retrocession of Texas to Spain, which extinguished all the slave territory south of the compromise line. Mr. Calhoun was then against slavery extension, and so much in favor of extinguishing slave territory as to be a favorite in the free States, and beat Mr. Adams himself in those States in the presidential election of 1824—receiving more of their votes for Vice-President than Mr. Adams did for President. After the failure in 1833 to unite the slave States against the free ones on the Tariff agitation, he took up the slavery agitation—pursuing it during his life, and leaving it at his death as a legacy to the disciples in his political school. Mr. Tyler was a follower in these amputations and extinction of slave territory in 1819-'20: he was now a follower in the slavery agitation to get back the province which was then given away, or to make it the means of a presidential election, or of Southern dismemberment. This scheme had been going on for two years before it appeared above the political horizon; and the right understanding of the Texas annexation movement in 1844, requires the hidden scheme to be uncovered from its source, and laid open through its long and crooked course: which will be the subject of the next chapter, as shown at the time in a speech from Senator Benton.

CHAPTER CXXXIX.

TEXAS ANNEXATION TREATY: FIRST SPEECH OF MR. BENTON AGAINST IT: EXTRACTS.

MR. BENTON. The President, upon our call, sends us a map and a memoir from the Topographical bureau to show the Senate the boundaries of the country he proposes to annex. This memoir is explicit in presenting the Rio Grande del Norte in its whole extent as a boundary of the republic of Texas, and that in conformity to the law of the Texian Congress establishing its boundaries. The boundaries on the map conform to those in the memoir: each takes for the western limit the Rio Grande from head to mouth; and a law of the Texian Congress is copied into the margin of the map, to show the legal, and the actual, boundaries at the same time. From all this it results that the treaty before us, besides the incorporation of Texas proper, also incorporates into our Union the left bank of the Rio Grande, in its whole extent from its head spring in the *Sierra Verde* (Green Mountain), near the South Pass in the Rocky Mountains, to its mouth in the Gulf of Mexico, four degrees south of New Orleans, in latitude 26°. It is a "*grand and solitary river,*" almost without affluents or tributaries. Its source is in the region of eternal snow; its outlet in the clime of eternal flowers. Its direct course is 1,200 miles; its actual run about 2,000. This immense river, second on our continent to the Mississippi only, and but little inferior to it in length, is proposed to be added in the whole extent of its left bank to the American Union! and that by virtue of a treaty for the *re*-annexation of Texas! Now, the real Texas which we acquired by the treaty of 1803, and flung away by the treaty of 1819, never approached the Rio Grande except near its mouth! while the whole upper part was settled by the Spaniards, and great part of it in the year 1694—just one hundred years before La Salle first saw Texas!—all this upper part was then formed into provinces, on both sides of the river, and has remained under Spanish, or Mexican authority ever since. These former provinces of the Mexican viceroyalty, now departments of the Mexican republic, lying on both sides of the Rio Grande from its head to its mouth, we now propose to incorporate, so far as they lie on the left bank of the river, into our Union, by virtue of a treaty of *re*-annexation with Texas. Let us pause and look at our new and important proposed acquisitions in this quarter. First: there is the department, formerly the province of New Mexico, lying on both sides of the river from its head spring to near the Paso del Norte—that is to say, half down the river. This department is studded with towns and villages—is populated—well cultivated—and covered with flocks and herds. On its left bank (for I only speak of the part which we propose to *re*-annex) is, first, the frontier village Taos, 3,000 souls, and where the custom-house is kept at which the Missouri caravans enter their goods. Then comes Santa Fé, the capital, 4,000 souls—then Albuquerque, 6,000 souls—then some scores of other towns and villages—all more or less populated, and surrounded by flocks and fields. Then come the departments of Chihuahua, Coahuila, and Tamaulipas, without settlements on the left bank of the river, but occupying the right bank, and commanding the left. All this—being parts of four Mexican departments—now under Mexican governors and governments—is permanently reannexed to this Union, if this treaty is ratified; and is actually reannexed from the moment of the signature of the treaty, according to the President's last message, to remain so until the acquisition is rejected by rejecting the treaty! The one-half of the department of New Mexico, with its capital, becomes a territory of the United States: an angle of Chihuahua, at the Paso del Norte, famous for its wine, also becomes ours: a part of the department of Coahuila, not populated on the left bank, which we take, but commanded from the right bank by Mexican authorities: the same of Tamaulipas, the ancient Nuevo San Tander (New St. Andrew), and which covers both sides of the river from its mouth for some hundred miles up, and all the left bank of which is in the power and possession of Mexico. These, in addition to the old Texas; these parts of four States—these towns and villages—these people and territory—these flocks and herds—this *slice* of the republic of Mexico, two thousand miles long, and some hundred broad—all this our President has cut off from its mother empire, and presents to us, and declares it is ours till the Senate rejects it! He calls it Texas! and the cutting off he calls *re*-annexation! Humboldt calls it New Mexico, Chihuahua, Coahuila, and Nuevo San Tander (now Tamaulipas); and the civilized world may qualify this *re*-annexation by the application of some odious and terrible epithet. Demosthenes advised the people of Athens not to take, but to *re*-take a certain city; and in that *re* laid the virtue which saved the act from the character of spoliation and robbery. Will it be equally potent with us? and will the *re*, prefixed to the annexation, legitimate the seizure of two thousand miles of a neighbor's dominion, with whom we have treaties of peace, and friendship, and commerce? Will it legitimate this seizure, made by virtue of a treaty with Texas, when no Texian force—witness the disastrous expeditions to Mier and to Santa Fé—have been seen near it without being killed or taken, to the last man?

The treaty, in all that relates to the boundary of the Rio Grande, is an act of unparalleled outrage on Mexico. It is the seizure of two thousand miles of her territory without a word of explanation with her, and by virtue of a treaty with Texas, to which she is no party. Our Secretary of State (Mr. Calhoun) in his letter to the United States chargé in Mexico, and seven days after the treaty was signed, and after the Mexican minister had withdrawn from our seat of government, shows full well that he was conscious of the enormity of this outrage; knew it was war; and proffered volunteer apologies to avert the consequences which he knew he had provoked.

The President, in his special message of Wednesday last, informs us that we have acquired a title to the ceded territories by his signature to the treaty, wanting only the action of the Senate to perfect it; and that, in the mean time, he will protect it from invasion, and for that purpose has detached all the disposable portions of the army and navy to the scene of action. This is a caper about equal to the mad freaks with which the unfortunate emperor Paul, of Russia, was accustomed to astonish Europe about forty years ago. By this declaration the thirty thousand Mexicans in the left half of the valley of the Rio del Norte are our citizens, and standing, in the language of the President's message, in a hostile attitude towards us, and subject to be repelled as invaders. Taos, the seat of the custom-house, where our caravans enter their goods, is ours: Santa Fé, the capital of New Mexico, is ours: Governor Armijo is our governor, and subject to be tried for treason if he does not submit to us: twenty Mexican towns and villages are ours; and their peaceful inhabitants, cultivating their fields and tending their flocks, are suddenly converted, by a stroke of the President's pen, into American citizens, or American rebels. This is too bad: and, instead of making themselves party to its enormities, as the President invites them to do, I think rather that it is the duty of the Senate to wash its hands of all this part of the transaction by a special disapprobation. The Senate is the constitutional adviser of the President, and has the right, if not the duty, to give him advice when the occasion requires it. I therefore propose, as an additional resolution, appliable to the Rio del Norte boundary only—the one which I will read and send to the Secretary's table—stamping as a spoliation this seizure of Mexican territory—and on which, at the proper time, I shall ask the vote of the Senate.

I now proceed a step further, and rise a step higher, Mr. President, in unveiling the designs and developing the conduct of our administration in this hot and secret pursuit after Texas. It is my business now to show that war with Mexico is a design and an object with it from the beginning, and that the treaty-making power was to be used for that purpose. I know the responsibility of a senator—I mean his responsibility to the moral sense of his country and the world—in attributing so grave a culpability to this administration. I know the whole extent of this responsibility, and shall therefore be careful to proceed upon safe and solid ground. I shall say nothing but upon proof—upon the proof furnished by the President himself—and ask for my opinions no credence beyond the strict letter of these proofs. For this purpose I have recourse to the messages and correspondence which the President has sent us, and begin with the message of the 22d of April—the one which communicated the treaty to the Senate. That message, after a strange and ominous declaration that no sinister means have been used—no intrigue set on foot—to procure the consent of Texas to the annexation, goes on to show exactly the contrary, and to betray the President's design to protect Texas by receiving her into our Union and adopting her war with Mexico.

I proceed to another piece of evidence to the same effect—namely, the letter of the present Secretary of State to Mr. Benjamin Green, our chargé at Mexico, under date of the 19th of April past. The letter has been already referred to, and will be only read now in the sentence which declares that the treaty has been made in the full view of war! for that alone can be the meaning of this sentence:

> "It has taken the step (to wit, the step of making the treaty) in full view of all possible consequences, but not without a desire and a hope that a full and fair disclosure of the causes which induced it to do so, would prevent the disturbance of the harmony subsisting between the two countries, which the United States is anxious to preserve."

This is part of the despatch which communicates to Mexico the fact of the conclusion of the treaty of annexation—that treaty, the conclusion of which the formal and reiterated declarations of the Mexican government informed our administration, during its negotiation, would be war. I will quote one of these declarations, the last one made by General Almonte, the Mexican minister, and in reply to the letter of our Secretary who considered the previous declarations as *threats*. General Almonte disclaims the idea of a *threat*—repeats his asseveration that it is a *notice* only, and that in a case in which it was the right and the duty of Mexico to give the *notice* which would apprise us of the consequences of carrying the treaty of annexation to a conclusion.

After receiving this notification from the Mexican minister, the letter of our present Secretary, of the 19th instant, just quoted, directing our chargé to inform the Mexican government of the conclusion of the treaty of annexation, must be considered as an official notification to Mexico that the war has begun! and so indeed it has! and as much to our astonishment as to that of the Mexicans! Who among us can ever forget the sensations produced in this chamber, on Wednesday last, when the marching and the sailing orders were read! and still more, when the message was read which had set the army and navy in motion!

These orders and the message, after having been read in this chamber, were sent to the printer, and have not yet returned: I can only refer to them as I heard them read, and from a brief extract which I took of the message; and must refer to others to do them justice. From all that I could hear, the war is begun; and begun by orders issued by the President before the treaty was communicated to the Senate! We are informed of a squadron, and an army of "*observation*," sent to the Mexican ports, and Mexican frontier, with orders to watch, remonstrate, and report; and to communicate with President Houston! Now, what is an army of *observation*, but an army in the field for war? It is an army whose name is known, and whose character is defined, and which is incident to war alone. It is to watch the ENEMY! and can never be made to watch a FRIEND! Friends cannot be watched by armed men, either individually or nationally, without open enmity. Let an armed man take a position before your door, show himself to your family, watch your movements, and remonstrate with you, and report upon you, if he judged your movements equivocal: let him do this, and what is it but an act of hostility and of outrage which every feeling of the heart, and every law of God and man, require you to resent and repulse? This would be the case with the mere individual; still more with nations, and when squadrons and armies are the watchers and remonstrants. Let Great Britain send an army and navy *to lie in wait* upon our frontiers, and before our cities, and then see what a cry of war would be raised in our country. The same of Mexico. She must feel herself outraged and attacked; she must feel our treaties broken; all our citizens within her dominions alien enemies; their commerce to be instantly ruined, and themselves expelled from the country. This must be our condition, unless the Senate (or Congress) saves the country. We are at war with Mexico now; and the message which covers the marching and sailing orders is still more extraordinary than they. The message assumes the republic of Texas to be part of the American Union by the mere signature of the treaty, and to remain so until the treaty is rejected, if rejected at all; and, in the mean time, the President is to use the army and the navy to protect the acquired country from invasion, like any part of the existing Union, and to treat as hostile all adverse possessors or intruders. According to this, besides what may happen at Vera Cruz, Tampico, Matamoros, and other ports, and besides what may happen on the frontiers of Texas proper, the Mexican population in New Mexico, and Governor Armijo, or in his absence the governor *ad interim*, Don Mariano Chaves, may find themselves pursued as rebels and traitors to the United States.

The war with Mexico, and its unconstitutionality, is fully shown: its injustice remains to be exhibited, and that is an easy task. What is done in violation of treaties, in violation of neutrality, in violation of an armistice, must be unjust. All this occurs in this case, and a great deal more. Mexico is our neighbor. We are at peace with her. Social, commercial, and diplomatic relations subsist between us, and the interest of the two nations requires these relations to continue. We want a country which was once ours, but which, by treaty, we have acknowledged to be hers. That country has revolted. Thus far it has made good its revolt, and not a doubt rests upon my mind that she will make it good for ever. But the contest is not over. An armistice, duly proclaimed, and not revoked, strictly observed by each in not firing a gun, though inoperative thus far in the appointment of commissioners to treat for peace: this armistice, only determinable upon notice, suspends the war. Two thousand miles of Texian frontier is held in the hands of Mexico, and all attempts to conquer that frontier have signally failed: witness the disastrous expeditions to Mier and to Santa Fé. We acknowledge the right—the moral and political right—of Mexico to resubjugate this province, if she can. We declare our neutrality: we profess friendship: we proclaim our respect for Mexico. In the midst of all this, we make a treaty with Texas for transferring herself to the United States, and that without saying a word to Mexico, while receiving notice from her that such transfer would be war. Mexico is treated as a nullity; and the province she is endeavoring to reconquer is suddenly, by the magic of a treaty signature, changed into United States domain. We want the country; but instead of applying to Mexico, and obtaining her consent to the purchase, or waiting a few months for the events which would supersede the necessity of Mexican consent—instead of this plain and direct course, a secret negotiation was entered into with Texas, in total contempt of the acknowledged rights of Mexico, and without saying a word to her until all was over. Then a messenger is despatched in furious haste to this same Mexico, the bearer of volunteer apologies, of deprecatory excuses, and of an offer of ten millions of dollars for Mexican acquiescence in what Texas has done. Forty days are allowed for the return of the messenger; and the question is, will he bring back the consent? That question is answered in the Mexican official notice of war, if the treaty of annexation was made! and it is answered in the fact of not applying to her for her consent before the treaty was made. The wrong to Mexico is confessed in the fact of sending this messenger, and in the terms of the letter of which he was the bearer. That letter of Mr. Secretary Calhoun, of the 19th of April, to Mr. Benjamin Green, the United States chargé in Mexico, is the most unfortunate in the annals of human diplomacy! By the fairest implications, it admits insult and injury to Mexico, and violation of her territorial boundaries! it admits that we should have had her previous consent—should have had her concurrence—that we have injured her as little as possible—and that we did all this in full view of all possible consequences! that is to say, in full view of war! in plain English, that we have wronged her, and will fight her for it. As an excuse for all this, the imaginary designs of a third power, which designs are four times solemnly disavowed, are brought forward as a justification of our conduct; and an incomprehensible terror of immediate destruction is alleged as the cause of not applying to her for her "*previous consent*" during the eight months that the negotiation continued, and during the whole of which time we had a minister in Mexico, and Mexico had a minister in Washington. This letter is surely the most unfortunate in the history of human diplomacy. It admits the wrong, and tenders war. It is a confession throughout, by the fairest implication, of injustice to Mexico. It is a confession that her "*concurrence*" and "*her previous consent*" were necessary.

It is now my purpose, Mr. President, to show that all this movement, which is involving such great and serious consequences, and drawing upon us the eyes of the civilized world, is bottomed upon a weak and groundless pretext, discreditable to our government, and insulting and injurious to Great Britain. We want Texas—that is to say, the Texas of La Salle; and we want it for great national reasons, obvious as day, and permanent as nature. We want it because it is geographically appurtenant to our division of North America, essential to our political, commercial, and social system, and because it would be detrimental and injurious to us to have it fall into the hands or to sink under the domination of any foreign power. For these reasons, I was against sacrificing the country when it was thrown away—and thrown away by those who are now so suddenly possessed of a fury to get it back. For these reasons, I am for getting it back whenever it can be done with peace and honor, or even at the price of just war against any intrusive European power: but I am against all disguise and artifice—against all pretexts—and especially against weak and groundless pretexts, discreditable to ourselves, offensive to others, too thin and shallow not to be seen through by every beholder, and merely invented to cover unworthy purposes. I am against the inventions which have been brought forward to justify the secret concoction of this treaty, and its sudden explosion upon us, like a ripened plot, and a charged bomb, forty days before the conventional nomination of a presidential candidate. In looking into this pretext, I shall be governed by the evidence alone which I find upon the face of the papers, regretting that the resolution which I have laid upon the table for the examination of persons at the bar of the Senate, has not yet been adopted. That resolution is in these words:

> "*Resolved*, That the AUTHOR of the '*private letter*' from London, in the summer of 1843 (believed to be Mr. Duff Green), addressed to the American Secretary of State (Mr. Upshur), and giving him the first intelligence of the (imputed) British anti-slavery designs upon Texas, and the contents of which '*private letter*' were made the basis of the Secretary's leading despatch of the 8th of August following, to our chargé in Texas, for procuring the annexation of Texas

to the United States, be SUMMONED to appear at the bar of the Senate, to answer on oath to all questions in relation to the contents of said *'private letter,'* and of any others in relation to the same subject: and also to answer all questions, so far as he shall be able, in relation to the origin and objects of the treaty for the annexation of Texas, and of all the designs, influences, and interests which led to the formation thereof.

"*Resolved, also*, That the Senate will examine at its bar, or through a committee, such other persons as shall be deemed proper in relation to their knowledge of any, or all, of the foregoing points of inquiry."

I hope, Mr. President, this resolution will be adopted. It is due to the gravity of the occasion that we should have facts and good evidence before us. We are engaged in a transaction which concerns the peace and the honor of the country; and extracts from private letters, and letters themselves, with or without name, and, it may be, from mistaken or interested persons, are not the evidence on which we should proceed. Dr. Franklin was examined at the bar of the British House of Commons before the American war, and I see no reason why those who wish to inform the Senate, and others from whom the Senate could obtain information, should not be examined at our bar, or at that of the House, before the Senate or Congress engages in the Mexican war. It would be a curious incident in the Texas drama if it should turn out to be a fact that the whole annexation scheme was organized before the reason for it was discovered in London! and if, from the beginning, the abolition plot was to be burst upon us, under a sudden and overwhelming sense of national destruction, exactly forty days before the national convention at Baltimore! I know nothing about these secrets; but, being called upon to act, and to give a vote which may be big with momentous consequences, I have a right to know the truth; and shall continue to ask for it, until fully obtained, or finally denied. I know not what the proof will be, if the examination is had. I pretend to no private knowledge; but I have my impressions; and if they are erroneous, let them be effaced—if correct, let them be confirmed.

In the absence of the evidence which this responsible and satisfactory examination might furnish, I limit myself to the information which appears upon the face of the papers—imperfect, defective, disjointed, and fixed up for the occasion, as those papers evidently are. And here I must remark upon the absence of all the customary information which sheds light upon the origin, progress, and conclusion of treaties. No minutes of conferences—no protocols—no propositions, or counter-propositions—no inside view of the nascent and progressive negotiation. To supply all this omission, the Senate is driven to the tedious process of calling on the President, day by day, for some new piece of information; and the endless necessity for these calls—the manner in which they are answered—and the often delay in getting any answer at all—become new reasons for the adoption of my resolution, and for the examination of persons at the bar of the Senate.

The first piece of testimony I shall use in making good the position I have assumed, is the letter of Mr. Upshur, our Secretary of State, to Mr. Murphy, our chargé in Texas dated the 8th day of August, in the year 1843. It is the first one, so far as we are permitted to see, that begins the business of the Texas annexation; and has all the appearance of beginning it in the middle, so far as the United States are concerned, and upon grounds previously well considered: for this letter of the 8th of August, 1843, contains every reason on which the whole annexation movement has been defended, or justified. And, here, I must repeat what I have already said: in quoting these letters of the secretaries, I use the name of the writer to discriminate the writer, but not to impute it to him. The President is the author: the secretary only his head clerk, writing by his command, and having no authority to write any thing but as he commands. This important letter, the basis of all Texian "*immediate*" annexation, opens thus:

"SIR: A private letter from a citizen of Maryland, then in London, contains the following passage:

"'I learn from a source entitled to the fullest confidence, that there is now here a Mr. Andrews, deputed by the abolitionists of Texas to negotiate with the British government. That he has seen Lord Aberdeen, and submitted his project for the abolition of slavery in Texas, which is, that there shall be organized a company in England, who shall advance a sum sufficient to pay for the slaves now in Texas, and receive in payment Texas lands; that the sum thus advanced shall be paid over as an indemnity for the abolition of slavery; and I am authorized by the Texian minister to say to you, that Lord Aberdeen has agreed that the British government will guarantee the payment of the interest on this loan, upon condition that the Texian government will abolish slavery.'

"The writer professes to feel entire confidence in the accuracy of this information. He is a man of great intelligence, and well versed in public affairs. Hence I have every reason to confide in the correctness of his conclusions."

The name of the writer is not given, but he is believed to be Mr. Duff Green—a name which suggests a vicarious relation to our Secretary of State—which is a synonym for intrigue—and a voucher for finding in London whatever he was sent to bring back—who is the putative recipient of the Gilmer letter to a friend in Maryland, destined for General Jackson—and whose complicity with this Texas plot is a fixed fact. Truly this "inhabitant of Maryland," who lived in Washington, and whose existence was as ubiquitous as his *rôle* was vicarious, was a very indispensable agent in all this Texas plot.

The letter then goes on, through a dozen elaborate paragraphs, to give every reason for the annexation of Texas, founded on the apprehension of British views there and the consequent danger to the slave property of the South, and other injuries to the United States, which have been so incontinently reproduced, and so tenaciously adhered to ever since.

Thus commenced the plan for the immediate annexation of Texas to the United States, as the only means of saving that country from British domination, and from the anti-slavery schemes attributed to her by Mr. Duff Green. Unfortunately, it was not deemed necessary to inquire into the truth of this gentleman's information; and it was not until four months afterwards, and until after the most extraordinary efforts to secure annexation had been made by our government, that it was discovered that the information given by Mr. Green was entirely mistaken and unfounded! The British minister (the Earl of Aberdeen) and the Texian chargé in London (Mr. Ashbel Smith), both of whom were referred to by Mr. Green, being informed in the month of November of the use which had been made of their names, availed themselves of the first opportunity to contradict the whole story to our minister, Mr. Everett. This minister immediately communicated these important contradictions to his own government, and we find them in the official correspondence transmitted to us by Mr. Everett, under dates of the 3d and 16th of November, 1843. I quote first from that of the 3d of November:

(Here was read Mr. Everett's account of his first conversation with the Earl of Aberdeen on this subject.)

I quote copiously, and with pleasure, Mr. President, from this report of Lord Aberdeen's conversation with Mr. Everett; it is frank and friendly, equally honorable to the minister as a man and a statesman, and worthy of the noble spirit of the great William Pitt. Nothing could dissipate more completely, and extinguish more utterly, the insidious designs imputed to Great Britain; nothing could be more satisfactory and complete; nothing more was wanting to acquit the British government of all the alarming designs imputed to her. It was enough; but the Earl of Aberdeen, in the fulness of his desire to leave the American government no ground for suspicion or complaint on this head, voluntarily returned to the topic a few days afterwards; and, on the 6th of November, again disclaims in the strongest terms the offensive designs imputed to his government. Mr. Everett thus relates, in his letter of the 16th of November, the substance of these renewed declarations:

(Here the letter giving an account of the second interview was read.)

Thus, twice, in three days, the British minister fully, formally, and in the broadest manner contradicted the whole story upon the faith of which our President had commenced (so far as the papers show the commencement of it) his immediate annexation project, as the only means of counteracting the dangerous designs of Great Britain! But this was not all. There was another witness in London who had been referred to by Mr. Duff Green; and it remained for this witness to confirm or contradict his story. This was the Texian chargé (Mr. Ashbel Smith): and the same letter from Mr. Everett, of the 16th of November, brought his contradiction in unequivocal terms. Mr. Everett thus recites it:

(The passage was read.)

Such was the statement of Mr. Ashbel Smith! and the story of Mr. Duff Green, which had been made the basis of the whole scheme for *immediate* annexation, being now contradicted by two witnesses—the two which he himself had named—it might have been expected that some halt or pause would have taken place, to give an opportunity for consideration and reflection, and for consulting the American people, and endeavoring to procure the consent of Mexico. This might have been expected: but not so the fact. On the contrary, the *immediate* annexation was pressed more warmly than ever, and the administration papers became more clamorous and incessant in their accusations of Great Britain. Seeing this, and being anxious (to use his own words) to put a stop to these misrepresentations, and to correct the errors of the American government, the Earl of Aberdeen, in a formal despatch to Mr. Pakenham, the new British minister at Washington, took the trouble of a third contradiction, and a most formal and impressive one, to all the evil designs in relation to Texas, and, through Texas, upon the United States, which were thus perseveringly attributed to his government. This paper, destined to become a great landmark in this controversy, from the frankness and fulness of its disavowals, and from the manner in which detached phrases, picked out of it, have been used by our Secretary of State [Mr. CALHOUN] since the treaty was signed, to justify its signature, deserves to be read in full, and to be made a corner-stone in the debate on this subject. I therefore, quote it in full, and shall read it at length in the body of my speech. This is it:

(The whole letter read.)

This was intended to stop the misrepresentations which were circulated, and to correct the errors of the government in relation to Great Britain and Texas. It was a reiteration, and that for the third time, and voluntarily, of denial of all the alarming designs attributed to Great Britain, and by means of which a Texas agitation was getting up in the United States. Besides the full declaration made to our federal government, as head of the Union, a special assurance was given to the slaveholding States, to quiet their apprehensions, the truth and sufficiency of which must be admitted by every person who cannot furnish proof to the contrary. I read this special assurance a second time, that its importance may be more distinctly and deeply felt by every senator:

> "*And the governments of the slaveholding States may be assured, that, although we shall not desist from those open and honest efforts which we have constantly made for procuring the abolition of slavery throughout the world, we shall neither openly nor secretly resort to any measures which can tend to disturb their internal tranquillity, or thereby to affect the prosperity of the American Union.*"

It was on the 26th day of February that this noble despatch was communicated to the (then) American Secretary of State. That gentleman lost his life by an awful catastrophe on the 28th, and it seems to be understood, and admitted all around, that the treaty of annexation was agreed upon, and virtually concluded before his death. Nothing, then, in Lord Aberdeen's declaration, could have had any effect upon its formation or conclusion. Yet, six days after the actual signature of the treaty by the present Secretary of State—namely, on the 18th day of April—this identical despatch of Lord Aberdeen is seized upon, in a letter to Mr. Pakenham, to justify the formation of the treaty, and to prove the necessity for the *immediate* annexation of Texas to the United States, as a measure of self-defence, and as the only means of saving our Union! Listen to the two or three first paragraphs of that letter: it is the long one filled with those negro statistics of which Mr. Pakenham declines the controversy. The secretary says:

(Here the paragraphs were read, and the Senate heard with as much amazement as Mr. Pakenham could have done, that comparative statement of the lame, blind, halt, idiotic, pauper and jail tenants of the free and the slave blacks, which the letter to the British minister contained, with a view to prove that slavery was their best condition.)

It is evident, Mr. President, that the treaty was commenced, carried on, formed, and agreed upon, so far as the documents show its origin, in virtue of the information given in the private letter of Mr. Duff Green, contradicted as that was by the Texian and British ministers, to whom it referred. It is evident from all the papers that this was the case. The attempt to find in Lord Aberdeen's letter a subsequent pretext for what had previously been done, is evidently an afterthought, put to paper, for the first time, just six days after the treaty had been signed! The treaty was signed on the 12th of April: the afterthought was committed to paper, in the form of a letter to Mr. Pakenham, on the 18th! and on the 19th the treaty was sent to the Senate! having been delayed seven days to admit of drawing up, and sending in along with it, this *ex post facto* discovery of reasons to justify it. The letter of Mr. Calhoun was sent in with the treaty: the reply of Mr. Pakenham to it, though brief and prompt, being written on the same day (the 19th of April), was not received by the Senate until ten days thereafter—to wit: on the 29th of April; and when received, it turns out to be a fourth disavowal, in the most clear and unequivocal terms, of this new discovery of the old designs imputed to Great Britain, and which had been three times disavowed before. Here is the letter of Mr. Pakenham, giving this fourth contradiction to the old story, and appealing to the judgment of the civilized world for its opinion on the whole transaction. I read an extract from this letter; the last one, it is presumed, that Mr. Pakenham can write till he hears from his government, to which he had immediately transmitted Mr. Calhoun's *ex post facto* letter of the 18th.

(It was read.)

Now what will the civilized world, to whose good opinion we must all look: what will Christendom, now so averse to war, and pretexted war: what will the laws of reason and honor, so just in their application to the conduct of nations and individuals: what will this civilized world, this Christian world, these just laws—what will they all say that our government ought to have done, under this accumulation of peremptory denials of all the causes which we had undertaken to find in the conduct of Great Britain for our "*immediate*" annexation of Texas, and war with Mexico? Surely these tribunals will say: *First,* That the disavowals should have been received as sufficient; *or Secondly,* They should be disproved, if not admitted to be true; *or Thirdly,* That reasonable time should be allowed for looking further into their truth.

One of these things should have been done: our President does neither. He concludes the treaty—retains it a week—sends it to the Senate—and his Secretary of State obtains a promise from the chairman of the Committee on Foreign Relations [Mr. ARCHER] to delay all action upon it—not to take it up for forty days— the exact time that would cover the sitting of the Baltimore democratic convention for the nomination of presidential candidates! This promise was obtained under the assurance that a special messenger had been despatched to Mexico for her consent to the treaty; and the forty days was the time claimed for the execution of his errand, and at the end of which he was expected to return with the required consent. Bad luck again! This despatch of the messenger, and delay for his return, and the *reasons* he was understood to be able to have offered for the consent of Mexico, were felt by all as an admission that the consent of Mexico must be obtained, cost what millions it might. This admission was fatal! and it became necessary to take another tack, and do it away! This was attempted in a subsequent message of the President, admitting, to be sure, that the messenger was sent, and sent to operate upon Mexico in relation to the treaty; but taking a fine distinction between obtaining her consent to it, and preventing her from being angry at it! This message will receive justice at the hands of others; I only heard it as read, and cannot quote it in its own words. But the substance of it was, that the messenger was sent to prevent Mexico from going to war with us on account of the treaty! as if there was any difference between getting her to consent to the treaty, and getting her not to dissent! But, here again, more bad luck. Besides the declarations of the chairman of Foreign Relations, showing what this messenger was sent for, there is a copy of the letter furnished to us of which he was the bearer, and which shows that the "*concurrence*" of Mexico was wanted, and that apologies are offered for not obtaining her "*previous consent*." But, of this hereafter. I go on with the current of events. The treaty was sent in, and forty days' silence upon it was demanded of the Senate. Now why send it in, if the Senate was not to touch it for forty days? Why not retain it in the Department of State until the lapse of these forty days, when the answer from Mexico would have been received, and a fifth disavowal arrived from Great Britain! if, indeed, it is possible for her to reiterate a disavowal already four times made, and not received? Why not retain the treaty during these forty days of required silence upon it in the Senate, and when that precious time might have been turned to such valuable account in interchanging friendly explanations with Great Britain and Mexico? Why not keep the treaty in the Secretary of State's office, as well as in the Secretary of the Senate's office, during these forty days? Precisely because the Baltimore convention was to sit in thirty-eight days from that time! and forty days would give time for the "*Texas bomb*" to burst and scatter its fragments all over the Union, blowing up candidates for the presidency, blowing up the *tongue-tied* Senate itself for not ratifying the treaty, and furnishing a new Texas candidate, anointed with gunpowder, for the presidential chair. This was the reason, and as obvious as if written at the head of every public document. In the mean time, all these movements give fresh reason for an examination of persons at the bar of the Senate. The determination of the President to conclude the treaty, before the Earl of Aberdeen's despatch was known to him—that is to say, before the 26th of February, 1844: the true nature of the messenger's errand to Mexico, and many other points, now involved in obscurity, may be cleared up in these examinations, to the benefit and well being of the Union. Perhaps it may chance to turn out in proof, that the secretary, who found his reasons for making the treaty and hastening the immediate annexation, had determined upon all that long before he heard of Lord Aberdeen's letter.

But to go on. Instead of admitting, disproving, or taking time to consider the reiterated disavowals of the British government, the messenger to Mexico is charged with our manifesto of war against that government, on account of the imputed designs of Great Britain, and in which they are all assumed to be true! and not only true, but fraught with such sudden, irresistible, and irretrievable ruin to the United States, that there was no time for an instant of delay, nor any way to save the Union from destruction but by the "*immediate*" annexation of Texas. Here is the letter. It is too important to be abridged; and though referred to several times, will now be read in full. Hear it:

(The letter read.)

This letter was addressed to Mr. Benjamin Green, the son of Mr. Duff Green; so that the beginning and the ending of this "*immediate*" annexation scheme, so far as the invention of the pretext, and the inculpation of Great Britain is concerned, is in the hands of father and son—a couple, of whom it may be said, in the language of Gil Blas, "These two make a pair." The letter itself is one of the most unfortunate that the annals of diplomacy ever exhibited. It admits the wrong to Mexico, and offers to fight her for that wrong; and not for any thing that she has done to the United States, but because of some supposed operation of Great Britain upon Texas. Was there ever such a comedy of errors, or, it may be, tragedy of crimes! Let us analyze this important letter; let us examine it, paragraph by paragraph.

The first paragraph enjoins the strongest assurances to be given to Mexico of our indisposition to wound the dignity or honor of Mexico in making this treaty, and of our regret if she should consider it otherwise. This admits that we have done something to outrage Mexico, and that we owe her a volunteer apology, to soften her anticipated resentment.

The same paragraph states that we have been driven to this step in self-defence, and to counteract the "*policy adopted*," and the "*efforts made*" by Great Britain to abolish slavery in Texas. This is an admission that we have done what may be offensive and injurious to Mexico, not on account of any thing she has done to us, but for what we fear Great Britain may do to Texas. And as for this plea of self-defence, it is an invasion of the homicidal criminal's prerogative, to plead it. All the murders committed in our country, are done in self-defence—a few through insanity. The choice of the defence lies between them, and it is often a nice guess for counsel to say which to take. And so it might have been in this case; and insanity would have been an advantage in the plea, being more honorable, and not more false.

The same paragraph admits that the United States has made this treaty in full view of war with Mexico; for the words "*all possible consequences*," taken in connection with the remaining words of the sentence, and with General Almonte's notice filed by order of his government at the commencement of this negotiation, can mean nothing else but war! and that to be made by the treaty-making power.

The second paragraph directs the despatch of Lord Aberdeen to be read to the Mexican Secretary of State, to show him our cause of complaint against Great Britain. This despatch is to be read—not delivered, not even a copy of it—to the Mexican minister. He may take notes of it during the reading, but not receive a copy, because it is a document to be sent to the Senate! Surely the Senate would have pardoned a departure from *etiquette* in a case where war was impending, and where the object was to convince the nation we were going to fight! that we had a right to fight her for fear of something which a third power might do to a fourth. To crown this scene, the reading is to be of a document in the English language, to a minister whose language is Spanish; and who may not know what is read, except through an interpreter.

The third paragraph of this pregnant letter admits that questions are to grow out of this treaty, for the settlement of which a minister will be sent by us to Mexico. This is a most grave admission. It is a confession that we commit such wrong upon Mexico by this treaty, that it will take another treaty to redress it; and that, as the wrong doer, we will volunteer an embassy to atone for our misconduct. Boundary is named as one of these things to be settled, and with reason; for we violate 2,000 miles of Mexican boundary which is to become ours by the ratification of this treaty, and to remain ours till restored to its proper owner by another treaty. Is this right? Is it sound in morals? Is it safe in policy? Would we take 2,000 miles of the Canadas in the same way? I presume not. And why not? why not treat Great Britain and Mexico alike? why not march up to "Fifty-Four Forty" as courageously as we march upon the Rio Grande? Because Great Britain is powerful, and Mexico weak—a reason which may fail in policy as much as in morals. Yes, sir! Boundary will have to be adjusted, and that of the Rio Grande; and until adjusted, we shall be aggressors, by our own admission, on the undisputed Mexican territory on the Rio Grande.

The last paragraph is the most significant of the whole. It is a confession, by the clearest inferences, that our whole conduct to Mexico has been tortuous and wrongful, and that she has "*rights*," to the settlement of which Mexico must be a party. The great admissions are, the want of the concurrence of Mexico; the want of her previous consent to this treaty; its objectionableness to her; the violation of her boundary; the "*rights*" of each, and of course the right of Mexico to settle questions of security and interest which are unsettled by the present treaty. The result of the whole is, that the war, in full view of which the treaty was made, was an unjust war upon Mexico.

Thus admitting our wrong in injuring Mexico, in not obtaining her concurrence; in not securing her previous consent; in violating her boundary; in proceeding without her in a case where her rights, security, and interests are concerned; admitting all this, what is the reason given to Mexico for treating her with the contempt of a total neglect in all this affair? And here strange scenes rise up before us. This negotiation began, upon the record, in August last. We had a minister in Mexico with whom we could communicate every twenty days. Mexico had a minister here, with whom we could communicate every hour in the day. Then why not consult Mexico before the treaty? Why not speak to her during these eight months, when in such hot haste to consult her afterwards, and so anxious to stop our action on the treaty till she was heard from, and so ready to volunteer millions to propitiate her wrath, or to conciliate her consent? Why this haste after the treaty, when there was so much time before? It was because the plan required the "*bomb*" to be kept back till forty days before the Baltimore convention, and then a storm to be excited.

The reason given for this great haste after so long delay, is that the safety of the United States was at stake: that the British would abolish slavery in Texas, and then in the United States, and so destroy the Union. Giving to this imputed design, for the sake of the argument, all the credit due to an uncontradicted scheme, and still it is a preposterous excuse for not obtaining the previous consent of Mexico. It turns upon the idea that this abolition of slavery in Texas is to be sudden, irresistible, irretrievable! and that not a minute was to be lost in averting the impending ruin! But this is not the case. Admitting what is charged—that Great Britain has adopted a policy, and made efforts to abolish slavery in Texas, with a view to its abolition in the United States—yet this is not to be done by force, or magic. The Duke of Wellington is not to land at the head of some 100,000 men to set the slaves free. No gunpowder plot, like that intended by Guy Fawkes, is to blow the slaves out of the country. No magic wand is to be waved over the land, and to convert it into the home of the free. No slips of magic carpet in the Arabian Nights is to be slipped under the feet of the negroes to send them all whizzing, by a wish, ten thousand miles through the air. None of these sudden, irresistible, irretrievable modes of operating is to be followed by Great Britain. She wishes to see slavery abolished in Texas, as elsewhere; but this wish, like all other human wishes, is wholly inoperative without works to back it: and these Great Britain denies. She denies that she will operate by works, only by words where acceptable. But admit it. Admit that she has now done what she never did before—*denied her design!* admit all this, and you still have to confess that she is a human power and has to work by human means, and in this case to operate upon the minds of people and of nations— upon Mexico, Texas, the United States, and slaves within the boundaries of these two latter countries. She has to work by moral means; that is to say, by operating on the mind and will. All this is a work of time—a work of years—the work of a generation! Slavery is in the constitution of Texas, and in the hearts, customs, and interests of the people; and cannot be got out in many years, if at all. And are we to be told that there was no time to consult Mexico? or, in the vague language of the letter, that *circumstances* did not permit the consultation, and that without disclosing what these circumstances were? It was last August that the negotiation began. Was there fear that Mexico would liberate Texian slaves if she found out the treaty before it was made? Alas! sir, she refused to have any thing to do with the scheme! Great Britain proposed to her to make emancipation of slaves the condition of acknowledging Texian independence. She utterly refused it; and of this our government was officially informed by the Earl of Aberdeen. No, sir, no! There is no reason in the excuse. I profess to be a man that can understand reason, and could comprehend the force of the circumstances which would show that the danger of delay was so imminent that nothing but *immediate* annexation could save the United States from destruction. But none such are named, or can be named; and the true reason is, that the Baltimore convention was to sit on the 27th of May.

Great Britain avows all she intends, and that is—a wish—TO SEE—slavery abolished in Texas; and she declares all the means which she means to use, and that is, advice where it is acceptable.

It will be a strange spectacle, in the nineteenth century, to behold the United States at war with Mexico, because Great Britain wishes—TO SEE—the abolition of slavery in Texas.

So far from being a just cause of war, I hold that the expression of such a wish is not even censurable by us, since our naval alliance with Great Britain for the suppression of the slave trade—since our diplomatic alliance with her to close the markets of the world against the slave trade—and since the large effusion of mawkish sentimentality on the subject of slavery, in which our advocates of the aforesaid diplomatic and naval alliance indulged themselves at the time of its negotiation and conclusion. Since that time, I think we have lost the right (if we ever possessed it) of fighting Mexico, because Great Britain says she wishes—TO SEE—slavery abolished in Texas, as elsewhere throughout the world.

The civilized world judges the causes of war, and discriminates between motives and pretexts: the former are respected when true and valid—the latter are always despised and exposed. Every Christian nation owes it to itself, as well as to the family of Christian nations, to examine well its grounds of war, before it begins one, and to hold itself in a condition to justify its act in the eyes of God and man. Not satisfied of either the truth or validity of the cause for our war with Mexico, in the alleged interference of Great Britain in Texian affairs, I feel myself bound to oppose it, and not the less because it is deemed a small war. Our constitution knows no difference between wars. The declaration of all wars is given to Congress—not to the President and Senate—much less to the President alone. Besides, a war is an ungovernable monster, and there is no knowing into what proportions even a small one may expand! especially when the interference of one large power may lead to the interference of another.

Great Britain disavows (and that four times over) all the designs upon Texas attributed to her. She disavows every thing. I believe I am as jealous of the encroaching and domineering spirit of that power, as any reasonable man ought to be; but these disavowals are enough for me. That government is too proud to lie! too wise to criminate its future conduct by admitting the culpability which the disavowal implies. Its fault is on the other side of the account—in its arrogance in avowing, and even overstating, its pretensions. Copenhagen is her style! I repeat it, then, the disavowal of all design to interfere with Texian Independence, or with the existence of slavery in Texas, is enough for me. I shall believe in it until I see it disproved by evidence, or otherwise falsified. Would to God that our administration could get the same disavowal in all the questions of real difference between the two countries! that we could get it in the case of the Oregon—the claim of search—the claim of visitation—the claim of impressment—the practice of liberating our fugitive and criminal slaves—the repetition of the Schlosser invasion of our territory and murder of our citizens—the outrage of the Comet, Encomium, Enterprise, and Hermosa cases!

And here, without regard to the truth or falsehood of this imputed design of British intentions to abolish slavery in Texas, a very awkward circumstance crosses our path in relation to its validity, if true: for, it so happens that we did that very thing ourselves! By the Louisiana treaty of 1803, Texas, and all the country, between the Red River and Arkansas, became ours, and was subject to slavery: by the treaty of 1819, made, as Mr. Adams assures us, by the majority of Mr. Monroe's cabinet, who were Southern men, this Texas, and a hundred thousand square miles of other territory between the Red River and Arkansas, were dismembered from our Union, and added to Mexico, a non-slaveholding empire. By that treaty of 1819, slavery was actually abolished in all that region in which we now only fear, contrary to the evidence, that there is a design to abolish it! and the confines of a non-slaveholding empire were then actually brought to the boundaries of Louisiana, Arkansas, and Missouri! the exact places which we now so greatly fear to expose to the contact of a non-slaveholding dominion. All this I exposed at the time the treaty of 1819 was made, and pointed out as one of the follies or crimes, of that unaccountable treaty; and now recur to it in my place here to absolve Mr. Adams, the negotiator of the treaty of 1819, from the blame which I then cast upon him. His responsible statement on the floor of the House of Representatives has absolved him from that blame, and transferred it to the shoulders of the majority of Mr. Monroe's cabinet. On seeing the report of his speech in the papers, I deemed it right to communicate with Mr. Adams, through a senator from his State, now in my eye, and who hears what I say (looking at Mr. BATES, of Massachusetts), and through him received the confirmation of the reported speech, that he (Mr. Adams) was the last of Mr. Monroe's cabinet to yield our true boundaries in that quarter. [Here Mr. Bates nodded assent.] Southern men deprived us of Texas, and made it non-slaveholding in 1819. Our present Secretary of State was a member of that cabinet, and counselled that treaty: our present President was a member of the House, and sanctioned it in voting against Mr. Clay's condemnatory resolution. They did a great mischief then: they should be cautious not to err again in the *manner* of getting it back.

I have shown you, Mr. President, that the ratification of this treaty would be war with Mexico—that it would be unjust war, unconstitutionally made—and made upon a weak and groundless pretext. It is not my purpose to show for what object this war is made—why these marching and sailing orders have been given—and why our troops and ships, as squadrons and corps of observation, are now in the Gulf of Mexico, watching Mexican cities; or on the Red River, watching Mexican soldiers. I have not told the reasons for this war, and warlike movements, nor is it necessary to do so. The purpose of the whole is plain and obvious. It is in every body's mouth. It is in the air, and we can see and feel it. Mr. Tyler wants to be President; and, different from the perfumed fop of Shakspeare, to whom the smell of gunpowder was so offensive, he not only wants to smell that compound, but also to smell of it. He wants an odor of the "*villanous compound*" upon him. He has become infected with the modern notion that gunpowder popularity is the passport to the presidency; and he wants that passport. He wants to play Jackson; but let him have a care. From the sublime to the ridiculous there is but a step; and, in heroic imitations, there is no middle ground. The hero missed, the harlequin appears; and hisses salute the ears which were itching for applause. Jackson was no candidate for the presidency when he acted the real, not the mock hero. He staked himself for his country—did nothing but what was just—and eschewed intrigue. His elevation to the presidency was the act of his fellow-citizens—not the machination of himself.

CHAPTER CXL.

TEXAS OR DISUNION: SOUTHERN CONVENTION: MR. BENTON'S SPEECH: EXTRACTS.

The senator from South Carolina (Mr. McDuffie) assumes it for certain, that the great meeting projected for Nashville is to take place: and wishes to know who are to be my bedfellows in that great gathering: and I on my part, would wish to know who are to be his! Misery, says the proverb, makes strange bedfellows: and political combinations sometimes make them equally strange. The fertile imagination of Burke has presented us with a view of one of these strange sights; and the South Carolina procession at Nashville (if nothing occurs to balk it) may present another. Burke has exhibited to us the picture of a cluster of old political antagonists (it was after the formation of Lord North's broad bottomed administration, and after the country's good and love of office had smothered old animosities)—all sleeping together in one truckle-bed: to use his own language, all pigging together (that is, lying like pigs, heads and tails, and as many together) in the same truckle-bed: and a queer picture he made of it! But if things go on as projected here, never did misery, or political combination, or the imagination of Burke, present such a medley of bedfellows as will be seen at Nashville. All South Carolina is to be there: of course General Jackson will be there, and will be good and hospitable to all. But let the travellers take care who goes to bed to him. If he should happen to find old tariff disunion, disguised as Texas disunion, lying by his side! then woe to the hapless wight that has sought such a lodging. Preservation of the Federal Union is as strong in the old Roman's heart now as ever: and while, as a Christian, he forgives all that is past (if it were past!), yet, no old tricks under new names. Texas disunion will be to him the same as tariff disunion: and if he detects a Texas disunionist nestling into his bed, I say again, woe to the luckless wight! Sheets and blankets will be no salvation. The tiger will not be toothless—the senator understands the allusion— nor clawless either. Teeth and claws he will have, and sharp use he will make of them! Not only skin and fur, but blood and bowels may fly, and double-quick time scampering may clear that bed! I shall not be there: even if the scheme goes on (which I doubt after this day's occurrences); if it should go on, and any thing should induce me to go so far out of my line, it would be to have a view of the senator from South Carolina, and the friends for whom he speaks, and their new bedfellows, or fellows in bed, as the case may be, all pigging together in one truckle-bed at Nashville.

But I advise the contrivers to give up this scheme. Polk and Texas are strong, and can carry a great deal, but not every thing. The oriental story informs us that it was the last ounce which broke the camel's back? What if a mountain had been put first on the poor animal's back? Nullification is a mountain! Disunion is a mountain! and what could Polk and Texas do with two mountains on their backs? And here, Mr. President, I must speak out. The time has come for those to speak out who neither fear nor count consequences when their country is in danger. Nullification and disunion are revived, and revived under circumstances which menace more danger than ever, since coupled with a popular question which gives to the plotters the honest sympathies of the patriotic millions. I have often intimated it before, but now proclaim it. Disunion is at the bottom of this long-concealed Texas machination. Intrigue and speculation co-operate; but disunion is at the bottom, and I denounce it to the American people. Under the pretext of getting Texas into the Union, the scheme is to get the South out of it. A separate confederacy, stretching from the Atlantic to the Californias (and hence the secret of the Rio Grande del Norte frontier), is the cherished vision of disappointed ambition; and for this consummation every circumstance has been carefully and artfully contrived. A secret and intriguing negotiation, concealed from Congress and the people: an abolition quarrel picked with Great Britain to father an abolition quarrel at home: a slavery correspondence to outrage the North: war with Mexico: the clandestine concentration of troops and ships in the southwest: the secret compact with the President of Texas, and the subjection of American forces to his command: the flagrant seizure of the purse and the sword: the contradictory and preposterous reasons on which the detected military and naval movement was defended— all these announce the prepared catastrophe; and the inside view of the treaty betrays its design. The whole annexed country is to be admitted as one territory, with a treaty-promise to be admitted as States, when we all know that Congress alone can admit new States, and that the treaty-promise, without a law of Congress to back it, is void. The whole to be slave States (and with the boundary to the Rio Grande there may be a great many); and the correspondence, which is the key to the treaty, and shows the design of its framers, wholly directed to the extension of slavery and the exasperation of the North. What else could be done to get up Missouri controversies and make sure of the non-admission of these States? Then the plot is consummated: and Texas without the Union, sooner than the Union without Texas (already the premonitory chorus of so many resolves), receives its practical application in the secession of the South, and its adhesion to the rejected Texas. Even without waiting for the non-admission of the States, so carefully provided for in the treaty and correspondence, secession and confederation with the foreign Texas is already the scheme of the subaltern disunionists. The subalterns, charged too high by their chiefs, are ready for this; but the more cunning chiefs, want Texas in as a territory—in by treaty—the supreme law of the land—with a void promise for admission as States. Then non-admission can be called a breach of the treaty. Texas can be assumed to be a part of the Union; and secession and conjunction with her becomes the rightful remedy. This is the design, and I denounce it; and blind is he who, occupying a position at this capitol, does not behold it!

I mention secession as the more cunning method of dissolving the Union. It is disunion, and the more dangerous because less palpable. Nullification begat it, and if allowed there is an end to the Union. For a few States to secede, without other alliances, would only put the rest to the trouble of bringing them back; but with Texas and California to retire upon, the Union would have to go. *Many persons would secede on the non-admission of Texian States who abhor disunion now.* To avoid all these dangers, and to make sure of Texas, pass my bill! which gives the promise of Congress for the admission of the new States—neutralizes the slave question—avoids Missouri controversies—pacifies Mexico—and harmonizes the Union.

The senator from South Carolina complains that I have been arrogant and overbearing in this debate, and dictatorial to those who were opposed to me. So far as this reproach is founded, I have to regret it, and to ask pardon of the Senate and of its members. I may be in some fault. I have, indeed, been laboring under deep feeling; and while much was kept down, something may have escaped. I marked the commencement of this Texas movement long before it was visible to the public eye; and always felt it to be dangerous, because it gave to the plotters the honest sympathies of the millions. I saw men who never cared a straw about Texas—one of whom gave it away—another of whom voted against saving it—and all of whom were silent and indifferent while the true friends of the sacrificed country were laboring to get it back: I saw these men lay their plot in the winter of 1842-'43, and told every person with whom I talked every step they were to take in it. All that has taken place, I foretold: all that is intended, I foresee. The intrigue for the presidency was the first act in the drama; the dissolution of the Union the second. And I, who hate intrigue, and love the Union, can only speak of intriguers and disunionists with warmth and indignation. The oldest advocate for the recovery of Texas, I must be allowed to speak in just terms of the criminal politicians who prostituted the question of its recovery to their own base purposes, and delayed its success by degrading and disgracing it. A western man, and coming from a State more than any other interested in the recovery of this country so unaccountably thrown away by the treaty of 1819, I must be allowed to feel indignant at seeing Atlantic politicians seizing upon it, and making it a sectional question, for the purposes of ambition and disunion. I have spoken warmly of these plotters and intriguers; but I have not permitted their conduct to alter my own, or to relax my zeal for the recovery of the sacrificed country. I have helped to reject the disunion treaty; and that obstacle being removed, I have brought in the bill which will insure the recovery of Texas (with peace, and honor, and with the Union) as soon as the exasperation has subsided which the outrageous conduct of this administration has excited in every Mexican breast. No earthly power but Mexico has a right to say a word. Civil treatment and consultation beforehand would have conciliated her; but the seizure of two thousand miles of her undisputed territory, an insulting correspondence, breach of the armistice, secret negotiations with Texas, and sending troops and ships to waylay and attack her, have excited feelings of resentment which must be allayed before any thing can be done.

The senator from South Carolina compares the rejected treaty to the slain Cæsar, and gives it a ghost, which is to meet me at some future day, as the spectre met Brutus at Philippi. I accept the comparison, and thank the senator for it. It is both classic and just; for as Cæsar was slain for the good of his country, so has been this treaty; and as the spectre appeared at Philippi on the side of the ambitious Antony and the hypocrite Octavius, and against the patriot Brutus, so would the ghost of this poor treaty, when it comes to meet me, appear on the side of the President and his secretary, and against the man who was struggling to save his country from their lawless designs. But here the comparison must stop; for I can promise the ghost and his backers that if the fight goes against me at this new Philippi, with which I am threatened, and the enemies of the American Union triumph over me as the enemies of Roman liberty triumphed over Brutus and Cassius, I shall not fall upon my sword, as Brutus did, though Cassius be killed, and run it through my own body; but I shall save it, and save myself for another day, and for another use—for the day when the battle of the disunion of these States is to be fought—not with words, but with iron—and for the hearts of the traitors who appear in arms against their country.

The comparison is just. Cæsar was rightfully killed for conspiring against his country; but it was not he that destroyed the liberties of Rome. That work was done by the profligate politicians, without him, and before his time; and his death did not restore the republic. There were no more elections. Rotten politicians had destroyed them; and the nephew of Cæsar, as heir to his uncle, succeeded to the empire on the principle of hereditary succession.

And here, Mr. President, History appears in her grand and instructive character, as Philosophy teaching by example: and let us not be senseless to her warning voice. Superficial readers believe it was the military men who destroyed the Roman republic. No such thing! It was the politicians who did it! factious, corrupt, intriguing, politicians! destroying public virtue in their mad pursuit after office! destroying their rivals by crime! deceiving and debauching the people for votes! and bringing elections into contempt by the frauds and violence with which they were conducted. From the time of the Gracchi there were no elections that could bear the name. Confederate and rotten politicians bought and sold the consulship. Intrigue, and the dagger, disposed of rivals. Fraud, violence, bribes, terror, and the plunder of the public treasury, commanded votes. The people had no choice: and long before the time of Cæsar nothing remained of republican government, but the name, and the abuse. Read Plutarch. In the life of Cæsar, and not three pages before the crossing of the Rubicon, he paints the ruined state of the elections—shows that all elective government was gone—that the hereditary form had become a necessary relief from the contests of the corrupt—and that in choosing between Pompey and Cæsar, many preferred Pompey, not because they thought him republican, but because they thought he would make the milder king. Even arms were but a small part of Cæsar's reliance when he crossed the Rubicon. Gold, still more than the sword, was his dependence: and he sent forward the accumulated treasures of plundered Gaul, to be poured into the laps of rotten politicians. There was no longer a popular government; and in taking all power to himself, he only took advantage of the state of things which profligate politicians had produced. In this he was culpable, and paid the forfeit with his life; but in contemplating his fate, let us never forget that the politicians had undermined and destroyed the republic, before he came to seize and to master it.

It was the same in our day. We have seen the conqueror of Egypt and Italy overturn the Directory, usurp all power, and receive the sanction of the people. And why? Because the government was rotten, and elections had become a farce. The elections of forty-eight departments, at one time, in the year 1798, were annulled, to give the Directory a majority in the legislative councils. All sorts of fraud and violence were committed at the elections. The people had no confidence in them, and submitted to Bonaparte.

All elective governments have failed in this manner; and, in process of time, must fail here, unless elections can be taken out of the hands of the politicians, and restored to the full control of the people. The plan which I have submitted this day, for dispensing with intermediate bodies, and holding a second election for President when the first fails, is designed to accomplish this great purpose; and will do much good if adopted. Never have politicians, in so young a country, shown such a thirst for office—such disregard of the popular will, such readiness to deceive and betray the people. The Texas treaty (for I must confine myself to the case before us) is an intrigue for the presidency, and a contrivance to get the Southern States out of the Union, instead of getting Texian States into it; and is among the most unscrupulous intrigues which any country every beheld. But we know how to discriminate. We know how to separate the wrong from the right. Texas, which the intriguers prostrated to their ambitious purposes (caring nothing about it, as their past lives show), will be rescued from their designs, and restored to this Union as naturally, and as easily, as the ripened pear falls to the earth. Those who prepared the result at the Baltimore convention, in which the will of the people was overthrown, will be consigned to oblivion; while the nominees of the convention will be accepted and sustained: and as for the plotters of disunion and secession, they will be found out and will receive their reward; and I, for one, shall be ready to meet them at Philippi, sword in hand, whenever they bring their parricidal scheme to the test of arms.

CHAPTER CXLI.

TEXAS OR DISUNION: VIOLENT DEMONSTRATIONS IN THE SOUTH: SOUTHERN CONVENTION PROPOSED.

The secret intrigue for the annexation of Texas was framed with a double aspect—one looking to the presidential election, the other to the separation of the Southern States; and as soon as the rejection of the treaty was foreseen, and the nominating convention had acted (Mr. Calhoun and Mr. Tyler standing no chance), the disunion aspect manifested itself over many of the Southern States—beginning of course with South Carolina. Before the end of May a great meeting took place (with the muster of a regiment) at Ashley, in the Barnwell district of that State, to combine the slave States in a convention to unite the Southern States to Texas, if Texas should not be received into the Union; and to invite the President to convene Congress to arrange the terms of the dissolution of the Union if the rejection of the annexation should be persevered in. At this meeting all the speeches and resolves turned upon the original idea in the Gilmer letter—that of British alliance with Texas—the abolition of slavery in Texas in consequence of that alliance, and a San Domingo insurrection of slaves in the Southern States; and the conjunction of the South and Texas in a new republic was presented as the only means of averting these dire calamities. With this view, and as giving the initiative to the movement, these resolutions were adopted:

> "*First*: To call upon our delegations in Congress, if in session, or our senators, if they be at the seat of government, to wait on the Texian Minister, and remonstrate with him against any negotiation with other powers, until the Southern States shall have had a reasonable time to decide upon their course.

> "*Second*: That object secured, a convention of the people of each State should be promptly called, to deliberate and decide, upon the action to be taken by the slave States on the question of annexation; and to appoint delegates to *a convention of the slave States*, with instructions to carry into effect the behests of the people.

> "*Third*: That a convention of the slave States by delegations from each, appointed as aforesaid, should be called, to meet at some central position, to take into consideration the question of annexing Texas to the Union, if *the Union will accept it*; or, if the Union *will not accept it*, then of *annexing Texas to the Southern States*!

> "*Fourth*: That the President of the United States be requested by the general convention of the slave States, to call Congress together immediately; when, *the final issue* shall be made up, and the alternative distinctly presented to the free States, either to *admit Texas into the Union*, or to proceed *peaceably and calmly* to *arrange the terms of a dissolution of the Union*!"

About the same time another large meeting was held at Beaufort, in the same State, in which it was

> "*Resolved*, That if the Senate of the United States—under the drill of party leaders—should reject the treaty of annexation, we appeal to the citizens of Texas, and urge them not to yield to a just resentment, and turn their eyes to other alliances, but to believe that they have the warm advocacy of a large portion of the American public, who are resolved, that sooner or later, the pledge in the treaty of 1803 shall be redeemed, and Texas be incorporated into our Union. But if—on the other hand—we are not permitted to bring Texas into our Union peacefully and legitimately, as now we may, then we solemnly announce to the world—that we will dissolve this Union, sooner than abandon Texas.

> "*Resolved*, That the chair, at his leisure, appoint a committee of vigilance and correspondence, to consist of twenty-one, to aid in carrying forward the cause of Texas annexation."

In the Williamsburg District in the same State another large meeting resolved:

> "That in the opinion of this meeting, the honor and integrity of our Union require the immediate annexation of Texas; and we hold it to be better and more to the interest of the

Southern and Southwestern portions of this confederacy 'to be out of the Union with Texas than in it without her.'

"That we cordially approve of the recommendation of a Southern convention composed of delegates from the Southern and Southwestern portions of this confederacy, to deliberate together, and adopt such measures as may best promote the great object of annexation; provided such annexation is not previously brought about by joint resolution of Congress, either at its present or an extra session."

Responsive resolutions were adopted in several States, and the 4th day of July furnished an occasion for the display of sentiments in the form of toasts, which showed both the depth of the feeling on this subject, and its diffusion, more or less, through all the Southern States. "Texas, or Disunion," was a common toast, and a Southern convention generally called for. Richmond, Virginia, was one of the places indicated for its meeting, by a meeting in the State of Alabama. Mr. Ritchie, the editor of the Enquirer, repulsed the idea, on the part of the Democracy, of holding the meeting there, saying, "*There is not a democrat in Virginia who will encourage any plot to dissolve the Union.*" The Richmond Whig, on the part of the whigs, equally repulsed it. Nashville, in the State of Tennessee, was proposed in the resolves of many of the public meetings, and the assembling of the convention at that place—the home of General Jackson—was still more formally and energetically repulsed. A meeting of the citizens of the town was called, which protested against "*the desecration of the soil of Tennessee by having any convention held there to hatch treason against the Union,*" and convoked a general meeting for the purpose of bringing out a full expression of public opinion on the subject. The meeting took place accordingly, and was most numerously and respectably attended, and adopted resolutions worthy of the State, worthy of the *home* of General Jackson, honorable to every individual engaged in it; and so ample as to stand for an authentic history of that attempt to dissolve the Union. The following were the resolves, presented by Dr. John Shelby:

"Whereas, at several public meetings recently held in the South, resolutions have been adopted urging with more or less directness the assembling of a convention of States friendly to the immediate annexation of Texas, at Nashville, some time in August next; and whereas it is apparent from the resolutions themselves and the speeches of some of its prime movers in those meetings, and the comments of public journals friendly to them, that the convention they propose to hold in this city was contemplated *as a means towards an end*—that end being to present deliberately and formally the issue, 'annexation of Texas or dissolution of this Union.'

"And whereas, further, it is manifested by all the indications given from the most reliable sources of intelligence, that there is a party of men in another quarter of this nation who—in declaring that 'the only true issue before the South should be Texas or disunion,' and in proposing the line of operation indicated by the South Carolinian, their organ published at Columbia, South Carolina, in the following words,

"That the President of the United States be requested by the general convention of the slave States to call Congress together immediately, when the final issue shall be made up, and the alternative distinctly presented to the free States, either to admit Texas into the Union, or to proceed peaceably and calmly to arrange the terms of a dissolution of the Union'—are influenced by sentiments and opinions directly at issue with the solemn obligation of the citizens of every State to our national Union—sentiments and opinions which, if not repressed and condemned, may lead to the destruction of our tranquillity and happiness, and to the reign of anarchy and confusion. Therefore, we, the citizens of Davidson County, in the State of Tennessee, feel ourselves called upon by these demonstrations to express, in a clear, decided, and unequivocal manner, our deliberate sentiments in regard to them. And upon the momentous question here involved, we are happy to believe there is no material division of sentiment among the people of this State.

"The citizens here assembled are *Tennesseans*; they are Americans. They glory in being citizens of this great confederate republic; and, whether friendly or opposed to the immediate annexation of Texas, they join with decision, firmness, and zeal in avowing their attachment to our glorious, and, we trust, impregnable Union, and in condemning every attempt to bring its preservation into issue, or its value into calculation.

"Under these impressions, and with these feelings, regarding with deep and solemn interest the circumstances under which this new issue may be ere long sprung upon us, and actuated by a sense of the high responsibility to his country imposed on every American citizen, in the language of the immortal Washington, 'to frown upon the first dawnings of every attempt to alienate any portion of our country from the rest, or to enfeeble the sacred ties which now link together the various parts,' we hereby adopt and make known, as expressing our deliberate sentiments, the following resolutions:

"*Resolved*, That while we never have interfered, and never will interfere with the arrangements of any of the parties divided on the general political questions of the day, and while we absolutely repel the charge of designing any such interference as totally unfounded and unjustifiable, yet when we see men of any party and any quarter of this nation announcing as their motto, 'Texas or Disunion,' and singling out the city of Nashville as a place of general gathering, in order to give formality and solemnity to the presentation of that issue, we feel it to be not only our sacred right, but our solemn duty to protest, as we now do protest, against the desecration of the soil of Tennessee, by any act of men holding within its borders a convention for any such object.

"*Resolved*, That when our fellow-citizens of any State come hither as Americans, loyal to our glorious Union, they will be received and welcomed by us with all the kindness and hospitality which should characterize the intercourse of a band of brothers, whatever may be our differences on political subjects; but when they avow their willingness to break up the Union rather than fail to accomplish a favorite object, we feel bound to tell them this is no fit place to concert their plans.

"*Resolved*, That we entertain for the people of South Carolina, and the other quarters in which this cry of 'Texas or Disunion' has been raised, feelings of fraternal regard and affection; that we sincerely lament the exhibition by any portion of them of disloyalty to the Union, or a disposition to urge its dissolution with a view to annexation with Texas, if not otherwise obtained; and that we hope a returning sense of what is due to themselves, to the other States of the Union, to the American people, and to the cause of American liberty, will prevent them from persevering in urging the issue they have proposed."

The energy with which this proposed convention was repulsed from Nashville and Richmond, and the general revolt against it in most of the States, brought the movement to a stand, paralyzed its leaders, and suppressed the disunion scheme for the time being—only to lie in wait for future occasions. But it was not before the people only that this scheme for a Southern convention with a view to the secession of the slave States, was matter of discussion: it was the subject of debate in the Senate. Mr. McDuffie mentioned it, and in a way to draw a reply from Mr. Benton—an extract from which has been given in a previous chapter, and which, besides some information on its immediate subject, and besides foreseeing the failure of *that* attempt to get up a disunion convention, also told that the design of the secessionists was to extend the new Southern republic to the Californias: and this was told two years before the declaration of the war by which California was acquired.

CHAPTER CXLII.

REJECTION OF THE ANNEXATION TREATY: PROPOSAL OF MR. BENTON'S PLAN.

The treaty was supported by all the power of the administration; but in vain. It was doomed to defeat, ignominious and entire, and was rejected by a vote of two to one against it, when it would have required a vote of two to one to have ratified it. The yeas were:

Messrs. Atchison, Bagby, Breese, Buchanan, Colquitt, Fulton, Haywood, Henderson, Huger, Lewis, McDuffie, Semple, Sevier, Sturgeon, Walker, Woodbury.—16.

The nays were:

Messrs. Allen, Archer, Atherton, Barrow, Bates, Bayard, Benton, Berrien, Choate, Clayton, Crittenden, Dayton, Evans, Fairfield, Foster, Francis, Huntington, Jarnagin, Johnson, Mangum, Merrick, Miller, Morehead, Niles, Pearce, Phelps, Porter, Rives, Simmons, Tallmadge, Tappan, Upham, White, Woodbridge, Wright.—35.

This vote was infinitely honorable to the Senate, and a severe rebuke upon those who had the hardihood to plot the annexation of Texas as an intrigue for the presidency, and to be consummated at the expense of war with Mexico, insults to Great Britain, breach of our own constitution, and the disgrace and shame of committing an outrage upon a feeble neighboring power. But the annexation was desirable in itself, and had been the unceasing effort of statesmen from the time the province had been retroceded to Spain. The treaty was a wrong and criminal way of doing a right thing. That obstacle removed, and the public mind roused and attracted to the subject, disinterested men who had no object but the public good, took charge of the subject, and initiated measures to effect the annexation in an honorable and constitutional manner. With this view Mr. Benton brought into the Senate a bill authorizing and advising the President to open negotiations with Mexico and Texas for the adjustment of boundaries between them, and the annexation of the latter to the United States. In support of his bill, he said:

"The return of Texas to our Union, and all the dismembered territory of 1819 along with it, is as certain as that the Red River and the Arkansas rise within our natural limits, and flow into the Mississippi. I wish to get it back, and to get it with peace and honor—at all events without unjust war, unconstitutionally made, on weak and groundless pretexts. I wish it to come back without sacrificing our trade even with Mexico, so valuable to us on account of the large returns of specie which it gave us, especially before the commencement of the Texian revolution, the events of which have alienated Mexican feeling from us, and reduced our specie imports from eleven millions of dollars per annum to one million and a half. I wish it to come back in a way to give as little dissatisfaction to any part of the Union as possible; and I believe it is very practicable to get it back without a shock to any part. The difficulty now is in the aspect which has been put upon it as a sectional, political, and slave question; as a movement of the South against the North, and of the slaveholding States for political supremacy. This is as unfounded in the true nature of the question, as it is unwise and unfortunate in the design which prompted it. The question is more Western than Southern, and as much free as slave. The territory to be recovered extends to the latitude of 38° in its north-east corner, and to latitude 42° in its north-west corner. One-half of it will lie in the region not adapted to slave labor; and, of course when regained, will be formed into non-slaveholding States. So far as slavery is concerned, then, the question is neutralized: it is as much free as slave; and it is greatly to be regretted—*regretted by all the friends of the Union*—that a different aspect has been given to it. I am southern by my birth—southern in my affections, interests, and connections—and shall abide the fate of the South in every thing in which she has right upon her side. I am a slaveholder, and shall take the fate of other slaveholders in every aggression upon that species of property, and in every attempt to excite a San Domingo insurrection among us. I have my eyes wide open to that danger, and fixed on the laboratories of insurrection, both in Europe and America; but I must see a real case of danger before I take the alarm. I am against the cry of wolf, when there is no wolf. I will resist the intrusive efforts of those whom it does not concern, to abolish slavery among us; but I shall not engage in schemes for its extension into regions where it was never known—into the valley of the Rio del Norte, for example, and along a river of two thousand miles in extent, where a slave's face was never seen."

The whole body of the people, South and West, a majority of those in the Middle States, and respectable portions of the Northern States, were in favor of getting back Texas; and upon this large mass the intriguers operated, having their feelings in their favor, and exciting them by fears of abolition designs from Great Britain, and the fear of losing Texas for ever, if not then obtained. Mr. Benton deemed it just to discriminate this honest mass from the intriguers who worked only in their own interest, and at any cost of war and dishonor, and even disunion to our own country. Thus:

"A large movement is now going on for the annexation of Texas; and I, who have viewed this movement from the beginning, believe that I have analyzed it with a just and discriminating eye. The great mass of it is disinterested, patriotic, reasonable, and moderate, and wishes to get back our lost territory, as soon as it can be done with peace and honor. This large mass is passive, and had just as lief have Texas next year as this year. A small part of this movement is interested, and is the active part, and is unreasonable, and violent, and must have Texas during the present presidential election, or never. For the former part—the great mass—I feel great respect, and wish to give them reasons for my conduct: to the latter part it would be lost labor in me to offer reasons. Political and interested parties have no ears; they listen only to themselves, and run their course upon their own calculations. All that I shall say is, that the present movement, prostituted as it evidently is, to selfish and sectional purposes, is injurious to the cause of annexation, and must end in delaying its consummation. But it will be delay only. Annexation is the natural and inevitable order of events, and will come! and when it comes, be it sooner or later, it will be for the national reasons stated in Mr. Van Buren's instructions of 1829, and in the rational manner indicated in his letter of 1844. It will come, because the country to be received is geographically appurtenant to our country, and politically, commercially, and socially connected with our people, and with our institutions: and it will come, not in the shape of a secret treaty between two Presidents, but as a *legislative* as well as an *executive* measure—as the act of two nations (the United States and Texas) and with the consent of Mexico, if she is wise, or without her consent, upon the lapse of her rights."

The wantonness of getting up a quarrel with Great Britain on this subject, was thus exposed:

"Our administration, and especially the negotiator of this treaty, has been endeavoring to pick a quarrel with England, and upon the slave question. Senators have observed this, and have remarked upon the improvidence of seeking a quarrel with a great power on a weak point, and in which we should be in the wrong, and have the sympathies of the world against us, and see divided opinions at home; and doing this when we have several great questions of real difficulty with that power, in any war growing out of which we should have right on our side, good wishes from other nations, and unity among ourselves. Senators have remarked this, and set it down to the account of a great improvidence. I look upon it, for my part, as a designed conclusion, and as calculated to promote an ulterior scheme. The disunion of these States is still desired by many, and the slave question is viewed as the instrument to effect it; and in that point of view, the multiplication of quarrels about slavery, both at home and abroad, becomes a natural part of the disunion policy. Hence the attempt to pick a quarrel with Great Britain for imputed anti-slavery designs in Texas, and among ourselves, and all the miserable correspondence to which that imputation has given birth; and that by persons who, two years ago, were emulating Great Britain in denunciation of the slave trade, and forming a naval and diplomatic alliance with her for closing the markets of the world against the introduction of slaves. Since then the disunion scheme is revived; and this accounts for the change of policy, and for the search after a quarrel upon a weak point, which many thought so improvident."

The closing sentences of this paragraph refer to the article in the Ashburton treaty which stipulated for a joint British and American squadron to guard the coast of Africa from slave-trading vessels: a stipulation which Mr. Calhoun and his friends supported, and which showed him at that time to be against the propagation of slavery, either in the United States or elsewhere. He had then rejoined the democratic party, and expected to be taken up as the successor to Mr. Van Buren; and, in that prospect of becoming President of the whole Union, had suspended his design for a separation, and for a new republic South, and was conciliating instead of irritating the free States; and in which scheme of conciliation he went so far as to give up all claim for reclamation for slaves liberated by the British authorities in their passage from one port of the United States to another, and even relinquished all opposition to the practice. The danger of an alliance offensive and defensive between Great Britain and Texas was still insisted upon by the President, and an attempt made upon the public sensibilities to alarm the country into immediate annexation as the means of avoiding that danger. The folly of such an apprehension was shown by the interest which Great Britain had in the commerce and friendship of Mexico, compared to which that of Texas was nothing:

"The President expresses his continued belief in a declaration previously made to the Senate, that an alliance, offensive and defensive, is to be formed between Texas and Great Britain, if the treaty is rejected. Well, the treaty is rejected! and the formidable alliance is not heard of, and never will be. It happens to take two to make a bargain; and the President would seem to have left out both parties when he expressed his belief, amounting almost to certainty, 'that instructions have already been given by the Texian government to propose to the government of Great Britain forthwith, on the failure (of the treaty) to enter into a treaty of commerce, and an alliance offensive and defensive. Alliance offensive and defensive, between Great Britain and Texas! a true exemplification of that famous alliance between the giant and the dwarf, of which we all read at the age of seven years. But let us see. First, Texas is to apply for this honor: and I, who know the people of Texas, and know them to be American and republican, instead of British and monarchical, know full well that they will apply for no such dependent alliance; and, if they did, would show themselves but little friendly to our country or its institutions. Next, Great Britain is to enter into this alliance; and how stands the account of profit and loss with her in such a contract for common cause against the friends and foes of each other? An alliance offensive and defensive, is a bargain to fight each other's enemies— each in proportion to its strength. In such a contract with Texas, Great Britain might receive a contingent of one Texian soldier for her Afghanistan and Asiatic wars: on the other hand she would lose the friendship of Mexico, and the twenty millions of silver dollars which the government or the merchants of Great Britain now annually draw from Mexico. Such would be the effect of the alliance offensive and defensive which our President so fully believes in— amounting, as he says his belief does, to an almost entire certainty. Incredible and absurd! The Mexican annual supply of silver dollars is worth more to Great Britain than all the Texases in the world. Besides the mercantile supply, the government itself is deeply interested in this trade of silver dollars. Instead of drawing gold from London to pay her vast establishments by sea and land throughout the NEW WORLD, and in some parts of the Old—instead of thus depleting herself of her bullion at home, she finds the silver for these payments in the Mexican mines. A commissary of purchases at $6,000 per annum, and a deputy at $4,000, are incessantly employed in these purchases and shipments of silver; and if interrupted, the Bank of England would pay the forfeit. Does any one suppose that Great Britain, for the sake of the Texian alliance, and the profit upon her small trade, would make an enemy of Mexico? would give up twenty millions annually of silver, deprive herself of her fountain of supply, and subject her bank to the drains which the foreign service of her armies and navies would require? The supposition is incredible: and I say no more to this scare-crow alliance, in which the President so fully believes."

The magnitude and importance of our young and growing trade with Mexico—the certainty that her carrying trade would fall into our hands, as her want of ports and ship timber would for ever prevent her from having any marine—were presented as a reason why we should cultivate peace with her.

"The legal state between the United States and Mexico is that of war; and the legal consequence is the abrogation of all treaties between the two powers, and the cessation of all commercial intercourse. This is a trifle in the eyes of the President; not sufficient to impede for an instant his intrigue for the presidency, and the ulterior scheme for the dissolution of the Union. But how is it in the eyes of the country? Is it a trifle in the eyes of those whose eyes are large enough to behold the extent of the Mexican commerce, and whose hearts are patriotic enough to lament its loss? Look at that commerce! The richest stream which the world beholds: for, of exports, silver is its staple article; of imports, it takes something of every thing, changed, to be sure, into the form of fine goods and groceries: of navigation, it requires a constant foreign supply; for Mexico neither has, nor can have, a marine, either commercial or military. The want of ports and timber deny her a marine now and for ever. This country, exporting what we want—(hard money)—taking something of all our exports—using our own ships to fetch and carry—lying at our door—with many inland streams of trade besides the great maritime stream of commerce—pouring the perennial product of her innumerable mines into our paper-money country, and helping us to be able to bear its depredations: this country, whose trade was so important to us under every aspect, is treated as a nullity by the American President, or rather, is treated with systematic outrage; and even the treaty which secures us her trade is disparagingly acknowledged with the contemptuous prefix of mere!— a mere commercial treaty. So styles it the appeal message. Now let us look to this commerce with our nearest neighbor, depreciated and repudiated by our President: let us see its origin, progress, and present state. Before the independence of Mexico, that empire of mines had no foreign trade: the mother country monopolized the whole. It was the Spanish Hesperides, guarded with more than the fabulous dragon's care. Mexican Independence was declared at Iguala, in the year 1821. In that year its trade with the United States began, humbly to be sure, but with a rapid and an immense development. In 1821, our exports to Mexico were about $100,000; our imports about the double of that small sum. In the year 1835, the year before the Texian revolution, our exports to the same country (and that independent of Honduras, Campeachy, and the Mosquito shore) amounted to $1,500,639; and that of direct trade, without counting exportations from other countries. Our imports were, for the same year, in merchandise, $5,614,819; of which the whole, except about $200,000 worth, was carried in American vessels. Our specie imports, for the same year, were $8,343,181. This was the state of our Mexican trade (and that without counting the inland branches of it), the year of the commencement of the Texian revolution—an event which I then viewed, as my speeches prove, under many aspects! And, with every sympathy alive in favor of the Texians, and with the full view of their return to our Union after a successful revolt, I still wished to conciliate this natural event with the great object of preserving our peaceful relations, and with them our commercial, political, social, and moral position in regard to Mexico, the second power of the New World after ourselves, and the first of the Spanish branch of the great American family."

Political and social considerations, and a regard for the character of republican government, were also urged as solid reasons for effecting the annexation of Texas without an outbreak or collision with Mexico:

"Mr. President, I have presented you considerations, founded in the relations of commerce and good neighborhood, for preserving not merely peace, but good-will with Mexico. We are the first—she the second power of the New World. We stand at the head of the Anglo-Saxon—she at the head of the South-European race—but we all come from the same branch of the human family—the white branch—which, taking its rise in the Caucasian Mountains, and circling Europe by the north and by the south, sent their vanguards to people the two

Americas—to redeem them from the savage and the heathen, and to bring them within the pale of the European systems. The independence of these vanguards from their metropolitan ancestors, was in the natural order of human events; and the precedence of the Anglo-Saxon branch in this assertion of a natural right, was the privilege and prerogative of their descent and education. The descendants of the English became independent first; those of the Spaniards followed; and, from the first dawn of their national existences, were greeted with applause, and saluted with the affection of brothers. They, on their part, showed a deference and an affection for us fraternal and affecting. Though speaking a different language, professing a different religion, bred in a different system of laws and of government, and guarded from all communication with us for centuries, yet they instantly took us for their model, framed their constitutions upon ours, and spread the great elements of old English liberty—elections, legislatures, juries, habeas corpus, face-to-face trials, no arrests but on special warrants!—spread all these essentials of liberty from the ancient capital of Montezuma to the end of the South American continent. This was honorable to us, and we felt it; it was beneficial to them, and we wished to cement the friendship they had proffered, and to perpetuate among them the institutions they had adopted. Conciliation, arising from justice and fairness, was our only instrument of persuasion; and it was used by all, and with perfect effect. Every administration—all the people—followed the same course; and, until this day— until the present administration—there has not been one to insult or to injure a new State of the South. Now it is done. Systematic insult has been practised; spoliation of two thousand miles of incontestable territory, over and above Texas, has been attempted; outrage to the perpetration of clandestine war, and lying in wait to attack the innocent by land and water, has been committed: and on whom? The second power of the New World after ourselves— the head of the Spanish branch—and the people in whose treatment at our hands the rest may read their own. Descended from the proud and brave Castilian—as proud and as brave now as in the time of Charles the Fifth, when Spain gave law to nations, and threatened Europe with universal domination—these young nations are not to be outraged with impunity. Broken and dispersed, the Spanish family has lost much of its power, but nothing of its pride, its courage, its chivalry, and its sensitiveness to insult.

"The head of the powers of the New World—deferred to as a model by all—the position of the United States was grand, and its vocation noble. It was called to the high task of uniting the American nations in the bonds of brotherhood, and in the social and political systems which cherish and sustain liberty. They are all republics, and she the elder sister; and it was her business to preserve harmony, friendship, and concord in a family of republics, occupying the whole extent of the New World. Every interest connected with the welfare of the human race required this duty at our hands. Liberty, religion, commerce, science, the liberal and the useful arts, all required it; and, until now, we had acted up to the grandeur of our position, and the nobleness of our vocation. A sad descent is now made; but the decision of the Senate arrests the plunge, and gives time to the nation to recover its place, and its character, and again to appear as the elder sister, the friendly head, and the model power of the cordon of republics which stretch from the north to the south, throughout the two Americas. The day will come when the rejection of this treaty will stand, uncontestedly, amongst the wisest and most patriotic acts of the American Senate.

"The bill which I have offered, Mr. President, is the true way to obtain Texas. It conciliates every interest at home and abroad, and makes sure of the accomplishment of its object. Offence to Mexico, and consequent loss of her trade and friendship, is provided against. If deaf to reason, the annexation would eventually come without her consent, but not without having conciliated her feelings by showing her a proper respect. The treaty only provided difficulties—difficulties at home and abroad—war and loss of trade with Mexico—slavery controversies, and dissolution of the Union at home. When the time came for admitting new States under the treaty, had it been ratified, then came the tug of war. The correspondence presented it wholly as a slave question. As such it would be canvassed at the elections; and here numerical strength was against us. If the new States were not admitted with slaves, they would not come in at all. Then Southern States might say they would stand out with them: and then came the crisis! So obviously did the treaty mode of acquisition, and the correspondence, lead to this result, that it may be assumed to have been their object; and thus a near period arranged for the dissolution of our Union. Happily, these dire consequences are averted, for the present; and the bill I have brought in provides the way of obviating them for ever, and, at the same time, making sure of the annexation."

This bill, by referring the question of annexation to the legislative and executive authorities combined, gave the right turn to the public mind, and led to the measure which was adopted by Congress at the ensuing session, and marred by Mr. Tyler's assuming to execute it in the expiring moments of his administration, when, forestalling his successor, he rejected the clause for peaceful negotiations, and rushed forward the part of the act which, taken alone, involved war with Mexico.

During the whole continuance of these debates in the Senate, the lobbies of the chamber were crowded with speculators in Texas scrip and lands, and with holders of Mexican claims, all working for the ratification of the treaty, which would bring with it an increase of value to their property, and war with Mexico, to be followed by a treaty providing for their demands. They also infested the Department of State, the presidential mansion, all the public places, and kept the newspapers in their interest filled with abuse and false accusations against the senators who stood between themselves and their prey. They were countenanced by the politicians whose objects were purely political in getting Texas, as well as by those who were in sympathy or complicity with their schemes. Persons employed by the government were known to be in the ranks of these speculators; and, to uncover them to the public, Mr. Benton submitted this resolution:

> "*Resolved*, That the Committee on Foreign Affairs be instructed to inquire whether any provisions are necessary in providing for the annexation of Texas, to protect the United States from speculating operations in Texas lands or scrip, and whether any persons employed by the government are connected with such speculations."

The resolve was not adopted, as it was well foreseen would be the case, there being always in every public body, a large infusion of gentle tempered men, averse to any strong measure, and who usually cast the balance between contending parties. The motion, however, had the effect of fixing public attention the more earnestly upon these operators; and its fate did not prevent the mover from offering other resolves of a kindred character. It had been well known that Mr. Calhoun's letter of slave statistics to Mr. Pakenham, as a cause for making the treaty of annexation, had been written after the treaty had been concluded and signed by the negotiators; and this fact was clearly deducible from the whole proceeding, as well as otherwise known to some. There was enough to satisfy close observers; but the mass want the proof, or an offer to prove; and for their benefit, Mr. Benton moved:

> "Also, that said committee be instructed to inquire whether the Texas treaty was commenced or agreed upon before the receipt of Lord Aberdeen's despatch of December 26, 1843, to Mr. Pakenham, communicated to our government in February, 1844."

This motion shared the fate of the former; but did not prevent a similar movement on another point. It will be remembered that this sudden commencement in the summer of 1843, was motived exclusively upon the communication of a British abolition plot in Texas, contained in a private letter from a citizen of Maryland in London, an "*extract*" from which had been sent to the Senate to justify the "*self-defence*" measures in the immediate annexation of Texas. The writer of that letter had been ascertained, and it lent no credit to the information conveyed. It had also been ascertained that he had been paid, and largely, out of the public Treasury, for that voyage to London—which authorized the belief that he had been sent for what had been found. An extract of the letter only had been sent to the Senate: a view of the whole was desired by the Senate in such an important case—and was asked for—but not obtained. Mr. Upshur was dead, and the President, in his answer, had supposed it had been taken away among his private papers—a very violent supposition after the letter had been made the foundation for a most important public proceeding. Even if so carried, it should have been pursued, and reclaimed, and made an archive in the Department: and this, not having been done by the President, was proposed to be done by the Senate; and this motion submitted:

> "Also, that it be instructed to obtain, if possible, the '*private letter*' from London, quoted in Mr. Upshur's first despatch on the Texas negotiation, and supposed by the President to have been carried away among his private papers; and to ascertain the name of the writer of said letter."

To facilitate all these inquiries an additional resolve proposed to clothe the committee with authority to send for persons and papers—to take testimony under oath—and to extend their inquiries into all subjects which should connect themselves with selfish, or criminal motives for the acquisition of Texas. And all these inquiries, though repulsed in the Senate, had their effect upon the public mind, already well imbued with suspicions and beliefs of sinister proceedings, marked with an exaggerated demonstration of zeal for the public good.

CHAPTER CXLIII.

OREGON TERRITORY: CONVENTIONS OF 1818 AND 1828: JOINT OCCUPATION: ATTEMPTED NOTICE TO TERMINATE IT.

These conventions provided for the joint occupation of the countries respectively claimed by Great Britain and the United States on the north-west coast of America—that of 1818 limiting the joint occupancy to ten years—that of 1828 extending it indefinitely until either of the two powers should give notice to the other of a desire to terminate it. Such agreements are often made when it is found difficult to agree upon the duration of any particular privilege, or duty. They are seductive to the negotiators because they postpone an inconvenient question: they are consolatory to each party, because each says to itself it can get rid of the obligation when it pleases—a consolation always delusive to one of the parties: for the one that has the advantage always resists the notice, and long baffles it, and often through menaces to consider it as an unfriendly proceeding. On the other hand, the party to whom it is disadvantageous often sees danger in change; and if the notice is to be given in a legislative body, there will always be a large per centum of easy temperaments who are desirous of avoiding questions, putting off difficulties, and suffering the evils they have in preference of flying to those they know not: and in this way these temporary agreements, to be terminated on the notice of either party, generally continue longer than either party dreamed of when they were made. So it was with this Oregon joint occupancy. The first was for ten years: not being able to agree upon ten years more, the usual delusive resource was fallen upon: and, under the second joint occupation had already continued in operation fourteen years. Western members of Congress now took up the subject, and moved the Senate to advise the government to give the notice. Mr. Semple, senator from Illinois, proposed the motion: it was debated many days—resisted by many speakers: and finally defeated. It was first resisted as discourteous to Great Britain—then as offensive to her—then as cause of war on her side—finally, as actual war on our side—and even as a conspiracy to make war. This latter accusation was so seriously urged as to call out a serious answer from one of the senators friendly to the notice, not so much in exculpation of himself, as that of a friend at whom the imputation was levelled. In this sense, Mr. Breese, of Illinois, stood up, and said:

> "His friend on the left (Mr. Benton) was accused of being at the head of a conspiracy, having no other object than the involving us in a war with Great Britain; and it was said with equal truth that his lever for moving the different elements was the northern boundary question. What foundation was there for so grave an accusation? None other than that he had fearlessly, from the beginning, resisted every encroachment, come from what quarter it might. He had stemmed the tide of British influence, if any such there was—he had rendered great and imperishable services to the West, and the West was grateful to him—he had watched her interests from the cradle; and now, when arrived at maturity, and able to take care of herself, he boldly stood forth her advocate. If devotion to his country, then, made him a conspirator, he was indeed guilty."

Upon all this talk of war the commercial interest became seriously alarmed, and looked upon the delivery of the notice as the signal for a disastrous depression in our foreign trade. In a word, the general uneasiness became so great that there was no chance for doing what we had a right to do, what the safety of our territory required us to do, and without the right to do which the convention of 1828 could not have been concluded. The motion for the notice was defeated by a vote of 28 against 18. The yeas were:

> "YEAS—Messrs. Allen, Atchison, Atherton, Bagby, Benton, Breese, Buchanan, Colquitt, Fairfield, Fulton, Hannegan, King, Semple, Sevier, Sturgeon, Walker, Woodbury, and Wright—18."

> "NAYS—Messrs. Archer, Barrow, Bates, Bayard, Berrien, Choate, Clayton, Crittenden, Dayton, Evans, Foster, Haywood, Huger, Huntington, Jarnagin, Johnson, McDuffie, Mangum, Merrick, Miller, Morehead, Phelps, Rives, Simmons, Tallmadge, Upham, White, and Woodbridge—28."

CHAPTER CXLIV.

PRESIDENTIAL ELECTION.

Mr. James Knox Polk, and Mr. George Mifflin Dallas, had been nominated, as shown, for President and Vice-President by the democratic convention: Mr. Calhoun had declined to suffer his name to go before that election for reasons which he published, and an attempt to get up a separate convention for him, entirely failed: Mr. Tyler, who had a separate convention, and received its unanimous nomination, and thankfully accepted it, soon withdrew, and without having had a vice-presidential candidate on his ticket. On the whig side, Mr. Clay and Mr. Theodore Frelinghuysen were the candidates, and the canvass was conducted without those appeals to "hard cider, log-cabins, and coon-skins" which had been so freely used by the whig party during the last canvass, and which were so little complimentary to the popular intelligence. The democratic candidates were elected—and by a large electoral vote—170 to 105. The States which voted the democratic ticket, were: Maine, New Hampshire, New York, Pennsylvania, Virginia, South Carolina, Georgia, Louisiana, Mississippi, Indiana, Illinois, Alabama, Missouri, Arkansas, Michigan. Those which voted the opposite ticket, were: Massachusetts, Rhode Island, Connecticut, Vermont, New Jersey, Delaware, Maryland, North Carolina, Kentucky, Tennessee, Ohio. The popular vote was, for the democratic candidate, 1,536,196: for the opposite ticket, 1,297,912. This was a large increase upon the popular vote of 1840—large as that vote was, and Mr. Clay, though defeated, receiving 22,000 votes more than General Harrison did—affording good evidence that he would have been elected if he had been the candidate at that time. The issue in the election was mainly the party one of whig and democrat, modified by the tariff and Texas questions—Mr. Clay being considered the best representative of the former interest, Mr. Polk of the latter.

The difference in the electoral vote was large—65: in the popular vote, not so considerable: and in some of the States (and in enough of them to have reversed the issue), the difference in favor of Mr. Polk quite small, and dependent upon causes independent of himself and his cause. Of these it is sufficient to mention New York. There the popular vote was about five hundred thousand: the difference in favor of Mr. Polk, about five thousand: and that difference was solely owing to the association of Mr. Silas Wright, with the canvass. Refusing the nomination for the vice-presidency, and seeing a person nominated for the presidency by a long intrigue at the expense of his friend, Mr. Van Buren, he suffered himself to be persuaded to quit the Senate, which he liked, to become the democratic candidate for governor of New York—a place to which he was absolutely averse. The two canvasses went on together, and were in fact one; and the name and popularity of Mr. Wright brought to the presidential ticket more than enough votes to make the majority that gave the electoral vote of the State to Mr. Polk, but without being able to bring it up to his own vote for governor; which was still five thousand more. It was a great sacrifice of feeling and of wishes on his part to quit the Senate to stand this election—a sacrifice purely for the good of the cause, and which became a sacrifice, in a more material sense for himself and his friends. The electoral vote of New York was 36, which, going all together, and being taken from one side and added to the other, would have made a difference of 72—being seven more than enough to have elected Mr. Clay. Mr. Polk was also aided by the withdrawal of Mr. Tyler, and by receiving the South Carolina vote; both of which contingencies depended upon causes independent of his cause, and of his own merits: but of this in another place. I write to show how things were done, more than what was done; and to save, if possible, the working of the government in the hands of the people whose interests and safety depend upon its purity, not upon its corruptions.

CHAPTER CXLV.

AMENDMENT OF THE CONSTITUTION: ELECTION OF PRESIDENT AND VICE-PRESIDENT: MR. BENTON'S PLAN.

Mr. Benton asked the leave for which he had given notice on Wednesday, to bring in a joint resolution for the amendment of the Constitution of the United States in relation to the election of President and Vice-President, and prefaced his motion with an exposition of the principle and details of the amendment which he proposed to offer. This exposition, referring to a speech which he had made in the year 1824, and reproducing it for the present occasion, can only be analyzed in this brief notice.

Mr. B. said he found himself in a position to commence most of his speeches with "*twenty years ago!*"—a commencement rather equivocal, and liable to different interpretations in the minds of different persons; for, while he might suppose himself to be displaying sagacity and foresight, in finding a medicine for the cure of the present disorders of the state in the remedies of prevention which he had proposed long since, yet others might understand him in a different character, and consider him as belonging to the category of those who, in that long time, had learned nothing, and had forgot nothing. So it might be now; for he was endeavoring to revive a proposition which he had made exactly twenty years before, and for the revival of which he deemed the present time eminently propitious. The body politic was now sick; and the patient, in his agony, might take the medicine as a cure, which he refused, when well, to take as a prevention.

Mr. B. then proceeded to state the object and principle of his amendment, which was, to dispense with all intermediate bodies in the election of President and Vice-President, and to keep the election wholly in the hands of the people; and to do this by giving them a direct vote for the man of their choice, and holding a second election between the two highest, in the event of a failure in the first election to give a majority to any one. This was to do away with the machinery of all intermediate bodies to guide, control, or defeat the popular choice; whether a Congress caucus, or a national convention, to dictate the selection of candidates; or a body of electors to receive and deliver their votes; or a House of Representatives to sanction or frustrate their choice.

Mr. B. spoke warmly and decidedly in favor of the principle of his proposition, assuming it as a fundamental truth to which there was no exception, *that liberty would be ruined by providing any kind of substitute for popular election!* asserting that all elections would degenerate into fraud and violence, if any intermediate body was established between the voters and the object of their choice, and placed in a condition to be able to control, betray, or defeat that choice. This fundamental truth he supported upon arguments, drawn from the philosophy of government, and the nature of man, and illustrated by examples taken from the history of all elective governments which had ever existed. He showed that it was the law of the few to disregard the will of the many, when they got power into their hands; and that liberty had been destroyed wherever intermediate bodies obtained the direction of the popular will. He quoted a vast number of governments, both ancient and modern, as illustrations of this truth; and referred to the period of direct voting in Greece and in Rome, as the grand and glorious periods of popular government, when the unfettered will of the people annually brought forward the men of their own choice to administer their own affairs, and when those people went on advancing from year to year, and produced every thing great in arts and in arms—in public and in private life—which then exalted them to the skies, and still makes them fixed stars in the firmament of nations. He believed in the capacity of the people for self-government, but they must have fair play—fair play at the elections, on which all depended; and for that purpose should be free from the control of any intermediate, irresponsible body of men.

At present (he said), the will of the people was liable to be frustrated in the election of their chief officers (and that at no less than three different stages of the canvass), by the intervention of small bodies of men between themselves and the object of their choice. First, at the beginning of the process, in the nomination or selection of candidates. A Congress caucus formerly, and a national convention now govern and control that nomination; and never fail, when they choose, to find pretexts for substituting their own will for that of the people. Then a body of electors, to receive and hold the electoral votes, and who, it cannot be doubted, will soon be expert enough to find reasons for a similar substitution. Then the House of Representatives may come in at the conclusion, to do as they have done heretofore, and set the will of the people at absolute defiance. The remedy for all this is the direct vote, and a second election between the two highest, if the first one failed. This would operate fairly and rightfully. No matter how many candidates then appeared in the field. If any one obtained a majority of the whole number of votes, the popular principle was satisfied; the majority had prevailed, and acquiescence was the part of the minority. If no one obtained the majority, then the first election answered the purpose of a nomination—a real nomination by the people; and a second election between the two highest would give effect to the real will of the people.

Mr. B. then exposed the details of his proposed amendment, as contained in the joint resolution which he intended to offer. The plan of election contained in that resolution, was the work of eminent men—of Mr. Macon, Mr. Van Buren, Mr. Hugh L. White, Mr. Findlay, of Pennsylvania, Mr. Dickerson, of New Jersey, Mr. Holmes, Mr. Hayne, and Mr. R. M. Johnson, and was received with great favor by the Senate and the country at the time it was reported. Subsequent experience should make it still more acceptable, and entitle its details to a careful and indulgent consideration from the people, whose rights and welfare it is intended to preserve and promote.

The detail of the plan is to divide the States into districts; the people to vote direct in each district for the candidate they prefer; the candidate having the highest vote for President to receive the vote of the district for such office, and to count one. If any candidate receives the majority of the whole number of districts, such person to be elected; if no one receives such majority, the election to be held over again between the two highest. To afford time for these double elections, when they become necessary, the first one is proposed to be held in the month of August—at a time to which many of the State elections now conform, and to which all may be made to conform—and to be held on the same days throughout the Union. To receive the returns of such elections, the Congress is required to be in session, on the years of such elections, in the month of October; and if a second election becomes necessary, it will be held in December. Two days are proposed for the first election, because most of the State elections continue two days: one day alone is allowed for the second election, it being a brief issue between two candidates. To provide for the possibility of remote and most improbable contingencies, that of an equality of votes between the two candidates—a thing which *cannot* occur where the whole number of votes is odd, and is utterly improbable when they are even—and to keep the election from the House of Representatives, while preserving the principle which should prevail in elections by the House of Representatives, it is provided that the candidate, in the case of such equality, having the majority of votes in the majority of the States, shall be the person elected President. To provide against the possibility of another almost impossible contingency (that of more than two candidates having the highest, and, of course, the same number of votes in the first election, by an equality of votes between several), the proposed amendment is so worded as to let all—that is, all having the two highest number of votes—go before the people at the second election.

Such are the details for the election of President: they are the same for that of Vice-President, with the single exception that, when the first election should have been effective for the election of President, and not so for Vice-President, then, to save the trouble of a second election for the secondary office only, the present provision of the constitution should prevail, and the Senate choose between the two highest.

Having made this exposition of the *principle* and of the *details* of the plan he proposed, Mr. B. went on to speak at large in favor of its efficacy and practicability in preserving the rights of the people, maintaining the purity of elections, preventing intrigue, fraud, and treachery, either in guiding or defeating the choice of the people and securing to our free institutions a chance for a prolonged and virtuous existence.

Mr. B. said he had never attended a nominating caucus or convention, and never intended to attend one. He had seen the last Congress caucus in 1824, and never wished to see another, or hear of another; he had seen the national convention of 1844, and never wished to see another. He should support the nominations of the last convention; but hoped to see such conventions rendered unnecessary, before the recurrence of another presidential election.

Mr. B. after an extended argument, concluded with an appeal to the Senate to favor his proposition, and send it to the country. His only object at present was to lay it before the country: the session was too far advanced to expect action upon it. There were two modes to amend the constitution—one by Congress proposing, and two-thirds of the State legislatures adopting, the amendment; the other by a national convention called by Congress for the purpose. Mr. B. began with the first mode: he might end with the second.

Disclaiming every thing temporary or invidious in this attempt to amend the constitution in an important point—referring to his labors twenty years ago for the elucidation of his motives—despising all pursuit after office, high or low—detesting all circumvention, intrigue, and management—anxious to restore our elections to their pristine purity and dignity—and believing the whole body of the people to be the only safe and pure authority for the selection as well as election of the first officers of the republic,—he confidently submitted his proposition to the Senate and the people, and asked for it the indulgent consideration which was due to the gravity and the magnitude of the subject.

Mr. B. then offered his amendment, which was unanimously received, and ordered to be printed.

The following is the copy of this important proposition:

"*Resolved by the Senate and House of Representatives of the United States of America in Congress assembled, two-thirds of both Houses concurring*, That the following amendment to the constitution of the United States be proposed to the legislatures of the several States, which, when ratified by the legislatures of three-fourths of the States, shall be valid to all intents and purposes as part of the constitution:

"That, hereafter, the President and Vice-President of the United States shall be chosen by the people of the respective States, in the manner following: Each State shall be divided, by the legislature thereof, into districts, equal in number to the whole number of senators and representatives to which such State may be entitled in the Congress of the United States; the said districts to be composed of contiguous territory, and to contain, as nearly as may be, an equal number of persons, entitled to be represented under the constitution, and to be laid off, for the first time, immediately after the ratification of this amendment, and afterwards, at the session of the legislature next ensuing the apportionment of representatives by the Congress of the United States; that, on the first Thursday in August, in the year 1848, and on the same day every fourth year thereafter, the citizens of each State who possess the qualifications requisite for electors of the most numerous branch of the State legislatures, shall meet within their respective districts, and vote for a President and Vice-President of the United States, one of whom at least shall not be an inhabitant of the same State with themselves; and the person receiving the greatest number of votes for President, and the one receiving the greatest number of votes for Vice-President in each district, shall be holden to have received one vote; which fact shall be immediately certified by the governor of the State, to each of the senators in Congress from such State, and to the President of the Senate and the Speaker of the House of Representatives. The Congress of the United States shall be in session on the second Monday in October, in the year 1848, and on the same day on every fourth year thereafter; and the President of the Senate, in the presence of the Senate and House of Representatives, shall open all the certificates, and the votes shall then be counted. The person having the greatest number of votes for President, shall be President, if such number be equal to a majority of the whole number of votes given; but if no person have such majority, then a second election shall be held on the first Thursday in the month of December then next ensuing, between the persons having the two highest numbers for the office of President; which second election shall be conducted, the result certified, and the votes counted, in the same manner as in the first; and the person having the greatest number of votes for President, shall be President. But, if two or more persons shall have received the greatest, and an equal number of votes, at the second election, then the person who shall have received the greatest number of votes in the greatest number of States, shall be President. The person having the greatest number of votes for Vice-President, at the first election, shall be Vice-President, if such number be equal to a majority of the whole number of votes given: and, if no person have such majority, then a second election shall take place between the persons having the two highest numbers on the same day that the second election is held for President; and the person having the highest number of votes for Vice-President, shall be Vice-President. But if there should happen to be an equality of votes between the persons so voted for at the second election, then the person having the greatest number of votes in the greatest number of States, shall be Vice-President. But when a second election shall be necessary in the case of Vice-President, and not necessary in the case of President, then the Senate shall choose a Vice-President from the persons having the two highest numbers in the first election, as is now prescribed in the constitution."

CHAPTER CXLVI.

THE PRESIDENT AND THE SENATE: WANT OF CONCORD: NUMEROUS REJECTIONS OF NOMINATIONS.

Mr. Tyler was without a party. The party which elected him repudiated him: the democratic party refused to receive him. His only resource was to form a Tyler party, at which he made but little progress. The few who joined him from the other parties were, most of them, importunate for office; and whether successful or not in getting through the Senate (for all seemed to get nominations), they lost the moral force which could aid him. The incessant rejection of these nominations, and the pertinacity with which they were renewed, presents a scene of presidential and senatorial oppugnation which had no parallel up to that time, and of which there has been no example since. Nominations and rejections flew backwards and forwards as in a game of shuttlecock—the same nomination, in several instances, being three times rejected in the same day (as it appears on the journal), but within the same hour, as recollected by actors in the scene. Thus: on the 3d day of March, 1843, Mr. Caleb Cushing having been nominated to the Senate for Secretary of the Treasury, was rejected by a vote of 27 nays to 19 yeas. The nays were: Messrs. Allen, Archer, Bagby, Barrow, Bayard, Benton, Berrien, Thomas Clayton, Conrad, Crafts, Crittenden, Graham, Henderson, Huntingdon, Kerr, Linn, Mangum, Merrick, Miller, Morehead, Phelps, Porter, Simmons, Smith of Indiana, Sprague, Tappan, White. This vote was taken after dark in the night of the last day of the session. The President, who according to the custom on such occasions, attended in an ante-chamber appropriated to the Vice-President, immediately sent back Mr. Cushing's name, re-nominated for the same office. He was immediately rejected again by the same 27 nays, and with a diminution of nine who had voted for him. Incontinently the private secretary of Mr. Tyler returned with another re-nomination of the same citizen for the same office; which was immediately rejected by a vote of 29 to 2. The two senators who voted for him on this last trial were, Messrs. Robert J. Walker and Cuthbert. The 19 who voted for the nomination on the first trial were: Messrs. Bates, Buchanan, Calhoun, Choate, Cuthbert, Evans, Fulton, King, McDuffie, McRoberts, Sevier, Sturgeon, Tallmadge, Walker, Wilcox, Williams, Woodbury, Wright. The message containing this second re-nomination was written in such haste and flurry that half the name of the nominee was left out. "I nominate *Cushing* as Secretary of the Treasury, in place of Walter Forward, resigned," was the whole message; but the Senate acted upon it as it was, without sending the message back for rectification, as the rule always has been in the case of clerical mistakes. These re-nominations by Mr. Tyler were the more notable because, as chairman of the committee which had the duty of reporting upon the nomination of the United States Bank directors in the time of the "*war*," as it was called of the government upon the bank, he had made the report against President Jackson on the re-nomination of the four government directors (Messrs. Gilpin, Sullivan, Wager and McEldery), who had been rejected for reporting to the President, at his request, the illegal and corrupt proceedings of the bank (such as were more fully established by a committee of the stockholders); and also voted against the whole four re-nominations.

The same night Mr. Henry A. Wise underwent three rejections on a nomination, and two re-nominations as minister plenipotentiary and envoy extraordinary to France. The first rejection was by a vote of 24 to 12—the second, 26 to 8—the third, 29 to 2. The two yeas in this case were the same as on the third rejection of Mr. Cushing. The yeas and nays in the first vote were, yeas: Messrs. Archer, Buchanan, Calhoun, Choate, Cuthbert, Evans, Fulton, King, McDuffie, Sturgeon, Tallmadge, Walker. The nays: Messrs. Bagby, Barrow, Benton, Berrien, Clayton (Thomas), Conrad, Crafts, Crittenden, Dayton, Graham, Henderson, Huntingdon, John Leeds Kerr, Mangum, Merrick, Miller, Phelps, Porter, Simmons, Smith of Indiana, Sprague, Tappan, White, Woodbridge. Mr. Wise had been nominated in the place of Lewis Cass, Esq., resigned.

At the ensuing session a rapid succession of rejections of nominations took place. Mr. George H. Proffit, of Indiana, late of the House of Representatives, was nominated minister plenipotentiary and envoy extraordinary to the Emperor of Brazil. He had been commissioned in the vacation, and had sailed upon his destination, drawing the usual outfit and quarter's salary, leaving the principal part behind, bet upon the presidential election. He was not received by the Emperor of Brazil, and was rejected by the Senate. Only eight members voted for his confirmation—Messrs. Breese, Colquitt, Fulton, Hannegan, King, Semple, Sevier, Walker. He had been nominated in the place of William Hunter, Esq., ex-senator from Rhode Island, recalled—a gentleman of education, reading, talent, and finished manners; and eminently fit for his place. It was difficult to see in Mr. Proffit, intended to supersede him, any cause for his appointment except his adhesion to Mr. Tyler.

Mr. David Henshaw, of Massachusetts, had been commissioned Secretary of the Navy in the recess, in place of Mr. Upshur, appointed Secretary of State. He was rejected—only eight senators voting for his nomination: they were: Messrs. Colquitt, Fulton, Haywood, King, Semple, Sevier, Walker, Woodbury. The same fate attended Mr. James M. Porter, of Pennsylvania, appointed in the recess Secretary at War, in the place of Mr. John C. Spencer, resigned. No more than three senators voted for his confirmation—Messrs. Haywood, Porter of Michigan, and Tallmadge. Mr. John C. Spencer himself, nominated an associate justice of the Supreme Court of the United States, in the place of Smith Thompson, Esq., deceased, was also rejected—26 to 21 votes. The negatives were: Messrs. Allen, Archer, Atchison, Barrow, Bates, Bayard, Benton, Berrien, Choate, Clayton, Crittenden, Dayton, Evans, Foster, Haywood, Henderson, Huntingdon, Jarnagin, Mangum, Merrick, Miller, Morehead, Pearce, Simmons, Tappan, Woodbridge.—Mr. Isaac Hill, of New Hampshire, was another subject of senatorial rejection. He was nominated for the place of the chief of the bureau of provisions and clothing of the Navy Department, to fill a vacancy occasioned by the death of Charles W. Goldsborough, Esq., and rejected by a vote of 25 to 11. The negatives were: Messrs. Allen, Archer, Atchison, Bagby, Barrow, Bates, Bayard, Benton, Berrien, Breese, Clayton (Thomas), Crittenden, Dayton, Evans, Foster, Huntingdon, Jarnagin, Mangum, Merrick, Morehead, Pearce, Sturgeon, Tappan, Walker, White.—Mr. Cushing was nominated at the same session for minister plenipotentiary and envoy extraordinary to China, the proceedings on which have not been made public.

CHAPTER CXLVII.

MR. TYLER'S LAST MESSAGE TO CONGRESS.

Texas was the prominent topic of this message, and presented in a way to have the effect, whatever may have been the intent, of inflaming and exasperating, instead of soothing and conciliating Mexico. Mr. Calhoun was now the Secretary of State, and was now officially what he had been all along actually, the master spirit in all that related to Texas annexation. Of the interests concerned in the late attempted negotiation, one large interest, both active and powerful, was for war with Mexico—not for the sake of the war, but of the treaty of peace which would follow it, and by which their Texas scrip and Texas land, now worth but little, would become of great value. Neither Mr. Tyler nor Mr. Calhoun were among these speculators, but their most active supporters were; and these supporters gave the spirit in which the Texas movement was conducted; and in this spirit the message, in all that related to the point, was conceived. The imperious notification given at the last session to cease the war, was repeated with equal arrogance, and with an intimation that the United States would come to the aid of Texas, if it went on. Thus:

> "In my last annual message, I felt it to be my duty to make known to Congress, in terms both plain and emphatic, my opinion in regard to the war which has so long existed between Mexico and Texas; and which, since the battle of San Jacinto, has consisted altogether of predatory incursions, attended by circumstances revolting to humanity. I repeat now, what I then said, that, after eight years of feeble and ineffectual efforts to recover Texas, it was time that the war should have ceased."

This was not the language for one nation to hold towards another, nor would such have been held towards Mexico, except from her inability to help herself, and our desire to get a chance to make a treaty of acquisitions with her. The message goes on to say, "*Mexico has no right to jeopard the peace of the world, by urging any longer a useless and fruitless contest.*" Very imperious language that, but entirely unfounded in the facts. Hostilities had ceased between Mexico and Texas upon an armistice under the guarantee of the great powers, and peace with Mexico was immediate and certain when Mr. Tyler's government effected the breach and termination of the armistice by the Texas negotiations, and by lending detachments of the army and navy to President Houston, to assist in the protection of Texas. This interposition, and by the lawless and clandestine loan of troops and ships, to procure a rupture of the armistice, and prevent the peace which Mexico and Texas were on the point of making, was one of the most revolting circumstances in all this Texas intrigue. Thus presenting a defiant aspect to Mexico, the President recommended the admission of Texas into the Union upon an act of Congress, to be passed for that purpose, and under the clause in the constitution which authorizes Congress to admit new States. Thus, a great constitutional point was gained by those who had opposed and defeated the annexation treaty. By that mode of annexation the treaty-making power—the President and Senate—made the acquisition: by the mode now recommended the legislative authority was to do it.

The remainder of the message presents nothing to be noted, except the congratulations of the President upon the restoration of the federal currency to what he called a sound state, but which was, in fact, a solid state—for it had become gold and silver; and his equal felicitations upon the equalization of the exchanges (which had never been unequal between those who had money to exchange), saying that exchange was now only the difference of the expense of transporting gold. That had been the case always with those who had gold; and what had been called inequalities of exchange before, was nothing but the different degrees of the depreciation of different bank notes. But what the President did not note, but which all others observed, was the obvious fact, that this restoration and equalization were attained without any of the remedies which he had been prescribing for four years! without any of those Fiscal Institutes—Fiscal Corporations—Fiscal Agents—or Fiscal Exchequers, which he had been prescribing for four years. It was the effect of the gold bill, and of the Independent Treasury, and the cessation of all attempts to make a national currency of paper money.

CHAPTER CXLVIII.

LEGISLATIVE ADMISSION OF TEXAS INTO THE UNION AS A STATE.

A joint resolution was early brought into the House of Representatives for the admission of Texas as a State of the Union. It was in these words:

"That Congress doth consent that the territory properly included within, and rightfully belonging to the republic of Texas, may be erected into a new State, to be called the State of Texas, with a republican form of government, to be adopted by the people of said republic, by deputies in convention assembled, with the consent of the existing government, in order that the same may be admitted as one of the States of this Union. And, that the foregoing consent of Congress is given upon the following conditions, and with the following guarantees:

"First. Said State to be formed, subject to the adjustment by this government of all questions of boundary that may arise with other governments; and the constitution thereof, with the proper evidence of its adoption by the people of said republic of Texas, shall be transmitted to the President of the United States, to be laid before Congress for its final action, on or before the 1st day of January, 1846.

"Second. Said State, when admitted into the Union, after ceding to the United States all public edifices, fortifications, barracks, ports and harbors, navy and navy-yards, docks, magazines, arms, armaments, and all other property and means pertaining to the public defence belonging to said republic of Texas, shall retain all the public funds, debts, taxes, and dues of every kind which may belong to, or be due and owing said republic; and shall also retain all the vacant and unappropriated lands lying within its limits, to be applied to the payment of the debts and liabilities of said republic of Texas; and the residue of said lands, after discharging said debts and liabilities, to be disposed of as said State may direct; but in no event are said debts and liabilities to become a charge upon the government of the United States.

"Third. New States, of convenient size, not exceeding four in number, in addition to said State of Texas, and having sufficient population, may hereafter by the consent of said State, be formed out of the territory thereof, which shall be entitled to admission under the provisions of the federal constitution. And such States as may be formed out of that portion of said territory lying south of thirty-six degrees thirty minutes north latitude, commonly known as the Missouri compromise line, shall be admitted into the Union, with or without slavery, as the people of each State asking admission may desire; and in such State or States as shall be formed out of said territory north of said Missouri compromise line, slavery or involuntary servitude (except for crime) shall be prohibited."

To understand the third, and last clause of this resolve, it must be recollected that the boundaries of Texas, by the treaty of 1819, which retroceded that province to Spain, were extended north across the Red River, and entirely to the Arkansas River; and following that river up to the 37th, the 38th, and eventually to the 42d degree of north latitude; so that all this part of the territory lying north of 36 degrees 30 minutes, came within the terms of the Missouri compromise line prohibiting slavery north of that line. Here then was an anomaly—slave territory, and free territory within the same State; and it became the duty of Congress to provide for each accordingly: and it was done. The territory lying south of that compromise line might become free or slave States as the inhabitants should decide: the States to be formed out of the territory north of it were to be bound by the compromise: and lest any question should arise on that point in consequence of Texas having been under a foreign dominion since the line was established, it was expressly re-enacted by this clause of the resolution, and in the precise words of the Missouri compromise act. Thus framed, and made clear in its provisions in respect to slavery, the resolutions, after ample discussion, were passed through the House by a good majority—120 to 97. The affirmatives were

"Archibald H. Arrington, John B. Ashe, Archibald Atkinson, Thomas H. Bayly, James E. Belser, Benjamin A. Bidlack, Edward J. Black, James Black, James A. Black, Julius W. Blackwell, Gustavus M. Bower, James B. Bowlin, Linn Boyd, Richard Brodhead, Aaron V. Brown, Milton Brown, William J. Brown, Edmund Burke, Armistead Burt, George Alfred Caldwell, John Campbell, Shepherd Carey, Reuben Chapman, Augustus A. Chapman, Absalom H. Chappell, Duncan L. Clinch, James G. Clinton, Howell Cobb, Walter Coles, Edward Cross, Alvan Cullom, John R. J. Daniel, John W. Davis, John B. Dawson, Ezra Dean, James Dellet, Stephen A. Douglass, George C. Dromgool, Alexander Duncan, Chesselden Ellis, Isaac G. Farlee, Orlando B. Ficklin, Henry D. Foster, Richard French, George Fuller, William H. Hammett, Hugh A. Haralson, Samuel Hays, Thomas J. Henley, Isaac E. Holmes, Joseph P. Hoge, George W. Hopkins, George S. Houston, Edmund W. Hubard, William S. Hubbell, James M. Hughes, Charles J. Ingersoll, John Jameson, Cave Johnson, Andrew Johnson, George W. Jones. Andrew Kennedy, Littleton Kirkpatrick, Alcée Labranche, Moses G. Leonard, William Lucas, John H. Lumpkin, Lucius Lyon, William C. McCauslen, William B. Maclay, John A. McClernand, Felix G. McConnel, Joseph J. McDowell, James J. McKay, James Mathews, Joseph Morris, Isaac E. Morse, Henry C. Murphy, Willoughby Newton, Moses Norris, jr., Robert Dale Owen, William Parmenter, William W. Payne, John Pettit, Joseph H. Peyton, Emery D. Potter, Zadock Pratt, David S. Reid, James H. Relfe, R. Barnwell Rhett, John Ritter, Robert W. Roberts, Jeremiah Russell, Romulus M. Saunders, William T. Senter, Thomas H. Seymour, Samuel Simons, Richard F. Simpson, John Slidell, John T. Smith, Thomas Smith, Robert Smith, Lewis Steenrod, Alexander H. Stephens, John Stewart, William H. Styles, James W. Stone, Alfred P. Stone, Selah B. Strong, George Sykes, William Taylor, Jacob Thomson, John W. Tibbatts, Tilghman M. Tucker, John B. Weller, John Wentworth, Joseph A. Woodward, Joseph A. Wright, William L. Yancey, Jacob S. Yost."

Members from the slave and free States voted for these resolutions, and thereby asserted the right of Congress to legislate upon slavery in territories, and to prohibit or prevent it as they pleased, and also exercised the right each way—forbidding it one side of a line, and leaving it optional with the State on the other—and not only acknowledging the validity of the Missouri compromise line, but enforcing it by a new enactment; and without this enactment every one saw that the slavery institution would come to the Arkansas River in latitude 37, and 38, and even 42. The vote was, therefore, an abolition of the institution legally existing between these two lines, and done in the formal and sacred manner of a compact with a foreign State, as a condition of its admission into the Union. One hundred and twenty members of the House of Representatives voted in favor of these resolutions, and thereby both asserted, and exercised the power of Congress to legislate upon slavery in territories, and to abolish it therein when it pleased: of the 97 voting against the resolution, not one did so from any objection to that power. The resolutions came down from the Department of State, and corresponded with the recommendation in the President's message.

Sent to the Senate for its concurrence, this joint resolution found a leading friend in the person of Mr. Buchanan, who was delighted with every part of it, and especially the re-enactment of the Missouri compromise line in the part where it might otherwise have been invalidated by the Texian laws and constitution, and which thus extinguished for ever the slavery question in the United States. In this sense he said:

"He was pleased with it, again, because it settled the question of slavery. These resolutions went to re-establish the Missouri compromise, by fixing a line within which slavery was to be in future confined. That controversy had nearly shaken this Union to its centre in an earlier and better period of our history; but this compromise, should it be now re-established, would prevent the recurrence of similar dangers hereafter. Should this question be now left open for one or two years, the country could be involved in nothing but one perpetual struggle. We should witness a feverish excitement in the public mind; parties would divide on the dangerous and exciting question of abolition; and the irritation might reach such an extreme as to endanger the existence of the Union itself. But close it now, and it would be closed for ever.

"Mr. B. said he anticipated no time when the country would ever desire to stretch its limits beyond the Rio del Norte; and, such being the case, ought any friend of the Union to desire to see this question left open any longer? Was it desirable again to have the Missouri question brought home to the people to goad them to fury? That question between the two great interests in our country had been well discussed and well decided; and from that moment Mr. B. had set down his foot on the solid ground then established, and there he would let the question stand for ever. Who could complain of the terms of that compromise?

"It was then settled that north of 36° 30' slavery should be for ever prohibited. The same line was fixed upon in the resolutions recently received from the House of Representatives, now before us. The bill from the House for the establishment of a territorial government in Oregon excluded slavery altogether from that vast country. How vain were the fears entertained in some quarters of the country that the slaveholding States would ever be able to control the Union! While, on the other hand, the fears entertained in the south and south-west as to the ultimate success of the abolitionists, were not less unfounded and vain. South of the compromise line of 36° 30' the States within the limits of Texas applying to come into the Union were left to decide for themselves whether they would permit slavery within their limits or not. And under this free permission, he believed, with Mr. Clay (in his letter on the subject of annexation), that if Texas should be divided into five States, two only of them would be slaveholding, and three free States. The descendants of torrid Africa delighted in the meridian rays of a burning sun; they basked and rejoiced in a degree of heat which enervated and would destroy the white man. The lowlands of Texas, therefore, where they raised cotton, tobacco, and rice, and indigo, was the natural region for the slave. But north of San Antonio, where the soil and climate were adapted to the culture of wheat, rye, corn, and cattle, the climate was exactly adapted to the white man of the North; there he could labor for himself without risk or injury. It was, therefore, to be expected that three out of the five new Texian States would be free States—certainly they would be so, if they but willed it. Mr. B. was willing to leave that question to themselves, as they applied for admission into the Union. He had no apprehensions of the result. With that feature in the bill, as it came from the House, he was perfectly content; and, whatever bill might ultimately pass, he trusted this would be made a condition in it."

It was in the last days of his senatorial service that Mr. Buchanan crowned his long devotion to the Missouri compromise by celebrating its re-enactment where it had been abrogated, taking a stand upon it as the solid ground on which the Union rested, and invoking a perpetuity of duration for it.

This resolution, thus adopted by the House, would make the admission a legislative act, but in the opinion of many members of the Senate that was only a step in the right direction: another in their opinion required to be taken: and that was to combine the treaty-making power with it—the Congress taking the initiative in the question, and the President and Senate finishing it by treaty, as done in the case of Louisiana and Florida. With this view Mr. Benton had brought in a bill for commissioners to treat for annexation, and so worded as to authorize negotiations with Mexico at the same time, and get her acquiescence to the alienation in the settlement of boundaries with her. His bill was in these terms:

"That a State, to be formed out of the present republic of Texas, with suitable extent and boundaries, and with two representatives in Congress until the next apportionment of representation, shall be admitted into the Union by virtue of this act, on an equal footing with the existing States, as soon as the terms and conditions of such admission, and the cession of the remaining Texian territory to the United States shall be agreed upon by the government of Texas and the United States.

"SEC. 2. *And be it further enacted*, That the sum of one hundred thousand dollars be, and the same is hereby appropriated, to defray the expenses of missions and negotiations to agree upon the terms of said admission and cession, either by treaty, to be submitted to the Senate, or by articles to be submitted to the two Houses of Congress, as the President may direct."

In support of this bill, Mr. Benton said:

"It was a copy, substantially, of the bill which he had previously offered, with the omission of all the terms and conditions which that bill contained. He had been induced to omit all these conditions because of the difficulty of agreeing upon them, and because it was now clear that whatever bill was passed upon the subject of Texas, the execution of it must devolve upon the new President, who had been just elected by the people with a view to this object. He had confidence in Mr. Polk, and was willing to trust the question of terms and conditions to his untrammelled discretion, certain that he would do the best that he could for the success of the object, the harmony of the Union, and the peace and honor of the country.

"The occasion is an extraordinary one, and requires an extraordinary mission. The voluntary union of two independent nations is a rare occurrence, and is worthy to be attended by every circumstance which lends it dignity, promotes its success, and makes it satisfactory. When England and Scotland were united, at the commencement of the last century, no less than thirty-one commissioners were employed to agree upon the terms; and the terms they agreed upon received the sanction of the Parliaments of the two kingdoms, and completed a union which had been in vain attempted for one hundred years. Extraordinary missions, nationally constituted, have several times been resorted to in our own country, and always with public approbation, whether successful or not. The first Mr. Adams sent Marshall, Gerry, and Pinckney to the French directory in 1798: Mr. Jefferson sent Ellsworth, Davie, and Murray to the French consular government of 1800: Mr. Madison sent Adams, Bayard, Gallatin, Clay, and Russell to Ghent in 1814. All these missions, and others which might be named, were nationally constituted—composed of eminent citizens taken from each political party, and from different sections of the Union; and, of course, all favorable to the object for which they were employed. An occasion has occurred which, in my opinion, requires a mission similarly constituted—as numerous as the missions to Paris or to Ghent—and composed of citizens from both political parties, and from the non-slaveholding as well as the slaveholding States. Such a commission could hardly fail to be successful, not merely in agreeing upon the terms of the union, but in agreeing upon terms which would be satisfactory to the people and the governments of the two countries. And here, to avoid misapprehension and the appearance of disrespect where the contrary is felt, I would say that the gentleman now in Texas as the chargé of the United States, is, in my opinion, eminently fit and proper to be one of the envoys extraordinary and ministers plenipotentiary which my bill contemplates.

"In withdrawing from my bill the terms and conditions which had been proposed as a basis of negotiation, I do not withdraw them from the consideration of those who may direct the negotiation. I expect them to be considered, and, as far as judged proper, to be acted on. The compromise principle between slave and non-slaveholding territory is sanctioned by the vote of the House of Representatives, and by the general voice of the country. In withdrawing it from the bill, I do not withdraw it from the consideration of the President: I only leave him free and untrammelled to do the best he can for the harmony of the Union on a delicate and embarrassing point.

"The assent of Mexico to the annexation is judged to be unnecessary, but no one judges her assent to a new boundary line to be unnecessary: no one judges it unnecessary to preserve her commerce and good will; and, therefore, every consideration of self-interest and national policy requires a fair effort to be made to settle this boundary and to preserve this trade and friendship; and I shall consider all this as remaining just as fully in the mind of the President as if submitted to him in a bill.

"The bill which I now offer is the same which I have presented heretofore, divested of its conditions, and committing the subject to the discretion of the President to accomplish the object in the best way that he can, and either negotiate a treaty to be submitted to the Senate, or to agree upon articles of union to be submitted to the two Houses of Congress. I deem this the best way of proceeding under every aspect. It is the safest way; for it will settle all questions beforehand, and leave no nest-eggs to hatch future disputes. It is the most speedy way; for commissioners conferring face to face will come to conclusions much sooner than two deliberative bodies sitting in two different countries, at near two thousand miles apart, and interchanging categorical propositions in the shape of law. It is the most satisfactory way; for whatever such a commission should agree upon, would stand the best chance to be satisfactory to all parts of the Union. It is the most respectful way to Texas, and the mode for which she has shown a decided preference. She has twice sent envoys extraordinary and ministers plenipotentiary here to treat with us; and the actual President, Mr. Jones, has authentically declared his willingness to engage in further negotiations. Ministers sent to confer and agree—to consult and to harmonize—is much more respectful than the transmission, by mail or messenger, of an inflexible proposition, in the shape of law, to be accepted or rejected in the precise words in which we send it. In every point of view, the mode which I propose seems to me to be the best; and as its execution will devolve upon a President just elected by the people with a view to this subject, I have no hesitation in trusting it to him, armed with full power, and untrammelled with terms and conditions."

It was soon ascertained in the Senate, that the joint resolution from the House could not pass—that unless combined with negotiation, it would be rejected. Mr. Walker, of Mississippi, then proposed to join the two together—the bill of Mr. Benton and the resolution from the House—with a clause referring it to the discretion of the President to act under them as he deemed best. It being then the end of the session, and the new President arrived so as to be ready to act immediately; and it being fully believed that the execution of the bill was to be left to him, the conjunction was favored by the author of the bill, and his friends; and the proposal of Mr. Walker was agreed to. The bill was added as an amendment, and then the whole was passed—although by a close vote—27 to 25. The yeas were: Messrs. Allen, Ashley, Atchison, Atherton, Bagby, Benton, Breese, Buchanan, Colquitt, Dickinson, Dix, Fairfield, Hannegan, Haywood, Henderson, Huger, Johnson, Lewis, McDuffie, Merrick, Niles, Semple, Sevier, Sturgeon, Tappan, Walker, Woodbury,—27. The nays were: Messrs. Archer, Barrow, Bates, Bayard, Berrien, Choate, Clayton, Crittenden, Dayton, Evans, Foster, Francis, Huntington, Jarnagin, Mangum, Miller, Morehead, Pearce, Phelps, Porter, Rives, Simmons, Upham, White, Woodbridge—25. The resolve of the House was thus passed in the Senate, and the validity of the Missouri compromise was asserted, and its re-enactment effected in the Senate, as well as in the House. But the amendment required the bill to go back to the House for its concurrence in that particular, which was found to increase the favor of the measure—an addition of thirty-six being added to the affirmative vote. Carried to Mr. Tyler for his approval, or disapproval, it was immediately approved by him, with the hearty concurrence of his Secretary of State (Mr. Calhoun), who even claimed the passage of the measure as a triumph of his own. And so the executive government, in the persons of the President and his cabinet, added their sanction to the validity of the Missouri compromise line, and the full power of Congress which it exercised, to permit or abolish slavery in territories. This was the month of March, 1845—so that a quarter of a century after the establishment of that compromise line, the dogmas of "squatter sovereignty"—"no power in Congress to legislate upon slavery in the territories"—and "the extension of slavery to the territories by the self-expansion of the constitution," had not been invented. The discovery of these dogmas was reserved for a later period, and a more heated state of the public mind.

The bill providing for the admission of Texas had undergone all its formalities, and became a law on Saturday, the first day of March; the second was Sunday, and a *dies non*. Congress met on Monday for the last day of its existence; and great was the astonishment of members to hear that the actual President had assumed the execution of the act providing for the admission of Texas—had adopted the legislative clause—and sent it off by a special messenger for the adoption of Texas. It was then seen that some senators had been cheated out of their votes, and that the passage of the act through the Senate had been procured by a fraud. At least five of the senators who voted affirmatively would have voted against the resolutions of the House, if Mr. Benton's bill had not been added, and if it had not been believed that the execution of the act would be left to the new President, and that he would adopt Mr. Benton's. The possibility of a contrary course had been considered, and, as it was believed, fully guarded against. Several senators and some citizens conversed with Mr. Polk, then in the city, and received his assurance that he would act on Mr. Benton's proposition, and in carrying it into effect would nominate for the negotiation a national commission, composed of safe and able men of both parties, such as Mr. Benton had suggested. Among those who thus conversed with Mr. Polk were two (senator Tappan, of Ohio, and Francis P. Blair, Esq., of Washington City), who published the result of their conversations, and the importance of which requires to be stated in their own words: which is here done. Mr. Tappan, writing to the editors of the New York Evening Post, says:

"When the joint resolution declaring the terms on which Congress will admit Texas into the Union as a State, was before the Senate, it was soon found that a number of the democratic members who were favorable to the admission of Texas, would vote against that resolution. I was one of them. In this stage of the matter it was proposed, that instead of rejecting the House resolution, we should amend it by adding, as an alternative proposition, the substance of Mr. Benton's bill to obtain Texas by negotiation. Mr. Polk was in the city; it was understood that he was very anxious that Congress should act on the subject before he came into office; it was also understood that the proposition to amend the House resolution originated with Mr. Polk. It had been suggested, that, if we did so amend the resolution, Mr. Calhoun would send off the House resolution to Texas, and so endeavor to forestall the action of Mr. Polk; but Mr. McDuffie, his friend, having met this suggestion by the declaration that he would not have the 'audacity' to do such a thing, it was no more thought of. One difficulty remained, and that was the danger of putting it into the power of Mr. Polk to submit the House resolution to Texas. We understood, indeed, that he intended to submit the Senate proposition to that government; but, without being satisfied that he would do this, I would not vote for the resolution, and it was well ascertained that, without my vote, it could not pass. Mr. Haywood, who had voted with me, and was opposed to the House resolution, undertook to converse with Mr. Polk on the subject, and did so. He afterwards told me that he was authorized by Mr. Polk to say to myself and other senators, that, if we could pass the resolution with the amendment proposed to be made, he would not use the House resolution, but would submit the Senate amendment as the sole proposition to Texas. Upon this assurance I voted for the amendment moved by Mr. Walker, containing the substance of Mr. Benton's bill, and voted for the resolution as it now stands on the statute book."

Mr. Francis P. Blair, in a letter addressed to Mr. Tappan, and conversing with Mr. Polk at a different time, gives his statement to the same effect:

"When the resolution passed by the House of Representatives for the annexation of Texas reached the Senate, it was ascertained that it would fail in that body. Benton, Bagby, Dix, Haywood, and as I understood, you also, were opposed to this naked proposition of annexation, which necessarily brought with it the war in which Texas was engaged with Mexico. All had determined to adhere to the bill submitted by Col. Benton, for the appointment of a commission to arrange the terms of annexation with Texas, and to make the attempt to render its accession to our Union as palatable as possible to Mexico before its consummation. It was hoped that this point might be effected by giving (as has been done in the late treaty of peace) a pecuniary consideration, fully equivalent in value for the territory desired by the United States, and to which Texas could justly assert any title. The Senate had been polled, and it was ascertained that any two of the democratic senators who were opposed to Brown's resolution, which had passed the House, could defeat it—the whole whig party preferring annexation by negotiation, upon Col. Benton's plan, to that of Brown. While the question was thus pending, I met Mr. Brown (late Governor of Tennessee, then a member or the House), who suggested that the resolution of the House, and the bill of Col. Benton, preferred by the Senate, might be blended, making the latter an alternative, and leaving the President elect (who alone would have time to consummate the measure), to act under one or the other at his discretion. I told Mr. Brown that I did not believe that the democratic senators opposed to the resolution of the House, and who had its fate in their hands, would consent to this arrangement, unless they were satisfied in advance by Mr. Polk that the commission and negotiation contemplated in Col. Benton's plan would be tried, before that of direct legislative annexation was resorted to. He desired me to see Colonel Benton and the friends of his proposition, submit the suggestions he had made, and then confer with Mr. Polk to know whether he would meet their views. I complied; and after several interviews with Messrs. Haywood, Dix, Benton, and others (Mr. Allen, of Ohio, using his influence in the same direction), finding that the two plans could be coupled and carried, if it were understood that the pacific project was first to be tried, I consulted the *President elect on the subject.* In the conference I had with him, *he gave me full assurance that he would appoint a commission, as contemplated in the bill prepared by Col. Benton, if passed in conjunction with the House resolution as an alternative.* In the course of my conversation with Mr. Polk, I told him that the friends of this plan were solicitous that the commission should be filled by distinguished men of both parties, and that Colonel Benton had mentioned to me the names of Crittenden and Wright, as of the class from which it should be formed. *Mr. Polk responded, by declaring with an emphasis, 'that the first men of the country should fill the commission.'* I communicated the result of this interview to Messrs. Benton, Dix, Haywood, &c. The two last met, on appointment, to adapt the phraseology of Benton's bill, to suit as an alternative for the resolution of the House, and it was passed, after a very general understanding of the course which the measure was to take. Both Messrs. Dix and Haywood told me they had interviews with Mr. Polk on the subject of the communication I had reported to them from him, and they were confirmed by his immediate assurance in pursuing the course which they had resolved on in consequence of my representation of his purpose in regard to the point on which their action depended. After the law was passed, and Mr. Polk inaugurated, he applied to Gen. Dix (as I am informed by the latter), to urge the Senate to act upon one of the suspended cabinet appointments, saying that he wished his administration organized immediately, as he intended the instant recall of the messenger understood to have been despatched by Mr. Tyler, and to revoke his orders given in the last moments of his power, to thwart the design of Congress in affording him (Mr. Polk) the means of instituting a negotiation, with a view of bringing Texas peaceably into the Union."

All this was perfectly satisfactory with respect to the President elect; but there might be some danger from the actual President, or rather, from Mr. Calhoun, his Secretary of State, and who had over Mr. Tyler that ascendant which it is the prerogative of genius to exercise over inferior minds. This danger was suggested in debate in open Senate. It was repulsed as an impossible infamy. Such a cheat upon senators and such an encroachment upon the rights of the new President, were accounted among the impossibilities: and Mr. McDuffie, a close and generous friend of Mr. Calhoun, speaking for the administration, and replying to the suggestion that they might seize upon the act, and execute it without regard to the Senate's amendment, not only denied it for them, but repulsed it in terms which implied criminality if they did. He said they would not have the "*audacity*" to do it. Mr. McDuffie was an honorable man, standing close to Mr. Calhoun; and although he did not assume to speak by authority, yet his indignant repulse of the suggestion was entirely satisfactory, and left the misgiving senators released from apprehension on account of Mr. Tyler's possible conduct. Mr. Robert J. Walker also, who had moved the conjunction of the two measures, and who was confidential both with the coming in and going out President, assisted in allaying apprehension in the reason he gave for opposing an amendment offered by Mr. Ephraim H. Foster, of Tennessee, which, looking to the President's adoption of the negotiating clause, required that he should make a certain "*stipulation*" in relation to slavery, and another in relation to the public debt. Mr. Walker objected to this proposition, saying it was already in the bill, "*and if the President proceeded properly in the negotiation he would act upon it.*" This seemed to be authoritative that negotiation was to be the mode, and consequently that Mr. Benton's plan was to be adopted. Thus quieted in their apprehensions, five senators voted for the act of admission, who would not otherwise have done so; and any two of whom voting against it would have defeated it. Mr. Polk did not despatch a messenger to recall Mr. Tyler's envoy; and that omission was the only point of complaint against him. Mr. McDuffie stood exempt from all blame, known to be an honorable man speaking from a generous impulsion.

Thus was Texas incorporated into the Union—by a deception, and by deluding five senators out of their votes. It was not a barren fraud, but one prolific of evil, and pregnant with bloody fruit. It established, so far as the United States was concerned, the state of war with Mexico: it only wanted the acceptance of Texas to make war the complete legal condition of the two countries: and that temptation to Texas was too great to be resisted. She desired annexation any way: and the government of the United States having broken up the armistice, and thwarted the peace prospects, and brought upon her the danger of a new invasion, she leaped at the chance of throwing the burden of the war on the United States. The legislative proposition sent by Mr. Tyler was accepted: Texas became incorporated with the United States: by that incorporation the state of war—*the status belli*—was established between the United States and Mexico: and it only became a question of time and chance, when hostilities were to begin. Mr. Calhoun, though the master spirit over Mr. Tyler, and the active power in sending off the proposition to Texas, was not in favor of war, and still believed, as he did when he made the treaty, that the weakness of Mexico, and a *douceur* of ten millions in money, would make her submit: but there was another interest all along working with him, and now to supersede him in influence, which was for war, not as an object, but as a means—as a means of getting a treaty providing for claims and indemnities, and territorial acquisitions. This interest, long his adjunct, now became independent of him, and pushed for the war; but it was his conduct that enabled this party to act; and this point became one of earnest debate between himself and Mr. Benton the year afterwards; in which he was charged as being the real author of the war; and in which Mr. Benton's speech being entirely historical, becomes a condensed view of the whole Texas annexation question; and as such is presented in the next chapter.

ADMINISTRATION OF JAMES K. POLK.

CHAPTER CXLIX.

THE WAR WITH MEXICO: ITS CAUSE: CHARGED ON THE CONDUCT OF MR. CALHOUN: MR. BENTON'S SPEECH.

Mr. BENTON: The senator from South Carolina (Mr. Calhoun) has boldly made the issue as to the authorship of this war, and as boldly thrown the blame of it upon the present administration. On the contrary, I believe himself to be the author of it, and will give a part of my reasons for believing so. In saying this, I do not consider the march to the Rio Grande to have been the cause of the war, any more than I consider the British march upon Concord and Lexington to have been the cause of the American Revolution, or the crossing of the Rubicon by Cæsar to have been the cause of the civil war in Rome. In all these cases, I consider the causes of war as pre-existing, and the marches as only the effect of these causes. I consider the march upon the Rio Grande as being unfortunate, and certainly should have advised against it if I had been consulted, and that without the least fear of diminishing my influence in the settlement of the Oregon question—a fear which the senator from South Carolina says prevented him from interposing to prevent the war which he foresaw. My opinion of Mr. Polk—and experience in that very Oregon case has confirmed it—did not authorize me to conjecture that any one would lose influence with him by giving him honest opinions; so I would have advised against the march to the Rio Grande if I had been consulted. Nor do I see how any opinion adverse to the President's was to have the effect of lessening his influence in the settlement of the Oregon question. That question was settled by us, not by the President. Half the democratic senators went contrary to the President's opinion, and none of them lost influence with him on that account; and so I can see no possible connection between the facts of the case and the senator's reason for not interfering to save his country from the war which, he says, he saw. His reason to me is unintelligible, incomprehensible, unconnectable with the facts of the case. But the march on the Rio Grande was not the cause of the war; but the causes of this event, like the causes of our own revolutionary war, were in progress long before hostilities broke out. The causes of this Mexican war were long anterior to this march; and, in fact, every circumstance of war then existed, except the actual collision of arms. Diplomatic intercourse had ceased; commerce was destroyed; fleets and armies confronted each other; treaties were declared to be broken; the contingency had occurred in which Mexico had denounced the existence of war; the incorporation of Texas, with a Mexican war on her hands, had produced, in legal contemplation, the *status belli* between the two countries: and all this had occurred before the march upon the Rio Grande, and before the commencement of this administration, and had produced a state of things which it was impossible to continue, and which could only receive their solution from arms or negotiation. The march to the Rio Grande brought on the collision of arms; but, so far from being the cause of the war, it was itself the effect of these causes. The senator from South Carolina is the author of those causes, and therefore the author of the war; and this I propose to show, at present, by evidence drawn from himself—from his public official acts—leaving all the evidence derived from other sources, from private and unofficial acts, for future production, if deemed necessary.

The senator from South Carolina, in his effort to throw the blame of the war upon the President, goes no further back in his search for causes than to this march upon the Rio Grande: upon the same principle, if he wrote a history of the American Revolution, he would begin at the march upon Lexington and Concord, leaving out of view the ten years' work of Lord North's administration which caused that march to be made. No, the march upon the Rio Grande was not the cause of the war: had it not been for pre-existing causes, the arrival of the American army on the Mexican frontier would have been saluted with military courtesy, according to the usage of all civilized nations, and with none so much as with the Spaniards. Complimentary visits, dinners, and fandangos, balls—not cannon balls—would have been the salutation. The causes of the war are long anterior; and I begin with the beginning, and show the senator from South Carolina an actor from the first. In doing this, I am acting in defence of the country, for the President represents the country. The senator from South Carolina charges the war upon the President: the whole opposition follow him: the bill under discussion is forgotten: crimination of the President is now the object: and in that crimination, the country is injured by being made to appear the aggressor in the war. This is my justification for defending the President, and showing the truth that the senator, in his manner of acquiring Texas, is the true cause of the war.

The cession of Texas to Spain in 1819 is the beginning point in the chain of causes which have led to this war; for unless the country had been ceded away, there could have been no quarrel with any power in getting it back. For a long time the negotiator of that treaty of cession (Mr. J. Q. Adams) bore all the blame of the loss of Texas; and his motives for giving it away were set down to hostility to the South and West, and a desire to clip the wings of the slaveholding States. At last the truth of history has vindicated itself, and has shown who was the true author of that mischief to the South and West. Mr. Adams has made a public declaration, which no one controverts, that that cession was made in conformity to the decision of Mr. Monroe's cabinet, a majority of which was slaveholding, and among them the present senator from South Carolina, and now the only survivor of that majority. He does not contradict the statement of Mr. Adams: he, therefore, stands admitted the co-author of that mischief to the South and West which the cession of Texas involved, and to escape from which it became necessary, in the opinion of the senator from South Carolina, to get back Texas at the expense of war with Mexico. This conduct of the senator in giving away Texas when we had her, and then making war to get her back, is an enigma which he has never yet condescended to explain, and which, until explained, leaves him in a state of self-contradiction, which, whether it impairs his own confidence in himself or not, must have the effect of destroying the confidence of others in him, and wholly disqualifies him for the office of champion of the slaveholding States. It was the heaviest blow they had ever received, and put an end, in conjunction with the Missouri compromise, and the permanent location of the Indians west of the Mississippi, to their future growth or extension as slave States beyond the Mississippi. The compromise, which was then in full progress, and established at the next session of Congress, cut off the slave States from all territory north and west of Missouri, and south of thirty-six and a half degrees of north latitude: the treaty of 1819 ceded nearly all south of that degree, comprehending not only all Texas, but a large part of the valley of the Mississippi on the Red River and the Arkansas, to a foreign power, and brought a non-slaveholding empire to the confines of Louisiana and Arkansas: the permanent appropriation of the rest of the territory for the abode of civilized Indians swept the little slaveholding territory west of Arkansas and lying between the compromise line and the cession line; and left the slave States without one inch of ground for their future growth. Nothing was left. Even the then territory of Arkansas was encroached upon. A breadth of forty miles wide, and three hundred long was cut off from her, and given to the Cherokees; and there was not as much slave territory left west of the Mississippi as a dove could have rested the sole of her foot upon. It was not merely a curtailment, but a total extinction of slaveholding territory; and done at a time when the Missouri controversy was raging, and every effort made by Northern abolitionists to stop the growth of slave States.[8]

I come now to the direct proofs of the senator's authorship of the war; and begin with the year 1836, and with the month of May of that year, and with the 27th day of that month, and with the first rumors of the victory of San Jacinto. The Congress of the United States was then in session: the senator from South Carolina was then a member of this body; and, without even waiting for the official confirmation of that great event, he proposed at once the immediate recognition of the independence of Texas, and her immediate admission into this Union. He put the two propositions together—recognition and admission: and allowed us no further time for the double vote than the few days which were to intervene before the official intelligence of the victory should arrive. Here are some extracts from his speech on that occasion, and which verify what I say, and show that he was then ready to plunge the country into the Texian war with Mexico, without the slightest regard to its treaties, its commerce, its duties, or its character.

(The extracts.)

Here, then, is the proof of the fact that, ten years ago, and without a word of explanation with Mexico, or any request from Texas—without the least notice to the American people, or time for deliberation among ourselves, or any regard to existing commerce—he was for plunging us into instant war with Mexico. I say, instant war; for Mexico and Texas were then in open war; and to incorporate Texas, was to incorporate the war at the same time. All this the senator was then for, immediately after his own gratuitous cession of Texas, and long before the invention of the London abolition plot came so opportunely to his aid. Promptness and unanimity were then his watchwords. Immediate action—action before Congress adjourned—was his demand.

No delay. Delays were dangerous. We must vote, and vote unanimously, and promptly. I well remember the senator's look and attitude on that occasion—the fixedness of his look, and the magisteriality of his attitude. It was such as he often favors us with, especially when he is in a "crisis," and brings forward something which ought to be instantly and unanimously rejected—as when he brought in his string of abstractions on Thursday last. So it was in 1836—prompt and unanimous action, and a look to put down opposition. But the Senate was not looked down in 1836. They promptly and unanimously refused the senator's motion! and the crisis and the danger—good-natured souls!—immediately postponed themselves until wanted for another occasion.

The peace of the country was then saved; but it was a respite only; and the speech of the senator from South Carolina, brief as it was, becomes momentous as foreshadowing every thing that has subsequently taken place in relation to the admission of Texas. In this brief speech we have the shadows of all future movements, coming in procession—in advance of the events. In the significant intimation, qualified with the if——"*the Texians prudently managed their affairs, they (the Senate) might soon be called upon to decide the question of admission.*" In that pregnant and qualified intimation, there was a visible doubt that the Texians might *not* be prudent enough to manage their own affairs, and might require help; and also a visible feeling of that paternal guardianship which afterward assumed the management of their affairs for them. In the admonitions to unanimity, there was that denunciation of any difference of opinion which afterwards displayed itself in the ferocious hunting down of all who opposed the Texas treaty. In the reference to southern slavery, and annoyance to slave property from Texas, we have the germ of the "*self-defence*" letter, and the first glimpse of the abolition plot of John Andrews, Ashbel Smith, Lord Aberdeen—I beg pardon of Lord Aberdeen for naming him in such a connection—and the World's Convention, with which Mexico, Texas, and the United States were mystified and bamboozled in April, 1844. And, in the interests of the manufacturing and navigating States of the north and east, as connected with Texas admission, we have the text of all the communications to the agent, Murphy, and of all the letters and speeches to which the Texas question, seven years afterwards, gave rise. We have all these subsequent events here shadowed forth. And now, the wonder is, why all these things were not foreseen a little while before, when Texas was being ceded to a non-slaveholding empire? and why, after being so imminent and deadly in May, 1836, all these dangers suddenly went to sleep, and never waked up again until 1844? These are wonders; but let us not anticipate questions, and let us proceed with the narrative.

The Congress of 1836 would not admit Texas. The senator from South Carolina became patient: the Texas question went to sleep; and for seven good years it made no disturbance. It then woke up, and with a suddenness and violence proportioned to its long repose. Mr. Tyler was then President: the senator from South Carolina was potent under his administration, and soon became his Secretary of State. All the springs of intrigue and diplomacy were immediately set in motion to resuscitate the Texas question, and to re-invest it with all the dangers and alarms which it had worn in 1836. Passing over all the dangers of annoyance from Texas as possibly non-slaveholding, *foreseen* by the senator in 1836, and not foreseen by him in 1819, with all the need for guardianship then foreshadowed, and all the arguments then suggested: all these immediately developed themselves, and intriguing agents traversed earth and sea, from Washington to Texas, and from London to Mexico:—passing over all this, as belonging to a class of evidence, not now to be used, I come at once to the letter of the 17th of January, from the Texian minister to Mr. Upshur, the American Secretary of State; and the answer to that letter by Mr. CALHOUN, of April 11th of the same year. They are both vital in this case; and the first is in these words:

(The letter.)

This letter reveals the true state of the Texian question in January, 1844, and the conduct of all parties in relation to it. It presents Texas and Mexico, weary of the war, reposing under an armistice, and treating for peace; Great Britain and France acting the noble part of mediators, and endeavoring to make peace: our own government secretly intriguing for annexation, acting the wicked part of mischief-makers, and trying to renew the war; and the issue of its machinations to be unsuccessful unless the United States should be involved in the renewed hostilities. That was the question; and the letter openly puts it to the American Secretary of State. The answer to that question, in my opinion, should have been, that the President of the United States did not know of the armistice and the peace negotiations at the time that he proposed to Texas to do an act which would be a perfidious violation of those sacred engagements, and bring upon herself the scourge of renewed invasion and the stigma of perfidy—that he would not have made such a proposal for the whole round world, if he had known of the armistice and the peace negotiations—that he wished success to the peace-makers, both for the sake of Mexico and Texas, and because Texas could then come into the Union without the least interruption to our friendly, commercial, and social relations with our sister republic of Mexico; and that, as to secretly lending the army and navy of the United States to Texas to fight Mexico while we were at peace with her, it would be a crime against God, and man, and our own constitution, for which heads might be brought to the block, if presidents and their secretaries, like constitutional kings and ministers, should be held capitally responsible for capital crimes. This, in my opinion, should have been the answer.

Mr. Nelson refused to lend the army and navy, because to do so was to violate our own constitution. This is very constitutional and proper language: and if it had not been reversed, there would have been no war with Mexico. But it was reversed. Soon after it was written, the present senator from South Carolina took the chair of the Department of State. Mr. Pinckney Henderson, whom Mr. Murphy mentions as coming on with full powers, on the faith of the pledge he had given, arrived also, and found that pledge entirely cancelled by Mr. Tyler's answer through Mr. Nelson; and he utterly refused to treat. The new secretary was in a strait; for time was short, and Texas must be had; and Messrs. Henderson and Van Zandt would not even begin to treat without a renewal of the pledge given by Mr. Murphy. That had been cancelled in writing, and the cancellation had gone to Texas, and had been made on high constitutional ground. The new secretary was profuse of verbal assurances, and even permitted the ministers to take down his words in writing, and read them over to him, as was shown by the senator from Texas (General Houston) when he spoke on this subject on Thursday last. But verbal assurances, or memoranda of conversations, would not do. The instructions under which the ministers acted required the pledge to be in writing, and properly signed. The then President, present senator from Texas, who had been a lawyer in Tennessee before he went to Texas, seemed to look upon it as a case under the statute of frauds and perjuries—a sixth case added to the five enumerated in that statute—in which the promise is not valid, unless reduced to writing, and signed by the person to be charged therewith, or by some other person duly authorized by him to sign for him. The firmness of the Texian ministers, under the instructions of President Houston, prevailed; and at last, and after long delay, the secretary wrote, and signed the pledge which Murphy had given, and in all the amplitude of his original promise.

The promise was clear and explicit to lend the army and navy to the President of Texas, to fight the Mexicans while they were at peace with us. That was the point—at peace with us. Mr. Calhoun's assumpsit was clear and explicit to that point; for the cases in which they were to fight were to be before the ratification of the treaty by the Senate, and consequently before Texas should be in our Union, and could be constitutionally defended as a part of it. And, that no circumstance of contradiction or folly should be wanting to crown this plot of crime and imbecility, it so happened that on the same day that our new secretary here was giving his written assumpsit to lend the army and navy to fight Mexico while we were at peace with her, the agent Murphy was communicating to the Texian government, in Texas, the refusal of Mr. Tyler, through Mr. Nelson, to do so, because of its unconstitutionality.

In conformity with the secretary's letter of April 11th, detachments of the army and navy were immediately sent to the frontiers of Texas, and to the coast of Mexico. The senator from South Carolina, in his colloquy with the senator from Texas (General Houston), on Thursday last, seemed anxious to have it understood that these land and naval forces were not to *repel* invasions, but only to *report* them to our government, for its report to Congress. The paper read by the senator from Texas, consisting of our secretary's words, taken down in his presence, and read over to him for his correction by the Texian ministers, establishes the contrary, and shows that the repulse of the invasion was in the mean time to be made. And in fact, any other course would have been a fraud upon the promise. For, if the invasion had to be made known at Washington, and the sense of Congress taken on the question of repelling it, certainly, in the mean time, the mischief would have been done—the invasion would have been made; and, therefore, to be consistent with himself, the President in the mean time was bound to repel the invasion, without waiting to hear what Congress would say about it. And this is what he himself tells us in his two messages to the Senate, of the 15th and 31st of May, doubtless written by his Secretary of State, and both avowing and justifying his intention to fight Mexico, in case of invasion, while the treaty of annexation was depending, without awaiting the action of Congress.

(The message.)

Here are the avowals of the fact, and the reasons for it—that honor required us to fight for Texas, if we intrigued her into a war. I admit that would be a good reason between individuals, and in a case where a big bully should involve a little fellow in the fight again after he had got himself parted; but not so between nations, and under our constitution. The engagement to fight Mexico for Texas, while we were at peace with Mexico, was to make war with Mexico!—a piece of business which belonged to the Congress, and which should have been referred to them! and which, on the contrary, was concealed from them, though in session, and present! and the fact only found out after the troops had marched, and then by dint of calls from the Senate.

The proof is complete that the loan of the land and naval forces was to fight Mexico while we were at peace with her! and this becomes a great turning point in the history of this war. Without this pledge given by our Secretary of State—without his reversal of Mr. Tyler's first decision—there could have been no war! Texas and Mexico would have made peace, and then annexation would have followed of itself. The victor of San Jacinto, who had gone forth and recovered by the sword, and erected into a new republic the beautiful domain given away by our secretary in 1819, was at the head of the Texas government, and was successfully and honorably conducting his country to peace and acknowledged independence. If let alone, he would have accomplished his object; for he had already surmounted the great difficulty of the first step—the armistice and the commencement of peace negotiations; and under the powerful mediation of Great Britain and France, the establishment of peace was certain. A heavenly benediction rests upon the labors of the peacemaker; and what is blessed of God must succeed. At all events, it does not lie in the mouth of any man—and least of all, in the mouth of the mischief-maker—to say that the peaceful mediation would not have succeeded. It was the part of all men to have aided, and wished, and hoped for success; and had it not been for our secretary's letter of April 11th, authentic facts warrant the assertion that Texas and Mexico would have made peace in the spring of 1844. Then Texas would have come into this Union as naturally, and as easily, and with as little offence to any body, as Eve went into Adam's bosom in the garden of Eden. There would have been no more need for intriguing politicians to get her in, by plots and tricks, than there was for some old hag of a match-making beldame, with her arts and allurements, her philters and her potions, to get Eve into Adam's bosom. And thus, the breaking up of the peace negotiations becomes the great turning point of the problem of the Mexican war.

The pledge of the 11th of April being *signed*, the treaty was *signed*, and being communicated to the Senate, it was *rejected*: and the great reason for the rejection was that the ratification of the treaty would have been WAR with Mexico! an act which the President and Senate together, no more than President Tyler and his Secretary of State together, had the power to make.

The treaty of annexation was signed, and in signing it the secretary knew that he had made war with Mexico. No less than three formal notices were on file in the Department of State, in which the Mexican government solemnly declared that it would consider annexation as equivalent to a declaration of war; and it was in allusion to these notices that the Secretary of State, in his notification to Mexico of the signature of the treaty, said it had been signed IN FULL VIEW OF ALL POSSIBLE CONSEQUENCES! meaning war as the consequence! At the same time, he suited the action to the word; he sent off detachments of the army and navy, and placed them under the command of President Houston, and made him the judge of the emergencies and exigencies in which they were to fight. This authority to the President of Texas was continued in full force until after the rejection of the treaty, and then only modified by placing the American diplomatic agent in Texas between President Houston and the naval and military commanders, and making him the medium of communication between a foreign President and our forces; but the forces themselves were not withdrawn. They remained on the Texian and Mexican frontier, waiting for the *exigencies* and *emergencies* in which they were to fight. During all that time a foreign President was commander-in-chief of a large detachment of the army and navy of the United States. Without a law of Congress—without a nomination from the President and confirmation by the Senate—without citizenship—without the knowledge of the American people—he was president-general of our land and sea forces, made so by the senator from South Carolina, with authority to fight them against Mexico with whom we were at peace—an office and authority rather above that of lieutenant-general!—and we are indebted to the forbearance and prudence of President Houston for not incurring the war in 1844, which fell upon us in 1846. This is a point—this secret and lawless appointment of this president-general to make war upon Mexico, while we were at peace with her—on which I should like to hear a constitutional argument from the senator from South Carolina, showing it to be constitutional and proper, and that of the proposed lieutenant-general unconstitutional and improper; and upon which he has erected himself into the *foreman* of the grand-jury of the whole American people, and pronounced a unanimous verdict for them before he had time to hear from the ten-thousandth part of them.

The treaty was rejected by the Senate; but so apprehensive was the senator of immediate war, that, besides keeping the detachments of the army and navy at their posts, a messenger was despatched with a deprecatory letter to Mexico, and the offer of a large sum of money (ten millions of dollars) to purchase peace from her, by inducing her to treat for a boundary which would leave Texas within our limits. This was report: and I would not mention it, if the senator was not present to contradict it, if not correct. Report at the time said from five to ten millions of dollars: from one of Mr. Shannon's letters, we may set it down at ten millions. Be it either sum, it will show that the senator was then secretly willing to pay an immense sum to pacify Mexico, although he now declares that he does not know how he will vote in relation to the three millions responsibly asked by Mr. Polk.

The secretary knew that he had made war with Mexico—that in accepting the gage three times laid down, he had joined an issue which that compound of Celtic and Roman blood, called Spanish, would redeem. I knew it, and said it on this floor, in secret session—for I did not then choose to say it in public—that if there was but one man of that blood in all Mexico, and he no bigger than General Tom Thumb, he would fight. Senators will recollect it. [Mr. Mangum nodded assent.]

I now come to the last act in this tragedy of errors—the alternative resolutions adopted by Congress in the last days of the session of 1844-'45, and in the last moments of Mr. Tyler's administration. A resolve, single and absolute, for the admission of Texas as a State of this Union, had been made by the House of Representatives; it came to this body; and an alternative resolution was added, subject to the choice of the President, authorizing negotiations for the admission, and appropriating one hundred thousand dollars to defray the expenses of these negotiations. A senator from North Carolina, not now a member of this body, but who I have the pleasure to see sitting near me (Mr. Haywood), knows all about that alternative resolution; and his country owes him good thanks for his labors about it. It was considered by every body, that the choice between these resolutions belonged to the new President, who had been elected with a special view to the admission of Texas, and who was already in the city, awaiting the morning of the 4th of March to enter upon the execution of his duties; and upon whose administration all the evils of a mistake in the choice of these resolutions were to fall. We all expected the question to be left open to the new President; and so strong was that expectation, and so strong the feeling against the decency or propriety of interference on the part of the expiring administration, to snatch this choice out of the hands of Mr. Polk, that, on a mere suggestion of the possibility of such a proceeding, in a debate on this floor, a senator standing in the relation personally, and politically, and locally to feel for the honor of the then Secretary of State, declared they would not have the audacity to do it. Audacity was his word: and that was the declaration of a gentleman of honor and patriotism, no longer a member of this body, but who has the respect and best wishes of all who ever knew him. I speak of Mr. McDuffie, and quote his words as heard at the time, and as since printed and published by others. Mr. McDuffie was mistaken! They did have the audacity! They did do it, or rather, HE did it (looking at Mr. Calhoun); for it is incontestable that Mr. Tyler was nothing, in any thing that related to the Texas question, from the time of the arrival of his last Secretary of State. His last act, in relation to Texas, was the answer which Mr. Nelson gave for him through the agent, Murphy, denying his right to lend our forces to the President of Texas to fight the Mexicans while we were at peace with them: the reversal of that answer by his new secretary was the extinction of his power over the Texas question. He, the then Secretary of State, the present senator from South Carolina, to whom I address myself, did it. On Sunday, the second day of March—that day which preceded the last day of his authority—and on that day, sacred to peace—the council sat that acted on the resolutions—and in the darkness of a night howling with the storm, and battling with the elements, as if Heaven warred upon the audacious act (for well do I remember it), the fatal messenger was sent off which carried the selected resolution to Texas. The exit of the secretary from office, and the start of the messenger from Washington, were coetaneous—twin acts—which come together, and will be remembered together. The act was then done: Texas was admitted: all the consequences of admission were incurred—and especially that consequence which Mr. de Bocanegra had denounced, and which our secretary had accepted—WAR. The state of war was established—the *status belli* was created—and that by the operation of our own constitution, as well as by the final declaration of Mexico: for Texas then being admitted into the Union, the war with her extended to the whole Union; and the duty of protecting her, devolved upon the President of the United States. The selection of the absolute resolution exhausted our action: the alternative resolution for negotiation was defunct: the only mode of admission was the absolute one, and it made war. The war was made to Mr. Polk's hands: his administration came into existence with the war upon its hands, and under the constitutional duty to protect Texas at the expense of war with Mexico: and to that point, all events rapidly tended. The Mexican minister, General Almonte, who had returned to Washington city after the rejection of the treaty of annexation, demanded his passports, and left the United States. The land forces which had been advanced to the Sabine, were further advanced to Corpus Christi; the Mexican troops moved towards the Rio Grande: the fleet which remained at Vera Cruz, continued there: commerce died out: the citizens of each country left the other, as far as they could: angry denunciations filled the press of each country: and when a minister was sent from the United States, his reception was refused. The state of war existed legally: all the circumstances of war, except the single circumstance of bloodshed, existed at the accession of Mr. Polk; and the two countries, Mexico and the United States, stood in a relation to each other impossible to be continued. The march upon the Rio Grande brought on the conflict—made the collision of arms—but not the war. The war was prepared, organized, established by the Secretary of State, before he left the department. It was his legacy to the democracy, and to the Polk administration—his last gift to them, in the moment of taking a long farewell. And now he sets up for a man of peace, and throws all the blame of war upon Mr. Polk, to whom he bequeathed it.

Cicero says that Antony, flying from Rome to the camp of Cæsar in Cisalpine Gaul, was the cause of the civil war which followed—as much so as Helen was of the Trojan war. *Ut Helena Trojanis, sic iste huic reipublica causa belli—causa pestis atque exitii fuit.* He says that that flight put an end to all chance of accommodation; closed the door to all conciliation; broke up the plans of all peaceable men; and by inducing Cæsar to break up his camp in Gaul, and march across the Rubicon, lit up the flames of civil war in Italy. In like manner, I say that the flight of the winged messenger from this capital on the Sunday night before the 3d of March, despatched by the then Secretary of State, in the expiring moment of his power, and bearing his fatal choice to the capital of Texas, was the direct cause of the war with Mexico in which we are now engaged. Like the flight of Antony, it broke up the plans of all peaceable men, slammed the door upon negotiations, put an end to all chance for accommodation, broke up the camp on the Sabine, sent the troops towards Mexico, and lit up the war. Like Antony and Helen, he made the war; unlike Antony, he does not stand to it; but, copying rather the conduct of the paramour of Helen, he flies from the conflict he has provoked! and, worse than Paris, he endeavors to draw along with him, in his own unhappy flight, the whole American host. Paris fled alone at the sight of Menelaus: the senator from South Carolina urges us all to fly at the sight of Santa Anna. And, it may be, that worse than Paris again, he may refuse to return to the field. Paris went back under the keen reproach of Hector, and tried to fight:

"For thee the soldier bleeds, the matron mourns, And wasteful war in all its fury burns."

Stung with this just and keen rebuke—this vivid picture of the ruin he had made—Paris returned to the field, and tried to fight: and now, it remains to be seen whether the senator from South Carolina can do the same, on the view of the ruin which he has made: and, if not, whether he cannot, at least, cease to obstruct the arms of others—cease to labor to involve the whole army in his own unmanly retreat.

Upon the evidence now given, drawn from his public official acts alone, he stands the undisputed author and architect of that calamity. History will so write him down. Inexorable HISTORY, with her pen of iron and tablets of brass, will so write him down: and two thousand years hence, and three thousand years hence, the boy at his lesson shall learn it in the book, that as Helen was the cause of the Trojan, and Antony the cause of the Roman civil war, and Lord North made the war of the Revolution, just so certainly is JOHN C. CALHOUN the author of the present war between the United States and Mexico.

He now sets up for the character of pacificator—with what justice, let the further fact proclaim which I now expose. Three hundred newspapers, in the summer of 1844, in the pay of the administration and Department of State, spoke the sentiments of the Department of State, and pursued as traitors to the United States all who were for the peaceable annexation of Texas by settling the boundary line of Texas with Mexico simultaneously with the annexation. Here is the instruction under which the three hundred acted:

"As the conductor of the official journal here, he has requested me to answer it (your letter), which request I comply with readily. With regard to the course of your paper, you can take the tone of the administration from the * * * *. I think, however, and would recommend that you would confine yourself to attacks upon Benton, showing that he has allied himself with the whigs on the Texas question. Quote Jackson's letter on Texas, where he denounces all those as traitors to the country who oppose the treaty. Apply it to Benton. Proclaim that Benton, by attacking Mr. Tyler and his friends, and driving them from the party, is aiding the election of Mr. Clay; and charge him with doing this to defeat Mr. Polk, and insure himself the succession in 1848; and claim that full justice be done to the acts and motives of John Tyler by the leaders. Harp upon these strings. Do not propose the union; 'it is the business of the democrats to do this, and arrange it to our perfect satisfaction.' *I quote here* from our leading friend at the South. Such is the course which I recommend, and which you can pursue or not, according to your real attachment to the administration. Look out for my leader of to-morrow as an indicator, and regard this letter as of the most strict and inviolate confidence of character."

I make no comment on this letter, nor read the other parts of it: a time will come for that. It is an original, and will keep, and will prove itself. I merely read a paragraph now, to show with what justice the person who was in the Department of State when these three hundred newspapers in its pay were thus attacking the men of peace, now sets up for the character of pacificator!

Mr. CALHOUN. Does he intend to say that I ever wrote such a letter?

Mr. BENTON. I read it. I say nothing.

Mr. CALHOUN. I never wrote such a letter as that!

Mr. BENTON. I have not said so.

Mr. CALHOUN. I take this occasion to say that I never exercised the slightest influence over that paper. I never had the slightest connection with it. I never was a subscriber to it, and I very rarely read it.

Mr. BENTON. It was the work of one of the organs of the administration, not John Jones, not the *Madisonian*; and the instruction was followed by three hundred newspapers in the pay of the Department of State.

I have now finished what I proposed to say, at this time, in relation to the authorship of this war. I confine myself to the official words and acts of the senator, and rely upon them to show that he, and not Mr. Polk, is the author of this calamity. But, while thus presenting him as the author of the war, I do not believe that war was his object, but only an incident to his object; and that all his conduct in relation to the admission of Texas refers itself to the periods of our presidential elections, and to some connection with those elections, and explains his activity and inactivity on those occasions. Thus, in May, 1836, when he was in such hot and violent haste for immediate admission, the election of that year was impending, and Mr. Van Buren the democratic candidate; and if the Texas question could then have been brought up, he might have been shoved aside just as easily as he was afterwards, in 1844. This may explain his activity in 1836. In 1840, the senator from South Carolina was a sort of a supporter of Mr. Van Buren, and might have thought that one good turn deserves another; and so nothing was said about Texas at that election—dangerous as was the least delay four years before; and this may explain the inactivity of 1840. The election of 1844 was coming on, and the senator from South Carolina was on the turf himself; and then the Texas question, with all its dangers and alarms, which had so accommodatingly postponed themselves for seven good years, suddenly woke up; and with an activity and vigor proportioned to its long repose. Instant admission, at all hazards, and at the expense of renewing hostilities between Mexico and Texas, and involving the United States in them, became indispensable—

necessary to our own salvation—a clear case of self-defence; and then commenced all those machinations which ended in the overthrow of Mr. Van Buren and Mr. Clay for the presidency, and in producing the present war with Mexico; but without making the senator President. And this may explain his activity in 1844. Now, another presidential election is approaching; and if there is any truth in the rule which interprets certain gentlemen's declarations by their contraries, he will be a candidate again: and this may explain the reasons of the production of that string of resolutions which the senator laid upon the table last week; and upon which he has required us to vote instantly, as he did in the sudden Texas movement of 1836, and with the same magisterial look and attitude. The Texas slave question has gone by—the Florida slave question has gone by—there is no chance for it now in any of its old haunts: hence the necessity for a new theatre of agitation, even if we have to go as far as California for it, and before we have got California. And thus, all the senator's conduct in relation to Texas, though involving his country in war, may have had no other object than to govern a presidential election.

Our northern friends have exceeded my hopes and expectations in getting themselves and the Union safe through the Texas and Florida slave questions, and are entitled to a little repose. So far from that, they are now to be plunged into a California slave question, long before it could arise of itself, if ever. The string of resolutions laid on the table by the senator from South Carolina is to raise a new slave question on the borders of the Pacific Ocean, which, upon his own principles, cannot soon occur, if ever. He will not take the country by conquest—only by treaty—and that treaty to be got by sitting out the Mexicans on a line of occupation. At the same time, he shows that he knows that Spanish blood is good at that game, and shows that they sat it out, and fought it out, for 800 years, against the Moors occupying half their country. By-the-by, it was only 700; but that is enough; one hundred years is no object in such a matter. The Spaniards held out 700 years against the Moors, holding half their country, and 300 against the Visigoths, occupying the half of the other half; and, what is more material, whipped them both out at the end of the time. This is a poor chance for California on the senator's principles. His five regiments would be whipped out in a fraction of the time; but no matter; men contend more violently for nothing than for something, and if he can get up a California slave question now, it will answer all the purposes of a reality, even if the question should never arise in point of fact.

The Senator from South Carolina has been wrong in all this business, from beginning to ending—wrong in 1819, in giving away Texas—wrong in 1836, in his sudden and hot haste to get her back—wrong in all his machinations for bringing on the Texas question of 1844—wrong in breaking up the armistice and peace negotiations between Mexico and Texas—wrong in secretly sending the army and navy to fight Mexico while we were at peace with her—wrong in secretly appointing the President of Texas president-general of the army and navy of the United States, with leave to fight them against a power with whom we were at peace—wrong in writing to Mexico that he took Texas in view of all possible consequences, meaning war—wrong in secretly offering Mexico, at the same time, ten millions of dollars to hush up the war which he had created—wrong now in refusing Mr. Polk three millions to aid in getting out of the war which he made—wrong in throwing the blame of this war of his own making upon the shoulders of Mr. Polk—wrong in his retreat and occupation line of policy—wrong in expelling old Father Ritchie from the Senate, who worked so hard for him during the Texas annexation—and more wrong now than ever, in that string of resolutions which he has laid upon the table, and in which, as Sylla saw in the young Cæsar many Mariuses, so do I see in them many nullifications.

In a picture of so many and such dreadful errors, it is hard to specify the worst, or to dwell upon any one to the exclusion of the rest; but there is one feature in this picture of enormities which seems entitled to that distinction: I allude to the pledge upon which the armistice and the peace negotiations between Mexico and Texas were broken up in 1844, and those two countries put back into a state of war, and ourselves involved in the contest. The story is briefly told, and admits of no dispute. The letter of 17th of January is the accusing record, from which there is no escape. Its awful words cannot be read now without freezing up the blood: "It is known to you that an armistice exists between Mexico and Texas, and that negotiations for peace are now going on under the mediation of two powerful sovereigns, mutually friendly. If we yield to your solicitation to be annexed to the United States, under these circumstances, we shall draw upon ourselves a fresh invasion from Mexico, incur the imputation of bad faith, and lose the friendship and respect of the two great mediating powers. Now, will you, in the event of our acceding to your request, step between us and Mexico and take the war off our hands?" This was the letter, and the terrible question with which it concluded. Mr. Upshur, to whom it was addressed, gave it no answer. In the forty days that his life was spared, he gave it no answer. Mr. Nelson, his temporary successor, gave it an answer; and, speaking for the President of the United States, positively refused to take annexation on the awful terms proposed. This answer was sent to Texas, and put an end to all negotiation for annexation. The senator from South Carolina came into the Department of State, procured the reversal of the President's decision, and gave the pledge to the whole extent that Texas asked it. Without, in the least denying the knowledge of the armistice, and the negotiations for peace, and all the terrible consequences which were to result from their breach, he accepts the whole, and gives the fatal pledge which his predecessors had refused: and follows it up by sending our troops and ships to fight a people with whom we were at peace—the whole veiled by the mantle of secrecy, and pretexted by motives as unfounded as they were absurd. Now, what says morality and Christianity to this conduct? Certainly, if two individuals were engaged in strife, and two others should part them, and put them under an agreement to submit to an amicable settlement: and while the settlement was going on, another man, lying behind a hedge, should secretly instigate one of the parties to break off the agreement and renew the strife, and promise to take the fight off his hands if he did: what would morality and Christianity say to this? Surely the malediction of all good men would fall upon the man who had interfered to renew the strife. And if this would be the voice of all good men in the case of mere individuals, what would it be when the strife was between nations, and when the renewal of it was to involve a third nation in the contest, and such a war as we now have with our sister republic of Mexico? This is the feature which stands out in the awful picture: this is the question which now presents itself to the moral sense of the civilized world, in judging the conduct of the senator from South Carolina in writing that letter of the 11th of April, 1844, aggravated by now throwing upon another the blame of a war for which he then contracted.

CHAPTER CL.

MR. POLK'S INAUGURAL ADDRESS, AND CABINET.

This was the longest address of the kind which had yet been delivered, and although condemned by its nature to declarations of general principles, there were some topics on which it dwelt with more particularity. The blessings of the Union, and the necessity of its preservation were largely enforced, and not without point, considering recent manifestations. Our title to the Oregon Territory was asserted as clear and indisputable, and the determination avowed to protect our settlers there. The sentiments were good, but the necessity or propriety of avowing them so positively, was quite questionable, seeing that this title was then a subject of negotiation with Great Britain, upon the harmony of which a declaration so positive might have an ill effect: and in fact did. The return voice from London was equally positive on the other side; and the inevitability of war became the immediate cry. The passage by Congress of the Texas annexation resolution was dwelt upon with great exultation, and the measure considered as consummated from the real disposition of Texas for the measure, and her great desire to get a partner in the war with Mexico, which would take its expenses and burdens off her hands.

The cabinet ministers were nominated and confirmed the same day—the Senate, as always, being convened on the 4th day of March for that purpose: James Buchanan, of Pennsylvania, Secretary of State; Robert J. Walker, of Mississippi, Secretary of the Treasury; William L. Marcy, of New York, Secretary at War; George Bancroft, of Massachusetts, Secretary of the Navy; Cave Johnson, of Tennessee, Postmaster-general; John Y. Mason, of Virginia, Attorney-general. The last was the only one retained of the late cabinet. Mr. Calhoun expected to be, and desired it, to prosecute, as he said, the Oregon negotiations, which he had commenced; and also to continue a certain diplomatic correspondence with France, on the subject of slavery, which he opened through Wm. R. King—greatly to the puzzle of the King, Louis Phillippe, and his ministers. In place of the State Department he was offered the mission to London, which he refused; and the same being offered to his friend, Mr. Francis W. Pickens, it was refused by him also: and the word became current, and was justified by the event, that neither Mr. Calhoun, nor any of his friends, would take office under this administration. In other respects, there was some balk and change after the cabinet had been agreed upon—which was done in Tennessee. General William O. Butler, the particular friend of General Jackson, had been brought on to receive the place of Secretary at War. He came in company with the President elect, at his special request, from Louisville, Kentucky, and was not spared to stop at his own house to get his wardrobe, though in sight of it: he was thrown out by the effect of a circuitous arrangement of which Mr. Polk was the dupe, and himself the victim. In the original cast of the cabinet, Mr. Silas Wright, the Governor elect of New York, and to whom Mr. Polk was indebted for his election, was to be Secretary of the Treasury. It was offered to him. He refused it, as he did all office: it was then intended for Mr. Azariah Flagg, the able and incorruptible comptroller of New York, the friend of Wright and Van Buren. He was superseded by the same intrigue which displaced General Butler. Mr. Robert J. Walker had been intended for Attorney-general: he brought an influence to bear upon Mr. Polk, which carried him into the Treasury. That displaced Mr. Flagg. But New York was not a State to be left out of the cabinet, and no place could be made for her except in the War Department; and Mr. Van Buren and Governor Wright were notified accordingly, with the intimation that the place belonged to one of their friends; and to name him. They did so upon the instant, and named Mr. Benjamin F. Butler; and, beginning to be a little suspicious, and to guard against all danger of losing, or delaying the name on the road, a special messenger was despatched to Washington, to travel day and night, and go straight to the President, and deposit the name in his hands. The messenger did so—and was informed that he was fifteen minutes too late! that the place had been assigned to Mr. Wm. L. Marcy. And that was the beginning of the material damage (not in Kossuth's sense of the word), which Mr. Polk's administration did to Mr. Van Buren, Governor Wright, and their friends.

CHAPTER CLI.

MR. BLAIR AND THE GLOBE SUPERSEDED AS THE ADMINISTRATION ORGAN: MR. THOMAS RITCHIE AND THE DAILY UNION SUBSTITUTED.

It was in the month of August, 1844, that a leading citizen of South Carolina, and a close friend of Mr. Calhoun—one who had been at the Baltimore presidential convention, but not in it—arrived at Mr. Polk's residence in Tennessee, had interviews with him, and made known the condition on which the vote of South Carolina for him might be dependent. That condition was to discontinue Mr. Blair as the organ of the administration if he should be elected. The electoral vote of the State being in the hands of the General Assembly, and not in the people, was disposable by the politicians, and had been habitually disposed of by them—and even twice thrown away in the space of a few years. Mr. Polk was certain of the vote of the State if he agreed to the required condition: and he did so. Mr. Blair was agreed to be given up. That was propitiation to Mr. Calhoun, to whom Mr. Blair was obnoxious on account of his inexorable opposition to nullification, and its author. Mr. Blair was also obnoxious to Mr. Tyler because of his determined opposition both to him, and to his administration. The Globe newspaper was a spear in his side, and would continue to be so; and to get it out had been one of the anxieties and labors of his presidential life. He had exhausted all the schemes to quiet, or to gain it, without success. A printing job of twenty thousand dollars had been at one time given to his office, with the evident design to soften him: to avoid that suspicion he struck the harder; and the job was taken away when partly executed. It now became the interest of Mr. Polk to assist Mr. Tyler in silencing, or punishing that paper; and it was done. Mr. Tyler had accepted the nomination of his convention for the presidency, and was in the field with an array of electoral candidates struggling for it. He stood no chance to obtain a single electoral vote: but Mr. Polk was in no condition to be able to lose any part of the popular vote. Mr. Tyler, now fully repudiated by the whigs, and carrying democratic colors, and with the power and patronage of the federal government in his hands, would take off some votes—enough in a closely contested State to turn the scale in favor of Mr. Clay. Hence it became essential to get Mr. Tyler out of the way of Mr. Polk; and to do that, the condition was, to get Mr. Blair out of the way of Mr. Tyler. Mr. Polk was anxious for this. A friend of his, who afterwards became a member of his cabinet, wrote to him in July, that the main obstacle to Mr. Tyler's withdrawal was the course of the Globe towards him and his friends. Another of those most interested in the result urged Mr. Polk to devise some mode of inducing Mr. Tyler to withdraw, and General Jackson was requested "*to ascertain the motives which actuated the course of the Globe towards Mr. Tyler and his friends.*" These facts appear in a letter from Mr. Polk to General Jackson, in which he says to him: "*The main object in the way of Mr. Tyler's withdrawal, is the course of the Globe towards himself and his friends.*" These communications took place in the month before the South Carolina gentleman visited Tennessee. Mr. Polk's letter to General Jackson is dated the 23d of July. In about as short time after that visit as information could come from Tennessee to Washington, Mr. Tyler publicly withdrew his presidential pretensions! and his official paper, the Madisonian, and his supporters, passed over to Mr. Polk. The inference is irresistible, that the consideration of receiving the vote of South Carolina, and of getting Mr. Tyler out of the way of Mr. Polk, was the agreement to displace Mr. Blair as government editor if he should be elected.

And now we come to another fact, in this connection, as the phrase is, about which also there is no dispute; and that fact is this: on the fourth day of November, 1844, being after Mr. Tyler had joined Mr. Polk, and when the near approach of the presidential election authorized reliable calculations to be made on its result, the sum of $50,000, by an order from the Treasury in Washington, was taken from a respectable bank in Philadelphia, where it was safe and convenient for public use, and transferred to a village bank in the interior of Pennsylvania, where there was no public use for it, and where its safety was questionable. This appears from the records of the Treasury. Authentic letters written in December following from the person who had control of this village bank (Simon Cameron, Esq., a senator in Congress), went to a gentleman in Tennessee, informing him that $50,000 was in his hands for the purpose of establishing a new government organ in Washington City, proposing to him to be its editor, and urging him to come on to Washington for the purpose. These letters were sent to Andrew Jackson Donelson, Esq., connection and ex-private Secretary of President Jackson, who immediately refused the proffered editorship, and turned over the letters to General Jackson. His (Jackson's) generous and high blood boiled with indignation at what seemed to be a sacrifice of Mr. Blair for some political consideration; for the letters were so written as to imply a cognizance on the part of Mr. Polk, and of two persons who were to be members of his cabinet; and that cognizance was strengthened by a fact unknown to General Jackson, *namely*, that Mr. Polk himself, in due season, proposed to Mr. Blair to yield to Mr. Donelson as actual editor—himself writing *sub rosa*; which Mr. Blair utterly refused. It was a contrivance of Mr. Polk to get rid of Mr. Blair in compliance with his engagement to Mr. Calhoun and Mr. Tyler, without breaking with Mr. Blair and his friends; but he had to deal with a man, and with men, who would have no such hugger-mugger work; and to whom an open breach was preferable to a simulated friendship: General Jackson wrote to Mr. Blair to apprise him of what was going on, and to assure him of his steadfast friendship, and to let him know that Mr. Ritchie, of the Richmond Enquirer, was the person to take place on the refusal of Andrew Jackson Donelson, and to foretell mischiefs to Mr. Polk and his party if he fell into these schemes, of which Mr. Robert J. Walker was believed to be the chief contriver, and others of the cabinet passive instruments. On the 14th of December, 1844, he (General Jackson) wrote to Mr. Blair:

"But there is another project on foot as void of good sense and benefit to the democratic cause as the other, but not as wicked, proceeding from weak and inexperienced minds. It is this: to bring about a partnership between you and Mr. Ritchie, you to continue proprietor, and Ritchie the editor. This, to me, is a most extraordinary conception coming from any well-informed mind or experienced politician. It is true, Mr. Ritchie is an experienced editor, but sometimes goes off at half cock before he sees the whole ground, and does the party great injury before he sees his error, and then has great difficulty to get back into the right track again. Witness his course on my removal of the deposits, and how much injury he did us before he got into the right track again. Another *faux pas* he made when he went off with Rives and the conservatives, and advocated for the safe keeping of the public revenue special deposits in the State banks, as if where the directory were corrupt there could be any more security in special deposits in corrupt banks than in general deposits, and it was some time before this great absurdity could be beat out of his mind.

"These are visionary measures of what I call weak politicians who suggest them, but who wish to become great by foolish changes. Polk, I believe, will stick by you faithfully; should he not, he is lost; but I have no fears but that he will, and being informed confidentially of this movement, may have it in his power to put it *all down*. There will be great intrigue going on at Washington this winter."—(*Dec. 14, 1844.*)

"I fear there are some of our democratic friends who are trying to bring about a partnership of which I wrote you, which shows a want of confidence, or something worse. Be on your guard—no partnership; you have the confidence of the great body of the democrats, and I have no confidence in shifting politicians."—(*December, 21.*)

"Another plan is to get Mr. Ritchie interested as editor of the Globe—all of which I gave you an intimation of, and which I thought had been put down. But that any leading Democrat here had any thought of becoming interested in the Madisonian, to make it the organ of the administration, was such a thing as I could not believe; as common sense at once pointed out, as a consequence that it would divide the democracy, and destroy Polk's administration. Why, it would blow him up. The moment I heard it, I adopted such measures as I trust have put an end to it, as I know nothing could be so injurious to Polk and his administration. The pretext for this movement will be the Globe's support of Mr. Wright. *Let me know if there is any truth in this rumor.* I guarded Colonel Polk against any abandonment of the Globe. If true, it would place Colonel Polk in the shoes of Mr. Tyler."—(*February 28, 1845.*)

"I have written a long, candid, and friendly letter to Mr. Polk, bringing to his view the dilemma into which he has got by some bad advice, and which his good sense ought to have prevented. I have assured him of your uniform declarations to me of your firm support, and of the destruction of the democratic party if he takes any one but you as the executive organ, until you do something to violate that confidence which the democracy reposes in you. I ask in emphatic terms, what cause can he assign for not continuing your paper, the organ that was mine and Mr. Van Buren's, whose administration he, Polk, and you hand to hand supported, and those great fundamental principles you and he have continued to support, and have told him frankly that you will never degrade yourself or your paper by submitting to the terms proposed. I am very sick, exhausted by writing to Polk, and will write you again soon. I can only add, that, although my letter to Mr. Polk is both friendly and frank, I have done justice to you, and I hope he will say at once to you, go on with my organ as you have been the organ of Jackson and Van Buren. Should he not, I have told him his fate—a divided democracy, and all the political cliques looking to the succession, will annoy and crush him—the fairest prospects of successful administration by folly and jealousy lost. I would wish you to inform me which of the heads of the Departments, if any, are hostile to you. If Polk does not look well to his course, the divisions in New York and Pennsylvania will destroy him."—(*April 4, 1845.*)

I wrote you and the President, on the 4th instant, and was in hopes that my views would open his eyes to his own interests and union of the democratic party. But from the letters before me, I suppose my letter to the President will not prevent that evil to him and the democratic party that I have used my voice to prevent. I am too unwell to write much to-day. I have read your letter with care and much interest. I know you would never degrade yourself by dividing the editorial chair with any one for any cause. I well know that you never can or will abandon your democratic principles. You cannot, under existing circumstances, do any thing to save your character and democratic principles, and your high standing with all classes of the democracy, but by selling out your paper. When you sell, have good security for the consideration money. Ritchie is greatly involved, if not finally broke; and you know Cameron, who boasts that he has $50,000 to invest in a newspaper. Under all existing circumstances, I say to you, sell, and when you do, I look to a split in the democratic ranks; which I will sorely regret, and which might have been so easily avoided."—(*April 7.*)

"I have been quite sick for several days. My mind, since ever I heard of the attitude the President had assumed with you as editor of the Globe,—which was the most unexpected thing I ever met with,—my mind has been troubled, and it was not only unexpected by me, but has shown less good common sense, by the President, than any act of his life, and calculated to divide instead of uniting the democracy; which appears to be his reason for urging this useless and foolish measure at the very threshold of his administration, and when every thing appeared to augur well for, to him, a prosperous administration. The President, here, before he set out for Washington, must have been listening to the secret counsels of some political cliques, such as Calhoun or Tyler cliques (for there are such here); or after he reached Washington, some of the secret friends of some of the aspirants must have gotten hold of his ear, and spoiled his common sense, or he never would have made such a movement, so uncalled for, and well calculated to sever the democracy by calling down upon himself suspicions, by the act of secretly favoring some of the political cliques who are looking to the succession for some favorite. I wrote him a long letter on the 4th, telling him there was but one safe course to pursue—review his course, send for you, and direct you and the *Globe* to proceed as the organ of his administration, give you all his confidence, and all would be well, and end well. *This is the substance*; and I had a hope the receipt of this letter, and some others written by mutual friends, would have restored all things to harmony and confidence again. I rested on this hope until the 7th, when I received yours of the 30th, and two confidential letters from the President, directed to be laid before me, from which it would seem that the purchase of the *Globe*, and to get clear of you, its editor, is the great absorbing question before the President. *Well, who is to be the purchaser?* Mr. Ritchie and Major A. J. Donelson its editors. *Query as to the latter.* The above question I have asked the President. Is that renegade politician, Cameron, who boasts of his $50,000 to set up a new paper, to be one of them? Or is Knox Walker to be the purchaser? Who is to purchase? and where is the money to come from? Is Dr. M. Gwinn, the satellite of Calhoun, the great friend of Robert J. Walker? a perfect bankrupt in property. I would like to know what portion of the cabinet are supporting and advising the President to this course, where nothing but injury can result to him in the end, and division in his cabinet, arising from jealousy. What political clique is to be benefited? My dear friend, let me know all about the cabinet, and their movements on this subject. How loathsome it is to me to see an old friend laid aside, principles of justice and friendship forgotten, and all for the sake of *policy*—and the great democratic party divided or endangered for *policy*—I cannot reflect upon it with any calmness; every point of it, upon scrutiny, turns to harm and disunion, and not one beneficial result can be expected from it. I will be anxious to know the result. If harmony is restored, and the *Globe* the organ, I will rejoice; if sold to whom, and for what. *Have, if you sell, the purchase money well secured.* This may be the last letter I may be able to write you; but live or die, I am your friend (and never deserted one from *policy*), and leave my papers and reputation in your keeping."—(*April 9.*)

From these letters it will be seen that General Jackson, after going through an agony of indignation and amazement at the idea of shoving Mr. Blair from his editorial chair and placing Mr. Ritchie in it (and which would have been greater if he had known the arrangement for the South Carolina vote and the withdrawal of Mr. Tyler), advised Mr. Blair to sell his Globe establishment, cautioning him to get good security; for, knowing nothing of the money taken from the Treasury, and well knowing the insolvency of all who were ostensible payers, he did not at all confide in their promises to make payment. Mr. Blair and his partner, Mr. John C. Rives, were of the same mind. Other friends whom they consulted (Governor Wright and Colonel Benton) were of the same opinion; and the Globe was promptly sold to Mr. Ritchie, and in a way to imply rather an abandonment of it than a sale—the materials of the office being offered at valuation, and the "name and good will" of the paper left out of the transaction. The materials were valued at $35,000, and the metamorphosed paper took the name of the "Daily Union;" and, in fact, some change of name was necessary, as the new paper was the reverse of the old one.—In all these schemes, from first to last, to get rid of Mr. Blair, the design was to retain Mr. Rives, not as any part editor (for which he was far more fit than either himself or the public knew), but for his extraordinary business qualities, and to manage the machinery and fiscals of the establishment. Accustomed to trafficking and trading politicians, and fortune being sure to the government editor, it was not suspicioned by those who conducted the intrigue that Mr. Rives would refuse to be saved at the expense of his partner. He scorned it! and the two went out together.—The letters from General Jackson show his appreciation of the services of the Globe to the country and the democratic party during the eight eventful years of his presidency: Mr. Van Buren, on learning what was going on, wrote to Mr. Rives to show his opinion of the same services during the four years of his arduous administration; and that letter also belongs to the history of the extinction of the Globe newspaper—that paper which, for twelve years, had fought the battle of the country, and of the democracy, in the spirit of Jackson: that is to say, victoriously and honorably. This letter was written to Mr. Rives, who, in spite of his modest estimate of himself, was classed by General Jackson, Mr. Van Buren, and all their friends, among the wisest, purest, and safest of the party.

"The Globe has run its career at too critical a period in our political history—has borne the democratic flag too steadily in the face of assaults upon popular sovereignty, more violent and powerful than any which had ever preceded them in this or any other country, not to have made impressions upon our history and our institutions, which are destined to be remembered when those who witnessed its discontinuance shall be no more. The manner in which it demeaned itself through those perilous periods, and the repeated triumphs which crowned its labors, will when the passions of the day have spent their force, be matters of just exultation to you and to your children. *None have had better opportunities to witness, nor more interest in observing your course, than General Jackson and myself; and I am very sure that I could not, if I were to attempt it, express myself more strongly in favor of the constancy, fidelity, and ability with which it was conducted, than he would sanction with his whole heart.* He would, I have no doubt, readily admit that it would have been exceedingly difficult, if not impossible, for his administration to have sustained itself in its contest with a money power (a term as well understood as that of democrat, and much better than that of whig at the present day), if the corruptions which were in those days spread broadcast through the length and breadth of the land, had been able to subvert the integrity of the Globe; and I am very certain that the one over which I had the honor to preside, could never, in such an event, have succeeded in obtaining the institution of an independent treasury, without the establishment of which, the advantages to be derived from the overthrow of the Bank of the United States will very soon prove to be wholly illusory. The Bank of the United States first, and afterwards those of the States, succeeded in obtaining majorities in both branches of the national legislature favorable to their views; but they could never move the Globe from the course which has since been so extensively sanctioned by the democracy of the nation. You gave to the country (and when I say you, I desire to be understood as alluding to Mr. Blair and yourself) at those momentous periods, the invaluable advantages of a press at the seat of the general government, not only devoted, root and branch, to the support of democratic principles, but independent in fact and in feeling, as well of bank influences as of corrupting pecuniary influences of any description. The vital importance of such an establishment to the success of our cause is incapable of exaggeration. Experience will show, if an opportunity is ever afforded to test the opinion, that, without it, the principles of our party can never be upheld in their purity in the administration of the federal government. Administrations professedly their supporters may be formed, but they will prove to be but whited sepulchres, appearing beautiful outward, but within full of dead men's bones, and all uncleanness—Administrations which, instead of directing their best efforts to advance the welfare and promote the happiness of the toiling millions, will be ever ready to lend a favorable ear to the advancement of the selfish few."

The Globe was sold, and was paid for, and how? becomes a question of public concern to answer; for it was paid for out of public money—those same $50,000 which were removed to the village bank in the interior of Pennsylvania by a Treasury order on the fourth day of November, 1844. Three annual instalments made the payment, and the Treasury did not reclaim the money for these three years; and, though travelling through tortuous channels, the sharpsighted Mr. Rives traced the money back to its starting point from that deposit. Besides, Mr. Cameron admitted before a committee of Congress, that he had furnished money for the payments—an admission which the obliging committee, on request, left out of their report. Mr. Robert J. Walker was Secretary of the Treasury during these three years, and the conviction was absolute, among the close observers of the course of things, that he was the prime contriver and zealous manager of the arrangements which displaced Mr. Blair and installed Mr. Ritchie.

In the opinions which he expressed of the consequences of that change of editors, General Jackson was prophetic. The new paper brought division and distraction into the party—filled it with dissensions, which eventually induced the withdrawal of Mr. Ritchie; but not until he had produced the mischiefs which abler men cannot repair.

CHAPTER CLII.

TWENTY-NINTH CONGRESS: LIST OF MEMBERS: FIRST SESSION: ORGANIZATION OF THE HOUSE.

Senators.

MAINE.—George Evans, John Fairfield.

NEW HAMPSHIRE.—Benjamin W. Jenness, Charles G. Atherton.

VERMONT.—William Upham, Samuel S. Phelps.

MASSACHUSETTS.—Daniel Webster, John Davis.

RHODE ISLAND.—James F. Simmons, Albert C. Green.

CONNECTICUT.—John M. Niles, Jabez W. Huntington.

NEW YORK.—John A. Dix, Daniel S. Dickinson.

NEW JERSEY.—Jacob W. Miller, John L. Dayton.

PENNSYLVANIA.—Simon Cameron, Daniel Sturgeon.

DELAWARE.—Thomas Clayton, John M. Clayton.

MARYLAND.—James A. Pearce, Reverdy Johnson.

VIRGINIA.—William S. Archer, Isaac S. Pennybacker.

NORTH CAROLINA.—Willie P. Mangum, William H. Haywood, jr.

SOUTH CAROLINA.—John C. Calhoun, George McDuffie.

GEORGIA.—John McP. Berrien, Walter T. Colquitt.

ALABAMA.—Dixon H. Lewis, Arthur P. Bagby.

MISSISSIPPI.—Joseph W. Chalmers, Jesse Speight.

LOUISIANA.—Alexander Barrow, Henry Johnson.

TENNESSEE.—Spencer Jarnagin, Hopkins L. Turney.

KENTUCKY.—James T. Morehead, John J. Crittenden.

OHIO.—William Allen, Thomas Corwin.

INDIANA.—Ed. A. Hannegan, Jesse D. Bright.

ILLINOIS.—James Semple, Sidney Breese.

MISSOURI.—David R. Atchison, Thomas H. Benton.

ARKANSAS.—Chester Ashley, Ambrose H. Sevier.

MICHIGAN.—William Woodbridge, Lewis Cass.

FLORIDA.—David Levy, James D. Westcott.

In this list will be seen the names of several new senators, not members of the body before, and whose senatorial exertions soon made them eminent;—Dix and Dickinson of New York, Reverdy Johnson of Maryland, Jesse D. Bright of Indiana, Lewis Cass of Michigan; and to these were soon to be added two others from the newly incorporated State of Texas, Messrs. General Sam Houston and Thomas F. Rusk, Esq., and of whom, and their State, it may be said they present a remarkable instance of mutual confidence and concord, neither having been changed to this day (1856).

House of Representatives.

MAINE.—John F. Scammon, Robert P. Dunlap, Luther Severance, John D. McCrate, Cullen Sawtelle, Hannibal Hamlin, Hezekiah Williams.

NEW HAMPSHIRE.—Moses Norris, jr., Mace Moulton, James H. Johnson.

VERMONT.—Solomon Foot, Jacob Collamer, George P. Marsh, Paul Dillingham, jr.

MASSACHUSETTS.—Robert C. Winthrop, Daniel P. King, Amos Abbot, Benjamin Thompson, Charles Hudson, George Ashmun, Julius Rockwell, John Quincy Adams, Joseph Grinnell.

RHODE ISLAND.—Henry Y. Cranston, Lemuel H. Arnold.

CONNECTICUT.—James Dixon, Samuel D. Hubbard, John A. Rockwell, Truman Smith.

NEW YORK.—John W. Lawrence, Henry I. Seaman, William S. Miller, William B. Maclay, Thomas M. Woodruff, William W. Campbell, Joseph H. Anderson, William W. Woodworth, Archibald C. Niven, Samuel Gordon, John F. Collin, Richard P. Herrick, Bradford R. Wood, Erastus D. Culver, Joseph Russell, Hugh White, Charles S. Benton, Preston King, Orville Hungerford, Timothy Jenkins, Charles Goodyear, Stephen Strong, William J. Hough, Horace Wheaton, George Rathbun, Samuel S. Ellsworth, John De Mott, Elias B. Holmes, Charles H. Carcoll, Martin Grover, Abner Lewis, William A. Mosely, Albert Smith, Washington Hunt.

NEW JERSEY.—James G. Hampton, George Sykes, John Runk, John Edsall, William Wright.

PENNSYLVANIA.—Lewis C. Levin, Joseph R. Ingersoll, John H. Campbell, Charles J. Ingersoll, Jacob S. Yost, Jacob Erdman, Abraham R. McIlvaine, John Strohm, John Ritter, Richard Brodhead, jr., Owen D. Leib, David Wilmot, James Pollock, Alexander Ramsay, Moses McLean, James Black, James Blanchard, Andrew Stewart, Henry D. Foster, John H. Ewing, Cornelius Darragh, William S. Garvin, James Thompson, Joseph Buffington.

DELAWARE.—John W. Houston.

MARYLAND.—John G. Chapman, Thomas Perry, Thomas W. Ligon, William F. Giles, Albert Constable, Edward Long.

VIRGINIA.—Archibald Atkinson, George C. Dromgoole, William M. Treadway, Edward W. Hubard, Shelton F. Leake, James A. Seddon, Thomas H. Bayly, Robert M. T. Hunter, John S. Pendleton, Henry Redinger, William Taylor, Augustus A. Chapman, George W. Hopkins, Joseph Johnson, William G. Brown.

NORTH CAROLINA.—James Graham, Daniel M. Barringer, David S. Reid, Alfred Dockery, James C. Dobbin, James J. McKay, John R. J. Daniels, Henry S. Clarke, Asa Biggs.

SOUTH CAROLINA.—James A. Black, Richard F. Simpson, Joseph A. Woodward, A. D. Sims, Armistead Burt, Isaac E. Holmes, R. Barnwell Rhett.

GEORGIA.—Thomas Butler King, Seaborn Jones, Hugh A. Haralson, John H. Lumpkin, Howell Cobb, Alex. H. Stephens, Robt. Toombs.

ALABAMA.—Samuel D. Dargin, Henry W. Hilliard, William L. Yancey, Winter W. Payne, George S. Houston, Reuben Chapman, Felix G. McConnell.

MISSISSIPPI.—Jacob Thompson, Stephen Adams, Robert N. Roberts, Jefferson Davis.

LOUISIANA.—John Slidell, Bannon G. Thibodeaux, J. H. Harmonson, Isaac E. Morse.

OHIO.—James J. Faran, F. A. Cunningham, Robert C. Schenck, Joseph Vance, William Sawyer, Henry St. John, Joseph J. McDowell, Allen G. Thurman, Augustus L. Perrill, Columbus Delano, Jacob Brinkerhoff, Samuel F. Vinton, Isaac Parish, Alexander Harper, Joseph Morris, John D. Cummins, George Fries, D. A. Starkweather, Daniel R. Tilden, Joshua R. Giddings, Joseph M. Root.

KENTUCKY.—Linn Boyd, John H. McHenry, Henry Grider, Joshua F. Bell, Bryan R. Young, John P. Martin, William P. Thomasson, Garrett Davis, Andrew Trumbo, John W. Tibbatts.

TENNESSEE.—Andrew Johnson, William M. Cocke, John Crozier, Alvan Cullom, George W. Jones, Barclay Martin, Meridith, P. Gentry, Lorenzo B. Chase, Frederick P. Stanton, Milton Brown.

INDIANA.—Robert Dale Owen, Thomas J. Henley, Thomas Smith, Caleb B. Smith, William W. Wick, John W. Davis, Edward W. McGaughey, John Petit, Charles W. Cathcart, Andrew Kennedy.

ILLINOIS.—Robert Smith, John A. McClernand, Orlando B. Ficklin, John Wentworth, Stephen A. Douglass, Joseph P. Hoge, Edward D. Baker.

MISSOURI.—James B. Bowlin, James H. Relf, Sterling Price, John S. Phelps, Leonard H. Simms.

ARKANSAS.—Archibald Yell.

MICHIGAN.—Robert McClelland, John S. Chapman, James B. Hunt.

The delegates from territories were:

FLORIDA.—Edward C. Cabell.

IOWA.—Augustus C. Dodge.

WISCONSIN.—Morgan L. Martin.

The election of Speaker was readily effected, there being a large majority on the democratic side. Mr. John W. Davis, of Indiana, being presented as the democratic candidate, received 120 votes; Mr. Samuel F. Vinton, of Ohio, received the whig vote, 72. Mr. Benjamin B. French, of New Hampshire, was appointed clerk (without the formality of an election), by a resolve of the House, adopted by a general vote. He was of course democratic. The House being organized, a motion was made by Mr. Hamlin, of Maine, to except the hour rule (as it was called) from the rules to be adopted for the government of the House—which was lost, 62 to 143.

CHAPTER CLIII.

MR. POLK'S FIRST ANNUAL MESSAGE TO CONGRESS.

The leading topic in the message was, naturally, the incorporation of Texas, then accomplished, and the consequent dissatisfaction of Mexico—a dissatisfaction manifested every way short of actual hostilities, and reason to believe they were intended. On our side, strong detachments of the army and navy had been despatched to Texas and the Gulf of Mexico, to be ready for whatever might happen. The Mexican minister, General Almonte, had left the United States: an American minister sent to Mexico had been refused to be received, and had returned home. All this was the natural result of the *status belli* between the United States and Mexico which the incorporation of Texas had established; and, that there were not actual hostilities was only owing to the weakness of one of the parties. These things were thus stated by the President:

> "Since that time Mexico has, until recently, occupied an attitude of hostility towards the United States—has been marshalling and organizing armies, issuing proclamations, and avowing the intention to make war on the United States, either by an open declaration, or by invading Texas. Both the Congress and convention of the people of Texas invited this government to send an army into that territory, to protect and defend them against the menaced attack. The moment the terms of annexation, offered by the United States, were accepted by Texas, the latter became so far a part of our own country, as to make it our duty to afford such protection and defence. I therefore deemed it proper, as a precautionary measure, to order a strong squadron to the coast of Mexico, and to concentrate an efficient military force on the western frontier of Texas. Our army was ordered to take position in the country between the Nueces and the Del Norte, and to repel any invasion of the Texian territory which might be attempted by the Mexican forces. Our squadron in the Gulf was ordered to co-operate with the army. But though our army and navy were placed in a position to defend our own, and the rights of Texas, they were ordered to commit no act of hostility against Mexico, unless she declared war, or was herself the aggressor by striking the first blow. The result has been, that Mexico has made no aggressive movement, and our military and naval commanders have executed their orders with such discretion, that the peace of the two republics has not been disturbed."

Thus the armed forces of the two countries were brought into presence, and the legal state of war existing between them was brought to the point of actual war. Of this the President complained, assuming that Texas and the United States had a *right* to unite, which was true as to the right; but asserting that Mexico had no right to oppose it, which was a wrong assumption. For, in taking Texas into the Union, she was taken with her circumstances, one of which was a state of war with Mexico. Denying her right to take offence at what had been done, the message went on to enumerate causes of complaint against her, and for many years back, and to make out cause of war against her on account of injuries done by her to our citizens. In this sense the message said:

> "But though Mexico cannot complain of the United States on account of the annexation of Texas, it is to be regretted that serious causes of misunderstanding between the two countries continue to exist, growing out of unredressed injuries inflicted by the Mexican authorities and people on the persons and property of citizens of the United States, through a long series of years. Mexico has admitted these injuries, but has neglected and refused to repair them. Such was the character of the wrongs, and such the insults repeatedly offered to American citizens and the American flag by Mexico, in palpable violation of the laws of nations and the treaty between the two countries of the 5th April, 1831, that they have been repeatedly brought to the notice of Congress by my predecessors. As early as the 8th February, 1837, the President of the United States declared, in a message to Congress, that 'the length of time since some of the injuries have been committed, the repeated and unavailing application for redress, the wanton character of some of the outrages upon the persons and property of our citizens, upon the officers and flag of the United States, independent of recent insults to this

government and people by the late extraordinary Mexican minister, would justify, in the eyes of all nations, immediate war.' He did not, however, recommend an immediate resort to this extreme measure, which he declared 'should not be used by just and generous nations, confiding in their strength, for injuries committed, if it can be honorably avoided;' but, in a spirit of forbearance, proposed that another demand be made on Mexico for that redress which had been so long and unjustly withheld. In these views, committees of the two Houses of Congress, in reports made in their respective bodies, concurred. Since these proceedings more than eight years have elapsed, during which, in addition to the wrongs then complained of, others of an aggravated character have been committed on the persons and property of our citizens. A special agent was sent to Mexico in the summer of 1838, with full authority to make another and final demand for redress. The demand was made; the Mexican government promised to repair the wrongs of which we complained; and after much delay, a treaty of indemnity with that view was concluded between the two powers on the 11th of April, 1839, and was duly ratified by both governments."

This treaty of indemnity, the message went on to show, had never yet been complied with, and its non-fulfilment, added to the other causes of complaint, the President considered as just cause for declaring war against her—saying:

"In the mean time, our citizens, who suffered great losses, and some of whom have been reduced from affluence to bankruptcy, are without remedy, unless their rights be enforced by their government. Such a continued and unprovoked series of wrongs could never have been tolerated by the United States, had they been committed by one of the principal nations of Europe. Mexico was, however, a neighboring sister republic, which, following our example, had achieved her independence, and for whose success and prosperity, all our sympathies were early enlisted. The United States were the first to recognize her independence, and to receive her into the family of nations, and have ever been desirous of cultivating with her a good understanding. We have, therefore, borne the repeated wrongs she has committed, with great patience, in the hope that a returning sense of justice would ultimately guide her councils, and that we might, if possible, honorably avoid any hostile collision with her."

Torn by domestic dissension, in a state of revolution at home, and ready to be crushed by the power of the United States, the Mexican government had temporized, and after dismissing one United States minister, had consented to receive another, who was then on his way to the City of Mexico. Of this mission, and the consequences of its failure, the President thus expressed himself:

"The minister appointed has set out on his mission, and is probably by this time near the Mexican capital. He has been instructed to bring the negotiation with which he is charged to a conclusion at the earliest practicable period; which, it is expected, will be in time to enable me to communicate the result to Congress during the present session. Until that result is known, I forbear to recommend to Congress such ulterior measures of redress for the wrongs and injuries we have so long borne, as it would have been proper to make had no such negotiation been instituted."

From this communication it was clear that a recommendation of a declaration of war was only deferred for the issue of this mission, which failing to be favorable, would immediately call forth the deferred recommendation. The Oregon question was next in importance to that of Texas and Mexico, and like it seemed to be tending to a warlike solution. The negotiations between the two governments, which had commenced under Mr. Tyler's administration, and continued for some months under his own, had come to a dead stand. The government of the United States had revoked its proposition to make the parallel of 49 degrees the dividing line between the two countries, and asserted the unquestionable title of the United States to the whole, up to the Russian boundary in 54 degrees 40 minutes; and the message recommended Congress to authorize the notice which was to terminate the joint occupancy, to extend our laws to the territory, to encourage its population and settlement; and cast upon Great Britain the responsibility of any belligerent solution of the difficulty which might arise. Thus, the issue of peace or war with Great Britain was thrown into the hands of Congress.

The finances, and the public debt, required a notice, which was briefly and satisfactorily given. The receipts into the Treasury for the past year had been $29,770,000: the payments from it $29,968,000; and the balance in the Treasury at the end of the year five millions—leaving a balance of $7,658,000 on hand. The nature of these balances, always equal to about one-fourth of the revenue even where the receipts and expenditures are even, or the latter even in some excess, has been explained in the first volume of this View, as resulting from the nature of great government transactions and payments, large part of which necessarily go into the beginning of the succeeding year, when they would be met by the accruing revenue, even if there was nothing in the Treasury; so that, in fact, the government may be carried on upon an income about one-fourth less than the expenditure. This is a paradox—a seeming absurdity, but true, which every annual statement of the Treasury will prove; and which the legislative, as well as the executive government, should understand. The sentiments in relation to the public debt (of which there would have been none had it not been for the distribution of the land revenue, and the surplus fund, among the States, and the absurd plunges in the descent of the duties on imports in the last two years of the compromise act of 1833), were just and wise, such as had been always held by the democratic school, and which cannot be too often repeated. They were these:

"The amount of the public debt remaining unpaid on the first of October last, was seventeen millions, seventy-five thousand, four hundred and forty-five dollars and fifty-two cents. Further payments of the public debt would have been made, in anticipation of the period of its reimbursement under the authority conferred upon the Secretary of the Treasury, by the acts of July twenty-first, 1841, and of April fifteenth, and of March third, 1843, had not the unsettled state of our relations with Mexico menaced hostile collision with that power. In view of such a contingency, it was deemed prudent to retain in the Treasury an amount unusually large for ordinary purposes. A few years ago, our whole national debt growing out of the revolution and the war of 1812 with Great Britain, was extinguished, and we presented to the world the rare and noble spectacle of a great and growing people who had fully discharged every obligation. Since that time the existing debt has been contracted; and small as it is, in comparison with the similar burdens of most other nations, it should be extinguished at the earliest practicable period. Should the state of the country permit, and especially if our foreign relations interpose no obstacle, it is contemplated to apply all the moneys in the Treasury as they accrue beyond what is required for the appropriations by Congress, to its liquidation. I cherish the hope of soon being able to congratulate the country on its recovering once more the lofty position which it so recently occupied. Our country, which exhibits to the world the benefits of self-government, in developing all the sources of national prosperity, owes to mankind the permanent example of a nation free from the blighting influence of a public debt."

The revision of the tariff was recommended, with a view to revenue as the object, with protection to home industry as the incident.

CHAPTER CLIV.

DEATH OF JOHN FORSYTH.

Like Mr. Crawford, he was a Virginian by birth Georgian by citizenship, republican in politics, and eminent in his day. He ran the career of federal honors—a member of the House and of the Senate, and a front rank debater in each: minister in Spain, and Secretary of State under Presidents Jackson and Van Buren; successor to Crawford in his State, and the federal councils; and the fast political and personal friend of that eminent citizen in all the trials and fortunes of his life. A member of the House when Mr. Crawford, restrained by his office, and disabled by his calamity, was unable to do any thing for himself, and assailed by the impersonation of the execrable A. B. plot, it devolved upon him to stand up for his friend; and nobly did he do it. The examination through which he led the accuser exterminated him in public opinion—showed every accusation to be false and malicious; detected the master spirit which lay behind the ostensible assailants, and greatly exalted the character of Mr. Crawford.

Mr. Forsyth was a fine specimen of that kind of speaking which constitutes a debater, and which, in fact, is the effective speaking in legislative assemblies. He combined the requisites for keen debate—a ready, copious, and easy elocution; ample knowledge of the subject; argument and wit; great power to point a sarcasm, and to sting courteously; perfect self-possession, and a quickness and clearness of perception to take advantage of every misstep of his adversary. He served in trying times, during the great contests with the Bank of the United States, with the heresy of nullification, and the dawning commencement of the slavery agitation. In social life he was a high exemplification of refined and courteous manners, of polite conversation, and of affability, decorum and dignity.

CHAPTER CLV.

ADMISSION OF FLORIDA AND IOWA.

At this time were admitted into the Union, and by a single bill, two States, which seem to have but few things in common to put them together—one the oldest, the other the newest territory—one in the extreme northwest of the Union, the other in the extreme southeast—one the land of evergreens and perpetual flowers, the other the climate of long and rigorous winter—one maintaining, the other repulsing slavery. It would seem strange that two territories so different in age, so distant from each other, so antagonistic in natural features and political institutions, should ripen into States at the same time, and come into the Union by a single act; but these antagonisms—that is, the antagonistic provisions on the subject of slavery—made the conjunction, and gave to the two young States an inseparable admission. It happened that the slave and free States had long before become equal in number, and a feeling of jealousy, or a calculation of policy operated to keep them so; and for that purpose to admit one of each character at the same time. Thus balancing and neutralizing each other, the bill for their admission was passed without a struggle, and furnished but little beyond the yeas and nays—these latter a scant minority in either House—to show the disposition of members. In the Senate the negatives were 9 to 36 yeas: in the House 48 to 144. Numerically the free and the slave States were thus kept even: in political power a vast inequality was going on—the increase of population being so much greater in the northern than in the southern region.

———————————————————

CHAPTER CLVI.

OREGON TREATY: NEGOTIATIONS COMMENCED, AND BROKEN OFF.

This was a pretermitted subject in the general negotiations which led to the Ashburton treaty: it was now taken up as a question for separate settlement. The British government moved in it, Mr. Henry S. Fox, the British minister in Washington, being instructed to propose the negotiation. This was done in November, 1842, and Mr. Webster, then Secretary of State under Mr. Tyler, immediately replied, accepting the proposal, and declaring it to be the desire of his government to have this territorial question immediately settled. But the movement stopped there. Nothing further took place between Mr. Webster and Fox, and the question slumbered till 1844, when Mr. (since Sir) Richard Pakenham, arrived in the United States as British minister, and renewed the proposition for opening the negotiation to Mr. Upshur, then Secretary of State. This was February 24th, 1844. Mr. Upshur replied promptly, that is to say, on the 26th of the same month, accepting the proposal, and naming an early day for receiving Mr. Pakenham to begin the negotiation. Before that day came he had perished in the disastrous explosion of the great gun on board the Princeton man-of-war. The subject again slumbered six months, and at the end of that time, July 22d, was again brought to the notice of the American government by a note from the British minister to Mr. Calhoun, successor to Mr. Upshur in the Department of State. Referring to the note received from Mr. Upshur the day before his death, he said:

> "The lamented death of Mr. Upshur, which occurred within a few days after the date of that note, the interval which took place between that event and the appointment of a successor, and the urgency and importance of various matters which offered themselves to your attention immediately after your accession to office, sufficiently explain why it has not hitherto been in the power of your government, sir, to attend to the important matters to which I refer. But, the session of Congress having been brought to a close, and the present being the season of the year when the least possible business is usually transacted, it occurs to me that you may now feel at leisure to proceed to the consideration of that subject. At all events it becomes my duty to recall it to your recollection, and to repeat the earnest desire of her majesty's government, that a question, on which so much interest is felt in both countries, should be disposed of at the earliest moment consistent with the convenience of the government of the United States."

Mr. Calhoun answered the 22d of August declaring his readiness to begin the negotiation and fixing the next day for taking up the subject. It was taken up accordingly, and conducted in the approved and safe way of conducting such negotiations, that is to say, a protocol of every conference signed by the two negotiators before they separated, and the propositions submitted by each always reduced to writing. This was the proper and satisfactory mode of proceeding, the neglect and total omission of which had constituted so just and so loud a complaint against the manner in which Mr. Webster and Lord Ashburton had conducted their conferences. Mr. Calhoun and Mr. Pakenham met seven times, exchanged arguments and propositions, and came to a balk, which suspended their labors. Mr. Calhoun, rejecting the usual arts of diplomacy, which holds in reserve the ultimate and true offer while putting forward fictitious ones for experiment, went at once to his ultimatum, and proposed the continuation of the parallel of the 49th degree of north latitude, which, after the acquisition of Louisiana, had been adopted by Great Britain and the United States as the dividing line between their possessions, from the Lake of the Woods (fixed as a land-mark under the treaty of Utrecht), to the summit of the Rocky Mountains—the United States insisting at the same time to continue that line to the Pacific Ocean under the terms of the same treaty. Mr. Pakenham declined this proposition in the part that carried the line to the ocean, but offered to continue it from the summit of the mountains, to the Columbia River, a distance of some three hundred miles; and then follow the river to the ocean. This was refused by Mr. Calhoun; and the ultimatum having been delivered on one hand, and no instructions being possessed on the other to yield any thing, the negotiations, after continuing through the month of September, came to a stand. At the end of four months (January 1845) Mr. Pakenham, by the direction of his government, proposed to leave the question to arbitration, which was declined by the American secretary, and very properly; for, while arbitrament is the commendable mode of settling minor questions, and especially those which arise from the construction of existing treaties, yet the boundaries of a country are of too much gravity to be so submitted.

Mr. Calhoun showed a manly spirit in proposing the line of 49, as the dominant party in the United States, and the one to which he belonged, were then in a high state of exultation for the boundary of 54 degrees 40 minutes, and the presidential canvass, on the democratic side, was raging upon that cry. The Baltimore presidential convention had followed a pernicious practice, of recent invention, in laying down a platform of principles on which the canvass was to be conducted, and 54-40 for the northern boundary of Oregon, had been made a canon of political faith, from which there was to be no departure except upon the penalty of political damnation. Mr. Calhoun had braved this penalty, and in doing so had acted up to his public and responsible duty.

The new President, Mr. Polk, elected under that cry, came into office on the 4th of March, and acting upon it, put into his inaugural address a declaration that our title to the whole of Oregon (meaning up to 54-40), was clear and indisputable; and a further declaration that he meant to maintain that title. It was certainly an unusual thing—perhaps unprecedented in diplomacy—that, while negotiations were depending (which was still the case in this instance, for the last note of Mr. Calhoun in January, declining the arbitration, gave as a reason for it that he expected the question to be settled by negotiation), one of the parties should authoritatively declare its right to the whole matter in dispute, and show itself ready to maintain it by arms. The declaration in the inaugural had its natural effect in Great Britain. It roused the British spirit as high as that of the American. Their excited voice came thundering back, to be received with indignation by the great democracy; and war— "*inevitable war*"—was the cry through the land. The new administration felt itself to be in a dilemma. To stand upon 54-40 was to have war in reality: to recede from it, might be to incur the penalty laid down in the Baltimore platform. Mr. Buchanan, the new Secretary of State, did me the honor to consult me. I answered him promptly and frankly, that I held 49 to be the right line, and that, if the administration made a treaty upon that line, I should support it. This was early in April. The secretary seemed to expect some further proposition from the British government; but none came. The rebuff in the inaugural address had been too public, and too violent, to admit that government to take the initiative again. It said nothing: the war cry continued to rage: and at the end of four months our government found itself under the necessity to take the initiative, and recommence negotiations as the means of avoiding war. Accordingly, on the 22d of July, Mr. Buchanan (the direction of the President being always understood) addressed a note to Mr. Pakenham, resuming the negotiation at the point at which it had been left by Mr. Calhoun; and, conforming to the offer that he had made, and because he had made it, again proposed the line of 49 to the ocean. The British minister again refused that line, and inviting a "fairer" proposition. In the mean time the offer of 49 got wind. The democracy was in commotion. A storm was got up (foremost in raising which was the new administration organ, Mr. Ritchie's Daily Union), before which the administration quailed—recoiled—and withdrew its offer of 49. There was a dead pause in the negotiation again; and so the affair remained at the meeting of Congress, which came together under the loud cry of war, in which Mr. Cass was the leader, but followed by the body of the democracy, and backed and cheered on by the democratic press—some hundreds of papers. Of course the Oregon question occupied a place, and a prominent one, in the President's message—(which has been noticed)—and, on communicating the failure of the negotiation to Congress, he recommended strong measures for the security and assertion of our title. The delivery of the notice which was to abrogate the joint occupation of the country by the citizens of the two powers, was one of these recommendations, and the debate upon that question brought out the full expression of the opinions of Congress upon the whole subject, and took the management of the questions into the hands of the Senate and House of Representatives.

CHAPTER CLVII.

OREGON QUESTION: NOTICE TO ABROGATE THE ARTICLE IN THE TREATY FOR A JOINT OCCUPATION: THE PRESIDENT DENOUNCED IN THE SENATE FOR A SUPPOSED LEANING TO THE LINE OF FORTY-NINE.

The proposition for the line of 49 having been withdrawn by the American government on its non-acceptance by the British, had appeased the democratic storm which had been got up against the President; and his recommendation for strong measures to assert and secure our title was entirely satisfactory to those who now came to be called the Fifty-Four Forties. The debate was advancing well upon this question of notice, when a sinister rumor—only sinister to the extreme party—began to spread, that the British government would propose 49, and that the President was favorable to it. This rumor was true, and by way of preparing the public mind for it, Mr. William H. Haywood, a senator from North Carolina, both personally and politically friendly to the President, undertook to show, not so much that the line of 49 was right in itself, but that the President was not so far committed against it as that he could not yet form a treaty upon it. In this sense he—

> "Took a view of the course which had been pursued by the President, approving of the offer of the parallel of 49° to Great Britain, and maintaining that there was nothing in the language of the President to render it improper in him to negotiate hereafter on that basis, notwithstanding this rejection. He regarded the negotiation as still open; and he would not do the President so much wrong as to suppose that, if we passed the notice, and thus put into his hand a great moral weapon, that he could be guilty of so miserable a trick as to use it to the dishonor of his country on the one hand, or to the reckless provocation of a war on the other. Believing that the administration stood committed to accept an offer of a division of the territory on the parallel of 49°—or substantially that—he should sustain the Executive in that position. He expressed his conviction that, whatever might be his individual opinions, the President—as General Washington did in 1796—would fulfil his obligations to the country; that, whenever the interests of the country required it, he would sacrifice his own opinions to the sense of his official duty. He rebuked the cry which had been set up by some of the friends of the President, which placed him in the position of being the mere organ of the Baltimore convention, and declared that, if he could believe that the Executive would permit the resolution of that convention to overrule his duty to his country, he would turn his back upon him. Mr. H. then proceeded to deduce, from the language and acts of the Executive, that he had not put himself in a position which imposed on him the necessity of refusing to negotiate on the parallel of 49°, should negotiation be resumed on that basis. In this respect, the President did not occupy that attitude in which some of his friends wished to place him. It ought to be borne in mind that Great Britain had held occupancy for above forty years; and it was absurd to suppose, that, if we turn suddenly upon her and tell her she must quit, that she will not make resistance. And he asked what our government would be likely to do if placed in a similar position and reduced to the same alternative. No one could contend for a moment that the rejection of the offer of 49° by Great Britain released the President from the obligation to accept that offer whenever it should again be made. The question was to be settled by compromise; and, on this principle, the negotiation was still pending. It was not to be expected that a negotiation of this kind could be carried through hastily. Time must be given for communication with the British government, for proper consideration and consultation; and true politeness requires that ample time should be given for this purpose. It is obvious that Great Britain does not consider the negotiation terminated, as she would have recalled her minister; and the President cannot deem it closed, or he would have made a communication to Congress to that effect. The acts of the President were not such as to justify any apprehensions of a rupture; and from that, he did not ask for the notice in order that he might draw the sword and throw away the scabbard. The falsehood of any such charge is proved by the fact that he has asked for no enlargement of the annual appropriations; on the other hand, his estimates are rather diminished. Knowing him to be honest, he (Mr. H.) would

acquit him of any such imputation of moral treason, which would subject him to the reprobation of man and the anger of his God. Mr. H. then referred to the divisions which had sprung up in the democratic party, the tendency of which is, to destroy the party, by cutting off its heads. This question of Oregon had been turned into a party question, for the purpose of President-making. He repudiated any submission to the commands of factious meetings, got up by demagogues, for the purpose of dictating to the Senate how to make a treaty, and felt thankful that North Carolina had never taken this course. He did not regard such proceedings as indicative of that true democracy which, like a potato, grew at the root, and did not, like the spurious democracy, show itself from the blossom. The creed of the Baltimore convention directs the party to re-annex Texas and to *re-occupy* Oregon. Texas had been re-annexed, and now we are to go for the *re-occupation* of Oregon. Now, Old Oregon, embracing all the territory on which American foot ever trod, comprised merely the valley of Willamette, which did not extend above 49°; and consequently this portion was all which could be contemplated in the expression "re-occupation," as it would involve an absurdity to speak of re-occupying what we had never occupied. Referring to the history of the annexation of Texas, he cited the impossibility of getting Texas through, until the two questions had been made twin sisters by the Baltimore convention. Then Texas passed the House, and came into the Senate, followed so closely by Oregon, that they seemed to be akin."

In all this Mr. Haywood spoke the sentiments of the President, personally confided to him, and to prepare the way for his action in conformity to them. The extreme party suspected this, and had their plan arranged to storm it down, and to force the President to repulse the British offer of 49, if now it should be made, as he had been stormed into a withdrawal of his own offer of that line by his own newspapers and party in the recess of Congress. This task fell upon Mr. Hannegan of Indiana, and Mr. William Allen of Ohio, whose temperaments were better adapted to the work than that of their chief, Mr. Cass. Mr. Hannegan began:

"I must apologize to the Senate for obtruding myself upon your attention at this advanced period of the day, particularly as I have already occupied your attention on several occasions in the course of this debate. My remarks now, however, will be very brief. Before I proceed to make any reply to the speech of the senator from North Carolina—the most extraordinary speech which I have ever listened to in the whole course of my life—I desire, through the Vice President, to put a question to him, which I have committed to writing. It is this: I ask him if he has the authority of the President, directly or indirectly, for saying to the Senate that it is his (the President's) wish to terminate the Oregon question by compromising with Great Britain on the 49th degree of north latitude?"

To this categorical demand, Mr. Haywood replied that it would be unwise and impolitic for the President to authorize any senator to make such a declaration as that implied in the question of Mr. Hannegan. Mr. Allen, of Ohio, then took up the demand for the answer, and said:

"I put the question, and demand an answer to it as a public right. The senator here has assumed to speak for the President. His speech goes to the world; and I demand, as a public right, that he answer the question; and if he won't answer it, I stand ready to deny that he has expressed the views of the President."

Mr. Westcott of Florida, called Mr. Allen to order for asking for the opinions of the President through a senator. The President could only communicate his opinions to the Senate responsibly, by message. It would be a breach of privilege for any senator to undertake to report such opinions, and consequently a breach of order for any senator to call for them. In this Mr. Westcott was right, but the call to order did not prevent Mr. Allen from renewing his demand:

"I do not demand an answer as any personal right at all. I demand it as a public right. When a senator assumes to speak for the President, every senator possesses a public right to demand his authority for so doing. An avowal has been made that he is the exponent of the views of the President, upon a great national question. He has assumed to be that exponent. And I ask him whether he has the authority of the President for the assumption?"

Mr. Westcott renewed his call to order, but no question was taken upon the call, which must have been decided against Mr. Allen. Mr. Haywood said, he denied the right of any senator to put questions to him in that way, and said he had not assumed to speak by the authority of the President. Then, said Mr. Allen, the senator takes back his speech. Mr. Haywood: "Not at all; but I am glad to see my speech *takes*." Mr. Allen: "With the British." Mr. Hannegan then resumed:

"I do not deem it material whether the senator from North Carolina gives a direct answer to my question or not. It is entirely immaterial. He assumes—no, he says there is no assumption about it—that there is no meaning in language, no truth in man, if the President any where commits himself to 54° 40', as his flattering friends assume for him. Now, sir, there is no truth in man, there is no meaning in language, if the President is not committed to 54° 40' in as strong language as that which makes up the Holy Book. From a period antecedent to that in which he became the nominee of the Baltimore convention, down to this moment, to all the world he stands committed for 54° 40'. I go back to his declaration made in 1844, to a committee of citizens of Cincinnati, who addressed him in relation to the annexation of Texas, and he there uses this language being then before the country as the democratic candidate for the chair which he now fills.

"Mr. CRITTENDEN. What is the date?

"Mr. HANNEGAN. It is dated the 23d of April.

[Mr. H. here read an extract from Mr. Polk's letter to the committee of the citizens of Cincinnati.]"

Mr. Hannegan then went on to quote from the President's message—the annual message at the commencement of the session—to show that, in withdrawing his proposition for a boundary on the 49th parallel, he had taken a position against ever resuming it. He read this paragraph:

"The extraordinary and wholly inadmissible demands of the British Government, and the rejection of the proposition made in deference alone to what had been done by my predecessors, and the implied obligation which their acts seemed to impose, afford satisfactory evidence that no compromise which the United States ought to accept can be effected. With this conviction, the proposition of compromise which had been made and rejected was, by my direction, subsequently withdrawn, and our title to the whole Oregon Territory asserted, and, as is believed, maintained by irrefragable facts and arguments."

Having read this paragraph, Mr. Hannegan proceeded to reply to it; and exclaimed—

"What does the President here claim? Up to 54° 40'—every inch of it. He has asserted that claim, and is, as he says, sustained by 'irrefragable facts and arguments.' But this is not all: I hold that the language of the Secretary of State is the language of the President of the United States; and has not Mr. Buchanan, in his last communication to Mr. Pakenham, named 54° 40' in so many words? He has. The President adopts this language as his own. He plants himself on 54° 40'."

Mr. Hannegan then proceeded to plant the whole democratic party upon the line of 54-40, and to show that Oregon to that extent, and Texas to her whole extent, were the watchwords of the party in the presidential election—that both were to be carried together; and Texas having been gained, Oregon, without treachery, could not be abandoned.

"The democratic party is thus bound to the whole of Oregon—every foot of it; and let the senator rise in his place who will tell me in what quarter of this Union—in what assembly of democrats in this Union, pending the presidential election, the names of Texas and Oregon did not fly together, side by side, on the democratic banners. Every where they were twins—

every where they were united. Does the senator from North Carolina suppose that he, with his appeals to the democracy, can blind our eyes, as he thinks he tickled our ears? He is mistaken. 'Texas and Oregon' cannot be divided; they dwell together in the American heart. Even in Texas, I have been told the flag of the lone star had inscribed on it the name of Oregon. Then, it was all Oregon. Now, when you have got Texas, it means just so much of Oregon as you in your kindness and condescension think proper to give us. You little know us, if you think the mighty West will be trodden on in this way."

Mr. Hannegan then undertook to disclaim for the President the sentiments attributed to him by Mr. Haywood, and to pronounce an anathema upon him if the attribution was right.

"The senator in his defence of the President, put language into his mouth which I undertake to say the President will repudiate, and I am not the President's champion. I wish not to be his champion. I would not be the champion of power. I defend the right, and the right only. But, for the President, I deny the intentions which the senator from North Carolina attributes to him—intentions, which, if really entertained by him, would make him an infamous man— ay, an infamous man. He [Mr. Haywood] told the Senate yesterday—unless I grossly misunderstood him, along with several friends around me—'that the President had occasionally stickings-in, parenthetically, to gratify—what?—the ultraisms of the country and of party; whilst he reposed in the White House with no intentions of carrying out these parenthetical stickings-in.' In plain words, he represents the President as parenthetically sticking in a few hollow and false words to cajole the 'ultraisms of the country?' What is this, need I ask, but charging upon the President conduct the most vile and infamous? If this allegation be true, these intentions of the President must sooner or later come to light, and when brought to light, what must follow but irretrievable disgrace? So long as one human eye remains to linger on the page of history, the story of his abasement will be read, sending him and his name together to an infamy so profound, a damnation so deep, that the hand of resurrection will never be able to drag him forth."

Mr. Mangum called Mr. Hannegan to order: Mr. Haywood desired that he might be permitted to proceed, which he did, disclaiming all disrespect to Mr. Haywood, and concluded with saying; that, "so far as the whole tone, spirit, and meaning of the remarks of the senator from North Carolina is concerned, if they speak the language of James K. Polk, then James K. Polk has spoken words of falsehood with the tongue of a serpent."

Mr. Reverdy Johnson came to the relief of the President and Mr. Haywood in a temperate and well-considered speech, in which he showed he had had great apprehension of war—that this apprehension was becoming less, and that he deemed it probable, and right and honorable in itself, that the President should meet the British on the line of 49 if they should come to it; and that line would save the territorial rights of the United States, and the peace and honor of the country.

"It is with unaffected embarrassment I rise to address the Senate on the subject now under consideration; but its great importance and the momentous issues involved in its final settlement are such as compel me, notwithstanding my distrust of my own ability to be useful to my country, to make the attempt. We have all felt that, at one time at least (I trust that time is now past), we were in imminent danger of war. From the moment the President of the United States deemed it right and becoming, in the outset of his official career, to announce to the world that our title to Oregon was clear and unquestionable, down to the period of his message to Congress in December last, when he reiterated the declaration, I could not see how it was possible that war should be averted. That apprehension was rendered much more intense from the character of the debates elsewhere, as well as from the speeches of some of the President's political friends within this chamber. I could not but listen with alarm and dismay to what fell from the very distinguished and experienced senator from Michigan (Mr. Cass) at an early period of this debate; to what I heard from the senator from Indiana (Mr. Hannegan); and, above all, to what was said by the senator from Ohio (Mr. Allen), the chairman of the Committee on Foreign Relations, who, in my simplicity, I supposed must necessarily be apprised of the views of the government in regard to the foreign concerns of the country. Supposing the condition of the country to be what it was represented to be by each and all of the three senators, I could not imagine how it could be possible that the most direful of all human calamities, war, was to be avoided; and I was accordingly prepared to say, on the hypothesis of the fact assumed by the senator from Michigan, that war was inevitable;—to use his own paraphrase of his own term, which, it would appear, has got out of favor with himself—'war must come.'

"What did they represent to be the condition of the nation? I speak now more particularly of the last two senators, from Indiana and Ohio. They told us that negotiation was at an end; that we were now thrown back on our original rights; that, by these original rights, as had been officially announced, our title to the whole country was beyond all question: and that the national honor must be forfeited, if that title should not be maintained by force of arms. I felt that he must have been a careless and a profitless reader of English history who could indulge the hope that, if such was to be the course and conduct of this country, war was not inevitable. Then, in addition to my own opinion, when I heard it admitted by the honorable senator from Michigan, with that perfect candor which always distinguishes him on this floor, that, in his opinion, England would never recede, I felt that war was inevitable.

"I now rejoice in hoping and believing, from what I have subsequently heard, that the fears of the Senate, as well as my own apprehensions, were, as I think, unfounded. Since then, the statesmanlike view taken by the senator from New York who first addressed us (Mr. Dix), and by the senator from Missouri (Mr. Benton), to whom this whole question is as familiar as a household term—and the spirit of peace which breathed in their every word—have fully satisfied me that, so far as depends upon them, a fair and liberal compromise of our difficulties would not be in want of willing and zealous advocates.

"And this hope has been yet more strengthened by the recent speech of the senator from North Carolina (Mr. Haywood), not now in his place. Knowing, as I thought I did, the intimate relations, both personal and political, which that senator bore to the Chief Magistrate—knowing, too, that, as chairman of the Committee on Commerce, it was his special duty to become informed in regard to all matters having a bearing on the foreign relations of the country; I did not doubt, and I do not now doubt, that in every thing he said as to the determination of the President to accept, if offered by the British government, the same terms which he had himself proposed in July last, the reasonable inference was, that such an offer, if made, would be accepted. I do not mean to say, because I did not so understand the senator, that, in addressing this body with regard to the opinions or purposes of the President, he spoke by any express or delegated authority. But I do mean to say, that I have no doubt, from his knowledge of the general views of the President, as expressed in his message, taken in connection with certain omissions on the part of the Executive, that when he announced to us that the President would feel himself in honor bound to accept his own offer, if now reciprocated by Great Britain, he spoke that which he knew to be true. And this opinion was yet more strengthened and confirmed by what I found to be the effect of his speech on the two senators I have named—the leaders, if they will permit me to call them so, of the ultraists on this subject—I mean the senator from Indiana (Mr. Hannegan), and the senator from Ohio (Mr. Allen). He was an undiscerning witness of the scene which took place in this chamber immediately after the speech of the senator from North Carolina (Mr. Haywood), who must not have seen that those two senators had consulted together with the view of ascertaining how far the senator from North Carolina spoke by authority, and that the result of their consultation was a determination to catechise that senator; and the better to avoid all mistake, that they reduced their interrogatory to writing, in order that it might be propounded to him by the senator from Indiana (Mr. Hannegan); and if it was not answered, that it was then to be held as constructively answered by the senator from Ohio (Mr. Allen). What the result of the manœuvre was I leave it to the Senate to decide; but this I will venture to say, that in the keen encounter of wits, to which their colloquy led, the two senators who commenced it got rather the worst of the contest. My hope and belief has been yet further strengthened by what has NOT since happened; I mean my belief in the pacific views of the Chief Magistrate. The speech of the senator from North Carolina was made on Thursday, and though a week has nearly elapsed since that time, notwithstanding the anxious solicitude of both those senators, and their evident desire to set the public right on that subject, we have, from that day to this, heard from neither of the gentlemen the slightest intimation that the construction given to the message by the senator from North Carolina was not a true one."

Mr. Johnson continued his speech on the merits of the question—the true line which should divide the British and American possessions beyond the Rocky Mountains; and placed it on the parallel of 49° according to the treaty of Utrecht, and in conformity with the opinions and diplomatic instructions of Mr. Jefferson, who had acquired Louisiana and sent an expedition of discovery to the Pacific Ocean, and had well studied the whole question of our territorial rights in that quarter. Mr. Benton did not speak in this incidental debate, but he knew that Mr. Haywood spoke with a knowledge of the President's sentiments, and according to his wishes, and to prepare the country for a treaty upon 49°. He knew this, because he was in consultation with the President, and was to speak for the same purpose, and was urged by him to speak immediately in consequence of the attempt to crush Mr. Haywood—the first of his friends who had given any intimation of his views. Mr. Benton, therefore, at an early day, spoke at large upon the question when it took another form—that of a bill to establish a territorial government for Oregon; some extracts from which constitute the next chapter.

CHAPTER CLVIII.

OREGON TERRITORIAL GOVERNMENT: BOUNDARIES AND HISTORY OF THE COUNTRY: FRAZER'S RIVER: TREATY OF UTRECHT: MR. BENTON'S SPEECH: EXTRACTS.

Mr. Benton then addressed the Senate. Mr. President, the bill before the Senate proposes to extend the sovereignty and jurisdiction of the United States over all our territories west of the Rocky Mountains, without saying what is the extent and what are the limits of this territory. This is wrong, in my opinion. We ought to define the limits within which our agents are to do such acts as this bill contemplates, otherwise we commit to them the solution of questions which we find too hard for ourselves. This indefinite extension of authority, in a case which requires the utmost precision, forces me to speak, and to give my opinion of the true extent of our territories beyond the Rocky Mountains. I have delayed doing this during the whole session, not from any desire to conceal my opinions (which, in fact, were told to all that asked for them), but because I thought it the business of negotiation, not of legislation, to settle these boundaries. I waited for negotiation: but negotiation lags, while events go forward; and now we are in the process of acting upon measures, upon the adoption of which it may no longer be in the power either of negotiation or of legislation to control the events to which they may give rise. The bill before us is without definition of the territory to be occupied. And why this vagueness in a case requiring the utmost precision? Why not define the boundaries of these territories? Precisely because we do not know them! And this presents a case which requires me to wait no longer for negotiation, but to come forward with my own opinions, and to do what I can to prevent the evils of vague and indefinite legislation. My object will be to show, if I can, the true extent and nature of our territorial claims beyond the Rocky Mountains, with a view to just and wise decisions; and, in doing so, I shall endeavor to act upon the great maxim, "Ask nothing but what is right—submit to nothing that is wrong."

It is my ungracious task, in attempting to act upon this maxim, to commence by exposing error at home, and endeavoring to clear up some great mistakes under which the public mind has labored.

It has been assumed for two years, and the assumption has been made the cause of all the Oregon excitement of the country, that we have a dividing line with Russia, made so by the convention of 1824, along the parallel of 54° 40', from the sea to the Rocky Mountains, up to which our title is good. This is a great mistake. No such line was ever established; and so far as proposed and discussed, it was proposed and discussed as a northern British, and not as a northern American line. The public treaties will prove there is no such line; documents will prove that, so far as 54° 40', from the sea to the mountains, was ever proposed as a northern boundary for any power, it was proposed by us for the British, and not for ourselves.

To make myself intelligible in what I shall say on this point, it is necessary to go back to the epoch of the Russian convention of 1824, and to recall the recollection of the circumstances out of which that convention grew. The circumstances were these: In the year 1821 the Emperor Alexander, acting upon a leading idea of Russian policy (in relation to the North Pacific Ocean) from the time of Peter the Great, undertook to treat that ocean as a close sea, and to exercise municipal authority over a great extent of its shores and waters. In September of that year, the emperor issued a decree, bottomed upon this pretension, assuming exclusive sovereignty and jurisdiction over both shores of the North Pacific Ocean, and over the high seas, in front of each coast, to the extent of one hundred Italian miles, from Behring's Straits down to latitude fifty-one, on the American coast, and to forty-five on the Asiatic; and denouncing the penalties of confiscation upon all ships, of whatsoever nation that should approach the coasts within the interdicted distances. This was a very startling decree. Coming from a feeble nation, it would have been smiled at; coming from Russia, it gave uneasiness to all nations.

Great Britain and the United States, as having the largest commerce in the North Pacific Ocean, and as having large territorial claims on the north-west coast of America, were the first to take the alarm, and to send remonstrances to St. Petersburg against the formidable ukase. They found themselves suddenly thrown together, and standing side by side in this new and portentous contest with Russia. They remonstrated in concert, and here the wise and pacific conduct of the Emperor Alexander displayed itself in the most prompt and honorable manner. He immediately suspended the ukase (which, in fact, had remained without execution), and invited the United States and Great Britain to unite with Russia in a convention to settle amicably, and in a spirit of mutual convenience, all the questions between them, and especially their respective territorial claims on the north-west coast of America. This magnanimous proposition was immediately met by the two powers in a corresponding spirit; and, the ukase being voluntarily relinquished by the emperor, a convention was quickly signed by Russia with each power, settling, so far as Russia was concerned, with each, all their territorial claims in North-west America. The Emperor Alexander had proposed that it should be a joint convention of the three powers—a tripartite convention—settling the claims of each and of all at the same time; and if this wise suggestion had been followed, all the subsequent and all the present difficulties between the United States and Great Britain, with respect to this territory, would have been entirely avoided. But it was not followed: an act of our own prevented it. After Great Britain had consented, the non-colonization principle—the principle of non-colonization in America by any European power—was promulgated by our government, and for that reason Great Britain chose to treat separately with each power, and so it was done.

Great Britain and the United States treated separately with Russia, and with each other; and each came to agreements with Russia, but to none among themselves. The agreements with Russia were contained in two conventions signed nearly at the same time, and nearly in the same words, limiting the territorial claim of Russia to 54° 40', confining her to the coasts and islands, and leaving the continent, out to the Rocky Mountains, to be divided between the United States and Great Britain, by an agreement between themselves. The emperor finished up his own business and quit the concern. In fact, it would seem, from the promptitude, moderation, and fairness with which he adjusted all differences both with the United States and Great Britain, that his only object of issuing the alarming ukase of 1821 was to bring those powers to a settlement; acting upon the homely, but wise maxim, that short settlements make long friends.

Well, there is no such line as 54° 40'; and that would seem to be enough to quiet the excitement which has been got up about it. But there is more to come. I set out with saying, that although this fifty-four forty was never established as a northern boundary for the United States, yet it was proposed to be established as a northern boundary, not for us, but for Great Britain—and that proposal was made to Great Britain by ourselves. This must sound like a strange statement in the ears of the fifty-four forties; but it is no more strange than true; and after stating the facts, I mean to prove them. The plan of the United States at that time was this: That each of the three powers (Great Britain, Russia, and the United States) having claims on the north-west coast of America, should divide the country between them, each taking a third. In this plan of partition, each was to receive a share of the continent from the sea to the Rocky Mountains, Russia taking the northern slice, the United States the southern, and Great Britain the centre, with fifty-four forty for her northern boundary, and forty-nine for her southern. The document from which I now read will say fifty-one; but that was the first offer—forty-nine was the real one, as I will hereafter show. This was our plan. The moderation of Russia defeated it. That power had no settlements on that part of the continent, and rejected the continental share which we offered her. She limited herself to the coasts and islands where she had settlements, and left Great Britain and the United States to share the continent between themselves. But before this was known, we had proposed to her fifty-four forty for the Russian southern boundary, and to Great Britain the same for her northern boundary. I say fifty-four forty; for, although the word in the proposition was fifty-five, yet it was on the principle which gave fifty-four forty—namely, running from the south end of Prince of Wales' Island, supposed to be in fifty-five, but found to have a point to it running down to fifty-four forty. We proposed this to Great Britain. She refused it, saying she would establish her northern boundary with Russia, who was on her north, and not with the United States, who was on her south. This seemed reasonable; and the United States then, and not until then, relinquished the business of pressing fifty-four forty upon Great Britain for her northern boundary. The proof is in the executive documents. Here it is—a despatch from Mr. Rush, our minister in London, to Mr. Adams, Secretary of State, dated December 19, 1823.

(The despatch read.)

> Here is the offer, in the most explicit terms, in 1823, to make fifty-five, which was in fact fifty-four forty, the northern boundary of Great Britain; and here is her answer to that proposition. It is the next paragraph in the same despatch from Mr. Rush to Mr. Adams.

(The answer read.)

> This was her answer, refusing to take, in 1823, as a northern boundary coming south for quantity, what is now prescribed to her, at the peril of war, for a southern boundary, with nothing north!—for, although the fact happens to be that Russia is not there, bounding us on the north, yet that makes no difference in the philosophy of our Fifty-four-Forties, who believe it to be so; and, on that belief, are ready to fight. Their notion is, that we go jam up to 54° 40', and the Russians come jam down to the same, leaving no place for the British lion to put down a paw, although that paw should be no bigger than the sole of the dove's foot which sought a resting-place from Noah's ark. This must seem a little strange to British statesmen, who do not grow so fast as to leave all knowledge behind them. They remember that Mr. Monroe and his cabinet—the President and cabinet who acquired the Spanish title under which we now propose to squeeze them out of the continent—actually offered them six degrees of latitude in that very place; and they will certainly want reasons for this so much compression now, where we offered them so much expansion then. These reasons cannot be given. There is no boundary at 54° 40'; and so far as we proposed to make it one, it was for the British and not for ourselves; and so ends this redoubtable line, up to which all true patriots were to march! and marching, fight! and fighting, die! if need be! singing all the while, with Horace—

> "Dulce et decorum est pro patria mori."

I come to the line of Utrecht, the existence of which is denied upon this floor by senators whose fate it seems to be to assert the existence of a line that is not, and to deny the existence of one that is. A clerk in the Department of State has compiled a volume of voyages and of treaties, and, undertaking to set the world right, has denied that commissioners ever met under the treaty of Utrecht, and fixed boundaries between the British northern and French Canadian possessions in North America. That denial has been produced and accredited on this floor by a senator in his place (Mr. Cass); and this production of a blundering book, with this senatorial endorsement of its blunder, lays me under the necessity of correcting a third error which the "fifty-four-forties" hug to their bosom, and the correction of which becomes necessary for the vindication of history, the establishment of a political right, and the protection of the Senate from the suspicion of ignorance. I affirm that the line was established; that the commissioners met and did their work; and that what they did has been acquiesced in by all the powers interested from the year 1713 down to the present time.

In the year 1805, being the second year after the acquisition of Louisiana, President Jefferson sent ministers to Madrid (Messrs. Monroe and Charles Pinckney) to adjust the southern and southwestern boundaries with her; and, in doing so, the principles which had governed the settlement of the northern boundary of the same province became a proper illustration of their ideas. They quoted these principles, and gave the line of Utrecht as the example; and this to Don Pedro Cevallos, one of the most accomplished statesmen of Europe. They say to him:

> "It is believed that this principle has been admitted and acted on invariably since the discovery of America, in respect to their possessions there, by all the European powers. It is particularly illustrated by the stipulations of their most important treaties concerning those possessions and the practice under them, viz., the treaty of Utrecht in 1713, and that of Paris in 1763. In conformity with the 10th article of the first-mentioned treaty, the boundary between Canada and Louisiana on the one side, and the Hudson Bay and Northwestern Companies on the other, was established by commissioners, by a line to commence at a cape or promontory on the ocean, in 58° 31' north latitude; to run thence, southwestwardly, to latitude 49° north from the equator; and along that line indefinitely westward. Since that time, no attempt has been made to extend the limits of Louisiana or Canada to the *north* of that line, or of those companies to the *south* of it, by purchase, conquest, or grants from the Indians."

This is what Messrs. Monroe and Charles Pinckney said to Don Pedro Cevallos—a minister who must be supposed to be as well acquainted with the treaties which settled the boundaries of the late Spanish province of Louisiana as we are with the treaties which settle the boundaries of the United States. The line of Utrecht, and in the very words which carry it from the Lake of the Woods to the Pacific Ocean, and which confine the British to the north, and the French and Spanish to the south of that line, are quoted to Mr. Cevallos as a fact which he and all the world knew. He received it as such; and thus Spanish authority comes in aid of British, French, and American, to vindicate our rights and the truth of history.

(The letter was read.)

Another contribution, which I have pleasure to acknowledge, is from a gentleman of Baltimore, formerly of the House of Representatives (Mr. Kennedy), who gives me an extract from the Journal of the British House of Commons, March 5th, 1714, directing a writ to be issued for electing a burgess in the place of Frederick Herne, Esq., who, since his election, hath accepted, as the Journal says, the office of one of his Majesty's commissioners for treating with commissioners on the part of France for settling the trade between Great Britain and France. The same entry occurs at the same time with respect to James Murray, Esq., and Sir Joseph Martyn. The tenth article of the treaty of Utrecht applies to limits in North America, the eleventh and fifteenth to commerce; and these commissioners were appointed under some or all of these articles. Others might have been appointed by the king, and not mentioned in the journals, as not being members of Parliament whose vacated seats were to be filled. All three of the articles of the treaty were equally obligatory for the appointment of commissioners; and here is proof that three were appointed under the commercial articles.

One more piece of testimony, and I have done. And, first, a little statement to introduce it. We all know that in one of the debates which took place in the British House of Commons on the Ashburton treaty, and after that treaty was ratified and past recall, mention was made of a certain map called the King's map, which had belonged to the late King (George III.), and hung in his library during his lifetime, and afterwards in the Foreign Office, from which said office the said map silently disappeared about the time of the Ashburton treaty, and which certainly was not before our Senate at the time of the ratification of that treaty. Well, the member who mentioned it in Parliament said there was a strong red line upon it, about the tenth of an inch wide, running all along where the Americans said the true boundary was, with these words written along it in four places in King George's handwriting: "*This is Oswald's line*," meaning, it is the line of the treaty of peace negotiated by Mr. Oswald on the British side, and therefore called *Oswald's line*.

Now, what I have to say is this: That whenever this royal map shall emerge from its retreat and resume its place in the Foreign Office, on it will be found another strong red line about the tenth of an inch wide, in another place, with these words written on it: Boundaries between the British and French possessions in America "*as fixed by the treaty of Utrecht*." To complete this last and crowning piece of testimony, I have to add that the evidence of it is in the Department of State, as is nearly the whole of the evidence which I have used in crushing this *pie-poudre* insurrection—"*this puddle-lane rebellion*"—against the truth and majesty of history, which, beginning with a clerk in the Department of State, spread to all the organs, big and little; then reached the Senate of the United States, held divided empire in this chamber for four months, and now dies the death of the ridiculous.[9]

We must now introduce the gentlemen of 54-40 to Frazer's River, an acquaintance which they will be obliged to make before they arrive at their inexorable line; for it lies in their course, and must be crossed—both itself and the British province of New Caledonia, which it waters. This, then, is the introduction to that inevitable acquaintance, hitherto ignored. It is a river of about a thousand miles in length (following its windings), rising in the Rocky Mountains, opposite the head of the Unjigah, or Peace River, which flows into the Frozen Ocean in latitude about 70. The course of this river is nearly north and south, rising in latitude 55, flowing south to near latitude 49, and along that parallel, and just north of it, to the Gulf of Georgia, into which it falls behind Vancouver's Island. The upper part of this river is good for navigation; the lower half, plunging through volcanic chasms in mountains of rock, is wholly unnavigable for any species of craft. This river was discovered by Sir Alexander Mackenzie in 1793, was settled by the Northwest Company in 1806, and soon covered by their establishments from head to mouth. No American or Spaniard had ever left a track upon this river or its valley. Our claim to it, as far as I can see, rested wholly upon the treaty with Spain of 1819; and her claim rested wholly upon those discoveries among the islands, the value of which, as conferring claims upon the continent, it has been my province to show in our negotiations with Russia in 1824. At the time that we acquired this

Spanish claim to Frazer's River, it had already been discovered twenty-six years by the British; had been settled by them for twelve years; was known by a British name; and no Spaniard had ever made a track on its banks. New Caledonia, or Western Caledonia, was the name which it then bore; and it so happens that an American citizen, a native of Vermont, respectably known to the senators now present from that State, and who had spent twenty years of his life in the hyperborean regions of Northwest America, in publishing an account of his travels and sojournings in that quarter, actually published a description of this New Caledonia, as a British province, at the very moment that we were getting it from Spain, and without the least suspicion that it belonged to Spain! I speak of Mr. David Harmon, whose Journal of Nineteen Years' Residence between latitudes 47 and 58 in Northwestern America, was published at Andover, in his native State, in the year 1820, the precise year after we had purchased this New Caledonia from the Spaniards. I read, not from the volume itself, which is not in the library of Congress, but from the London Quarterly Review January No., 1822, as reprinted in Boston; article, WESTERN CALEDONIA.

(The extract.)

This is the account given by Mr. Harmon of New Caledonia, and given of it by him at the exact moment that we were purchasing the Spanish title to it! Of this Spanish title, of which the Spaniards never heard, the narrator seems to have been as profoundly ignorant as the Spaniards were themselves; and made his description of New Caledonia as of a British possession, without any more reference to an adverse title than if he had been speaking of Canada. So much for the written description: now let us look at the map, and see how it stands there. Here is a map—a 54° 40' map—which will show us the features of the country, and the names of the settlements upon it. Here is Frazer's River, running from 55° to 49° and here is a line of British posts upon it, from Fort McLeod, at its head, to Fort Langley, at its mouth, and from Thompson's Fork, on one side, to Stuart's Fork on the other. And here are clusters of British names, imposed by the British, visible every where—Forts George, St. James, Simpson, Thompson, Frazer, McLeod, Langley, and others: rivers and lakes with the same names, and others: and here is Deserter's Creek, so named by Mackenzie, because his guide deserted him there in July, 1793; and here is an Indian village which he named Friendly, because the people were the most friendly to strangers that he had ever seen; and here another called Rascals' village, so named by Mackenzie fifty-three years ago, because its inhabitants were the most rascally Indians he had ever seen; and here is the representation of that famous boundary line 54° 40', which is supposed to be the exact boundary of American territorial rights in that quarter, and which happens to include the whole of New Caledonia, except McLeod's fort, and the whole of Stuart's lake, and a spring, which is left to the British, while we take the branch which flows from it. This line takes all in—river, lakes, forts, villages. See how it goes! Starting at the sea, it gives us, by a quarter of an inch on the map, Fort Simpson, so named after the British Governor Simpson, and founded by the Hudson Bay Company. Upon what principle we take this British fort I know not—except it be on the assumption that our sacred right and title being adjusted to a minute, by the aid of these 40 minutes, so appositely determined by the Emperor Paul's charter to a fur company in 1799, to be on this straight line, the bad example of even a slight deviation from it at the start should not be allowed even to spare a British fort away up at Point McIntyre, in Chatham Sound. On this principle we can understand the inclusion, by a quarter of an inch on the map, of this remote and isolated British post. The cutting in two of Stuart's lake, which the line does as it runs, is quite intelligible: it must be on the principle stated in one of the fifty-four-forty papers, that Great Britain should not have one drop of our water; therefore we divide the lake, each taking their own share of its drops. The fate of the two forts, McLeod and St. James, so near each other and so far off from us, united all their lives, and now so unexpectedly divided from each other by this line, is less comprehensible; and I cannot account for the difference of their fates, unless it is upon the law of the day of judgment, when, of two men in the field, one shall be taken and the other left, and no man be able to tell the reason why. All the rest of the inclusions of British establishments which the line makes, from head to mouth of Frazer's River, are intelligible enough: they turn upon the principle of all or none!—upon the principle that every acre and every inch, every grain of sand, drop of water, and blade of grass in all Oregon, up to fifty-four forty, is ours! and have it we will.

This is the country which geography and history five-and-twenty years ago called New Caledonia, and treated as a British possession; and it is the country which an *organized* party among ourselves of the present day call "*the whole of Oregon or none*," and every inch of which they say belongs to us. Well, let us proceed a little further with the documents of 1823, and see what the men of that day—President Monroe and his cabinet—the men who made the treaty with Spain by which we became the masters of this large domain: let us proceed a little further, and see what they thought of our title up to fifty-four forty. I read from the same document of 1823:

Mr. Adams to Mr. Middleton, July, 22, 1823.

"The right of the United States, from the forty-second to the forty-ninth parallel of latitude on the Pacific Ocean we consider as unquestionable, being founded, first, on the acquisition by the treaty of 22d February, 1819, of all the rights of Spain; second, by the discovery of the Columbia River, first from the sea at its mouth, and then by land, by Lewis and Clarke; and, third, by the settlement at its mouth in 1811. This territory is to the United States of an importance which no possession in North America can be of to any European nation, not only as it is but the continuity of their possessions from the Atlantic to the Pacific Ocean, but as it offers their inhabitants the means of establishing hereafter water communications from the one to the other."

From 42° to 49° is here laid down by Mr. Monroe and his cabinet as the extent of our unquestionable title, and on these boundaries they were ready to settle the question. Five other despatches the same year from Mr. Adams to Mr. Rush, our minister in London, offer the same thing. They all claim the valley of the Columbia River, and nothing more. They claim the land drained by its waters, and no more; but as the Columbia had a northern prong, drawing water just under the mountains from as far north as 51°—yes! 51—not 54-40, they offered to cut off the head of that prong, and take the line of 49, which included all that was worth having of the waters of the Columbia, and left out, but barely left out, Frazer's River—coming within three miles of it at its mouth.

On Friday, Mr. President, I read one passage from the documents of 1823, to let you see that fifty-four forty (for that is the true reading of fifty-five) had been offered to Great Britain for her northern boundary: to-day I read you six PASSAGES from the same documents, to show the same thing. And let me remark once more— the remark will bear eternal repetition—these offers were made by the men who had acquired the Spanish title to Oregon! and who must be presumed to know as much about it as those whose acquaintance with Oregon dates from the epoch of the Baltimore convention—whose love for it dates from the era of its promulgation as a party watchword—whose knowledge of it extends to the luminous pages of Mr. Greenhow's horn-book!

Six times Mr. Monroe and his cabinet renounced Frazer's River and its valley, and left it to the British! They did so on the intelligible principle that the British had discovered it, and settled it, and were in the actual possession of it when we got the Spanish claim; which claim Spain never made! Upon this principle, New Caledonia was left to the British in 1823. Upon what *principle* is it claimed now?

This is what Mr. Monroe and his cabinet thought of our title to the whole of Oregon or none, in the year 1823. They took neither branch of this proposition. They did not go for all or none, but for some! They took some, and left some; and they divided by a line right in itself, and convenient in itself, and mutually suitable to each party. That President and his cabinet carry their "unquestionable right" to Oregon as far as 49°, and no further. This is exactly what was done six years before. Mr. Gallatin and Mr. Rush offered the same line, as being a continuation of the line of Utrecht (describing it by that name in their despatch of October 20th, 1818), and as covering the valley of the Columbia River, to which they alleged our title to be indisputable. Mr. Jefferson had offered the same line in 1807. All these offers leave Frazer's River and its valley to the British, because they discovered and settled it. All these offers hold on to the Columbia River and its valley, because we discovered and settled it; and all these offers let the principle of contiguity or continuity work equally on the British as on the American side of the line of Utrecht.

This is what the statesmen did who made the acquisition of the Spanish claim to Oregon in 1819. In four years afterwards they had freely offered all north of 49 to Great Britain; and no one ever thought of arraigning them for it. Most of these statesmen have gone through fiery trials since, and been fiercely assailed on all the deeds of their lives; but I never heard of one of them being called to account, much less lose an election, for the part he acted in offering 49 to Great Britain in 1823, or at any other time. For my part, I thought they were right then, and I think so now; I was senator then, as I am now. I thought with them that New Caledonia belonged to the British; and thinking so still, and acting upon the first half of the great maxim—Ask nothing but what is right—I shall not ask them for it, much less fight them for it now.

CHAPTER CLIX.

OREGON JOINT OCCUPATION: NOTICE AUTHORIZED FOR TERMINATING IT: BRITISH GOVERNMENT OFFERS THE LINE OF 49: QUANDARY OF THE ADMINISTRATION: DEVICE: SENATE CONSULTED: TREATY MADE AND RATIFIED.

The abrogation of the article in the conventions of 1818 and 1828, for the joint occupation of the Columbia, was a measure right in itself, indispensable in the actual condition of the territory—colonies from two nations planting themselves upon it together—and necessary to stimulate the conclusion of the treaty which was to separate the possessions of the two countries. Every consideration required the notice to be given, and Congress finally voted it; but not without a struggle in each House, longer and more determined than the disparity of the vote would indicate. In the House of Representatives, the vote in its favor was 154—headed by Mr. John Quincy Adams: the nays were 54. The resolution as adopted by the House, then went to the Senate for its concurrence, where, on the motion of Mr. Reverdy Johnson, of Maryland, it underwent a very material alteration in form, without impairing its effect, adopting a preamble containing the motives for the notice, and of which the leading were to show that amicable settlement of the title by negotiation was an object in view, and intended to be promoted by a separation of interests between the parties. Thus amended, the resolution was passed by a good majority—40 to 14. The yeas and nays were:

> Messrs. Archer, Ashley, Atherton, Bagby, Barrow, Benton, Berrien, Calhoun, Cameron, Chalmers, John M. Clayton, Corwin, Crittenden, Davis, Dayton, Dix, Greene, Haywood, Houston, Huntington, Jarnagin, Johnson of Maryland, Johnson of Louisiana, Lewis, McDuffie, Mangum, Miller, Morehead, Niles, Pearce, Pennybacker, Phelps, Rusk, Sevier, Simmons, Speight, Turney, Upham, Webster, Woodbridge.

The nays were:

> Messrs. Allen, Atchison, Breese, Bright, Cass, Thomas Clayton, Dickinson, Evans, Fairfield, Hannegan, Jenness, Semple, Sturgeon, Westcott.

These nays were not all opposed to the notice itself, but to the form it had adopted, and to the clause which left it discretional with the President to give it when he should think proper. They constituted the body of the extreme friends of Oregon, standing on the Baltimore platform—"the whole of Oregon or none"—looking to war as inevitable, and who certainly would have made it if their course had been followed. In the House the Senate's amendment was substantially adopted, and by an increased vote; and the authority for terminating the joint occupancy—a great political blunder in itself, and fraught with dangerous consequences—was eventually given, but after the lapse of a quarter of a century, and after bringing the two countries to the brink of hostilities. The President acted at once upon the discretion which was given him—caused the notice for the abrogation of the joint occupant article to be immediately given to the British government—and urged Congress to the adoption of the measures which were necessary for the protection of the American citizens who had gone to the territory.

The news of the broken off negotiations was received with regret in Great Britain. Sir Robert Peel, with the frankness and integrity which constitute the patriotic statesman, openly expressed his regret in Parliament that the offer of 49, when made by the American government, had not been accepted by the British government; and it was evident that negotiations would be renewed. They were so: and in a way to induce a speedy conclusion of the question—being no less than a fair and open offer on the side of the British to accept the line we had offered. The administration was in a quandary (qu'en dirai-je? what shall I say to it?), at this unexpected offer. They felt that it was just, and that it ought to be accepted: at the same time they had stood upon the platform of the Baltimore convention—had helped to make it—had had the benefit of it in the election; and were loth to show themselves inconsistent, or ignorant. Besides the fifty-four forties were in commotion against it. A specimen of their temper has been shown in Mr. Hannegan's denunciation of the President. All the government newspapers—the official organ at Washington City, and the five hundred democratic papers throughout the Union which followed its lead, were all vehement against it. Underhandedly they did what they could to allay the storm which was raging—encouraging Mr. Haywood, Mr. Benton, and others to speak; but the pride of consistency, and the fear of reproach, kept them in the background, and even ostensibly in favor of 54-40, while encouraging the events which would enable them to settle on 49. Mr. Pakenham made his offer: it was not a case for delay: and acceptance or rejection became inevitable. It was accepted; and nothing remained but to put the treaty into form. A device was necessary, and it was found in the early practice of the government—that of the President asking the advice of the Senate upon the articles of a treaty before the negotiation. Mr. Benton proposed this course to Mr. Polk. He was pleased with it, but feared its feasibility. The advice of the Senate would be his sufficient shield: but could it be obtained? The chances seemed to be against it. It was an up-hill business, requiring a vote of two-thirds: it was a novelty, not practised since the time of Washington: it was a submission to the whigs, with the risk of defeat; for unless they stood by the President against the dominant division of his own friends, the advice desired would not be given; and the embarrassment of the administration would be greater than ever. In this uneasy and uncertain state of mind, the President had many conferences with Mr. Benton, the point of which was to know, beyond the chance of mistake, how far he could rely upon the whig senators. Mr. Benton talked with them all—with Webster, Archer, Berrien, John M. Clayton, Crittenden, Corwin, Davis of Massachusetts, Dayton, Greene of Rhode Island, Huntington of Connecticut, Reverdy Johnson, Henry Johnson of Louisiana, Miller of New Jersey, Phelps, Simmons, Upham, Woodbridge,—and saw fully that they intended to act for their country, and not for their party: and reported to the President that he would be safe in trusting to them—that their united voice would be in favor of the advice, which, added to the minority of the democracy, would make the two-thirds which were requisite. The most auspicious mode of applying for this advice was deemed to be the submission of a *projet* of a treaty, presented by the British minister, and to be laid before the Senate for their opinion upon its acceptance. The *projet* was accordingly received by Mr. Buchanan, a message drawn up, and the desired advice was to be asked the next day, 10th of June. A prey to anxiety as to the conduct of the whigs, the mere absence of part of whom would defeat the measure, the President sent for Mr. Benton the night before, to get himself re-assured on that point. Mr. Benton was clear and positive that they would be in their places, and would vote the advice, and that the measure would be carried. The next day the *projet* of the treaty was sent in, and with it a message from the President, asking the advice which he desired. It stated:—

> "In the early periods of the government, the opinion and advice of the Senate were often taken in advance upon important questions of our foreign policy. General Washington repeatedly consulted the Senate, and asked their previous advice upon pending negotiations with foreign powers; and the Senate in every instance responded to his call by giving their advice, to which he always conformed his action. This practice, though rarely resorted to in later times, was, in my judgment, eminently wise, and may, on occasions of great importance, be properly revived. The Senate are a branch of the treaty-making power; and, by consulting them in advance of his own action upon important measures of foreign policy which may ultimately come before them for their consideration, the President secures harmony of action between that body and himself. The Senate are, moreover, a branch of the war-making power, and it may be eminently proper for the Executive to take the opinion and advice of that body in advance upon any great question which may involve in its decision the issue of peace or war. On the present occasion, the magnitude of the subject would induce me, under any circumstances, to desire the previous advice of the Senate; and that desire is increased by the recent debates and proceedings in Congress, which render it, in my judgment, not only respectful to the Senate, but necessary and proper, if not indispensable, to insure harmonious action between that body and the Executive. In conferring on the Executive the authority to give the notice for the abrogation of the convention of 1827, the Senate acted publicly so large a part, that a decision on the proposal now made by the British government, without a definite knowledge of the views of that body in reference to it, might render the question still more complicated and difficult of adjustment. For these reasons I invite the consideration of the Senate to the proposal of the British government for the settlement of the Oregon question, and ask their advice on the subject."

This statement and expression of opinion were conformable to the early practice of the government and the theory of the constitution, which, in requiring the President to take the advice of the Senate in the formation of treaties, would certainly imply a consultation before they were made; and this interpretation had often been asserted by members of the Senate. As an interpretation deemed right in itself, and being deferential to the Senate, and being of good example for the future, and of great immediate practical good in taking the question of peace or war with Great Britain out of the hands of an administration standing upon the creed of the Baltimore convention, and putting it into the hands of the whigs to whom it did not apply, and that part of the democracy which disregarded it, this application of the President was most favorably received. Still, however, dominated by the idea of consistency, the President added a salvo for that sensitive point in the shape of a reservation in behalf of his previous opinions, thus:

> "My opinions and my action on the Oregon question were fully made known to Congress in my annual message of the second of December last; and the opinions therein expressed remain unchanged."

With this reservation, and with a complete devolution of the responsibility of the act upon the Senate, he proceeded to ask their advice in these terms:

> "Should the Senate, by the constitutional majority required for the ratification of treaties, advise the acceptance of this proposition, or advise it with such modifications as they may, upon full deliberation, deem proper, I shall conform my action to their advice. Should the Senate, however, decline by such constitutional majority to give such advice, or to express an opinion on the subject, I shall consider it my duty to reject the offer."

It was clear, then, that the fact of treaty or no treaty depended upon the Senate—that the whole responsibility was placed upon it—that the issue of peace or war depended upon that body. Far from shunning this responsibility, that body was glad to take it, and gave the President a faithful support against himself, against his cabinet, and against his peculiar friends. These friends struggled hard, and exhausted parliamentary tactics to defeat the application, and though a small minority, were formidable in a vote where each one counted two against the opposite side. The first motion was to refer the message to the Committee on Foreign Relations, where the fifty-four forties were in the majority, and from whose action delay and embarrassment might ensue. Failing in that motion, it was moved to lay the message on the table. Failing again, it was moved to postpone the consideration of the subject to the next week. That motion being rejected, the consideration of the message was commenced, and then succeeded a series of motions to amend and alter the terms of the proposition as submitted. All these failed, and at the end of two days the vote was taken and the advice given. The yeas were:

> "Messrs. Archer, Ashley, Bagby, Benton, Berrien, Calhoun, Chalmers, Thomas Clayton, John M. Clayton, Colquitt, Davis, Dayton, Dix, Evans, Greene, Haywood, Houston, Huntington, Johnson of Maryland, Johnson of Louisiana, Lewis, McDuffie, Mangum, Miller, Morehead, Niles, Pearce, Pennybacker, Phelps, Rusk, Sevier, Simmons, Speight, Turney, Upham, Webster, Woodbridge, Yulee."—38.

The nays:

> "Messrs. Allen, Atherton, Breese, Cameron, Cass, Dickinson, Fairfield, Hannegan, Jarnagin, Jenness, Semple, Sturgeon."—12.

The advice was in these words:

> "*Resolved* (two-thirds of the Senators present concurring), That the President of the United States be, and he is hereby, advised to accept the proposal of the British government, accompanying his message to the Senate dated 10th June, 1846, for a convention to settle boundaries, &c., between the United States and Great Britain west of the Rocky or Stony mountains.
>
> "*Ordered*, That the Secretary lay the said resolution before the President of the United States."

Four days afterwards the treaty was sent in in due form, accompanied by a message which still left its responsibility on the advising Senate, thus:

"In accordance with the resolution of the Senate of the 12th instant, that 'the President of the United States be, and he is hereby, advised to accept the proposal of the British government, accompanying his message to the Senate dated 10th June, 1846, for a convention to settle boundaries, &c., between the United States and Great Britain west of the Rocky or Stony mountains,' a convention was concluded and signed on the 15th instant, by the Secretary of State on the part of the United States, and the envoy extraordinary and minister plenipotentiary of her Britannic Majesty on the part of Great Britain. This convention I now lay before the Senate for their consideration, with a view to its ratification."

Two days more were consumed in efforts to amend or alter the treaty in various of its provisions, all of which failing, the final vote on its ratification was taken, and carried by an increased vote on each side—41 to 14.

YEAS.—"Messrs. Archer, Ashley, Bagby, Barrow, Benton, Berrien, Calhoun, Chalmers, Thomas Clayton, John M. Clayton, Colquitt, Corwin, Crittenden, Davis, Dayton, Dix, Evans, Greene, Haywood, Houston, Huntington, Johnson of Maryland, Henry Johnson of Louisiana, Lewis, McDuffie, Mangum, Miller, Morehead, Niles, Pearce, Pennybacker, Phelps, Rusk, Sevier, Simmons, Speight, Turney, Upham, Webster, Woodbridge, Yulee.

NAYS.—"Messrs. Allen, Atchison, Atherton, Breese, Bright, Cameron, Cass, Dickinson, Fairfield, Hannegan, Jenness, Semple, Sturgeon, Westcott."

An anomaly was presented in the progress of this question—that of the daily attack, by all the government papers, upon the senators who were accomplishing the wishes of the President. The organ at Washington, conducted by Mr. Ritchie, was incessant and unmeasured in these attacks, especially on Mr. Benton, whose place in the party, and his geographical position in the West, gave him the privilege of being considered the leader of the forty-nines, and therefore the most obnoxious. It was a new thing under the sun to see the senator daily assailed, in the government papers, for carrying into effect the wishes of the government—to see him attacked in the morning for what the President was hurrying him to do the night before. His course was equally independent of the wishes of the government, and the abuse of its papers. He had studied the Oregon question for twenty-five years—had his mind made up upon it—and should have acted according to his convictions without regard to support or resistance from any quarter.—The issue was an instructive commentary upon the improvidence of these party platforms, adopted for an electioneering campaign, made into a party watch-word, often fraught with great mischief to the country, and often founded in ignorance or disregard of the public welfare. This Oregon platform was eminently of that character. It was a party platform for the campaign: its architects knew but little of the geography of the north-west coast, or of its diplomatic history. They had never heard of the line of the treaty of Utrecht, and denied its existence: they had never heard of the multiplied offers of our government to settle upon that line, and treated the offer now as a novelty and an abandonment of our rights: they had never heard that their 54-40 was no line on the continent, but only a point on an island on the coast, fixed by the Emperor Paul as the southern limit of the charter granted by him to the Russian Fur Company: had never heard of Frazer's River and New Caledonia, which lay between Oregon and their indisputable line, and ignored the existence of that river and province. The pride of consistency made them adhere to these errors; and a desire to destroy Mr. Benton for not joining in the *hurrahs* for the "whole of Oregon, or none," and for the "immediate annexation of Texas without regard to consequences," lent additional force to the attacks upon him. The conduct of the whigs was patriotic in preferring their country to their party—in preventing a war with Great Britain—and in saving the administration from itself and its friends. Great Britain acted magnanimously, and was worthily represented by her minister, Mr. (now Sir Richard) Pakenham. Her adoption and renewal of our own offer, settled the last remaining controversy between the countries—left them in a condition which they had not seen since the peace of 1783—without any thing to quarrel about, and with a mutuality of interest in the preservation of peace which promised a long continuance of peace. But, alas, Great Britain is to the United States now what Spain was for centuries to her—the raw-head and bloody-bones which inspires terror and rage. During these centuries a ministry, or a public man that was losing ground at home, had only to raise a cry of some insult, aggression, or evil design on the part of Spain to have Great Britain in arms against her. And so it is in the United States at present, putting Great Britain in the place of Spain, and ourselves in hers. We have periodical returns of complaints against her, each to perish when it has served its turn, and to be succeeded by another, evanescent as itself. Thus far, no war has been made; but politicians have gained reputations; newspapers have taken fire; stocks have vacillated, to the profit of jobbers; great expense incurred for national defence in ships and forts, when there is nothing to defend against: and if there was, the electric telegraph and the steam car would do the work with little expense either of time or money.

CHAPTER CLX.

MEETING OF THE SECOND SESSION OF THE 29TH CONGRESS: PRESIDENT'S MESSAGE: VIGOROUS PROSECUTION OF THE WAR RECOMMENDED: LIEUTENANT-GENERAL PROPOSED TO BE CREATED.

Congress met at the regular annual period, the first Monday in December; and being the second session of the same body, there was nothing to be done, after the assembling of a quorum, before the commencement of business, but to receive the President's message. It was immediately communicated, and, of course, was greatly occupied with the Mexican war. The success of our arms, under the command of General Taylor, was a theme of exultation; and after that, an elaborate argument to throw the blame of the war on Mexico. The war was assumed, and argued to have been made by her, and its existence only recognized by us after "American blood had been spilled upon American soil." History is bound to pronounce her judgment upon these assumptions, and to say that they are unfounded. In the first place, the legal state of war, the *status belli*, was produced by the incorporation of Texas, with which Mexico was at war. In the next place, the United States' government understood that act to be the assumption of the war in fact, as well as in law, by the immediate advance of the army to the frontier of Texas, and of the navy to the Gulf of Mexico, to take the war off the hands of the Texians. In the third place, the actual collision of arms was brought on by the further advance of the American troops to the left bank of the Lower Rio Grande, then and always in the possession of Mexico, and erecting field works on the bank of the river, and pointing cannon at the town of Matamoras on the opposite side, the seat of a Mexican population, and the head-quarters of their army of observation. It was under these circumstances that the Mexican troops crossed the river, and commenced the attack. And this is what is called spilling American blood on American soil. The laws of nations and the law of self-defence, justify that spilling of blood; and such will be the judgment of history. The paragraph in the original message asking for a provisional territorial government to be established by Congress for the conquered provinces was superseded, and replaced by one asserting the right of the United States to govern them under the law of nations, according to the recommendation of Mr. Benton, and expressed in these words:

> "By the laws of nations a conquered territory is subject to be governed by the conqueror during his military possession, and until there is either a treaty of peace, or he shall voluntarily withdraw from it. The old civil government being necessarily superseded, it is the right and duty of the conqueror to secure his conquest, and provide for the maintenance of civil order and the rights of the inhabitants. This right has been exercised and this duty performed by our military and naval commanders, by the establishment of temporary governments in some of the conquered provinces in Mexico, assimilating them as far as practicable to the free institutions of our country. In the provinces of New Mexico and of the Californias, little, if any further resistance is apprehended from the inhabitants of the temporary governments which have thus, from the necessity of the case, and according to the laws of war, been established. It may be proper to provide for the security of these important conquests, by making an adequate appropriation for the purpose of erecting fortifications, and defraying the expenses necessarily incident to the maintenance of our possession and authority over them."

Having abandoned the idea of conquering by "a masterly inactivity," and adopted the idea of a vigorous prosecution of the war, the President also adopted Mr. Benton's plan for prosecuting it, which was to carry the war straight to the city of Mexico—General Taylor, for that purpose, to be supplied with 25,000 men, that, advancing along the table land by San Luis de Potosi, and overcoming all the obstacles in his way, and leaving some garrisons, he might arrive at the capital with some 10,000 men:—General Scott to be supplied with 15,000, that, landing at Vera Cruz, and leaving some battalions to invest (with the seamen) that town, he might run up the road to Mexico, arriving there (after all casualties) with 10,000 men. Thus 20,000 men were expected to arrive at the capital, but 10,000 were deemed enough to master any Mexican force which could meet it—no matter how numerous. This plan (and that without any reference to dissensions among generals) required a higher rank than that of major-general. A lieutenant-general, representing the constitutional commander-in-chief, was the proper commander in the field: and as such, was a part of Colonel Benton's plan; to which negotiation was to be added, and much relied on, as it was known that the old republican party—that which had framed a constitution on the model of that of the United States, and sought its friendship—were all in favor of peace. All this plan was given to the President in writing, and having adopted all that part of it which depended on his own authority, he applied to Congress to give him authority to do what he could not without it, namely, to make the appointment of a lieutenant-general—the appointment, it being well known, intended for Senator Benton, who had been a colonel in the army before either of the present generals held that rank. The bill for the creation of this office readily passed the House of Representatives, but was undermined and defeated in the Senate by three of the President's cabinet ministers, Messrs. Marcy, Walker, and Buchanan—done covertly, of course, for reasons unconnected with the public service. The plan went on, and was consummated, although the office of lieutenant-general was not created. A major-general, in right of seniority, had to command other major-generals; while every one accustomed to military, or naval service, knows that it is rank, and not seniority, which is essential to harmonious and efficient command.

CHAPTER CLXI.

WAR WITH MEXICO: THE WAR DECLARED, AND AN INTRIGUE FOR PEACE COMMENCED THE SAME DAY.

The state of war had been produced between the United States and Mexico by the incorporation of Texas: hostilities between the two countries were brought on by the advance of the American troops to the left bank of the Lower Rio Grande—the Mexican troops being on the opposite side. The left bank of the river being disputed territory, and always in her possession, the Mexican government had a right to consider this advance an aggression—and the more so as field-works were thrown up, and cannon pointed at the Mexican town of Matamoros on the opposite side of the river. The armies being thus in presence, with anger in their bosoms and arms in their hands, that took place which every body foresaw must take place: collisions and hostilities. They did so; and early in May the President sent in a message to the two Houses of Congress, informing them that American blood had been spilt upon American soil; and requesting Congress to recognize the existence of war, as a fact, and to provide for its prosecution. It was, however, an event determined upon before the spilling of that blood, and the advance of the troops was a way of bringing it on. The President in his message at the commencement of the session, after an enumeration of Mexican wrongs, had distinctly intimated that he should have recommended measures of redress if a minister had not been sent to effect a peaceable settlement; but the minister having gone, and not yet been heard from, "he should forbear recommending to Congress such ulterior measures of redress for the wrongs and injuries we have so long borne, as it would have been proper to make had no such negotiation been instituted." This was a declared postponement of war measures for a contingency which might quickly happen; and did. Mr. Slidell, the minister, returned without having been received, and denouncing war in his retiring despatch. The contingency had therefore occurred on which the forbearance of the President was to cease, and the ulterior measures to be recommended which he had intimated. All this was independent of the spilt blood; but that event producing a state of hostilities in fact, fired the American blood, both in and out of Congress, and inflamed the country for immediate war. Without that event it would have been difficult—perhaps impossible—to have got Congress to vote it: with it, the vote was almost unanimous. Duresse was plead by many members—duresse in the necessity of aiding our own troops. In the Senate only two senators voted against the measure, Mr. Thomas Clayton of Delaware, and Mr. John Davis of Massachusetts. In the House there were 14 negative votes: Messrs. John Quincy Adams, George Ashmun, Henry Y. Cranston, Erastus D. Culver, Columbus Delano, Joshua R. Giddings, Joseph Grinnell, Charles Hudson, Daniel P. King, Joseph M. Root, Luther Severance, John Strohm, Daniel R. Tilden and Joseph Vance. Mr. Calhoun spoke against the bill, but did not vote upon it. He was sincerely opposed to the war, although his conduct had produced it—always deluding himself, even while creating the *status belli*, with the belief that money, and her own weakness, would induce Mexico to submit, and yield to the incorporation of Texas without forcible resistance: which would certainly have been the case if the United States had proceeded gently by negotiation. He had despatched a messenger, to offer a douceur of ten millions of dollars at the time of signing the treaty of annexation two years before, and he expected the means, repulsed then, to be successful now when the incorporation should be effected under an act of Congress. Had he remained in the cabinet to do which he had not concealed his wish, his labors would have been earnestly directed to that end; but his associates who had co-operated with him in getting up the Texas question for the presidential election, and to defeat Mr. Van Buren and Mr. Clay, had war in view as an object within itself from the beginning: and these associates were now in the cabinet, and he not—their power increased: his gone. Claims upon Mexico, and speculations in Texas land and scrip, were with them (the active managing part of the cabinet) an additional motive, and required a war, or a treaty under the menace of war, or at the end of war, to make these claims and speculations available. Mr. Robert J. Walker had the reputation of being at the head of this class.

Many members of Congress, of the same party with the administration, were extremely averse to this war, and had interviews with the administration, to see if it was inevitable, before it was declared. They were found united for it, and also under the confident belief that there would be no war—not another gun fired: and that in "ninety" or "one hundred and twenty days," peace would be signed, and all the objects gained. This was laid down as a certainty, and the President himself declared that Congress would be "responsible if they did not vote the declaration." Mr. Benton was struck with this confident calculation, without knowing its basis; and with these 90 and 120 days, the usual run of a country bill of exchange; and which was now to become the run of the war. It was enigmatical, and unintelligible, but eventually became comprehensible. Truth was, an intrigue was laid for a peace before the war was declared! and this intrigue was even part of the scheme for making the war. It is impossible to conceive of an administration less warlike, or more intriguing, than that of Mr. Polk. They were men of peace, with objects to be accomplished by means of war; so that war was a necessity and an indispensability to their purpose; but they wanted no more of it than would answer their purposes. They wanted a small war, just large enough to require a treaty of peace, and not large enough to make military reputations, dangerous for the presidency. Never were men at the head of a government less imbued with military spirit, or more addicted to intrigue. How to manage the war was the puzzle. Defeat would be ruin: to conquer vicariously, would be dangerous. Another mode must be fallen upon; and that seemed to have been devised before the declaration was resolved upon, and to have been relied upon for its immediate termination—for its conclusion within the 90 and the 120 days which had been so confidently fixed for its term. This was nothing less than the restoration of the exiled Santa Anna to power, and the purchase of a peace from him. The date of the conception of this plan is not known: the execution of it commenced on the day of the declaration of war. It was intended to be secret, both for the honor of the United States, the success of the movement, and the safety of Santa Anna; but it leaked out: and the ostentation of Captain Slidell Mackenzie in giving all possible *eclat* to his secret mission, put the report on the winds, and sent it flying over the country. At first it was denied, and early in July the Daily Union (the government paper) gave it a formal and authoritative contradiction. Referring to the current reports that paper said:

"We deem it our duty to state in the most positive terms, that our government has no sort of connection with any scheme of Santa Anna for the revolution of Mexico, or for any sort of purpose. Some three months ago some adventurer was in Washington, who wished to obtain their countenance and aid in some scheme or other connected with Santa Anna. They declined all sort of connection, co-operation, or participation in any effort for the purpose. The government of this country declines all such intrigues or bargains. They have made war openly in the face of the world. They mean to prosecute it with all their vigor. They mean to force Mexico to do us justice at the point of the sword. This, then, is their design—this is their plan; and it is worthy of a bold, high-minded, and energetic people."

The only part of this publication that retains a surviving interest, is that which states that, some three months before that time (which would have been a month before the war was declared), some adventurer was in Washington who wished to obtain the government countenance to some scheme connected with Santa Anna. As for the rest, and all the denial, it was soon superseded by events—by the actual return of Santa Anna through our fleet, and upon an American passport! and open landing at Vera Cruz. Further denial became impossible: justification was the only course: and the President essayed it in his next annual message. Thus:

"Before that time (the day of the declaration of the war) there were symptoms of a revolution in Mexico, favored, as it was understood to be, by the more liberal party, and especially by those who were opposed to foreign interference and to the monarchical government. Santa Anna was then in exile in Havana, having been expelled from power and banished from his country by a revolution which occurred in December, 1844; but it was known that he had still a considerable party in his favor in Mexico. It was also equally well known, that no vigilance which could be exerted by our squadron would, in all probability, have prevented him from effecting a landing somewhere on the extensive gulf coast of Mexico, if he desired to return to his county. He had openly professed an entire change of policy; had expressed his regret that he had subverted the federal constitution of 1824, and avowed that he was now in favor of its restoration. He had publicly declared his hostility, in the strongest terms, to the establishment of a monarchy, and to European interference in the affairs of his country. Information to this effect had been received, from sources believed to be reliable, at the date of the recognition of the existence of the war by Congress, and was afterwards fully confirmed by the receipt of the despatch of our consul in the city of Mexico, with the accompanying documents, which are herewith transmitted. Besides, it was reasonable to suppose that he must see the ruinous consequences to Mexico of a war with the United States, and that it would be his interest to favor peace. It was under these circumstances and upon these considerations that it was deemed expedient not to obstruct his return to Mexico, should he attempt to do so. Our object was the restoration of peace; and with that view, no reason was perceived why we should take part with Paredes, and aid him, by means of our blockade, in preventing the return of his rival to Mexico. On the contrary, it was believed that the intestine divisions which ordinary sagacity could not but anticipate as the fruit of Santa Anna's return to Mexico, and his contest with Paredes, might strongly tend to produce a disposition with both parties to restore and preserve peace with the United States. Paredes was a soldier by profession, and a monarchist in principle. He had but recently before been successful in a military revolution, by which he had obtained power. He was the sworn enemy of the United States, with which he had involved his country in the existing war. Santa Anna had been expelled from power by the army, was known to be in open hostility to Paredes, and publicly pledged against foreign intervention and the restoration of monarchy in Mexico. In view of these facts and circumstances, it was, that, when orders were issued to the commander of our naval forces in the Gulf, on the thirteenth day of May last, the day on which the existence of the war was recognized by Congress, to place the coasts of Mexico under blockade, he was directed not to obstruct the passage of Santa Anna to Mexico, should he attempt to return."

So that the return of Santa Anna, and his restoration to power, and his expected friendship, were part of the means relied upon for obtaining peace from the beginning—from the day of the declaration of war, and consequently before the declaration, and obviously as an inducement to it. This knowledge, subsequently obtained, enabled Mr. Benton (to whom the words had been spoken) to comprehend the reliance which was placed on the termination of the war in ninety or one hundred and twenty days. It was the arrangement with Santa Anna! we to put him back in Mexico, and he to make peace with us; of course an agreeable peace. But Santa Anna was not a man to promise any thing, whether intending to fulfill it or not, without receiving a consideration; and in this case some million of dollars was the sum required—not for himself, of course, but to enable him to promote the peace at home. This explains the application made to Congress by the President before the end of its session—before the adjournment of the body which had declared the war—for an appropriation of two millions as a means of terminating it. On the 4th of August a confidential message was communicated to the Senate, informing them that he had made fresh overtures to Mexico for negotiation of a treaty of peace, and asking for an appropriation of two millions to enable him to treat with the better prospect of success, and even to pay the money when the treaty should be ratified in Mexico, without waiting for its ratification by our own Senate. After stating the overture, and the object, the message went on to say:

"Under these circumstances, and considering the exhausted and distracted condition of the Mexican republic, it might become necessary, in order to restore peace, that I should have it in my power to advance a portion of the consideration money for any cession of territory which may be made. The Mexican government might not be willing to wait for the payment of the whole until the treaty could be ratified by the Senate, and an appropriation to carry it into effect be made by Congress; and the necessity for such a delay might defeat the object altogether. I would, therefore, suggest whether it might not be wise for Congress to appropriate a sum such as they might consider adequate for this purpose, to be paid, if necessary, immediately upon the ratification of the treaty by Mexico."

A similar communication was made to the House on the 8th day of the month (August), and the dates become material, as connecting the requested appropriation with the return of Santa Anna, and his restoration to power. The dates are all in a cluster—Santa Anna landing at Vera Cruz on the 8th of August, and arriving at the capital on the 15th—the President's messages informing the Senate that he had made overtures for peace, and asking the appropriations to promote it, being dated on the 4th and the 8th of the same month. The fact was, it was known at what time Santa Anna was to leave Havana for Mexico, and the overture was made, and the appropriations asked, just at the proper time to meet him. The appropriation was not voted by Congress, and at the next session the application for it was renewed, increased to three millions—the same to which Mr. Wilmot offered that *proviso* which Mr. Calhoun privately hugged to his bosom as a fortunate event for the South, while publicly holding it up as the greatest of outrages, and just cause for a separation of the slave and the free States.

An intrigue for peace, through the restored Santa Anna, was then a part of the war with Mexico from the beginning. They were simultaneous concoctions. They were twins. The war was made to get the peace. Ninety to one-hundred and twenty days was to be the limit of the life of the war, and that pacifically all the while, and to be terminated by a good treaty of indemnities and acquisitions. It is probably the first time in the history of nations that a secret intrigue for peace was part and parcel of an open declaration of war! the first time that a war was commenced upon an agreement to finish it in so many days! and that the terms of its conclusion were settled before its commencement. It was certainly a most unmilitary conception: and infinitely silly, as the event proved. Santa Anna, restored by our means, and again in power, only thought of himself, and how to make Mexico his own, after getting back. He took the high military road. He roused the war spirit of the country, raised armies, placed himself at their head, issued animating proclamations; and displayed the most exaggerated hatred to the United States—the more so, perhaps, to cover up the secret of his return. He gave the United States a year of bloody and costly work! many thousands killed—many more dead of disease—many ten millions of money expended. Buena Vista, Cerro Gordo, Contreras, Churubusco, Chepultepec, were the fruit of his return! honorable to the American arms, but costly in blood and money. To the Mexicans his return was not less inauspicious: for, true to his old instincts, he became the tyrant of his country—ruled by fraud, force, and bribes—crushed the liberal party—exiled or shot liberal men—became intolerable—and put the nation to the horrors of another civil war to expel him again, and again: but not finally until he had got another milking from the best cow that ever was in his pen—more money from the United States. It was all the natural consequence of trusting such a man: the natural consequence of beginning war upon an intrigue with him. But what must history say of the policy and morality of such doings? The butcher of the American prisoners at Goliad, San Patricio, the Old Mission and the Alamo; the destroyer of republican government at home; the military dictator aspiring to permanent supreme power: this man to be restored to power by the United States, for the purpose of fulfilling speculating and indemnity calculations on which a war was begun.

CHAPTER CLXII.

BLOODLESS CONQUEST OF NEW MEXICO: HOW IT WAS DONE: SUBSEQUENT BLOODY INSURRECTION, AND ITS CAUSE.

General Kearney was directed to lead an expedition to New Mexico, setting out from the western frontier of Missouri, and mainly composed of volunteers from that State; and to conquer the province. He did so, without firing a gun, and the only inquiry is, how it was done? how a province nine hundred miles distant, covered by a long range of mountain which could not well be turned, penetrable only by a defile which could not be forced, and defended by a numerous militia—could so easily be taken? This work does not write of military events, open to public history, but only of things less known, and to show how they were done: and in this point of view the easy and bloodless conquest of New Mexico, against such formidable obstacles, becomes an exception, and presents a proper problem for intimate historical solution. That solution is this: At the time of the fitting out that expedition there was a citizen of the United States, long resident in New Mexico, on a visit of business at Washington City—his name James Magoffin;—a man of mind, of will, of generous temper, patriotic, and rich. He knew every man in New Mexico and his character, and all the localities, and could be of infinite service to the invading force. Mr. Benton proposed to him to go with it: he agreed. Mr. Benton took him to the President and Secretary at War, who gladly availed themselves of his agreement to go with General Kearney. He went: and approaching New Mexico, was sent ahead, with a staff officer—the officer charged with a mission, himself charged with his own plan: which was to operate upon Governor Armijo, and prevent his resistance to the entrance of the American troops. That was easily done. Armijo promised not to make a stand at the defile, after which the invaders would have no difficulty. But his second in command, Col. Archuletti, was determined to fight, and to defend that pass; and if he did, Armijo would have to do the same. It became indispensable to quiet Archuletti. He was of different mould from the governor, and only accessible to a different class of considerations—those which addressed themselves to ambition. Magoffin knew the side on which to approach him. It so happened that General Kearney had set out to take the left bank of the Upper Del Norte—the eastern half of New Mexico—as part of Texas, leaving the western part untouched. Magoffin explained this to Archuletti, pointed to the western half of New Mexico as a derelict, not seized by the United States, and too far off to be protected by the central government: and recommended him to make a *pronunciamiento*, and take that half to himself. The idea suited the temper of Archuletti. He agreed not to fight, and General Kearney was informed there would be no resistance at the defile: and there was none. Some thousands of militia collected there (and which could have stopped a large army), retired without firing a gun, and without knowing why. Armijo fled, and General Kearney occupied his capital: and the conquest was complete and bloodless: and this was the secret of that facile success—heralded in the newspapers as a masterpiece of generalship, but not so reported by the general.

But there was an after-clap, to make blood flow for the recovery of a province which had been yielded without resistance. Mr. Magoffin was sincere and veracious in what he said to Col. Archuletti; but General Kearney soon (or before) had other orders, and took possession of the whole country! and Archuletti, deeming himself cheated, determined on a revolt. Events soon became favorable to him. General Kearney proceeded to California, leaving General Sterling Price in command, with some Missouri volunteers. Archuletti prepared his insurrection, and having got the upper country above Santa Fé ready, went below to prepare the lower part. While absent, the plot was detected and broke out, and led to bloody scenes in which there was severe fighting, and many deaths on both sides. It was in this insurrection that Governor Charles Bent, of New Mexico, and Captain Burgwin of the United States army, and many others were killed. The insurgents fought with courage and desperation; but, without their leader, without combination, without resources, they were soon suppressed; many being killed in action, and others hung for high treason—being tried by some sort of a court which had no jurisdiction of treason. All that were condemned were hanged except one, and he recommended to the President of the United States for pardon. Here was a dilemma for the administration. To pardon the man would be to admit the legality of the condemnation: not to pardon was to subject him to murder. A middle course was taken: the officers were directed to turn loose the condemned, and let him run. And this was the cause of the insurrection, and its upshot.

Mr. Magoffin having prepared the way for the entrance of General Kearney into Santa Fé, proceeded to the execution of the remaining part of his mission, which was to do the same by Chihuahua for General Wool, then advancing upon that ancient capital of the Western Internal Provinces on a lower line. He arrived in that city—became suspected—was arrested—and confined. He was a social, generous-tempered man, a son of Erin: loved company, spoke Spanish fluently, entertained freely, and where it was some cost to entertain—claret $36 00 a-dozen, champagne $50 00. He became a great favorite with the Mexican officers. One day the military judge advocate entered his quarters, and told him that Dr. Connolly, an American, coming from Santa Fé, had been captured near El Paso del Norte, his papers taken, and forwarded to Chihuahua, and placed in his hands, to see if there were any that needed government attention: and that he had found among the papers a letter addressed to him (Mr. Magoffin). He had the letter unopened, and said he did not know what it might be; but being just ordered to join Santa Anna at San Luis Potosi, and being unwilling that any thing should happen after he was gone to a gentleman who had been so agreeable to him, he had brought it to him, that he might destroy it if there was any thing in it to commit him. Magoffin glanced his eyes over the letter. It was an attestation from General Kearney of his services in New Mexico, recommending him to the acknowledgments of the American government in that invasion!—that is to say, it was his death warrant, if seen by the Mexican authorities. A look was exchanged: the letter went into the fire: and Magoffin escaped being shot.

But he did not escape suspicion. He remained confined until the approach of Doniphan's expedition, and was then sent off to Durango, where he remained a prisoner to the end of the war. Returning to the United States after the peace, he came to Washington in the last days of Mr. Polk's administration, and expected remuneration. He had made no terms, asked nothing, and received nothing, and had expended his own money, and that freely, for the public service. The administration had no money applicable to the object. Mr. Benton stated his case in secret session in the Senate, and obtained an appropriation, couched in general terms, of fifty thousand dollars for secret services rendered during the war. The appropriation, granted in the last night of the expiring administration, remained to be applied by the new one—to which the business was unknown, and had to be presented unsupported by a line of writing. Mr. Benton went with Magoffin to President Taylor, who, hearing what he had done, and what information he had gained for General Kearney, instantly expressed the wish that he had had some person to do the same for him—observing that he got no information but what he obtained at the point of the bayonet. He gave orders to the Secretary at War to attend to the case as if there had been no change in the administration. The secretary (Mr. Crawford, of Georgia), higgled, required statements to be filed, almost in the nature of an account; and, finally, proposed thirty thousand dollars. It barely covered expenses and losses; but, having undertaken the service patriotically, Magoffin would not lower its character by standing out for more. The paper which he filed in the war office may furnish some material for history—some insight into the way of making conquests—if ever examined. This is the secret history of General Kearney's expedition, and of the insurrection, given because it would not be found in the documents. The history of Doniphan's expedition will be given for the same reason, and to show that a regiment of citizen volunteers, without a regular officer among them, almost without expense, and hardly with the knowledge of their government, performed actions as brilliant as any that illustrated the American arms in Mexico; and made a march in the enemy's country longer than that of the ten thousand under Xenophon. This history will constitute the next chapter, and will consist of the salutatory address with which the heroic volunteers were saluted, when, arriving at St. Louis, they were greeted with a public reception, and the Senator of Thirty Years required to be the organ of the exulting feelings of their countrymen.

CHAPTER CLXIII.

MEXICAN WAR: DONIPHAN'S EXPEDITION: MR. BENTON'S SALUTATORY ADDRESS, ST. LOUIS, MISSOURI.

COLONEL DONIPHAN AND OFFICERS AND MEN:—I have been appointed to an honorable and a pleasant duty—that of making you the congratulations of your fellow-citizens of St. Louis, on your happy return from your long, and almost fabulous expedition. You have, indeed, marched far, and done much, and suffered much, and well entitled yourselves to the applauses of your fellow-citizens, as well as to the rewards and thanks of your government. A year ago you left home. Going out from the western border of your State, you re-enter it on the east, having made a circuit equal to the fourth of the circumference of the globe, providing for yourselves as you went, and returning with trophies taken from fields, the names of which were unknown to yourselves and your country, until revealed by your enterprise, illustrated by your valor, and immortalized by your deeds. History has but few such expeditions to record; and when they occur, it is as honorable and useful as it is just and wise, to celebrate and commemorate the events which entitle them to renown.

Your march and exploits have been among the most wonderful of the age. At the call of your country you marched a thousand miles to the conquest of New Mexico, as part of the force under General Kearney, and achieved that conquest, without the loss of a man, or the fire of a gun. That work finished, and New Mexico, itself so distant, and so lately the ultima thule—the outside boundary of speculation and enterprise—so lately a distant point to be attained, becomes itself a point of departure—a beginning point, for new and far more extended expeditions. You look across the long and lofty chain—the Cordilleras of North America—which divide the Atlantic from the Pacific waters; and you see beyond that ridge, a savage tribe which had been long in the habit of depredations upon the province which had just become an American conquest. You, a part only of the subsequent Chihuahua column, under Jackson and Gilpin, march upon them—bring them to terms—and they sign a treaty with Colonel Doniphan, in which they bind themselves to cease their depredations on the Mexicans, and to become the friends of the United States. A novel treaty, that! signed on the western confines of New Mexico, between parties who had hardly ever heard each other's names before, and to give peace and protection to Mexicans who were hostile to both. This was the meeting, and this the parting of the Missouri volunteers, with the numerous and savage tribe of the Navaho Indians living on the waters of the Gulf of California, and so long the terror and scourge of Sonora, Sinaloa, and New Mexico.

This object accomplished, and impatient of inactivity, and without orders (General Kearney having departed for California), you cast about to carve out some new work for yourselves. Chihuahua, a rich and populous city of near thirty thousand souls, the seat of government of the State of that name, and formerly the residence of the captains-general of the Internal Provinces under the vice-regal government of New Spain, was the captivating object which fixed your attention. It was a far distant city—about as far from St. Louis as Moscow is from Paris; and towns and enemies, and a large river, and defiles and mountains, and the desert whose ominous name, portending death to travellers—*el jornada de los muertos*—the journey of the dead—all lay between you. It was a perilous enterprise, and a discouraging one, for a thousand men, badly equipped, to contemplate. No matter. Danger and hardship lent it a charm, and the adventurous march was resolved on, and the execution commenced. First, the ominous desert was passed, its character vindicating its title to its mournful appellation—an arid plain of ninety miles, strewed with the bones of animals perished of hunger and thirst—little hillocks of stone, and the solitary cross, erected by pious hands, marking the spot where some Christian had fallen, victim of the savage, of the robber, or of the desert itself—no water—no animal life—no sign of habitation. There the Texian prisoners, driven by the cruel Salazar, had met their direst sufferings, unrelieved, as in other parts of their march in the settled parts of the country, by the compassionate ministrations (for where is it that *woman* is not compassionate?) of the pitying women. The desert was passed, and the place for crossing the river approached. A little arm of the river, Bracito (in Spanish), made out from its side. There the enemy, in superior numbers, and confident in cavalry and artillery, undertook to bar the way. Vain pretension! Their discovery, attack, and rout, were about simultaneous operations. A few minutes did the work! And in this way our Missouri volunteers of the Chihuahua column spent their Christmas day of the year 1846.

The victory of the Bracito opened the way to the crossing of the river Del Norte, and to admission into the beautiful little town of the Paso del Norte, where a neat cultivation, a comfortable people, fields, orchards, and vineyards, and a hospitable reception, offered the rest and refreshment which toils and dangers, and victory had won. You rested there till artillery was brought down from Sante Fé; but the pretty town of the Paso del Norte, with all its enjoyments, and they were many, and the greater for the place in which they were found, was not a Capua to the men of Missouri. You moved forward in February, and the battle of the Sacramento, one of the military marvels of the age, cleared the road to Chihuahua; which was entered without further resistance. It had been entered once before by a detachment of American troops; but under circumstances how different! In the year 1807, Lieutenant Pike and his thirty brave men, taken prisoners on the head of the Rio del Norte, had been marched captives into Chihuahua: in the year 1847, Doniphan and his men enter it as conquerors. The paltry triumph of a captain-general over a lieutenant, was effaced in the triumphal entrance of a thousand Missourians into the grand and ancient capital of all the Internal Provinces! and old men, still alive, could remark the grandeur of the American spirit under both events—the proud and lofty bearing of the captive thirty—the mildness and moderation of the conquering thousand.

Chihuahua was taken, and responsible duties, more delicate than those of arms, were to be performed. Many American citizens were there, engaged in trade; much American property was there. All this was to be protected, both life and property, and by peaceful arrangement; for the command was too small to admit of division, and of leaving a garrison. Conciliation, and negotiation were resorted to, and successfully. Every American interest was provided for, and placed under the safeguard, first, of good will, and next, of guarantees not to be violated with impunity.

Chihuahua gained, it became, like Santa Fé, not the terminating point of a long expedition, but the beginning point of a new one. General Taylor was somewhere—no one knew where—but some seven or eight hundred miles towards the other side of Mexico. You had heard that he had been defeated, that Buena Vista had not been a *good prospect* to him. Like good Americans, you did not believe a word of it; but, like good soldiers, you thought it best to go and see. A volunteer party of fourteen, headed by Collins, of Boonville, undertake to penetrate to Saltillo, and to bring you information of his condition. They set out. Amidst innumerable dangers they accomplish their purpose, and return. Taylor is conqueror; but will be glad to see you. You march. A vanguard of one hundred men, led by Lieutenant-colonel Mitchell, led the way. Then came the main body (if the name is not a burlesque on such a handful), commanded by Colonel Doniphan himself.

The whole table land of Mexico, in all its breadth, from west to east, was to be traversed. A numerous and hostile population in towns—treacherous Camanches in the mountains—were to be passed. Every thing was to be self-provided—provisions, transportation, fresh horses for remounts, and even the means of victory— and all without a military chest, or even an empty box, in which government gold had ever reposed. All was accomplished. Mexican towns were passed, in order and quiet: plundering Camanches were punished: means were obtained from traders to liquidate indispensable contributions: and the wants that could not be supplied, were endured like soldiers of veteran service.

The long march from Chihuahua to Monterey, was made more in the character of protection and deliverance than of conquest and invasion. Armed enemies were not met, and peaceful people were not disturbed. You arrived in the month of May in General Taylor's camp, and about in a condition to vindicate, each of you for himself, your lawful title to the double *sobriquet* of the general, with the addition to it which the colonel commanding the expedition has supplied—ragged—as well as rough and ready. No doubt you all showed title, at that time, to that third *sobriquet*; but to see you now, so gayly attired, so sprucely equipped, one might suppose that you had never, for a day, been strangers to the virtues of soap and water, or the magic ministrations of the *blanchisseuse*, and the elegant transformations of the fashionable tailor. Thanks perhaps to the difference between pay in the lump at the end of the service, and driblets along in the course of it.

You arrived in General Taylor's camp ragged and rough, as we can well conceive, and ready, as I can quickly show. You arrived: you reported for duty: you asked for service—such as a march upon San Luis de Potosi, Zacatecas, or the "halls of the Montezumas;" or any thing in that way that the general should have a mind to. If he was going upon any excursion of that kind, all right. No matter about fatigues that were passed, or expirations of service that might accrue: you came to go, and only asked the privilege. That is what I call ready. Unhappily the conqueror of Palo Alto, Resaca de la Palma, Monterey, and Buena Vista, was not exactly in the condition that the lieutenant-general, that might have been, intended him to be. He was not at the head of twenty thousand men! he was not at the head of any thousands that would enable him to march! and had to decline the proffered service. Thus the long-marched and well-fought volunteers—the rough, the ready, and the ragged—had to turn their faces towards home, still more than two thousand miles distant. But this being mostly by water, you hardly count it in the recital of your march. But this is an unjust omission, and against the precedents as well as unjust. "The ten thousand" counted the voyage on the Black Sea as well as the march from Babylon; and twenty centuries admit the validity of the count. The present age, and posterity, will include in "the going out and coming in" of the Missouri-Chihuahua volunteers, the water voyage as well as the land march; and then the expedition of the one thousand will exceed that of the ten by some two thousand miles.

The last nine hundred miles of your land march, from Chihuahua to Matamoros, you made in forty-five days, bringing seventeen pieces of artillery, eleven of which were taken from the Sacramento and Bracito. Your horses, travelling the whole distance without United States provender, were astonished to find themselves regaled, on their arrival on the Rio Grande frontier, with hay, corn, and oats from the States. You marched further than the farthest, fought as well as the best, left order and quiet in your train; and cost less money than any.

You arrive here to-day, absent one year, marching and fighting all the time, bringing trophies of cannon and standards from fields whose names were unknown to you before you set out, and only grieving that you could not have gone further. Ten pieces of cannon, rolled out of Chihuahua to arrest your march, now roll through the streets of St. Louis, to grace your triumphal return. Many standards, all pierced with bullets while waving over the heads of the enemy at the Sacramento, now wave at the head of your column. The black flag, brought to the Bracito, to indicate the refusal of that quarter which its bearers so soon needed and received, now takes its place among your trophies, and hangs drooping in their nobler presence. To crown the whole—to make public and private happiness go together—to spare the cypress where the laurel hangs in clusters—this long, perilous march, with all its accidents of field and camp, presents an incredibly small list of comrades lost. Almost all return: and the joy of families resounds, intermingled with the applause of the State.

I have said that you made your long expedition without government orders: and so, indeed, you did. You received no orders from your government, but, without knowing it, you were fulfilling its orders—orders which, though issued for you, never reached you. Happy the soldier who executes the command of his government: happier still he who anticipates command, and does what is wanted before he is bid. This is your case. You did the right thing, at the right time, and what your government intended you to do, and without knowing its intentions. The facts are these: Early in the month of November last, the President asked my opinion on the manner of conducting the war. I submitted a plan to him, which, in addition to other things, required all the disposable troops in New Mexico, and all the American citizens in that quarter who could be engaged for a dashing expedition, to move down through Chihuahua, and the State of Durango, and, if necessary, to Zacatecas, and get into communication with General Taylor's right as early as possible in the month of March. In fact, the disposable forces in New Mexico were to form one of three columns destined for a combined movement on the city of Mexico, all to be on the table-land and ready for a combined movement in the month of March. The President approved the plan, and the Missourians being most distant, orders were despatched to New Mexico to put them in motion. Mr. Solomon Sublette carried the order, and delivered it to the commanding officer at Santa Fé, General Price, on the 22d day of February—just five days before you fought the marvellous action of Sacramento. I well remember what passed between the President and myself at the time he resolved to give this order. It awakened his solicitude for your safety. It was to send a small body of men a great distance, into the heart of a hostile country, and upon the contingency of uniting in a combined movement, the means for which had not yet been obtained from Congress. The President made it a question, and very properly, whether it was safe or prudent to start the small Missouri column, before the movement of the left and the centre was assured: I answered that my own rule in public affairs was to do what I thought was right, and leave it to others to do what they thought was right; and that I believed it the proper course for him to follow on the present occasion. On this view he acted. He gave the order to go, without waiting to see whether Congress would supply the means of executing the combined plan; and for his consolation I undertook to guarantee your safety. Let the worst come to the worst, I promised him that you would take care of yourselves. Though the other parts of the plan should fail—though you should become far involved in the advance, and deeply compromised in the enemy's country, and without support—still I relied on your courage, skill, and enterprise to extricate yourselves from every danger—to make daylight through all the Mexicans that should stand before you—cut your way out—and make good your retreat to Taylor's camp. This is what I promised the President in November last; and what I promised him you have done. Nobly and manfully you have made one of the most remarkable expeditions in history, worthy to be studied by statesmen, and showing what citizen volunteers can do; for the crowning characteristic is that you were all citizens—all volunteers—not a regular bred officer among you: and if there had been, with power to control you, you could never have done what you did.

CHAPTER CLXIV.

FREMONT'S THIRD EXPEDITION, AND ACQUISITION OF CALIFORNIA.

In the month of May 1845, Mr. Frémont, then a brevet captain of engineers (appointed a lieutenant-colonel of Rifles before he returned), set out on his third expedition of geographical and scientific exploration in the Great West. Hostilities had not broken out between the United States and Mexico; but Texas had been incorporated; the preservation of peace was precarious, and Mr. Frémont was determined, by no act of his, to increase the difficulties, or to give any just cause of complaint to the Mexican government. His line of observation would lead him to the Pacific Ocean, through a Mexican province—through the desert parts first, and the settled part afterwards of the Alta California. Approaching the settled parts of the province at the commencement of winter, he left his equipment of 60 men and 200 horses on the frontier, and proceeded alone to Monterey, to make known to the governor the object of his coming, and his desire to pass the winter (for the refreshment of his men and horses) in the uninhabited parts of the valley of the San Joaquin. The permission was granted; but soon revoked, under the pretext that Mr. Frémont had come into California, not to pursue science, but to excite the American settlers to revolt against the Mexican government. Upon this pretext troops were raised, and marched to attack him. Having notice of their approach, he took a position on the mountain, hoisted the flag of the United States, and determined, with his sixty brave men, to defend himself to the last extremity—never surrendering; and dying, if need be, to the last man. A messenger came into his camp, bringing a letter from the American consul at Monterey, to apprise him of his danger: that messenger, returning, reported that 2,000 men could not force the American position: and that information had its effect upon the Mexican commander. Waiting four days in his mountain camp, and not being attacked, he quit his position, descended from the mountain, and set out for Oregon, that he might give no further pretext for complaint, by remaining in California.

Turning his back on the Mexican possessions, and looking to Oregon as the field of his future labors, Mr. Frémont determined to explore a new route to the Wah-lah-math settlements and the tide-water region of the Columbia, through the wild and elevated region of the Tla-math lakes. A romantic interest attached to this region from the grandeur of its features, its lofty mountains, and snow-clad peaks, and from the formidable character of its warlike inhabitants. In the first week of May, he was at the north end of the Great Tla-math lake, and in Oregon—the lake being cut near its south end by the parallel of 42 degrees north latitude. On the 8th day of that month, a strange sight presented itself—almost a startling apparition—two men riding up, and penetrating a region which few ever approached without paying toll of life or blood. They proved to be two of Mr. Frémont's old *voyageurs*, and quickly told their story. They were part of a guard of six men conducting a United States officer, who was on his trail with despatches from Washington, and whom they had left two days back, while they came on to give notice of his approach, and to ask that assistance might be sent him. They themselves had only escaped the Indians by the swiftness of their horses. It was a case in which no time was to be lost, or a mistake made. Mr. Frémont determined to go himself; and taking ten picked men, four of them Delaware Indians, he took down the western shore of the lake on the morning of the 9th (the direction the officer was to come), and made a ride of sixty miles without a halt. But to meet men, and not to miss them, was the difficult point in this trackless region. It was not the case of a high road, where all travellers must meet in passing each other: at intervals there were places—defiles, or camping grounds—where both parties must pass; and watching for these, he came to one in the afternoon, and decided that, if the party was not killed, it must be there that night. He halted and encamped; and, as the sun was going down, had the inexpressible satisfaction to see the four men approaching. The officer proved to be a lieutenant of the United States marines, who had been despatched from Washington the November previous, to make his way by Vera Cruz, the City of Mexico, and Mazatlan to Monterey, in Upper California, deliver despatches to the United States' consul there; and then find Mr. Frémont, wherever he should be. His despatches for Mr. Frémont were only a letter of introduction from the Secretary of State (Mr. Buchanan), and some letters and slips of newspapers from Senator Benton and his family, and some verbal communications from the Secretary of State. The verbal communications were that Mr. Frémont should watch and counteract any foreign scheme on California, and conciliate the good will of the inhabitants towards the United States. Upon this intimation of the government's wishes, Mr. Frémont turned back from Oregon, in the edge of which he then was, and returned to California.

The letter of introduction was in the common form, that it might tell nothing if it fell into the hands of foes, and signified nothing of itself; but it accredited the bearer, and gave the stamp of authority to what he communicated; and upon this Mr. Frémont acted: for it was not to be supposed that Lieutenant Gillespie had been sent so far, and through so many dangers, merely to deliver a common letter of introduction on the shores of the Tlamath lake.

The events of some days on the shores of this wild lake, sketched with the brevity which the occasion requires, may give a glimpse of the hardships and dangers through which Mr. Frémont pursued science, and encountered and conquered perils and toils. The night he met Mr. Gillespie presented one of those scenes to which he was so often exposed, and which nothing but the highest degree of vigilance and courage could prevent from being fatal. The camping ground was on the western side of the lake, the horses picketed with long halters on the shore, to feed on the grass; and the men (fourteen in number) sleeping by threes at different fires, disposed in a square; for danger required them so to sleep as to be ready for an attack; and, though in the month of May, the elevation of the place, and the proximity of snow-clad mountains, made the night intensely cold. His feelings joyfully excited by hearing from home (the first word of intelligence he had received since leaving the U. S. a year before), Mr. Frémont sat up by a large fire, reading his letters and papers, and watching himself over the safety of the camp, while the men slept. Towards midnight, he heard a movement among the horses, indicative of alarm and danger. Horses, and especially mules, become sensitive to danger under long travelling and camping in the wilderness, and manifest their alarm at the approach of any thing strange. Taking a six-barrelled pistol in his hand, first making sure of their ready fire, and, without waking the camp, he went down among the disturbed animals. The moon shone brightly: he could see well, but could discover nothing. Encouraged by his presence, the horses became quiet—poor dumb creatures that could see the danger, but not tell what they had seen; and he returned to the camp, supposing it was only some beast of the forest—a bear or wolf—prowling for food, that had disturbed them. He returned to the camp fire. Lieutenant Gillespie woke up, and talked with him awhile, and then lay down again. Finally nature had her course with Mr. Frémont himself. Excited spirits gave way to exhausted strength. The day's ride, and the night's excitement demanded the reparation of repose. He lay down to sleep, and without waking up a man to watch—relying on the loneliness of the place, and the long ride of the day, as a security against the proximity of danger. It was the second time in his twenty thousand miles of wilderness explorations that his camp had slept without a guard: the first was in his second expedition, and on an island in the Great Salt Lake, and when the surrounding water of the lake itself constituted a guard. The whole camp was then asleep. A cry from Carson roused it. In his sleep he heard a groan: it was the groan of a man receiving the tomahawk in his brains. All sprung to their feet. The savages were in the camp: the hatchet and the winged arrow were at work. Basil Lajeunesse, a brave and faithful young Frenchman, the follower of Frémont in all his expeditions, was dead: an Iowa was dead: a brave Delaware Indian, one of those who had accompanied Frémont from Missouri, was dying: it was his groan that awoke Carson. Another of the Delawares was a target for arrows, from which no rifle could save him—only avenge him. The savages had waited till the moon was in the trees, casting long shadows over the sleeping camp: then approaching from the dark side, with their objects between themselves and the fading light, they used only the hatchet and the formidable bow, whose arrow went to its mark without a flash or a sound to show whence it came. All advantages were on the side of the savages: but the camp was saved! the wounded protected from massacre, and the dead from mutilation. The men, springing to their feet, with their arms in their hands, fought with skill and courage. In the morning, Lieutenant Gillespie recognized, in the person of one of the slain assailants, the Tlamath chief who the morning before had given him a salmon, in token of friendship, and who had followed him all day to kill and rob his party at night—a design in which he would certainly have been successful had it not been for the promptitude and precision of Mr. Frémont's movement. Mr. Frémont himself would have been killed, when he went to the horses, had it not been that the savages counted upon the destruction of the whole camp, and feared to alarm it by killing one, before the general massacre.

It was on the 9th of May—a day immortalized by American arms at Resaca de la Palma—that this fierce and bloody work was done in the far distant region of the Tlamath lakes.

The morning of the 10th of May was one of gloom in the camp. The evening sun of the 9th had set upon it full of life and joy at a happy meeting: the same sun rose upon it the next morning, stained with blood, ghastly with the dead and wounded, and imposing mournful duties on the survivors. The wounded were to be carried—the dead to be buried; and so buried as to be hid and secured from discovery and violation. They were carried ten miles, and every precaution taken to secure the remains from the wolf and the savage: for men, in these remote and solitary dangers, become brothers, and defend each other living and dead. The return route lay along the shore of the lake, and during the day the distant canoes of the savages could be seen upon it, evidently watching the progress of the party, and meditating a night attack upon it. All precautions, at the night encampment, were taken for security—horses and men enclosed in a breastwork of great trees, cut down for the purpose, and half the men constantly on the watch. At leaving in the morning, an ambuscade was planted—and two of the Tlamaths were killed by the men in ambush—a successful return of their own mode of warfare. At night the main camp, at the north end of the lake, was reached. It was strongly intrenched, and could not be attacked; but the whole neighborhood was infested, and scouts and patrols were necessary to protect every movement. In one of these excursions the Californian horse, so noted for spirit and docility, showed what he would do at the bid of his master. Carson's rifle had missed fire, at ten feet distance. The Tlamath long bow, arrow on the string, was bending to the pull. All the rifles in the party could not have saved him. A horse and his rider did it. Mr. Frémont touched his horse; he sprang upon the savage! and the hatchet of a Delaware completed the deliverance of Carson. It was a noble horse, an iron gray, with a most formidable name—el Toro del Sacramento: and which vindicated his title to the name in all the trials of travel, courage, and performance to which he was subjected. It was in the midst of such dangers as these, that science was pursued by Mr. Frémont; that the telescope was carried to read the heavens; the barometer to measure the elevations of the earth; the thermometer to gauge the temperature of the air; the pencil to sketch the grandeur of mountains, and to paint the beauty of flowers; the pen to write down whatever was new, or strange, or useful in the works of nature. It was in the midst of such dangers, and such occupations as these, and in the wildest regions of the Farthest West, that Mr. Frémont was pursuing science and shunning war, when the arrival of Lieutenant Gillespie, and his communications from Washington, suddenly changed all his plans, turned him back from Oregon, and opened a new and splendid field of operations in California itself. He arrived in the valley of the Sacramento in the month of May, 1846, and found the country alarmingly, and critically situated. Three great operations, fatal to American interests, were then going on, and without remedy, if not arrested at once. These were: 1. The massacre of the Americans, and the destruction of their settlements, in the valley of the Sacramento. 2. The subjection of California to British protection. 3. The transfer of the public domain to British subjects. And all this with a view to anticipate the events of a Mexican war, and to shelter California from the arms of the United States.

The American settlers sent a deputation to the camp of Mr. Frémont, in the valley of the Sacramento, laid all these dangers before him, and implored him to place himself at their head and save them from destruction. General Castro was then in march upon them: the Indians were incited to attack their families, and burn their wheat fields, and were only waiting for the dry season to apply the torch. Juntas were in session to transfer the country to Great Britain: the public domain was passing away in large grants to British subjects: a British fleet was expected on the coast: the British vice consul, Forbes, and the emissary priest, Macnamara, ruling and conducting every thing: and all their plans so far advanced as to render the least delay fatal. It was then the beginning of June. War had broken out between the United States and Mexico, but that was unknown in California. Mr. Frémont had left the two countries at peace when he set out upon his expedition, and was determined to do nothing to disturb their relations: he had even left California to avoid giving offence; and to return and take up arms in so short a time was apparently to discredit his own previous conduct as well as to implicate his government. He felt all the responsibilities of his position; but the actual approach of Castro, and the immediate danger of the settlers, left him no alternative. He determined to put himself at the head of the people, and to save the country. To repulse Castro was not sufficient: to overturn the Mexican government in California, and to establish Californian Independence, was the bold resolve, and the only measure adequate to the emergency. That resolve was taken, and executed with a celerity that gave it a romantic success. The American settlers rushed to his camp—brought their arms, horses and ammunition—were formed into a battalion; and obeyed with zeal and alacrity the orders they received. In thirty days all the northern part of

California was freed from Mexican authority—Independence proclaimed—the flag of Independence raised—Castro flying to the south—the American settlers saved from destruction; and the British party in California counteracted and broken up in all their schemes.

This movement for Independence was the salvation of California, and snatched it out of the hands of the British at the moment they were ready to clutch it. For two hundred years—from the time of the navigator Drake, who almost claimed it as a discovery, and placed the English name of New Albion upon it—the eye of England has been upon California; and the magnificent bay of San Francisco, the great seaport of the North Pacific Ocean, has been surveyed as her own. The approaching war between Mexico and the United States was the crisis in which she expected to realize the long-deferred wish for its acquisition; and carefully she took her measures accordingly. She sent two squadrons to the Pacific as soon as Texas was incorporated—well seeing the actual war which was to grow out of that event—a small one into the mouth of the Columbia, an imposing one to Mazatlan, on the Mexican coast, to watch the United States squadron there, and to anticipate its movements upon California. Commodore Sloat commanding the squadron at Mazatlan, saw that he was watched, and pursued, by Admiral Seymour, who lay alongside of him, and he determined to deceive him. He stood out to sea, and was followed by the British Admiral. During the day he bore west, across the ocean, as if going to the Sandwich Islands: Admiral Seymour followed. In the night the American commodore tacked, and ran up the coast towards California: the British admiral, not seeing the tack, continued on his course, and went entirely to the Sandwich Islands before he was undeceived. Commodore Sloat arrived before Monterey on the second of July, entering the port amicably, and offering to salute the town, which the authorities declined on the pretext that they had no powder to return it—in reality because they momentarily expected the British fleet. Commodore Sloat remained five days before the town, and until he heard of Frémont's operations: then believing that Frémont had orders from his government to take California, he having none himself, he determined to act himself. He received the news of Frémont's successes on the 6th day of July: on the 7th he took the town of Monterey, and sent a despatch to Frémont. This latter came to him in all speed, at the head of his mounted force. Going immediately on board the commodore's vessel, an explanation took place. The commodore learnt with astonishment that Frémont had no orders from his government to commence hostilities—that he had acted entirely on his own responsibility. This left the commodore without authority for having taken Monterey; for still at this time, the commencement of the war with Mexico was unknown. Uneasiness came upon the commodore. He remembered the fate of Captain Jones in making the mistake of seizing the town once before in time of peace. He resolved to return to the United States, which he did—turning over the command of the squadron to Commodore Stockton, who had arrived on the 15th. The next day (16th) Admiral Seymour arrived; his flagship the Collingwood, of 80 guns, and his squadron the largest British fleet ever seen in the Pacific. To his astonishment he beheld the American flag flying over Monterey, the American squadron in its harbor, and Frémont's mounted riflemen encamped over the town. His mission was at an end. The prize had escaped him. He attempted nothing further, and Frémont and Stockton rapidly pressed the conquest of California to its conclusion. The subsequent military events can be traced by any history: they were the natural sequence of the great measure conceived and executed by Frémont before any squadron had arrived upon the coast, before he knew of any war with Mexico, and without any authority from his government, except the equivocal and enigmatical visit of Mr. Gillespie. Before the junction of Mr. Frémont with Commodore Sloat and Stockton, his operations had been carried on under the flag of Independence—the Bear Flag, as it was called—the device of the bear being adopted on account of the courageous qualities of that animal (the white bear), which never gives the road to men,—which attacks any number,—and fights to the last with increasing ferocity, with amazing strength of muscle, and with an incredible tenacity of the vital principle—never more formidable and dangerous than when mortally wounded. The Independents took the device of this bear for their flag, and established the independence of California under it: and in joining the United States forces, hauled down this flag, and hoisted the flag of the United States. And the fate of California would have been the same whether the United States squadrons had arrived, or not; and whether the Mexican war had happened, or not. California was in a revolutionary state, already divided from Mexico politically as it had always been geographically. The last governor-general from Mexico, Don Michel Toreno, had been resisted—fought—captured—and shipped back to Mexico, with his 300 cut-throat soldiers. An insurgent government was in operation, determined to be free of Mexico, sensible of inability to stand alone, and looking, part to the United States, part to Great Britain, for the support which they needed. All the American settlers were for the United States protection, and joined Frémont. The leading Californians were also joining him. His conciliatory course drew them rapidly to him. The Picos, who were the leading men of the revolt (Don Pico, Don Andres, and Don Jesus), became his friends. California, become independent of Mexico by the revolt of the Picos, and independent of them by the revolt of the American settlers, had its destiny to fulfil—which was, to be handed over to the United States. So that its incorporation with the American Republic was equally sure in any, and every event.

CHAPTER CLXV.

PAUSE IN THE WAR: SEDENTARY TACTICS: "MASTERLY INACTIVITY."

Arriving at Washington before the commencement of the session of '46-'47, Mr. Benton was requested by the President to look over the draught of his proposed message to Congress (then in manuscript), and to make the remarks upon it which he might think it required; and in writing. Mr. Benton did so, and found a part to which he objected, and thought ought to be omitted. It was a recommendation to Congress to cease the active prosecution of the war, to occupy the conquered part of the country (General Taylor had then taken Monterey) with troops in forts and stations, and to pass an act establishing a temporary government in the occupied part; and to retain the possession until the peace was made. This recommendation, and the argument in support of it, spread over four pages of the message—from 101 to 105. Mr. Benton objected to the whole plan, and answered to it in an equal, or greater number of pages, and to the entire conviction and satisfaction of the President. 1. The sedentary occupation was objected to as being entirely contrary to the temper of the American people, which was active, and required continual "going ahead" until their work was finished. 2. It was a mode of warfare suited to the Spanish temper, which loved procrastination, and could beat the world at it, and had sat-out the Moors seven hundred years in the South of Spain and the Visigoths three hundred years in the north of it; and would certainly out-sit us in Mexico. 3. That he could govern the conquered country under the laws of nations, without applying to Congress, to be worried upon the details of the act, and rousing the question of annexation by conquest, and that beyond the Rio Grande; for the proposed line was to cover Monterey, and to run east and west entirely across the country. These objections, pursued through their illustrations, were entirely convincing to the President, and he frankly gave up the sedentary project.

But it was a project which had been passed upon in the cabinet, and not only adopted but began to be executed. The Secretary at War, Mr. Marcy, had officially refused to accept proffered volunteers from the governors of several States, saying to them—"*A sufficient amount of force for the prosecution of the war had already been called into service:*" and a premium of two dollars a head had been offered to all persons who could bring in a recruit to the regular army—the regulars being the reliance for the sedentary occupation. The cabinet adhered to their policy. The President convoked them again, and had Mr. Benton present to enforce his objections; but without much effect. The abandonment of the sedentary policy required the adoption of an active one, and for that purpose the immediate calling out of ten regiments of volunteers had been recommended by Mr. Benton; and this call would result at once from the abandonment of the sedentary scheme. Here the pride of consistency came in to play its part. The Secretary at War said he had just refused to accept any more volunteers, and informed the governors of two States that the government had troops enough to prosecute the war; and urged that it would be contradictory now to call out ten regiments. The majority of the cabinet sided with him; but the President retained Mr. Benton to a private interview—talked the subject all over—and finally came to the resolution to act for himself, regardless of the opposition of the major part of his cabinet. It was then in the night, and the President said he would send the order to the Secretary at War in the morning to call out the ten regiments—which he did: but the Secretary, higgling to the last, got one regiment abated: so that nine instead of ten were called out: but these nine were enough. They enabled Scott to go to Mexico, and Taylor to conquer at Buena Vista, and to finish the war victoriously.

A comic mistake grew out of this change in the President's message, which caused the ridicule of the sedentary line to be fastened on Mr. Calhoun—who in fact had counselled it. When the message was read in the Senate, Mr. Westcott, of Florida, believing it remained as it had been drawn up, and induced by Mr. Calhoun, with whose views he was acquainted, made some motion upon it, significant of approbatory action. Mr. Benton asked for the reading of the part of the message referred to. Mr. Westcott searched, but could not find it: Mr. Calhoun did the same. Neither could find the passage. Inquiring and despairing looks were exchanged: and the search for the present was adjourned. Of course it was never found. Afterwards Mr. Westcott said to Mr. Benton that the President had deceived Mr. Calhoun—had told him that the sedentary line was recommended in the message, when it was not. Mr. Benton told him there was no deception—that the recommendation was in the message when he said so, but had been taken out (and he explained how) and replaced by an urgent recommendation for a vigorous prosecution of the war. But the secret was kept for the time. The administration stood before the country vehement for war, and loaded with applause for their spirit. Mr. Calhoun remained mystified, and adhered to the line, and incurred the censure of opposing the administration which he professed to support. He brought forward his plan in all its detail—the line marked out—the number of forts and stations necessary—and the number of troops necessary to garrison them: and spoke often, and earnestly in its support: but to no purpose. His plan was entirely rejected, nor did I ever hear of any one of the cabinet offering to share with him in the ridicule which he brought upon himself for advocating a plan so preposterous in itself, and so utterly unsuited to the temper of our people. It was in this debate, and in support of this sedentary occupation that Mr. Calhoun characterized that proposed inaction as "*a masterly inactivity:*" a fine expression of the Earl of Chatham—and which Mr. Calhoun had previously used in the Oregon debate in recommending us to do nothing there, and leave it to time to perfect our title. Seven years afterwards the establishment of a boundary between the United States and Mexico was attempted by treaty in the latitude of this proposed line of occupation—a circumstance,—one of the circumstances,—which proves that Mr. Calhoun's plans and spirit survive him.

In all that passed between the President and Mr. Benton about this line, there was no suspicion on the part of either of any design to make it permanent; nor did any thing to that effect appear in Mr. Calhoun's speeches in favor of it; but the design was developed at the time of the ratification of the treaty of peace, and has since been attempted by treaty; and is a design which evidently connects itself with, what is called, *preserving the equilibrium of the States* (free and slave) by adding on territory for slave States—and to increase the Southern margin for the "UNITED STATES SOUTH," in the event of a separation of the two classes of States.

CHAPTER CLXVI.

THE WILMOT PROVISO; OR, PROHIBITION OF SLAVERY IN THE TERRITORIES: ITS INUTILITY AND MISCHIEF.

Scarcely was the war with Mexico commenced when means, different from those of arms, were put in operation to finish it. One of these was the return of the exiled Santa Anna (as has been shown) to his country, and his restoration to power, under the belief that he was favorable to peace, and for which purpose arrangements began to be made from the day of the declaration of the war—or before. In the same session another move was made in the same direction, that of getting peace by peaceable means, in an application made to Congress by the President, to place three millions of dollars at his disposal, to be used in negotiating for a boundary which should give us additional territory: and that recommendation not having been acted upon at the war session, was renewed at the commencement of the next one. It was recommended as an "important measure for securing a speedy peace;" and as an argument in favor of granting it, a sum of two millions similarly placed at the disposition of Mr. Jefferson when about to negotiate for Florida (which ended in the acquisition of Louisiana), was plead as a precedent; and justly. Congress, at this second application, granted the appropriation; but while it was depending, Mr. Wilmot, a member of Congress, from Pennsylvania, moved a proviso, *that no part of the territory to be acquired should be open to the introduction of slavery.* It was a proposition not necessary for the purpose of excluding slavery, as the only territory to be acquired was that of New Mexico and California, where slavery was already prohibited by the Mexican laws and constitution; and where it could not be carried until those laws should be repealed, and a law for slavery passed. The proviso was nugatory, and could answer no purpose but that of bringing on a slavery agitation in the United States; for which purpose it was immediately seized upon by Mr. Calhoun and his friends, and treated as the greatest possible outrage and injury to the slave States. Congress was occupied with this proviso for two sessions, became excessively heated on the subject, and communicated its heat to the legislatures of the slave States—by several of which conditional disunion resolutions were passed. Every where, in the slave States, the Wilmot Proviso became a Gorgon's head—a chimera dire—a watchword of party, and the synonyme of civil war and the dissolution of the Union. Many patriotic members were employed in resisting the proviso as a *bona fide* cause of breaking up the Union, if adopted; many amiable and gentle-tempered members were employed in devising modes of adjusting and compromising it; a few, of whom Mr. Benton was one, produced the laws and the constitution of Mexico to show that New Mexico and California were free from slavery; and argued that neither party had any thing to fear, or to hope—the free soil party nothing to fear, because the soil was now free; the slave soil party nothing to hope, because they could not take a step to make it slave soil, having just invented the dogma of "No power in Congress to legislate upon slavery in territories." Never were two parties so completely at loggerheads about nothing: never did two parties contend more furiously against the greatest possible evil. Close observers, who had been watching the progress of the slavery agitation since its inauguration in Congress in 1835, knew it to be a game played by the abolitionists on one side and the disunionists on the other, to accomplish their own purposes. Many courageous men denounced it as such—as a game to be kept up for the political benefit of the players; and deplored the blindness which could not see their determination to keep it agoing to the last possible moment, and to the production of the greatest possible degree of national and sectional exasperation. It was while this contention was thus raging, that Mr. Calhoun wrote a confidential letter to a member of the Alabama legislature, hugging this proviso to his bosom as a fortunate event—as a means of "*forcing the issue*" between the North and the South; and deprecating any adjustment, compromise, or defeat of it, as a misfortune to the South: and which letter has since come to light. Gentle and credulous people, who believed him to be in earnest when he was sounding the *tocsin* to rouse the States, instigating them to pass disunion resolutions, and stirring up both national and village orators to attack the proviso unto death: such persons must be amazed to read in that exhumed letter, written during the fiercest of the strife, these ominous words:

> "*With this impression I would regard any compromise or adjustment of the proviso, or even its defeat, without meeting the danger in its whole length and breadth, as very unfortunate for us. It would lull us to sleep again, without removing the danger, or materially diminishing it.*"

This issue to be forced was a separation of the slave and the free States; the means, a commercial non-intercourse, in shutting the slave State seaports against the vessels of the free States; the danger to be met, was in the trial of this issue, by the means indicated; which were simply high treason when pursued to the overt act. Mr. Calhoun had flinched from that act in the time of Jackson, but he being dead, and no more Jacksons at the head of the government, he rejoiced in another chance of meeting the danger—meeting it in all its length and breadth; and deprecated the loss of the proviso as the loss of this chance.

Truly the abolitionists and the nullifiers were necessary to each other—the two halves of a pair of shears, neither of which could cut until joined together. Then the map of the Union was in danger; for in their conjunction, that map was cloth between the edges of the shears. And this was that Wilmot Proviso, which for two years convulsed the Union, and prostrated men of firmness and patriotism—a thing of nothing in itself, but magnified into a hideous reality, and seized upon to conflagrate the States and dissolve the Union. The Wilmot Proviso was not passed: that chance of forcing the issue was lost: another had to be found, or made.

CHAPTER CLXVII.

MR. CALHOUN'S SLAVERY RESOLUTIONS, AND DENIAL OF THE RIGHT OF CONGRESS TO PROHIBIT SLAVERY IN A TERRITORY.

On Friday, the 19th of February, Mr. Calhoun introduced into the Senate his new slavery resolutions, prefaced by an elaborate speech, and requiring an immediate vote upon them. They were in these words:

"*Resolved*, That the territories of the United States belong to the several States composing this Union, and are held by them as their joint and common property.

"*Resolved*, That Congress, as the joint agent and representative of the States of this Union, has no right to make any law, or do any act whatever, that shall directly, or by its effects, make any discrimination between the States of this Union, by which any of them shall be deprived of its full and equal right in any territory of the United States acquired or to be acquired.

"*Resolved*, That the enactment of any law which should directly, or by its effects, deprive the citizens of any of the States of this Union from emigrating, with their property, into any of the territories of the United States, will make such discrimination, and would, therefore, be a violation of the constitution, and the rights of the States from which such citizens emigrated, and in derogation of that perfect equality which belongs to them as members of this Union, and would tend directly to subvert the Union itself.

"*Resolved*, That it is a fundamental principle in our political creed, that a people, in forming a constitution, have the unconditional right to form and adopt the government which they may think best calculated to secure their liberty, prosperity, and happiness; and that, in conformity thereto, no other condition is imposed by the federal constitution on a State, in order to be admitted into this Union, except that its constitution shall be republican; and that the imposition of any other by Congress would not only be in violation of the constitution, but in direct conflict with the principle on which our political system rests."

These resolutions, although the sense is involved in circumlocutory phrases, are intelligible to the point, that Congress has no power to prohibit slavery in a territory, and that the exercise of such a power would be a breach of the constitution, and leading to the subversion of the Union. Ostensibly the complaint was, that the emigrant from the slave State was not allowed to carry his slave with him: in reality it was that he was not allowed to carry the State law along with him to protect his slave. Placed in that light, which is the true one, the complaint is absurd: presented as applying to a piece of property instead of the law of the State, it becomes specious—has deluded whole communities; and has led to rage and resentment, and hatred of the Union. In support of these resolutions the mover made a speech in which he showed a readiness to carry out in action, to their extreme results, the doctrines they contained, and to appeal to the slave-holding States for their action, in the event that the Senate should not sustain them. This was the concluding part of his speech:

"Well, sir, what if the decision of this body shall deny to us this high constitutional right, not the less clear because deduced from the whole body of the instrument and the nature of the subject to which it relates? What, then, is the question? I will not undertake to decide. It is a question for our constituents—the slave-holding States. A solemn and a great question. If the decision should be adverse, I trust and do believe that they will take under solemn consideration what they ought to do. I give no advice. It would be hazardous and dangerous for me to do so. But I may speak as an individual member of that section of the Union. There I drew my first breath. There are all my hopes. There is my family and connections. I am a planter—a cotton planter. I am a Southern man, and a slave-holder; a kind and a merciful one, I trust—and none the worse for being a slave-holder. I say, for one, I would rather meet any extremity upon earth than give up one inch of our equality—one inch of what belongs to us as members of this great republic. What, acknowledge inferiority! The surrender of life is nothing to sinking down into acknowledged inferiority.

"I have examined this subject largely—widely. I think I see the future if we do not stand up as we ought. In my humble opinion, in that case, the condition of Ireland is prosperous and happy—the condition of Hindostan is prosperous and happy—the condition of Jamaica is prosperous and happy, to what the Southern States will be if they should not now stand up manfully in defence of their rights".

When these resolutions were read, Mr. Benton rose in his place, and called them "firebrand." Mr. Calhoun said he had expected the support of Mr. Benton "as the representative of a slave-holding State." Mr. Benton answered that it was impossible that he could have expected such a thing. Then, said Mr. Calhoun, I shall know where to find the gentleman. To which Mr. Benton: "I shall be found in the right place—on the side of my country and the Union." This answer, given on that day, and on the spot, is one of the incidents of his life which Mr. Benton will wish posterity to remember.

Mr. Calhoun demanded the prompt consideration of his resolutions, giving notice that he would call them up the next day, and press them to a speedy and final vote. He did call them up, but never called for the vote, nor was any ever had: nor would a vote have any practical consequence, one way or the other. The resolutions were abstractions, without application. They asserted a constitutional principle, which could not be decided, one way or the other, by the separate action of the Senate; not even in a bill, much less in a single and barren set of resolves. No vote was had upon them. The condition had not happened on which they were to be taken up by the slave States; but they were sent out to all such States, and adopted by some of them; and there commenced the great slavery agitation, founded upon the dogma of "*no power in Congress to legislate upon slavery in the territories,*" which has led to the abrogation of the Missouri compromise line—which has filled the Union with distraction—and which is threatening to bring all federal legislation, and all federal elections, to a mere sectional struggle, in which, one-half of the States is to be arrayed against the other. The resolves were evidently introduced for the mere purpose of carrying a question to the slave States on which they could be formed into a unit against the free States; and they answered that purpose as well on rejection by the Senate as with it; and were accordingly used in conformity to their design without any such rejection, which—it cannot be repeated too often—could in no way have decided the constitutional question which they presented.

These were new resolutions—the first of their kind in the (almost) sixty years' existence of the federal government—contrary to its practice during that time—contrary to Mr. Calhoun's slavery resolutions of 1838—contrary to his early and long support of the Missouri compromise—and contrary to the re-enactment of that line by the authors of the Texas annexation law. That re-enactment had taken place only two years before, and was in the very words of the anti-slavery ordinance of '87, and of the Missouri compromise prohibition of 1820; and was voted for by the whole body of the annexationists, and was not only conceived and supported by Mr. Calhoun, then Secretary of State, but carried into effect by him in the despatch of that messenger to Texas in the expiring moments of his power. The words of the re-enactment were: "*And in such State, or States as shall be formed out of said territory north of the said Missouri compromise line, slavery or involuntary servitude (except for crime) shall be prohibited.*" This clause re-established that compromise line in all that long extent of it which was ceded to Spain by the treaty of 1819, which became Texian by her separation from Mexico, and which became slave soil under her laws and constitution. So that, up to the third day of March, in the year 1845—not quite two years before the date of these resolutions—Mr. Calhoun by authentic acts, and the two Houses of Congress by recorded votes, and President Tyler by his approving signature, acknowledged the power of Congress to prohibit slavery in a territory! and not only acknowledged the power, but exerted it! and actually prohibited slavery in a long slip of country, enough to make a "State or States," where it then legally existed. This fact was formally brought out in the chapter of this volume which treats of the legislative annexation of Texas; and those who wish to see the proceeding in detail may find it in the journals of the two Houses of Congress, and in the congressional history of the time.

These resolutions of 1847, called fire-brand at the time, were further characterized as nullification a few days afterwards, when Mr. Benton said of them, that, "*as Sylla saw in the young Cæsar many Mariuses, so did he see in them many nullifications.*"

CHAPTER CLXVIII.

THE SLAVERY AGITATION: DISUNION: KEY TO MR. CALHOUN'S POLICY: FORCING THE ISSUE: MODE OF FORCING IT.

In the course of this year, and some months after the submission of his resolutions in the Senate denying the right of Congress to abolish slavery in a territory, Mr. Calhoun wrote a letter to a member of the Alabama Legislature, which furnishes the key to unlock his whole system of policy in relation to the slavery agitation, and its designs, from his first taking up the business in Congress in the year 1835, down to the date of the letter; and thereafter. The letter was in reply to one asking his opinion "*as to the steps which should be taken*" to guard the rights of the South; and was written in a feeling of personal confidence to a person in a condition to take steps; and which he has since published to counteract the belief that Mr. Calhoun was seeking the dissolution of the Union. The letter disavows such a design, and at the same time proves it—recommends forcing the issue between the North and the South, and lays down the manner in which it should be done. It opens with this paragraph:

> "I am much gratified with the tone and views of your letter, and concur entirely in the opinion you express, that instead of shunning, we ought to court the issue with the North on the slavery question. I would even go one step further, and add that it is our duty—due to ourselves, to the Union, and our political institutions, to *force* the issue on the North. We are now stronger relatively than we shall be hereafter, politically and morally. Unless we bring on the issue, delay to us will be dangerous indeed. It is the true policy of those enemies who seek our destruction. Its effects are, and have been, and will be to weaken us politically and morally, and to strengthen them. Such has been my opinion from the first. Had the South, or even my own State backed me, I would have *forced* the issue on the North in 1835, when the spirit of abolitionism first developed itself to any considerable extent. It is a true maxim, to meet danger on the frontier, in politics as well as war. Thus thinking, I am of the impression, that if the South act as it ought, the Wilmot Proviso, instead of proving to be the means of successfully assailing us and our peculiar institution, may be made the occasion of successfully asserting our equality and rights, by enabling us to *force* the issue on the North. Something of the kind was indispensable to rouse and unite the South. On the contrary, if we should not meet it as we ought, I fear, greatly fear, our doom will be fixed. It would prove that we either have not the sense or spirit to defend ourselves and our institutions."

The phrase "forcing the issue" is here used too often, and for a purpose too obvious, to need remark. The reference to his movement in 1835 confirms all that was said of that movement at the time by senators from both sections of the Union, and which has been related in chapter 131 of the first volume of this View. At that time Mr. Calhoun characterized his movement as defensive—as done in a spirit of self-defence: it was then characterized by senators as aggressive and offensive: and it is now declared in this letter to have been so. He was then openly told that he was playing into the hands of the abolitionists, and giving them a champion to contend with, and the elevated theatre of the American Senate for the dissemination of their doctrines, and the production of agitation and sectional division. All that is now admitted, with a lamentation that the South, and not even his own State, would stand by him then in forcing the issue. So that chance was lost. Another was now presented. The Wilmot Proviso, so much deprecated in public, is privately saluted as a fortunate event, giving another chance for forcing the issue. The letter proceeds:

> "But in making up the issue, we must look far beyond the proviso. It is but one of many acts of aggression, and, in my opinion, by no means the most dangerous or degrading, though more striking and palpable."

In looking beyond the proviso (the nature of which has been explained in a preceding chapter) Mr. Calhoun took up the recent act of the General Assembly of Pennsylvania, repealing the slave sojournment law within her limits, and obstructing the recovery of fugitive slaves—saying:

"I regard the recent act of Pennsylvania, and laws of that description, passed by other States, intended to prevent or embarrass the reclamation of fugitive slaves, or to liberate our domestics when travelling with them in non-slaveholding States, as unconstitutional. Insulting as it is, it is even more dangerous. I go further, and hold that if we have a right to hold our slaves, we have a right to hold them in peace and quiet, and that the toleration, in the non-slaveholding States, of the establishment of societies and presses, and the delivery of lectures, with the express intention of calling in question our right to our slaves, and of seducing and abducting them from the service of their masters, and finally overthrowing the institution itself, as not only a violation of international laws, but also of the Federal compact. I hold, also, that we cannot acquiesce in such wrongs, without the certain destruction of the relation of master and slave, and without the ruin of the South."

The acts of Pennsylvania here referred to are justly complained of, but with the omission to tell that these injurious acts were the fruit of his own agitation policy, and in his own line of forcing issues; and that the repeal of the sojournment law, which had subsisted since the year 1780, and the obstruction of the fugitive slave act, which had been enforced since 1793, only took place twelve years after he had commenced slavery agitation in the South, and were legitimate consequences of that agitation, and of the design to force the issue with the North. The next sentence of the letter reverts to the Wilmot Proviso, and is of momentous consequence as showing that Mr. Calhoun, with all his public professions in favor of compromise and conciliation, was secretly opposed to any compromise or adjustment, and actually considered the defeat of the proviso as a misfortune to the South. Thus:

"With this impression, I would regard any compromise or adjustment of the proviso, or even its defeat, without meeting the danger in its whole length and breadth, as very unfortunate for us. It would lull us to sleep again, without removing the danger, or materially diminishing it."

So that, while this proviso was, publicly, the Pandora's box which filled the Union with evil, and while it was to Mr. Calhoun and his friends the theme of endless deprecation, it was secretly cherished as a means of keeping up discord, and forcing the issue between the North and the South. Mr. Calhoun then proceeds to the serious question of disunion, and of the manner in which the issue could be forced.

"This brings up the question, how can it be so met, *without resorting to the dissolution of the Union?* I say without its dissolution, for, in my opinion, a high and sacred regard for the constitution, as well as the dictates of wisdom, make it our duty in this case, as well as all others, not to resort to, or even to look to that extreme remedy, until all others have failed, and then only in defence of our liberty and safety. There is, in my opinion, but one way in which it can be met; and that is the one indicated in my letter to Mr. ——, and to which you allude in yours to me, viz., by retaliation. Why I think so, I shall now proceed to explain."

Then follows an argument to justify retaliation, by representing the constitution as containing provisions, he calls them stipulations, some in favor of the slaveholding, and some in favor of the non-slaveholding States, and the breach of any of which, on one side, authorizes a retaliation on the other; and then declaring that Pennsylvania, and other States, have violated the provision in favor of the slave States in obstructing the recovery of fugitive slaves, he proceeds to explain his remedy—saying:

"There is and can be but one remedy short of disunion, and that is to retaliate on our part, by refusing to fulfil the stipulations in their favor, or such as we may select, as the most efficient. Among these, the right of their ships and commerce to enter and depart from our ports is the most effectual, and can be enforced. That the refusal on their part would justify us to refuse to fulfil on our part those in their favor, is too clear to admit of argument. That it would be effectual in compelling them to fulfil those in our favor can hardly be doubted, when the immense profit they make by trade and navigation out of us is regarded; and also the advantages we would derive from the direct trade it would establish between the rest of the world and our ports."

Retaliation by closing the ports of the State against the commerce of the offending State: and this called a constitutional remedy, and a remedy short of disunion. It is, on the contrary, a flagrant breach of the constitution, and disunion itself, and that at the very point which caused the Union to be formed. Every one acquainted with the history of the formation of the federal constitution, knows that it grew out of the single question of commerce—the necessity of its regulation between the States to prevent them from harassing each other, and with foreign nations to prevent State rivalries for foreign trade. To stop the trade with any State is, therefore, to break the Union with that State; and to give any advantage to a foreign nation over a State, would be to break the constitution again in the fundamental article of its formation; and this is what the retaliatory remedy of commercial non-intercourse arrives at—a double breach of the constitution—one to the prejudice of sister States, the other in favor of foreign nations. For immediately upon this retaliation upon a State, and as a consequence of it, a great foreign trade is to grow up with all the world. The letter proceeds with further instructions upon the manner of executing the retaliation:

> "My impression is, that it should be restricted to *sea-going* vessels, which would leave open the trade of the valley of the Mississippi to New Orleans by river, and to the other Southern cities by railroad; and tend thereby to detach the North-western from the North-eastern States."

This discloses a further feature in the plan of forcing the issue. The North-eastern States were to be excluded from Southern maritime commerce: the North-western States were to be admitted to it by railroad, and also allowed to reach New Orleans by the Mississippi River. And this discrimination in favor of the North-western States was for the purpose of detaching them from the North-east. Detach is the word. And that word signifies to separate, disengage, disunite, part from: so that the scheme of disunion contemplated the inclusion of the North-western States in the Southern division. The State of Missouri was one of the principal of these States, and great efforts were made to gain her over, and to beat down Senator Benton who was an obstacle to that design. The letter concludes by pointing out the only difficulty in the execution of this plan, and showing how to surmount it.

> "There is but one practical difficulty in the way; and that is, to give it force, it will require the co-operation of all the slave-holding States lying on the Atlantic Gulf. Without that, it would be ineffective. To get that is the great point, and for that purpose a convention of the Southern States is indispensable. Let that be called, and let it adopt measures to bring about the co-operation, and I would underwrite for the rest. The non-slaveholding States would be compelled to observe the stipulations of the constitution in our favor, or abandon their trade with us, or to take measures to coerce us, which would throw on them the responsibility of dissolving the Union. Which they would choose, I do not think doubtful. Their unbounded avarice would, in the end, control them. Let a convention be called—let it recommend to the slaveholding States to take the course advised, giving, say one year's notice, before the acts of the several States should go into effect, and the issue would fairly be made up, and our safety and triumph certain."

This the only difficulty—the want of a co-operation of all the Southern Atlantic States; and to surmount that, the indispensability of a convention of the Southern States is fully declared. This was going back to the starting point—to the year 1835—when Mr. Calhoun first took up the slavery agitation in the Senate, and when a convention of the slaveholding States was as much demanded then as now, and that twelve years before the Wilmot Proviso—twelve years before the Pennsylvania unfriendly legislation—twelve years before the insult and outrage to the South, in not permitting them to carry their local laws with them to the territories, for the protection of their slave property. A call of a Southern convention was as much demanded then as now; and such conventions often actually attained: but without accomplishing the object of the prime mover. No step could be got to be taken in those conventions towards dividing and sectionalizing the States, and after a vain reliance upon them for seventeen years, a new method has been fallen upon: and this confidential letter from Mr. Calhoun to a member of the Alabama legislature of 1847, has come to light, to furnish the key which unlocks his whole system of slavery agitation which he commenced in the year 1835. That system was to force issues upon the North under the pretext of self-defence, and to sectionalize the South, preparatory to disunion,

through the instrumentality of sectional conventions, composed wholly of delegates from the slaveholding States. Failing in that scheme of accomplishing the purpose, a new one was fallen upon, which will disclose itself in its proper place.

CHAPTER CLXIX.

DEATH OF SILAS WRIGHT, EX-SENATOR AND EX-GOVERNOR OF NEW YORK.

He died suddenly, at the early age of fifty-two, and without the sufferings and premonitions which usually accompany the mortal transit from time to eternity. A letter that he was reading, was seen to fall from his hand: a physician was called: in two hours he was dead—apoplexy the cause. Though dying at the age deemed young in a statesman, he had attained all that long life could give—high office, national fame, fixed character, and universal esteem. He had run the career of honors in the State of New York—been representative and senator in Congress—and had refused more offices, and higher, than he ever accepted. He refused cabinet appointments under his fast friend, Mr. Van Buren, and under Mr. Polk, whom he may be said to have elected: he refused a seat on the bench of the federal Supreme Court; he rejected instantly the nomination of 1844 for Vice-President of the United States, when that nomination was the election. He refused to be put in nomination for the presidency. He refused to accept foreign missions. He spent that time in declining office which others did in winning it; and of those he did accept, it might well be said they were "*thrust*" upon him. Office, not greatness, was thrust upon him. He was born great, and above office, and unwillingly descended to it; and only took it for its burthens, and to satisfy an importunate public demand. Mind, manners, morals, temper, habits, united in him to form the character that was perfect, both in public and private life, and to give the example of a patriot citizen—of a farmer statesman—of which we have read in Cincinnatus and Cato, and seen in Mr. Macon, and some others of their stamp—created by nature—formed in no school: and of which the instances are so rare and long between.

His mind was clear and strong, his judgment solid, his elocution smooth and equable, his speaking always addressed to the understanding, and always enchaining the attention of those who had minds to understand. Grave reasoning was his forte. Argumentation was always the line of his speech. He spoke to the head, not to the passions; and would have been disconcerted to have seen any body laugh, or cry, at any thing he said. His thoughts evolved spontaneously, in natural and proper order, clothed in language of force and clearness; all so naturally and easily conceived that an extemporaneous speech, or the first draught of an intricate report, had all the correctness of a finished composition. His manuscript had no blots—a proof that his mind had none; and he wrote a neat, compact hand, suitable to a clear and solid mind. He came into the Senate, in the beginning of General Jackson's administration, and remained during that of Mr. Van Buren; and took a ready and active part in all the great debates of those eventful times. The ablest speakers of the opposition always had to answer him; and when he answered them, they showed by their anxious concern, that the adversary was upon them whose force they dreaded most. Though taking his full part upon all subjects, yet finance was his particular department, always chairman of that committee, when his party was in power, and by the lucidity of his statements making plain the most intricate moneyed details. He had a just conception of the difference between the functions of the finance committee of the Senate, and the committee of ways and means of the House— so little understood in these latter times: those of the latter founded in the prerogative of the House to originate all revenue bills; those of the former to act upon the propositions from the House, without originating measures which might affect the revenue, so as to coerce either its increase or prevent its reduction. In 1844 he left the Senate, to stand for the governorship of New York; and never did his self-sacrificing temper undergo a stronger trial, or submit to a greater sacrifice. He liked the Senate: he disliked the governorship, even to absolute repugnance. But it was said to him (and truly, as then believed, and afterwards proved) that the State would be lost to Mr. Polk, unless Mr. Wright was associated with him in the canvass: and to this argument he yielded. He stood the canvass for the governorship—carried it—and Mr. Polk with him; and saved the presidential election of that year.

Judgment was the character of Mr. Wright's mind: purity the quality of the heart. Though valuable in the field of debate, he was still more valued at the council table, where sense and honesty are most demanded. General Jackson and Mr. Van Buren relied upon him as one of their safest counsellors. A candor which knew no guile— an integrity which knew no deviation—which worked right on, like a machine governed by a law of which it was unconscious—were the inexorable conditions of his nature, ruling his conduct in every act, public and private. No foul legislation ever emanated from him. The jobber, the speculator, the dealer in false claims, the plunderer, whose scheme required an act of Congress; all these found in his vigilance and perspicacity a detective police, which discovered their designs, and in his integrity a scorn of corruption which kept them at a distance from the purity of his atmosphere.

His temper was gentle—his manners simple—his intercourse kindly—his habits laborious—and rich upon a freehold of thirty acres, in much part cultivated by his own hand. In the intervals of senatorial duties this man, who refused cabinet appointments and presidential honors, and a seat upon the Supreme Bench—who measured strength with Clay, Webster, and Calhoun, and on whose accents admiring Senates hung: this man, his neat suit of broadcloth and fine linen exchanged for the laborer's dress, might be seen in the harvest field, or meadow, carrying the foremost row, and doing the cleanest work: and this not as recreation or pastime, or encouragement to others, but as work, which was to count in the annual cultivation, and labor to be felt in the production of the needed crop. His principles were democratic, and innate, founded in a feeling, still more than a conviction, that the masses were generally right in their sentiments, though sometimes wrong in their action; and that there was less injury to the country from the honest mistakes of the people, than from the interested schemes of corrupt and intriguing politicians. He was born in Massachusetts, came to man's estate in New York, received from that State the only honors he would accept; and in choosing his place of residence in it gave proof of his modest, retiring, unpretending nature. Instead of following his profession in the commercial or political capital of his State, where there would be demand and reward for his talent, he constituted himself a village lawyer where there was neither, and pertinaciously refused to change his locality. In an outside county, on the extreme border of the State, taking its name of St. Lawrence from the river which washed its northern side, and divided the United States from British America—and in one of the smallest towns of that county, and in one of the least ambitious houses of that modest town, lived and died this patriot statesman—a good husband (he had no children)—a good neighbor—a kind relative—a fast friend—exact and punctual in every duty, and the exemplification of every social and civic virtue.

CHAPTER CLXX.

THIRTIETH CONGRESS: FIRST SESSION: LIST OF MEMBERS: PRESIDENT'S MESSAGE.

Senate.

MAINE.—Hannibal Hamlin, J. W. Bradbury.

NEW HAMPSHIRE.—Charles G. Atherton, John P. Hale.

VERMONT.—William Upham, Samuel S. Phelps.

MASSACHUSETTS.—Daniel Webster, John Davis.

RHODE ISLAND.—Albert C. Greene, John H. Clarke.

CONNECTICUT.—John M. Niles, Roger S. Baldwin.

NEW YORK.—John A. Dix, Daniel S. Dickinson.

NEW JERSEY.—William L. Dayton, Jacob W. Miller.

PENNSYLVANIA.—Simon Cameron, Daniel Sturgeon.

DELAWARE.—John M. Clayton, Presley Spruance.

MARYLAND.—James A. Pearce, Reverdy Johnson.

VIRGINIA.—James M. Mason, R. M. T. Hunter.

NORTH CAROLINA.—George. E. Badger, Willie P. Mangum.

SOUTH CAROLINA.—A. P. Butler, John C. Calhoun.

GEORGIA.—Herschell V. Johnson, John M. Berrien.

ALABAMA.—William R. King, Arthur P. Bagley.

MISSISSIPPI.—Jefferson Davis, Henry Stuart Foote.

LOUISIANA.—Henry Johnson, S. U. Downs.

TENNESSEE.—Hopkins L. Turney, John Bell.

KENTUCKY.—Thomas Metcalfe, Joseph R. Underwood.

OHIO.—William Allen, Thomas Corwin.

INDIANA.—Edward A. Hannegan, Jesse D. Bright.

ILLINOIS.—Sidney Breese, Stephen A. Douglass.

MISSOURI.—David R. Atchison, Thomas H. Benton.

ARKANSAS.—Solon Borland, William K. Sebastian.

MICHIGAN.—Thomas Fitzgerald, Alpheus Felch.

FLORIDA.—J. D. Westcott, Jr., David Yulee.

TEXAS.—Thomas J. Rusk, Samuel Houston.

IOWA.—Augustus C. Dodge, George W. Jones.

WISCONSIN.—Henry Dodge, I. P. Walker.

House of Representatives.

MAINE.—David Hammonds, Asa W. H. Clapp, Hiram Belcher, Franklin Clark, E. K. Smart, James S. Wiley, Hezekiah Williams.

NEW HAMPSHIRE.—Amos Tuck, Charles H. Peaslee, James Wilson, James H. Johnson.

MASSACHUSETTS.—Rob't C. Winthrop, Daniel P. King, Amos Abbott, John G. Palfrey, Chas. Hudson, George Ashmun, Julius Rockwell, Horace Mann, Artemas Hale, Joseph Grinnell.

RHODE ISLAND.—R. B. Cranston, B. B. Thurston.

CONNECTICUT.—James Dixon, S. D. Hilliard, J. A. Rockwell, Truman Smith.

VERMONT.—William Henry, Jacob Collamer, George P. Marsh, Lucius B. Peck.

NEW YORK.—Frederick W. Lloyd, H. C. Murphy, Henry Nicoll, W. B. Maclay, Horace Greeley, William Nelson, Cornelius Warren, Daniel B. St. John, Eliakim Sherrill, P. H. Sylvester, Gideon Reynolds, J. I. Slingerland, Orlando Kellogg, S. Lawrence, Hugh White, George Petrie, Joseph Mullin, William Collins, Timothy Jenkins, G. A. Starkweather, Ausburn Birdsall, William Duer, Daniel Gott, Harmon S. Conger, William T. Lawrence, Ebon Blackman, Elias B. Holmes, Robert L. Rose, David Ramsay, Dudly Marvin, Nathan K. Hall, Harvey Putnam, Washington Hunt.

NEW JERSEY.—James G. Hampton, William A. Newell, Joseph Edsall, J. Van Dyke, D. S. Gregory.

PENNSYLVANIA.—Lewis C. Levin, J. R. Ingersoll, Charles Brown, C. J. Ingersoll, John Freedly, Samuel A. Bridges, A. R. McIlvaine, John Strohm, William Strong, R. Brodhead, Chester Butler, David Wilmot, James Pollock, George N. Eckert, Henry Nes, Jasper E. Brady, John Blanchard, Andrew Stewart, Job Mann, John Dickey, Moses Hampton, J. W. Farrelly, James Thompson, Alexander Irvine.

DELAWARE.—John W. Houston.

MARYLAND.—J. G. Chapman, J. Dixon Roman, T. Watkins Ligon, R. M. McLane, Alexander Evans, John W. Crisfield.

VIRGINIA.—Archibald Atkinson, Richard K. Meade, Thomas S. Flournoy, Thomas S. Bocock, William L. Goggin, John M. Botts, Thomas H. Bayly, R. T. L. Beale, J. S. Pendleton, Henry Bedinger, James McDowell, William B. Preston, Andrew S. Fulton, R. A. Thompson, William G. Brown.

NORTH CAROLINA.—Thomas S. Clingman, Nathaniel Boyden, D. M. Berringer, Aug. H. Shepherd, Abm. W. Venable, James J. McKay, J. R. J. Daniel, Richard S. Donnell, David Outlaw.

SOUTH CAROLINA.—Daniel Wallace, Richard F. Simpson, J. A. Woodward, Artemas Burt, Isaac E. Holmes, R. Barnwell Rhett.

GEORGIA.—T. Butler King, Alfred Iverson, John W. Jones, H. A. Harralson, J. A. Lumpkin, Howell Cobb, A. H. Stephens, Robert Toombs.

ALABAMA.—John Gayle, H. W. Hilliard, S. W. Harris, William M. Inge, G. S. Houston, W. R. W. Cobb, F. W. Bowdon.

MISSISSIPPI.—Jacob Thompson, W. S. Featherston, Patrick W. Tompkins, Albert G. Brown.

LOUISIANA.—Emile La Sere, B. G. Thibodeaux, J. M. Harmansan, Isaac E. Morse.

FLORIDA.—Edward C. Cabell.

OHIO.—James J. Faran, David Fisher, Robert C. Schenck, Richard S. Canby, William Sawyer, R. Dickinson, Jonathan D. Morris, J. L. Taylor, T. O. Edwards, Daniel Duncan, John K. Miller, Samuel F. Vinton, Thomas Richey, Nathan Evans, William Kennon, Jr., J. D. Cummins, George Fries, Samuel Lahm, John Crowell, J. R. Giddings, Joseph M. Root.

INDIANA.—Elisha Embree, Thomas J. Henley, J. L. Robinson, Caleb B. Smith, William W. Wick, George G. Dunn, R. W. Thompson, John Pettit, C. W. Cathcart, William Rockhill.

MICHIGAN.—R. McClelland, Cha's E. Stewart, Kinsley S. Bingham.

ILLINOIS.—Robert Smith, J. A. McClernand, O. B. Ficklin, John Wentworth, W. A. Richardson, Thomas J. Turner, A. Lincoln.

IOWA.—William Thompson, Shepherd Leffler.

KENTUCKY.—Linn Boyd, Samuel O. Peyton, B. L. Clark, Aylett Buckner, J. B. Thompson, Green Adams, Garnett Duncan, Charles S. Morehead, Richard French, John P. Gaines.

TENNESSEE.—Andrew Johnson, William M. Cocke, John H. Crozier, H. L. W. Hill, George W. Jones, James H. Thomas, Meredith P. Gentry, Washington Barrow, Lucien B. Chase, Frederick P. Stanton, William T. Haskell.

MISSOURI.—James B. Bowlin, John Jamieson, James S. Green, Willard P. Hall, John S. Phelps.

ARKANSAS.—Robert W. Johnson.

TEXAS.—David S. Kaufman, Timothy Pillsbury.

WISCONSIN.—Mason C. Darling, William Pitt Lynde.

Robert C. Winthrop, Esq., of Massachusetts, was elected Speaker of the House, and Benjamin B. French, Esq., clerk, and soon after the President's message was delivered, a quorum of the Senate having appeared the first day. The election of Speaker had decided the question of the political character of the House, and showed the administration to be in a minority:—a bad omen for the popularity of the Mexican war. The President had gratifying events to communicate to Congress—the victories of Cerro Gordo, Contreras and Churubusco, the storming of Chepultepec, and the capture of the City of Mexico: and exulted over these exploits with the pride of an American, although all these advantages had to be gained over the man whom he handed back into Mexico under the belief that he was to make peace. He also informed Congress that a commissioner had been sent to the head-quarters of the American army to take advantage of events to treat for peace; and that he had carried out with him the draught of the treaty, already prepared, which contained the terms on which alone the war was to be terminated. This commissioner was Nicholas P. Trist, Esq., principal clerk in the Department of State, a man of mind and integrity, well acquainted with the state of parties in Mexico, subject to none at home, and anxious to establish peace between the countries. Upon the capture of the city, and the downfall of Santa Anna, commissioners were appointed to meet Mr. Trist; but the Mexican government, far from accepting the treaty as drawn up and sent to them, submitted other terms still more objectionable to us than ours to them; and the two parties remained without prospect of agreement. The American commissioner was recalled, "*under the belief*," said the message, "*that his continued presence with the army could do no good*." This recall was despatched from the United States the 6th of October, immediately after information had been received of the failure of the attempted negotiations; but, as will be seen hereafter, the notice of the recall arriving when negotiations had been resumed with good prospect of success, Mr. Trist remained at his post to finish his work.

In the course of the summer a "*female*," fresh from Mexico, and with a masculine stomach for war and politics, arrived at Washington, had interviews with members of the administration, and infected some of them with the contagion of a large project—nothing less than the absorption into our Union of all Mexico, and the assumption of all her debts (many tens of millions *in esse*, and more *in posse*), and all to be assumed at par, though the best were at 25 cents in the dollar, and the mass ranging down to five cents. This project was given out, and greatly applauded in some of the administration papers—condemned by the public feeling, and greatly denounced in a large opposition meeting in Lexington, Kentucky, at which Mr. Clay came forth from his retirement to speak wisely and patriotically against it. The "*female*" had gone back to Mexico, with high letters from some members of the cabinet to the commanding general, and to the plenipotentiary negotiator; both of whom, however, eschewed the proffered aid. A party in Mexico developed itself for this total absorption, and total assumption of debts, and the scheme acquired so much notoriety, and gained such consistency of detail, and stuck so close to some members of the administration, that the President deemed it necessary to clear himself from the suspicion; which he did in a decisive paragraph of his message:

"It has never been contemplated by me, as an object of the war, to make a permanent conquest of the republic of Mexico, or to annihilate her separate existence as an independent nation. On the contrary, it has ever been my desire that she should maintain her nationality, and, under a good government adapted to her condition, be a free, independent, and prosperous republic. The United States were the first among the nations to recognize her independence, and have always desired to be on terms of amity and good neighborhood with her. This she would not suffer. By her own conduct we have been compelled to engage in the present war. In its prosecution, we seek not her overthrow as a nation, but, in vindicating our national honor, we seek to obtain redress for the wrongs she has done us, and indemnity for our just demands against her. We demand an honorable peace; and that peace must bring with it indemnity for the past, and security for the future."

While some were for total absorption, others were for half; and for taking a line (provisionally during the war), preparatory to its becoming permanent at its close, and giving to the United States the northern States of Mexico from gulf to gulf. This project the President also repulsed in a paragraph of his message:

"To retire to a line, and simply hold and defend it, would not terminate the war. On the contrary, it would encourage Mexico to persevere, and tend to protract it indefinitely. It is not to be expected that Mexico, after refusing to establish such a line as a permanent boundary when our victorious army are in possession of her capital, and in the heart of her country, would permit us to hold it without resistance. That she would continue the war, and in the most harassing and annoying forms, there can be no doubt. A border warfare of the most savage character, extending over a long line, would be unceasingly waged. It would require a large army to be kept constantly in the field stationed at posts and garrisons along such a line, to protect and defend it. The enemy, relieved from the pressure of our arms on his coasts and in the populous parts of the interior, would direct his attention to this line, and selecting an isolated post for attack, would concentrate his forces upon it. This would be a condition of affairs which the Mexicans, pursuing their favorite system of guerilla warfare, would probably prefer to any other. Were we to assume a defensive attitude on such a line, all the advantages of such a state of war would be on the side of the enemy. We could levy no contributions upon him, or in any other way make him feel the pressure of the war; but must remain inactive, and wait his approach, being in constant uncertainty at what point on the line, or at what time, he might make an assault. He may assemble and organize an overwhelming force in the interior, on his own side of the line, and, concealing his purpose, make a sudden assault on some one of our posts so distant from any other as to prevent the possibility of timely succor or reinforcements; and in this way our gallant army would be exposed to the danger of being cut off in detail; or if by their unequalled bravery and prowess every where exhibited during this war, they should repulse the enemy, their number stationed at any one post may be too small to pursue him. If the enemy be repulsed in one attack, he would have nothing to do but to retreat to his own side of the line, and being in no fear of a pursuing army, may reinforce himself at leisure, for another attack on the same or some other post. He may, too, cross the line between our posts, make rapid incursions into the country which we hold, murder the inhabitants, commit depredations on them, and then retreat to the interior before a sufficient force can be concentrated to pursue him. Such would probably be the harassing character of a mere defensive war on our part. If our forces, when attacked, or threatened with attack, be permitted to cross the line, drive back the enemy, and conquer him, this would be again to invade the enemy's country, after having lost all the advantages of the conquests we have already made by having voluntarily abandoned them. To hold such a line successfully and in security, it is far from being certain that it would not require as large an army as would be necessary to hold all the conquests we have already made, and to continue the prosecution of the war in the heart of the enemy's country. It is also far from being certain that the expense of the war would be diminished by such a policy."

These were the same arguments which Senator Benton had addressed to the President the year before, when the recommendation of this line of occupation had gone into the draught of his message, as a cabinet measure, and was with such difficulty got out of it; but without getting it out of the head of Mr. Calhoun and his political friends. To return to the argument against such a line, in this subsequent message, bespoke an adherence to it on the part of some formidable interest, which required to be authoritatively combated: and such was the fact. The formidable interest which wished a separation of the slave from the free States, wished also as an extension of their Southern territory, to obtain a broad slice from Mexico, embracing Tampico as a port on the east, Guaymas as a port on the Gulf of California, and Monterey and Saltillo in the middle. Mr. Polk did not sympathize with that interest, and publicly repulsed their plan—without, however, extinguishing their scheme—which survives, and still labors at its consummation in a different form, and with more success.

The expenses of the government during that season of war, were the next interesting head of the message, and were presented, all heads of expenditure included, at some fifty-eight millions of dollars; or a quarter less than those same expenses now are in a state of peace The message says:

> "It is estimated that the receipts into the Treasury for the fiscal year ending on the 30th of June, 1848, including the balance in the Treasury on the 1st of July last, will amount to forty-two millions eight hundred and eighty-six thousand five hundred and forty-five dollars and eighty cents; of which thirty-one millions, it is estimated, will be derived from customs; three millions five hundred thousand from the sale of the public lands; four hundred thousand from incidental sources; including sales made by the solicitor of the Treasury; and six millions two hundred and eighty-five thousand two hundred and ninety-four dollars and fifty-five cents from loans already authorized by law, which, together with the balance in the Treasury on the 1st of July last, make the sum estimated. The expenditures for the same period, if peace with Mexico shall not be concluded, and the army shall be increased as is proposed, will amount, including the necessary payments on account of principal and interest of the public debt and Treasury notes, to fifty-eight millions six hundred and fifteen thousand and sixty dollars and seven cents."

An encomium upon the good working of the independent treasury system, and the perpetual repulse of paper money from the federal Treasury, concluded the heads of this message which retain a surviving interest:

> "The financial system established by the constitutional Treasury has been, thus far, eminently successful in its operations; and I recommend an adherence to all its essential provisions; and especially to that vital provision, which wholly separates the government from all connection with banks, and excludes bank paper from all revenue receipts."

An earnest exhortation to a vigorous prosecution of the war concluded the message.

CHAPTER CLXXI.

DEATH OF SENATOR BARROW: MR. BENTON'S EULOGIUM.

MR. BENTON. In rising to second the motion for paying to the memory of our deceased brother senator the last honors of this body, I feel myself to be obeying the impulsions of an hereditary friendship, as well as conforming to the practice of the Senate. Forty years ago, when coming to the bar at Nashville, it was my good fortune to enjoy the friendship of the father of the deceased, then an inhabitant of Nashville, and one of its most respected citizens. The deceased was then too young to be noted amongst the rest of the family. The pursuits of life soon carried us far apart, and long after, and for the first time to know each other, we met on this floor. We met not as strangers, but as friends—friends of early and hereditary recollections; and all our intercourse since—every incident and every word of our lives, public and private—has gone to strengthen and confirm the feelings under which we met, and to perpetuate with the son the friendship which had existed with the father. Up to the last moments of his presence in this chamber—up to the last moment that I saw him—our meetings and partings were the cordial greetings of hereditary friendship; and now, not only as one of the elder senators, but as the early and family friend of the deceased, I come forward to second the motion for the honors to his memory.

The senator from Louisiana (Mr. H. Johnson) has performed the office of duty and of friendship to his deceased friend and colleague. Justly, truly and feelingly has he performed it. With deep and heartfelt emotion he has portrayed the virtues, and sketched the qualities, which constituted the manly and lofty character of Alexander Barrow. He has given us a picture as faithful as it is honorable, and it does not become me to dilate upon what he has so well presented; but, in contemplating the rich and full portrait of the high qualities of the head and heart which he has presented, suffer me to look for an instant to the source, the fountain, from which flowed the full stream of generous and noble actions which distinguished the entire life of our deceased brother senator. I speak of the heart—the noble heart—of Alexander Barrow. Honor, courage, patriotism, friendship, generosity—fidelity to his friend and his country—the social affections—devotion to the wife of his bosom, and the children of their love: all—all, were there! and never, not once, did any cold, or selfish, or timid calculation ever come from his manly head to check or balk the noble impulsions of his generous heart. A quick, clear, and strong judgment found nothing to restrain in these impulsions; and in all the wide circle of his public and private relations—in all the words and acts of his life—it was the heart that moved first, and always so true to honor that judgment had nothing to do but to approve the impulsion. From that fountain flowed the stream of the actions of his life; and now what we all deplore—what so many will join in deploring—is, that such a fountain, so unexpectedly, in the full tide of its flow, should have been so suddenly dried up. He was one of the younger members of this body, and in all the hope and vigor of meridian manhood. Time was ripening and maturing his faculties. He seemed to have a right to look forward to many years of usefulness to his country and to his family. With qualities evidently fitted for the *field* as well as for the Senate, a brilliant future was before him; ready, as I know he was, to serve his country in any way that honor and duty should require.

CHAPTER CLXXII.

DEATH OF MR. ADAMS.

"Just after the yeas and nays were taken on a question, and the Speaker had risen to put another question to the House, a sudden cry was heard on the left of the chair, 'Mr. Adams is dying!' Turning our eyes to the spot, we beheld the venerable man in the act of falling over the left arm of his chair, while his right arm was extended, grasping his desk for support. He would have dropped upon the floor had he not been caught in the arms of the member sitting next him. A great sensation was created in the House: members from all quarters rushing from their seats, and gathering round the fallen statesman, who was immediately lifted into the area in front of the clerk's table. The Speaker instantly suggested that some gentleman move an adjournment, which being promptly done, the House adjourned."

So wrote the editors of the National Intelligencer, friends and associates of Mr. Adams for forty years, and now witnesses of the last scene—the sudden sinking in his chair, which was to end in his death. The news flew to the Senate chamber, the Senate then in session, and engaged in business, which Mr. Benton interrupted, standing up, and saying to the President of the body and the senators:

"I am called on to make a painful announcement to the Senate. I have just been informed that the House of Representatives has this instant adjourned under the most afflictive circumstances. A calamitous visitation has fallen on one of its oldest and most valuable members—one who has been President of the United States, and whose character has inspired the highest respect and esteem. Mr. Adams has just sunk down in his chair, and has been carried into an adjoining room, and may be at this moment passing from the earth, under the roof that covers us, and almost in our presence. In these circumstances the whole Senate will feel alike, and feel wholly unable to attend to any business. I therefore move the immediate adjournment of the Senate."

The Senate immediately adjourned, and all inquiries were directed to the condition of the stricken statesman. He had been removed to the Speaker's room, where he slightly recovered the use of his speech, and uttered in faltering accents, the intelligible words, "*This is the last of earth;*" and soon after, "*I am composed.*" These were the last words he ever spoke. He lingered two days, and died on the evening of the 23d—struck the day before, and dying the day after the anniversary of Washington's birth—and attended by every circumstance which he could have chosen to give felicity in death. It was on the field of his labors—in the presence of the national representation, presided by a son of Massachusetts (Robert C. Winthrop, Esq.), in the full possession of his faculties, and of their faithful use—at octogenarian age—without a pang—hung over in his last unconscious moments by her who had been for more than fifty years the worthy partner of his bosom. Such a death was the "crowning mercy" of a long life of eminent and patriotic service, filled with every incident that gives dignity and lustre to human existence.

I was sitting in my library-room in the twilight of a raw and blustering day, the lamp not yet lit, when a note was delivered to me from Mr. Webster—I had saved it seven years, just seven—when it was destroyed in that conflagration of my house which consumed, in a moment, so much which I had long cherished. The note was to inform me that Mr. Adams had breathed his last; and to say that the Massachusetts delegation had fixed upon me to second the motion, which would be made in the Senate the next day, for the customary funeral honors to his memory. Seconding the motion on such an occasion always requires a brief discourse on the life and character of the deceased. I was taken by surprise, for I had not expected such an honor: I was oppressed; for a feeling of inability and unworthiness fell upon me. I went immediately to Mr. Winthrop, who was nearest, to inquire if some other senator had been named to take my place if I should find it impossible to comply with the request. He said there was none—that Mr. Davis, of Massachusetts, would make the motion, and that I was the only one named to second him. My part was then fixed. I went to the other end of the city to see Mr. Davis, and so to arrange with him as to avoid repetitions—which was done, that he should speak of events, and I of characteristics. It was late in the night when I got back to my house, and took pen and paper to note the heads of what I should say. Never did I feel so much the weight of Cicero's admonition—"*Choose with discretion out of the plenty that lies before you.*" The plenty was too much. It was a field crowded with fruits and flowers, of which you could only cull a few—a mine filled with gems, of which you could only snatch a handful. By midnight I had finished the task, and was ready for the ceremony.

Mr. Adams died a member of the House, and the honors to his memory commenced there, to be finished in the Senate. Mr. Webster was suffering from domestic affliction—the death of a son and a daughter—and could not appear among the speakers. Several members of the House spoke justly and beautifully; and of these, the pre-eminent beauty and justice of the discourse delivered by Mr. James McDowell, of Virginia (even if he had not been a near connection, the brother of Mrs. Benton), would lead me to give it the preference in selecting some passages from the tributes of the House. With a feeling and melodious delivery, he said:

"It is not for Massachusetts to mourn alone over a solitary and exclusive bereavement. It is not for her to feel alone a solitary and exclusive sorrow. No, sir; no! Her sister commonwealths gather to her side in this hour of her affliction, and, intertwining their arms with hers, they bend together over the bier of her illustrious son—feeling as she feels, and weeping as she weeps, over a sage, a patriot, and a statesman gone! It was in these great characteristics of individual and of public man that his country reverenced that son when living, and such, with a painful sense of her common loss, will she deplore him now that he is dead.

"Born in our revolutionary day, and brought up in early and cherished intimacy with the fathers and founders of the republic, he was a living bond of connection between the present and the past—the venerable representative of the memories of another age, and the zealous, watchful, and powerful one of the expectations, interests, and progressive knowledge of his own.

"There he sat, with his intense eye upon every thing that passed, the picturesque and rare one man, unapproachable by all others in the unity of his character and in the thousand-fold anxieties which centred upon him. No human being ever entered this hall without turning habitually and with heart-felt deference first to him, and few ever left it without pausing, as they went, to pour out their blessings upon that spirit of consecration to the country which brought and which kept him here.

"Standing upon the extreme boundary of human life, and disdaining all the relaxations and exemptions of age, his outer framework only was crumbling away. The glorious engine within still worked on unhurt, uninjured, amid all the dilapidations around it, and worked on with its wonted and its iron power, until the blow was sent from above which crushed it into fragments before us. And, however appalling that blow, and however profoundly it smote upon our own feelings as we beheld its extinguishing effect upon his, where else could it have fallen so fitly upon him? Where else could he have been relieved from the yoke of his labors so well as in the field where he bore them? Where else would he himself have been so willing to have yielded up his life, as upon the post of duty, and by the side of that very altar to which he had devoted it? Where but in the capitol of his country, to which all the throbbings and hopes of his heart had been given, would the dying patriot be so willing that those hopes and throbbings should cease? And where but from this mansion-house of liberty on earth, could this dying Christian more fitly go to his mansion-house of eternal liberty on high?"

Mr. Benton concluded in the Senate the ceremonies which had commenced in the House, pronouncing the brief discourse which was intended to group into one cluster the varied characteristics of the public and private life of this most remarkable man:

"The voice of his native State has been heard, through one of the senators of Massachusetts, announcing the death of her aged and most distinguished son. The voice of the other senator from Massachusetts is not heard, nor is his presence seen. A domestic calamity, known to us all, and felt by us all, confines him to the chamber of grief while the Senate is occupied with the public manifestations of a respect and sorrow which a national loss inspires. In the absence of that senator, and as the member of this body longest here, it is not unfitting or unbecoming in me to second the motion which has been made for extending the last honors of the Senate to him who, forty-five years ago, was a member of this body, who, at the time of his death, was among the oldest members of the House of Representatives, and who, putting the years of his service together, was the oldest of all the members of the American government.

"The eulogium of Mr. Adams is made in the facts of his life, which the senator from Massachusetts (Mr. Davis) has so strikingly stated, that from early manhood to octogenarian age, he has been constantly and most honorably employed in the public service. For a period of more than fifty years, from the time of his first appointment as minister abroad under Washington, to his last election to the House of Representatives by the people of his native district, he has been constantly retained in the public service, and that, not by the favor of a sovereign, or by hereditary title, but by the elections and appointments of republican government. This fact makes the eulogy of the illustrious deceased. For what, except a union of all the qualities which command the esteem and confidence of man, could have insured a public service so long, by appointments free and popular, and from sources so various and exalted? Minister many times abroad; member of this body; member of the House of Representatives; cabinet minister; President of the United States; such has been the galaxy of his splendid appointments. And what but moral excellence the most perfect; intellectual ability the most eminent; fidelity the most unwavering; service the most useful; would have commanded such a succession of appointments so exalted, and from sources so various and so eminent? Nothing less could have commanded such a series of appointments; and accordingly we see the union of all these great qualities in him who has received them.

"In this long career of public service, Mr. Adams was distinguished not only by faithful attention to all the great duties of his stations, but to all their less and minor duties. He was not the Salaminian galley, to be launched only on extraordinary occasions; but he was the ready vessel, always under sail when the duties of his station required it, be the occasion great or small. As President, as cabinet minister, as minister abroad, he examined all questions that came before him, and examined all, in all their parts—in all the minutiæ of their detail, as well as in all the vastness of their comprehension. As senator, and as a member of the House of Representatives, the obscure committee-room was as much the witness of his laborious application to the drudgery of legislation, as the halls of the two Houses were to the ever-ready speech, replete with knowledge, which instructed all hearers, enlightened all subjects, and gave dignity and ornament to all debate.

"In the observance of all the proprieties of life, Mr. Adams was a most noble and impressive example. He cultivated the minor as well as the greater virtues. Wherever his presence could give aid and countenance to what was useful and honorable to man, there he was. In the exercises of the school and of the college—in the meritorious meetings of the agricultural, mechanical, and commercial societies—in attendance upon Divine worship—he gave the punctual attendance rarely seen but in those who are free from the weight of public cares.

"Punctual to every duty, death found him at the post of duty; and where else could it have found him, at any stage of his career, for the fifty years of his illustrious public life? From the time of his first appointment by Washington to his last election by the people of his native town, where could death have found him but at the post of duty? At that post, in the fulness of age, in the ripeness of renown crowned with honors, surrounded by his family, his friends, and admirers, and in the very presence of the national representation, he has been gathered to his fathers, leaving behind him the memory of public services which are the history of his country for half a century, and the example of a life, public and private, which should be the study and the model of the generations of his countrymen."

The whole ceremony was inconceivably impressive. The two Houses of Congress were filled to their utmost capacity, and of all that Washington contained, and neighboring cities could send—the President, his cabinet, foreign ministers, judges of the Supreme Court, senators and representatives, citizens and visitors.

CHAPTER CLXXIII.

DOWNFALL OF SANTA ANNA: NEW GOVERNMENT IN MEXICO: PEACE NEGOTIATIONS: TREATY OF PEACE.

The war was declared May 13th, 1846, upon a belief, grounded on the projected restoration of Santa Anna (then in exile in Havana), that it would be finished in ninety to one hundred and twenty days, and that, in the mean time, no fighting would take place. Santa Anna did not get back until the month of August; and, simultaneously with his return, was the President's overture for peace, and application to Congress for two millions of dollars—with leave to pay the money in the city of Mexico on the conclusion of peace there, without waiting for the ratification of the treaty by the United States. Such an overture, and such an application, and the novelty of paying money upon a treaty before it was ratified by our own authorities, bespoke a great desire to obtain peace, even by extraordinary means. And such was the fact. The desire was great—the means unusual; but the event baffled all the calculations. Santa Anna repulsed the peace overture, put himself at the head of armies, inflamed the war spirit of the country, and fought desperately. It was found that a mistake had been made—that the sword, and not the olive branch had been returned to Mexico; and that, before peace could be made, it became the part of brave soldiers to conquer by arms the man whom intrigue had brought back to grant it. Brought back by politicians, he had to be driven out by victorious generals before the peace he was to give could be obtained. The victories before the city of Mexico, and the capture of the city, put an end to his career. The republican party, which abhorred him, seized upon those defeats to depose him. He fled the country, and a new administration being organized, peaceful negotiations were resumed, and soon terminated in the desired pacification. Mr. Trist had remained at his post, though recalled, and went on with his negotiations. In three months after his downfall, and without further operation of arms, the treaty was signed, and all the desired stipulations obtained. New Mexico and Upper California were ceded to the United States, and the lower Rio Grande, from its mouth to El Paso, taken for the boundary of Texas. These were the acquisitions. On the other hand, the United States agreed to pay to Mexico fifteen millions of dollars in five instalments, annual after the first; which first instalment, true to the original idea of the efficacy of money in terminating the war, was to be paid down in the city of Mexico as soon as the articles of pacification were signed, and ratified there. The claims of American citizens against Mexico were all assumed, limited to three and a quarter millions of dollars, which, considering that the war ostensibly originated in these claims, was a very small sum. But the largest gratified interest was one which did not appear on the face of the treaty, but had the full benefit of being included in it. They were the speculators in Texas lands and scrip, now allowed to calculate largely upon their increased value as coming under the flag of the American Union. They were among the original promoters of the Texas annexation, among the most clamorous for war, and among the gratified at the peace. General provisions only were admitted into the treaty in favor of claims and land titles. Upright and disinterested himself, the negotiator sternly repulsed all attempts to get special, or personal provisions to be inserted in behalf of any individuals or companies. The treaty was a singular conclusion of the war. Undertaken to get indemnity for claims, the United States paid those claims herself. Fifteen millions of dollars were the full price of New Mexico and California—the same that was paid for all Louisiana; so that, with the claims assumed, the amount paid for the territories, and the expenses of the war, the acquisitions were made at a dear rate. The same amount paid to Mexico without the war, and by treating her respectfully in treating with her for a boundary which would include Texas, might have obtained the same cessions; for every Mexican knew that Texas was gone, and that New Mexico and Upper California were going the same way, both inhabited and dominated by American citizens, and the latter actually severed from Mexico by a successful revolution before the war was known of, and for the purpose of being transferred to the United States.

The treaty was a fortunate event for the United States, and for the administration which had made it. The war had disappointed the calculation on which it began. Instead of brief, cheap, and bloodless, it had become long, costly, and sanguinary: instead of getting a peace through the restoration of Santa Anna, that formidable chieftain had to be vanquished and expelled, before negotiations could be commenced with those who would always have treated fairly, if their national feelings had not been outraged by the aggressive and defiant manner in which Texas had been incorporated. Great discontent was breaking out at home. The Congress elections were going against the administration, and the aspirants for the presidency in the cabinet were struck with terror at the view of the great military reputations which were growing up. Peace was the only escape from so many dangers, and it was gladly seized upon to terminate a war which had disappointed all calculations, and the very successes of which were becoming alarming to them.

Mr. Trist signed his treaty in the beginning of February, and it stands on the statute-book, as it was in fact, the sole work on the American side, of that negotiator. Two ministers plenipotentiary and envoys extraordinary were sent out to treat after he had been recalled. They arrived after the work was done, and only brought home what he had finished. His name alone is signed to the treaty on the American side, against three on the Mexican side: his name alone appears on the American side in the enumeration of the ministers in the preamble to the treaty. In that preamble he is characterized as the "*plenipotentiary*" of the United States, and by that title he was described in the commission given him by the President. His work was accepted, communicated to the Senate, ratified; and became a supreme law of the land: yet he himself was rejected! recalled and dismissed, without the emoluments of plenipotentiary; while two others received those emoluments in full for bringing home a treaty in which their names do not appear. Certainly those who served the government well in that war with Mexico, fared badly with the administration. Taylor, who had vanquished at Palo Alto, Resaca de la Palma, Monterey, and Buena Vista, was quarrelled with: Scott, who removed the obstacles to peace, and subdued the Mexican mind to peace, was superseded in the command of the army: Frémont, who had snatched California out of the hands of the British, and handed it over to the United States, was court-martialled: and Trist, who made the treaty which secured the objects of the war, and released the administration from its dangers, was recalled and dismissed.

CHAPTER CLXXIV.

OREGON TERRITORIAL GOVERNMENT: ANTI-SLAVERY ORDINANCE OF 1787 APPLIED TO OREGON TERRITORY: MISSOURI COMPROMISE LINE OF 1820, AND THE TEXAS ANNEXATION RENEWAL OF IT IN 1845, AFFIRMED.

It was on the bill for the establishment of the Oregon territorial government that Mr. Calhoun first made trial of his new doctrine of, "No power in Congress to abolish slavery in territories;" which, so far from maintaining, led to the affirmation of the contrary doctrine, and to the discovery of his own, early as well as late support, of what he now condemned as a breach of the constitution, and justifiable cause for a separation of the slave from the free States. For it was on this occasion that Senator Dix, of New York, produced the ample proofs that Mr. Calhoun, as a member of Mr. Monroe's cabinet, supported the constitutionality of the Missouri compromise at the time it was made; and his own avowals eighteen years afterwards proved the same thing—all to be confirmed by subsequent authentic acts. On the motion of Mr. Hale, in the Senate, the bill (which had come up from the House without any provision on the subject of slavery) was amended so as to extend the principle of the anti-slavery clause of the ordinance of '87 to the bill. Mr. Douglass moved to amend by inserting a provision for the extension of the Missouri compromise line to the Pacific Ocean. His proposed amendment was specific, and intended to be permanent, and to apply to the organization of all future territories established in the West. It was in these words:

> "That the line of thirty-six degrees and thirty minutes of north latitude, known as the Missouri compromise line, as defined by the eighth section of an act entitled 'An act to authorize the people of the Missouri territory to form a constitution and State government, and for the admission of such State into the Union on an equal footing with the original States, and to prohibit slavery in certain territories, approved March 6, 1820,' be, and the same is hereby, declared to extend to the Pacific Ocean; and the said eighth section, together with the compromise therein effected, is hereby revived, and declared to be in full force and binding, for the future organization of the territories of the United States, in the same sense, and with the same understanding, with which it was originally adopted."

The yeas and nays were demanded on the adoption of this amendment, and resulted, 33 for it, 22 against it. They were:

> "YEAS—Messrs. Atchison, Badger, Bell, Benton, Berrien, Borland, Bright, Butler, Calhoun, Cameron, Davis of Mississippi, Dickinson, Douglass, Downs, Fitzgerald, Foote, Hannegan, Houston, Hunter, Johnson of Maryland, Johnson of Louisiana, Johnson of Georgia, King, Lewis, Mangum, Mason, Metcalfe, Pearce, Sebastian, Spruance, Sturgeon, Turney, Underwood.

> "NAYS—Messrs. Allen, Atherton, Baldwin, Bradbury, Breese, Clark, Corwin, Davis of Massachusetts, Dayton, Dix, Dodge, Felch, Greene, Hale, Hamlin, Miller, Niles, Phelps, Upham, Walker, Webster."

The vote here given by Mr. Calhoun was in contradiction to his new doctrine, and excused upon some subtle distinction between a vote for an amendment, and a bill, and upon a reserved intent to vote against the bill itself if adopted. Considering that his objections to the matter of the amendment were constitutional and not expedient, and that the votes of others might pass the bill with the clause in it without his help, it is impossible to see the validity of the distinction with which he satisfied himself. His language was that, "though he had voted for the introduction of the Missouri compromise, he could not vote for the bill which he regarded as artificial." Eventually the bill passed through both Houses with the anti-slavery principle of the ordinance embraced in it; whereat Mr. Calhoun became greatly excited, and assuming to act upon the new doctrine that he had laid down, that the exclusion of slavery from any territory was a subversion of the Union, openly proclaimed the strife between the North and the South to be ended, and the separation of the States accomplished; called upon the South to do her duty to herself, and denounced every Southern representative who would not follow the same course that he did. He exclaimed:

"The great strife between the North and the South is ended. The North is determined to exclude the property of the slaveholder, and of course the slaveholder himself, from its territory. On this point there seems to be no division in the North. In the South, he regretted to say, there was some division of sentiment. The effect of this determination of the North was to convert all the Southern population into slaves; and he would never consent to entail that disgrace on his posterity. He denounced any Southern man who would not take the same course. Gentlemen were greatly mistaken if they supposed the presidential question in the South would override this more important one. The separation of the North and the South is completed. The South has now a most solemn obligation to perform—to herself—to the constitution—to the Union. She is bound to come to a decision not to permit this to go on any further, but to show that, dearly as she prizes the Union, there are questions which she regards as of greater importance than the Union. She is bound to fulfil her obligations as she may best understand them. This is not a question of territorial government, but a question involving the continuance of the Union. Perhaps it was better that this question should come to an end, in order that some new point should be taken."

This was an open invocation to disunion, and from that time forth the efforts were regular to obtain a meeting of the members from the slave States, to unite in a call for a convention of the slave States to redress themselves. Mr. Benton and General Houston, who had supported the Oregon bill, were denounced by name by Mr. Calhoun after his return to South Carolina, "as traitors to the South:" a denunciation which they took for a distinction; as, what he called treason to the South, they knew to be allegiance to the Union. The President, in approving the Oregon bill, embraced the opportunity to send in a special message on the slavery agitation, in which he showed the danger to the Union from the progress of that agitation, and the necessity of adhering to the principles of the ordinance of 1787—the terms of the Missouri compromise of 1820—and the Texas compromise (as he well termed it) of 1845, as the means of averting the danger. These are his warnings:

"The fathers of the constitution—the wise and patriotic men who laid the foundation of our institutions—foreseeing the danger from this quarter, acted in a spirit of compromise and mutual concession on this dangerous and delicate subject; and their wisdom ought to be the guide of their successors. Whilst they left to the States exclusively the question of domestic slavery within their respective limits, they provided that slaves, who might escape into other States not recognizing the institution of slavery, shall 'be delivered up on the claim of the party to whom such service or labor may be due.' Upon this foundation the matter rested until the Missouri question arose. In December, 1819, application was made to Congress by the people of the Missouri territory for admission into the Union as a State. The discussion upon the subject in Congress involved the question of slavery, and was prosecuted with such violence as to produce excitements alarming to every patriot in the Union. But the good genius of conciliation which presided at the birth of our institutions finally prevailed, and the Missouri compromise was adopted. This compromise had the effect of calming the troubled waves, and restoring peace and good-will throughout the States of the Union. I do not doubt that a similar adjustment of the questions which now agitate the public mind would produce the same happy results. If the legislation of Congress on the subject of the other territories shall not be adopted in a spirit of conciliation and compromise, it is impossible that the country can be satisfied, or that the most disastrous consequences shall fail to ensue. When Texas was admitted into our Union, the same spirit of compromise which guided our predecessors in the admission of Missouri, a quarter of a century before, prevailed without any serious opposition. The 'joint-resolution for annexing Texas to the United States,' approved March the first, one thousand eight hundred and forty-five, provides that 'such States as may be formed out of that portion of said territory lying south of thirty-six degrees thirty minutes north latitude, commonly known as the Missouri compromise line, shall be admitted into the Union with or without slavery, as the people of each State asking admission may desire. And in such State or States as shall be formed out of said territory north of the Missouri compromise line, slavery or involuntary servitude (except for crime) shall be prohibited. The territory of Oregon lies far north of thirty-six degrees thirty minutes, the Missouri and Texas compromise line. Its southern boundary is the parallel of forty-two, leaving the intermediate distance to be three hundred and thirty geographical miles. And it is because the provisions of this bill are not inconsistent with the terms of the Missouri compromise, if extended from the Rio Grande to the Pacific Ocean, that I have not felt at liberty to withhold my sanction. Had it embraced territories south of that compromise, the question presented for my consideration would have been of a far different character, and my action upon it must have corresponded with my convictions.

"Ought we now to disturb the Missouri and Texas compromises? Ought we at this late day, in attempting to annul what has been so long established and acquiesced in, to excite sectional divisions and jealousies; to alienate the people of different portions of the Union from each other; and to endanger the existence of the Union itself?"

To the momentous appeals with which this extract concludes, a terrible answer has just been given. To the question—Will you annul these compromises, and excite jealousies and divisions, sectional alienations, and endanger the existence of this Union? the dreadful answer has been given—WE WILL! And in recording that answer, History performs her sacred duty in pointing to its authors as the authors of the state of things which now alarms and afflicts the country, and threatens the calamity which President Polk foresaw and deprecated.

CHAPTER CLXXV.

MR. CALHOUN'S NEW DOGMA ON TERRITORIAL SLAVERY: SELF-EXTENSION OF THE SLAVERY PART OF THE CONSTITUTION TO THE TERRITORIES.

The resolutions of 1847 went no further than to deny the power of Congress to prohibit slavery in a territory, and that was enough while Congress alone was the power to be guarded against: but it became insufficient, and even a stumbling-block, when New Mexico and California were acquired, and where no Congress prohibition was necessary because their soil was already free. Here the dogma of '47 became an impediment to the territorial extension of slavery; for, in denying power to legislate upon the subject, the denial worked both ways—both against the admission and exclusion. It was on seeing this consequence as resulting from the dogmas of 1847, that Mr. Benton congratulated the country upon the approaching cessation of the slavery agitation—that the Wilmot Proviso being rejected as unnecessary, the question was at an end, as the friends of slavery extension could not ask Congress to pass a law to carry it into a territory. The agitation seemed to be at an end, and peace about to dawn upon the land. Delusive calculation! A new dogma was invented to fit the case—that of the transmigration of the constitution—(the slavery part of it)—into the territories, overriding and overruling all the anti-slavery laws which it found there, and planting the institution there under its own wing, and maintaining it beyond the power of eradication either by Congress or the people of the territory. Before this dogma was proclaimed efforts were made to get the constitution extended to these territories by act of Congress: failing in those attempts, the difficulty was leaped over by boldly assuming that the constitution went of itself—that is to say, the slavery part of it. In this exigency Mr. Calhoun came out with his new and supreme dogma of the transmigratory function of the constitution in the *ipso facto*, and the instantaneous transportation of itself in its slavery attributes, into all acquired territories. This dogma was thus broached by its author in his speech upon the Oregon territorial bill:

> "*But I deny that the laws of Mexico can have the effect attributed to them (that of keeping slavery out of New Mexico and California). As soon as the treaty between the two countries is ratified, the sovereignty and authority of Mexico in the territory acquired by it become extinct, and that of the United States is substituted in its place, carrying with it the constitution, with its overriding control over all the laws and institutions of Mexico inconsistent with it.*"

History cannot class higher than as a vagary of a diseased imagination this imputed self-acting and self-extension of the constitution. The constitution does nothing of itself—not even in the States, for which it was made. Every part of it requires a law to put it into operation. No part of it can reach a territory unless imparted to it by act of Congress. Slavery, as a local institution, can only be established by a local legislative authority. It cannot transmigrate—cannot carry along with it the law which protects it: and if it could, what law would it carry? The code of the State from which the emigrant went? Then there would be as many slavery codes in the territory as States furnishing emigrants, and these codes all varying more or less; and some of them in the essential nature of the property—the slave, in many States, being only a chattel interest, governed by the laws applicable to chattels—in others, as in Louisiana and Kentucky, a real-estate interest, governed by the laws which apply to landed property. In a word, this dogma of the self-extension of the slavery part of the constitution to a territory is impracticable and preposterous, and as novel as unfounded.

It was in this same debate, on the Oregon territorial bill, that Mr. Calhoun showed that he had forgotten the part which he had acted on the Missouri compromise question, and also forgotten its history, and first declared that he held that compromise to be unconstitutional and void. Thus:

> "After an arduous struggle of more than a year, on the question whether Missouri should come into the Union, with or without restrictions prohibiting slavery, a compromise line was adopted between the North and the South; but it was done under circumstances which made it nowise obligatory on the latter. It is true, it was moved by one of her distinguished citizens (Mr. Clay), but it is equally so, that it was carried by the almost united vote of the North against the almost united vote of the South; and was thus imposed on the latter by superior numbers, in opposition to her strenuous efforts. The South has never given her sanction to

it, or assented to the power it asserted. She was voted down, and has simply acquiesced in an arrangement which she has not had the power to reverse, and which she could not attempt to do without disturbing the peace and harmony of the Union—to which she has ever been adverse."

All this is error, and was immediately shown to be so by Senator Dix of New York, who produced the evidence that Mr. Monroe's cabinet, of which Mr. Calhoun was a member, had passed upon the question of the constitutionality of that compromise, and given their opinions in its favor. It has also been seen since that, as late as 1838, Mr. Calhoun was in favor of that compromise, and censured Mr. Randolph for being against it; and, still later, in 1845, he acted his part in re-enacting that compromise, and re-establishing its line, in that part of it which had been abrogated by the laws and constitution of Texas, and which, if not re-established, would permit slavery in Texas, to spread south of 36° 30'. Forgetting his own part in that compromise, Mr. Calhoun equally forgot that of others. He says Mr. Clay moved the compromise—a clear mistake, as it came down to the House from the Senate, as an amendment to the House restrictive bill. He says it was carried by the almost united voice of the North against the almost united voice of the South—a clear mistake again, for it was carried in the Senate by the united voice of the South, with the aid of a few votes from the North; and in the House, by a majority of votes from each section, making 134 to 42. He says it was imposed on the South: on the contrary, it was not only voted for, but invoked and implored by its leading men—by all in the Senate, headed by Mr. Pinkney of Maryland; by all in the House, headed by Mr. Lowndes, with the exception of Mr. Randolph, whom Mr. Calhoun has since authentically declared he blamed at the time for his opposition. So far from being imposed on the South, she re-established it when she found it down at the recovery of Texas. Every member of Congress that voted for the legislative admission of Texas in 1845, voted for the re-establishment of the prostrate Missouri compromise line: and that vote comprehended the South, with Mr. Calhoun at its head—not as a member of Congress, but as Secretary of State, promoting that legislative admission of Texas, and seizing upon it in preference to negotiation, to effect the admission. This was on the third day of March, 1845; so that up to that day, which was only two years before the invention of the "no power" dogma, Mr. Calhoun is estopped by his own act from denying the constitutionality of the Missouri compromise: and in that estoppel is equally included every member of Congress that then voted for that admission. He says the South never gave her sanction to it: on the contrary, she did it twice—at its enactment in 1820, and at its re-establishment in 1845. He says she was voted down: on the contrary, she was voted up, and that twice, and by good help added to her own exertions—and for which she was duly grateful both times. All this the journals and legislative history of the times will prove, and which any person may see that will take the trouble to look. But admit all these errors of fact, Mr. Calhoun delivered a sound and patriotic sentiment which his disciples have disregarded and violated: He would not attempt to reverse the Missouri compromise, because it would disturb the peace and harmony of the Union. What he would not attempt, they have done: and the peace and harmony of the Union are not only disturbed, but destroyed.

In the same speech the dogma of squatter sovereignty was properly repudiated and scouted, though condemnation was erroneously derived from a denial, instead of an assertion, of the power of Congress over it. "Of all the positions ever taken on the subject, he declared this of squatter sovereignty to be the most absurd:" and, going on to trace the absurdity to its consequences, he said:

> "The first half-dozen of squatters would become the sovereigns, with full dominion and sovereignty over the territories; and the conquered people of New Mexico and California would become the sovereigns of the country as soon as they become territories of the United States, vested with the full right of excluding even their conquerors."

Mr. Calhoun concluded this speech on the Oregon bill, in which he promulgated his latest dogmas on slavery, with referring the future hypothetical dissolution of the Union, to three phases of the slavery question: 1. The ordinance of '87. 2. The compromise of 1820. 3. The Oregon agitation of that day, 1848. These were his words:

> "Now, let me say, Senators, if our Union and system of government are doomed to perish, and we to share the fate of so many great people who have gone before us, the historian, who, in some future day, may record the events tending to so calamitous a result, will devote his

first chapter to the ordinance of 1787, as lauded as it and its authors have been, as the first in that series which led to it. His next chapter will be devoted to the Missouri compromise, and the next to the present agitation. Whether there will be another beyond, I know not. It will depend on what we may do."

These the three causes: The ordinance of 1787, which was voted for by every slave State then in existence: The compromise of 1820, supported by himself, and the power of the South: The Oregon agitation of 1848, of which he was the sole architect—for he was the founder of the opposition to free soil in Oregon. But the historian will have to say that neither of these causes dissolved the Union: and that historian may have to relate that a fourth cause did it—and one from which Mr. Calhoun recoiled, "*because it could not be attempted without disturbing the peace and the harmony of the Union.*"

CHAPTER CLXXVI.

COURT-MARTIAL ON LIEUTENANT-COLONEL FREMONT.

Columbus, the discoverer of the New World, was carried home in chains, from the theatre of his discoveries, to expiate the crime of his glory: Frémont, the explorer of California and its preserver to the United States, was brought home a prisoner to be tried for an offence, of which the penalty was death, to expiate the offence of having entered the army without passing through the gate of the Military Academy.

The governor of the State of Missouri, Austin A. King, Esq., sitting at the end of a long gallery at Fort Leavenworth, in the summer of 1846, where he had gone to see a son depart as a volunteer in General Kearney's expedition to New Mexico, heard a person at the other end of the gallery speaking of Frémont in a way that attracted his attention. The speaker was in the uniform of a United States officer, and his remarks were highly injurious to Frémont. He inquired the name of the speaker, and was told it was Lieutenant Emory, of the Topographical corps; and he afterwards wrote to a friend in Washington that Frémont was to have trouble when he got among the officers of the regular army: and trouble he did have: for he had committed the offence for which, in the eyes of many of these officers, there was no expiation except in ignominious expulsion from the army. He had not only entered the army intrusively, according to their ideas, that is to say, without passing through West Point, but he had done worse: he had become distinguished. Instead of seeking easy service about towns and villages, he had gone off into the depths of the wilderness, to extend the boundaries of science in the midst of perils and sufferings, and to gain for himself a name which became known throughout the world. He was brought home to be tried for the crime of mutiny, expanded into many specifications, of which one is enough to show the monstrosity of the whole. At page 11 of the printed record of the trial, under the head of "Mutiny" stands this specification, numbered 6:

> "In this, that he, Lieutenant-colonel John C. Frémont, of the regiment of mounted riflemen, United States army, did, at Ciudad de los Angeles, on the second of March, 1847, in contempt of the lawful authority of his superior officer, Brigadier-general Kearney, assume to be and act as governor of California, in executing a deed or instrument of writing in the following words, to wit: '*In consideration of Francis Temple having conveyed to the United States a certain island, commonly called White, or Bird Island, situated near the mouth of San Francisco Bay, I, John C. Frémont, Governor of California, and in virtue of my office as aforesaid, hereby oblige myself as the legal representative of the United States, and my successors in office, to pay the said Francis Temple, his heirs or assigns, the sum of $5,000, to be paid at as early a day as possible after the receipt of funds from the United States. In witness whereof, I have hereunto set my hand, and caused the seal of the Territory of California to be affixed, at Ciudad de los Angeles, the capital of California, this 2d day of March, A. D. 1847.—John C. Frémont.*'"

And of this specification, as well as of all the rest, two dozen in number, Frémont was duly found guilty by a majority of the court. Now this case of mutiny consisted in this: That there being an island of solid rock, of some hundred acres extent, in the mouth of the San Francisco bay, formed by nature to command the bay, and on which the United States are now constructing forts and a light-house to cost millions, which island had been granted to a British subject and was about to be sold to a French subject, Colonel Frémont bought it for the United States, subject to their ratification in paying the purchase money: all which appears upon the face of the papers. Upon this transaction (as upon all the other specifications) the majority of the court found the accused guilty of "mutiny," the appropriate punishment for which is death; but the sentence was moderated down to dismission from the service. The President disapproved the absurd findings (seven of them) under the mutiny charge, but approved the finding and sentence on inferior charges; and offered a pardon to Frémont: which he scornfully refused. Since then the government has taken possession of that island by military force, without paying any thing for it; Frémont having taken the purchase on his own account since his conviction for "mutiny" in having purchased it for the government—a conviction about equal to what it would have been on a specification for witchcraft, heresy, or "flat burglary." And now annual appropriations are made for forts and the light-house upon it, under the name of Alcatraz, or Los Alcatrazes—that is to say, Pelican Island; so called from being the resort of those sea birds.

Justice to the dead requires it to be told that these charges, so preposterously wicked, were not the work of General Kearney, but had been altered from his. At page 64 of the printed record, and not in answer to any question on that point, but simply to place himself right before the court, and the country, General Kearney swore in these words, and signed them: "*The charges upon which Colonel Frémont is now arraigned, are not my charges. I preferred a single charge against Lieutenant-colonel Frémont. These charges, upon which he is now arraigned, have been changed from mine.*" The change was from one charge to three, and from one or a few specifications to two dozen—whereof this island purchase is a characteristic specimen. No person has ever acknowledged the authorship of the change, but the caption to the charges (page 4 of the record) declares them to have been preferred by order of the War Department. The caption runs thus: "*Charges against Lieutenant-colonel Frémont, of the regiment of mounted riflemen, United States army, preferred against him by order of the War Department, on information of Brigadier-general Kearney.*" The War Department, at that time, was William L. Marcy, Esq.; in consequence of which Senator Benton, chairman for twenty years of the Senate's committee on Military Affairs, refused to remain any longer at the head of that committee, because he would not hold a place which would put him in communication with that department.

The gravamen of the charge was, that Frémont had mutinied because Kearney would not appoint him governor of California; and the answer to that was, that Commodore Stockton, acting under full authority from the President, had already appointed him to that place before Kearney left Santa Fé for New Mexico: and the proof was ample, clear, and pointed to that effect: but more has since been found, and of a kind to be noticed by a court of West Point officers, as it comes from graduates of the institution. It so happens that two of General Kearney's officers (Captain Johnston, of the First Dragoons, and Lieutenant Emory, of the Topographical corps), both kept journals of the expedition, which have since been published, and that both these journals contain the same proof—one by a plain and natural statement—the other by an unnatural suppression which betrays the same knowledge. The journal of Captain Johnston, of the first dragoons, under the date of October 6th, 1846, contains this entry:

> "Marched at 9, after having great trouble in getting some ox carts from the Mexicans: after marching about three miles we met Kit Carson, direct on express from California, with a mail of public letters for Washington. He informs us that Colonel Frémont is probably civil and military governor of California, and that about forty days since, Commodore Stockton with the naval forces, and Colonel Frémont, acting in concert, commenced to revolutionize that country, and place it under the American flag: that in about ten days this was done, and Carson having received the rank of lieutenant, was despatched across the country by the Gila, with a party to carry the mail. The general told him that he had just passed over the country which we were to traverse, and he wanted him to go back with him as a guide: he replied that he had pledged himself to go to Washington, and he could not think of not fulfilling his promise. The general told him he would relieve him of all responsibility, and place the mail in the hands of a safe person to carry it on. He finally consented, and turned his face towards the West again, just as he was on the eve of entering the settlements, after his arduous trip, and when he had set his hopes on seeing his family. It requires a brave man to give up his private feelings thus for the public good; but Carson is one: such honor to his name for it."

This is a natural and straightforward account of this meeting with Carson, and of the information he gave, that California was conquered by Stockton and Frémont, and the latter governor of it; and the journal goes on to show that, in consequence of this information, General Kearney turned back the body of his command, and went on with an escort only of one hundred dragoons. Lieutenant Emory's journal of the same date opens in the same way, with the same account of the difficulty of getting some teams from the Mexicans, and then branches off into a dissertation upon peonage, and winds up the day with saying: "*Came into camp late, and found Carson with an express from California, bearing intelligence that the country had surrendered without a blow, and that the American flag floated in every part.*" This is a lame account, not telling to whom the country had surrendered, eschewing all mention of Stockton and Frémont, and that governorship which afterwards became the point in the court-martial trial. The next day's journal opens with Carson's news, equally lame at the same point, and redundant in telling something in New Mexico, under date of Oct. 7th, 1846, which took place the next year in old Mexico, thus: "*Yesterday's news caused some changes in our camp: one hundred dragoons, officered, &c., formed the party for California. Major Sumner, with the dragoons, was ordered to retrace his steps.*" Here the news brought by Carson is again referred to, and the consequence of receiving it is stated; but still no mention of Frémont and Stockton, and that governorship, the question of which became the whole point in the next year's trial for mutiny. But the lack of knowledge of what took place in his presence is more than balanced by a foresight into what took place afterwards and far from him—exhibited thus in the journal: "*Many friends here parted that were never to meet again: some fell in California, some in New Mexico, and some at Cerro Gordo.*" Now, no United States troops fell in New Mexico until after Lieutenant Emory left there, nor in California until he got there, nor at Cerro Gordo until April of the next year, when he was in California, and could not know it until after Frémont was fixed upon to be arrested for that mutiny of which the governorship was the point. It stands to reason, then, that this part of the journal was altered nearly a year after it purports to have been written, and after the arrest of Frémont had been resolved upon; and so, while absolutely proving an alteration of the journal, explains the omission of all mention of all reference to the governorship, the ignoring of which was absolutely essential to the institution of the charge of mutiny.—Long afterwards, and without knowing a word of what Captain Johnston had written, or Lieutenant Emory had suppressed, Carson gave his own statement of that meeting with General Kearney, the identity of which with the statement of Captain Johnston, is the identity of truth with itself. Thus:

"I met General Kearney, with his troops, on the 6th of October, about —— miles below Santa Fé. I had heard of their coming, and when I met them, the first thing I told them was that they were 'too late'—that California was conquered, and the United States flag raised in all parts of the country. But General Kearney said he would go on, and said something about going to establish a civil government. I told him a civil government was already established, and Colonel Frémont appointed governor, to commence as soon as he returned from the north, some time in that very month (October). General Kearney said that made no difference—that he was a friend of Colonel Frémont, and he would make him governor himself. He began from the first to insist on my turning back to guide him into California. I told him I could not turn back—that I had pledged myself to Commodore Stockton and Colonel Frémont to take their despatches through to Washington City, and to return with despatches as far as New Mexico, where my family lived, and to carry them all the way back if I did not find some one at Santa Fé that I could trust as well as I could myself—that I had promised them I would reach Washington in sixty days, and that they should have return despatches from the government in 120 days. I had performed so much of the journey in the appointed time, and in doing so had already worn out and killed thirty-four mules—that Stockton and Frémont had given me letters of credit to persons on the way to furnish me with all the animals I needed, and all the supplies to make the trip to Washington and back in 120 days; and that I was pledged to them, and could not disappoint them; and besides, that I was under more obligations to Colonel Frémont than to any other man alive. General Kearney would not hear of any such thing as my going on. He told me he was a friend to Colonel Frémont and Colonel Benton, and all the family, and would send on the despatches by Mr. Fitzpatrick, who had been with Colonel Frémont in his exploring party, and was a good friend to him, and would take the despatches through, and bring back despatches as quick as I could. When he could not persuade me to turn back, he then told me that he had a right to make me go with him, and insisted on his right; and I did not consent to turn back till he had made me believe that he had a right to order me; and then, as Mr. Fitzpatrick was going on with the despatches and General Kearney seemed to be such a good friend of the colonel's, I let him take me back; and I guided him through, but went with great hesitation, and had prepared every thing to escape the night before they started, and made known my intention to Maxwell, who urged me not to do so. More than twenty times on the road, General Kearney told me about his being a friend of Colonel Benton and Colonel Frémont, and all their family, and that he intended to make Colonel Frémont the governor of California; and all this of his own accord, as we were travelling along, or in camp, and without my saying a word to him about it. I say, more than twenty times, for I cannot remember how many times, it was such a common thing for him to talk about it."

Such was the statement of Mr. Carson, made to Senator Benton; and who, although rejected for a lieutenancy in the United States army because he did not enter it through the gate of the military academy, is a man whose word will stand wherever he is known, and who is at the head, as a guide, of the principal military successes in New Mexico. But why back his word? The very despatches he was carrying conveyed to the government the same information that he gave to General Kearney, to wit, that California was conquered and Frémont to be governor. That information was communicated to Congress by the President, and also sworn to by Commodore Stockton before the court-martial: but without any effect upon the majority of the members.

Colonel Frémont was found guilty of all the charges, and all the specifications; and in the secrecy which hides the proceedings of courts-martial, it cannot be told how, or whether the members divided in their opinions; but circumstances always leak out to authorize the formation of an opinion, and according to these leakings, on this occasion four members of the court were against the conviction: to wit, Brigadier-general Brooke, President; Lieutenant-colonel Hunt; Lieutenant-colonel Taylor, brother of the afterwards President; and Major Baker, of the Ordnance. The proceedings required to be approved, or disapproved, by the President; and he, although no military man, was a rational man, and common reason told him there was no mutiny in the case. He therefore disapproved that finding, and approved the rest, saying:

"Upon an inspection of the record, I am not satisfied that the facts proved in this case constitute the military crime of 'mutiny.' I am of opinion that the second and third charges are sustained by the proof, and that the conviction upon these charges warrants the sentence of the court. The sentence of the court is therefore approved; but in consideration of the peculiar circumstances of the case—of the previous meritorious and valuable services of Lieutenant-colonel Frémont, and of the foregoing recommendation of a majority of the court, to the clemency of the President, the sentence of dismissal from the service is remitted. Lieutenant-col. Frémont will accordingly be released from arrest, will resume his sword, and report for duty." (Dated, February 17, 1848.)

Upon the instant of receiving this order, Frémont addressed to the adjutant-general this note:

"I have this moment received the general order, No. 7 (dated the 17th instant), making known to me the final proceedings of the general court-martial before which I have been tried; and hereby send in my resignation of lieutenant-colonel in the army of the United States. In doing this I take the occasion to say, that my reason for resigning is, that I do not feel conscious of having done any thing to deserve the finding of the court; and, this being the case, I cannot, by accepting the clemency of the President, admit the justice of the decision against me."

General Kearney had two misfortunes in this court-martial affair: he had to appear as prosecutor of charges which he swore before the court were not his: and he had been attended by West Point officers envious and jealous of Frémont, and the clandestine sources of poisonous publications against him, which inflamed animosities, and left the heats which they engendered to settle upon the head of General Kearney. Major Cooke and Lieutenant Emory were the chief springs of these publications, and as such were questioned before the court, but shielded from open detection by the secret decisions of the majority of the members.

The secret proceedings of courts-martial are out of harmony with the progress of the age. Such proceedings should be as open and public as any other, and all parties left to the responsibility which publicity involves.

CHAPTER CLXXVII.

FREMONT'S FOURTH EXPEDITION, AND GREAT DISASTER IN THE SNOWS AT THE HEAD OF THE RIO GRANDE DEL NORTE: SUBSEQUENT DISCOVERY OF THE PASS HE SOUGHT.

No sooner freed from the army, than Frémont set out upon a fourth expedition to the western slope of our continent, now entirely at his own expense, and to be conducted during the winter, and upon a new line of exploration. His views were practical as well as scientific, and tending to the establishment of a railroad to the Pacific, as well as the enlargement of geographical knowledge. He took the winter for his time, as that was the season in which to see all the disadvantages of his route; and the head of the Rio Grande del Norte for his line, as it was the line of the centre, and one not yet explored, and always embraced in his plan of discovery. The mountain men had informed him that there was a good pass at the head of the Del Norte. Besides other dangers and hardships, he had the war ground of the Utahs, Apaches, Navahoes, and other formidable tribes to pass through, then all engaged in hostilities with the United States, and ready to prey upon any party of whites; but 33 of his old companions, 120 picked mules, fine rifles—experience, vigilance and courage—were his reliance; and a trusted security against all evil. Arrived at the *Pueblos* on the Upper Arkansas, the last of November, at the base of the first sierra to be crossed, luminous with snow and stern in their dominating look, he dismounted his whole company, took to their feet, and wading waist-deep in the vast unbroken snow field, arrived on the other side in the beautiful valley of San Luis; but still on the eastern side of the great mountain chain which divided the waters which ran east and west to the rising and the setting sun. At the head of that valley was the pass, described to him by the old hunters. With his glasses he could see the depression in the mountain which marked its place. He had taken a local guide from the Pueblo San Carlos to lead him to that pass. But this precaution for safety was the passport to disaster. He was behind, with his faithful draughtsman, Preuss, when he saw his guide leading off the company towards a mass of mountains to the left: he rode up and stopped them, remonstrated with the guide for two hours; and then yielded to his positive assertion that the pass was there. The company entered a tortuous gorge, following a valley through which ran a head stream of the great river Del Norte. Finally they came to where the ascent was to begin, and the summit range crossed. The snow was deep, the cold intense, the acclivity steep, and the huge rocks projecting. The ascent was commenced in the morning, struggled with during the day, an elevation reached at which vegetation (wood) ceased, and the summit in view, when, buried in snow, exhausted with fatigue, freezing with cold, and incapable of further exertion, the order was given to fall back to the line of vegetation where wood would afford fire and shelter for the night. With great care the animals were saved from freezing, and at the first dawn of day the camp, after a daybreak breakfast, were in motion for the ascent. Precautions had been taken to make it more practicable. Mauls, prepared during the night, were carried by the foremost division to beat down a road in the snow. Men went forward by relieves. Mules and baggage followed in long single file in the track made in the snow. The mountain was scaled: the region of perpetual congelation was entered. It was the winter solstice, and at a place where the summer solstice brought no life to vegetation—no thaw to congelation. The summit of the sierra was bare of every thing but snow, ice and rocks. It was no place to halt. Pushing down the side of the mountain to reach the wood three miles distant, a new and awful danger presented itself: a snow storm raging, the freezing winds beating upon the exposed caravan, the snow become too deep for the mules to move in, and the cold beyond the endurance of animal life. The one hundred and twenty mules, huddling together from an instinct of self-preservation from each other's heat and shelter, froze stiff as they stood, and fell over like blocks, to become hillocks of snow. Leaving all behind, and the men's lives only to be saved, the discomfited and freezing party scrambled back, recrossing the summit, and finding under the lee of the mountain some shelter from the driving storm, and in the wood that was reached the means of making fires.

The men's lives were now saved, but destitute of every thing, only a remnant of provisions, and not even the resource of the dead mules which were on the other side of the summit; and the distance computed at ten days of their travel to the nearest New Mexican settlement. The guide, and three picked men, were despatched thither for some supplies, and twenty days fixed for their return. When they had been gone sixteen days, Frémont, preyed upon by anxiety and misgiving, set off after them, on foot, snow to the waist, blankets and some morsels of food on the back: the brave Godey, his draughtsman Preuss, and a faithful servant, his only company. When out six days he came upon the camp of his guide, stationary and apparently without plan or object, and the men haggard, wild and emaciated. Not seeing King, the principal one of the company, and on whom he relied, he asked for him. They pointed to an older camp, a little way off. Going there he found the man dead, and partly devoured. He had died of exhaustion, of fatigue, and his comrades fed upon him. Gathering up these three survivors, Frémont resumed his journey, and had not gone far before he fell on signs of Indians—two lodges, implying 15 or 20 men, and some 40 or 50 horses—all recently passed along. At another time this would have been an alarm, one of his fears being that of falling in with a war party. He knew not what Indians they were, but all were hostile in that quarter, and evasion the only security against them. To avoid their course was his obvious resource: on the contrary, he followed it! for such was the desperation of his situation that even a change of danger had an attraction. Pursuing the trail down the Del Norte, then frozen solid over, and near the place where Pike encamped in the winter of 1807-'8, they saw an Indian behind his party, stopped to get water from an air hole. He was cautiously approached, circumvented, and taken. Frémont told his name: the young man, for he was quite young, started, and asked him if he was the Frémont that had exchanged presents with the chief of the Utahs at Las Vegas de Santa Clara three years before? He was answered, yes. Then, said the young man, we are friends: that chief was my father, and I remember you. The incident was romantic, but it did not stop there. Though on a war inroad upon the frontiers of New Mexico, the young chief became his guide, let him have four horses, conducted him to the neighborhood of the settlements, and then took his leave, to resume his scheme of depredation upon the frontier.

Frémont's party reached Taos, was sheltered in the house of his old friend Carson—obtained the supplies needed—sent them back by the brave Godey, who was in time to save two-thirds of the party, finding the other third dead along the road, scattered at intervals as each had sunk exhausted and frozen, or half burnt in the fire which had been kindled for them to die by. The survivors were brought in by Godey, some crippled with frozen feet. Frémont found himself in a situation which tries the soul—which makes the issue between despair and heroism—and leaves no alternative but to sink under fate, or to rise above it. His whole outfit was gone: his valiant mountain men were one-third dead, many crippled: he was penniless, and in a strange place. He resolved to go forward—*nulla vestigia retrorsum*: to raise another outfit, and turn the mountains by the Gila. In a few days it was all done—men, horses, arms, provisions—all acquired; and the expedition resumed. But it was no longer the tried band of mountain men on whose vigilance, skill and courage he could rely to make their way through hostile tribes. They were new men, and to avoid danger, not to overcome it, was his resource. The Navahoes and Apaches had to be passed, and eluded—a thing difficult to be done, as his party of thirty men and double as many horses would make a trail, easy to be followed in the snow, though not deep. He took an unfrequented course, and relied upon the secrecy and celerity of his movements. The fourth night on the dangerous ground the horses, picketed without the camp, gave signs of alarm: they were brought within the square of fires, and the men put on the alert. Daybreak came without visible danger. The camp moved off: a man lagged a little behind, contrary to injunctions: the crack of some rifles sent him running up. It was then clear that they were discovered, and a party hovering round them. Two Indians were seen ahead: they might be a decoy, or a watch, to keep the party in view until the neighboring warriors could come in. Evasion was no longer possible: fighting was out of the question, for the whole hostile country was ahead, and narrow defiles to be passed in the mountains. All depended upon the address of the commander. Relying upon his ascendant over the savage mind, Frémont took his interpreter, and went to the two Indians. Godey said he should not go alone, and followed. Approaching them, a deep ravine was seen between. The Indians beckoned him to go round by the head of the ravine, evidently to place that obstacle between him and his men. Symptoms of fear or distrust would mar his scheme: so he went boldly round, accosted them confidently, and told his name. They had never heard it. He told them they ought to be ashamed, not to know their best friend; inquired for their tribe, which he wished to see: and took the whole air of confidence and friendship. He saw they were staggered. He then invited them to go to his camp where the men had halted, and take breakfast with him. They said that might be dangerous—that they had shot at one of his men that morning, and might have killed him, and now be punished for it. He ridiculed the idea of their hurting his men, charmed them into the camp, where they ate, and smoked, and told their secret, and became messengers to lead their tribe in one direction, while Frémont and his men escaped by another; and the whole expedition went through without loss, and without molestation. A subsequent winter expedition completed the design of this one, so disastrously frustrated by the mistake of a guide. Frémont went out again upon his own expense—went to the spot where the guide had gone astray—followed the course described by the mountain men—and found safe and easy passes all the way to California, through a good country, and upon the straight line of 38 and 39 degrees. It is the route for the Central Pacific Railroad, which the structure of the country invites, and every national consideration demands.

CHAPTER CLXXVIII.

PRESIDENTIAL ELECTION.

Party conventions for the nomination of presidential candidates, had now become an institution, and a power in the government; and, so far as the party was concerned, the nomination was the election. No experience of the evils of this new power had yet checked its sway, and all parties (for three of them now appeared in the political field) went into that mode of determining the election for themselves. The democratic convention met, as heretofore, at Baltimore, in the month of May, and was numerously attended by members of Congress, and persons holding office under the federal government, who would be excluded by the constitution from the place of electors, but who became more than electors, having virtually supreme power over the selection of the President, as well as his election, so far as the party was concerned. The two-thirds rule was adopted, and that put the nomination in the hands of the minority, and of the trained intriguers. Every State was to be allowed to give the whole number of its electoral votes, although it was well known, now as heretofore, that there were many of them which could not give a democratic electoral vote at the election. The State of New York was excluded from voting. Two sets of delegates appeared from that State, each claiming to represent the true democracy: the convention settled the question by excluding both sets: and in that exclusion all the States which were confessedly unable to give a democratic vote, were allowed to vote; and most of them voted for the exclusion. Massachusetts, which had never given a democratic vote, now gave twelve votes; and they were for the exclusion of New York, which had voted democratically since the time of Mr. Jefferson; and whose vote often decided the fate of the election. The vote for the exclusion was 157 to 95: and in this collateral vote, as well as in the main one, the delegates generally voted according to their own will, without any regard to the people; and that *will*, with the most active and managing, was simply to produce a nomination which would be most favorable to themselves in the presidential distribution of offices. After four days work a nomination was produced. Mr. Lewis Cass, of Michigan, for President: General Wm. O. Butler, of Kentucky, for Vice-President. The construction of the platform, or party political creed for the campaign, was next entered upon, and one was produced, interminably long, and long since forgotten. The value of all such constructions may be seen in comparing what was then adopted, or rejected as political test, with what has since been equally rejected or adopted for the same purpose. For example: the principle of squatter sovereignty, that is to say, the right of the inhabitants of the *territories* to decide the question of slavery for themselves, was then repudiated, and by a vote virtually unanimous: it is since adopted by a vote equally unanimous. Mr. Yancy, of Alabama, submitted this resolution, as an article of democratic faith to be inserted in the creed; to wit: "*That the doctrine of non-interference with the rights of property of any portion of this confederation, be it in the States or in the Territories, by any other than the parties interested in them, is the true republican doctrine recognized by this body.*" This article of faith was rejected; 246 against 36: so that, up to the month of May, in the year 1848, squatter sovereignty, or the right of the inhabitants of a *territory* to determine the question of slavery for themselves, was rejected and ignored by the democratic party.

The whig nominating convention met in Philadelphia, in the month of June, and selected General Zachary Taylor, and Millard Fillmore, Esq., for their candidates. On their first balloting, the finally successful candidates lacked much of having the requisite number of votes, there being 22 for Mr. Webster, 43 for General Scott, 97 for Mr. Clay, and 111 for General Taylor. Eventually General Taylor received the requisite majority, 171—making his gains from the friends of Mr. Clay, whose vote was reduced to 32. The nomination of General Taylor was avowedly made on the calculation of availability—setting aside both Mr. Clay and Mr. Webster, in favor of the military popularity of Buena Vista, Monterey, Palo Alto, and Resaca de la Palma. In one respect the whig convention was more democratic than that of the democracy: it acted on the principle of the majority to govern.

But there was a third convention, growing out of the rejection of the Van Buren democratic delegates at the Baltimore democratic convention—for the exclusion, though ostensibly against both, was in reality to get rid of them—which met first at Utica, and afterwards at Buffalo, in the State of New York, and nominated Mr. Van Buren for President, and Mr. Charles Francis Adams (son of the late John Quincy Adams), for Vice-President. This convention also erected its platform, its distinctive feature being an opposition to slave institutions, and a desire to abolish, or restrain slavery wherever it constitutionally could be done. Three principles were laid down: First, That it was the duty of the federal government to abolish slavery wherever it could constitutionally be done. Second, That the States within which slavery existed had the sole right to interfere with it. Thirdly, That Congress alone can prevent the existence of slavery in the territories. By the first of these principles it would be the duty of Congress to abolish slavery in the District of Columbia; by the second, to let it alone in the States; by the third, to restrain and prevent it in the territories then free; the dogma of squatter sovereignty being abjured by this latter principle. The watchwords of the party, to be inscribed on their banner, were: "*Free soil*"—"*Free speech*"—"*Free labor*"—"*Free men*"—from which they incurred the appellation of Free-soilers. It was an organization entirely to be regretted. Its aspect was sectional—its foundation a single idea—and its tendency, to merge political principles in a slavery contention. The Baltimore democratic convention had been dominated by the slavery question, but on the other side of that question, and not openly and professedly: but here was an organization resting prominently on the slavery basis. And deeming all such organization, no matter on which side of the question, as fraught with evil to the Union, this writer, on the urgent request of some of his political associates, went to New York, to interpose his friendly offices to get the Free-soil organization abandoned. The visit was between the two conventions, and before the nominations and proceedings had become final: but in vain. Mr. Van Buren accepted the nomination, and in so doing, placed himself in opposition to the general tenor of his political conduct in relation to slavery, and especially in what relates to its existence in the District of Columbia. I deemed this acceptance unfortunate to a degree far beyond its influence upon persons or parties. It went to impair confidence between the North and the South, and to narrow down the basis of party organization to a single idea; and that idea not known to our ancestors as an element in political organizations. The Free-soil plea was, that the Baltimore democratic convention had done the same; but the answer to that was, that it was a general convention from all the States, and did not make its slavery principles the open test of the election, while this was a segment of the party, and openly rested on that ground. Mr. Van Buren himself was much opposed to his own nomination. In his letter to the Buffalo convention he said: "*You all know, from my letter to the Utica convention, and the confidence you repose in my sincerity, how greatly the proceedings of that body, in relation to myself, were opposed to my earnest wishes.*" Yet he accepted a nomination made against his earnest wishes; and although another would have been nominated if he had refused, yet no other nomination could have given such emphasis to the character of the convention, and done as much harm. Senator Henry Dodge, of Wisconsin, had first been proposed for Vice-President; but, although opposed to the extension of slavery, he could not concur in the Buffalo platform; and declined the nomination. Of the three parties, the whig party, so far as slavery was concerned, acted most nationally; they ignored the subject, and made their nomination on the platform of the constitution, the country, and the character of their candidate.

The issue of the election did not disappoint public expectation. The State of New York could not be spared by the democratic candidate, and it was quite sure that the division of the party there would deprive Mr. Cass of the vote of that State. It did so: and these 36 votes, making a difference of 72, decided the election. The vote was 163 against 127, being the same for the vice-presidential candidates as for their principals. The States voting for General Taylor, were: Massachusetts, 12; Rhode Island 4; Connecticut, 6; Vermont, 7; New York, 36; New Jersey, 7; Pennsylvania, 26; Delaware, 3; Maryland, 8; North Carolina, 11; Georgia, 10; Kentucky, 12; Tennessee, 13; Louisiana, 6; Florida, 3. Those voting for Mr. Cass, were: Maine, 9; New Hampshire, 6; Virginia, 17; South Carolina, 9; Ohio, 23; Mississippi, 6; Indiana, 12; Illinois, 9; Alabama, 9; Missouri, 7; Arkansas, 3; Michigan, 5; Texas, 4; Iowa, 4; Wisconsin, 4. The Free-soil candidates received not a single electoral vote.

The result of the election was not without its moral, and its instruction. All the long intrigues to govern it, had miscarried. None of the architects of annexation, or of war, were elected. A victorious general overshadowed them all; and those who had considered Texas their own game, and made it the staple of incessant plots for five years, saw themselves shut out from that presidency which it had been the object of so many intrigues to gain. Even the slavery agitation failed to govern the election; and a soldier was elected, unknown to political machinations, and who had never even voted at an election.

CHAPTER CLXXIX.

LAST MESSAGE OF MR. POLK.

The message opened with an encomium on the conquest of Mexico, and of the citizen soldiers who volunteered in such numbers for the service, and fought with such skill and courage—saying justly:

> "Unlike what would have occurred in any other country, we were under no necessity of resorting to draughts or conscriptions. On the contrary, such was the number of volunteers who patriotically tendered their services, that the chief difficulty was in making selections, and determining who should be disappointed and compelled to remain at home. Our citizen soldiers are unlike those drawn from the population of any other country. They are composed indiscriminately of all professions and pursuits: of farmers, lawyers, physicians, merchants, manufacturers, mechanics, and laborers; and this, not only among the officers, but the private soldiers in the ranks. Our citizen soldiers are unlike those of any other country in other respects. They are armed, and have been accustomed from their youth up to handle and use fire-arms; and a large proportion of them, especially in the western and more newly settled States, are expert marksmen. They are men who have a reputation to maintain at home by their good conduct in the field. They are intelligent, and there is an individuality of character which is found in the ranks of no other army. In battle, each private man, as well as every officer, fights not only for his country, but for glory and distinction among his fellow-citizens when he shall return to civil life."

And this was the case in a foreign war, in which a march of two thousand miles had to be accomplished before the foe could be reached: how much more so will it be in defensive war—war to defend our own borders—the only kind in which the United States should ever be engaged. That is the kind of war to bring out all the strength and energy of volunteer forces; and the United States have arrived at the point to have the use of that force with a promptitude, a cheapness, and an efficiency, never known before, nor even conceived of by the greatest masters of the art of war. The electric telegraph to summon the patriotic host: the steam car to precipitate them on the point of defence. The whole art of defensive war, in the present condition of the United States, and still more, what it is hereafter to be, is simplified into two principles—accumulation of masses, and the system of incessant attacks. Upon these two principles the largest invading force would be destroyed—shot like pigeons on their roost—by the volunteers and their rifles, before the lumbering machinery of a scientific army could be got into motion.

The large acquisition of new territory was fiercely lighting up the fires of a slavery controversy, and Mr. Polk recommended the extension of the Missouri compromise line to the Pacific Ocean, as the most effectual and easy method of averting the dangers to the Union, which he saw in that question. He said:

> "Upon a great emergency, however, and under menacing dangers to the Union, the Missouri compromise line in respect to slavery was adopted. The same line was extended further west on the acquisition of Texas. After an acquiescence of nearly thirty years in the principle of compromise recognized and established by these acts, and to avoid the danger to the Union which might follow if it were now disregarded, I have heretofore expressed the opinion that that line of compromise should be extended on the parallel of thirty-six degrees thirty minutes from the western boundary of Texas, where it now terminates, to the Pacific Ocean. This is the middle line of compromise, upon which the different sections of the Union may meet, as they have hitherto met."

This was the compromise proposition of the President, but there were arrayed against it parties and principles which repelled its adoption. First, the large party which denied the power of Congress to legislate upon the subject of slavery in territories. Some of that class of politicians, and they were numerous and ardent, though of recent conception, were, from the necessity of their position, compelled to oppose a proposition which involved, to the greatest extent, the exercise of that denied power. Next, the class who believed in the still newer doctrine of the self-extension of slavery into all the territories, by the self-expansion of the constitution over them. This class would have nothing to do with any law upon the subject—equally repulsing congressional legislation, squatter sovereignty, or territorial law. A third class objected to the extension of the Missouri compromise line, because in its extension that line, astronomically the same, became politically different. In all its original extent it passed through territory all slave, and therefore made one side free: in its extension it would pass through territory all free, and therefore make one side slave. This was the reverse of the principle of the previous compromises, and although equal on its face, and to shallow observers the same law, yet the transfer and planting of slavery in regions where it did not exist, involved a breach of principle, and a shock of feeling, in those conscientiously opposed to the extension of slavery, which it was impossible for them to incur. Finally, those who wanted no compromise—no peace—no rest on the slavery question: These were of two classes; first, mere political demagogues on each side of the agitation, who wished to keep the question alive for their own political elevation; next, the abolitionists, who denied the right of property in slaves, and were ready to dissolve the Union to get rid of association with slave States; and the nullifiers, who wished to dissolve the Union, and who considered the slavery question the efficient means of doing it. Among all these parties, the extension of the Missouri compromise line became an impossibility.

The state of the finances, and of the expenditures of the government for the last year of the war, and the first year of peace, was concisely stated by the President, and deserves to be known and considered by all who would study that part of the working of our government. Of the first period it says:

> "The expenditures for the same period, including the necessary payment on account of the principal and interest of the public debt, and the principal and interest of the first instalment due to Mexico on the thirtieth of May next, and other expenditures growing out of the war, to be paid during the present year, will amount, including the reimbursement of treasury notes, to the sum of fifty-four millions one hundred and ninety-five thousand two hundred and seventy-five dollars and six cents; leaving an estimated balance in the Treasury on the first of July, 1849, of two millions eight hundred and fifty-three thousand six hundred and ninety-four dollars and eighty-four cents."

Deducting the three heads of expense here mentioned, and the expenses for the year ending the 30th of June, 1848, were about twenty-five millions of dollars, and about the same sum was estimated to be sufficient for the first fiscal year of entire peace, ending the 30th of June, 1849. Thus:

> "The Secretary of the Treasury will present, as required by law, the estimate of the receipts and expenditures for the next fiscal year. The expenditures, as estimated for that year, are thirty-three millions two hundred and thirteen thousand one hundred and fifty-two dollars and seventy-three cents, including three millions seven hundred and ninety-nine thousand one hundred and two dollars and eighteen cents, for the interest on the public debt, and three millions five hundred and forty thousand dollars for the principal and interest due to Mexico on the thirtieth of May, 1850; leaving the sum of twenty-five millions eight hundred and seventy-four thousand and fifty dollars and thirty-five cents; which, it is believed, will be ample for the ordinary peace expenditures."

About 25 millions of dollars for the future expenditures of the government: and this the estimate and expenditure only seven years ago. Now, three times that amount, and increasing with frightful rapidity.

CHAPTER CLXXX.

FINANCIAL WORKING OF THE GOVERNMENT UNDER THE HARD MONEY SYSTEM.

The war of words was over: the test of experiment had come: and the long contest between the hard money and the paper money advocates ceased to rage. The issue of the war with Mexico was as disastrous to the paper money party, as it was to the Mexicans themselves. The capital was taken in each case, and the vanquished submitted in quiet in each case. The virtue of a gold and silver currency had shown itself in its good effects upon every branch of business—upon the entire pursuits of human industry, and above all, in assuring to the working man a solid compensation, instead of a delusive cheat for his day's labor. Its triumph was complete: but that triumph was limited to a home experiment in time of peace. War, and especially war to be carried on abroad, is the great test of currency; and the Mexican war was to subject the restored golden currency of the United States to that supreme test: and here the paper money party—the national bank sound-currency party—felt sure of the victory. The first national bank had been established upon the war argument presented by General Hamilton to President Washington: the second national bank was born of the war of 1812: and the war with Mexico was confidently looked to as the trial which was to show inadequacy of the hard money currency to its exigencies, and the necessity of establishing a national paper currency. Those who had asserted the inadequacy of all the gold and silver in the world to do the business of the United States, were quite sure of the insufficiency of the precious metals to carry on a foreign war in addition to all domestic transactions. The war came: its demands upon the solid currency were not felt in its diminution at home. Government bills were above par! and every loan taken at a premium! and only obtained upon a hard competition! How different from any thing which had ever been seen in our country, or in almost any country before. The last loan authorized (winter of '47-'48) of sixteen millions, brought a premium of about five hundred thousand dollars; and one-half of the bidders were disappointed and chagrined because they could get no part of it. Compare this financial result to that of the war of 1812, during which the federal government was a mendicant for loans, and paid or suffered a loss of forty-six millions of dollars to obtain them, and the virtue of the gold currency will stand vindicated upon the test of war, and foreign war, as well as upon the test of home transactions. The war was conducted upon the hard money basis, and found the basis to be as ample as solid. Payments were regular and real: and, at the return of peace, every public security was above par, the national coffers full of gold; and the government having the money on hand, and anxious to pay its loans before they were due, could only obtain that privilege by paying a premium upon it, sometimes as high as twenty per centum—thus actually giving one dollar upon every five for the five before it was due. And this, more or less, on all the loans, according to the length of time they had yet to run. And this is the crown and seal upon the triumph of the gold currency.

CHAPTER CLXXXI.

COAST SURVEY: BELONGS TO THE NAVY: CONVERTED INTO A SEPARATE DEPARTMENT: EXPENSE AND INTERMINABILITY: SHOULD BE DONE BY THE NAVY, AS IN GREAT BRITAIN: MR. BENTONS SPEECH: EXTRACT.

MR. BENTON. My object, Mr. President, is to return the coast survey to what the law directed it to be, and to confine its execution, after the 30th of June next, to the Navy Department. We have now, both by law and in fact, a bureau for the purpose—that of Ordnance and Hydrography—and to the hydrographical section of this bureau properly belongs the execution of the coast survey. It is the very business of hydrography; and in Great Britain, from whom we borrow the idea of this bureau, the hydrographer, always a naval officer, and operating wholly with naval forces, is charged with the whole business of the coast survey of that great empire. One hydrographer and with only ten vessels until lately, conducts the whole survey of coasts under the laws of that empire—surveys not confined to the British Isles, but to the British possessions in the four quarters of the globe—and not merely to their own possessions, but to the coasts of all countries with which they have commerce, or expect war, and of which they have not reliable charts—even to China and the Island of Borneo. Rear Admiral Beaufort is now the hydrographer, and has been for twenty years; and he has no civil astronomer to do the work for him, or any civil superintendent to overlook and direct him. But he has somebody to overlook him, and those who know what they are about—namely, the Lords of the Admiralty—and something more besides—namely, the House of Commons, through its select committees—and by which the whole work of this hydrographer is most carefully overlooked, and every survey brought to the test of law and expediency in its inception, and of economy and speed in its execution. I have now before me one of the examinations of this hydrographer before a select committee of the House of Commons, made only last year, and which shows that the British House of Commons holds its hydrographer to the track of the law—confines him to his proper business—and that proper business is precisely the work which is required by our acts of 1807 and 1832. Here is the volume which contains, among other things, the examination of Rear Admiral Beaufort [showing a huge folio of more than a thousand pages]. I do not mean to read it. I merely produce it to show that, in Great Britain, the hydrographer, a naval officer, is charged with the whole business of the coast survey, and executes it exclusively with the men and ships of the navy; and having produced it for this purpose, I read a single question from it, not for the sake of the answer, but for the sake of the facts in the question. It relates to the number of assistants retained by the rear admiral, and the late increase in their number. The question is in these words:

> "In 1834 and 1835 you had three assistants—one at three pounds a week, and two at two guineas a week; now you have five assistants—one at four pounds a week, three at three pounds, and one at three guineas: why has this increase been made?"

The answer was that these assistants had to live in London, where living was dear, and that they had to do much work—for example, had printed 61,631 charts the year before. I pass over the answer for the sake of the question, and the facts of the question, and to contrast them with something in our own coast survey. The question was, why he had increased the number of the assistants from three to five, and the compensation of the principal one from about $800 to about $1,000, and of the others from about $600 to about $800 a year? And turning to our Bluc Book, under the head of coast survey, I find the number of the assistants of our superintendent rather more than three, or five, and their salaries rather more than six, or eight, or even ten and twelve hundred dollars. They appear thus in the official list: One assistant at $3,500 per annum; one at $2,500; three at $2,000 each; three at $1,500 each; four at $1,300 each; two at $1,000 each; two at $600 each; one draughtsman at $1,500; another at $600; one computer at $1,500; two ditto at $1,000 each; one disbursing officer at $2,000. All this in addition to the superintendent himself at $4,500 as superintendent of coast survey, and $1,500 as superintendent of weights and measures, with an assistant at $2,000 to aid him in that business; with all the paraphernalia of an office besides. I do not know what law fixes either the number or compensation of these assistants, nor do I know that Congress has ever troubled itself to inquire into their existence: but if our superintendent was in England, with his long catalogue of assistants, the question which I have read shows that there would be an inquiry there.

Mr. President, the cost of this coast survey has been very great, and is becoming greater every year, and, expanding as it does, must annually get further from its completion. The direct appropriations out of the Treasury exceed a million and a half of dollars (1,509,725), besides the $186,000 now in the bill which I propose to reduce to $30,000.

These are the direct appropriations; but they are only half, or less than half the actual expense of this survey. The indirect expenses are much greater than the direct appropriations; and without pretending to know the whole extent of them, I think I can show a table which will go as high as $210,000 for the last year. It has been seen, that the superintendent (for I suppose that astronomer is no longer the recognized title, although the legal one) is authorized to get from the Treasury Department *quantum sufficit* of men and ships. Accordingly, for the last year the number of vessels was thirteen—the number of men and officers five hundred and seventy-six—and the cost of supporting the whole about $210,000 a year; and this coming from the naval appropriations proper.

Thus, sir, the navy does a good deal, and pays a good deal, towards this coast survey; and my only objection is, that it does not do the whole, and pay the whole, and get the credit due to their work, instead of being, as they now are, unseen and unnoticed—eclipsed and cast into the shade by the civil superintendent and his civil assistants.

I have shown you that, in Great Britain, the Bureau of Ordnance and Hydrography is charged with the coast survey; we have the same bureau, both by law and in fact; but that bureau has only a divided, and, I believe, subordinate part of the coast survey. We have the expense of it, and that expense should be added to the expense of the coast survey. Great Britain has no civil superintendent for this business. We have her law, but not her practice, and my motion is, to come to her practice. We should save by it the whole amount of the direct appropriations, saving and excepting the small appropriations for the extra expense which it would bring upon the navy. The men and officers are under pay, and would be glad to have the work to do. Our naval establishment is now very large, and but little to do. The ships, I suppose, are about seventy; the men and officers some ten thousand: the expense of the whole establishment between eight and nine millions of dollars a year. We are in a state of profound peace, and no way to employ this large naval force. Why not put it upon the coast survey? I know that officers wish it—that they feel humiliated at being supposed incompetent to it—and if found to be so, are willing to pay the penalty, by being dismissed the service. Incompetency is the only ground upon which a civil superintendent and a list of civil assistants can be placed over them. And is that objection well founded? Look to Maury, whose name is the synonym of nautical and astronomical science. Look to that Dr. Locke, once on the medical staff of the navy, and now pursuing a career of science in the West, from which has resulted that discovery of the magnetic clock and telegraph register which the coast survey now uses, and which an officer of the navy (Captain Wilkes) was the first to apply to the purposes for which it is now used.

And are we to presume our naval officers incompetent to the conduct of this coast survey, when it has produced such men as these—when it may contain in its bosom we know not how many more such? In 1807 we had no navy—we may say none, for it was small, and going down to nothing. Then, it might be justifiable to employ an astronomer. In 1832, the navy had fought itself into favor; but Mr. Hassler, the father of the coast survey, was still alive, and it was justifiable to employ him as an astronomer. But now there is no need for a civil astronomer, much less for a civil superintendent; and the whole work should go to the navy. We have naval schools now for the instruction of officers; we have officers with the laudable ambition to instruct themselves. The American character, ardent in every thing, is pre-eminently ardent in the pursuit of knowledge. In every walk of life, from the highest to the lowest, from the most humble mechanical to the highest professional employment, knowledge is a pursuit, and a laudable object of ambition with a great number. We are ardent in the pursuit of wealth—equally so in the pursuit of science. The navy partakes of this laudable ambition. You will see an immense number of the naval officers, of all ages and of all ranks, devoting themselves, with all the ardor of young students, for the acquisition of knowledge: and are all these—the whole naval profession—to be told that none of them are able to conduct the coast survey, none of them able to execute the act of 1807, none of them able to find shoals and islands within twenty leagues of the coast, to sound a harbor, to take the distance and bearings of headlands and capes—and all this within sixty miles of the shore? Are they to be told this? If they are, and it could be told with truth, it would be time to go to reducing. But it cannot be said with truth. The naval officers can not only execute the act of 1807 but they can do any thing, if it was proper to do it, which the present coast survey is engaged in over and beyond that act. They can do any thing that the British officers can do; and the British naval officers conduct the coast survey of that great empire. We have many that can do any thing that Rear Admiral Beaufort can do, and he has conducted the British coast survey for twenty years, and has stood examinations before select committees of the British House of Commons, which have showed that no civil superintendent was necessary to guide him.

Mr. President, we have a large, and almost an idle navy at present. We have a home squadron, like the British, though we do not live on an island, nor in times subject to a descent, like England from Spain in the time of the Invincible Armada, or from the Baltic in the times of Canute and Hardicanute. Our home squadron has nothing to do, unless it can be put on the coast survey. We have a Mediterranean squadron; but there are no longer pirates in the Mediterranean to be kept in check. We have a Pacific squadron, and it has no enemy to watch in the Pacific Ocean. Give these squadrons employment—a part of them at least. Put them on the coast survey, as many as possible, and have the work finished—finished for the present age as well as for posterity. We have been forty years about it; and, the way we go on, may be forty more. The present age wants the benefit of these surveys, and let us accelerate them by turning the navy upon them—as much of it as can be properly employed. Let us put the whole work in the hands of the navy, and try the question whether or not they are incompetent to it.

CHAPTER CLXXXII.

PROPOSED EXTENSION OF THE CONSTITUTION OF THE UNITED STATES TO THE TERRITORIES, WITH A VIEW TO MAKE IT CARRY SLAVERY INTO CALIFORNIA, UTAH AND NEW MEXICO.

The treaty of peace with Mexico had been ratified in the session of 1847-'48, and all the ceded territory became subject to our government, and needing the immediate establishment of territorial governments: but such were the distractions of the slavery question, that no such governments could be formed, nor any law of the United States extended to these newly acquired and orphan dominions. Congress sat for six months after the treaty had been ratified, making vain efforts to provide government for the new territories, and adjourning without accomplishing the work. Another session had commenced, and was coming to a close with the same fruitless result. Bills had been introduced, but they only gave rise to heated discussion. In the last days of the session, the civil and diplomatic appropriation bill, commonly called the general appropriation bill—the one which provides annually for the support of the government, and without the passage of which the government would stop, came up from the House to the Senate. It had received its consideration in the Senate, and was ready to be returned to the House, when Mr. Walker, of Wisconsin, moved to attach to it, under the name of amendment, a section providing a temporary government for the ceded territories, and extending an enumerated list of acts of Congress to them. It was an unparliamentary and disorderly proposition, the proposed amendment being incongruous to the matter of the appropriation bill, and in plain violation of the obvious principle which forbade extraneous matter, and especially that which was vehemently contested, from going into a bill upon the passage of which the existence of the government depended. The proposition met no favor: it would have died out if the mover had not yielded to a Southern solicitation to insert the extension of the constitution into his amendment, so as to extend that fundamental law to those for whom it was never made, and where it was inapplicable, and impracticable. The novelty and strangeness of the proposition called up Mr. Webster, who said:

> "It is of importance that we should seek to have clear ideas and correct notions of the question which this amendment of the member from Wisconsin has presented to us; and especially that we should seek to get some conception of what is meant by the proposition, in a law, to 'extend the constitution of the United States to the territories.' Why, sir, the thing is utterly impossible. All the legislation in the world, in this general form, could not accomplish it. There is no cause for the operation of the legislative power in such a manner as that. The constitution—what is it? We extend the constitution of the United States by law to territory! What is the constitution of the United States? Is not its very first principle, that all within its influence and comprehension shall be represented in the legislature which it establishes, with not only a right of debate and a right to vote in both Houses of Congress, but a right to partake in the choice of the President and Vice-President? And can we by law extend these rights, or any of them, to a territory of the United States? Every body will see that it is altogether impracticable. It comes to this, then, that the constitution is to be extended as far as practicable; but how far that is, is to be decided by the President of the United States, and therefore he is to have absolute and despotic power. He is the judge of what is suitable, and what is unsuitable; and what he thinks suitable is suitable, and what he thinks unsuitable is unsuitable. He is '*omnis in hoc*;' and what is this but to say, in general terms, that the President of the United States shall govern this territory as he sees fit till Congress makes further provision. Now, if the gentleman will be kind enough to tell me what principle of the constitution he supposes suitable, what discrimination he can draw between suitable and unsuitable which he proposes to follow, I shall be instructed. Let me say, that in this general sense there is no such thing as extending the constitution. The constitution is extended over the United States, and over nothing else. It cannot be extended over any thing except over the old States and the new States that shall come in hereafter, when they do come in. There is a want of accuracy of ideas in this respect that is quite remarkable among eminent gentlemen, and especially professional and judicial gentlemen. It seems to be taken for granted

that the right of trial by jury, the *habeas corpus*, and every principle designed to protect personal liberty, is extended by force of the constitution itself over every new territory. That proposition cannot be maintained at all. How do you arrive at it by any reasoning or deduction? It can be only arrived at by the loosest of all possible constructions. It is said that this must be so, else the right of the *habeas corpus* would be lost. Undoubtedly these rights must be conferred by law before they can be enjoyed in a territory."

It was not Mr. Walker, of Wisconsin, the mover of the proposition, that replied to Mr. Webster: it was the prompter of the measure that did it, and in a way to show immediately that this extension of the constitution to territories was nothing but a new scheme for the extension of slavery. Denying the power of Congress to legislate upon slavery in territories—finding slavery actually excluded from the ceded territories, and desirous to get it there—Mr. Calhoun, the real author of Mr. Walker's amendment, took the new conception of carrying the constitution into them; which arriving there, and recognizing slavery, and being the supreme law of the land, it would over-ride the anti-slavery laws of the territory, and plant the institution of slavery under its Ægis, and above the reach of any territorial law, or law of Congress to abolish it. He, therefore, came to the defence of his own proposition, and thus replied to Mr. Webster:

"I rise, not to detain the Senate to any considerable extent, but to make a few remarks upon the proposition first advanced by the senator from New Jersey, fully endorsed by the senator from New Hampshire, and partly endorsed by the senator from Massachusetts, that the constitution of the United States does not extend to the territories. That is the point. I am very happy, sir, to hear this proposition thus asserted, for it will have the effect of narrowing very greatly the controversy between the North and the South as it regards the slavery question in connection with the territories. It is an implied admission on the part of those gentlemen, that, if the constitution does extend to the territories, the South will be protected in the enjoyment of its property—that it will be under the shield of the constitution. You can put no other interpretation upon the proposition which the gentlemen have made, than that the constitution does not extend to the territories. Then the simple question is, does the constitution extend to the territories, or does it not extend to them? Why, the constitution interprets itself. It pronounces itself to be the supreme law of the land."

When Mr. Webster heard this syllogistic assertion, that the constitution being the supreme law of the land, and the territories being a part of the land, *ergo* the constitution being extended to them would be their supreme law: when he heard this, he called out from his seat—"*What land?*" Mr. Calhoun replied, saying:

"The land; the territories of the United States are a part of the land. It is the supreme law, not within the limits of the States of this Union merely, but wherever our flag waves—wherever our authority goes, the constitution in part goes, not all its provisions certainly, but all its suitable provisions. Why, can we have any authority beyond the constitution? I put the question solemnly to gentlemen; if the constitution does not go there, how are we to have any authority or jurisdiction whatever? Is not Congress the creature of the constitution; does it not hold its existence upon the tenure of the continuance of the constitution; and would it not be annihilated upon the destruction of that instrument, and the consequent dissolution of this confederacy? And shall we, the creature of the constitution, pretend that we have any authority beyond the reach of the constitution? Sir, we were told, a few days since, that the courts of the United States had made a decision that the constitution did not extend to the territories without an act of Congress. I confess that I was incredulous, and am still incredulous that any tribunal, pretending to have a knowledge of our system of government, as the courts of the United States ought to have, could have pronounced such a monstrous judgment. I am inclined to think that it is an error which has been unjustly attributed to them; but if they have made such a decision as that, I for one say, that it ought not and never can be respected. The territories belong to us; they are ours; that is to say, they are the property of the thirty States of the Union; and we, as the representatives of those thirty States, have the right to exercise all that authority and jurisdiction which ownership carries with it."

Mr. Webster replied, with showing that the constitution was made for States, not territories—that no part of it went to a territory unless specifically extended to it by act of Congress—that the territories from first to last were governed as Congress chose to govern them, independently of the constitution and often contrary to it, as in denying them representatives in Congress, a vote for President and Vice-President, the protection of the Supreme Court—that Congress was constantly doing things in the territories without constitutional objection (as making mere local roads and bridges) which could not be attempted in a State. He argued:

"The constitution as the gentleman contends, extends over the territories. How does it get there? I am surprised to hear a gentleman so distinguished as a strict constructionist affirming that the constitution of the United States extends to the territories, without, showing us any clause in the constitution in any way leading to that result; and to hear the gentleman maintaining that position without showing us any way in which such a result could be inferred, increases my surprise.

"One idea further upon this branch of the subject. The constitution of the United States extending over the territories, and no other law existing there! Why, I beg to know how any government could proceed, without any other authority existing there than such as is created by the constitution of the United States? Does the constitution of the United States settle titles to land? Does it regulate the rights of property? Does it fix the relations of parent and child, guardian and ward? The constitution of the United States establishes what the gentleman calls a confederation for certain great purposes, leaving all the great mass of laws which is to govern society to derive their existence from State enactments. That is the just view of the state of things under the constitution. And a State or territory that has no law but such as it derives from the constitution of the United States, must be entirely without any State or territorial government. The honorable senator from South Carolina, conversant with the subject as he must be, from his long experience in different branches of the government, must know that the Congress of the United States have established principles in regard to the territories that are utterly repugnant to the constitution. The constitution of the United States has provided for them an independent judiciary; for the judge of every court of the United States holds his office upon the tenure of good behavior. Will the gentleman say that in any court established in the territories the judge holds his office in that way? He holds it for a term of years, and is removable at Executive discretion. How did we govern Louisiana before it was a State? Did the writ of *habeas corpus* exist in Louisiana during its territorial existence? Or the right to trial by jury? Who ever heard of trial by jury there before the law creating the territorial government gave the right to trial by jury? No one. And I do not believe that there is any new light now to be thrown upon the history of the proceedings of this government in relation to that matter. When new territory has been acquired it has always been subject to the laws of Congress, to such laws as Congress thought proper to pass for its immediate government, for its government during its territorial existence, during the preparatory state in which it was to remain until it was ready to come into the Union as one of the family of States."

All this was sound constitutional law, or, rather, was veracious history, showing that Congress governed as it pleased in the territories independently of the constitution, and often contrary to it; and consequently that the constitution did not extend to it. Mr. Webster then showed the puerility of the idea that the constitution went over the territories because they were "*land*," and exposed the fallacy of the supposition that the constitution, even if extended to a territory, could operate there of itself, and without a law of Congress made under it. This fallacy was exposed by showing that Mr. Calhoun, in quoting the constitution as the supreme law of the land, had omitted the essential words which were part of the same clause, and which couples with that supremacy the laws of Congress made in pursuance of the constitution. Thus:

"The honorable senator from South Carolina argues that the constitution declares itself to be the law of the land, and that, therefore, it must extend over the territories. 'The land,' I take it, means the land over which the constitution is established, or, in other words, it means the

States united under the constitution. But does not the gentleman see at once that the argument would prove a great deal too much? The constitution no more says that the constitution itself shall be the supreme law of the land, than it says that the laws of Congress shall be the supreme law of the land. It declares that the constitution and the law of Congress passed under it shall be the supreme law of the land."

The question took a regular slavery turn, Mr. Calhoun avowing his intent to be to carry slavery into the territories under the wing of the constitution, and openly treated as enemies to the South all that opposed it. Having taken the turn of a slavery question, it gave rise to all the dissension of which that subject had become the parent since the year 1835. By a close vote, and before the object had been understood by all the senators, the amendment was agreed to in the Senate, but immediately disagreed to in the House, and a contest brought on between the two Houses by which the great appropriation bill, on which the existence of the government depended, was not passed until after the constitutional expiration of the Congress at midnight of the third of March, and was signed by Mr. Polk (after he had ceased to be President) on the 4th of March—the law and his approval being antedated of the 3d, to prevent its invalidity from appearing on the face of the act. Great was the heat which manifested itself, and imminent the danger that Congress would break up without passing the general appropriation bill; and that the government would stop until a new Congress could be assembled— many of the members of which remained still to be elected. Many members refused to vote after midnight— which it then was. Mr. Cass said:

"As I am among those who believe that the term of this session has expired, and that it is incompetent for us now to do business, I cannot vote upon any motion. I have sat here as a mere looker on. I merely desire to explain why I took no part in the proceedings."

Mr. Yulee, of Florida, moving an adjournment, said:

"I should be very sorry, indeed, to make any proposition which may in any degree run counter to the general sentiment of the Senate; but I feel bound, laboring under the strong conviction that I do, to arrest at every step, and by every means, any recorded judgment of the Senate at a time when we are not legally engaged in the discharge of our senatorial duties. I agree entirely in the view taken by the senator from Michigan."

Mr. Turney, of Tennessee, said:

"I am one of those who believe that we have no right to sit here. The time has expired; one-third of this body are not present at all, and the others have no right to sit here as a part of Congress. But a motion has been made for adjournment, and the presiding officer has refused to entertain that motion. This being the case, I must regard all that is done as done in violation of the constitution, or, rather, not in pursuance of it. It appears to me that we sit here more in the character of a town meeting than as the Senate of the United States, and that what we do is no more binding on the American people than if we did it at a town meeting. I shall express no opinion by saying yea or nay on the question before the Senate. At the same time, I protest against it, as being no part of the constitutional proceedings of the Senate of the United States."

Mr. Benton, and many others, declined to vote. The House of Representatives had ceased to act, and sent to the Senate the customary message of adjournment. The President who, according to the usage, had remained in the capitol till midnight to sign bills, had gone home. It was four o'clock in the morning of the fourth, and the greatest confusion and disorder prevailed. Finally, Mr. Webster succeeded in getting a vote, by which the Senate receded from the amendment it had adopted, extending the constitution to the territories; and that recession leaving the appropriation bill free from the encumbrance of the slavery question, it was immediately passed.

This attempt, pushed to the verge of breaking up the government in pursuit of a newly invented slavery dogma, was founded in errors too gross for misapprehension. In the first place as fully shown by Mr. Webster, the constitution was not made for territories, but for States. In the second place, it cannot operate any where, not even in the States for which it was made without acts of Congress to enforce it. This is true of the constitution in every particular. Every part of it is inoperative until put into action by a statute of Congress. The constitution allows the President a salary: he cannot touch a dollar of it without an act of Congress. It allows the recovery of fugitive slaves: you cannot recover one without an act of Congress. And so of every clause it contains. The proposed extension of the constitution to territories, with a view to its transportation of slavery along with it, was then futile and nugatory, until an act of Congress should be passed to vitalize slavery under it. So that, if the extension had been declared by law, it would have answered no purpose except to widen the field of the slavery agitation—to establish a new point of contention—to give a new phase to the embittered contest— and to alienate more and more from each other the two halves of the Union. But the extension was not declared. Congress did not extend the constitution to the Territories. The proposal was rejected in both Houses; and immediately the crowning dogma is invented, that the constitution goes of itself to the territories without an act of Congress, and executes itself, so far as slavery is concerned, not only without legislative aid, but in defiance of Congress and the people of the territory. This is the last slavery creed of the Calhoun school, and the one on which his disciples now stand—and not with any barren foot. They apply the doctrine to existing territories, and make acquisitions from Mexico for new applications. It is impossible to consider such conduct as any thing else than as one of the devices for "*forcing the issue with the North*," which Mr. Calhoun in his confidential letter to the member of the Alabama legislature avows to have been his policy since 1835, and which he avers he would then have effected if the members from the slave States had stood by him.

CHAPTER CLXXXIII.

PROGRESS OF THE SLAVERY AGITATION: MEETING OF MEMBERS FROM THE SLAVE STATES: INFLAMMATORY ADDRESS TO THE SOUTHERN STATES.

The last days of Mr. Polk's administration were witness to an ominous movement—nothing less than nightly meetings of large numbers of members from the slave States to consider the state of things between the North and the South—to show the aggressions and encroachments (as they were called), of the former upon the latter—to show the incompatibility of their union—and to devise measures for the defence and protection of the South. Mr. Calhoun was at the bottom of this movement, which was conducted with extraordinary precautions to avoid publicity. None but slave State members were admitted. No reporters were permitted to be present; nor any spectators, or auditors. As many as seventy or eighty were assembled; but about one half of this number were inimical to the meeting, and only attended to prevent mischief to the Union, and mostly fell off from their attendance before the work was concluded. At the first meeting a grand committee of 15 (Mr. Calhoun one) were appointed to consider of resolutions: when they met, a sub-committee of five (Mr. Calhoun at their head) was carved out of the 15 to report an address to the slave States: and when they met, Mr. Calhoun produced the address ready written. So that the whole contrivance of the grand and petty committees was a piece of machinery to get Mr. Calhoun's own manifesto before the public with the sanction of a meeting. Mr. Calhoun's manifesto, sanctioned by the sub-committee, was only saved from condemnation in the committee of 15 by one vote, and that vote his own. Saved by one vote, and got before the meeting itself, it there underwent condemnation, and was recommitted for amendment. Four of the grand committee, consisting of those who were averse to the whole proceeding, were excused upon their own request from serving longer upon it. Got back into the grand committee, it was superseded *in toto* by an entire new address, not to the slave States, but to the people of the whole Union, and addressed not to their angry, but to their good feelings. That address was reported to an adjourned meeting of the members; and those opposed to the whole proceeding having nearly ceased to attend, the original manifesto of Mr. Calhoun was adopted in place of it: and thus, after a tedious and painful process, and defeated half the time, and only succeeding when the meeting had become thin and nearly reduced to his own partisans, that gentleman succeeded in getting his inflammatory composition before the public as the voice of the Southern members. But even then not as he first drew it up. In the primitive draft the introductory clause asserted that the present wrongs of the North upon the South were equal to those which produced the separation of these States, when colonies, from the British empire: that clause was softened down, and generalized in the amended and adopted manifesto into the assertion of a dangerous conflict between the two sections of the Union, and the perpetration of encroachments and aggressions upon the slave States which their safety would no longer allow them to stand, and for which a cure must be found. In the original it stood thus: "*Not excepting the declaration which separated you and the United Colonies from the parent country. That involved your independence; but this your all, not excepting your safety.*" As softened it ran thus:

> "We, whose names are hereunto annexed, address you in the discharge of what we believe to be a solemn duty on the most important subject ever presented for your consideration. We allude to the conflict between the two great sections of the Union, growing out of a difference of feeling and opinion in reference to the relation existing between the two races, the European and African, which inhabit the Southern section, and the acts of aggression and encroachment to which it has led. The conflict commenced not long after the acknowledgment of our Independence, and has gradually increased until it has arrayed the great body of the North against the South on this most vital subject. In the progress of this conflict, aggression has followed aggression, and encroachment encroachment, until they have reached a point when a regard for peace and safety will not permit us to remain longer silent. The object of this address is to give you a clear, correct, but brief account of the whole series of aggression and encroachments on your rights, with a statement of the dangers to which they expose you. Our object in making it, is not to cause excitement, but to put you in full possession of all the facts and circumstances necessary to a full and just conception of a deep-seated disease, which threatens great danger to you and the whole body politic. We act on the

impression, that in a popular government like ours, a true conception of the actual character and state of a disease is indispensable to effecting a cure."

The manifesto was modelled upon that of the Declaration of the Independence of the United States; and, by its authors, was soon saluted as the second Declaration of Independence. After the motive clause, showing the inducements to the act, followed a long list of grievances, as formidable in number as those which had impelled the separation from Great Britain, but so frivolous and imaginary in substance, that no one could repeat them now without recourse to the paper. Strange to see, they have become more remarkable for what they omitted than contained. That Missouri compromise, since become an outrage which the constitution and the slave States could no longer endure, was then a good thing, of which the slave States wished more, and claimed its extension to the Pacific Ocean. The Wilmot proviso, which had been the exasperation of the slave States for three years, was skipped over, the great misfortune having happened to the South which had been deprecated in the letter to the Alabama member of the General Assembly: it had been defeated! and for the express purpose of taking a handle of agitation out of the hands of the enemies of the Union: but without benefit, as others were seized upon immediately, and the slavery contention raged more furiously than ever. But past, or present, "encroachments and aggressions" were too light and apocryphal to rouse a nation. Something more stirring was wanted; and for that purpose, Time, and Imagination—the Future, and Invention—were to be placed in requisition. The abolition of slavery in the States—the emancipation of slaves, all over the South—the conflict between the white and the black races—the prostration of the white race, as in San Domingo: the whites the slaves of the blacks: such were the future terrors and horrors to be visited upon the slave States if not arrested by an instant and adequate remedy. Some passages from this conglomeration of invented horrors will show the furious zeal of the author, and the large calculation which he made upon the gullibility of the South when a slavery alarm was to be propagated:

"Such, then, being the case, it would be to insult you to suppose you could hesitate. To destroy the existing relation between the free and servile races at the South would lead to consequences unparalleled in history. They cannot be separated, and cannot live together in peace or harmony, or to their mutual advantage, except in their present relation. Under any other, wretchedness, and misery, and desolation would overspread the whole South. The example of the British West Indies, as blighting as emancipation has proved to them, furnishes a very faint picture of the calamities it would bring on the South. The circumstances under which it would take place with us would be entirely different from those which took place with them, and calculated to lead to far more disastrous results. There, the government of the parent country emancipated slaves in her colonial possessions—a government rich and powerful, and actuated by views of policy (mistaken as they turned out to be) rather than fanaticism. It was, besides, disposed to act justly towards the owners, even in the act of emancipating their slaves, and to protect and foster them afterwards. It accordingly appropriated nearly $100,000,000 as a compensation to them for their losses under the act, which sum, although it turned out to be far short of the amount, was thought at that time to be liberal. Since the emancipation it has kept up a sufficient military and naval force to keep the blacks in awe, and a number of magistrates, and constables, and other civil officers, to keep order in the towns and plantations, and enforce respect to their former owners. It can only be effected by the prostration of the white race; and that would necessarily engender the bitterest feelings of hostility between them and the North. But the reverse would be the case between the blacks of the South and the people of the North. Owing their emancipation to them, they would regard them as friends, guardians, and patrons, and centre, accordingly, all their sympathy in them. The people of the North would not fail to reciprocate and to favor them, instead of the whites. Under the influence of such feelings, and impelled by fanaticism and love of power, they would not stop at emancipation. Another step would be taken—to raise them to a political and social equality with their former owners, by giving them the right of voting and holding public offices under the federal government. But when once raised to an equality, they would become the fast political associates of the North, acting and voting with them on all questions, and by this political union between them, holding the white race at the South in complete subjection. The blacks, and the profligate whites that might unite with them, would become the principal recipients of federal offices and patronage, and would, in consequence, be raised above the whites of the South in the political and social scale. We would, in a word, change conditions with them—a degradation greater than has ever yet fallen to the lot of a free and enlightened people, and one from which we could not escape, should emancipation take place (which it certainly will if not prevented), but by fleeing the homes of ourselves and ancestors, and by abandoning our country to our former slaves, to become the permanent abode of disorder, anarchy, poverty, misery and wretchedness."

Emancipation, with all these accumulated horrors, is here held to be certain, "if not prevented:" certain, so far as it depended upon the free States, which were rapidly becoming the majority; and only to be prevented by the slave States themselves. Now, this certain emancipation of slaves in the States, was a pure and simple invention of Mr. Calhoun, not only without evidence, but against evidence—contradicted by every species of human action, negative and positive, before and since. Far from attacking slavery in the States, the free States have co-operated to extend the area of slavery within such States: witness the continued extinctions of Indian title which have so largely increased the available capacity of the slave States. So far from making war upon slave States, several such States have been added to the Union, as Texas and Florida, by the co-operation of free States. Far from passing any law to emancipate slaves in the States no Congress has ever existed that has seen a man that would make such a motion in the House; or, if made, would not be as unanimously rejected by one side of the House as the other—as if the unanimity would not be the same whether the whole North went out, and let the South vote alone! or the whole South went out, and let the North alone vote. Yet, this incendiary cry of abolishing slavery in the States has become the staple of all subsequent agitators. Every little agitator now jumps upon it—jumps into a State the moment a free territory is mentioned—and repeats all the alarming stuff invented by Mr. Calhoun; and as much more as his own invention can add to it. In the mean time events daily affix the brand of falsehood on these incendiary inventions. Slave State Presidents are continually elected by free State votes: the price of slaves themselves, instead of sinking, as it would if there was any real danger, is continually augmenting, and, in fact, has reached a height the double of what it was before the alarming story of emancipation had begun.

Assuming this emancipation of the slaves in the States to be certain and inevitable, with all its dreadful consequences, unless prevented by the slave States, the manifesto goes on seriously to bring the means of prevention most closely to the consideration of the slave States—to urge their unity and concert of action on the slavery question—to make it the supreme object of their labors, before which all other subjects are to give way—to take the attitude of self-defence; and, braving all consequences, throw the responsibility on the other side. Thus:

"With such a prospect before us, the gravest and most solemn question that ever claimed the attention of a people is presented for your consideration: What is to be done to prevent it? It is a question belonging to you to decide. All we propose is to give you our opinion. We, then, are of the opinion that the first and indispensable step, without which nothing can be done, and with which every thing may be, is to be united among yourselves on this great and most vital question. The want of union and concert in reference to it has brought the South, the Union, and our system of government to their present perilous condition. Instead of placing it above all others, it has been made subordinate not only to mere questions of policy, but to the preservation of party ties and insuring of party success. As high as we hold a due respect for these, we hold them subordinate to that and other questions involving our safety and happiness. Until they are so held by the South, the North will not believe that you are in earnest in opposition to their encroachments, and they will continue to follow, one after another, until the work of abolition is finished. To convince them that you are, you must prove by your acts that you hold all other questions subordinate to it. If you become united, and prove yourselves in earnest, the North will be brought to a pause, and to a calculation of consequences; and that may lead to a change of measures, and to the adoption of a course of policy that may quietly and peaceably terminate this long conflict between the two sections.

If it should not, nothing would remain for you but to stand up immovably in defence of rights involving your all—your property, prosperity, equality, liberty, and safety. As the assailed, you would stand justified by all laws human and divine, in repelling a blow so dangerous, without looking to consequences, and to resort to all means necessary for that purpose. Your assailants, and not you, would be responsible for consequences. Entertaining these opinions, we earnestly entreat you to be united, and for that purpose adopt all necessary measures. Beyond this, we think it would not be proper to go at present."

The primitive draft of the manifesto went further, and told what was to be done: opinions and counsels are as far as the signers thought it proper to go then. But something further was intimated; and that soon came in the shape of a Southern convention to dissolve the Union, and a call from the legislatures of two of the most heated States (South Carolina and Mississippi), for the assembling of a "Southern Congress," to put the machinery of the "United States South" into operation: but of this hereafter. Following the Declaration of Independence in its mode of adoption, as well in its exposition of motives as in its enumeration of grievances, the manifesto was left with the secretary of the meeting for the signature of the slave-holding members who concurred in it. The signers were the following:

"Messrs. Atchison of Missouri; Hunter and Mason of Virginia; Calhoun and Butler of South Carolina; Downs of Louisiana; Foote and Jefferson Davis of Mississippi; Fitzpatrick of Alabama; Borland and Sebastian of Arkansas; Westcott and Yulee of Florida; Atkinson, Bayley, Bedinger, Bocock, Beale, W. G. Brown, Meade, R. A. Thompson of Virginia; Daniel, Venable of North Carolina; Burt, Holmes, Rhett, Simpson, Woodward of South Carolina; Wallace, Iverson, Lumpkin of Georgia; Bowdon, Gayle, Harris of Alabama; Featherston, I. Thompson of Mississippi; La Sere, Morse of Louisiana; R. W. Johnson of Arkansas; Santon of Kentucky."

ADMINISTRATION OF ZACHARY TAYLOR.

CHAPTER CLXXXIV.

INAUGURATION OF PRESIDENT TAYLOR: HIS CABINET.

On the 4th of March the new President was inaugurated with the customary formalities, Chief Justice Taney administering the oath of office. He delivered an address, as use and propriety required, commendably brief, and confined to a declaration of general principles. Mr. Millard Fillmore, the Vice-President elect, was duly installed as President of the Senate, and delivered a neat and suitable address on taking the chair. Assembled in extraordinary session, the Senate received and confirmed the several nominations for the cabinet. They were: John M. Clayton, of Delaware, to be Secretary of State; William M. Meredith, of Pennsylvania, to be Secretary of the Treasury; George W. Crawford, of Georgia, to be Secretary at War; William Ballard Preston, of Virginia, to be Secretary of the Navy; Thomas Ewing, of Ohio, to be Secretary of the Home Department—a new department created at the preceding session of Congress; Jacob Collamer, of Vermont, to be Postmaster General; Reverdy Johnson, of Maryland, to be Attorney General. The whole cabinet were, of course, of the whig party.

CHAPTER CLXXXV.

DEATH OF EX-PRESIDENT POLK.

He died at Nashville, Tennessee, soon after he returned home, and within three months after his retirement from the presidency. He was an exemplary man in private life, moral in all his deportment, and patriotic in his public life, aiming at the good of his country always. It was his misfortune to have been brought into the presidency by an intrigue, not of his own, but of others, and the evils of which became an inheritance of his position, and the sole cause of all that was objectionable in his administration. He was the first President put upon the people without their previous indication—the first instance in which a convention assumed the right of disposing of the presidency according to their own will, and of course with a view to their own advantage. The scheme of these intriguers required the exclusion of all independent and disinterested men from his councils and confidence—a thing easily effected by representing all such men as his enemies, and themselves as his exclusive friends. Hence the ejection of the Globe newspaper from the organship of the administration, and the formation of a cabinet too much dominated by intrigue and selfishness. All the faults of his administration were the faults of his cabinet: all its merits were his own, in defiance of them. Even the arrangement with the Calhoun and Tyler interest by which the Globe was set aside before the cabinet was formed, was the work of men who were to be of the cabinet. His own will was not strong enough for his position, yet he became firm and absolute where his judgment was convinced and patriotism required decision. Of this he gave signal proof in overruling his whole cabinet in their resolve for the sedentary line in Mexico, and forcing the adoption of the vigorous policy which carried the American arms to the city of Mexico, and conquered a peace in the capital of the country. He also gave a proof of it in falling back upon the line of 49° for the settlement of the Oregon boundary with Great Britain, while his cabinet, intimidated by their own newspapers, and alarmed at the storm which themselves had got up, were publicly adhering to the line of 54° 40', with the secret hope that others would extricate them from the perils of that forlorn position. The Mexican war, under the impulse of speculators, and upon an intrigue with Santa Anna, was the great blot upon his administration; and that was wholly the work of the intriguing part of his cabinet, into which he entered with a full belief that the intrigue was to be successful, and the war finished in "ninety or one hundred and twenty days;" and without firing another gun after it should be declared. He was sincerely a friend to the Union, and against whatever would endanger it, especially that absorption of the whole of Mexico which had advocates in those who stood near him; and also against the provisional line which was to cover Monterey and Guaymas, when he began to suspect the ultimate object of that line. The acquisition of New Mexico and California were the distinguishing events of his administration—fruits of the war with Mexico; but which would have come to the United States without that war if the President had been surrounded by a cabinet free from intrigue and selfishness, and wholly intent upon the honor and interest of the country.

CHAPTER CLXXXVI.

THIRTY-FIRST CONGRESS: FIRST SESSION: LIST OF MEMBERS: ORGANIZATION OF THE HOUSE.

The Senate, now consisting of sixty members was composed as follows:

MAINE.—Hannibal Hamlin, James W. Bradbury.

NEW HAMPSHIRE.—John P. Hale, Moses Norris, jr.

MASSACHUSETTS.—Daniel Webster, John Davis.

RHODE ISLAND.—Albert C. Greene, John H. Clarke.

CONNECTICUT.—Roger S. Baldwin, Truman Smith.

VERMONT.—Samuel S. Phelps, William Upham.

NEW YORK.—Daniel S. Dickinson, William H. Seward.

NEW JERSEY.—William L. Dayton, Jacob W. Miller.

PENNSYLVANIA.—Daniel Sturgeon, James Cooper.

DELAWARE.—John Wales, Presley Spruance.

MARYLAND.—David Stuart, James A. Pearce.

VIRGINIA.—James M. Mason, Robert M. T. Hunter.

NORTH CAROLINA.—Willie P. Mangum, George E. Badger.

SOUTH CAROLINA.—John C. Calhoun, Arthur P. Butler.

GEORGIA.—John M. Berrien, William C. Dawson.

KENTUCKY.—Joseph R. Underwood, Henry Clay.

TENNESSEE.—Hopkins L. Turney, John Bell.

OHIO.—Thomas Corwin, Salmon P. Chase.

LOUISIANA.—Solomon W. Downs, Pierre Soulé.

INDIANA.—Jesse D. Bright, James Whitcomb.

MISSISSIPPI.—Jefferson Davis, Henry S. Foote.

ILLINOIS.—Stephen A. Douglass, James Shields.

ALABAMA.—Jeremiah Clemens, William R. King.

MISSOURI.—Thomas H. Benton, David R. Atchison.

ARKANSAS.—William R. Sebastian, Solon Borland.

FLORIDA.—David L. Yulee, Jackson Morton.

MICHIGAN.—Lewis Cass, Alpheus Felch.

TEXAS.—Thomas J. Rusk, Sam Houston.

WISCONSIN.—Henry Dodge, Isaac P. Walker.

IOWA.—George W. Jones, Augustus C. Dodge.

In this list the reader will not fail to remark the names of Mr. Clay, Mr. Webster, and Mr. Calhoun, all of whom, commencing their congressional career nearly a generation before, and after several retirings, had met again, and towards the close of their eventful lives, upon this elevated theatre of their long and brilliant labors. The House, consisting of two hundred and thirty members, was thus composed:

MAINE.—Thomas J. D. Fuller, Elbridge Gerry, Rufus K. Goodenow, Nathaniel S. Littlefield, John Otis, Cullen Sawtelle, Charles Stetson.

NEW HAMPSHIRE.—Harry Hibbard, Charles H. Peaslee, Amos Tuck, James Wilson.

VERMONT.—William Hebard, William Henry, James Meacham, Lucius B. Peck.

MASSACHUSETTS.—Charles Allen, George Ashmun, James H. Duncan, Orin Fowler, Joseph Grinnell, Daniel P. King, Horace Mann, Julius Rockwell, Robert C. Winthrop, Daniel Webster.

RHODE ISLAND.—Nathan F. Dixon, George G. King.

CONNECTICUT.—Walter Booth, Thomas B. Butler, Chauncey F. Cleveland, Loren P. Waldo.

NEW YORK.—Henry P. Alexander, George R. Andrews, Henry Bennett, David A. Bokee, George Briggs, James Brooks, Lorenzo Burrows, Charles E. Clarke, Harmon S. Conger, William Duer, Daniel Gott, Herman D. Gould, Ransom Halloway, William T. Jackson, John A. King, Preston King, Orsamus B. Matteson, Thomas McKissock, William Nelson, J. Phillips Phœnix, Harvey Putnam, Gideon Reynolds, Elijah Risley, Robert L. Rose, David Rumsey, jr., William A. Sackett, Abraham M. Schermerhorn, John L. Schoolcraft, Peter H. Silvester, Elbridge G. Spaulding, John R. Thurman, Walter Underhill, Hiram Walden, Hugh White.

NEW JERSEY.—Andrew K. Hay, James G. King, William A. Newell, John Van Dyke, Isaac Wildrick.

PENNSYLVANIA.—Chester Butler, Samuel Calvin, Joseph Casey, Joseph R. Chandler, Jesse C. Dickey, Milo M. Dimmick, John Freedley, Alfred Gilmore, Moses Hampton, John W. Howe, Lewis C. Levin, Job Mann, James X. McLanahan, Henry D. Moore, Henry Nes, Andrew J. Ogle, Charles W. Pitman, Robert R. Reed, John Robbins, jr., Thomas Ross, Thaddeus Stevens, William Strong, James Thompson, David Wilmot.

DELAWARE.—John W. Houston.

MARYLAND.—Richard I. Bowie, Alexander Evans, William T. Hamilton, Edward Hammond, John B. Kerr, Robert M. McLane.

VIRGINIA.—Thomas H. Averett, Thomas H. Bayly, James M. H. Beale, Thomas S. Bocock, Henry A. Edmundson, Thomas S. Haymond, Alexander R. Holladay, James McDowell, Fayette McMullen, Richard K. Meade, John S. Millson, Jeremiah Morton, Richard Parker, Paulus Powell, James A. Seddon.

NORTH CAROLINA.—William S. Ashe, Joseph P. Caldwell, Thomas L. Clingman, John R. J. Daniel, Edmund Deberry, David Outlaw, Augustine H. Shepperd, Edward Stanly, Abraham W. Venable.

SOUTH CAROLINA.—Armistead Burt, William F. Colcock, Isaac E. Holmes, John McQueen, James L. Orr, Daniel Wallace, Joseph A. Woodward.

GEORGIA.—Howell Cobb, Thomas C. Hackett, Hugh A. Haralson, Thomas Butler King, Allen F. Owen, Alexander H. Stephens, Robert Toombs, Marshall J. Wellborn.

ALABAMA.—Albert J. Alston, Franklin W. Bowdon, Williamson R. W. Cobb, Sampson W. Harris, Henry W. Hilliard, David Hubbard, Samuel W. Inge.

MISSISSIPPI.—Albert G. Brown, Winfield S. Featherston, William McWillie, Jacob Thompson.

LOUISIANA.—Charles M. Conrad, John H. Harmanson, Emile La Sère, Isaac E. Morse.

OHIO.—Joseph Cable, Lewis D. Campbell, David K. Carter, Moses B. Corwin, John Crowell, David T. Disney, Nathan Evans, Joshua R. Giddings, Moses Hoagland, William F. Hunter, John K. Miller, Jonathan D. Morris, Edson B. Olds, Emery D. Potter, Joseph M. Root, Robert C. Schenck, Charles Sweetser, John L. Taylor, Samuel F. Vinton, William A. Whittlesey, Amos E. Wood.

KENTUCKY.—Linn Boyd, Daniel Breck, Geo A. Caldwell, James L. Johnson, Humphrey Marshall, John C. Mason, Finis E. McLean, Charles S. Morehead, Richard H. Stanton, John B. Thompson.

TENNESSEE.—Josiah M. Anderson, Andrew Ewing, Meredith P. Gentry, Isham G. Harris, Andrew Johnson, George W. Jones, John H. Savage, Frederick P. Stanton, Jas. H. Thomas, Albert G. Watkins, Christopher H. Williams.

INDIANA.—Nathaniel Albertson, William J. Brown, Cyrus L. Dunham, Graham N. Fitch, Willis A. Gorman, Andrew J. Harlan, George W. Julian, Joseph E. McDonald, Edward W. McGaughey, John L. Robinson.

ILLINOIS.—Edward D. Baker, William H. Bissell, Thomas L. Harris, John A. McClernand, William A. Richardson, John Wentworth, Timothy R. Young.

MISSOURI.—William V. N. Bay, James B. Bowlin, James S. Green, Willard P. Hall, John S. Phelps.

ARKANSAS.—Robert W. Johnson.

MICHIGAN.—Kinsley S. Bingham, Alexander W. Buel, William Sprague.

FLORIDA.—E. Carrington Cabell.

TEXAS.—Volney E. Howard, David S. Kaufman.

IOWA.—Shepherd Leffler, William Thompson.

WISCONSIN.—Orsamus Cole, James D. Doty, Charles Durkee.

Delegates from Territories.

OREGON.—S. R. Thurston.

MINNESOTA.—Henry S. Sibley.

The election of a Speaker is the first business of a new Congress, and the election which decided the political character of the House while parties divided on political principles. Candidates from opposite parties were still put in nomination at this commencement of the Thirty-first Congress, but it was soon seen that the slavery question mingled with the election, and gave it its controlling character. Mr. Robert Winthrop, of Massachusetts (whig), and Mr. C. Howell Cobb, of Georgia (democratic), were the respective candidates; and in the vain struggle to give either a majority of the House near three weeks of time was wasted, and above sixty ballotings exhausted. Deeming the struggle useless, resort was had to the plurality rule, and Mr. Cobb receiving 102 votes to the 99 for Mr. Winthrop—about twenty votes being thrown away—he was declared elected, and led to the chair most courteously by his competitor, Mr. Winthrop, and Mr. James McDowell, of Virginia. Mr. Thomas I. Campbell was elected clerk, and upon his death during the session, Richard M. Young, Esq., of Illinois, was elected in his place.

CHAPTER CLXXXVII.

FIRST AND ONLY ANNUAL MESSAGE OF PRESIDENT TAYLOR.

This only message of one of the American Presidents, shows that he comprehended the difficulties of his position, and was determined to grapple with them—that he saw where lay the dangers to the harmony and stability of the Union, and was determined to lay these dangers bare to the public view—and, as far as depended on him, to apply the remedies which their cure demanded. The first and the last paragraphs of his message looked to this danger, and while the first showed his confidence in the strength of the Union, the latter admitted the dangers to it, and averred his own determination to stand by it to the full extent of his obligations and powers. It was in these words:

> "But attachment to the Union of the States should be habitually fostered in every American heart. For more than half a century, during which kingdoms and empires have fallen, this Union has stood unshaken. The patriots who formed it have long since descended to the grave; yet still it remains the proudest monument to their memory, and the object of affection and admiration with every one worthy to bear the American name. In my judgment its dissolution would be the greatest of calamities, and to avert that should be the study of every American. Upon its preservation must depend our own happiness, and that of countless generations to come. Whatever dangers may threaten it, I shall stand by it, and maintain it in its integrity, to the full extent of the obligations imposed and the power conferred upon me by the constitution."

This paragraph has the appearance where it occurs of being an addition to the message after it had been written: and such it was. It was added in consequence of a visit from Mr. Calhoun to the Department of State, and expressing a desire that nothing should be said in the message about the point to which it relates. The two paragraphs were then added—the one near the beginning, the other at the end of the message; and it was in allusion to these passages that Mr. Calhoun's last speech, read in the Senate by Mr. Mason, of Virginia, contained those memorable words, so much noted at the time:

> "It (the Union) cannot, then, be saved by eulogies on it, however splendid or numerous. The cry of 'Union, Union, the glorious Union!' can no more prevent disunion than the cry of 'Health, Health, glorious Health!' on the part of the physician can save a patient from dying that is lying dangerously ill."

President Taylor surveyed the difficulties before him, and expressed his opinion of the remedies they required. California, New Mexico, and Utah had been left without governments: Texas was asserting a claim to one half of New Mexico—a province settled two hundred years before Texian independence, and to which no Texian invader ever went except to be killed or taken, to the last man. Each of these presented a question to be settled, in which the predominance of the slavery agitation rendered settlement difficult and embarrassing. President Taylor frankly and firmly presented his remedy for each one. California, having the requisite population for a State, and having formed her constitution, and prepared herself for admission into the Union, was favorably recommended for that purpose to Congress:

> "No civil government having been provided by Congress for California, the people of that territory, impelled by the necessities of their political condition, recently met in convention, for the purpose of forming a constitution and State government, which the latest advices give me reason to suppose has been accomplished; and it is believed they will shortly apply for the admission of California into the Union as a sovereign State. Should such be the case, and should their constitution be conformable to the requisitions of the constitution of the United States, I recommend their application to the favorable consideration of Congress."

New Mexico and Utah, without mixing the slavery question with their territorial governments, were recommended to be left to ripen into States, and then to settle that question for themselves in their State constitutions—saying:

"By awaiting their action, all causes of uneasiness may be avoided, and confidence and kind feeling preserved. With the view of maintaining the harmony and tranquillity so dear to all, we should abstain from the introduction of those exciting topics of a sectional character which have hitherto produced painful apprehensions in the public mind; and I repeat the solemn warning of the first and most illustrious of my predecessors, against furnishing 'any ground for characterizing parties by geographical discriminations!'"

This reference to Washington was answered by Calhoun in the same speech read by Mr. Mason, denying that the Union could be saved by invoking his name, and averring that there was "*nothing in his history to deter us from seceding from the Union should it fail to fulfil the objects for which it was instituted.*" which failure the speech averred—as others had averred for twenty years before: for secession was the off-shoot of nullification, and a favorite mode of dissolving the Union. With respect to Texas and New Mexico, it was the determination of the President that their boundaries should be settled by the political, or judicial authority of the United States, and not by arms.

In all these recommendations the message was wise, patriotic, temperate and firm; but it encountered great opposition, and from different quarters, and upon different grounds—from Mr. Clay, who wished a general compromise; from Mr. Calhoun, intent upon extending slavery; and holding the Union to be lost except by a remedy of his own which he ambiguously shadowed forth—a dual executive—two Presidents: one for the North, one for the South: which was itself disunion if accomplished. In his reference to Washington's warnings against geographical and sectional parties, there was a pointed rebuke to the daily attempts to segregate the South from the North, and to form political parties exclusively on the basis of an opposition of interest between the Southern and the Northern States. As a patriot, he condemned such sectionalism: as a President, he would have counteracted it.

After our duty to ourselves the President spoke of our duty to others—to our neighbors—and especially the Spanish possession of Cuba. An invasion of that island by adventurers from the United States had been attempted, and had been suppressed by an energetic proclamation, backed by a determination to carry it into effect upon the guilty. The message said:

"Having been apprised that a considerable number of adventurers were engaged in fitting out a military expedition, within the United States, against a foreign country, and believing, from the best information I could obtain, that it was destined to invade the island of Cuba, I deemed it due to the friendly relations existing between the United States and Spain; to the treaty between the two nations; to the laws of the United States; and, above all, to the American honor, to exert the lawful authority of this government in suppressing the expedition and preventing the invasion. To this end I issued a proclamation, enjoining it upon the officers of the United States, civil and military, to use all lawful means within their power. A copy of that proclamation is herewith submitted. The expedition has been suppressed. So long as the act of Congress of the 20th of April, 1818, which owes its existence to the law of nations and to the policy of Washington himself, shall remain on our statute book, I hold it to be the duty of the Executive faithfully to obey its injunctions."

This was just conduct, and just language, worthy of an upright magistrate of a Republic, which should set an example of justice and fairness towards its neighbors. The Spanish government had been greatly harassed by expeditions got up against Cuba in the United States, and put to enormous expense in ships and troops to hold herself in a condition to repulse them. Thirty thousand troops, and a strong squadron, were constantly kept on foot to meet this danger. A war establishment was kept up in time of peace in the island of Cuba to protect the island from threatened invasions. Besides the injury done to Spain by these aggravations, and the enormous expense of a war establishment to be kept in Cuba, there was danger of injury to ourselves from the number and constant recurrence of these expeditions, which would seem to speak the connivance of the people, or the negligence of the government. Fortunately for the peace of the countries during the several years that these expeditions were most undertaken, the Spanish government was long represented at Washington by a minister of approved fitness for his situation—Don Luis Calderon de la Barca: a fine specimen of the old Castilian character—frank, courteous, honorable, patriotic—whose amiable manners enabled him to mix intimately with

American society, and to see that these expeditions were criminally viewed by the government and the immense majority of the citizens; and whose high character enabled him to satisfy his own government of that important fact, and to prevent from being viewed as the act of the nation, what was only that of lawless adventurers, pursued and repressed by our own laws.

CHAPTER CLXXXVIII.

MR. CLAY'S PLAN OF COMPROMISE.

Early in the session Mr. Clay brought into the Senate a set of resolutions, eight in number, to settle and close up once and for ever, all the points of contestation in the slavery question, and to consolidate the settlement of the whole into one general and lasting compromise. He was placed at the head of a grand committee of thirteen members to whom his resolutions were to be referred, with a view to combine them all into one bill, and make that bill the final settlement of all the questions connected with slavery. Mr. Benton opposed this whole plan of pacification, as mixing up incongruous measures—making one measure dependent upon another—tacking together things which had no connection—as derogatory and perilous to the State of California to have the question of her admission confounded with the general slavery agitation in the United States—as being futile and impotent, as no such conglomeration of incongruities (though christened a compromise) could have any force:—as being a concession to the spirit of disunion—a capitulation to those who threatened secession—a repetition of the error of 1833:—and itself to become the fruitful source of more contentions than it proposed to quiet. His plan was to settle each measure by itself, beginning with the admission of California, settling every thing justly and fairly, in the spirit of conciliation as well as of justice—leaving the consequences to God and the country—and having no compromise with the threat of disunion. The majority of the Senate were of Mr. Benton's opinion, which was understood also to be the plan of the President: but there are always men of easy or timid temperaments in every public body that delight in temporizations, and dread the effects of any firm and straightforward course; and so it was now, but with great difficulty—Mr. Clay himself only being elected by the aid of one vote, given to him by Mr. Webster after it was found that he lacked it. The committee were: Mr. Clay, chairman: Messrs. Cass, Dickinson, Bright, Webster, Phelps, Cooper, King, Mason, Downs, Mangum, Bell, and Berrien, members. Mr. Clay's list of measures was referred to them; and as the committee was selected with a view to promote the mover's object, a bill was soon returned embracing the comprehensive plan of compromise which he proposed. The admission of California, territorial governments for Utah and New Mexico, the settlement of the Texas boundary, slavery in the District of Columbia, a fugitive slave law—all—all were put together in one bill, to be passed or rejected by the same vote! and to be called a system. United they could not be. Their natures were too incongruous to admit of union or mixture. They were simply tied together—called one measure; and required to be voted on as such. They were not even bills drawn up by the committee, but existing bills in the Senate—drawn up by different members—occupying different places on the calendar—and each waiting its turn to be acted on separately. Mr. Clay had made an ample report in favor of his measure, and further enforced it by an elaborate speech: the whole of which Mr. Benton contested, and answered in an ample speech, some extracts from which constitute a future chapter.

CHAPTER CLXXXIX.

EXTENSION OF THE MISSOURI COMPROMISE LINE TO THE PACIFIC OCEAN: MR. DAVIS, OF MISSISSIPPI, AND MR. CLAY: THE WILMOT PROVISO.

In the resolutions of compromise submitted by Mr. Clay there was one declaring the non-existence of slavery in the territory recently acquired from Mexico, and affirming the "inexpediency" of any legislation from Congress on that subject within the said territories. His resolution was in these words:

> "*Resolved*, That as slavery does not exist by law, and is not likely to be introduced into any of the territory acquired by the United States from the Republic of Mexico, it is inexpedient for Congress to provide by law either for its introduction into or exclusion from any part of the said territory; and that appropriate territorial governments ought to be established by Congress in all of the said territory, not assigned as the boundaries of the proposed State of California, without the adoption of any restriction or condition on the subject of slavery."

This proposition, with some half-dozen others, formed the system of compromise with which Mr. Clay expected to pacify the slavery agitation in the United States. Mr. Davis, of Mississippi, did not perceive any thing of a compromise in a measure which gave nothing to the South in the settlement of the question, and required the extension of the Missouri compromise line to the Pacific ocean as the least that he would be willing to take. Thus:

> "But, sir, we are called on to receive this as a measure of compromise! Is a measure in which we of the minority are to receive nothing, a measure of compromise? I look upon it as but a modest mode of taking that, the claim to which has been more boldly asserted by others; and that I may be understood upon this question, and that my position may go forth to the country in the same columns that convey the sentiments of the senator from Kentucky, I here assert that never will I take less than the Missouri compromise line extended to the Pacific ocean, with the specific recognition of the right to hold slaves in the territory below that line; and that, before such territories are admitted into the Union as States, slaves may be taken there from any of the United States at the option of their owners."

This was a manly declaration in favor of extending slavery into the new territories, and in the only way in which it could be done—that is to say, by act of Congress. Mr. Clay met it by a declaration equally manly, and in conformity to the principles of his whole life, utterly refusing to plant slavery in any place where it did not previously exist. He answered:

> "I am extremely sorry to hear the senator from Mississippi say that he requires, first, the extension of the Missouri compromise line to the Pacific, and also that he is not satisfied with that, but requires, if I understood him correctly, a positive provision for the admission of slavery south of that line. And now, sir, coming from a slave State, as I do, I owe it to myself, I owe it to truth, I owe it to the subject, to say that no earthly power could induce me to vote for a specific measure for the introduction of slavery where it had not before existed, either south or north of that line. Coming as I do from a slave State, it is my solemn, deliberate and well matured determination that no power, no earthly power, shall compel me to vote for the positive introduction of slavery either south or north of that line. Sir, while you reproach, and justly too, our British ancestors for the introduction of this institution upon the continent of America, I am, for one, unwilling that the posterity of the present inhabitants of California and of New Mexico shall reproach us for doing just what we reproach Great Britain for doing to us. If the citizens of those territories choose to establish slavery, and if they come here with constitutions establishing slavery, I am for admitting them with such provisions in their constitutions; but then it will be their own work, and not ours, and their posterity will have to reproach them, and not us, for forming constitutions allowing the institution of slavery to exist among them. These are my views, sir, and I choose to express them; and I care not how extensively or universally they are known."

These were manly sentiments, courageously expressed, and taking the right ground so much overlooked, or perverted by others. The Missouri compromise line, extending to New Mexico and California, though astronomically the same with that in Louisiana, was politically directly the opposite. One went through a territory all slave, and made one-half free; the other would go through territory all free, and make one-half slave. Mr. Clay saw this difference, and acted upon it, and declared his sentiments honestly and boldly; and none but the ignorant or unjust could reproach him with inconsistency in maintaining the line in the ancient Louisiana, where the whole province came to us with slavery, and refusing it in the new territories where all came to us free.

Mr. Seward, of New York, proposed the renewal of the Wilmot proviso:

> "Neither slavery nor involuntary servitude, otherwise than by conviction for crime, shall ever be allowed in either of said territories of Utah and New Mexico."

Upon the adoption of which the yeas and nays were:

> "YEAS.—Messrs. Baldwin, Bradbury, Bright, Chase, Clarke, Cooper, Corwin, Davis of Massachusetts, Dayton, Dodge of Wisconsin, Douglas, Felch, Greene, Hale, Hamlin, Miller, Norris, Seward, Shields, Smith, Upham, Whitcomb, and Walker—23.

> "NAYS.—Messrs. Atchison, Badger, Bell, Benton, Berrien, Butler, Cass, Clay, Clemens, Davis of Mississippi, Dawson, Dickinson, Dodge of Iowa, Downs, Foote, Houston, Hunter, Jones, King, Mangum, Mason, Morton, Pearce, Pratt, Rusk, Sebastian, Soulé, Spruance, Sturgeon, Turney, Underwood, Webster, and Yulee—33."

CHAPTER CXC.

MR. CALHOUN'S LAST SPEECH: DISSOLUTION OF THE UNION PROCLAIMED UNLESS THE CONSTITUTION WAS AMENDED, AND A DUAL EXECUTIVE APPOINTED—ONE PRESIDENT FROM THE SLAVE AND ONE FROM THE FREE STATES.

On the 4th of March Mr. Calhoun brought into the Senate a written speech, elaborately and studiously prepared, and which he was too weak to deliver, or even to read. Upon his request it was allowed to be read by his friend, Mr. James M. Mason of Virginia, and was found to be an amplification and continuation of the Southern manifesto of the preceding year; and, like it, occupied entirely with the subject of the dissolution of the Union, and making out a case to justify it. The opening went directly to the point, and presented the question of Union, or disunion with the formality and solemnity of an actual proposition, as if its decision was the business on which the Senate was convened. It opened thus:

> "I have, senators, believed from the first that the agitation of the subject of slavery would, if not prevented by some timely and effective measure, end in disunion. Entertaining this opinion, I have, on all proper occasions, endeavored to call the attention of each of the two great parties which divide the country to adopt some measure to prevent so great a disaster but without success. The agitation has been permitted to proceed, with almost no attempt to resist it, until it has reached a period when it can no longer be disguised or denied that the Union is in danger. You have thus had forced upon you the greatest and the gravest question that can ever come under your consideration: How can the Union be preserved?"

Professing to proceed like a physician who must find out the cause of a disease before he can apply a remedy, the speech went on to discover the reasons which now rendered disunion inevitable, unless an adequate remedy to prevent it should be administered. The first of these causes was the anti-slavery ordinance of 1787, which was adopted before the constitution was formed, and had its origin from the South, and the unanimous support of that section. The second was the Missouri compromise line, which also had its origin in the South, the unanimous support of the Southern senators, the majority of the Southern representatives, the unanimous support of Mr. Monroe's cabinet, of which Mr. Calhoun was a member; and his own approbation of it for about twenty-five years. The long continued agitation of the slave question was another cause of disunion, dating the agitation from the year 1835—which was correct; for in that year he took it up in the Senate, and gave the abolitionists what they wanted, and could not otherwise acquire—an antagonist to cope with, an elevated theatre for the strife, and a national auditory to applaud or censure. Before that time he said, and truly, the agitation was insignificant; since then it had become great; and (he might have added), that senators North and South told him that would be the case when he entered upon the business in 1835. Repeal of the slave sojournment laws by New York and Pennsylvania, was referred to, and with reason, except that these repeals did not take place until after his own conduct in the Senate had made the slavery agitation national, and given distinction and importance to the abolitionists. The progressive increase of the two classes of States, rapid in one, slow in the other, was adverted to as leading to disunion by destroying, what he called, the *equilibrium* of the States—as if that difference of progress was not mainly in the nature of things, resulting from climate and soil; and in some degree political, resulting from the slavery itself which he was so anxious to extend. The preservation of this equilibrium was to be effected by acquiring Southern territory and opening it to slavery. The *equality* of the States was held to be indispensable to the continuance of the Union; and that equality was to be maintained by admitting slavery to be carried into all the territories—even Oregon—equivocally predicated on the right of all persons to carry their "*property*" with them to these territories. The phrase was an equivocation, and has been a remarkable instance of delusion from a phrase. Every citizen can carry his property now wherever he goes, only he cannot carry the State law with him which makes it property, and for want of which it ceases to be so when he gets to his new residence. The New Englander can carry his bank along with him, and all the money it contains, to one of the new territories; but he cannot carry the law of incorporation with him; and it ceases to be the property he had in New England. All this complaint about inequality in a slave-holder in not being allowed to carry his "*property*" with him to a territory, stript of the ambiguity of phraseology, is nothing but a complaint that he cannot carry the law with him which makes it property; and in that there is no inequality between the States. They are all equal in the total inability of their citizens to carry the State laws with them. The result of the whole, the speech went on to say, was that the process of disruption was then going on between the two classes of States, and could not be arrested by any remedy proposed—not by Mr. Clay's compromise plan, nor by President's plan, nor by the cry of "Union, Union, Glorious Union!" The speech continues:

> "Instead of being weaker, all the elements in favor of agitation are stronger now than they were in 1835, when it first commenced, while all the elements of influence on the part of the South are weaker. Unless something decisive is done, I again ask what is to stop this agitation, before the great and final object at which it aims—the abolition of slavery in the States—is consummated? Is it, then, not certain that if something decisive is not now done to arrest it, the South will be forced to choose between abolition and secession? Indeed, as events are now moving, it will not require the South to secede to dissolve the Union."

The speech goes on to say that the Union could not be dissolved at a single blow: it would require many, and successive blows, to snap its cords asunder:

> "It is a great mistake to suppose that disunion can be effected by a single blow. The cords which bind these States together in one common Union are far too numerous and powerful for that. Disunion must be the work of time. It is only through a long process, and successively, that the cords can be snapped, until the whole fabric falls asunder. Already the agitation of the slavery question has snapped some of the most important, and has greatly weakened all the others, as I shall proceed to show."

The speech goes on to show that cords have already been snapt, and others weakened:

> "The cords that bind the States together are not only many, but various in character. Some are spiritual or ecclesiastical; some political; others social. Some appertain to the benefit conferred by the Union, and others to the feeling of duty and obligation.

> "The strongest of those of a spiritual and ecclesiastical nature consisted in the unity of the great religious denominations, all of which originally embraced the whole Union. All these denominations, with the exception, perhaps, of the Catholics, were organized very much upon the principle of our political institutions; beginning with smaller meetings correspondent with the political divisions of the country, their organization terminated in one great central assemblage, corresponding very much with the character of Congress. At these meetings the principal clergymen and lay members of the respective denominations from all parts of the Union met to transact business relating to their common concerns. It was not confined to what appertained to the doctrines and discipline of the respective denominations, but extended to plans for disseminating the Bible, establishing missionaries, distributing tracts, and of establishing presses for the publication of tracts, newspapers, and periodicals, with a view of diffusing religious information, and for the support of the doctrines and creeds of the denomination. All this combined, contributed greatly to strengthen the bonds of the Union. The strong ties which held each denomination together formed a strong cord to hold the whole Union together; but, as powerful as they were, they have not been able to resist the explosive effect of slavery agitation.

> "The first of these cords which snapped, under its explosive force, was that of the powerful Methodist Episcopal Church. The numerous and strong ties which held it together are all broke, and its unity gone. They now form separate churches, and, instead of the feeling of attachment and devotion to the interests of the whole church which was formerly felt, they are now arrayed into two hostile bodies, engaged in litigation about what was formerly their common property.

> "The next cord that snapped was that of the Baptists, one of the largest and most respectable of the denominations. That of the Presbyterian is not entirely snapped, but some of its strands

have given way. That of the Episcopal Church is the only one of the four great Protestant denominations which remains unbroken and entire.

"The strongest cord of a political character consists of the many and strong ties that have held together the two great parties, which have, with some modifications, existed from the beginning of the government. They both extended to every portion of the Union, and strongly contributed to hold all its parts together. But this powerful cord has fared no better than the spiritual. It resisted for a long time the explosive tendency of the agitation, but has finally snapped under its force—if not entirely, in a great measure. Nor is there one of the remaining cords which have not been greatly weakened. To this extent the Union has already been destroyed by agitation, in the only way it can be, by snapping asunder and weakening the cords which bind it together."

The last cord here mentioned, that of political parties, founded upon principles not subject to sectional, or geographical lines, has since been entirely destroyed, snapped clean off by the abrogation of the Missouri compromise line, and making the extension, or non-extension of slavery, the foundation of political parties. After that cord should be snapped, the speech goes on to consider "*force*" the only bond of Union, and justly considers that as no Union where power and violence constitute the only bond.

"If the agitation goes on, the same force, acting with increased intensity, as has been shown, will finally snap every cord, when nothing will be left to hold the States together except force. But surely that can, with no propriety of language, be called a Union, when the only means by which the weaker is held connected with the stronger portion is *force*. It may, indeed, keep them connected; but the connection will partake much more of the character of subjugation, on the part of the weaker to the stronger, than the union of free, independent, and sovereign States, in one confederation, as they stood in the early stages of the government, and which only is worthy of the sacred name of Union."

The admission of the State of California, with her free constitution, was the exciting cause of this speech from Mr. Calhoun. The Wilmot proviso was disposed of. That cause of disunion no longer existed; but the admission of California excited the same opposition, and was declared to be the "*test*" question upon which all depended. The President had communicated the constitution of that State to Congress, which Mr. Calhoun strongly repulsed.

"The Executive has laid the paper purporting to be the Constitution of California before you, and asks you to admit her into the Union as a State; and the question is, will you or will you not admit her? It is a grave question, and there rests upon you a heavy responsibility. Much, very much, will depend upon your decision. If you admit her, you endorse and give your sanction to all that has been done. Are you prepared to do so? Are you prepared to surrender your power of legislation for the territories—a power expressly vested in Congress by the constitution, as has been fully established? Can you, consistently with your oath to support the constitution, surrender the power? Are you prepared to admit that the inhabitants of the territories possess the sovereignty over them, and that any number, more or less, may claim any extent of territory they please, may form a constitution and government, and erect it into a State, without asking your permission? Are you prepared to surrender the sovereignty of the United States over whatever territory may be hereafter acquired to the first adventurers who may rush into it? Are you prepared to surrender virtually to the Executive Department all the powers which you have heretofore exercised over the territories? If not, how can you, consistently with your duty and your oaths to support the constitution, give your assent to the admission of California as a State, under a pretended constitution and government?"

Having shown that all the cords that held the Union together had snapped except one (political party principle), and that one weakened and giving way, the speech came to the solemn question: "*How can the Union be saved?*" and answered it (after some generalities) by coming to the specific point—

"To provide for the insertion of a provision in the Constitution, by an amendment, which will restore to the South in substance the power she possessed of protecting herself, before the equilibrium between the sections was destroyed by the action of this government."

The speech did not tell of what this amendment was to consist, which was to have the effect of saving the Union, by protecting the slave States, and restoring the equilibrium between the two classes of States; but an authentic publication soon after disclosed it, and showed it to be the election of two Presidents, one from the free and the other from the slave States, and each to approve of all the acts of Congress before they became laws. Upon this condition alone, the speech declared the Union could be saved! which was equivalent to pronouncing its dissolution. For, in the first place, no such amendment to the constitution could be made; in the second place, no such double-headed government could work through even one session of Congress, any more than two animals could work together in the plough with their heads yoked in opposite directions.

This last speech of Mr. Calhoun becomes important, as furnishing a key to his conduct, and that of his political friends, and as connecting itself with subsequent measures.

CHAPTER CXCI.

DEATH OF MR. CALHOUN: HIS EULOGIUM BY SENATOR BUTLER.

"MR. PRESIDENT: Mr. Calhoun has lived in an eventful period of our Republic and has acted a distinguished part. I surely do not venture too much when I say, that his reputation forms a striking part of a glorious history. Since 1811 until this time, he has been responsibly connected with the federal government. As representative, senator, cabinet minister, and Vice President, he has been identified with the greatest events in the political history of our country. And I hope I may be permitted to say that he has been equal to all the duties which were devolved upon him in the many critical junctures in which he was placed. Having to act a responsible part, he always acted a decided part. It would not become me to venture upon the judgment which awaits his memory. That will be formed by posterity before the impartial tribunal of history. It may be that he will have had the fate, and will have given to him the judgment that has been awarded to Chatham.

"Mr. Calhoun was a native of South Carolina, and was born in Abbeville district, on the 18th March, 1782. He was of an Irish family. His father, Patrick Calhoun, was born in Ireland, and at an early age came to Pennsylvania, thence moved to the western part of Virginia, and after Braddock's defeat moved to South Carolina, in 1756. He and his family gave a name to what is known as the Calhoun settlement in Abbeville district. The mother of my colleague was a Miss Caldwell, born in Charlotte County, Virginia. The character of his parents had no doubt a sensible influence on the destiny of their distinguished son. His father had energy and enterprise, combined with perseverance and great mental determination. His mother belonged to a family of revolutionary heroes. Two of her brothers were distinguished in the Revolution. Their names and achievements are not left to tradition, but constitute a part of the history of the times.

"He became a student in Yale College, in 1802, and graduated two years afterwards with distinction—as a young man of great ability, and with the respect and confidence of his preceptors and fellows. What they have said and thought of him, would have given any man a high reputation. It is the pure fountain of a clear reputation. If the stream has met with obstructions, they were such as have only shown its beauty and majesty.

"Mr. Calhoun came into Congress at a time of deep and exciting interest—at a crisis of great magnitude. It was a crisis of peril to those who had to act in it, but of subsequent glory to the actors, and the common history of the country. The invincibility of Great Britain had become a proverbial expression, and a war with her was full of terrific issues. Mr. Calhoun found himself at once in a situation of high responsibility—one that required more than speaking qualities and eloquence to fulfil it. The spirit of the people required direction; the energy and ardor of youth were to be employed in affairs requiring the maturer qualities of a statesman. The part which Mr. Calhoun acted at this time, has been approved and applauded by contemporaries, and now forms a part of the glorious history of those times.

"The names of Clay, Calhoun, Cheves, and Lowndes, Grundy, Porter, and others, carried associations with them that reached the *heart of the nation*. Their clarion notes penetrated the army; they animated the people, and sustained the administration of the government. With such actors, and in such scenes—the most eventful of our history—to say that Mr. Calhoun did not play a second part, is no common praise. In debate he was equal with Randolph, and in council he commanded the respect and confidence of Madison. At this period of his life he had the quality of Themistocles—*to inspire confidence*—which, after all, is the highest of earthly qualities: it is a mystical something which is felt, but cannot be described. The events of the war were brilliant and honorable to both statesmen and soldiers, and their history may be read with enthusiasm and delight. The war terminated with honor; but the measures which had to be taken, in a transition to a peace establishment, were full of difficulty and embarrassment. Mr. Calhoun, with his usual intrepidity, did not hesitate to take a responsible part. Under the influence of a broad patriotism, he acted with an uncalculating liberality to all the interests that were involved, and which were brought under review of Congress. His personal adversary at this time, in his admiration for his genius, paid Mr. Calhoun a beautiful compliment for his noble and national sentiments.

"At the termination of Mr. Madison's administration, Mr. Calhoun had acquired a commanding reputation; he was regarded as one of the sages of the Republic. In 1817 Mr. Monroe invited him to a place in his cabinet;

Mr. Calhoun's friends doubted the propriety of his accepting it, and some of them thought he would put a high reputation at hazard in this new sphere of action. Perhaps these suggestions fired his high and gifted intellect; he accepted the place, and went into the War Department, under circumstances that might have appalled other men. His success has been acknowledged; what was complex and confused, he reduced to simplicity and order. His organization of the War Department, and his administration of its undefined duties, have made the impression of an *author*, having the interest of originality and the sanction of trial.

"While he was Vice-President he was placed in some of the most trying scenes of any man's life. I do not now choose to refer to any thing that can have the elements of controversy; but I hope I may be permitted to speak of my friend and colleague in a character in which all will join in paying him sincere respect. As a presiding officer of this body, he had the undivided respect of its members. He was punctual, methodical, and accurate, and had a high regard for the dignity of the Senate, which, as a presiding officer, he endeavored to preserve and maintain. He looked upon debate as an honorable contest of intellect for truth. Such a strife has its incidents and its trials; but Mr. Calhoun had, in an eminent degree, a regard for parliamentary dignity and propriety.

"Upon General Hayne's leaving the Senate to become Governor of South Carolina, Mr. Calhoun resigned the Vice-Presidency, and was elected in his place. All will now agree that such a position was environed with difficulties and dangers. His own State was under the ban, and he was in the national Senate to do her justice under his constitutional obligations. That part of his life posterity will review, and will do justice to it.

"After his senatorial term had expired, he went into retirement by his own consent. The death of Mr. Upshur—so full of melancholy association—made a vacancy in the State Department; and it was by the common consent of all parties, that Mr. Calhoun was called to fill it. This was a tribute of which any public man might well be proud. It was a tribute to truth, ability, and experience. Under Mr. Calhoun's counsels, Texas was brought into the Union. His name is associated with one of the most remarkable events of history—that of one Republic being annexed to another by the voluntary consent of both. Mr. Calhoun was but the agent to bring about this fraternal association. It is a conjunction under the sanction of his name, and by an influence exerted through his great and intrepid mind. Mr. Calhoun's connection with the Executive Department of the government terminated with Mr. Tyler's administration. As Secretary of State, he won the confidence and respect of foreign ambassadors, and his despatches were characterized by clearness, sagacity, and boldness.

"He was not allowed to remain in retirement long. For the last five years he has been a member of this body, and has been engaged in discussions that have deeply excited and agitated the country. He has died amidst them. I had never had any particular association with Mr. Calhoun, until I became his colleague in this body. I had looked on his fame as others had done, and had admired his character. There are those here who know more of him than I do. I shall not pronounce any such judgment as may be subject to a controversial criticism. But I will say, as a matter of justice, from my own personal knowledge, that I never knew a fairer man in argument or a juster man in purpose. His intensity allowed of little compromise. While he did not qualify his own positions to suit the temper of the times, he appreciated the unmasked propositions of others. As a senator, he commanded the respect of the ablest men of the body of which he was a member; and I believe I may say, that where there was no political bias to influence the judgment, he had the confidence of his brethren. As a statesman, Mr. Calhoun's reputation belongs to the history of the country, and I commit it to his countrymen and posterity.

"In my opinion, Mr. Calhoun deserves to occupy the first rank as a parliamentary speaker. He had always before him the dignity of purpose, and he spoke to an end. From a full mind he expressed his ideas with clearness, simplicity, and force and in language that seemed to be the vehicle of his thoughts and emotions. His thoughts leaped from his mind, like arrows from a well-drawn bow. They had both the aim and force of a skilful archer. He seemed to have had little regard for ornament; and when he used figures of speech, they were only for illustration. His manner and countenance were his best language; and in these there was an exemplification of what is meant by action, in that term of the great Athenian orator and statesman. They served to exhibit the moral elevation of the man.

"In speaking of Mr. Calhoun as a man and a neighbor, I hope I may speak of him in a sphere in which all will like to contemplate him. Whilst he was a gentleman of striking deportment, he was a man of primitive tastes and simple manners. He had the hardy virtues and simple tastes of a republican citizen. No one disliked ostentation and exhibition more than he did. When I say he was a *good neighbor*, I imply more than I have expressed. It is summed up under the word *justice*. I will venture to say, that no one in his private relations could ever say that Mr. Calhoun treated him with injustice, or that he deceived him by professions. His private character was characterized by a beautiful propriety, and was the exemplification of truth, justice, temperance, and fidelity to his engagements."

CHAPTER CXCII.

MR. CLAY'S PLAN OF SLAVERY COMPROMISE: MR. BENTON'S SPEECH AGAINST IT: EXTRACTS.

MR. BENTON. It is a bill of thirty-nine sections—forty, save one—an ominous number; and which, with the two little bills which attend it, is called a compromise, and is pressed upon us as a remedy for the national calamities. Now, all this labor of the committee, and all this remedy, proceed upon the assumption that the people of the United States are in a miserable, distracted condition; that it is their mission to relieve this national distress, and that these bills are the sovereign remedy for that purpose. Now, in my opinion, all this is a mistake, both as to the condition of the country, the mission of the committee, and the efficacy of their remedy. I do not believe in this misery and distraction, and distress, and strife, of the people. On the contrary, I believe them to be very quiet at home, attending to their crops, such of them as do not mean to feed out of the public crib; and that they would be perfectly happy if the politicians would only permit them to think so. I know of no distress in the country, no misery, no strife, no distraction, none of those five gaping wounds of which the senator from Kentucky made enumeration on the five fingers of his left hand, and for the healing of which, all together, and all at once, and not one at a time, like the little Doctor Taylor, he has provided this capacious plaster in the shape of five old bills tacked together. I believe the senator and myself are alike, in this, that each of us has but five fingers on the left hand; and that may account for the limitation of the wounds. When the fingers gave out, they gave out; and if there had been five more fingers, there might have been more wounds—as many as fingers—and, toes also. I know nothing of all these "gaping wounds," nor of any distress in the country since we got rid of the Bank of the United States, and since we got possession of the gold currency. Since that time I have heard of no pecuniary or business distress, no rotten currency, no expansions and contractions, no deranged exchanges, no decline of public stocks, no laborers begging employment, no produce rotting upon the hands of the farmer, no property sacrificed at forced sales, no loss of confidence, no three per centum a month interest, no call for a bankrupt act. Never were the people—the business-doing and the working people—as well off as they are to-day. As for political distress, "*it is all in my eye.*" It is all among the politicians. Never were the political blessings of the country greater than at present: civil and religious liberty eminently enjoyed; life, liberty, and property protected; the North and the South returning to the old belief that they were made for each other; and peace and plenty reigning throughout the land. This is the condition of the country—happy in the extreme; and I listen with amazement to the recitals which I have heard on this floor of strife and contention, gaping wounds and streaming blood, distress and misery. I feel mystified. The senator from Kentucky (Mr. Clay), chairman of the committee, and reporter of the bill, and its pathetic advocate, formerly delivered us many such recitals, about the times that the tariff was to be increased, the national bank charter to be renewed, the deposits to be restored, or a bankrupt act to be passed. He has been absent for some years; and, on returning among us, seems to begin where he left off. He treats us to the old dish of distress! Sir, it is a mistake. There is none of it; and if there was, the remedy would be in the hands of the people—in the hearts of the people—who love their country, and mean to take care of it—and not in the contrivances of politicians, who mistake their own for their country's distresses. It is all a mistake. It looks to me like a joke. But when I recollect the imposing number of the committee, and how "distinguished" they all were, and how they voted themselves free from instructions, and allowed the Senate to talk, but not to vote, while they were out, and how long they were deliberating: when I recollect all these things, I am constrained to believe the committee are in earnest. And as for the senator himself, the chairman of the committee, the perfect gravity with which he brought forward his remedy—these bills and the report—the pathos with which he enforced them, and the hearty congratulations which he addressed to the Senate, to the United States, and all mankind on the appointment of his committee, preclude the idea of an intentional joke on his part. In view of all this, I find myself compelled to consider this proceeding as serious, and bound to treat it parliamentarily; which I now proceed to do. And, in the first place, let us see what it is the committee has done, and what it is that it has presented to us as the sovereign remedy for the national distempers, and which we are to swallow whole—in the lump—all or none—under the penalty of being treated by the organs as enemies to the country.

Here are a parcel of old bills, which have been lying upon our tables for some months, and which might have been passed, each by itself, in some good form, long ago; and which have been carried out by the committee, and brought back again, bundled into one, and altered just enough to make each one worse; and then called a compromise—where there is nothing to compromise—and supported by a report which cannot support itself. Here are the California State admission bill, reported by the committee on territories three months ago—the two territorial government bills reported by the same committee at the same time—the Texas compact bill, originated by me six years ago, and reproduced at the present session—the fugitive slave recovery bill, reported from the judiciary committee at the commencement of the session—and the slave trade suppression bill for this District of Columbia, which is nothing but a revival of an old Maryland law, in force before the District was created, and repealed by an old act of Congress. These are the batch—five bills taken from our files, altered just enough to spoil each, then tacked together, and christened a compromise, and pressed upon the Senate as a sovereign remedy for calamities which have no existence. This is the presentation of the case: and now for the case itself.

The committee has brought in five old bills, bundled into one, and requires us to pass them. Now, how did this committee get possession of these bills? I do not ask for the manual operation. I know that each senator had a copy on his table, and might carry his copy where he pleased; but these bills were in the possession of the Senate, on its calendar—for discussion, but not for decision, while the committee was out. Two sets of resolutions were referred to the committee—but not these bills. And I now ask for the law—the parliamentary law—which enables a committee to consider bills not referred to it? to alter bills not in their legal power or possession? to tack bills together which the Senate held separate on its calendar? to reverse the order of bills on the calendar? to put the hindmost before, and the foremost behind? to conjoin incongruities, and to conglomerate individualities? This is what I ask—for this is what the committee has done; and which, if a point of order was raised, might subject their bundle of bills to be ruled off the docket. Sir, there is a custom—a good-natured one—in some of our State legislatures, to convert the last day of the session into a sort of legislative saturnalia—a frolic—something like barring out the master—in which all officers are displaced, all authorities disregarded, all rules overturned, all license tolerated, and all business turned topsy-turvy. But then this is only done on the last day of the session, as a prelude to a general break-up. And the sport is harmless, for nothing is done; and it is relieved by adjournment, which immediately follows. Such license as this may be tolerated; for it is, at least, innocent sport—the mere play of those "children of a larger growth" which some poet, or philosopher, has supposed men to be. And it seems to me that our committee has imitated this play without its reason—taken the license of the saturnalia without its innocence—made grave work of their gay sport—produced a monster instead of a merry-andrew—and required us to worship what it is our duty to kill.

I proceed to the destruction of this monster. The California bill is made the scape-goat of all the sins of slavery in the United States—that California which is innocent of all these sins. It is made the scape-goat; and as this is the first instance of an American attempt to imitate that ancient Jewish mode of expiating national sins, I will read how it was done in Jerusalem, to show how exactly our committee have imitated that ancient expiatory custom. I read from an approved volume of Jewish antiquities:

> "The goat being tied in the north-east corner of the court of the temple, and his head bound with scarlet cloth to signify sin; the high-priest went to him, and laid his hands on his head, and confessed over it all the iniquities of the children of Israel, and all their transgressions in all their sins, putting them all on the head of the goat. After which, he was given to the person appointed to lead him away, who, in the early ages of the custom, led him into the desert, and turned him loose to die; but as the goat sometimes escaped from the desert, the expiation, in such cases, was not considered complete; and, to make sure of his death, the after-custom was to lead him to a high rock, about twelve miles from Jerusalem, and push him off of it backwards, to prevent his jumping, the scarlet cloth being first torn from his head, in token that the sins of the people were taken away."

This was the expiation of the scape-goat in ancient Jerusalem: an innocent and helpless animal, loaded with sins which were not his own, and made to die for offences which he had never committed. So of California. She is innocent of all the evils of slavery in the United States, yet they are all to be packed upon her back, and herself sacrificed under the heavy load. First, Utah and New Mexico are piled upon her, each pregnant with all the transgressions of the Wilmot Proviso—a double load in itself—and enough, without further weight, to bear down California. Utah and New Mexico are first piled on; and the reason given for it by the committee is thus stated in their authentic report:

> "The committee recommend to the Senate the establishment of those territorial governments; and, in order more effectually to secure that desirable object, they also recommend that the bill for their establishment be incorporated in the bill for the admission of California, and that, united together, they both be passed."

This is the reason given in the report: and the first thing that strikes me, on reading it, is its entire incompatibility with the reasons previously given for the same act. In his speech in favor of raising the committee, the senator from Kentucky [Mr. Clay] was in favor of putting the territories upon California for her own good, for the good of California herself—as the speedy way to get her into the Union, and the safe way to do it, by preventing an opposition to her admission which might otherwise defeat it altogether. This was his reason then, and he thus delivered it to the Senate:

> "He would say now to those who desired the speedy admission of California, the shortest and most expeditious way of attaining the desired object was to include her admission in a bill giving governments to the territories. He made this statement because he was impelled to do so from what had come to his knowledge. If her admission as a separate measure be urged, an opposition is created which may result in the defeat of any bill for her admission."

These are the reasons which the senator then gave for urging the conjunction of the State and the territories— quickest and safest for California: her admission the supreme object, and the conjunction of the territories only a means of helping her along and saving her. And, unfounded as I deemed these reasons at the time, and now know them to be, they still had the merit of giving preference where it was due—to the superior object—to California herself, a State, without being a State of the Union, and suffering all the ills of that anomalous condition. California was then the superior object: the territories were incidental figures and subordinate considerations, to be made subservient to her salvation. Now all this is reversed. The territories take the superior place. They become the object: the State the incident. They take the first—she the second place! And to make sure of their welfare—make more certain of giving governments to them—*innuendo*, such governments as the committee prescribe—the conjunction is now proposed and enforced. This is a change of position, with a corresponding change of reasons. Doubtless the senator from Kentucky has a right to change his own position, and to change his reasons at the same time; but he has no right to ask other senators to change with him, or to require them to believe in two sets of reasons, each contradictory to the other. It is my fortune to believe in neither. I did not believe in the first set when they were delivered; and time has shown that I was right. Time has disposed of the argument of speed. That reason has expired under the lapse of time. Instead of more speedy, we all now know that California has been delayed three months, waiting for this conjunction: instead of defeat if she remained single, we all know now that she might have been passed singly before the committee was raised, if the senator from Kentucky had remained on his original ground, on my side; and every one knows that the only danger to California now comes from the companionship into which she has been forced. I do not believe in either set of reasons. I do not admit the territorial governments to be objects of superior interest to the admission of California. I admit them to be objects of interest, demanding our attention, and that at this session; but not at the expense of California, nor in precedence of her, nor in conjunction with her, nor as a condition for her admission. She has been delayed long, and is now endangered by this attempt to couple with her the territories, with which she has no connection, and to involve her in the Wilmot Proviso question, from which she is free. The senator from Kentucky has done me the favor to blame me for this delay. He may blame me again when he beholds the catastrophe of his attempted conjunctions; but all mankind will see that the delay is the result of his own abandonment of the position which he originally took with me. The other reason which the senator gave in his speech for the conjunction is not repeated in the report—the one which addressed itself to our nervous system, and menaced total defeat to California if urged in a bill by herself. He has not renewed that argument to our fears, so portentously exhibited three months ago; and it may be supposed that that danger has passed by, and that Congress is now free. But California is not bettered by it, but worsted. Then it was only necessary to her salvation that she should be joined to the territories; so said the speech. Now she is joined to Texas also; and must be damned if not strong enough to save Texas, and Utah, and New Mexico, and herself into the bargain!

United together, the report says, the bills will be passed together. That is very well for the report. It was natural for it to say so. But, suppose they are rejected together, and in consequence of being together: what is, then, the condition of California? First, she has been delayed three months, at great damage to herself, waiting the intrusive companionship of this incongruous company. Then she is sunk under its weight. Who, then, is to blame—the senator from Kentucky or the senator from Missouri? And if opposition to this indefinite postponement shall make still further delay to California, and involve her defeat in the end, who then is to be blamed again? I do not ask these questions of the senator from Kentucky. It might be unlawful to do so: for, by the law of the land, no man is bound to criminate himself.

Mr. CLAY (from his seat). I do not claim the benefit of the law.

Mr. BENTON. No; a high-spirited man will not claim it. But the law gives him the privilege; and, as a law-abiding and generous man, I give him the benefit of the law whether he claims it or not. But I think it is time for him to begin to consider the responsibility he has incurred in quitting his position at my side for California single, and first, to jumble her up in this crowd, where she is sure to meet death, come the vote when it will. I think it is time for him to begin to think about submitting to a mis-trial! withdraw a juror, and let a *venire facias de novo* be issued.

But I have another objection to this new argument. The territorial government bills are now the object; and to make more certain of these bills they are put into the California bill, to be carried safe through by it. This is the argument of the report; and it is a plain declaration that one measure is to be forced to carry the other. This is a breach of parliamentary law—that law upon the existence of which the senator from Kentucky took an issue with me, and failed to maintain his side of it. True, he made a show of maintaining it—ostentatiously borrowing a couple of my books from me, in open Senate, to prove his side of the case; and taking good care not to open them, because he knew they would prove my side of it. Then he quoted that bill for the "relief of John Thompson, and for other purposes," the reading of which had such an effect upon the risible susceptibilities of that part of our spectators which Shakspeare measures by the quantity, and qualifies as barren! Sir, if the senator from Kentucky had only read us Dr. Franklin's story of John Thompson and his hat-sign, it would have been something—a thing equally pertinent as argument, and still more amusing as anecdote. The senator, by doing that much, admitted his obligation to maintain his side of the issue: by doing no more, he confessed he could not. And now the illegality of this conjunction stands confessed, with the superaddition of an avowed condemnable motive for it. The motive is—so declared in the report—to force one measure to carry the other—the identical thing mentioned in all the books as the very reason why subjects of different natures should not be tacked together. I do not repeat what I have heretofore said on this point: it will be remembered by the Senate: and its validity is now admitted by the attempt, and the failure, to contest it. It is compulsory legislation, and a flagrant breach of parliamentary law, and of safe legislation. It is also a compliment of no equivocal character to a portion of the members of this Chamber. To put two measures together for the avowed purpose of forcing one to carry the other, is to propose to force the friends of the stronger measure to take the weak one, under the penalty of losing the stronger. It implies both that these members cannot be trusted to vote fairly upon one of the measures, or that an unfair vote is wanted from them; and that they are coercible, and ought to be coerced. This is the compliment which the compulsory process implies, and which is as good as declared in this case. It is a rough compliment, but such a one as "distinguished senators"—such as composed this committee—may have the prerogative to offer to the undistinguished ones: but then these undistinguished may have the privilege to refuse to receive it—may refuse to sanction the implication, by refusing to vote as required—may take the high ground that they are not coercible, that they owe allegiance, not to the committee, but to honor and duty; and that they can trust themselves for an honest vote, in a bill by itself, although the committee cannot trust them! But, stop! Is it *a* government or *the* government which the committee propose to secure by coercion? Is it *a* government, such as a majority of the Senate may agree upon? or is it *the* government, such as a majority of the committee have prescribed? If the former, why not leave the Senate to free voting in a separate bill? if the latter, will the Senate be coerced? will it allow a majority of the committee to govern the Senate?—seven to govern sixty? Sir! it is the latter—so avowed; and being the first instance of such an avowal, it should meet a reception which would make it the last.

Mr. President: all the evils of incongruous conjunctions are exemplified in this conjunction of the territorial government bills with the California State admission bill. They are subjects not only foreign to each other, but involving different questions, and resting upon principles of different natures. One involves the slavery and anti-slavery questions: the other is free from them. One involves constitutional questions: the other does not. One is a question of right, resting upon the constitution of the United States and the treaty with Mexico: the other is a question of expediency, resting in the discretion of Congress. One is the case of a State, asking for an equality of rights with the other States: the other is a question of territories, asking protection from States. One is a sovereignty—the other a property. So that, at all points, and under every aspect, the subjects differ; and it is well known that there are senators here who can unite in a vote for the admission of California, who cannot unite in any vote for the territorial governments; and that, because these governments involve the slavery questions, from all which the California bill is free. That is the rock on which men and parties split here. Some deny the power of Congress *in toto* over the subject of slavery in territories: such as these can support no bill which touches that question one way or the other. Others admit the power, but deny the expediency of its exercise. Others again claim both the power and the exercise. Others again are under legislative instructions— some to vote one way, some the other. Finally, there are some opposed to giving any governments at all to these territories, and in favor of leaving them to grow up of themselves into future States. Now, what are the senators, so circumstanced, to do with these bills conjoined? Vote for all—and call it a compromise! as if oaths, duty, constitutional obligation, and legislative instructions, were subjects of compromise. No! rejection of the whole is the only course; and to begin anew, each bill by itself, the only remedy.

The conjunction of these bills illustrates all the evils of joining incoherent subjects together. It presents a revolting enormity, of which all the evils go to an innocent party, which has done all in its power to avoid them. But, not to do the Committee of Thirteen injustice, I must tell that they have looked somewhat to the interest of California in this conjunction, and proposed a compensating advantage to her; of which kind consideration they are entitled to the credit in their own words. This, then, is what they propose for her:

> "As for California—far from feeling her sensibility affected by her being associated with other kindred measures—she ought to rejoice and be highly gratified that, in entering into the Union, she may have contributed to the tranquillity and happiness of the great family of States, of which it is to be hoped she may one day be a distinguished member."

This is the compensation proposed to California. She is to rejoice, and be highly gratified. She is to contribute to the tranquillity and happiness of the great family of States, and thereby become tranquil and happy herself. And she is one day, it is hoped, to become a distinguished member of this confederacy. This is to be her compensation—felicity and glory! Prospective felicity, and contingent glory. The felicity rural—rural felicity— from the geographical position of California—the most innocent and invigorating kind of felicity. The glory and distinction yet to be achieved. Whether California will consider these anticipations ample compensation for all the injuries of this conjunction—the long delay, and eventual danger, and all her sufferings at home in the mean time—will remain for herself to say. For my part, I would not give one hour's duration of actual existence in this Union for a whole eternity of such compensation; and such, I think, will be the opinion of California herself. Life, and present relief from actual ills, is what she wants. Existence and relief, is her cry! And for these she can find no compensation in the illusions of contributing to the tranquillity of States which are already tranquil, the happiness of people who are already happy, the settlement of questions in which she has no concern, and the formation of compromises which breed new quarrels in assuming to settle old ones.

With these fine reasons for tacking Utah and New Mexico to California, the committee proceed to pile a new load upon her back. Texas next appears in the committee's plan, crammed into the California bill, with all her questions of debt and boundary, dispute with New Mexico, division into future States, cession of territory to the United States, amount of compensation to be given her, thrust in along with her! A compact with one State put into a law for the life of another! And a veto upon the admission of California given to Texas! This is a monstrosity of which there is no example in the history of our legislation, and for the production of which it is fair to permit the committee to speak for themselves.

These are the reasons of the committee, and they present grave errors in law, both constitutional and municipal, and of geography and history. They assume a controversy between New Mexico and Texas. No such thing. New Mexico belongs to the United States, and the controversy is with the United States. They assume there is no way to settle this controversy but by a compact with Texas. This is another great mistake. There are three ways to settle it: first, and best, by a compact; secondly, by a suit in the Supreme Court of the United States; thirdly, by giving a government to New Mexico according to her actual extent when the United States acquired her, and holding on to that until the question of title is decided, either amicably by compact, or legally by the Supreme Court. The fundamental error of the committee is in supposing that New Mexico is party to this controversy with Texas. No such thing. New Mexico is only the *John Doe* of the concern. That error corrected, and all the reasoning of the committee falls to the ground. For the judicial power of the United States extends to all controversies to which the United States are party; and the original jurisdiction of the Supreme Court extends to all cases to which a State is a party. This brings the case bang up at once within the jurisdiction of the Supreme Court, without waiting for the consent of Texas, or waiting for New Mexico to grow up into a State, so as to have a suit between two States; and so there is no danger of collision, as the committee suppose, and make an argument for their bill, in the danger there is to New Mexico from this apprehended collision. If any takes place it will be a collision with the United States, to whom the territory of New Mexico belongs; and she will know how to prevent this collision, first, by offering what is not only just, but generous to Texas; and next, in defending her territory from invasion, and her people from violence.

These are the reasons for thrusting Texas, with all her multifarious questions, into the California bill; and, reduced to their essence, they argue thus: Utah must go in, because she binds upon California; New Mexico must go in, because she binds upon Utah; and Texas must go in, because she binds upon New Mexico. And thus poor California is crammed and gorged until she is about in the condition that Jonah would have been in, if he had swallowed the whale, instead of the whale swallowing him. This opens a new chapter in legislative ratiocination. It substitutes contiguity of territory for congruity of matter, and makes geographical affinities the rule of legislative conjunctions. Upon that principle the committee might have gone on, cramming other bills into the California bill, all over the United States; for all our territory is binding in some one part upon another. Upon that principle, the District of Columbia slave trade suppression bill might have been interjected; for, though not actually binding upon Texas, yet it binds upon land that binds upon land that does bind upon her. So of the fugitive slave bill. For, let the fugacious slave run as far as he may, he must still be on land; and that being the case, the territorial contiguity may be established which justifies the legislative conjunction.

Mr. President, the moralist informs us that there are some subjects too light for reason—too grave for ridicule; and in such cases the mere moralist may laugh or cry, as he deems best. But not so with the legislator—his business is not laughing or crying. Whimpering, or simpering, is not his mission. Work is his vocation, and gravity his vein; and in that vein I proceed to consider this interjection of Texas, with all her multifarious questions, into the bowels of the California bill.

In the first place, this Texas bill is a compact, depending for its validity on the consent of Texas, and is put into the California bill as part of a compromise and general settlement of all the slavery questions; and, of course, the whole must stand together, or fall together. This gives Texas a veto upon the admission of California. This is unconstitutional, as well as unjust; for by the constitution, new States are to be admitted by Congress, and not by another State; and, therefore, Texas should not have a veto upon the admission of California. In the next place, Texas presents a great many serious questions of her own—some of them depending upon a compact already existing with the United States, many of them concerning the United States, one concerning New Mexico, but no one reaching to California. She has a question of boundary nominally with New Mexico, in reality with the United States, as the owner of New Mexico; and that might be a reason for joining her in a bill, so far as that boundary is concerned, with New Mexico; but it can be no reason for joining her to California. The western boundary of Texas is the point of collision with New Mexico; and this plan of the committee, instead of proposing a suitable boundary between them adapted to localities, or leaving to each its actual possessions, disturbing no interest, until the decision of title upon the universal principle of *uti possidetis*; instead of these obvious and natural remedies, the plan of the committee cuts deep into the actual possessions of the United States in New Mexico—rousing the question which the committee professes to avoid, the question of extending slavery, and so disturbing the whole United States.

And here I must insist on the error of the committee in constitutional and municipal law, before I point out their mistakes in geography and history. They treat New Mexico as having a controversy with Texas—as being in danger of a collision with her—and that a compact with Texas to settle the boundary between them is the only way to settle that controversy and prevent that collision. Now, all this is a mistake. The controversy is not with New Mexico, but with the United States, and the judicial power of the United States has jurisdiction of it. Again, possession is title until the right is tried; and the United States having the possession, may give a government at once according to the possession; and then wait the decision of title.

I avoid all argument about right—the eventual right of Texas to any part of what was New Mexico before the existence of Texas. I avoid that question. Amicable settlement of contested claim, and not adjudication of title, is now my object. I need no argument from any quarter to satisfy me that the Texas questions ought to be settled. I happened to know that before Texas was annexed, and brought in bills and made speeches for that purpose at that time. I brought in such bills six years ago, and again at the present session; and whenever presented single, either by myself or any other person, I shall be ready to give it a generous consideration; but, as part of the California bill, I wash my hands of it.

I am against disturbing actual possession, either that of New Mexico or of Texas; and, therefore, am in favor of leaving to each all its population, and an ample amount of compact and homogeneous territory. With this view, all my bills and plans for a divisional line between New Mexico and Texas—whether of 1844 or 1850—left to each all its settlements, all its actual possessions, all its uncontested claim; and divided the remainder by a line adapted to the geography and natural divisions of the country, as well as suitable to the political and social condition of the people themselves. This gave a longitudinal line between them; and the longitude of 100 degrees in my bill of 1844, and 102 degrees in my bill of 1850—and both upon the same principle of leaving possessions intact, Texas having extended her settlements in the mean time. The proposed line of the committee violates all these conditions. It cuts deep and arbitrarily into the actual possessions of New Mexico, such as she held them before Texas had existence; and so conforms to no principle of public policy, private right, territorial affinity, or local propriety. It begins on the Rio del Norte, twenty miles in a straight line above El Paso, and thence, diagonally and northeastwardly, to the point where the Red River crosses the longitude of 100°. Now this beginning, twenty miles above El Paso, is about three hundred miles in a straight line (near six hundred by the windings of the river) above the ancient line of New Mexico; and this diagonal line to the Red River cuts about four hundred miles in a straight line through the ancient New Mexican possessions, cutting off about seventy thousand square miles of territory from New Mexico, where there is no slavery, and giving it to Texas where there is. This constitutes a more serious case of *tacking* than even that of sticking incongruous bills together, and calls for a most considerate examination of all the circumstances it involves. I will examine these circumstances, first making a statement, and then sustaining it by proof.

El Paso, above which the Texas boundary is now proposed to be placed by the committee, is one of the most ancient of the New Mexican towns, and to which the Spaniards of New Mexico retreated in the great Indian revolt in 1680, and made their stand, and thence recovered the whole province. It was the residence of the lieutenant-governor of New Mexico, and the most southern town of the province, as Taos was the most northern. Being on the right bank of the river, the dividing line between the United States and the Republic of Mexico leaves it out of our limits, and consequently out of the present limits of New Mexico; but New Mexico still extends to the Rio del Norte at the Paso; and therefore this beginning line proposed by the committee cuts into the ancient possession of New Mexico—a possession dating from the year 1595. That line in its course to the Red River, cuts the river and valley of the Puerco (called Pecos in the upper part) into two parts, leaving the lower and larger part to Texas; the said Rio Puerco and its valley, from head to mouth, having always been a part of New Mexico, and now in its actual possession. Putting together what is cut from the Puerco, and from the Del Norte above and below El Paso, and it would amount to about seventy thousand square miles, to be taken by the committee's line from its present and ancient possessor, and transferred to a new claimant.

This is what the new line would do, and in doing it would raise the question of the extension of slavery, and of its existence at this time, by law, in New Mexico as a part of Texas.

To avoid all misconception, I repeat what I have already declared, that I am not occupying myself with the question of title as it may exist and be eventually determined between New Mexico and Texas; nor am I questioning the power of Congress to establish any line it pleases in that quarter for the State of Texas, with the consent of the State, and any one it pleases for the territory of New Mexico without her consent. I am not occupying myself with the questions of title or power, but with the question of possession only—and how far the possession of New Mexico is to be disturbed, if disturbed at all, by the committee's line; and the effect of that disturbance in rousing the slavery question in that quarter. In that point of view the fact of possession is every thing: for the possessor has a right to what he holds until the question of title is decided—by law, in a question between individuals or communities in a land of law and order—or by negotiation or arms between independent Powers. I use the phrase, possession by New Mexico; but it is only for brevity, and to give locality to the term possession. New Mexico possesses no territory; she is a territory, and belongs to the United States; and the United States own her as she stood on the day of the treaty of peace and cession between the United States and the Republic of Mexico; and it is into that possession that I inquire, and all which I assert that the United States have a right to hold until the question of title is decided. And to save inquiry or doubt, and to show that the committee are totally mistaken in law in assuming the consent of Texas to be indispensable to the settlement of the title, I say there are three ways to settle it; the first and best by compact, as I proposed before Texas was annexed, and again by a bill of this year: next, by a suit in the Supreme Court, under that clause in the constitution which extends the judicial power of the United States to all controversies to which the United States is a party, and that other clause which gives the Supreme Court original jurisdiction of all cases to which a State is a party: the third way is for the United States to give a government to New Mexico according to the territory she possessed when she was ceded to the United States. These are the three ways to settle the question—one of them totally dependent on the will of Texas—one totally independent of her will— and one independent of her will until she chooses to go into court. As to any thing that Texas or New Mexico may do in taking or relinquishing possession, it is all moonshine. New Mexico is a territory of the United States. She is the property of the United States; and she cannot dispose of herself, or any part of herself; nor can Texas take her or any part of her. She is to stand as she did the day the United States acquired her; and to that point all my examinations are directed.

And in that point of view it is immaterial what are the boundaries of New Mexico. The whole of the territory obtained from Mexico, and not rightfully belonging to a State, belongs to the United States; and, as such, is the property of the United States, and to be attended to accordingly. But I proceed with the possession of New Mexico, and show that it has been actual and continuous from the conquest of the country by Don Juan de Onate, in 1595 to the present time. That ancient actual possession has already been shown at the starting point of the line—at El Paso del Norte. I will now show it to be the same throughout the continuation of the line across the Puerco and its valley, and at some points on the left bank of the Del Norte below El Paso. And first, of the Puerco River. It rises in the latitude of Santa Fé, and in its immediate neighborhood, only ten miles from it, and running south, falls into the Rio del Norte, about three hundred miles on a straight line below El Paso, and has a valley of its own between the mountain range on the west, which divides it from the valley of the Del Norte, to which it is parallel, and the high arid table land on the east called El Llano Estacado—the Staked Plain—which divides it from the head waters of the Red River, the Colorado, the Brasos, and other Texian streams. It is a long river, its head being in the latitude of Nashville—its mouth a degree and a half south of New Orleans. It washes the base of the high table land, and receives no affluents, and has no valley on that side; on the west it has a valley, and many bold affluents, coming down from the mountain range (the Sierra Obscura, the Sierra Blanca, and the Sierra de los Organos), which divides it from the valley of the upper Del Norte. It is valuable for its length, being a thousand miles, following its windings—from its course, which is north and south—from the quality of its water, derived from high mountains—from its valley, timbered and grassy, part prairie, good for cultivation, for pasturage, and salt. It has two climates, cold in the north from its altitude (seven thousand feet)—mild in the south from its great descent, not less than five thousand feet, and with a general amelioration of climate over the valley of the Del Norte from its openness on the east, and mountain shelter on the west. It is a river of New Mexico, and is so classified in geography. It is an old possession of New Mexico and the most valuable part of it, and has many of her towns and villages upon it. Las Vegas, Gallinas, Tecolote Abajo, Cuesta, Pecos, San Miguel, Anton Chico, Salinas, Gran Quivira, are all upon it. Some of these towns date their origin as far back as the first conquest of the Taos Indians, about the year 1600, and some have an historical interest, and a special relation to the question of title between New Mexico and Texas. Pecos is the old village of the Indians of that name, famous for the sacred fire so long kept burning there for the return of Montezuma. Gran Quivira was a considerable mining town under the Spaniards before the year 1680, when it was broken up in the great Indian revolt of that year.

San Miguel, twenty miles from Santa Fé, is the place where the Texian expedition, under Colonel Cooke, were taken prisoners in 1841.

To all these evidences of New Mexican possession of the Rio Puerco and its valley, is to be added the further evidence resulting from acts of ownership in grants of land made upon its upper part, as in New Mexico, by the superior Spanish authorities before the revolution, and by the Mexican local authorities since. The lower half was ungranted, and leaves much vacant land, and the best in the country, to the United States.

The great pastoral lands of New Mexico are in the valley of the Puerco, where millions of sheep were formerly pastured, now reduced to about two hundred thousand by the depredation of the Indians. The New Mexican inhabitants of the Del Norte send their flocks there to be herded by shepherds, on shares; and in this way, and by taking their salt there, and in addition to their towns and settlements, and grants of lands, the New Mexicans have had possession of the Puerco and its valley since the year 1600—that is to say, for about one hundred years before the shipwreck of La Salle, in the bay of San Bernardo, revealed the name of Texas to Europe and America.

These are the actual possessions of New Mexico on the Rio Puerco. On the Rio del Norte, as cut off by the committee's bill, there are, the little town of Frontera, ten miles above El Paso, a town begun opposite El Paso, San Eleazario, twenty miles below, and some houses lower down opposite El Presidio del Norte. Of all these, San Eleazario is the most considerable, having a population of some four thousand souls, once a town of New Biscay, now of New Mexico, and now the property of the United States by avulsion. It is an island; and the main river, formerly on the north and now on the south of the island, leaves it in New Mexico. When Pike went through it, it was the most northern town, and the frontier garrison of New Biscay; and there the then lieutenant-governor of New Mexico, who had escorted him from El Paso, turned him over to the authorities of a new province. It is now the most southern town of New Mexico, without having changed its place, but the river which disappeared from its channel in that place, in 1752, has now changed it to the south of the island.

I reiterate: I am not arguing title; I am only showing possession, which is a right to remain in possession until title is decided. The argument of title has often been introduced into this question; and a letter from President Polk, through Secretary Buchanan, has often been read on the Texian side. Now, what I have to say of that letter, so frequently referred to, and considered so conclusive, is this: that, however potent it may have been in inducing annexation, or how much soever it may be entitled to consideration in fixing the amount to be paid to Texas for her Mexican claim, yet as an evidence of title, I should pay no more regard to it than to a chapter from the life and adventures of Robinson Crusoe. Congress and the judiciary are the authorities to decide such claims to titles, and not Presidents and secretaries.

I rest upon the position, then, that the Rio Puerco, and its valley, is and was a New Mexican possession, as well as the left bank of the Del Norte, from above El Paso to below the mouth of the Puerco; and that this possession cannot be disturbed without raising the double question, first, of actual extension of slavery; and, secondly, of the present legal existence of slavery in all New Mexico east of the Rio Grande, as a part of Texas. These are the questions which the proposed line of the committee raise, and force us to face. They are not questions of my seeking, but I shall not avoid them. It is not a new question with me, this extension of slavery in that quarter. I met it in 1844, before the annexation of Texas. On the 10th day of June, of that year, and as part of a bill for a compact with Texas, and to settle all questions with her—the very ones which now perplex us—before she was annexed, I proposed, as article V. in the projected compact:

ART. V. "The existence of slavery to be for ever prohibited in that part of the annexed territory which lies west of the hundredth degree of longitude west from the meridian of Greenwich."

This is what I proposed six years ago, and as one in a series of propositions to be offered to Texas and Mexico for settling all questions growing out of the projected annexation beforehand. They were not adopted. Immediate annexation, without regard to consequences, was the cry; and all temperate counsels were set down to British traitors, abolitionists, and whigs. Well! we have to regard consequences now—several consequences: one of which is this large extension of slavery, which the report and conglomerate bills of the Committee of Thirteen force us to face. I did so six years ago, and heard no outbreak against my opinions then. But my opposition to the extension of slavery dates further back than 1844—forty years further back; and as this is a suitable time for a general declaration, and a sort of general conscience delivery, I will say that my opposition to it dates from 1804, when I was a student at law in the State of Tennessee, and studied the subject of African slavery in an American book—a Virginia book—Tucker's edition of Blackstone's Commentaries. And here it is (holding up a volume and reading from the title-page): "*Blackstone's Commentaries, with notes of reference to the Constitution and laws of the Federal Government of the United States, and of the Commonwealth of Virginia, in five volumes, with an appendix to each volume containing short tracts, as appeared necessary to form a connected view of the laws of Virginia as a member of the Federal Union. By St. George Tucker, Professor of Law in the University of William and Mary, and one of the Judges of the General Court in Virginia.*" In this American book—this Virginia edition of an English work—I found my principles on the subject of slavery. Among the short tracts in the appendices, is one of fifty pages in the appendix to the first volume, second part, which treats of the subject of African slavery in the United States, with a total condemnation of the institution, and a plan for its extinction in Virginia. In that work—in that school—that old Virginia school which I was taught to reverence—I found my principles on slavery: and adhere to them. I concur in the whole essay, except the remedy—gradual emancipation—and find in that remedy the danger which the wise men of Virginia then saw and dreaded, but resolved to encounter, because it was to become worse with time: the danger to both races from so large an emancipation. The men of that day were not enthusiasts or fanatics: they were statesmen and philosophers. They knew that the emancipation of the black slave was not a mere question between master and slave—not a question of property merely—but a question of white and black—between races; and what was to be the consequence to each race from a large emancipation.[10] And there the wisdom, not the philanthropy, of Virginia balked fifty years ago; there the wisdom of America balks now. And here I find the largest objection to the extension of slavery—to planting it in new regions where it does not now exist—bestowing it on those who have it not. The incurability of the evil is the greatest objection to the extension of slavery. It is wrong for the legislator to inflict an evil which can be cured: how much more to inflict one that is incurable, and against the will of the people who are to endure it for ever! I quarrel with no one for supposing slavery a blessing: I deem it an evil: and would neither adopt it nor impose it on others. Yet I am a slaveholder, and among the few members of Congress who hold slaves in this District. The French proverb tells us that nothing is new but what has been forgotten. So of this objection to a large emancipation. Every one sees now that it is a question of races, involving consequences which go to the destruction of one or the other: it was seen fifty years ago, and the wisdom of Virginia balked at it then. It seems to be above human wisdom. But there is a wisdom above human! and to that we must look. In the mean time, not extend the evil.

In refusing to extend slavery into these seventy thousand square miles, I act in conformity not only to my own long-established principles, but also in conformity to the long-established practice of Congress. Five times in four years did Congress refuse the prayer of Indiana for a temporary suspension of the anti-slavery clause of the ordinance of '87. On the 2d of March, 1803, Mr. Randolph, of Roanoke, as chairman of the committee to which the memorial praying the suspension was referred, made a report against it, which was concurred in by the House. This is the report:

> "That the rapid population of the State of Ohio, sufficiently evinces, in the opinion of your committee, that the labor of slaves is not necessary to promote the growth and settlement of colonies in that region. That this labor, demonstrably the dearest of any, can only be employed to advantage in the cultivation of products more valuable than any known to that quarter of the United States: that the committee deem it highly dangerous and inexpedient to impair a

provision wisely calculated to promote the happiness and prosperity of the north-western country, and to give strength and security to that extensive frontier. In the salutary operation of this sagacious and benevolent restraint, it is believed that the inhabitants of Indiana will, at no very distant day, find ample remuneration for a temporary privation of labor and of emigration."

This report of Mr. Randolph was in 1803: the next year, March, 1804, a different report, on the same prayer, was made by a committee of which Mr. Rodney, of Delaware, was chairman. It recommended a suspension of the anti-slavery clause for ten years: it was not concurred in by the House. Two years afterwards, February, 1806, a similar report, recommending suspension for ten years, was made by a committee of which Mr. Garnett, of Virginia, was chairman: it met the same fate—non-concurrence. The next year, 1807, both Houses were tried. In February of that year, a committee of the House, of which Mr. Parke was chairman, reported in favor of the indefinite suspension of the clause: the report was not concurred in. And in November of that year, Mr. Franklin, of North Carolina, as chairman of a committee of the Senate, made a report against the suspension, which was concurred in by the Senate, and unanimously, as it would seem from the journal, there being no division called for. Thus, five times in four years, the respective Houses of Congress refused to admit even a temporary extension, or rather re-extension of slavery into Indiana territory, which had been before the ordinance of '87 a slave territory, holding many slaves at Vincennes. These five refusals to suspend the ordinance of '87, were so many confirmations of it. All the rest of the action of Congress on the subject, was to the same effect or stronger. The Missouri compromise line was a curtailment of slave territory; the Texas annexation resolutions were the same; the ordinance of '87 itself, so often confirmed by Congress, was a curtailment of slave territory—in fact, its actual abolition; for it is certain that slavery existed in fact in the French settlements of the Illinois at that time; and that the ordinance terminated it. I acted then in conformity to the long, uniformly established policy of Congress, as well as in conformity to my own principles, in refusing to vote the extension of slavery, which the committee's line would involve.

And here, it does seem to me that we, of the present day, mistake the point of the true objection to the extension of slavery. We look at it as it concerns the rights, or interests, of the inhabitants of the States! and not as it may concern the people to whom it is to be given! and to whom it is to be an irrevocable gift—to them, and posterity! Mr. Randolph's report, in the case of Indiana, took the true ground. It looked to the interests of the people to whom the slavery was to go, and refused them an evil, although they begged for it.

This is a consequence which the committee's bill involves, and from which there is no escape but in the total rejection of their plan, and the adoption of the line which I propose—the longitudinal line of 102—which, corresponding with ancient title and actual possession, avoids the question of slavery in either country: which, leaving the population of each untouched, disturbs no interest, and which, in splitting the high sterile table land of the Staked Plain, conforms to the natural division of the country, and leaves to each a natural frontier, and an ample extent of compact and homogeneous territory. To Texas is left all the territory drained by all the rivers which have their mouths within her limits, whether those mouths are in the Gulf of Mexico, the Mississippi, or the Rio Grande: to New Mexico is left the whole course of the Rio Puerco and all its valley: and which, added to the valley of the Del Norte, will make a State of the first class in point of territory, susceptible of large population and wealth, and in a compact form, capable of defence against Indians. The Staked Plain is the natural frontier of both countries. It is a dividing wall between systems of waters and systems of countries. It is a high, sterile plain, some sixty miles wide upon some five hundred long, running north and south, its western declivity abrupt, and washed by the Puerco at its base: its eastern broken into chasms—cañones— from which issue the myriad of little streams which, flowing towards the rising sun, form the great rivers— Red River, Brasos, Colorado, Nueces, which find their outlet in the Mississippi or in the Gulf of Mexico. It is a salient feature in North American geography—a table of land sixty miles wide, five hundred long, and some thousands of feet above the level of the sea—and sterile, level, without a shrub, a plant, or grass, and presenting to the traveller a horizon of its own like the ocean. Without a landmark to guide the steps of the traveller across it, the early hunters and herdsmen of New Mexico staked their course across it, and hence its name, *El Llano Estacado*—the Staked Plain. It is a natural frontier between New Mexico and Texas; and for such a line, quieting all questions between them, all with the United States, yielding near two hundred thousand square miles of territory to the United States and putting into her hands the means of populating and defending New Mexico by giving lands to settlers and defenders—I am ready to vote the fifteen millions which my bill fairly and openly proposes. For the line in this bill I would not give a copper. But it would be a great error to suppose I would give fifteen millions for the territory in dispute between New Mexico and Texas. That disputed territory is only a small part of what the Texian cession would be. It would embrace four degrees of latitude on the north of Texas, and a front of a thousand miles on the Arkansas, and would give to the United States territory indispensable to her—to the population and defence both of New Mexico and Utah, in front of both which this part of Texas lies.

The committee, in their report, and the senator from Kentucky [Mr. Clay], in his speech, are impressive in their representations in favor of giving governments to New Mexico and the remaining part of California. I join them in all they say in favor of the necessity of these governments, and the duty of Congress to give them. But this bill is not the way to give it. These governments are balked by being put into this bill. They not only impede California, but themselves. The conjunction is an injury to both. They mutually delay and endanger each other. And it is no argument in favor of the conjunction to say that the establishment of a government for New Mexico requires the previous settlement of her eastern boundary with Texas. That is no argument for tacking Texas, with all her multifarious questions, even to New Mexico, much less to California. It is indeed very desirable to settle that boundary, and to settle it at once, and for ever; but it is not an indispensability to the creation of a government for New Mexico. We have a right to a government according to her possession; and that we can give her, to continue till the question of title is decided. The *uti possidetis*—as you possess—is the principle to govern our legislation—the principle which gives the possessor a right to the possession until the question of title is decided. This principle is the same both in national and municipal law—both in the case of citizens or communities of the same government and between independent nations. The mode of decision only is different. Between independent nations it is done by negotiation or by arms: between citizens or communities of the same government, it is done by law. Independent nations may invade and fight each other for a boundary: citizens or communities of the same government cannot. And the party that shall attempt it commits a violation of law and order; and the government which permits such violation is derelict of its duty.

I have now examined, so far as I propose to do it on a motion for indefinite postponement, the three bills which the committee have tacked together—the California, Utah, New Mexico and Texas bills. There are two other bills which I have not mentioned, because they are not tacked, but only hung on; but which belong to the system, as it is called, and without some mention of which, injustice would be done to the committee in the presentation of their scheme. The fugitive slave recovery bill, and the District of Columbia slave trade suppression bill, are parts of the system of measures which the committee propose, and which, taken together, are to constitute a compromise, and to terminate for ever and most fraternally all the dissensions of the slavery agitation in the United States. They apply to two out of the five gaping wounds which the senator from Kentucky enumerated on the five fingers of his left hand, and for healing up all which at once he had provided one large plaster, big enough to cover all, and efficacious enough to cure all; while the President only proposed to cure one, and that with a little plaster, and it of no efficacy. I do not propose to examine these two attendant or sequacious bills, which dangle at the tail of the other three.

This is the end of the committee's labor—five old bills gathered up from our table, tacked together, and christened a compromise! Now compromise is a pretty phrase at all times, and is a good thing in itself, when there happens to be any parties to make it, any authority to enforce it, any penalties for breaking it, or any thing to be compromised. The compromises of the constitution are of that kind; and they stand. Compromises made in court, and entered of record, are of that kind; and they stand. Compromises made by individuals on claims to property are likewise of that character; and they stand. I respect all such compromises. But where there happens to be nothing to be compromised, no parties to make a compromise, no power to enforce it, no penalty for its breach, no obligation on any one—not even its makers—to observe it, and when no two human beings can agree about its meaning, then a compromise becomes ridiculous and pestiferous. I have no respect for it, and eschew it. It cannot stand, and will fall; and in its fall will raise up more ills than it was intended to cure. And of this character I deem this farrago of incongruous matter to be, which has been gathered up and stuck together, and offered to us "all or none," like "fifty-four forty." It has none of the requisites of a compromise, and the name cannot make it so.

In the first place, there are no parties to make a compromise. We are not in convention, but in Congress; and I do not admit a geographical division of parties in this chamber, although the Committee of Thirteen was formed upon that principle—six from the South, half a dozen from the North, and one from the borders of both—sitting on a ridge-pole, to keep the balance even. The senator from Kentucky chairman of this committee of a baker's dozen and the illustrious progenitor of that committee, sits on that ridge-pole. It is a most critical position, and requires a most nice adjustment of balance to preserve the equilibrium—to keep the weight from falling on one side or the other—something like that of the Roman emperor, in his apotheosis, who was required to fix himself exactly in the middle of the heavens when he went up among the gods, lest, by leaning on one side or the other, he might overset the universe:

"Press not too much on any part the sphere, Hard were the task thy weight divine to bear! O'er the mid orb more equal shalt thou rise, And with a juster balance fix the skies."—LUCAN.

I recognize no such parties—no two halves in this Union, separated by a ridge-pole, with a man, or a god, sitting upon it, to keep the balance even. I know no North, and I know no South; and I repulse and repudiate, as a thing to be for ever condemned, this first attempt to establish geographical parties in this chamber, by creating a committee formed upon that principle. In the next place, there is no sanction for any such compromise—no authority to enforce it—none to punish its violation. In the third place, there is nothing to be compromised. A compromise is a concession, a mutual concession of contested claims between two parties. I know of nothing to be conceded on the part of the slaveholding States in regard to their slave property. Their rights are independent of the federal government, and admitted in the constitution—a right to hold their slaves *as property*, a right to pursue and recover them *as property*, a right to it as a *political element* in the weight of these States, by making five count three in the national representation. These are our rights by an instrument which we are bound to respect, and I will concede none of them, nor purchase any of them. I never purchase as a concession what I hold as a right, nor accept an inferior title when I already hold the highest. Even if this congeries of bills was a compromise, in fact, I should be opposed to it for the reasons stated. But the fact itself is to me apocryphal. What is it but the case of five old bills introduced by different members as common legislative measures—caught up by the senator from Kentucky, and his committee, bundled together, and then called a compromise! Now, this mystifies me. The same bills were ordinary legislation in the hands of their authors; they become a sacred compromise in the hands of their new possessors. They seemed to be of no account as laws: they become a national panacea as a compromise. The difference seems to be in the change of name. The poet tells us that a rose will smell as sweet by any other name. That may be true of roses, but not of compromises. In the case of the compromise, the whole smell is in the name; and here is the proof. The senator from Illinois (Mr. Douglass) brought in three of these bills: they emitted no smell. The senator from Virginia (Mr. Mason) brought in another of them—no smell in that. The senator from Missouri, who now speaks to the Senate, brought in the fifth—*ditto*, no smell about it. The olfactory nerve of the nation never scented their existence. But no sooner are they jumbled together, and called a compromise, than the nation is filled with their perfume. People smell it all over the land, and, like the inhalers of certain drugs, become frantic for the thing. This mystifies me; and the nearest that I can come to a solution of the mystery is in the case of the two Dr. Townsends and their sarsaparilla root. They both extract from the same root, but the extract is a totally different article in the hands of the two doctors. Produced by one it is the universal panacea: by the other, it is of no account, and little less than poison. Here is what the old doctor says of this strange difference:

"We wish it understood, because it is the *absolute truth*, that S. P. Townsend's article and Old Dr. Jacob Townsend's sarsaparilla are *heaven-wide apart, and infinitely dissimilar*, that they are unlike in every particular, having not one single thing in common."

And accounts for the difference thus:

"The sarsaparilla root, it is well known to medical men, contains many medicinal properties, and some properties which are inert or useless, and others which, if retained in preparing it for use, produce *fermentation and acid*, which is injurious to the system. Some of the properties of sarsaparilla are so *volatile* that they entirely evaporate, and are lost in the preparation, if they are not preserved by a *scientific process*, known only to the experienced in its manufacture. Moreover, those *volatile principles*, which fly off in vapor, or as an exhalation, under heat, are the very *essential medical properties* of the root, which give to it all its value."

Now, all this is perfectly intelligible to me. I understand it exactly. It shows me precisely how the same root is either to be a poison or a medicine, as it happens to be in the hands of the old or the young doctor. This may be the case with these bills. To me it looks like a clue to the mystery; but I decide nothing, and wait patiently for the solution which the senator from Kentucky may give when he comes to answer this part of my speech. The old doctor winds up in requiring particular attention to his name labelled on the bottle, to wit, "Old Doctor Jacob Townsend," and not Young Doctor Samuel Townsend. This shows that there is virtue in a name when applied to the extract of sarsaparilla root; and there may be equal virtue in it when applied to a compromise bill. If so, it may show how these self-same bills are of no force or virtue in the hands of the young senator from Illinois (Mr. Douglass), and become omnipotently efficacious in the hands of the old senator from Kentucky.

This is the end of the grand committee's work—five old bills tacked together, and presented as a remedy for evils which have no existence, and required to be accepted under a penalty—the penalty of being gazetted as enemies of compromise, and played at by the organs! The old one, to be sure, is dreadfully out of tune—the strings all broken, and the screws all loose, and discoursing most woful music, and still requiring us to dance to it! And such dancing it would be!—nothing but turn round, cross over, set-to, and back out! Sir, there was once a musician—we have all read of him—who had power with his lyre (but his instrument was spelt *l y r e*)—not only over men, but over wild beasts also, and even over stones, which he could make dance into their places when the walls of Ilion were built. But our old organist was none of that sort, even in his best day; and since the injury to his instrument in playing the grand national symphony of the four F's—the fifty-four forty or fight—it is so out of tune that its music will be much more apt to scare off tame men than to charm wild beasts or stones.

No, sir! no more slavery compromises. Stick to those we have in the constitution, and they will be stuck to! Look at the four votes—those four on the propositions which I submitted. No abolition of slavery in the States: none in the forts, arsenals, navy-yards, and dock-yards: none in the District of Columbia: no interference with the slave trade between the States. These are the votes given on this floor, and which are above all Congress compromises, because they abide the compromises of the constitution.

The committee, besides the ordinary purpose of legislation, that of making laws for the government of the people, propose another object of a different kind, that of acting the part of national benefactors, and giving peace and happiness to a miserable and distracted people—*innuendo*, the people of the United States. They propose this object as the grand result and crowning mercy of their multifarious labors. The gravity with which the chairman of the committee has brought forward this object in his report, and the pathetic manner in which he has enforced it in his speech, and the exact enumeration he has made of the public calamities upon his fingers' ends, preclude the idea, as I have heretofore intimated, of any intentional joke to be practised upon us by that distinguished senator; otherwise I might have been tempted to believe that the eminent senator, unbending from his serious occupations, had condescended to amuse himself at our expense. Certain it is that the conception of this restoration of peace and happiness is most jocose. In the first place, there is no contention to be reconciled, no distraction to be composed, no misery to be assuaged, no lost harmony to be restored, no lost happiness to be recovered! And, if there was, the committee is not the party to give us these blessings. Their example and precept do not agree. They preach concord, and practise discord. They recommend harmony to others, and disagree among themselves. They propose the fraternal kiss to us, and give themselves rude rebuffs. They set us a sad example. Scarcely is the healing report read, and the anodyne bills, or pills, laid on our tables, than fierce contention breaks out in the ranks of the committee itself. They attack each other. They give and take fierce licks. The great peacemaker himself fares badly—stuck all over with arrows, like the man on the first leaf of the almanac. Here, in our presence, in the very act of consummating the marriage of California with Utah, New Mexico, Texas, the fugacious slaves of the States, and the marketable slaves of this District—in this very act of consummation, as in a certain wedding feast of old, the feast becomes a fight—the festival a combat—and the amiable guests pummel each other.

When his committee was formed, and himself safely installed at the head of it, conqueror and pacificator, the senator from Kentucky appeared to be the happiest of mankind. We all remember that night. He seemed to ache with pleasure. It was too great for continence. It burst forth. In the fulness of his joy, and the overflowing of his heart, he entered upon that series of congratulations which we all remember so well, and which seemed to me to be rather premature, and in disregard of the sage maxim which admonishes the traveller never to halloo till he is out of the woods. I thought so then. I was forcibly reminded of it on Saturday last, when I saw that senator, after vain efforts to compose his friends, and even reminding them of what they were "threatened" with this day—*innuendo*, this poor speech of mine—gather up his beaver and quit the chamber, in a way that seemed to say, the Lord have mercy upon you all, for I am done with you! But the senator was happy that night—supremely so. All his plans had succeeded—Committee of Thirteen appointed—he himself its chairman—all power put into their hands—their own hands untied, and the hands of the Senate tied—and the parties just ready to be bound together for ever. It was an ecstatic moment for the senator, something like that of the heroic Pirithous when he surveyed the preparations for the nuptial feast—saw the company all present, the lapithæ on couches, the centaurs on their haunches—heard the *Io hymen* beginning to resound, and saw the beauteous Hippodamia, about as beauteous I suppose as California, come "glittering like a star," and take her stand on his left hand. It was a happy moment for Pirithous! and in the fulness of his feelings he might have given vent to his joy in congratulations to all the company present, to all the lapithæ and to all the centaurs, to all mankind, and to all horsekind, on the auspicious event. But, oh! the deceitfulness of human felicity. In an instant the scene was changed! the feast a fight—the wedding festival a mortal combat—the table itself supplying the implements of war!

"At first a medley flight, Of bowls and jars supply the fight; Once implements of feasts, but now of fate."

You know how it ended. The fight broke up the feast. The wedding was postponed. And so may it be with this attempted conjunction of California with the many ill-suited spouses which the Committee of Thirteen have provided for her.

Mr. President, it is time to be done with this comedy of errors. California is suffering for want of admission. New Mexico is suffering for want of protection. The public business is suffering for want of attention. The character of Congress is suffering for want of progress in business. It is time to put an end to so many evils; and I have made the motion intended to terminate them, by moving the indefinite postponement of this unmanageable mass of incongruous bills, each an impediment to the other, that they may be taken up one by one, in their proper order, to receive the decision which their respective merits require.

CHAPTER CXCIII.

DEATH OF PRESIDENT TAYLOR.

He died in the second year of his presidency, suddenly, and unexpectedly, of violent fever, brought on by long exposure to the burning heat of a fourth of July sun—noted as the warmest of the season. He attended the ceremonies of the day, sitting out the speeches, and omitting no attention which he believed the decorum of his station required. It cost him his life. The ceremony took place on Friday: on the Tuesday following, he was dead—the violent attack commencing soon after his return to the presidential mansion. He was the first President elected upon a reputation purely military. He had been in the regular army from early youth. Far from having ever exercised civil office, he had never even voted at an election, and was a major-general in the service, at the time of his election. Palo Alto, Resaca de la Palma, Monterey, and Buena Vista, were his titles to popular favor—backed by irreproachable private character, undoubted patriotism, and established reputation for judgment and firmness. His brief career showed no deficiency of political wisdom for want of previous political training. He came into the administration at a time of great difficulty, and acted up to the emergency of his position. The slavery agitation was raging; the Southern manifesto had been issued: California, New Mexico, Utah, were without governments: a Southern Congress was in process of being called, the very name of which implied disunion: a Southern convention was actually called, and met, to consult upon disunion. He met the whole crisis firmly, determined to do what was right among all the States, and to maintain the Federal Union at all hazards. His first, and only annual message, marked out his course. The admission of California as a State was recommended by him, and would avoid all questions about slavery. Leaving Utah and New Mexico to ripen into State governments, and then decide the question for themselves, also avoided the question in those territories where slavery was then extinct under the laws of the country from which they came to the United States. Texas had an unsettled boundary on the side of New Mexico. President Taylor considered that question to be one between the United States and New Mexico, and not between New Mexico and Texas; and to be settled by the United States in some legal and amicable way—as, by compact, by mutual legislation, or judicial decision. Some ardent spirits in Texas proposed to take possession of one half of New Mexico, in virtue of a naked pretension to it, founded in their own laws and constitution. President Taylor would have resisted that pretension, and protected New Mexico in its ancient actual possession until the question of boundary should have been settled in a legal way. His death was a public calamity. No man could have been more devoted to the Union, or more opposed to the slavery agitation; and his position as a Southern man, and a slave-holder—his military reputation, and his election by a majority of the people and of the States—would have given him a power in the settlement of these questions which no President without these qualifications could have possessed. In the political division he classed with the whig party, but his administration, as far as it went, was applauded by the democracy, and promised to be so to the end of his official term. Dying at the head of the government, a national lamentation bewailed his departure from life and power, and embalmed his memory in the affections of his country.

ADMINISTRATION OF MILLARD FILLMORE.

CHAPTER CXCIV.

INAUGURATION AND CABINET OF MR. FILLMORE.

Wednesday, July the tenth, witnessed the inauguration of Mr. Fillmore, Vice-President of the United States, become President by the death of President Taylor. It took place in the Hall of the House of Representatives, in the presence of both Houses of Congress, in conformity to the wish of the new President, communicated in a message. The constitution requires nothing of the President elect, before entering on the duties of his station, except to take the oath of office, *faithfully to execute his duties, and do his best to preserve, protect, and defend the constitution*; and that oath might be taken any where, and before any magistrate having power to administer oaths, and then filed in the department of State; but propriety and custom have made it a ceremony to be publicly performed, and impressively conducted. A place on the great eastern portico of the Capitol, where tens of thousands could witness it, and the Chief Justice of the Supreme Court of the United States to administer the oath, have always been the place and the magistrate for this ceremony, in the case of Presidents elected to the office—giving the utmost display to it—and very suitably as in such cases there is always a feeling of general gratification and exultation. Mr. Fillmore, with great propriety, reduced the ceremony of his inauguration to an official act, impressively done in Congress, and to be marked by solemnity without joy. A committee of the two Houses attended him—Messrs. Soulé, of Louisiana, Davis, of Massachusetts, and Underwood, of Kentucky, on the part of the Senate; Messrs. Winthrop, of Massachusetts, Morse, of Louisiana, and Morehead, of Kentucky, on the part of the House; and he was accompanied by all the members of the late President's cabinet. The Chief Justice of the Circuit Court of the District of Columbia, the venerable William Cranch, appointed fifty years before, by President John Adams, administered the oath; which being done, the President, without any inaugural address, bowed, and retired; and the ceremony was at an end.

The first official act of the new President was an immediate message to the two Houses, recommending suitable measures to be taken by them for the funeral of the deceased President—saying:

> "A great man has fallen among us, and a whole country is called to an occasion of unexpected, deep, and general mourning.

> "I recommend to the two Houses of Congress to adopt such measures as in their discretion they may deem proper, to perform with due solemnities the funeral obsequies of ZACHARY TAYLOR, late President of the United States; and thereby to signify the great and affectionate regard of the American people for the memory of one whose life has been devoted to the public service; whose career in arms has not been surpassed in usefulness or brilliancy; who has been so recently raised by the unsolicited voice of the people to the highest civil authority in the government—which he administered with so much honor and advantage to his country; and by whose sudden death, so many hopes of future usefulness have been blighted for ever.

> "To you, senators and representatives of a nation in tears, I can say nothing which can alleviate the sorrow with which you are oppressed. I appeal to you to aid me, under the trying circumstances which surround me, in the discharge of the duties, from which, however much I may be oppressed by them, I dare not shrink; and I rely upon Him, who holds in his hands the destinies of nations, to endow me with the requisite strength for the task, and to avert from our country the evils apprehended from the heavy calamity which has befallen us.

> "I shall most readily concur in whatever measures the wisdom of the two Houses may suggest, as befitting this deeply melancholy occasion."

The two Houses readily complied with this recommendation, and a solemn public funeral was unanimously voted, and in due time, impressively performed. All the members of the late President's cabinet gave in their resignations immediately, but were requested by President Fillmore to retain their places until successors could be appointed; which they did. In due time, the new cabinet was constituted: Daniel Webster, of Massachusetts,

Secretary of State; Thomas Corwin, of Ohio, Secretary of the Treasury; Alexander H. H. Stuart, of Virginia, Secretary of the Interior; Charles M. Conrad, of Louisiana, Secretary at War; William A. Graham, of North Carolina, Secretary of the Navy (succeeded by John P. Kennedy, of Maryland); John J. Crittenden, of Kentucky, Attorney-General; Nathan K. Hall, of New York (succeeded by Samuel D. Hubbard, of Connecticut).

CHAPTER CXCV.

REJECTION OF MR. CLAY'S PLAN OF COMPROMISE.

The Committee of Thirteen had reported in favor of Mr. Clay's plan. It was a committee so numerous, almost a quarter of the Senate, that its recommendation would seem to insure the senatorial concurrence. Not so the fact. The incongruities were too obvious and glaring to admit of conjunction. The subjects were too different to admit of one vote—yea or nay—upon all of them together. The injustice of mixing up the admission of California, a State which had rejected slavery for itself, with all the vexations of the slave question in the territories, was too apparent to subject her to the degradation of such an association. It was evident that no compromise, of any kind whatever, on the subject of slavery, under any one of its aspects separately, much less under all put together, could possibly be made. There was no spirit of concession—no spirit in which there could be giving and taking—in which a compromise could be made. Whatever was to be done, it was evident would be done in the ordinary spirit of legislation, in which the majority gives law to the minority. The only case in which there was even forbearance, was in that of rejecting the Wilmot proviso. That measure was rejected again as heretofore, and by the votes of those who were opposed to extending slavery into the territories, because it was unnecessary and inoperative—irritating to the slave States without benefit to the free States—a mere work of supererogation, of which the only fruit was to be discontent. It was rejected, not on the principle of non-intervention—not on the principle of leaving to the territories to do as they pleased on the question; but because there had been intervention! because Mexican law and constitution had intervened! had abolished slavery by law in those dominions! which law would remain in force, until repealed by Congress. All that the opponents to the extension of slavery had to do then, was to do nothing. And they did nothing.

The numerous measures put together in Mr. Clay's bill were disconnected and separated. Each measure received a separate and independent consideration, and with a result which showed the injustice of the attempted conjunction. United, they had received the support of the majority of the committee: separated, and no two were passed by the same vote: and only four members of the whole grand committee that voted alike on each of the measures.

CHAPTER CXCVI.

THE ADMISSION OF THE STATE OF CALIFORNIA: PROTEST OF SOUTHERN SENATORS: REMARKS UPON IT BY MR. BENTON.

This became the "*test*" question in the great slavery agitation which disturbed Congress and the Union, and as such was impressively presented by Mr. Calhoun in the last and most intensely considered speech of his life— read for him in the Senate by Mr. Mason of Virginia. In that speech, and at the conclusion of it, and as the resulting consequence of the whole of it, he said:

"It is time, senators, that there should be an open and manly avowal on all sides, as to what is intended to be done. If the question is not now settled, it is uncertain whether it ever can hereafter be; and we, as the representatives of the States of this Union, regarded as governments, should come to a distinct understanding as to our respective views, in order to ascertain whether the great questions at issue can be settled or not. If you, who represent the stronger portion, cannot agree to settle them on the broad principle of justice and duty, say so; and let the States we both represent agree to separate and part in peace. If you are unwilling that we should part in peace, tell us so, and we shall know what to do, when you reduce the question to submission or resistance. If you remain silent, you will compel us to infer by your acts what you intend. In that case, California will become the *test* question. If you admit her, under all the difficulties that oppose her admission, you compel us to infer that you intend to exclude us from the whole of the acquired territories, with the intention of destroying irretrievably the equilibrium between the two sections. We would be blind not to perceive, in that case, that your real objects are power and aggrandizement, and infatuated not to act accordingly."

Mr. Calhoun died before the bill for the admission of California was taken up: but his principles did not die with him: and the test question which he had proclaimed remained a legacy to his friends. As such they took it up, and cherished it. The bill was taken up in the Senate, and many motions made to amend, of which the most material was by Mr. Turney of Tennessee, to limit the southern boundary of the State to the latitude of 36° 30', and to extend the Missouri line through to the Pacific, so as to authorize the existence of slavery in all the territory south of that latitude. On this motion the yeas and nays were:

"YEAS—Messrs. Atchison, Badger, Barnwell, Bell, Berrien, Butler, Clemens, Davis of Mississippi, Dawson, Downs, Foote, Houston, Hunter, King, Mangum, Mason, Morton, Pearce, Pratt, Rusk, Sebastian, Soulé, Turney, and Yulee—24.

"NAYS—Messrs. Baldwin, Benton, Bradbury, Bright, Cass, Clarke, Cooper, Davis of Massachusetts, Dayton, Dickinson, Dodge of Wisconsin, Dodge of Iowa, Douglass, Ewing, Felch, Greene, Hale, Hamlin, Jones, Norris, Phelps, Seward, Shields, Smith, Spruance, Sturgeon, Underwood, Upham, Wales, Walker, Whitcomb, and Winthrop—32."

The amendments having all been disposed of, the question was taken upon the passage of the bill, and resulted in its favor, 34 yeas to 18 nays. The vote was:

"YEAS—Messrs. Baldwin, Bell, Benton, Bradbury, Bright, Cass, Chase, Cooper, Davis of Massachusetts, Dickinson, Dodge of Wisconsin, Dodge of Iowa, Douglass, Ewing, Felch, Greene, Hale, Hamlin, Houston, Jones, Miller, Norris, Phelps, Seward, Shields, Smith, Spruance, Sturgeon, Underwood, Upham, Wales, Walker, Whitcomb, and Winthrop—34.

"NAYS—Messrs. Atchison, Barnwell, Berrien, Butler, Clemens, Davis of Mississippi, Dawson, Foote, Hunter, King, Mason, Morton, Pratt, Rusk, Sebastian, Soulé, Turney, and Yulee—18."

Immediately upon the passage of the bill through the Senate, ten of the senators opposed to it offered a protest against it, which was read at the secretary's table, of which the leading points were these:

"We, the undersigned senators, deeply impressed with the importance of the occasion, and with a solemn sense of the responsibility under which we are acting, respectfully submit the following protest against the bill admitting California as a State into this Union, and request that it may be entered upon the Journal of the Senate. We feel that it is not enough to have resisted in debate alone a bill so fraught with mischief to the Union and the States which we represent, with all the resources of argument which we possessed; but that it is also due to ourselves, the people whose interest have been intrusted to our care, and to posterity, which even in its most distant generations may feel its consequences, to leave in whatever form may be most solemn and enduring, a memorial of the opposition which we have made to this measure, and of the reasons by which we have been governed, upon the pages of a journal which the constitution requires to be kept so long as the Senate may have an existence. We desire to place the reasons upon which we are willing to be judged by generations living and yet to come, for our opposition to a bill whose consequences may be so durable and portentous as to make it an object of deep interest to all who may come after us.

"We have dissented from this bill because it gives the sanction of law, and thus imparts validity to the unauthorized action of a portion of the inhabitants of California, by which an odious discrimination is made against the property of the fifteen slaveholding States of the Union, who are thus deprived of that position of equality which the constitution so manifestly designs, and which constitutes the only sure and stable foundation on which this Union can repose.

"Because the right of the slaveholding States to a common and equal enjoyment of the territory of the Union has been defeated by a system of measures which, without the authority of precedent, of law, or of the constitution, were manifestly contrived for that purpose, and which Congress must sanction and adopt, should this bill become a law.

"Because to vote for a bill passed under such circumstances would be to agree to a principle, which may exclude for ever hereafter, as it does now, the States which we represent from all enjoyment of the common territory of the Union; a principle which destroys the equal rights of their constituents, the equality of their States in the Confederacy, the equal dignity of those whom they represent as men and as citizens in the eye of the law, and their equal title to the protection of the government and the constitution.

"Because all the propositions have been rejected which have been made to obtain either a recognition of the rights of the slaveholding States to a common enjoyment of all the territory of the United States, or to a fair division of that territory between the slaveholding and non-slaveholding States of the Union—every effort having failed which has been made to obtain a fair division of the territory proposed to be brought in as the State of California.

"But, lastly, we dissent from this bill, and solemnly protest against its passage, because, in sanctioning measures so contrary to former precedent, to obvious policy, to the spirit and intent of the constitution of the United States, for the purpose of excluding the slaveholding States from the territory thus to be erected into a State, this government in effect declares, that the exclusion of slavery from the territory of the United States is an object so high and important as to justify a disregard not only of all the principles of sound policy, but also of the constitution itself. Against this conclusion we must now and for ever protest, as it is destructive of the safety and liberties of those whose rights have been committed to our care, fatal to the peace and *equality* of the States which we represent, and must lead, if persisted in, to the *dissolution* of that confederacy, in which the slaveholding States have never sought more than *equality*, and in which they will not be content to *remain* with less."

This protest was signed by Messrs. Mason and Hunter, senators from Virginia; Messrs. Butler and Barnwell, senators from South Carolina; Mr. Turney, senator from Tennessee; Mr. Pierre Soulé, senator from Louisiana; Mr. Jefferson Davis, senator from Mississippi; Mr. Atchison, senator from Missouri; and Messrs. Morton and

Yulee, senators from Florida. It is remarkable that this protest is not on account of any power exercised by Congress over the subject of slavery in a territory, but for the non-exercise of such power, and especially for not extending the Missouri compromise line to the Pacific Ocean; and which non-extension of that line was then cause for the dissolution of the Union.

Mr. Winthrop, newly appointed senator from Massachusetts, in place of Mr. Webster, appointed Secretary of State, immediately raised the question of reception upon this protest, for the purpose of preventing it from going upon the Journal, where, he alleged, the only protest that could be entered by a senator (and that was a sufficient one) was his peremptory "no:" and then said:

> "Sir, does my honorable friend from Virginia (Mr. Hunter), know that there is but one parliamentary body in the world—so far as my own knowledge, certainly, goes—which acknowledges an inherent right in its members to enter their protests upon the Journals? That body is the British House of Lords. It is the privilege of every peer, as I understand it, to enter upon the Journals his protest against any measure which may have been passed contrary to his own individual views or wishes. But what has been the practice in our own country? You, yourself, Mr. President, have read to us an authority upon this subject. It seems that in the earliest days of our history, when there may have been something more of a disposition than I hope prevails among us now, to copy the precedents of the British government, a rule was introduced into this body for the purpose of securing to the senators of the several States this privilege which belongs to the peers of the British Parliament. That proposition was negatived. I know not by what majority, for you did not read the record; I know not by whose votes; but that rule was rejected. It was thus declared in the early days of our history that this body should not be assimilated to the British House of Lords in this respect, however it may be in any other; and that individual senators should not be allowed this privilege which belongs to British peers, of spreading upon the Journals the reasons which may have influenced their votes."

Mr. Benton spoke against the reception of the protest, denying the right of senators to file any reasons upon the Journal for their vote; and said:

> "In the British House of Lords, Mr. President, this right prevails, but not in the House of Commons; and I will show you before I have done that the attempt to introduce it into the House of Commons gave rise to altercation, well-nigh led to bloodshed on the floor of the House, and caused the member who attempted to introduce it, though he asked leave to do so, to be committed to the Tower for his presumption. And I will show that we begin the practice here at a point at which the British Parliament had arrived, long after they commenced the business of entering the dissents. It will be my business to show that, notwithstanding the British House of Lords in the beginning entered the protestor's name under the word 'dissent,' precisely as our names are entered here under the word 'nay,' it went on until something very different took place, and which ended in authorizing any member who pleased to arraign the sense of the House, and to reproach the House whenever he pleased. Now, how came the lords to possess this right? It is because every lord is a power within himself. He is his own constituent body. He represents himself; and in virtue of that representation of himself, he can constitute a representative, and can give a proxy to any lord to vote for him on any measure not judicial. Members of the House of Commons cannot do it, because they are themselves nothing but proxies and representatives of the people. The House of Lords, then, who have this privilege and right of entering their dissent, have it by virtue of being themselves, each one, a power within himself, a constituent body to himself, having inherent rights which he derives from nobody, but which belong to him by virtue of being a peer of the realm; and by virtue of that he enters his protest on the Journal, if he pleases. It is a privilege belonging to every lord, each for himself, and is an absolute privilege; and although the form is to ask leave of the House, yet the House is bound to grant the leave."

Mr. Benton showed that there was no right of protest in the members of the British House of Commons—that the only time it was attempted there was during the strifes of Charles the First with the Parliament, and by Mr. Hyde (afterwards Lord Clarendon), who was committed prisoner to the Tower for presuming to insult the House, by proposing to set up his judgment against the act of the House after the House had acted. Having spoken against the right of the senators to enter a protest on the Journal against an act of the Senate, Mr. Benton proceeded to speak against the protest itself, and especially the concluding part of it, in which a dissolution of the Union was hypothetically predicated upon the admission of California.

"I now pass over what relates to the body or matter of the protest, and come to the concluding sentence, where, sir, I see a word which I am sorry to see, or hear used even in the heat of debate in this chamber. It is one which I believe I have not pronounced this session, not even hypothetically or historically, in speaking of every thing which has taken place. But I find it here, and I am sorry to see it. It is qualified, it is true; yet I am sorry to see it any where, and especially in a paper of such solemn import. It is in the concluding sentence:

'Against this conclusion we must now and for ever *protest*, as it is destructive of the safety and liberties of those whose rights have been committed to our care, fatal to the peace and *equality* of the States which we represent, and must lead, if persisted in, to the *dissolution* of that confederacy in which the slaveholding States have never sought more than an *equality*, and in which they will not be content to *remain* with less.'

"I grieve to see these words used with this deliberation; still more do I grieve to see an application made to enter them on the Journal of the Senate. Hypothetically they use the words; but we all know what this word "if" is—a great peacemaker, the poet tells us, between individuals, but, as we all know, a most convenient introduction to a positive conclusion. The language here is used solemnly, and the word protest is one of serious import. Protest is a word known to the law, and always implies authority, and one which is rarely used by individuals at all. It is a word of grave and authoritative import in the English language, which implies the testification of the truth! and a right to testify to it! and which is far above any other mode of asseveration. It comes from the Latin—*testari*, to be a witness—*protestari*, to be a public witness, to publish, avouch, and testify the truth; and can be only used on legal or on the most solemn occasions. It has given a name to a great division of the Christian family, who took the title from the fact of their '*protesting*' against the imperial edicts of Charles V., which put on a level with the Holy Scriptures the traditions of the church and the opinions of the commentators. It was a great act of *protesting*, and an act of conscience and duty. It was a proper occasion to use the word *protest*; and it was used in the face of power, and maintained through oceans and seas of blood, until it has found an immortality in the name of one division of the Christian family.

"I have read to you from British history—history of 1640—the most eventful in the British annals—to show the first attempt to introduce a protest in the House of Commons—to show you how the men of that day—men in whose bosoms the love of liberty rose higher than love of self—the Puritans whose sacrifices for liberty were only equalled by their sacrifices to their religion—these men, from whom we learned so much, refused to suffer themselves to be arraigned by a minority—refused to suffer an indictment to be placed on their own Journals against themselves. I have shown you that a body in which were such men as Hampden, and Cromwell, and Pym, and Sir Harry Vane, would not allow themselves to be arraigned by a minority, or to be impeached before the people, and that they sent the man to the Tower who even asked leave to do it. This period of British history is that of the civil wars which deluged Great Britain with blood; and, sir, may there be no analogy to it in our history!—may there be no omen in this proceeding—nothing ominous in this attempted imitation of one of the scenes which preceded the outbreak of civil war in Great Britain. Sir, this protest is treated by some senators as a harmless and innocent matter; but I cannot so consider it. It is a novelty, but a portentous one, and connects itself with other novelties, equally portentous. The Senate must bear with me for a moment. I have refrained hitherto from alluding to the painful subject, and would not now do it if it was not brought forward in such a manner as to compel me. This is a novelty, and it connects itself with other novelties of a most important character. We have seen lately what we have never before seen in the history of the country—sectional meetings of members of Congress, sectional declarations by legislative bodies, sectional meetings of conventions, sectional establishment of a press here! and now the introduction of this protest, also sectional, and not only connecting itself in time and circumstances, but connecting itself by its arguments, by its facts, and by its conclusions, with all these sectional movements to which I have referred. It is a sectional protest.

"All of these sectional movements are based upon the hypothesis, that, if a certain state of things is continued, there is to be a dissolution of the Union. The Wilmot proviso, to be sure, is now dropped, or is not referred to in the protest. That cause of dissolution is dead; but the California bill comes in its place, and the system of measures of which it is said to be a part. Of these, the admission of California is now made the prominent, the salient point in that whole system, which hypothetically it is assumed may lead to a dissolution of the Union. Sir, I cannot help looking upon this protest as belonging to the series of novelties to which I have referred. I cannot help considering it as part of a system—as a link in a chain of measures all looking to one result, hypothetically, to be sure, but all still looking to the same result—that of a dissolution of the Union. It is afflicting enough to witness such things out of doors; but to enter a solemn protest on our Journals, looking to the contingent dissolution of the Union, and that for our own acts—for the acts of a majority—to call upon us of the majority to receive our own indictment, and enter it, without answer, upon our own Journals—is certainly going beyond all the other signs of the times, and taking a most alarming step in the progress which seems to be making in leading to a dreadful catastrophe. '*Dissolution*' to be entered on our Journal! What would our ancestors have thought of it? The paper contains an enumeration of what it characterizes as unconstitutional, unjust, and oppressive conduct on the part of Congress against the South, which, if persisted in, must lead to a dissolution of the Union, and names the admission of California as one of the worst of these measures. I cannot consent to place that paper on our Journals. I protest against it—protest in the name of my constituents. I have made a stand against it. It took me by surprise; but my spirit rose and fought. I deem it my sacred duty to resist it—to resist the entrance upon our Journal of a paper hypothetically justifying disunion. If defeated, and the paper goes on the Journal, I still wish the present age and posterity to see that it was not without a struggle—not without a stand against the portentous measure—a stand which should mark one of those eras in the history of nations from which calamitous events flow."

The reception of the protest was refused, and the bill sent to the House of Representatives, and readily passed; and immediately receiving the approval of the President, the senators elect from California, who had been long waiting (Messrs. William M. Gwinn and John Charles Frémont), were admitted to their seats; but not without further and strenuous resistance. Their credentials being presented, Mr. Davis, of Mississippi, moved to refer them to the Committee on the Judiciary, to report on the law and the facts of the case; which motion led to a discussion, terminated by a call for the yeas and nays. The yeas were 12 in number; to wit: Messrs. Atchison, Barnwell, Berrien, Butler, Davis of Mississippi, Hunter, Mason, Morton, Pratt, Sebastian, Soulé, Turney. Only 12 voting for the reference, and 36 against it; the two senators elect were then sworn in, and took their seats.

CHAPTER CXCVII.

FUGITIVE SLAVES—ORDINANCE OF 1787: THE CONSTITUTION: ACT OF 1793: ACT OF 1850.

It is of record proof that the anti-slavery clause in the ordinance of 1787, could not be passed until the fugitive slave recovery clause was added to it. That anti-slavery clause, first prepared in the Congress of the confederation by Mr. Jefferson in 1784, and rejected, remained rejected for three years—until 1787; when receiving the additional clause for the recovery of fugitives, it was unanimously passed. This is clear proof that the first clause, prohibiting slavery in the Northwest territory, could not be obtained without the second, authorizing the recovery of slaves which should take refuge in that territory. It was a compromise between the slave States and the free States, unanimously agreed to by both parties, and founded on a valuable consideration—one preventing the spread of slavery over a vast extent of territory, the other retaining the right of property in the slaves which might flee to it. Simultaneously with the adoption of this article in the ordinance of 1787 was the formation of the constitution of the United States—both formed at the same time, in neighboring cities, and (it may be said) by the same men. The Congress sat in New York—the Federal Convention in Philadelphia—and, while the most active members of both were members of each, as Madison and Hamilton, yet, from constant interchange of opinion, the members of both bodies may be assumed to have worked together for a common object. The right to recover fugitive slaves went into the constitution, as it went into the ordinance, simultaneously and unanimously; and it may be assumed upon the facts of the case, and all the evidence of the day, that the constitution, no more than the ordinance, could have been formed without the fugitive slave recovery clause contained in it. A right to recover slaves is not only authorized by the constitution, but it is a right without which there would have been no constitution, and also no anti-slavery ordinance.

One of the early acts of Congress, as early as February, '93, was a statute to carry into effect the clause in the constitution for the reclamation of fugitives from justice, and fugitives from labor; and that statute, made by the men who made the constitution, may be assumed to be the meaning of the constitution, as interpreted by men who had a right to know its meaning. That act consisted of four sections, all brief and clear, and the first two of which exclusively applied to fugitives from justice. The third and fourth applied to fugitives from labor, embracing apprentices as well as slaves, and applying the same rights and remedies in each case: and of these two, the third alone contains the whole provision for reclaiming the fugitive—the fourth merely containing penalties for the obstruction of that right. The third section, then, is the only one essential to the object of this chapter, and is in these words:

> "That when a person held to labor in any of the United States, or in either of the territories on the north-west, or south of Ohio, under the laws thereof, shall escape into any other of said States or territories, the person to whom such labor is due, his agent or attorney, is hereby empowered to seize or arrest such fugitive from labor, and to take him or her before any judge of the circuit or district courts of the United States, residing or being within the State, or before any magistrate of a county, city, or town corporate, wherein such seizure or arrest shall be made, and upon proof to the satisfaction of such judge or magistrate, either by oral testimony, or affidavit taken before and certified by a magistrate of any such State or territory, that the person so seized and arrested, doth under the laws of the State or territory from which he or she fled, owe service to the person claiming him or her, it shall be the duty of such judge or magistrate to give a certificate thereof to such claimant, his agent or attorney, which shall be sufficient warrant for removing the said fugitive from labor, to the State or territory from which he or she fled."

This act was passed on the recommendation of President Washington, in consequence of a case having arisen between Pennsylvania and Virginia, which showed the want of an act of Congress to carry the clause in the constitution into effect. It may be held to be a fair interpretation of the constitution, and by it the party claiming the service of the fugitive in any State or territory, had the right to seize his slave wherever he saw him, and to carry him before a judicial authority in the State; and upon affidavit, or oral testimony, showing his right, he was to receive a certificate to that effect, by virtue of which he might carry him back to the State from which he had fled. This act, thus fully recognizing the right of the claimant to seize his slave by mere virtue of ownership, and then to carry him out of the State upon a certificate, and without a trial, was passed as good as unanimously by the second Congress which sat under the constitution—the proceedings of the Senate showing no division, and in the House only seven voting against the bill, there being no separate vote on the two parts of it, and two of these seven from slave States (Virginia and Maryland). It does not appear to what part these seven objected—whether to the fugitive slave sections, or those which applied to fugitives from justice. Such unanimity in its passage, by those who helped to make the constitution, was high evidence in its favor: the conduct of the States, and both judiciaries, State and federal, were to the same effect. The act was continually enforced, and the courts decided that this right of the owner to seize his slave, was just as large in the free State to which he had fled as in the slave State from which he had run away—that he might seize, by night as well as by day, of Sundays as well as other days; and, also, in a house, provided no breach of the peace was committed. The penal section in the bill was clear and heavy, and went upon the ground of the absolute right of the master to seize his slave by his own authority wherever he saw him, and the criminality of any obstruction or resistance in the exercise of that right. It was in these words:

> "That any person who shall knowingly and wilfully obstruct or hinder such claimant, his agent or attorney, in so seizing or arresting such fugitive from labor, or shall rescue such fugitive from such claimant, his agent or attorney, when so arrested pursuant to the authority herein given or declared; or shall harbor or conceal such person after notice that he or she was a fugitive from labor as aforesaid, shall, for either of the said offences, forfeit and pay the sum of five hundred dollars. Which penalty may be recovered by and for the benefit of such claimant, by action of debt in any court proper to try the same, saving moreover to the person claiming such labor or service his right of action for or on account of the said injuries, or either of them."

State officers, the magistrates and judges, though not bound to act under the law of Congress, yet did so; and State jails, though not obligatory under a federal law, were freely used for the custody of the re-captured fugitive. This continued till a late day in most of the free States—in all of them until after the Congress of the United States engaged in the slavery agitation—and in the great State of Pennsylvania until the 20th of March, 1847: that is to say, until a month after the time that Mr. Calhoun brought into the Senate the slavery resolutions, stigmatized by Mr. Benton as "fire-brand," at the moment of their introduction, and which are since involving the Union in conflagration. Then Pennsylvania passed the act forbidding her judicial authorities to take cognizance of any fugitive slave case—granted a habeas corpus remedy to any fugitive arrested—denying the use of her jails to confine any one—and repealing the six months' slave sojourning law of 1780.

Some years before the passage of this harsh act, and before the slavery agitation had commenced in Congress, to wit, 1826 (which was nine years before the commencement of the agitation), Pennsylvania had passed a most liberal law of her own, done upon the request of Maryland, to aid the recovery of fugitive slaves. It was entitled, "*An act to give effect to the Constitution of the United States in reclaiming fugitives from justice.*" Such had been the just and generous conduct of Pennsylvania towards the slave States until up to the time of passing the harsh act of 1847. Her legal right to pass that act is admitted; her magistrates were not bound to act under the federal law—her jails were not liable to be used for federal purposes. The sojourning law of 1780 was her own, and she had a right to repeal it. But the whole act of '47 was the exercise of a mere right, against the comity which is due to States united under a common head, against moral and social duty, against high national policy, against the spirit in which the constitution was made, against her own previous conduct for sixty years; and injurious and irritating to the people of the slave States, and parts of it unconstitutional. The denial of the intervention of her judicial officers, and the use of her prisons, though an inconvenience, was not insurmountable, and might be remedied by Congress; the repeal of the act of 1780 was the radical injury and for which there was no remedy in federal legislation.

That act was passed before the adoption of the constitution, and while the feelings of conciliation, good will, and entire justice, prevailed among the States; it was allowed to continue in force near sixty years after the constitution was made; and was a proof of good feeling towards all during that time. By the terms of this act, a discrimination was established between sojourners and permanent residents, and the element of time—the most obvious and easy of all arbiters—was taken for the rule of discrimination. Six months was the time allowed to discriminate a sojourner from a resident; and during that time the rights of the owner remained complete in his slave; after the lapse of that time, his ownership ceased. This six months was equally in favor of all persons; but there was a further and indefinite provision in favor of members of Congress, and of the federal government, all of whom, coming from slave States, were allowed to retain their ownership as long as their federal duties required them to remain in the State. Such an act was just and wise, and in accordance with the spirit of comity which should prevail among States formed into a Union, having a common general government, and reciprocating the rights of citizenship. It is to be deplored that any event ever arose to occasion the repeal of that act. It is to be wished that a spirit would arise to re-enact it; and that others of the free States should follow the example. For there were others, and several which had similar acts, and which have repealed them in like manner, as Pennsylvania—under the same unhappy influences, and with the same baleful consequences. New York, for example—her law of discrimination between the sojourner and the resident, being the same in principle, and still more liberal in detail, than that of Pennsylvania—allowing nine months instead of six, to determine that character.

This act of New York, like that of Pennsylvania, continued undisturbed in the State, until the slavery agitation took root in Congress; and was even so well established in the good opinion of the people of that State, as late as thirteen years after the commencement of that agitation, as to be boldly sustained by the candidates for the highest offices. Of this an eminent instance will be given in the canvass for the governorship of the State, in the year 1838. In that year Mr. Marcy and Mr. Seward were the opposing candidates, and an anti-slavery meeting, held at Utica, passed a resolve to have them interrogated (among other things) on the point of repealing the slave sojournment act. Messrs. Gerritt Smith, and William Jay, were nominated a committee for that purpose, and fulfilled their mission so zealously as rather to overstate the terms of the act, using the word "importation" as applied to the coming of these slaves with their owners, thus: "Are you in favor of the repeal of the law which now authorizes the importation of slaves into this State, and their detention here as such for the time of nine months?" Objecting to the substitution of the term importation, and stating the act correctly, both the candidates answered fully in the negative, and with reasons for their opinion. The act was first quoted in its own terms, as follows:

> "Any person, not being an inhabitant of this State, who shall be travelling to or from, or passing through this State, may bring with him any person lawfully held by him in slavery, and may take such person with him from this State; but the person so held in slavery shall not reside or continue in this State more than nine months; and if such residence be continued beyond that time, such person shall be free."

Replying to the interrogatory, Mr. Marcy then proceeds to give his opinion and reasons in favor of sustaining the act, which he does unreservedly:

> "By comparing this law with your interrogatory, you will perceive at once that the latter implies much more than the former expresses. The discrepancy between them is so great, that I suspected, at first, that you had reference to some other enactment which had escaped general notice. As none, however, can be found but the foregoing, to which the question is in any respect applicable, there will be no mistake, I presume, in assuming it to be the one you had in view. The deviation, in putting the question, from what would seem to be the plain and obvious course of directing the attention to the particular law under consideration, by referring to it in the very terms in which it is expressed, or at least in language showing its objects and limitations, I do not impute to an intention to create an erroneous impression as to the law, or to ascribe to it a character of odiousness which it does not deserve; yet I think that it must be conceded that your question will induce those who are not particularly acquainted with the section of the statute to which it refers, to believe that there is a law of this State which allows a free importation of slaves into it, without restrictions as to object, and without limitation as to the persons who may do so; yet this is very far from being true. This law does not permit any inhabitant of this State to bring into it any person held in slavery,

under any pretence or for any object whatsoever; nor does it allow any person of any other State or country to do so, except such person is actually travelling to or from, or passing through this State. This law, in its operation and effect, only allows persons belonging to States or nations where domestic slavery exists, who happen to be travelling in this State, to be attended by their servants whom they lawfully hold in slavery when at home, provided they do not remain within our territories longer than nine months. The difference between it and the one implied by your interrogatory is so manifest, that it is perhaps fair to presume, that if those by whose appointment you act in this matter had not misapprehended its character, they would not have instructed you to make it the subject of one of your questions. It is so restricted in its object, and that is so unexceptionable, that it can scarcely be regarded as obnoxious to well-founded objections when viewed in its true light. Its repeal would, I apprehend, have an injurious effect upon our intercourse with some of the other States, and particularly upon their business connection with our commercial emporium. In addition to this, the repeal would have a tendency to disturb the political harmony among the members of our confederacy, without producing any beneficial results to compensate for these evils. I am not therefore in favor of it."

This is an explicit answer, meeting the interrogatory with a full negative, and impliedly rebuking the phrase "importation," by supposing it would not have been used if the Utica convention had understood the act. Mr. Seward answered in the same spirit, and to the same effect, only giving a little more amplitude to his excellent reasons. He says:

"Does not your inquiry give too broad a meaning to the section? It certainly does not confer upon any citizen of a State, or of any other country, or any citizen of any other State, except the owner of slaves in another State by virtue of the laws thereof, the right to bring slaves into this State or detain them here under any circumstances as such. I understand your inquiry, therefore to mean, whether I am in favor of a repeal of the law which declares, in substance, that any person from the southern or south-western States, who may be travelling to or from or passing thrugh the State, may bring with him and take with him any person lawfully held by him in slavery in the State from whence he came, provided such slaves do not remain here more than nine months. The article of the constitution of the United States which bears upon the present question, declares that no person held to service or labor in one State, under the laws thereof, escaping to another State, shall, in consequence of any law or regulation therein, be discharged from such service or labor, but such persons shall be delivered up on claim of the party to whom such service or labor may be due. I understand that, in the State of Massachusetts, this provision of the constitution has been decided by the courts not to include the case of a slave brought by his master into the State, and escaping thence. But the courts of law in this State have uniformly given a different construction to the same article of the constitution, and have always decided that it does embrace the case of a slave brought by his master into this State, and escaping from him here. Consequently, under this judicial construction of the constitution, and without, and in defiance of any law or regulation of this State, if the slave escape from his master in this State, he must be restored to him, when claimed at any time during his master's temporary sojournment within the State, whether that sojournment be six months, nine months, or longer. It is not for me to say that this decision is erroneous, nor is it for our legislature. Acting under its authority, they passed the law to which you object, for the purpose, not of conferring new powers or privileges on the slave-owner, but to prevent his abuse of that which the constitution of the United States, thus expounded, secures to him. The law, as I understand it, was intended to fix a period of time as a test of transient passage through, or temporary residence in the State, within the provisions of the constitution. The duration of nine months is not material in the question, and if it be unnecessarily long, may and ought to be abridged. But, if no such law existed, the right of the master (under the construction of the constitution before mentioned) would be indefinite, and the slave must be surrendered to him in all cases of travelling through, or passage to or from the State. If I have correctly apprehended the subject, this law is not one conferring a right upon any person to import slaves into the State, and hold them here as such; but is an attempt at restriction upon the constitutional right of the master; a qualification, or at least a definition of it, and is in favor of the slave. Its repeal, therefore, would have the effect to put in greater jeopardy the class of persons you propose to benefit by it. While the construction of the constitution adopted here is maintained, the law, it would seem, ought to remain upon our statute book, not as an encroachment upon the rights of man, but a protection for them.

"But, gentlemen, being desirous to be entirely candid in this communication, it is proper I should add, that I am not convinced it would be either wise, expedient or humane, to declare to our fellow-citizens of the southern and south-western States, that if they travel to or from, or pass through the State of New York, they shall not bring with them the attendants whom custom, or education, or habit, may have rendered necessary to them. I have not been able to discover any good object to be attained by such an act of inhospitality. It certainly can work no injury to us, nor can it be injurious to the unfortunate beings held in bondage, to permit them, once perhaps in their lives, and at most, on occasions few and far between, to visit a country where slavery is unknown. I can even conceive of benefits to the great cause of human liberty, from the cultivation of this intercourse with the South. I can imagine but one ground of objection, which is, that it may be regarded as an implication that this State sanctions slavery. If this objection were well grounded, I should at once condemn the law. But, in truth, the law does not imply any such sanction. The same statute which, in necessary obedience to the constitution of the United States as expounded, declares the exception, condemns, in the most clear and definite terms, all human bondage. I will not press the considerations flowing from the nature of our Union, and the mutual concessions on which it was founded, against the propriety of such an exclusion as your question contemplates, apparently for the purpose only of avoiding an implication not founded in fact, and which the history of our State so nobly contradicts. It is sufficient to say that such an exclusion could have no good effect practically, and would accomplish nothing in the great cause of human liberty."

These answers do not seem to have affected the election in any way. Mr. Seward was elected, each candidate receiving the full vote of his party. Since that time the act has been repealed, and no voice has yet been raised to restore it. Just and meritorious as were the answers of Messrs. Marcy and Seward in favor of sustaining the sojourning act, their voice in favor of its restoration would be still more so now. It was a measure in the very spirit of the constitution, and in the very nature of a union, and in full harmony with the spirit of concession, deference and good-will in which the constitution was founded. Several other States had acts to the same effect, and the temper of the people in all the free States was accordant. It was not until after the slavery question became a subject of *political* agitation, in the national legislature, that these acts were repealed, and this spirit destroyed. Political agitation has done all the mischief.

The act of Pennsylvania, of March 3d, 1847, besides repealing the slave sojournment act of 1780—(an act made in the time of Dr. Franklin, and which had been on her statute-book near seventy years), besides repealing her recent act of 1826, and besides forbidding the use of her prisons, and the intervention of her officers in the recovery of fugitive slaves—besides all this, went on to make positive enactments to prevent the exercise of the rights of forcible recaption of fugitive slaves, as regulated by the act of Congress, under the clause in the constitution; and for that purpose contained this section:

"That if any person or persons claiming any negro or mulatto, as fugitive from servitude or labor, shall, under any pretence of authority whatever, violently and tumultuously seize upon and carry away in a riotous, violent, and tumultuous manner, and so as to disturb and endanger the public peace, any negro or mulatto within this commonwealth, either with or without the intention of taking such negro or mulatto before any district or circuit judge, the person or persons so offending against the peace of this commonwealth, shall be deemed guilty of a misdemeanor; and on conviction thereof, shall be sentenced to pay a fine of not less than one hundred nor more than two thousand dollars; and, further, be confined in the county jail for any period not exceeding three months, at the discretion of the court."

The granting of the *habeas corpus* writ to any fugitive slave completed the enactments of this statute, which thus carried out, to the full, the ample intimations contained in its title, to wit: "*An act to prevent kidnapping, preserve the public peace, prohibit the exercise of certain powers heretofore exercised by judges, justices of the peace, aldermen, and jailers in this commonwealth; and, to repeal certain slave laws.*" This act made a new starting-point in the anti-slavery movements North, as the resolutions of Mr. Calhoun, of the previous month, made a new starting-point in the pro-slavery movements in the South. The first led to the new fugitive slave recovery act of 1850—the other has led to the abrogation of the Missouri Compromise line; and, between the two, the state of things has been produced which now afflicts and distracts the country, and is working a sectional divorce of the States.

A citizen of Maryland, acting under the federal law of '93, in recapturing his slave in Pennsylvania, was prosecuted under the State act of 1826—convicted—and sentenced to its penalties. The constitutionality of this enactment was in vain plead in the Pennsylvania court; but her authorities acted in the spirit of deference and respect to the authorities of the Union, and concurred in an "*agreed case,*" to be carried before the Supreme Court of the United States, to test the constitutionality of the Pennsylvania law. That court decided fully and promptly all the points in the case, and to the full vindication of all the rights of a slaveholder, under the recaption clause in the constitution. The points decided cover the whole ground, and, besides, show precisely in what particular the act of 1793 required to be amended, to make it work out its complete effect under the constitution, independent of all extrinsic aid. The points were these:

"The provisions of the act of 12th of February, 1793, relative to fugitive slaves, is clearly constitutional in all its leading provisions, and, indeed, with the exception of that part which confers authority on State magistrates, is free from reasonable doubt or difficulty. As to the authority so conferred on State magistrates, while a difference of opinion exists, and may exist on this point, in different States, whether State magistrates are bound to act under it, none is entertained by the court, that State magistrates may, if they choose, exercise that authority, unless forbid by State legislation." "The power of legislation in relation to fugitives from labor is exclusive in the national legislature." "The right to seize and retake fugitive slaves, and the duty to deliver them up, in whatever State of the Union they may be found, is under the constitution recognized as an absolute, positive right and duty, pervading the whole Union with an equal and supreme force, uncontrolled and uncontrollable by State sovereignty or State legislation. The right and duty are co-extensive and uniform in remedy and operation throughout the whole Union. The owner has the same exemption from State regulations and control, through however many States he may pass with the fugitive slaves in his possession *in transitu* to his domicil." "The act of the legislature of Pennsylvania, on which the indictment against Edward Prigg was founded, for carrying away a fugitive slave, is unconstitutional and void. It purports to punish, as a public offence against the State, the very act of seizing and removing a slave by his master, which the constitution of the United States was designed to justify and uphold." "The constitutionality of the act of Congress (1793), relating to fugitives from labor, has been affirmed by the adjudications of the State tribunals, and by those of the courts of the United States."

This decision of the Supreme Court—so clear and full—was further valuable in making visible to the legislative authority what was wanting to give efficacy to the act of 1793; it was nothing but to substitute federal commissioners for the State officers forbidden to act under it; and that substitution might have been accomplished in an amendatory bill of three or four lines—leaving all the rest of the act as it was. Unfortunately Congress did not limit itself to an amendment of the act of 1793; it made a new law—long and complex—and striking the public mind as a novelty. It was early in the session of 1849-'50 that the Judiciary Committee of the Senate reported a bill on the subject; it was a bill long and complex, and distasteful to all sides of the chamber, and lay upon the table six months untouched. It was taken up in the last weeks of a nine months' session, and substituted by another bill, still longer and more complex. This bill also was very distasteful to the

Senate (the majority), and had the singular fate of being supported in its details, and passed into law, with less than a quorum of the body in its favor, and without ever receiving the full senatorial vote of the slave States. The material votes upon it, before it was passed, were on propositions to give the fugitive a jury trial, if he desired it, upon the question of his condition—free or slave; and upon the question of giving him the benefit of the writ of *habeas corpus*. The first of these propositions originated with Mr. Webster, but was offered in his absence by Mr. Dayton, of New Jersey. He (Mr. Webster) drew up a brief bill early in the session, to supply the defect found in the working of the act of '93; it was short and simple; but it contained a proviso in favor of a jury trial when the fugitive denied his servitude. That would have been about always; and this jury trial, besides being incompatible with the constitution, and contradictory to all cases of proceeding against fugitives, would have been pretty sure to have been fatal to the pursuer's claim; and certainly both expensive and troublesome to him. It was contrary to the act of 1793, and contrary to the whole established course of reclaiming fugitives, which is always to carry them back to the place from which they fled to be tried. Thus, if a man commits an offence in one country, and flies to another, he is carried back; so, if he flies from one State to another; and so in all the extradition treaties between foreign nations. All are carried back to the place from which they fled, the only condition being to establish the flight and the probable cause; and that in the case of fugitives from labor, as well as from justice, both of which classes are put together in the constitution of the United States, and in the fugitive act of 1793. The proposition was rejected by a vote of eleven to twenty-seven. The yeas were: Messrs. Davis of Massachusetts, Dayton, Dodge of Wisconsin, Greene, Hamlin, Phelps, Smith, Upham, Walker of Wisconsin, and Winthrop. The nays were: Messrs. Atchison, Badger, Barnwell, Bell, Benton, Berrien, Butler, Cass, Davis of Mississippi, Dawson, Dodge of Iowa, Downs, Houston, Jones of Iowa, King, Mangum, Mason, Morton, Pratt of Maryland, Rusk, Sebastian, Soulé, Sturgeon, Turney, Underwood, Wales, Yulee. The motion in favor of granting the benefit of the writ of habeas corpus to the fugitive was made by Mr. Winthrop, and rejected by the same vote of eleven yeas and twenty-seven nays. Other amendments were offered and disposed of, and the question coming on the passing of the bill, Mr. Cass, in speaking his own sentiments in favor of merely amending the act of 1793, also spoke the sentiments of many others, saying:

"When this subject was before the compromise committee, there was a general wish, and in that I fully concurred, that the main features of the act of 1793 upon this subject, so far as they were applicable, should be preserved, and that such changes as experience has shown to be necessary to a fair and just enforcement of the provisions of the constitution for the surrender of fugitive slaves, should be introduced by way of amendment. That law was approved by Washington, and has now been in force for sixty years, and lays down, among others, four general principles, to which I am prepared to adhere: 1. The right of the master to arrest his fugitive slave wherever he may find him. 2. His duty to carry him before a magistrate in the State where he is arrested, and that claim may be adjudged by him. 3. The duty of the magistrate to examine the claim, and to decide it, like other examining magistrates, without a jury, and then to commit him to the custody of the master. 4. The right of the master then to remove the slave to his residence. At the time this law was passed, every justice of the peace throughout the Union was required to execute the duties under it. Since then, as we all know, the Supreme Court has decided that justices of the peace cannot be called upon to execute this law, and the consequence is, that they have almost every where refused to do so. The master seeking his slave found his remedy a good one at the time, but now very ineffectual; and this defect is one that imperiously requires a remedy. And this remedy I am willing to provide, fairly and honestly, and to make such other provisions as may be proper and necessary. But I desire for myself that the original act should remain upon the statute book, and that the changes shown to be necessary should be made by way of amendment."

The vote on the passing of the bill was 27 to 12, the yeas being: Messrs. Atchison, Badger, Barnwell, Bell, Berrien, Butler, Davis of Miss., Dawson, Dodge of Iowa, Downs, Foote, Houston, Hunter, Jones of Iowa, King, Mangum, Mason, Pearce, Rusk, Sebastian, Soulé, Spruance, Sturgeon, Turney, Underwood, Wales, and Yulee. The nays were: Messrs. Baldwin, Bradbury, Cooper, Davis of Mass., Dayton, Dodge of Wisconsin, Greene of Rhode Island, Smith, Upham, Walker, and Winthrop. Above twenty senators did not vote at all upon the bill, of whom Mr. Benton was one. Nearly the whole of these twenty would have voted for an amendment to the act of 1793, supplying federal officers in place of the State officers who were to assist in its execution. Some three or four lines would have done that; but instead of this brief enactment to give effect to an ancient and well-known law, there was a long bill of ten sections, giving the aspect of a new law; and with such multiplied and complex provisions as to render the act inexecutable, except at a cost and trouble which would render the recovery of little or no value; and to be attended with an array and machinery which would excite disturbance, and scenes of force and violence, and render the law odious. It passed the House, and became a law, and has verified all the objections taken to it.

Mr. Benton did not speak upon this bill at the time of its passage; he had done that before, in a previous stage of the question, and when Mr. Clay proposed to make it a part of his compromise measures. He (Mr. Benton) was opposed to confounding an old subject of constitutional obligation with new and questionable subjects, and was ready to give the subject an independent consideration, and to vote for any bill that should be efficient and satisfactory. He said:

> "We have a bill now—an independent one—for the recovery of these slaves. It is one of the oldest on the calendar, and warmly pressed at the commencement of the session. It must be about ripe for decision by this time. I am ready to vote upon it, and to vote any thing under the constitution which will be efficient and satisfactory. It is the only point, in my opinion, at which any of the non-slaveholding States, as States, have given just cause of complaint to the slaveholding States. I leave out individuals and societies, and speak of States in their corporate capacity; and say, this affair of the runaway slaves is the only case in which any of the non-slaveholding States, in my opinion, have given just cause of complaint to the slaveholding States. But, how is it here? Any refusal on the part of the northern members to legislate the remedy? We have heard many of them declare their opinions; and I see no line of east and west dividing the north from the south in these opinions. I see no geographical boundary dividing northern and southern opinions. I see no diversity of opinion but such as occurs in ordinary measures before Congress. For one, I am ready to vote at once for the passage of a fugitive slavery recovery bill; but it must be as a separate and independent measure."

Mr. Benton voted upon the amendments, and to make the bill efficient and satisfactory; but failed to make it either, and would neither vote for it nor against it. It has been worth but little to the slave States in recovering their property, and has been annoying to the free States from the manner of its execution, and is considered a new act, though founded upon that of '93, which is lost and hid under it. The wonder is how such an act came to pass, even by so lean a vote as it received—for it was voted for by less than the number of senators from the slave States alone. It is a wonder how it passed at all, and the wonder increases on knowing that, of the small number that voted for it, many were against it, and merely went along with those who had constituted themselves the particular guardians of the rights of the slave States, and claimed a lead in all that concerned them.

Those self-constituted guardians were permitted to have their own way; some voting with them unwillingly, others not voting at all. It was a part of the plan of "compromise and pacification," which was then deemed essential to save the Union: and under the fear of danger to the Union on one hand, and the charms of pacification and compromise on the other, a few heated spirits got the control, and had things their own way. Under other circumstances—in any season of quiet and tranquillity—the vote of Congress would have been almost general against the complex, cumbersome, expensive, annoying, and ineffective bill that was passed, and in favor of the act (with the necessary amendment) which Washington recommended and signed—which State and Federal judiciaries had sanctioned—which the people had lived under for nearly sixty years, and against which there was no complaint until slavery agitation had become a political game to be played at by parties from both sides of the Union. All public men disavow that game. All profess patriotism. All applaud the patriotic spirit of our ancestors. Then imitate that spirit. Do as these patriotic fathers did—the free States by reviving the sojournment laws which gave safety to the slave property of their fellow-citizens of other States passing through them—the slave States by acting in the spirit of those who enacted the anti-slavery ordinance of 1787, and the Missouri Compromise line of 1820. New York and Pennsylvania are the States to begin, and to revive the sojournment laws which were in force within them for half a century. The man who would stand up in each of these States and propose the revival of these acts, for the same reasons that Messrs. Marcy and Seward opposed their repeal, would give a proof of patriotism which would entitle him to be classed with our patriotic ancestors.

CHAPTER CXCVIII.

DISUNION MOVEMENTS: SOUTHERN PRESS AT WASHINGTON: SOUTHERN CONVENTION AT NASHVILLE: SOUTHERN CONGRESS CALLED FOR BY SOUTH CAROLINA AND MISSISSIPPI.

"When the future historian shall address himself to the task of portraying the rise, progress, and decline of the American Union, the year 1850 will arrest his attention, as denoting and presenting the first marshalling and arraying of those hostile forces and opposing elements which resulted in dissolution; and the world will have another illustration of the great truth, that forms and modes of government, however correct in theory, are only valuable as they conduce to the great ends of all government—the peace, quiet, and conscious security of the governed."

So wrote a leading South Carolina paper on the first day of January, 1850—and not without a knowledge of what it was saying. All that was said was attempted, and the catastrophe alone was wanting to complete the task assigned to the future historian.

The manifesto of the forty-two members from the slave States, issued in 1849, was not a *brutum fulmen*, nor intended to be so. It was intended for action, and was the commencement of action; and regular steps for the separation of the slave from the free States immediately began under it. An organ of disunion, entitled "The Southern Press," was set up at Washington, established upon a contribution of $30,000 from the signers to the Southern manifesto, and their ardent adherents—its daily occupation to inculcate the advantages of disunion, to promote it by inflaming the South against the North, and to prepare it by organizing a Southern concert of action. Southern cities were to recover their colonial superiority in a state of sectional independence; the ships of all nations were to crowd their ports to carry off their rich staples, and bring back ample returns; Great Britain was to be the ally of the new "United States South;" all the slave States were expected to join, but the new confederacy to begin with the South Atlantic States, or even a part of them; and military preparation was to be made to maintain by force what a Southern convention should decree. That convention was called—the same which had been designated in the first manifesto, entitled THE CRISIS, published in the Charleston Mercury in 1835; and the same which had been repulsed from Nashville in 1844. Fifteen years of assiduous labor produced what could not be started in 1835, and what had been repulsed in 1844. A disunion convention met at Nashville! met at the home of Jackson, but after the grave had become his home.

This convention (assuming to represent seven States) took the decisive step, so far as it depended upon itself, towards a separation of the States. It invited the assembling of a "Southern Congress." Two States alone responded to that appeal—South Carolina and Mississippi; and the legislatures of these two passed solemn acts to carry it into effect—South Carolina absolutely, by electing her quota of representatives to the proposed congress; Mississippi provisionally, by subjecting her law to the approval of the people. Of course, each State gave a reason, or motive for its action. South Carolina simply asserted the "aggressions" of the slaveholding States to be the cause, without stating what these aggressions were; and, in fact, there were none to be stated. For even the repeal of the slave sojournment law in some of them, and the refusal to permit the State prisons to be used for the detention of fugitives from service, or State officers to assist in their arrest, though acts of unfriendly import, and a breach of the comity due to sister States, and inconsistent with the spirit of the constitution, were still acts which the States, as sovereign within their limits upon the subjects to which they refer, had a right to pass. Besides, Congress had readily passed the fugitive slave recovery bill, just as these Southern members wished it; and left them without complaint against the national legislature on that score. All other matters of complaint which had successively appeared against the free States were gone—Wilmot Proviso, and all. The act of Mississippi gave two reasons for its action:

"*First.* That the legislation of Congress, at the last session, was controlled by a dominant majority regardless of the constitutional rights of the slaveholding States: and,

"*Secondly.* That the legislation of Congress, such as it was, affords alarming evidence of a settled purpose on the part of said majority to destroy the institution of slavery, not only in the State of Mississippi, but in her sister States, and to subvert the sovereign power of that and other slaveholding States."

Waiving the question whether these reasons, if true, would be sufficient to justify this abrupt attempt to break up the Union, an issue of fact can well be taken on their truth: and first, of the dominant majority of the last session, ending September 1850: that majority, in every instance, was helped out by votes from the slave States, and generally by a majority of them. The admission of California, which was the act of the session most complained of, most resisted, and declared to be a "test" question, was supported by a majority of the members from the slave States: so that reason falls upon the trial of an issue of fact. The second set of reasons have for their point, an assertion that the majority in Congress have a settled purpose to destroy the institution of slavery in the State of Mississippi, and in the other slave States, and to subvert the sovereignty of all the slave States. It is the duty of history to deal with this assertion, thus solemnly put in a legislative act as a cause for the secession of a State from the Union—and to say, that it was an assertion without evidence, and contrary to the evidence, and contrary to the fact. There was no such settled purpose in the majority of Congress, nor in a minority of Congress, nor in any half-dozen members of Congress—if in any one at all. It was a most deplorable assertion of a most alarming design, calculated to mislead and inflame the ignorant, and make them fly to disunion as the refuge against such an appalling catastrophe. But it was not a new declaration. It was part and parcel of the original agitation of slavery commenced in 1835, and continued ever since. To destroy slavery in the States has been the design attributed to the Northern States from that day to this, and is necessary to be kept up in order to keep alive the slavery agitation in the slave States. It has received its constant and authoritative contradiction in the conduct of those States at home, and in the acts of their representatives in Congress, year in and year out; and continues to receive that contradiction, continually; but without having the least effect upon its repetition and incessant reiteration. In the mean time there is a fact visible in all the slave States, which shows that, notwithstanding these twenty years' repetition of the same assertion, there is no danger to slavery in any slave State. Property is timid! and slave property above all: and the market is the test of safety and danger to all property. Nobody gives full price for anything that is insecure, either in title or possession. All property, in danger from either cause, sinks in price when brought to that infallible test. Now, how is it with slave property, tried by this unerring standard? Has it been sinking in price since the year 1835? since the year of the first alarm manifesto in South Carolina, and the first of Mr. Calhoun's twenty years' alarm speeches in the Senate? On the contrary, the price has been constantly rising the whole time—and is still rising, although it has attained a height incredible to have been predicted twenty years ago.

But, although the slavery alarm does not act on property, yet it acts on the feelings and passions of the people, and excites sectional animosity, hatred for the Union, and desire for separation. The Nashville convention, and the call for the Southern Congress, were natural occasions to call out these feelings; and most copiously did they flow. Some specimens, taken from the considered language of men in high authority, and speaking advisedly, and for action, will show the temper of the whole—the names withheld, because the design is to show a danger, and not to expose individuals.

In the South Carolina Legislature, a speaker declared:

> "We must secede from a Union perverted from its original purpose, and which has now become an engine of oppression to the South. He thought our proper course was for this legislature to proceed directly to the election of delegates to a Southern Congress. He thought we should not await the action of all the Southern States; but it is prudent for us to await the action of such States as Alabama, Georgia, Mississippi, and Florida; because these States have requested us to wait. If we can get but one State to unite with us, then we must act. Once being independent, we would have a strong ally in England. But we must prepare for secession."

Another:

> "The friends of the Southern movement in the other States look to the action of South Carolina; and he would make the issue in a reasonable time, and the only way to do so is by secession. There would be no concert among the Southern States until a blow is struck. And

if we are sincere in our determination to resist, we must give the South some guarantee that we are in earnest. He could not concur with the gentleman from Greenville in his expressions of attachment to the Union. He hated and detested the Union, and was in favor of cutting the connection. He avowed himself a disunionist—a disunionist *per se*. If he had the power, he would crush this Union to-morrow."

Another:

"Denied the right or the power of the general government to coerce the State in case of secession. This State is sovereign and independent, so soon as she sees proper to assert that sovereignty. And when can we be stronger than we are now? If we intend to wait until we become superior to the federal government in numerical strength, we will wait for ever. In the event of an attempt to coerce her, sacrifices might be made, but we are willing and ready to make those sacrifices. But he did not believe one gun would be fired in this contest. South Carolina would achieve a bloodless victory. But, should there be a war, all the nations of Europe would be desirous of preserving their commercial intercourse with the Southern States, and would make the effort to do so. He thought there never would be a union of the South until this State strikes the blow, and makes the issue."

Another:

"Would not recapitulate the evils which had been perpetrated upon the South. Great as they have been, they are comparatively unimportant, when compared with the evils to which they would inevitably lead. We must not consider what we have borne, but what we must bear hereafter. There is no remedy for these evils in the government; we have no alternative left us, then, but to come out of the government."

Another:

"He was opposed to calling a convention, because he thought it would impede the action of this State on the questions now before the country. He thought it would impede our progress towards disunion. All his objections to a convention of the people applied only to the proposition to call it now. He thought conventions dangerous things, except when the necessities of the country absolutely demand them. He said that he had adopted the course he had taken on these weighty matters simply and entirely with the view of hastening the dissolution of this Union."

Another:

"Would sustain the bill for electing delegates to a Southern Congress, because he thought it would bring about a more speedy dissolution of the Union."

In the Nashville convention a delegate said:

"I shall enumerate no more of the wrongs that we have suffered, or the dangers with which we are threatened. If these, so enormous and so atrocious, are not sufficient to arouse the Southern mind, our case is desperate. But, supposing that we shall be roused, and that we shall act like freemen, and, knowing our rights and our wrongs, shall be prepared to sustain the one and redress the other, what is the remedy? I answer secession—united secession of the slaveholding States, or a large number of them. Nothing else will be wise—nothing else will be practicable. The Rubicon is passed. The Union is already dissolved. Instead of wishing the perpetuity of any government over such vast boundaries, the rational lover of liberty should wish for its speedy dissolution, as dangerous to all just and free rule. Is not all this exemplified in our own case? In nine months, in one session of Congress, by a great *coup d'etat*, our constitution has been completely and for ever subverted. Instead of a well balanced government, all power is vested in one section of the country, which is in bitter hostility with the other. And this is the glorious Union which we are to support, for whose eternal duration we are to pray, and before which the once proud Southron is to bow down. He ought to perish rather."

"They have not, however, been satisfied with taking all (the territory). They have made that all a wicked instrument for the abolition of the constitution, and of every safeguard of our property and our lives. I have said they have made the appropriation of this territory an instrument to abolish the constitution. There is no doubt that they have abolished the constitution. The carcass may remain, but the spirit has left it. It is now a fetid mass, generating disease and death. It stinks in our nostrils."

"A constitution means *ex vi termini*, a guarantee of the rights, liberty, and security of a free people, and can never survive in the shape of dead formalities. It is a thing of life, and just and fair proportions; not the *caput mortuum* which the so-called Constitution of the United States has now become. Is there a Southern man who bears a soul within his ribs, who will consent to be governed by this vulgar tyranny," &c.

From public addresses:

"Under the operation of causes beyond the scan of man, we are rapidly approaching a great and important crisis in our history. The shadow of the sun has gone back upon the dial of American liberty, and we are rapidly hastening towards the troubled sea of revolution. A dissolution of the Union is our inevitable destiny, and it is idle for man to raise his puny arm to stem the tide of events," &c.

Another:

"We must form a separate government. The slaveholding States must all yet see that their only salvation consists in uniting, and that promptly too, in organizing a Southern confederacy. Should we be wise enough thus to unite, all California, with her exhaustless treasures, would be ours; all New Mexico also, and the sun would never shine upon a country so rich, so great and so powerful, as would be our Southern republic."

Another:

"By our physical power," said one of the foremost of those leaders, in a late speech to his constituents, "we can protect ourselves against foreign nations, whilst by our productions we can command their peace or support. The keys of their wealth and commerce are in our hands, which we will freely offer to them by a system of free trade, making our prosperity their interest—our security their care. The lingering or decaying cities of the South, which before our Revolution carried on all their foreign commerce, buoyant with prosperity and wealth, but which now are only provincial towns, sluggish suburbs of Boston and New York, will rise up to their natural destiny, and again enfold in their embraces the richest commerce of the world. Wealth, honor, and power, and one of the most glorious destinies which ever crowned a great and happy people, awaits the South, if she but control her own fate; but, controlled by another people, what pen shall paint the infamous and bloody catastrophe which must mark her fall?"

From fourth of July toasts:

"The Union: A splendid failure of the first modern attempt, by people of different institutions, to live under the same government.

"The Union: For it we have endured much; for it we have sacrificed much. Let us beware lest we endure too much; lest we sacrifice too much.

"Disunion rather than degradation.

"South Carolina: She struck for the Union when it was a blessing; when it becomes a curse, she will strike for herself.

"The Compromise: 'The best the South can get.' A cowardly banner held out by the *spoilsman* that would sell his country for a mess of pottage.

"The American Eagle: In the event of a dissolution of the Union, the South claims as her portion, the heart of the noble bird; to the Yankees we leave the feathers and carcass.

"The South: Fortified by right, she considers neither threats nor consequences.

"The Union: Once a holy alliance, now an accursed bond."

Among the multitude of publications most numerous in South Carolina and Mississippi, but also appearing in other slave States, all advocating disunion, there were some (like Mr. Calhoun's letter to the Alabama member which feared the chance might be lost which the Wilmot Proviso furnished) also that feared agitation would stop in Congress, and deprive the Southern politicians of the means of uniting the slave States in a separate confederacy. Of this class of publications here is one from a leading paper:

"The object of South Carolina is undoubtedly to dissolve this Union, and form a confederacy of slaveholding States. Should it be impossible to form this confederacy, then her purpose is, we believe conscientiously, to disconnect herself from the Union, and set up for an independent Power. Will delay bring to our assistance the slaveholding States? If the slavery agitation, its tendencies and objects, were of recent origin, and not fully disclosed to the people of the South, delay might unite us in concerted action. We have no indication that Congress will soon pass obnoxious measures, restricting or crippling directly the institution of slavery. Every indication makes us fear that a pause in fanaticism is about to follow, to allow the government time to consolidate her late acquisitions and usurpations of power. Then the storm will be again let loose to gather its fury, and burst upon our heads. We have no hopes that the agitation in Congress, this or next year, will bring about the union of the South."

Enough to show the spirit that prevailed, and the extraordinary and unjustifiable means used by the leaders to mislead and exasperate the people. The great effort was to get a "Southern Congress" to assemble, according to the call of the Nashville convention. The assembling of that "Congress" was a turning point in the progress of disunion. It failed. At the head of the States which had the merit of stopping it, was Georgia—the greatest of the South-eastern Atlantic States. At the head of the presses which did most for the Union, was the National Intelligencer at Washington City, long edited by Messrs. Gales & Seaton, and now as earnest against Southern disunion in 1850 as they were against the Hartford convention disunion of 1814. The Nashville convention, the Southern Congress, and the Southern Press established at Washington, were the sequence and interpretation (so far as its disunion-design needed interpretation), of the Southern address drawn by Mr. Calhoun. His last speech, so far as it might need interpretation, received it soon after his death in a posthumous publication of his political writings, abounding with passages to show that the Union was a mistake—the Southern States ought not to have entered into it, and should not now re-enter it, if out of it, and that its continuance was impossible as things stood: Thus:

"All this has brought about a state of things hostile to the continuance of this Union, and the duration of the government. Alienation is succeeding to attachment, and hostile feelings to alienation; and these, in turn, will be followed by revolution, or a disruption of the Union, unless timely prevented. But this cannot be done by restoring the government to its *federal* character—however necessary that may be as a first step. What has been done cannot be undone. The equilibrium between the two sections has been permanently destroyed by the measures above stated. The Northern section, in consequence, will ever concentrate within itself the two majorities of which the government is composed; and should the Southern be excluded from all the territories, now acquired, *or to be hereafter acquired*, it will soon have so decided a preponderance in the government and the Union, as to be able to mould the constitution to its pleasure. Against this the restoration of the *federal* character of the government can furnish no remedy. So long as it continues there can be no safety for the weaker section. It places in the hands of the stronger and the *hostile* section, the power to crush

- 890 -

her and her *institutions*; and leaves no alternative but to *resist*, or sink down into a colonial condition. This must be the consequence, if some effectual and appropriate remedy is not applied.

"The nature of the disease is such, that nothing can reach it, short of some organic change—a change which will so modify the constitution as to give to the weaker section, in some one form or another, a *negative* on the action of the government. Nothing short of this can protect the weaker, and restore harmony and tranquillity to the Union by arresting effectually the tendency of the dominant section to oppress the weaker. When the constitution was formed, the impression was strong that the tendency to conflict would be between the larger and smaller States; and effectual provisions were accordingly made to guard against it. But experience has proved this to be a mistake; and that instead of being as was then supposed, the conflict is between the two great sections which are so strongly distinguished by their institutions, geographical character, productions and pursuits. Had this been then as clearly perceived as it now is, the same jealousy which so vigilantly watched and guarded against the danger of the larger States oppressing the smaller, would have taken equal precaution to guard against the same danger between the two sections. It is for *us*, who see and feel it, to do, what the framers of the constitution would have done, had they possessed the knowledge, in this respect, which experience has given to us; that is, to provide against the dangers which the system has practically developed; and which, had they been foreseen at the time, and left without guard, would undoubtedly have *prevented* the States forming the *Southern* section of the confederacy, from ever *agreeing* to the constitution; and which, under like circumstances, were they now out of, would for ever *prevent* them *entering* into the Union. How the constitution could best be modified, so as to effect the object, can only be authoritatively determined by the amending power. It may be done in various ways. Among others, it might be effected through a re-organization of the Executive Department; so that its powers, instead of being vested, as they now are, in a single officer, should be vested in two, to be so elected, as that the two should be constituted the special organs and representatives of the respective sections in the Executive Department of the government; and requiring each to *approve* of all the acts of Congress before they become laws. One might be charged with the administration of matters connected with the foreign relations of the country; and the other, of such as were connected with its domestic institutions: the selection to be decided by lot. Indeed it may be doubted, whether the framers of the constitution did not commit a great *mistake*, in constituting a single, instead of a plural executive. Nay, it may even be doubted whether a single magistrate, invested with all the powers properly appertaining to the Executive Department of the government, as is the President, is compatible with the *permanence* of a popular government; especially in a wealthy and populous community, with a large revenue, and a numerous body of officers and employées. Certain it is, that there is no instance of a popular government so constituted which has long endured. Even ours, thus far, furnishes no evidence in its favor, and not a little against it: for, to it the present disturbed and dangerous state of things, which threaten the country with *monarchy* or *disunion*, may be justly attributed."

The observing reader, who may have looked over the two volumes of this View, in noting the progress of the slavery agitation, and its successive alleged causes for disunion, must have been struck with the celerity with which these causes, each in its turn, as soon as removed, has been succeeded by another, of a different kind; until, at last, they terminate in a cause which ignores them all, and find a new reason for disunion in the constitution itself! in that constitution, the protection of which had been invoked as sufficient, during the whole period of the alleged "aggressions and encroachments." In 1835, when the first agitation manifesto and call for a Southern convention, and invocation to unity and concert of action, came forth in the Charleston Mercury, entitled "*The Crisis*," the cause of disunion was then in the abolition societies established in some of the free States, and which these States were required to suppress. Then came the abolition petitions presented in Congress; then the mail transmission of incendiary publications; then the abolition of slavery in the District of Columbia; then the abolition of the slave trade between the States; then the exclusion of slavery from Oregon;

then the Wilmot Proviso; then the admission of California with a free constitution. Each of these, in its day, was a cause of disunion, to be effected through the instrumentality of a Southern convention, forming a sub-confederacy, in flagrant violation of the constitution, and effecting the disunion by establishing a commercial non-intercourse with the free States. After twenty years' agitation upon these points, they are all given up. The constitution, and the Union, were found to be a "mistake" from the beginning—an error in their origin, and an impossibility in their future existence, and to be amended into another impossibility, or broken up at once.

The regular inauguration of this slavery agitation dates from the year 1835; but it had commenced two years before, and in this way: nullification and disunion had commenced in 1830 upon complaint against protective tariff. That being put down in 1833 under President Jackson's proclamation and energetic measures, was immediately substituted by the slavery agitation. Mr. Calhoun, when he went home from Congress in the spring of that year, told his friends, *That the South could never be united against the North on the tariff question—that the sugar interest of Louisiana would keep her out—and that the basis of Southern union must be shifted to the slave question.* Then all the papers in his interest, and especially the one at Washington, published by Mr. Duff Green, dropped tariff agitation, and commenced upon slavery; and, in two years, had the agitation ripe for inauguration on the slavery question. And, in tracing this agitation to its present stage, and to comprehend its rationale, it is not to be forgotten that it is a mere continuation of old tariff disunion; and preferred because more available.

In June, 1833, at the first transfer of Southern agitation from tariff to slavery, Mr. Madison wrote to Mr. Clay:

> "*It is painful to see the unceasing efforts to alarm the South, by imputations against the North of unconstitutional designs on the subject of slavery. You are right, I have no doubt, in believing that no such intermeddling disposition exists in the body of our Northern brethren. Their good faith is sufficiently guaranteed by the interest they have as merchants, as ship-owners, and as manufacturers in preserving a union with the slaveholding States. On the other hand, what madness in the South to look for greater safety in disunion. It would be worse than jumping into the fire for fear of the frying-pan. The danger from the alarms is, that pride and resentment excited by them may be an overmatch for the dictates of prudence; and favor the project of a Southern convention, insidiously revived, as promising by its counsels the best security against grievances of every kind from the North.*"

Nullification, secession, and disunion were considered by Mr. Madison as Synonymous terms, dangerous to the Union as fire to powder, and the danger increasing in all the Southern States, even Virginia. "*Look at Virginia herself, and read in the Gazettes, and in the proceedings of popular meetings, the figure which the anarchical principle now makes, in contrast with the scouting reception given to it but a short time ago.*" Mr. Madison solaced himself with the belief that this heresy would not reach a majority of the States; but he had his misgivings, and wrote them down in the same paper, entitled, "Memorandum on nullification," written in his last days and published after his death. "*But a susceptibility of the contagion in the Southern States is visible, and the danger not to be concealed, that the sympathy arising from known causes, and the inculcated impression of a permanent incompatibility of interests between the North and the South, may put it in the power of popular leaders, aspiring to the highest stations, to unite the South on some critical occasion, in a course that will end in creating a theatre of great though inferior extent. In pursuing this course, the first and most obvious step is nullification—the next, secession—and the last, a farewell separation. How near has this course been lately exemplified! and the danger of its recurrence, in the same or some other quarter, may be increased by an increase of restless aspirants, and by the increasing impracticability of retaining in the Union a large and cemented section against its will.*"—So wrote Mr. Madison in the year 1836, in the 86th year of his age, and the last of his life. He wrote with the pen of inspiration, and the heart of a patriot, and with a soul which filled the Union, and could not be imprisoned in one half of it. He was a Southern man! but his Southern home could not blind his mental vision to the origin, design, and consequences of the slavery agitation. He gives to that agitation, a Southern origin—to that design, a disunion end—to that end, disastrous consequences both to the South and the North.

Mr. Calhoun is dead. Peace to his manes. But he has left his disciples who do not admit of peace! who "*rush in*" where their master "*feared to tread.*" He recoiled from the disturbance of the Missouri compromise: they expunge it. He shuddered at the thought of bloodshed in civil strife: they demand three millions of dollars to prepare arms for civil war.

CHAPTER CXCIX.

THE SUPREME COURT: ITS JUDGES, CLERK, ATTORNEY-GENERALS, REPORTERS AND MARSHALS DURING THE PERIOD TREATED OF IN THIS VOLUME.

CHIEF JUSTICE:—Roger Brooke Taney, of Maryland, appointed in 1836: continues, 1850.

JUSTICES:—Joseph Story, of Massachusetts, appointed, 1811: died 1845.—John McLean, of Ohio, appointed, 1829: continues, 1850.—James M. Wayne, of Georgia, appointed, 1835: continues, 1850.—John Catron, of Tennessee, appointed, 1837: continues, 1850.—Levi Woodbury, of New Hampshire, appointed, 1845: continues, 1850.—Robert C. Grier, of Pennsylvania, appointed, 1846: continues, 1850.

ATTORNEY-GENERALS:—Henry D. Gilpin, of Pennsylvania, appointed, 1840.—John J. Crittenden, of Kentucky, appointed, 1841.—Hugh S. Legare, of South Carolina, appointed, 1841.—John Nelson, of Maryland, appointed, 1843.—John Y. Mason, of Virginia, appointed, 1846.—Nathan Clifford, of Maine, appointed, 1846.—Isaac Toucey, of Connecticut, appointed, 1848.—Reverdy Johnson, of Maryland, appointed, 1849.—John J. Crittenden, of Kentucky, appointed, 1850.

CLERK:—William Thomas Carroll, of the District of Columbia, appointed, 1827: continues, 1850.

REPORTERS OF DECISIONS:—Richard Peters, jr., of Pennsylvania, appointed, 1828.—Benjamin C. Howard, appointed, 1843: continues, 1850.

MARSHALS:—Alexander Hunter, appointed, 1834.—Robert Wallace, appointed, 1848.—Richard Wallach, appointed, 1849.

CHAPTER CC.

CONCLUSION.

I have finished the View which I proposed to take of the Thirty Years' working of the federal government during the time that I was a part of it—a task undertaken for a useful purpose and faithfully executed, whether the object of the undertaking has been attained or not. The preservation of what good and wise men gave us, has been the object; and for that purpose it has been a duty of necessity to show the evil, as well as the good, that I have seen, both of men and measures. The good, I have exultingly exhibited! happy to show it, for the admiration and imitation of posterity: the evil, I have stintedly exposed, only for correction, and for the warning example.

I have seen the capacity of the people for self-government tried at many points, and always found equal to the demands of the occasion. Two other trials, now going on, remain to be decided to settle the question of that capacity. 1. The election of President! and whether that election is to be governed by the virtue and intelligence of the people, or to become the spoil of intrigue and corruption? 2. The sentiment of political nationality! and whether it is to remain co-extensive with the Union, leading to harmony and fraternity; or, divide into sectionalism, ending in hate, alienation, separation and civil war?

An irresponsible body (chiefly self-constituted, and mainly dominated by professional office-seekers and office-holders) have usurped the election of President (for the nomination is the election, so far as the party is concerned); and always making it with a view to their own profit in the monopoly of office and plunder.

A sectional question now divides the Union, arraying one-half against the other, becoming more exasperated daily—which has already destroyed the benefits of the Union, and which, unless checked, will also destroy its form.

Confederate republics are short-lived—the shortest in the whole family of governments. Two diseases beset them—corrupt election of the chief magistrate, when elective; sectional contention, when interest or ambition are at issue. Our confederacy is now laboring under both diseases: and the body of the people, now as always, honest in sentiment and patriotic in design, remain unconscious of the danger—and even become instruments in the hands of their destroyers.

If what is written in these chapters shall contribute to open their eyes to these dangers, and rouse them to the resumption of their electoral privileges and the suppression of sectional contention, then this View will not have been written in vain. If not, the writer will still have one consolation—the knowledge of the fact that he has labored in his day and generation, to preserve and perpetuate the blessings of that Union and self-government which wise and good men gave us.

THE END.

FOOTNOTES

[1] *Preamble to the act of 34th of* HENRY VIII.

Whereas divers and sundry persons craftily obtained into their hands great substance of other men's goods, do suddenly flee to parts unknown, or keep their houses, not minding to pay or restore to any of their creditors, their debts and duties, but at their own wills and own pleasures consume the substance obtained by credit of other men for their own pleasures and delicate living, against all reason, equity, and good conscience.

[2] The following was the vote:

YEAS—Messrs. Benton, Buckner, Calhoun, Dallas, Dickerson, Dudley, Forsyth, Johnston, Kane, King, Rives, Robinson, Seymour, Tomlinson, Webster, White, Wilkins, and Wright—18.

NAYS—Messrs. Bell, Bibb, Black, Clay, Clayton, Ewing, Foot, Grundy, Hendricks, Holmes, Knight, Mangum, Miller, Moore, Naudain, Poindexter, Prentiss, Robbins, Silsbee, Smith, Sprague, Tipton, Troup, Tyler—24.

[3] About four and a quarter millions taken since; and still taking.

[4] He has waged cruel war against human nature itself, violating its most sacred rights of life and liberty in the persons of a distant people who never offended him, captivating and carrying them into slavery in another hemisphere, or to incur miserable death in their transportation thither. This piratical warfare—the opprobrium of *infidel* powers—is the warfare of the Christian king of Great Britain, determined to keep open a market where *men* should be bought and sold. He has prostituted his negative for suppressing every legislative attempt to prohibit or restrain this execrable commerce; and, that this assemblage of horrors might want no fact of distinguished dye, he is now exciting the very people to rise in arms among us, and to purchase that liberty of which he has deprived them, by murdering the people on whom he has obtruded them; thus paying off former crimes committed against the *liberties* of one people, with crimes which he urges them to commit against the *lives* of another.—[*Original draught of the Declaration of Independence, as drawn by Mr. Jefferson, and before it was altered by the committee.*]

[5] General now Senator Henry Dodge.

[6] General Jackson.

[7] "Mr. Granger observed that he had a few words to say to the gentleman from Massachusetts [Mr. CUSHING]. When he reflected that that gentleman had voted for every bill that the President had vetoed, and had then defended every veto which the President had sent them, he had been not a little puzzled to know how to defend his position. The gentleman was like a man he saw a short time since in the circus, who came forward ready dressed and equipped to ride any horse that might be brought out for him. First the gentleman from Massachusetts rode the bank pony; and that having run to death, he mounted the veto charger. The second bank roadster, then the tariff palfrey, and lastly, the stout-limbed tariff hunter, were mounted in their turn; and the veto animals were as complacently mounted, and were seated with as much self-satisfaction. The gentleman had voted for every bill, and then had justified every veto, and every act of executive encroachment on this House."

[8] At the presidential election of 1824, the Northern States voted pretty much in a body for Mr. Calhoun, as Vice-President, giving him near the same vote which they gave Mr. Adams for President. Thus:

	For Mr. Adams.	*For Mr. Calhoun.*
New Hampshire,	8	7
Massachusetts,	15	15
Rhode Island,	4	3
Vermont,	7	7
New York,	26	29

[9] Since the delivery of this speech a copy of a paragraph of a despatch from Mr. Edward Everett, United States minister in London, dated 31st March, 1843, has been obtained, giving an account of this map as shown to him by Lord Aberdeen, containing the two red lines upon it, one for our northeast boundary, called "Oswald's line," the other for the northwest, called the line of the "treaty of Utrecht." The paragraph is in these words:

"The above was chiefly written before I had seen Mr. Oswald's map, which I have since by the kindness of Sir Robert Peel and Lord Aberdeen, been permitted to do. It is a copy of Mitchell in fine preservation. The boundaries between the British and French possessions in America, 'as fixed by the treaty of Utrecht,' are marked upon it in a very full distinct line, at least a tenth of an inch broad, and those words written in several places. In like manner the line giving our boundary as we have always claimed it, that is, carrying the northeastern angle of Nova Scotia far to the north of the St. Johns, is drawn very carefully in a bold red line, full a tenth of an inch broad: and in four different places along the line distinctly written 'the boundary described by Mr. Oswald.' What is very noticeable is, that a line narrower, but drawn with care with an instrument, from the lower end of Lake Nipissing to the source of the Mississippi, as far as the map permits such a line to run, had once been drawn on the map, and has since been partially erased, though still distinctly visible."

[10] "It may be asked why not retain the blacks among us, and incorporate them into the State. Deep-rooted prejudices entertained by the whites; ten thousand recollections of the blacks of the injuries they have sustained; new provocations; the real distinctions which nature has made; and many other circumstances, will divide us into parties, and produce convulsions, which will probably never end but in the extermination of one or the other race."—*Jefferson.*

Milton Keynes UK
Ingram Content Group UK Ltd.
UKHW021428160324
439374UK00013B/559